Visual Basic® .NET Bible

Bill Evjen, Jason Beres, et. al.

Hungry Minds™

Best-Selling Books • Digital Downloads • e-Books • Answer Networks • e-Newsletters • Branded Web Sites • e-Learning

New York, NY ✦ Cleveland, OH ✦ Indianapolis, IN

Visual Basic® .NET Bible

Published by
Hungry Minds, Inc.
909 Third Avenue
New York, NY 10022
www.hungryminds.com

Library of Congress Catalog Card No.: 2001118284

ISBN: 0-7645-4826-3

Printed in the United States of America

10 9 8 7 6 5 4 3 2

1B/RU/RS/QR/IN

Distributed in the United States by Hungry Minds, Inc.

Distributed by CDG Books Canada Inc. for Canada; by Transworld Publishers Limited in the United Kingdom; by IDG Norge Books for Norway; by IDG Sweden Books for Sweden; by IDG Books Australia Publishing Corporation Pty. Ltd. for Australia and New Zealand; by TransQuest Publishers Pte Ltd. for Singapore, Malaysia, Thailand, Indonesia, and Hong Kong; by Gotop Information Inc. for Taiwan; by ICG Muse, Inc. for Japan; by Intersoft for South Africa; by Eyrolles for France; by International Thomson Publishing for Germany, Austria, and Switzerland; by Distribuidora Cuspide for Argentina; by LR International for Brazil; by Galileo Libros for Chile; by Ediciones ZETA S.C.R. Ltda. for Peru; by WS Computer Publishing Corporation, Inc., for the Philippines; by Contemporanea de Ediciones for Venezuela; by Express Computer Distributors for the Caribbean and West Indies; by Micronesia Media Distributor, Inc. for Micronesia; by Chips Computadoras S.A. de C.V. for Mexico; by Editorial Norma de Panama S.A. for Panama; by American Bookshops for Finland.

For general information on Hungry Minds' products and services please contact our Customer Care department within the U.S. at 800-762-2974, outside the U.S. at 317-572-3993 or fax 317-572-4002.

For sales inquiries and reseller information, including discounts, premium and bulk quantity sales, and foreign-language translations, please contact our Customer Care department at 800-434-3422, fax 317-572-4002 or write to Hungry Minds, Inc., Attn: Customer Care Department, 10475 Crosspoint Boulevard, Indianapolis, IN 46256.

For information on licensing foreign or domestic rights, please contact our Sub-Rights Customer Care department at 212-884-5000.

For information on using Hungry Minds' products and services in the classroom or for ordering examination copies, please contact our Educational Sales department at 800-434-2086 or fax 317-572-4005.

For press review copies, author interviews, or other publicity information, please contact our Public Relations department at 317-572-3168 or fax 317-572-4168.

For authorization to photocopy items for corporate, personal, or educational use, please contact Copyright Clearance Center, 222 Rosewood Drive, Danvers, MA 01923, or fax 978-750-4470.

Hungry Minds is a trademark of Hungry Minds, Inc.

About the Authors

Bill Evjen has been programming in Web development since 1996. Though raised in Seattle, Bill is presently an Internet Applications developer in St. Louis, Missouri. His abilities in Microsoft-centric Web technologies have led him to develop a number of large Internet-based applications for Fortune 500 companies and others. Bill's love of the new .NET platform led him to be the Founder and President of the St. Louis .NET User Group (http://www.stlnet.org/), and has helped in bringing prominent .NET speakers to the Midwest. Bill graduated from Western Washington University in Bellingham, Washington with a Russian Linguistics degree, and when he isn't tinkering on the computer, he enjoys spending his free time in his summer place in Toivakka, Finland. You can reach Bill at evjen@yahoo.com.

Jason Beres has been a software developer for 10 years. He is currently a consultant in south Florida and works exclusively with Microsoft technologies. Jason holds the MCT, MCSD, and MCDBA certifications from Microsoft. When he is not teaching, consulting, or writing, he is formatting his hard drive and installing the latest beta products from Microsoft and keeping up with the latest episodes of *Star Trek*.

About the Series Editor

Michael Lane Thomas is an active development community and computer industry analyst who currently spends a great deal of time spreading the gospel of Microsoft .NET in his current role as a .NET Technology Evangelist for Microsoft. In working with over a half-dozen publishing companies, Michael has written numerous technical articles and authored/contributed to almost 20 books on numerous technical topics including Visual Basic, Visual C++, and .NET technologies. He is a prolific supporter of the Microsoft certification programs, having earned his MCSD, MCSE+I, MCT, MCP+SB, and MCDBA.

In addition to technical writing, Michael can also be heard over the airwaves from time to time, including two previous weekly radio programs on Entercom stations, most often in Kansas City on News Radio 980KMBZ. He can also occasionally be caught on the Internet doing an MSDN Webcast discussing .NET, the Next Generation of Web application technologies.

Michael started his journey through the technical ranks back in college at the University of Kansas, where he earned his stripes and a couple of degrees. After a brief stint as a technical and business consultant to Tokyo-based Global Online Japan, he returned to the states to climb the corporate ladder. He has held assorted roles including IT Manager, Field Engineer, Trainer, Independent Consultant, and even a brief stint as Interim CTO of a successful dot com, although he believes his current role as .NET Evangelist for Microsoft is the best of the lot. He can be reached via email at mlthomas@microsoft.com.

About the Contributors

Jim Chandler is an independent consultant with extensive experience in architecting and developing custom, integrated software solutions for small- to medium-sized businesses in the Midwest. Before focusing his career on the Windows platform, Jim was a Graphics Partner at Digital Equipment Corporation, evangelizing X11 and Motif. Jim is a coauthor of an upcoming ASP book from Hungry Minds and an active member of the St. Louis .NET Users Group. He has delivered presentations on such topics as ASP.NET, XML, and Web Services to the St. Louis developer community. His research interests include everything .NET as well as COM+ and the Total Cost of Ownership initiatives. Outside the daily challenges of developing applications and fulfilling his research interests, Jim shares his spare time with his wife, Rhonda, and their two sons, Sam and Thomas.

Jacob Grass is currently a Software Engineer at Abiliti Solutions, Inc., an industry leader in customer care and billing solutions for the Telecommunications Industry. His professional experience includes Quality Assurance, Research Analysis, Application Development, and instruction. Jacob currently specializes in development and instruction with Visual Basic .Net. This is his first publication.

Kevin Grossnicklaus works as an Enterprise Application Architect for SSE in St. Louis, Missouri. He is responsible for assisting development teams in designing, architecting, and building enterprise scale, distributed Web applications using the latest in Web development tools and technologies. He spends a lot of time evangelizing Microsoft technologies through presentations and talks and pushing the use of XML throughout the enterprise. What spare time he has, he spends with his wife, Lynda, and his two (soon to be three) little girls.

Yancey Jones is a full-time programmer with a small consulting firm in southern Ohio. He recently received his B.S. in Information Engineering Technology from the University of Cincinnati's College of Applied Science, where he graduated summa cum laude. Yancey has also done development work for various companies, including a leading airport consulting firm, a national provider of healthcare insurance, an online real estate agency, and a multimedia development company. When not at work Yancey enjoys spending time with his three daughters, playing EverQuest, and reading science fiction (in that order). Yancey can be reached at ybjones@msn.com.

Uday Kranti, NIIT, is an MCSD and MCDBA. He is currently employed with NIIT Ltd. as a consultant and has been with NIIT for the last three years. He has been involved in the development of applications in technologies such as Microsoft Visual Basic 5.0, Microsoft Visual Basic 6.0, Microsoft Visual InterDev, ASP, MS office automation, JavaScript, VBScript, XML, WML, VC++ (ATL), Flash + generator, Install Shield, C, C++ and COBOL. His responsibilities also include training development executives, managing projects, and instructionally and technically reviewing training material.

Rob Teixeira is a Florida-based consultant who has been involved with Windows development for over a decade. He has worked with every version of Visual Basic, including VB for DOS, and is pleased and amazed at how the language has evolved to fit the needs of the programming community. His favorite aspect of the job is teaching, and he has taught many private corporate classes, as well as several semesters at the University of Southern Florida, Tampa. Rob is looking forward to the new era of programming that will be ushered in by .NET. You can reach him at RobTeixeira@msn.com.

NIIT is a global IT solutions company that creates customized multimedia training products and has more than 2,000 training centers worldwide. NIIT has more than 4,000 employees in 37 countries and has strategic partnerships with a number of major corporations including Microsoft and AT&T.

Credits

Senior Acquisitions Editor
Sharon Cox

Senior Project Editor
Jodi Jensen

Technical Editors
Bill Evjen
Sundar Rajan
Shervin Shakibi

Development Editors
Sydney Jones
Anne L. Owen
Valerie Haynes Perry

Copy Editors
Kim Cofer
Sean Medlock
Nancy E. Sixsmith

Project Coordinator
Jennifer Bingham

Graphics and Production Specialists
Beth Brooks
Sean Decker
LeAndra Johnson
Kristin McMullan
Barry Offringa
Laurie Petrone
Jill Piscitelli
Betty Schulte

Quality Control Technicians
Laura Albert
David Faust

Proofreading and Indexing
TECHBOOKS Production Services

Special Help
Sara Shlaer
Jeremy Zucker

Cover Image
Murder By Design

Preface

Visual Basic .NET is one of four .NET languages that Microsoft is providing to build the latest in .NET components, applications, and services. This is the newest version of the language, following Visual Basic 6, and it's the greatest generational leap the language has taken in its history. Now, Visual Basic .NET is a true object-oriented language! With this new version, developers can build everything from ASP.NET applications to XML Web Services. Like all the other .NET languages, Visual Basic .NET can take advantage of everything the .NET Framework has to offer.

This book is written to show you what you need to know to get started right away building .NET applications. Visual Basic .NET has changed dramatically from its predecessor, and you will find everything here that you need to make the transition to the newest version of one of the world's most popular programming languages.

This book shows you exactly how to build everything from traditional console applications, ASP.NET applications, and XML Web Services. Along with these various applications, we deal with the issues of security, data access (ADO.NET), and the new Visual Studio .NET IDE, and we introduce you to everything you need to know to fully understand the .NET Framework.

Who Should Read This Book?

This book is aimed at Visual Basic 6 developers looking to make the transition to this new version of the language. The changes are many, and in some cases, they're quite dramatic. We spend a good deal of time alerting you to all that has changed and explaining what you need to know to make the transition to Visual Basic .NET.

This book can also help Active Server Pages (ASP) developers make the transition from VBScript to Visual Basic .NET and discover what it has to offer for developing ASP.NET pages. This new framework is going to shatter boundaries that have been the norm in Web application development in the past.

If you are new to developing, you should read this book to help you get started in the .NET Revolution!

What Hardware and Software Do You Need?

This book utilizes everything from the .NET Framework provided by Microsoft. You will need to download the latest version of the .NET Framework, as well as the latest version of Visual Studio .NET. Visual Studio .NET is the development environment that you use to build all the sample applications that are provided in the book. Please note, though, that it is possible to use Notepad and compile your code on the command line with the compilers that are provided with the framework, thus avoiding using Visual Studio .NET.

Hardware Specifics

Here are the minimum requirements for running the .NET Framework and Visual Studio .NET are

- ✦ Intel Pentium processor; 450 MHz or equivalent processor
- ✦ Microsoft Windows 2000, Windows NT 4.0 or Windows XP
- ✦ 128MB of available RAM
- ✦ 3GB of available disk space
- ✦ Color monitor capable of 800 × 600 resolution
- ✦ CD-ROM drive

Microsoft recommends the following requirements for running the .NET Framework:

- ✦ Intel Pentium processor; 733 MHz or equivalent processor
- ✦ Microsoft Windows 2000, Windows NT 4.0 or Windows XP
- ✦ 256MB of available RAM
- ✦ 3GB of available disk space
- ✦ Color monitor capable of 1024 × 768 resolution
- ✦ CD-ROM drive

Note   Please note that these are the minimum requirements. More capability is definitely better for using the .NET Framework and Visual Studio .NET, especially in terms of memory and processor speed. The authors recommend running .NET with 512MB of available RAM.

How This Book Is Organized

This book is divided into eight parts. The following sections explain what you'll find.

Part I: Introduction

Part I begins with an overview of the .NET Framework and what it's all about. Part I explains why Microsoft made this dramatic change in application development with the introduction of .NET. This part introduces you to the building blocks of the .NET Framework and everything you need to understand in order to get the overall picture. This section also reviews the main changes that have taken place between Visual Basic 6 and Visual Basic .NET.

Part II: The VB .NET Programming Language

Part II of the book covers the entire Visual Basic .NET language. The language has changed dramatically from its predecessor, and there are lots of new features that you'll want to use in your programming. This section starts with the basics of the language and works its way up to more complex issues, such as threading and COM interoperability.

Part III: Visual Studio .NET: The IDE for VB .NET

Part III introduces you to the new IDE — Visual Studio .NET. We advise everyone to use this environment when developing new .NET applications. Beyond the general introduction to the IDE, Part III also covers compiling and debugging, as well as customization and source control features.

Part IV: Data Access

Part IV of the book covers data access, one of the most important features in all application development projects. Applications are built on data, and this section shows you everything you need to know to access and manipulate your data using ADO.NET and XML.

Part V: Windows Forms

Part V is an explanatory section on Windows Forms and all the new features that have taken place with the introduction of Visual Basic .NET. There has been a lot of talk about all the changes that have taken place with ASP.NET and Web Services, and Windows Forms is a significant element. The chapters in this part discuss everything you need to know to create rich .NET Windows Forms.

Part VI: VB .NET and the Web

Part VI provides a thorough overview of how to use Visual Basic .NET for ASP.NET development. VBScript is no more; now Visual Basic .NET is one of the language options available for Web application development.

In Part VI, you're introduced to building Web applications in an object-oriented manner, with overviews and introductions to ASP.NET, User controls, security, and Web application configuration. ASP.NET has shattered a lot of the boundaries that existed in VB 6. Part VI helps you take these next steps in your Web applications.

Part VII: Web Services

Part VII explains everything you need to know to use Visual Basic .NET to build and utilize Web Services.

Appendixes

Appendix A reviews globalization and Appendix B helps you use the VB Migration Tool to upgrade your VB 6 code to .NET.

Conventions Used in This Book

The following sections explain the conventions used in this book.

Menu commands

When you're instructed to select a command from a menu, you see the menu and the command separated by an arrow symbol. For example, when you're asked to choose the Open command from the File menu, you see the notation File ⇨ Open.

Typographical conventions

We use *italic* type to indicate new terms or to provide emphasis. We use **boldface** type to indicate text that you need to type directly from the keyboard.

Code

We use a special typeface to indicate code, as demonstrated in the following example of Visual Basic .NET code:

```
<script language="VB" runat="server">
Sub SubmitBtn_Click(sender As Object, e As EventArgs)
    Page.DataBind
```

```
End Sub
</script>
```

This special code font is also used within paragraphs to make elements such as XML tags (`</name>`) stand out from the regular text.

Italic type is also used in code syntax definitions to indicate that you must substitute an actual parameter in place of the italicized word(s):

```
<asp:Label [attributes] >Hello World!</asp:Label>
```

Navigating This Book

This book is highly modular. You can read most of the chapters without reading earlier chapters. Part II goes over the Visual Basic .NET language in detail. If you are not familiar with this language, I suggest you read this section before reading through other sections of the book, but otherwise, you can read the book in just about any order you find most useful.

Icons appear in the text to indicate important or especially helpful items. Here's a list of the icons and their functions:

Tips provide you with extra knowledge that separates the novice from the pro.

Notes provide additional or critical information and technical data on the current topic.

Cross-Reference icons indicate places where you can find more information on a particular topic.

The Caution icon is your warning of a potential problem or pitfall.

Companion Web Site

This book provides a companion Web site where you can download the code from various chapters. All the code listings reside in a single WinZip file that you can download by going to www.HungryMinds.com/extras and selecting the **Visual Basic .NET Bible** link. After you download the file (VBNetBible.zip), and if you have WinZip already on your system, you can open it and extract the contents by double-clicking. If you don't currently have WinZip, you can download an evaluation version from www.WinZip.com.

When extracting the files, use WinZip's default options (confirm that the Use Folder Names option is checked) and extract the `VBNetBible.zip` file to a drive on your system that has about 3MB of available space. The extraction process creates a folder called `VBNetBible`. As long as the Use Folder Names option is checked in the Extract dialog box, an entire folder structure is created within the `VBNetBible` folder. You'll see folders arranged by chapter number, and some of those chapter folders will contain subfolders.

If you'd rather download just the code you need from a particular chapter — when you need it — simply click the separate chapter link on the Web site instead of downloading the entire Winzip file.

Further Information

You can find more help for specific problems and questions by investigating several Web sites. Microsoft's own .NET Web site is a good place to start:

`msdn.microsoft.com/net`

We also recommend visiting the following support sites:

`www.gotdotnet.com`

`www.asp.net`

`www.aspng.com`

`www.123aspx.com`

`www.ibuyspy.com`

`www.stlnet.org`

`www.computerways.com`

`www.vbxml.net`

Feel free to contact the authors with any questions or comments. We would really like to hear anything you have to say about the book (good or bad), so we can always make sure you have the information you need to write the best applications you can.

Bill Evjen — `evjen@yahoo.com`

Jason Beres — `jberes@jberes.com`

Acknowledgments

From Bill Evjen: Writing books may seem like a great solo effort, but the author is just one of the contributors to what is really a team project. This book would not have been possible without the hard work and dedication of Hungry Mind's Senior Acquisition Editor, Sharon Cox. The timeline and scope of the book seemed quite daunting at the beginning of the project, and I told her that I would applaud her if it all happened that fast. Well, Sharon, hopefully you can hear me applauding!

The other people that made my life easier include Jodi Jensen, Valerie Perry, and Sydney Jones. I also want to thank all the copy and technical editors who worked on this project to produce this great book.

Special thanks go to the Microsoft .NET team for answering questions when needed. From this group, I would like to point out Rob Howard for all he has done in promoting .NET outside of Redmond. I would also like to thank Michael Lane Thomas from Microsoft for his help and support.

Many thanks go to the other authors of this book. All of them are great programmers and writers and have worked hard to bring readers a one-stop solution to learning VB .NET and everything it has to offer.

Most importantly, I would like to thank my wife, Tuija. Without her and her continuing support, I would never have made it to this point in my life. Finally, I want to thank my two kids, Henri and Sofia — and thank you, Sofia, for not asking to play the "Chicken Game" on the computer more than 150 times.

From Jason Beres: I would first like to thank Hungry Minds for giving me the opportunity to contribute to this book. Although writing always seems like the hard part, the real work is done behind the scenes to make this book the best it can possibly be. I would like to thank Kim Cofer who made it seem like I have a handle on the English language, and Jodi Jensen for all her hard work and effort in making this book a reality.

I would also like to thank my friends at Computer Ways Inc. and Homnick Systems in Florida for their support and encouragement for my writing. And I can't forget everyone at Diversified Data in Michigan, where I got my start down this path more than 10 years ago.

Last, and most important, without the endless support of my Mom and Dad and my brothers, Justin, Jude, and Brett, I would never have been able to do this. Thanks for always being there no matter what.

Contents

Part II: The VB .NET Programming Language 33

Part IV: Data Access — 449

Chapter 21: Introduction to Data Access in .NET 451

Chapter 22: ADO.NET 471

Chapter 23: Data Access in Visual Studio .NET 503

Part V: Windows Forms   547

Introduction

Introduction to .NET

by Jason Beres

What is .NET? That is the question everyone has been asking since Microsoft announced this new idea at the PDC in 2000. If you were at Tech-Ed before the PDC, you might have heard about something called NGWS, or Next Generation Web Services. About year before that, there were rumors that Microsoft was inventing a new language called "Cool." Or was it a development platform? I am not sure; I didn't pay much attention to it way back then. I was more worried about how my Web sites were going to scale with COM components and ASP. Because Windows DNA was the end-all for building robust, *n*-tier, Web-based solutions, I figured that there would be nothing *that* revolutionary to replace all that amazing technology.

I was wrong.

It became obvious to me that .NET was "the next big thing" when I received a book from a friend about something called ASP+. Although it would be at least 12 months before ASP+ was available to the public, there was already a book about it. As I read the foreword of the book, which was written by the developers of ASP.NET at Microsoft, it seemed they knew from the beginning that there had to be a better way to write Web-based applications.

So while the paint was still wet on the latest release of ASP more than three years ago, they started to work on the next version, which is today called ASP.NET. I thought that these guys were pretty smart because they listened to and understood all the things that developers complained about, and they decided to do something about it.

That may have been the beginning of .NET; I am not sure. It's hard to say where it all began, but one thing is for certain: .NET is a massive collaboration between many product groups at Microsoft. From the COM+ team to Windows 2000 to Developer Tools to SQL Server, everything is somehow tied together through .NET.

When you read about .NET, there are .NET servers, .NET languages, .NET specifications, .NET platforms, and probably more items suffixed with ".NET" than you could have ever imagined. In this chapter, you will learn exactly what .NET is, and what it means to you. In this book, you will learn about Visual Basic .NET, or VB .NET, how it fits into .NET, and how you can use this new language and the tools that come with it to transform the way you write applications today.

.NET Defined

There have been many articles, books, and conversations on what .NET really means, and depending on whom you talk to, the answer could be different every time. In reality, the answer is very simple:

.NET is Microsoft's platform for building XML Web Services.

More important, however, is what .NET does for you. No matter what your definition of .NET might be, or what you read about in magazines and on the Web, the end goal is to provide a platform for developing and deploying Web-based services, or Web Services, in a simple, secure, and consistent manner. This does not mean, however, that you will only be writing web services for all of your new .NET coding. There are great technological achievements in .NET that go far beyond the ability to create and consume web services, and throughout this chapter and throughout this book this will become very clear.

Software as a service

The software as a service paradigm has become more popular over the past few years. I saw an interview with the CEO of Oracle on CNET sometime in 2000, and he mentioned that off-the-shelf software was a thing of the past. The only way to distribute software was through the Internet.

He was kind of right, but I wasn't really sure where he was coming from. The last time I tried to download the latest Oracle version from the Web, it took 27 hours, even on my high-speed 128KB Dual ISDN line. After the interview was finished, I realized that he was talking about selling services through the Internet, the types of services that portals offer. Yahoo, Excite, and the other major portal services all offer services for free, and eventually the technology will need to be in place so these companies can actually make money doing some of this cool stuff. I never understood how selling ads could generate profit on these huge sites, and in the end, that business model has proven not to work. So there needs to be a way to offer services and make money from those services.

The tools to develop for this type of technology may have existed years ago, but not in the mainstream. There needed to be a common method of communication between platforms and servers over the Internet, or the HTTP protocol, so that the consumer and the provider were not limited to what types of transactions could take place based on the type of hardware or operating system they were using. Or worse yet, what type of browser they were using.

Enter SOAP. The Simple Object Access Protocol, or SOAP, was the first effort in enabling a common and consistent mechanism for moving data over HTTP to any type of computer. SOAP is a set of XML specifications that describes how data can be sent and received over the Internet. A SOAP message contains information about itself. There are "parts" to a SOAP message that define the message content, the intent of the message, and how to send data back to the sender of the SOAP request.

In order to have a consistent and common platform for building Web Services, there needed to be a consistent and common way of communicating over the Internet. With SOAP, XML can be used to handle any request, and because XML is just a self-describing text file, any type of operating system or browser can consume SOAP-based Web Services.

The software as a service paradigm can be accomplished by using SOAP as the common protocol. Any Web site can offer a service, and the server on the back end can accept the request for that service through the standard port 80 that HTTP uses. It can then send the results back down to the client as XML, and the client can manipulate the data is it sees fit.

The .NET experience

While watching the marketing videos for .NET that Microsoft produces, you see a common message of the .NET experience: The .NET experience is from an end-user perspective. Granted, .NET experiences will be developed by people like you, but ultimately .NET is about getting information to the user in a cleaner, faster, more accessible fashion.

When the PocketPC was released, I thought it was the coolest thing on earth. The advertisements had visions of wireless access to the Internet, downloading movies, viewing contact information from my Outlook at the office, and all kinds of cool things that were so new and exciting I was amazed they were ready for prime time. In the end, it has taken about two years for any of those things to be ready for pre-game, let alone prime time; but with .NET, it is more evident that devices like the PocketPC can be useful devices. Up until now, I have used my PocketPC for reading e-Books. But with Web Services and the ASP.NET Mobile SDK, the Web sites that are being developed for full-scale browsers can now be scaled down to devices like the PocketPC and even the cell phone with little or no change to the underlying source code. Figure 1-1 gives you a visual representation of what the .NET experience could mean to you.

Once useful services can be consumed from many devices, the typical end user will find them more useful, and their acceptance will become more widespread. If you can offer customers the same solution that can be used in the office or on the cell phone when they are away from the office, I think the selling part will not be how much, but when.

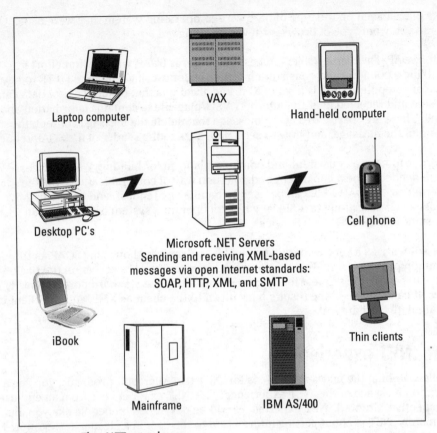

Figure 1-1: The .NET experience

From the developer viewpoint, the .NET experience is equally as important as the end user. If this stuff is going to be a pain in the neck to develop, you will never use it. The good news is that Microsoft realized that, and created the tools that developers like yourself need to create great Web- and Windows-based applications faster and easier than you have ever developed applications before.

With Visual Studio .NET, you have the tools you need to leverage your existing knowledge to create applications for .NET. Visual Basic has always been known for providing the developer with the most efficient IDE for developing Windows-based applications. With the introduction of Visual InterDev, Microsoft tried to create the same ease-of-use GUI for creating Web-based applications. If you have ever used InterDev, you know that it fell short in being the Rapid Application Development (RAD) tool for the Internet it was promised to be. Visual Studio .NET is truly RAD for the Internet. With the best of all worlds, from Visual Basic to InterDev to FrontPage to any other GUI tool you have ever used, Visual Studio .NET is a combination of everything great Microsoft has ever produced in a development environment.

If you are like me, you do not have time to learn brand new stuff. You have enough to do at work as it is, let alone learn about SOAP and how to make it work with .NET. With Visual Studio .NET, XML is "baked" in; it is everywhere, and you do not have to know where or how. Everything to the developer is transparent; all you need to worry about is coding. The plumbing that goes into marshalling XML from client to server is not an issue. I mentioned RAD for the Internet, but VS .NET is also RAD for the server. It is a unified environment for developing client- and server-based applications and services, in just about any language you choose to use, faster and easier than ever. And best of all, it is based on standards that are in place today, such as XML, SOAP, HTTP, and HTML.

Let's get into some details about what makes up .NET and how you can actually use it.

The .NET Framework

The .NET Framework is the plumbing of .NET. The framework provides the services necessary to develop and deploy applications for the loosely coupled, disconnected Internet environment. Figure 1-2 shows the key components of the framework.

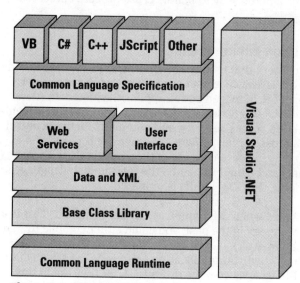

Figure 1-2: The .NET Framework

The two main components that make up the framework are the Common Language Runtime (CLR) and the Base Class Libraries (BCL). Everything in this book relates to the BCL. As a developer, you are coding against class libraries, which are all derived from the BCL. In the future, you may be using third-party class libraries that are not part of the base classes, but they must still be based on the CLR specifications.

Other core services include cross-language interoperability, security, managed execution, and the Common Type System (CTS). Together, these services make up the .NET Framework.

Common Language Runtime

The CLR is the foundation of the framework. The goals of the CLR are as follows:

✦ Secure and robust execution environment

✦ Simplified development process

✦ Multilanguage support

✦ Simplified management and simplified deployment

As I mentioned earlier, I always thought Windows DNA was the end-all to programming concepts. In my world of Windows only, I never ran into any interoperability issues, but in reality, that was a major drawback of the COM technology. COM provided a great way for applications to integrate, but each application had to supply the underlying infrastructure, and the objects had no direct interaction. This does not make for a very global concept. In order for any application to consume any type of service, there needed to be a better way to handle cross-process and cross-platform communication.

Secure and robust execution environment

The CLR provides the environment that manages code when it is executed. Code that runs inside the framework is known as managed code, which runs under certain rules provided by the CLR. Managed code supplies the Metadata (data about data) necessary for the CLR to provide services such as memory management, cross-language integration, code access security, and automatic lifetime control of objects. Code based on Microsoft Intermediate Language (MSIL) executes as managed code. Managed code is the core concept of the framework. With managed code, CPU-specific compilers can be built to handle the intermediate language's request. In this type of scenario, the COM model is outdated.

The MSIL is the output produced when .NET applications are compiled. This is a semi-new concept for VB developers. In the past, you could either compile to "native" code (which wasn't really native at all), or you could compile to P-Code, which was interpreted by the VB runtime when your application executed. The MSIL is the language that all of the .NET languages compile down to. After they are in this intermediate language, a process called Just-In-Time (JIT) compilation occurs when resources are used from your application at runtime. JIT allows "parts" of your application to execute when they are needed, which means that if something is never needed, it will never compile down to the PE (portable executable) file that is the native code. By using JIT, the CLR can cache the code that is used more than once and reuse it for subsequent calls, without going through the compilation process again. Figure 1-3 describes the JIT process.

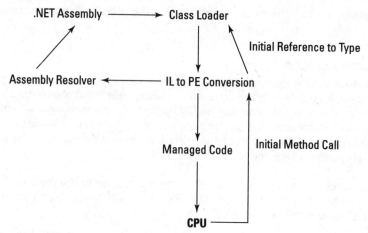

Figure 1-3: JIT compilation process

The JIT process enables a secure environment by making certain assumptions:

✦ Type references are compatible with the type being referenced.

✦ Operations are invoked on an object only if they are within the execution parameters for that object.

✦ Identities within the application are accurate.

By following these rules, the managed execution can guarantee that code being executed is type safe; the execution will only take place in memory that it is allowed to access. This is possible by the verification process that occurs when the MSIL is converted into CPU-specific code. During this verification, the code is examined to ensure it is not corrupt, it is type safe, and the code does not interfere with existing security policies that are in place on the system.

Exception handling

The framework supports Structured Exception Handling (SEH) across languages and processes. When you compile you applications, tables are created based on the methods in the classes and the errors that can occur are mapped to handlers in your method calls. In an unmanaged environment, errors were passed through HRESULTs and Boolean return values, and there was no common way to handle an error if it did occur. In .NET, error handing is integrated with the framework; it is not an afterthought.

Garbage collection

Object lifetime is managed through a process called garbage collection (GC). Through GC, released object references are automatically reclaimed by the operating system. In VB6, you had to explicitly set objects equal to nothing to ensure that memory was regained, and in C++, overlooking the release of objects caused nasty memory leaks. In .NET, memory management is automatic, and memory is reclaimed when the runtime decides that the object references are no longer in use.

Simplified development

Simplified development could mean a lot of different things to a lot of different people. In some cases, it could mean the computer reading your mind, saving you a lot of typing. In other cases, it could mean winning the lottery and retiring to a beach somewhere in the South Pacific, or maybe even a 20-million-dollar (586,440,010.07 Russian rubles) ride to Alpha, that cool space station circling the earth. In .NET, simplified development means more than any of that.

One of the biggest changes in the framework is the elimination of the registry. The registry is the enemy of all developers. GUIDs, IDL files, HRESULTs, and all other COM-related nightmares go away in .NET.

The good news is that you can still use your COM components in .NET.

Just like adding a reference to a DLL in VB6, you can add a reference to a COM DLL in .NET, and it will create a wrapper for the DLL that .NET can use to access the members in the DLL in a managed environment. You can also call .NET assemblies from an unmanaged environment, such as VB6. Both of these features require no additional work on your part, so you have a very flexible environment to use your existing code in a .NET application, or to use .NET assemblies in a VB6 environment.

Object-oriented features

A new concept to VB developers is object-oriented OO programming. OO simplifies the reuse and interoperability between components. The classes in the framework are all 100% object-oriented. The nice thing about the BCL being 100% OO is that you can implement OO features across languages, such as inheritance and polymorphism. This is a key factor to simplified development in large shops where some programmers might be using VB .NET, whereas other developers could be using COBOL .NET or C#. No matter what your language choice, the same features are available to everyone.

Visual Studio .NET

The Visual Studio .NET IDE is the best part of simplified development. The tools available in VS .NET allow you to quickly and easily develop large-scale, distributed applications. Chapter 17 delves into the features of the VS .NET IDE, and I am sure you will be very impressed as you start to use it in the real world to develop applications.

Multilanguage support

As of today, there are roughly 18 languages that the framework supports. From Pascal to COBOL to JScript, you have complete freedom over the tool you use to develop your applications. As the CLR gains more acceptance, there are sure to be additional languages added by other companies besides Microsoft.

Out of the VS .NET box, Microsoft ships with compilers for JScript .NET, Visual Basic .NET, C#, and Managed C++. .All of these languages are fully supported in the VS .NET IDE, and there are command-line compilers for each of these languages. The other 15 or so languages are coming from third parties, and they will either have their own IDE or they will hook into the VS .NET IDE.

How is this possible? The .NET Framework defines a subset of rules that defines how a language can be consumed by the CLR. The set of rules is called the Common Language Specification (CLS). The CLS allows any third party to create a language that can target the .NET Framework, as long as the specifications laid out in the CLS are followed.

Because of the CLS, language interoperability is possible. Components written in VB .NET can be consumed from C# or Managed C++, no extra code required. Passing strings from Managed C++ to VB .NET does not require strange conversion functions that will allow VB .NET to use the data. In .NET, a string is a string, the same in all languages. This is possible by the Common Type System employed by the framework, defined in the CLS.

The CTS defines what types are allowed to run inside the framework. A type can be defined as a value type or a reference type. Value types are stored as a representation of their value, such as data types. Reference types are stored as a reference to a type, such as an object. Reference types in .NET are based on the `System.Object` type, and they can be further broken down into classes that derive from the `System.Object` type. Figure 1-4 describes the CTS as implemented in the .NET Framework.

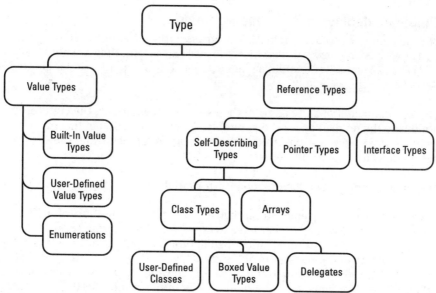

Figure 1-4: Common Type System

Debugging, tracing, and profiling are available across languages and across machines. Since these processes are based on what occurs at runtime, a single debugger can be used across all languages because it is interacting with the MSIL, not the specifics of a particular language.

All languages, no matter what developer-specific features the language offers, still have to compile down to the MSIL, and then get interpreted by the CPU-specific execution engine. This means that all languages are on a level playing field. All languages support the features of the .NET Framework, or else they would not be considered a .NET language.

There are language-specific features based on your language choice, which could include built-in functions, keywords, or language semantics, but when the file is built, it is built to the MSIL. The language-specific compiler will ensure that the code is type safe and will pass the MSIL verification process. This is not to say that certain rules cannot be broken, so you should investigate the CLS and CTS to make sure you are using CLS-compliant types.

VB .NET is an example of a language that has special features that other languages do not. Because there are roughly 12 million VB developers who have 10,000 times that in lines of code written, Microsoft has included an upgrade path for existing applications. This upgrade path uses a compatibility library that contains many of the same keywords and functions you are used to using in VB6. When you are coding in VB .NET, functions such as `MsgBox` are still valid, even though the BCL has a `MessageBox` class that is more robust and should be used. Essentially, the Msgbox function has a compatibility wrapper that actually calls the native BCL MessageBox class members.

Simplified deployment and management

The main unit of deployment in .NET is an assembly. Although assemblies can have a `.dll` extension (they can also have the .exe extension), they are not traditional COM DLLs. Assemblies contain a manifest, which is Metadata that is "emitted" to the callers of the assembly.

The Metadata contains the name of the assembly, the version, the culture, and optionally the public key for the assembly. Other information in the assembly includes what types are exported, what types are referenced, and the security permissions for each type.

Assemblies come in two flavors: *private* or *shared*.

Private assemblies are deployed through a "zero impact install" process. Zero impact install means that you no longer have to cross your fingers when you deploy an application, because the application installation is not affecting the state of the machine. Because the registry is not involved, you simply copy the files that your application needs to execute to the directory in which it will run. This process is called XCopy deployment. That's right, XCopy from the old DOS days. You are just copying files, and it all just works.

Shared assemblies are copied to the Global Assembly Cache (GAC). The GAC is a repository for files that can be shared across multiple processes. When assemblies are installed to the GAC, they are bound by version and policies defined by the publisher of the assembly.

Side-by-side DLLs, introduced with the release of Windows 2000, have come full circle in .NET. On the same machine, in the same exact process, DLLs with the same name but different versions can be executing at the same time.

Base Class Libraries

The .NET Framework provides a set of hierarchical objects, broken down by functionality, called the Base Class Libraries (BCL). The classes provide a set of common, object-oriented interfaces that can be accessed from any .NET language.

The BCL is divided into namespaces, which define a naming scheme for classes, such as webclasses, Data classes, Windows Forms, XML classes, Enterprise services, and System classes. By implementing a naming scheme, it is easy to categorize what functionality the classes are actually going to provide. For example, the Data classes provide the following top-level namespaces:

- ✦ System.Data
- ✦ System.Data.Common
- ✦ System.Data.OLEDB
- ✦ System.Data.SQLClient
- ✦ System.Data.SQLTypes

Each one of the data namespaces is broken down further into more granular classes, which define the methods, fields, structures, enumerations, and interfaces that are provided by each type.

The System class provides the base services that all languages would include, such as IO, arrays, collections, security, and globalization.

Because the class system is unified for all languages, it is not important what language is attempting to access the base classes, all of the features are available to all languages, and the way in which the code is implemented is the same. This actually makes it very easy to understand code written in other languages. Because the class libraries in use are the same, the only difference in the code is the semantics of each specific language. After you figure out those semantics, you can fully understand what is going on in other languages. Consider the differences in the following VB .NET and C# code.

```
' VB.NET CodePublic Sub ReadMyData(strCN As String)

    Dim strQuery As String = "SELECT * FROM Orders"
    Dim cn As New SqlConnection(strCN)
    Dim cmd As New SqlCommand(strQuery, cn)
```

```
        cn.Open()

        Dim rdr As SqlDataReader
        rdr = cmd.ExecuteReader()

        While rdr.Read()
            Console.WriteLine(rdr.GetString(1))
        End While

        rdr.Close()

        cn.Close()

    End Sub 'ReadMyData

    // C# Codepublic void ReadMyData(string strCN) {

        string strQuery = "SELECT * FROM Orders";
        SqlConnection cn = new SqlConnection(strCN);
        SqlCommand cmd = new SqlCommand(strQuery,cn);

        cn.Open();

        SqlDataReader rdr;
        rdr = cmd.ExecuteReader();

        while (rdr.Read()) {
            Console.WriteLine(rdr.GetString(1));
        }

        rdr.Close();

        cn.Close();
    }
```

The code is almost identical, except for the squiggly braces at the end of the lines of code in C#, and the way that variables are declared.

Visual Basic .NET

Now that you have an idea of what the .NET Framework is and the features it provides, what does this mean to you as a VB .NET developer? The key components to VB .NET that will make your life as a developer easier are the language innovations, RAD features, the new forms models for the Web-based applications and Windows-based applications, and most importantly the ability to create Web Services.

Language innovations

VB .NET is finally a first-class language. Every feature that is provided by the framework is available in VB .NET. VB .NET is a fully object-oriented language, providing inheritance, polymorphism, encapsulation, overloading, and overriding. With structured exception handling, there is a clean and consistent method of handling errors not only within a method, but also in a calling chain of multiple methods, and even across components written in other languages.

RAD features

The VS .NET tool provides the most RAD tool ever developed to assist you in every possible way while writing code. With improved designers, server explorers, data designers, and XML designers, you have all the external tools at your fingertips to write client- and server-based applications. All of this without having to learn anything new, because the VS .NET IDE will be familiar to you if you have used any of the previous VB versions, or even Visual InterDev. IDE features such as auto complete and auto-list members have been improved to make is easier than ever to verify your code as you are developing.

Web Forms

Web Forms allow the development of scalable Web-based applications in a familiar VB-like IDE. Features such as code behind minimize the spaghetti code produced by Visual InterDev, and with down-level browser support, no special code is needed to target specific browser types or versions. The IDE is the same for Windows-based applications, so all of the features available to developing Windows-based applications are available when building Web-based applications.

Web Services

By prefixing a method with the `<webmethod>` identifier, which is an example of attribute-based programming, you have just created a Web Service callable method. The underlying plumbing is handled by the IDE, and deployment is as easy as copying a file to the Web server. Creating a Web Service is as easy as creating any other type of application.

Windows Forms

Windows Forms are a rewritten forms engine targeted specifically for the .NET platform. The same classes that are used in VB .NET are shared across all languages, and Windows Forms can even run as a semi-trusted or fully trusted browser component. So who needs applets!

Summary

As you can see, .NET has a lot to offer, not only from a framework standpoint, but also from a tools standpoint. By taking advantage of features of the Common Language Runtime, you have the ability to write applications that are object-oriented to the core, and that can interact with any other .NET application, written in any of the 18 or so .NET languages. .NET is truly a revolution in the way VB developers like you can write code, not only in a "Next Generation" fashion, but also faster than before because of the robust toolset provided by Microsoft. It is a very exciting time, and by reading this book, you will have a solid foundation on which to proceed in your next .NET application.

✦   ✦   ✦

VB6 and VB .NET Differences

by Jason Beres

Visual Basic .NET is the most exciting upgrade to the Basic language since the GW-Basic upgrade to Visual Basic 1.0. As with anything brand new, there will be changes that are made that are supposed to make you life easier, but seem to make it harder in the beginning. This will be the case for most of you when moving to VB .NET. The reason for this, among others, is the shift not only to a new language, but also to a new platform in the .NET Framework. Everything that you learned over the past 4 or 5 years with Windows DNA, COM+, and ASP will all shift to this new way of writing applications. When I first looked at VB .NET, it seemed strange and didn't make sense; I was still thinking like a VB6 developer. I didn't understand why all the samples seemed to be console applications; I never did those in VB6. I had a hard time with the new idea of classes, and CodeBehind when it came to where all of my code was going. I was worried about learning SOAP and XML, since that is everywhere in .NET. But like anything else, I had to start somewhere. So by first understanding the changes that were made to the language, and then writing some small applications, I soon realized that VB .NET was the coolest thing since sliced bread. This is where we start in this chapter.

As you read through this book, you will see that there are definitely some changes in the way the VB code looks. Once you start coding, you will quickly see that this is not a big deal. The syntax changes make sense, and with features like auto complete, auto-list members, and dynamic help, writing the code is easier than ever. The outdated or unused statements and functions, and statements that look the same but mean something different, are the first things you will need to fully understand.

Data Type Changes

The .NET Framework has classes that define the Common Type System that allow for data types to be consistent across applications written in different .NET languages. Because of this, Visual Basic needed to change the types of data it supports and the numeric ranges of existing data types. The following section covers the differences.

 Cross-Reference   To get a full explanation of all data types and their ranges, see Chapter 5.

Variant not supported

In VB6, the `Variant` data type was the default universal data type; this was replaced by the `Object` data type in VB .NET. The default value for `Object` data types is `Nothing`, whereas the default value for `Variant` data types was `Empty`.

```
Dim var1 as Variant
```

Changes to:

```
Dim var1 as Object
```

Integer and Long

In VB6, the `Integer` data type was a 16-bit number, ranging in value from –32,767 to 32,767. The `Short` data type replaces `Integer` as a 32-bit number in VB .NET, and the `Integer` data type now ranges from –2,147,483,648 to 2,147,483,647. The `Long` data type is now a 64-bit number. Using `Integer` for 32-bit operations is the most efficient data type.

```
Dim X as Integer
Dim Y as Long
```

Changes to:

```
Dim X as Short
Dim Y as Integer
```

Currency not supported

The `Currency` data type is changed to decimal in VB .NET. Decimal is more accurate for rounding numbers, so the `Decimal` data type was created to handle currency operations. `Currency` was a 64-bit number, with 4 digits to the right of the decimal place. The new `Decimal` data type is a 96-bit signed integer and can have up to 28 digits to the right of the decimal place.

```
Dim X as Currency
```

Changes to:

```
Dim X as Decimal
```

Date changes

The `Date` data type is now a 64-bit integer, whereas in VB6 it was 64-bit double. To accommodate the code used in the `Date` data type, you have the `ToOADate` and `FromOADate` functions to convert between `Double` and `Date` data types.

```
Dim X as Double
```

Changes to:

```
Dim X as Double, Y as Date
Y = X.ToOADate
```

Strings

Fixed-length strings are no longer supported. SDK documentation states that this functionality will be added in future versions. There is a compatibility layer that allows for fixed-length strings, but they are not directly supported by the CLR.

DefType not supported

The `DefType` statement, which gives a default type for all variables declared without a type, is no longer supported. `DefInt`, `DefStr`, `DefBool`, and `DefLng` are no longer supported.

VarPtr, StrPtr, ObjPtr

These functions, which return the integer addresses of variables in API calls, are no longer supported. The `AddrOfPinnedHandle` method of the `GCHandle` class can provide similar functionality.

Arrays

One of the biggest issues when Microsoft announced the language changes in VB .NET was the lower-dimension arrays. From the beginning, Visual Basic has always allowed the lower bound of an array to be either 0 or 1. The `Option Base` statement, which is no longer supported, dictated whether all arrays should be treated as 0-based or 1-based. In the end, Microsoft decided that all arrays will have a default lower bound of 0, meaning that existing code using the `Option Base 1` statement will need to be revisited to ensure that there is no data loss or corruption, because the size of the array will be different.

Arrays cannot be fixed

Arrays cannot be declared as fixed sizes by specifying the lower and upper bounds at design time. You now declare just the upper bound to the array, with zero being the default lower bound.

```
Dim x(0 to 5) as string ' 6 item array
```

Changes to:

```
Dim x(5) as string ' 6 item array
```

Or

```
Dim X as String = new String(5) ' 6 item array
```

Option Base not supported

The `Option Base` statement to specify the lower bounds for all arrays in a module or form is no longer supported. The default lower bound for all arrays is zero.

ReDim changed

The `ReDim` statement cannot be used in the declaration of an array variable. In VB .NET, you declare an array using `Dim`, and then use the `ReDim` statement to alter the bounds of the array.

The Value of True

In VB6, the value of true is –1. This is the same in VB .NET, however, in the Common Language Runtime; the value of true is equal to 1. When passing Boolean variables between languages in the .NET Framework, –1 will be true in VB, and 1 in all other languages.

Operators

Some of the most exciting language changes in VB .NET have come in the category of operators. Table 2.1 lists the new assignment operators, which will mean less typing for you when you are using operators. Be sure the study Chapter 5, which covers in detail all of the operators and has great examples of what you can do with them.

EQV

The `EQV` operator is replaced with the "=" assignment operator.

Short-circuiting

The `AndAlso` and `OrElse` operators have been added to handle short-circuiting. All other operators will remain the same. In short circuiting, if the first part of an expression returns false, then the remainder of the expression is ignored, and false is returned.

```
Dim X as Integer = 5
Dim Y as Integer = 6
Dim Z as Integer = 7
ret = X > Y AndAlso Z > Y ' Return False, 5 is not greater than 6
```

Assignment

VB .NET offers some cool new assignment operators.

```
Dim intX as Integer
intX = intX + 1
```

Can now be changed to:

```
Dim intX as Integer
intX += 1
```

Table 2-1 lists other assignment operators that will save you a few lines of code.

Table 2-1 New Assignment Operators	
Operator	**Action**
+=	Addition and concatenation
-=	Subtraction
*=	Multiplication
/= and \=	Division
^=	Exponentiation
&=	String concatenation

User Defined Types

User defined types are no longer supported in VB .NET. They are replaced with structures, which have similar syntax but much greater power and flexibility.

```
Public Type MyCust
    strName as String
    strEMail as string
End Type
```

Changes to:

```
Public Struct MyCust
    Private strName as String
    Private strEMail as String
End Struct
```

Null Values

Null propagation is not supported. Value types that are null are passed to functions as the `DBNull` data types. To test for null values, the `IsNull` statement is no longer supported. It is replaced with the `DBNull` statement.

```
If IsNull(field) then ..
```

Changes to:

```
If IsDBNull(field) then ...
```

The `IsEmpty` statement is not supported. In VB6, the values `NULL` and `Empty` could be used to check for a variable that has not been initialized or for a variable that contains no data. `NULL` and `Empty` are no longer a valid means to check for this information, making `IsEmpty` obsolete. The `nothing` keyword should now be used to check for these conditions.

Variable Scoping

Variables can be declared within statement blocks and are only available within that block. In this example, the variable `intX` is only available within the `If...End If` statement, whereas the variable `intY` is available to the whole procedure.

```
Private Sub Test()
    Dim intY as Integer
    If intY > 5 then
            Dim intX as Integer
            ' Do Something
    End if
    IntX = 5
            ' Causes an error. intX cannot be used outside of the If block.
    intY = 10
            ' OK.  intY is not decalred within the If block.
End Sub
```

Variable Initialization

Variables can now be initialized to a value on the same line in which they are declared.

```
Dim intX as integer
intX = 5
```

Can be changed to:

```
Dim intX as Integer = 5
```

Instantiating objects can also be done with the `New` keyword on the same line as the object declaration. This behaves exactly opposite of VB6, where it was frowned upon because of the way in which COM had to ensure that an object was created before it could use its properties and methods.

```
Dim cn As Connection
Set Cn = New Connection
```

Can be changed to:

```
Dim cn as SQLConnection = New SQLConnection ' more efficient
```

You can now declare multiple variables on the same line, with a single type. Consider the following code:

```
Dim str1, str2, str3 as String
```

In VB6, the variables `str1` and `str2` would be `Variant` data types, and `str3` would be a `String` data type. In VB .NET, all of the variables will be of the `String` data type.

ParmArray Variables

`ParmArray` variables are not passed `ByRef` anymore. `ParmArray`s are passed by value, and the receiving function can modify the values of the `ParmArray` as it would a regular array.

Language Issues

One of the biggest challenges when upgrading to VB .NET will be learning the replacements for existing functions. This section covers specific functions that are replaced with newer syntax. Chapter 8 goes into detail on working with dates and times, which is very important to understand because they are common functions you will work with all the time.

IsMissing

The `IsMissing` function is no longer supported and should be replaced with the `IsNothing` statement.

Date$ and Time$

The `Date$` and `Time$` functions in VB6 to return a string representation of the current date or time are replaced by the `DateString` and `TimeString` methods in VB .NET.

Atn, Sgn, and Sqr

The `Atn`, `Sgn`, and `Sqr` functions are replaced by the `System.Math` methods `Atan`, `Sign`, and `Sqrt`.

MsgBox

The `MsgBox` function is replaced with the `Show` method, the `MessageBox` class.

```
MsgBox "VB6 is Great"
```

Changes to:

```
MessageBox.Show "VB.NET is Greater"
```

Although `MsgBox` is still supported through the compatibility library, you should consider using the new `MessageBox` classes since the `MsgBox` function is simply a wrapper which calls the `MessageBox` classes.

Procedures

Because VB .NET fully supports object-oriented features, there have been critical changes in procedure scope, returning values, and the types of procedures you can use. Beyond the changes mentioned here, Chapter 8 and Chapter 14 will give you the full explanation on what you can do with procedures in VB .NET.

Calling procedures

Calling procedures, either subs or functions, now require parentheses for the argument list, even if there are no arguments.

```
Sub Test()
        ' code
End Sub
Call Test
```

Changes to:

```
Call Test()
```

Static procedures

Static procedures are no longer supported. If you use static procedures, you should change them to regular subprocedures and define the variables within the static procedure as `Static`.

```
Static Sub Test()
  Dim X as integer
End Sub
```

Changes to:

```
Sub Test()
  Static X as Integer
End Sub
```

ByVal, ByRef, and As Any

The default behavior of `ByVal` and `ByRef` has changed. In VB6, the default for passing parameters was `ByRef`. In VB .NET, `ByVal` is the default mechanism for passing variables to procedures. The `As Any` statement in the `Declare` statement for API calls is not supported.

Properties

The syntax for declaring property procedures has been changed to accommodate the object-oriented features in VB .NET. Chapter 14 has real-world examples of using properties and defines the specific syntax that you will need to implement.

Let, Get, and Set

The `Let` keyword is no longer supported. When using `Set` and `Get`, the scope of the property must be the same in VB .NET. In VB6, the `Get` could have been scoped as `Private`, whereas the `Set` could have been scoped as `Public`. This is easily noticed in the way that the property must be declared.

```
Friend Property strName() As String

    Get

    End Get
```

```
      Set(ByVal Value As String)

      End Set

   End Property
```

Default properties

Default properties for any object are no longer supported. In VB6, custom classes could have default properties, and visual objects, such as text boxes, list boxes, and combo boxes could have default properties.

```
strName = Text1 ' Text1 is the name of a textbox on a form
Me.Caption = "Hello World"
```

Changes to:

```
strName = Text1.Text ' must use the Text property
Me.Text = "Hello World"
```

> **Note**   Default properties can still be created. Refer to Chapter 14 for information on how this can be accomplished.

Control Flow

The changes in control flow are not that drastic. The biggest change is the GoSub keyword, but because most developers have not used this since VB 2.0, it will not really be missed that much. The Return statement is the new way to return values from function procedures.

While...Wend

The While...Wend construct is no longer supported. It is replaced with While...End While.

```
While X < 5
     'Code
Wend
```

Changes to:

```
While X < 5
     'Code
End While
```

GoSub...Return

The `GoSub` branching to another subroutine within a procedure is no longer supported. The following code will no longer be valid.

```
Sub Test
     Return
End Sub
Sub Test2
     GoSub Test
End Sub
```

Return

The `Return` statement now returns control back to the caller of the function. If the function is of a certain type, it can return the value back to the caller also.

```
Private Function GetNames() as String
     Dim strName as string
     strName = "Seven Of Nine"
     GetNames = strName
End Function
```

Changes to:

```
Private Function GetNames() as String
     Dim strName as string
     strName = "Seven Of Nine"
     Return strName
End Function
```

Forms-based Application Changes

Windows Forms applications have a completely different subsystem in which forms are drawn on the page, making it necessary to remove some of the functionality you might be used to for painting information on a form. One if the best new features in VB .NET is the IDE for adding menus to forms, and the printing controls that allow full print preview in Windows Forms applications.

PrintForm

The `PrintForm` method is no longer supported. The .NET Framework has a new printing subsystem, with features such as Print Preview, which allow a more robust handling of screen shots and forms printing.

Circle, Cls, PSet, Line, and Point

These methods are no longer supported in VB .NET. The graphics methods of VB6 are replaced with the System.Drawing namespace, which uses the new GDI+ classes for drawing.

Caption property

The Caption property of label controls and forms is no longer supported. The Text property replaces the Caption property.

```
Label1.Caption = "VB.NET"
Form1.Caption = "My Form"
```

Changes to:

```
Label1.Text = "VB.NET"
Form1.Text = "My Form"
```

Twips on forms

The twips measurement in forms is replaced by pixels.

Fonts

Fonts in VB6 forms could be any font supported by Windows. Windows Forms support only True Type or Open Type fonts.

Control arrays

Multiple controls with the same name, but a different Index property could share the same event procedures in VB6. In VB .NET, controls cannot be grouped in arrays, but the same procedure can be used for multiple controls with the Handles keyword.

Context menus and main menus

In VB6, a menu added to a form could be used for both the main menu on the top of a form and a context menu that appeared with the right-click action. In VB .NET, you can have a menu be a main menu or a context menu, but not both.

DDE

DDE is no longer supported. Other means of communication between applications can be accomplished using OLE, Web Services, or in-process components.

Clipboard object

The Clipboard class replaces the Clipboard object.

Controls changes

When you create a new Windows Forms application, you will notice some new and exciting controls in the Toolbox. The controls listed in this section are no longer supported, and they will not appear in the Toolbox.

OLE control

The OLE Container control that allowed the adding of OLE objects to forms is no longer supported.

Image control

The Image control is replaced with the PictureBox control in VB .NET.

Line control

The Line control has been replaced by GDI+ Draw methods.

Shape control

The Shape control has been replaced by GDI+ Draw methods.

Application Types

Many of the templates that you might have been used to in previous VB versions no longer exist, and some application types do not even have an upgrade path.

Webclasses

Webclass applications are no longer supported. Web Forms applications should be used to write Web-based applications. The power and functionality provided in using Web Services and ASP.NET applications will give you much more flexibility than programming Webclasses applications ever did

ActiveX documents

ActiveX document applications are no longer supported. You can, however, write Windows Forms applications that run through the browser as safe code and mimic ActiveX documents, yet you will have the full Windows Forms object model and controls support.

DHTML applications

DHTML applications are no longer supported. Web Forms applications should be used to write Web-based applications.

User controls

User controls created in VB6 are usable in VB .NET, but there is no design time support for editing or modifying the controls.

Property pages

Property pages are no longer supported and there is no upgrade path. This is not a very big deal, since property pages were used in ActiveX control applications, and in .NET, you will be creating user controls instead of ActiveX controls.

Data Access

ADO.NET is the new library for accessing data from any source. More than just an upgrade, it is an actual rewrite from the previous version of ADO that you might have used. A big issue for upgrading applications is the elimination of data binding. When performing an upgrade using the Upgrade Wizard, you will be notified of code that cannot be migrated if you are using data binding of any sort.

Data Binding, RDO, and ADO

Data Binding to an RDO or ADO data source is no longer supported. The following code is obsolete.

```
Text1.DataField = "Customer_Name"
Set Text1.Datasource = rs
```

There are extremely powerful and more advanced data binding capabilities in VB .NET, and they are just implemented differently.

DAO

Data Access Objects is not supported in VB .NET. Because you can access data through ADO.NET, the loss of DAO is not earth shattering. It will just mean that you need to convert DAO code to ADO.NET code.

Debugging

Visual Basic has always been at the forefront in support for debugging. The
`Debug.Print` method has been replaced, but this is minor compared to all of
the new features that make debugging easier than ever. Chapters 18 and 42 cover
debugging techniques for Windows-based as well as Web-based applications.

Debug.Print

`Debug.Print` is replaced by the `Debug.Write` or the `Debug.Writeline` methods.
The `Debug` class provides a complete set of methods and properties that help
debug your code.

```
Debug.Print Err.number
```

Changes to:

```
Debug.Writeline Err.Number ' includes Line Feed
```

Or

```
Debug.Write Err.Number ' does NOT include Line Feed
```

Debug.Assert

The `Debug.Assert` method is no longer supported. It is replaced with the `Assert`
and `Fail` methods of the `Debug` class.

Summary

This chapter looked at the differences of VB6 and VB .NET. Most of the major
changes are probably seldom-used function calls, but when upgrading, you will
need to know why your code is "broken."

VB .NET includes the Microsoft.VisualBasic namespace, which includes most of the
legacy VB functions and keywords that are still supported in .NET, but you should
avoid using the Microsoft.VisualBasic namespace in favor of the System namespaces
that will make your code compatible across all .NET languages.

✦   ✦   ✦

The VB .NET Programming Language

Object-Oriented Programming and VB .NET

by Jason Beres

✦ ✦ ✦ ✦

In This Chapter

Encapsulation

Inheritance

Polymorphism

✦ ✦ ✦ ✦

Visual Basic has always been looked at as a toy language by C and C++ developers. Their main gripe was that VB was not an OO (object-oriented) programming language. VB was a Rapid Application Development (RAD) tool, and good for creating demo versions and quick user interface examples, but it was not the right tool to actually write code with. With the introduction of Visual Basic .NET, this is no longer the case. VB .NET is now a full-fledged first-class player in the world of OO programming languages. Previous versions of VB did have some OO concepts, but these concepts come full circle in .NET and allow VB developers to take full advantage of OO development techniques.

True OO languages support *encapsulation*, *inheritance*, and *polymorphism*. In this chapter and throughout this book, you are introduced to these concepts and how you can correctly implement them in your applications. I think you will see that even though these are new concepts to VB, you will recognize the concepts and be able to get up and running with OO very quickly.

Cross-Reference To fully understand the concepts in this chapter, see Chapter 8, which discusses procedures and functions, and Chapter 14, which explains classes, fields, members, properties, and scope.

Encapsulation

Through encapsulation, you can conceal the actual implementation of properties and methods in your classes. The end goal is to be able to give the user interface a set of statements that it must execute, while hiding the behind-the-scenes details. By implementing encapsulation, you can hide the implementation details, and modify code without affecting or modifying the front-end application. In Listing 3-1, three fields are declared as private. When the Contact class is instantiated from the client application, the private fields are not accessible. The properties are accessible, and the client can set and retrieve values for the private fields through the public properties. There are also three read-only properties, which return to the client different flavors of the FirstName and LastName properties. By hiding the actual data stored in the private fields, you are encapsulating the implementation of the data. Users do not care what happens to the data or how is stored, they just know there is a FirstName, LastName, and Email field they have access to.

Listing 3-1: **Encapsulation Example**

```
Public Class Contact

    Private _FirstName As String
    Private _LastName As String
    Private _Email As String

    Public Property FirstName()
      Get
          Return _FirstName
      End Get

      Set(ByVal Value)
        _FirstName = Value
      End Set
End Property

    Public Property Email()
      Get
          Return _Email
      End Get

      Set(ByVal Value)
        _Email = Value
      End Set
End Property

    Public Property LastName()
      Get
          Return _LastName
      End Get

      Set(ByVal Value)
        _LastName = Value
      End Set
End Property
```

```
Public ReadOnly Property NameHi()
    Get
        Return _FirstName.ToUpper & " " & _LastName.ToUpper
    End Get
End Property

Public ReadOnly Property NameLo()
    Get
        Return _FirstName.ToLower & " " & _LastName.ToLower
    End Get
End Property

Public ReadOnly Property NameProper()
Get
 Return StrConv(_FirstName, VbStrConv.ProperCase) & " " _
    & StrConv(_LastName, VbStrConv.ProperCase)
End Get   End Property

End Class
```

From the client application, when the `Contact` class is instantiated, the `FirstName`, `LastName`, and `Email` properties can be set and retrieved, and the read-only properties `NameHi`, `NameLo`, and `NameProper` returns the private fields in various forms. The following code demonstrates using the `Contact` class from a client application:

```
' Create an instance on the Contact class
Dim c As New Contact()

' set properties
c.FirstName = "Luke"
c.LastName = "Skywalker"

Console.WriteLine(c.NameLo)
' Returns luke skywalker

Console.WriteLine(c.NameHi)
' Returns LUKE SKYWALKER

Console.WriteLine(c.NameProper)
' Returns Luke Skywalker
```

Inheritance

Inheritance is the ability to create new classes based on an existing class. The new class inherits all the properties, methods, and events of the base class, and can be customized with additional properties and methods. Inheritance is used everywhere in the .NET Framework. Every time you create an object, you are inheriting from a base class and using its properties and methods.

Note   Chapter 27 dicusses visual inheritance, which is inheriting forms and controls. This section covers inheritance from a class standpoint.

The goal behind inheritance is to provide a framework for a class that you can use and modify. When members of a class are defined, they can specifically be coded to allow for inheritance. Two terms that are used when referring to classes used in inheritance are *derived* and *base*. The base class is the original class, or the framework class. A derived class is a class based on a base class. The Inherits keyword used inside a class derives, or inherits, the functionality of that class.

In .NET, all classes are inheritable by default unless they are defined with the NotInheritable keyword. In the Contact class you created earlier, the class was defined as

```
Public Class Contact
```

To make the class not inheritable, you would define it as follows:

```
Public NotInheritable Class Contact
```

By defining the Contact class as NotInheritable, it does not affect the client-side declaration. It does, however, affect how the class can be used in other classes. An instance of Contact can be created with the New keyword, but a class cannot use the Inherits keyword to implement the Contact class functionality.

The exact opposite of the NotInheritable keyword is the MustInherit keyword. If you define a class with the MustInherit keyword, it cannot be created with the New keyword. The base class can only be inherited from other classes. If the Contact class was defined as MustInherit, as the following code demonstrates:

```
Public MustInherit Class Contact
```

Then the following code from the client application would be invalid:

```
Dim c as New Customer
```

This means that in order to get to any of the members in the Contact class, you need to create another class, and using the Inherits keyword, inherit the Contact class.

To make sense of inheritance, you can expand on the Contact class that you created earlier. Imagine that you are creating a contact management application for your company. This application needs to track contacts. There are several types of contacts, and based on the type of contact, you may need to implement different functionality. You have already created the Contact class, which has information that all contacts require, such as a first name, a last name, and an e-mail address. You now need to implement code to handle employees and customers.

Employees and customers share the same base information that any contact would have, but other implementation details are specific to each type, such as salary and Social Security number for an employee, or category for a customer. You could go ahead and just add public functions to the Contact class that will handle the different types on contacts, but that will make it unmanageable and not reusable.

The base class Contact has already been debugged and you know it works; you just need to inherit its functionality in other classes, and extend the functionality of those classes for your specific needs. In Listing 3-2, you can see the additional classes that have been added to Listing 3-1, and the use of the Inherits keyword.

Listing 3-2: **Customer and Employee Classes**

```
Public Class Customer

  ' Use the Inherits keyword to inherit the
  ' base class Contact

  Inherits Contact

  Private _Category As String

  Public Property Category() As String
    Get
       Return _Category
    End Get

    Set(ByVal Value As String)
       _Category = Value
    End Set
  End Property

End Class

Public Class Employee

  Inherits Contact

  Private _Salary As Double
  Private _SSN As String

  Public Property Salary() As Double
    Get
       Return _Salary
    End Get

    Set(ByVal Value As Double)
       _Salary = Value
```

Continued

Listing 3-2 *(continued)*

```
      End Set
   End Property

   Public Property SSN() As String
      Get
         Return _SSN
      End Get

      Set(ByVal Value As String)
         _SSN = Value
      End Set
   End Property

End Class
```

From the client code, you do not create an instance of Contact class anymore. Because the Employee class and the Customer class inherit the Contact class, all of the methods and properties are available to you when you declare new instances of those classes. From the client, your code looks like the following:

```
'   Create an instance on the Employee class
'   which inherits all of the Contact class
'   methods and properties

Dim emp As New Employee()

' set properties
emp.FirstName = "Luke"
emp.LastName = "Skywalker"
emp.Salary = 30000.5
emp.SSN = "111-11-1111"
'
Console.WriteLine(emp.NameLo)
' Returns luke skywalker

Console.WriteLine(emp.NameHi)
' Returns LUKE SKYWALKER

Console.WriteLine(emp.NameProper)
' Returns Luke Skywalker

Console.WriteLine(emp.Salary)
' Returns 30000.5

Console.WriteLine(emp.SSN)
' Returns 111-11-1111
```

```
'   Create an instance on the Customer class
'   which inherits all of the Contact class
'   methods and properties

Dim cust As New Customer()
cust.Category = "Buyer"
cust.FirstName = "Jabba"
cust.LastName = "The Hut"
'
Console.WriteLine(cust.NameLo)
' Returns jabba the hut

Console.WriteLine(cust.NameHi)
' Returns JABBA THE HUT

Console.WriteLine(cust.NameProper)
' Returns Jabba The Hut

Console.WriteLine(cust.Category)
' Returns Buyer
```

Polymorphism

Polymorphism is the capability to have methods and properties in multiple classes that have the same name and can be used interchangeably, even though each class implements the same properties or methods in different ways. In VB .NET, this is known as *inheritance-based polymorphism*. It is easy to get inheritance and polymorphism mixed up because they appear to be very similar, and they actually are. The idea behind polymorphism is that when inheriting classes, you may need to override the functionality of a method or property.

In the Contact class, it would defeat the concept of reusability if you had to define a SaveContact, SaveEmployee, and SaveCustomer method. Using polymorphism, each class can implement its own Save method, and the compiler can figure out which one to use based on the members in the derived class. You may also want to have specific code to handle the LastName or Email property. Say, for example, that all employees must have an e-mail that ends with "@msn.com". Instead of adding specific code to the base class Contact, which handles the Email property, you could override the functionality of the Email property in the Employee class.

The following list gets you up to speed on some of the syntax you can use when implementing polymorphism:

✦ Overridable: Allows a property or method in a class to be overridden in a derived class.

✦ Overrides: Overrides an Overridable property or method defined in the base class.

✦ NotOverridable: Prevents a property or method from being overridden in an inheriting class. Public methods are NotOverridable by default.

✦ MustOverride: Requires that a derived class override the property or method. When the MustOverride keyword is used, the method definition consists of just the Sub, Function, or Property statement. No other statements are allowed, and specifically there is no End Sub or End Function statement. MustOverride methods must be declared in MustInherit classes.

Cross-Reference   Chapter 14 goes into greater detail on these concepts.

In Listing 3-3, you add a Save method to the base class Contact. You also add a Save method to the Employee class and the Customer class. The Save method in the Contact class is defined as Overridable. The Save methods in the Employee and Customer classes are defined as Overrides. This ensures that no matter what type of object is created — Contact, Customer, or Employee — when the Save method is called, the correct code executes. The Email property in the Contact class is defined as Overridable. By implementing an Email property in the Employee class, you can write code specific to employees, and not affect any other type of contact. You also see how to handle the case where the e-mail address might be incorrect.

Note   To learn more about exceptions, see Chapter 12.

Listing 3-3 Polymorphism Example

```
Public Class Contact

    Private _FirstName As String
    Private _LastName As String
    Private _Email As String

    Public Property FirstName()
        Get
            Return _FirstName
        End Get

        Set(ByVal Value)
            _FirstName = Value
        End Set
    End Property

    Public Property LastName()
        Get
            Return _LastName
        End Get
```

```
                Set(ByVal Value)
                    _LastName = Value
                End Set
            End Property

        Public Overridable Property Email()
            Get
                Return _Email
            End Get
            Set(ByVal Value)
                _Email = Value
            End Set
        End Property

        Public ReadOnly Property NameHi()
            Get
                Return _FirstName.ToUpper & " " & _LastName.ToUpper
            End Get
        End Property

        Public ReadOnly Property NameLo()
            Get
                Return _FirstName.ToLower & " " & _LastName.ToLower
            End Get
        End Property

        Public ReadOnly Property NameProper()
            Get
                Return StrConv(_FirstName, VbStrConv.ProperCase) & " " _
                        & StrConv(_LastName, VbStrConv.ProperCase)
            End Get
        End Property

        Public Overridable Function Save() As String
            Return "Contact Saved"
        End Function

End Class

Public Class Customer

    Inherits Contact

    Private _Category As String

    Public Property Category() As String
        Get
            Return _Category
        End Get
```

Continued

Listing 3-3 *(continued)*

```
        Set(ByVal Value As String)
            _Category = Value
        End Set
    End Property
    Public Overrides Function Save() As String
        Return "Customer Saved"
    End Function

End Class

Public Class Employee

    Inherits Contact

    Private _Salary As Double
    Private _SSN As String
    Private _Email As String

    Public Property Salary() As Double
        Get
            Return _Salary
        End Get
        Set(ByVal Value As Double)
            _Salary = Value
        End Set
    End Property

    Public Property SSN() As String
        Get
            Return _SSN
        End Get

        Set(ByVal Value As String)
            _SSN = Value
        End Set
    End Property

    Public Overrides Property Email()
        Get
            Return _Email
        End Get
        Set(ByVal Value)
            ' Check the email address
            ' if it is incorrect, throw an exception
            If Right(Value, 8) <> "@msn.com" Then
                Throw New Exception("Invalid email address")
            Else
                _Email = Value
            End If
        End Set
    End Property
```

```
       Public Overrides Function Save() As String
            Return "Employee Saved"
       End Function

End Class
```

From the client, your code looks exactly the same as it did before, with the addition of the calling the Save methods and setting the value of the Email property in the Employee class that was created:

```
'  Create an instance on the Employee class
'  which inherits all of the Contact class
'  methods and properties

Dim emp As New Employee()

' set properties
emp.FirstName = "Luke"
emp.LastName = "Skywalker"
emp.Salary = 30000.5
emp.SSN = "111-11-1111"
emp.Email = "Test@msn.com"
MessageBox.Show(emp.Save())
' Returns "Employee Saved"

'
Console.WriteLine(emp.NameLo)
' Returns luke skywalker

Console.WriteLine(emp.NameHi)
' Returns LUKE SKYWALKER

Console.WriteLine(emp.NameProper)
' Returns Luke Skywalker

Console.WriteLine(emp.Salary)
' Returns 30000.5

Console.WriteLine(emp.SSN)
' Returns 111-11-1111

'  Create an instance on the Customer class
'  which inherits all of the Contact class
'  methods and properties

Dim cust As New Customer()
cust.Category = "Buyer"
cust.FirstName = "Jabba"
cust.LastName = "The Hut"
'
```

```
Console.WriteLine(cust.NameLo)
' Returns jabba the hut

Console.WriteLine(cust.NameHi)
' Returns JABBA THE HUT

Console.WriteLine(cust.NameProper)
' Returns Jabba The Hut

Console.WriteLine(cust.Category)
' Returns Buyer

MessageBox.Show(Cust.Save())
' Returns "Customer Saved"
```

Summary

This chapter introduced you to some of the object-oriented features in Visual Basic .NET. You can write code that can be reused in multiple applications by carefully designing your applications using the OO techniques you learned here.

By using OO design, your code is easier to maintain and debug. In the samples you created in this chapter, each class can be thoroughly tested and debugged on its own, and when the classes are inherited by other classes, you know that they will work. This is your first step in writing solid, reusable code.

✦   ✦   ✦

Hello World

by Uday Kranti

As already mentioned in the previous chapters, the Microsoft .NET Framework supports many programming languages, such as Visual Basic .NET, C++, C#, and JScript .NET. For the existing Visual Basic developers, Visual Basic .NET has come as a natural progression as they move to the .NET environment.

With the .NET Framework, you can create three types of applications — Windows applications, Web applications, and Console applications. Because the classes to create these applications are included with the .NET Framework, you can use any .NET programming language to create these applications. The flexibility to use any .NET programming language gives a lot of freedom to application developers because they can use the language according to their proficiency levels and still use the same environment.

Windows Forms provide users with a basic set of classes to create a graphical user interface for Win32 desktop applications. They use the same drag-and-drop technique to create a rich user interface. On the other hand, Web Forms provide a browser-based user interface. Web Forms also allow you to create a user interface by using the drag-and-drop method.

In addition to the graphical user interface (GUI) applications, the .NET Framework also allows developers to create character user interface (CUI) applications. Creating CUI applications is possible through Console applications.

This chapter introduces you to Windows Forms and Web Forms, and you will learn to create your first Hello World application by using both Windows Forms and Web Forms.

In This Chapter

A Hello World application using Windows Forms

A Hello World application using Web Forms

✦ ✦ ✦ ✦

Creating a Windows Forms Application

Windows Forms, which are based on the .NET Framework, allow you to develop Windows applications. You can develop Visual Basic .NET Windows applications by using the Windows Forms Designer provided with Visual Studio .NET. Visual Studio .NET provides a common Integrated Development Environment (IDE) for developing applications in all .NET programming languages.

Cross-Reference For detailed information about Windows Forms, see Chapter 25.

Creating a Windows Application project

The first step to create a Windows Forms application is to create a Visual Basic Windows Application project. To do so, follow these steps.

1. Select File ➪ New ➪ Project to open the New Project dialog box.

Tip Alternatively, you can use hot keys to access different options. In the preceding step, press Alt + F to open the File menu. Then, press N to open the New submenu. Finally, to open the New Project dialog box, press P.

You can also open the New Project dialog box by pressing Ctrl + Shift +N.

2. From the Project Types pane, select Visual Basic.

3. From the Templates pane, select Windows Application to create a Visual Basic Windows Application project.

4. In the Name box, enter the name of the project. In the Location box, specify the directory where you want to store the project. To do so, you can use the Browse button. In this case, specify the name of the project as WinHelloWorld and the location as C:\VBProjects. At this stage, the New Project dialog box appears, as shown in Figure 4-1.

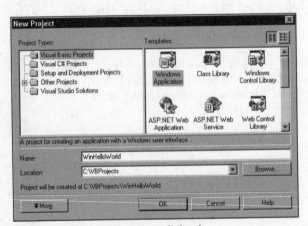

Figure 4-1: The New Project dialog box.

After the Visual Basic Windows Application project is created, Visual Studio .NET displays the interface, as shown in Figure 4-2.

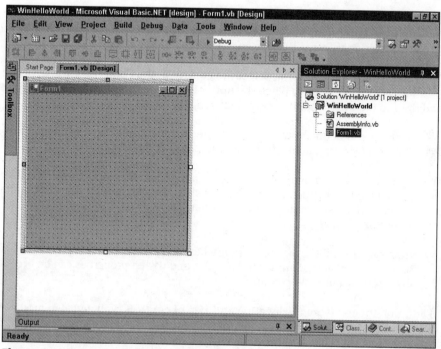

Figure 4-2: A sample Windows Application project.

As you can see in the figure, the Solution Explorer window is displayed to the extreme right of the Visual Studio .NET window. The Solution Explorer window can consist of multiple projects, which could be created in multiple languages. When a Windows Application project is created, the Form1.vb file is selected by default, and the form is displayed in Design mode.

Using Windows controls

Visual Studio .NET provides a Toolbox that you can use to design the user interface for your applications. You can display the Toolbox by selecting Toolbox from the View menu. By default, the Toolbox is placed to the extreme left of the window. The Toolbox opens only when you move your mouse over it. This feature is called *autohide*.

Note

The way the Toolbox is displayed depends on how the VS .NET environment is set up. When you set up your VS .NET environment, you can choose different options for the setup. If you choose the Visual Studio Developer setup, you will have the Toolbox hidden. If you choose the Visual Basic Developer environment, the Toolbox will be locked open.

The Toolbox contains different controls, categorized according to their functionality. For example, the standard Windows controls — such as Label, Button, and TextBox — are categorized under Windows controls.

You can either drag or draw controls on the form from the Toolbox. To drag a control, click the control in the Toolbox and drag it to the form at the location where you want to add the control. The control will be added in its default size.

To draw a control on the form, select the control in the Toolbox. Then click the location where you want to place the upper-left corner of the control on the form, and drag to create the control of the desired size.

Tip   You can also double-click a control in the Toolbox to add the control to a form in its default size and at the default location (0,0) of the form.

When you design a form, you need to move and resize the controls so that they are properly aligned and appear in the desired size. You can modify the location and size of a control by specifying various properties, such as X, Y (for location) and Height, Width (for size).

Note   You can access the X and Y properties of a control only by accessing the `Location` property. Similarly, the `Height` and `Width` properties can be accessed by accessing the `Size` property.

In addition to modifying the location and size of controls, you can also modify the various other attributes, such as the font, size, text, or color. Visual Studio .NET provides the Properties window to access or set the properties of forms and controls.

Tip   You can move a control by selecting the control and dragging it to the position where you want to position it. To resize a control, select the control, point to one of the corners of the control, and drag it to resize it.

Usually, the Properties window is visible. If it is not visible, however, you can display it by choosing Properties Window from the View menu or by pressing F4. Alternatively, you can use hot keys to access the Properties window. To do so, press Alt +V, and then press W. The Properties window displays the properties of a selected object, such as a form or a control. The property that appears highlighted is the default property of the selected control or the form.

Tip   To view or modify the properties of an object, you can also select the object from the Object drop-down list in the Properties window.

Tip   It is good programming practice to set the `Default` property and the `Name` property of controls first.

Figure 4-3 displays the Properties window when a Label control is selected. As you can see in the figure, the `Default` property of the Label control is highlighted.

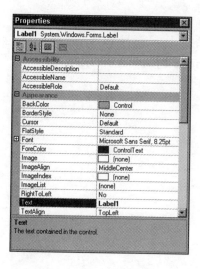

Figure 4-3: A Label control is selected in the Properties window.

In the Properties window, you can view the properties of a selected object in a categorized or an alphabetical manner.

Cross-Reference For detailed information about Windows controls, see Chapter 26.

To create a simple Hello World Windows application, create a form that contains a Label and a Button. Specify the properties, as described in Table 4-1.

Table 4-1
Properties of Controls in the Sample Windows Form

Control	Property	Value
Label	Text	Welcome to Windows Forms
	Name	MessageLabel
	ForeColor	Blue
	Font.Bold	True
	TextAlign	TopCenter
Button	Text	Say Hello
	Name	HelloButton
	Forecolor	Blue
	Font.Bold	True

Figure 4-4 shows the sample form.

Figure 4-4: A sample form for the Hello World Windows application.

Using the Code window

After you design a form, the next step is writing the code to provide the desired functionality for the controls. You write the code in the Code window, which you can open by selecting Code from the View menu or by pressing F7. You can also open the Code window by double-clicking the button control or right-clicking the form and selecting View Code. The Code window already contains some Visual Basic code, as shown in Figure 4-5.

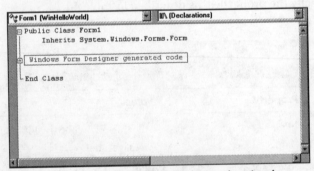

Figure 4-5: The Code window displaying the Visual Basic code.

The top of the Code window contains two drop-down lists: Class Name and Method Name. The Class Name list contains the names of all the classes in the current project. Currently, the Class Name list displays Form1 [WinHelloWorld]. The Method Name list contains the names of the methods of the class that is selected in the Class Name list. Currently, the Method Name list displays [Declarations].

The first line of the Code window displays the following code:

```
Public Class Form1
     Inherits System.Windows.Forms.Form
```

The preceding code indicates that Form1 is a class that is inherited from the Form class.

The Form class is included in the System namespace of the .NET Framework. System.Windows.Forms.Form indicates the class hierarchy in the System name-space. *Namespaces* are a way to group the related classes together. They provide proper organization of classes, so that they are convenient to use.

Cross-Reference For detailed information on namespaces, see Chapter 13.

The next line displays Windows Form Designer generated code. To display the entire code, click the + (plus) button on the left. When you expand the code, the entire code within the Windows Form Designer generated code section is displayed. The code is enclosed between #Region and #End Region. The #Region directive allows the organization of a part of the code in sections. The code that is included between #Region and #End Region is displayed or hidden when the section is expanded or collapsed. This directive allows an easy organization and management of code.

The Windows Forms generated code contains the instances of the various controls on the form, along with their positions and initial values on the form. In addition, it contains the constructor named New and destructor named Dispose. You write the initialization code in the constructor and de-initialization code in the destructor.

As mentioned earlier, Form1 is a class that is inherited from the Form class. Since every class has a constructor and a destructor, Form1 class also has a constructor and a destructor. The constructor is called automatically as soon as the form is instantiated. Because the constructor is called first, all the common initialization tasks, such as initializing variables or opening a file can be included in the construc-tor. In VB .NET, constructor methods are always named "New." The New() method is called automatically when the Form1 class is instantiated; i.e., when the instance of the Form1 class is created. You cannot call the New() method explicitly. VB .NET automatically generates code for the New() method, which is shown here:

```
Public Sub New()
MyBase.New()

'This call is required by the Windows Form Designer.
InitializeComponent()

'Add any initialization after the InitializeComponent() call
End Sub
```

As you can see in the preceding code, the first line calls the constructor of the base class. The `MyBase` keyword is used to refer to the base class.

The `New()` method then calls the `InitializeComponent()` method, which initializes the form and all the components in the form. The code of the `InitializeComponent()` method is also contained within the #Region directive. Although the code contained in the `InitializeComponent()` method can be written in the `New()` method directly, the idea behind having the `InitializeComponent()` method is the reusability of code. By grouping the initialization code in the `InitializeComponent()` method, you can get your application back to the initial state at any point of time. If this method did not exist, and the initialization code existed in the `New()` method directly, you would not be able to re-initialize the application. To re-initialize the application, you would then need to create a new instance of the application.

When objects are destroyed (set to `Nothing`) or are no longer in scope, the .NET Framework automatically calls the `Finalize` destructor. However, the only drawback with this destructor is that you do not know when the destructor is called. This is known as non-deterministic finalizers. Also, certain objects might remain active for longer than necessary. To manage your application resources well, VB .NET automatically generates code for the destructor named `Dispose`. The automatically generated code for the `Dispose()` method is shown here:

```
Protected Overloads Overrides Public Sub Dispose(ByVal
disposing As Boolean)
  If disposing Then
    If Not(components Is Nothing) Then
      components.Dispose()
    End If
  End If
  MyBase.Dispose(disposing)
End Sub
```

As you can see in the preceding code, the `Dispose()` method takes a `Boolean` parameter. If the `Boolean` parameter is true and the components are not de-initialized, the `Dispose` method is called for the components. On the other hand, if the `Boolean` parameter of the `Dispose()` method is false, the `Dispose()` method of the base class is called.

You can associate the code that you want with an object in the Code window. For example, to write the code for the `Click` event of the Button named Hello, select Hello from the Class Name list. Then select Click from the Method Name list. The code is automatically generated for the `Click` event of the Button. Then write the code to set the `Text` property of the Label control to Hello World. The complete code is as follows:

```
Private Sub HelloButton_Click (ByVal sender As Object, ByVal
e As System.EventArgs) Handles HelloButton.Click
  MessageLabel.Text =
"Hello World"
End Sub
```

Tip   You can also associate a code with a form or a control by double-clicking the form or control in the Design window.

After you finish designing and coding, you can build and run your application. To do so, press F5. The form is displayed. When you click the button, the text on the Label control changes to `Hello World`.

Creating a Web Forms Application

Web Forms is a feature of ASP.NET that creates rich Web applications. ASP.NET is a programming framework used to develop Web applications, and is a part of the .NET Framework. Web Forms provide Rapid Application Development techniques that enable you to create a rich user interface for Web applications.

Cross-Reference   For more information about ASP.NET, see Chapter 32.

Web Forms consist of a page that is used to design the user interface and a code file that provides functionality to the user interface. The *page* consists of a file containing a markup language, such as HTML or XML, and controls. A page file has `.aspx` as its extension.

The functionality to respond to user interactions with the Web Forms pages is implemented by using programming languages, such as Visual Basic and Visual C#. You can implement the functionality in the `.aspx` file or in a separate file written in Visual Basic .NET or C#. This separate file, called the *CodeBehind* class file, has `.aspx.cs` or `.aspx.vb` as its extension. Thus, a Web Forms page consists of a page (an `.aspx` file) and a code behind class file (an `.aspx.vb` file or an `.aspx.cs` file).

Cross-Reference   For detailed information about the page framework, see Chapter 33.

Creating a Web Application project

The first step to create a Visual Basic Web Forms application is to create a Web Application project. To do so, follow these steps:

1. Select File ⇨ New ⇨ Project to open the New Project dialog box.

2. From the Project Types pane, select Visual Basic.

3. From the Templates pane, select ASP.NET Web Application to create a Visual Basic Web Application project.

4. In the Name box, enter the name of the project. In the Location box, specify the name of a Web server in which you want to store the project. In this case, specify the name of the project as WebHelloWorld and the location as `http://<computer name>/`. Here, `<computer name>` in the Location box represents the name of the computer that hosts the IIS Server.

Note   You must have an IIS Server installed on the development computer. Otherwise, you cannot create Web applications.

After the Visual Basic Web Application project is created, Visual Studio .NET displays the number of files in the Solution Explorer window. The `WebForm1.aspx` is selected by default and is displayed in the designer.

Using the Web Forms Server controls

After you create a Web Application project, you can design the user interface of the Web Forms page by using the Web Forms designer provided by Visual Studio .NET. The designer provides a Toolbox that contains various Web Forms Server controls that can be added on the page to design a rich user interface. These Server controls differ from the usual Windows controls. Unlike the Windows controls, the Web Forms Server controls work within the ASP.NET Framework and are available to be programmed at the server end.

Cross-Reference   For detailed information about Web Forms Server controls, see Chapter 35.

The way controls are added to the Web Forms pages is similar to the way you add them to the Windows Forms. You can access or assign the properties of a control in the Properties window the same way as you do with Windows Forms.

To create a simple Hello World Web application, add a Label and Button to the page. Then set the properties, as shown in Table 4-2.

Table 4-2		
Properties of Controls in the Sample Web Form		
Control	**Property**	**Value**
Label	Text	Welcome to Web Forms
	ID	MessageLabel
	ForeColor	Blue
	Font.Bold	True
Button	Text	Say Hello
	ID	HelloButton
	Forecolor	Blue
	Font.Bold	True

The form should appear as shown in Figure 4-6.

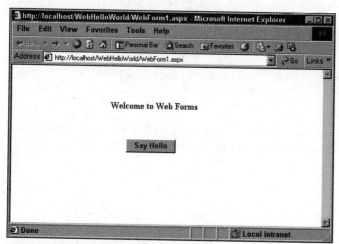

Figure 4-6: A sample Web Forms page.

Using the Code window

After the visual component is designed, you can use the CodeBehind file to implement the desired functionality with the user interface. You can view the CodeBehind file by selecting Code from the View menu or by pressing F7.

The first line of the Code window contains the following code:

```
Public Class WebForm1
    Inherits System.Web.UI.Page
```

The preceding code indicates that the Web Forms page, WebForm1, is a class inherited from the Page class, which is included in the System.Web.UI namespace of the .NET Framework.

Just as Windows Forms generates code automatically, Web Forms also generates code, which appears collapsed under the section Web Form Designer generated code. This code contains the Page_Init() method, which is called when a page is initialized while accessing it from a Web server. The Page_Init() method in turn calls the InitializeComponent() method. The Page_Load() method is also displayed in the Code window. This method gets executed as soon as the page is loaded in the memory.

You can write a code for an event of a control by selecting the control from the Class Name list and the event from the Method Name list. For example, to write the code in the `Click` event of the Button having ID Hello, select Hello from the Class Name list and Click from the Method Name list. Then write the code to set the `Text` property of the Label control to Hello World. The complete code follows:

```
Private Sub HelloButton_Click (ByVal sender As Object, ByVal
e As System.EventArgs) Handles HelloButton.Click
    MessageLabel.Text = "Hello World"
End Sub
```

When you save and run the application (by pressing F5), the page is displayed in a Web browser. When you click the button, the text on the label changes to Hello World.

Summary

This chapter introduced you to the basic features of Windows Forms and Web Forms. In this chapter, you learned how to create a Windows Application project, design a Windows Form, and associate code with a control on the form. In the process of learning the basics of Windows Forms, you developed a Hello World Windows application. Finally, you learned how to create an ASP.NET Web Application project, design a Web Forms page, and write code for a control on the page. In the process, you developed a Hello World Web application.

✦   ✦   ✦

Data Types, Variables, and Operators

by Uday Kranti and Jason Beres

To begin learning how to code in VB .NET, you need to understand the types of data that you can work with, how you can store that data in variables, and how you can convert from one type of data to another.

In this chapter, you begin to understand the core concepts of the VB .NET language. Every language has data types, conversion functions, and data manipulation functions. VB .NET is no different. If you are an experienced VB developer, do not skip this chapter; many new items are covered that can make your programming life much simpler in the long run. I point out changes that are important as you read along. If you are a newbie, this chapter is a must-read. In order to do any VB .NET development, you need to thoroughly understand everything in this chapter. If you don't use the correct types in your applications, you're opening yourself up to future headaches that you could have easily avoided.

Data Types and Variables

A *variable* is a pointer to a block of memory that stores information. The information that is stored in a variable is of a certain *data type*. In all programming languages, you define a real-world object that refers to some type of information that you need to work with. The information that you are working with needs to be understood by the compiler. This data you work with could be a number, a string, a date, a user defined type, or it could even be a generic type of data. The compiler of your language has rules that define the types of data that are allowed, and the real-world representations that you define must live within the parameters of the defined types that the compiler can understand.

The .NET Framework uses the concept of Common Language Specification (CLS) compliant data types. This means that *any* .NET compiler you are using must at least allow for certain data types. If it does not, the compiler is not CLS compliant and, in turn, the language cannot be considered a CLR-compliant language. If you write an application in VB .NET, and the types of data you use are CLS compliant, any other language in the .NET Framework can exchange information with your application, because it understands the type of data you are using. This is important to the interoperability of the languages in the framework that has been an elusive goal for VB developers in the past. If you have ever attempted to receive or send string data to a DLL written in C++, then you know that the task is not trivial. C++ and VB 6 do not look at the string data type the same way, so there has to be some massaging of the data in order to effectively communicate with C++ applications.

VB .NET data types

In VB .NET, all data types allowed are CLS-compliant. The .NET Framework, all data types are derived from the System namespace. Each type is defined as a structure within the System namespace. Because all objects in .NET are derived from the base type System.Object, the data types you are using are actually classes and structures derived from the System.Object type. All classes have members, properties, and fields; the data types defined in the System namespace are no different. Table 5-1 lists the data types, the CLS type and the allowable ranges for each type defined in the System namespace.

Table 5-1
VB .NET Data Types

Type	CLS Type	Bytes	Value
Boolean	System.Boolean	4	True or False
Byte	System.Byte	1	0 to 255 unsigned
Char	System.Char	2	0 to 65,535 unsigned
Date	System.DateTime	8	January 1, 1 to December 31, 9999
Decimal	System.Decimal	12	+/− 79,228,162,514,264,337,593,950, 335 with no decimal point. +/− 7.9228162514264337593543950335 with 28 places to the right of the decimal point. The smallest nonzero number would be a 1 in the 28th position to the right of the decimal point.

Type	CLS Type	Bytes	Value
Double	System.Double	8	−1.797693134862231E308 to −4.94065645841247 for negative values to 4.94065645841247 to 1.797693134862231E308 for positive values
Integer	System.Int32	4	−2,147,483,648 to 2,147,483,648
Long	System.Int64	8	−9,223,372,036,854,775,808 to 9,223,372,036,854,775,807
Short	System.Int16	2	−32,768 to 32,767
Object	System.Object	4	An object can hold any variable type
Single	System.Single	4	−3.402823E38 to −1.401298E-45 for negative values to 1.401298E-45 to 3.402823E38 for positive values
String	System.String	10+ (2*Length)	0 to 2 billion Unicode characters (approximately).
User Defined Type (structure)	System. ValueType		Sum of the size of its members Each member of the structure has a range determined by its data type and independent of the ranges of the other members

An important thing to notice for VB developers is the differences between .NET data types and pre-.NET data types. In VB 6, the Short data type did not exist, and the Integer data type had a range of −32,768 to +32767. In .NET, the Short data type replaces the Integer data type, and the Integer data type replaces the Long data type. The new Long data type is a 64-bit, 8-byte number, a very large number. Table 5-2 summarizes the data type changes in VB .NET from previous VB versions.

Table 5-2
Data Type Changes

Data Type	Pre VB.NET	VB.NET
System.Int16	Integer	Short
System.Int32	Long	Integer
System.int64	Did not exist	Long
Variant	Variant	Does not exist
Currency	Currency	Decimal
Date	Date	Long

If you plan on porting applications to VB .NET, you need to consider the data type changes. In VB 6, it was common to declare numeric types as integers that were used for looping and counters. In VB .NET, this might be a bad idea. The `Integer` data type is a very large number, so using the correct type for the correct operation still needs to be considered. You might want to change the `Integer` data types to `Short` data types in the conversion process. The .NET Framework SDK points out that 32-bit numbers run faster on 32-bit systems and 64-bit numbers run better on 64-bit systems. This makes sense, because the OS doesn't need to do any internal conversion to process the types. However, in the end, you consume way too much memory if you declare all your variables as 64-bit numbers just to be prepared for 64-bit Windows in 2004.

In Visual Basic .NET, the *variant* data type no longer exists. If you developed applications in VB 6, the variant data type was the default data type. VB Script, the language of choice for many ASP developers, is a typeless language. This means that no data types exist, except for the default type. Everything in VB Script is a variant data type. If you decide to declare variables without a type in .NET, the default is the *object* type. When porting, you need to consider that if you don't change the variables declared without a type, you are forcing the object type to be used, which uses late binding. Late binding means that the compiler does not know the type at runtime, and it is forced to convert the data in order to use it. There is a performance penalty when this occurs.

Reference types versus Value types

In .NET, there are two variations of types: reference and value. What matters when you are developing is whether the data you are working on is in its own memory space, or if it is simply a pointer or reference to another area of memory holding the value of the data. Table 5-3 defines the rules for value and reference types.

Table 5-3 Reference Types and Value Types	
Value Types	*Reference Types*
Numeric, Boolean, Char and Date data types.	String data type
Structures	Arrays
Enumerations	Classes

To determine if the data you are working on is a reference type or a value type, the `Microsoft.VisualBasic.Information.IsReference` method returns a True or False to help you determine the type. The following code segments make this clearer.

```
Dim x As Single
MsgBox(Microsoft.VisualBasic.Information.IsReference(x)) ' Returns False
Dim x As Object
MsgBox(Microsoft.VisualBasic.Information.IsReference(x)) ' Returns True
```

Types as classes

As mentioned earlier in the discussion on the ranges and values of data types, data types are actually derived from the System namespace. When you declared X as Object earlier, you could have used this code with the same results:

```
Dim x as System.Object
```

All objects are derived from a class, and that class can have methods, properties, fields, and events, which collectively are referred to as members. In .NET, this includes data types. This is evident in the following code:

```
Dim x as Single = 123.45
Msgbox(X.ToString)
```

The variable X has a method call to the member ToString(). This is a new concept for VB developers, and a very cool one. In pre-.NET VB, developers acted on numeric data types with built-in functions such as CStr, CInt, and CDate. In .NET, those conversion functions are still valid, but you can take advantage of the various .NET methods and properties from which the types are derived. In the preceding example, if I had written this in the VS .NET IDE, after I typed the "X." a whole list of methods and properties would have appeared.

Declaring variables

Now that you have an understanding of the allowable types in VB .NET, you need to learn how to use these types in your code. When you begin working with any type in VB .NET, you declare a variable of that type, and then assign a value to that variable. The following is a simple declaration of a variable of the type Integer:

```
Dim intX as Integer
```

Depending on where you use the variable, you can declare the variable in any number of ways. If the variable is local to a procedure, it is a procedure-level variable, meaning the variable is *private* to that procedure. If the variable needs to be used across many procedures within a module, you could declare the variable as private as well, but the variable declaration must be kept outside of any procedures within the module. If a variable will be accessed across multiple modules or classes, you could declare it a *public*. The accessibility of your variables within your application is known as *scope*. Depending on the scope of a variable, you may or may not be able to access the variable in certain sections of your application.

The allowable scope for any variable in VB .NET can be Public, Protected, Friend, Private, Shared, or Static. To declare a variable, you use a variable declaration statement. The following is the basic syntax for variable declaration in VB .NET:

```
[ Dim | Public | Protected | Friend | Protected Friend |
Private | Static ] variablename As [ New ] type =
[expression]
```

The following would be an example of the variations of the declaration statement:

```
Dim intX as Integer
Private intX as Integer
Public intX as Integer
Static intX as Integer
Protected intX as Integer
Friend intX as Integer
```

I use the term *basic* syntax of the declare statement because as you learn more about object-oriented programming, events, arrays, collections, and properties, you expand on how you can declare different types of variables. For now, the discussion concentrates on the basics of declaring variables. You see how the scope of variables can affect their availability to your application later in this section, but first it covers some of the differences in the behavior of variables and how they are different in VB .NET compared to previous VB versions.

Note   Dim and Private are both considered Private. The Dim keyword is allowed within a procedure block. Public, Private, Shared, and Friend are not allowed when declaring variables within a procedure block.

One of the most noticeable changes when moving to Visual Basic .NET is how you can declare variables. The following two code snippets are identical in VB .NET:

```
Dim intX as Integer, intY as Integer
Dim intX, intY as integer
```

In both cases, intX and intY are of the integer data type. This, of course, was not the case in previous Visual Basic versions. In VB 6, the second line of code intX would be of variant data type, and intY would be Integer.

Another major change is assignment of variables. The following VB 6 code assigns the number 6 to the variable intX:

```
Dim intX as Integer
IntX = 6
```

In .NET, you can declare a variable and explicitly assign it to an expression in the same line of code. The following code is equivalent to the previous VB 6 code:

```
Dim intX as Integer = 6
```

Where you declare your variables is also important. If a variable is declared within a statement block of any type, such as an If...End If statement, a

`Try...Catch...Finally` block, or a `Do...Loop` statement, the variable is only available within the block that it is declared. The following code causes an error in VB .NET: because the variable `strX` is declared within the `If` block, it cannot be accessed outside of the `If` block.

```
Dim intX as integer
For intX = 0 to 10
   If intX = 5 then
         Dim strX as string = Cstr(intX)
         Exit For
   End If
Next
Msgbox(strX)
```

If you change the code to the following, the error doesn't occur:

```
Dim intX as integer
For intX = 0 to 10
   If intX = 5 then
         Dim strX as string = intX.ToString
         Console.Writeline(strX)
         Exit For
   End If
Next
```

Most developers do not declare variables within loops, but if you do, you need to make that minor modification.

Variable defaults

When you declare a variable of a type without assigning a value to it, the variable has a default value based on the type of variable you have assigned as the type. The following are the default values for different types:

✦ **Numbers:** 0 (zero)

✦ **Boolean:** False

✦ **String:** Nothing

✦ **Object:** Nothing

✦ **Date:** 12:00:00 AM

Option Explicit statement

The `Option Explicit` statement forces you to declare variables before you reference them in your code. This statement works the same way as it did in previous VB versions. In VB .NET, you can set the `Option Explicit` statement on the project level, in the properties dialog box, or you can use the `Option Explicit` statement at the top of your class files or modules. The usage for the `Option Explicit` statement is as follows:

```
Option Explicit { On | Off }
```

If you specify `Option Explicit On` and attempt to reference a variable that is not declared, the IDE notifies you of the error as you are coding.

I highly recommend leaving `Option Explicit On`, which is the default. You can avoid many headaches when you're debugging.

Identifier and literal type characters

I cringe that I need to cover this, but identifier type characters are still allowed when declaring variables in VB .NET. Identifier type characters are shortcuts when declaring variables. Instead of using the actual data type when declaring a variable, you can use the shortcut characters that represent the data types you are referring to.

The following code is still valid in .NET:

```
Dim I%, AM#, LAZY$
```

> **Note**   Identifier-type characters make your code very difficult to read and are available for backward compatibility.

You may choose to declare all variables as type `Object`. If this is the case, you can force literals to be of a certain data type by using the literal type character immediately following the literal type. An example of forcing a literal type would be:

```
Dim Price as Object = 992.4D
' forces the Decimal data type
Dim intX as Object = 445S
' forces the Short data type
```

Table 5-4 lists data types and their respective literal type character and identifier type character.

Table 5-4
Literal and Identifier Type Characters

Data Type	Literal	Identifier
Short	(none)	S
Integer	%	I
Long	&	L
Decimal	@	D
Single	!	F
Double	#	R
String	$	C

If you run into code where the variables are declared with a literal, you can use the TypeName function to determine the type of the variable.

```
Dim Price as Object = 993.56D
MessageBox.Show(Price)' returns 993.56
MessageBox.Show(TypeName(Price))' returns Decimal
```

Constants

A constant allows you to use a friendly name for a variable value that does not change throughout the execution of your application. Constants in Visual Basic .NET act exactly as they did in previous versions. To declare a constant, you use the Const keyword within a procedure or at the declarations section of your classes or modules. Constants can be declared with the scope of Private, Public, Friend, Protected, or Protected Friend. The following is the usage of the Const statement.

```
[ Public | Private | Friend | Protected | Protected Friend ]
    Const constantname[ As type ] = expression
```

When you declare a constant, you must declare it as a certain type. Constants can be declared as Boolean, Byte, Char, DateTime, Decimal, Double, Integer, Long, Short, Single, or String data types. In the following code, you are declaring several constants and then using them in the procedure within the module.

```
Module Module1
    Private Const BillsSalary As Double = 1000000000
    Private Const MySalary As Byte = 100
    Private Const strMsg As String = "Try Again Please"

    Private Function Test_Salary() As Boolean

        If MySalary > BillsSalary Then
            Console.WriteLine(strMsg)
        End If

    End Function
End Module
```

After a variable is declared as a constant, its value cannot be changed. The purpose is to improve the readability of your code. It is much easier to refer to a friendly name than a long number or string every time you need to use a particular variable.

Variable scope

The scope of a variable can be declared as Private, Public, Static, Shared, Protected, or Friend. Here is some familiar looking code, declaring different variable types with different scopes:

```
Public v, b as Double
Static i, s as Long
Dim c, o, o, l as String
Private n, e, a, t, o as Integer
```

Private variables

Private variables are available to the module, class, or structure in which they are declared. As with previous Visual Basic version, `Dim` and `Private` act in the same manner, with the exception that the `Private` keyword cannot be used to declare variables within a subprocedure or function.

Here is an example of how you could use `Private` and `Dim` within a class:

```
Public Class Var1

    Private Shared intJ as Integer

    Shared Sub Main()
            Dim intY as Integer = 100
            Call DoSomething
            Console.Writeline(intJ)
            ' returns 100
            Console.Writeline(intY)
    End Sub

    Private Shared Sub DoSomething()
            IntJ = 100
    End Sub
End Class
```

In this example, `intJ` is shared throughout all members of the class, since you used the `Private Shared` declaration. When you declared `intY` within the `Sub Main` procedure, the scope of that variable is the `Sub Main` procedure only; any attempt to use it outside of `Sub Main` results in an error. This behavior is identical to previous VB versions. The following code is invalid:

```
Sub EatDinner() as Boolean
    Private intX as integer = 100
End Sub
```

`Private` is not allowed to declare local variables within a subprocedure.

Public variables

Public variables are available to all procedures in all classes, modules, and structures in your application. It is important to note that in most cases, method and variable declaration is public by default in VB .NET. In previous versions of Visual Basic, the default was private, so you may want to consider where you need to access methods and variables before declaring everything as public. The following example demonstrates the use of a public variable used in multiple classes. Notice that both `intX` and `intY` are in the `Public` scope, and are accessible to the classes in the module.

```
Module ModMain

    ' This is our public variable, available to everything
    Public intX, intY As Integer

    Public Class Dog
        Sub X()
            intX = 100
        End Sub

        Sub Y()
            intY = 300
        End Sub
    End Class

    Private Class Animals
        Sub Z()
            intX = 500
        End Sub
    End Class

End Module
```

Static variables

Static variables are special variable types that retain their values within the scope of the method or class in which they are declared. A static variable retains its value until the value of the variable is reset, or until the application ends.

```
Static intS As Integer = 100

Sub Test()
    intS = intS + 1
    If intS = 105 Then
        intS = 100
    End If
End Sub
```

In this example, each time the sub is executed, the value of intS is retained until the value reaches 105, then the value of intX is reset to 100, and this happens forever until the application ends. Static variables can only be declared at the procedure level. If you attempt to declare a variable at the class or module level, you get a compiler error.

Shared variables

Shared members are properties, procedures, or fields that are shared by all instances of a class. This makes it easy to declare a new instance of a class, but maintain a shared, public variable throughout all instances of the class. Here is some code that explains this:

```
Module ModMain
    Class Animal
```

```
            Public Shared Eyes As Boolean
            Private strDesc As String

            Property Friendly() As String
                Get
                    Friendly = strDesc
                End Get

                Set(ByVal Value As String)
                    strDesc = Value
                End Set
            End Property

        End Class

        Sub Main()
            Dim Cat As Animal = New Animal()
            Dim Rat As Animal = New Animal()

            Cat.Friendly = "Yes"
            Cat.Eyes = True
            Rat.Friendly = "No"
            console.WriteLine(Rat.Eyes)
        End Sub

    End Module
```

The result written to the console is True. Because you declared Eyes as shared,
you don't have to set it for each instance of the class created. The variable is
shared throughout all instances of the class. This could also cause you problems
if you are expecting variables to be initialized to empty or null when a class is
instantiated, so you should use caution when implementing shared variables.

Protected variables

Protected variables are only available to the class in which they are declared, or
classes that derive from the same class. In the following code, the variable X is
available only to the class in which it is declared. The attempt to access it in the
Class B results in an error.

```
    Module Module1
        Class A
            ' Declare protected variable
            Protected X As Integer

            Private Function TestX() As Boolean
                ' Set value of protected variable
                X = 5
            End Function
        End Class
```

```
     Class B
         Private Function TestX() As Boolean
             X = 5
         End Function
     End Class
End Module
```

Friend variables

Friend variables are accessible from any class or module within the assembly that they are declared in. In the following code, a friend variable is declared at the module level, and the variable is available to all classes within this module.

```
Module Module1
    ' Declare Friend variable
    Friend X As Integer

    Class A
        Private Function TestX() As Boolean
            ' Set value of protected variable
            X = 5
        End Function
    End Class

    Class B
        Private Function TestX() As Boolean
            X = 5
        End Function
    End Class
End Module
```

Type Conversion

Data type conversion in VB .NET is very similar to earlier VB versions. When you convert types, you can use built-in functions to convert from one type to another. There are two types of data conversion: widening and narrowing.

✦ **Widening:** Conversion is able to maintain the original data value, without data loss.

✦ **Narrowing:** Conversion attempts to convert data from a larger type to a smaller type (in bytes or precision) that may not be able to maintain the original value.

An example of narrowing conversion would be the following:

```
Dim X as Single = 123.45
Dim Y as Integer
Y = X
```

In this case, the decimal places are lost; an integer value does not have precision, so it cannot hold numbers to the right of the decimal place. In VS .NET, if you turn `Option Strict` to `ON` the application doesn't compile unless you perform an explicit conversion between the data types. This is a good thing; the compiler in all earlier VB versions did not offer this catch, and bugs were easily introduced due to conversion errors. Table 5-5 lists the allowable ranges for widening when converting data types.

Table 5-5
Allowable Type Conversion Ranges

Data Type	Allowable Conversion Range
Byte	Byte, Short, Integer, Long, Decimal, Single, Double, Object
Short	Short, Integer, Long, Decimal, Single, Double, Object
Integer	Integer, Long, Decimal, Single, Double, Object
Long	Long, Decimal, Single, Double, Object
Decimal	Decimal, Single, Double, Object
Single	Single, Double, Object
Double	Double, Object
Char	Char, String, Object
Derived Types	Any base type from which it is derived
Any Type	Any Interface the Type implements

Built-in type conversion functions

The following built-in conversion keywords are still available in VB .NET:

```
CBool, CByte, CChar, CDate, CDbl, CDec, CInt, CLng, CObj,
CShort, CSng, CStr and CType.
```

The keywords take an expression as a parameter and return a specific data type.

Note   The next section covers the System.Convert namespace, which should be used when doing data conversion because it can handle all .NET data types. The built-in functions covered in this section are left over from previous versions of VB for backward compatibility only.

This example uses `CInt` to convert a `Double` value to `Integer`:

```
Dim dblX as Double = 123.45
MessageBox.Show(Cint(dblX)) ' returns 123
```

This next example converts from `Double` to `Single` using the `CSng` function. Notice the returned results; `dblX` is rounded up and `dblY` is rounded down, based on the value of the decimal places.

```
Dim dblX As Double = 25.921987
Dim dblY As Double = 25.959234
MessageBox.Show(CSng(dblX))    ' Returns 25.92199
MessageBox.Show(CSng(dblY))    ' Returns 25.95923
```

You can also use explicit casting when narrowing data types. Here is an example of using two conversion functions that do not do any rounding, `Fix` and `Int`, so you are explicitly narrowing the values:

```
Dim dblX as Double = 123.45
MessageBox.Show(Fix(dblX)) ' returns 123
Dim dblX as double = 123.45
MessageBox.Show(Int(dblX)) ' returns 123
```

You can convert strings to the `Char` data type with `CChar`; not the best usage, but it shows you that the `Char` data type truncates to a single byte.

```
Dim strName as string = "Bill Gates"
MessageBox.Show(CChar(strName)) ' Returns "B"
```

The next sample illustrates as an `Overflow Exception` (exceptions are explained in detail in Chapter 12), which occurs if you are not careful in determining your data types before conversion. The `Short` data type can only hold values up to 32,768.

```
Dim lngX As Long = 234985
MessageBox.Show(CShort(lngX))    ' Returns Overflow Exception
```

Date conversion is accomplished with `CDate`. This example takes string input and converts it properly to a date format and does a comparison to the current date:

```
Dim strDate as string
strDate = Textbox1.Text
If CDate(strDate) < Now() then
  MessageBox.Show("Please enter a date after today")
End If
```

The `CType` conversion takes a type and converts it to another type, not just a new value. In this example, you use `CType` to convert from a `Double` to an `Integer` data type:

```
Dim dblX As Double = 100.56
Dim intX As Integer = CType(dblX, Integer)
MessageBox.Show CStr(intX)) ' Returns 101
```

A few more important notes on changes to conversion functions in Visual Basic .NET:

✦ CChar() can no longer be passed a numeric type. Use Chr() to convert a number to a character.

✦ Numeric conversion functions CShort(), CInt(), CLng(), CDbl(), and CDec() do not support conversion of a char to the numeric data types. Use Asc() instead.

System.Convert namespace

The System.Convert class supports similar functionality of the built-in conversion functions of VB .NET. The difference is that System.Convert handles narrowing conversions without throwing exceptions and it can handle all .NET data types, even those not supported by VB .NET, such as unsigned integers. Table 5-6 lists the most common members of the System.Convert class.

	Table 5-6 System.Convert Members
Method	**Converts Value to**
ToBoolean	Boolean type
ToByte	8 bit unsigned integer
ToChar	Unicode Character
ToDateTime	DateTime
ToDecimal	Decimal
ToDouble	Double precision floating point number
ToInt16	16-bit signed integer
ToInt32	32-bit signed integer
ToInt64	64-bit signed integer
ToSByte	8-bit signed integer
ToSingle	Single precision floating point number
ToString	Equivalent string representation
ToUInt16	16-bit unsigned integer
ToUInt32	32-bit unsigned integer
ToUInt64	64-bit unsigned integer

The nice thing about the System.Convert class is that you do not have to remember the built-in conversion functions of VB. For an experienced VB developer, this is not a big deal, but for a new developer, this makes life much easier, all complements of the VS .NET IDE's auto-complete mechanism.

Here is an example of using the System.Convert class to convert a 64-bit number to a 32-bit number, or in VB-Speak, a Long to an Integer.

```
Dim lngX As Long = 150
Dim intX As Integer
intX = Convert.ToInt32(lngX) ' intX = 150
```

In this example, you perform another narrowing conversion from a Single type to an Integer:

```
Dim sngX As Single = 123.4567
Dim intX As Integer
intX = Convert.ToInt32(sngX) ' intX = 123
```

When performing the conversion from a Date type to a String, the ToString() method does the trick.

```
Dim dteDate as Date = Now()
Dim strDate as string = Convert.ToString(dteDate)
' strDate now contains a string representation of the current
date
```

Here is a cool example of how smart System.Convert is, using to the ToBoolean() method with a string argument:

```
Dim strX as string = "False"
MessageBox.Show(Convert.ToBool(strX)) ' Returns False
Dim strY as string = "True"
MessageBox.Show(Convert.ToBool(strY)) ' Returns True
```

The legacy conversion functions such as CInt and CDbl and the System.Convert namespace conversion methods do pretty much the same thing. If you have a specific need to do narrowing conversions with more ease, use the System.Convert class. If you are a hardcore VB programmer from 1990, you can still use your built-in functions. It boils down to a few factors:

✦ Preference

✦ Interaction with other developers — C# does not have CInt, but it has Convert.ToInt32

✦ Specific functionality that exists in one method or the other

This brings me to another point about why .NET is so great. The System.Convert class is available to all CLS-compliant languages, so when your friend asks you to look at his COBOL .NET code, and you see Convert.ToString or Convert.ToInt64, it makes it very easy to pick up on other languages. As you progress in your .NET development, converting a C# to VB .NET application and back isn't a problem at all. The classes are the same in all languages, so the syntax is pretty much identical in all .NET languages.

Option Strict statement

To ensure that conversion errors are avoided in your code, set the Option Strict option to On. The Option Strict statement allows widening conversion statements, but a compiler error occurs if a narrowing conversion is attempted that will cause data loss. The usage for Option Strict is as follows:

```
Option Strict { On | Off }
```

Like the Option Explicit statement, the Option Strict option can be set at the top line of your class files or modules, or on a project level by modifying the project's properties. By default, Option Strict is Off, so it might be a good idea to change that default in the properties of your projects to avoid any nasty conversion errors.

Structures

In previous VB versions, the User Defined Type (UDT) was an extremely useful way of defining your own types. I used it all the time to store global data, and to store rows from a database that were mostly static. An example of a UDT in VB 6 would be:

```
Public Customer as Type
   strName as string
   strAddress as string
   strEmail as string
End Type
Public CCustomer() as Customer
```

The variable CCustomer was declared as an array of type Customer. In VB .NET, Structures replace UDTs. This is not a trivial name change. Structures offer increased functionality and object-oriented features. My example of the Customer type would be converted to a structure in VB .NET like this:

```
Structure Customer
   Public strName as string
   Public strAddress as string
   Private strTaxIDNumber as string
End Structure
Public CCustomer as Customer
```

Both examples look similar, and they are. It's what happens under the hood that gives us the advantages of structures in VB .NET.

You can define a structure as a way to group like data. Structures are declared with the Structure...End Structure statement. Between the declarations, you list your variables with the Public, Private, Protected, or Shared scope. Inside of a

structure, variables declared with `Dim` are `Public` by default; this is the exact opposite behavior in classes and modules. When you declare a variable to be an instance
of a structure, all of the structure's members are initialized automatically, which
means you do not need to initialize individual members of a structure. When you
decide that you need to use the structure, you declare a variable as the type of that
structure. You can declare the variable in one of two ways:

```
Dim varname as StructureName
Dim  varname as StructureName = New StructureName
```

You do not access the structure directly; you create an instance of the structure
through a variable.

You might say that you could use global variables to accomplish the same thing,
and that is true, but there is no grouping of like data in that case. So it is more
difficult to manage multiple arrays than possibly a single array stored in a structure.
It is also very nice syntax when referencing types within a structure, similar to a
property in a class. Another thing to keep in mind is that global variable should be
avoided whenever possible. Sharing fields between classes as structures or properties is cleaner and more consistent with OO design.

> **Note**   Structures are value types, not reference types.

After you define a structure, and declare a variable to reference the structure, you
can use the following syntax to reference the members of the structure:

```
CCusotmer.strAddress = "1234 Main Street"
CCustomer.strName = "Bill Gates"
```

To make your structure more robust, and to give you an idea of how far you can take
it, consider this structure, which stores a SQL DataSet, an array of names, and a Word
document, and has a method to combine variables defined within the structure.

```
Structure MyData

    Private strName as string
    Private strEmail as string
    Private retVal as string
    Public dsData as DataSet
    Public strNames() as string
    Public Docs as Word.Document

    Function DoName() as String
        retVal = strName & strEMail
        Return retVal
    End Function

End Structure
```

```
Public Function ProcessMyData(TheData as MyData) as Boolean
  strName1 = TheData.strNames(0)
  strName2 = TheData.strNames(1)
  ' .... Process DataSet
  ' ... Process Word Documents
End Function
```

Structures can also be nested. In this example, you define a structure of addresses, and then nest it inside the Customers structure.

```
Structure Addresses
   Public Location as string
   Public Description as string
End Structure

Structure Customers
   Dim Name as string
   Dim Email as string
   Dim Address()  as   Addresses
End Structure
```

I mentioned earlier that structures have OO features. Here is a summary of how structures can fit into your OO design:

✦ Structures can implement interfaces.

✦ Structures have constructors, methods, properties, fields, constants, and events.

✦ Structures can have shared constructors.

Numeric Parsing

The .NET runtime provides powerful new parsing features previously unavailable to Visual Basic developers. In particular, the new Parse method; which gives you flexibility on what you can do with incoming data, what you can return to the caller, and the control you have over the manipulation of the data. The Parse method is a member of the NumberStyles enumeration, which lives in the System.Globalization namespace. Consider the following example:

```
Dim strX as string = "$123,456,789"
' Now we need to do some math
Dim intX as integer =
intX.Parse(Globalization.NumberStyles.Currency)
Console.Writeline(intX * 3)' returns 7037034
```

Parse essentially takes a string value that represents a numeric value, and converts it to a numeric base type. The idea is that you need to convert or manipulate data that is not necessarily in the perfect format. With the Parse method, you can use its members to tell the compiler that certain rules apply to the data before you act upon it. Table 5-7 lists the available members in the `Parse` method.

Table 5-7 Parse Members	
Member	**Description**
AllowCurrencySymbol	Currency symbol is allowed.
AllowDecimalPoint	Decimal point is allowed.
AllowExponent	An exponent is allowed. The format of the number should be {e|E} [(+|-)] n, where n is a number.
AllowHexSpecifier	Hexadecimal numbers are allowed.
AllowLeadingSign	Leading sign is allowed.
AllowLeadingWhite	Leading whitespace character is allowed.
AllowParentheses	Parentheses are allowed.
AllowThousands	Group separators are allowed.
AllowTrailingSign	Trailing sign is allowed.
AllowTrailingWhite	Trailing whitespace character is allowed.
Any	All the AllowXXX bit styles are permitted.
Currency	All styles except AllowExponent are allowed.
Float	AllowLeadingWhite, AllowTrailingWhite, AllowLeadingSign, AllowDecimalPoint, and AllowExponent styles are allowed.
HexNumber	AllowLeadingWhite, AllowTrailingWhite, and AllowHexSpecifier styles are allowed.
Integer	AllowLeadingWhite, AllowTrailingWhite, and AllowLeadingSign styles are allowed.
None	None of the bit styles are allowed.
Number	AllowLeadingWhite, AllowTrailingWhite, AllowLeadingSign, AllowTrailingSign, AllowDecimalPoint, and AllowThousands styles are allowed.

In previous VB versions, you would use a custom parsing method or a built-in function like `Replace` to get rid of invalid characters. In .NET, you can use the numeric parse members to alleviate much of your custom parsing code.

System.String Class

VB .NET has tons of cool new features that are worth switching from pre-.NET VB to VB .NET right away, but one of the best features, in the category of "making your life easy" is the System.String class. Never before have VB developers been able to manipulate strings with such ease. Strings in VB .NET are immutable, which means that after they are created, they cannot be changed. You can copy strings, and clone strings, but most of the time you are creating new strings. This might seem a little confusing, but the behavior of string manipulation is exactly how you would expect, and what is happening under the hood does not really affect how you write your code.

Table 5-8 lists the methods of the System.String class, and what each method does.

Table 5-8
System.String Members

Method	Description
Clone( )	Makes an exact copy of an object
Compare( ),CompareOrdinal( )	Compares two strings
CompareTo( )	Compares a string to this string object
Concat( )	Joins one string to another string
Copy( )	Copies one string object to another string object
CopyTo( )	Copies characters into an array
EndsWith( ), StartsWith( )	Tests the beginning and ends of a string
Equals( )	Tests the equality of one object to another
Format( )	Formats numeric strings
GetHashCode( )	Gets the hash code of the string
IndexOf( ), LastIndexOf( )	Gets the index location of characters in a string
Insert( )	Inserts substrings into a string
Intern( ), IsInterned	Obtains a reference to a string
Join( ), Split( )	Joins or splits strings based on a parameter
PadLeft( ), PadRight( )	Pads a string with additional characters
Remove( )	Removes characters from a string
Replace( )	Replaces characters in a string
SubString( )	Isolates a substring from a string
Trim( ), TrimEnd( ), TrimStart( )	Trims characters from the beginning and ends of strings

The methods in Table 5-8 make perfect sense when you look at them, although a few might be a little strange looking and need a little explaining.

When I first started looking at System.String, I had thousands of ideas running through my head. Nothing is more exciting than easy string manipulation. The Split, Join, and Replace functions introduced in VB 6 changed my life, so imagine how elated I was when I saw this new System.String namespace.

The Replace() method is very similar to its VB 6 little brother.

```
Dim strName As String = "USS Voyager"
MsgBox(strName.Replace("USS", "United Space Ship"))
' returns "United Space Ship Voyager"
' The Equals methods will return a Boolean value indicating '
equality.

Dim strName1 as string = "Jar Jar Binks"
Dim strName2 as string = "jar jar binks"
Msgbox(strName1.Equals(strName2)) ' returns FALSE
```

If your goal is not necessarily the case (upper or lower) of the values, then try using the ToUpper() or ToLower() functions to check equality.

```
Dim strName1 As String = "Jar Jar Binks"
Dim strName2 As String = "jar jar binks"

If strName1.ToUpper.Equals(strName2.ToUpper) Then
   MessageBox.Show("The case might be different, " & _
         "but the values are the same")
End If
```

If you are not concerned with the case of the strings, always do an uppercase or lowercase conversion. Forgetting to do this brings up hard-to-find errors.

The following code is VB 6 compliant, performing the same uppercase conversion and string comparison:

```
Dim strName1 As String = "Jar Jar Binks"
Dim strName2 As String = "jar jar binks"
If UCase(strName1) = UCase(strName2) then
    MsgBox("The case might be different, but the values are the same")
End If
```

I like the first example better. Is the performance better? No. It is the same. Is the first example more fun to code? The answer to that is Yes.

The Concat() method takes 2 strings and concatenates them:

```
Dim strName1 As String = "I wish it w"
Dim strName2 As String = "ere Friday"

MsgBox(String.Concat(strName1, strName2)) ' returns "I wish it were Friday"
```

StartsWith() will test the beginning of a string:

```
Dim strPhrase As String = "Your bonus was rejected"

If strPhrase.EndsWith("rejected") Then
    strPhrase = strPhrase.Replace("rejected", "approved")
    MsgBox(strPhrase) ' returns "Your bonus was approved"
End If
```

I think you get the idea. The System.String namespace opens a ton of new options for you in VB .NET.

Operators

Visual Basic offers a host of operator options that you use daily in your coding, and many of these operators have been sprinkled throughout the code you have seen in first several chapters, but now you get the official explanation. The operators can fall into one of these categories: arithmetic, assignment, bitwise, comparison, concatenation, and logical.

The basic purpose of an operator is to assign or retrieve values based on expressions or statements.

In the following example, you are assigning the value of the variable X equal to whatever the value of Y might be. This is an example of an assignment operator; you are assigning the value of one expression to the value of another.

```
X = Y
```

The following is another example of an assignment operator, except that in this case, you are evaluating the return value of the SquareIt function, which is a statement, and assigning the value from the function call to the variable intX.

```
X = SquareIt(5)
```

In the next example you are combining two strings with the concatenation operator, setting the value of the variable on the left to the evaluation of the statement on the right side of the equals (=) sign.

```
TheCarIWishIHad = "Mercedes " & "Benz 500SL"
```

I think you are getting the basic idea. Let's go over each category of operator type and examine further samples.

Arithmetic operators

In grade school, we all learned how to add, subtract, multiply, and divide. These are basic life functions, just like watching Star Trek or eating pizza. Visual Basic .NET offers the arithmetic operators listed in Table 5-9 that handle the dirty work of doing math.

Table 5-9 **Arithmetic Operators**	
Operator	*Action*
+	Addition
-	Subtraction
*	Multiplication
/ and \	Division
%	Modulo
^	Exponentiation

Arithmetic operators supply basic algebraic functions. Let's examine some code that walks through these operators.

Addition operator

The +, or addition operator, sums or concatenates two expressions. Concatenation is discussed a little later in this chapter, as well as what you have to look out for when using the + operator. The usage for addition operator is as follows:

```
Result = Expression + Expression
```

The following example shows the simplest form of the addition operator possible, adding two values together:

```
Dim intX As Integer
intX = intX + 5
Console.Writeline(intX.ToString)
```

The variable intX, declared as integer value, has the initial value of zero. To add 5 to the value intX, you simply use the addition operator (+) and the assignment operator (=) to derive the new value. The following code accomplishes the same thing:

```
Dim intX As Integer
Dim intY As Integer
intY = intX + 5
Console.Writeline(intY.ToString)
```

The only difference is that you create a new variable called intY to hold the value of intX plus the number 5. Creating variables just for the heck of it is not efficient, so if the value of intX has the sole purpose of being an integer with 5 added to it, then use the first example as a guide. New to Visual Basic .NET are special assignment operators that perform an action on a variable, such as addition. The preceding addition code can also be represented as

```
Dim intX As Integer
intX += 5
Console.Writeline(intX.ToString)
```

Assignment operators are covered in more detail in the next section. Even though they look like mathematical operators, they are actually not; because you are using the equals sign (=), it indicates an assignment. In the previous code, you declared variables of the type Integer, which the compiler understood, and added the values together. Consider this example:

```
Dim intX As Integer = 10
MessageBox.Show(intX + "9")
```

The result in this example is 109. Addition did not occur. Because the value of "9" is enclosed in double quotes, the compiler understands it as a string data type, so the values are concatenated, and not added. If you are not sure of the type of data you are dealing with, and you need to make sure that addition occurs, use the conversion functions discussed earlier in the chapter. The following code takes care of this problem:

```
Dim intX As Integer = 10
MessageBox.Show(intX + CInt("9"))
```

Understanding the data you are dealing with is very important; as you can see, the results can vary significantly if you are not careful. The following rules apply when using the addition operator:

✦ Addition occurs if both expressions are of the same numeric data type.

✦ Concatenation occurs if one or both expressions are strings.

✦ If Option Strict is ON, implicit conversion between types is not allowed, so the previous example using CInt throws an exception, and neither concatenation nor addition occurs.

✦ If Option Strict is OFF, implicit conversion is allowed, and the expressions are added if implicit conversion is used. This conversion can be to numeric or string data types, and the result varies based on the conversion of the expression.

✦ Narrowing or widening conversions occur if the numeric data types used in expressions are different than the numeric data type of the result.

The following code rounds up an example of using the addition operand, and the results that can occur, assuming the default Option Strict of OFF. The inline comments in the code can help you understand what we're trying to accomplish.

```
Dim dblX As Double = 6.54
Dim dblY As Double = 9.32
Dim strX As String = "6"
Dim strY As String = "5"
Dim intX As Short
intX = CShort(strX) + CShort(strY)
MessageBox.Show(intX)
' Result is Short Data Type with a value of 11
MessageBox.Show(strX + strY)
' Result is String Data Type with a value of 65
intX = dblX + dblY
MessageBox.Show(intX)
' Result is 16, Integer data type cannot have a decimal place,
' so the narrowing conversion takes place
strX = dblX + dblY
MessageBox.Show(strX)
' Result is 15.86, Double data types are added, since they are
' of the same type, and the String will hold the result without
' an error
strX = dblX.ToString + dblY.ToString
MessageBox.Show(strX)
' Result is the concatenation of 6.549.43, since the ToString
' convert the Double values to strings, all values are strings,
' and concatenation occurs
```

Subtraction operator

The subtraction operator (–), indicating subtraction or negations, returns the difference between two numbers or expressions, or it negates a numeric value. Here are the two possible uses:

```
result = number1 - number2
variable = - number
```

You have been doing subtraction since you opened your first bank account and the teller gave you the little account balance booklet. There are no real gotchas here with the way the operator works.

```
Dim intX as Integer
Dim intY as Integer = 500
intX = intY - 100
```

In this example, you are subtracting 100 from the value of intY, which is 500, and assigning this value to the variable intX. In this case, the new value of intX is 400. If intY is less than 100, the value returned to intX is negative. So if the code was modified to

```
Dim intY as Integer = 5
```

the result would now be –95.

To simply negate a value, you can assign it to the negative value of itself or to a new variable. You could refer to the – operator as the unary negation operator in this case, as in the following example:

```
Dim intX as Integer = 100
intX = -intX
```

When using subtraction, make sure that the data types in use support the type of operation that you are attempting to accomplish. This rule stands for all operators. For example, if you are balancing your checkbook, and the result variable is declared as an integer data type, then you are definitely losing money, because the decimal places are getting lost in the process.

```
Dim dblVal1 As Double = 100.54
Dim dblVal2 As Double = 23.45
Dim intY As Integer
intY = dblVal1 - dblVal2
MessageBox.Show(intY) 'Returns 77
MessageBox.Show(dblVal1 - dblVal2) ' Returns 77.09
```

If this were your checkbook, you just lost 9 cents. The .09 gets cut off the end of the resulting integer variable intY. How can you avoid this pitfall? Turn the Option Strict option to ON. This causes a compile error in the preceding code statement, and your error gets caught before the application goes into production. In previous versions of Visual Basic, this error would have never been caught by the compiler, and you would have found out about it when you ran those year-end reports the boss wanted and he wondered why all the numbers were nice and rounded.

Multiplication operator

The multiplication operator (*) multiplies two numbers and returns a result.

The usage is

```
Result = Number1 * Number2
5 * 5 = 25
```

When you use a calculator, the logical process is taking the two numbers you want to multiply and then press the equals sign. When you code, you do the opposite — you declare the variable, and set that value to the resulting value of the operation you are attempting to accomplish.

```
Dim intX as Integer = 5
Dim intY as Integer = 5
Dim intResult as Integer
intResult = intX * intY
```

In this example, you multiply two variables and assign the value of intResult to the result of your multiplication. If you did this the opposite way, as you would type it into a calculator or adding machine, the value of intResult would be zero.

```
intX * intY = intResult
```

`intResult` is initialized as zero, and by setting the value of `intX * intY` to the value of zero, you have done the exact opposite of what you are trying to accomplish.

```
Dim intX as Short
intX = 56000 * 998
```

What happens in the preceding example? Two things, actually. First, a squiggly blue line appears underneath the `intX` assignment. The message indicates that the result is not representable in the data type `Short`. The second thing that happens, if you attempt to compile, is that the overflow exception occurs. When performing multiplication, it's important to understand the data you're dealing with. Overflows can occur if the variable you are attempting to assign the evaluated expression to does not allow the type you are attempting to create. When you do things in your head, it's easy to understand, but when you write applications, you are passing variables all over the place, and possibly receiving variables from other services that you did not write, so make sure you always consider this.

Division operator

The regular division (/) and the integer division (\) operators divide two numbers and return a result.

The usage is

```
RegularResult = Number1 / Number2
IntegerResult = Number1 \ Number2
```

The difference between the two types of division is how the numbers on the right-hand side of the equals sign are treated before the division operation takes place. In integer division, integral data types must be used. These are the data types that do not allow decimal places, such as `Integer`, `Long`, `Bit`, and `Short`. The result of an integer division is how many times one number can evenly divide into another number.

```
25 \ 5 = 5
```

The number 5 evenly divides into 25 five times.

```
26 \ 5 <> 5
```

In this case, 26 divided by 5 obviously does not equal 5.

Here is the long case example of several scenarios of choosing the correct or incorrect type of division:

```
Dim intX As Integer = 100
Dim intY As Integer = 50
MessageBox.Show(intX / intY) ' Returns 2
MessageBox.Show(intX \ intY) ' Returns 2
intX = 101 ' Modify variable so division is not even
MessageBox.Show(intX / intY) ' Returns 2.02
MessageBox.Show(intX \ intY) ' Returns 2
' Use floating point variables
Dim dblX As Double = 103.435
Dim dblY As Double = 50
MessageBox.Show(dblX / dblY) ' Returns 2.0687
MessageBox.Show(dblX \ dblY) ' Returns 2
```

As you can see, choosing the correct angle of the division operator can definitely influence the results.

Modulo operator

The modulo operator (%) divides two numbers and returns the remainder.

The usage is

```
Result = Number1 MOD Number2
```

If either of the numbers being divided are floating-point numbers, the result is the floating-point remainder. If the both of the numbers being divided are integers, the return value is an integer data type.

Here is a summary of samples using the mod operand:

```
Dim intX As Integer = 100
Dim intY As Integer = 50
MessageBox.Show(intY Mod intX) ' Returns 50
MessageBox.Show(intX Mod intY) ' Returns 0
intX = 101 ' Modify variable so division is not even
MessageBox.Show(intX Mod intY) ' Returns 1
' Use floating point variables
Dim dblX As Double = 103.435
Dim dblY As Double = 50.74
MessageBox.Show(dblX Mod dblY) ' Returns 1.955
MessageBox.Show(dblY Mod dblX) ' Returns 50.74
```

As you can see, once again, using the correct data types and understanding how your division should take place alters the outcome of your results.

Exponentiation operator

The exponentiation operator (^) returns the exponent of two numbers.

The usage is

```
Result = Number1 ^ Number2
```

The first number is raised to the power of the second number. Normally the data type of the result is double, unless you explicitly define the result as an integral data type. Here are a few samples of the exponential operand:

```
Dim intX As Integer = 50
Dm intY As Integer = 5
Dim intZ As Integer
Console.WriteLine(intY ^ intX) ' Returns 8.88178419700125E34
Console.WriteLine(intX ^ intY) ' Returns 312500000
intZ = intY ^ intX
Console.WriteLine(intZ)
' Overflow exception occurs
' The exponent of the 2 floating point
' numbers cannot fit into an integer data type
Dim dblX As Double = 3
Dim dblY As Double = 3
Console.WriteLine(dblX ^ dblY) ' Returns 27
```

In the preceding examples, I threw in an example of an exception, so you can see that when dealing with raising numbers to the power of another number, the return data type should be Double, because the numbers have a tendency to be quite large.

Concatenation operators

Concatenation operators (&) combine string variables with string expressions.

The usage is

```
Variable = expression & expression

Dim X as Integer = 3
Dim intY as Integer = 15
intX = intX & intY ' Returns 315
```

Or, you do not have to assign the value immediately:

```
Dim str1 as string = "NCC "
Dim str2 as string = "D"
str1 = str1 & "1701" & str2 ' Returns NCC 1701D
```

When you combine strings in Visual Basic, you can use the variable on the left-hand side of the equals sign as a string variable in the expression on the right-hand side of the equals sign. So the str1 variable in the preceding example can be used in your expression as well as in the result.

The addition operator (+) can also be used for concatenation, if any of the values in the expression on the right-hand side of the equals sign are string data types. The previous sections on arithmetic operators showed several examples of this behavior.

Assignment operators

Assignment operators are almost as common as arithmetic operators. The equals (=) sign is used whenever you need to set the value of a variable. When you declare variables, you can use assignment to set the value of the variable in the same line that you are declaring it.

```
Dim X as Integer = 3
```

Or, you do not have to assign the value immediately:

```
Dim X as Integer
```

It all depends on what you plan on doing with the variable. If you plan on using other operators, such as arithmetic, the value of the variable is assigned in your code. The bottom line is that assignment operators take a value from the right-hand side of the operator you choose to use and assign it to the value on the left-hand side of the operator. Table 5-10 lists the assignment operators and the actions they perform.

Table 5-10 Assignment Operators	
Operator	*Action*
=	Equals assignment
+=	Addition/concatenation assignment
-=	Subtraction assignment
*=	Multiplication assignment
/= and \=	Division assignment
^=	Exponentiation assignment
&=	String Concatenation assignment

If you have used Visual Basic before, you are probably scratching your head. There are some new operators that were never available to you before. These operators can be confused with arithmetic operators, but they are actually classified as assignment operators, even though they also perform arithmetic functions too. The first time you use these new assignment operators, it might be a little confusing because of the new syntax, but I think you'll agree that they are very cool and very powerful. Let's go over the assignment variables and some samples of each type.

Equals operator

The equals operator (=) is probably the most widely used operator in any development language. You are always assigning a variable or object to the result of arithmetic, or a function call return value, or any value that you need to assign. The = operator is also used to compare one expression of variable to another, returning a Boolean value.

The usage is

```
Variable = Expression
```

The expression on the right-hand side of the = is evaluated, and assigned to the variable on the left-hand side of the operator.

```
Dim strFirstName as String = "Billion Dollar "
Dim strLastName as String = "Bill"
Dim strFullName as string
strFullName = strFirstName & strLastName ' Returns Billion Dollar Bill
```

In the preceding example, you are taking two string variables and assigning them to the variable strFullName.

```
Dim lngResult as Long
lngResult = DoTheMath()
```

In this example, the return value from the DoTheMath function is assigned to the variable lngResult.

In all of the examples so far, you have been evaluating an expression on the right-hand side of the operator and assigning a value to the left-hand side. You can also compare variables with the assignment operator:

```
If bNotEmpty = True Then
  Messagebox.Show("Please fill in a value for name")
End if
If strName = "SMITH" then
  Messagebox.show("Your name is not Gates")
End if
```

In the first example, if the Boolean variable bNotEmpty has a value of True, then you notify the user that they must fill in a value into a text box or whatever control you might be using. In the second example, you check the value of the strName variable, and if it equals SMITH, you raise a message to the user. Both of these examples use the = operator to check for the value of an operator, and not necessarily assign a value to an operator.

Addition/concatenation assignment operator

The addition/concatenation assignment operator (+=) adds the value of an expression to the value of a variable and assigns the result to that same variable. The type of operation that occurs is based on the type of data that is being evaluated.

The usage is

```
Variable += Expression
```

If the expression is numeric, then addition occurs; if the expression is a string, then concatenation occurs.

```
Dim strFName as string = "Romeo"
Dim strLName as string = " Must Die"
```

Here you have the strFName variable that holds a value of "Romeo". You then use that same variable as the recipient of the expression += strLName. This evaluation takes the contents of strFName, and concatenates strLName to it. See the "&=" operator later in this section to accomplish the same thing in a cleaner fashion. You should always avoid using the addition (+) operator for string concatenation.

```
strFName += strLName 'Returns Romeo Must Die

Dim intX as Integer = 100
intX += 1 ' Returns 101
```

Here you are incrementing the value of intX. The original value of intX was 100, and using the assignment concatenation operator, you can increment the value and assign it back to intX. You can accomplish the same thing with this line of code:

```
intX = intX + 1
```

I think that the shortcut way is cooler and newer, but for developers who have never used Java or C, the syntax may be a little confusing at first. There does not seem to be any performance difference between the two syntaxes.

```
Do While intX < 100
      intX += 1 ' Increment integer value by 1
Loop
MessageBox.Show(intX) ' Displays 100
```

When discussing the addition operator in the beginning of the section, you saw some of the errors that could arise if you are attempting addition and the data type is not numeric.

```
Dim Val1 as Integer = 100
Dim Val2 as Integer = 50
Val1 += Val2 '  Returns 150
Dim Val1 as String = 100
Dim Val2 as string = 50
Val1 += Val2 ' Returns 10050
```

Here you can see that based on the data type, either addition or concatenation may occur. You have obviously declared your own variables here, but as I mentioned before, you might not always know the data type of the variables you are dealing with, so use caution and make sure you can determine the actual data types before performing any operations that include arithmetic.

Subtraction assignment operator

The subtraction assignment operator (–=) subtracts the value of an expression from the value of a variable and assigns the result to that same variable.

The usage is

```
Variable -= Expression
```

The same rules apply for the subtraction assignment operator as for the subtraction arithmetic operator.

```
Dim intX as integer = 100
intX -= 25 ' Returns 75
```

or

```
intX -= 100 + 34 ' Returns -34
```

Both statements are fairly straightforward. The variable intX is initialized with a value of 100, and the expression on the right-hand side of the operand is evaluated, subtracted from the variable on the left, and then assigned to the variable on the left.

Multiplication assignment operator

The multiplication assignment operator (*=) multiplies the value of an expression by the value of a variable and assigns the result to that same variable.

The usage is

```
Variable *= Expression
```

The same rules apply for the multiplication assignment operator as for the multiplication arithmetic operator.

```
Dim intX as integer = 3
intX *= 3 ' Returns 9
intX *=15 ' Returns 45
Dim intY as Integer = 7
intX *= intY ' Returns 21
```

You are doing simple multiplication here, taking the value on the right, multiplying it by the variable on the left, and assigning the result to the variable on the left.

```
Dim intX as integer = 10
intX *= DoTheMath()
```

In this example, you are evaluating the expression `DoTheMath`, a function call, multiplying it by `intX`, and assigning to `intX`. If the function `DoTheMath` returned 10, your result would be 100; if it returned 3, your result would be 30, or 3 * 10.

```
Dim intX as integer = 27000
intX *= 129093482 ^ 45
```

Here you have the same issue you ran into with the multiplication operator — the danger of not having a large enough data type to hold the result. This example results in an exception overflow, because the result of 27000 * 129093482 to the 45th power is larger than the integer data type can hold.

Division assignment operator

The floating-point division (/=) and integer division (\=) assignment operators divide the value of an expression by the value of a variable and assign the result to that same variable.

The usage is

```
FloatingPointVariable /= Expression
integralVariabe \= Expression
```

The same rules that you learned earlier in the chapter regarding floating-point and integral division apply. Here is a summary of examples using the division assignment operators:

```
Dim intX as integer = 5
Dim intY as integer = 25
intY /= intX   ' Returns 5
Dim dblX as Double = 234.6
Dim dblY as Double = 23.928
dblX /= dblY ' Returns 9.80441323971916
Dim intX as Integer = 200
Dim dblY as Double = 5.34
intX \= dblY ' Returns 40
```

Exponentiation assignment operator

The exponentiation operator (^=) raises the value of a variable to the power of an expression and assigns it to that variable.

The usage is

```
Variable ^= Expression
```

The variable on the left-hand side of the operator is raised to the power of the expression on the right-hand side of the operator.

```
Dim intX as Integer = 3
Dim intY as Integer = 5
intX ^= intY ' Returns 243
Dim intX = 10
Dim intY = 3
intX ^= intY ' Returns 1000
```

This example is the same as 10 * 10 * 10. If you were to make that somewhat generic, you could code like this:

```
Dim intVar1 as Integer
For intVar1 = 0 to intY - 1
   intX = intX * intX
Next
```

Obviously using the correct operator simplifies your code, and does not leave room for any errors.

Concatenation assignment operator

The concatenation operator (&=) concatenates a string expression to a string variable and assigns it to the string variable.

The usage is

```
Variable &= Expression
```

The variable on the left-hand side of the operator is concatenated to the expression on the right-hand side of the operator.

```
Dim strName as string = "Dr. "
Dim strVar as string = "Evil"
strName &= strVar ' Returns Dr. Evil
Dim intX as Integer = 3
Dim intY as integer = 5
intX &= intY ' Returns 35
```

The inclusion of the integer example in the preceding code is to demonstrate that the &= operator always treats the variables and expressions as strings, so no addition occurs as with the += operator if the variable and expression are actual numbers.

Comparison operators

Comparison operators evaluate an expression on the right-hand side of the equals sign and return a Boolean True or False based on the comparison of the expressions.

The usage is

```
result = expression1 comparisonoperator expression2
result = object1 Is object2
result = string Like pattern
```

```
Dim intX As Integer = 3
Dim intY As Integer = 5
Console.WriteLine(intX < intY)
```

This example returns True, because the integer value 3 is less than the integer value 5.

```
Dim intX As String = "A"
Dim intY As String = "a"
Console.WriteLine(intX > intY) ' Returns False
Console.WriteLine(Asc("A")) ' Returns 65
Console.WriteLine(Asc("a")) ' Returns 97
```

This comparison is based on strings, which is a little different than numeric comparison. You have compared "A" and "a", which the compiler converts to their respective ASCII equivalent to do the comparison based on the sort order of the ASCII value. The ASCII value for "A" is 65, and the ASCII value for "a" is 97, which is why False is returned from the comparison; 65 is not greater than 97. When comparison operators are used with strings, the ASCII equivalent of the string values is compared to evaluate the expressions. Table 5-11 lists the comparison operators and the actions they perform.

Table 5-11
Comparison Operators

Operator	Action
Is	Object comparison
Like	String pattern comparison
<	Less than
<=	Less than or equal to
>	Greater than
>=	Greater than or equal to
=	Equal to

Is operator

The Is operator compares two object types and tests whether they are the same, always returning a Boolean value.

The usage is

```
Result = objectX Is objectY
```

The only way to get a True value back from the comparison is if the objects refer to the same object. If there are two objects that are of the same type but do not refer back to the same object, that is, the object was not created from that object, the result is always False. Here is a summary of examples using the Is operator:

```
Dim x As System.String
Dim y As New Object()
Dim v As Object
v = y
Console.Write(v Is y) ' Returns True
Console.Write(x Is y) ' Returns False
```

Like operator

The Like operator returns a Boolean value based on the evaluation of a string and a pattern. If the pattern matches the string, True is returned; otherwise False is returned.

The usage is

```
Result = String Like Pattern
```

The results can also vary based on the Option Compare statement. If Option Compare is set to TEXT, then a case insensitive, text sort is used to determine the result. If Option Compare BINARY (default) is set, the pattern matching is based on the binary representation of the characters, based on locale, and not the textual representation of the characters.

Table 5-12 lists the pattern matching syntax for character, numeric, and wildcard character matching.

	Table 5-12
	Pattern Matching Syntax

Character	*Meaning*
?	Matches any single character.
*	Matches zero or more characters.
#	Matches any single digit (0–9).
[...]	Character list surrounded by brackets can match any character in the list. For example: [bilgates] .
[!...]	Character list surrounded by brackets prefixed by exclamation point match any single character not in the list.
X – X	Characters separated by a hyphen specify a range of Unicode characters.

```
Console.Writeline("DOG" Like "D*") ' Returns True
Console.Writeline("a" LIKE "A") ' Returns False
Console.Writeline("XYZ" LIKE "X[ACY]?") Returns True
```

The preceding examples give a summary of the pattern matching syntax.

Comparing strings and numbers

The remaining comparison operators are covered as a group rather than one at a time because they all follow the same rules, and they all act exactly as you would expect. The only thing that you need to worry about is the data type that you are comparing: strings or numbers. Either way, you are returning a Boolean value. Table 5-13 lists the remaining numeric comparison operators and the possible values the evaluated expressions can return.

<table>
<tr><th colspan="4">Table 5-13
Comparison Operators</th></tr>
<tr><th>Operator</th><th>Usage</th><th>True Example</th><th>False Example</th></tr>
<tr><td><</td><td>Expr1 < Expr2</td><td>27 < 45</td><td>45 < 27</td></tr>
<tr><td><=</td><td>Expr1 <= Expr2</td><td>45 <= 45</td><td>16 <=6</td></tr>
<tr><td>></td><td>Expr1 > Expr2</td><td>98 > 97</td><td>98 > 98</td></tr>
<tr><td>>=</td><td>Expr1 >= Expr2</td><td>98 >=98</td><td>97 >= 98</td></tr>
<tr><td>=</td><td>Expr1 = Expr2</td><td>98 = 98</td><td>98 = 100</td></tr>
<tr><td><></td><td>Expr1 <> Exp2</td><td>98 <> 97</td><td>98 <> 98</td></tr>
</table>

Logical/bitwise operators

The operators used for either the logical evaluation of the Boolean expressions or bitwise evaluation of the numeric expressions are called logical/bitwise operators. The syntax for using the logical/bitwise operator is

```
Var_result = Expr1 Operator Expr2
```

where

✦ Var_result is any Boolean or numeric variable.

✦ Expr1 and Expr2 are Boolean or numeric expressions.

✦ Operator is any logical/bitwise operator, such as And, Or, Not, or XOR.

To more easily understand how these operators work, in this section their operation is broken into logical and bitwise. Table 5-14 explains the logical operation of these operators.

Table 5-14
Logical Operation

Operation	Description
And	Used to perform logical joining on two Boolean expressions. It returns True if both the Boolean expressions are True.
Or	Used to perform logical disjoining on two Boolean expressions. It returns True if any of the Boolean expressions is True.
Not	Used to perform logical negation on a Boolean expressions. It returns False if the Boolean expression is True and vice-versa.
Xor	Used to perform logical exclusion on two Boolean expressions. It returns True only if one of the Boolean expression is True.
AndAlso	Used to perform logical joining of two Boolean expressions in a short-circuit manner. It returns True if both the expressions are True. However, if the first expression is False, the second expression is not evaluated.
OrElse	Used to perform logical disjoining on two Boolean expressions in a short-circuit manner. It returns True if any of the given expressions is True. However, if the first expression is True, the second expression is not evaluated.

To understand the logical operation of these operators, consider the following example:

```
'Declare three Integer variables
Dim intVar1 As Integer = 16
Dim intVar2 As Integer = 14
Dim intVar3 As Integer = 12

'Declare a Boolean variable
Dim bResult As Boolean

'Use And Operator
bResult = intVar1 > intVar2 And intVar2 > intVar3      'Returns True
bResult = intVar1 > intVar2 And intVar3 > intVar2      'Returns False

'Use Or Operator
bResult = intVar1 > intVar2 Or intVar2 > intVar3       'Returns True
bResult = intVar1 > intVar2 Or intVar3 > intVar2       'Returns True
bResult = intVar2 > intVar1 Or intVar3 > intVar2       'Returns False
```

```
'Use Not Operator
bResult = Not(intVar1 > intVar2)      'Returns False
bResult = Not(intVar1 < intVar2)      'Returns True

'Use Xor Operator
bResult = intVar1 > intVar2 Xor intVar2 > intVar3    'Returns False
bResult = intVar1 > intVar2 Xor intVar3 > intVar2    'Returns True
bResult = intVar2 > intVar1 Xor intVar3 > intVar2    'Returns False

'Use AndAlso Operator
bResult = intVar1 > intVar2 AndAlso intVar2 > intVar3
'Returns True

bResult = intVar2 > intVar1 AndAlso intVar2 > intVar3
'Returns False - Second Condition is not evaluated

'Use OrElse Operator
bResult = intVar1 > intVar2 OrElse intVar2 > intVar3
'Returns True

bResult = intVar1 > intVar2 OrElse intVar3 > intVar2
'Returns True - Second Condition is not evaluated
```

Table 5-15 explains the bitwise operation of these operators.

Table 5-15 Bitwise Operation		
Operation	**Description**	
And	Used to perform bitwise joining of two numeric expressions. The And operator compares the identical bits in the two numeric expressions and stores the corresponding bit in the result according to the following table:	
	Expr1 **Expr2** **Result**	
	0 0 0	
	0 1 0	
	1 0 0	
	1 1 1	

Operation	Description		
Or	Used to perform bitwise disjoining of two numeric expressions. The Or operator compares the identical bits in two numeric expressions and stores the corresponding bit in the result according to the following table:		
	Expr1	**Expr2**	**Result**
	0	0	0
	0	1	1
	1	0	1
	1	1	1
Not	Used to invert the bit values of a numeric expression.It stores the bit values in the result according to the following table:		
	Expr	**Result**	
	0	1	
	1	0	
Xor	Used to perform logical exclusion on two Boolean expressions. It compares the identical bits in the two numeric expressions and stores the corresponding bit in the result according to the following table:		
	Expr1	**Expr2**	**Result**
	0	0	0
	0	1	1
	1	0	1
	1	1	0

Operator precedence

In all of the examples, you have seen fairly simple expressions. This is not always the case when you are writing your applications, and you may have several different operators being used to evaluate a single expression or series of expressions.

```
Dim dblRet as Integer
dblRet = 5 * 4 / 6 ^ 4 + 9 - 100
Console.Writeline(dblRet) ' Returns -90.9845679012346
```

In this statement, five operators are being used to retrieve the value of intRet. The precedence in which the operators are evaluated affects the outcome.

```
Dim dblRet As Double
dblRet = ((5 * 4) / 6) ^ 4 + 9 - 100
Console.WriteLine(dblRet) ' Returns 32.4567901234568
```

You can see the difference in the two examples. Although they both are using the same numbers, the results are different based on the usage of parentheses on the code. So two things are actually affecting the outcome:

1. The location of the parentheses in the expression.

2. The order of the operators in the expression.

Table 5-16 lists the precedence of operators when evaluating expressions.

Table 5-16
Operator Precedence

Arithmetic	Comparison	Logical
^	=	Not
- (Negation)	<>	And
*, /	<	Or
\	>	XOR
Mod	<=	
+, -	>=	
Bitwise Operators	Like, Is, TypeOf .. Is	
&		

When parentheses are used in expressions, they are always evaluated first. So in the previous example, there are two different results for the same numbers because the parentheses have overridden the precedence of the operators, causing a portion or portions of the expression to be evaluated by others.

Here is a summary of the rules:

✦ Operator evaluation begins from the left to the right.

✦ Arithmetic operators are always evaluated first, then comparison operators, followed by logical operators.

✦ Comparison operators all have equal precedence.

✦ Operations enclosed with parentheses are evaluated before expressions outside of the parentheses.

✦ Concatenation (&) operator precedes all comparison operators and follows mathematical operators.

These rules are very easy to understand; they follow the logical order in which you would process these expressions on paper or using a calculator. You always figure out your grouping, process those instructions and then move on to the math, and finally you compare the results of the expressions and come up with the answer.

Summary

This chapter covered a lot of material. As you can see, understanding the types of data that you can use and what you can do with that data is very important in any programming language. For new developers, this chapter is your first step to understanding the power of VB .NET. For the experienced developer, you probably saw some very cool new things that you want to take advantage of right away. Here is my list of cool new things that I think you should take advantage of right away in your new VB .NET applications:

✦ System.String namespace

✦ System.Convert namespace

✦ New assignment operators, such as += and -=

✦ Structures

✦ AndAlso and OrElse operators

✦ Option Strict statement

There is much to learn, and this chapter started you on the path toward grasping some of the cool new concepts available to you as a VB .NET developer.

✦   ✦   ✦

Arrays

by Uday Kranti

You have seen the arrangements of books in a library. A bookshelf contains books on a particular subject, such as science, mathematics, and English. All the books in a bookshelf are numbered in a continuous pattern. To locate a particular science book, you need to know two things: the bookshelf containing science books and the book number. This kind of arrangement makes locating a book easier. In the same manner, you can store similar data in an application in an organized manner by using arrays. You can then locate this data by the array name and the position at which the data is stored.

Arrays help you store data in a contiguous memory area. In this chapter, you learn to create single- and multidimensional arrays. You also learn about dynamic arrays.

Introducing Arrays

In the previous chapter, you learned about variables. You use variables to store values. However, you might face situations when you need to store multiple values of similar type, such as names of 100 employees in an organization. One way to do this is to declare 100 variables and store all the names. However, in that case you need to remember the names of all the variables. A much more simple and efficient way of storing these values is using *arrays*. An array is a memory location that is used to store multiple values.

All the values in an array are of same type, such as `Integer` or `String` and are referenced by their index or subscript number, which is the order in which these values are stored in the array. These values are called the *elements* of an array. The number of elements that an array contains is called the *length* of the array. In VB .NET, all the arrays are inherited from the `System.Array` class. The `Array` class is a member of the System namespace. The `Array` class provides methods for creating, searching, sorting, and modifying arrays. Some of the commonly used methods of the `Array` class are `GetUpperBound`, `GetLowerBound`, and `GetLength`.

Note You learn more about the methods of the `Array` class in the later sections of this chapter.

Arrays can be single- or multidimensional. You can determine the dimensions of an array by the number of subscripts that are used to identify the position of an array element. For example, an element in a single-dimensional array is identified by only a single subscript and an element in a two-dimensional array is identified by two subscripts.

You need to declare arrays before using them in a program. The array declaration comprises the name of the array and the number of elements the array can contain. The syntax for declaring a single-dimensional array is as follows:

```
Dim Array_Name (Num_Elements) [As Element_Type]
```

where

✦ `Array_Name` refers to the name of the array.

✦ `Num_Elements` refers to the number of elements the array can contain.

✦ `Element_Type` refers to the data type of elements. This parameter is optional. If you do not specify the `Element_Type`, the array is of type `Object`.

For example,

```
Dim Emp_Name(100) as String
```

This statement declares an array named `Emp_Name` of type `String`, and it can store 101 values of type `String`. This is because the starting index of an array is zero.

You can also rewrite the preceding statement as follows:

```
Dim Emp_Name() As String = New String(100) {}
```

After declaring an array, you need to assign values to it. Consider the following example, which illustrates assigning values to an array:

```
Emp_Name(0) = "Jack"
Emp_Name(1) = "Peter"
Emp_Name(2) = "John"
. . .
. . .
Emp_Name(100) = "Michelle"
```

In this example, Jack is stored at the index 0 of the array `Emp_Name`. Similarly, Peter, John, and Michelle are stored at indices 1, 2, and 100, respectively. This implies that the array can store 101 elements. Here, 0 is the starting index or the *lower bound* of the array. The lower bound is fixed for all the arrays. Here, 100 is the *upper bound* of the array and it can differ from array to array depending on the size specified.

The lower bound of an array is always zero. The upper bound of an array is one less than the number of elements in the array.

You can also assign values to an array at the time of declaring it. The following example illustrates how to do so:

```
Dim Emp_Name() As String = {"Jack", "Peter", "John",
"Michelle"}
```

Multidimensional Arrays

In the previous section, you used arrays to store data, such as names of employees. But, you might need to store related data together, such as employee codes along with their salaries. In such a situation, you use multidimensional arrays, such as two- or three-dimensional arrays. To understand this better, consider the following statements:

```
Dim arr(10,2) as String
```

The preceding statement declares a two-dimensional array, arr, of type String. A two-dimensional array has two indices, which helps you to specify the position of elements in the array.

```
Dim arr1(10,10,10) as Integer
```

The preceding statement declares a three-dimensional array, arr1, of type Integer. The number of dimensions in an array is called the *rank* of an array. So the array mentioned in the preceding statement has a rank of 3. Each dimension in an array can have a different length.

Consider the following example, which describes the process of creating a two-dimensional array and storing the data in it.

```
Dim Emp_Details(10,6) As String
```

The preceding statement creates an array, Emp_Details, of type String. Now, consider the following statements to initialize values in this array:

```
Emp_Details(0,0) = "John"
```

The preceding statement stores the value John at the index position (0, 0).

```
Emp_Details(0,1) = "$10000"
```

The preceding statement stores the value $10000 at the index position (0, 1).

```
MessageBox.Show (Emp_Details(0,1))
```

The preceding statement displays the value stored at the index position (0, 1) of the array Emp_Details.

Cross-Reference The Show method of the MessageBox class is used to display a message to the user. You will learn more about the MessageBox class in Chapter 9.

Dynamic Arrays

You might face situations in which you don't know the number of elements to be stored in an array. For example, consider an application that uses an array to store names of the candidates who apply for a job. You cannot specify a size for this array because you would not know the number of candidates who will apply for the job. In such a situation, you use *dynamic arrays*. The size of a dynamic array can vary during the execution of a program.

You create a dynamic array by not specifying the size of the array at the time of the array declaration. To understand it better, consider the following example:

```
Dim Cand_Name() as String
```

In the preceding example, Cand_Name is a dynamic array of type String. Note that the number of elements in the array is not specified. You use the ReDim statement to specify the size of this array.

The ReDim statement

You use the ReDim statement to specify or change the size of one or more dimensions of an array that has already been declared. However, the ReDim statement cannot change the number of dimensions in an array. When the ReDim statement is executed, the existing contents of the array are lost. This is because the ReDim statement releases the array resources and creates a new array.

Some of the features of the ReDim statement are

✦ The ReDim statement does not change the data type of the array or initialize new values for the array elements. The elements of the new array are initialized with the default values of their data type.

✦ The ReDim statement can be used at the procedure level only and not at the class or module level.

The following statement illustrates the use of the ReDim statement:

```
Dim Cand_Name() as String
ReDim Cand_Name(10)
```

In the preceding example, `Cand_Name` is a dynamic array of type `String`. The `ReDim` statement resizes the array `Cand_Name` to 10. You can now store 11 strings in the array.

The `ReDim` statement can also be used for resizing multidimensional arrays. However, you cannot change the number of dimensions in an array. To understand this better, consider the following example:

```
'Declares a multidimensional array
Dim Arry(10, 20) As String

'Resizing the array
ReDim Arry(15, 25)
```

In the preceding example, `Arry` is a multidimensional array. The size of the first dimension is changed from 10 to 15 and the second dimension is changed from 20 to 25 by using the `ReDim` statement.

The Preserve keyword

In most situations, you might not want to lose the contents of an array while resizing it. To do so, you use the `Preserve` keyword with the `ReDim` statement. If you include the `Preserve` keyword, VB .NET copies the elements of the old array to the new one before modifying the dimension of the array. The following statements illustrate the use of the `Preserve` keyword:

```
Dim Cand_Name() as String
ReDim Preserve Cand_Name(15)
```

The preceding statements resize the array `Cand_Name` without losing the existing contents of the array.

In multidimensional arrays, if you use the `Preserve` keyword with the `ReDim` statement, only the size of the last dimension can be modified. For example, if you use the `Preserve` keyword for a one-dimensional array, you can resize that array and still preserve its contents because the array has only one dimension. However, if the array has two or more dimensions, you can change the size of only the last dimension by using the `Preserve` keyword.

Consider the following example:

```
'Declares a multidimensional array
Dim Arry(10, 20) As String

'Resizing the array
ReDim Preserve Arry(15, 25)
```

The preceding code will generate an error, because it is trying to change the size of the first dimension.

Consider the following example, which illustrates the use of ReDim and Preserve statements:

```
Dim Arry() as String = {"John"}

'Displaying the contents of the array
MessageBox.Show(Arry(0))        'Displays John

'Specifying the size of array
ReDim Arry(2)

'Displaying the contents of array
MessageBox.Show(Arry(0))        'Displays a blank message box

'Initializing the array
Arry(0) = "John"
Arry(1) = "Harry"

'Displaying the contents of array
MessageBox.Show(Arry(0))        'Displays John
MessageBox.Show(Arry(1))        'Displays Harry

'Modifying the size of array using Preserve
ReDim Preserve Arry(3)

'Displaying the contents
MessageBox.Show(Arry(0))        'Displays John
MessageBox.Show(Arry(1))        'Displays Harry

'Adding more contents
Arry(2) = "Jim"

'Displaying the new content
MessageBox.Show(Arry(2))        'Displays Jim
```

In the preceding example, Arry is a dynamic array of type String. Initially, it contains John. The array is then resized using the ReDim statement. All the contents of the array are lost. Then, the values John and Harry are stored in the array. Now the size of the array is further increased. However, this time the Preserve keyword is used along with the ReDim statement. As a result, the initial contents are retained.

The Erase statement

The Erase statement is used to release the memory assigned to array variables. The syntax is

```
Erase Array_names
```

Here, Array_names refers to the names of the arrays to be erased. You can specify multiple names in a single Erase statement by separating them with commas.

For example,

```
Erase Array1, Array2
```

The preceding statement erases `Array1` and `Array2`.

Having discussed arrays, we will now look at the members of the `Array` class.

The Array Class Members

The `Array` class provides various methods that help you in manipulating the arrays. Some of the commonly used functions are mentioned in the following sections.

The GetUpperBound function

The `GetUpperBound` function returns the upper bound of the specified dimension of an array. It takes the dimension for which the upper bound is to be found as a parameter. The syntax is

```
Array_name.GetUpperBound(Dimension)
```

In the preceding syntax

- ✦ `Array_name` refers to the name of the array for which the upper bound is to be found.

- ✦ `Dimension` refers to the dimension number for which the upper bound is to be found. You use 0 for the first dimension, 1 for the second dimension, and so on.

Consider the following example, which uses the `GetUpperBound` function:

```
Dim var1(10, 20, 30) as String
Dim Result as Integer
Result = var1.GetUpperBound(0)      'Returns 10
Result = var1.GetUpperBound(1)      'Returns 20
Result = var1.GetUpperBound(2)      'Returns 30
```

The GetLowerBound function

You use the `GetLowerBound` function to find the lower bound of the specified dimension of an array. However, because the lower bound of an array is always 0, this function will always return 0. It also takes the dimension for which the lower bound is to be found as a parameter. The syntax is

```
Array_name.GetLowerBound(Dimension)
```

In the preceding syntax

- ✦ `Array_name` refers to the name of the array for which the lower bound is to be found.
- ✦ `Dimension` refers to the dimension number for which the lower bound is to be found. You use 0 for the first dimension, 1 for the second dimension, and so on.

Consider the following example, which uses the `GetLowerBound` function:

```
Dim var1(10, 20, 30) as String
Dim Result as Integer

Result = var1.GetLowerBound (0)      'Returns 0
Result = var1.GetLowerBound (1)      'Returns 0
Result = var1.GetLowerBound (2)      'Returns 0
```

The GetLength function

You use the `GetLength` function to find the number of elements in the specified dimension of an array. The syntax is

```
Array_name.GetLength(Dimension)
```

In the preceding syntax

- ✦ `Array_name` refers to the name of the array whose length is to be found.
- ✦ `Dimension` refers to the dimension number for which the length is to be found. You use 0 for the first dimension, 1 for the second dimension, and so on.

Consider the following example, which uses the `GetLength` function:

```
Dim var1(10,20) as String
Dim Result as Integer

Result = var1.GetLength(0)      'Returns 11
Result = var1.GetLength(1)      'Returns 21
```

The `GetLength` function returns one more than the specified index because arrays are zero based.

The SetValue function

You use the `SetValue` function to set a value for a specific array element. You can use this function to set values in single- or multidimensional arrays.

The syntax of the `SetValue` function for storing values in a single-dimensional array is

```
Array_name.SetValue(Value, Pos)
```

In the preceding syntax:

- ✦ `Array_name` refers to the name of a single-dimensional array for which the value of the element is to be set.
- ✦ `Value` is the value to be stored or set at the specified position.
- ✦ `Pos` is the index number at which the value is to be stored.

The syntax of the `SetValue` function for storing values in a two-dimensional array is

```
Array_name.SetValue(Value, Pos1, Pos2)
```

In the preceding syntax:

- ✦ `Array_name` refers to the name of a two-dimensional array for which the value of the element is to be set.
- ✦ `Value` is the value to be stored or set at the specified position.
- ✦ `Pos1` and `Pos2` are the index numbers specifying the row and the column at which the value is to be stored.

The syntax of the `SetValue` function for storing values in a three-dimensional array is

```
Array_name.SetValue(Value, Pos1, Pos2, Pos3)
```

In the preceding syntax:

- ✦ `Array_name` refers to the name of a three-dimensional array for which the value of the element is to be set.
- ✦ `Value` is the value to be stored or set at the specified position.
- ✦ `Pos1`, `Pos2`, and `Pos3` are the first-, second-, and third-dimension index numbers of the array.

The syntax of the `SetValue` function for storing values in a multidimensional array is

```
Array_name.SetValue(Value, Pos())
```

In the preceding syntax:

- ✦ `Array_name` refers to the name of a multidimensional array for which the value of the element is to be set.

✦ `Value` is the value to be stored or set at the specified position.

✦ `Pos()` is a one-dimensional array that contains the index numbers at which the values are to be stored.

To understand this better, consider the following example:

```
Dim var1(10,10) as String

'Store Hello at index position (0,0)
var1.SetValue("Hello",0,0)

'Store World at index position (0,1)
var1.SetValue("World",0,1)
'Display the value
MessageBox.Show( var1(0,0) & " " & var1(0,1))
```

 Note   The concatenation operator (&) is used to join two strings.

An Example

The following example illustrates the use of arrays. A number is accepted from the user; the program declares an array by using the number entered by the user as the size of the array. The example uses the `GetLength`, `GetLowerBound`, and `GetUpperBound` functions to calculate the length, lower bound, and upper bound of the array. The program then accepts the values from the user and stores them in the array by using the `SetValue` function. It then displays all the values stored by using the `Show` function of the `MessageBox` class.

To test the functionality of this code, attach it to the `click` event of a button on a form.

```
Dim acceptval As Integer
'Accept a number from the user
acceptval = CInt(InputBox("Enter a number:", "Accepting
value"))

'Declare an array of the size specified by the user
Dim myarry(acceptval) As Integer
Dim length, upbound, lobound As Integer

'Find the length of array
length = myarry.GetLength(0)

'Find the lower bound of array
lobound = myarry.GetLowerBound(0)
```

```
'Find the upper bound of array
upbound = myarry.GetUpperBound(0)

'Display the length, lower bound, and upper bound of the
array
MessageBox.Show("You declared an array of size " & length)
MessageBox.Show("The lower bound of this array is " &
lobound)
MessageBox.Show("You upper bound of this array is " &
upbound)

Dim ctr As Integer
Dim str As Integer

'Store the values in the array
For ctr = lobound To upbound
   If ctr = lobound Then
      MessageBox.Show("You are at the lower bound of the
array")
   End If
   'Accept a value
   str = CInt(InputBox("Enter any number"))

   'Set the value at the specified position
   myarry.SetValue(str, ctr)
   If ctr = upbound Then
      MsgBox("You reached the upper bound of the array")
   End If
Next ctr

'Display all the values stored
For ctr = lobound To upbound
   MessageBox.Show("Number Stored at " & ctr & " is " &
myarry(ctr), "Array Contents")
Next ctr
```

 Cross-Reference You learn about the `For...Next` **loop and** `If...Then...Else` **statements in** Chapter 7.

Arrays of Arrays

VB .NET allows you to create an array containing sub-arrays. This concept is useful in situations where you need to store related data but of different data types, for example, storing the employee name and the salary of an employee within the same array. You can do this only when the base array is of type `Object`. You can also use a multidimensional array to store related data. However, the data stored in a multi-dimensional array can be of a single data type.

For example,

```
'Declare the base array
Dim myArray()() As Integer = New Integer(2)() {}

'Assign first sub array at the index position 0
myArray(0) = New Integer(5) {1, 3, 5, 7, 9, 10}

'Assign second sub array at the index position 1
myArray(1) = New Integer(4) {2, 4, 6, 8, 20}
```

In this example, myArray is an Integer array. This array contains two Integer sub-arrays.

Consider the following statement, which explains how to access the elements of these arrays:

```
MessageBox.Show(myArray(1)(4))
```

The first subscript specified with the array name points to the sub-array and the second subscript points to the specified element of that sub-array. Thus, in the preceding statement, the message box displays 20, which is the fourth element of the second sub-array.

To store the elements of different data types in an array, create an array of type Object and store arrays of other data types in it. The advantage of doing so is that you can maintain the functionality specific to a particular data type. For example, you can store strings and integers together and then you can perform calculations on integers.

To understand this better, consider an example where you need to store the names of the employees along with their salaries. You also need to calculate deductions on the salary, which is 10% of the salary. To execute this code, create a form with a text box and a button. You also need to make the following changes:

✦ Set Option Strict to Off. If the Option Strict is On, then the following code gives an error. This is because the Visual Basic compiler does not allow late binding when the Option Strict is On. *Late binding* is the process of binding objects with their classes at runtime.

✦ Set the Name property of the text box to txtSummary.

✦ Set the Multiline property of the text box to true.

```
Dim arrObj(2) As Object
Dim iVal, Ctr As Integer
iVal = CInt(InputBox("Enter the number of Employees:"))
```

```
If iVal <= 0 Then
    MessageBox.Show("Enter details of atleast one student",
"Error")
End If

Dim arrName(iVal) As String
Dim arrDed(iVal) As Integer
Dim arrSalary(iVal) As Integer

Do While Ctr < iVal
    arrName(Ctr) = InputBox("Enter the name of the Employee"
& Ctr + 1 & ":", "Enter Details")
    arrSalary(Ctr) = InputBox("Enter the salary of the
Employee" & Ctr + 1 & ":", "Enter Details")
    Ctr = Ctr + 1
Loop

arrObj(0) = arrName
arrObj(1) = arrSalary

For Ctr = 0 To iVal - 1
    arrDed(Ctr) = 0.1 * arrObj(1)(Ctr)
Next Ctr

For Ctr = 0 To iVal - 1

    If txtSummary.Text = "" Then
        txtSummary.Text = "Employee Name : " &
arrObj(0)(iCtr) & " Salary : " & arrObj(1)(iCtr) & "
Deductions : " & arrDed(iCtr)
    Else
        txtSummary.Text = txtSummary.Text & Chr(13) & Chr(10)
& "Employee Name : " & arrObj(1)(iCtr) & " Salary : " &
arrObj(0)(iCtr) & "Deductions : " & arrDed(iCtr)
    End If

Next Ctr
```

Note

The IsArray function returns a Boolean value that determines whether the given variable is an array. If the given variable is an array, the function returns True, else it returns False. You supply the variable name as an argument to the function.

Consider the following example, which illustrates the use of the IsArray function:

```
Dim var1(10) as String
Dim var2 as Integer
Dim Result as Boolean
Result = IsArray(var1)      'IsArray returns True
Result = IsArray(var2)      'IsArray return False
```

Summary

In this chapter, you learned about arrays. First, you learned about declaring arrays. Next, you learned about the various types of arrays, such as fixed arrays, multidimensional arrays, and dynamic arrays. You also learned about the `ReDim` and `Erase` statements and the `Preserve` keyword. Finally, you learned about the members of the `Array` class, such as `GetUpperBound`, `GetLowerBound`, `GetLength`, and `SetValue`.

✦　　✦　　✦

Conditional Logic

by Uday Kranti

Y ou write programs to carry out a set of tasks, such as entering data into a database, validating data, and performing calculations. In all these tasks, the program code comprises a set of statements, which contains logic related to the program. But a program should also be capable of handling unexpected situations, such as the user not entering data or entering incorrect data. In other words, the program must be able to adjust its behavior depending on the user input.

VB .NET has statements, such as If...Then...Else and Select...Case, which help you to conditionally execute your program . VB .NET also provides you with various looping statements, such as Do...Loop, While...End While, and For...Next, which help your program to repeat a set of statements, conditionally. In this chapter, you learn about the syntax and implementation of these statements.

The If...Then...Else Statement

Consider a sales and invoicing application that is used by a department store to calculate the total order value. Now, the store decides to offer a discount of 20 percent to all the customers buying more than 10 articles and a 10 percent discount to the remaining customers. In situations in which you need to execute some code based on a condition, you use If...Then...Else statements. There are two types of If...Then...Else statements: single-line and multiple-line. You use the single-line statement to execute a single statement based on a condition. The syntax of the single-line If...Then...Else statement is

```
If condition Then statement [Else statement]
```

In the preceding syntax, *condition*, which is a Boolean expression, is evaluated. If the condition is true, the statement following `Then` is executed. If the condition is false, the statement following `Else` is executed. However, the `Else` part is optional.

 Note   All the statements enclosed in square brackets in the syntax are optional; that is, you can omit them.

The following example illustrates the use of single-line `If...Then...Else` statement:

```
If QtyOrdered > 10 Then Discount = 20 Else Discount = 10
```

In this example, the value of the variable `QtyOrdered` is evaluated. If it is greater than 10, the value of `Discount` is set to 20; otherwise, it is set to 10.

You can have multiple statements in the single-line form of the `If...Then...Else` statement. However, all the statements need to be on the same line and should be separated by a colon. The syntax is

```
If condition Then statement:[statement]:[statement]
```

The following example illustrates the use of multiple statements in a single-line `If...Then...Else` statement:

```
If QtyOrdered > 10 Then Discount = 20 : MsgBox ("Discount is"
& iDiscount)
```

In this example, the value of the variable `QtyOrdered` is evaluated. If it is greater than 10, the value of `Discount` is set to 20 and a message box is displayed. However, multiple statements in a single line might affect the readability of the code. In such a situation, you can break a single-line `If...Then...Else` statement to multiple lines. The syntax for a multiple-line `If...Then...Else` statement is as follows:

```
If condition Then
   statement(s)
[Else
   [statement(s)]]
End If
```

In a multiple-line `If...Then...Else` statement, the `End If` statement is used to mark the end of an `If...Then...Else` statement.

The following example illustrates the point:

```
If QtyOrdered > 10 Then
   Discount = 20
Else
   Discount = 10
End If
```

This example does not check for any quantity less than or equal to zero. You can do this in the preceding example by adding multiple conditions. To do so, you use logical operators, such as AND and OR. You can modify the preceding code as

```
If QtyOrdered >0 And QtyOrdered < 10 Then
   Discount = 10
Else
   Discount = 20
End If
```

You might have situations in which you need to check an expression for multiple values. For example, a company might decide to offer different discounts depending on the quantity ordered. In addition, the program should also check for any invalid entry. In such situations, you use the ElseIf statement in the If...Then...Else statement. The syntax for the If statement with the ElseIf statement is

```
If condition1 Then
   statement1
[ElseIf condition2 [Then]
   [statement2]]
[Else
   [statement3]]
End If
```

In the preceding syntax, if *condition1* is false, then control moves to *condition2*. If *condition2* is true, the *statement2* following ElseIf is executed; otherwise, the control moves to the statements following the Else.

For example:

```
If QtyOrdered > 0 And QtyOrdered <= 10 Then
   Discount = 10
ElseIf QtyOrdered > 10 And QtyOrdered <= 20 Then
   Discount = 20
ElseIf QtyOrdered > 20 Then
   Discount = 30
Else
   Msgbox ("Please check the quantity entered")
End If
```

In this example, a discount is offered in three slabs. If the quantity ordered is less than or equal to 10, the discount offered is 10 percent. If the quantity ordered is greater than 10 and less than or equal to 20, the discount offered is 20 percent. If the quantity ordered is greater than 20, the discount offered is 30 percent. It also checks for any quantity less than or equal to zero and displays an error message.

Note   You can have as many ElseIf statements within an If...Then...Else statement as you require. However, all the ElseIf statements should come before the Else statement. You need only one End If statement for the entire If block.

You can also have nested If statements in your program. You can nest the If statements to any number of levels. But you need to have a separate End If for each If statement. To understand this better, consider the following example:

```
Dim Type As String
Dim Size, Discount As Integer

'Accept the type of drive
Type = InputBox("Enter the type of Drive (CD/DVD/Floppy): ")

'Accept the size of RAM
Size = CInt(InputBox("Enter the size of RAM: "))

If Type = "CD" Then
    Discount = 10
    MessageBox.Show("Discount is " & Discount & "%")
ElseIf Type = "DVD" Then
    If Size <= 128 Then
       Discount = 20
       MessageBox.Show("Discount is " & Discount & "%")
    Else
       Discount = 30
       MessageBox.Show("Discount is " & Discount & "%")
    End If
Else
    MessageBox.Show("No Discount")
End If
```

The Select...Case Statement

You use the Select...Case statement to execute different sets of statements based on the value of an expression. The Select...Case statement is similar to the If...Then...Else statement. The only difference between the two is that If and ElseIf can evaluate different expressions in each statement, whereas the Select statement can evaluate only one expression. The Select statement then uses the result of this expression to execute different sets of statements. However, the Select...Case statement is preferred over If and ElseIf statement when you need to use multiple conditions because it makes the code easy to read and understand. The syntax for the Select...Case statement is

```
Select Case expression
  Case expressionlist
        statement(s)
  [Case Else
        [statement(s)]]
End Select
```

In the preceding syntax, expressionlist refers to the constants or expressions that are compared with the result of the expression mentioned with the Select...Case statement. When the Select...Case statement is executed, the expression is evaluated and the result is compared with each constant specified with the Case statement. If the result of the expression is equal to any of the Case constants, statements following that Case statement are executed. However, if no match is found for the expression result, statements following the Case Else statement (if it is present) are executed. The End Select statement marks the end of the Select...Case statement.

For example:

```
Select Case Month
  Case 1
        Msgbox ("January")
  Case 2
        MsgBox ("February")
   . . .
   . . .
  Case 12
        MsgBox ("December")
  Case Else
        MsgBox ("Incorrect number")
End Select
```

In this example, the value of the variable Month is evaluated and is then compared with the values mentioned with the various Case statements. In this case, none of the values match and a message box informing that an incorrect number was entered is displayed.

Consider the sales and invoicing application again. In this application, it is practically impossible to write Case statements for each and every value of quantity ordered. In such a situation, you can specify a conditional expression in the Case statement instead of specifying a value. You use the Is keyword to specify this conditional expression.

For example:

```
Select Case QtyOrdered
  Case Is <=10
        Discount = 10
  Case Is <=15
        Discount = 15
  Case Is <=20
        Discount = 20
  Case Is <=25
        Discount = 25
  Case Is >25
        Discount = 30
  Case Else
        MsgBox ("Incorrect Quantity Entered")
End Select
```

In this example, the value of QtyOrdered is evaluated and is checked against each Case. If QtyOrdered is less than or equal to 10, the Discount is set to 10.

You can specify ranges in each of the Case statements given. To do so, you use the To keyword.

For example:

```
Select Case QtyOrdered
   Case 1 To 10
           Discount = 10
   Case 11 To 15
           Discount = 15
   Case 16 To 20
           Discount = 20
   Case 21 To 25
           Discount = 25
   Case Is >30
           Discount = 30
   Case Else
           MsgBox ("Incorrect Quantity Entered")
End Select
```

You might need to have the same set of statements for more than one value of the expression. In such a situation, you can specify multiple values or ranges in a single Case statement. To understand this better, consider the following example:

```
Dim Num as Integer
Num = CInt.(InputBox ("Enter a number between 10 and 20:"))
Select Case Num
   Case 11, 13, 17, 19
           MsgBox (" Prime Number")
   Case 10, 12, 14 To 16, 18, 20
           MsgBox ("Not a Prime Number")
   Case Else
           MsgBox "Incorrect Number"
End Select
```

In this example, a number between 10 and 20 is accepted from the user. The value of the expression is evaluated and if it is 11, 13, 17, or 19, a message box informing that these are prime numbers is displayed. If the numbers are 10, 12, 14, 15, 16, or 20, a message box informing that these are not prime numbers is displayed. Otherwise, an error message is displayed.

Do...Loop Statement

You might need to execute a set of statements repetitively. For example, to calculate the total order value, you want the user to enter a valid value (that is, greater than zero) for quantity ordered. In such a situation, you can display a message box until the user enters a valid value. You can do this by using the Do...Loop statements. The Do...Loop statements are used to execute a set of statements repeatedly. The syntax of the Do...Loop statement is

```
Do While|Until condition
   [statements]
   [Exit Do]
   [statements]
Loop
```

or

```
Do
   [statements]
   [Exit Do]
   [statements]
Loop While|Until condition
```

In the preceding syntax

✦ While|Until are the keywords that are used to repeat the loop. You can use only one of them at a time. Use While to repeat the loop until the condition becomes false and use Until to repeat the loop until the condition becomes true.

✦ The Exit Do statement is used to exit the Do loop. As a result, the statement following the Loop statement is executed. If you place the While or Until after the Loop statement, the loop will be executed at least once.

For example:

```
Dim Ctr as Integer = 1
Do While Ctr <= 10
   MsgBox ("The value of counter is " & Ctr)
   Ctr = Ctr + 1
Loop
```

In this example, the set of statements within the Do...Loop statement is repeated 10 times.

Sometimes, during execution your application might run into an infinite or endless loop. This problem occurs if you do not specify the condition correctly or you forget to increment the counter variable.

For example:

```
Dim Ctr as Integer = 1
Do While Ctr <= 10
   MsgBox ("The value of counter is " & Ctr)

Loop
```

The preceding code will run into an infinite loop because the value of the variable Ctr will always remain the same and the condition will never become false. In this situation, you need to close the VB .NET application. As a result, all the unsaved information will be lost. You can avoid infinite loops by carefully examining the code before actually executing it.

While...End While Statement

You use the `While...End While` statements to repeat a set of statements as long as the condition is true. The syntax for the `While...End While` statement is

```
While condition
   statements
End While
```

In the preceding syntax, if the condition is true, the statements are executed. The `End While` statement marks the end of the `While` statement.

For example:

```
Dim Ctr as Integer = 1
While Ctr <= 10
   MsgBox ("The value of counter is " & Ctr)
   Ctr = Ctr + 1
End While
```

In this example, the set of statements within `While...End While` statement is repeated 10 times.

For...Next Statement

The `For...Next` statements are used to repeat a set of statements a specified number of times. The syntax for the `For...Next` statement is

```
For Counter = <StartValue> To <EndValue> [StepValue]
   [Statement(s)]
   [Exit For]
Next [Counter]
```

In the preceding syntax

✦ `Counter` is any numeric variable.

✦ `StartValue` is the initial value of the counter. `EndValue` is the final value of the counter.

✦ `StepValue` is the value by which the counter is incremented. It can be positive or negative and is optional. If you omit the step value, the default is set to 1.

✦ *Statements* refers to the code that is executed the given number of times. The Exit For statement is used to exit the For loop. As a result, the statement following the Next statement is executed.

✦ The Next statement marks the end of the For statement. As soon as the program encounters the Next statement, the step value is added to the counter and the next iteration of the loop takes place. It is good programming practice to specify the name of the counter in the Next statement.

For example:

```
Dim Ctr as Integer
For Ctr = 1 To 10
  MsgBox ("The value of counter is " & Ctr)
Next Ctr
```

In this example, the statement within the For...Next statement is repeated 10 times.

You can use variables instead of specifying numbers. This makes the application more user-friendly because your application can loop the number of times specified by the user.

For example:

```
Dim Ctr, Value as Integer
Value = CInt("How many times should the loop execute")
For Ctr = 1 To Value
  MsgBox ("The value of counter is " & Ctr)
Next Ctr
```

For Each...Next Statement

The For Each...Next statement is used to repeat a set of statements for each element in an array or collection. The For Each...Next statement is executed if there is at least one element in an array or collection. The loop repeats for each element. The syntax of the For Each...Next statement is

```
For Each Component In Set
  [Statement(s)]
  [Exit For]
Next [Counter]
```

In the preceding syntax

✦ *Component* is the variable used to refer to the elements of an array or a collection.

✦ *Set* refers to an array or an object collection.

For example:

```
Dim Arr() as String = {"Mon", "Tues", "Wed", "Thurs", "Fri", "Sat"}
Dim Arrelement as String
For Each Arrelement in Arr
  MsgBox (Arrelement)
Next
```

In this example, Arr is an array of type String that stores weekdays. Arrelement is a string. Here, the For Each...Next statement is used to display all the elements of the array Arr.

Note   A collection is a set of similar items. These items are objects having properties and methods.

A Complete Example

Now, create a VB .NET application that accepts the name of the students and their grades. Depending on the grade of the student, the application assigns remarks to them, such as Excellent and Good. The summary of the performance of all the students is then displayed in a text box. The application also checks the user for entering any incorrect data, such as incorrect grades. To execute this code, design a form as shown in Figure 7-1. You also need to make the following changes:

✦ Set the Name property of the text box to txtSummary.

✦ Set the Multiline property of the text box to true.

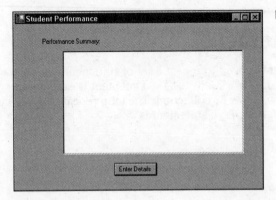

Figure 7-1: A sample form

In the following example, the number of students is accepted from the user. This number is used to define the length of two arrays, arrName and arrRemarks. Now, a Do...While loop is used to prompt the user for the names and grades of the students. The name entered by the user is stored in the array arrName. Depending on the grade of the student, the remarks are generated (by using the Select...Case statement) and are stored in the array `arrRemarks`. The values stored in these arrays are then displayed in the text box `txtSummary` by using a `For...Next` loop. See Figure 7-2 for the sample output of this code.

```
'Clear the text box
txtSummary.Text = ""

Dim Value, Ctr As Integer

'Accept a number from the user
Value = CInt(InputBox("Enter the number of students:"))

'Check the validity of the number
If Value <= 0 Then
    MessageBox.Show("Enter details of atleast one student",
"Error")
End If

Dim arrName(Value) As String
Dim sGrade As String
Dim arrRemarks(Value) As String

Do While Ctr < Value

    'Accept the name of students
    arrName(Ctr) = InputBox("Enter the name of Student " &
Ctr + 1 & ":", "Enter Details")

    'Accept the grade of students
    Grade = InputBox("Enter the grade of Student " & Ctr + 1
& ":" & Chr(10) & Chr(13) & "(A/B/C/D/F)", "Enter Details")

'Assign remarks to students
    Select Case Grade
      Case "A"
        arrRemarks(Ctr) = "Excellent"
      Case "B"
        arrRemarks(Ctr) = "Good"
      Case "C"
        arrRemarks(Ctr) = "Fair"
      Case "D"
        arrRemarks(Ctr) = "Poor"
      Case "F"
        arrRemarks(Ctr) = "Fail"
      Case Else
        MessageBox.Show("Incorrect Value Entered", "Error")
        Exit Sub
    End Select
    Ctr = Ctr + 1
Loop

'Display the summary in the text box
For Ctr = 0 To Value - 1
```

```
'Check whether the text box is empty or not
    If txtSummary.Text = "" Then

      If arrRemarks(Ctr) = "Fail" Then
        txtSummary.Text = arrName(Ctr) & " has Failed in
the exams"
      Else
        txtSummary.Text = arrName(Ctr) & "'s performance
is " & arrRemarks(Ctr)
      End If

    Else

      If arrRemarks(Ctr) = "Fail" Then
        txtSummary.Text = txtSummary.Text & Chr(13) +
Chr(10) & arrName(Ctr) & " has Failed in the exams"
      Else
        txtSummary.Text = txtSummary.Text & Chr(13) &
Chr(10) & arrName(Ctr) & "'s performance is " &
arrRemarks(Ctr)
      End If

    End If
Next
```

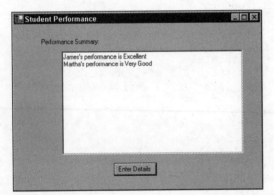

Figure 7-2: The sample output

 Note   The Chr function is used to get the character for the specified character code. Chr(10) returns the linefeed character and Chr(13) returns carriage return. Both of these are used simultaneously to move the text to a new line.

Summary

In this chapter, you learned the concepts related to conditional logic. First, you learned implementing If...Then...Else statements and Select...Case statements. Next, you learned about the various looping statements, such as Do...Loop, While...End While, For...Next, and For Each...Next.

✦   ✦   ✦

Procedures

by Uday Kranti and Jason Beres

Up until now, you have learned the basics of the VB .NET programming language. All of the executable VB .NET code that you write will be in procedures. Procedures give you the ability to logically group code that will perform certain tasks.

In this chapter, you learn about two types of procedures that you can write in VB .NET: the Sub procedure and the Function procedure.

Cross-Reference For more information on all of the possibilities and new functionality of procedures in VB .NET, see Chapter 3 and Chapter 15.

Visual Basic has always supplied built-in functions that do many complex and simple tasks. Although they are not necessarily "procedures," you will use these built-in functions in the procedures that you write to alleviate some of the tedious coding that you would otherwise need to do. It is important to note that these functions are geared towards developers who have used Visual Basic before. The .NET framework provides the same capabilities that the built-in functions did in Visual Basic through the base class libraries, and a new developer should consider using only the System namespaces in application development and not rely on the compatibility layer provided for legacy Visual Basic functions.

Procedures Overview

Procedures contain all of the executable code in your application. During the design phase of any application, you can have a team of developers working on the user interface, and another team of developers working on the application logic flow. The team working on the application logic determines how to logically group tasks that need to make the program work. A task can be getting data from a database, checking the status of an order, or authenticating a user to your Web site. Each one of these tasks can be separated and put into procedures. If you design your application correctly, and split the processes and tasks logically, you can reuse that same code across the application you are working on or even across other applications. This should be the goal of every developer. There is no sense in having a block of code behind a button and then having the same exact code behind another button on another form in the same application. This creates room for bugs. If you change something in one place, you will need to change it in another place. This is a bad thing, because it is very easy to forget where things are when an application gets very large. You could have hundreds of classes and forms in your application, and it would be impossible to remember where you changed what and how. To avoid this, you group your code in logical tasks and put that code inside of procedures.

Procedure access modifiers

A procedure is created within a class or a module. You can always call a procedure from the same class or module in which it is created. However, you can call the procedure from different classes and modules depending on the access modifier used while creating the procedure. The *access modifiers* determine the scope within which a procedure can be called. The following lists the valid access modifiers for all Sub and Function procedures:

✦ **Public:** Procedures that can called from any class or module in the application.

✦ **Private:** Procedures that can be called only from the class or module where they are declared.

✦ **Shared:** Procedures that are not associated with an instance of a class.

✦ **Protected:** Procedures that can be called from the class or module where they are declared or from the derived classes.

✦ **Friend:** Procedures that can be called from any class or module in the application that contains its declaration.

✦ **Protected Friend:** Procedures that have both Protected and Friend access.

Advantages of procedures

As mentioned earlier, procedures allow logical grouping of code into tasks. When a complex application is divided into procedures, the code is more flexible and easier to maintain and debug. Creating procedures to perform a single task has the following benefits:

✦ The code in a procedure is reusable. After a procedure is created and tested, it can be called from different places in an application.

✦ The application is easier to debug and maintain, because you can easily trace the source of an error in a procedure instead of checking the entire application for errors.

Types of Procedures

The two types of procedures covered in this chapter are Sub procedures and Function procedures.

✦ Sub procedures perform specific tasks, such as generating an Order ID or connecting to a database. However, these procedures do not return a value to the calling statement.

✦ last:Function procedures perform specific tasks and return a value to the calling statement.

Cross-Reference   For information on Property procedures, see Chapter 14.

Sub procedures

You can create a Sub procedure in modules and classes. The default access modifier for Sub procedures is Public, indicating that Sub procedures can be called from anywhere in an application. This is the exact opposite of previous versions of Visual Basic, where the default access modifier was Private. The syntax for creating a Sub procedure is

```
[ <attrlist> ] [{ Overloads | Overrides | Overridable |
NotOverridable | MustOverride | Shadows | Shared }]
[{ Public | Protected | Friend | Protected Friend | Private
}]
Sub name [(arglist)]
    [ statements ]
    [ Exit Sub ]
    [ statements ]
End Sub
```

In the preceding syntax

✦ Overloads indicates that there are other procedures in the class with the same name, but with different arguments.

✦ Overrides indicates that the procedure can "override" an identically named procedure in the base class.

✦ Overridable indicates that the procedure can be overridden by an identically named procedure in a derived class.

✦ NotOverridable indicates that this procedure cannot be overridden in a derived class.

✦ MustOverride indicates that the procedure is not implemented in the class and must be implemented in a derived class for the class to be creatable.

Cross-Reference `Overloads, Overrides, Overridable, NotOverridable,` **and** `MustOverride` **are covered in Chapter 14.**

✦ `[Public | Protected | Friend | Protected Friend | Private]` represents the access modifier for the Sub procedure. If you do not specify any access modifier, `Public` is used by default.

✦ `Sub` indicates that the procedure is a `Sub` procedure.

✦ `<ProcedureName>` represents the name of the procedure.

✦ `([Argument list])` represents the list of arguments to be passed to the procedure.

Note If the `Sub` procedure does not take any arguments, the `Sub` statement must include an empty set of parantheses.

✦ `End Sub` indicates the end of the `Sub` procedure.

To understand the usage of the preceding syntax, consider the following procedure. The `CalculateDiscount` `Sub` procedure takes the quantity and unit price of a product and calculates the sales discount.

```
Public Sub CalculateDiscount(dblQuantity As Double, _
                       dblPrice As Double)

    Dim dblAmount As Double
    Dim dblDiscount As Double

    dblAmount = dblQuantity * dblPrice
    If dblAmount >= 150 And dblAmount < 250 Then
      dblDiscount = 0.1
    ElseIf dblAmount >=250 Then
      dblDiscount = 0.15
    End If

    Console.Writeline(dblDiscount)

End Sub
```

After creating a `Sub` procedure, it is invoked explicitly by a calling statement. The syntax used to call a `Sub` procedure is

```
[Call] <ProcedureName> ([Arguments list])
```

The `Call` keyword can be used to execute the code inside of a `Sub` procedure. However, the use of this keyword is optional. For example, to call the `CalculateDiscount` procedure that you created, use one of the following statements:

```
Call CalculateDiscount(20, 10.5)
```

or

```
CalculateDiscount(20, 10.5)
```

Argument passing mechanisms

As mentioned earlier, procedures are used to perform specific tasks. With each call to a procedure, the result differs depending on the data passed as arguments. Procedure arguments can be variables, constants, or expressions. While creating a procedure, you declare an argument for the procedure in the same way you declare a variable.

The default data type of a procedure argument is the Object. However, you can specify a different data type by using the As clause:

```
Varname As data type
```

Arguments can be passed to a procedure in two ways: by value and by reference. When an argument is passed *by value*, a copy of the argument is passed when the procedure is called. On the other hand, when an argument is passed *by reference*, a reference to the original variable is passed. Table 8-1 compares the two mechanisms.

Table 8-1 **Comparison Between the By Value and By Reference Mechanisms**	
By Value	*By Reference*
An argument is passed by value by using the ByVal keyword.	An argument is passed by reference by using the ByRef keyword
In this mechanism, since only a copy of the orginal variable is passed, the value of the original variable remains unchanged even if the procedure modifies the value that is passed.	In this mechanism, since a reference to the original variable is passed, the value of the original variable is affected immediately if the procedure modifies the value that is passed.
This is the default mechanism.	This is not the default mechanism.

To understand the difference between the ByVal and ByRef mechanism of parameter passing, consider the following example. In this example, the SwapByVal procedure takes two integer parameters, which are passed by value. The procedure then swaps the integer values that are passed. Another procedure called SwapByRef also takes two integer parameters, which are then swapped. But, the parameters are passed by reference.

The two procedures are then called in the Click event of a command button. In the Click event of the command button, two numbers are accepted from the user.

These two numbers are passed to the SwapByVal procedure. Because the numbers are passed by value, the original numbers are not affected. However, when the same numbers are passed to the SwapByRef procedure, the original numbers are also swapped.

```
' The SwapByVal Sub procedure
Public Sub SwapByVal (ByVal intNum1 As Integer, ByVal intNum2
As Integer)

    Dim temp As Integer

    Temp = intNum1
    intNum1 = intNum2
    intNum2 = temp

     Messagebox.Show("The swapped ByVal numbers are: " & _
                  CStr(intNum1) & _
              " And " & CStr (intNum2))
End Sub

' The SwapByRef Sub procedure
Public Sub SwapByRef (ByRef intNum1 As Integer, ByRef intNum2
As Integer)

    Dim temp As Integer

    Temp = intNum1
    intNum1 = intNum2
    intNum2 = temp

     Messagebox.Show("The swapped ByRef numbers are: " & _
                  CStr(intNum1) & _
              " And " & CStr (intNum2))
End Sub
```

The following code calls the SwapByVal and SwapByRef **procedures:**

```
Dim intMyNum1, intMyNum2 As Integer

intMyNum1 = InputBox("Please enter the first number:")
intMyNum2 = InputBox("Please enter the second number:")

' Calling the SwapByVal procedure

SwapByVal(intMyNum1,intMyNum2)

' The same numbers that you entered are displayed.
' Thus, the original numbers are not changed.

    MessageBox.Show("The original numbers are: " _
        & " + CStr(intMyNum1) & " And " & CStr(intMyNum2))

' Calling the SwapByRef procedure
```

```
SwapByRef(intMyNum1, intMyNum2)

' The original numbers are swapped.

MessageBox.Show("The original numbers are: " _
    & " + CStr(intMyNum1) & " And " & CStr(intMyNum2))
```

The Sub Main procedure

The `Sub` procedure that is executed first when a Visual Basic program is run is the `Main` procedure. The syntax of this procedure is

```
Sub Main()
'Code here
End Sub
```

The `Sub Main` procedure is the starting point of every application. Every Visual Basic .NET application must contain a `Sub Main` procedure. You can include any initialization code that you might have in the `Sub Main` procedure, such as connection to a database or authenticating a user.

Function procedures

Like `Sub` procedures, `Function` procedures (or functions), perform a specific task and are created in classes and modules. However, unlike `Sub` procedures, `Function` procedures can return a value. Because `Function` procedures return a value, you need to define the data type for the return value while creating a `Function` procedure. The syntax for creating a `Function` procedure is

```
[ <attrlist> ] [{ Overloads | Overrides | Overridable |
NotOverridable | MustOverride | Shadows | Shared }]
[{ Public | Protected | Friend | Protected Friend | Private
}] Function name[(arglist)] [ As type ]
    [ statements ]
    [ Exit Function ]
    [ statements ]
End Function
```

In the preceding syntax

- ✦ `Overloads` indicates that there are other procedures in the class with the same name, but with different arguments.

- ✦ `Overrides` indicates that the procedure can "override" an identically named procedure in the base class.

- ✦ `Overridable` indicates that the procedure can be overridden by an identically named procedure in a derived class.

- ✦ `NotOverridable` indicates that this procedure cannot be overridden in a derived class.

✦ `MustOverride` indicates that the procedure is not implemented in the class and must be implemented in a derived class for the class to be creatable.

Cross-Reference
`Overloads`, `Overrides`, `Overridable`, `NotOverridable`, **and** `MustOverride` are covered in Chapter 14.

✦ `[Public | Protected | Friend | Protected Friend | Private]` represents the access modifier for the `Sub` procedure. If you do not specify any access modifier, `Public` is used by default.

✦ `Function` indicates that the procedure is a `Function` procedure.

✦ `<Function Name>` represents the name of the `Function` procedure.

✦ `([Arguments list])` represents the list of arguments to be passed to the `Function` procedure. The arguments can be passed by value or by reference.

✦ `[As <type>]` represents the data type of the return value of the `Function` procedure.

✦ `Exit Function` explicitly exits a function. There can be more than one `Exit Function` statement in a function.

✦ `End Function` indicates the end of the Function procedure.

Now create a `Function` procedure called `CalculateDiscount` (the one created as a `Sub` procedure earlier) that returns the calculated discount. If the data type of the calculated discount is `Double`, you need to declare the `Function` as follows:

```
Function CalculateDiscount (ByVal dblQuantity As Double,
ByVal dblPrice As Double) As Double
    'Code here
End Function
```

To return a value from a `Function` procedure, you can use the `Return` statement or assign the return value to the name of the `Function` procedure. For example, if the calculated discount is stored in a variable `dblDiscount`, use one of the following statements to return the calculated discount from the `CalculateDiscount` `Function` procedure:

```
CalculateDiscount = dblDiscount
```

or

```
Return dblDiscount
```

Note
The statement that returns a value can appear any number of times in the `Function` procedure. If the `Function` procedure contains no statement that returns a value, the procedure returns a default value. For example, if the procedure returns a numeric value, 0 is returned. If the return type of the procedure is `String`, the value returned is a zero-length string ("").

The complete code for the `CalculateDiscount Function` procedure is as follows:

```
Public Function CalculateDiscount(dblQuantity As Double, _
                        dblPrice As Double) As Double

    Dim dblAmount As Double
    Dim dblDiscount As Double

    dblAmount = dblQuantity * dblPrice

    If dblAmount >= 150 And dblAmount < 250 Then
        dblDiscount = 0.1
    ElseIf dblAmount >=250 Then
        dblDiscount = 0.15
    End If

    Return dblDiscount

End Function
```

To call a function, you create a variable to accept the return value from the function, as the following code demonstrates:

```
ReturnValue = <FunctionName>([Arguments list])
```

To call the `CalculateDiscount` function, you use the following code:

```
Dim dblqty As Double = 10
Dim dblprice As Double = 10
Dim dbldiscount As Double
dbldiscount = CalculateDiscount(dblqty, dblprice)
MessageBox.Show(dbldiscount)
```

You can also call a function within an expression. For example, consider the following code, which checks the discount returned from the `CalculateDiscount` function against a specific value:

```
If CalculateDiscount(dblqty, dblprice) = 0.15 Then
    ' Execute statements
End If
```

Built-in Functions

Visual Basic has many built-in functions that are very useful in easing your development. Although the .NET Framework has many System namespaces that provide built-in functionality, it is also important to know that the Microsoft.VisualBasic namespace has functions that you can use in your applications as well. This chapter is not a comprehensive list of every built-in function, but it gives you the most commonly used functions that are important when you write your applications. For a complete list of functions in Visual Basic .NET, refer to the Platform SDK.

In this section, you learn about the functions and properties in the following namespaces:

✦ Microsoft.VisualBasic.Conversion

✦ Microsoft.VisualBasic.DateAndTime

✦ Microsoft.VisualBasic.Strings

 Cross-Reference More namespaces are covered in other chapters. See Chapters 6, 7, 9, 10, 11, and 12 to understand the full range of built-in functions that you can use.

Microsoft.VisualBasic.Conversion

The Microsoft.VisualBasic.Conversion namespace handles basic conversion functions for strings and numbers. For a broader range of conversion functionality, including types not allowed in VB .NET, refer the to System.Convert namespace in the Platform SDK.

ErrorToString

The `ErrorToString` function returns a human-readable string representing the numeric error number passed to it. When using Unstructured Exception Handling, this will be the last number reported by number property of the `err` object. In previous versions of Visual Basic, the same functionality was provided by the `Error` function.

```
MessageBox.Show(ErrorToString(13))
' Returns "Type Mismatch"
```

Fix and Int

The `Fix` and `Int` functions remove the fractional part of a number. For positive numbers, both functions behave the same; the fraction is removed. There is no rounding of numbers. The difference is when dealing with negative numbers. The `Int` function returns the first negative integer less than or equal to the number, whereas the `Fix` function returns the first negative integer greater than or equal to the number.

```
Dim x, y as single
Y = -99.4
X = -99.4
Messagebox.show cstr(fix(y)) ' Returns -99
Messagebox.show cstr(int(x)) ' Returns -100
```

If the number passed to the functions were a positive 99.4, both `Messagebox` functions would return 99.

Hex

The Hex function returns the string representation of the hexadecimal value of a number. The value passed to the Hex function can be the Short, Byte, Integer, Long, or Object data type.

```
MessageBox.Show(Hex(10)) ' Returns A
MessageBox.Show(Hex(16)) ' Returns 10
MessageBox.Show(Hex("T"))' Error - Cannot pass a String value
```

Oct

The Oct function returns the string representation of the octal value of a number. The value passed to the Oct function can be the Short, Byte, Integer, Long, or Object data type.

```
MessageBox.Show(Oct(10)) ' Returns 12
MessageBox.Show(Oct(16)) ' Returns 20
MessageBox.Show(Oct("T"))' Error - Cannot pass a String value
```

Str

The Str function returns the string representation of a number. A leading space is returned to represent the sign.

```
MessageBox.Show(Str(10)) ' Returns " 10"
MessageBox.Show(Str(-10))' Returns "-10"
MessageBox.Show(Str("T"))' Error - Cannot pass a String value
```

Val

The Val function returns the numbers contained in a string as a numeric value of the type Integer or Double, depending on whether there is a decimal place in the string value. The Val function evaluates a string and stops at the first character that cannot be represented as a number or space.

```
MessageBox.Show(Val("123"))
'Returns 123
MessageBox.Show(Val("123 4"))
' Returns "1234"
MessageBox.Show(Val("123.4"))
' Returns "123.4"
MessageBox.Show(Val("123 4 Main Street Suite 194"))
' Returns "1234"
```

Microsoft.VisualBasic.DateAndTime

The Microsoft.VisualBasic.DataAndTime namespace covers everything you could ever need to accomplish when manipulating dates and times. This namespace is very comprehensive in date and time functionality.

Note

Depending on the settings in the control panel or in application-specific settings, the format of the default date and time might be different than listed here. The setting used here is English – United States.

DateAdd

The `DateAdd` function returns a date value to which a time interval has been added. The `DateAdd` function contains three parts:

- ✦ `Interval`: The `DateInterval` enumeration value or string equivalent representing the type of interval you are adding.
- ✦ `Number`: Positive or negative `Double` data type representing the number of intervals you are adding.
- ✦ `DateValue`: The date expression representing the date and time to which the interval is added.

If the *number* passed to the `DateAdd` function is negative, the function subtracts from the *date value* expression. Table 8-2 lists the values of the `DateInterval` enumeration.

Table 8-2
DateInterval Enumeration

Value	String	Interval Added
DateInterval.Day	D	Day (integer)
DateInterval.DayOfYear	Y	Day (integer)
DateInterval.Hour	H	Hour rounded to nearest millisecond
DateInterval.Minute	N	Minute rounded to nearest millisecond
DateInterval.Month	M	Month (integer)
DateInterval.Quarter	Q	Quarter (integer)
DateInterval.Second	S	Second rounded to nearest millisecond
DateInterval.Weekday	W	Day (integer)
DateInterval.WeekOfYear	www	Week (integer)
DateInterval.Year	yyyy	Year (integer)

```
Dim ret As Date

ret = DateAdd(DateInterval.Day, 5, #1/1/2001#)
' Returns 1/6/2001 12:00:00 AM
```

```
ret = DateAdd(DateInterval.Quarter, 2, #1/1/2001#)
' Returns 7/1/2001 12:00:00 AM

ret = DateAdd(DateInterval.Year, 25, #1/1/2001#)
' Returns 1/1/2026 12:00:00 AM
```

DateDiff

The DateDiff function returns a long value representing the number of time intervals specified between two date values. The DateDiff function has the following four arguments:

✦ Interval: DateInterval enumeration value or string expression representing the unit of time between the date1 and date2 values. Table 8-2 lists the values of the DateInterval enumeration.

✦ Date1, Date2: The date and time values used in the calculation. This first date value is subtracted from the second date value.

✦ DayOfWeek: An optional value from the FirstDayOfWeek enumeration that specifies what day to use as the first day of the week. The default value is Sunday. Table 8-3 lists the values of the FirstDayOfWeek enumeration.

✦ WeekOfYear: An optional value from the FirstWeekOfYear enumeration that specifies the first week of the year. The default value is Jan1. Table 8-4 lists the values of the WeekOfYear enumeration.

Table 8-3 FirstDay Of Week Enumeration		
Enumeration	**Value**	**Description**
FirstDayOfWeek.System	0	First day of the week as specified in the system settings in the control panel.
FirstDayOfWeek.Sunday	1	Sunday
FirstDayOfWeek.Monday	2	Monday
FirstDayOfWeek.Tuesday	3	Tuesday
FirstDayOfWeek.Wednesday	4	Wednesday
FirstDayOfWeek.Thursday	5	Thursday
FirstDayOfWeek.Friday	6	Friday
FirstDayOfWeek.Saturday	7	Saturday

Table 8-4
Week Of Year Enumeration

Enumeration Value	Value	Description
FirstWeekOfYear.System	0	First week of the year as specified in the system settings in the control panel.
FirstWeekOfYear.Jan1	1	The week in which January 1st occurs.
FirstWeekOfYear.FirstFourDays	2	The first week that has at least four days in the new year.
FirstWeekOfYear.FirstFullWeek	3	The first full week of the year.

```
Dim ret As Long

ret = DateDiff(DateInterval.Day, #1/1/1970#, Now)
' Returns 11575

ret = DateDiff(DateInterval.Year, #1/1/1970#, Now)
' Returns 31

ret = DateDiff(DateInterval.Second, #1/1/1970#, Now)
' Returns 1000108077

ret = DateDiff(DateInterval.Day, #1/1/1970#, Now, _
        FirstDayOfWeek.Monday, _
        FirstWeekOfYear.FirstFourDays)
' Returns 11575
```

DatePart

The `DatePart` function returns an integer value representing the requested part of a date. The `DatePart` function takes four arguments:

+ `Interval`: `DateInterval` enumeration value or string expression representing the unit of time you are requesting. Table 8-2 lists the values of the `DateInterval` enumeration.

+ `DateValue`: The date and time value used in the calculation.

+ `DayOfWeek`: An optional value from the `FirstDayOfWeek` enumeration that specifies what day to use as the first day of the week. The default value is `Sunday`. Table 8-3 lists the values of the `FirstDayOfWeek` enumeration.

+ `WeekOfYear`: An optional value from the `FirstWeekOfYear` enumeration that specifies the first week of the year. The default value is `Jan1`. Table 8-4 lists the values of the `WeekOfYear` enumeration.

```
Dim ret As Integer
```

```
ret = DatePart(DateInterval.Day, #1/1/1970#)
' Returns 1

ret = DatePart(DateInterval.Year, #1/1/1970#)
' Returns 1970
```

DateSerial

The `DateSerial` function returns a date value representing the year, month, and day. The time value is set to 00:00. The `DateSerial` function has three required arguments:

✦ `Year`: Integer value ranging from 1 to 9999. In Windows 98 and greater, the two-digit values 00 through 29 are considered the year 2000 through the year 2029, and the two-digit values 30 through 99 are considered 1930 through 1999. For all other year values, you should always use the four-digit year value. To be safe, you should always use the four-digit year value.

✦ `Month`: Integer value ranging from 1 to 12. If the month value is outside of this range, the month value is offset by 1 and applied to January of the calculated year, which is recalculated if necessary.

✦ `Day`: Integer value ranging from 1 to 31. If the day value is outside of this range, the day value is offset by 1 and applied to the first day of the calculated month, which is recalculated if necessary.

```
Dim d As Date

d = DateSerial(2001, -14, 1)
' Returns 10/1/1999 12:00:00 AM

d = DateSerial(2001, -14, 1)
' Returns 10/1/1999 12:00:00 AM

d = DateSerial(2001, 7, -18)
' Returns 6/12/2001 12:00:00 AM

d = DateSerial(2001, 7, 18)
' Returns 7/18/2001 12:00:00 AM

d = DateSerial(29, 12, 1)
' Returns 12/1/2029 12:00:00 AM
```

DateString

The `DateString` property returns or sets a string value representing the current date on your system.

```
Console.WriteLine(DateString())
' Returns 09-07-2001
```

DateValue

The DateValue function returns a Date data type value containing the date represented by a string. The time value of the date is set to 00:00. The DateValue function has one required argument:

✦ DateString: String value representing a valid date/time ranging from 1/1/1 00:00:00 to 12/31/9999 23:59:59.

```
Dim d As Date

d = DateValue("January 15, 2001")
' Returns 1/15/2001 12:00:00 AM

d = DateValue("1/15")
' Returns 1/15/2001 12:00:00 AM
' If Year is omitted, than the current
' year on the system is used
```

Day

The Day function returns an integer value ranging from 1 to 31 representing the day of the month of the date passed. The Day function has one required argument:

✦ DateValue: Date value from which you want to extract the day.

```
Dim intDay As Integer

intDay = Day("1/15/01")
' Returns 15

intDay = Day("Jan 15 2001")
' Returns 15
```

Hour

The Hour function returns an integer value ranging from 0 to 23 representing the hour of the day. The Hour function has one required argument:

✦ TimeValue: The date value from which you want to extract the hour.

```
Dim d As Date
Dim intHour As Integer

d = #1/15/2001 1:45:00 PM#

intHour = Hour(d)
' Returns 13
```

Minute

The Minute function returns an integer value ranging from 0 to 59 representing the minute of the hour. The Minute function has one required argument:

✦ `TimeValue`: The date value from which you want to extract the minute.

```
Dim d As Date
Dim intMinute As Integer

d = #1/15/2001 1:45:15 PM#

intMinute = Minute(d)
' Returns 45
```

Month

The `Month` function returns an integer value ranging from 0 to 12 representing the month of the year of the date passed. The `Month` function has one required argument:

✦ `TimeValue`: The date value from which you want to extract the month.

```
Dim d As Date
Dim intMonth As Integer

d = #1/15/2001 1:45:15 PM#

intMonth = Month(d)
' Returns 1
```

MonthName

The `MonthName` function returns a string value containing the name of the specified integer value of the month of the date passed. The `MonthName` function has the following two arguments:

✦ `Month`: The numeric value of the month ranging from 1 to 13. If the calendar you are using is a 12-month calendar and you pass the number 13, an empty string is returned.

✦ `Abbreviate`: Optional Boolean value indicating whether the return value should be abbreviated. The default value is false.

```
Dim strMonth As String

strMonth = MonthName(8)
' Returns August

strMonth = MonthName(8, True)
' Returns Aug
```

Now

The `Now` property returns a date value containing the current date and time of your system.

```
Console.WriteLine(Now)
' Retuns 9/7/2001 6:59:40 AM
```

Second

The `Second` function returns an integer value ranging from 0 to 59 representing the second of the minute of the date passed. The `Second` function has one required argument:

✦ `TimeValue`: The date/time value from which you want to extract the second.

```
Dim d As Date
Dim intSecond As Integer

d = #1/15/2001 1:45:15 PM#

intSecond = Second(d)
' Returns 15
```

TimeOfDay

The `TimeOfDay` property returns a time value containing the current date and time of your system. In the following example, notice the difference in output from the `Now` property and the `TimeOfDay` property. The date value of the `TimeOfDay` property is set to all 1s.

```
Console.WriteLine(TimeOfDay)
' Retuns 1/1/0001 6:59:40 AM

Console.WriteLine(Now)
' Retuns 9/7/2001 6:59:40 AM
```

Timer

The `Timer` property returns a double value representing the number of seconds elapsed since midnight.

```
Console.WriteLine(TimeOfDay)
' Returns 1/1/0001 7:08:56 AM

Console.WriteLine(Timer)
' Returns 25736.4829728
```

TimeSerial

The `TimeSerial` function returns a date value representing the hour, minute, and second of the values passed. The `TimeSerial` function has three required arguments:

✦ `Hour`: An integer value ranging from 0 to 23.

✦ `Minute`: An integer value ranging from 0 to 99. If a value is passed outside of this range, the value is calculated as minutes to the next hour, and the hour is recalculated. If the number passed is negative, the minutes are subtracted and the hour is decremented if necessary.

✦ Second: An integer value ranging from 0 to 99. If a value is passed outside of this range, the value is calculated as seconds in the next minute, and the minute value is recalculated. If the number value passed is negative, the seconds are subtracted and the minute value is decremented if necessary.

```
Dim d1 As Date

d1 = TimeSerial(6, 15, 10)
' Returns 1/1/0001 6:15:10 AM

d1 = TimeSerial(6, -15, -10)
' Returns 1/1/0001 5:44:50 AM

d1 = TimeSerial(6, -115, 0)
' Returns 1/1/0001 4:05:00 AM
```

TimeString

The TimeString property returns or sets a string value representing the current time of day according to your system.

```
Console.WriteLine(TimeString)
' Returns 07:56:03
```

TimeValue

The TimeValue function returns a date value representing the time of a string passed. The TimeValue function has one argument:

✦ TimeString: String value representing a valid date/time ranging from 1/1/1 00:00:00 to 12/31/9999 23:59:59.

```
Dim d1 As Date
d1 = TimeValue(Now)
' Returns 1/1/0001 7:58:42 AM
```

Today

The Today property returns or sets a date value containing the current date according to your system.

```
Console.WriteLine(Today)
' Returns 9/7/2001 12:00:00 AM
```

WeekDay

The WeekDay function returns an integer value containing a number representing the day of the week. The WeekDay function has two arguments:

✦ `DateValue`: A required date value that you need to get the day of the week.

✦ `DayOfWeek`: An optional value chosen from the `FirstDayOfWeek` enumeration that specifies the first day of the week. `Sunday` is the default. Table 8-3 lists the values of the `FirstDayOfWeek` enumeration.

```
Dim d1 As Date
Dim intWeekDay As Integer

d1 = #5/15/2001#
Console.Write(Weekday(d1))
' Returns 3

Console.Write(Weekday(d1, FirstDayOfWeek.Monday))
' Returns 2
```

WeekDayName

The `WeekDayName` function returns a string value containing the name of the specified weekday. The `WeekDayName` function has three arguments:

✦ `WeekDay`: A required integer value ranging from 1 to 7 representing the day of the week.

✦ `Abbreviate`: An optional Boolean value that indicating if the weekday name is to be abbreviated. False is the default.

✦ `FirstDayOfWeekValue`: An optional value chosen from the `FirstDayOfWeek` enumeration that specifies the first day of the week. If not specified, `FirstDayOfWeek.System` is used. Table 8-3 lists the values in the `FirstDayOfWeek` enumeration.

```
Dim d1 As Date

d1 = #5/15/2001#

Console.Write(WeekdayName(3, False))
' Returns Tuesday

Console.Write(WeekdayName(3, False, FirstDayOfWeek.Monday))
'Returns Wednesday
```

Year

The `Year` function returns an integer value ranging from 0 to 9999 representing the year of the date passed. The `Year` function has one required argument:

✦ `TimeValue`: The date value from which you want to extract the year.

```
Dim d As Date
Dim intYear As Integer

d = #1/15/2001 1:45:15 PM#
```

```
intYear = Year(d)
' Returns 2001
```

Microsoft.VisualBasic.Strings

The Microsoft.VisualBasic.Strings namespace handles string manipulation and formatting. From simple upper-to-lowercase conversion to more complex joining and splitting of strings, the namespace is extremely comprehensive.

ASC

The ASC function returns the integer character code value of the first letter in a string.

```
Messagebox.Show ASC("A")
' Returns 97
Messagebox.Show ASC("a")
' Returns 65
```

Chr

The Chr function takes an ANSI value and converts to a string containing the character code.

```
Messagebox.Show Chr(65)
' Returns A

Messagebox.Show ASC(97)
' Returns a
```

Filter

The Filter function returns a zero-based array containing a subset of a string array based on specified filter criteria. The Filter function has four arguments:

✦ Source: A required one-dimensional array of strings to be searched.

✦ Match: A required string to search for.

✦ Include: An optional Boolean value indicating whether to return substrings that include or exclude Match.

✦ Compare: An optional numeric value indicating the kind of string comparison to use. The CompareMethod.Binary or CompareMethod.Text constants can be passed to indicate a text or binary match on the match string.

```
Dim intX As Integer
Dim strArr(2) As String
strArr(0) = "We"
strArr(1) = "were"
strArr(2) = "Relaxing"
```

```
Dim subArr1() As String = Filter(strArr, "we", True, _
   CompareMethod.Text)
For intX = 0 To UBound(subArr1)
   MessageBox.Show(subArr1(intX))
Next
' Returns "We", "were"

Dim subArr2() As String = Filter(strArr, "we", True, _
   CompareMethod.Binary)
For intX = 0 To UBound(subArr2)
   MessageBox.Show(subArr2(intX))
Next
' Returns "were"

Dim subArr3() As String = Filter(strArr, "we", False, _
   CompareMethod.Text)
For intX = 0 To UBound(subArr3)
   MessageBox.Show(subArr3(intX))
Next
' Returns "Relaxing"

Dim subArr4() As String = Filter(strArr, "we", False, _
   CompareMethod.Binary)
For intX = 0 To UBound(subArr4)
   MessageBox.Show(subArr4(intX))
Next
' Returns "We", "Relaxing"
```

FormatNumber, FormatCurrency, FormatPercent

The FormatNumber, FormatPercent, and FormatCurrency functions all return an expression formatted as a number of the specified type. The FormatCurrency function returns a value using the currency symbol defined in the system control panel, whereas the FormatPercent returns a value with a trailing percent sign. All of the functions have the same five arguments:

✦ Expression: The expression to be formatted.

✦ NumDigitsAfterDecimal: An optional numeric value indicating how many places are displayed to the right of the decimal. The default value is –1, which indicates that the computer's regional settings are used.

✦ IncludeLeadingDigit: An optional value of the Tristate enumeration (see Table 8-5) indicating whether a leading zero is displayed for fractional values.

✦ UseParensForNegativeNumbers: An optional value of the Tristate enumeration (see Table 8-5) indicating whether to place negative values within parentheses.

✦ GroupDigits: An optional value of the Tristate enumeration (see Table 8-5) indicating whether numbers should be grouped using the group delimiter specified in the computer's regional settings.

Table 8-5	
Tristate Enumeration	
Value	*Description*
Tristate.True	True
Tristate.False	False
Tristate.UseDefault	Use the computer's regional settings.

Example:

```
Dim dblX As Double = 1234.5678

' FormatNumber Function
Console.WriteLine(FormatNumber(dblX, 4, _
                TriState.UseDefault, _
                TriState.UseDefault, TriState.True))
' Returns 1,234.5678

Console.WriteLine(FormatNumber(dblX, 4, _
                TriState.UseDefault, _
                TriState.UseDefault, TriState.True))
' Returns 1,234.57

' FormatCurrency Function
Console.WriteLine(FormatCurrency(dblX, 4, _
                TriState.UseDefault, _
                TriState.UseDefault, TriState.True))
' Returns $1,234.5678

Console.WriteLine(FormatCurrency(dblX, 2, _
                TriState.UseDefault, _
                TriState.UseDefault, TriState.True))
' Returns $1,234.57

' FormatPercent Function
Console.WriteLine(FormatPercent(dblX, 4, _
                TriState.UseDefault, _
                TriState.UseDefault, TriState.True))
' Returns 123,456.7800%

Console.WriteLine(FormatPercent(dblX, 2, _
                TriState.UseDefault, _
                TriState.UseDefault, TriState.True))
' Returns 123,456.78%
```

FormatDateTime

The FormatDateTime function returns an expression formatted as a date or time.
The FormatDateTime function has two arguments:

✦ Expression: The date expression to be formatted.

✦ NamedFormat: An optional numeric value that indicates the date or time format used. If value is omitted, the GeneralDate (seeTable 8-6) format is used.

Table 8-6
NameFormat Constants

Constant	Description
DateFormat.GeneralDate	Displays the date as a short date and time as a long time if they are present.
DateFormat.LongDate	Displays the date using the long date format as specified in the control panel's regional settings.
DateFormat.ShortDate	Displays the date using the short date format as specified in the control panel's regional settings.
DateFormat.LongTime	Displays the time using the long time format as specified in the control panel's regional settings.
DateFormat.ShortTime	Displays the time using the 24-hour format (hh:mm).

```
Dim d As DateTime = #5/15/2001 10:30:00 AM#

Console.WriteLine(FormatDateTime(d, DateFormat.GeneralDate))
' Returns 5/15/2001

Console.WriteLine(FormatDateTime(d, DateFormat.LongDate))
' Returns Tuesday, May 15, 2001

Console.WriteLine(FormatDateTime(d, DateFormat.LongTime))
' Returns 10:30:00 AM

Console.WriteLine(FormatDateTime(d, DateFormat.ShortDate))
' Returns 5/15/2001

Console.WriteLine(FormatDateTime(d, DateFormat.ShortTime))
' Returns 10:30
```

GetChar

The GetChar function returns a char value representing the character from the specified index in the supplied string. The GetChar function has two arguments:

✦ Str: A required string expression.

✦ Index: A required integer expression. The (1-based) index of the character in Str to be returned.

```
Dim strIn As String = "Mr. Spock"

Console.Writeline(GetChar(strIn, 6))
' Return "p"
```

InStr

The InStr function returns an integer specifying the start position of the first occurrence of one string within another. The InStr function has four arguments:

✦ Start: An optional numeric expression that sets the starting position for each search. If omitted, search begins at the first character position. The start index is 1-based.

✦ String1: The string expression being searched.

✦ String2: The string expression sought.

✦ Compare: An optional setting indicating whether to do a textual- or binary-based search.

```
Dim strSearch, strChar As String

' String to search in.
strSearch = "AaAaBbBbCcDdEe"
' String to seach for
strChar = "a"

' A textual comparison starting at position 1
Console.WriteLine(InStr(1, strSearch, strChar,
CompareMethod.Text))
' Returns 1

' A binary comparison starting at position 1
Console.WriteLine(InStr(1, strSearch, strChar,
CompareMethod.Binary))
' Returns 2
```

The return value from the InStr function returns a zero if

✦ String1 is zero length

✦ String2 is not found

✦ Start is greater than String2

InStrRev

The InStr function returns an integer specifying the start position of the first occurrence of one string within another starting from the right side of the string. InStrRev has four arguments:

✦ StringCheck: A required string expression being searched.

✦ StringMatch: A required string expression being searched for.

✦ Start: An optional numeric expression that sets the 1-based starting position for each search, starting from the left side of the string. If Start is omitted, –1 is used, which means that the search begins at the last character position. Search then proceeds from right to left.

✦ Compare: Optional value indicating whether to perform a textual or binary search. If omitted, a binary search is performed.

```
Dim strSearch, strChar As String, intRet As Integer

' String to search in.
strSearch = "AaAaBbBbCcDdEe"
' String to seach for
strChar = "a"

intRet = InStrRev(strSearch, strChar, 1, CompareMethod.Text)
' Returns 1

intRet = InStrRev(strSearch, strChar, 1,
CompareMethod.Binary)
' Returns 0
```

The return value from the InStrRev function returns a zero if

✦ StringCheck is zero-length

✦ StringMatch is not found

✦ Start is greater than the length of StringMatch

Join

The Join function returns a string created by joining a number of substrings contained in an array. Join has two arguments:

✦ SourceArray(): A required one-dimensional array containing substrings to be joined.

✦ Delimiter: An optional string used to separate the substrings in the returned string. If omitted, the space character is used. If Delimiter is a zero-length string, the items in the list are concatenated with no delimiters.

```
Dim strArr(7), strOut As String
strArr(0) = "You"
strArr(1) = "are"
strArr(2) = "the"
strArr(3) = "finest"
strArr(4) = "crew"
strArr(5) = "in the"
strArr(6) = "fleet"

strOut = Join(strArr, "~")
Console.WriteLine(strOut)
' Returns You~are~the~finest~crew~in the~fleet~
```

LCase

The LCase function converts a string to lowercase.

```
Console.Writeline(LCase("THIS IS COOL"))
' Returns "this is cool"
```

Left

The Left function returns a string containing a specified number of characters from the left side of a string. The Left function has two arguments:

✦ Str: A required string expression from which the leftmost characters are returned.

✦ Length: A required integer expression indicating how many characters to return. If 0, a zero-length string is returned. If greater than or equal to the number of characters in Str, the entire string is returned.

```
Dim strIn, strOut As String
strIn = "C:\My Documents\Document1.Doc"
strOut = Microsoft.VisualBasic.Left(strIn, 5)
Console.WriteLine(strOut)
' Returns "C:\My"
```

Len

The Len function returns an integer containing either the number of characters in a string or the number of bytes required to store a variable.

```
Dim strIn, strOut As String
strIn = "C:\My Documents\Document1.Doc"
strOut = Len(strIn)
Console.WriteLine(strOut)
' Returns 29
```

LSet, RSet

The LSet and RSet functions pad either the left or right side of a string.

```
Dim strIn As String = "Left"

Console.WriteLine("~" & LSet(strIn, 10) & "~")
' Returns ~Left      ~

strIn = "Right"
Console.WriteLine("~" & RSet(strIn, 10) & "~")
' Returns ~      Right~
```

LTrim, Trim, RTrim

These functions return a string containing a copy of a specified string with no leading spaces (LTrim), no trailing spaces (RTrim), or no leading or trailing spaces (Trim).

```
Dim strIn as String = "   This is That   "

Console.Writeline(Trim(strIn))
' Returns "This is That"


Console.Writeline(LTrim(strIn))
' Returns "This is That   "

Console.Writeline(RTrim(strIn))
' Returns "   This is That"
```

Mid

The Mid function returns a string containing a specified number of characters from a string. The Mid function has three arguments:

- ✦ Str: The string expression from which characters are returned.

- ✦ Start: A 1-based integer representing the position in Str at which the part to be taken starts. If Start is greater than the number of characters in Str, the Mid function returns a zero-length string.

- ✦ Length: An optional integer expression indicating the number of characters to return. If omitted or if there are fewer than Length characters in the text (including the character at position Start), all characters from the start position to the end of the string are returned.

```
Console.WriteLine(Mid("USS Voyager", 5))
' Returns "Voyager"
```

Replace

The Replace function returns a string in which a specified substring has been replaced with another substring a specified number of times. The Replace function has six arguments:

- ✦ Expression: The string expression containing substring to replace.

- ✦ Find: The substring you are searching for.

- ✦ Replacement: The replacement substring.

- ✦ Start: An optional numeric value indicating the position with the Expression where to begin the search.

- ✦ Count: An optional numeric value indicating the number of substitutions to perform. If omitted, the default value is –1, which means make all possible substitutions.

✦ Compare: An optional numeric value indicating whether to do a textual or binary search.

```
Dim strIn As String = "This is the way it works"

Console.WriteLine(Replace(strIn, " ", "="))
' Returns "This=is=the=way=it=works"

Console.WriteLine(Replace(strIn, " ", "=", 10, 1,
CompareMethod.Text))
' Returns "he=way it works"
```

Space

The Space function returns a string consisting of the specified number of spaces.

```
Console.Writeline "~" & Spc(5) & "~"
' Returns "~     ~"
```

Split

The Split function returns a zero-based, one-dimensional array containing a specified number of substrings. The Split function has four arguments:

✦ Expression: The string expression containing substrings and delimiters.

✦ Delimiter: An optional character used to identify substring limits.

✦ Limit: An optional numeric value indicating the number of substrings to be returned. The default value of –1 indicates that all substrings are returned.

✦ Compare: An optional numeric value indicating whether to use a textual or binary search for the substring.

```
Dim strIn As String = "This is the way it works"
Dim strArr() As String, intX As Integer

strArr = Split(strIn, " ")

For intX = 0 To strArr.Length - 1
    Console.WriteLine(strArr(intX))
Next

' Returns
This
is
the
way
it
works
```

StrComp

The StrComp function returns –1, 0, or 1 (see Table 8-7), based on the result of a string comparison. The strings are compared by alphanumeric sort values beginning with the first character. The StrComp function has three arguments:

✦ String1: Any valid string expression.

✦ String2: Any valid string expression.

✦ Compare: An optional numeric value indicating whether to use a textual or binary compare.

Table 8-7
Return Values from StrComp Function

Return Value	Function
-1	String1 sorts ahead of String2
0	String1 is equal to String2
1	String1 sorts after String2

```
Dim str1 As String = "THEY ARE THE SAME"
Dim str2 As String = "they are the same"

Console.WriteLine(StrComp(str1, str2, CompareMethod.Text))
' Returns 0

Console.WriteLine(StrComp(str1, str2, CompareMethod.Binary))
' Returns -1
```

StrConv

The StrConv function returns a converted string based on the specified conversion enumeration. The StrConv function has three arguments:

✦ Str: The string expression to be converted.

✦ Conversion: The Microsoft.VisualBasic.VbStrConv specifying the type of conversion. Table 8-8 lists the members of this enumeration.

✦ LocaleID: An optional LocaleID value, if different from the system LocaleID value.

Table 8-8
VbStrConv Enumeration

Value	Description
VbStrConv.None	Performs no conversion.
VbStrConv.LinguisticCasing	Uses linguistic rules for casing, rather than File System (default). Valid with UpperCase and LowerCase only.
VbStrConv.UpperCase	Converts the string to uppercase characters.
VbStrConv.LowerCase	Converts the string to lowercase characters.
VbStrConv.ProperCase	Converts the first letter of every word in string to uppercase.
VbStrConv.Wide	Converts narrow (half-width) characters in the string to wide (full-width) characters.
VbStrConv.Narrow	Converts wide (full-width) characters in the string to narrow (half-width) characters.
VbStrConv.Katakana	Converts Hiragana characters in the string to Katakana characters.
VbStrConv.Hiragana	Converts Katakana characters in the string to Hiragana characters.
VbStrConv.SimplifiedChinese	Converts Traditional Chinese characters to Simplified Chinese.
VbStrConv.TraditionalChinese	Converts Traditional Chinese characters to Simplified Chinese.

The following lists the valid word separators for proper casing:

✦ Null — Chr$(0)

✦ Tab — Chr$(9)

✦ Linefeed — Chr$(10)

✦ Vertical tab — Chr$(11)

✦ Form feed — Chr$(12)

✦ Carriage return — Chr$(13)

✦ Space (single-byte character set) — Chr$(32)

```
Dim strOut As String = "this is all the wrong case"
Console.WriteLine(StrConv(strOut, VbStrConv.ProperCase))
' Returns This Is All The Wrong Case
```

StrReverse

The `StrReverse` function returns a string in which the character order is reversed.

```
Dim strIN As String = "Wow, this is really smart"

Console.WriteLine(StrReverse(strIN))
' Returns "trams yllaer si siht ,woW"
```

UCase

The `UCase` function converts a string to uppercase.

```
Messagebox.show UCase("enterprise nx-01")
' Returns ENTERPRISE NX-01
```

Working with the registry

The registry is always a dangerous place to visit, but as a developer it is a great place to store application settings. VB .NET provides built-in functions that handle all of the registry manipulation functions that you need.

SaveSetting

The `SaveSetting` function creates an application entry in the registry for the current application. The `SaveSetting` function has four arguments:

✦ `AppName`: A required string expression containing the name of the application or project to which the setting applies.

✦ `Section`: A required string expression containing the name of the section in which the key setting is being saved.

✦ `Key`: A required string expression containing the name of the key setting to be saved.

✦ `Setting`: A required expression containing the value to which the key is being set. This is your actual data value you want to save.

```
' This following code tells the registry that
' for the HelloWorld application (HelloWorld.exe),
' I want a retrievable value called "Main Icon"
' with the value of "HappyFace.ico" in the "C:\" directory.

SaveSetting("HelloWorld", "Icon", "Main", "C:\HappyFace.ico")
```

GetSetting

The `GetSetting` function returns a key setting from an application entry in the registry. The `GetSetting` function has four arguments:

✦ `AppName`: A required string expression containing the name of the application whose setting is requested.

✦ `Section`: A required string expression containing the name of the section in which the key setting will be found.

✦ `Key`: A required string expression containing the name of the key setting to return.

✦ `Default`: Optional value to return if no value is set in the key setting. If omitted, the value returned is a zero-length string.

```
' Returns "C:\HappyFace.ico" based on the
' previous SaveSetting example.

GetSetting("HelloWorld", "Icon", "Main")
```

DeleteSetting

The `DeleteSetting` statement deletes a section or a key setting from an application entry in the registry. The `DeleteSetting` has three arguments:

✦ `AppName`: A required string expression containing the name of the application to which the section or key setting applies.

✦ `Section`: A required string expression containing the name of the section from which the setting is being deleted.

✦ `Key`: An optional string expression containing the name of the key setting to be deleted. If this is not specified, the section is deleted along with all related key settings.

```
' Deletes the "main" key and the
' "C:\HappyFace.ico" setting.

DeleteSetting("HelloWorld", "Icon")
```

GetAllSettings

The `GetAllSettings` function returns a list of key settings and their respective values, which were created with the `SaveSetting` statement, from the application entry in the registry. The `GetAllSettings` function has two arguments:

✦ `AppName`: A required string expression containing the name of the application whose key settings are to be retrieved.

✦ `Section`: A required string expression containing the name of the section whose key settings are requested. The return value is an object containing a two-dimensional array, the key settings and their respective values.

```
' This will retrieve the "main" value in the
' two-dimensional array x(,)

Dim x as string(,)

X  = GetAllSettings("HelloWorld", "Icon")
```

Summary

In this chapter, you learned how to create Sub procedures and Function procedures. If you need to return a value back to procedure, you use a Function. If your procedure simply processes information and does not need to return any data to the caller, you can use a Sub procedure to execute your code.

The Microsoft.VisualBasic namespace supplies you with many built-in functions that you can use in place of writing custom procedures. Using this built-in functionality will expedite the writing of your application, but it should not be at the expense of learning the namespaces in the .NET framework. If you are a new developer, learn the functionality provided in the System namespaces in the .NET framework; if you are an experienced Visual Basic developer, you can still use the functions that you are used to using, but you should take the time to learn the new and vastly improved functionality in the .NET framework.

✦   ✦   ✦

Dialog Boxes

by Uday Kranti

While working in the Windows environment, you have seen a number of dialog boxes. These dialog boxes are used for a variety of purposes, such as displaying values, prompting values, and performing file operations. VB .NET provides you with various functions and controls to implement dialog boxes in your application.

In this chapter, you learn to use the MessageBox class and the MsgBox and InputBox functions. You also learn about the CommonDialog class.

Introduction to Dialog Boxes

A *dialog box* adds interactivity to your application. You can use a dialog box to accept some value from a user, display some error message to a user, or perform some input/output operation, such as opening, saving, or printing a file. A dialog box is simply a form with its own set of controls, such as labels, text boxes, and buttons. However, unlike forms you cannot resize a dialog box. You can create your own dialog boxes or use the standard dialog boxes. Dialog boxes are of two types, *modal* and *modeless*.

✦ A modal dialog box must be closed before you can continue your work with the same application or switch to another application. A modal dialog box can be further classified into two types, *application modal* and *system modal*.

  • An application modal dialog box does not allow the user to continue working in the same application before closing the dialog box. However, the user can switch to other applications.

  • A system modal dialog box does not allow the user to work in any application before closing the dialog box.

✦ A modeless dialog box allows users to switch between applications or continue to work with the rest of the application without closing the dialog box.

.NET provides the `CommonDialog` class to display the standard dialog boxes, such as the Open, Save, and Print dialog boxes. It also provides the `MessageBox` class to display a message to the user. In addition, VB .NET provides the `MsgBox` function to display a message box. This function provides compatibility with previous versions of Visual Basic, thereby providing a familiar environment to developers who have worked in older versions. VB .NET provides you with the `InputBox` function to accept a value from the user. The following section looks at the `MessageBox` class.

The MessageBox Class

You have seen a number of message boxes in an application. These message boxes are used to display an error message or the result of a calculation, or provide tips and warnings. They can also be used for confirming operations, such as confirming the deletion of a file. To carry out these operations efficiently, the message box provides the user with different buttons, such as OK, Cancel, Yes, and No.

You too can display message boxes in your applications by using the `MessageBox` class. This message can contain text, buttons, and icons.

The Show method

You use the `Show` method of the `MessageBox` class to display a message box. This method exists in twelve different forms. These forms differ from each other on the basis of the parameters passed in each form. Look at all these forms:

✦ MessageBox.Show(*Text*)

✦ MessageBox.Show(*Owner, Text*)

✦ MessageBox.Show(*Text, Caption*)

✦ MessageBox.Show(*Owner, Text, Caption*)

✦ MessageBox.Show(*Text, Caption, Buttons*)

✦ MessageBox.Show(*Owner, Text, Caption, Buttons*)

✦ MessageBox.Show(*Text, Caption, Buttons, Icon*)

✦ MessageBox.Show(*Owner, Text, Caption, Buttons, Icon*)

✦ MessageBox.Show(*Text, Caption, Buttons, Icon, DefaultButton*)

✦ MessageBox.Show(*Owner, Text, Caption, Buttons, Icon, DefaultButton*)

✦ MessageBox.Show(*Text, Caption, Buttons, Icon, DefaultButton, Options*)

✦ MessageBox.Show(*Owner, Text, Caption, Buttons, Icon, DefaultButton, Options*)

In all the preceding variations of the MessageBox.Show method:

✦ `Owner` specifies the window in front of which the message box will be displayed.

✦ `Text` is the message to be displayed in the message box.

✦ `Caption` is the text to be displayed in the title bar of the message box.

✦ `Buttons` specifies the buttons to be displayed in the message box. You use the `MessageBoxButtons` enumeration to specify the buttons. An enumeration is a list of constants.

✦ `Icon` specifies the icons to be displayed in the message box. You use the `MessageBoxIcon` enumeration to specify the icon.

✦ `DefaultButton` specifies the default button for the message box. You use the `MessageBoxDefaultButton` enumeration to specify the default button.

✦ `Options` specifies the display and association options for the message box. You use the `MessageBoxOptions` enumeration to specify the options.

The following statement displays the use of the `Show` method:

```
MessageBox.Show("Hello World", "Sample")
```

This statement displays a message box with the message `Hello World`. `Sample` is displayed in the title bar of the message box.

The MessageBoxButtons enumeration

The `MessageBoxButtons` enumeration contains constants that are used to specify the buttons for the message box. Some of the commonly used constants are `OK`, `OKCancel`, `YesNo`, and `YesNoCancel`. Consider the following statement to understand the usage of the `MessageBoxButtons` enumeration:

```
MessageBox.Show("Hello World", "Sample",
  MessageBoxButtons.OKCancel)
```

The preceding statement displays a message box with OK and Cancel buttons. Table 9-1 lists the constants contained in the `MessageBoxButtons` enumeration.

Table 9-1
MessageBoxButtons Enumeration Constants

Constant	Used To
OK	Display only the OK button.
OKCancel	Display the OK and Cancel buttons.
AbortRetryIgnore	Display the Abort, Retry, and Ignore buttons.
YesNoCancel	Display the Yes, No, and Cancel buttons.
YesNo	Display the Yes and No buttons.
RetryCancel	Display the Retry and Cancel buttons.

The MessageBoxIcon enumeration

The MessageBoxIcon enumeration contains constants that are used to specify the icons for the message box. Some of the commonly used constants are Error, Exclamation, and Information. Consider the following statement to understand the usage of the MessageBoxIcon enumeration.

```
MessageBox.Show("Hello World", "Sample",
    MessageBoxButtons.OKCancel, MessageBoxIcon.Exclamation)
```

The preceding statement displays a message box with an Exclamation icon. Table 9-2 lists some of the constants contained in the MessageBoxIcon enumeration.

Table 9-2
MessageBoxIcon Enumeration Constants

Constant	Used To
Error	Display an icon that contains a white X in a circle with red background.
Question	Display an icon that contains a question in a circle.
Exclamation	Display an icon that contains an exclamation mark in a triangle with yellow background.
Information	Display an icon that contains a lowercase "i" in a circle.

The MessageBoxDefaultButton enumeration

The MessageBoxDefaultButton enumeration contains constants that are used to specify the default button in a message box. The commonly used constants are

Button1, Button2, and Button3. The Button1 constant makes the first button of the message box the default button. Similarly, Button2 and Button3 specify the second and the third button as default, respectively. Consider the following statement to understand the usage of the MessageBoxDefaultButton enumeration:

```
MessageBox.Show("Hello World", "Sample",
    MessageBoxButtons.OKCancel, MessageBoxIcon.Exclamation,
    MessageBoxDefaultButton.Button1)
```

The preceding statement displays a message box with OK as the default button.

The MessageBoxOptions enumeration

The MessageBoxOptions enumeration contains constants that are used to specify options, such as RightAlign and RtlReading, for the message box. The RightAlign constant right aligns the text and RtlReading constant sets the reading order of the message box from right to left. Consider the following statement to understand the usage of the MessageBoxOptions enumeration:

```
MessageBox.Show("Hello World", "Sample",
    MessageBoxButtons.OKCancel, MessageBoxIcon.Exclamation,
    MessageBoxDefaultButton.Button1,
    MessageBoxOptions.RightAlign)
```

The preceding statement displays a message box with right-aligned text. The output of this statement is shown in Figure 9-1.

Figure 9-1: The sample output

You can also use the MsgBox function to display a message box to the user.

The MsgBox function

The MsgBox function is a shared member of the Microsoft.VisualBasic. Interaction class. The Interaction class contains procedures and methods that are used to interact with objects, applications, and systems. Because it is a shared member, you can use the MsgBox function directly like a system function, as was used in previous versions of Visual Basic, or by specifying the complete class hierarchy. The following code will help you understand this better.

```
Microsoft.VisualBasic.Interaction.MsgBox("Hello World")
```

is similar to,

```
MsgBox("Hello World")
```

The `MsgBox` function takes three parameters: the message to be displayed, a constant representing the buttons and icons to be displayed, and the title of the message box.

The `MsgBox` function returns an integer value, which corresponds to the button clicked by the user. The syntax is

```
Dim retValue as Integer
retValue = MsgBox ( sMessage, [nConst], [sTitle])
```

In the preceding syntax

✦ *sMessage* is the message to be displayed. It can contain up to 1,024 characters.

✦ *nConst* is a numeric or named constant used to specify the number and type of buttons, icon to be displayed, default button, and modality of the message box. To do so, you use the `MsgBoxStyle` enumeration. Actually, all the previously mentioned items, such as buttons and icons, are represented by a number and this parameter contains the sum of all these numbers. You can also use named constants to specify this. This parameter is optional. If you skip it, only the OK button is displayed in the message box.

✦ *sTitle* is the string used as a title for the message box. This parameter is also optional. If you skip this parameter, the name of the application is displayed in the title bar of the message box.

✦ *retValue* is an integer that contains the value of the button clicked by the user. You can use this to trap the button clicked by the user. You can use the `MsgBoxResult` enumeration to trap these values.

The MsgBoxStyle enumeration

The `MsgBoxStyle` enumeration is used to specify the buttons, icons, and modality of the message box. This enumeration contains certain members, such `OKOnly` and `OKCancel`, which in turn represent some constants, such as `vbOKOnly` and `vbOKCancel`. These constants determine the style of the message box. Consider the following statement to understand the usage of `MessageBoxOptions` enumeration:

```
MsgBox("Hello World", MsgBoxStyle.OKOnly, "Sample")
```

The preceding statement displays the message `Hello World`. `Sample` is displayed in the title bar of the message box. The message box contains only the OK button.

You can add two or more named constants to get a constant numeric expression for the second parameter. To understand this better, consider the following statement:

```
MsgBox("Hello World", MsgBoxStyle.OKCancel +
MsgBoxStyle.Critical, "Sample")
```

The preceding statement displays a message box with OK and Cancel buttons along with an icon.

Some of the members of the `MsgBoxStyle` enumeration are similar to the ones discussed in `MessageBoxButtons` and `MessageBoxIcon` enumeration. Table 9-3 describes the `MsgBoxStyle` enumeration members other than those discussed in Tables 9-1 and 9-2.

Table 9-3
MsgBoxStyle Enumeration Members

Member	Constant	Used To
ApplicationModal	VbApplicationModal	Specify the type of the message box as application modal, which means that the user cannot continue working in the current application before responding to the message box.
SystemModal	VbSystemModal	Specify the type of the message box as system modal, which means that the user cannot work in any application before responding to the message box.
MsgBoxSetForeGround	VbMsgBoxSetForeGround	Set the message box window as the foreground window.
MsgBoxHelp	VbMsgBoxHelp	Set the help text.

The MsgBoxResult enumeration

The `MsgBoxResult` enumeration contains all the constants that you need to find the button that was clicked by the user. The commonly used `MsgBoxResult` enumeration constants are `vbOK`, `vbCancel`, `vbAbort`, `vbRetry`, `vbIgnore`, `vbYes`, and `vbNo`.

Consider the following example to understand the use of the `MsgBox` function, the `MsgBoxStyle`, and the `MsgBoxResult` enumerations. To make this code work, create a button on a form. Now, attach this code to the `Click` event of the button:

```
'Declare a variable to store the value returned by MsgBox
Dim iType As Integer

'Using the MsgBox function
iType = MsgBox("This is a sample message", MsgBoxStyle.YesNo
  + MsgBoxStyle.Information, "My Message")
'Check for the button clicked
```

```
'If the user clicks the Yes button
If iType = MsgBoxResult.Yes Then
    'Display another message box
    MsgBox ("You clicked the Yes button")
    'Note only one parameter is passed

'If the user clicks the No button
Else

    'Display another message box
    MsgBox ("You clicked the No Button")
End If
```

This code displays a message box as shown in Figure 9-2. This message box contains the Yes and the No buttons along with the Information icon. The value returned by the `MsgBox` function is stored in the variable `iType`. This value is checked by using the `MsgBoxResult` enumeration and a corresponding message box is displayed.

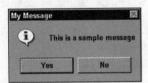

Figure 9-2: The sample output

The InputBox Function

The `InputBox` function is a shared member of the `Microsoft.VisualBasic.Interaction` class. Like the MsgBox function, the `InputBox` function can also be used directly like a system function instead of specifying the complete class hierarchy.

```
Microsoft.VisualBasic.Interaction.InputBox("Enter your name")
```

The preceding statement is similar to the following statement:

```
InputBox ("Enter your name")
```

You use the `InputBox` function to accept a value from the user. It returns the value entered by the user. The syntax is

```
InputBox(sPrompt, [sTitle], [sDefaultValue], [nX], [nY])
```

In the preceding syntax

✦ *sPrompt* is the prompt to be displayed to the user. It can hold a maximum of 1,024 characters.

✦ *sTitle* is the text to be displayed in the title bar of the input box. It is optional. If you skip it, the name of the application is displayed in the title bar.

✦ *sDefaultValue* is the value displayed in the text box (contained in the input box) as the default value. It is optional and if you omit it, an empty text box is displayed.

✦ *nX* is the horizontal distance between the left edge of the input box and the left of the screen. It is optional. If you omit this parameter, the input box is displayed in the horizontal center of the screen.

✦ *nY* is the vertical distance between the top edge of the dialog box and the top of the screen. It is optional. If you skip this parameter, the input box is displayed at a position approximately one-third of the way down the screen.

Note If you skip any of the positional arguments, you need to retain the corresponding comma delimiter.

To understand the usage of the InputBox function, consider the following example:

```
Dim sVar, sResult As String
sVar = "Enter the user name"
sResult = InputBox(sVar, "Logon", "User", 50, 50)
```

You can see the output of this code in Figure 9-3.

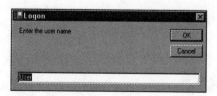

Figure 9-3: The sample output

In the preceding example, the application prompts the user for the username. The input box contains Logon in its title bar and the value User is displayed in the text box, by default.

If you do not specify any of the optional parameters, you need to retain the corresponding delimiter (that is, comma). For example:

```
Dim sVar As String
sVar = InputBox("Enter the user name", "Logon", , 50, 50)
```

In the preceding example, the default value is not specified in the InputBox function. However, the corresponding delimiter (,) is specified. You can see the output of this example in Figure 9-4.

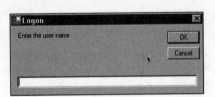

Figure 9-4: The sample output

The CommonDialog Class

While working in Windows, you have seen a number of standard dialog boxes, such as Open, Save, and Print. You can implement these dialog boxes in your VB .NET application as well. The CommonDialog class provides you with the functionality to do so. The CommonDialog class consists of various classes, each of which is used to provide a specific functionality. The classes included in the CommonDialog class are

✦ FileDialog

✦ ColorDialog

✦ FontDialog

✦ PageSetupDialog

✦ PrintDialog

The details of these classes are discussed in the following sections.

The FileDialog class

The FileDialog class is used to handle file operations, such as opening and saving a file. This class displays a dialog box from which the user can select a file. The dialog box shown by the FileDialog class is a modal dialog box.

The FileDialog class further consists of the OpenFileDialog class and the SaveFileDialog classes that help you to display Open and Save dialog boxes, respectively.

The OpenFileDialog class

The OpenFileDialog class provides you the standard Open dialog box provided by Windows. You use this dialog box to provide users with the file selection capability. The OpenFileDialog class provides various properties and methods to manipulate the Open dialog box. Table 9-4 describes some of the properties and methods of the OpenFileDialog class.

Table 9-4
OpenFileDialog Class Properties and Methods

Property Or Method	Description
ShowDialog	Displays the dialog box.
Multiselect	Determines whether the dialog box allows selecting multiple files.
ShowReadOnly	Determines whether the dialog box displays a read-only check box.
ReadOnlyChecked	Determines whether the read-only check box is checked.
Filter	Determines the types of files that will appear in the "Files of Type" box in the dialog box.
FilterIndex	Determines the index of the filter selected in the dialog box.

This class provides only the functionality to display a dialog box and allows the user to specify a file to open. You need to write the code for opening a file manually.

You can open a file in *Input*, *Output*, and *Append* mode. The Input mode is used to read characters from a file. The Output mode is used to write characters to a file. The Append mode is used to append characters to a file. The following steps specify how to open a file:

1. To retrieve the contents of a file, you need to get a file number that is free or is not associated with any file. This file number is used to uniquely identify a file. The `FreeFile` funtion helps you to get a file number that is not in use. The following statement illustrates the use of `FreeFile` function:

```
Dim FileNumber As Integer
FileNumber = FreeFile()
```

2. After getting a free file number, you need to open the file for input. The `FileOpen` function helps you to do this. It takes the file number, file name, and mode of opening the file as parameters. The following statement illustrates the use of `FileOpen` function:

```
FileOpen(FileNumber, FileName, OpenMode.Input)
```

In this statement, `FileName` is the name of the file to be opened. The `OpenMode` enumeration helps you to specify the mode of the file. Some of the constants of this enumeration are `Input`, `Output`, and `Append`.

3. After specifying the name and the mode of the file, you need to open the file. The `Input` function helps you to do this. This function takes the file number and the name of the variable in which the file is to be copied as the parameters. The following statement illustrates the use of `Input` method:

```
Input(FileNumber, MyChar)
```

In this statement, contents of the file are copied to the variable `MyChar`. You can then display the contents of this variable in a message box or a text box.

The following example illustrates the use of `OpenFileDialog` class. To make this code work, design a form with a text box and a button. Add the OpenFileDialog control to the form. To add this control, double-click OpenFileDialog control in the Toolbox. You also need to make the following changes:

- ✦ Set the `Name` property of the text box to `DisplayText`.
- ✦ Set the `Multiline` property of the text box to `True`. Also, increase the size of the text box.
- ✦ Set the `Text` property of the button to `Open File`.

Attach the following code to the `Click` event of the Open File button:

```
'Allow users to select multiple files
OpenFileDialog1.Multiselect = True

'Display a read-only check box
OpenFileDialog1.ShowReadOnly = True

'Specify the files for Files of type list
OpenFileDialog1.Filter = "All Files|*.*|Text Files|*.txt"

'Make All Files the default selection
OpenFileDialog1.FilterIndex = 1

'Check whether the user clicked the OK button in the Open dialog box
'Select a .txt file to open
If OpenFileDialog1.ShowDialog() = DialogResult.OK Then
    Dim MyChar As String
    Dim FileNumber As Integer

'Get a file number that is not in use
    FileNumber = FreeFile()

'Open the file in the input mode
    FileOpen(FileNumber, OpenFileDialog1.FileName, OpenMode.Input)

'Read the data from the file and store it in a variable
    Input(FileNumber, MyChar)

'Display the contents of the file in the text box
    DisplayText.Text = MyChar
End If
```

In this code, the `DialogResult` enumeration contains constants that indicate the return value of a dialog box. Some of the members of this enumeration are `Abort`, `Retry`, `OK`, and `Cancel`.

Figure 9-5 shows a sample Open dialog box.

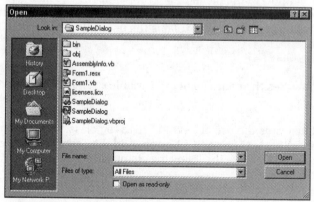

Figure 9-5: A sample Open dialog box

The SaveFileDialog class

The `SaveFileDialog` class offers you the standard Save dialog box provided by Windows. You use this dialog box to provide users with file-saving capability. The `SaveFileDialog` class provides you with methods to manipulate this dialog.

Table 9-5 describes some of the properties and methods of the `SaveFileDialog` class.

Table 9-5	
SaveFileDialog Class Properties and Methods	
Property Or Method	**Description**
ShowDialog	Displays the message box.
CheckFileExists	Determines whether the file specified by the user exists.
FileName	Determines the file name selected by the user in the dialog box.
Filter	Determines the types of files that will appear in the "Save as file Type" box in the dialog box.
FilterIndex	Determines the index of the filter selected in the dialog box.

While saving a file, some of the steps performed are similar to the ones used in opening a file. First, you need to get a free file number. Then, you specify the file name and mode (that is, Output) of the file in the `FileOpen` method. Finally, you need to save the specified contents with the specified file name. To do so, you use the `Write` method. The following statement explains the use of `Write` method:

```
Write(FileNumber,myChar)
```

The preceding statement writes the contents of the variable `myChar` to the specified `FileNumber`.

The following example illustrates the use of `SaveFileDialog` class. To make this code work, design a form with a text box and a button. Add the SaveFileDialog control to the form. You also need to make the following changes:

✦ Set the `Name` property of the text box to `DisplayText`.

✦ Set the `Multiline` property of the text box to `True`. Also, increase the size of the text box.

✦ Set the `Text` property of the button to `Save File`.

✦ Add some text to the text box.

Attach the following code to the `Click` event of the Save File button:

```
'Specify the files for Files of type list
SaveFileDialog1.Filter = "All Files|*.*|Text Files|*.txt"

'Make All Files the default selection
SaveFileDialog1.FilterIndex = 1

'Display the dialog box
'Also check the whether the user clicked OK button in the dialog box
If SaveFileDialog1.ShowDialog() = DialogResult.OK Then
    Dim FileNumber As Integer
    FileNumber = FreeFile()

'Create a file with the specified name in the output mode
    FileOpen(FileNumber, SaveFileDialog1.FileName, OpenMode.Output)

'Write the specified data to a file
'Here the data is the contents of the text box
    Write(FileNumber, DisplayText.Text)
End If
```

Figure 9-6 shows a sample Save As dialog box.

Figure 9-6: A sample Save As dialog box

The ColorDialog class

The ColorDialog class provides a dialog box that allows the user to select a color from the palette and to add colors to that palette. Table 9-6 describes some of the properties and methods of the ColorDialog class.

Table 9-6
ColorDialog class Properties and Methods

Property Or Method	Description
ShowDialog	Displays the dialog box.
Color	Determines the color selected by the user.
AllowFullOpen	Determines whether the user can add custom colors to the dialog box.
SolidColorOnly	Determines whether the user can use dithered colors.

The following example illustrates the use of ColorDialog class. For making this code work, design a form with a text box and a button. Add the ColorDialog control to the form. You also need to make the following changes:

✦ Set the Name property of the text box to DisplayText.

✦ Set the Multiline property of the text box to True. Also, increase the size of the text box. However, you can skip this step.

✦ Set the Text property of the button to Change Color.

✦ Add some text to the text box.

Attach this code to the Click event of the Change Color button:

```
'Enable the Define Custom Colors button
ColorDialog1.AllowFullOpen = True

'Users can use dithered colors
ColorDialog1.SolidColorOnly = False

'Display the dialog box
ColorDialog1.ShowDialog()

'Change the forecolorof the text box
DisplayText.ForeColor = ColorDialog1.Color
```

Figure 9-7 shows a sample Color dialog box.

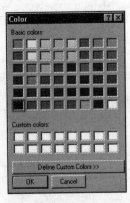

Figure 9-7: A sample Color dialog box

The FontDialog class

The FontDialog class provides a dialog box that allows you to alter the font, font style, and size. This dialog box displays the currently installed fonts on your system. Table 9-7 describes some of the properties of the FontDialog class.

Table 9-7 FontDialog Class Properties and Methods	
Property Or Method	*Description*
ShowDialog	Displays the dialog box.
Color	Determines font color selected by the user.
Font	Determines the font, style, size, script, and effects.

The following example illustrates the use of FontDialog class. To make this code work, design a form with a text box and a button. Add the FontDialog control to the form. You also need to make the following changes:

✦ Set the Name property of the text box to DisplayText.

✦ Set the Multiline property of the text box to True. Also, increase the size of the text box. However, you can skip this step.

✦ Set the Text property of the button to Change Font.

✦ Add some text to the text box.

Attach this code to the Click event of the Change Font button:

```
'Display list of colors in the dialog box
FontDialog1.ShowColor = True

'Display the dialog box
FontDialog1.ShowDialog()


'Apply color selected by the user to the font in the text box
DisplayText.ForeColor = FontDialog1.Color

'Apply font properties selected by the user
DisplayText.Font = FontDialog1.Font
```

Figure 9-8 shows a sample Font dialog box.

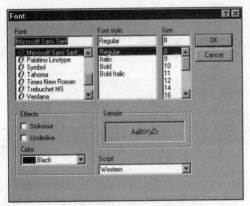

Figure 9-8: A sample Font dialog box

The PageSetupDialog class

The PageSetupDialog class displays a dialog box that you can use to manipulate page settings, such as margins and orientations and the printer settings of a document. The page settings of a single page are represented by the PageSettings class. The information for printing a document is represented by the PrinterSettings class. The PrinterSettings class can also manipulate the settings of the printer used for printing the document.

Table 9-8 describes some of the properties and methods of the PageSetupDialog class.

	Table 9-8 PageSetupDialog Class Properties and Methods
Property Or Method	**Description**
ShowDialog	Displays the dialog box.
AllowMargins	Determines whether the margins section of the dialog box is enabled.
AllowOrientations	Determines whether the orientation section of the dialog box is enabled.
AllowPaper	Determines whether the paper section of the dialog box is enabled.
Document	Determines the document to get page settings from. The PrintDocument class defines an object that is used to send output to a printer.

The following code illustrates the use of PageSetupDialog class. To make this code work, create a button on the form. Set the Text property of the button to Page Setup. Also, add the PageSetupDialog control to the form. Attach the following code to the Click event of Page Setup button:

```
Dim prnDoc As New PrintDocument()

'Specify the document
prnDoc.DocumentName = "c:\test.txt"

Dim prnName As String

'Accept the name of the printer
prnName = InputBox("Enter the Name of the Printer:")

'Create a PageSettings object
Dim pgSettings As New PageSettings()

'Specify the printer name for page settings
pgSettings.PrinterSettings.PrinterName = prnName

PageSetupDialog1.PageSettings = pgSettings

PageSetupDialog1.PageSettings.PrinterSettings.PrinterName =
prnName

'Specify the document for page setup
PageSetupDialog1.Document = prnDoc
PageSetupDialog1.ShowDialog()
```

Figure 9-9 shows a sample Page Setup dialog box.

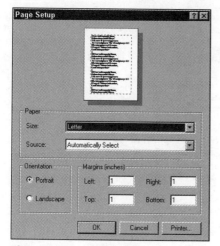

Figure 9-9: A sample Page Setup dialog box

The PrintDialog class

The `PrintDialog` class provides the standard Print dialog box provided by the Windows. You use this dialog box to handle print-related operations, such as specifying the printer name or pages to print. The `PrintDialog` class enables the user to print all the pages in a file, print the specified page range, or print the selected region. You use the `ShowDialog` method of this class to display the Print dialog box.

You can manipulate the properties of this class to specify the settings of a single print job or an individual printer. Table 9-9 describes some of the properties and methods of the `PrintDialog` class.

Table 9-9
PrintDialog Class Properties and Methods

Property Or Method	Description
ShowDialog	Displays the dialog box.
AllowPrintToFile	Determines whether the Print to File check box is enabled.
AllowSelection	Determines whether the From...To...Page option button is enabled.
AllowSomePages	Determines whether the Pages option button is enabled.

The following example illustrates the use of `PrintDialog` class. To make this code work, design a form with a button. Add the PrintDialog control to the form. Set the `Text` property of the button to `Print`. Also, add the PrintDialog control to the form. Attach the following code to the `Click` event of the Print button:

```
Dim prnName As String

'Accept the name of the printer
prnName = InputBox("Enter the Name of the Printer:")

'Create a new PrinterSettings object
Dim prnSettings As New PrinterSettings()

'Specify the printer name
prnsettings.PrinterName = prnName

'Specify the printer settings for the PrintDialog class
PrintDialog1.PrinterSettings = prnsettings
'Display the dialog box
PrintDialog1.ShowDialog()
```

Figure 9-10 shows a sample Print dialog box.

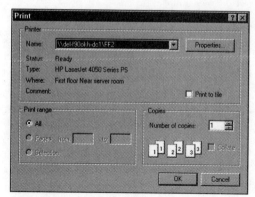

Figure 9-10: A sample Print dialog box

Note

You can also preview a document before actually printing it. To do so, you use the PrintPreviewDialog control, which provides the dialog box that displays how a document will appear when printed. In addition, the PrintPreviewDialog control allows user to print, zoom in, display one or multiple pages, and close the dialog box. The two most commonly used properties of this control are `Document` and `UseAntiAlias`. The `Document` property is used to specify the document to be previewed. The `UseAntiAlias` property is used to set antialiasing on or off. Antialiasing makes text appear smoother.

Summary

In this chapter, you learned about dialog boxes. First, you learned about the `MessageBox` class. Then, you learned about the `MsgBox` and the `InputBox` functions that you can use to add interactivity to your program. Finally, you learned about the `CommonDialog` class provided by VB .NET that allows you to display and manipulate various standard dialog boxes, such as Open, Save, or Print File, in your application. You also learned about the `ColorDialog` and the `FontDialog` classes.

✦   ✦   ✦

File IO and System Objects

by Jason Beres

Visual Basic .NET opens up new file and directory options previously unavailable in Visual Basic. In the old days, you had the Open, Print, and Write statements. With the introduction of the FileSystemObject in VB6 and VBScript, you had a better way to handle file access, but you were still limited. In .NET, you have the System.IO namespace, which has more options than you would ever need to manipulate files, directories, and system objects.

In this chapter, you explore all the possibilities of File IO, Directory Access, and File Access available in .NET. You also get a peek at the System.XML namespace to read and write XML files without using the Document Object Model. I don't cover the legacy Visual Basic statements such as FreeFile, Open, Put, Get, and Print. My assumption is that if you're new to Visual Basic, you'll want (and need) to learn the System.IO classes; if you're an experienced Visual Basic developer, you'll never want to use those built-in functions again once you see what the System.IO namespace has to offer.

Introduction to IO

From the early days of pre-orchestrated wire input to punch cards to files on hard drives in PCs, the need to access data has been the only way to truly embrace the power of the computer. When you design applications today, you are most likely using a database to store information. The database might be Microsoft Access, SQL Server, Oracle, DB2, or any number of relational data stores. Although your needs might warrant something robust such as a relational database, there are still many situations in which simple File IO and directory access is necessary. XML is the hottest buzzword since Yuppie, and XML files are nothing but text documents readable in plain English. So having a simple way to retrieve data out of those files is imperative.

The .NET framework gives you this power of file access through the System.IO namespace. The System.IO namespace runs the gamut in options for all things IO. The following list summarizes what the System.IO namespace offers:

✦ Creating directory listings

✦ Creating, deleting, renaming, and moving directory objects

✦ Setting and retrieving file properties

✦ Reading, writing, and appending to strings, binary files, and text files

✦ Reading, writing, and appending to network streams

✦ Watching for file system changes

✦ Reading, writing, and appending data and files in structured storage

This is all accomplished through the abstract classes available in the System.IO namespace. Figure 10-1 shows a partial hierarchy of the System.IO namespace classes covered in this chapter.

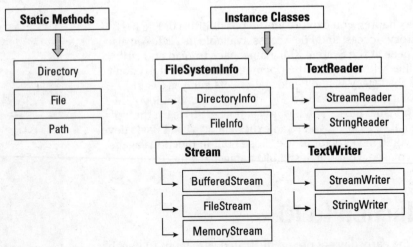

Figure 10-1: Classes in the System.IO namespace covered in this chapter

Directory and DirectoryInfo Class

The `Directory` and `DirectoryInfo` classes provide similar functionality. Both classes allow complete control over directory objects on a system. The main differences between the two classes are

✦ `DirectoryInfo` is an instance class; `Directory` is static.

✦ `DirectoryInfo` does perform permission checks on objects each time it attempts access.

Directory class

The Directory class is a static class, meaning that an instance of the class does not need to be created in order for you to access its methods and properties. Table 10-1 lists the members of the Directory class.

Table 10-1 Directory Class Members	
Member	**Description**
CreateDirectory	Creates directories and subdirectories as specified in the path argument.
Delete	Deletes a directory and its contents.
Exists	Determines if a directory exists.
GetCreationTime	Gets the date and time of the directory's creation.
GetCurrentDirectory	Gets the current directory.
GetDirectories	Gets an array of directories in the current directory.
GetDirectoryRoot	Returns the root of the specified path.
GetFiles	Gets the files in the specified directory.
GetFileSystemEntries	Returns an array of system entries in the specified directory.
GetLastAccessTime	Gets the date and time the directory was last accessed.
GetLastWriteTime	Gets the data and time the directory was last written to.
GetLogicalDrives	Gets the logical drives on the computer.
GetParent	Gets the parent directory of the specified path.
Move	Moves a directory and its contents to the specified path.
SetCreationTime	Sets the creation date and time for the specified directory.
SetCurrentDirectory	Sets the current directory.
SetLastAccessTime	Sets the date and time the directory was last accessed.
SetLastWriteTime	Sets the date and time the directory was last written to.

All of the members of the Directory class can be used to start the creation of a robust file management application. By the end of the next few sections, you will have everything to create an application that mimics the functionality of the File Explorer or My Computer.

To create a listing of the drives on your system, use the `GetLogicalDrives` method, which returns an array of drives.

```
Dim str() as string, intX as integer
Str() = Directory.GetLogicalDrives
For intX = 0 to str.length - 1
  Console.writeline str(intx)
Next
```

To get the properties on individual drives, use the `GetCreationTime`, `GetLastAccessTime`, `GetLastWriteTime` properties.

```
Console.WriteLine(Directory.GetCreationTime("C:\"))
Console.WriteLine(Directory.GetLastAccessTime("C:\"))
Console.WriteLine(Directory.GetLastWriteTime("C:\"))
```

Returns:

```
7/21/2001 12:48:03 PM
7/30/2001 12:50:30 AM
7/30/2001 12:13:37 AM
```

To create a new directory, delete a directory, move a directory, or check if a directory exists, use the `Delete`, `Exists`, `Move`, and `CreateDirectory` methods.

```
Directory.CreateDirectory("C:\DirTest")
Directory.CreateDirectory("C:\DirTest\Sub1")
Directory.CreateDirectory("C:\DirTest\Sub2")
'Check to see if the directory exists, and Delete it or Move it
If Directory.Exists("C:\DirTest\Sub2") Then
    If MsgBox("Delete", MsgBoxStyle.YesNo) = MsgBoxResult.Yes Then
        Directory.Delete("C:\DirTest\Sub2")
    Else
        Directory.Move("C:\DirTest\Sub1", "C:\Program Files\Sub1")
    End If
End If
```

Note   If a directory exists and you attempt to create one with the same name, the command is ignored. The directory is not deleted and re-created, and no exception is raised. The preceding code shows you how to avoid this by using the `Exists` method or the `Directory` class to check for the existence of a directory.

The `Delete` method fails if the directory you are attempting to delete contains files or subdirectories. To get around this, use the Boolean parameter `True` to delete everything, as the following code demonstrates. Notice also the exception that is being caught. I show you the exceptions for IO later in the chapter.

```
Try
    Directory.Delete("C:\testDir")
Catch ex1 As IOException
    If MessageBox.Show("Directory is not empty, " _
```

```
      & " delete sub directories too?", "", _
      MessageBoxButtons.YesNo, _
      MessageBoxIcon.Question) = DialogResult.Yes Then
      ' Delete directory and all contents
    Directory.Delete("C:\TestDir", True)
  End If
End Try
```

To get the current directory, its root and parent, and the directories it contains, you would use GetCurrentDirectory, GetParent, GetDirectoryRoot, and GetFiles.

```
Console.Writeline(Directory.GetCurrentDirectory)
Console.Writeline(Directory.GetDirectoryRoot _
    (Directory.GetCurrentDirectory))
Dim str() As String, intX As Integer
str = Directory.GetFiles(Directory.GetCurrentDirectory)
For intX = 0 To str.Length - 1
    Console.Writeline(str(intX))
Next
```

Returns:

```
C:\Temp\FileIO\bin
C:\
C:\Temp\FileIO\bin\FileIO.exe
C:\Temp\FileIO\bin\FileIO.pdb
```

If you need to search for specific files, the GetFiles method has a constructor that supports filtering. The following example returns all files with the .txt extension:

```
Dim str() As String
str = Dire
ctory.GetFiles("C:\", *.txt")
```

To set the current directory, you can use the SetCurrentDirectory method:

```
Directory.SetCurrentDirectory("C:\TestDir")
```

To place properties on a directory, you can use the SetCurrentDirectory, SetCreationTime, SetLastWriteTime, and SetLastAccessTime methods along with the path of the directory you wish to manipulate.

```
Directory.SetCreationTime("C:\TestDir", Now)
Directory.SetLastAccessTime("C:\TestDir", Now)
Directory.SetLastWriteTime("C:\TestDir", Now)
```

GetDirectories returns an array of directories in the current path, and it also has a search constructor that allows you to look for specific directories based on a search pattern.

```
Dim str() As String, intX As Integer
str = Directory.GetDirectories("C:\")
For intX = 0 To str.Length - 1
    MsgBox(str(intX))
Next
' Look for Directories starting with "d"
str = Directory.GetDirectories("C:\", "d*")
For intX = 0 To str.Length - 1
    MsgBox(str(intX))
Next
```

To get all of the entries in a given path, use the GetFileSystemEntries method, which also supports a search pattern.

```
Dim str() As String, intX As Integer
str = Directory.GetFileSystemEntries("C:\")
For intX = 0 To str.Length - 1
    MsgBox(str(intX))
Next
' Look for Directories and Files starting with "d"
str = Directory.GetFileSystemEntries("C:\", "d*")
For intX = 0 To str.Length - 1
    MsgBox(str(intX))
Next
```

DirectoryInfo class

The DirectoryInfo class and the Directory class are very similar in functionality. As mentioned earlier, the DirectoryInfo class is an instance class, so you will need to create an instance of the class and assign it to a variable. This has an effect on the way you can reference properties within the class. For example, in the sample for the Directory class, you retrieved the arrays as strings, so the name was the only real property you could look at. By using DirectoryInfo, you can retrieve multiple properties on objects, since you are creating an instance of all properties and methods for the specified directory. The following is an example of creating an instance of the DirectoryInfo class and retrieving a few properties on the object.

```
' create an instance and specify the Path
Dim d As DirectoryInfo = New DirectoryInfo("C:\")
MsgBox(d.FullName)
MsgBox(d.LastAccessTime)
MsgBox(d.LastWriteTime)
```

Table 10-2 lists the members in the DirectoryInfo class. If you take a look at this table and compare it to Table 10-1, you will notice that the Directory class has a CreateDirectory member, while the DirectoryInfo class has a Create member, both providing the same functionality. The class that you use will depend on your needs, such as taking advantage of the security checks on each method class, as in the Directory class.

Table 10-2
DirectoryInfo Class Members

Member	Description
Attributes	Gets or sets the attributes of the current file.
CreationTime	Gets or sets the creation time of the current file.
Exists	Determines if a directory exists.
Extension	Gets the file name extension.
FullName	Gets the full path of the directory or file.
LastAccessTime	Gets or sets the last access time of the current file or directory.
LastWriteTime	Gets or sets the last write time of the current file or directory.
Name	Gets the name of the DirectoryInfo instance.
Parent	Gets the parent of a specified directory.
Root	Gets the root portion of the path specified.
Create	Creates the specified directory.
CreateSubDirectory	Creates a subdirectory or subdirectories on the specified path.
Delete	Deletes the DirectoryInfo and its contents from the specified path.
GetDirectories	Returns the subdirectories of the current directory.
GetFiles	Returns a file list from the current directory.
GetFileSystemInfos	Retrieves an array of strongly typed FileSystemInfo objects.
MoveTo	Moves the DirectoryInfo object and its contents to a new path.
Refresh	Refreshes the state of the DirectoryInfo object.

The following code creates an instance of the DirectoryInfo class to retrieve the directory names and when they were created:

```
Dim d As DirectoryInfo = New DirectoryInfo("C:\")
Dim di As DirectoryInfo
For Each di In d.GetDirectories
    Console.WriteLine(di.Name & "-" & di.CreationTime)
Next
```

This results in the following:

```
DirTest-7/28/2001 10:20:36 PM
Documents and Settings-7/21/2001 12:56:05 PM
drivers-7/21/2001 5:36:53 PM
Inetpub-7/22/2001 4:17:16 PM
Program Files-7/21/2001 12:57:41 PM
Proof-7/23/2001 9:10:32 AM
```

```
RECYCLER-7/23/2001 3:57:48 PM
System Volume Information-7/21/2001 5:31:03 PM
testdir-7/29/2001 5:14:53 PM
WINDOWS-7/21/2001 12:48:45 PM
winnt-7/21/2001 5:36:54 PM
```

Path Class

The Path class allows the processing of path strings in a multiplatform way. Like the Directory class, the Path class is static, so you do not need an instance variable to use the Path members. Table 10-3 lists the static fields of the Path class. Keep in mind that all of these fields are platform specific, so based on your operating system, they will be different, which allows a more robust way of determining what is and is not allowed on a particular system.

Table 10-3
Path Class Fields

Field	Description
AltDirectorySeparatorChar	Returns the alternate directory separator character.
DirectorySeparatorChar	Returns the directory separator character.
InvalidPathChars	Returns a list of invalid characters allowed in a path.
PathSeparator	Returns the directory separator character.
VolumeSeparatorChar	Returns the volume separator character.

Take a look at a procedure that uses the Path class fields. I am using Windows XP Professional, so the results I get may differ on your machine.

```
Console.WriteLine("AltDirectorySeparatorChar: " & _
    Path.AltDirectorySeparatorChar)
Console.WriteLine("PathSeparator: " & _
    Path.PathSeparator)
Console.WriteLine("DirectorySeparatorChar: " & _
    Path.DirectorySeparatorChar)
Console.WriteLine("VolumeSeparatorChar: " & _
    Path.VolumeSeparatorChar)
Console.WriteLine("InvalidPathChars: " & _
    Path.InvalidPathChars)
```

Returns the following:

```
AltDirectorySeparatorChar: /
PathSeparator: ;
DirectorySeparatorChar: \
VolumeSeparatorChar: :
InvalidPathChars: "<>|
```

The Path class has shared methods that perform path operations. These methods will all be useful once you need to go beyond the directory methods from the Directory classes and need to get more specific on a file level. Table 10-4 lists the methods of the Path class.

Table 10-4
Path Class Methods

Method Name	Description
ChangeExtension	Changes the file name extension.
Combine	Combines two file paths.
GetDirectoryName	Returns the directory path of a file.
GetExtension	Returns the extension of a file.
GetFileName	Returns the name and extension parts of a path.
GetFileNameWithoutExtension	Gets the file name without the extension.
GetFullPath	Expands the path to a fully qualified path.
GetPathRoot	Gets the root of the specified path.
GetTempFileName	Returns a unique temporary file name on disk with a zero byte size.
GetTempPath	Gets the path of the Temp folder.
HasExtension	Determines whether a path includes a file name extension.
IsPathRooted	Gets a value determining whether the specified path includes the root.

The following are a few code snippets using the Path methods. Notice the File.Create method. I'll explain that in more detail in the next section.

```
File.Create("C:\Test.txt")
Path.ChangeExtension("C:\Test.txt", "doc")
Console.WriteLine(Path.GetFileNameWithoutExtension("C:\Test.doc"))
Console.WriteLine(Path.GetFileName("C:\Test.doc"))
Console.WriteLine(Path.GetTempPath())
Console.WriteLine(Path.GetDirectoryName(Path.GetTempPath))
Console.WriteLine(Path.GetTempFileName)
Console.WriteLine(Path.GetTempFileName)
```

Returns the following:

```
Test
Test.doc
C:\DOCUME~1\JASONB~1\LOCALS~1\Temp\
C:\DOCUME~1\JASONB~1\LOCALS~1\Temp
C:\DOCUME~1\JASONB~1\LOCALS~1\Temp\tmp191.tmp
C:\DOCUME~1\JASONB~1\LOCALS~1\Temp\tmp192.tmp
```

The following code uses the Directory method GetFiles to retrieve an array of files in my Windows\System32 directory. I wanted to find all of the DLLs and OCXs, so I used the Path.GetExtension method to determine if the file in the array was what I needed.

```
Dim str() As String, intX As Integer
str = Directory.GetFiles("C:\Windows\System32")
For intX = 0 To str.Length - 1
  If Path.GetExtension(str(intX)) = ".dll" Or _
    Path.GetExtension(str(intX)) = ".ocx" Then
    Console.WriteLine(str(intX))
  End If
Next
```

The following are partial results; the total number was pretty high.

```
C:\Windows\System32\dpvoice.dll
C:\Windows\System32\dpvvox.dll
C:\Windows\System32\dpwsock.dll
C:\Windows\System32\dpwsockx.dll
C:\Windows\System32\drmclien.dll
C:\Windows\System32\drmstor.dll
C:\Windows\System32\drmv2clt.dll
C:\Windows\System32\drprov.dll
C:\Windows\System32\ds32gt.dll
C:\Windows\System32\dsauth.dll
```

File and FileInfo Class

The File and FileInfo classes in the System.IO namespace provide all options for the creation, deletion, moving, and opening of files. Like the Directory and DirectoryInfo classes, the File class is a static class, and the FileInfo class is an instance class. The File classes do not read and write actual data to files. This is done with the stream classes. The FileStream, NetworkStream, and BufferedStream are all classes that give you a *handle* to files that you are opening, and then you use the methods of the stream classes to manipulate the actual data in the files. You will see more information on the stream classes in the next section, but it is worth mentioning here because some of the examples will use the FileStream class to work with the File members. Table 10-5 lists the shared methods of the File class.

Table 10-5
File Class Methods

Field	Description
AppendText	Creates a StreamWriter that appends text to a file. The file will be created if it does not exist.
Copy	Copies an existing file to a new file.
Create	Creates a file at the specified path.
CreateText	Creates a StreamWriter that writes to a new text file at the specified path.
Delete	Deletes the specified file.
Exists	Determines whether a file exists.
GetAttributes	Gets the FileAttributes of the specified file.
GetCreationTime	Gets the date and time the specified file was created.
GetLastAccessTime	Gets the date and time the file was last accessed.
GetLastWriteTime	Get the date and time the file was last written to.
Move	Moves the file to a new location, with the option of specifying a new file name.
Open	Opens a FileStream at the specified path.
OpenRead	Creates a read-only file at the specified path.
OpenText	Creates a StreamReader that reads from an existing text file at the specified path.
OpenWrite	Creates a read-write Stream at the specified path.
SetAttributes	Sets the FileAttributes of the file at the specified path.
SetCreationTime	Sets the date and time the specified file was created.
SetLastAccessTime	Sets the date and time the specified file was last accessed.
SetLastWriteTime	Sets the date and time the specified file was last written to.

Before you get into using the FileStream class, I show you some of the simpler methods of the File class. Although the File methods are powerful, when it comes to working with data in files, you need to use streams.

In this example, you create a new file and copy it to another file. Before you copy it, you check to see if a file with the existing name is already on the system, and if there is an existing file, you will delete it.

```
File.Create("C:\Test.txt")
If File.Exists("C:\TestDir\test.txt") Then
```

```
    File.Delete("C:\TestDir\Test.txt")
    File.Copy("C:\Test.txt", "C:\TestDir\Test.txt")
End If
```

The Copy method takes two parameters: Source and Destination. Make sure you remember to include the fully qualified path of the files. The Copy method also has a third parameter: Overwrite. To accomplish the same create, delete, and copy routine, you could use this code:

```
File.Create("C:\Test.txt")
If File.Exists("C:\TestDir\test.txt") Then
    File.Copy("C:\Test.txt", "C:\TestDir\Test.txt", True)
End If
```

To move a file, using either the original file name or a new name, use the Move method as this code demonstrates:

```
File.Move("C:\Test.txt", "C:\TestDir\Test.doc")
```

Often you will want to know the attributes of a file before working with it. The following code returns the attributes of a file. Notice the FileNotFoundException that is added into the mix. This is very important for all of the file manipulation that you do. If a file does not exist, an exception occurs, and if you are not looking for exceptions, your application could crash. Most classes give you a full range of exceptions to look out for, but they also give methods that aid you in avoiding exceptions. In the Copy code you saw before, you used the File.Exists method to check for the file before copying. You should do this instead of using exceptions if at all possible, but there are situations in which you will still need to look out for exceptions.

```
Try
    MsgBox(File.GetAttributes("C:\test_attr.txt"))
Catch ex As FileNotFoundException
    MsgBox("File Not Found")
End Try
```

I added this file to my system, and I manually modified the properties to read-only. Figure 10-2 shows the result.

Figure 10-2: File attributes of Test_attr.txt

Looking at Figure 10-2 does not really give you a good idea of the attributes on the file. You need to use the ToString method of the GetAttributes method to retrieve the human readable file attributes, so modify your code to look like this:

```
Try
    MsgBox(File.GetAttributes("C:\test_attr.txt").ToString)
Catch ex As FileNotFoundException
    MsgBox("File Not Found")
End Try
```

And your new results will look like Figure 10-3.

Figure 10-3: Attributes using the ToString method

Although it may seem like magic, it is not. The FileAttributes enumeration gives the bitwise equivalent of the results you achieved in Figure 10-3. Table 10-6 lists the FileAttributes enumeration for files and directories.

Table 10-6	
FileAttributes Enumeration Members	

Field	Description
Archive	The file's archive status. Applications can use this to mark files for backup or removal.
Compressed	The file is compressed.
Device	Reserved for future use.
Directory	The file is a directory.
Encrypted	The file or directory is encrypted. If the object is a file, the data in the file is encrypted. If the object is a directory, then encryption is the default for newly created files.
Hidden	The file is hidden.
Normal	No attributes are set on the file. Can only be used alone with no other attributes.
NotContentIndexed	The file is not indexed by the content indexing service on the operating system.
Offline	The file is offline. Data in the file is not immediately available.
ReadOnly	The file is read-only.
ReparsePoint	The file contains a reparse point, which is a block of user-defined data associated with a file or directory.
SparseFile	The file is a sparse file. Sparse files are normally large files that contain mostly zeros.
System	System file. Either the file is part of the operating system or is used exclusively by the operating system.

The attributes are pretty straightforward. You have probably been dealing with attributes since DOS days and the `attrib` command.

Note   Not all attributes are for files and not all attributes are for directories.

To retrieve properties on file objects, you can use the following file methods: `GetAttributes`, `GetCreationTime`, `GetLastAccessTime`, and `GetLastWriteTime`. To set properties on the file objects, use the `SetCreationTime`, `SetLastAccessTime`, and `SetLastWriteTime` methods. Notice that the same methods are available in the `Directory` class I covered earlier.

```
' Look at the file properties
MsgBox(File.GetAttributes("C:\odbcconf.log"))
MsgBox(File.GetCreationTime("C:\odbcconf.log"))
MsgBox(File.GetLastAccessTime("C:\odbcconf.log"))
MsgBox(File.GetLastWriteTime("C:\odbcconf.log"))
' Set the file properties
File.SetCreationTime("C:\odbcconf.log", Now())
File.SetLastAccessTime("C:\odbcconf.log", Now())
File.SetLastWriteTime("C:\odbcconf.log", Now())
```

I used the various get methods on the `odbcconf.log` file in my root directory, and Figures 10-4 and 10-5 display the before and after effect.

The following code uses the `AppendText` method of the `File` class to append text to an existing file. I talk more about streams in the next section, but it's important to see how you can use the `File` methods with the `Stream` class to create files.

```
' Create a StreamWriter object, and use
' the AppendText method of the File class
Dim stream As StreamWriter = File.AppendText("C:\Bones.txt")
stream.WriteLine("I'm a Doctor")
stream.WriteLine("Not a Brick Layer")
stream.Close()

' Create a reader object, and use
' the OpenText method of the File class
Dim reader As StreamReader = File.OpenText("C:\Bones.txt")
MsgBox(reader.ReadToEnd)
reader.Close()
```

The results are displayed in Figure 10-6.

WINNT		File Folder	7/28/2001 4:16 PM
xp		File Folder	7/20/2001 5:02 PM
HMIWin2K.reg	5 KB	Registration Entries	6/14/2001 12:31 PM
odbcconf.log	7 KB	Text Document	7/19/2001 12:44 PM

Figure 10-4: Before setting properties on the odbcconf.log file

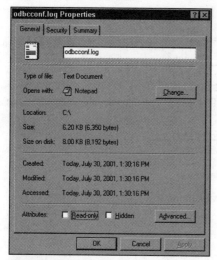

Figure 10-5: After setting properties on the odbcconf.log file

Figure 10-6: StreamWriter results

The `File.AppendText` method creates a new file if the one specified in the path argument doesn't exist. It appends to an existing file, so if you run the example more than once, the text is repeated as you execute the code.

It's important to note that the `File` methods, when opening or creating files, are all dealing with a specific type of stream. Streams can be text, binary, network, or buffered. This leads us into the next section, where you learn more about streams and how to use them with or without the `File` class.

Reading and Writing Files

File streams provide complete synchronous and asynchronous file input and output manipulation. The `FileStream`, `MemoryStream`, `NetworkStream`, and `BufferedStream` all derive from the `Stream` base class, which is primarily used for byte IO. The `TextReader` and `TextWriter` classes facilitate the reading and writing of text data. The `TextReader` class uses a `StreamReader` or `StringReader` to read text, and the `TextWriter` class uses a `StreamWriter` or `StringWriter` to write text data. Figure 10-7 displays the hierarchy of the `Stream` class.

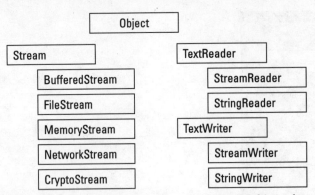

Figure 10-7: Stream, TextReader, and TextWriter hierarchy

File streams

In order to read and write data from files, you begin with the `FileStream` class. The `FileStream` class is instantiated by passing a file name or a file handle created by one of the `Stream` classes, to the `FileStream` constructor. To create an instance of the `FileStream`, use the `new` keyword:

```
Dim fs as FileStream = New FileStream (path, mode, access,
share, buffersize, useAsync, msgPath)
```

The following arguments are optional for the `FileStream`, with the exception of the *path* argument:

- ✦ `Path`: Relative or absolute path for the file that the current instantiation is attempting to encapsulate.

- ✦ `Mode`: A `FileMode` constant that determines how the file will be opened or created (see Table 10-6).

- ✦ `Access`: A `FileAccess` constant that determines how the `FileStream` object will access the file. This argument sets the `CanRead`, `CanWrite`, and `CanSeek` properties (see Table 10-6).

- ✦ `Share`: A `FileShare` constant that determines how processes will share the file (see Table 10-6).

- ✦ `BufferSize`: Desired buffer size in bytes.

- ✦ `UseAsync`: Specifies synchronous or asynchronous IO. Asynchronous IO is only supported if the operating system supports it.

The following example demonstrates the usage of the `FileStream` object. In this example, you create a `FileStream` object and a `StreamWriter` object and write a few lines of text to a file:

```
Dim fs As New FileStream("C:\NewFile.txt", _
    FileMode.CreateNew, FileAccess.Write, FileShare.Write)
Dim w As New StreamWriter(fs)
w.WriteLine("Line1")
w.Close()
fs.Close()
```

The `FileStream` class only supports binary IO. If you are not reading or writing text data, you don't need to create a `StreamWriter` or `StreamReader`, as the following code demonstrates:

```
Dim fs As FileStream = New FileStream("C:\Test1.txt",
    FileMode.OpenOrCreate)
fs.WriteByte(0)
fs.WriteByte(1)
fs.Close()
Dim fsr As FileStream = New FileStream("C:\Test1.txt", FileMode.Open)
MsgBox(fsr.ReadByte.ToString)
MsgBox(fsr.ReadByte.ToString)
```

Notice the use of the `FileMode`, `FileAccess`, and `FileShare` constants. Table 10-7 describes these constants.

Table 10-7
FileMode, FileAccess, and FileShare Constants

Constant	Description
FileMode.Append	Creates a new file, or opens an existing file and moves to the end of the file. FileAccess.Write must be used in conjunction with FileMode.Append. An *ArgumentException* is thrown if FileAccess.ReadWrite is specified with the FileMode.Append argument.
FileMode.Create	Creates a new file or overwrites an existing file.
FileMode.CreateNew	Creates a new file.
FileMode.Open	Opens an existing file.
FileMode.OpenOrCreate	Opens an existing file; if the file does not exist, creates a new file.
FileMode.Truncate	Opens an existing file and truncates to a size of zero bytes once open.
FileAccess.Read	Specifies read access to a file. Data can be read from the file and the file pointer can be moved.
FileAccess.ReadWrite	Specifies read and write access to a file. Data can be read from and written to the file and the file pointer can be moved.

Continued

Constant	Description
FileAccess.Write	Specifies write access to a file. Data can be written to the file and the file pointer can be moved.
FileShare.None	Sharing is not allowed on the current file. Attempts to open the file by any process will fail until the file is closed.
FileShare.Read	Subsequent opening of the file for reading is allowed. If not specified, any request to open the file for reading will fail until the file is closed.
FileShare.ReadWrite	Subsequent opening of the file for reading or writing is allowed. If not specified, any request to read or write to the file will fail until the file is closed.
FileShare.Write	Subsequent opening of the file for writing is allowed. If not specified, any request to open the file for writing will fail until the file is closed.

Table 10-7 *(continued)*

When attempting to open files or create files, you need to make sure that a path, directory, or file exists before you attempt to access the resource. The following code demonstrates how to catch the exceptions that could occur when dealing with file IO. Read the comments for each type of exception to get a handle on what they actually mean.

```
Public Shared Function WriteFile() As Boolean
   Try
      Dim fs As New FileStream("C:\NewFile.txt", _
      FileMode.CreateNew, FileAccess.Write, FileShare.Write)
      Dim w As New StreamWriter(fs)
      w.WriteLine("Line1")
      w.Close()
      fs.Close()
   Catch e1 As ArgumentNullException
      ' Path is NULL
   Catch e2 As ArgumentException
      ' Path is an Empty String
   Catch e3 As ArgumentOutOfRangeException
      ' Mode is NOT a field of FileMode
      ' Access is NOT a field of FileAccess
      ' Share is NOT a field of FileShare
      ' BufferSize is Not a Positive Number
   Catch e4 As FileNotFoundException
      ' The file cannot be found
   Catch e5 As IOException
      ' An IO error has occurred
   Catch e6 As FileLoadException
      ' The File was Found but could not be Loaded
   End Try
End Function
```

After a FileStream is opened, you have random access to the file. Using the Seek method, you can position the pointer in the file to where you want to read or write. The following code demonstrates using the Seek method to append data to an existing file:

```
Dim fs As FileStream = New FileStream("C:\Test1.txt",
    FileMode.OpenOrCreate)
fs.Seek(0, SeekOrigin.End)
fs.WriteByte(3)
fs.WriteByte(4)
fs.Close()
```

The SeekOrigin.End argument tells the stream to go to the end of the file before writing. SeekOrigin.Begin would start writing at the beginning of the stream, and SeekOrigin.Current would write at the current pointer in the stream. Table 10-8 lists the core FileStream members.

Table 10-8
Core FileStream Members

Member	Description
IsAsync	Gets a value indicating whether the FileStream was opened asynchronously or synchronously.
CanRead	Returns whether the stream supports reading.
CanSeek	Returns whether the stream supports seeking.
CanWrite	Returns whether the stream supports writing.
Length	Length in bytes of the stream.
Position	Gets or sets the current position in the stream.
BeginRead	Begins an async read.
BeginWrite	Begins an async write.
Close	Closes the file and releases related resources.
EndRead	Waits for the pending async read to complete.
EndWrite	Ends an async write, blocking until the IO operation has completed.
Flush	Clears all buffers for the stream and forces buffered data to be written to the device.
Lock	Prevents access to all or part of the file.
Handle	Gets the operating system file handle for the file that the current FileStream object encapsulates.

Continued

Table 10-8 *(continued)*	
Member	**Description**
Read	Reads a block of bytes from the stream and writes them to the given buffer.
Name	Gets the name of the FileStream that was passed to the constructor.
ReadByte	Reads a byte from the file and advances the pointer one position.
Seek	Sets the current position of the stream to the given value.
SetLength	Sets the length of this stream to the given value.
Unlock	Allows access by other processes to all or part of a file that was previously locked.
Write	Writes a block of bytes to the stream with data from the buffer.
WriteByte	Writes a byte to the current posistion in the stream.

TextReader class

The TextReader class is an abstract class that defines how you read and write textual information. The StreamReader and StringReader classes are derived from the TextReader class to do the actual implementation of reading the text.

StreamReader

The StreamReader class implements a TextReader that reads data from a byte stream in a specific encoding. Whereas the Stream class is for byte I/O, the StreamReader is designed for character input in a particular encoding. The default encoding for the StreamReader class is UTF-8, not the default ANSI code page for the operating system that it is running. The reason for this is that UTF-8 can handle Unicode characters in a consistent manner based on the localized settings of the operating system.

You can implement a StreamReader class in two ways: through the *path* of a physical disk file or through an existing *stream*. The syntax is identical for creating both types of StreamReader objects with the exception of the first argument, *path* or *stream*:

```
(path As String[, encoding As Encoding[, bufferSize As
Integer[, detectEncodingFromByteOrderMarks As Boolean]]])
```

Or for implementing a *stream* class:

```
(stream As Stream[, encoding As Encoding[, bufferSize As
Integer[, detectEncodingFromByteOrderMarks As Boolean]]])
```

For example:

```
Dim s as new StreamReader("C:\MyFile.txt")
```

The optional arguments are as follows:

- ✦ Encoding : Specified character encoding to use.
- ✦ BufferSize: Suggested minimum buffer size.
- ✦ DetectEncodingFromByteOrderMarks: Encoding type indicator.

When you read data from the StreamReader for the first time, you can change the encoding by changing the encoding flag.

The detectEndcodingFromByteOrderMarks argument detects the encoding from the first three bytes of the stream. The big endian, little endian, and UTF-8 Unicode text are automatically recognized. If the encoding cannot be determined, the user-defined encoding is implemented.

Table 10-9 lists the core members of the StreamReader class.

Table 10-9 StreamReader Members	
Member	**Description**
Close	Closes the StreamReader and releases any resources associated with the object.
DiscardBufferedData	Allows a StreamReader to discard its current data.
Peek	Returns the next available character without reading it from the stream.
Read	Reads the next character(s) from the stream.
ReadBlock	Reads the maximum of count characters from the current stream and writes the data to the buffer at the specified index.
ReadLine	Reads a line of characters from the current stream and returns the data as a string.
ReadToEnd	Reads the stream from the current posistion to the end of the stream.

The following example uses some of the methods you just looked at to read the text file you created earlier and then write the output to the system console.

```
Dim fsIn As FileStream = New FileStream("C:\MyFile.txt", FileMode.Open,
  FileAccess.Read, FileShare.Read)
Dim sr As StreamReader = New StreamReader(fsIn)
While sr.Peek() > -1
console.WriteLine(CStr(sr.ReadLine))
End While
sr.Close()
```

To iterate the text in the file, you use the `Peek` method, which returns a –1 until the end of the file is reached. If you need to read the whole file at once, and not line by line, use the `ReadToEnd` method as shown here:

```
Dim fs As FileStream = New FileStream("C:\test.txt", FileMode.Open)
Dim sr As New StreamReader(fs)
MsgBox(sr.ReadToEnd)
```

Returns Figure 10-8.

Figure 10-8: Results from ReadToEnd method

Figure 10-9 displays the text file that the `StreamReader` was reading from.

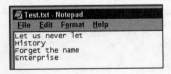

Figure 10-9: Text input to StreamReader

To accomplish the same feat without using a `FileStream` class, you can create a `StreamReader` from a file on the file system:

```
Dim sr As StreamReader = New StreamReader("C:\Test.txt")
MsgBox(sr.ReadToEnd)
```

Or you can read the file line by line as this code demonstrates:

```
Dim sr As StreamReader = New StreamReader("C:\Test.txt")
While sr.Peek <> -1
    sr.ReadLine()
End While
```

StringReader

The `StringReader` class implements a `TextReader` that reads data from a string. The `StringReader` takes one parameter, a string variable, which can be a string or a file.

```
Dim s as new StringReader(string variable)
```

The `StringReader` class shares some of the same methods as the `StreamReader` class. So, once the `StringReader` is instantiated, use the same methods as you would with the `StreamReader` to manipulate the string file you are reading. The following commented code demonstrates a usage of the `StringReader` class.

```
' Declare a string variable and stick some data in it
Dim str As String = "Red Alert ... Raise Shields"
' Declare an array of type Char for the length of the string
Dim x(str.Length) As Char
' Create a new StringReader to hold the String
Dim sr As New StringReader(str)
' Read the array using the Read method, starting in the Zero
    position for 14 characters
sr.Read(x, 0, 14)
' Display the results
MsgBox(x)
' Close the StringReader
sr.Close()
```

The following are common methods that the `StringReader` and `StreamReader` share: `Close`, `Peek`, `Read`, `ReadBlock`, `ReadLine`, and `ReadToEnd`.

TextWriter class

The `TextWriter` is an abstract class that represents a *writer* that can write a sequential stream of characters. The `StreamWriter` and the `StringWriter` are the actual class implementations that you use to interact with the files themselves. Just as the `TextReader` has the `StringWriter` and `StreamWriter` classes that invoke methods to read data from files or streams based on the encoding of the file, the `StreamWriter` and `StringWriter` invoke methods that write data to files or streams.

StreamWriter

The `StreamWriter` class is for character output in a particular `Encoding`. The `StreamWriter` class default is to write UTF-8 unless specified otherwise when the class is instantiated. UTF-8 will handle the Unicode characters correctly based on localized versions of the operating system. Similar to the `StreamReader` class, a `StreamWriter` can be instantiated based on the path of an existing file or a based on an existing stream. The following are the constructors for the `StreamWriter` class depending on whether the input is a file from the path or a stream.

```
(path As String[, append As Boolean[, encoding As Encoding[,
bufferSize As Integer]]])
```

And this creates a `StreamWriter` based on a stream:

```
(stream As Stream [, encoding As Encoding[, bufferSize As
Integer]]])
```

The following is a breakdown of the optional arguments.

✦ Append: This determines whether data is appended to the file. If the file exists and append is false, the file will be overwritten. If the file exists and append is true, the data is appended to the file, otherwise a new file is created.

✦ Encoding: Specifies the character encoding to use.

✦ BufferSize: Sets the buffer size of the stream.

The following example creates a `StreamWriter` and adds a few lines of text to the newly created file.

```
Dim sr As StreamWriter = New StreamWriter("C:\Writer.txt")
sr.WriteLine("You are the finest")
sr.WriteLine("crew in the")
sr.WriteLine("Fleet")
sr.Close()
```

Table 10-10 lists the core members of the `StreamWriter` class.

Table 10-10 StreamWriter Members	
Member	**Description**
Close	Closes the StreamWriter and releases any resources associated with the object.
Write	Writes the specified data to the text stream.
WriteLine	Writes some data as specified by the overloaded parameters, followed by a line terminator.
Encoding	Gets the encoding of the stream being written.
Flush	Clears the buffer for the current writer and causes any buffered data to be written to the underlying stream.

Note   `StreamWriter` **is not thread safe. Look up** `TextWriter.Synchronized` **in the SDK for a thread-safe wrapper example.**

The following example creates a `StreamWriter` using a `FileStream`, writes some data to the writer, and then reads the data back out with the `StreamReader`.

```
Dim fs as FileStream fs = new FileStream("MyFile.txt", FileMode.Open)
Dim s As StreamWriter = New SteamWriter(fs)
Dim intX as Integer
For intX = 0 to 11
     s.Write( CStr (intX))
Next intX
Dim r As StreamReader =  new StreamReader(fs)
s.BaseStream.Seek(0, SeekOrigin.Begin)
For intX = 0 to 11
     Console.Write cstr(r.Read)
Next intX
```

StringWriter

The `StringWriter` class, similar to the `StringReader`, is a very simple implementation of writing textual data to a string file. The `StringReader` shares the same methods of the `StreamWriter`. The only difference is the default encoding, which is the ANSI encoding of the current system and not the Unicode UTF-8 default of the `StreamWriter` class. The `StringWriter` constructor has two optional parameters: the `IFormatProvider` and the `StringBuilder`.

StringBuilder

The `StringBuilder` member provides a means of string modification, by adding, removing, or replacing characters to an existing string without creating a new string with each modification. This class is meant to optimize the handling of string data, since the overhead of creating a new string to handle the string operations is not necessary. The `StringBuilder` is a member of the System.Text namespace. Table 10-11 lists the core methods allowed on the `StringBuilder` member.

Table 10-11
StringBuilder Methods

Method	Description
Append	Appends a typed object to the end of the current StringBuilder.
AppendFormat	Replaces one or more format specifications with the appropriately formatted value of an obejct.
EnsureCapacity	Ensures that the capacity of the current StringBuilder is at least the value specified.
Insert	Inserts the specified object into the StringBuilder at the specified position.
Remove	Removes the specified characters from the StringBuilder.
Replace	Replaces all instances of characters with another character.
ToString	Converts the StringBuilder to a string.

IFormatProvider

The `IFormatProvider` provides culture-specific numeric and date formatting for a specific locale. When used in conjunction with the `StringWriter`, you can control how the data is written and that it is written in the correct fashion.

`IFormatProvider` has a single method, `GetType`, which returns the format object of the specified type.

StringWriter in action

The following example uses the `StringBuilder` and the `StringWriter` to write and modify string data and returns the result in a message box.

```
Dim sb As New StringBuilder("Warp 9.5 ... ")
Dim arr As Char() = {"E", "n", "g", "a", "g", "e"}
Dim sw As New StringWriter(sb)
sw.Write(arr, 0, arr.Length)
Console.WriteLine(sb.ToString)
sw.Close()
```

Outputs to the command window:

```
Warp 9.5 ... Engage
```

XML IO

The System.XML namespace provides us with robust XML functionality. In this section, you look at the `XMLTextReader` and the `XMLTextWriter` and how you can use these classes to read and write XML files as plain old text, and do a little manipulation along the way. For more details on using XML thru the `DataSet` classes, see Chapter 24.

Reading XML files

The `XMLTextReader` class provides the parsing and tokenizing functionality you need to read XML files. The XML Document Object Model (DOM) provides great flexibility for loading XML files as documents, but there is still the need to read XML as a file-based stream and perform basic manipulation. Because loading XML thru the DOM does require some overhead, loading XML files through the `XMLTextReader` is normally faster and more efficient.

To read an XML file, you declare an instance of the `XMLTextReader`; then you call the `read` method until you hit the end of the XML file. Here is a simple implementation of this example, where the `"xml file"` argument is the path to a valid XML file.

Note   The XML classes are in the System.XML namespace, not the System.IO namespace.

```
Dim r as XmlTextReader = new XxmlTextReader ("Xml File Name")
Do while r.read()
     ' manipulate XML file
Loop
```

When you read the file, the XMLTextReader class that you instantiated has the NodeType property, which returns the type of node you're reading. The Name property returns element and attribute names, and the Value property returns the text value that the node contains. Table 10-12 describes the node types and their equivalents in the W3C DOM.

Table 10-12
XMLNode Type Enumeration

Member Name	Description	Numeric Value
None		0
Element	<name>	1
Attribute	Id='123'	2
Text	'123'	3
CDATA	<![CDATA[...]]>	4
EntityReference	&foo;	5
Entity	<!ENTITY...>	6
ProcessingInstruction	<?pi test?>	7
Comment	<!— comment -->	8
Document		9
DocumentType	<!DOCTYPE...>	10
DocumentFragment		11
Notation	<!NOTATION...>	12
Whitespace	Whitespace	13
SignificantWhiteSpace	Whitespace between markup in a mixed content model.	14
EndTag	</foo>	15
EndEntity	Returned when the reader is at the end to the entity replacement as a result of a call to ExpendEntry().	16
CharacterEntity	Returned when the reader has been told to report character entities.	17

Not only is it important to understand what the node value types equate to, but you also need to know the methods supported by the XMLTextReader. There are many methods and properties. The XMLTextReader properties are listed in Table 10-13 and the XMLTextReader methods are listed in Table 10-14.

Table 10-13 XMLTextReader Properties	
Property	**Description**
AttributeCount	Gets the number of attributes in the current node.
BaseURI	Gets the base URI of the current node.
CanResolveEntity	Gets a value indicating whether this reader can parse and resolve entities.
Depth	Gets the depth of the current node in the XML document.
Encoding	Gets the encoding attribute for the document.
EOF	Gets a value indicating whether XmlReader is positioned at the end of the stream.
HasAttributes	Gets a value indicating whether the current node has any attributes.
HasValue	Gets a value indicating whether the node can have a Value.
IsDefault	Gets a value indicating whether the current node is an attribute that was generated from the default value defined in the DTD or schema.
IsEmptyElement	Gets a value indicating whether the current node is an empty element (for example, <MyElement/>).
Item	Gets the value of the attribute.
LineNumber	Gets the current line number.
LinePosition	Gets the current line position.
LocalName	Gets the name of the current node without the namespace prefix.
Name	Gets the qualified name of the current node.
Namespaces	Gets or sets a value indicating whether to do namespace support.
NamespaceURI	Gets the namespace URI (as defined in the W3C Namespace Specification) of the node the reader is positioned on.
NameTable	Gets the XmlNameTable associated with this implementation.
NodeType	Gets the type of the current node.

Property	Description
Normalization	Gets or sets a value indicating whether to do whitespace normalization as specified in the WC3 XML recommendation version 1.0 (see http://www.w3.org/TR/1998/REC-xml-19980210).
Prefix	Gets the namespace prefix associated with the current node.
QuoteChar	Gets the quotation mark character used to enclose the value of an attribute node.
ReadState	Gets the state of the reader.
Value	Gets the text value of the current node.
WhitespaceHandling	Gets or sets a value that specifies how whitespace is handled.
XmlLang	Gets the current xml:lang scope.
XmlResolver	Sets the XmlResolver used for resolving DTD references.
XmlSpace	Gets the current xml:space scope.

Table 10-14
XMLTextReader Methods

Method	Description
Close	Changes the ReadState to Closed.
GetAttribute	Gets the value of an attribute.
GetHashCode	Serves as a hash function for a particular type, suitable for use in hashing algorithms and data structures like a hash table.
GetRemainder	Gets the remainder of the buffered XML.
IsStartElement	Tests if the current content node is a start tag.
LookupNamespace	Resolves a namespace prefix in the current element's scope.
MoveToAttribute	Move to the specified attribute.
MoveToContent	Checks whether the current node is a content (non-whitespace text, CDATA, Element, EndElement, EntityReference, or EndEntity) node. If the node is not a content node, then the method skips ahead to the next content node or end of file. Skips over nodes of type ProcessingInstruction, DocumentType, Comment, Whitespace, or SignificantWhitespace.
MoveToElement	Moves to the element that contains the current attribute node.

Continued

Table 10-14 *(continued)*

Method	Description
MoveToFirstAttribute	Moves to the first attribute.
MoveToNextAttribute	Moves to the next attribute.
Read	Reads the next node from the stream.
ReadAttributeValue	Parses the attribute value into one or more Text and/or EntityReference node types.
ReadBase64	Decodes Base64 and returns the decoded binary bytes.
ReadBinHex	Decodes BinHex and returns the decoded binary bytes.
ReadChars	Reads the text contents of an element into a character buffer. This method is designed to read large streams of embedded text by calling it successively.
ReadElementString	This is a helper method for reading simple text-only elements.
ReadEndElement	Checks that the current content node is an end tag and advances the reader to the next node.
ReadInnerXml	Reads all the content, including markup, as a string.
ReadOuterXml	Reads the content, including markup, representing this node and all its children.
ReadStartElement	Checks that the current node is an element and advances the reader to the next node.
ReadString	Reads the contents of an element or a text node as a string.
ResolveEntity	Resolves the entity reference for EntityReference nodes.
Skip	Skips the current element.

The following code creates an XMLTextReader class, opens an existing file called C:\MyFile.Xml and iterates through the XML, using the NodeType property to determine what to do with the data. In this example, you display only the data in the output window; but in real life, you could have complex processing for node types based on their names or values.

The XML file reads:

```
<name>
  <fname>James</fname>
  <mname>Tiberius</mname>
  <lname>Kirk</lname>
  <specs position="Captain" Ship="Enterprise" />
</name>
```

The code to process to the file, as described earlier:

```
Dim xr As XmlTextReader = New XmlTextReader("C:\MyFile.Xml")
While xr.Read()
   Select Case (xr.NodeType)
     Case XmlNodeType.Comment
         Console.WriteLine("Comment:" & xr.Value)
     Case XmlNodeType.Element
         Console.WriteLine("Element:" & xr.Value)
         If (xr.HasAttributes) Then
             Console.WriteLine("Attribute Count:" & _
                   xr.AttributeCount)
             Dim intX As Integer
             For intX = 0 To xr.AttributeCount - 1
                 Console.WriteLine(xr.GetAttribute(intX))
             Next
         End If
     Case XmlNodeType.Text

         Console.WriteLine("Text:" & xr.Value)
     Case XmlNodeType.Whitespace
         Console.WriteLine("Whitespace:")
   End Select
End While
```

Outputs the following:

```
Element:name
Whitespace
Element:fname
Text: James
Whitespace
Element:mname
Text: Tiberius
Whitespace
Element:lname
Text: Kirk
Whitespace
Element:specs
Attribute Count: 2
Captain
Enterprise
Whitespace
```

Writing XML files

Writing data as an XML file is implemented through the XMLTextWriter class. The XMLTextWriter class, similar to the XMLTextReader class, allows forward-only generation of XML files without the overhead of loading the XML Document Object Model (DOM). To create XML output, you use the WriteElementString and the WriteAttribute methods. For nesting elements, you use the WriteStartElement and the WriteEndElement methods, and for more complex attribute handling, the

`WriteStartAttribute` and `WriteEndAttribute` methods are available. Of course, you need to create well-formed XML, so you must have the correct document structure. Table 10-15 lists the core methods of the XMLTextWriter class.

Table 10-15
XMLTextWriter Methods

Method	Description
Close	Closes this stream and the underlying stream.
Flush	Flushes whatever is in the buffer to the underlying streams and also flushes the underlying stream.
GetHashCode	Serves as a hash function for a particular type, suitable for use in hashing algorithms and data structures like a hash table.
LookupPrefix	Returns the closest prefix defined in the current namespace scope for the namespace URI.
WriteAttributes	When overridden in a derived class, writes out all the attributes found at the current position in the XmlReader.
WriteAttributeString	When overridden in a derived class, writes an attribute with the specified value.
WriteBase64	Encodes the specified binary bytes as base64 and writes out the resulting text.
WriteBinHex	Encodes the specified binary bytes as binhex and writes out the resulting text.
WriteCData	Writes out a <![CDATA[...]]> block containing the specified text.
WriteCharEntity	Forces the generation of a character entity for the specified Unicode character value.
WriteChars	Writes text a buffer at a time.
WriteComment	Writes out a comment <!--...--> containing the specified text.
WriteDocType	Writes the DOCTYPE declaration with the specified name and optional attributes.
WriteElementString	When overridden in a derived class, writes an element containing a string value.
WriteEndAttribute	Closes the previous WriteStartAttribute call.
WriteEndDocument	Closes any open elements or attributes and puts the writer back in the Start state.
WriteEndElement	Closes one element and pops the corresponding namespace scope.

Method	Description
WriteEntityRef	Writes out an entity reference as follows: & *name*;.
WriteFullEndElement	Closes one element and pops the corresponding namespace scope.
WriteName	Writes out the specified name, ensuring it is a valid Name according to the XML specification (http://www.w3.org/TR/1998/REC-xml-19980210#NT-Name).
WriteNmToken	Writes out the specified name, ensuring it is a valid NmToken according to the XML specification (http://www.w3.org/TR/1998/REC-xml-19980210#NT-Name).
WriteNode	When overridden in a derived class, copies everything from the reader to the writer and moves the reader to the start of the next sibling.
WriteProcessingInstruction	Writes out a processing instruction with a space between the name and text as follows: <?name text?>.
WriteQualifiedName	Writes out the namespace-qualified name. This method looks up the prefix that is in scope for the given namespace.
WriteRaw	Writes raw markup manually.
WriteStartAttribute	Writes the start of an attribute.
WriteStartDocument	Writes the XML declaration with the version "1.0".
WriteStartElement	Writes the specified start tag.
WriteString	Writes the given text content.
WriteSurrogateCharEntity	Generates and writes the surrogate character entity for the surrogate character pair.
WriteWhiteSpace	Writes out the given whitespace.

The following example creates a new XML file using the XMLTextWriter class.

```
' Declare a new XMLTextWriter object
' the Nothing parameter will force the
' default UTF-8 Endcoding of the XML output
Dim xtw As XmlTextWriter = _
    New XmlTextWriter("C:\ncc1701.xml", Nothing)
With xtw
    ' Make the XML look pretty automatically
    .Formatting = System.Xml.Formatting.Indented
    .WriteStartDocument(False)
    .WriteComment("Confidential")
    .WriteStartElement("name")
    .WriteElementString("fname", "Jean-Luc")
```

```
       .WriteElementString("lname", "Picard")
       .WriteStartElement("specs", Nothing)
       .WriteAttributeString("rank", "Captain")
       .WriteAttributeString("ship", "Enterprise")
       .WriteEndElement()
       .WriteEndElement()
       .Flush()
       .Close()
    End With
```

Figure 10-10 displays the XML file created.

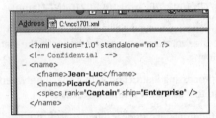

Figure 10-10: XML file created with XMLTextWriter class

Watching the File System

I have saved the best for last. Probably the coolest thing I have seen when it comes to IO is the `FileSystemWatcher` class. As its name implies, this class will watch the file system for you and raise events when changes are made to directories or files. About a year ago, I spent a couple thousand dollars on a single-threaded application that kept track of files that were added to a directory on an NT4 system. It was painfully slow and locked the computer every time it "synced" directories based on changes made. The same feat can now be accomplished in a multithreaded, super fast way with the `FileSystemWatcher` class.

Event watching

File system events are raised when events occur in the file system. The whole concept of Windows is that it reacts to messages, or events, that are fired directly by the user or indirectly by applications that may be running. These messages are essentially events; they could be a user clicking a button on a form, clicking the Start menu, copying a file, or creating a directory. In previous versions of VB, it was very difficult to listen for system events to occur because VB has always been a single threaded application. This is not the case anymore. In VB .NET, you have the capability to watch for any type of event that occurs in the operating system, in a multithreaded way. Table 10-16 lists the events that the `FileSystemWatcher` will track.

Event	Raised When
	Table 10-16 **File System Events**

Event	Raised When
Created	Directory or file is created.
Deleted	Directory or file is deleted.
Renamed	Directory name or file name is changed.
Changed	Changes are made to the size, system attributes, last write time, last access time, or security permissions of a directory or file.

 Note The `FileSystemWatcher` works only in Windows NT4, Windows 2000, or Windows XP. You can't monitor Windows 95 or Windows 98.

To watch for events in the file system, you need to create an instance of the `FileSystemWatcher` class.

```
Dim watcher as new FileSystemWatcher
```

After the watcher is created, you set several properties to determine what the watcher should do. The properties and their definitions are as follows:

✦ `Filter`: A wildcard expression that determines the files to watch. This could be "*.*" for all files or "*.txt" for files with the .txt extension.

✦ `IncludeSubDirectories`: Boolean value whether to include or exclude subdirectories in the specified path.

✦ `NotifyFilter`: Enumeration dictating the events to watch for. Figure 10-11 displays the intellitype for the `NotifyFilter` enumeration.

✦ `Path`: Path to watch.

 Figure 10-11: NotifyFilters enumeration

After you have set your properties, set the `EnableRaisingEvents` property to True, and your `FileSystemWatcher` is in action.

Creating a custom watcher application

Creating a custom watcher is one of the easiest tasks on earth. This section has all of the code you need to create your own watcher.

The first step is to create a new `FileSystemWatcher` class. The new instance needs to be created with `WithEvents` so you can handle the event from procedures when individual events are raised.

```
Dim WithEvents Watcher As New FileSystemWatcher()
```

It is kind of cheesy, but I used a Windows Form to start my watcher. You will proba-bly create a service or something like that, unless you want to add list box that lists items as they are added, changed, or deleted to have a running log file on the screen. You can go ahead and create a Windows Service application and try the same code, but I want to stick to one concept at a time here. The following code blocks are pretty self-explanatory.

After you create an instance of the watcher, you set a few properties telling the watcher what you want it to do. Notice the use of the `Or` operator to specify multi-ple `NotifyFilters`. The `Watcher.EnableRaisingEvents` is probably the most important line of code here, since no events are raised if you don't specify that property. Depending on what events you're watching, you add code that specifies what to do when the event occurs. In the `Changed`, `Created`, and `Deleted` events for this `Watcher` instance, the `Name` and `ChangeType` arguments are being passed to a `WriteLog` function, which takes advantage of what you learned earlier in appending text to a file. That's pretty much it. Have a look at the code. Figure 10-12 displays the results of my log file.

```
Private Sub Form1_Load(ByVal sender As System.Object, _
        ByVal e As System.EventArgs) Handles MyBase.Load
        Watcher.Path = "C:\Files"
        Watcher.Filter = "*.*"
        Watcher.IncludeSubdirectories = True
        Watcher.NotifyFilter = NotifyFilters.LastWrite
        Watcher.NotifyFilter = NotifyFilters.LastAccess Or _
                        NotifyFilters.Size Or _
                        NotifyFilters.FileName
        Watcher.EnableRaisingEvents = True
End Sub

Private Sub Watcher_Changed(ByVal sender As System.Object, _
        ByVal e As System.IO.FileSystemEventArgs) Handles
            Watcher.Changed
        WriteLog(e.Name, e.ChangeType.ToString)
    End Sub

Private Sub Watcher_Created(ByVal sender As System.Object, _
        ByVal e As System.IO.FileSystemEventArgs) Handles
            Watcher.Created
        WriteLog(e.Name, e.ChangeType.ToString)
    End Sub
```

```
Private Sub Watcher_Deleted(ByVal sender As Object, _
        ByVal e As System.IO.FileSystemEventArgs) Handles
            Watcher.Deleted
            WriteLog(e.Name, e.ChangeType.ToString)
    End Sub

    Private Function WriteLog(ByVal strFile As String, _
        ByVal strChange As String) As Boolean
    ' Create a StreamWriter class with the True constructor to
    ' Append to the file each time.
        Dim sw As StreamWriter = New
            StreamWriter("C:\Log.txt", True)
        sw.WriteLine(strFile & "-" & strChange)
        sw.Close()
    End Function
```

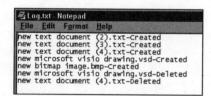

Figure 10-12: Watcher log file

Summary

As you can see, there are many options for IO and system object access in the .NET framework. In this chapter, you experienced the System.IO class and a little bit of the System.XML class for reading and writing XML files.

I didn't cover the legacy Visual Basic IO methods such as Open, Put, Write, and Print, but they're all still available in .NET. I would encourage you to use the System.IO classes you learned in this chapter rather than the old-style methods. They are easier to use and a whole lot more fun.

✦   ✦   ✦

Dictionary Object

by Yancey Jones

The Dictionary Object in Visual Basic 6 was accessed through the Microsoft Scripting Runtime Dynamic Link Library (Scrrun.dll). In Visual Basic .NET, the Scrrun.dll can still be referenced but there is a new, .NET way of creating a Dictionary style collection. A Dictionary style collection is similar in function to a standard collection except that it stores information in key and value pairs instead of just the value.

Visual Basic .NET includes a class named DictionaryBase that is defined as MustInherit and it implements three interface classes: IDictionary, ICollection, and IEnumerable. The DictionaryBase class is part of the System.Collections namespace. Inheriting this class makes it easy to create a strongly typed collection consisting of associated keys and values. A strongly typed Dictionary collection accepts only a specific key type and a specific value type and exposes the same specific key type and specific value type

Note

A MustInherit class can only be used as a base class. It cannot be instantiated and will give an error if an attempt is made to use the New constructor on it.

Most of the DictionaryBase class members are declared Protected, therefore they can only be accessed through a derived class. This means that in order to gain access to them from outside the derived class, the code must be added.

This chapter demonstrates how to implement the DictionaryBase class as well as its properties and methods. The code examples are intended to provide an idea of how to build a DictionaryBase collection class for use in personal projects.

This chapter also takes a brief look at the interfaces implemented by the DictionaryBase class.

Cross-Reference For more on inheritance and other object-oriented features of Visual Basic .NET, see Chapter 14.

Getting Started Using the DictionaryBase

The DictionaryBase class is intended to be extended to give it more than limited functionality. As mentioned previously, the DictionaryBase class implements three interfaces. Looking at the properties and methods of these interfaces provides some idea of what properties and methods are available when creating a Dictionary style collection and also provides some insight on how to use them to extend the DictionaryBase class.

Implemented classes

The three interfaces implemented by the DictionaryBase class are the IDictionary, ICollection, and IEnumerable interfaces. Each of these interfaces has certain public properties and methods that are accessible through the DictionaryBase class.

IDictionary

The IDictionary interface is used for storing associated key and value objects. The key object must be a unique non-null object, but the associated value object may contain a null reference.

The properties and methods of the IDictionary interface are accessed through the Dictionary property of the DictionaryBase class. The following list shows the public properties and methods available via the IDictionary interface.

✦ IsFixedSize: Returns a Boolean value indicating whether or not the IDictionary instance is fixed size. A fixed-size collection does not allow elements to be added or deleted, but existing elements can be modified. (Property)

✦ IsReadOnly: Returns a Boolean value indicating whether the IDictionary instance is read-only. (Property)

✦ Item: Accepts one parameter, a key object, and returns the element with the specified key. (Property)

✦ Keys: Returns an ICollection of the keys in the current instance of IDictionary. (Property)

✦ `Values`: Returns an `ICollection` of the values in the current instance of `IDictionary`. (Property)

✦ `Add`: Adds an element with the provided key object and value object to the instance of `IDictionary`. (Method)

✦ `Clear`: Removes all entries from the instance of `IDictionary`. (Method)

✦ `Contains`: Returns a Boolean value indicating whether the provided key object exists in the instance of `IDictionary`. (Method)

✦ `GetEnumerator`: Returns an `IDictionaryEnumerator` for the instance of `IDictionary`. The `IDictionaryEnumerator` can then be used to iterate through the elements in the `IDictionary` instance. (Method)

✦ `Remove`: Removes the element associated with the provided key object from the instance of the `IDictionary` collection. (Method)

ICollection

`ICollection` is the base interface for all collections. The `DictionaryBase` class and `IDictionary` interface implement the `ICollection` interface. Access to the `ICollection` properties and methods can be made through the `Dictionary` property of the `DictionaryBase` class or limited access is available through an instance of the `DictionaryBase` derived class.

The following list shows the public properties and methods available in the `ICollection` interface.

✦ `Count`: Returns the number of elements in the `ICollection`. It can be accessed directly from an instance of the derived class or through the `Dictionary` property of the `DictionaryBase` class. (Property)

✦ `IsSynchronized`: Returns a Boolean value indicating the syncronized state of the `ICollection` instance. It is accessible through the `Dictionary` property of the `DictionaryBase` class. (Property)

✦ `SynchRoot`: Returns an object that is capable of synchronizing access to the `ICollections` instance. It is accessible through the `Dictionary` property of the `DictionaryBase` class. (Property)

✦ `CopyTo`: Copies the elements of the collection to an array starting at the specified array index. It can be accessed directly from an instance of the derived class or through the `Dictionary` property of the `DictionaryBase` class. (Method)

IEnumerable

`IEnumerable` exposes an object that can be used to iterate through a collection. It is implemented by the `DictionaryBase` class and inherited by both the `IDictionary` and `ICollection` interfaces.

The IEnumerable interface has one public method available called
GetEnumerator. GetEnumerator returns an object that can be used to iterate
through a collection. It can be accessed directly from an instance of the derived
class or through the Dictionary property of the DictionaryBase class. In the
case of the DictionaryBase class, it returns a DictionaryEntry type.

Creating a functional DictionaryBase collection

Implementing the DictionaryBase class is relatively simple. In this section, two
classes for a Visual Basic project will be created. The first class is a fictional class
that holds some of the properties that could be associated with a small airplane,
such as tail number and manufacturer. The second inherits from the
DictionaryBase class and is used to hold a collection of the airplane class.

Start up Visual Studio .NET and create a new Visual Basic Windows Application
named DictionaryDemo. Once the project is created, add two class files to it. Name
the first AirplaneCollection.vb and the second Airplane.vb.

Note   In Visual Basic .NET the physical class file names are arbitrary, and Visual Basic
.NET is not limited to having only one class per file as in Visual Basic Version 6. All
the code being generated for this project could be put in the Form1.vb file that is
created by default with the project. All the code samples in this chapter use
AirplaneCollection.vb as the DictionaryBase collection class and
Airplane.vb as the object being stored in the DictionaryBase collection.

Cross-Reference   For more information on Visual Basic .NET classes, see Chapter 14.

Add the code in bold from Listing 11-1 to the Airplane class and the code in bold
from Listing 11-2 to the AirplaneCollection class.

Listing 11-1: **Airplane Class**

```
Public Class Airplane

    Private mTailNumber As String
    Private mManufacturer As String


    Public Property TailNumber() As String
        Get
            Return mTailNumber
        End Get
        Set(ByVal Value As String)
            mTailNumber = Value
```

```
        End Set
    End Property

    Public Property Manufacturer() As String
        Get
            Return mManufacturer
        End Get
        Set(ByVal Value As String)
            mManufacturer = Value
        End Set
    End Property

End Class
```

Listing 11-2: **AirplaneCollection Class**

```
Public Class AirplaneCollection
    Inherits System.Collections.DictionaryBase

End Class
```

By inheriting the `DictionaryBase` class, all of its exposed properties and methods can now be accessed from the `AirplaneCollection` class.

 Note   As stated at the beginning of this chapter, most of the `DictionaryBase` class members are protected. Only the public properties and methods are accessible from outside of the `AirplaneCollection` class.

Adding Functionality

Now you have created two classes, one that represents an airplane and another that inherits the `DictionaryBase` class. The `AirplaneCollection` class can be instantiated at this time but has only a few public members available for use. The `Dictionary` property, which is an `IDictionary` type, is protected so direct access to it is not possible from outside its class. This is probably the most important property of the `DictionaryBase` class because it is what actually stores the associated `Key` objects and `Value` objects.

In order to gain basic functionality from the `AirplaneCollection` class, an Add method, a `Remove` method, and an `Item` property must be created.

Creating the Add method

The first method is a subroutine that adds an item to the `DictionaryBase` collection. Add the code in bold in Listing 11-3 to the `AirplaneCollection` class.

Listing 11-3: **The Add Method**

```
Class AirplaneCollection
    Inherits System.Collections.DictionaryBase

  Public Sub Add _
        (ByVal Key As String, ByVal Item As Airplane)

        'Invokes the Dictionary Property's Add method
        Dictionary.Add(Key, Item)
  End Sub

End Class
```

The subroutine just added invokes the Add method of the `IDictionary` interface. If the inside of the `DictionaryBase` class could be seen at the `Dictionary` property declaration, it would reveal something like the following:

```
Protected ReadOnly Property Dictionary As IDictionary
```

The `IDictionary` interface contains several public properties and methods. The following is the declaration for the Add method:

```
Sub Add(ByVal Key As Object, ByVal Value As Object)
```

Notice that the `IDictionary`'s Add method actually allows the use of a generic object type for both the `Key` and the `Value`. The Add method in the `AirplaneCollection` class can be modified to accept any object type for the Key and Value pair. Since the AirplaneCollection class is being created as a strong typed class, the Add method in Listing 11-3 specifies the type for the `Key` and `Value` pair.

Note   Even though the properties and methods of `IDictionary` are public, they are not available from outside the derived class because the `Dictionary` property was declared protected in `DictionaryBase`.

Creating the Remove method

Objects can now be added to the AirplaneCollection class. A method must now be provided for removing an item. The IDictionary interface also contains a Remove method with the following declaration:

```
Sub Remove(ByVal key As Object)
```

The Remove method in IDictionary, like the Add method, accepts any object type. Because a string type was used in the AirplaneCollection Add method, a string type for the AirplaneCollection Remove method is used.

Add the code in bold in Listing 11-4 to the AirplaneCollection class.

Listing 11-4: **The Remove Method**

```
Public Class AirplaneCollection
    Inherits System.Collections.DictionaryBase

    Public Sub Add _
        (ByVal Key As String, ByVal Item As Airplane)

        'Invokes the Dictionary Add method
        Dictionary.Add(Key, Item)
    End Sub


    Public Sub Remove(ByVal Key As String)
        Dictionary.Remove(Key)
    End Sub
End Class
```

Creating the Item property

The last thing to add to the AirplaneCollection class in order to give it basic functionality is an Item property. Once again, looking at IDictionary, there is an Item property with the following declaration:

```
Default Property Item(ByVal Key As Object) As Object
```

Add the code in bold in Listing 11-5 to the Dictionary class.

Listing 11-5: **The Item Property**

```
Public Class AirplaneCollection
    Inherits System.Collections.DictionaryBase

  Public Sub Add _
        (ByVal Key As String, ByVal Item As Airplane)

        'Invokes the Dictionary Add method
        Dictionary.Add(Key, Item)
  End Sub


  Public Sub Remove(ByVal Key As String)
        Dictionary.Remove(Key)
  End Sub


  Default ReadOnly Property Item _
        (ByVal Key As String) As Airplane

      Get
        'Invokes the Dictionary Item property
        Return CType(Dictionary.Item(Key), Airplane)
      End Get
  End Property

End Class
```

Because a strong typed `DictionaryBase` collection is being created, the returned object must be cast into the `Airplane` type even though it was stored as that type of an object. If the `CType` keyword is omitted, it returns an error when the `Item` property is invoked.

Note   Unlike Visual Basic Version 6, Visual Basic .NET only allows parameterized properties to be a default property. By declaring the `Item` property as `Default`, there are now two ways to access it. The first way is by explicitly calling the `Item` property, `Airplanes.Item(Key)`. Because the `Item` property is the default, you can implicitly call it using `Airplanes(Key)`.

Putting It All Together

Now it's time to test the `DictionaryBase` collection. Add a button named Button1 to Form1, and then switch to Code View and add the code in bold from Listing 11-6.

Listing 11-6: **Testing the AirplaneCollection Class**

```
Public Class Form1
    Inherits System.Windows.Forms.Form

    Windows Form Designer generated code

    Private Airplanes As New AirplaneCollection()

    Private Sub Button1_Click _
        (ByVal sender As System.Object, _
        ByVal e As System.EventArgs) _
        Handles Button1.Click

        'Set up the airplane
        Dim arrAirplane(1) As Airplane
        arrAirplane(0) = New Airplane()
        With arrAirplane(0)
            .Manufacturer = "Cessna"
            .TailNumber = "OH2236"
        End With

        arrAirplane(1) = New Airplane()
        With arrAirplane(1)
            .Manufacturer = "Mooney"
            .TailNumber = "OH2212"
        End With

        Airplanes.Add(arrAirplane(0).TailNumber, _
            arrAirplane(0))

        Airplanes.Add(arrAirplane(1).TailNumber, _
            arrAirplane(1))

        MessageBox.Show _
            (Airplanes.Item("OH2236").Manufacturer _
            & vbCrLf & _
            Airplanes.Item("OH2236").TailNumber)

        MessageBox.Show _
            (Airplanes.Item("OH2212").Manufacturer _
            & vbCrLf & _
            Airplanes.Item("OH2212").TailNumber)

    End Sub

End Class
```

Save and run the application. If everything was entered correctly, two message boxes pop up with two lines of text in each when Button1 is clicked. The `AirplaneCollection` class now has very basic functionality as a strong typed `DictionaryBase` collection.

The next part of this chapter goes over the members of the `DictionaryBase` class so that additional functionality can be added to the collection.

DictionaryBase Members

Five categories of `DictionaryBase` members are covered:

   Public properties

   Public methods

   Protected properties

   Protected methods

   Protected constructors

Only those that are not inherited directly from the `Object` class are listed. The `DictionaryBase` declaration of each of the properties, methods, and constructors are given in the descriptions. Looking at the way they are declared in the `DictionaryBase` class gives an idea of how to make use of them.

Note   The `System.Object` class is the base class for all classes in the .NET Framework. All classes implicitly inherit from the `Object` class and all the methods defined in the `Object` class are available to all objects on the system. One such method is `ToString`. To illustrate this, go into any method of the application and type **MessageBox.Show(1.ToString)**. In .NET, even numbers are derived from the `Object` class.

Public properties

`DictionaryBase` public properties are available outside of the derived class without adding any additional code. But their use is really limited without having at least an `Add` method (see Listing 11-3) in the derived class.

Count
The `Count` property is read-only and it returns the number of items in the `DictionaryBase` collection. It is declared in the `DictionaryBase` class in the following manner:

```
Public ReadOnly Property Count As Integer
```

As with all public properties of the DictionaryBase class, it can be called from outside of the derived class. Add a second button to Form1 named Button2. Switch to Code View and add the code from Listing 11-7.

Listing 11-7: **Accessing the Count Property**

```
Private Sub Button2_Click _
  (ByVal sender As System.Object, _
  ByVal e As System.EventArgs) _
  Handles Button2.Click

      MessageBox.Show(Airplanes.Count.ToString)
End Sub
```

The DictionaryBase Count property can also be overridden in the class by adding the code from Listing 11-8 to the AirplaneCollection class. You don't need to override it unless you want to change the way it counts or what it counts.

Listing 11-8: **Overriding the Count Property**

```
Public Overrides ReadOnly Property Count() As Integer
    Get
         Return MyBase.Count
    End Get
End Property
```

Note   When running the application with the code in Listing 11-8, remember that the Airplane objects do not get added to the AirplaneCollection until Button1 is clicked. If Button2 is clicked before Button1, the message box shows the number zero.

Public methods

As with public properties, public methods are available by default from outside the derived class and have limited use without adding basic functionality.

Clear

The Clear method clears the contents of the DictionaryBase collection. It is declared in the DictionaryBase class in the following manner:

```
NotOverridable Public Sub Clear()
```

The code in listing 11-9 demonstrates the use of the `Clear` method.

Listing 11-9: **Clearing the DictionaryBase**

```
Private Sub Button2_Click _
(ByVal sender As System.Object, _
  ByVal e As System.EventArgs) _
  Handles Button2.Click
    Airplanes.Clear()
    MessageBox.Show(Airplanes.Count.ToString)
End Sub
```

CopyTo

The `CopyTo` method copies all the `DictionaryEntries` in the `DictionaryBase`
class into a one-dimensional array of `DictionaryEntries`. It is declared in the
`DictionaryBase` class in the following manner:

```
NotOverridable Public Sub CopyTo _
  (ByVal array As Array, _
  ByVal index As Integer)
```

The code in Listing 11-10 demonstrates how to use the `CopyTo` method. The variable `Airplane` is used to iterate through the array and is declared as a
`DictionaryEntry` type.

Listing 11-10: **The CopyTo Method**

```
Private Sub CopyToTest()
  Dim Airplane As System.Collections.DictionaryEntry
  Dim arrAirplanes(Airplanes.Count - 1) As _
        System.Collections.DictionaryEntry

  'Copies the DictionaryEntries starting at
  'index 0
  Airplanes.CopyTo(arrAirplanes, 0)
  For Each Airplane In arrAirplanes
        MessageBox.Show(Airplane.Key & vbCrLf & _
              Airplane.Value.Manufacturer)
  Next

End Sub
```

GetEnumerator

The GetEnumerator method is used to return an object that allows iteration through the DictionaryBase instance. It is declared in the DictionaryBase class in the following manner:

```
NotOverridable Public Function GetEnumerator() As _
    IDictionaryEnumerator
```

Listing 11-11 demonstrates how to use the GetEnumerator method. The code demonstrates two ways to use this method. The first iteration uses the For Each method available to all objects while the second uses the MoveNext method of the IEnumerator interface.

Note   The IDictionaryEnumerator has a Current property, which returns the current element in the DictionaryBase. It also has a MoveNext and Reset method. If the Dictionary collection changes in any way after the GetEnumerator method is called, then calling the Current property or the MoveNext method will raise an exception. Calling the MoveNext method when the Current property is on the last element will also raise an exception. Before the Current property can be accessed, the MoveNext method must be called.

Listing 11-11: **The GetEnumerator Method**

```
Private Sub GetEnumeratorTest()
        Dim i As Object
        Dim j As System.Collections.IEnumerator
        i = Airplanes.GetEnumerator
        For Each i In Airplanes
            MessageBox.Show(i.Key & vbCrLf & _
                i.Value.Manufacturer)
        Next
        j = Airplanes.GetEnumerator
        While True
            Try
                j.MoveNext()
                MessageBox.Show(j.Current.Key & vbCrLf _
                    & j.Current.Value.Manufacturer)
            Catch
                Exit While
            End Try
        End While

    End Sub
```

Protected properties

The protected properties of the `DictionaryBase` class are not directly accessible from outside the derived class.

Dictionary

By shadowing the `Dictionary` property, access to the properties and methods of the `DictionaryBase`'s `Dictionary` property can be gained. This includes the `Add` and `Remove` methods as well as the `Item` property. Accessing these properties and methods this way is not recommended because it does not enforce strong typing. A better way of accessing this property is by using the `Add` method created earlier in this chapter. It is declared in the `DictionaryBase` class in the following manner:

```
Protected ReadOnly Property Dictionary As IDictionary
```

Note   By shadowing the `Dictionary` property, any access made to that property from within the scope of the derived class uses the shadowed property instead of the base property. It does not remove the base property but rather makes it unavailable from within the scope of the derived class. A shadowed property or method cannot be inherited.

The code in Listing 11-12 would be added to the `AirplaneCollection` class and the public methods and properties if `IDictionary` could then be accessed from the Form1 code, as shown in Listing 11-13.

Listing 11-12: **The Dictionary Property**

```
Shadows ReadOnly Property Dictionary() As IDictionary
  Get
          Return MyBase.Dictionary
  End Get
End Property
```

To test the code in Listing 11-13, make a call to the `AccessShadowedDictionary` method from the `Button2_Click` method.

Listing 11-13: **Accessing the Dictionary Property**

```
Private Sub AccessShadowedDictionary()
  Airplanes.Dictionary.Add("TEST", "TEST")
  MessageBox.Show(Airplanes.Dictionary.Item _
        ("TEST").ToString())
End Sub
```

InnerHashTable

By shadowing the InnerHashTable property, access to the properties and methods of the DictionaryBase's InnerHastable property, a Hashtable type, are gained. It is declared in the DictionaryBase class in the following manner:

```
Protected ReadOnly Property InnerHashtable As Hashtable
```

The code in Listing 11-14 shows how to make the InnerHashTable property accessible outside of the derived class and how it would be added to the AirplaneCollection class. Listing 11-15 demonstrates how to access it from inside the Form1 code.

Listing 11-14: **The InnerHashTable**

```
Shadows ReadOnly Property InnerHashtable()
    Get
          Return MyBase.InnerHashtable
    End Get
End Property
```

Listing 11-15: **Accessing the InnerHashTable Property**

```
Private Sub AccessShadowedInnerHashTable()

    Dim myHT As Hashtable
    myHT = Airplanes.InnerHashtable
    MessageBox.Show(myHT.Count.ToString)

End Sub
```

Protected methods

Just like the protected properties, protected methods are not directly accessible from outside the derived class.

OnClear

The OnClear method gets executed before the DictionaryBase's Clear method. This gives the opportunity to run code before the items are cleared. An exception can be thrown to cancel the Clear method or an event can be raised back to the instantiating object. It is declared in the DictionaryBase class in the following manner:

```
Overridable Protected Sub OnClear()
```

Listing 11-16 shows an example of using the OnClear method to create and raise an event in the AirplaneCollection class. Listing 11-17 gives an example of a possible way to handle the raised event from the Form1 code. No rule says that raising an event is the only way to use the OnClear method or any other method.

Listing 11-16: **The OnClear Method**

```
Public Event BeforeClear()
Protected Overrides Sub OnClear()
   RaiseEvent BeforeClear()
End Sub
```

Listing 11-17: **Handling the Event**

```
Dim WithEvents Airplanes As New AirplaneCollection()

Private Sub Button2_Click(ByVal sender As System.Object, _
        ByVal e As System.EventArgs) Handles Button2.Click

   Try
        Airplanes.Clear()
   Catch err As Exception
        'Throwing an exception here will
        'cancel the Clear method
        If err.Message <> "Cancel" Then Throw err
   Finally
        MessageBox.Show(Airplanes.Count.ToString)
   End Try

End Sub

Private Sub Airplanes_BeforeClear() _
        Handles Airplanes.BeforeClear

   If MessageBox.Show("Are you sure?", _
        "Clear DictionaryBase", _
        MessageBoxButtons.YesNo) = DialogResult.No Then
```

```
            Dim exc As New System.Exception("Cancel")
            Throw exc
        End If

    End Sub
```

Note The `AirplaneCollection` class is now being instansiated by using the `WithEvents` keyword. This allows for receipt and handling of the events from the `AirplaneCollection` class.

OnClearComplete

The `OnClearComplete` method is executed after the `Clear` method is complete. It is declared in the `DictionaryBase` class in the following manner:

```
Overridable Protected Sub OnClearComplete()
```

Listing 11-18 shows an example of using the `OnClearComplete` method to create and raise an event in the `AirplaneCollection` class. Listing 11-19 gives an example of a possible way to handle the raised event from the Form1 code.

Listing 11-18: **The OnClearComplete Method**

```
Public Event AfterClear()
Protected Overrides Sub OnClearComplete()
  RaiseEvent AfterClear()
End Sub
```

Listing 11-19: **Handling the Event**

```
Dim WithEvents Airplanes As New AirplaneCollection()

Private Sub Airplanes_AfterClear() _
        Handles Airplanes.AfterClear

  MessageBox.Show("Items Cleared")
End Sub
```

OnGet

The OnGet method gets executed before the Item property is retrieved. It is declared in the DictionaryBase class in the following manner:

```
Overridable Protected Function OnGet( _
    ByVal key As Object, _
    ByVal currentValue As Object) _
    As Object
```

If a DictionaryEntry does not exist for the passed-in key object, the key gets added to the collection with its associated value set to NULL. This is not necessarily a desirable feature. The OnGet method could be used to check for the existence of the given key and throw an exception if it does not exist. The code in Listing 11-20 shows how to implement this from within the AirplaneCollection class.

Listing 11-20: The OnGet Method

```
Protected Overrides Function OnGet( _
            ByVal key As Object, _
            ByVal currentValue As Object _
            ) As Object

    Dim exc As System.Exception
    If Not Dictionary.Contains(key) Then
        exc = New System.Exception("Does not exist")
        Throw exc
    End If
End Function
```

OnInsert

The OnInsert method gets executed before the element gets inserted into the DictionaryBase collection. It is declared in the DictionaryBase class in the following manner:

```
Overridable Protected Sub OnInsert( _
    ByVal key As Object, _
    ByVal value As Object)
```

The code in Listing 11-21 shows how to implement the OnInsert method from within the AirplaneCollection class to validate the type of the object being inserted.

Listing 11-21: **The OnInsert Method**

```
Protected Overrides Sub OnInsert _
  (ByVal key As Object, _
  ByVal value As Object)

  Dim exc As System.Exception
  'Check to see if the value is the correct type
  If Not value.GetType Is New Airplane().GetType() Then
        exc = New System.Exception("Not a valid Airplane")
        Throw exc
  End If
End Sub
```

OnInsertComplete

The OnInsertComplete method gets executed after the element gets inserted into the DictionaryBase collection. It is declared in the DictionaryBase class in the following manner:

```
Overridable Protected Sub OnInsertComplete( _
  ByVal key As Object, _
  ByVal value As Object)
```

The code in Listing 11-22 shows how to create and raise an event associated with the OnInsertComplete method from within the AirplaneCollection class. The code in Listing 11-23 shows how to handle the event from the Form1 code.

Listing 11-22: **The OnInsertComplete Method**

```
Public Event ElementInserted()
Protected Overrides Sub OnInsertComplete _
  (ByVal key As Object, _
  ByVal value As Object)

  RaiseEvent ElementInserted()

End Sub
```

Listing 11-23: **Handling the Event**

```
Dim WithEvents Airplanes As New AirplaneCollection()

Private Sub Airplanes_ElementInserted() _
        Handles Airplanes.ElementInserted

  MessageBox.Show("Item inserted")
End Sub
```

OnRemove

The OnRemove method gets executed before an element is removed from the DictionaryBase collection. It is declared in the DictionaryBase class in the following manner:

```
Overridable Protected Sub OnRemove( _
  ByVal key As Object, _
  ByVal value As Object)
```

The code in Listing 11-24 shows how to create and raise an event associated with the OnRemove method inside the AirplaneCollection class. The code in Listing 11-25 shows how to handle the event from the Form1 code.

Listing 11-24: **The OnRemove Method**

```
Public Event RemovingItem(Key as String)
Protected Overrides Sub OnRemove _
  (ByVal key As Object, _
  ByVal value As Object)

  RaiseEvent RemovingItem(Key.ToString)

End Sub
```

Listing 11-25: **Handling the Event**

```
Dim WithEvents Airplanes As New AirplaneCollection()

Private Sub Airplanes_RemovingItem _
        (ByVal Key As String) _
        Handles Airplanes.RemovingItem
```

```
   Dim exc As System.Exception
   If MessageBox.Show("Remove Item: " & Key, "Remove", _
         MessageBoxButtons.YesNo) = DialogResult.No Then
      exc = New System.Exception("Cancel")
      Throw exc
   End If
End Sub
```

OnRemoveComplete

This method gets executed after an element is removed from the DictionaryBase collection. It is declared in the DictionaryBase class in the following manner:

```
Overridable Protected Sub OnRemoveComplete( _
   ByVal key As Object, _
   ByVal value As Object)
```

The code in Listing 11-26 shows how to create and raise an event associated with the OnRemoveComplete method inside the AirplaneCollection class. The code in Listing 11-27 shows how to handle the event from the Form1 code.

Listing 11-26: **The OnRemoveComplete Method**

```
Public Event ItemRemoved(Key as String)
Protected Overrides Sub OnRemove _
   (ByVal key As Object, _
   ByVal value As Object)

   RaiseEvent ItemRemoved(Key.ToString)

End Sub
```

Listing 11-27: **Handling the Event**

```
Dim WithEvents Airplanes As New AirplaneCollection()

Private Sub Airplanes_ItemRemoved _
        (ByVal Key As String) _
        Handles Airplanes.ItemRemoved

  MessageBox.Show("Item " & Key & " Successfully Removed")

End Sub
```

OnSet

The OnSet method gets executed before an element is updated in the DictionaryBase collection. It does not, however, get executed before the Add method. It is declared in the DictionaryBase class in the following manner:

```
Overridable Protected Sub OnSet( _
    ByVal key As Object, _
    ByVal oldValue As Object, _
    ByVal newValue As Object)
```

The code in Listing 11-28 shows how to use the OnSet method to verify that an item exists before trying to update the value. This code would be added to the AirplaneCollection class.

Listing 11-28: **The OnSet Method**

```
Protected Overrides Sub OnSet _
        (ByVal key As Object, _
        ByVal oldValue As Object, _
        ByVal newValue As Object)

    Dim exc as System.Exception
    If oldValue Is Nothing Then
            exc = New System.Exception("No current value")
            Throw exc
    End If
End Sub
```

OnSetComplete

The OnSetComplete method gets executed after an element is updated in the DictionaryBase collection but not after the Add method is invoked. It is declared in the DictionaryBase class in the following manner:

```
Overridable Protected Sub OnSetComplete( _
    ByVal key As Object, _
    ByVal oldValue As Object, _
    ByVal newValue As Object)
```

Listing 11-29 shows how to use OnSetComplete to raise an event from within the AirplaneCollection class. The code in Listing 11-30 handles the event in the Form1 code.

Note If the Item property is declared as ReadOnly, the DictionaryBase elements cannot be updated by using the DictionaryBase.Item(Key) = NewValue. What this means is that the OnSet and OnSetComplete methods will never get executed unless the Item property is made setable or the Dictionary property is shadowed.

Listing 11-29: **The OnSetComplete Method**

```
Public Event UpdateComplete(Key as String)

Protected Overrides Sub OnSetComplete _
    (ByVal key As Object, _
    ByVal oldValue As Object, _
    ByVal newValue As Object)

    RaiseEvent UpdateComplete(key.ToString)

End Sub
```

Listing 11-30: **Handling the Event**

```
Dim WithEvents Airplanes As New AirplaneCollection()

Private Sub Airplanes_UpdateComplete _
        (ByVal Key As String) _
        Handles Airplanes.UpdateComplete

    MessageBox.Show("Item " & Key & " Successfully Updated")

End Sub
```

OnValidate

The OnValidate method runs before any of the other DictionaryBase methods listed previously and gives the developer the chance to provide validation of the objects. It is declared in the DictionaryBase class in the following manner:

```
Overridable Protected Sub OnValidate( _
    ByVal key As Object, _
    ByVal value As Object)
```

The code in Listing 11-31 shows how to use the OnValidate method to provide simple validation of the value object from within the AirplaneCollection class.

Listing 11-31: The OnValidate Method

```
Protected Overrides Sub OnValidate _
        (ByVal key As Object, _
        ByVal value As Object)

   Dim exc as System.Exception
   If value Is Nothing Then
          exc = New System.Exception("No object")
          Throw exc
   End If
End Sub
```

Protected constructors

A *constructor* is simply a procedure used to control the initialization of a new object. Visual Basic 6 used the Class_Initialize method for this, whereas Visual Basic .NET uses the New method.

New

The New constructor is called to initialize state in the derived class. It is declared in the DictionaryBase class in the following manner:

```
Protected Sub New()
```

Both parameterized and parameterless constructors can coexist in a single class. The code in Listing 11-32 shows two New constructors that would be added to the AirplaneCollection class. They both create a new instance of the DictionaryBase class, however, the parameterized constructor also adds the passed-in Key and Value to the DictionaryBase class.

Note   In order to use both a paramerterized and a parameterless constructor in the same derived class, they both have to be declared in the derived class. Notice also the absence of an Overrides or Overloads keyword. Constructors cannot be declared with the Overrides or Overloads keywords.

The only place that a constructor can be explicitly called is from the first line of code in another constructor that exists in the base class or a derived class. To demonstrate this, try adding MyBase.NEW() after the MyBase.Dictionary. Add(Key, Value) in Listing 11-32.

Listing 11-32: **The New Constructor**

```
Sub New()
  MyBase.New()
End Sub

Sub New(ByVal Key As String, ByVal Value As Airplane)
  MyBase.New()
  MyBase.Dictionary.Add(Key, Value)
End Sub
```

 See Chapter 14 for a more in-depth look at parameterized constructors.

Summary

By implementing the methods demonstrated in this chapter, the `DictionaryBase` class can be used to create strongly typed collections that are based on associated key objects and value objects. There are many available properties and methods, but to get the basic Dictionary style functionality, the `Add`, `Remove`, and `Item` methods need to be created in the derived class.

✦   ✦   ✦

Error Handling

by Jason Beres

Bugs are an unfortunate evil in software. This is not because developers are necessarily bad, or that we write bad code, it's just that sometimes we can't think of everything that could possibly happen when users are involved. And as you know, users are the main reason that your programs might crash, not the code. Besides, what would all the Quality Assurance people do if we all wrote perfect code?

To alleviate the complexity of error handling in your applications, VB .NET now supports Structured Exception Handling. This does not mean that your 8 million `On Error GoTo` statements are not supported; it means that you now have a better and more robust way of handling exceptions. This translates into happier users because their applications will not suddenly fail because of a forgotten runtime error not trapped, and it means that you can now handle errors in a more consistent manner across all of your applications. This chapter looks at the types of errors that can occur, and how you can handle exceptions in VB .NET with the new Structured Exception Handling syntax or with the old Unstructured Exception Handling syntax of the `On Error Goto` statement.

Errors in Programming

When writing code, there are several types of errors, or exceptions, that can occur. Depending on how your Visual Studio .NET environment is set up, these errors may or may not get caught. Table 12-1 lists the types of errors that can occur.

	Table 12-1 Types of Errors	
Type	**Reason**	
Syntax Errors	Misspelled keywords or variables. The VB .NET compiler will normally catch these errors while you are coding, but you have control over how much checking you want the IDE to do.	
Logic Errors	Code does not act as expected because of a flaw in the logic you have applied.	
Runtime Errors	Occur once your application is in production. The result of not handling an unexpected error.	

The worst types of errors that can possibly occur are logic errors. Logic errors normally crop up after your application has been rolled out, and the accounting department is doing year-end reports. You get an e-mail about missing money and inaccurate figures, and you realize that you had the wrong code in your number-rounding routine. You then start praying that the accounting department was also doing things manually for the year. Once you clean out your desk and bid farewell to your ex-employer, you realize the importance of understanding how to avoid logic errors at all costs.

Syntax errors are the easiest types of errors to catch. If you use the VS .NET IDE to write all of your code, and not Notepad, the IDE will notify you of syntax errors with a nice squiggly line under the offending line of code. The way to avoid any syntax errors is to set the `Option Explicit` setting to `ON` in your project settings. `Option Explicit` forces you to declare all of your variables before referencing them so if there is an accidental typo somewhere, the IDE will notify you and the project will not compile successfully.

Figure 12-1 gives an example of the IDE notifying you of a syntax error. In this example, the variable `strNme` is declared, but in the project, the code is attempting to use a variable called `strName`. Because the variable is not declared, a blue squiggly line appears, and you know that something is amiss. If you hover your mouse over the squiggly line, you will get a definition for the error.

```
 1  Public Class Form1
 2      Inherits System.Windows.Forms.Form
 3  Windows Form Designer generated code
55      Private Sub Button1_Click(ByVal sender As System.Object, E
56          Dim strNme As String
57          strName = "James T. Kirk"
58      End Sub    The name 'strName' is not declared.
59  End Class
60
```

Figure 12-1: Error notification using Option Explicit

`Option Strict` is another project-level setting that can help you avoid errors. With `Option Strict` set to `ON`, the IDE will notify you if the data conversion you are attempting is illegal. For example, if you are multiplying numbers and those numbers are greater than the amount allowed for the variable you have declared, the compiler will let you know. Figure 12-2 shows the error that will occur if you attempt to set the value of an arithmetic operation using a short data type to hold a non-integral number.

```
 1 ⊟ Public Class Form1
 2        Inherits System.Windows.Forms.Form
 3 ⊞  Windows Form Designer generated code
55 ⊟    Private Sub Button1_Click(ByVal sender As System.Object, ByVal e A
56          Dim x As Double = 100.5
57          Dim z As Short = x * 5
58      End Sub          Option Strict disallows implicit conversions from Double to Short.
59  └ End Class
60 |
```

Figure 12-2: Option Strict error notification

Note   In Visual Studio, `Option Explicit` is on `ON` by default and `Option Strict` is `OFF` by default.

As you can see, it is very easy to create errors. Using the features in the Visual Studio IDE can make your life much easier and accelerate your coding.

Structured Exception Handling

Now that you have a grasp of the types of errors that can occur, you need to know how to trap errors that the IDE does not catch. After all, it cannot do everything for you. A typical scenario for catching errors might be code that asks the user to open a file. Your program will pop up a box, and the user will have to type in a file name. If the file does not exist, or possibly it was misspelled, your application will have to react to that somehow. If you are not trapping for exceptions, a runtime error will occur, and your application will crash. Trapping errors in Visual Basic was always done with the `On Error Goto` statement. You will see that later in the chapter, but now you need to look at a new and better way to handle errors. Using the `Try...End Try` blocks of Structured Exception Handling, you have a more object-oriented approach to handle errors. The following code demonstrates our File ⇨ Open scenario:

```
Private Sub Button1_Click(ByVal sender As System.Object, _
    ByVal e As System.EventArgs) Handles Button1.Click

    GetFileName(Textbox1.Text)

End Sub
```

```
Private Function GetFileName(ByVal strName As String) As
  String

Try
     If strName <> "" Then
         Return "Everything is OK"
     End If
Catch
         Return "Please enter a valid file name"
Finally
     ' Do some cleanup code
End Try

End Function
```

You will notice several new things here; the `Try...End Try` block, the `Catch` statement, and the `Finally` statement. This is the backbone of Structured Exception Handling.

Exceptions

Before I get into the details about `Try...End Try`, you need to first know what exceptions are and what you can do with them. Exceptions are objects that are raised at runtime to abnormal behavior in your application. Like the `Error` object in previous VB versions, exceptions notify you if something goes wrong. The difference between the way the .NET runtime handles exceptions and the way previous VB versions handled errors are as follows:

✦ Exceptions can cross process boundaries and machine boundaries.

✦ Exceptions are handled the same way regardless of what language the application was written in or what language the exception will be handled in.

✦ Exceptions are based on the `System.Exception` class.

✦ Exceptions can be traced to the offending procedure and line of code in the calling chain using the `StackTrace` property.

So what does this really mean? In short, you are given a very robust way to ensure that your applications do not crash. In previous versions of VB, you could really control only what happened in your application. When you wrote procedures, they had error-handling mechanisms using the `On Error Goto` statement, which contained information about what just may have happened, but there was no way to interoperate with other applications with 100% success when it came to errors cropping up. With Structured Exception Handling, there is a standard way to handle and throw, or raise, exceptions in all .NET languages. You know what to expect, and you know what other applications expect. Table 12-2 lists the common properties in the `Exception` class. You will notice similarities to the `Err` object.

Table 12-2
Exception Class Properties

Property	Description
HelpLink	Gets or sets the location of the help file associated with the exception.
HResult	Gets or sets HRESULT, a coded numerical value that is assigned to a specific exception.
InnerException	Gets a reference to the inner exception.
Message	Gets the string representation of the error message associated with the exception.
Source	Gets or sets the name of the application or object that caused the exception.
StackTrace	Gets the stack trace identifying the location in the code where the exception occurred.
TargetSite	Gets the method that threw the exception.

When you are investigating classes for use in your application, you will notice that most of them have an exception class derived from the System.Exception class that describes the possible exceptions that can occur within this class. When you are working with File IO, there is the IOException class that contains exceptions for that class, such as FileNotFoundException or EndOfStreamException. When working with the System.Net classes for Web access, you have exceptions such as CookieException or WebException. The gist is that exceptions are *built in*, not an afterthought. When you create your own namespaces, you can create exception classes that notify users of exceptions that occur within your object. And the cool thing is the user of your classes can be writing in COBOL .NET, and the exceptions will be understood and handled by the framework correctly.

Getting inside the runtime and understanding how it manages exceptions will help you understand why you are using Structured Exception Handling. You will see how to actually handle exceptions later in this chapter; this section gives you a background on what is happening on the inside

The CLR creates an internal exception table with an array for every method in your application. This array contains information about what the runtime should do if an exception occurs in a method. If you have exception-handling code, it is called *protected* code. Each block of protected code has corresponding exception handlers or filters that tell the runtime what to do in the event something goes wrong. If you do not have exception-handling code, the array in the exception table for that method call will be empty, so the exceptions will bubble up to the caller in the stack that has an exception handler. If none of the procedures in the stack has an exception handler, a runtime error will occur, crashing your application. This is not a good thing for the end user.

For an exception to be caught and handled gracefully, the runtime searches the array in the exception table looking for the protected code for the current instruction that is executing. If it finds a protected code block, and that code block has an exception hander, and that exception handler has a filter, the runtime will create a new Exception object that describes the exception, the exception will be handled, and the Finally statement for that block is executed. You will see the Finally statement in the next section.

Try...Catch...Finally

Knowing that exceptions will happen is one thing, but knowing what to do when they appear is another. In Structured Exception Handling, you use the Try...Catch...Finally block to handle exceptions. When reading the online help, the Try...Catch...Finally block will appear under "Handling Program Flow," or something similar. This is true because you are actually controlling the flow of your procedures while implementing exception handling. Here are the rules for handling exceptions with Try...Catch...Finally:

✦ Code that can cause an exception should be placed in a Try...End Try block.

✦ Within the Try...End Try block, you write one or more Catch blocks that respond to exceptions that may occur in the Try block, attempting to handle the exception.

✦ If you want code to always execute, regardless of an exception, you write code in a Finally block.

This is made clearer in the following example. Here you are attempting to open a text file located somewhere on the system. The code that attempts to open the text file is in the Try block. Within the Try block, there are two Catch blocks looking for the FileNotFoundException or the DirectoryNotFoundException. If these exceptions are raised, the Catch blocks handle the error by raising a descriptive message to the user. In a real-life scenario, you may prompt the user to look for another file, or write a message to the event log. The Finally block displays a message box that simply informs you that this block of code will always occur. This is very important to remember: code in the Finally block will always execute, whether there is an exception or not. Here you have attempted to catch two specific exceptions, a missing file or invalid directory. If you are not sure of the specific exceptions in the class you are using, in this case the IOException class of the System.IO namespace, you can use a generic Catch block, which is the third Catch block in the code example.

```
Imports System.IO
Public Class ExceptionTest
    Shared Sub Main()
        Dim strError As String
        Try
            Dim fStream As New FileStream("V:\XFiles.Txt", FileMode.Open)
            Dim sReader As New StreamReader(fStream)
```

```
                Dim strOut As String
                strOut = sReader.ReadLine()
                MsgBox(strOut)
                fStream.Close()
            Catch e1 As FileNotFoundException
                strError = "The FileNotFoundException has occurred" & vbCrLf _
                    & "The message is: " & e1.Message & vbCrLf _
                    & "The stack trace is: " & e1.StackTrace & vbCrLf _
                    & "The source is: " & e1.Source
                MsgBox(strError)
            Catch e2 As DirectoryNotFoundException
                strError = "The DirectoryNotFoundException occurred" & vbCrLf _
                    & "The message is: " & e2.Message & vbCrLf _
                    & "The stack trace is: " & e2.StackTrace & vbCrLf _
                    & "The source is: " & e2.Source
                MsgBox(strError)
            Catch e3 As Exception ' Generic Exception Handler
                MsgBox(e3.Message())
            Finally
                MsgBox("This will always happen, exception or no exception")
            End Try
        End Sub
End Class
```

The message box for the exception is displayed in Figure 12-3.

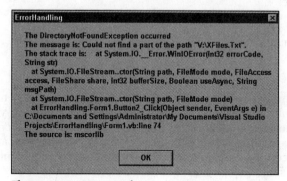

Figure 12-3: Message box

The examples of the Try statement are pretty straightforward, and I think they are pretty clear. There are some other things about the Try statement that you need to be aware of. The Try statement can be used in one of three ways:

1. A Try statement followed with one or more Catch blocks

2. A Try statement followed by a Finally block

3. A Try statement followed by one or more Catch blocks followed by a Finally block

In the following code block, each one of the Try blocks is valid. Notice too that you can have more than one Try block within a procedure.

```
Public Function TestingTryBlocks() As String
        'Example #1 - Try - Finally
        Try
            ' Try some code
        Finally
            ' Do something no matter what
        End Try

        ' Example #2 - Try-Catch
        Try
            ' Try some code
        Catch e As Exception
            ' Catch an exception
        End Try

        'Example #3 - Try-Many Catches-Finally
        Try
            'Try some code
        Catch e1 As Exception
            ' Catch exception declared by
            ' variable e1
        Catch e2 As Exception
            ' Catch Exception declared by
            ' variable e2
        Finally
            ' Execute code no matter what exceptions
            ' occur or do not occur
        End Try
End Function
```

In the preceding code, the third example demonstrates multiple Catch statements. When you are trapping for multiple errors by using multiple Catch statements, you should have only a single generic trap for an exception, and the remaining Catch statements should look for a specific exception that can occur in the class you are working with. The generic exception handler should be the last Catch statement in your handler. This works the same way as a Select Case statement; the Case Else clause is always the "fallback" statement. Once you have attempted to catch all of the possible exceptions, and none of them have actually occurred, the generic Catch will trap the error and your application will not crash. Consider the following generic Catch statement:

```
Catch e as Exception
```

And this specific exception:

```
Catch e as FileNotFoundException
```

Both are fine. You would use a generic exception in two situations:

1. You do not know any of the exception classes for the namespace you are using.

2. You do not care to trap specific exceptions; you just want a single Catch statement looking for any exception.

You will also see that you are actually declaring variables to hold the exception information. In previous VB versions, because all you had was the Err object, you would look at its properties to find out error information. In .NET, because everything is a class, you are creating a new variable to hold the information of the class that you are deriving from. So when there are multiple Catch statements, each one needs a unique variable name to hold the information about that exception.

 Note   When using multiple Catch statements, the generic exception handler should always be in the the last Catch block, or it may be executed before the code block for an actual exception you are attempting to catch has a chance to execute.

Most classes expose properties that indicate whether an action was a success or a failure, or whether an action is even allowed. The FileStream class has properties such as CanRead or CanWrite, and supports the While statement to check for the EndOfFile marker while reading a file. It is much more efficient to code in this manner than to include all of your code in Try...End Try blocks. The following code uses an If statement to check the CanRead property, and if it returns true, the file is read while the EOF marker <> True.

```
Dim fStream As New FileStream("V:\XFiles.Txt", FileMode.Open)
Dim sReader As New StreamReader(fStream)
Dim bOut As Byte
If fStream.CanRead Then
   While bOut = fStream.ReadByte <> True
      ' Do some processing
   End While
End If
```

VB .NET extensions

VB .NET supports two extensions to exceptions that C# and other languages do not: the When clause and the Exit Try statement. You use the When clause in a situation like this:

```
Try
   Dim strName as string
   strName = "Spock"
Catch e as Exception When strName = "Kirk"
   ' Exception Code
Catch e as Exception
   ' Exception Code
End Try
```

The `Exit Try` statement is used in a conditional situation, such as the following:

```
Dim strName As String = "Scotty"
Try
   If strName = "Uhura" Then
         Exit Try
   Else
         Call PromoteToEnginerr()
  End If
Finally
        ' This code will still ALWAYS Execute
End Try
```

The `Exit Try` statement is similar to the `Exit For` and `Exit Do` statements. The difference is the `Finally` statement again. Even if you use `Exit Try`, the `Finally` code will execute before the `End Try` is reached.

Note   Do not use `Try...Catch...Finally` for normal flow control; use it only when the chances of an exception occurring are 30% or greater. Performance will improve if you use this as a guideline.

Throwing exceptions

Similar to raising errors with `Err` object, you can *throw* exceptions implicitly with the `throw` statement. The `Throw` statement allows you to raise an exception in your procedures that will be passed up the calling chain to the closest exception handler, or you may want to re-throw a previously caught exception, adding information to the object so it makes more sense to the user or application. The following example demonstrates the `Throw` statement:

```
Dim strName As String = "Scotty"
Try
    If strName = "Uhura" Then
        Exit Try
    Else
        Throw New Exception("Enter a Valid Rank")
    End If
Finally
End Try
```

In its simplest form, you throw a new exception, pass it a string indicating the error text, and the exception will be handled by the calling procedure. You can customize the exception further, and even declare a new exception based on an existing exception, and modify the properties, as I do here:

```
Dim strName As String = "Scotty"
Try
    If strName = "Uhura" Then
        Exit Try
    Else
```

```
        Dim e1 As New _
            System.ArgumentException("Scotty is already an Engineer")
        e1.HelpLink = "http://www.vbxml.net/help123"
        e1.Source = "X1 Sub Procedure in ExceptionText Class"
        Throw e1
    End If
Finally
End Try
```

Note   Do not throw exceptions for normal or expected errors, such as hitting the EOF marker while reading a file or a database.

On Error Statement

Visual Basic has long supported the use of Goto statements for handling program flow and enabling error traps. On Error Goto has always had a bad name compared to the Structured Error Handling of object-oriented languages, but nevertheless, it is firmly embedded in billions of lines of existing Visual Basic code. If you are new to VB, you should definitely use the newer Structured Exception Handling techniques mentioned earlier to handle error trapping in your code. If you choose to use Unstructured Exception Handling, you will be using the On Error Goto statement, which is still fully supported in VB .NET.

The Err object

When errors occur, the Err object contains information about the error, which helps you to determine whether you can attempt to fix the error or ignore the error. The Err object also has several methods that allow you to raise errors or clear the state of the Err object. The Err object is available for backward compatibility, so if you are migrating code from previous versions of VB to VB .NET, you will not have to modify all of your code to enable error handling. Table 12-3 lists the properties and methods of the Err object.

Table 12-3	
Types of Errors	
Type	*Description*
Clear	Clears the Err object.
GetException	Gets the exception that represents the error that occurred.
GetType	Returns the type of the current instance.
Raise	Raises an error.

Continued

Table 12-3 *(continued)*

Type	Description
Description	Returns or sets a descriptive string for the current error number.
Erl	Returns an integer indicating the line number of the last executed statement.
HelpContext	Returns or sets an integer value that contains the Context ID in the help file.
HelpFile	Returns or sets the fully qualified path to the help file.
LastDLLError	Returns a system error code produced by a call to an external DLL.
Source	Returns or sets the application or object name from which the error occurred.
Number	Returns the numeric value of the error.

To retrieve the numeric value of the error that has occurred, you would query the `Err.Number` property, and to get the descriptive string value of the number in the `Err.Number` property, you would check the `Err.Description` property. As you move through this section, all of this will become clearer. For now, just understand the `Err` object contains all of the information you need to handle an error.

Note   You must use either stuctured or unstructured error handling in your procedures. You cannot use both.

Error trapping

Error trapping is enabled by using the `On Error` statement. Once the error trap is enabled, any errors that occur will be handled by the line label indicated by the `Goto` statement in the `On Error` statement. The following code block demonstrates the use of the `On Error` statement.

```
Private Sub ErrorHandlerTest()
        On Error Goto errHandler
        ' Code
        ' Code
        Exit Sub
errHandler:
        MsgBox("An Error Occurred")
End Sub
```

The `On Error` statement tells the compiler that if an error does occur within this procedure, to jump to the line label indicated by the `Goto` statement. In the preceding example, you created a *line label* called `errHandler`. If an error occurs, execution will stop on the offending line and jump to the `errHandler` label. The code following the `errHandler` label will then execute. Once this code is executed and the procedure is out of scope, the error trap for this procedure is no longer in use. The next time you call this method, the error trap will be enabled, and the process will repeat itself. If no errors occur in your code, the error code in the error handler will never execute, but you need to explicitly tell the compiler to exit the procedure before the error code begins. That is why you include the `Exit Sub` statement immediately before the error handler.

> **Note** The `On Error Goto` statement should be the first line of code in your procedures.

To disable an error trap within a procedure, use the `On Error Goto 0` statement. This will disable any previous error trap that might be enabled. The `On Error Goto -1` statement will disable any exception in the current procedure. The following example demonstrates the use of the `On Error Goto 0` statement:

```
Private Sub DisableHandler()
        On Error Goto errHandler
        Dim cn As SqlConnection
        Dim cmd As SqlCommand
        cn.Open()
        ' Connection is open with no error
        On Error Goto 0
        ' Disable any further error trap
        ' code statements
        Exit Sub
errHandler:
        ' Handle the error
End Sub
```

In this example, you want to make sure the connection gets opened. If that is all okay, your `On Error Goto 0` statement disables the error trap, and the code will execute without the checking of errors. If an error does occur after the `On Error Goto 0` statement, a runtime error will occur and your application will crash. Use `On Error Goto 0` with great caution. If you choose to use `On Error Goto 0`, you should also consider using `On Error Resume Next` immediately following the `On Error Goto 0` statement, and then check the value of the `err.number` each time you execute code that may cause an error. You will learn about `On Error Resume Next` later in this chapter.

Handling errors

The error handler is the code you write to handle errors that are trapped by your `On Error Goto` statement. The code in the error handler can attempt to fix the error, it can ignore the error, or it can instruct the compiler to perform another task. The error handler can be written in one of two ways: with the `Goto` statement or *inline*.

Goto statement

To write an error handler using the `Goto` statement, you add a line label to your code, normally at the bottom of the procedure. A line label is a word followed by a colon. Line labels allow you to use the `Goto` statement to jump to a section of code. In the case of trapping errors, you need a line label to tell the compiler where to jump to when an error occurs. The `Exit Sub` or `Exit Function` statement should immediately precede the line label, so the procedure will exit gracefully if no errors occur. The following code gives you an example of the `Goto` statement with a line label:

```
Private Sub GetName()
On Error Goto errHandler
[code]
Exit Sub
errHandler:
    ' Handle error
End Sub
```

In this example, the line label is called `errHandler`.

Note   You can use the same line label name in all of your procedures because they are only in the scope of the procedure you are in. You cannot jump to line labels in other procedures.

Inline error handling

You can employ inline error handling by using the `On Error Resume Next` statement. When `On Error Resume Next` is used in your procedures, an offending line of code is ignored, and execution continues on the next line of code. This type of error handling is the *only* way to handle errors in scripting languages, such as VBScript. If you are used to writing Active Server Pages, you would use `On Error Resume Next` in your procedures, and then check the value of the `err.number` property after each line of code executes. The following code is an example of inline error handling:

```
Private Sub DeleteAndCopyFile()
        On Error Resume Next
        If Dir("C:\file.txt") <> "" Then
            Kill("C:\file.txt")
            If Err.Number <> 0 Then Err.Clear()
        End If
        FileCopy("E:\File.txt", "C:\File.txt")
        If Err.Number <> 0 Then
            MsgBox("Cannot Copy File, Please Try Again")
        End If
    End Sub
```

After each line of code is executed, you check the value of Err.Number property. If the value of Err.Number does not equal 0, an error has occurred. At this point, you can decide to notify the user of the error, ignore the error and continue processing, or attempt to fix the error. Once the Err.Number is filled, you need to clear the contents of the Err object with the Err.Clear method before continuing processing within the procedure. If you do not clear the value of the Err object, the Err.Number property will always contain the number of the last error that occurred, even though you may have chosen to ignore it. This could get you into trouble because an error might be reported on the first or second line of code, and if the object does not get cleared, each check of the Err.Number property will be something other than 0.

On Error Resume Next **is valid only for the procedure that is executing. If you call other procedures within your procedure, each procedure must specify** On Error Resume Next **to use inline error handling.**

Exiting the error handler

The Resume statement enables you to tell the application where to resume processing if the error is handled. The Resume statement has three variations: Resume, Resume Next, **and** Resume *Line Number* or *Label*.

✦ Resume: Execution returns to the line of code that caused the error. If you have corrected the offending line, it will re-execute and hopefully get to the next line. If the error still exists, the error handler will be re-executed.

✦ Resume Next: Execution continues on the line of code immediately following the offending line of code. You will use Resume Next if the error encountered can be ignored.

✦ Resume *Line Number* or *Label*: Execution will continue at a specific label or line number within the procedure.

The following code samples illustrate how to use each one of the Resume statement options in the same error handler, based on the value of the Err.Number property.

```
Private Sub CopyFile()
      On Error Goto errHandler
      Dim strSource, strDest As String
GetFileName:
      strSource = InputBox("Please enter source file name")
      strDest = InputBox("Please enter destination file name")
      If strSource <> "" And strDest <> "" Then
          FileCopy(strSource, strDest)
          MsgBox("File Copied Successfully")
      Else
          Err.Raise(53)
```

```
            End If
            Exit Sub
errHandler:
        Select Case Err.Number
            Case 53 ' File Not Found Error
                MsgBox("File Does Not Exist, Please Try Again")
                Err.Clear()
                Resume GetFileName ' Jump to the GetFileName label
            Case 71 ' Drive Not Ready Error
                If MsgBox("Please Insert Disk In Drive",
                    MsgBoxStyle.RetryCancel) = MsgBoxResult.Retry Then
                        Resume ' If the user clicks RETRY button, the same
                        ' line of code will get executed
                End If
            Case Else
                MsgBox(Err.Number & "-" & Err.Description)
                Resume Next
        End Select
End Sub
```

You can see the variations of the Resume statement. To determine how to handle the error, you use the Select...Case statement in the error handler, and check the value of the Err.Number property. Based on the error number, you take a certain action. You can also see the Err.Raise statement used in this procedure. The Err.Raise statement forces an error to occur, so essentially you're causing the error yourself. In this case, you raise the error so the user will re-enter the file names, but in a real-world scenario, you would use Err.Raise to test your error handler or your inline error handling code.

Note   If an error occurs within your error handler, a runtime error occurs, causing program execution to stop altogether.

The chains of errors

Most of your applications are not as simple as a single button on a form calling the Click event. Most of the time, you have procedures that call procedures that call other procedures. You have a chain of events that occur to accomplish the task at hand. If you have error handling in each procedure that you write, the errors are handled as they occur in the procedures and the execution is returned to the calling procedure. If you do not have error handling in every procedure, when an error occurs, it passes it up the chain to the procedure that does have an error handler. If none of your procedures has an error handler, a runtime error will occur and program execution will stop. Figure 12-4 demonstrates the path an error will take if error handling is not used in each procedure.

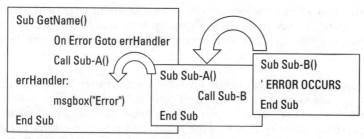

Figure 12-4: Errors and the calling chain

You can see that if the original caller is the only procedure that has an error handler, the error will bubble all the way up to its own error handler. This is one of the biggest problems with unstructured error handling. An error can be very deep within an application, and if each procedure does not handle errors as they arise, it is extremely difficult to debug and find the reason for the error. Even worse, if one of the procedures in the calling chain uses On Error Resume Next, the error may never get caught because the original caller's error handler will never get notified of an error. For example, if Sub-A used On Error Resume Next, once an error occurred in Sub-B the execution would continue in Sub-A and not return the error to GetName(), which is really what you want. The best way to avoid these issues is to use the Structured Exception Handling routines discussed earlier in the chapter.

Custom Made Errors

In the pre- .NET world of unmanaged code, every DLL and COM component and ActiveX control had its own way of returning errors and handling errors in a clear, consistent manner. Because it will be years before the whole world is a managed environment, you still need to worry about properly notifying a calling application if an error occurred in your object. You do this with the vbObjectError constant. The Err.Number and Err.Description properties are read/write, which means that you can modify the value of the number that it contains in order to pass back custom error information to a calling client. The reason you do not just set the err.number to the first figure that pops in your head is because you will most likely step on a real error code, and that would confuse the calling client. The vbObjectError ensures that the number you are passing back as an error is unique. The following code shows the vbObjectError usage.

```
Err.Number = vbObjectError + 2050
Err.Descrption = "Error Occurred in Method X"
```

You will find that when writing components, your customers or users will need to look up error codes if they occur. By using your own error numbering scheme, you can document and publish your SDK with meaningful error codes, and your errors will mean something to you and they will not be a generic VB error code.

Visual Basic cannot trap errors that occur when calls are made to Windows DLLs. For this reason, you are always checking return code values. The return code is different for almost every DLL; there is no consistency between what a particular return code represents. So when checking the return codes of a function call into a DLL, make sure that you verify the meaning of the return codes before writing too much code. Normally, if there is no SDK documentation handy, I will test various inputs to the method calls, see what return codes I am getting back, and then use those for the actions that I will take on a method call. If you want to check for a particular error in an error handler, you can look at the `err.LastDLLError` property, and it may contain the error code coming from the DLL. This cannot be guaranteed, so use with caution.

Summary

In this chapter, you learned everything you will ever need to know about errors and how to handle them. Here are the two most important things to remember:

✦ Always check for errors

✦ Use Structured Exception Handling

There is nothing worse than getting phone calls from users saying that the application just "disappeared." Runtime errors are the root of all evil, and they are easy to avoid. All you need to do is check for errors.

Do not wait until your application is ready to roll out into production to add error-handling code. It should be something that is carefully thought out and included from the first day of the project. With VB .NET's new Structured Exception Handling, you have a modern, robust error-handling scheme that helps application flow and solidifies the VB .NET language's position as a first-class object-oriented language.

✦   ✦   ✦

Namespaces

by Jason Beres

To understand how the framework is making your applications work, how auto-list members are possible, and how your classes are organized, you need to understand the concept of namespaces. In this chapter, you learn what a namespace is, how you can create your own namespaces, and some of the more common .NET namespaces.

Introduction to Namespaces

Namespaces allow classes to be categorized in a consistent, hierarchical manner. The .NET Framework is comprised of hundreds of namespaces that all derive from the base class `System`. A namespace is essentially a phone book for functionality in the framework and is comprised of types that you use in your applications. The types can be classes, enumerations, structures, delegates, or interfaces.

The convention for naming namespaces is as follows:

+ The first part of the namespace, up to the right-most dot, is the name of the namespace.

+ The last part of the namespace name is the typename.

If you need to perform data access, you would look to the System.Data namespace. To access SQL Server-specific functionality, you would reference the System.Data.SQLClient namespace.

To use a namespace in your application, you use the `Imports` statement at the very top of your class file. Each `Imports` statement defines the namespaces for that specific file; if you need to use System.Data in more that on class file, you must specify it in each class file.

A namespace can contain classes, structures, enumerations, delegates, interfaces, and other namespaces. Namespaces can also be nested, meaning that a namespace called B can be inside a namespace called A, and each namespace can have any number of members. The following could represent the System namespace. Notice how the IO namespace is nested within System.

```
Namespace System
   Namespace IO
         Public Class FileStream
                    ' Functions that
                    ' implement stream IO
         End Class
   End Namespace
End Namespace
```

In the client code, you would reference this namespace like this:

```
Imports System.IO
Class Class1
   Sub New()
          Dim fs as new FileStream
   End Sub
End Class
```

In .NET, all namespaces shipped by Microsoft will begin with either System or Microsoft. Namespaces prefixed with System will come from the .NET SDK team, whereas namespaces prefixed with Microsoft will come from the product groups at Microsoft. The Office team may ship a namespace called Microsoft.Office, Microsoft.Word, or possibly Microsoft.Office.Word.

When you create your own namespaces, they should be prefixed by your company name or application name. This will ensure that your namespace does not conflict with an existing namespace, or with a namespace that you might use in the future.

The idea of uniqueness for the namespace name allows for scope to occur in classes. For example, if you create a namespace called System, and a nested namespace called IO, there will be a conflict with the existing System.IO namespace provided by Microsoft. Your goal is to have some kind of uniqueness in the names of your namespaces so they will not conflict with other namespaces, especially if you plan on selling your namespaces as a third-party tool.

If there is a conflict in a namespace prefix, or a namespace class, you can use the fully qualified name in your code. For example, if you are using the System.IO namespace, and someone else has created a System.IO namespace, in order to guarantee that the correct methods are being called, you would need to use the fully qualified name in your code. But, in the case of a complete conflict, you will be unable to use the namespace, so if there were a class called `System.IO.Create` in both namespaces, the compiler would not be able to resolve the conflict. I think the chances of this happening are slim to none, but it is something to be aware of.

Creating Namespaces

To create a namespace, you use the `Namespace...End Namespace` block. Within the namespace block, you create classes, enumerations, structures, delegates, interfaces, or other namespaces. You do not have to include all of your code in a single, physical file. A namespace can span multiple files, and even multiple assemblies. This makes it easy for many developers to build a single application using the same namespace. For example, if you are writing a book, and the book has lots of source code, you may decide to give the namespace the same name as your book. The namespace you will build here will be called VBBible. It will look like this:

```
Namespace VBBible

End Namespace
```

Throughout this book, there is lots of code that you might want to test to see how it works. To keep it separate from your real work, just use the `Namespace` identifier at the top of each source file.

There are some guidelines you should follow when naming your namespaces:

✦ Attempt to maintain uniqueness against other published namespaces.

✦ Use Pascal casing; that is, the first character is uppercase, and the remaining characters are lowercase. If it does not make sense, as in the example of VBBible, then use your discretion on casing.

✦ Separate components with a dot.

✦ Use plural names where it makes sense to do so.

To start building a new namespace, create a new class library project called HungryMinds. In the default `Class1.vb` file, add some code that looks similar to what is listed here. The goal behind this is to use the `Namespace` block, and within the block, to have more than one `Class` block.

```
Namespace VBBible
    Public Class Chapter10
        Public Function Test_StreamReader() As String

            ' Streamreader code
        End Function
        '
        Public Function Test_StreamWriter() As String

            ' Streamwriter code
        End Function
    End Class

    Public Class Chapter11
```

```
            Public Function Test_Errors() As Boolean

                    ' error testing code
            End Function
        End Class

        Public Enum ChapterRef
            Chapter1 = 1
            Chapter2 = 2
            Chapter3 = 3
        End Enum
    End Namespace
```

Now add a test project to your solution. It can be a class project, a Windows Forms-based application, or a Web Forms-based application. It does not matter, because you reference the namespace the same way across all project types.

From the client perspective, the form file or class file would have an Imports statement, like this:

```
    Imports HungryMinds.VBBible
```

The Imports statement lets your file know that the namespace members should be listed in the auto-list members when you reference the class members. By using the Imports statement, you are not including any additional overhead in your application when it compiles. You are simply allowing early binding to occur, and you are making your coding easier by having the members auto-listed for you.

To use a class in the test client, you would simply reference the type like any other namespace:

```
    Dim x As New Chapter10()
    x.Test_StreamReader()
```

If you used an Imports statement like this:

```
    Imports HungryMinds
```

The test client code would look like this:

```
    Dim x as New VBBible.Chapter10
```

Earlier I mentioned that namespaces could be nested. If you felt the need to create a more hierarchical namespace, based on the book name and each individual chapter, you might nest the namespace like this:

```
    Namespace VBBible
        Namespace Chapter10
            Public Class Sample1
                Public Function Test_StreamReader() As String
```

```
                    ' Streamreader code
                End Function
                '
                Public Function Test_StreamWriter() As String
                    ' Streamwriter code
                End Function
            End Class
        End Namespace
    End Namespace
```

The `Imports` statement would look like this:

```
Imports HungryMinds.VBBible.Chapter10
```

And the client test code would look like this:

```
Dim x As New Sample1()
x.Test_StreamReader()
```

Finding assemblies

Because .NET does not use the registry, there is no automatic way to bind an assembly to an application. Once you create your application, you select Build Solution or Rebuild Solution from the Build menu. This creates a DLL, but it is not a COM DLL. It is a .NET assembly. Assemblies contain the classes, namespaces, DLLs, bitmaps, EXE files, and so on that your application consumes, or that other applications might consume.

To notify your application of the existence of an assembly, you use the `Imports` statement. The `Imports` statement will list the commonly used assemblies that the framework offers. Third-party or custom assemblies will not be in the auto-list members of the `Imports` statement. You will need to add a reference to the assembly in your application.

You can do this either by right-clicking your project and selecting Add Reference, or selecting Add Reference from the Project menu.

You will be presented with a dialog box that lists the available .NET components, COM components, and active projects. By selecting the assembly you want to import, the name will appear in the auto-list members of the `Imports` statement, and the assembly name will appear in the References list in your application.

If you do not go through this process, you will receive an error when attempting to reference your assembly. Figure 13-1 shows the test client application after adding the `HungryMinds` assembly from the Add Reference dialog box.

Once the assembly is imported, all members of the assembly are available to your application.

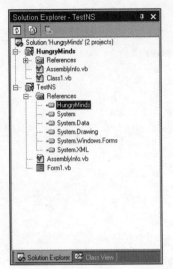

Figure 13-1: References list in Solution Explorer

References and auto-List members

Because there are so many assemblies, it is not prudent to display all of them all the time in the auto-list members. You may find that something you know exists is not showing up through the IDE. If this is the case, you will need to manually add the reference through the Add Reference dialog box, which you saw earlier. If you find that this is happening all the time, you can tell the IDE to always list all members by default. In the Options dialog box under the Tools menu, uncheck the Hide Advanced Members option. Figure 13-2 shows the section that you need to look for.

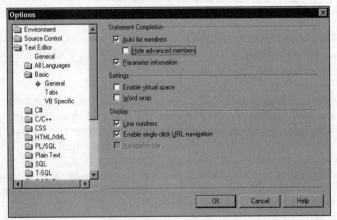

Figure 13-2: Options dialog box for hiding advanced members

Namespaces in .NET

Because namespaces are your front door into the functionality of types in .NET, it is a good idea to familiarize yourself with some of the common namespaces, and how to read the SDK help when you are looking up namespace details.

In the .NET SDK, you will find the details on every namespace and class in the framework. Namespaces are broken up by their functionality, and they are all derived from the base class `System`. Because the framework needs to be cross language compatible, the `System` base class defines the common types that are allowed across languages and platforms. The CTS or Common Type System is the backbone of the framework's ability to run across languages and across platforms, which is defined by the CLS or Common Language Specification. To get a refresher on the CTS and CLS, check out Chapter 1.

The .NET Framework is meant to be run on the Windows platform, but by providing a set of rules that define what is allowed and what is not allowed, there may be a day in the future when other vendors provide similar frameworks on other operating systems. By sticking to the rules defined in the Common Language Specification, you are guaranteed that your code will be accessible by all languages and platforms in the framework.

Help on help

If you drill into the SDK under the .NET Framework Classes, you will get a listing of the available namespaces and classes in the framework. To give you an idea of how much functionality is provided, Figure 13-3 displays the `System.IO` class from the SDK help.

As you can see, there are a ton of classes in System.IO. When you need to find specific functionality, you drill into the class you are looking for, such as IO, and attempt to find a class that best fits your need. If you know that you need to read and write text files, you would find the classes `TextReader` and `TextWriter`. If you are interested only in file system manipulation, you might look to the `Path` class or the `Directory` class. The names of the classes make sense based on the kind of functionality they offer.

Once you determine that a certain class is what you need, you can drill further into the definition and start examining its members. Members of a class define the methods, fields, properties, and structures that are exposed by the class. The SDK will list all members for every class, and define the functionality of each member. Figure 13-4 is a partial list of the `BinaryReader` members in the `BinaryReader` class.

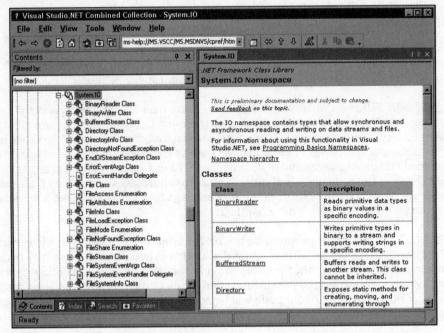

Figure 13-3: System.IO class in the SDK

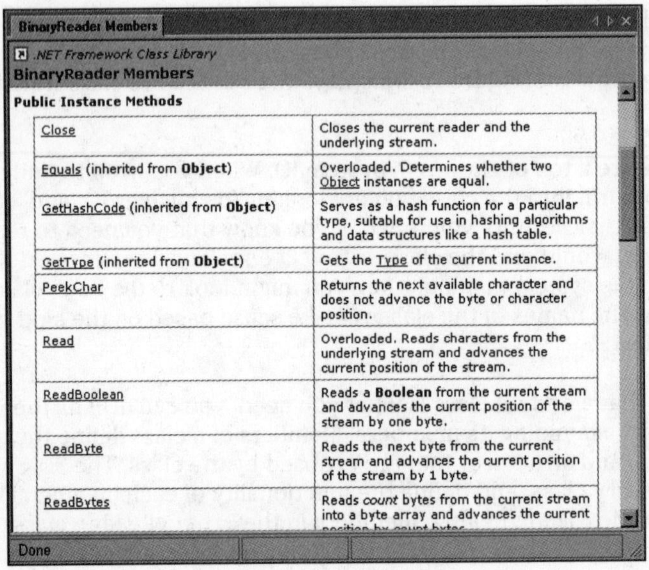

Figure 13-4: BinaryReader public members

Working with namespaces

So now you have found that the functionality you need is in the System.IO namespace, in a class called `BinaryReader`. To start working with this namespace, you would import it into your application, and then declare an instance of the `BinaryReader` class. The following code demonstrates this:

```
Imports System.IO
Public Class MP3Reader
    Public Function ReadMP3() As Boolean
        Dim fs As New FileStream("C:\mymusic.mp3", _
        FileMode.Open)
        Dim br As New BinaryReader(fs)
        While br.Read
            ' do something
        End While
    End Function
End Class
```

But how do you even know how to get that far? First, you could buy a book like this one and hope there are great samples on using the IO namespace (see Chapter 10). Or, there could be samples in the SDK or you could go the hard way and figure out what each of the members in the class represent, and start coding.

If you choose the latter, your first step will be to understand how to read the members in the classes.

Figure 13-4 shows a partial list of the public members. The first member, `Close`, will close the current reader and the underlying stream. Where does the underlying stream come from? When you declare a new instance of the `BinaryReader` class, you will notice that it is expecting a parameter of the type `System.IO.Stream`. Figure 13-5 shows the pop-up help when you declare the new instance of the `BinaryReader`.

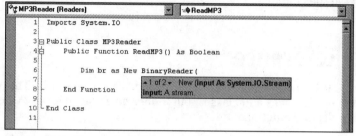

Figure 13-5: Pop-up help for a new BinaryReader instance

Now you need to determine what a System.IO.Stream is. If you go back to the SDK, you will find that the BinaryReader has a constructor definition that looks like this:

```
[Visual Basic]
Public Sub New( _
    ByVal input As Stream _
)
```

The Stream parameter has a hyperlink to the FileStream class. When you click the hyperlink, you are taken to a new listing of the FileStream class namespace, which defines its classes and the members of its classes.

By reading the SDK documentation on each of the classes, you can determine that in order to successfully read the file, you need to create a new FileStream that will point to the physical file name, and then pass that FileStream handle to the BinaryReader instance that was created. This is how you can come up with code that looks like this:

```
Dim fs As New FileStream("C:\mymusic.mp3", _
        FileMode.Open)
Dim br As New BinaryReader(fs)
```

It sounds like a lot of work, but the functionality and organization of the namespaces will make sense to you once you start using them more.

In general, the namespaces and classes as defined by the SDK are named in a logical fashion, and in the SDK help, there are hyperlinks everywhere to assist you in getting from point A to point B very quickly, which makes learning the functionality of the classes fairly simple.

By studying the implementation of the namespaces and classes and their respective members in the framework, you will have a good idea of how to proceed with the creation of your own namespaces, and how to avoid the name collisions that were mentioned earlier in the chapter.

Namespace Reference

This section covers the common namespaces provided in the framework. This will not cover all of the namespaces and classes, but it does give you an idea of where to start looking for desired functionality.

Component model

System.ComponentModel —Licensing and design time implementation of components.

Data

`System.Data` — Data access

`System.Data.SQLClient` — SQL Server data access

`System.Data.OLEDB` — OLE DB data access

`System.Data.XML` — XML Processing

`System.XML.Serialization` — Bidirectional object to XML mapping

Services

`System.Diagnostics` — Provides debugging and tracing services

`System.DirectoryServices` — Active Directory provider

`System.Messaging` — Microsoft Message Queue management

`System.ServiceProcess` — Services to install and run service-based applications

Networking

`System.Net` — Programmable access to network protocols

`System.Net.Sockets` — Managed access to Windows Sockets

GUI

`System.Drawing` — Access to GDI+ functions

`System.Windows.Forms` — Classes that create Windows Forms based–applications

Security

`System.Security` — Access to .NET Framework security mechanisms

`System.Security.Cryptography` — Cryptography services, such as encoding, decoding, hashing, authentication and digital signatures

Web Services

`System.Web` — ASP.NET and Web Forms support

`System.Web.Mail` — SMTP mail send functionality

`System.Web.Caching` — Caching frequently used resources on the Web server

`System.Web.Services` — Build and maintain Web Services

General application

`System.Collections` — Collection support

`System.IO` — File IO support

`System.Text` — String manipulation and character encoding

`System.Threading` — Multithreading support

Globalization

`System.Globalization` — Internationalization classes

Summary

In this chapter, you saw how namespaces are the core method of accessing .NET types. Namespaces are your Yellow Pages to the functionality of .NET. By organizing namespaces into human-understandable functions, you can decipher fairly quickly which namespaces you will need to use and how to use them.

You also learned how to create your own namespaces, which will become important when you decide to redistribute your code and allow others to use it.

The section on understanding how to read the SDK and decipher what goes where and how will make your coding life much easier as you delve into .NET development. You can always use the old-style `File` methods of VB6 to manipulate and read files, or even the old ADO methods in ADO 2.6, since they are available in the VB6 compatibility namespace, but you should learn how to use the newer namespaces for all of your .NET development. They are CLS-compliant and will work across languages and CPUs, which is the ultimate goal of using the .NET Framework.

✦   ✦   ✦

Classes and Objects

by Jason Beres

Classes, or reference types, are the backbone of .NET Common Language Runtime. The .NET Framework is built upon classes, and everything you code will derive from the base class System.Object. You are using classes in everything from dragging controls onto forms to adding forms to projects to creating server controls. In .NET *everything* is an object, and objects are instances of classes, so you could really say that everything is a class, right down to the instance of the IDE that you are running right now!

When you built your first house, there were many pieces of the pie that needed to be in place before everything worked the way it was supposed to. You certainly could not wash the dishes or flush the toilet without having the proper plumbing in place. Writing your VB.NET applications is the exact same scenario. You need to carefully plan out what is going to go into your application, get all those pieces together, and build the final product. When users click on a Save button in your application, they expect something to happen, just like when you flick a light switch, you expect certain things to occur.

All of the code that makes up the actions that will take place in your applications is going to be in classes. Those classes will be created, or instantiated, into an object. You will set properties, call methods, and even raise events, causing your applications to do what they are supposed to do.

In this chapter, you will learn everything you need to know about classes and how those classes become objects. You will learn what classes are and what they can do, and you will learn how to create methods, properties, constants, events, and fields. You will also see how some of the new object-oriented (OO) features can be used when you write your classes, such as overloading, overriding, and shadowing. I won't rehash what you learned about OO programming in Chapter 3, but this chapter along with Chapter 27 will help tie together many concepts on your road to learning OO programming.

Introduction to Classes

When you started the VS .NET IDE for the first time, you most likely took the default WindowsApplication1 project name, waited for it to load up, and went immediately to the Toolbox and started looking at the new controls and dragging them onto the Form1.vb that was supplied. After the first button was dragged onto the form, you double-clicked it, saw there was a `Click` event of some sort, typed in some code, such as `MsgBox "Here"`, and pressed the F5 key. You saw the results, and breathed a sigh of relief that the changes to VB .NET were not as dramatic as everyone said they were.

This is typical VB programming. You write applications that are event driven and forms based. To some degree, this is still true in VB .NET, but the underlying infrastructure is very different from previous versions of VB. When you write your applications in .NET, you will be using things that look the same, but they really are not. In VB6 and earlier, everything was hidden from you; all of the complexities of what the application was really doing were not important most of the time. It was all done magically through the MSVBVM60.DLL. That DLL did everything that you now have to learn more about, which is a good thing, because you have much more control now over everything that happens in your applications.

This is why you need to understand classes. Classes are the bricks that make up the building. You are writing your own classes, or you are using someone else's classes, when you are developing your applications. Take this code as an example:

```
Dim myStream as FileStream = New FileStream
```

You are creating an object called `myStream`, which is an instance of the pre-built `FileStream` class. `myStream` is now your object, and you are free to do whatever you want with it. When the programmers at Microsoft decided to implement File IO in .NET, they had a conversation about what needed to go into reading and writing files, and what developers like you might need beyond just simple text input and output. So they started to make a brick that makes up the File IO part of your building. One of those bricks is called the `FileStream` class. You will go through this same process when you create your classes.

In the previous example, you created a variable called `myStream`. This variable was *instantiated* as the type `FileStream`, and then set to a new instance of `FileStream`. Consider the following two definitions, courtesy of www.dictionary.com.

1. **Instantiate** (in-stan-she-ate): To represent an abstract concept by a concrete or tangible example.

2. **Instantiation:** Producing a more defined version of some object by replacing variables with values or other variables.

Other variations of the word include *instantiated, instantiating,* and *instantiates.*

When you need to do something tangible with a class, such as the `FileStream` class, you instantiate a variable to hold an instance of that class; thus producing a tangible object with which you can work. The object that is created is an exact duplicate of the base class `FileStream`. When you instantiate a variable as a certain type, you are deriving from that particular class.

You can then write code that modifies your instance of that class or uses other members of that class. This is where auto-list members and auto-complete come into play. When you type the "." after your variable name and a list of properties, methods, and events is displayed in the handy drop-down list, it is listing shared and public members of the derived class.

If you need to use more than one instance of a class, you simply declare another variable and instantiate it as that class all over again. In this example, you are creating three separate instances of the `FileStream` class, each assigned to a separate variable that works independently of the other variable instantiation.

```
Dim fs1 as New FileStream("C:\File1.txt", FileMode.CreateNew)
Dim fs2 as New FileStream("C:\File2.txt", FileMode.CreateNew)
Dim fs3 as New FileStream("C:\File3.txt", FileMode.CreateNew)
```

Instance and static classes

When you are reading the SDK, and reading this book, you will see two types of classes mentioned, *instance* and *static*. An instance class is instantiated with the `New` keyword, producing a new instance of the class with which you can work. A static class does not need to be instantiated with the `New` keyword, you can just reference the class and set properties and execute method calls.

This is possible because of the way the code inside the class is written. You will learn more about how to create static classes and instance classes later, but in the meantime, just remember that static classes do not have a `MyBase.New` method call, and the code inside of the class contains shared methods and fields. An example of a static class would be the `Path` class. Once you have imported the System.IO namespace to your class, you do not need to create a new `Path` instance; you can just reference the class.

Consider this code:

```
Imports System.IO
Class MyClass
   Public Function GetVolumeSeparators() as string
         Dim strChars As String = Path.VolumeSeparatorChar
         Return strChars
   End Function
End Class
```

You are not doing this:

```
Imports System.IO
Class MyClass
    Public Function GetVolumeSeparators() as string
            Dim P as new Path
            Dim strChars As String = P.VolumeSeparatorChar
            Return strChars
    End Function
End Class
```

That code will cause an error that states, "No accessible overloaded 'New' is callable". Path is static, so the New keyword is illegal.

If you want to save some typing, you can assign the static class to a variable without the New keyword, as this code shows:

```
Imports System.IO
Class MyClass
    Public Function GetVolumeSeparators() as string
            Dim P as Path
            Dim strChars As String = P.VolumeSeparatorChar
            Return strChars
    End Function
End Class
```

FileStream, on the other hand, is an instance class. A new instance of FileStream needs to be created before you can reference its members.

```
Imports System.IO
Class MyClass
    Public Function CreateFile(strFile as string) as Boolean
            Dim fs as New FileStream(strFile,FileMode.CreateNew)
    End Function
End Class
```

This code is also valid for creating the FileStream instance:

```
Imports System.IO
Class MyClass
  Public Function CreateFile(strFile as string) as Boolean
    Dim fs as FileStream = New FileStream("C:\test.txt",FileMode.CreateNew)
  End Function
End Class
```

Both instantiations of the FileStream class are the same.

Creating a Class

There are several ways to create a class, and it all depends on what you are trying accomplish.

- ✦ To add a class that will be used within an existing application, you can right-click on your project name in the Solution Explorer and select Add ... and then Add Class from the pop-up menu.

- ✦ Create a new solution using the Class Library template.

- ✦ Open Notepad, and in your new text file, type `Class`, press Enter, type `End Class`, and save the file with a `.vb` extension.

Because I'm not that hard core, I won't go any further into using Notepad (you need auto-complete).

If you go ahead and create a new Class Library solution called StarFleetCommand, you should have something that looks similar to Figure 14-1.

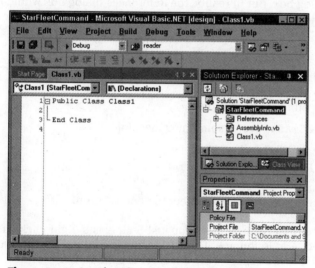

Figure 14-1: StarFleetCommand class project

When VB .NET creates class projects, the name you specify is simply the name of the project, not the name of the class. If you recall creating DLLs in VB6, you had a project name, and within the project you had any number of classes. The concept is the same here. In VB6, you would do the following:

1. Create a new ActiveX DLL project.

2. Rename the default `class1.cls` to something meaningful.

3. Add properties and methods to your class.

Once that was accomplished, you needed to test your new code, so you would add a new forms-based project to the project group. Once the forms project was created, you went to the Project menu and selected References, and added the ActiveX DLL project name as a reference to your test client. Your test code would have looked something like this:

```
Sub Form_Load
    Dim x as Project1.Class1
    Set x = New Project1.Class1
    x.AddName strName
    ' assuming you had a function called AddName was expecting
      ' a string parameter
End Sub
```

VB6 was really smart; you did not have to compile your DLL in order for it to show up in the References dialog box. But in reality, the References dialog box would read through the registry and find all of the available components on your computer that were properly registered. That is why it took a while for that References dialog box to pop up.

In VB .NET, you follow similar steps:

1. Create a new Class Library application.

2. Rename the default `Class1.vb` to something meaningful.

3. Change the class name in the class file.

4. Add properties and methods to your class.

Once that is accomplished, you add a test project to your solution.

To notify your test project that the new class you just built exists, right-click on your test client and select Add Reference. This dialog box is a little different than the VB6 References dialog box. Because .NET does not use the registry for its assemblies, you have to tell the client where to find the DLL. Microsoft was kind enough to include a tab named Projects, which lists the active projects in your solution. By selecting your active project in the list, you are making its classes available to your test client application so you can use your newly created class members.

The following is how your code would look in your client application:

```
Imports ClassLibrary1 ' Name of your class project
Class TestClient
  Sub TestNewReference
        Dim x as New Class1() ' Name of the file
        x.AddName("Microsoft")
  End Sub
End Class
```

Two items are worth noting. First, the use of the `Set` keyword is obsolete in .NET. All variable assignment is done with the equals sign, even if the variable is an object. Second, the `Imports` statement in your test client notifies this class that the members of a namespace named ClassLibrary1 should be available.

The `Imports` statement allows types in a namespace to be referenced without using the fully qualified name in your source code. It does not create any object from those namespaces unless you explicitly reference a member of one of the namespaces used in the `Imports` statement. You can also add a namespace reference through the VS .NET IDE by right-clicking on the project name in the solution explorer and selecting Add Reference.

Cross-Reference To learn more about namespaces, see Chapter 13.

You can import as many namespaces as you need to. In the same test client, if you need to use ADO .NET and FILE IO, it would look like this:

```
Imports ClassLibrary1 ' Name of your class project
Imports System.IO
Imports System.Data
Imports System.Data.SQLClient

Class TestClient
  Sub TestNewReference
        Dim x as New Class1() ' Name of the file
        x.AddName("Microsoft")
  End Sub
End Class
```

By default, when you create a new Windows Forms application in the Visual Studio .NET IDE, the following namespaces are automatically included:

System, System.Data, System.Drawing, System.Windows.Forms, and System.XML.

When you create an ASP.NET Web Application in the Visual Studio .NET IDE, the following namespaces are added by default:

System, System.Data, System.Drawing, System.Web, System.Web.Services, and System.XML.

If you decide not to use the Imports statement, you will need to use the fully qualified name of your class to instantiate it.

```
Class TestClient
   Sub TestNewReference
          Dim x as New ClassLibrary1.Class1()
          x.AddName("Microsoft")
   End Sub
End Class
```

Component classes

When you add new items to your solution, you will notice an item called a Component Class in the Add New Item dialog box. A component class is that same as a regular class, except for the inclusion of the following Inherits statement.

```
Inherits System.ComponentModel.Component
```

By inheriting the ComponentModel.Component class, you are given a nice designer surface, almost like a forms designer, but it is called a component designer. You can then drag and drop controls from the Toolbox onto the designer surface.

One of the main goals of .NET is to make client- and server-side programming quicker and easier (remember RAD for the Server from Chapter 1), and with inclusion of designers such as the component class, you can rapidly add server controls to your classes, saving coding time.

To give you an idea of the coding it can save, go ahead and right-click on your solution, and select Add Component. If you switch to Code View, you will see something like this:

```
Public Class Component1
    Inherits System.ComponentModel.Component
End Class
```

Now, switch to the Designer View, and drag the FileSystemWatcher and EventLog controls from the Toolbox onto the surface. When you switch back to Code View, you will see this in the Component Designer generated code section:

```
Public Class Component1
    Inherits System.ComponentModel.Component
#Region " Component Designer generated code "
    Public Sub New(Container As System.ComponentModel.IContainer)
        MyClass.New()
        'Required for Windows.Forms Class Composition Designer support
        Container.Add(me)
    End Sub
    Friend WithEvents EventLog1 As System.Diagnostics.EventLog
    Friend WithEvents FileSystemWatcher1 As System.IO.FileSystemWatcher

    Public Sub New()
        MyBase.New()
        'This call is required by the Component Designer.
        InitializeComponent()
        'Add any initialization after the InitializeComponent() call
    End Sub

    'Required by the Component Designer

    Private components As System.ComponentModel.Container

    'NOTE: The following procedure is required by the Component Designer
    'It can be modified using the Component Designer.
    'Do not modify it using the code editor.

    <System.Diagnostics.DebuggerStepThrough()> Private Sub
      InitializeComponent()
        Me.EventLog1 = New System.Diagnostics.EventLog()
        Me.FileSystemWatcher1 = New System.IO.FileSystemWatcher()
        CType(Me.EventLog1,
    System.ComponentModel.ISupportInitialize).BeginInit()
        CType(Me.FileSystemWatcher1,
    System.ComponentModel.ISupportInitialize).BeginInit()
        '
        'FileSystemWatcher1
        '
        Me.FileSystemWatcher1.EnableRaisingEvents = True
        Me.FileSystemWatcher1.NotifyFilter =
    ((System.IO.NotifyFilters.FileName Or
    System.IO.NotifyFilters.DirectoryName) _
                Or System.IO.NotifyFilters.LastWrite)
        CType(Me.EventLog1,
    System.ComponentModel.ISupportInitialize).EndInit()
        CType(Me.FileSystemWatcher1,
    System.ComponentModel.ISupportInitialize).EndInit()
    End Sub

#End Region

End Class
```

That is a fair amount of code that you did not have to write. The cool thing about .NET is that when you drag a control from the Toolbox onto your forms and designers, it is really just adding the code that creates the object instance class and sets some default properties. You have a lot of control over what can go on, and you have complete control over what you can do next with the classes. In VB6 and Visual InterDev, everything was a black box that you couldn't really do anything about.

What about standard modules?

When teaching VB classes, new developers have a hard time understanding the difference between class modules and standard modules. This is not surprising, because the Microsoft Official Curriculum for VB Fundamentals states that "Class Modules are beyond the scope of this course." It kind of leaves you hanging. Here is the two-bullet answer:

✦ Data in class modules is unique to each new instance of the class created, whereas data in standard modules is global to the application or to methods within the standard module.

✦ Data in class modules is destroyed when the class instance is destroyed, or goes in garbage collection, whereas data in standard modules is alive for the lifetime of the application, only being released when the application ends.

If you create a standard module in your application, and in the module you add a public variable named strName, the value of that variable is available to every bit in your application, even instance classes. If you create a public variable in a class, that variable is only available to the variable referencing that particular instance of the class.

The Class Block

The Class block defines the name of that class that you are creating. The following is the usage of the Class statement:

```
[ <attrlist> ] [ Public | Private | Protected | Friend | Protected
Friend ] [ Shadows ] [ MustInherit | NotInheritable ]
Class name
  [ Implements interfacename ]
    [ statements ]
End Class
```

The Class, name, and End Class are required. The name is the meaningful description of the objects that you create in your code, so it is important to think through your application and decide what the class names will be so that when your classes are being created, it makes sense to the consumers of your class. The name of the class follows standard variable naming convention; refer to Chapter 4 for a refresher on how to name variables. Table 14-1 lists the remaining options for the Class block, which define accessibility of members within the class.

Table 14-1 Class Statement Modifiers	
Part	**Description**
Public	Public, unrestricted access to entities within the class.
Private	Members are accessible only within their declaration context, including nested entities.
Protected	Members are accessible only within their own class or from a derived class.
Friend	Members are accessible only from within the program that contains the entity.
Protected Friend	Combination of Protected and Friend.
Shadows	Indicates that the class shadows an identically named programming element within the class.
MustInherit	Indicates that the class contains methods that must be implemented by a deriving class.
NotInheritable	The class is a class that does not allow any further inheritance.
Interface	The name of the interface implemented by the class.
Statements	Events, properties and fields that exist within this class.

Inside Classes

What is a class comprised of? The answer may seem obvious veteran VB developers, but in the OO world of VB .NET, there are some differences to classes from previous VB versions. Classes describe the methods, properties, events, and fields (or constants) of an object. These are collectively known as *members*. To access the members of an object, you type the name of your variable, type a period (.), and then type the member you are attempting to reference. This is easy in the VS .NET IDE thanks to auto-list members. Figure 14-2 demonstrates the members of the FileStream class.

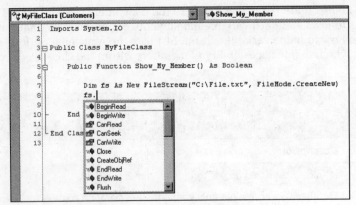

Figure 14-2: Members of the FileStream class

Methods

Methods are procedures that contain application logic. They can either be sub procedures or function procedures, the only difference being that functions will return a value back to the caller.

If you add a method called Set_Rank to your class1.vb in the StarFleetCommand project, it will look like this:

```
Class Class1
    Public Function Set_Rank(ByVal strRank As String) _
        As Boolean
        ' public function code
    End Function
End Class
```

The Public modifier for the function tells the class that this function is available to any consumer of the class. If the function were Private, only members of the class could access this method. The same rules apply for the Friend and Protected modifiers of a method.

Earlier, I discussed static instances. To make a method static, use the Shared modifier.

```
Class Class1
    Shared Function Set_Rank(ByVal strRank As String) _
        As Boolean

    End Function
End Class
```

When referenced from code, you do not have to instantiate the class to access the Set_Rank member:

```
Class SetRank
   Sub PromoteOrNotPromote()
          Class1.Set_Rank("Ensign")
   End Sub
End Class
```

Private, Protected, and Friend modifiers exist to support encapsulation. By planning your classes carefully, you will expose to the outside word only what is necessary, hiding implementation details in the class itself. Even though this is not COM, it is still important to be able to modify the implementation of a class without changing public details.

Note   Shared members cannot be declared as Overridable, NotOverridable or MustOverride.

Properties

Properties are used to store variables in a class. Properties exist to give you an object-oriented way of setting and getting variables. In VB6, you declared variables on a global scope to store information. You can do something similar in classes, called fields, but for each class you create, you will need to encapsulate properties for that specific instance. To create a property, you use a Property...End Property block, set a scope modifier, and set the name of the property.

```
Class Class1
   Private strRank as String
   Public Property Rank() as String
          Get
                  Return strRank
          End Get
          Set (ByVal Value As String)
                  strRank = value
          End Set
   End Property
End Class
```

From the client code, the property would be referenced like this:

```
Dim x as New Class1
If x.Rank = "Captain" then
   ' do something
Else
   x.Rank = "Engineer"
End if
```

Properties are cool because they can also implement code within the Get and Set identifiers, controlling what happens to the property when it is accessed or set. When a person's rank is set to Captain, for example, let's say you need to perform some special action, such as update the calendar for the big promotion celebration. You could modify the code to look like this:

```
Class Class1
   Private strRank as String
   Public Property Rank() as String
         Get
                  Return strRank
         End Get
         Set (ByVal Value As String)
                  strRank = value
                  If value = "Captain" then
                           'Call the update calendar method
                           'Call the send-invitation method
                  End If
         End Set
   End Property
End Class
```

This code is close enough to VB6 property syntax, which would look like this:

```
Public Property Get Rank() As Variant

End Property

Public Property Let Rank(ByVal vNewValue As Variant)

End Property
```

The very major and important difference is the *scope* of properties declared in .NET. You cannot set the access modifier for the Get and Set to a different scope. In VB6, your class could contain a private property Let, which would allow only members in that class access to setting the value of that property.

In .NET, Set and Get both need to be the same scope. This at first seems a little odd, but in the end, it will ensure that your application logic flows smoothly. And because this is a CLS issue, not a VB issue, it affects all languages in the CLR. To make your Rank property read-only, your code would look like this:

```
Public ReadOnly Property Rank() As String
   Get
            Rank = strRank
   End Get
End Property
```

If you are an old-timer OO type, you are probably thinking that this is not OO programming. In OO, you use `Getter` and `Setter` method calls to set and retrieve variable values within a class.

So in the `Rank` example, your code inside the class would look like this:

```
Class Class1
  Private Rank as String
  Public Function Set_Rank(strRank as String) as Boolean
       Rank = strRank
  End Function
  Public Function Get_Rank() as String
       Return Rank
  End Function
End Class
```

And your client code would look like this:

```
Function PromoteOrDemote()
  Dim x as New Class1
  Dim strRank as string
  strRank = x.Get_Rank()
  x.Set_Rank(strRank)
End Function
```

So what is the difference? You could say preference, or you could say that properties should be used for nouns and methods should be used for verbs. Both answers are fine. It is really up to you. But keep this in mind: The whole idea of `Getter` and `Setter` methods is to hide the implementation of variables within a class, and properties do that in a much cleaner way, with less code.

I would strongly suggest that you use properties in place of `Getter` and `Setter` methods because the Microsoft implementation of OO has more features than other languages you might be used to, and property procedures will be much more prevalent in new .NET code.

In VB6, classes could implement default properties. This was especially evident in ActiveX controls and Intrinsic controls. When you add a control to a form in VB6, you can use its default property to save yourself a little bit of coding. For example, when you drag a text box to a form, the following code is valid:

```
Text1 = "I'm a doctor, not a magician"
```

In VB .NET, when you drag a text box to a form, you need specify the property that you are using:

```
Textbox1.Text = "Yes, I Know, The Borg"
```

So for controls, there are no longer default properties. This is not the case when you create a class. By using the `Default` identifier, you can indicate that a property in your class is the default. The following code is an example of what is needed to implement a default property in a class file:

```
Dim strID As String()
Default Public Property ID(ByVal Index As Integer) As String
    Get
        Return strID(Index)
    End Get

    Set(ByVal Value As String)
        If strID Is Nothing Then
            ReDim strID(0)
        Else
            ReDim Preserve strID(UBound(strID) + 1)
        End If
        strID(Index) = Value
    End Set
End Property
```

In this case, you are creating an array of strings that the class is maintaining. This is very cool. Now, from the client, you create an instance of the class as normal, and then use the "shortcut" syntax to reference the default property:

```
Dim x As New Class1()
x(0) = "NX01 Enterprise"
x(1) = "NCC 1701 Enterprise"
MsgBox(x(0))
MsgBox(x(1))
```

If you choose not to use a default property, you can just use the normal syntax to reference the property:

```
Dim x As New Class1()
x.ID(0) = "NX01 Enterprise"
x.ID(1) = "NCC 1701 Enterprise"
MsgBox(x.ID(0))
MsgBox(x.ID(1))
```

Note   Only one default property is allowed per class.

Fields

Fields are variables declared with a public scope that are available to consumers of your class. Fields can be used in place of properties if the variable is read-write, it contains no restrictions, and you decide that the implementation of the field will not hurt any security measures in the class, such as making visible something you would rather hide.

To add a field that is exposed to a consumer application, just declare a public variable in your class:

```
Shared Class Class1
   Public Rank as String
End Class
```

From the client application, you would access the field like any other variable:

```
Dim x as Class1
x.Rank = "Doctor"
If x.Rank = "Captain" then
   ' Conditional logic
End If
```

If you need help deciding whether to use properties or fields, here are some guidelines to follow:

✦ Use properties when the variable needs to be read-only.

✦ Use properties if validation beyond data type validation is needed.

✦ Use properties if the variable changes the state of the object.

✦ Use properties if other variables within the class need to change if this variable changes.

Events

Events are notifications that cause something to happen or occur in response to something happening. Inside your classes, you can raise and consume events. Events are raised with the RaiseEvent statement, and handled with either the AddHandler or Handles statements. In the following code, you will raise an event when a crewmember is promoted to captain, which will then update the party calendar.

```
Public Class Class1
    Private strRank As String
    Event Promoted(ByVal newRank As String)
    Public Property Rank() As String
        Get
            Return strRank
        End Get
        Set(ByVal Value As String)
            strRank = Value
            If Value = "Captain" Then
```

```
                    RaiseEvent Promoted(strRank)
              End If
        End Set
    End Property
End Class

' Client Application
Class Class2
    Dim WithEvents NewRank As Class1
    Private Sub NewRank_Promoted(ByVal newRank As String) _
          Handles NewRank.Promoted
        ' Update Calendar
    End Sub
End Class
```

Using the AddHandler statement, you do not have to declare a variable with events. Within your client applications, you can use the AddHandler statement to connect to one or more event handlers at runtime. To remove an event handler at runtime, you use RemoveHandler statement.

Overloading and Overriding

The overloading and overriding properties and methods are part of the new object-oriented features of VB .NET. Their names are a good indication of what you can do with these two keywords, with the definitions being:

✦ Overload: Multiple methods, constructors, or properties that have the same name but different parameter lists.

✦ Override: You can provide a new implementation of on existing method in another class.

Overloading

To overload a method, you simply define two or more methods with the same name but different parameters, which must have different data types, using the Overloads keyword. When you read the .NET SDK, you will constantly see members that are "overloaded," meaning that there is more than one implementation for that member.

The following code demonstrates this by implementing a Search function. A common application feature is a search screen, where users can input data in some or all of the fields that you give them to search by.

```
Class Class1
Public Overloads Function Search(ByVal strName As String) As String
   Return "You searched by Name only"
```

```
End Function

Public Overloads Function Search(ByVal strName As String, _
                        ByVal strShip As String) As String
    Return "You searched for Name and Ship"
End Function

Public Overloads Function Search(ByVal strName As String, _
                        ByVal strShip As String, _
                        ByVal strRank As String) As String
    Return "You searched for Name, Ship and Rank"
End Function
End Class
```

From the client, you do not have to specify anything special; just call the method as you normally would and pass the parameters. This code demonstrates executing each of the overloaded functions.

```
Dim x As New StarFleetCommand.Class1()
MsgBox(x.Search("Kirk"))
MsgBox(x.Search("Kirk", "Enterprise"))
MsgBox(x.Search("Kirk", "Enterprise", "Captain"))
```

When you use the VS .NET IDE, after you get a reference to an object, you get the auto-list members and parameter information listed when you type the "." after you reference your variable. When there is more than one option for the specific member, the tool tip tells you how many options you have, and you can press the down arrow on your keyboard to get to the correct method calling list you need. Figure 14-3 shows the list for the overloaded `Search` function.

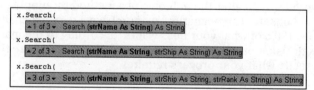

Figure 14-3: Search options

Implementing a `Search` function is one very useful example of implementing a versatile user interface for your users. You might also need to only have a single parameter, but of different data types. The following code demonstrates the same method with a single parameter, but different data type.

```
Public Overloads Function Get_StarDate(ByVal sYear As Short) As String
        ' Calculate based on SHORT datatype
End Function

Public Overloads Function Get_Stardate(ByVal iYear As Integer) As String
```

```
          ' Calculate based on INTEGER datatype
End Function

Public Overloads Function Get_Stardate(ByVal lYear As Long) As String
          ' Calculate based on LONG datatype
End Function
```

Now, from the client application, any number can be passed, and the correct method will be used based on the size of the number.

When using the `Overloads` keyword, it is important to note that only the number of parameters or their data types can be used to differentiate between methods of the same name. For example, you cannot use a single parameter of type `string`, but with different names:

```
Public Overloads Function Test(strName as string) as String
Public Overloads Function Test(strCompany as string) as string
```

This would cause an error. The `Return` type cannot be used to differentiate an overloaded method either, so the following code will also cause an error:

```
Public Overloads Function Test(strName as string) as Double
Public Overloads Function Test(strName as string) as string
```

Because the parameter is still a single string input, there is no overloading occurring.

Overriding

Overriding is a very powerful way to alter the outcome of a method by supplying your own implementation. Consider this scenario: You purchase a very expensive software product that does 100% of what your boss wants (according to the marketing material he based his decision on), but there are a couple instances where the methods do not match exactly what your process requires.

If the software is a black box, there is nothing you can do, but if the software gives you an API to work with that contains `Overridable` methods, you can *override* the existing implementations where you need to and bring the package up to spec for your needs.

You can do this if the methods in a class are declared as `Overridable`.

The default for all members is `NotOverridable`, so the method must specifically state that it is `Overridable` when it is declared. If you are overriding a member from a base class, you must specify the same number of arguments in your implementation for the method. If you choose to implement methods with the `MustOverride` identifier, the base class will have no code in the method implementation, and you must override the method in your class and provide the implementation.

If this is the case, you must use the `MustInherit` identifier in the base class name to ensure that the methods are overridden correctly.

In the next scenario, you are going to override the implementation of the `Add_New` method in a base class. This example shows how simple this process really is. Remember, as long as the methods in the class you are deriving from are marked as `Overridable`, you can write you own implementation of that particular method.

```
Public Class Class4

    Public Overridable Function Add_New(ByVal strName As String) _
                                        As String
        ' Original Implementation of the Add New method
        Return "Overridable Add New"
    End Function

    Public Function Set_Speed(ByVal intSpeed As Int16) As String
        Return "Speed Set"
    End Function

End Class

Public Class Class5
    Inherits Class4
    Public Overrides Function Add_New(ByVal strName As String) _
                                      As String
        ' Your implementation of the Add New method
        Return "Overridden Add New"
    End Function
End Class
```

The method `Add_New` in `Class5` is overriding the `Add_New` method in `Class4`. From the client application, you are declaring a variable as type `Class5`, and then setting that variable to an instance of `Class4`. The following would be the client code:

```
Dim x As New Class5()
Dim y As Class4 = x

MsgBox(y.Add_New("Enterprise"))
MsgBox(y.Set_Speed(10))

MsgBox(x.Add_New("Enterprise"))
MsgBox(x.Set_Speed(10))
```

Either way, you will never get a return value that says "Overridable Add New". It is impossible. Because `Class5` is inheriting `Class4`, and you are setting `Class4` equal to an instance of `Class5`, the overriding method will always execute.

This is inheritance and polymorphism in its truest form. So you might say that you could just as easily have created a new class and added a method, and just called that method without all this OO stuff.

This is true, but the idea is that you do not want to do the following:

- ✦ Change the client implementation.
- ✦ Lose the other methods in the base class.
- ✦ Declare more instances of another nonderived class.

Here are a few rules to follow when implementing this type of functionality:

- ✦ NotOverridable **cannot be used with** MustOverride.
- ✦ Overridable, NotOverridable, **and** MustOverride **methods cannot be of a** Private **scope.**
- ✦ Overridable **and** MustOverride **cannot be used in classes marked as** NotInheritable.

Constructors and Destructors

Earlier, you created instances of classes using the New keyword. In .NET, classes can have initialization code every time they are instantiated using *constructors*. When the class is destroyed, or set to nothing, the *destructor* code is run. With the use of constructors and destructors, you can implement code that needs to be run when a class is created or when a class is destroyed.

Constructors

To create a constructor for a class, you create a procedure called New. When the class is instantiated, New is called automatically. The client code does not specify ClassName.New in its code.

The following code creates a constructor for Class4 in the previous code example:

```
Public Class Class5
    Inherits Class4
    Public Overrides Function Add_New(ByVal strName As String) _
                                      As String
        ' Your implementation of the Add New method
        Return "Overridden Add New"
    End Function

    Sub New()
        MsgBox("New Executed")
    End Sub
End Class
```

Every time an instance of Class5 is created, the Sub New() will execute.

Destructors

Destructors are run when a class is no longer needed. This mechanism is handled through a process called *garbage collection*. With garbage collection, .NET can determine on its own when a resource is no longer needed and then reclaim the memory that the resource was using. In VB6, you set objects to nothing, and that forced the memory handle to be released. In .NET, when an object is set to nothing, the reference is not actually released until the garbage collection process occurs.

When writing classes, you may want to control when resources should be released. You can do this by using the Dispose destructor. Using Dispose, you can write code that frees resources from the class and have some control when the memory gets released back to the operating system. After Dispose is called, you may decide to set the object equal to nothing. Once this occurs, the garbage collector will reclaim allocated resources the next time it runs. This is known as *non-deterministic finalization*. You know that resources will be reclaimed by the OS, but you really do not know when.

When garbage collection occurs, the Finalize method of your class is run. Finalize may have further cleanup code that you have implemented, or it may contain no code at all. When you implement code in a Finalize method, you are overriding the Finalize method of the class that you derived from.

The following code demonstrates the use of the Finalize destructor.

```
Public Class Class5
    Inherits Class4
    Public Overrides Function Add_New(ByVal strName As String) _
                                     As String
        ' Your implementation of the Add New method
        Return "Add New"
    End Function

    Sub New()
        MsgBox("New Executed")
    End Sub

    Protected Overrides Sub Finalize()
        MsgBox("Finalize is Occurring")
        ' Close connections, write log files
        ' Perform cleanup code
    End Sub
End Class
```

To test the Finalize method, use the following client code:

```
        Dim x As New Class5()
        MsgBox(x.Add_New("Enterprise"))
        x = Nothing
        System.GC.Collect()
```

Calling the `System.GC.Collect` method forces garbage collection to occur. You should not call this in real life; you should let the system handle when garbage collection occurs. By calling the `Collect` method, you will see that the `Finalize` code in the class is executing.

Summary

In this chapter, you learned about classes and some of the new OO features that VB .NET offers. Just as it was important to carefully plan your components in VB6, it is equally important to plan the implementation of your .NET classes. Do not haphazardly define methods as `Overridable`; it could affect the results that you expect. Also, plan your inheritance carefully. If you are going to allow your classes to be inherited by others, be sure to write cleanup code for the objects that your class is responsible for. Although garbage collection will ensure that the object of your derived class is destroyed, the individual objects within the base class must be released to garbage collection also.

✦   ✦   ✦

Multithreading

by Jason Beres

Multithreading, or free threading, has always been one of the items on the list of many things that "superior" languages such as C++ had and Visual Basic did not. With VB .NET, that list of unsupported "stuff" has pretty much disappeared, and multithreading is fully supported. This means that now, as a VB .NET developer, you can do all those multithreaded things you could not do before.

When I first heard this, I though it was awesome. Finally, I had the chance to write multithreaded applications. My mind was filled with visions of threads processing data and doing processor-intensive tasks magically in the background while the user interface was going on in the foreground. Then, the more I read, and the more I heard, I really wondered why I needed multithreaded applications. Ever since the earliest versions of Visual Basic, I never really sat up at night and wished I could spawn a new thread to do some great thing while the users of my applications continued on with their work. Maybe it would have been cool to somehow get that "Cancel" button to work correctly on my forms, but other than that, I had to start digging.

In fact, if I did write multithreaded applications, my users would probably get upset at me because they wouldn't have to wait around for things such as long print jobs to finish, thus causing them to actually have to do work while they are sitting at their desks.

It doesn't really matter anymore; writing multithreaded applications in VB .NET is here to stay. In this chapter, you will learn the ins and outs of threading. We'll start with an overview the different types of threading and how threading works in the .NET Framework, and then you'll see what you can do with multithreading in your own applications. Read this chapter carefully and consider the dangers of adding multiple threads to your applications before implementing them, because you will see that multithreading is not a trivial concept.

Threading Background

Before you start writing multithreaded applications, you should have an understanding of what happens when threads are created, and how the operating system handles them.

When an application executes, a primary thread is created, and the application scope is based on this thread. Within the application, additional threads can be created to perform additional tasks. An example of creating a primary thread would be firing up Microsoft Word. The application execution starts the main thread. Within the Word application, background printing a document would be an example of an additional thread being created to handle another task. While you are still interacting with the main thread, the Word document, the system is carrying out your printing request. Once the main application thread is killed, all other threads created as a result of that thread are also killed.

Consider these two definitions from the MFC SDK:

✦ **Process:** An executing instance of an application.

✦ **Thread:** A path of execution within a process.

C++ and the MFC have long supported the concept of developing multithreaded applications. Because the core of the Windows operating system is written using these tools, it is important that they support the ability to create threads in which tasks can be assigned and executed. In the early days of Windows 3.1, there was not a whole lot of multitasking going on; this concept was more a reality in Windows NT 3.5, and NT 4.0, and then Windows 95, 98, 98SE, ME, 2000, and XP. In order to take advantage of the operating system features, multithreaded applications became more important. The concept of doing more than one thing at a time became a feature of an application. Visual Basic 6.0 and earlier compiled down to single threaded applications, which meant that no matter what was going on, the VB application could only do one thing at a time.

In reality, on a single processor system, it does not matter what tool you used to write your application, everything was still happening in a linear process. Sure, C++ developers could create new threads and perform a task while something else was going on, but it was really just sharing the same time with everything else that was running on the system. If there is only one processor, only one thing can happen at a time. This concept is called *preemptive multitasking*.

Preemptive multitasking

Preemptive multitasking splits the processor time between running tasks, or threads. When a task is running, it is using a time slice. When the time slice has expired for the running task (approximately 20 milliseconds), it gets preempted and another task is given a time slice. The system saves the current context of the preempted task, and when the task is allocated another time slice, the context is restored and the process continues. This circle of life for a task continues over and over until the thread is aborted or the task ends. Preemptive multitasking gives the user the appearance that more than one thing is happening at a time. Why do some tasks seem to finish before others, even though you started the one that finished last first?

Threading priorities and locking

When threads are created, they are assigned a priority either by the programmer or by the operating system. If an application seems to be locking up your system, it has the highest priority, and it is blocking other threads from getting any time slices. Priorities determine what happens, and in what order. Your application might be 90% complete with a certain process, but all of a sudden a brand new thread starts and races ahead of your thread, causing your work to go into a low priority process. This happens all the time in Windows. On my computer, I am running Windows XP Professional. Certain tasks take priority over others, such as starting up the new Windows Media Player. The Media Player basically stops anything that is running until it is finished loading and the Media Guide page is displayed.

Last night, I was watching a Dave Matthews video in my Windows Media Player, and I decided to see what was new on the Media Guide page. Sure enough, there was the new Nelly video I hadn't seen yet, so I clicked the link, and the browser took me to a Web site that was going to play the video inside the browser, not the Media Player. Now, you would normally have no problem doing this; I do it all the time. But for some reason, this time my computer started getting real sluggish when the video inside my browser started to play. I could hear the music, but I couldn't see Nelly in the video. It was a black square inside the browser. At the same time, my Dave Matthews video stopped playing. The music was still going, but not the picture. Of course, panic set in, because I had not saved the Word document I had been writing in for the last two hours or so. I couldn't close my browser, and I couldn't close my Media Player. Eventually my computer would barely bring up the Task Manager, so my last resort was turning it off, and then praying that my Word document would be recovered.

There could be 100 different reasons why this happened, but it could have to do with the way the threads were programmed into the video portion of Windows Media. Under normal circumstances, there can be multiple videos running using Windows Media technology on the same machine. In my case, the circumstances were perfect for a thread lock. A *thread lock* occurs when a shared resource is being accessed by a thread and another thread attempts to access that same shared resource. If both threads are the same priority, and the lock is not coded correctly, the system slowly dies because it cannot release either of the high-priority threads that are running. This is one of the larger dangers in writing multithreaded applications, and can easily happen. When you assign thread priorities and are sharing global data, you must lock the context correctly in order for the operating system to handle the time slicing correctly.

Symmetrical Multiprocessing (SMP)

On a multiprocessor system, more than one task can truly occur at the same time. Because each processor can assign time slices to tasks that are requesting work, you are doing more than one thing at a time. This sounds more reasonable when you need to run a processor-intensive, long running thread, such as when a user decides to sort 10 million records by first name, address, zip code, middle name, and country. If you could stick that job on another processor, then the running application would not be affected at all. Having more than one processor on a system allows symmetrical multiprocessing. Figure 15-1 shows the processor options for SQL Server 2000.

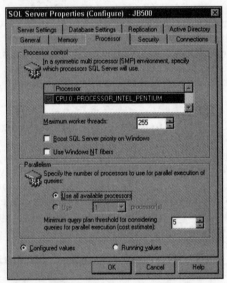

Figure 15-1: SQL Server 2000 Processor options dialog box

If you are running SQL Server on a multiprocessor machine, you can define how many processors it should use for large, long running tasks, like the sorting task just mentioned. SQL takes this a step further and will even perform queries across different processors, bring the data together once the last thread is completed, and output the data to the user. This is known as *thread synchronization*. The main thread that creates multiple threads must wait for all of the threads to complete before it can continue the process. SQL Server is pretty smart, and it probably took more than one pretty smart programmer to figure this one out.

When using an SMP system, it is important to note that a single thread still runs only on a single processor. Your single threaded VB6 application will not perform one iota better if you throw another processor at it. Your 16-bit Access 2.0 application will not run any better either; 16 bit = single process. You need to actually create processes on the other processors to take advantage of them. This means that you do not design a multiprocessor GUI; you create a GUI that creates other processes and can react when those processes are completed or interrupted, while still allowing the user to use the GUI for other tasks.

Resources – The more the merrier

Threads take up resources. When too many resources are being used, the system slows down, acts tired, and in turn, you get tired. If you attempt to open 80 instances of Visual Studio .NET while installing Exchange 2000 on a computer with 96MB of RAM, you will notice that the screen does not paint correctly, and the mouse doesn't move very fast, and your Nelly video is not playing anymore. This is caused by too many threads running at the same time. The operating system cannot handle this type of work based on the hardware that is installed. If you attempt the same action on your new server, the 32-processor Unisys box with 1 terabyte of RAM, you will not see any performance degradation at all. The more memory, the more physical address space there is for threads to run. When you start writing applications that create threads, you need to take this into consideration. The more threads you create, the more resources your application consumes. This could actually cause poorer performance than a single threaded application. The more the merrier does not include threads, so use caution when haphazardly creating threads in the new version of Multithreaded-Tetris you are writing in VB .NET.

Threading in VB6

In VB6, when you created standard EXE applications, they were obviously single threaded. When you created ActiveX DLL projects, whose ultimate destination was COM+ Services or MTS, you had the ability to specify Apartment Model Threading as the threading model when the DLL was compiled. Figure 15-2 will refresh your memory on the Project Properties dialog box in VB6.

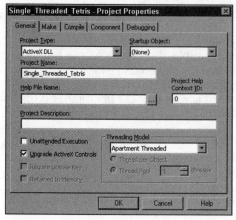

Figure 15-2: Project Properties dialog box in VB6

COM+ offers scalability. By creating components and installing them to COM+ Services, you are guaranteed a more robust multiuser application than if the component was running outside of the COM+ environment. This is because COM+ could take your single threaded DLL and treat is as a multithreaded DLL. By compiling a DLL as Apartment Model threaded, COM+ can create a thread-safe environment for many instances of your component. Consider this code:

```
Dim x as MyObject
Set x = New MyObject
x.FavoriteColor = "Yellow"
x.FavoriteFood = "Pizza"
x.Save
```

If the MyObject DLL is running inside COM+, there needs to be a guarantee that another creator of the MyObject instance will not overwrite the FavoriteColor property before the Save method gets called. COM+ will guarantee this by marshalling only calls created on the same thread, or in the same apartment, between the client and the server. When the object is created, it is accessed on the same thread in which it was created, no matter what, so each call can be serialized and not overwritten by another thread. Each apartment isolates data from other apartments, so there is no danger of one thread clobbering another thread.

Application domains

Earlier, you read that the MFC SDK defines a process as an executing instance of an application. Each application that is executing creates a new main thread, which lasts the lifetime of that application instance. Because each application is a process, each instance of an application must have process isolation. Two separate instances of Microsoft Word act independently of each other. When you click Spell Check, InstanceA of Word does not decide to spell check the document running in InstanceB of Word. Even if InstanceA of Word attempted to pass a memory pointer to InstanceB of Word, InstanceB would not know what to do with it, or even know where to look for it, because memory pointers are only relative to the process in which they are running.

In the .NET Framework, application domains are used to provide security and application isolation for managed code. Several application domains can run on a single process, or thread, with the same protection that would exist if the applications were running on multiple processes. Overhead is reduced with this concept because calls do not need to be marshaled across process boundaries if the applications need to share data. Conversely, a single application domain can run across multiple threads.

This is possible because of the way the CLR executes code. Once code is ready to execute, it has already gone through the process of verification by the JIT compiler. By passing this verification process, the code is guaranteed not to do invalid things, such as access memory it is not supposed to, thus causing a page fault.

The concept of type-safe code means that your code will not violate the rules once the verifier has approved it passing from MSIL to PE code. In typical Win32 applications, there was no guarantee that your code would not step on my code, so each application needed process isolation. In .NET, because type safety is guaranteed, it is safe to run multiple applications from multiple providers within the same application domain.

Benefits of multithreaded applications

There are several types of applications that can take advantage of multithreading.

Applications with long processes

Applications with long processes that the user does not need to interact with can benefit from multithreading because the long running process can be created on a worker thread that goes off and does a job. In the meantime, the user is not kept waiting, staring at an hourglass cursor, to move on to the next task.

Polling and listening applications

Polling applications and listening applications could benefit from multithreading. If you have an application that has created threads that are listening or polling, when something happens, a thread can consume that particular event, and the other threads could still be polling or listening for events to occur. An example of this would be a service that listens for requests on a network port, or a polling application that checks the state of Microsoft Message Queue for messages. The best off-the-shelf polling application is Microsoft BizTalk Server. BizTalk is constantly polling for things, such as files in a directory or files on an SMTP server. It cannot accomplish all of this on a single thread, so there are multiple threads polling different resources. Microsoft Message Queue has an add-on for Windows 2000 and a feature in Windows XP called Message Queue Triggers. With MSMQ Triggers, you can set properties that cause a trigger to fire an event. This is a multithreaded service that can handle thousands of simultaneous requests.

Cancel buttons

Any application that has a Cancel button on a form should follow this process:

1. Load and show the form modally.

2. Start the process that is occurring on a new thread.

3. Wait for the thread to complete.

4. Unload the form.

By following these steps, the Click event of your Cancel button will occur if the user clicks on the button while the other thread is executing. If the user does click on the Cancel button, it will actually click, since the process is running on another thread, and your code should then abort the thread. This is a GUI feature that makes a good application a great application.

Missile defense systems

Missile defense systems would benefit the most from multithreading. You can compare this to the polling and listening applications, but I want to make sure that if anyone from the Department of Defense is reading this chapter, the missile shield tracks more than one missile at a time. This is very important.

Creating Multithreaded Applications

Let's get down to creating multithreaded applications. Threading is handled through the System.Threading namespace. The core members of the Thread class that you will use are listed in Table 15-1.

| Table 15-1 | |
| Common Thread Class Members | |
Member	**Description**
CurrentContext	Returns the current context the thread is executing on.
CurrentCulture	Gets the CultureInfo instance that represents the culture used by the current thread.
CurrentUICulture	Gets the CultureInfo instance that represents the current culture used by the ResourceManager to look up culture-specific resources at run time.
CurrentPrincipal	Gets and sets the thread's current principal (for role-based security).
CurrentThread	Returns a reference to the currently running thread.
ResetAbort	Resets an abort request.
Sleep	Suspends the current thread for a specified time.
ApartmentState	Gets or sets the apartment state of the thread.
IsAlive	Gets a value that indicates whether the thread has been started and is not dead.
IsBackground	Gets or sets a value indicating whether the thread is a background thread.
Name	Gets or sets the name of the thread.

Member	Description
Priority	Gets or sets the thread priority.
Threadstate	Gets the state of the thread.
Abort	Raises the ThreadAbortException, which can end the thread.
Interrupt	Interrupts a thread that is in the WaitSleepJoin thread state.
Join	Waits for a thread.
Resume	Resumes a thread that has been suspended.
Start	Begins the thread execution.
Suspend	Suspends the thread.

Creating new threads

Creating a variable of the System.Threading.Thread type will allow you to create a new thread to start working with. Because the concept of threading is that you go off and do another task, the Thread constructor requires the address of a procedure that will do the work for the thread you are creating. The AddressOf delegate is the only parameter the constructor needs to begin using the thread.

To test this code, create a new project with the Console application template.

The following code will create two new threads and call the Start method of the Thread class to get the thread running.

```
Imports System
Imports System.Threading
Module Module1
    ' private variables of type THREAD
    Private t1 As Thread
    Private t2 As Thread

    Sub Main()
        ' new instance of Thread variables
        t1 = New Thread(AddressOf Threader1)
        t2 = New Thread(AddressOf Threader2)
        ' give threads a name
        t1.Name = "Threader1"
        t2.Name = "Threader2"
        ' start both threads
        t1.Start()
        t2.Start()
        ' wait for enter key to be hit
        Console.ReadLine()
    End Sub
End Module
```

When you create a variable of type `Thread`, the procedure that handles the thread must exist for the `Address of` delegate. If it does not, an error will occur and your application will not compile.

The `Name` property will set or retrieve the name of a thread. This allows you to use a meaningful name instead of an address or hash code to reference the running threads.

Now that the thread variables are declared, named, and started, you need to do something on the threads you have created. The procedure names that were passed to the thread constructor were called `Threader1` and `Threader2`. Add two procedures with those respective names, and use the properties of the `Thread` class to return some information about the threads that are running. Your code should now look something like this:

```
Imports System
Imports System.Threading
Module Module1
    ' private variables of type THREAD
    Private t1 As Thread
    Private t2 As Thread

    Sub Main()
        ' new instance of Thread variables
        t1 = New Thread(AddressOf Threader1)
        t2 = New Thread(AddressOf Threader2)
        ' give threads a name
        t1.Name = "Threader1"
        t2.Name = "Threader2"
        ' start both threads
        t1.Start()
        t2.Start()
        ' wait for enter key to be hit
        Console.ReadLine()
    End Sub

    Sub Threader1()
        Console.WriteLine("*** Threader1 Information ***")
        Console.WriteLine("Name = " & t1.Name)
        Console.WriteLine(t1.CurrentThread)
        Console.WriteLine("State = " & t1.ThreadState.ToString)
        Console.WriteLine("Priority = " & t1.Priority)
        Console.WriteLine("*** End Threader1 Information ***")
        Console.WriteLine()
        Console.WriteLine()
    End Sub

    Sub Threader2()
        Console.WriteLine("*** Threader2 Information ***")
```

```
        Console.WriteLine("Name = " & t2.Name)
        Console.WriteLine(t2.CurrentThread)
        Console.WriteLine("State = " & t2.ThreadState.ToString)
        Console.WriteLine("Priority = " & t2.Priority)
        Console.WriteLine("*** End Threader2 Information ***")
    End Sub
End Module
```

When you run the application, your console output should look something like Figure 15-3.

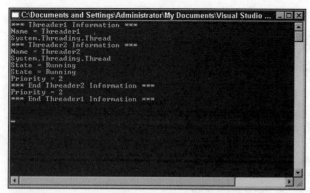

Figure 15-3: Threading application output

It is not very pretty. If you recall, we are working with threads. And without setting a property or two, our `Threader1` procedure will never complete before `Threader2` starts.

When this code executes

```
t1.Start()
```

it begins the execution of the `Threader1` code. Because it is a thread, it has roughly 20 milliseconds of the time slice. In that time period, it reached the second line of code in the function, passed control back to the operating system, and executed this line of code:

```
t2.start()
```

The `Threader2` procedure then executed for its slice of time, and was preempted by the t1 thread. This goes back and forth until both procedures can finish.

Thread priority

In order for the `Threader1` procedure to finish before the `Threader2` procedure begins, you need to set the `Priority` property to the correct `ThreadPriority` enumeration to ensure that the `t1` thread will have priority over any other thread. Before the `t1.Start` method call, add this code:

```
t1.Priority  = ThreadPriority.Highest
```

By setting the priority to highest, `t1` will now finish before `t2`. If you run the application again, your output should look similar to Figure 15-4.

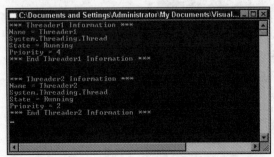

Figure 15-4: Output after setting the thread priority

The `ThreadPriority` enumeration dictates how a given thread will be scheduled based on other running threads. `ThreadPriority` can be any one of the following: `AboveNormal`, `BelowNormal`, `Highest`, `Lowest`, or `Normal`. Depending on the operating system that the threads are running on, the algorithm that determines the thread scheduling can be different. By default, when a new thread is created, it is given a priority of `2`, which is `Normal` in the enumeration.

Thread state

When you create a new thread, you call the `Start` method. At this point in time, the operating system will allocate time slices to the address of the procedure passed in the thread constructor. Although the thread may live for a very long time, it is still passing between different states while other threads are being processed by the operating system. This state may be useful to you in your application. Based on the state of a thread, you could determine that something else might need to be processed. Besides `Start`, the most common thread states you will use are `Sleep` and `Abort`. By passing a number of milliseconds to the `Sleep` constructor, you are instructing the thread to give up the remainder of its time slice for the given period of time. Calling the `Abort` method will stop the execution of the thread. Here is some code that will use both `Sleep` and `Abort`.

```
Imports System.Threading
Imports System

Module Module1

    Private t1 As Thread
    Private t2 As Thread

    Sub Main()
        t1 = New Thread(AddressOf Threader1)
        t2 = New Thread(AddressOf Threader2)
        t1.Priority = ThreadPriority.Highest
        t1.Start()
        t2.Start()
        Console.ReadLine()
        t1.Abort()
        t2.Abort()
    End Sub

    Sub Threader1()
        Dim intX As Integer
        For intX = 0 To 50
            Console.WriteLine("1")
            If intX = 5 Then
                Console.Write("T1 Sleeping")
                t1.Sleep(500)
            End If
        Next
    End Sub

    Sub Threader2()
        Dim intX As Integer
        For intX = 0 To 50
            Console.WriteLine("2")
        Next
    End Sub

End Module
```

If you notice, the Priority is set to highest for the t1 thread. This means that no matter what, it will execute before t2 starts. But, in the Threader1 procedure, you have the following If block:

```
If intX = 5 Then
        Console.Write("T1 Sleeping")
        t1.Sleep(500)
    End If
Next
```

This tells the t1 thread to sleep for 500 milliseconds, giving up its current time slice, allowing the t2 thread to begin. Once both threads are complete, the Abort method is called, and the threads are killed.

The `Thread.Suspend` method call will suspend a thread, indefinitely, until another thread wakes it back up. I remember back when I used Access 97 on Windows NT 4.0, the processor meter in the Task Manager would spike at 100%, but I wasn't losing any memory. That is what happens when a thread is suspended. To get the thread back on track, you need to call the `Resume` method from another thread so it can restart itself. The following code demonstrates `Suspend` and `Resume`.

```
Imports System.Threading
Imports System

Module Module1

    Private t1 As Thread
    Private t2 As Thread

    Sub Main()
        t1 = New Thread(AddressOf Threader1)
        t2 = New Thread(AddressOf Threader2)
        t1.Priority = ThreadPriority.Highest
        t1.Start()
        t2.Start()
        Console.ReadLine()
        t1.Abort()
        t2.Abort()
    End Sub

    Sub Threader1()
        Dim intX As Integer
        For intX = 0 To 50
            Console.WriteLine("1")
            If intX = 5 Then
                Console.Write("T1 Suspended")
                t1.Suspend()
            End If
        Next
    End Sub

    Sub Threader2()
        Dim intX As Integer
        For intX = 0 To 50
            Console.WriteLine("2")
            If intX = 5 Then
                Console.WriteLine("T1 is resuming")
                t1.Resume()
            End If
        Next
    End Sub

End Module
```

Suspending threads can cause undesirable results. You must make sure that the thread will be resumed by another thread. Figure 15-5 demonstrates the issues I had. Notice in the figure that the console window is at the "T1 Suspended" line of code. I was testing, so I got rid of the resume. The Task Manager results speak for the state of the system.

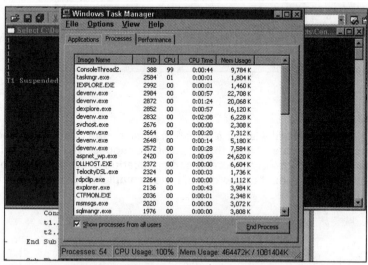

Figure 15-5: Spiked processor

ThreadState is a bitwise combination of the FlagsAttribute enumeration. At any given time, a thread can be in more than one state. For example, if a thread is a background thread, and it is currently running, the state would be Running and Background. Table 15-2 lists the FlagsAttribute of the ThreadState enumeration.

Table 15-2
FlagsAttribute Members

Member	Description
Aborted	Thread has aborted.
AbortRequested	A request has been made to abort a thread.
Background	The thread is executing as a backgroung thread.
Running	The thread is being executed.
Suspended	The thread has been suspended.
SuspendRequested	The thread is being requested to suspend.
Unstarted	The thread has not been started.

Continued

<table>
<tr><td colspan="2">Table 15-2 (continued)</td></tr>
</table>

Member	Description
Stopped	The Thread has stopped. This is for internal use only.
StopRequested	The Thread is being requested to stop. This is for internal use only.
WaitSleepJoin	The thread is blocked on a call to Wait, Sleep, or Join.

Joining threads

The Thread.Join method will wait for a thread to finish before continuing processing. This is useful if you create several threads that are supposed to accomplish a certain task, but before you want the foreground application to continue, you need to make sure all of the threads that you created were completed. In the following code, switch the

```
T2.Join()
```

with

```
Console.Writeline("Writing")
```

You will get two sets of results; the second time you run the code, the console output of "Writing" will not show up until both threads have finished.

```
Imports System.Threading
Imports System

Module Module1

    Private t1 As Thread
    Private t2 As Thread

    Sub Main()
        t1 = New Thread(AddressOf Threader1)
        t2 = New Thread(AddressOf Threader2)
        t1.Start()
        t2.Start()
        Console.WriteLine("Writing")
        t2.Join()
        Console.ReadLine()
        t1.Abort()
        t2.Abort()
    End Sub

    Sub Threader1()
        Dim intX As Integer
        For intX = 0 To 50
            Console.WriteLine("1")
```

```
        Next
    End Sub

    Sub Threader2()
        Dim intX As Integer
        For intX = 0 To 50
            Console.WriteLine("2")
        Next
    End Sub

End Module
```

Earlier, you saw the SQL Server 2000 properties dialog box for determining how many processors you could tell the service to use for processing. Using the `Join` statement, you can create your own "poor man's" multiprocessor query engine.

Consider that you may have data on different servers. You allow your users to select data from each one of these data sources, and once it gets down to the client; you do some sort of processing.

By creating two threads that the queries can execute on, you will get the data back down to the client that much quicker. And with the new `DataSet` object in ADO.NET, your job is even easier. Once the threads have completed, you create a `DataRelation` object based on the data returned from the two threads, and manipulate as you wish. In Listing 15-1, you are creating an XML file output.

As you read through the code in Listing 15-1, if there are ADO.NET items you are unfamiliar with, check out Part IV of this book to learn everything about ADO.NET.

Listing 15-1: **Poor Man's Multithreaded Query Processor**

```
Imports System.Data
Imports System.Data.SqlClient
Imports System.Threading

Class PoorMansQueryProcessor

    ' Global DataSet object
    Dim ds As DataSet

    Sub Main()
        ' Create the new data set here,
        ' otherwise the threads will try to create it
        ' this is "shared", so you need to be careful
        ' that the threads do not hose the instance

        ds = New DataSet("Customers")
```

Continued

Listing 15-1 *(continued)*

```
        ' Create t1 and t2 threads
        Dim t1 As New Thread(AddressOf Get_Suppliers)
        Dim t2 As New Thread(AddressOf Get_Products)

        ' Start new threads
        t1.Start()
        t2.Start()
        ' Wait for threads to finish up
        t1.Join()

        ' Created the realtionship
        ' between the two data sources
        ' with the DataRelation object
        Dim dr As DataRelation
        Dim dc1, dc2 As DataColumn

        ' Get the parent and child columns of the two tables.
        dc1 = ds.Tables("Suppliers").Columns("SupplierID")
        dc2 = ds.Tables("Products").Columns("SupplierID")
        dr = New System.Data.DataRelation("match", dc1, dc2)

        ' Add the relationship
        ds.Relations.Add(dr)

        ' Write out to XML file
        ds.WriteXml("C:\ADO.xml")
        MsgBox("Finito")

    End Sub

    Sub Get_Suppliers()
        ' ***
        ' Connection to SERVER A
        ' ***
        Dim strCN As String
        strCN = "uid=sa;pwd=;database=northwind;" & _
                " server=jb500\NetSDK;"
        Dim cn As SqlConnection = New SqlConnection(strCN)
        Dim adpSuppliers As _
                SqlDataAdapter = New SqlDataAdapter()
        adpSuppliers.TableMappings.Add("Table", "Suppliers")
        cn.Open()
        Dim cmdSuppliers As SqlCommand = _
                New SqlCommand("SELECT * FROM Suppliers", cn)
        cmdSuppliers.CommandType = CommandType.Text
        adpSuppliers.SelectCommand = cmdSuppliers
        adpSuppliers.Fill(ds)
    End Sub
```

```
    Sub Get_Products()
        ' ***
        ' Connection to SERVER B
        ' ***
        Dim strCN As String
        strCN = "uid=sa;pwd=;database=northwind;" & _
                " server=jb500\NetSDK;"
        Dim cn As SqlConnection = New SqlConnection(strCN)
        Dim adpProducts As _
                SqlDataAdapter = New SqlDataAdapter()
        adpProducts.TableMappings.Add("Table", "Products")
        Dim cmdProducts As SqlCommand = _
        New SqlCommand("SELECT * FROM Products", cn)
        adpProducts.SelectCommand = cmdProducts
        adpProducts.Fill(ds)
        cn.Close()
    End Sub
End Class
```

SyncLock statement

The SyncLock statement is also a way to force the joining of threads. Its implementation is a little different than the Join method. With SyncLock, you are evaluating an expression passed to the SyncLock block. When a thread reaches the SyncLock block, it will wait until it can get an exclusive lock on the expression being evaluated until it attempts any further processing. This ensures that multiple threads cannot corrupt shared data.

Returning Values from Threads

Up until now, your threading has been fairly simple. Hopefully you have a good understanding on the basic ins and outs of threading.

Now, you have to use the threading in a real-life situation.

Earlier, I mentioned the background-printing scenario in Microsoft Word. This idea can be expanded to include any type of background process, not just printing. If you create a new thread to handle a truly long-running process, you will most likely not want to use Thread.Join or SyncLock to determine when the process is complete.

These statements both block until either the Join or Lock occurs. If you need to spawn a new thread, and go on your merry way, and then get a notification later, you will need an event to be raised that lets you know that the thread has completed.

In this next example, you will create a class that handles the processing of a print job. The print job consists of console.writeline statements, but you'll get the idea that the method that is doing the printing can be doing anything. Complex math, missile tracking, it does not matter. When the thread is created, it executes a method in another class. To demonstrate the fact that you can still do something while the print job is running, the Form1.Text property is updated with the current time. So the clock is ticking along happily while the print job is running in the background. Once the print job is completed, an event is raised back to the form, which displays a message box letting you know that the print job has completed, and it returns the number of pages. In this case, the counter goes up to 801, so the return value will be 801.

Listing 15-2 is the complete code for the PrintPreview application.

Listing 15-2: Multithreaded Print Preview

```
Imports System.Threading
Public Class Form1
    Inherits System.Windows.Forms.Form

#Region " Windows Form Designer generated code "

    Public Sub New()
        MyBase.New()

        'This call is required by the Windows Form Designer.
        InitializeComponent()

        'Add any initialization after the InitializeComponent() call

    End Sub

    'Form overrides dispose to clean up the component list.
    Protected Overloads Overrides Sub Dispose(ByVal disposing As Boolean)
        If disposing Then
            If Not (components Is Nothing) Then
                components.Dispose()
            End If
        End If
        MyBase.Dispose(disposing)
    End Sub
    Friend WithEvents Button1 As System.Windows.Forms.Button

    'Required by the Windows Form Designer
    Private components As System.ComponentModel.Container

    'NOTE: The following procedure is required by the Windows Form Designer
    'It can be modified using the Windows Form Designer.
    'Do not modify it using the code editor.
    <System.Diagnostics.DebuggerStepThrough()> Private Sub InitializeComponent()
        Me.Button1 = New System.Windows.Forms.Button()
```

```
        Me.SuspendLayout()
        '
        'Button1
        '
        Me.Button1.Font = New System.Drawing.Font("Microsoft Sans Serif",
14.25!, System.Drawing.FontStyle.Regular, System.Drawing.GraphicsUnit.Point,
CType(0, Byte))
        Me.Button1.Location = New System.Drawing.Point(40, 20)
        Me.Button1.Name = "Button1"
        Me.Button1.Size = New System.Drawing.Size(120, 40)
        Me.Button1.TabIndex = 0
        Me.Button1.Text = "Print"
        '
        'Form1
        '
        Me.AutoScaleBaseSize = New System.Drawing.Size(5, 13)
        Me.ClientSize = New System.Drawing.Size(202, 73)
        Me.Controls.AddRange(New System.Windows.Forms.Control() {Me.Button1})
        Me.Name = "Form1"
        Me.Text = "Print Preview"
        Me.ResumeLayout(False)

    End Sub

#End Region

    Dim WithEvents objPrinter As PrintClass

    Sub PrintJobDone(ByVal Pages As Integer) Handles objPrinter.ThreadDone
        MsgBox("The job has printed " & CStr(Pages))
    End Sub

    Private Sub Button1_Click(ByVal sender As System.Object, ByVal e As
System.EventArgs) Handles Button1.Click
        objPrinter = New PrintClass()
        Dim Thread As New Thread _
                    (AddressOf objPrinter.DoPrint)
        Thread.Start()
        Dim intX As Integer
    End Sub
End Class

Class PrintClass
    Public Event ThreadDone(ByVal Pages As Integer)
    Sub DoPrint()
        Dim intX As Integer
        For intX = 0 To 800
            Form1.ActiveForm.Text = Now()
            Console.WriteLine(intX)
        Next
        RaiseEvent ThreadDone(intX)
    End Sub
End Class
```

Polling and Listening

Polling and listening are two more instances that represent the usefulness of multithreading. Class libraries such as `System.Net.Sockets` include a full range of multithreaded classes that can aid you in creating TCP listeners, UDP listeners, and a bevy of other network-related tasks that require multithreading. Earlier, I mentioned MSMQ as a perfect candidate for creating an MSMQ listener. There is an excellent example of how to accomplish this in the .NET SDK, and taking what you have learned in Listing 15-2 and what you will learn in Chapter 16 about MSMQ, you can easily create your own MSMQ listener.

What I want you to be aware of here is the `TimerCallBack` delegate of the System.Threading namespace. This delegate is very similar to what you have been doing so far, with the exception that a timer period is part of the constructor, which allows you to poll for something to happen at certain intervals.

The same thing can be accomplished by adding a timer control to your form, but by using the `TimerCallBack` delegate, the timing and the callback to the addressed procedure are automatic.

The following code uses a timer call back to poll for files in a directory. If a file is found, it is promptly deleted. I would suggest you only run this code against a test directory. The constructor for the `TimerCallBack` expects an address for the thread to execute on; an object data type representing the state of the timer; a due time, which represents a period of time to poll until; and a period, which is the millisecond variable that the polling interval will occur.

```
Imports System.IO
Imports System.Threading

Module Module1
    Dim thisTimer As Timer
    Dim str() As String, intX As Integer

    Sub Main()
        thisTimer = New Timer(New TimerCallback _
            (AddressOf CheckDirectory), Nothing, 0, 5000)
        Console.ReadLine()
    End Sub

    Sub CheckDirectory(ByVal state As Object)
        str = Directory.GetFiles("C:\Poll")
        If str.Length > 0 Then
            For intX = 0 To UBound(str)
                Console.WriteLine(str(intX))
                File.Delete(str(intX))
            Next
        Else
            Console.WriteLine("Directory is empty")
```

```
        End If
    End Sub

End Module
```

After running this for a while and periodically copying a few files into the C:\Poll directory, my console output is represented in Figure 15-6.

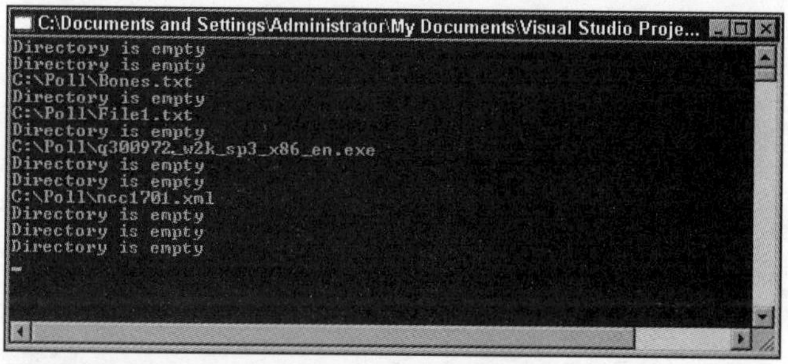

Figure 15-6: Output from TimerCallBack

Summary

In this chapter, you learned about how to implement multithreading in VB .NET with the System.Thread namespace.

With threads, the basic idea is that you need to create more than one thread to get more than one thing done at a time. Too many threads, however, might cause resource issues and not enough threads might cause your application to perform below its full potential.

How many threads you create will have to be determined by solid testing. There is not a magic number.

With the examples that you created here, you should be well on your way to implementing threading in your own applications. Just make sure that you do not start running with scissors, because before you know it, your multithreaded applications might turn into a multithreaded headache.

Remember, just because it's there does not mean you have to use it. As with anything else, careful planning should go into your applications, and deciding if you will implement multithreading needs to be part of this planning process.

✦ ✦ ✦

COM Interop and MSMQ

by Jason Beres

W hen I first started reading about .NET in the fall of 2000, it all seemed really cool. I was not sure what it really was, but everything I read said that the investment in current applications would not be lost. In other words, the millions of COM components floating around the world would still be usable in .NET. As more documentation became available, and more samples of .NET features became available, it seemed pretty clear to me that COM was still usable, but not the "new" way of doing things. The new way, or the Managed Code, CLR Compliant way of doing things, is a different technology than COM. It is definitely easy to use and has great features, but if you upgrade to .NET, you will need a compelling reason to get your boss to authorize such a big transformation, while ensuring that your existing code will not *all* need to be rewritten. That is what we cover in this chapter. There are two important features of the old Windows DNA marketing scheme: COM components and Message Queue Services (MSMQ).

In this chapter, you learn how truly simple it is to consume your VB 6 COM components from a VB .NET application, and you learn how to leverage the new class libraries for MSMQ in your applications.

Consuming COM from .NET

The CLR exposes COM objects to callers through the Runtime Callable Wrapper (RCW) proxy. The RCW exposes metadata to the CLR, which allows the CLR to successfully marshal calls between managed .NET code and COM components.

When you decide you need to use a COM component in your .NET application, you add a reference to your project just as you did in VB 6. When the component is added, metadata is created from the type library of the component that is being referenced. When the object is instantiated in your .NET application, it is treated as any other .NET class library. Your code acts and looks the same. Under the hood, the CLR is creating the RCW for the COM object and the COM object itself is marshaling calls back and forth between the managed and unmanaged processes. Figure 16-1 represents an outside look at the process of interoperability between unmanaged and managed code.

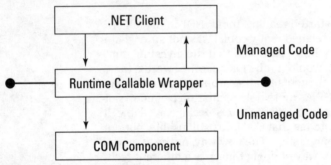

Figure 16-1: Com interoperability path

Getting this process rolling is quite simple. To start, create a VB 6 ActiveX DLL project called Math, and rename the Class1 to Square. In the Square class, add a public function called SquareIt. If you have taken the Microsoft VB courses, you have done this example many times. The SquareIt function should look like the following:

```
Public Function SquareIt(intX As Integer, intY As Integer) As Long
    SquareIt = intX * intY
End Function
```

When that is all squared away, go ahead and compile the DLL. This will register it and make it available to our VB .NET application. If you are using another machine to compile the DLL, you will need to register it using REGSVR32.EXE on the .NET machine. To register a component using the REGSVR32.EXE utility, simply open the command prompt and pass the *path* argument to the utility. If you copied the DLL to the C:\Winnt\System32 directory, then to register the DLL, type the following:

```
C:\Winnt\System32\Regsvr32.exe C:\Winnt\System32\Math.Dll
```

You will be notified with a message box that the DLL was successfully registered.

Next, create a VB .NET Windows Forms application. On the default Form1, add two text boxes, a label, and a button. The form should look like Figure 16-2.

Figure 16-2: The SquareIt form

Now you need to add a reference to the Math DLL that you compiled earlier. You can do this in one of two ways:

1. From the Project menu, select Add Reference.

2. Right-click the Project name and select Add Reference.

Once the Add Reference dialog is open, click the COM tab, find your Math.DLL in the list, highlight it with your mouse, click the Select button, and then click OK. You will receive a message box similar to Figure 16-3.

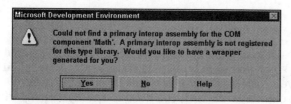

Figure 16-3: Wrapper generation notification

This is the process of creating the RCW for this component. Click Yes on the dialog box, and let the IDE generate the RCW for this COM object. You will now see your Math object in the references list.

All that is left is to consume the object, which is no different than consuming any other .NET component, thanks to the RCW. In the `click` event for the button on your form, add the following code:

```
Dim x As New Math.Square()
Label1.Text = x.SquareIt(TextBox1.Text, TextBox2.Text)
```

Run your application, enter a value in each of the text boxes, and click the button. The label will display your newly squared number. It does not get much easier than that.

The next example is just to show you that something *can* be done. The Math DLL is very simple, and you are probably looking for something a little more complex. The following code is regular old ADO code running inside the managed .NET environment. I would highly recommend that you use ADO.NET for all data access, but by running through this process, you get a better idea of the power that the RCW gives you.

The first step is to add a reference to the Microsoft ActiveX Data Object 2.6 library to your VB .NET application. In the `click` event for the button, add the following code:

```
Dim rs As New ADODB.Recordset()
Dim cn As New ADODB.Connection()
With cn
    .Provider = "SQLOLEDB"
    .CursorLocation = ADODB.CursorLocationEnum.adUseClient
    .ConnectionString = "uid=sa;pwd=;database=pubs;server=."
    .Open()
End With
rs = cn.Execute("Select * from authors")
While Not rs.EOF
    Dim strName As String
    strName = Convert.ToString(rs.Fields("au_fname").Value) & " " _
            & Convert.ToString(rs.Fields("au_lname").Value)
    Console.WriteLine(strName)
    rs.MoveNext()
End While
rs.Close()
cn.Close()
```

This code should look very familiar. It is the same ADO code you have plastered all over your VB 6 applications. When you were typing the code, you had the full ADO 2.6 type library available to you. This is all made available through the RCW. Remember when referencing objects in VB .NET, you need to specify which part of the object you are referring to, so when using components that are returning values, remember to use the fully qualified object name, such as `rs.Fields ("au_fname").Value`, not just `rs.Fields("au_fname")`. Otherwise, you will not see any data.

Error Handling in COM Interoperability

Because .NET manages errors through Exception classes, and COM returns errors via HRESULTs, the RCW maps managed exceptions to failure HRESULTs. The `IErrorInfo` interface of the COM component contains information that is passed to the RCW if an error occurs, so you do not need to do any special coding if an error does occur. If you look up HRESULTS in the SDK, you will get a table with about 75 specific COM error codes and the .NET Exceptions they map to.

Microsoft Message Queue

MSMQ is probably one of the greatest (and least used) servers, making it possible to write truly disconnected and scalable applications. In the next part of this chapter, you learn the major components of writing applications that use MSMQ and how to manipulate MSMQ objects.

What is Message Queue?

MSMQ is essentially an application that guarantees sending and receiving messages reliably. Messages can be anything from XML files to ADO Recordsets to Microsoft Word documents. It does not matter what you send to MSMQ, you just know that once the message is in a queue, its delivery is guaranteed. A scenario that I teach in class is the airline ticket counter and the food provider. When you call the airline to make a reservation, they will ask you if you have a food preference. The airline itself is not making the food; they have it contracted out to someone else. Once the ticket person takes all of your information and clicks the submit button, the airline data is updated and the food data is sent to the food provider. But what happens if the food provider database is not up, or if the connection to the food provider is not robust and fails? The airline ticket person will never tell you that he cannot take your reservation because the connection to the food provider is down. So the airline application uses MSMQ to send the food information to the food provider, and whenever the food provider wants to pick up the messages, they can just connect in and grab whatever they choose. This is a guaranteed delivery mechanism that will never fail (except for an act of God, such as an administrator deleting a queue). Figure 16-4 describes this process visually.

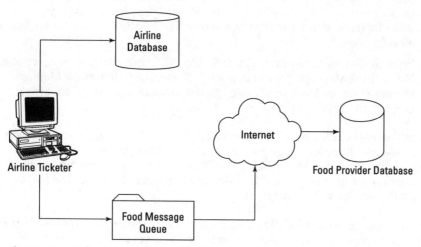

Figure 16-4: Client to MSMQ to Food Provider Database

Why MSMQ?

The need for MSMQ needs to be built in to the design phase of your applications. It is not something that should be an afterthought because it is the backbone of a disconnected, robust application. The following are a few factors that will make you choose to implement MSMQ into your design:

✦ Direct calls between clients and servers over connections can fail. MSMQ gives you mechanism in which this will never be an issue.

✦ Messages can be sent to queues when resources are not available, such as other queues, and retrieved when the resource becomes available.

✦ Messages can be prioritized, so certain messages such as food orders will be delivered before log files or something of a noncritical nature.

✦ MSMQ is 100% transactional, so it can be part of a COM+ transaction, giving you the guarantee of an all or nothing delivery mechanism.

✦ MSMQ access is based on Windows Security, so you are guaranteed to be working within a secure environment.

Getting started with MSMQ

Before you decide to implement MSMQ, you need to make sure that it is installed on the server that you intend to send the messages to. Unless you did a custom setup when you installed Windows, MSMQ will not be installed. There are two ways to check that MSMQ is installed:

1. Right-click My Computer and select Computer Management. In the tree view under Services and Applications, you will see Message Queue. If you can drill into that node without receiving an error that MSMQ is not installed, you are all set.

2. From the Server Explorer in Visual Studio .NET, drill into the Servers node. You will see Message Queues in the list. If you can drill into the Message Queues node, and you see Public Queues, Private Queues, and Journal Queues, then MSMQ is properly installed.

If these processes fail, you will need to install MSMQ. To do this, open up Control Panel, select Add/Remove Programs, and select the Add/Remove Windows Components button on the left-hand side. When the options come up for what is installed on your machine, select the Message Queues option from the list. Click OK, and the service will be installed.

When the service is successfully installed, make sure the queues are visible through computer management or the Server Explorer. The queues that are visible fall into two categories: user-created queues and system-created queues. Table 16-1 defines the user-created queues and Table 16-2 defines the system-created queues.

Table 16-1
User-Created Queues

Name	Description
Public Queue	Queues that are replicated throughout the network and can be accessed by other connected sites.
Private Queue	Queues that are available only on the local computer.
Administration Queue	Contains acknowledgment receipts of messages sent in the network.
Response Queue	Contains response messages that are returned to the sending application when the message is received by the destination application.

Table 16-2
System-Created Queues

Name	Description
Journal Queue	Optionally stores copies of messages that are sent and copies of messages that are removed from a queue.
Dead-Letter Queue	Stores copies of undeliverable or expired messages.
Report Queue	Stores the route a message has taken.
Private System Queue	Stores administrative and notification messages that the system needs to process.

Programming MSMQ

Implementing messaging into your application is quite easy. Using the System.Messaging namespace, you have all of the members that incorporate messaging. Using System.Messaging, you are going to do one of the following tasks:

✦ Create a new queue

✦ Find an existing queue

✦ Send messages to a queue

✦ Read messages from a queue

✦ Retrieve information about messages in a queue without actually reading the message

Once a queue is created, either programmatically or through the Computer Management snap-in, it exists until it is physically deleted through the Computer Management snap-in or by calling a `Delete` method of a queue object that you created. A queue can be created and live forever and it is a durable store for messages. When messages are sent to a queue, they live there forever until they are read or deleted. Once a message is read, it is gone out of the queue. If the reading of a message is part of a transaction and the transaction fails, the message will go back into the queue, as long as the queue is set up as transactional. If you need to look into the queue and see what messages exist, you "peek" at the queue. This will allow you to get information on messages without actually reading them, which ensures that the message will stay in the queue. When working with private queues, you must specify the name of the queue when you create the queue object. If you are attempting to access queues across the network, you can use enumeration methods that will return queues that are available, and based on the properties returned, you may or may not want to use a specific queue.

The fact that you can enumerate available queues adds to the durability of the MSMQ solution. If you are in a 24 x 7 environment, with servers all over the place, the chances are you will have machines that serve as backup queues. If your application queries for queue information and returns an error, you can decide to use another queue that might be available. This concept ensures delivery of data. If your SQL server is down, you are not going to send data to another SQL server. This would create massive data inconsistency, and it is not a robust solution.

The System.Messaging namespace is quite large, and it would not make sense in this instance to list all of the members and their definitions. We will go through the main concepts of messaging that were listed earlier: creating queues, sending messages to queues, reading messages from queues, and peeking into queues. This will give you a background on the main functions of MSMQ, and when you decide to implement your messaging solution, read through all of the members in the SDK to see what we missed here.

To start off, create a new Windows Forms application called MSMQ. Figure 16-5 displays how the form should look. You can get an idea of what you will be doing by looking at the labels and captions of the buttons. If you want to create a Web Forms application, that is great, nothing will be different in the code you write. The code for all of this is in Listing 16-1 at the end of the chapter.

Note   Make sure to import the System.Messaging namespace to get your auto-list members and auto-complete features for MSMQ properties and methods. You may need to add the System.Messaging.DLL reference if it is not in the list of available namespaces.

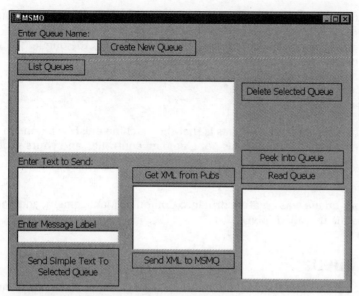

Figure 16-5: MSMQ project form

Creating queues

The `Create` constructor of System.Messaging handles the creation of new queues. If you are attempting to simply send messages to a queue, you will not use the `Create` method, but you will use the `Send` method. In most environments, I would imagine that your administrator might manually create queues through the Computer Management snap-in, but it is possible that your application will need to create new queues on the fly. The `Create` method is overloaded, with a Boolean parameter indicating whether the queue will be transactional. To create a new queue, use the following code:

```
If txtQueueName.Text.Length > 0 Then
    Dim q As New MessageQueue()
    Dim strQ As String = ".\Private$\" & txtQueueName.Text
    q.UseJournalQueue = True
    q.Create(strQ, True)
    q.Close()
End If
```

You will notice that the path that was created to create the new queue:

```
".\Private$\queuename"
```

The "." refers to the local machine; you could replace the "." with your computer name. The `Private$` means that the queue you are creating is a local private queue; no other machines on the network will be able to access the queue. To create a public queue, use the following `Create` method:

```
strQ = "MachineName\QueueName"
Q.Create(strQ, True)
```

The problem with creating public queues is that the machine must be a domain controller. My development computer is not a domain controller, and yours probably is not either, so for the sake of time, we will use private queues in these exercises.

To verify that your queue was created, drill into Computer Management, and you should see a new queue called "MyQ".

Accessing queues

If you create queues through the `Create` method, or if you manually create them through Computer Management, you will need a way to reference queues in your code. There are several enumeration members in the System.Messaging namespace, depending on what type of queues you are looking for. Table 16-3 shows common members of the System.Messaging.MessageQueue class used for queue enumeration.

Table 16-3
Enumeration Members

Member	Description
GetMessageQueueEnumerator	Creates an enumerator object for a dynamic listing of public queues on the network.
GetPrivateQueuesByMachineName	Retrieves private queues on a machine.
GetPublicQueues	Retrieves public queues on the network.
GetPublicQueuesByLabel	Retrieves public queues on the network that match a specific label.
GetPublicQueuesByMachine	Retrieves public queues for a specified machine.
GetPublicQueuesByCategory	Retrieves public queues on the network that match a specific category.

Because you are working with a public queue, you will use the `GetPrivateQueuesByMachineName` member. The following code demonstrates this usage.

```
Dim LocalQueues() As MessageQueue = _
    MessageQueue.GetPrivateQueuesByMachine("JB650")
Dim Q As MessageQueue
For Each Q In LocalQueues
  Console.Writeline(Q.FormatName)
  Console.Writeline(Q.QueueName)
Next
```

Note   JB650 is the name of my computer. You can use "." to specify the local machine, or the name of your machine to reference the queue.

The `For...Each` statement loops through the array returned by the `Get` method, with all of the properties available of an actual message queue. Some common properties of the `MessageQueue` object are listed in Table 16-4.

	Table 16-4
	MessageQueue Properties

Property	Description
Path	Gets or sets the queue's path.
Label	Gets or sets the queue's description.
QueueName	Gets or sets the friendly name that identifies the queue.
CreateTime	Gets the date and time that the queue was created.
Category	Gets or sets the queue category.
ID	Gets the unique identifier for the queue.

Deleting queues

To delete a queue, you use the `Delete` method after you have gotten a reference to a `MessageQueue` object. The parameter of the `Delete` method will take either a fully qualified private or fully qualified public queue name, so make sure you reference the machine name and the queue name. The following code will delete a private and public queue named "MyQ".

```
Dim q As MessageQueue
' Deletes Private Queue
q.Delete("Server1\Private$\MyQ")
' Deletes Public Queue
q.Delete("Server1\MyQ")
```

If you are automating the deletion of a queue, and not hard-coding queue names, you can use the `QueueName` property or the `FormatName` property to retrieve the values of the queue names on your machine or network. The following code returns those properties:

```
Console.WriteLine("FormatName = " & Q.FormatName)
Console.WriteLine("QueueName = " & Q.QueueName)
```

Returns:

```
FormatName = DIRECT=OS:jb650\private$\myq
QueueName = private$\myq
```

In Listing 16-1, the delete queue code takes the `FormatName` property and uses the `Split` function to return the fully qualified name, so you will never be wrong on the machine name or the queue name. Alternatively, you could also use the `MachineName` property and the `QueueName` property to build the fully qualified path. As a note to you, I had success with the `MachineName` property on Windows XP, but it returned an empty string on Windows 2000 Server.

Referencing queues

To reference a queue, either for sending messages or retrieving messages, you will need to use the `Path`, `Label`, or `FormatName` property to tell the queue object where to look.

The `Path` property uses the same syntax to refer to the queue as the `Create` method.

```
Dim q as New MessageQueue
q.Path = "jb650\Private$\MyQ" ' Private Queue
q.Path = "jb650\MyQ" ' Public Queue
```

The `FormatName` property is the fastest, most efficient way to refer to a queue. This is an internal optimization to the way queue names are resolved by the servers. The `FormatName` property is assigned to a queue when it is created, you do not set this property. The `FormatName` for MyQ on my machine is:

```
DIRECT=OS:jb650\private$\myq
```

Using the `Label` property to reference a queue can be a little dangerous. When you created your queue earlier, you did not set the `Label` property, which is 100% legal. If you are going to reference a queue by its label, make sure you use one of the enumeration methods mentioned earlier to ensure that the queue has a label.

Sending messages to queues

You send messages to a queue using the Send method. The Send constructor is overloaded, having parameters such as Body, Label, and Transaction. To send a message, you will need to create an instance of a queue, and set the Path property, so the Send will know where to go. The following code will accomplish this feat.

```
Dim q As New MessageQueue()
q.Path = "jb650\Private$\MyQ"
If q.Exists(q.Path) Then
    q.Send("This is the message", "TestLabel")
    q.Close()
Else
    MsgBox("The Queue you are writing to does not exist")
End If
```

Notice that you use the Exists method to check whether the queue is even there. This is a good idea; do not let the exception occur if a queue is not created or at the location specified.

If you drill into the queues in Computer Management, you will see a message with the label "TestLabel". If you double-click the message, or right-click and select Properties, you will be able to see the properties of the message and the message text in hex format.

Reading queue messages

To read messages from a queue, you will either Peek into a queue or Receive from a queue. The Peek method reads the first message in the queue, all the time. You would peek into a queue to test for the existence of messages and check message properties. Peeking into a queue does not remove the message. If you peek into the same queue multiple times, the same message will always be read unless a new message has been added with a higher priority than the message that was looked at previously. The Receive method will read a message from a queue and remove it from the queue. So once a message is received, it will no longer exist in the queue.

Peeking into a queue

The following code shows the Peek method in action.

```
Dim strQ As String = ".\Private$\MyQ"
Dim q As New MessageQueue()
q.Path() = strQ
If q.Exists(q.Path) Then
    Dim msg As Message
    Dim formatter As XmlMessageFormatter = _
        CType(q.Formatter, XmlMessageFormatter)
```

```
            formatter.TargetTypeNames = New String() _
                {"System.String,mscorlib"}
            msg = q.Peek
            Console.Writeline(msg.Label)
            Console.Writeline(msg.Body)
        End If
```

In this example, you used the Peek method and assigned the result to an object declared as a message. Because messages are what live in a queue, you are retrieving properties of the message itself, not the queue that the message lives in.

You are probably scratching your head over the following two lines of code:

```
        Dim formatter As XmlMessageFormatter = _
            CType(q.Formatter, XmlMessageFormatter)
        formatter.TargetTypeNames = New String() _
            {"System.String,mscorlib"}
```

I was too when I first tried to read messages from a queue. In VB 6, when you read queue messages, they were returned in a text format. In .NET, formatters are used to serialize and de-serialize messages from message queues. In the framework, there are three types of formatters:

✦ **XMLMessageFormatter:** Default formatter for MSMQ. Persists objects as human readable XML.

✦ **BinaryMessageFormatter:** Persists one or more connected objects into serialized streams. This is very fast and compact, but not human readable.

✦ **ActiveXMessageFormatter:** Persists primitive data types, allowing for interoperability with components that use previous versions of MSMQ.

To successfully read a message from the queue, you need to set the TargetType or TargetTypeNames of the XMLMessageFormatter object.

Receiving messages from a queue

Receiving messages works almost like the Peek method, except you use the Receive method and you specify a timeout period for the Receive method to fail if nothing is in the queue. The following code will attempt to receive a message from the queue for three seconds.

```
    If q.Exists(q.Path) Then
        Dim formatter As XmlMessageFormatter = _
            CType(q.Formatter, XmlMessageFormatter)
        formatter.TargetTypeNames = New String() _
            {"System.String,mscorlib"}
        Dim msg As Message = q.Receive(New TimeSpan(0, 0, 3))
        Console.Writeline(msg.Label)
        Console.Writeline(msg.Body)
    End If
```

The Receive method will take days, hours, minutes, seconds, and milliseconds in the constructor. If a timeout occurs, an exception will be raised that notifies you of the timeout. The following Catch statement will trap the timeout error and allow you to handle it gracefully. For the full receive code, look at the Receive function in Listing 16-1 at the end of the chapter.

```
Catch ex As MessageQueueException
   If ex.MessageQueueErrorCode = MessageQueueErrorCode.IOTimeout Then
     Msgbox("There are no messages in the Queue"
   Else
       MsgBox(ex.Source)
       MsgBox(ex.MessageQueueErrorCode.ToString)
   End If
```

To ensure that another process is not attempting to retrieve messages from the queue while your process is, you should set the DenySharedReceive property to True before reading any messages.

```
  If q.Exists(q.Path) then
    q.DenySharedReceive = True
```

Up until now, you have seen how to read a single message from a queue. If there are multiple messages in a queue, you would need to call the Receive method until there was nothing left in the queue to receive. This might not always be practical. If you need to retrieve all queue messages in one fell swoop, use the GetAllMessages method.

```
  Dim intX as Integer
  q.Path = "jb650\Private$\MyQ"
  Dim msg() As Message = q.GetAllMessages()
  For intX = 0 to msg.Upperbound
    Console.Writeline msg(intx).Body
  Next
```

There are several ways to handle reading messages from a queue without sitting there at your server and clicking the Receive button. You could use a timer to poll a queue, you could create a Windows Service Application that checks queue properties to see if anything has changed since the last read attempt, or you could set up an asynchronous class that checks for queue messages when system events fire. As you develop your message queue applications, you will have to test which method of retrieval best fits your needs. The QuickStart tutorials in the .NET Framework SDK have an excellent example of creating an asynchronous queue reader, so I would encourage you to check out the SDK when you are done testing these samples.

Deleting queue messages

To delete messages that exist in a queue, you call the `Purge` method on the `MessageQueue` object. The following code will delete all of the messages in the queue named "MyQ".

```
Dim q as MessageQueue
q.Path = "jb650\Private$\MyQ"
q.Purge()
```

It is unlikely that you will delete messages in an actual queue. The more common usage of `Purge` would be to delete the messages in a *journal* queue. If you remember, when the `UseJournalQueue` property is set to true during queue creation, an exact duplicate of every message in the queue is kept as a journal entry. To delete the journal queue for the queue named "MyQ", you would use the following code:

```
Dim q as MessageQueue
q.Path = "jb650\Private$\MyQ\Journal$"
q.Purge()
```

Listing 16-1: **The MSMQ Project**

```
Imports System.Messaging
Imports System.Data
Imports System.Data.SqlClient
Imports System.IO
Imports System.Xml

Public Class frmMSMQ
    Inherits System.Windows.Forms.Form

    Private Sub cmdCreateQueue_Click(ByVal sender As System.Object, _
            ByVal e As System.EventArgs) Handles cmdCreateQueue.Click
        Try
            If txtQueueName.Text.Length > 0 Then
                Dim q As New MessageQueue()
                Dim strQ As String = ".\Private$\" & txtQueueName.Text
                q.Create(strQ)
                q.Close()
            End If
        Catch ex As Exception
            MsgBox(ex.Message)
        Finally
            ListQueues()
        End Try
    End Sub

    Private Sub cmdListQueues_Click(ByVal sender As System.Object, _
            ByVal e As System.EventArgs) Handles cmdListQueues.Click
```

```
        ListQueues()
    End Sub

    Private Sub cmdDeleteQueue_Click(ByVal sender As System.Object, _
            ByVal e As System.EventArgs) Handles cmdDeleteQueue.Click

        Dim strQ() As String = Split(ListBox1.SelectedItem, ":")
        Dim q As MessageQueue
        q.Delete(strQ(1))
        ListQueues()

    End Sub

    Private Sub ListQueues()
        ListBox1.Items.Clear()
        Dim LocalQueues() As MessageQueue = _
          MessageQueue.GetPrivateQueuesByMachine(".")
        Dim Q As MessageQueue
        For Each Q In LocalQueues
            ListBox1.Items.Add(Q.FormatName)
        Next
    End Sub

    Private Sub frmMSMQ_Load(ByVal sender As System.Object, _
            ByVal e As System.EventArgs) Handles MyBase.Load
        ListQueues()
    End Sub

    Private Sub cmdGetXMLADO_Click(ByVal sender As System.Object, _
            ByVal e As System.EventArgs) Handles cmdGetXMLADO.Click

        Dim strCn As String = "server=.;uid=sa;pwd=;database=pubs"
        Dim cn As SqlConnection = New SqlConnection(strCn)
        Dim cmd As SqlCommand = New SqlCommand("select * from authors " & _
                    " FOR XML AUTO, XMLDATA", cn)
        cn.Open()
        Dim ds As DataSet = New DataSet()
        ds.ReadXml(cmd.ExecuteXmlReader(), XmlReadMode.Fragment)
        txtXMLText.Text = ds.GetXml
        cn.Close()
    End Sub


    Private Sub cmdSendText_Click(ByVal sender As System.Object, _
            ByVal e As System.EventArgs) Handles cmdSendText.Click
        Dim strQ() As String = Split(ListBox1.SelectedItem, ":")
        Dim strMsg As String = txtSimpleText.Text
        Dim strLabel As String = txtMsgLabel.Text
        Send_To_MSMQ(strMsg, strLabel, strQ(1))
    End Sub
```

Continued

Listing 16-1 *(continued)*

```
Private Sub cmdPeek_Click(ByVal sender As System.Object, _
        ByVal e As System.EventArgs) Handles cmdPeek.Click
    lstMessages.Items.Clear()
    If ListBox1.SelectedItem = "" Then
        MsgBox("Please select a Queue to Peek")
    Else
        Try
            Dim strQ() As String = Split(ListBox1.SelectedItem, ":")
            Dim q As New MessageQueue()
            q.Path() = strQ(1)
            If q.Exists(q.Path) Then
                Dim msg As Message
                Dim formatter As XmlMessageFormatter = _
                    CType(q.Formatter, XmlMessageFormatter)
                formatter.TargetTypeNames = New String() _
                    {"System.String,mscorlib"}
                msg = q.Peek
                lstMessages.Items.Add(msg.Label)
                lstMessages.Items.Add(Space(5) & msg.Body)
            End If
        Catch ex1 As Exception
            MsgBox(ex1.Message)
        End Try
    End If

End Sub


Private Sub cmdRead_Click(ByVal sender As System.Object, _
        ByVal e As System.EventArgs) Handles cmdRead.Click
    Read_Queue()
End Sub

Private Sub Read_Queue()
    lstMessages.Items.Clear()
    If ListBox1.SelectedItem = "" Then
        lstMessages.Items.Add("Please select a Queue to Read")
    Else
        Try
            Dim strQ() As String = Split(ListBox1.SelectedItem, ":")
            Dim q As New MessageQueue()
            q.Path() = strQ(1)
            If q.Exists(q.Path) Then
                Dim formatter As XmlMessageFormatter = _
                    CType(q.Formatter, XmlMessageFormatter)
                formatter.TargetTypeNames = New String() _
                    {"System.String,mscorlib"}
                Dim msg As Message = q.Receive(New TimeSpan(0, 0, 2))
```

```vb
                        lstMessages.Items.Add(msg.Label)
                        lstMessages.Items.Add(Space(5) & msg.Body)
                    End If
            Catch ex As MessageQueueException
                If ex.MessageQueueErrorCode = _
    MessageQueueErrorCode.IOTimeout Then
                        lstMessages.Items.Add("No Messages in Queue")
                        lstMessages.Items.Add(Now())
                Else
                        MsgBox(ex.Source)
                        MsgBox(ex.MessageQueueErrorCode.ToString)
                End If
            Catch ex1 As Exception
                MsgBox(ex1.Message)
            End Try
        End If
    End Sub

    Private Function Send_To_MSMQ(ByVal strMsg As String, _
            ByVal strLabel As String, ByVal strQ As String) As Boolean
        If strQ.Length > 0 Then
            Try
                Dim q As New MessageQueue()
                q.Path = strQ
                If q.Exists(q.Path) Then
                    q.Send(strMsg, strLabel)
                    q.Close()
                Else
                    MsgBox("The Queue you are writing to does not exist")
                End If
            Catch ex As Exception
                MsgBox(ex.Message)
            End Try
        Else
            MsgBox("Please select a Queue to Send To!")
        End If
    End Function

    Private Sub cmdSendXMLToQueue_Click(ByVal sender As System.Object, _
            ByVal e As System.EventArgs) Handles cmdSendXMLToQueue.Click
        Dim strQ() As String = Split(ListBox1.SelectedItem, ":")
        Dim strMsg As String = txtXMLText.Text
        Dim strLabel As String = "ADO-XML Data"
        Send_To_MSMQ(strMsg, strLabel, strQ(1))
    End Sub

End Class
```

Summary

In this chapter you learned how to consume VB 6 COM components from a .NET client and how to use the new System.Messaging class to take full advantage of Microsoft Message Queue features.

There is not a whole lot to consuming VB 6 components as a .NET client, because it seems that the hard workers at Microsoft have hidden most of the plumbing for us, so it looks easy. The important thing to take away is that it is 100% possible to use all of the code written in components over the years in your new VB .NET applications.

MSMQ is a cornerstone of scalable, robust, forward-thinking applications. I would encourage you to read the SDK very carefully after going through the sample application you built here to learn everything possible about System.Messaging. I think that as the world becomes a more disconnected, Internet-centric place, applications that use MSMQ will become more and more prevalent.

✦   ✦   ✦

Visual Studio .NET: The IDE for VB .NET

Visual Basic .NET IDE

by Jason Beres

♦ ♦ ♦ ♦

In This Chapter

Visual Studio .NET IDE

Creating a Windows Forms application

Windows management basics

Project structure

Designers

♦ ♦ ♦ ♦

Since it was first released in 1991, Visual Basic has been the cornerstone in rapid application development. Every Visual Basic upgrade gave developers improvements in an already incredible development environment. Visual Studio .NET is no different. From IntelliType to AutoComplete to Drag and Drop Database access to Dynamic Help, you will be most amazed at how productive this development environment is.

This chapter walks you through the new features of the IDE and looks at how you can use the IDE to make your work more efficient and your job easier.

The Start Page

After you have installed Visual Studio .NET, you will notice that the program group consists only of the icon for MSDN Library for Visual Studio .NET and an icon for Visual Studio .NET itself. This convergence of the IDE to include all of the Visual Studio .NET languages into a single development environment will facilitate the RAD (Rapid Application Development) features that Microsoft has been promising. Because the development of Web applications and Win32 Forms–based applications is equally important, the goal of integrating the IDE into a single workspace will allow developers to create any type of application faster than ever. The Start page is the first page you will see when the IDE loads. The Start page is essentially an HTML-based GUI with several options on the left menu that include customizing the IDE, linking to the MSDN Web site for news and events, and even options for Web hosting. Figure 17-1 displays the IDE the first time you fire it up.

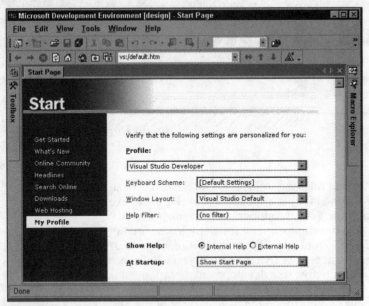

Figure 17-1: VS .NET Start page

My Profile

Based on the type of development that you will be doing, you can customize the IDE to specific keyboard schemes, window layouts, and help filters. If you are a previous VB developer, you might want to select the Visual Basic Developer profile so that the IDE is familiar. The following are the settings that I chose based on my development needs:

- ✦ **Profile:** (Custom)
- ✦ **Keyboard Scheme:** Visual Basic 6
- ✦ **Window Layout:** Visual Studio Default
- ✦ **Help Filter:** Visual Basic Documentation
- ✦ **Show Help:** Outside the IDE
- ✦ **At Startup Show:** Visual Studio Home Page

The cool thing is that if you feel the preferences you have selected do not do you justice, you can change them later at any time. I think that one of the most important options is the Help Filter. There is so much information in the MSDN Library that it makes life a lot easier when the help is filtered to just the Visual Basic information that you need.

Get Started

The most recent application list is offered. A single click with the mouse on a recent project will open your development so you can begin using the selected project. You can also select Open Existing Project if an application that you have worked on is not in the list. Create New Project will start a new project, and Report a Visual Studio .NET Issue will take you to the Web to report a problem or to submit a bug report.

What's New

This page offers links to the latest service pack updates for Visual Studio .NET, links to partner resources on the Web, and product information on Visual Studio .NET products.

Online Community

For years, the best resource for Visual Basic developers has been the online offerings. From the MSDN Web site to newsgroups, if you ever run into a serious issue, expert help is always online somewhere. The new IDE now integrates important Web sites and newsgroups for you, so expert help is just a single click away.

Headlines

The MSDN Online home page is integrated into the IDE, so all of the latest technical articles, news, and training information are at your doorstep.

Search Online

The MSDN Online Library in available for quick access when the answers might not be in the help files installed on your machine.

Downloads

The latest downloads and add-ons available for Visual Studio and related products are available here. This feature is great because you only need to look at a single area for anything new that is available.

Web Hosting

Links to ISPs that offer .NET hosting are offered in this option. A very strong word of caution: You get what you pay for, so be wary of "free" hosting and very low-priced hosting. The service may not be what you are used to (I am speaking from personal experience using this feature).

Your First Visual Basic .NET Solution

Now that we have explored the Visual Studio .NET home page, let's go through the IDE and discuss its features. The best way to accomplish this is to create a new solution, and then drill into the features Visual Studio offers.

To create a new solution:

1. From the File menu, click New ➪ Project (see Figure 17-2). The New Project dialog box will appear. The New Project dialog box is broken up into two panes, Project Types and Templates. For our purposes, we will concentrate on the Visual Basic Projects folder in the Project Types pane.

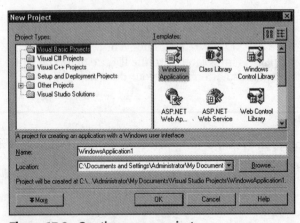

Figure 17-2: Creating a new project

The following templates are available through the Templates pane:

- **Windows Application:** Create a Windows Forms-based application
- **Class Library:** Create a Class Library to use in another application
- **Windows Control Library:** Create Windows Forms-based controls

- **Web Application:** Create a Web Server–based ASP.NET-based application comprised of static or dynamic HTML pages
- **Web Service:** Create a Web-based Service to be consumed by any application that can communicate over the HTTP protocol
- **Web Control Library:** Create Web-based controls
- **Console Application:** Create a command-line application
- **Windows Service:** Create a Windows Service
- **Empty Project:** Empty Windows Application project
- **Empty Web Project:** Empty Web server-based application
- **Import Folder Wizard:** Create a new project based on an existing application

2. Select the Windows Application template.

3. Type a Name for your application. For our purposes, type `HelloWorld`, the de facto standard for all first-time projects.

4. For the Location, you can accept the default, which is your My Documents folder. If you want to store your project files elsewhere, simply click the Browse... button and select a new location.

5. Click Add to Solution or Close Solution. This option allows you to either add your new project to the existing solution, or close the existing solution and start a new one. An example would be adding a new Web Service application to your existing VB .NET solution.

6. If you are adding to an existing solution, you can specify an alternate directory and solution name for your new project by entering a value in the New Solution Name text box.

7. Click OK.

As your hard drive churns in circles creating your new HelloWorld project, let's go over the structure of files and where they are stored when new projects and solutions are created, and what the file extensions mean.

Solution directory structure

Your projects are stored in the My Documents folder by default. You can change this in the Options dialog box, which we will cover in detail later in the chapter. Each solution has its own directory created. For the HelloWorld project, a HelloWorld directory was created. In the HelloWorld directory, there are six files and two subdirectories created. Table 17-1 lists the files created and their purpose.

Table 17-1
File Structure of New Project

File/Directory	Description
HelloWorld.**sln**	Solution file. Contains details about the individual projects and their locations in the solution.
HelloWorld.**vbproj**	Visual Basic project file. Contains information about all of the files contained with a specific project within a solution.
HelloWorld.**suo**	Solutions options file used by the project.
Form1.**vb**	Default Form1 for project. This file is in plain text and can be edited with any text editor.
Form1.**resx**	XML Metadata file containing default project references.
Bin directory	Binary files.
Obj directory	Object files.

File extensions

All of the file extensions for Visual Basic .NET have been changed from previous versions of Visual Basic. It is important to understand what the extensions are and what they mean. Table 17-2 describes each file extension.

Table 17-2
File Extensions

File Extension	Description
XML	XML Document.
XSD	XML Schema File without generated classes.
TDL	Template Description Language File.
VB	Windows Form, Control, Class, or Code file.
RPT	Crystal Reports Designer file.
HTML	HTML source file.
XSLT	XML file containing transformation instructions for XML and XSD documents.
CSS	Cascading Style Sheet used for HTML pages to apply styles.
VBS	VB Script source file.

File Extension	Description
WSF	Windows Scripting source file.
JS	Jscript.NET source file.
CS	C# source file.
ASPX	Web Application form.
ASP	Active Server Page source file.
ASMX	Web Service source file.
DISCO	Dynamic Discovery Document, source file that enumerates Web Services and Schemas in a Web project.
ASCX	ASP.NET user control.
CONFIG	Application specific configuration file.
ASAX	ASP.NET configuration file that handles Session_OnStart, Session_OnEnd, Application_OnStart, and Application_OnEnd script. Similar to Global.ASA in Visual InterDev 6.0.

Back to the IDE

Now that you understand the solution and project structure, and the files that are part of a project, let's go back to the IDE and go into details while exploring our HelloWorld application.

Window management basics

The new Visual Studio .NET has a revolutionary new way of handling windows. Understanding how to manage windows will make your life easy as you build very simple or very complex projects. I believe that the best screen resolution for having as much real estate as possible is 1024×768. This will allow maximum space for your dialogs as well as code windows and forms designers. The following breakdown of window management basics will get you on your way to understanding the IDE a little better.

Auto Hide

The new Auto Hide feature allows you to "hide" windows from the main IDE while you are developing applications. Every window that appears in the IDE has the Auto Hide feature. To toggle Auto Hide on and off, click the pushpin button (see Figure 17-3) on the toolbar for each window you want to hide. When a window is hidden, a tab replaces the location of the window, which allows you to click the tab to view the window.

 **Figure 17-3:** Auto Hide pushpin

Tabbed documents

In the past, you had the Window pull-down menu to switch between open windows in the IDE. With Visual Studio .NET, there is the tabbed document theme that adds a tab to the top of the main window for each document or file that you have open (see Figure 17-4). This includes the MSDN Help topics that we previously looked at, the object browser, the Start page, Code File, forms, or any previously opened window. To switch between open documents, simply click on the tab that represents the document you want to open. To close a document, or to navigate forward and backward within open documents, use the buttons on the upper right-hand corner of the main window, which give further navigation control. The Ctrl+Tab key combination will navigate open windows in the main workspace. This technique is identical to the Alt+Tab key combination that we use to navigate open windows in the operating system.

Figure 17-4: Tabbed document feature

Dockable windows

All windows within the IDE are dockable to any edge of the IDE. Simply drag any window to whatever location you want it to reside, and it will lock into place. If you have previously made the window auto-hide, it will now auto-hide in its new location. The combination of Auto Hide with dockable windows allows complete customization of your IDE workspace.

Favorites

Similar to Favorites in your Web browser, any document in your IDE can be added to your Favorites, as well as any Web-based document.

Multiple monitor support

This cool new feature allows multiple monitor support with the IDE. You can now have windows spread across multiple screens, further enhancing your productivity. This is, of course, based on the type of video card that you are using. You cannot run a crossover cable between two computers and like magic have multiple monitors; you will need to invest in a fancy video card with multiple video outputs.

Windows, dialogs, and more windows

We now drill into the windows that make up the IDE, the toolbars, the drop-down menus, and all the cool things that make up our new environment. Because we have the HelloWorld application open, everything that you are about to read about should be visible. If any of the following windows that we drill into are not visible, you can get to them by selecting the View menu, as Figure 17-5 demonstrates.

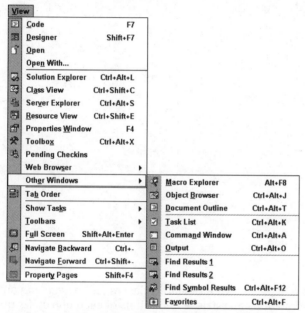

Figure 17-5: View Menu with other windows

If you refer to Figure 17-4, you can see all of the possible windows that you can open in the IDE. Let's go through each one and give some background and details.

Solution Explorer

Similar to the Project Explorer in VB 6, the Solution Explorer (see Figure 17-6) contains a list of all of the files associated with your current solution. Through the Solution Explorer, you have total management of your project and its corresponding files. Solutions may contain several projects, written in several languages, using several different technologies. It is truly a global view of your solution. As in Visual Studio 6, all project options are available by right-clicking within the Solution Explorer and bringing up the context menu. Because each part of a solution is different, the options available to you will be different depending on what you select and right-click. If you right-click on a Project name, then Project options such as Build, Add Reference, and Save As will appear. If you right-click on a Form or a Code module, options such as Open, View Code, or View Designer will be available to you. It is a good idea to explore each of the options when you first start using this new IDE to become more proficient in Solution Management.

Figure 17-6: Solution Explorer

Class View

The Class View window is a high-level view of all the classes and objects in your solution. From the Class View, you can retrieve definitions of each object, its properties, and methods with a simple double-click. If the class has methods that exist in your application, double-clicking on the object will bring its code window up in the main workspace. There is a handy toolbar on the Class View window that allows different sort options for fast access to objects.

Server Explorer

The Server Explorer (see Figure 17-7) is a central location to manage all servers and server-based services from within the Visual Studio .NET IDE. Because the whole idea of the .NET platform is shared services among many different servers, there needs to be a place to locate and manage these servers. The Server Explorer allows a central view of all server resources, any data connections that you have for your current solution, e-mail configuration — particularly Exchange 2000 configuration — and Web Service management.

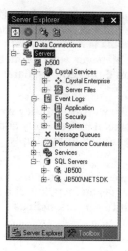

Figure 17-7: Server Explorer

The following is a list of the top-level nodes in the Server Explorer and the purpose of each node:

✦ **Crystal Services:** Installed Crystal Report options.

✦ **Event Logs:** Application, Security, and System Event logs for the attached server.

✦ **Loaded Modules:** List of the processes and loaded DLLs on the selected server. The very cool thing here is that through the System.Diagnostics.Process class library, you are exposed to the properties of the processes. So if you feel it necessary, you can modify any of the exposed read/write properties through Properties windows.

✦ **Management Data:** List of interfaces available through Windows Management Instrumentation. Again, an insight to services and read/write properties of the connected server. For example, I drilled into Win32_Server, Logical Disk Manager, all the way into my Computer Name, and modified the SystemStartupDelay property to 10. Now when I reboot, the OS Choices menu is at 10 seconds instead of 30.

✦ **Message Queues:** List of available queues and their corresponding messages. Message Queue must be installed for this to work. This would be the same view that you can retrieve from Computer Management snap-in.

✦ **Performance Counters:** List of all available Performance Counters for the selected server. The list is huge compared to what we are used to. There are hundreds of new counters for .NET alone. For example, we now have a counter to track .NET CLR LOCKS and IL Bytes JITted/sec.

✦ **Processes:** List of running processes on the selected server.

✦ **Services:** List of running services on the selected server.

✦ **SQL Server Databases:** List of databases on the selected server. Like the Data View window of past Visual Studio versions, you are opened up to all of the functionality of the SQL Server Enterprise Manager. This is a very robust COM interface that alleviates the need to have Enterprise Manager open. From this view, you can add, edit, and delete tables, views, stored procedures, database diagrams, and functions.

✦ **Web Services:** List of Web Services by Project and File with which they were published on the selected server. From this view, you can immediately add a reference to a Web Service to your project with a right-click or by simply using drag and drop into your code window.

✦ **Data Connections:** Similar to the SQL Server Databases node, you can add connections to any database or server provider that has an installed OLE DB provider on your system. This allows you to connect to servers such as Oracle, DB2, Exchange, and Active Directory.

Properties window

The Properties window allows you to modify at design time the properties of any object that is currently selected in the main workspace. If you are a VB 6 developer, you will be familiar with working with the Properties window. It is the single most important window in the IDE for customizing your application at design time. The default view for the Properties window is to display properties by Category; this can be changed to an alphabetical view of properties by clicking the alphabetic toolbar button on the Properties window. You can also view the properties of any control on the current form by selecting it from the drop-down list just above the toolbar. As a VB developer, regardless of whether you are developing a Windows Forms–based application or a Web Forms–based application, you are always modifying properties of objects to maintain the desired look and feel of your application. Using the Properties window is something that you do about 10,000 times a day. Get yourself familiar with the Properties window and each object's properties, especially if you are an experienced VB developer, because the changes to properties of all objects in Visual Studio .NET will surprise you.

Toolbox

The Toolbox (see Figure 17-8) contains the objects and controls that can be added to Windows Forms applications and Web Forms applications. The Toolbox has a vertical tabbed theme that allows quick navigation between the different types of objects or controls that you want to add to your forms. By default, the Toolbox displays the Data, Components, Windows Forms, Clipboard Ring, and General tabs. A right-click on the Toolbox will display options for the Toolbox. Show All Tabs will display the remainder of the tabs that are not displayed. If you select this option, you will see that there are about 20 different tabs, ranging from XSD Schemas to UML Shapes. To place a Toolbox item onto a form, simply drag the selected control to the location of the form where you want the control to reside. You can also double-click on a control to place it at the last cursor position on the form. Once the control is on the form, you can then move it to any location on the form by clicking on the control and dragging it with your mouse.

Figure 17-8: The Toolbox

If you have code snippets that you use across many projects, or there is code that you don't want to type every time you need it, you can add that code to the Toolbox. My goal in life is to write as little code as possible, so I have tons of code snippets stored in the Toolbox.

To add code snippets to the Toolbox:

1. In the Code window, highlight the code you want to add to the Toolbox.

2. Drag the selected code to the General tab.

3. Right-click on the Toolbox and select Rename, and give the newly added code snippet a meaningful name.

You can do all Toolbox customization with a right-click, so go ahead and look at the menu options available when you right-click on the Toolbox.

Macro Explorer

With the Macro Explorer, you can write macros that customize your IDE or automate tasks. The Visual Studio .NET IDE has its own object model, which is very complete, so you can automate processes within the IDE using the Macro IDE. To get to the Macro IDE, you can double-click on any of the macros that already exist in the Macro Explorer, or you can select Add, Edit, or Delete from the right-click context menu within the Macro Explorer. Figure 17-9 displays the Macro IDE.

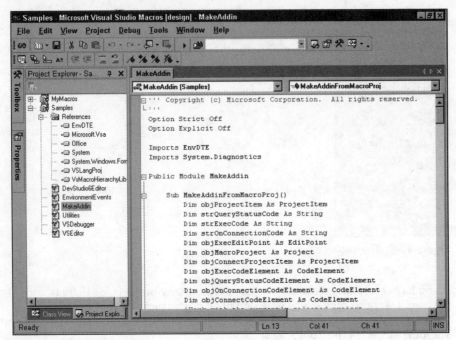

Figure 17-9: Macro IDE

Object Browser

The Object Browser (see Figure 17-10) is one of the most powerful windows in the Visual Studio IDE. The Object Browser allows you to view every object in the current solution and their properties and methods. Broken up into two panes, the left pane, or Objects Pane, displays a hierarchical list of all objects in your solution (classes, interfaces, structures, types, namespaces, and so on). The right pane, or Members Pane, displays the properties, methods, classes, enumerated items, variables, and constants. When you select a member in the right pane, the Description Pane at the bottom of the Object Browser describes the member and gives you an example of the syntax that you will use if you plan on using the member. This includes any dependencies, variables, and additional help description that may have been compiled with the object. The Browse drop-down on the top of the Object Browser enables quick navigation to the loaded objects in your project, so you can limit the list of objects in the left pane to a specific object in your project. The Customize button enables you to add additional components to the Object Browser or to remove components that currently exist in the project. If you choose to add new components to the Object Browser, all of the .NET Framework and COM components will be offered to you in an alphabetical list. The Find button on the Object Browser toolbar gives you a quick search functionality to sift through the hundreds of objects that may be in your project.

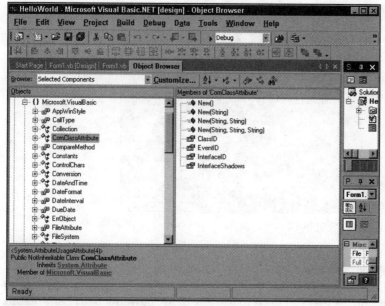

Figure 17-10: Object Browser

Task list

The task list is a familiar site for Visual InterDev developers. It is a centralized area that helps you to manage tasks within your solution, give you error details when you compile your code or as you enter code, and it helps you self-document your projects. There are several predefined tokens that help you self-document your code. They are TODO, UPGRADE_TODO, and UPGRADE_WARNING. By entering these tokens after the comment symbol (the single quote), tasks are automatically added to the task list for you. When you need to go back to a token that you added, just double-click the item in the task list and the appropriate section of code is brought up in the main workspace. For errors, the behavior is the same. If there are errors listed, simply double-click the task list item and you are taken to the offending line. You can add custom tokens by selecting Tools ➪ Options and drilling into the Tasks options as Figure 17-11 shows.

Command window

The Command window is used for executing commands directly in the Visual Studio .NET environment, bypassing the menu system, or for executing commands that do not appear on any menu.

Output window

The Output window displays compiler-specific information when you build your project or solution. The Output window will display build errors, libraries that are loaded, and other details of the build process.

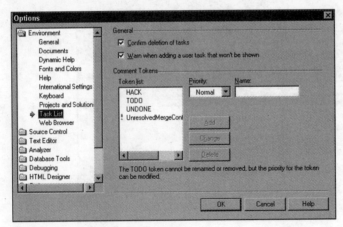

Figure 17-11: Task list options

Debugging windows

If you are like me, you consistently amaze yourself by writing error-free code. If the slight chance arises that you need to use any of the powerful debugging features in Visual Studio .NET, there are five windows that assist you with this at runtime. Figure 17-12 displays the available windows for debugging: the Breakpoints, Autos, Locals, Watch, and Call Stack windows. Chapter 18 talks about debugging in detail, so we will not duplicate that effort here.

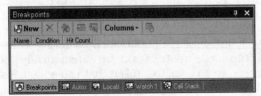

Figure 17-12: Debugging windows

The Code Editor

The code editor (see Figure 17-13) is where you spend most of your time writing VB .NET functions and procedures. The code editor is probably the most impressive feature of Visual Studio. With features such as spell checking, Auto-complete, word and statement completion, and Auto-list members, the code editor assists you in every facet of your coding.

You can open the code editor in several ways, based on your preference:

✦ You can double-click on an object on a form in the Windows Forms designer, which will bring up the code editor.

✦ You can click the "view code" button on the Solution Explorer toolbar, which is the first button on that toolbar.

✦ You can right-click anywhere in the forms designer and select View Code from the context menu.

Because the IDE has the tabbed documents feature, you can have as many code editor windows open as you like. When a file is open, such as a class file, form, or XML document, they are listed in tabs across the top of the editor window. Figure 17-4 earlier in the chapter showed the tabbed document feature.

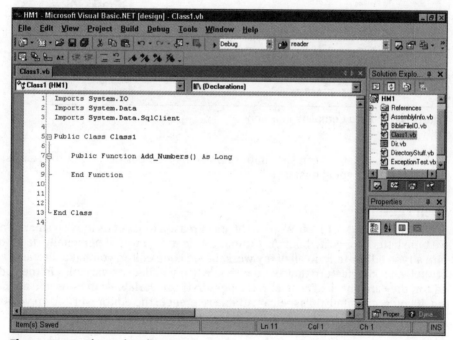

Figure 17-13: The code editor

With the invention of Auto-complete, Auto-list members, and spell checking in the code editor, you do not even have to know even 70% of the language to get applications written.

Auto List Members and Auto Complete

Auto List Members and Auto Complete are features that help you discover object members and finish off object references while coding. This feature works in conjunction with the `Imports` statements at the top of your class files, and with the built-in namespaces that are part of each class file. By importing a namespace into your class, the editor becomes aware of its existence and makes its properties, methods, and events available in the form of drop-down lists as you reference those objects. Once a list of members for an object appears, you can scroll through the list, or start typing the member you are looking for, and once it is highlighted, pressing the space bar or the Enter key will complete the statement for you. Figure 17-14 is an example of Auto Complete in action.

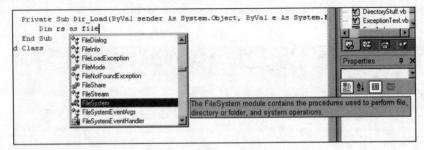

Figure 17-14: Auto Complete in action

With Auto Complete, it is nearly impossible to make incorrect object references, declarations, or typing mistakes.

Spell checking

Spell checking in Microsoft Word is the main reason most of us look so smart when we type letters (or write books). Without this feature, I would personally need to hire a typo editor to redo all of my work. In the code editor, you have the same sort of spell-checking feature that Word offers. When you declare variables in the code editor, they are checked against references to those variable names as you are coding. If you accidentally misspell a variable reference, the editor will inform you of this mistake with a squiggly line under the offending code. Figure 17-15 gives an example of the spell checker in action.

```
Private Sub Spell_Check_ME()
    Dim intX As Integer
    inX = 50
        The name 'inX' is not declared.

End Sub
```

Figure 17-15: The spell checker
in action

Designers

There are several designers that make up the "visual" part of working in the IDE. Designers give you a surface to create the graphical front end of ASP.NET applications and Windows Forms applications. There are also designers that aid in database creation, query generation, and XML editing.

Windows Forms designer

The Windows Forms designer is used to create forms-based applications. By adding a new form to your project, you can drag and drop controls such as text boxes or list boxes onto the form to visually create your GUI. When working on the Forms designer, selecting objects on the form, or the form itself, changes the Properties windows to display the properties for that object.

Web Forms designer

The Web Forms designer behaves exactly like the Windows Forms designer. The difference is the type of application you are developing. If you are developing an ASP.NET application, you will be using the Web Forms designer to modify the look and feel of your ASPX files, which make up the user interface of an ASP.NET application.

XML designer

The XML designer is used to edit and create XML and XSD files. The XML designer has three views: Schema View, XML Source View, and Data View.

Schema View

The Schema View allows you to visually design and edit XML schemas. You can create schemas by dragging and dropping tables from database connections in the Server Explorer, or you can add new attributes and elements in the editor. The Schema View also allows the creation of ADO.NET datasets.

XML Source View

The XML Source View is the editor for viewing and creating XML files. The editor also shares the same features of the code editor, such as auto-complete and auto-list members.

Data View

The Data View is similar to the Table View of a database tool such as Microsoft Access or SQL Server. Using the Data View, you can view and edit XML data in a familiar table-like fashion. You can also generate and view schema definitions based on XML data being displayed or edited in the data view window.

Database designer

The Database designer is a full-fledged database creation tool. With the Database designer, you can add, edit, and delete tables, indexes, views, stored procedures, and table relationships in a SQL Server, Oracle, or any database for which you have the correct OLEDB providers.

Query designer

The Query designer allows the creation of complex queries by dragging and dropping tables from a database connection onto the designer surface. The look and feel is the same as the view designer in SQL Server Enterprise Manager and the Query designer in previous versions of Visual Studio.

Component designer

The Component designer allows for the creation of non-graphical middle-tier components. Dragging objects from the Components tab of the Toolbox onto the designer surface allows rapid development of server-based objects by setting properties on objects through the designer, avoiding some of the coding that would normally be needed for middle-tier and server components.

User Control Designer

The User Control designer allows for the visual creation of controls that can be reused throughout your ASP.NET applications. Like `include` files in ASP, a user control can be placed onto an ASPX page and its functionality is completely encapsulated within the control itself. The difference between `include` files and user controls is that a user control can be visually created using the designer, and has its own code-behind pages.

Summary

In this chapter you saw the power of the Visual Studio .NET tool and what it can provide you in your development tasks. The Visual Studio .NET IDE takes the concept of Rapid Application Development to new levels, providing you with all of the tools you need to write robust applications without the hassle of learning complex tools. From creating forms, components, and databases, to features such as autocomplete and auto-list members, you will never need to leave the IDE to write your applications, and your applications will be more robust and error free because of the tools and features provided with Visual Studio .NET.

✦   ✦   ✦

Compiling and Debugging

by Rob Teixeira

When you're done creating all the marvelous code that constitutes your project, it's time to make to make it run. Turning your text code into something that can execute is called compiling. Compiling VB source code in the .NET environment is the job of Visual Basic .NET compiler: VBC.EXE.

If you're familiar with previous versions of Visual Basic, you will notice some differences in the new process. The most apparent is that all .NET languages now share the same environment, and because of that, you will see more integrated compiling features. Another big difference is that previous versions of Visual Basic compiled to either P-Code, an interpreted code, or to a Windows native binary code. VB .NET compiles to IL (Intermediate Language). This IL code is platform and processor neutral. The advantage is that it can run on many platforms without you needing to change your code and recompile. The first implementations of this feature are the two runtimes currently available: a single processor version and a multiprocessor version. Each is optimized for its environment. Because a large part of the specifications for the Type System, the Language Specifications, and IL have been submitted as standards, a number of third-party groups are working on runtimes for a number of platforms running operating systems other than Windows. Note that IL does not run interpreted, as did the P-Code from earlier versions of VB. A VB .NET program always runs as native binary code. The key to making this work is a JIT (Just-In-Time Compiler) that reads the IL and produces native code. The JIT can be invoked at the time of install, rendering the entire codebase to native code, or on an as-needed basis at runtime.

Another vital concept in VB .NET is the assembly. An assembly is the sum of all the pieces needed to run an application, and is self-descriptive. In other words, an assembly doesn't require external information, such as entries in the registry, in order for it to run. This is possible because Metadata is embedded in the assembly manifest, which contains all relevant information about the name, permission settings, and version. An assembly installation could be as simple as copying all the files and subdirectory structure. Assemblies also take on a big role in defining versioning for your project. The technology involved in making assemblies work allows multiple versions of an assembly to run on a computer. This allows other programs that are dependent on an assembly to continue to use an older version even if a newer version is present in order to avoid problems in execution.

Compiling Your Code

Two scenarios exist for running your code. One is running your code from the development environment so that you can test what you are writing (running in Debug mode), and the other is producing the binary files that will be placed into production or release. In either case, the source code files must be compiled. This process is called building.

Builds are controlled by build configurations. There are two levels of build configurations. One is the solution level, which affects a build of all the projects in the solution, and the other is project level, which affects build settings for the individual projects in the solution.

Solution build configurations

There is always one active build configuration for the open solution. This is shown in a drop-down list on the Standard toolbar, which also allows you to select the active build configuration.

You can also select the active build configuration, as well as define new configurations, by selecting the Configuration Manager command in the Build menu. This same command is available from the context menu (opened by a secondary click) of the solution item in the Solution Explorer. This command displays the Configuration Manager dialog box (see Figure 18-1).

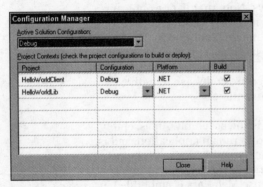

Figure 18-1: Configuration Manager dialog box

You can select the Active Solution Configuration with the drop-down list, or create a new configuration by clicking the New item in the list. All projects come with two default solution configurations: Debug and Release. The list shows the project-level build configuration settings for each project in the solution for this solution configuration. Note that here, the Debug solution configuration sets the two project build configurations to Debug, sets the Platform to .NET, and rebuilds all the projects.

For each project in the list, you can set the project-level configuration, which defaults to either Build or Release, or you can create a new project-level configuration by clicking the New item in the Configuration drop-down list. You can then select the target Platform for the build. Note that VB .NET lists only .NET because it targets .NET managed code only. Other languages such as C++ can show other entries, such as Win32. Finally, you can check the Build column if you want a particular project to be built under this configuration, or uncheck it if you want to exclude this project from a build.

So, for example, I can go to the Active Solution Configuration drop-down list and create a new solution build configuration, which I will call Client Test. I can then build HelloWorldClient in Debug configuration while excluding HelloWorldLib from the build in this configuration or build its Release mode instead.

When you want to compile your solution, you can select the Build Solution command from the Build menu. This command honors your build configuration settings. You can also select the Rebuild Solution command, which performs a complete build on all projects in the solution from.

If you want to build individual projects, you can select a project in Solution Explorer, and then select the Build *ProjectName* command from the Build menu (the text of the menu item changes to reflect the actual name of the selected project). The Rebuild *ProjectName* command performs a full build on the project. You can get the same commands from the context menu of a project node in Project Explorer.

If you want to perform a quick batch build on several projects without going through all the configuration steps, you can select Batch Build from the Build menu. This opens the Batch Build dialog box (see Figure 18-2).

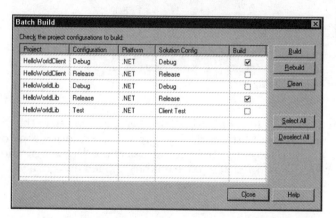

Figure 18-2: Batch Build dialog box

This dialog box shows all the combinations of project and solution configurations, and allows you to check which ones you want to build. You can then click Build to build all changes, Rebuild to build fully from scratch, or Clean to wipe out any intermediate and temporary files for that build.

Project configurations

Each project in the solution has two sets of properties, one set that is common and one set that is defined for each configuration. Initially, all VB .NET projects start out with only Debug and Release project configurations. As a general rule in Visual Studio .NET, there is one project property set for each combination of Configuration and Platform. However, as I mentioned earlier, VB .NET only lists one Platform, which is .NET. Therefore, if you have a Debug and Release configuration for a project, you will have two project property sets, whereas Visual C++ could have four because it would also list a Win32 platform option in addition to .NET.

To access the properties for a project, select a project and click the Properties command in the Project menu. Alternately, you can use the Properties command in the context menu of any project item in the Solution Explorer. This opens the Project Properties dialog box as shown in Figure 18-3. The caption of the dialog box is in the form of *Project Name* Property Pages.

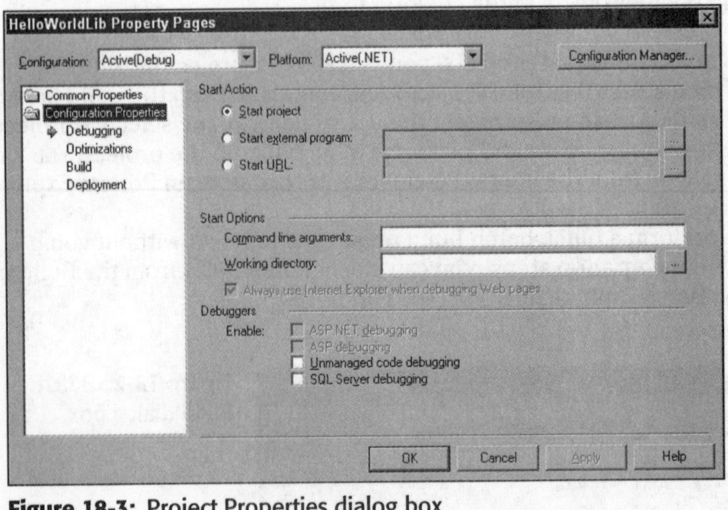

Figure 18-3: Project Properties dialog box

Use the Configuration drop-down list at the top of the dialog box to select the project configuration to which you want the options to apply. The Platform drop-down list isn't applicable to VB .NET projects. Also, you can select the All Configurations entry in the Configuration drop-down list to have options applied universally.

All items that appear under the Common Properties folder on the left pane of the dialog box are common to all configurations. These are options such as the Assembly Name, the Application Icon, and project Imports. The options that apply to specific configurations appear under the Configuration Properties folder.

Debugging options

Use the Start Action to tell the environment what to do when running a project from within the design environment. Start Project simply runs the project. Start External Program is useful for library type projects, and starts another program that uses this library project, allowing you to debug the library with the other program as the client. Start URL opens the browser and navigates to the given URL. The given page or ASP script then acts as the client to the library project.

If you are writing an executable or console program, you can additionally provide Command Line Arguments that will be used when the project is launched from within the design environment. You can also specify a Working Directory in much the same way as you can with a Windows PIF file or shortcut.

Furthermore, you can enable debuggers for types of code other than VB .NET managed code.

Optimizations

The optimization options help you tune your code for better performance. To display this options view, select the Optimizations node under the Configuration Properties folder.

Remove Integer Overflow prevents math operations from raising errors such as Overflow and Divide by Zero. Removing these checks makes the operations run faster, but also incurs a risk of the calculations being incorrect.

The broad term Enable Optimizations allows the compiler to rearrange instructions and create results that are different from a standard compile in order to make the code smaller and more efficient. You should always debug with this option turned off, because the rearrangement of code can confuse the debugger.

Enable Incremental Build allows the compiler to leave pieces of the previous build alone and attempt to build only what's changed since the last build. This can speed up the build processes for large amounts of code. If the changes are too overwhelming for VS to safely determine what changed, a full compile occurs.

The DLL Base Address option applies to library projects. This allows you to specify the virtual address of where the DLL will be initially loaded for a process at runtime. When a process loads a DLL, if the DLL's base address is already being occupied by something else, the DLL is moved to the next available space in memory. This causes what's called a *ReBase*, where address offsets for the DLL will have to be recalculated. Therefore, selecting an address that will likely keep the base address from conflicting with other DLLs makes the load process faster.

Build

This property page allows you to specify general build options for the project. Select the Build node under Configuration Properties to display this page. These build options are dependent on the project configuration, in contrast with the Build options on the Common Properties folder.

Specify the directory you want the resulting compiled file to be placed in by typing it in the Output Path.

Check Generate Debugging Information if you want the compiler to add debug information to your compile. This generates a PDB file (program database) and inserts information that allows you to step through code, add breakpoints, synchronize the execution with the source code files, and so on.

Caution If you uncheck this option, you will not be able to utilize these debug features; however, your executable will be bloated with the debug information if you do check it. Therefore, this option is checked by default for Debug configurations, and unchecked for Release configurations.

Register for COM Interop specifies that your code will expose objects that can be called from COM clients. This option by itself does not physically make your classes callable from COM clients. Your project output type must be Class Library in order for you to set this option.

Enable Build Warning specifies that you want warnings generated by the compiler to be added to your Task List.

Warnings aren't fatal and typically won't stop the code from running, but they can introduce bugs down the road, for example. Check Treat Compiler Warning as Errors if you want the compiler to treat a warning as a compile error. When the compiler encounters the first warning of its type, it treats that warning as an error and no output file is generated.

Checking Define DEBUG Constant and Define TRACE Constant allows you to access these symbols from a conditional compile statement, such as

```
#If DEBUG Then
    Console.WriteLine("I'm running in debug mode")
#End If
```

Define Constants allows you to specify additional condition compile constants that are configuration dependent. These constants can only be used in condition compile statements and are not regular constants.

Deployment

This property page has one field that allows you to enter a Web configuration file that will be used to compile your project. This comes in handy if you have different Web settings (such as permissions and URLs) for use in testing and debugging.

Build dependencies

Sometimes a solution has multiple projects, and one project requires that another be built first. In my example here, I have a library project called HelloWorldLib, and a Console project called HelloWorldClient that uses the library. The client project has a dependency on the library. When you run into this type of scenario, you can specify the build order by selecting the project dependencies. To do this, select the Project Dependencies command from the Project menu. This opens the Project Dependencies dialog box (see Figure 18-4).

Figure 18-4: Project Dependencies dialog box

Select the project you want in the drop-down list, and then check the projects it depends on. Visual Studio then creates a build order list based on the dependencies. Click the Build Order tab to see this list. When you select certain projects, other projects may be grayed out in the list. This is done to prevent circular dependencies between projects. For example, if Project1 depends on Project2, then Project2 can't depend on Project1. The compiler would be unable to determine which to build first. An entry can also be grayed out if the system creates the dependency for you. For example, if I add a reference to the HelloWorldLib project from my HelloWorldClient project, the HelloWorldLib project will be checked automatically, and VS will prevent me from unchecking this dependency.

Project item build properties

One further level of build options exists, and that is at the project item. If you look at the Solution Explorer window, you see that a `Solution` node represents the container for all the open projects. You can more or less think of this as the Project Group in VB 6. All the open projects are listed underneath it as `Project` nodes. Underneath a `Project` node are the Project Items. These items represent files and other items associated with that project. Some of those files are code, whereas others may be supplementary files such as XML files, HTML files, text files, resources, configuration files, and so on. The Visual Studio build manager needs to know what to do with any given file when you run a build. Therefore, each Project Item has a Build Action. If you select a Project Item and then look at the property sheet for that item, you see a drop-down list that specifies the current Build Action for that Project Item.

The Build Action property can be one of four values, as specified in Table 18-1.

Table 18-1
Build Action Values

Value	Description
None	This Project Item will be tracked as part of the project, but no action is taken on this Project Item during a build.
Compile	This Project Item will be compiled.
Content	No action is taken on this Project Item during a build, but this item will be deployed with the project as a content item.
Embedded Resource	This Project Item will be embedded in the output file (for example, EXE) as a resource.

Most of the time, you won't have to play with these settings. VB .NET recognizes the most common project file extensions and applies a default action. For example, .vb files are understood to be source code, and have the Compile value by default.

The Custom Tool property tells the build manager to run the specified tool, which in turn processes that Project Item. This allows a flat data file to be processed by a custom tool into an XML file or proprietary format file, for example.

The Custom Tool Namespace property is passed by the build manager to the custom tool, and specifies what namespace the processed results of the Project Item should be added to (if appropriate).

Conditional Compilation

When you write your program, you can add logic that tells the compiler what to compile and what not to compile based on a condition. This is called conditional compilation. Use the #If...#End If directive when you want to tell the compiler to compile a piece of code depending upon a condition. This statement works almost identically to the regular If...End If statement, except that it is used by the compiler and not at runtime. The most common example is when you need to tell whether you are in Debug mode. For example:

```
#If DEBUG Then
    Console.WriteLine("Running in debug mode")
#Else
    Console.WriteLine("Running in release mode")
#End If
```

In this case, the code does not branch execution, as would be the case with a regular If statement. Instead, only one of the lines is compiled.

The expressions used in the #If directive must utilize conditional compile constants. You can't use normal constants or variables. To define a conditional compile constant, you must use the #Const directive. For example:

```
#Const Win32 = True
#Const Win64 = False
```

You can then code the following:

```
#If Win64 Then
    Console.WriteLine("- 64-bit Version -")
    ' 64-bit specific code starts here...
#End If
```

Caution   Conditional compile constants apply only to the source code file they are defined in. In order to create constants that are global to your project, you must use the Custom Constants field in the Build page of the Project Properties dialog box as shown previously in this chapter. The DEBUG and TRACE constants are special cases and are turned on by checking the appropriate field in the same dialog box.

Debugging

As you write your source code, you need to be able to run it and test its execution for problems. These problems are called bugs. They can be errors and exceptions, or a condition that leads to unexpected results, bad calculations, and logic failures. Hopefully, you catch these problems as early in the project cycle as possible. A good and thorough design process often eliminates potential problems before they can be made. Statistics prove that problems found this early in the development cycle cost many times less in time and money to fix than if they are found later. In addition, it should be the goal of every developer to release robust and error-free programs. The cost of fixing a problem when it is in production can be enormous and it can have a very negative impact on the end users, not to mention the potential risk these errors have on the integrity of the data a program may use.

When you are working in the design environment, you have several options and tools that aid you in looking for problems and solving them. Central to your debugging efforts is the environment's capability to utilize debug information that is compiled along with your source code when you build in Debug mode. For maximum flexibility, make sure you have this feature turned on when you're still developing the application.

The best way to see the behavior of the application is to run it. If you run it from within the design environment, the design environment hooks into the debug information from the build. This allows you to set breakpoints, which temporarily halt the program when the program executes the line with the breakpoint. It also allows you to step through code; that is, execute one line of source code at a time. Halting your code with breakpoints and stepping through code allows you to see where the program may be having problems and also lets you check the values of the data the program is using while it executes. To run a project from within the design environment, press F5, select the Start command from the Debug menu, or press the Start button on the Standard or Debug toolbars.

To begin stepping through the code, press F11, and select the Step Into command from the Debug menu, or the Step Into button on the Debug toolbar. You can also press F10 or use the Step Over command. Both allow you to step through your code one line at a time, pressing F10 or F11 to proceed with the next line. The difference between the two is that Step Into steps into a function call, whereas Step Over executes a function at its call, but does not step into its code.

Breakpoints

Most of the time, stepping through the program in its entirety is very impractical because of the program's size. Setting a breakpoint somewhere in the code allows the program to run normally until the breakpoint is reached. The program temporarily halts when the execution comes to the line of code with the breakpoint. When this happens, the program is in what's called Break mode. This allows you to examine the data, check the logic, and so on, and then either continue execution by pressing F5 (or Start) again, or step through the code (F10 or F11). To insert a breakpoint, place the cursor on the line of code where you want to break the execution and press F9. You can also click on the margin to the left of your code. A breakpoint symbol then displays on that line as shown in Figure 18-5.

If you want to remove a breakpoint, place the cursor on the line with the breakpoint you want to remove and press F9 again, or click on the breakpoint symbol you want to remove. You can also remove a breakpoint by using the Remove Breakpoint command on the context menu when you use a secondary click on the breakpoint symbol. This context menu also allows you to Disable or Enable a breakpoint. By disabling a breakpoint, the breakpoint remains as a point of reference, but it does not affect the execution.

This demonstrates the simplest form of breakpoints. Breakpoints have more advanced features, such as breaking only on certain conditions. To use the more advanced breakpoint features, set the cursor on the line of code where you want to insert a new breakpoint, and press Ctrl+B or use the New Breakpoint command from the Debug menu. This opens the Breakpoint dialog box (see Figure 18-6). This dialog box allows you to insert a breakpoint based on one of four criteria: a function, a source code file, an address, or data values.

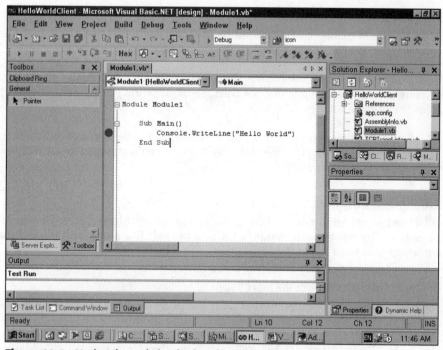

Figure 18-5: Notice the red circular breakpoint symbol on the left margin.

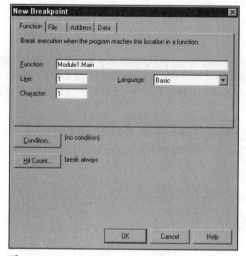

Figure 18-6: Inserting a breakpoint based on a function name

Breakpoints on functions

When you want to insert a breakpoint by finding a section of code based on a function name, select the Function tab on the dialog box.

Here, you specify the function name. Keep the language set to Basic. Visual Studio must be able to locate a line of code with the information you entered in order to place the breakpoint.

Note
Setting the Line number to 1 causes the breakpoint to be placed at the first line of the function, not the first line of the file. Only the first line is valid for VB .NET if you set function breakpoints.

Breakpoints on files

Click the File tab on the dialog box to insert a breakpoint based on a file rather than a function. You can type the name of the source code file, along with the line number where you want to set the breakpoint.

Breakpoints on memory addresses

You can also place a breakpoint that halts the program when execution reaches a certain memory address. Click the Address tab to do this.

This feature isn't as useful in VB .NET as it is in other languages, such as Visual C++, where you would have access to a function pointer or virtual function table.

This dialog box has one other tab, called Data. Visual Basic does not support this feature.

Conditional breakpoints

If you want to break based on a variable's value, you can add a conditional breakpoint. Notice that all the tabs on this dialog box have a button captioned Condition. When you click it, the Breakpoint Condition dialog box appears (see Figure 18-7).

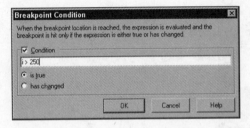

Figure 18-7: Breakpoint Condition dialog box

If you select the Is True option, the breakpoint causes the program to halt only when the specified condition evaluates to True. In this case, the breakpoint only causes the program to halt when the variable i is greater than 250. Alternately, you can select the Has Changed option, which evaluates the expression you entered, and breaks if the result is different from the result produced the last time this breakpoint was reached.

Hit count condition breakpoint

The other button on this dialog box is Hit Count. This button can be used to specify conditional breaks based on how many times this breakpoint has been reached during the execution of the program. For example, you can halt the code when a line has been executed 10 times. This is especially helpful in determining the cause of infinite loop bugs and recursive functions that fail to unwind. Clicking this button opens the Breakpoint Hit Count dialog box (see Figure 18-8).

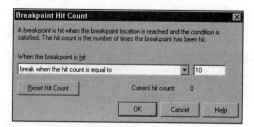

Figure 18-8: Breakpoint Hit Count dialog box

The default is to Break Always. The other entries in the list are Break When Hit Count is Equal To, Break When Hit Count is a Multiple Of, and Break When Hit Count is Greater Than or Equal To. Selecting an entry other than Break Always makes another text field visible where you can specify a number.

If you want to review all your breakpoints, you can display the Breakpoints window by pressing Ctrl+Alt+B. This window lists all the breakpoints, their status (enabled/disabled, error), and allows you to remove, add, or edit any of them (see Figure 18-9).

You can also make the Breakpoints window visible by selecting the Breakpoints command from the windows tool of the Debug toolbar.

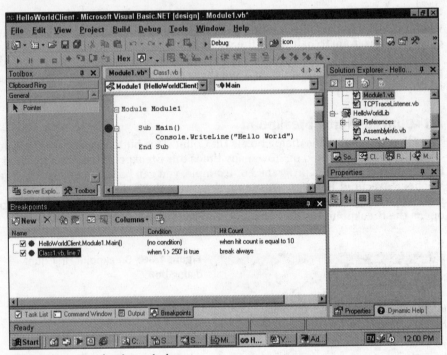

Figure 18-9: Breakpoints window

Debugging Tools

Now that you can execute code in Debug mode with the Visual Studio debugger environment, and selectively halt the execution into Break mode, you can then use several other tools to view the current state of the application and its data.

Call stack

The Call Stack is a stack list that contains the information for each function call leading up to the current function. The current function is at the top, and every function down the call chain is listed beneath it. This is a powerful tool for determining which route the program took to a function that is having a potential problem. This is especially true when you are working with components, where a number of clients can be calling into your component's methods. It's possible that some of them may not be passing correct information or aren't using your component properly. To display the Call Stack window, press Ctrl+Alt+C or select the Call Stack command from the window tool of the Debug toolbar (same place as the

Breakpoint window command). The call stack is only available when you run a program.

You can also programmatically obtain a stack trace. The Exception class has a StackTrace property that dumps the current stack trace as a string. This shows all functions leading up to the current function where the exception is being handled. The following code dumps the stack trace to the console window if an error occurs:

```
Try
    ' Program code here
Catch e As Exception
    Console.WriteLine(e.StackTrace)
End Try
```

If you want a stack trace without an exception, you can call Environment.StackTrace instead.

Note   The stack trace can only display some information, such as source code file names and line numbers, if you compile with Debug information turned on.

Autos

When the execution has halted at a breakpoint, or you are stepping through code, you have several tools from which to check the value of the current data being used by the program. The Autos window (see Figure 18-10) displays all the variables in the current statement of execution, as well as those in the previous line of code. To display the Autos window, press Ctrl+Alt+V,A, or select the Autos command from the window tool of the Debug toolbar. The Autos window is only available when you run a program and are either at a breakpoint or are stepping through the code—in other words, Break mode.

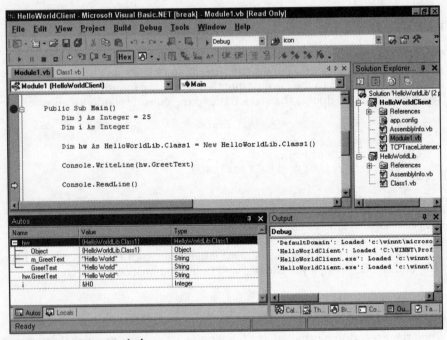

Figure 18-10: Autos window

The Autos window shows the names of the variables, their values, and their data type. In this case, there is an integer variable called i with a value of zero, and an object reference called hw with a class type of HelloWorldLib.Class1. Object references and structures have an expandable tree to show properties and fields of that type. HelloWorldLib.Class1 has a private m_GreetText string field, and a public GreetText property.

Locals

The Locals window functions identically to the Autos window, except that it lists all the variables in the current scope. Press Ctrl+Alt+V,L or select the Locals command from the window tool of the Debug toolbar to display the Locals window (see Figure 18-11).

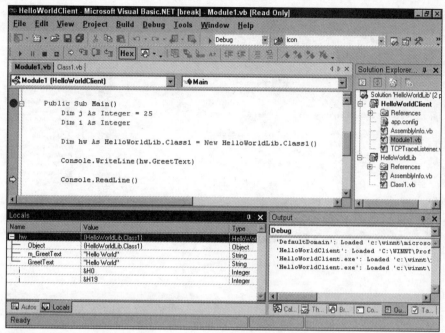

Figure 18-11: Locals window

Here, in addition to showing the i and hw variables from the Autos window sample, the integer variable j is also shown, with a value of 25 (&H19).

Tip   The Hex button on the Debug toolbar toggles the display of numbers in the debug tools between decimal and hexadecimal.

Me window

The Me window works in much the same way as the previous two windows, but it shows the current state of the instance of the class whose code you are debugging (the "Me" reference, or "this" in C#). To display the Me window, press Ctrl+Alt+V,T or select the Me command from the window tool of the Debug toolbar (see Figure 18-12).

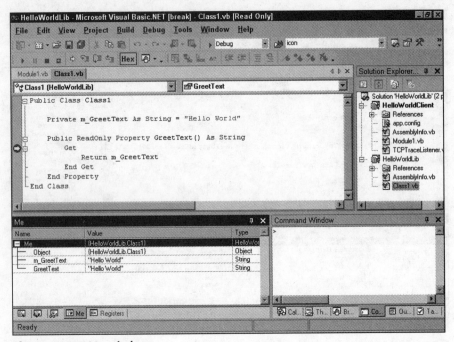

Figure 18-12: Me window

In this case, the code is showing the contents of the current instance of the HelloWorldLib.Class1 code.

Watch windows

Sometimes it is useful to track the values of certain variables while running a program from the design environment debugger. When you want keep track of a variable, you can add it to a Watch window (see Figure 18-13). There are four Watch windows in Visual Studio. NET. You can display them by pressing Ctrl+Alt+W,*n* where *n* is a number from 1 to 4. For example Ctrl+Alt+W,2 displays Watch window number 2. You can also select the Watch 1, Watch 2, Watch 3, or Watch 4 commands from the Window tool of the Debug toolbar.

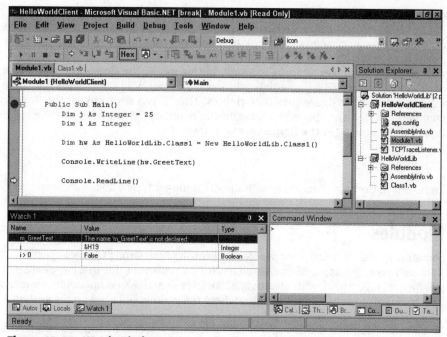

Figure 18-13: Watch window

All four Watch windows work identically. In this example, I've added the variable j to the Watch window, and the Watch window shows its value to be 25 (&H19 in hex). I have also added the m_GreetText field of my HelloWorldLib.Class1 class. The m_GreetText field is not in scope, and therefore not visible to the currently running code, so the value displays as "The name 'm_GreetText' is not declared". Also note that I added the expression i > 0, which is currently False. Unlike the other data viewing windows shown previously in this chapter, the contents of the Watch windows do not change unless you add or remove variables or expressions from the Watch window.

To add a variable to a Watch window, highlight the variable in your code and bring up the context menu by using a secondary click. You can then select the Add Watch command. You can also add variables and expressions to a Watch window by opening the Quick Watch dialog box. To display this dialog box, press Ctrl+Alt+Q or select the Quick Watch command from the Debug menu.

Command window

Press Ctrl+Alt+A or select Other Windows ➪ Command Window from the View menu to view the Command window.

The Command window has two modes: Command mode and Immediate mode. In Command mode, you see a ">" prompt before each line. You can type Visual Studio commands that affect the development environment, such as `SaveAll`, `Close`, and `Build.CurrentSelection`. When you are running a program from within the environment, you can change to Immediate mode by typing the `Immed` command. In Immediate mode, the word "Immediate" appears at the top of the Command window and you no longer see a ">" prompt. In this mode, the Command window works very much like the VB 6 Immediate windows. You can type statements, evaluate expressions, and assign values to variables. The "?" is a shortcut for the `Print` command. So for example, you can print the result of the expression j <= 30 by typing the following in the Immediate window:

```
? j <= 30
```

To return to Command mode from Immediate mode, type `>Cmd`.

Modules

Sometimes, you can encounter problems because of the wrong DLL being used. Although managed assemblies created in .NET help prevent this to a large extent, it can still happen if you work with unmanaged libraries—ActiveX components, for example. This tool is also useful for determining where the various DLLs are on the system.

To view the Modules window, press Ctrl+Alt+U or select the Modules command from the window tool of the Debug toolbar (see Figure 18-14).

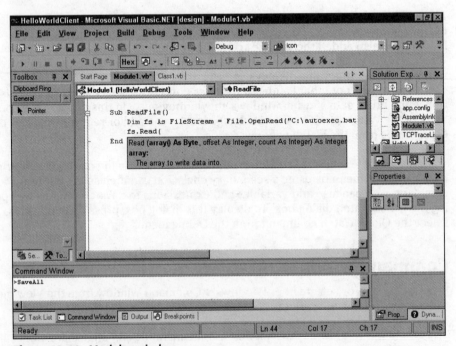

Figure 18-14: Modules window

The list contains the name of the executable or library, the address the DLL occupies, the path to the executable or library, the order it was loaded, the version, the program using the library, and the timestamp. If debug information is included with the executable or library, you see "Symbols loaded" in the Information column; otherwise you see "No symbols loaded." If an item appears with a red exclamation point, this library attempted to load in an address that was already being used, and had to be ReBased. You typically want to avoid this because it can slow your application, so go back to your projects and set the Base Address field to another value in the Optimizations property page for the project.

Edit and Continue

Edit and Continue is a term used to name the feature that allows programmers to run code from within the design environment, go into Break mode, alter code in the source file, and continue with the execution. The SDK has several documents with some very intricate details on how Visual Studio implements Edit and Continue. It's very tricky because a function, which is already compiled, needs to be replaced by a newly compiled snippet, and the stack frame adjusted properly with any data synchronized to what it was before the change. Edit and Continue is a bit more complicated in VB .NET as compared to VB 6, because unlike VB 6, the code does not run in an interpreted mode. To make a long story short, Edit and Continue will not be available in Version 1, although Microsoft has stated that it is one of the priority tasks for the next version. In the meantime, utilize the other debugging tools to their full potential, because if you need to alter code, you will have to restart the execution.

Microsoft CLR Debugger

Although Visual Studio .NET is by far the most flexible and efficient tool used to debug your VB .NET applications, you aren't limited to using only VS for debugging. The Microsoft CLR Debugger is included with the .NET Framework SDK, and is available even if you don't install Visual Studio .NET. The debugger looks like a mini version of Visual Studio, and reminds me a lot of the Windows Scripting Debugger (see Figure 18-15). You can't edit code in the debugger, but you can use all the debugging tools described in this chapter. To launch the CLR Debugger, run the DbgCLR.EXE program found in the `Program Files\Microsoft.NET\FrameworkSDK\GuiDebug` folder.

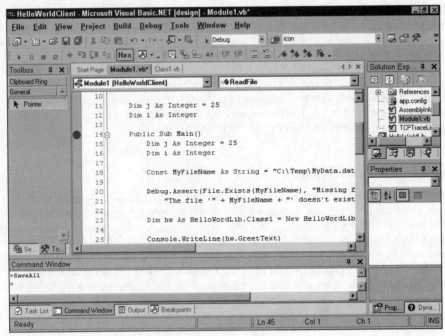

Figure 18-15: The Microsoft CLR Debugger application

Before you start, you need to connect to the executable file you want to debug. That executable must be built with the proper debug information in order for the debugging features to be available. The alternative is to connect to a program that is already running. If you want to debug an executable file, you can select the file by using the Program to Debug command from the Debug menu (see Figure 18-16).

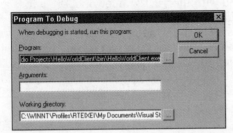

Figure 18-16: Program To Debug dialog box

If you want to connect the debugger to a program that is already running, press Ctrl+Alt+P or select the Debug Processes command from the Tools menu (see Figure 18-17).

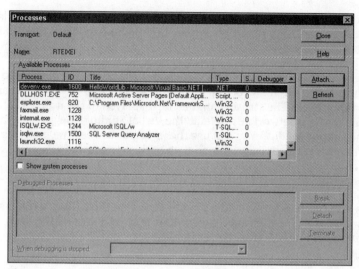

Figure 18-17: Debug Processes dialog box

In this dialog box, you can select the processes you want to attach the debugger to, and click the Attach button. The selections appear in the Debugged Processes list at the bottom of the dialog. If any of these processes break or cause an assertion or fail, you will be able to view the code provided the process has the proper debug information and source code is available.

If you use the previous method instead — selecting the executable file — you can then start the execution, set breakpoints, or step through the code. In order to set breakpoints initially, you need to be able to view the source files. You can open as many source code files as are necessary by using the Open ⇨ File command from the File menu. This is a very useful tool for debugging applications where the full Visual Studio environment is not available.

Debug and Trace Objects

Another nice thing about VB .NET is that it has access to the Debug and Trace classes. This means you can programmatically use the debug information and communicate with any debuggers that may be attached to your processes. VB .NET makes it a breeze with the classes in the System.Diagnostics namespace.

Debug class

The Debug class allows your program to selectively emit debugging information as it runs. All debug code is executed only if you compile with debugging information turned on (check Generate Debugging Information in the Build section of the Project Configuration Properties — this is turned on by default for Debug configuration, and turned off by default for Release configurations). With this class, you can emit information to any debugger application (including Visual Studio) that is attached to your process.

A number of listeners can be attached to the Debug and Trace classes in order to monitor the output. These listeners contain an output stream, and the process can write text out to this stream. The stream can then be displayed to the user, written to a file, or even sent across a network. By default, the Visual Studio debugger displays that stream in the Output window. You can use the Write or WriteLine methods of the Debug class to have your application send data to this stream. For example:

```
Debug.WriteLine("Now starting batch file processing...")
```

The Debug class also has a WriteIf and a WriteLineIf method. They work just like the Write and WriteLine methods, except that they only write if the first Boolean parameter evaluates to True. For example:

```
Debug.WriteLineIf((MyCount > 250), _
    "Unexpected large number of items returned.")
```

You can also affect the indenting of the messages to help format the output. The Debug class has an IndentSize and IndentLevel property, as well as Indent and Unindent methods. The IndentSize is the number of spaces occupied by an indent, and is defaulted to 4. IndentLevel is the current level of indenting, which you can also affect by calling the Indent and Unindent methods. These methods increase the indent by one level and decrease the indent by one level, respectively. So the following code

```
Debug.WriteLine("The following problems have occurred:")
Debug.Indent()
Debug.WriteLine("* Too many items returned.")
Debug.WriteLine("* Buffer too small.")
```

produces this output in the debugger:

```
The following problems have occurred:
    * Too many items returned.
    * Buffer too small.
```

The Debug class also has an AutoFlush property and a Flush method. Calling the Flush method forces a flush of the output stream. This is useful if a listener is utilizing a buffered stream. If the AutoFlush property is set to True, a Flush is invoked after every write. There is also a Close method. Calling Close invokes a Flush and closes the listeners.

The last two methods in the Debug class are Assert and Fail. The Assert method displays a message if the Boolean parameter is False. This method has several overrides. If you pass only an expression that results in a Boolean value, such as

```
Debug.Assert(File.Exists(MyFileName))
```

then the `Assert` method displays the current call stack if the expression is False. You can also provide an optional message by passing an extra string parameter as follows:

```
Debug.Assert(File.Exists(MyFileName), "Missing file.")
```

You can display a more detailed message (as seen in Figure 18-18) by adding yet another string argument:

```
Debug.Assert(File.Exists(MyFileName), "Missing file.", _
    "The file '" + MyFileName + "' doesn't exist.")
```

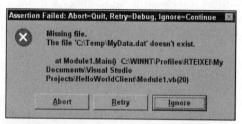

Figure 18-18: Message dialog box that the default listener displays from a debug Assert

You can use the `Fail` method to display an error message. The `Fail` method works identically to the `Assert` method, except that there is no Boolean test; the assertion always fails and produces the message

```
Debug.Fail("Can't connect to server.")
```

The last property of the `Debug` class is the `Listeners` property, which is a collection of attached `TraceListeners`. `TraceListeners` is covered in a following section.

Trace class

The `Debug` class works only if you have an executable file with debug information. However, if you want to monitor Release mode executables (executables with no debug information), you can use the `Trace` class. `Trace` is enabled by default for both Debug and Release build configurations. The `Trace` class has exactly the same methods as the `Debug` class.

Debugger class

The `Debugger` class allows you to communicate directly to any attached debuggers, such as the Visual Studio environment. Calling `Debugger.IsAttached` returns True if a debugger is attached to the process. To launch a debugger and attach it to the process, call `Debugger.Launch`. This method returns True if the launch was successful. You can use `Debugger.IsLogging` to check whether the debugger is reporting errors, and if so, you can then call `Debugger.Log` to emit a message directly to the debugger, as shown here:

```
If Not Debugger.IsAttached Then Debugger.Launch()
If Debugger.IsLogging Then Debugger.Log(1, "Info", _
    "Report this message")
```

The `Log` method has three parameters; a `Level` parameter, which is a number indicating the importance of the message; a `Category` parameter, which you can use to categorize your messages; and finally the message itself.

You can also call `Debugger.Break` to break the execution, creating a sort of dynamic breakpoint. The user is asked if he wants the debugger to launch if no debugger is attached.

TraceListeners

`TraceListeners` monitor output from both the `Debug` and `Trace` classes and provide streams that the `Debug` and `Trace` classes can write to. The `TraceListener` class is a base class for deriving new types of listeners. Both `Debug` and `Trace` classes have a `Listeners` property, which is a collection of attached listener objects. This allows you to add new listeners that will pick up information emitted by `Debug` or `Trace`, or replace listeners by removing the ones you don't want. The framework provides three listeners.

DefaultTraceListener

This listener is automatically attached to the `Debug.Listeners` and `Trace.Listeners` collections. Anytime the `Debug` or `Trace` classes invoke a `Write`, the `DefaultTraceListener` invokes `Debugger.Log`, which causes an attached debugger to display the output. At the same time, it directs the output to `OutputDebugString` for compatibility with legacy debuggers. If an `Assert` is invoked, the `DefaultTraceListener` displays a message dialog box and calls `WriteLine`.

TextWriterTraceListener

This listener directs the output of the `Debug` or `Trace` class to a text stream, such as a `FileStream`, or `Console.Out` (the console window output stream). The following code shows how to create a trace log file using this method:

```
Const MyFilename As String = "C:\MyTraceLog.txt"
Dim tl As TextWriterTraceListener

'Create a log file if needed and instantiate the listener
If File.Exists(MyFilename) Then
    tl = New TextWriterTraceListener(File.Open(MyFilename, _
        FileMode.Append))
Else
```

```
        tl = New TextWriterTraceListener(File.Open(MyFilename, _
            FileMode.Create))
End If

'Attach the listener
Trace.Listeners.Add(tl)

'Write to the log
Trace.WriteLine("This message reported at: " + _
    DateTime.Now.ToString)

'Close the log
Trace.Close()
```

Remember that the TextWriterListener can work on any output stream. Expanding on this idea, it's possible to do something such as create a TCP connection, and attach TCP socket's stream to the TextWriterListener. This would allow you to send the trace messages across your network to a monitoring application on a different computer.

EventLogTraceListener

The third TraceListener provided by the framework is an event log listener. This directs the output of Debug or Trace to the Windows event log. You can then monitor the messages with the Event Viewer application. Here's an example of how to write to the event log:

```
'Create a new event log and listener based on that log
Dim el As EventLog = New EventLog("Application", ".", _
    "HelloWorldClient")
Dim ell As EventLogTraceListener = New _
    EventLogTraceListener(el)

'Attach the listener
Trace.Listeners.Add(ell)

'Write to the log
Trace.WriteLine("This message reported at: " +
    DateTime.Now.ToString)

'Close the log
Trace.Close()
```

If you are creating application instrumentation, you will have more flexibility if you use the Event Log directly, but this gives you a generic way of working with Debug and Trace output.

Creating Your Own TraceListener

You can also inherit from the TraceListener base class, and create your own custom listener. For example, you can establish a program in a monitoring station that receives trace information from a program running on a server. The server-side program can utilize a custom listener that directs the trace output to the monitoring application by using a TCP stream over the network. This is demonstrated by the sample in Listing 18-1.

Listing 18-1: Creating a Custom TCP TraceListener Sample

```
Imports System.Net
Imports System.Net.Sockets
Imports System.IO

Public NotInheritable Class TCPTraceListener
    Inherits TraceListener

    Dim tcpc As TcpClient
    Dim sw As StreamWriter

    Public Sub New(ByVal RemoteHostName As String, _
        ByVal port As Integer)

        MyBase.New()
        Dim tcpc As TcpClient = New _
            TcpClient(RemoteHostName, port)
        sw = New StreamWriter(tcpc.GetStream)
        sw.AutoFlush = True
    End Sub

    Public Sub New(ByVal RemoteHostName As String, _
        ByVal port As Integer, ByVal Name As String)

        MyBase.New(Name)
        Dim tcpc As TcpClient = New _
            TcpClient(RemoteHostName, port)
        sw = New StreamWriter(tcpc.GetStream)
        sw.AutoFlush = True
    End Sub

    Public Overloads Overrides Sub Write(ByVal o As Object)
        sw.Write(o)
    End Sub

    Public Overloads Overrides Sub Write( _
        ByVal Message As String)
        sw.Write(Message)
    End Sub

    Public Overloads Overrides Sub Write( _
        ByVal o As Object, ByVal Category As String)
        Write(o.ToString, Category)
    End Sub
```

```vb
        Public Overloads Overrides Sub Write( _
            ByVal Message As String, ByVal Category As String)
            sw.Write("[" + Category + "] " + Message)
        End Sub

        Public Overloads Overrides Sub WriteLine( _
            ByVal o As Object)
            sw.WriteLine(o)
        End Sub

        Public Overloads Overrides Sub WriteLine( _
            ByVal Message As String)
            sw.WriteLine(Message)
        End Sub

        Public Overloads Overrides Sub WriteLine( _
            ByVal o As Object, ByVal Category As String)
            WriteLine(o.ToString, Category)
        End Sub

        Public Overloads Overrides Sub WriteLine( _
            ByVal Message As String, ByVal Category As String)
            sw.WriteLine("[" + Category + "] " + Message)
        End Sub

        Public Overloads Overrides Sub Fail( _
            ByVal Message As String)

            WriteLine("--- ASSERTION FAILED ---")
            WriteLine("Message: " + Message)
        End Sub

        Public Overloads Overrides Sub Fail( _
            ByVal Message As String, ByVal Details As String)

            WriteLine("--- ASSERTION FAILED ---")
            WriteLine("Message: " + Message)
            WriteLine("Details:")
            WriteLine(Details)
        End Sub

        Public Overrides Sub Close()
            sw.Close()
            MyBase.Close()
        End Sub

        Public Overloads Overrides Sub Dispose()
            Close()
            MyBase.Dispose()
        End Sub

End Class
```

To attach this listener to a `Trace`, use the code in Listing 18-2.

Listing 18-2: Attaching Trace to a TCP Listener

```
Try
    'Create a new TCP trace listener based
    '(pass remote IP and port, I'm using my
    ' local system as a test here)
    Dim tcpl As TCPTraceListener = New _
        TCPTraceListener("127.0.0.1", 7010)

    'Attach the listener
    Trace.Listeners.Add(tcpl)

    'Write to the log
    Trace.WriteLine("This message reported at: " + _
        DateTime.Now.ToString)
Catch e As Exception
    ' error occurred
    Console.WriteLine(e.Message)
Finally
    'Close the log
    Trace.Close()
End Try
```

In this case, there would be an application on the remote side that listens to the specified port (7010 in our example), and outputs the incoming data to the screen or file on the remote monitoring machine.

Trace switches

When you want to dynamically configure the way in which your trace information is displayed, you can set up a `TraceSwitch`. This `TraceSwitch` can be defined in your application's configuration file, so that an end user or administrator can toggle the settings. To add a configuration file to your project, select the Add New Item command from the File menu. Scroll down in the dialog box and select Application Configuration File as shown in Figure 18-19.

This inserts a file called `app.config` to your project. When you build the project, this file is copied to the build output directory, and renamed as the name of the application with a `.config` extension. In my case, this is `HelloWorldClient.exe.config`. This file contains all your application settings in XML. An end user of administrator can then modify these values. Think of it as a super INI file.

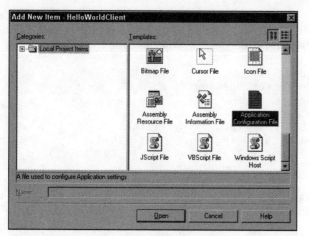

Figure 18-19: Adding a configuration file to your project

Note Configuration files are valid (strict) XML. Make sure you carefully follow XML formatting rules, which includes valid tag nesting. You must be very careful about text case—you can't substitute upper- or lowercase letters.

In order to provide a `TraceSwitch`, you can add the following section to your configuration file:

```
<system.diagnostics>
     <trace autoflush="true" indentsize="7" />
     <switches>
             <add name="HellowWorldTrace" value="2" />
     </switches>
</system.diagnostics>
```

Every switch needs a name, and I'm calling this one "HelloWorldTrace". The value corresponds to the trace level. The `TraceSwitch` supports the following levels:

    0 — Off

    1 — Error

    2 — Warning

    3 — Info

    4 — Verbose

In order to use a switch from your code, you need to create a new instance of that switch, for example:

```
Private Shared ts As TraceSwitch = New _
    TraceSwitch("HellowWorldTrace", _
    "Global App Trace Switch")
```

The `Level` property reflects the `TraceLevel` as shown. The `TraceError`, `TraceWarning`, `TraceInfo`, and `TraceVerbose` properties return True or False depending on the level. Using this information, you can code the following:

```
If ts.TraceError Then
    Trace.WriteLine("Error opening file.")
End If
If ts.TraceVerbose Then
    Trace.WriteLine("The file '" + MyFilename + _
    "' could not be located in the '" + MyPath + _
    "' directory, is currently locked, or is corrupt.")
End If
```

This technique also allows you to turn tracing off completely, which can speed up a process when it's not needed.

Summary

In this chapter, you saw how to compile your code and set build options and configurations. You also saw how to run the program in Debug mode, and utilize a host of tools that help you pinpoint bugs and errors. Finally, you saw how to work with the `Debug` and `Trace` classes to monitor the execution of your application.

✦   ✦   ✦

Customizing

by Rob Teixeira

This is one of the biggest and most powerful releases of Visual Studio yet. Finally, you get all the languages and tools you need in one place. In fact, as this is being written, there are well over a dozen languages in the works for .NET. Each language, each tool, and even each developer has unique quirks and twists, so luckily Visual Studio .NET is extremely flexible in terms of customization.

Start Page and Profiles

The first place you can see evidence of customization is the Start Page, which is the first open window you see when you launch Visual Studio.

On the navigation area to the left of this screen, you can select from among the following view panes:

+ Get Started
+ What's New
+ Online Community
+ Headlines
+ Search Online
+ Downloads
+ Web Hosting
+ My Profile

Getting Started

The Get Started view consists of a list of recently used projects, as well as an Open Project button and a New Project button. You can click a project to open it, click the Open Project to browse for a project that isn't listed, or click New Project to create a project.

Up-to-date content

The What's New view shows you the latest additions and updates to Visual Studio tools and third-party tools. The Online Community view displays Visual Studio-related Web sites and newsgroups. The Headlines view displays the latest news and articles from Microsoft's MSDN online site. You can customize each of these views by selecting an item from the Filter drop-down list, as shown in Figure 19-1. This allows you to keep current on the things you are interested in.

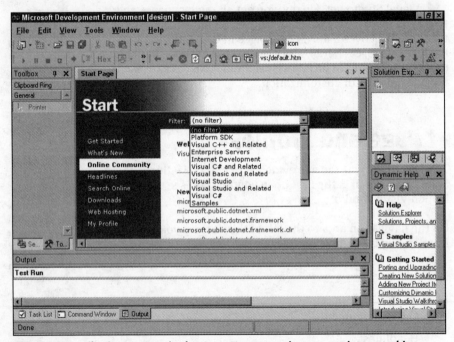

Figure 19-1: Filtering content in the Start Page to topics you are interested in

My Profile

The biggest area of customization in the Start Page is the My Profile view (see Figure 19-2). The first time you launch Visual Studio .NET, you will be prompted for a profile. If you need to change this information at some point, you can return to this view.

The Profile drop-down list contains general default settings for keyboard scheme, window layout, and documentation filters. Selecting entries such as the Visual Basic Developer profile or Visual Interdev Developer profile sets the environment layout and keyboard shortcuts to a scheme that is more familiar to users of the previous versions of those products.

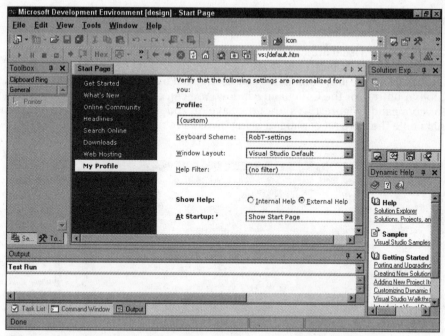

Figure 19-2: Customizing environment options in the My Profile screen

You can also select custom combinations of Keyboard Scheme, Window Layout, and Help Filter.

Tip   The MSDN help and documentation for .NET is enormous. Selecting a Help Filter can save you a lot of time by focusing only on topics you are interested in until you get more familiar with the documentation layout.

The Show Help section contains two options: Internal Help and External Help. Selecting Internal Help allows the help system to work inside the IDE, whereas selecting External Help opens a new window for help and documentation.

The At Startup section allows you to select what is displayed when Visual Studio .NET is launched. Your options are the following:

✦ Show Start Page

✦ Load Last Loaded Solution

✦ Show Open Project dialog box

✦ Show New Project dialog box

✦ Show Empty Environment

Commands

Commands in Visual Studio .NET work in much the same way as they do in Microsoft Office. In fact, they share a common object model for command display and usage. In the IDE, commands can be invoked from a menu, a context menu, a toolbar button, or the Command window. You can also set up a keyboard shortcut for commands. Figure 19-3 shows the Save All command from the main File menu. Also note the Save All command being invoked in the Command window.

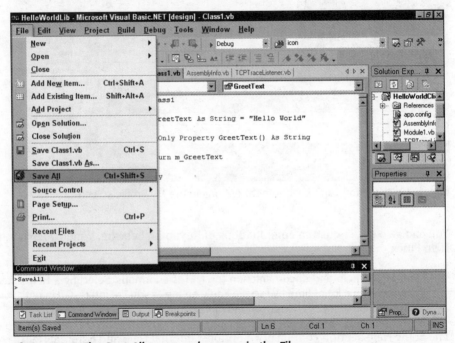

Figure 19-3: The Save All command as seen in the File menu

There are quite a few toolbars in Visual Studio .NET. It's often helpful to select the ones with the tool buttons you use the most. If you bring up the context menu on the toolbar (with a secondary click), you can check the toolbars you want to make visible and uncheck the ones you want to hide. The same menu can be displayed under the View ➪ Toolbars menu. The initial toolbars are as follows:

✦ Analyzer

✦ Analyzer Windows

✦ Build

✦ Crystal Reports – Insert

✦ Crystal Reports – Main

✦ Data Design

✦ Database Diagram

✦ Debug

✦ Debug Location

✦ Design

✦ Dialog Editor

✦ Diff-Merge Viewer

✦ Formatting

✦ Full Screen

✦ HTML Editor

✦ Image Editor

✦ Layout

✦ MenuBar

✦ Query

✦ Recorder

✦ Source Control

✦ Standard

✦ Style Sheet

✦ Table

✦ Text Editor

✦ View

✦ Visio UML

✦ Web

✦ XML Data

✦ XML Schema

The last command on this context menu is Customize. You can also get to the Customize command in the Tools menu. Clicking this command displays the Customize dialog box, as shown in Figure 19-4.

Figure 19-4: Choose the toolbars to display from the Toolbars tab of the Customize dialog box

The Toolbars tab on this dialog box lists all the toolbars, allows you to check the ones you want to make visible, and uncheck the ones you wish to hide — exactly like the toolbar context menu. In addition, you can add new custom toolbars. Click the New button to add a custom toolbar, which you can name anything you want. You can only delete and rename custom toolbars. Custom toolbars start with no buttons, and are a convenient way to group all your most commonly used commands.

The second tab is the Commands view. This view contains all the commands in Visual Studio .NET according to their category (see Figure 19-5).

Figure 19-5: Commands tab of the Customize dialog box

Selecting a category in the Categories list displays all the commands belonging to that category in the list to the right. You can then drag a command from the Commands list to a toolbar or menu. While this dialog box is showing, you can also drag commands that are already on a toolbar or menu to a different toolbar or menu, or remove a command from a toolbar or menu by dragging it off the toolbar or menu.

When you highlight an instance of a command on a toolbar or menu, you can then click the Modify Selection button to change the characteristics of that command button or menu item. This allows you to change the settings for an instance of a command. The following options are available:

✦ Selecting Reset will restore all the default settings for that command.

✦ Selecting Delete will remove the command from that context (a toolbar, for example).

✦ Selecting the Name field allows you to type a new name for the command. (You actually type in the Name field on the menu. Selecting it doesn't really do anything.)

✦ Selecting the Copy/Paste Button Image commands allow you to copy images from one button and apply them to another.

✦ Selecting Reset Image will restore only the image for a command instance.

✦ Selecting the Change Button Image displays another submenu with some stock images you can choose from. The next group of menu items allows you to set the visible display characteristics for the command instance.

✦ Selecting Default Style uses button images if they are available, and displays those images on toolbars while displaying the text in menus.

✦ Selecting Text Only (Always) displays text regardless of where the command is placed.

✦ Selecting Text Only (in Menus) shows text only when the command is in a menu, but not if the command is in a toolbar.

✦ Selecting Image and Text will display both the image and text for the command. Finally, we get to a command we skipped earlier:

✦ Selecting the Edit Button Image command displays the Button Editor dialog box, which is a mini-paint program that allows you to edit the image manually.

The last tab is the Options tab (see Figure 19-6). The Options view is used to modify the appearance and behavior of the toolbars and menu items.

Figure 19-6: The Options view of the Customize dialog box enables you to change the appearance and behavior of toolbars and menu items.

The Reset my usage data button clears the settings that are created automatically, such as the selection of menu items that will be visible by default if the full menu is not shown. Other toolbar and menu item settings, such as the addition of toolbars and commands, are not affected. The Large icons option will display bigger toolbar images if checked. List font names in their font will display font entries in a font drop-down list as the font actually appears. The Show ScreenTips on toolbars option displays ToolTips for commands if you hover above toolbar buttons with the mouse pointer. The Show shortcut keys in ScreenTips will include the shortcut combination in the ToolTip text if it is available. The Menu animations drop-down list specifies how you want your menu animations to appear when you open a menu, such as Unfold or Fade. The (System default) entry uses the Windows display settings for the animation.

The Customize dialog box also has a Keyboard button at the bottom. Clicking this button displays the Keyboard Options view in the Options dialog box (see Figure 19-7). You also get to this dialog box from the Options command in the Tools menu.

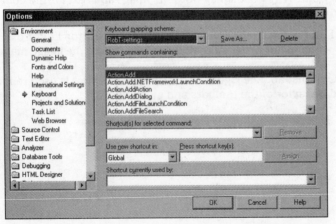

Figure 19-7: The keyboard view of the Options dialog box allows you to assign shortcuts to any available command.

I'll get to the Options dialog box soon, but because the Keyboard view affects commands, I'll address it here. The Keyboard mapping scheme drop-down list shows a list of all current keyboard schemes. Each scheme holds a complete set of keyboard options. This is the same information you saw in the My Profile view of the Start Page. You can't overwrite the default schemes, so if you make modifications, you must click the Save As button, which allows you to create and name a new custom keyboard scheme. The list box shows all commands in Visual Studio .Net. You can use the edit field above it to specify a filter, so only a smaller set of commands is displayed. Selecting a command in the list box displays the command shortcut assigned to it for this scheme in the Shortcut(s) for selected command drop-down list. You can select a shortcut in this drop-down list and click the Remove button to get rid of the assigned shortcut. To create a new shortcut, press the key (combination) in the Press shortcut key(s) edit field. You can then assign the context for this shortcut in the Use new shortcut in drop-down list. Global means the shortcut works in any context within Visual Studio .NET. Alternately, you can select to have the shortcut work only in certain editor/design windows, such as the HTML Editor or XML Editor. Click the Assign button to apply the new shortcut to the selected command. If you select a key (combination) that is already in use, you will see the command it is assigned to in the Shortcut currently used by drop-down list.

Windows

Visual Studio .NET has a host of tool, editor, and designer windows. The profile you select in the My Profile page affects the default window layout — displaying certain windows in certain locations and hiding others. You can make new windows visible or hide them from the View menu.

Some tool windows appear directly under the View menu, whereas others are in the Other Windows submenu.

Editor and Design windows appear when you open certain types of documents and other project items. Because Editor and Design windows represent main documents, they are opened in the main portion of the workspace by default. You have several options for displaying these windows, which you can change by selecting the Options command from the Tools menu and then selecting the General view, as shown in Figure 19-8.

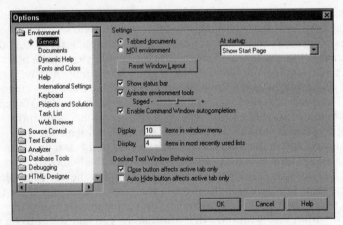

Figure 19-8: The General view of the Options dialog box lets you control basic options for the IDE.

You can toggle these windows to display either in Tabbed documents or in an MDI environment. In Tabbed document mode, these windows are all maximized, and you can switch between them using the tabs at the top of the document display, as shown in Figure 19-9.

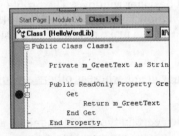

Figure 19-9: Tabs at the top of the Tabbed document display area allow you to select which open document you wish to view.

In MDI environment mode, the document windows appear as normal MDI windows within the development environment. The following options are available:

✦ The At startup drop-down list displays the same options as the My Profiles view in the Start Page.

✦ The Reset Window Layout button restores the default settings for window layout to the defaults specified the first time you opened Visual Studio .NET. You can show or hide the status bar by selecting or unselecting the Show status bar option.

✦ The Animate environment tools option allows you to turn the window transition animations on and off. You can use the slider to affect the speed of these animations.

✦ The Enable Command Window autocompletion option actually affects commands, which we covered earlier. If you turn this option on, some of the tool windows, such as the Command Window, will utilize text autocompletion similar to that of Internet Explorer.

✦ The Display [x] items in the window menu field allows you to enter the default number of menu items representing open windows that appear in the Window menu.

✦ The Display [x] items in the most recently used lists field is used to specify how many menu items appear in the various MRU lists, such as the File ⇨ Recent Files, or Recent Projects menu.

✦ The various tool windows all have a Close and Auto Hide button, and the Close button affects active tab only is used to specify whether you want the Close button on these windows to close only the active tab (if checked) or close all tabs. For example, if you are currently viewing the Command Window and Task List window on the same tab group, both tool windows will be closed if this option is not checked. The Auto Hide button (which looks like a thumbtack) is used to autohide a tool window. In other words, setting the button to Auto Hide mode (a horizontal thumbtack versus a vertical one) causes the tool window to shrink out of view when it's not in use.

✦ The Auto Hide button affects active tab only option is used to specify whether you want the Auto Hide button to hide all tool windows in a tab group (unchecked) or to hide only the tool window represented by the active tab.

The last few items of the Window menu show a numbered list of open document windows (up to the number specified in the General Options view). Selecting an item from this list activates that window. The last item is captioned Windows, and is used to display the Windows dialog box, as shown in Figure 19-10.

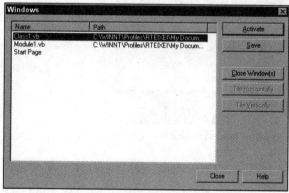

Figure 19-10: The Windows dialog box, in which you can control all opened windows

The Windows dialog box lists all the open project item windows. You can select one or more windows in the list. The Activate button makes that window the active window. The Save button saves the document that window represents. The Close Window(s) button closes the selected windows. The Tile Horizontally and Tile Vertically buttons only work in MDI mode, and will evenly tile the windows vertically or horizontally within the environment.

The top two items in the View menu are Code and Open. Select a project item in Solution Explorer, and click Open to open the default editor or designer. Selecting Code opens the document's code in a code editor window.

Customizing Editors and Designers

Every project item in Solution Explorer represents a document or item belonging to the current project. Opening a project item opens its associated Designer window by default. For example, when you open a file that defines a Form, you will see the Form designer. Opening an XML file displays the XML editor window. All the default editors have options you can specify in the Option dialog box. Select the Options command from the Tools menu to view this dialog box. The first view in the Options dialog box that allows customization is the Fonts and Colors view, as shown in Figure 19-11.

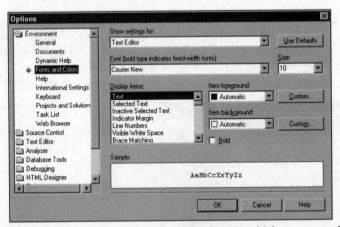

Figure 19-11: Fonts and Colors dialog box, in which you control the look of text features for editor windows

Select the editor or designer in the Show settings for drop-down list, and you can subsequently change the font and foreground/background colors for each display item supported by that editor. The Text Editor is used to edit all source code for the default languages and HTML/XML.

Next, you can select the Text Editor folder, and the General view under it, as shown in Figure 19-12.

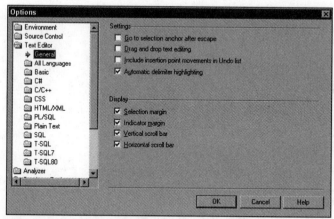

Figure 19-12: Basic text operations and formatting options in the Text Editor/General view of the Options dialog box

The General options affect all display items in a text editor and include the following:

✦ The Go to selection anchor after escape option causes the Esc key to move the insertion point back to the selection start when checked. For example, if you select four words from the middle of a sentence starting with the end of the fourth word, pressing the Esc key moves the insertion point after the fourth word, where the selection started.

✦ The Drag and drop text editing option allows you to select a block of text and drag the text to a new location in the document.

✦ The Include insertion point movements in Undo list option causes the movements of the cursor (insertion point) to be recorded for undo.

✦ The Automatic delimiter highlighting option causes delimiters between commands to be highlighted in a different color.

✦ The Selection margin option turns the selection margin space to the left of the text on or off. When turned on, the margin appears, in which the cursor changes from the I-beam to an arrow, and in which you can drag to select an entire line of text.

✦ The Indicator margin option toggles the display of the gray indicator strip to the left of the selection margin, where symbols such as breakpoints and execution lines are shown.

✦ The Horizontal/Vertical scroll bar options toggle the Text Editor's scroll bars on and off. You can still use the cursor keys to navigate within the document if the scroll bars are not visible.

The views under the All Languages folder affect the default settings for display items of all languages in the Text Editor. There are two views under the All Languages folder: General (see Figure 19-13) and Tabs.

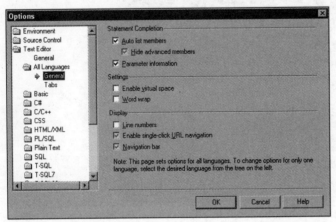

Figure 19-13: The General view under the All Languages folder of the Options dialog box.

Checking or unchecking an option in this view defaults the setting for all languages. Grayed-out check boxes mean that certain options are different for specific languages. The options in the Statement Completion section in the General view affect autocompletion. The Auto list members option toggles the displaying of a list of all available members for a reference or class in your code when you press the delimiter (period in VB) after a reference or class identifier.

If checked, the Hide advanced members option will prohibit the display of members in the auto member list if they are considered "advanced," such as the Handle property of a Form.

Tip If you can't find a property you're looking for in the Auto list members list, uncheck this option and try again.

The Parameter information option will display the parameter information in a ScreenTip when you write a call to a function or procedure in code, as shown in Figure 19-14.

The Enable virtual space option allows you to move past the last line of text in the text editor if checked (refer to Figure 19-14). If you begin typing, the lines between the last line and the new line will be populated with white space. If you check the Word wrap option, lines going beyond the right margin will wrap to the next line; otherwise, they will continue to the right and cause the horizontal scroll bar range to grow. The Line numbers option displays the row number for text in the Text Editor, as shown in Figure 19-15.

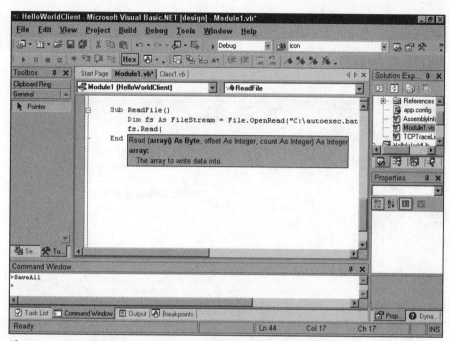

Figure 19-14: The parameter information ScreenTip for the Read method pops up when you type the open parenthesis for that method call.

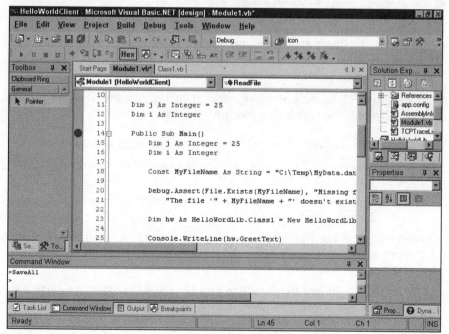

Figure 19-15: Line numbers displayed in the Text Editor margin

Turning on the Enable single-click URL navigation option allows you to navigate to a URL that is embedded in your code with a single click (refer to Figure 19-13). Otherwise, it requires a double-click. The Navigation bar option displays the Object and Procedures header at the top of the Text Editor, as shown in Figure 19-16.

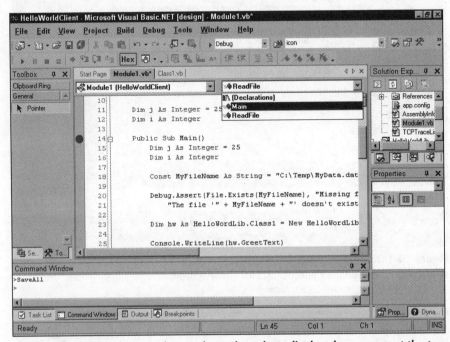

Figure 19-16: The Object and Procedures drop-down list header appears at the top of the Text Editor.

Moving on to the Tabs view of the Options dialog box, the first options you have are the Indenting options, which give you the following choices:

✦ Selecting None doesn't format the text after the Enter key is pressed.

✦ Selecting Block automatically indents the new line to the same tab as the preceding line.

✦ Selecting Smart indents the lines according to the indenting default rules for a particular language.

✦ Selecting the Tab size determines the number of spaces a Tab character is represented by. You must type the number in this field; it is not a "select" operation

✦ Selecting the Indent size field specifies the number of spaces to insert after an indenting operation, which can have a combination of spaces and tabs. See comment on previous item – the same applies here

✦ Selecting the Insert spaces option inserts spaces instead of tab characters when you press the Tab key.

✦ Selecting Keep tabs maintains tab characters instead of substituting them with spaces.

The other folders beneath All Languages represent the very same settings for particular languages. Because this is a VB .NET book, you'll look at the Basic folder. This folder contains a General and Tabs view identical to the All Languages folder, except this view affects settings for files with Basic code only. In addition, there is a VB Specific view, as shown in Figure 19-17.

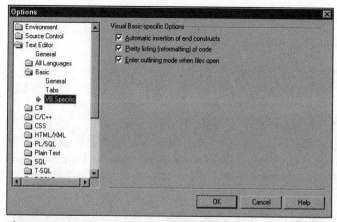

Figure 19-17: The VB Specific view in the Basic folder of the Options dialog box shows options that apply only to Visual Basic.

Checking the Automatic insertion of end constructs option causes the editor to automatically add the End portion of a code block when the beginning portion is typed and the Enter key is pressed. For example, typing the following

```
If i > 200 Then
```

and pressing the Enter key causes the editor to automatically insert the following beneath that line:

```
End If
```

Checking the Pretty listing (reformatting) of code option causes the editor to align the blocks of code with the correct indentation. Checking the Enter outlining mode when files open option automatically places the editor in outlining mode. This means that begin and end blocks are identified by a line grouping the code block lines. The beginning line has a "+" or "-" indicator, which you can click to expand or collapse the block of code (see Figures 19-18 and 19-19).

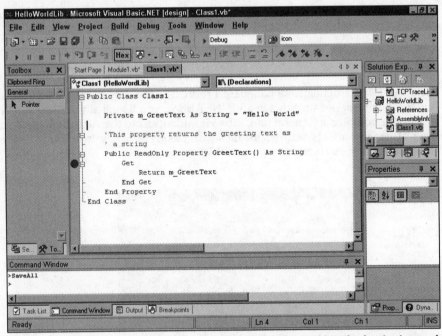

Figure 19-18: Notice the outline on the left of the code marking the beginning and end of the Class block, the Comment block, the Property block, and the Get block.

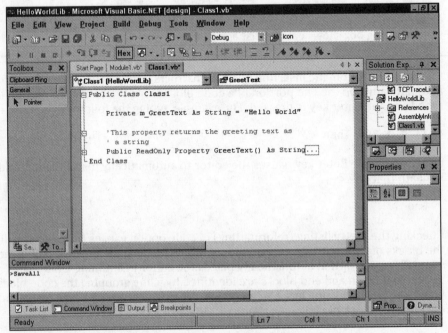

Figure 19-19: Notice the display when you collapse the Property block.

Tip   You can use the collapsing feature to quickly identify parts of code in large nested blocks. You can also use the #Region keyword to create a collapsible block. For example, you can type the following:

```
#Region " My Constants "
    Const i As Integer = 10
    Const j As Integer = 50
#End Region
```

You can now collapse this section of code to get the constants out of the way when you want to concentrate on the rest of the code.

Integrating external tools

Visual Studio .NET allows you to easily integrate external tools into the environment. The next-to-last group in the Tools menu shows some default external tools that ship with VS .NET, such as Spy++ and GuidGen (Create Guid). To insert new tools into the menu, select the External Tools command in the Tools menu. This displays the External Tools dialog box, as seen in Figure 19-20.

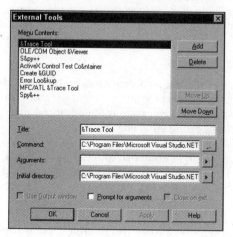

Figure 19-20: The External Tools dialog allows you to launch external development tool programs from the IDE.

Within the External Tools dialog box, you can perform the following actions:

✦ Add and Delete buttons to add new tools to the menu. Use the mnemonic & character, which underlines a letter to use as a menu shortcut when typing the caption in the Title edit field.

✦ The Move Up and Move Down buttons switch the ordinal positions of the menu items.

✦ The Command edit field specifies the complete filename to the external tool; for example, `C:\Winnt\Notepad.EXE`. The Arguments field allows you to add command-line arguments to the command. Alternately, you can click the button to the right of this field to select special arguments. So for example, you can invoke the external tool and pass the filename of the currently selected project item.

✦ The Initial directory field allows you to specify the working directory of the external tool when you invoke it. You can also select special paths by clicking the button to the right of this field.

✦ The Use Output window option reroutes the output of a console tool, a bat file, or a com file to the Output window, instead of opening a new console window.

✦ The Prompt for arguments option causes an Argument dialog box to prompt you for arguments when the tool is launched.

✦ The Close on exit option automatically closes a console window used by an external tool.

Macros

Probably the most powerful customizing aspect of Visual Studio .NET is the fact that it can be completely controlled from a class hierarchy that starts with the DTE (Development Tools Extensibility) class. This class represents the environment, and has members representing windows, tools, code, commands, and so on. You can take advantage of this Automation capability by writing macros against the DTE class and its members.

Tip   The object model is quite extensive, so I suggest recording macros at first in order to get used to the syntax, objects, methods, and properties. As you get more comfortable with the DTE classes and objects, you can code more advanced macros that control aspects of the environment beyond what you can record.

In order to work with macros, select the Macros submenu from the Tools menu. Selecting the Macro Explorer command from this menu displays the Macro Explorer tool window. This window lists all the currently loaded macro projects, and (below them) all the macro modules and macros. The following options are available:

✦ Selecting the New Macro Project command allows you to create a new top-level macro project.

✦ Selecting the Load Macro Project command allows you to load an existing macro project from disk.

✦ Selecting the Unload Macro Project command removes a macro project from the environment.

✦ Selecting a macro project in the Macro Explorer window enables you to then select the Set as Recording Project command to make that project the default for where newly recorded macros are inserted.

✦ Selecting the New Macro Module command inserts a module into the selected project.

✦ Selecting the New Macro command inserts a new macro into the selected module.

✦ Selecting the Run Macro command executes the selected macro.

✦ Selecting the Macros IDE command brings up the macro development environment, which looks a bit like a cross between Visual Studio .NET and the Office VBA macro development environment.

✦ Selecting the Edit command takes you into the macro IDE and the selection point will be the selected macro.

The first group of commands in the Macro menu relates to macro recording. If you select the Record TemporaryMacro command, a new macro will be created. This macro will be named TemporaryMacro and will be inserted into whatever project is set as the recording project. Anything you do in the environment, such as invoke commands, type code, and manipulate windows, will be recorded in this macro's code. This command will then be replaced with the Stop Recording command, which ends the macro recording. You can also select the Cancel Recording command to undo the recording. The Run TemporaryMacro command executes the current recorded macro.

Note There can only be one current recorded macro per project. This macro is always recorded as TemporaryMacro. If you record again, this macro will be overwritten with the new TemporaryMacro. In order to keep the recording, select the Save TemporaryMacro command, which allows you to rename the TemporaryMacro.

In order to put this all into a practical perspective, you can create a new sample macro. The following sample will demonstrate how to add automatically generated comments into your code. One typical application of this is code maintenance comments, which state who added or modified code, and when. To create this sample, follow the steps below:

1. First, create a new macro project by selecting the New Macro Project command in the Macro Explorer tool window.

2. In the prompt, call the new project MyMacros. You should now see an entry in Macro Explorer call MyMacros.

3. Next, select this project and select the New Macro Module command. In the prompt, call this module CommentMacros. Select this module and then select New Macro Command. This brings you into the macro IDE to a new macro procedure called Macro1.

4. Rename the procedure InsertAddComment. Inside the body of this procedure, type the following line of code:

```
DTE.ActiveDocument.Selection.Text = " ' Added by " + _
System.Environment.UserName + " : " + _
System.DateTime.Now.ToShortDateString
```

5. While you're in the macro IDE, you can create another macro. Add the following procedure to this module:

```
Sub InsertModComment()
    DTE.ActiveDocument.Selection.Text = " ' Modified by " +
    System.Environment.UserName + " : " + _
    System.DateTime.Now.ToShortDateString _
End Sub
```

6. You can click the Close and Return command from the File menu to return to Visual Studio .NET. If you open a code window and run these macros, a comment will be added to your code wherever the current insertion point is. For the `InsertAddComment` macro, the following comment will be added:

```
' Added by RTEIXEI : 8/24/2001
```

For the `InsertModComment` macro, this will be inserted in your code:

```
' Modified by RTEIXEI : 8/24/2001
```

The logon name of the current user and the current date will be used. You can execute the macros by selecting one in the Macro Explorer window and then selecting the `Run Macro` command, or by double-clicking the macro node in the Macro Explorer window. You can also invoke the macro from the Command window by typing the following:

```
>Macros.MyMacros.CommentMacros.InsertAddComment
```

You can take this one step further and create some toolbar buttons for your macros by performing the following steps:

1. First, select the Customize command. Next, click on the New button to insert a new toolbar. Name this toolbar `MyCommands`. At this point, you should see a small empty toolbar floating within the environment. You can dock this toolbar to the main toolbar area.

2. Now, select the Commands tab in the Customize dialog box, and then select the Macros category. You should now see all the available macros in the Commands list.

3. Drag both of the new macro commands you created to the new toolbar you just created.

4. Next, click the Modify Selection button, and select the Default Style command. This allows the button to display an image instead of the text.

5. You can then select the Change Button Image command, select a custom image for each of the buttons, and finally click the Close button on the dialog box.

Now, you can invoke the macros by clicking on the toolbar buttons.

Summary

In this chapter, you've seen how powerful the customization features of Visual Studio .NET are.

You learned how to customize your profile options, window layout, and keyboard/shortcut settings, as well as customize editor and designer windows. You also learned how to customize menu and toolbar commands. In addition, you learned how to modify and add external tools to the environment. And finally, you learned how to customize and create macros that interact with the environment.

✦   ✦   ✦

Source Control

by Yancey Jones

S ource control can be an invaluable tool for any application development project, whether it involves a single developer or many. Unfortunately, source control is often neglected or incorrectly used.

This chapter provides a basic introduction to Microsoft's Visual SourceSafe. This is in no way intended to be an all-inclusive reference for SourceSafe usage; such a reference would require an entire volume. However, an overview of what source control is, the necessary steps for the installation of Visual SourceSafe, and basic instructions on how to perform fundamental source control operations from within both Microsoft Visual SourceSafe and the Microsoft Visual Basic .NET IDE are provided.

What Is Source Control?

Source control can be described simply as code and documentation management. Source control software helps to maintain source code and document integrity, it tracks changes, it allows multiple developers to work on the same application while using the same code base, and it provides file and document security. Anyone who has ever had to manage or work on a project with multiple developers has probably used one variety of source control software or another.

Code is only one part of an application project. There are also many others, such as artwork, database diagrams, and other supporting documentation. Having to manage all of this manually would be a nightmare, even if there were only a single developer. Adding more developers rapidly increases the complexity. Source control software takes the burden of code and document management off the developers and project managers, and allows them to focus on other tasks.

CHAPTER 20

In This Chapter

What is source control?

Microsoft Visual SourceSafe

Installing SourceSafe

Visual SourceSafe administration

Visual SourceSafe Explorer

Accessing SourceSafe functions from within the Visual Studio .NET IDE

Good SourceSafe practices

Understanding Microsoft Visual SourceSafe

The latest version of Microsoft Visual SourceSafe is 6.0c, and it ships with the Enterprise Edition of Visual Studio .NET. All examples here assume SourceSafe Version 6.0c, but they should also work on earlier 6.0 versions.

SourceSafe tracks file changes by doing a reverse delta save to the SourceSafe database. What this means is that only one copy of the file exists in its entirety. Future saves include only the changes made.

In order for a file under source control to be changed, it must be checked out. The act of checking out a file accomplishes two things. First, the developer's local copy (also called the working copy) of the file is marked writable. Second, the file is marked as being checked-out in the SourceSafe database. When a file is marked as checked out, by default, no further checkouts are permitted. This allows the file to be edited by only one developer at a time. Each developer must have a working directory for each project in order to check files out. The working directory is where the temporary working copies are stored and can be located on a local or network drive.

After a developer finishes working on the file, it is then checked back in. Checking a file in saves any changes made into the SourceSafe database, marks the file as being available for check out, and makes the working copy read-only.

The SourceSafe administrator has the option of changing the default option to allow multiple checkouts on a file. Multiple developers can then work on the same file at the same time. The first time the file is checked in, it updates the database and creates a new version of the file. All subsequent checkins are merged into the new version.

Files can be checked in or out from the Visual SourceSafe Explorer application or directly from within the Visual Studio .NET IDE.

Installing SourceSafe

Three installation options are available when installing SourceSafe: SHARED DATABASE SERVER, CUSTOM, or STAND-ALONE (see Figure 20-1). To change the location of the SourceSafe install, click the Change Folder button. A SourceSafe database can be created on any local or network drives, regardless of where the SourceSafe program files are located. The default location should be used unless you have specific reasons for choosing another location.

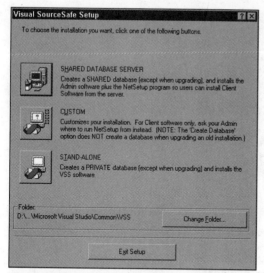

Figure 20-1: Choose one of the Visual SourceSafe Installation options.

The following installation types are available:

✦ **SHARED DATABASE SERVER:** Using the SHARED DATABASE SERVER installation creates a shared copy of a SourceSafe database, and copies the necessary setup files into the SourceSafe path. SourceSafe can then be installed on client workstations by running the NETSETUP.EXE program located in the SourceSafe path. This installation option automatically installs SourceSafe integration, which allows SourceSafe to be used from within the Visual Studio .NET IDE. Clicking the SHARED DATABASE SERVER installation button starts the SourceSafe installation (see Figure 20-3). For Shared Database Server installations, the folder location should be accessible to client workstations.

✦ **CUSTOM:** A CUSTOM SourceSafe installation allows the user to choose which options are installed (see Figure 20-2). If using this installation option, the Enable SourceSafe Integration option should be checked to allow SourceSafe operations to occur from within the Visual Studio .NET IDE. Clicking the Continue button starts the SourceSafe installation (see Figure 20-2).

✦ **STAND-ALONE:** A STAND-ALONE installation creates a private SourceSafe database, and does not copy any setup files. It is intended to be used by a single developer. As with the SHARED DATABASE SERVER option, this installation also installs SourceSafe integration. Pressing the STAND-ALONE button starts the installation.

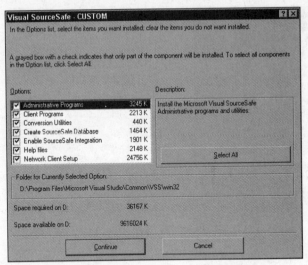

Figure 20-2: Custom installation setup options

Using the Visual SourceSafe Administration Program

Before the clients can access SourceSafe, they must have user accounts set up. This is done via the Visual SourceSafe 6.0 Admin application located in Start ⇨ Programs ⇨ Microsoft Visual SourceSafe. Two users are created by default with the installation: Admin and Guest (see Figure 20-3).

The Admin user is the account for the SourceSafe Administrator. This is the only user that can run the Visual SourceSafe Admin program and add or remove other users. The Admin account cannot be deleted or have its name changed. The Administrator has full rights to the SourceSafe database, and also has the right to undo a checkout by another user.

The Guest account provides a default template that can be used to create other users. It provides users with a temporary means of access while awaiting creation of their own account. This account can be deleted, and if project security is implemented, this account should be either deleted or have rights restricted.

Adding, editing, and deleting users

To add a user to SourceSafe, click the Users menu, and select Add User. Type the user's name and password into the pop-up box, check the Read only box to restrict this user's rights, and click OK (see Figure 20-4). The user is now added to the user list.

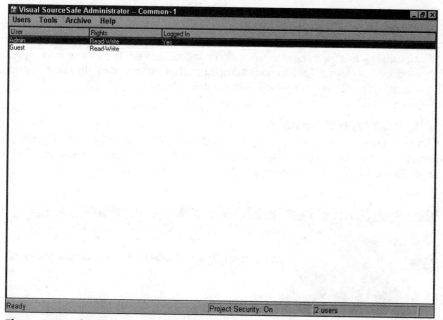

Figure 20-3: The Visual SourceSafe Administrator program creates Admin users and Guest users by default.

Figure 20-4: Type the username in the User name text box. Checking Read only restricts this user's rights.

To edit a SourceSafe username or read only access, select the user from the list of current users on the main program screen, and select the Edit User option under the Users menu item. The Edit User dialog box appears.

To change the user's password, select the user from the list of current users on the main program screen and select the Change Password option on the Users menu. The Change Password dialog box appears. Type the new password in twice (once in the New password text box, and again in the Verify text box), and click OK.

To delete a user's account, select the user from the list of current users on the main program screen and select the Delete User option on the Users menu. A confirmation box pops up; click Yes to delete the user or No to cancel the delete.

Note   Many of the menu options have keyboard shortcuts, an associated button on the toolbar, and/or a right mouse click pop-up menu. If a keyboard shortcut is available, it is given next to the menu option. Hovering the mouse over a toolbar button displays a ToolTip, indicating what that button does. To see if a pop-up menu is available, try right-clicking the item.

Setting up project security

On installation, project security is disabled by default (see Figure 20-5). Until project level security is enabled, the only available security from SourceSafe is the Read only option that can be selected when creating a new user.

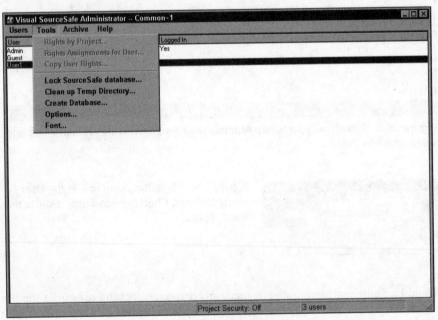

Figure 20-5: Project level security is disabled by default.

To enable project security, select Options from the Tools menu. Click the Project Security tab, and check the Enable project security check box. Select the desired default user properties for all projects (see Figure 20-6). The default rights are assigned to any new user that is created and they apply to all projects.

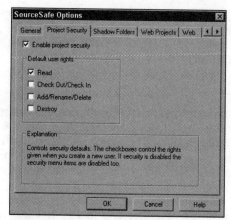

Figure 20-6: Check the Enable project security box to enable project level security.

Assigning rights by project

Once project level security is enabled, rights can be assigned on a per-project basis or per user basis. To assign user rights to a project, select the Rights by Project option from the Tools menu. A Project Rights dialog box with a list of the projects and users opens (see Figure 20-7). Select the project and the user to assign rights to; then check the appropriate rights for that user. Do the same for each project and user. When done, click the Close button.

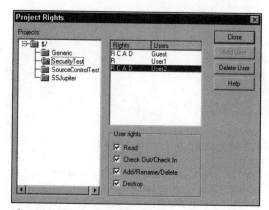

Figure 20-7: To assign rights on a per-project basis, select the project to assign rights to from the list and then place check marks beside the appropriate user rights.

If a user is set up with read-only access, the only right available is Read. To allow all rights to be edited, Edit the user (editing a user was covered previously in this chapter), and uncheck the Read only check box, as demonstrated earlier in the "Adding, Editing, and Deleting Users" section.

Assigning rights per user

Rights to projects can also be assigned on a per-user basis. To do this, select the user to assign rights to, and click the Rights Assignments for User option on the Tools menu. The Assignments for User dialog box that pops up (see Figure 20-8) contains a list of the current projects and the user's project rights. There may not be any projects listed for the user, but at least the root project is probably listed.

> **Note** $/ refers to the root project of a SourceSafe database. Projects are arranged in hierarchical order in a tree view, much like the files and folders in Windows Explorer. The root project would be the equivalent of $C:\backslash$ in Windows Explorer.

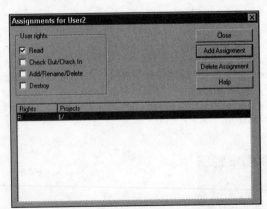

Figure 20-8: To modify the user's rights for a project, select the project from the list, and check the appropriate user's rights.

To add rights to a project, click the Add Assignment button in the Assignments for User dialog box. Another dialog box opens (see Figure 20-9) with the available projects listed. Select the project, check the appropriate rights for the user, and click OK. The new project and associated rights are then listed for the user.

Copying user rights

Rights can also be copied from one user to another. To do this, select the user to copy the rights to, and click the Copy User Rights option on the Tools menu. Select the user to copy the rights from in the pop-up dialog box and then click OK. The selected user's rights are now the same as that user who was selected in the pop-up dialog box. Only users not created with Read only access show up in the dialog box.

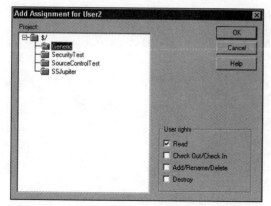

Figure 20-9: To add a project assignment and rights to a user's account, select the project and check the appropriate rights.

Creating a new database

To create a new SourceSafe database, click the Create Database option on the Tools menu. The Create New VSS Database window (see Figure 20-10) pops up. Type in the location of the new database, and click OK. SourceSafe creates a new database at that location.

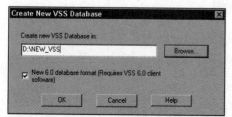

Figure 20-10: Type the location of the new SourceSafe database in the text box.

To administer this new database, you must open it from the Open SourceSafe Database dialog box, which you access from the Open SourceSafe Database option on the Users menu (see Figure 20-11). If it is a newly created database, it isn't listed in the Available databases list. Click the Browse button to locate the database. Find the location that it was created in (see Figure 20-12), click the srcsafe.ini file, and click the Open button. The Browse for Visual SourceSafe Database dialog box provides an opportunity to give the database a name that shows in the Name column on the Open SourceSafe Database dialog box (see Figure 20-11).

Note Even if the name assigned to any given database is arbitrary and can be different for each developer, it is a good idea to give the database a name that has meaning to the user.

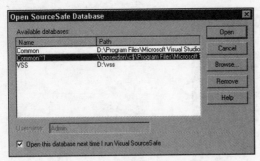

Figure 20-11: If you are opening a new SourceSafe database, click the Browse button to find it.

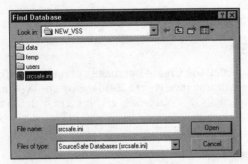

Figure 20-12: When browsing for a new SourceSafe database, type the filename and select the file type.

Using Visual SourceSafe Explorer

The Visual SourceSafe Explorer program is the built-in user interface for SourceSafe. All SourceSafe nonadministrative operations can be performed in this interface.

Creating a project

To create a project in SourceSafe, click the parent project in the project list in Visual SourceSafe Explorer (see Figure 20-13). After selecting the parent project, select the Create Project option on the File menu, or click the Create Project button on the toolbar. A Create Project in dialog box opens. Enter the project name and any desired comment, and click OK. The project is then listed under the selected parent project. Even if most new projects are likely to fall under the root, it is possible to create a project within a project.

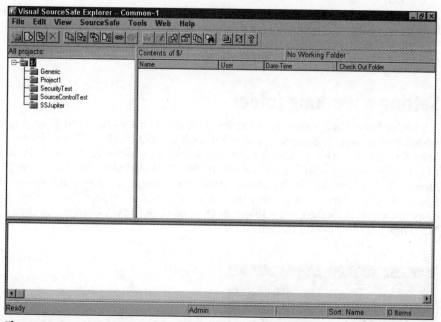

Figure 20-13: Projects are selected from the All projects list in the upper-left section of the Visual SourceSafe Explorer main screen.

Adding files to a project

Select the project to add files to from the project list, and select the Add Files option from the File menu. The Add File dialog box opens (see Figure 20-14). Find the current location of the files to add, either select each file individually or type in a wildcard in the File name text box, and then click the Add button. When the next dialog box opens, type in a comment if desired, and click OK. When all the files have been added, click the Close button.

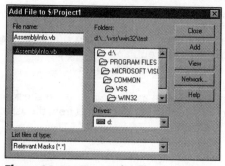

Figure 20-14: Locate the files you want to add. Type in the name (wildcards are OK) and click the Add button.

A dialog box may pop up, asking whether to set the folder that the files were added from as the current working folder. Clicking Yes sets the working folder to that directory. Clicking No keeps the working folder unset. Files cannot be checked out as long as no working folder is set.

Setting a working folder

A *working folder* for SourceSafe is the location the files are copied to when being edited by the user. The working folder for each project can be different for each user. To set the working folder for the user logged in to SourceSafe, click the project to set the working folder for, and select the Set Working Folder option on the File menu. The Set Working Folder dialog box opens. Type in the name of the working folder or select it from the Folders list; then click OK (see Figure 20-15). If the folder does not exist, click the Create folder button, or click the OK button and then click Yes when asked to create the new folder.

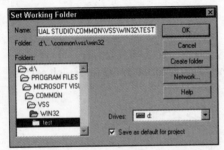

Figure 20-15: To set the project's working folder, type the folder name or select it from the list.

Checking out files

Select the project to check the files out from. A list of files associated with the selected project are displayed in the right frame of the SourceSafe Explorer screen. Select those files from the contents to check out and select the Check Out option on the SourceSafe menu, and the Check Out dialog box opens. Enter a comment, if desired, for the file(s) being checked out, and click OK. Notice that when a file is checked out, the file icon has a red check mark in it.

Note   A check out, as well as several other actions such as check in or undo check out, can also be done on an entire project by selecting just the project from the list and then performing the desired action.

Checking in files

Select the checked-out file, and click the Check In option on the SourceSafe menu. The Check In dialog box opens. Enter a comment if desired, and click OK (see Figure 20-16). Checking a file back in saves any changes made to that file in the SourceSafe database. Checking the Keep checked out option checks the file back in, saves the current version in the SourceSafe database, but maintains the check out status of that file. Checking the Remove local copy option deletes the copy in the working folder.

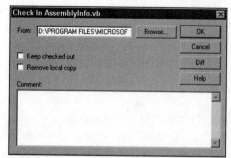

Figure 20-16: You can choose to keep the file checked out or to remove the local copy.

Undoing check out

Select the checked-out file, and select the Undo Check Out option on the SourceSafe menu. The Undo Checkout dialog box opens. Choose the action to perform on the local copy (see Figure 20-17), and click OK. Undoing a check out checks the file back in, but no changes are saved. Replace the local copy overwrites it with the version from SourceSafe; Leave local copy keeps it as is; Delete deletes it from the working folder.

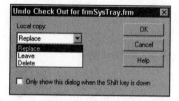

Figure 20-17: Select the action to take on the local copy of the file when undoing a check out.

Getting latest version of a file

To get the latest version of a file or project, select the file or project from the list, and select the Get Latest Version option on the SourceSafe menu. The Get dialog box opens (see Figure 20-18). By default, it copies the latest version into the current working directory. SourceSafe compares the version located in the working directory with the latest version in its database. If the files are identical, no action is taken.

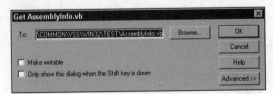

Figure 20-18: Type in or browse to the location to get the latest version. By default, this location is set to the working folder.

Sharing files

Sharing project files allows the same file to be used across multiple projects. When that file gets changed in any project, the change affects all projects that share that file. When a file is shared, the file icon changes to that shown in the highlighted file in Figure 20-19. To share a file, select the project to share a file with and then select the Share option on the SourceSafe menu. The Share With dialog box opens. In the pop-up window, select the file(s) to share, and click Share (see Figure 20-20). The selected file(s) are then shared with the selected project. When one copy of the shared file is checked out, it is shown as being checked out in all locations. A file can be shared with multiple projects.

Name	User	Date-Time	Check Out Folder
Web.config		8/09/01 12:28p	
WebForm1.aspx		8/09/01 12:28p	
WebForm1.aspx.resx		8/09/01 12:28p	
WebForm1.aspx.vb		8/09/01 12:28p	

Figure 20-19: Shared files have a different icon.

Branching files

Branching a file is similar to sharing a file except that the change made in one branch does not affect other branches. Each branch is edited independently. The branches can be merged together, but a merge in one location does not merge all branches.

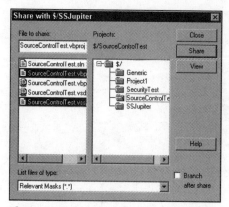

Figure 20-20: Select the file you want to
share from the list, and click the Share button.

If a file is already shared, it can be branched by selecting it and then clicking the
Branch option on the SourceSafe menu. The Branch dialog box displays. Enter a
comment for the branch, if desired. This branches the selected shared file only. If
the file is shared in multiple locations, the other locations continue as shared.

If the file is not shared, branching a file follows the same steps as sharing a file,
except that the Branch after share check box should be checked in the dialog box
(see Figure 20-21).

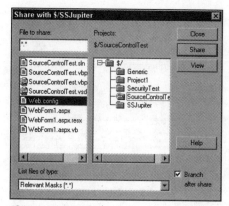

Figure 20-21: To branch an unshared file,
you access the same dialog box shown
in Figure 20-20.

To merge a one-branched file with another, select the branched file and then select
the Merge Branches option from the SourceSafe menu. A pop-up box (see Figure
20-22) opens and shows the branch locations of the file. Select the location of the
branch to merge in, and click the Merge button to open the comment box. If
desired, enter a comment and then click OK.

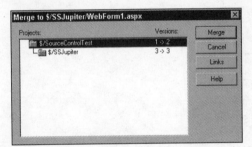

Figure 20-22: Select the branched file you want to merge and then click the Merge button.

If no conflicts are found, a message is displayed in a pop-up box to notify the user, and the program asks to check the file back in. If the file was checked out before the merge, it doesn't ask to check it back in.

If conflicts are found, a window should then open up with three panes. In the top-left pane is the selected file. The top-right pane is the file being merged into the selected file. The bottom pane shows what the merged file looks like after the merge is complete. Any conflicts between the files are highlighted with a border signifying the conflicting text. Clicking one of the highlighted conflicting areas adds that text into the final version (see Figure 20-23). Both changes can be kept by right-clicking one of the conflicts and selecting Apply Both Changes (see Figure 20-24). Once all conflicts are resolved, save the new file and close the window.

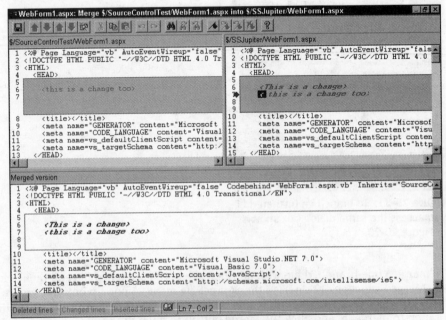

Figure 20-23: Click a highlighted area to add the text to the final version.

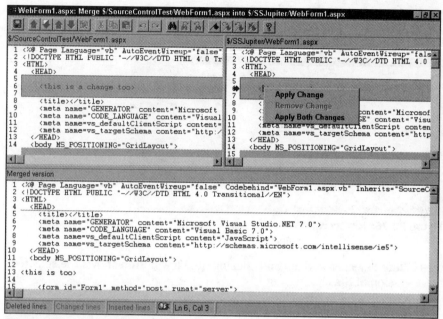

Figure 20-24: Right-clicking opens a context menu giving the option to apply the current change or both changes.

Using Show History

Selecting the file and selecting the Show History option on the Tools menu brings up the history of the file. The file history shows all check-in times and dates for the file, and allows the developer to see any changes made between checkouts. Enter any parameters to filter the history list by in the History Options dialog box that displays, and click OK. The file history can be filtered by a date range, by the user making the change, or both. To see the entire history, leave all the fields blank and click OK (see Figure 20-25).

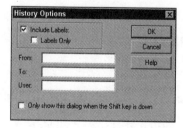

Figure 20-25: To filter the file history, enter a date range, a user, or both.

From the pop-up window that displays, a number of options are available (see Figure 20-26).

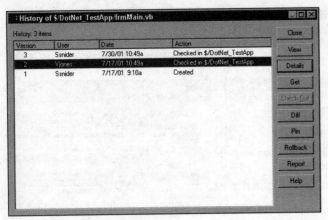

Figure 20-26: History window

- ✦ **View:** Selects a version and clicking the View button shows the selected version of the file.

- ✦ **Details:** Clicks the Details button shows the comments associated with the selected version.

- ✦ **Get:** Gets the latest version of the file.

- ✦ **Check Out:** Checks the file out.

- ✦ **Diff:** Selects two versions and then clicking the Diff button shows the differences between the two selected versions.

- ✦ **Pin/Unpin:** Pins or unpins the file. When a file is pinned, performing a Get Latest Version retrieves the pinned version. Unpinning the version reverts to using the latest version of the file.

- ✦ **Rollback:** Performs a rollback on a file discards all versions after the selected one. This command cannot be undone. Rolling back to a version that is earlier than a pinned version is not allowed.

Accessing SourceSafe through the Visual Studio .NET IDE

Most of the functionality of SourceSafe can be accessed through the Visual Studio .NET IDE through the Source Control submenu located on the File menu. The options available from here perform the same functions that they do inside of Visual SourceSafe Explorer (see Tables 20-1 and 20-2, and Figure 20-27). Many of the functions are also available by right-clicking a file in the Solutions Explorer window.

Table 20-1
SourceSafe Options for Visual Studio .NET Projects Already in SourceSafe

Command	Function
Open Project From Source Control	Copies a SourceSafe project into a working directory, and opens it in the Visual Studio .NET IDE.
Add Project From Source Control	Adds a project from SourceSafe into the current solution.
Exclude From Source Control	Excludes the selected file from being under source control. Files excluded from source control have a red circle with a line through it next to the filename (see Figure 20-27).
Change Source Control	Allows the project SourceSafe provider to be changed to a new resource location, such as from a primary server to a backup server.
Get Latest Version	Gets the latest version of the selected file.
Get	Gets the latest version of the selected file.
Check Out	Checks the selected file out. A checked-out file has a red check mark next to its filename in the solution explorer window (see Figure 20-27).
Check In	Checks the selected file in. A checked-in file has a blue lock next to its filename in the Solution Explorer window (see Figure 20-27).
Undo Check Out.	Performs an Undo Checkout on the currently selected file.
History	Brings up the history for the selected file.
Share	Brings up a dialog box to share files with the current project and then adds the shared file(s) to the current project.
Compare Versions	Shows the differences between the local copy and the copy in the SourceSafe database.
SourceSafe Properties	Shows the properties for the selected file, including any comments, the check-out status, any shares of the file, and its location in the SourceSafe database.
Microsoft Visual SourceSafe	Runs the Visual SourceSafe Explorer.
Refresh Status	Refreshes the SourceSafe status of the solution files.

Table 20-2
SourceSafe Options for Visual Studio .NET Projects Not Yet in SourceSafe

Command	Function
Add Solution to Source Control	Adds the current solution, including each project, to the SourceSafe database.
Add Selected Projects to Source Control	Adds only the selected project to the SourceSafe database.

Figure 20-27: Checked-out, checked-in, and excluded files

Good SourceSafe Practices

Source control makes the jobs of the developer and project manager easier, but its effectiveness is lessened when it is used incorrectly. Following are some good practices to follow when using SourceSafe:

✦ Check out only those files that are to be modified, not the entire project. This is especially important in multiple developer projects. Unless the SourceSafe administrator allows for multiple checkouts, checking out an entire project makes all the project files unavailable to other developers.

✦ Check files back in on a regular basis. Checking the file in saves the changes to the SourceSafe database providing a backup of the file. A file can be checked in to save changes only by selecting the Keep Checked Out option when checking the file in (refer to Figure 20-16).

✦ Files should always be checked in at the end of the workday or when leaving the workstation unattended for extended periods of time.

✦ Comment files when checking out or checking in. Identifying which bug was fixed or what enhancements were made helps to track progress, and it is valuable for future developers who may not be familiar with the project.

✦ Back up the SourceSafe database regularly.

✦ When making changes to shared files, communicate those changes to other developers so that they are aware of any possible problems that may arise in their projects that use the shared file.

✦ Add any new projects to SourceSafe as soon as they are created.

Summary

This chapter described only a small part of the capabilities of Microsoft's Visual SourceSafe. SourceSafe is a powerful tool for developers and project managers, and it has many more features not covered in this chapter. As with any tool, however, it should be used correctly to get the maximum benefit.

✦   ✦   ✦

Data Access

Introduction to Data Access in .NET

by Kevin Grossnicklaus

◆ ◆ ◆ ◆

In This Chapter

A history of Microsoft data access technologies

Data access today

An overview of ADO.NET

◆ ◆ ◆ ◆

With the release of Visual Basic .NET and the .NET Framework, Microsoft has provided the foundation and services to allow Visual Basic developers to develop applications with a wide degree of complexity that target a variety of business problems. This variety of applications brings with it the need to access and manipulate an equally diverse array of data sources and formats. Although data access has typically been associated with relational databases such as SQL Server and Oracle, the rise of the Internet and a computing environment built on much more open standards has brought about the need to think of data in a much more abstract format, such as that provided by XML.

It is upon this principle, thinking of data as XML and XML as data, that Microsoft has designed and built its next generation of data access technologies called ADO.NET. ADO.NET serves as not only a major evolutionary step from a decade of experience providing data access solutions, but also a complete new way of looking at data access. In this chapter, you look at Microsoft's history of providing solutions for data access and how these solutions have evolved into what has become ADO.NET. You also see how ADO.NET provides a standard and uniform method for accessing and manipulating very diverse and complex data through a single object model.

A History of Microsoft Data Access Technologies

Since the release of SQL Server 1.0 in 1989, Microsoft has played a key role in providing developers with the tools necessary to develop database applications. These tools targeted not only their own ever-evolving database products, but also thousands of other databases and data sources that have appeared throughout the industry. By providing a widely adopted set of APIs and COM implementations that database vendors could implement, Microsoft has made it possible for thousands of data sources to be made accessible through a uniform set of data access clients.

It is also important to realize that the features and functionality available today in ADO.NET are not only the direct result of Microsoft's many years of experience developing these types of solutions, but also the inherent evolution of data from a platform-dependant aggregation of data through such technologies as ODBC drivers or OLEDB providers to a platform-agnostic format represented in an industry-standard XML format.

To truly understand the inherent evolution of data into a common format and the power and simplicity behind this concept, you must first take a look back at Microsoft's history of providing the technologies that have become ADO.NET.

Open database connectivity

After the initial release of the Microsoft SQL Server product, which was developed in tandem with Sybase SQL Server, Microsoft saw the need to address the issue of providing a standard method of connectivity that would provide developers the means to utilize SQL Server from their applications. To address this need, as well as the much greater and industry-wide problem of having a large variety of disparate data sources and APIs, Microsoft, IBM, and a number of other manufacturers teamed up to develop a standard API that would simplify interoperability between their various database products. As a result of its work towards this end, Microsoft provided what was called the Open Database Connectivity API, or ODBC.

The ODBC specification provided database vendors with a standard low-level API for which they could provide database specific "drivers." By developing against a driver specific to a particular database, application developers were provided with a standard interface with which to interact with that database. This allowed developers much greater freedom when selecting a database to use for a particular application because they weren't tying themselves into an extremely proprietary and cryptic API, and the possibility existed for changing databases without a major rewrite of the API specific code.

Since its inception, ODBC has grown to become the most widely accepted interface for accessing not only nearly every popular relational database, but also a wide variety of nonrelational data sources. As time passed, the primary drawback of using the ODBC API was the fact that, as development tools such as Visual Basic evolved and allowed a much more rapid software lifecycle, it was not always easy to use a low-level API such as ODBC to provide data access. And although the existence of a standard API for direct data access to all data sources meant a much more standardized development community, as you see, it wasn't until the introduction of higher-level, object-oriented, and available means of accessing the ODBC API that the dream of simplified data access came closer to reality.

Visual Basic 3.0

Many of the developers who were fortunate enough to be using version 2.0 of Visual Basic to develop applications would agree that the adoption of Visual Basic by corporate developers really began in 1993 with the release of Visual Basic 3.0. It was with this release that Microsoft first provided Visual Basic developers with a method to easily connect to a variety of data sources and build much more robust, data-driven applications. With this new capability, corporations could take advantage of Visual Basic's inherent rapid application development strengths to quickly build solutions that utilized new and existing databases throughout their organizations. With VB 3.0, the two primary technologies that made this possible were the Jet database engine and a revolutionary new object model called Data Access Objects.

Jet database engine

The Jet database engine was initially developed as the core database engine built into the Microsoft Access database, and all development from within Access used the Jet engine to interact with the underlying database objects. Until the release of VB 3.0, this engine was specific to Access, and its features could not be used from any other product. Included with the release of VB 3.0, Microsoft shipped a version of the Jet engine that allowed developers to utilize the services provided by Jet to interact with any database that provided an ODBC driver. Although certain restrictions did apply to the types of databases and functionality a developer could expect, the Jet engine provided the perfect tool for VB developers to utilize data from any ODBC data source without having to resort to low-level API programming.

 Note ISAM, an acronym for Indexed Sequential Access Method, is a method for accessing database records based on an index. Although all records are stored sequentially, indexes are available that provide quick data access, regardless of whether data is accessed sequentially or randomly.

The initial focus of the Jet engine was on ISAM databases, such as Microsoft Access, Foxpro, or DBase. Although these databases did not support many of the advanced features available in a large, enterprise-wide RDMS such as stored procedures or server-side queries, they provide the basis for countless database solutions built with Visual Basic.

Because the Jet engine did allow the flexibility of utilizing any underlying ODBC driver, it provided a standard interface to a growing number of data sources, which allowed it to become an extremely popular data-access solution, even with its noticeable drawbacks.

One of the primary problems of early adoption of the Jet database engine through VB was its sheer size, which came in at more than one megabyte in memory during use. Due to the power of the average desktop computer in the early '90s, this was a hefty chunk to bite off for your standard database application. As its size implies, the Jet engine also provided a *thick* layer between the client application and the database that served to add a large amount of overhead to even the most basic database functions. Another serious architectural flaw imposed by this early version of Jet was the fact that all query processing occurred on the client, which meant that any client request for a small subset of data required that the entire table's data be moved across the network and onto the client computer, where the filtering occurred within the Jet engine itself. Although this type of client-side processing is usually imposed by the ISAM database itself if it doesn't provide support for performing this type of filtering on the server, Jet did not provide the capability to take advantage of the server-side queries where they were available. As the size and complexity of database applications grew, this was often an unacceptable solution for most projects.

DAO

One of the key reasons why VB 3.0 and this early version of the Jet Engine, version 1.1, gained such widespread acceptance was the inclusion of an abstract object model for interacting with the Jet engine. This object model, called Data Access Objects (DAO), provided a simple and flexible method for connecting to and manipulating data in any data source compatible with the Jet engine. Although the use of DAOs was still subject to the architectural limitations imposed by the Jet engine, the simplicity of data access through the DAO structure allowed developers to quickly develop robust and powerful database applications in VB.

DAO provided developers with more than just a standard object model; it provided a platform for third-party vendors to begin building what would turn into a huge market of data-bound controls and widgets. This new capability to rapidly build database applications using DAO served to increase demand for tools and controls that made many of the more difficult development tasks easier.

As new versions of Access and Visual Basic were released, and new features and functionality were added to the underlying Jet engine, the DAO object model also grew to become a much more powerful data-access tool utilized by millions of VB developers worldwide.

Visual Basic 4.0

As the popularity of Visual Basic in the corporate environment began to skyrocket with the release of VB 3.0 and the sudden availability of data-access tools, Microsoft began to build on those tools and address the architectural and functional limitations they imposed. And with the next release of VB 4.0, Microsoft not only extended the functionality already available through the DAO/Jet paradigm, but also delivered two new database-access methods that enabled developers to take advantage of the growing power of full RDMS systems.

VBSQL

Visual Basic 4.0 included support for a SQL Server-specific API, called VBSQL, which provided VB developers with a low-level API for connecting directly to a SQL Server database. This API, built around the C-Based DB-Library, served as a lightweight and high-speed interface that was relatively easy to code when using VB. Although VBSQL provided a great solution in specific situations, the fact that it could be used only to connect to a SQL Server database, which didn't have a significant market share in the early '90s, severely hindered its acceptance by the development community. Also, as more object-oriented and database-neutral methods for database access became available, developers became less likely to code directly in a database-specific API.

RDO

Also included in VB 4.0 was a new object model for data access called Remote Data Objects, or RDO. The inclusion of RDO was an attempt to address a number of design and scalability issues that developers were currently facing when developing large distributed client/server applications with DAO and Jet. Although the use of DAO and Jet required a heavy amount of processing and memory to be utilized on the client, RDO provided a much smaller and faster client-side object model while allowing the RDMS system to bear the brunt of all the processing. This type of architecture was not intended to replace the DAO/Jet data access method, which was still suitable for Access and other ISAM databases; instead it, allowed developers to take advantage of the features provided by more powerful and full-featured databases such as SQL Server and Oracle.

To provide its functionality, RDO served as a thin object interface directly to the underlying ODBC drivers. The RDO object model consisted of just 10 objects, as compared to the 17 objects provided by DAO. This significant decrease in the number of objects is related to the fact that RDO allowed the back-end data store to handle a lot of database-specific tasks, such as user accounts and security. By allowing the database to handle this type of functionality, the RDO object model did not need to include specific object interfaces to expose them to developers.

OLEDB

In late 1996, after years of relying on underlying ODBC drivers and the complexity that such an implementation imposed, Microsoft announced the next key technology in its quest for a unified data access paradigm. This technology, called OLEDB, was built on Microsoft's new COM architecture. It took a somewhat different approach to providing a standard interface to data sources than ODBC.

Whereas the ODBC method of data access required that database vendors provide a product-specific driver that exposed a standard API that would, in turn, translate all API calls into the appropriate database-specific actions, the OLEDB method focused on presenting data in a standard format. The implementation of OLEDB was based on the basic idea of implementing data *providers* and data *consumers*. With OLEDB, database vendors provide high-performance providers implemented as COM objects. These providers organize their underlying data into a consistent view of data and then make this data available as tables, rows, and columns. After the data was aggregated into this common view, data consumers could be developed to provide a consistent interface to this data. By providing the capability to view both structured and unstructured data in a common format, OLEDB allows consumers to use a standard syntax, such as SQL, to interact with a wide variety of disparate data sources and types.

Although the new OLEDB providers offered a significant performance increase over the older ODBC driver method due to much less overhead, Microsoft could not ignore the significant number of existing ODBC drivers on the market. Realizing this, and in an attempt to help speed adoption of this new data-access paradigm, the first OLEDB provider developed by Microsoft was for ODBC drivers. This additional layer allowed any OLEDB-compliant consumer to take advantage of all the existing ODBC-compliant data sources (albeit with an additional level of overhead) until a much faster database-specific OLEDB provider could be developed.

Due to the widespread adoption of Microsoft's ActiveX Data Objects, or ADO, the associated increase in available OLEDB drivers has grown significantly. The following is a just small list of some of the many data sources that can be accessed through a provided OLEDB provider today:

- ✦ Microsoft SQL Server databases
- ✦ Oracle databases
- ✦ Jet databases
- ✦ Microsoft OLAP servers
- ✦ Active Directory
- ✦ Microsoft Exchange Web Folders
- ✦ Microsoft Index Server
- ✦ Sybase databases
- ✦ Btrieve databases
- ✦ AS/400 (through Host Integration Server 2000)
- ✦ Text files
- ✦ Sharepoint Portal Server Document Storage (WSS)

It is important to note that by providing an OLEDB driver for all the data sources in the previous list, developers using ActiveX Data Objects (Microsoft's primary OLEDB consumer) can connect to and manipulate the underlying information in a consistent manner while utilizing the same object model. This extremely powerful concept has served as the basis for Microsoft's theory of Unified Data Access throughout the enterprise.

Visual Basic 6.0

By standardizing on OLEDB providers as the core technology for interacting with any type of relational or nonrelational data stores, Microsoft's next step was to provide developers with the necessary data consumer to be used by a multitude of client applications. This new consumer would have to build on the standard OLEDB provider concept by providing a powerful yet simple object-oriented interface to any OLEDB-exposed data source.

ADO

Since their introduction in 1996 as the de facto OLEDB consumer, ActiveX Data Objects, or ADO, have became the most widely adopted and most popular object-oriented, data-access technology ever developed by Microsoft.

The initial release of Microsoft's ActiveX Data Objects, or ADO 1.0, was initially used heavily only from Active Server Pages (ASP) to develop dynamic Web sites. By the time VB 6 was released, Microsoft included both its current OLEDB providers and the newest version of its ADO objects in a single data-access package called Microsoft Data Access Components (MDAC). The MDAC package, currently on version 2.7, continues to be a key redistributable package that contains the latest versions of OLEDB providers, as well as the latest versions of ADO. Microsoft also makes use of the MDAC package to distribute new versions of ODBC drivers and any additional data-access technologies required by developers to make the most of the tools and platforms available from Microsoft.

The ADO object model, consisting of just seven objects, provides developers the ability to query and manipulate data from any OLEDB-compliant provider. One key difference between the ADO object model and either DAO or RDO is the lack of a deep object hierarchy. Although DAO forced developers who wanted to retrieve even a small subset of data to traverse a deep object model down to the actual data, ADO developers can create and manipulate ADO `Recordset`-type objects directly, which allows them immediate access to the underlying data. This architecture requires developers to actually write much less plumbing code and get straight to the work of manipulating data, which means much less complexity in the data access itself. Also, because both OLEDB providers and the ADO objects themselves are built around Microsoft's COM and DCOM technologies, they are easily accessible from any development platform that supports COM automation.

Because the OLEDB providers offer a much more consisted view of data sources regardless of their underlying structure, Microsoft could develop a much cleaner and simpler object model in ADO than was previously available through DAO or RDO. Also, due to its rapid adoption and use in a wide variety of architecturally diverse applications, the ADO object model has evolved over the last few years to help address the growing disconnected nature of the Internet by providing such functionality as Remote Data Services, disconnected `Recordsets`, and XML-based persistence. Still, even with the addition of these new features, ADO does not always provide the optimal solution for data access in the disconnected world of the Internet.

Because most developers today think of their data in terms of the widely accepted ADO `Recordset` objects, and due to the fact that Microsoft has presented ADO.NET as the predecessor to ADO, this chapter takes some time to drill into one of the most key objects in the ADO architecture: the `Recordset`. For those developers who have no experience developing with the ADO object model, it is important to have a basic understanding of the ADO structure to appreciate the architectural decisions made in ADO.NET. And within the ADO architecture, no object plays as key a role as the `Recordset` when it comes to providing developers the flexibility to solve their data access needs with a single object model.

Recordsets

The entire development paradigm presented by ADO (and OLEDB) centers around the `Recordset` object. The `Recordset` object serves as a developer's primary interface when using ADO to interact with a database, effectively serving as a developer's window into the data store. All manipulation of the underlying data using ADO occurs through this window, and the ADO subsystem itself handles the details of making sure all changes are made back to the database. In essence, the `Recordset` object allows you to programmatically manipulate a subset of data from a database by using a variety of different objects, techniques, and cursor models. Each `Recordset` exposes a set of rows and columns that you can traverse to get or set the information you need. Because ADO serves to expose the functionality of the underlying OLEDB providers, the `Recordset` object provides a consistent and familiar interface regardless of the origin of a particular set of data.

One of the key drawbacks in the implementation of the ADO `Recordset` object has been the lack of a simple way to expose the extended types and features provided by any individual database or product in a standard fashion for developers to work with. Because multiple databases can have different underlying data structures for common data types such as strings and dates, the `Recordset` object simply manipulates all actual data values as *Variant data types*. This allows a great amount of flexibility and neutrality to the `Recordset` object when dealing with diverse data sources, but it has also provided ADO with its single biggest performance hit. By forcing every value of every field in an ADO `Recordset` to be accessed as a late bound Variant data type, a significant performance loss is incurred. This is a key feature that has been addressed in the implementation of ADO.NET.

> **Note**   In the initial versions of ADO, every object that needed a persistent database connection, such as the `Recordset` object, needed to keep a constant reference to an ADO connection object during the entire lifetime of the object. With the latest versions of ADO, Microsoft has provided the capability to disconnect a `Recordset` from a data source by removing the reference to its open database connection. This feature allows a `Recordset` to be viewed or modified away from the database while keeping track of all changes on the client. Once a reference to an open ADO connection object is restored, all the changes made to the `Recordset` while disconnected can be propagated back into the database in a single batch call.

Because most current Web applications developed on the Microsoft platform make use of ADO for their data access needs, Microsoft has evolved the current iteration of ADO to address some of the issues facing developers. ADO has served as a key piece in Microsoft's DNA platform strategy for highly distributed Web-based application development. And because the DNA platform has promoted the idea of distributed processing in logical components across machines, developers have needed a way to pass sets of data between processes and computers. This problem was initially addressed by providing the capability to use disconnected Recordsets in ADO. Although this solution had its advantages, it was still left with the overhead imposed by passing the thick object implementation of a Recordset across the network, which requires the overhead required by COM marshalling. This type of architecture also runs into significant barriers when dealing with Internet firewalls that do not easily accept such traffic as ADO Recordsets.

Another solution presented for this problem was Remote Data Services, or RDS. Although RDS allowed a proxy, stub method for performing database updates across the network, it was a very complicated solution with its own limitations that did not gain wide acceptance among developers. Another feature added to later versions of ADO to help address the transfer of data between machines was the capability to easily convert an entire ADO Recordset into an industry-standard XML format. Although this feature allowed the underlying data to be passed between processes and machines in a format that was much friendlier in a Web-based environment, it wasn't the cleanest implementation, and became a feature that few developers could take full advantage of. That said, it was this capability to transfer a set of data to and from an industry-standard XML format that eventually became the foundation for what would become ADO.NET.

Although this chapter hasn't spent a lot of time diving into the specifics of any object models (with the exception of the ADO Recordset), it is important to realize that there are a lot of similarities between DAO, RDO, and ADO. All three of these technologies share a lot of common characteristics in regards to the object models and interfaces exposed to developers. As you have seen, most of the key differences between each of the technologies lie in the underlying infrastructure that serves to provide their capabilities to connect to and manipulate data from a variety of sources.

When dealing with all Microsoft's previous implementations of data-access technologies, it is important to understand that they are all tied to the Microsoft Windows platform. Both the object models and the ODBC drivers or OLEDB providers that serve up the data are tied to Windows-specific implementations. Although the Windows platform provides an enormous base of users and applications to target with these kinds of technologies, the Internet has given rise to a more open and platform-agnostic environment built on standards such as HTML and XML. For these reasons, as well as to build upon the lessons learned from developers using previous Microsoft data-access technologies, it was important that Microsoft take a step back and assess the current development community and the types of issues facing developers today.

Data Access Today

Now that you have looked back at Microsoft's history of providing developers with the tools and technologies to manipulate data from its applications, you must look at the types of applications developers are focusing on today. The development of ADO.NET was not only focused on solving the problems that existed with the currently available methods of data access, but also on looking forward to see what types of applications developers will be building in the future.

With this goal in mind, most people would agree that the basic development community and focus have taken a dramatic shift toward the Internet and Web-based development for the better part of the last decade. Whereas client/server applications within an organization once targeted a single database with a consistent number of users, today's applications target a Web-server environment with possibly thousands of disconnected users who perform updates to one or more back-end databases. This Web-based environment has been built heavily on a large number of industry-adopted standards, such as TCP/IP, HTTP, HTML, and XML. The adoption of standards such as these has allowed the Internet, and applications built upon the Internet, to essentially transcend beyond a single platform or development tool. Not only has the Internet bridged a large number of platforms and operating systems, but with the wider availability of handheld devices, the Internet also provides a common platform for devices such as cell phones or PDAs to communicate. Also, with the rise in popularity of handheld devices, which are usually disconnected from any type of powerful database and are limited in the amount of available resources typically available on a desktop, the need has increased for a thinner, more disconnected form to manipulate relational data away from the server. This type of environment presents an entire new set of challenges than those specifically addressed by DAO, RDO, or even ADO.

Visual Basic and the Internet

For most VB developers, the nature of the Internet itself has probably created the most dramatic shift in their development structure. Whereas most VB developers have became familiar with building applications consisting of multiple forms and controls, all tied together by common variables and an extremely event-driven paradigm, the Web works on an entire different development model. Prior to the introduction of .NET, Web developers historically pieced applications together through a set of related but stateless pages that posted information from page to page to maintain a consistent programmatic flow. And until the release of the ASP.NET programming model as part of the .NET Framework, the differences in the basic development paradigm presented by both VB and the standard ASP Web structure provided a steep learning curve for most VB developers. Not only was the basic development model a significant change, but also finding the best way to utilize data access within each of these models presented a significant challenge to most developers. With traditional data-access methods, such as DAO, RDO, or ADO, this stateless environment required all the base objects (`Connections`, `Recordsets`, and so on) to be rebuilt during each call to a page. This overhead was unavoidable due to the need to maintain a stateless and scalable Web-based architecture. Also, as the concept of Web *farms* (applications running on a large number of identical Web servers) evolved, a large majority of the information an application requires from page to page was pushed back to the database. This required even more database interaction for applications that didn't generally use the database for the bulk of their work.

Enterprise Application Integration (EAI)

Another key concept being addressed by developers today is that of Enterprise Application Integration (EAI). As more diverse and powerful applications are being deployed throughout the corporate enterprise, a common interface for integration has became an integral piece to the enterprise puzzle. The complexity of integrating such disparate applications is only increased by the many hardware and software platforms that make up today's corporate environment. Manipulating and relating data from such a wide range of applications and platforms was another key feature Microsoft needed to address with its next generation of data access technology. Also, with products such as BizTalk Server 2000, Microsoft has begun to provide a standard platform for such things as EAI, which are built heavily on an XML-messaging paradigm. Knowing this direction, it became imperative that the next generation of data access tools provide developers with a way to easily manipulate XML documents from such products as BizTalk Server without requiring developers to learn an entire new set of development technologies.

With so many new directions for software development, Microsoft's next evolutionary step in data-access technologies would need to build on its past successes and solutions while providing the flexibility for developers to take advantage of the technologies and platforms available today. Although a new disconnected paradigm shift would be required, it needed a solution that still provided the type of connected access developers have become familiar with. It is with this flexibility in mind that Microsoft has presented the first release of its new ADO.NET Framework for data access.

Overview of ADO.NET

With the release of ADO.NET in the .NET Framework, Microsoft has provided not only an object model and infrastructure to facilitate data access, but also a complete new mindset for data access that differs from anything previously available. Before you begin examining the details of using the ADO.NET Framework in the next chapter, it is important to have an overview of the major pieces of the .NET data-access Framework to help provide a big picture of the architecture behind this technology.

XML = data, data = XML

As you have seen, prior versions of ADO relied on OLEDB providers to manipulate data into a consistent view. Although this was a revolutionary architecture at the time, it forced database vendors to standardize on Microsoft's specification for the format and structure of an OLEDB provider, as well as on the view in which the data should be presented. Also, these providers could be implemented only as COM objects on a Windows platform, which limited their use in cross platform scenarios. With the rise of XML as an industry-adopted standard for representing structured and hierarchical information, Microsoft saw the opportunity to see data in a way that would not impose such platform-specific implementation details.

The basic principle behind the ADO.NET implementation lies in the fact that all data is represented in an XML-based format. This allows vendors wishing to provide integration with relational databases or nonrelational structures to simply implement a new type of provider that manipulates their respective data stores into XML, and handles manipulating the returned XML back into a format understandable by the data store. This capability to consume XML as data also allows ADO.NET understand data from any XML-compliant application or platform.

Because XML has gained such wide industry adoption, ADO.NET supports viewing and manipulating XML data from any source through a very database-like object model. Most XML developers, prior to the .NET Framework, became accustomed to manipulating XML documents through an object structure modeled around the W3C specified Document Object Model, or DOM. With this structure, developers writing applications that edit XML documents have become familiar with utilizing a tree structure of various XML *nodes*. By traversing these nodes, developers have enjoyed complete control over the entire underlying XML document. In contrast, the DAO, RDO, and ADO object models presented a number of variations of a table/row/field metaphor for viewing data, which presented database developers a structure which was, hopefully, very similar to the way they viewed the underlying data that was being manipulated. As you see in the next couple of chapters, the .NET Framework offers a number of different possibilities for developers when manipulating XML documents. Because all underlying data in the .NET Framework is represented in a simple XML document, the choice of the object model for interacting with that data falls to the developers. ADO.NET provides a `DataSet` object that exposes a very simple table/row/field-like interface that should be familiar to database developers, whereas the XML objects provided by the .NET Framework allow a more DOM-like metaphor for manipulating the same data. Microsoft has provided a high level of overlap between these two methods for editing XML documents, which provides developers with a tightly integrated environment that offers complete control over the structure of and the data stored in the underlying XML document.

ADO.NET structure

The basic structure of the ADO.NET object model revolves around two separate groups of objects: `DataSets` and data providers. `DataSets` and their related groups of objects provide a database-neutral view of any data that can be exposed as an XML document. This structure allows developers to manipulate a disconnected and hierarchical view of data in a manner that should be very familiar to ADO developers. Appropriately, data providers serve as the low-level integration and mapping between XML documents, such as those manipulated by `DataSets`, and the underlying databases. Data providers essentially serve as the "bridge" between `DataSets` and data sources, which allow `DataSets` to essentially remain isolated from any specific data implementation or source. Beyond this "bridge" functionality between databases and `DataSets`, data providers also serve to provide all additional data source-specific functionality such as data types and commands.

As mentioned earlier, the ADO.NET structure not only differs significantly from the previous versions of ADO, the underlying mindset involved in taking full advantage of the ADO.NET Framework requires a new way of thinking about how applications are designed and built. Whereas ADO `Recordsets` allow developers to manipulate a single table or view at a time, a single ADO.NET `DataSet` can encapsulate a large group of disparate tables (possibly from different databases) while maintaining a consistent relationship between them all. It is possible to think of an ADO.NET `DataSet` as a complete disconnected relational database complete with tables, columns, constraints, and relationships. Developers have the ability to add tables, rows, and columns programmatically without any direct contact with an underlying data store. The `DataSet` even offers a host of other database-like features, such as the capability to define columns as being auto-generated, and handle all the implementation details on the client side without having to use the database for this type of functionality. To top it off, the entire relational structure can be passed safely from machine to machine as a simple XML stream, while retaining all structures and integrity. Clients can spend hours modifying any of the tables or data stored in a single `DataSet` without the need to ever open a database connection. Upon completion of all required changes, all modifications to each `DataSet` table can be propagated back to its own database. As you see, it is this kind of flexibility, which wasn't trivial in ADO, that provides developers with the tools to develop the next generation of distributed applications on the .NET Framework.

Although the next chapter focuses on how these two major halves of ADO.NET work together to provide a complete data access solution, you now take a high-level look at each of these major features to understand their importance in the overall ADO.NET design.

DataSets

Easily the most dramatic new addition to the ADO.NET architecture (and one that lacks easy comparisons to any specific feature in previous data access solutions) is the `DataSet`. As mentioned earlier, the `DataSet` provides an object model to manipulate one or more tables of data. The `DataSet` also provides the means to track and maintain relationships between tables, and enforce such constraints such as unique values and calculated fields.

Because the most obvious use of a `DataSet` is to hold and manipulate data, you must be aware of just how data gets into a `DataSet`. Although the most common scenario for populating a `DataSet` is through the use of a data provider, it is important to realize that a data provider is only one of many ways in which a `DataSet` can be loaded. Nor does a `DataSet` require any particular implementation of a driver, a provider, or anything else to be populated with data. A `DataSet`'s functionality is not tied to the existence of any other technology, and is available to be used whenever the need arises. As you begin to explore the details of the ADO.NET implementation in the next chapter, you see that there are many scenarios in which you may find that a `DataSet` is the optimum data structure to solve a specific problem, even when there is no database being used. `DataSets` can be used to manipulate any data that can be exposed as XML. For example, file-based configuration files can be loaded and manipulated quickly and easily by using an XML file format and a `DataSet`. It is also easily possible to load certain tables from one or more databases, certain tables from text files, and even programmatically create certain tables — all within the same DataSet.

DataSet object model

The root of the DataSet object model is the DataSet object itself, which handles all the base services for the entire underlying structure, such as serializing to and from XML. It is through the DataSet object that developers gain access to the many objects that work together to make up the entire DataSet object model. The following list gives an overview of each of the key objects that make up the DataSet object model:

✦ **DataTable:** This object represents a single table of data within a DataSet. A DataSet may contain multiple DataTable objects, each representing a logical table of data.

✦ **DataRow:** Each DataTable object in a DataSet contains a collection of zero or more DataRow objects representing the data within that table. Each DataRow object serves as an array of fields that are defined by the DataColumn collection discussed as follows.

✦ **DataColumn:** The DataColumn collection of a DataTable specifies information about the individual columns of data in each table. This schema information consists of a large number of properties beyond the standard name and data type of a specific column.

✦ **DataRelation:** The DataRelation collection exists directly off the root DataSet object, and specifies information regarding the specific table and column relationships that need to be maintained between two DataTable objects in a single DataSet.

✦ **DataConstraint:** A DataConstraint object provides a means for developers to specify constraints that must be enforced on a particular column in a DataTable.

All these objects work together to provide a very robust and dynamic object model that provides you with a powerful data-access solution. Although the next chapter provides much more detail about how they all work together and the function that each object adds to the structure, it is important now to realize how the structure is maintained as a whole.

DataSets and XML schema

When designing ADO.NET, one of the key pieces of information Microsoft gleaned from developers using its prior data-access technologies was the fact that most developers knew the schema of their databases at design time, and rarely needed to derive anything at runtime. For this reason, the ADO.NET Framework goes to great lengths to allow you to specify all you know about a data source at design time, and forego any unnecessary overhead when you actually need to interact with the database.

One of the most important concepts to grasp when dealing with `DataSets` and their schema is that they have no notion of databases. When dealing with a `DataSet`, there is no means to identify where the data came from or where the data goes when you are done editing it. This is an important concept to understand because it tells you that a `DataSet` behaves the same way, regardless of where the data originated. This is also important to note because it is dramatically different from the functionality provided by an ADO `Recordset`. When dealing with an ADO `Recordset`, the type of database you were currently connected to significantly affected your performance as well as the functionality available.

Now that you understand that a `DataSet` has no tie to a database and does not require a database for anything directly, you need to look at how a `DataSet` works with data and how it maintains a consistent schema for its data. A `DataSet` can be thought of as a database-like wrapper around an XML document that allows developers to manipulate that document, or data, in a fashion familiar to database developers. Put simply, a `DataSet` provides an XML parser that looks like a database object model.

Because a `DataSet` is simply a wrapper around an underlying XML document, you need to address how a `DataSet` derives its structure and then maps that structure to a database-like view for you to manipulate. If an XML document simply maintains structured data in an XML format, a `DataSet` needs a method to relate these various levels of elements and nodes into the tables, rows, and fields that a database developer would be familiar with.

To accomplish this task, the `DataSet` relies on an XML schema document (`www.w3.org/XML/Schema`) that describes the data the `DataSet` is currently manipulating. An *XML schema document* is an XML document that defines the structure and constraints of another set of one or more XML documents. An XML schema document defines which elements are included in an XML document, the structure and relationship between those elements, the data types of those elements, and a wealth of more detailed information about the document's structure. By relying on an industry-standard format such as XML schema to define the structure of the underlying XML document, a `DataSet` needs to maintain no database specific information to perform its function.

> **Note** Although an ADO.NET `DataSet` can represent the majority of its schema in an industry-standard XML schema document, it is important to realize that certain custom attributes are added to the document to help identify certain ADO.NET-specific features, such as which elements map to `DataTables` and which map to columns. When viewing the XML schema document, these ADO.NET-specific attributes can be identified with the `msdata:` prefix before the attribute name.

The first thing you need to identify about an XML schema document as it relates to a `DataSet` is where it comes from. This is an important issue to understand because it can have serious performance implications on any application built on the ADO.NET Framework. The structure of an ADO.NET `DataSet` can come from one of two possible places: It can be designed and built at design time, or the

`DataSet` can take a best guess at runtime through a process called *inference*. As you see in the next couple of chapters, the Visual Studio .NET development environment provides a powerful set of wizards and tools to design and build `DataSets`. The wizards can also be used to automatically generate all the XML schema documents required to utilize a `DataSet` at runtime, and these XML schema documents are added to your Visual Studio .NET projects with the `XSD` extension.

Before you decide on which of the two methods for determining the schema of a `DataSet` to use, you must examine the implications of each. First, you examine a little about the process that a `DataSet` must go through to infer the schema of an XML document. Given an XML document with no specified schema, the `DataSet` passes through the data to make its best guess as to which elements should be treated as `DataTables`, which should be treated as `DataRows`, and which should be treated as `DataColumns`. This process consists of an algorithm that makes decisions based on the XML document given, and applies a number of rules based on its content. This algorithm can determine structural properties such as multiple tables, as well as the relationships between them if enough of an XML structure exists. For those of you familiar with XML schema, the following list provides a little insight as to the decisions made by the `DataSet` when inferring schema:

- ✦ ComplexTypes map to DataTables
- ✦ Nested ComplexTypes map to Nested DataTables
- ✦ Key/Unique Constraints map to UniqueConstraints
- ✦ KeyRef values map to ForeignKeyConstraints
- ✦ Elements map to a DataTable if they repeat
- ✦ Elements map to a DataTable if they contain more than simple content
- ✦ Attributes become columns
- ✦ Relations are created for nested table-mapped elements
- ✦ Relations are created using hidden columns for parent/child relationships

As with any fairly detailed algorithm, it should be noted that this inference of schema imposes a significant amount of overhead on the process of loading a `DataSet`. This overhead becomes especially important if the process is something that occurs hundreds or thousands of times within a short timeframe in your application. Even if the overhead imposed by this schema inference is acceptable in certain situations, you should also realize that the capability to infer the schema of an XML document is entirely dependent on the specific instance of an XML document for which the schema is inferred. To demonstrate this point, review the following two XML documents:

```
<person>
    <name>Kevin Grossnicklaus</name>
    <address>123 East Main</address>
    <city>Shelby</city>
    <state>NE</state>
    <zip>12345</zip>
</person>
```

```
<person>
    <name>Kevin Grossnicklaus</name>
    <address>123 East Main</address>
    <address>P.O. Box 111</address>
    <city>Shelby</city>
    <state>NE</state>
    <zip>12345</zip>
</person>
```

Although each of these examples contains a very similar XML structure, the ADO.NET DataSet would infer the schema of each of them in a very different way. The first example would be inferred as a DataTable called person, with five DataColumns: name, address, city, state, and zip. This seems pretty straightforward, and behaves very much as it appears it should. The second XML document would also create a DataTable called person, but this DataTable would contain only four DataColumns: name, city, state, and zip. The major difference lies in the existence of two address elements in the second XML document. Because the DataSet perceives the existence of two of the same element to constitute a complex type, it creates a child DataTable called address, which infers a significantly different structure than that of the first document. For this reason, it is important to understand the implications of allowing a DataSet to infer its own schema at runtime. Also, in situations in which certain pieces of schema are missing from a DataSet, it is possible to allow the appropriate data provider to query a specific data store for the pieces of schema when filling a DataTable. This type of schema usually consists of primary key information as well as maximum field length. Allowing the data provider to query the database for this information again provides such a significant hit to performance that it sometimes takes the underlying data provider longer to query the system tables for schema than it does to query and return the actual requested data. It is considerations such as these that make the alternative method of determining the structure of a DataSet all the more attractive.

That alternative method of providing structure for a DataSet is to provide the XML schema document at design time. It is also, as you find out, very easy to allow the tools provided by Visual Studio .NET to infer the schema of a DataSet at design time and then save the schema file with your project. This allows you to modify the schema by hand, should you need to, and saves you the overhead of runtime inference. The generated code simply has the DataSet load the schema from a file at runtime, and can configure the entire DataSet in one call. It is this capability to infer the schema at runtime that provides the Visual Studio .NET development environment with the means to provide strongly "typed" DataSets through a basic code-generation function.

Another of the biggest benefits of using XML schema to represent the structure of a DataSet is the fact that all of a DataSet's structure and data can be persisted into a single XML document. This provides an extremely powerful data-access paradigm when dealing with applications that are distributed amongst n-tiers. Whereas it was not considered an architecturally sound solution to pass ADO Recordsets from process to process and machine to machine, there is very little overhead required to do the same with an ADO.NET DataSet.

Data providers

Because `DataSets` have no notion of databases, and they maintain all their schema information and data in a disconnected object model, the ADO.NET Framework needed an object or set of objects to serve as the translation of specific databases and data sources to and from `DataSets`.

The solution to this problem was presented in the implementation of data providers, or the set of objects and interfaces that provide all of the database-specific implementations used to access data. Another one of the key design considerations behind the ADO.NET implementation was to develop a factored set of components that placed more of the specific implementation details back into the hands of the developers. Due to the inherent object-oriented nature of the .NET Framework, this idea allowed database vendors to provide their own set of managed classes, which extended the functionality of the base services. This opportunity to provide a specific implementation that targeted a specific data source allows database and tools vendors to extend and optimize the Framework with extensions specific to a tool or product. The most obvious example of this concept can be seen with the implementation of data providers.

As you have seen, the entire foundation of ADO.NET as a data access tool is built on the fact that all data can be represented by XML. In the past, implementations such as OLEDB served as the intermediary layer that converted structured data from any source into a common structure that was usable by the front-end data "consumer". Because the .NET Framework views data in a disconnected format, ADO.NET required a set of base components that could accomplish the following tasks:

✦ Open a connection to the targeted data source

✦ Retrieve any requested data from the data source, and parse the results into the appropriate format (including, as you have seen, schema information)

✦ Accept data, and map the results into the appropriate insert, update, or delete actions to the underlying data store

✦ Read data quickly through a high-performance, forward-only stream when needed

✦ Raise the appropriate data source specific error information to the client should the need arise

✦ Provide object-oriented implementations of data source-specific data types

Although implementations such as OLEDB hid most of these details from the developers, ADO.NET data providers expose them programmatically, so the developer has more control over a specific implementation—both at design time and at runtime. For this reason, ADO.NET data providers can be thought of as managed equivalents of OLEDB providers.

To accomplish the tasks, Microsoft implemented the base data provider through six distinct objects:

✦ `Connection`: A data source connection similar to the `Connection` object exposed in ADO. Used to maintain information required by a provider to connect to a particular data source.

✦ `Command`: An object representing a single SQL command to be executed against a data source. Used by both the `DataReader` and the `DataSet` to retrieve or update information from the data source.

✦ `Parameter`: A `Parameter` object used to modify the `Command` object with con-text-specific information. It is similar to the `Parameter` object utilized by ADO `Connection` and `Command` objects.

✦ `DataReader`: A high-performance, forward-only cursor for quickly retrieving and viewing data from a data source

✦ `DataAdapter`: A multipurpose object used as a standard method to populate a `DataSet` with data from a specific `DataCommand` object, as well as to recon-cile all changes made to a disconnected `DataSet` by mapping each returned row to the appropriate insert, update, or delete `DataCommand` object.

✦ `Transaction`: An object controlled by the `Connection` object that allows the programmatic control of transactions through ADO.NET.

These six objects provide the base functionality and structure required by an ADO.NET data provider when dealing with database access through the .NET Framework. With the initial release of the .NET Framework, Microsoft is providing three derived implementations of this provider model, each optimized to target a specific database or driver. The first, the SQL managed provider, is an implementa-tion that bypasses all intermediary APIs, such as ODBC and OLEDB, and provides access to Microsoft SQL Server (Versions 7+) directly. As the next chapter dis-cusses, by providing an implementation such as this that can expose the same interface and bypass these layers of overhead, there are significant performance gains when dealing with a SQL Server database. The remaining two providers, an OLEDB provider and an ODBC direct provider, allow you access to any data sources supported by either of these two industry-standard protocols. It is by providing support such as this for all ODBC- and OLEDB-supported data sources that Microsoft hopes to help speed adoption of the revolutionary new data tools pro-vided in ADO.NET.

Although the next chapter goes into great detail about the details of implementing solutions utilizing these objects, it is appropriate here to point out how different data providers are delivered in ADO.NET. First, the ADO.NET Framework specifies only the interfaces that make up the base implementation of a data provider. Each implementation provides its own set of objects that implement these base inter-faces. Even though the .NET Framework provides namespaces to shield developers from ambiguous object names, each of the initial data providers provides object implementations with a unique set of names.

To help understand this point, you can examine the SQL Server data provider that ships with the .NET Framework. All data provider objects specific to the SQL Server data provider reside in the `System.Data.SqlClient` namespace, but each of the objects provided as part of this provider also has the SQL prefix before its name. For example, the `Command` object is implemented as `SQLCommand` in the SQL Server provider, and the `Connection` object is implemented as `SQLConnection`. It should come as no great shock, then, to realize that the OLEDB data provider resides in the `System.Data.OleDB` namespace, and each object is implemented with the OleDB prefix: `OleDBCommand`, `OleDBConnection`, `OleDBDataAdapter`, and so on.

It is important to realize that each of these data providers implements a set of base interfaces. Although it is possible and encouraged to provide functionality beyond these base sets of interfaces that allow vendors to provide their own specific implementation details, it is important to realize that when true database neutrality is a priority, you can develop against the interfaces themselves, and maintain the ability to plug and play different providers at any time. Although most of the code examples presented in the next chapter utilize the SQL Server provider for speed purposes, examples demonstrate development directly against the interfaces.

Summary

As you have seen in this chapter, the ADO.NET Framework of data access technologies has been designed to allow you to implement an entire new breed of distributed technologies built on open standards such as XML. The chapter helped to set the stage for the change in the overall data-access mindset that needs to occur to take full advantage of the features offered by the exciting new Framework. And although this chapter served to provide a high-level view of the objects and technologies that work together to make up the ADO.NET architecture, you spend the next chapter diving into the technical aspects of building solutions upon this Framework.

✦   ✦   ✦

ADO.NET

by Kevin Grossnicklaus

◆   ◆   ◆   ◆

In This Chapter

Accessing ADO.NET
features and
namespaces

Using ADO.NET

Data providers

DataSets

◆   ◆   ◆   ◆

As you learned in the last chapter, to take full advantage
of the powerful features provided by the ADO.NET
Framework, you have to develop an entirely new mindset in
regards to data access. Although many of the most common
data-access techniques required in today's development environment have been greatly simplified, it requires a strong
familiarity with a new set of objects and the manner in which
they interoperate. It is important to note, however, that even
with an entirely new manner for accessing data, Microsoft has
put a lot of effort into making the migration to ADO.NET from
ADO as simple as possible. ADO developers should have little
trouble adjusting to the objects and interfaces exposed by
ADO.NET, but might have a more difficult time determining
the best use of these tools.

Although a complete reference of these features is beyond the
scope of this book, this chapter attempts to serve as a detailed
introduction to many of the more powerful and commonly
used features associated with the ADO.NET Framework. Also,
all data access in this chapter occurs in code, not through the
use of the Visual Studio .NET wizards or other data tools.
Taking full advantage of these timesaving features requires a
firm understanding of the underlying objects and functions
that the Visual Studio .NET environment can help automate.
For this reason, this chapter develops everything the hard
way; the next chapter demonstrates how to use all the tools
available to help automate some of the more tedious programming tasks associated with ADO.NET.

Accessing ADO.NET Features
and Namespaces

Before you can start to take advantage of the features
provided by ADO.NET, you must know how to make these
features available from your VB .NET applications.

Because the ADO.NET objects are provided as part of the base classes of the .NET Framework, they can be made available to a Visual Basic .NET program by adding reference to the `System.Data.dll` from within your application.

Adding a reference to an application can be done in a variety of ways, but the easiest is probably to right-click the `Resources` folder of your project under the Solution Explorer window. After doing this, a context menu appears, in which you may select Add Reference. From the following dialog box, you may add the reference to the `System.Data.dll` by selecting it from the list of .NET components.

Now that you have added a reference to the ADO.NET objects to your project, you need to be aware of the .NET namespaces that make up this collection of tools. By being familiar with the locations of each of the various pieces of the ADO.NET objects within the .NET namespace hierarchy, you have an easier time locating the pieces you need. The root of the ADO.NET objects lies in the System.Data namespace.

Table 22-1 provides a brief description of the .NET namespaces that contain the ADO.NET structures.

Table 22-1 ADO.NET Namespaces	
Namespace	*Description*
System.Data	This namespace contains all major components of the DataSet object model.
System.Data.SqlTypes	A collection of Microsoft SQL Server-specific data types.
System.Data.SqlClient	A Microsoft SQL Server-specific data provider.
System.Data.OleDb	A managed data provider optimized for OleDB providers.
System.Data.ODBC	A managed data provider optimized for ODBC drivers.

Using ADO.NET

Now that you know where to find the objects in ADO.NET, you can begin by taking a look at some of the more common tasks available from this technology. As you see in the next chapter, the Visual Studio .NET IDE provides a number of tools to automate a large number of data access tasks, such as adding ADO.NET connections to your project. Although using these tools might be the quickest and easiest way to perform some of the more basic data access tasks, this section demonstrates how to perform these tasks without the use of these tools.

Understanding data providers

Before you get into how to manipulate and change data through a `DataSet` object, you should focus on the objects that make up a data provider. The majority of the samples provided in this chapter make use of the SQL Server provider (`System.Data.SqlClient`). Although some of the examples demonstrate using other providers, it is important to realize that all the providers implement the same functionality and base set of objects.

Because each data provider targets a different type of data connection, each implements its own set of objects that expose a standard interface. Also, it is important to note that each provider provides a separate set of objects, each having a unique name. What this means is that the SQL provider implements a set of objects with names preceded by a `SQL` prefix, and the OleDB provider implements a similar set of objects exposing the same interfaces, but with names preceded by an `OleDB` prefix. These sets of objects are also located within unique namespaces. Thus, when you wish to target a SQL server database, you can use the SQL provider located in the System.Data.SqlClient namespace and containing objects such as `SqlCommand` and `SqlConnection`. When targeting a database to which there is only an existing OleDB connection, you can use the OleDB provider that is located in the System.Data.OleDB namespace. The same objects in the OleDB namespace would be called `OleDBCommand` and `OleDBConnection`.

Table 22-2 presents each of the base ADO.NET data provider interfaces and their associated implementation for the two major providers:

Table 22-2 Provider Interfaces and Objects			
Object	**Base Interface**	**SQL Server Provider**	**OLEDB Provider**
Connection	IDBConnection	SQLConnection	OleDBConnection
Command	IDBCommand	SQLCommand	OleDBCommand
DataReader	IDataReader	SQLDataReader	OleDBDataReader
DataAdapter	IDataAdapter	SQLDataAdapter	OleDBDataAdapter
Transaction	IDBTransaction	SQLTransaction	OleDBTransaction

Throughout the rest of this chapter, generic provider objects, such as the Command and Connection objects, are simply called Command and Connection. When you need to implement these objects in code, this chapter specifies object names such as `SQLCommand` and `SQLConnection` to identify the correct provider.

Connections

When dealing with ADO.NET data providers, the obvious starting point is the Connection object, which provides the basis for which all the other ADO.NET data provider objects acquire and maintain their connections with their associated data stores. If you are familiar with ADO Connection objects, you should be instantly familiar with the Connection objects implemented in ADO.NET.

The Connection objects included by data providers each provide at least two constructor overrides. Listing 22-1 demonstrates connecting to databases in .NET using the ADO.NET Connection object.

Listing 22-1: Connecting to .NET Databases with the ADO.NET SQLConnection Object

```
'Create a Connection object setting it's location in the _
    constructor
Dim oConnection As New SqlClient.SqlConnection("Data _
    Source=(local); Initial Catalog=Northwind;User id=sa")

'Create an empty Connection object
Dim oConnection2 As New SqlClient.SqlConnection()
'Set it's location
oConnection2.ConnectionString = "Data Source=(local);Initial _
    Catalog= Northwind;User id=sa"
```

Notice that the `oConnection` and the `oConnection2` objects are identical, but you simplify the configuration of the first one by specifying the connection string when you instantiate your instance of the object. This type of override is a common occurrence in the .NET Framework, and taking advantage of it can greatly simplify your code.

As mentioned in the last chapter, each data provider provided in the .NET Framework must implement certain interfaces to make them consistent for all developers. But it is important to realize that this does not restrict the data provider vendors from extending the functionality of their providers beyond these interfaces to provide database-specific functionality and information. For example, the `SqlClient.SqlConnection` object exposes a method allowing runtime access to the `WorkstationID` of the client connecting to that data source through the `SqlConnection` object.

Also, although you are still using a connection string to specify the location of your database, certain features of the connection string are different — based on the current data provider. For example, when using the SQL Server data provider, you do not need to specify a specific driver implementation such as a DSN or OLEDB provider because this provider uses its own internal provider. Others, such as the .NET OLEDB data provider, require that an OLEDB provider be specified in the connection string.

Commands

Now that you have seen the simplicity of connecting to a data source through the Connection object, the chapter discusses Command objects. ADO.NET data providers use a Command object whenever data source-specific commands need to be executed against a specific data source. The most common types of commands to be executed against a data source are SQL commands, but the data provider model allows for a separate Command object to be implemented whenever this isn't possible.

In the following example, you create a simple Command object to execute a single `Select` statement against a server by using the `SqlCommand` implementation provided in the `System.Data.SqlClient` provider namespace.

```
'Create a new command object to be used to select all Customers
Dim oCommand As New _
    SqlClient.SqlCommand("Select * From Customers", oConnection)
```

In the previous example, you simply created a new `SqlCommand` object, and passed a valid SQL statement and a connection to its constructor. A Command object is actually a very basic, yet powerful, object that serves to associate valid commands (and their parameters) with data store connections and possibly transactions.

You created an instance of a new Command object directly in the previous example and associated it with the appropriate Connection object in the constructor. However, the Connection object also exposes a `CreateCommand` method that returns a new Command object that is already associated with that Connection object.

It is also important to note here that a Command object, as implemented by .NET data providers, offers no way to view any possible results of executing its command. Viewing and manipulating the results of executing a query fall to objects such as `DataReader` or `DataSet`. Command objects and SQL commands in general fall into two basic categories: those that return results and those that do not. When working with a Command object in ADO.NET, you are provided with a number of ways to execute a particular command. Some return object models you can use to view and manipulate the results; some do not return such objects.

Listing 22-2 provides a demonstration of one of the simplest methods for retrieving results from a Command object: creating a `DataReader` object. A `DataReader` object, as you see in the next section, provides a very fast, forward-only method for iterating through a view of data, such as is provided by executing a Command object.

Listing 22-2: Using DataReader to Retrieve Results from the Command Object

```
'Create a new command object to be used to select all Customers
Dim oCommand As New _
     SqlClient.SqlCommand("Select Top 5 CustomerID, ContactName _
     From Customers", oConnection)

'Execute the command and return the results in a datareader object
Dim oDataReader As SqlClient.SqlDataReader = _
     oCommand.ExecuteReader(CommandBehavior.CloseConnection)

'Iterate through all the resulting rows and debug.print the results
While oDataReader.Read()
     Debug.WriteLine(oDataReader.GetSqlValue(0))
     Debug.WriteLine(oDataReader.GetSqlValue(1))
End While
```

As shown in Listing 22-2, a Command object can be executed and a DataReader created with the resulting values by utilizing the ExecuteReader function to create the DataReader object. The Command object uses this same paradigm to execute queries that return other views of the data, or even provides an ExecuteNonQuery method that executes the Command object and does not return any data, as shown in Listing 22-3.

Listing 22-3: Using the ExecuteNonQuery Method of a Command Object

```
'Create a Connection object and set it's connection string _
 through the constructor
Dim oConnection As New _
     SqlClient.SqlConnection("Data Source=(local);Initial _
     Catalog=Northwind;User id=sa")
oConnection.Open()

'Create a Command object with a simple Select statement
Dim oCommand As New _
     SqlClient.SqlCommand("Delete From Customers Where CustomerID _
     Like 'A%'", oConnection)

'Execute the command
Dim nRowsDeleted As Integer = oCommand.ExecuteNonQuery()

'Close the connection
oConnection.Close()
```

Now that you understand the basics of how a Command object encapsulates a single SQL command into an object, you need to address some of the more common scenarios in which you would use this type of functionality in your applications. First, you would generally utilize a SQL Select statement with various parameters to retrieve a subset of data. Also, invoking SQL Insert, Update, and Delete statements directly require you to set certain parameters on the command before executing the statement. Another common use of the Command object is to execute stored procedures and pass the appropriate parameters to the database for the stored procedure.

In a fashion very similar to previous versions of ADO, the ADO.NET Command object exposes a collection of Parameter objects that can be used to build dynamic statements. Each Parameter object allows you to specify the parameter name, data type, length, and value. When the Command object is executed, the parameter names and values represented in the Command object's Parameters collection are used to replace the appropriate values in the Command objects text or to add the values to the end of a stored procedure call.

Listing 22-4 demonstrates the basic use of the Parameters collection.

Listing 22-4: **The Parameters Collection of a Command Object**

```
'Create a Connection object and set it's connection string _
 through the constructor
Dim oConnection As New _
    SqlClient.SqlConnection("Data Source=(local);Initial _
    Catalog=Northwind;User id=sa")
oConnection.Open()

'Create a Command object with parameters (Notice the parameter _
 has a name: @CustomerID)
Dim oCommand As New _
    SqlClient.SqlCommand("Select * From Customers Where _
    CustomerID Like @CustomerID", oConnection)

'Add a Parameter object to replace our single parameter _
 (@CustomerID)
Dim oCustomerIDParam As SqlClient.SqlParameter = _
    oCommand.Parameters.Add("@CustomerID", SqlDbType.NVarChar, 4)
oCustomerIDParam.Value = "A%"

'Execute the command
Dim oDataReader As SqlClient.SqlDataReader = _
    oCommand.ExecuteReader(CommandBehavior.CloseConnection)

'output the first column of each row
While oDataReader.Read
    Debug.WriteLine(oDataReader.GetSqlValue(0).ToString())
End While
```

Continued

Listing 22-4 *(continued)*

```
'Close the data reader and connection
oDataReader.Close()
oConnection.Close()
```

A key concept is the fact that the `Command.Text` property (which you set in the Command constructor) includes a SQL statement that contains a named parameter. The named parameter in Listing 22-4, `@CustomerID`, is replaced when the Command object is executed by the value of the Parameter object with the name of `@CustomerID`. Although this is a fairly straightforward concept, this is one of the places in the ADO.NET Framework in which there is significant difference between the functionality of the SQL data provider and the OleDB data provider. To demonstrate this difference, Listing 22-5 shows an example of a command with two parameters executed using the OleDB data provider:

Listing 22-5: **OleDBCommand Object with Two Parameters**

```
'Create a Connection object and set it's connection string _
 through the constructor
Dim oOleDbConnection As New _
    OleDb.OleDbConnection("Data Source=(local);Initial _
    Catalog=Northwind;User id=sa")
oOleDbConnection.Open()

'Create a Command object with two parameters
Dim oOleDbCommand As New _
    OleDb.OleDbCommand("Select * From Customers Where City = ? _
    And Region = ?", oOleDbConnection)

'Add a Parameter object to replace our first parameter (@City)
Dim oOleDbParam As OleDb.OleDbParameter = _
    oOleDbCommand.Parameters.Add("@City", _
    Data.OleDb.OleDbType.VarChar, 30)
oOleDbParam.Value = "St. Louis"

'Add another Parameter object to replace our second _
 parameter (@Region)
oOleDbParam = oOleDbCommand.Parameters.Add("@Region", _
             Data.OleDb.OleDbType.VarChar, 2)
oOleDbParam.Value = "MO"

'Execute the command
Dim oOleDbDataReader As OleDb.OleDbDataReader = _
    oOleDbCommand.ExecuteReader(CommandBehavior.CloseConnection)
```

```
'output the first column of each row
While oOleDbDataReader.Read
    Debug.WriteLine(oOleDbDataReader.GetValue(0).ToString())
End While

'Close the data reader and connection
oOleDbDataReader.Close()
oOleDbConnection.Close()
```

Although this sample appears very similar to Listing 22-4, albeit with two parameters and making use of the OleDB data provider, few significant differences exist. For example, the command text in Listing 22-4 (using the SQL provider) specified the parameter by name, or @CustomerID. In the previous example, you use question marks (?) in place of parameters. Although this is a key difference in the way parameters are represented in the command text between each of the data providers, it is even more important when adding parameters to the Parameters collection of the Command object. Although the SQL server provider specifies parameters by name, and the SqlParameter objects can be added with a specified name, the order in which they are added is arbitrary. This is not the case with the OleDBCommand and the OleDBParameters collection. Because the OleDBCommand object does not support named parameters, the order in which the question marks are replaced is directly related to the order in which the OleDBParameter objects are added to the OleDBParameters collection. This means that if you expect the first question mark to be replaced with the @City parameter, you need to add the @City Parameter object to the Parameters collection first.

One important use of the Parameters collection is to handle any output parameters returned by stored procedures. Listing 22-6 demonstrates how to specify a parameter as being an output parameter, and how to access its value after executing the stored procedure.

Listing 22-6: Using Output Parameters with the Command Object

```
'Create a Connection object and set it's connection string _
  through the constructor
Dim oConnection As New _
    SqlClient.SqlConnection("Data Source=(local);Initial _
    Catalog=Northwind;User id=sa")
oConnection.Open()

'Create a Command object with two named parameters
Dim oCommand As New _
    SqlClient.SqlCommand("spStoredProcedure @Input1, @Output1", _
    oConnection)
```

Continued

Listing 22-6 *(continued)*

```
'Add a Parameter object to replace our input parameter (@Input1)
Dim oParam As SqlClient.SqlParameter = _
    oCommand.Parameters.Add("@Input1", SqlDbType.Int)
oParam.Value = 123

'Add another Parameter object to replace our output _
 parameter (@Output1)
oParam = oCommand.Parameters.Add("@Output1", SqlDbType.Int)
oParam.Direction = ParameterDirection.Output

'Execute the command
Dim oDataReader As SqlClient.SqlDataReader = _
    oCommand.ExecuteReader(CommandBehavior.CloseConnection)

'Print the result of our query
Debug.WriteLine(oParam.Value)

'Close the data reader and connection
oDataReader.Close()
oConnection.Close()
```

Through the use of the Parameter.Direction property, the Command object supports the following types of parameters: Input, Output, InputOutput, and Return Value.

Before moving on to `DataReaders`, several more functions of the Command objects need to be demonstrated. First, at some point, most development projects require a single value out of a database. This is not a single row, but a single value. Most commonly the result of some aggregated SQL statement such as `Select Count(*) From Customers`. Historically, when developers wanted the results of such a query, they would instantiate a `Recordset` object and simply retrieve the first column out of the first row. Listing 22-7 shows a simpler technique using the `ExecuteScalar` method of a Command object.

Listing 22-7: **The ExecuteScalar Method**

```
'Create a Connection object and set it's connection string _
 through the constructor
Dim oConnection As New _
    SqlClient.SqlConnection("Data Source=(local);Initial _
    Catalog=Northwind;User id=sa")
oConnection.Open()

'Create a Command object with a simple Select statement using _
 an aggregate
Dim oCommand As New _
```

```
SqlClient.SqlCommand("Select Count(*) From Customers", _
oConnection)

'Execute the command that retrieves the value of the first _
 column in the first row only
Dim sCountOfCustomers As String = oCommand.ExecuteScalar().ToString

'Close the connection
oConnection.Close()
```

The ExecuteScalar method of the DataReader object returns the column value as an instance of a base Object class, without any specific type. As shown in Listing 22-7, it is possible to immediately convert this value to a string using the ToString method of a base Object class. Although this solution has the advantage of being very fast and simple for retrieving a single value from a database, you see in the next section that a DataReader object offers another alternative to this problem that provides you with strong typing.

DataReader objects

Now that you have become familiar with both Connection and Command objects, you take a look at the first of two major methods for viewing the results of your Command queries. These two methods, DataSets and DataReaders, provide solutions to two very different problems for the developer. It is important to realize that each of these objects is the best choice for certain situations, and neither provides a catchall solution (as was the case with the ADO Recordset).

The DataReader object, the first of the two you examine, is provided as part of a specific data provider. This means that a SQL Server-specific implementation of the DataReader (SQLDataReader) exists, as well as an OLEDB-specific implementation (OleDBDataReader). Any vendor implementing a set of data provider objects of the ADO.NET Framework for data access provides an application-specific implementation of the DataReader interface.

The DataReader object provides you with a very high-speed, forward-only method for iterating through a resulting set of data. The DataReader also accomplishes this task while using very few computer resources because it keeps only the current row in memory at any given point. Because it also does not expose each column or row as a separate object, little overhead or complexity when using a DataReader exists.

Although the more dynamic and flexible DataSet object has became much more synonymous with the ADO.NET Framework, the DataReader should be considered the best choice for any scenarios in which you need high-speed data access to a single table or view, and no modifications need to be made to the data. Although other architectural considerations exist when deciding between the two objects, as you work through the implementations of each, you become familiar with the strengths and weaknesses of both.

As you saw in the last section, the easiest and most-used method of creating a DataReader object is to use the Command.ExecuteReader function to return a new instance of a filled DataReader containing the results of the Command query.

Listing 22-8 demonstrates how easy it is to create a DataReader object using a Command object.

Listing 22-8: **The DataReader Object**

```
'Create a Connection object and set it's connection string _
 through the constructor
Dim oConnection As New _
    SqlClient.SqlConnection("Data Source=(local);Initial _
    Catalog=Northwind;User id=sa")
oConnection.Open()

'Create a Command object with a simple Select statement
Dim oCommand As New _
    SqlClient.SqlCommand("Select * From Customers", oConnection)

'Execute the command
Dim oDataReader As SqlClient.SqlDataReader = _
    oCommand.ExecuteReader()

'Iterate throught the results
While oDataReader.Read()
    'Write out the name of the first column (Column index 0)
    Debug.WriteLine(oDataReader.GetName(0).ToString())

    'Write out the value of the first column (Column index 0)
    Debug.WriteLine(oDataReader.GetValue(0).ToString())
End While

'Close the data reader and connection
oDataReader.Close()
oConnection.Close()
```

Listing 22-8 shows some important concepts. First, it is important to understand the method in which you move from row to row through the DataReader's data. The Read function of a DataReader moves sequentially from row to row in a forward-only fashion. The Read function also returns a single Boolean result, indicating whether there was actually another row to retrieve from the underlying data. As shown in the previous example, this makes it easy to iterate through all rows of a DataReader until the Read function returns a False. Also important to realize is that because of the fact that a DataReader maintains only a copy of a single row in memory at any given point in time, no programmatic way to determine the total number of rows returned by a Command object when using a DataReader object exists. This is just one of the major differences (and sacrifices) you must understand when deciding whether to use a `DataReader` or `DataSet` object to solve a specific development problem.

For the next example, you take a little deeper look at some of the more useful methods of a `DataReader` object. Another key concept that needs addressed when using a `DataReader` is how it returns data. Two main methods are available to developers retrieving specific field values out of a `DataReader`.

The first and easiest method for getting data out of a `DataReader` is to use the `Item` property, and pass either the name of the requested column or a column index. The `Item` property returns a base object class representing the value of the requested column in the current row. This method provides the option of specifying a column by name, but does not provide a way to return a strongly typed result. The best you can hope for is to return a reference to an instance of an Object class and then convert it to the appropriate type from there. This is similar to what is required when retrieving data using previous versions of ADO through the `Recordset` object.

The second method for retrieving column values from a `DataReader` is to use a set of methods that each `DataReader` provides to return typed values from specific rows given the column index. In the previous example, you used two methods, `GetName` and `GetValue`, to return a specific field's name and its value. Although the `GetValue` method returns an Object reference exactly as the Item property did, every `DataSet` implementation provides a number of typed methods that allow you to return a strongly typed value of a field's content. Each of these methods accepts an integer index into the array of columns. This means that to retrieve the typed value of a specific row in a result set, you need to know the index of that column, and cannot easily index specific field values by the name of the column (as is possible in the `Item` property). As the previous example demonstrated, it is possible to retrieve the name and data type of a specific column, given an index into the columns collection. These tasks can be performed using the `GetName` and `GetFieldType` methods of the `DataReader`. Also, it would not be difficult to write a wrapper class that allows you to retrieve strongly typed values for a column by specifying the column name. Listing 22-9 shows a simple implementation of a method for one such class.

Listing 22-9: Function to Retrieve DataReader Column Values as Strings

```
Public Function GetString(ByVal pDataReader As IDataReader, ByVal _
                  pFieldName As String) As String
     Dim iIndex As Integer

     'Loop through each column until we find the one with the name _
     we need
```

Continued

Listing 22-9 *(continued)*

```
        For iIndex = 0 To pDataReader.FieldCount - 1
            If pDataReader.GetName(iIndex) = pFieldName Then
                'Once we found the correct column, stop looping and _
                 return it's string value
                Return pDataReader.GetString(iIndex)
            End If
        Next

        'If we fell through to here, we didn't find the named field in _
         the DataReader
        Dim eNotFound As New _
            Exception("Field Not Found in DataReader: " + pFieldName)
        Throw eNotFound
End Function
```

Although a full implementation in Listing 22-9 would allow easy access to strongly typed data, as well as the ability to index data by the specific column names, it imposes a certain amount of overhead. One of the key benefits of using the DataReader object is its sheer speed and low memory overhead. To be forced to loop through a subset of columns to retrieve each value would work against those benefits. From an architectural standpoint, the example in Listing 22-9 allows easy access to strongly typed data, but it might be a much better solution to simply implement a solution with known column offsets that can be used to bypass any unnecessary looping when retrieving data.

Another useful feature of the DataReader lies in the GetSchemaTable method. This method allows you to quickly get a DataTable object that contains all the schema information for the DataReader. The features of a DataTable object are covered in the next section on the DataSet object.

As you see in the next chapter, one of the key uses of the DataReader is when performing data binding to controls or objects. This provides a powerful, high-speed solution for certain situations in which you can justify the tradeoffs between using a DataReader over a DataSet. Because all the controls and objects provided in the .NET Framework provide data-binding capabilities to either DataReaders or DataSets, it is easy for you to use the correct object for a particular situation without losing the flexibility of the tool and object support on the front end.

DataAdapter objects

The next and most complex major component of a data provider is the DataAdapter object. DataAdapter objects provide the means for a disconnected DataSet object, which is examined in detail in the next section, to interact with a database. DataAdapter objects provide the entire mapping from the database into the XML format understood by the DataSet; they also map the XML returned by a DataSet into the appropriate Insert, Update, and Delete Command objects, and set all parameters accordingly. This allows any database-specific implementation and SQL details to be preconfigured at design time by the developer, and abstracted into a DataAdapter. This paradigm, as you see, allows the DataSet object to be completely hidden from any of the behind-the-scenes details about where its data came from and where it goes when it is updated.

Also, another key point to understand when examining DataAdapter objects and DataSet objects is that DataSet objects provide the capability to have many inter-related tables in a single DataSet object. Each of these tables can be filled and updated through a separate DataAdapter, which means they can each come from a different database or at least have a completely different set of Command objects handling the Select, Insert, Update, and Delete commands for each.

The basic concept behind the implementation of a DataAdapter is that it serves as host to four ADO.NET Command objects. Each of these Command objects contains the appropriate SQL statement and parameters required to perform one of the four major SQL actions against a database. The four major actions are as follows: Select, Insert, Update, and Delete. Thus, each DataAdapter exposes each of its four main Command objects as properties called SelectCommand, InsertCommand, UpdateCommand, and DeleteCommand. Through preconfiguring each of these four Command objects, developers have complete control over a particular set of data's interaction with a database.

Listing 22-10 provides a demonstration of the most basic task of a DataAdapter object that is to select data out of a database and populate a DataSet.

Listing 22-10: **Filling a DataSet Using a DataAdapter**

```
'Create a Connection object and set it's connection string _
  through the constructor
Dim oConnection As New _
    SqlClient.SqlConnection("Data Source=KVGROSSW2K-NOTE;Initial _
    Catalog=Northwind;User id=sa")
oConnection.Open()

'Create a Command object with a simple Select statement
Dim oSelectCommand As New _
    SqlClient.SqlCommand("Select * From Customers", oConnection)

'Create a data adapter
Dim oDataAdapter As New SqlClient.SqlDataAdapter(oSelectCommand)

'Create a fill an empty dataset
Dim oDataSet As New DataSet()
```

Continued

Listing 22-10 *(continued)*

```
'Use the data adapter to create a fill a new DataTable called _
 Customers
oDataAdapter.Fill(oDataSet, "Customers")

'Write out the number of lines returned
Debug.WriteLine(oDataSet.Tables(0).Rows.Count)

oConnection.Close()
```

Although not required, in the Listing 22-10 example, you created the Select Command object prior to creating the DataAdapter. Then, when you created the DataAdapter, you passed the Select Command to the constructor. The DataAdapter constructor provides a number of overloads that allow you to optimize how you create a DataAdapter, and the one you use becomes a thing of personal preference as well as a factor of how much code you wish to write.

Listing 22-10 also makes use of the DataAdapter Fill command that is one of the only three points of interaction between a DataSet and a DataAdapter. The Fill command serves the purpose of executing the Select command against the database and populating the appropriate DataTable in the DataSet with the results of the query. You see the results of the fill later when you examine the details of a DataSet.

The FillSchema method is used primarily to configure a DataTable within a particular DataSet with the database-specific schema and constraint information before actually filling a DataTable using the DataAdapter. For example, certain database constraint information, such as primary key information, must be known by a DataTable before it can successfully update or delete information. Without a primary key, it cannot find the appropriate rows to perform these actions on. Because this type of information needs to be added to the schema of a particular DataTable, four methods exist for adding it:

✦ As noted in the previous chapter, you can specify it at design time in the XML schema document loaded into the DataSet.

✦ You can infer the schema from an existing XML document.

✦ You can fill it using the FillSchema method, which uses the SQL statement specified in the SelectCommand object to derive the database-specific schema information that can determine any schema that is explicitly defined in the database, such as primary key information and autonumbered fields.

✦ You fill in missing schema information when filling a DataSet with a DataAdapter.

Note   It is important to understand these four methods. Each is demonstrated in the "DataSets" section later in this chapter.

The final point of interaction between the `DataAdapter` and the `DataSet` is the `Update` method. The `Update` method accepts a `DataTable` as a parameter, and iterates through each `DataRow` in the `DataTable`. For each row in the `DataTable`, the `Update` method maps it to the appropriate `Insert`, `Update`, or `Delete` method, depending on the state of the row. In essence, the `Update` method handles the entire batch updating of data in a single call. You can work against a disconnected set of data in a `DataSet` object, and have all their changes propagated back to the database using preconfigured Command objects with a single call to the `Update` method of the appropriate `DataAdapter`.

Listing 22-11 demonstrates the creation of a `DataAdapter` object and each of its Command objects, and shows how it can be used to load and update data through a `DataSet`.

Listing 22-11: Configuring a DataAdapter by Manually Associating Command Objects

```
'Create a Connection object and set it's connection string _
  through the constructor
Dim oConnection As New _
    SqlClient.SqlConnection("Data Source=KVGROSSW2K-NOTE;Initial _
    Catalog=Northwind;User id=sa")
oConnection.Open()

'Create a blank data adapter
Dim oDataAdapter As New SqlClient.SqlDataAdapter()

'Create our select statement
Dim oSelectCommand As New _
    SqlClient.SqlCommand("Select CustomerID, CompanyName, _
    ContactName From Customers", oConnection)

'Create our Insert statement and add the appropriate parameters
Dim oInsertCommand As New _
    SqlClient.SqlCommand("Insert into Customers(CompanyName, _
    ContactName) Values (@CompanyName, @ContactName)", Connection)

oInsertCommand.Parameters.Add(New _
    SqlClient.SqlParameter("@CompanyName", _
    System.Data.SqlDbType.NVarChar, 20, _
    System.Data.ParameterDirection.Input, True, CType(0, Byte), _
    CType(0, Byte), "CompanyName", _
    System.Data.DataRowVersion.Current, Nothing))

oInsertCommand.Parameters.Add(New _
    SqlClient.SqlParameter("@ContactName", _
    System.Data.SqlDbType.NVarChar, 20, _
    System.Data.ParameterDirection.Input, True, CType(0, Byte), _
```

Continued

Listing 22-11 *(continued)*

```
        CType(0, Byte), "ContactName", _
        System.Data.DataRowVersion.Current, Nothing))

'Create our Update statement and add the appropriate parameters
Dim oUpdateCommand As New _
    SqlClient.SqlCommand("Update Customers Set CompanyName = _
    @CompanyName, ContactName = @ContactName Where CustomerID = _
    @CustomerID", oConnection)

oUpdateCommand.Parameters.Add(New _
    SqlClient.SqlParameter("@CompanyName", _
    System.Data.SqlDbType.NVarChar, 20, _
    System.Data.ParameterDirection.Input, True, CType(0, Byte), _
    CType(0, Byte), "CompanyName", _
    System.Data.DataRowVersion.Current, Nothing))

oUpdateCommand.Parameters.Add(New _
    SqlClient.SqlParameter("@ContactName", _
    System.Data.SqlDbType.NVarChar, 20, _
    System.Data.ParameterDirection.Input, True, CType(0, Byte), _
    CType(0, Byte), "ContactName", _
    System.Data.DataRowVersion.Current, Nothing))

oUpdateCommand.Parameters.Add(New _
    SqlClient.SqlParameter("@CustomerID", _
    System.Data.SqlDbType.Int, 5, _
    System.Data.ParameterDirection.Input, True, CType(0, Byte), _
    CType(0, Byte), "CustomerID", _
    System.Data.DataRowVersion.Current, Nothing))

'Create our Delete command with the single parameter (CustomerID)
Dim oDeleteCommand As New _
    SqlClient.SqlCommand("Delete From Customers Where _
    CustomerID = @CustomerID", oConnection)

oDeleteCommand.Parameters.Add(New _
    SqlClient.SqlParameter("@CustomerID", _
    System.Data.SqlDbType.Int, 5, _
    System.Data.ParameterDirection.Input, True, CType(0, Byte), _
    CType(0, Byte), "CustomerID", _
    System.Data.DataRowVersion.Current, Nothing))

'Set the appropriate object references on our DataAdapter
oDataAdapter.SelectCommand = oSelectCommand
oDataAdapter.InsertCommand = oInsertCommand
oDataAdapter.UpdateCommand = oUpdateCommand
oDataAdapter.DeleteCommand = oDeleteCommand

'Create a fill an empty dataset
Dim oDataSet As New DataSet()
```

```
'Use the data adapter to create a fill a new DataTable _
 called Customers
oDataAdapter.Fill(oDataSet, "Customers")

Dim sNewName As String = "Kevin Grossnicklaus"

oDataSet.Tables(0).Rows(0).Item("ContactName") = sNewName

oDataAdapter.Update(oDataSet)

oConnection.Close()
```

Listing 22-11 demonstrates the level of control that developers have over the specific SQL implementations of all four of the Command objects used by the `DataProvider`. Although the section on Command objects demonstrated the basic usage of the Parameters collection, Listing 22-11 uses a few additional features of the Parameter object. For example, you'll notice that it specifies a number of additional parameters in the constructor when creating a new Parameter object. One of the key parameters specified in this new format is the `ColumnName` parameter. This parameter allows you to associate a Parameter object with a specific column of a row being returned in the `DataSet`. This greatly simplifies the creation of `Insert`, `Update`, and `Delete` commands because it allows you to simply associate replaceable parameters in the SQL statement with the current values being returned for a particular row in a `DataSet`.

CommandBuilder

As you can see in Listing 22-11, this seems like a lot of code to have to write to provide the basic capability to load data, update some columns, and reconcile all changes back to the database. This task was very simple with prior versions of ADO when using a `Recordset`. A `Recordset` object abstracted all the functionality away from the developers, and generated all the SQL statements required for such things as inserting, updating, and deleting automatically. Although this abstraction was good for some situations, other situations called for a manual tweaking of the SQL statements that couldn't be done using a `Recordset`. Fortunately, ADO.NET `DataAdapter` objects provide the ability to configure your Command objects in three ways:

✦ You can configure and code them manually, as shown in Listing 22-11. This method provides you with great control over your database interaction, but also requires a large amount of manual coding to provide even the most basic database interactions.

✦ You can make use of the `CommandBuilder` object that is provided as part of each data provider. The `CommandBuilder` object is basically a "Black Box" that looks at the provided `Select` statement in the `SelectCommand` object, and automatically generates the appropriate insert, update, and delete commands and all associated Parameter objects. Listing 22-12 demonstrates using the `CommandBuilder` object to perform the exact same function that was performed in Listing 22-11.

✦ You can use the wizards available in Visual Studio .NET to configure your Command objects graphically.

Listing 22-12: **Using the CommandBuilder to Configure a DataAdapter**

```
'Create a Connection object and set it's connection string _
 through the constructor
Dim oConnection As New _
    SqlClient.SqlConnection("Data Source=KVGROSSW2K-NOTE;Initial _
    Catalog=Northwind;User id=sa")
oConnection.Open()

'Create the data adapter and configure the Select command _
 through the constructor
Dim oDataAdapter As New _
    SqlClient.SqlDataAdapter("Select CompanyName, ContactName, _
    CustomerID From Customers", oConnection)

Dim oCommandBuilder As New _
    SqlClient.SqlCommandBuilder(oDataAdapter)

'Create a fill an empty dataset
Dim oDataSet As New DataSet()

'Use the data adapter to create a fill a new DataTable _
 called Customers
oDataAdapter.Fill(oDataSet, "Customers")

Dim sNewName As String = "Kevin Grossnicklaus"

oDataSet.Tables(0).Rows(0).Item("ContactName") = "Test"

oDataAdapter.Update(oDataSet, "Customers")

oConnection.Close()
```

Although a CommandBuilder object greatly simplified your code in this situation, it is important to realize the implications of using such an object. First, a CommandBuilder object works only with the most basic SQL statements. This means that the CommandBuilder object does not work when using any type of stored procedure to retrieve or update data. It also does not work when using any type of join or advanced SQL in the Select statement of the SelectCommand object. Although this limitation might exempt it from certain situations, situations in which the CommandBuilder would still work exist. This is where you need to address the biggest drawback of using the CommandBuilder: speed. By using the CommandBuilder, you are required to execute an algorithm that parses your Select statement and dynamically decides on the appropriate statements to perform for the insert, update, and delete actions based on the single Select statement. After it has derived and built the SQL statement as a string for each of the remaining three actions, it must add the appropriate parameters to the Parameters collection in the order in which they appear in the SQL string (to account for OleDB parameters). Also, unless it is cached or pooled, the component that uses this CommandBuilder object to configure a DataAdapter must use it each time it creates a new instance of that DataAdapter. In the disconnected world you are striving for with ADO.NET, that means that the DataAdapter must be reconfigured using this "Black Box" each time you need to insert, update, or delete data from a table. If this seems pretty complicated and resource-intensive to you, you're right — there *is* a lot to it. It still must be noted that this is, in essence, what ADO Recordsets have done for years, but if there is an alternative that could bypass all this work each time you need to update the database, why not use it?

This is where you come to the third alternative to configuring DataAdapter objects: wizards. If possible, you don't want to turn control of your configuration over to the CommandBuilder for every database interaction, but you also don't want to be forced to write a horrendous amount of code each time you want to load and update something. So, as you see in the next chapter, to provide the best of both worlds, Microsoft provided a set of wizards in Visual Studio .NET that allow you to graphically configure a DataAdapter. These wizards handle generating a large amount of the "plumbing" you saw in the first example while using a CommandBuilder object to generate the SQL required for each DataAdapter action behind the scenes. This allows all the overhead of a CommandBuilder to be performed once at design time while still taking advantage of its simplicity. It also provides the means for a developer to generate the baseline "plumbing" code required for a specific database interaction and then go tweak the resulting code to gain more control over the specific interaction and SQL statements. When you begin to look at Visual Studio .NET's data wizards and tools in the next chapter, you see a better picture of the type of options available to you when using the Visual Studio .NET data wizards.

TableMappings

One additional feature provided by the DataAdapter is the ability to provide a set of table and column mappings through which it associates all table names and column names provided by the DataSet against those actually used by the data store. This allows DataAdapter developers the ability to provide a separate set of names for tables and columns to the front-end developers and users of the DataSet while maintaining all mappings in a consistent place.

As you begin to look at the structure and features of a DataSet object in the next section, you also look back a few more times at the interaction between a DataSet and a DataAdapter and how a DataAdapter serves as the "bridge" between a DataSet and the database.

DataSets

As presented in the last chapter, the DataSet serves as a database-neutral, disconnected collection of data that you can use for a wide variety of client-side purposes.

You were introduced to some of the more basic features of the DataSet in the last section on data providers; in this section you dig into the structure and usage of the DataSet objects and how they provide a simple, reusable data structure that can be utilized to solve a large number of development problems.

Creating DataTables

The core of the DataSet architecture is centered on the DataTable object. A single DataSet can contain many DataTable objects, and a DataSet provides the capability to enforce relationships between any two DataTables. The Tables collection of a DataSet contains each of the DataTables within the DataSet. Using the Tables collection, you can access a specific DataTable by either using an index or the name of the table.

The structure of each DataTable is defined by a collection of DataColumn objects. This collection can be accessed directly from a DataTable object using the Columns property. Each DataColumn object exposes a large amount of information defining the structure of that particular column. By manipulating a DataColumn object, you can configure exactly how a column of data behaves in a particular DataTable. The basic column features, such as name, data type, length, and initial value are easily available, as well as a host of more advanced properties. Properties such as AutoNumber, ReadOnly, Caption, and Unique provide a host of powerful features that you can use to make a DataTable behave more like a client-side database. Another handy property of the DataColumn object is the ColumnMapping property, which allows you to control how a specific column is added to the underlying XML. The available ColumnMapping types are Element, Attribute, Hidden, and SimpleContent. These settings affect how a DataColumn is written out when using WriteXML method of a DataSet to write its contents out as XML.

Programmatically creating a DataSet

One of the key features of a DataSet that makes it useful in such a wide range of scenarios is the ease in which one can be created and configured programmatically. This feature allows you to create each of the individual objects that make up a dataset and programmatically add them to the object model. Such an implementation as this allows the use of DataSets in situations that do not include a database and in which you want to take advantage of the .NET features that integrate tightly with the DataSet, such as data binding.

Listing 22-13 demonstrates how to programmatically create a DataSet and a DataTable with three DataColumns, and then add a new row.

Listing 22-13: **Programmatically Creating a DataSet**

```
'Create a new DataSet object
Dim oDataSet As New DataSet()

'Use the Tables.Add method to add a DataTable named "Persons"
Dim oPersonTable As DataTable = oDataSet.Tables.Add("Persons")
```

```
'Add three columns to our table
oPersonTable.Columns.Add("Name_First", _
    System.Type.GetType("System.String"))
oPersonTable.Columns.Add("Name_Last", _
    System.Type.GetType("System.String"))
oPersonTable.Columns.Add("PersonID", _
    System.Type.GetType("System.Int16"))

'Set the column "PersonID" to be an autogenerated primary key _
 type field
oPersonTable.Columns(2).AutoIncrement = True
oPersonTable.Columns(2).AutoIncrementStep = 1
oPersonTable.Columns(2).Unique = True
oPersonTable.Columns(2).ReadOnly = True

'Use the NewRow method to add a new row to the table
Dim oRow As DataRow = oPersonTable.NewRow()

'Set the values for our new row
oRow.Item("Name_First") = "Kevin"
oRow.Item("Name_Last") = "Grossnicklaus"

'Add the row to our table
oPersonTable.Rows.Add(oRow)

'Write our the last Name_Last column of our first row

Debug.WriteLine(oDataSet.Tables("Persons").Rows(0) _
("Name_First").ToString())
```

Listing 22-13 not only demonstrates how simple it is to programmatically create a DataSet and add DataTables, but it also demonstrates a few of the more powerful features of the DataColumn object by configuring the PersonID column to be the equivalent of a SQL Server AutoNumber field. This functionality is completely isolated from any database, and its implementation is managed by the DataSet itself (which is important to note because setting a column as AuthIncrement in a DataTable and then attempting to persist the data into an AutoNumber field in a SQL Server database causes problems).

Finally, Listing 22-13 demonstrates how to add a new row to a DataTable using the NewRow method. The NewRow method returns an instance of a DataRow object whose schema matches that defined in the DataColumns collection. After you have an instance of a DataRow, you can quickly and easily modify any of the data by setting the values of a specific item. It is important to realize that the DataRow implementation allows for strongly typed data. This means that when you set the value of a specific field in a DataRow object, the DataRow enforces such things as data type and maximum length, as is defined in the DataColumn definition for that column. Because the DataSet can enforce such strong typing, it is much easier to work in a very disconnected environment and not be as concerned with such typing issues being raised when changes are persisted to the data store.

Filling DataSets from files

While programmatically creating a DataSet provides you with the ability to use a DataSet structure for a variety of tasks, this feature is only extended by the ability to load dataset schema and data from files or any source that serves XML. As was presented in the previous chapter, the DataSet itself can accept only an XML document containing data and then "infer" its schema, or it can accept both data and schema to build its structure and populate it with data.

Before you look at how you can load an XML document from code and allow the DataSet to "infer" its schema, look at the following XML document:

```
<?xml version="1.0" encoding="UTF-8"?>
<person>
   <first_name>Hanna</first_name>
   <last_name>Grossnicklaus</last_name>
   <address>123 East Drive St. Louis, MO   63146</address>
   <gender>Female</gender>
</person>
```

This is a simple XML document with no attributes that has a root node called person and four simple elements. The next snippet of code demonstrates loading the XML document into a DataSet:

```
Dim oDataSet As New DataSet()

oDataSet.ReadXml("C:\Kevin's Stuff\Book\Samples\Sample.XML")

Debug.WriteLine(oDataSet.Tables("person").Rows(0)("first_name").ToString())
```

As you can see, you can read in an XML document from a file and have the DataSet perform all the work of deciding on the best schema with a single line of code. But, as discussed in the previous chapter, requiring the DataSet to perform this extra work each time you want to load the data is appropriate only in certain situations. To fully realize the amount of work that has to occur when "inferring" the structure of a DataSet, examine the following code:

```
Dim oDataSet As New DataSet()

oDataSet.ReadXml("C:\Kevin's Stuff\Book\Samples\Sample.XML")

Debug.WriteLine(oDataSet.Tables("person").Rows(0)("first_name").ToString())

oDataSet.WriteXmlSchema("C:\Kevin's Stuff\Book\Samples\Sample.XSD")

Dim oNewDataSet As New DataSet()

oNewDataSet.ReadXmlSchema("C:\Kevin's Stuff\Book\Samples\Sample.XSD")

oNewDataSet.ReadXml("C:\Kevin's Stuff\Book\Samples\Sample.XML")

Debug.WriteLine(oNewDataSet.Tables("person").Rows(0)("first_name").
   ToString())
```

Notice that after the structure of the first `DataSet` has been inferred, you use the `WriteXMLSchema` method to write it back out to a file. After the second `DataSet` has been created, you immediately use `ReadXMLSchema` to configure the second dataset. After the second `DataSet` is configured, you use the `ReadXML` method to read in the same file. The difference between loading data into the first `DataSet` and into the second `DataSet` is that the second `DataSet` doesn't have to worry about the overhead required to derive its structure off of the XML document.

Although this method of inferring schema seems complex, as you see in the next chapter, the Visual Studio .NET design time environment makes this type of `DataSet` configuration trivial.

Using DataSets with DataAdapters

The final method for loading data into a `DataSet` is through the use of a `DataAdapter`. As you learned in the previous section, a `DataAdapter` serves as the bridge between the database and the `DataSet`. The following code demonstrates the most basic method for filling a `DataSet` using a `DataAdapter`.

```
'Create a new DataAdapter and configure with our Select _
  statement and Connection object
Dim oDataAdapter As New _
    SqlClient.SqlDataAdapter("Select * From Customers", _
    oConnection)

'Populate a DataSet using the Fill method of the DataAdapter
oDataAdapter.Fill(oDataSet, "Customers")
```

You'll notice that a single `DataAdapter` is usually used for filling a single `DataTable` within a `DataSet`. Because it is relatively trivial to fill a `DataTable` using a `DataSet`, as you saw in the previous section, you focus on how to get the best performance when synchronizing your modified data back into the database using the `DataAdapter` Update method.

Because the data in `DataSets` can be manipulated in a disconnected fashion for an extended period of time, one of the key pieces of functionality provided by a `DataAdapter` is to map all modifications to a `DataSet` back to the appropriate Command objects encapsulated by the `DataSet`.

Although you can filter which results you retrieve from a `DataAdapter` through basic SQL, you usually don't need to send the entire contents of a `DataSet` back to the `DataAdapter` when you need to reconcile changes. When reconciling data with the database, you only need to be concerned with rows that need to be updated (rows that have been edited since they were loaded from the database), inserted (new rows that have been added while the `DataSet` was disconnected), and deleted (rows that have been flagged for deletion while the `DataSet` was disconnected). To handle these changes, the `DataSet` offers the ability to easily extract all modified rows into a new `DataSet`, a new `DataTable`, or a new collection of `DataRows`. This functionality, as presented in Listing 22-14, occurs through the use of the `GetChanges` method on a `DataSet`.

Listing 22-14: The GetChanges Method of a DataSet

```
'Fill the DataSet using the appropriate DataAdapter
oDataAdapter.Fill(oDataSet, "Person")

'...Make all necessary changes to the "person" table while _
 the database is disconnected

'Retrieve a new DataSet containing only the modified rows from _
 the first DataSet
Dim oChangedRows As DataSet = oDataSet.GetChanges()

'Use the DataAdapter to make all necessary changes to the _
 database per the changes in the DataSet
oDataAdapter.Update(oChangedRows, "Person")

'Merge the changes between the two DataSets back into the _
 first DataSet
'...This is done to preserve any changes made to the data by _
 the database
oDataSet.Merge(oChangedRows)
```

As you can see in Listing 22-14, you used a GetChanges method to create a new DataSet that was then passed to the Update method of the DataAdapter. Because it is possible that a DataAdapter could make changes to the dataset, such as set autonumber fields, you assume that the DataSet that was returned contains changes that need to be merged with your original DataSet. For this purpose, you use the Merge method on the original DataSet to synchronize all the data.

The capability to pass a DataSet only between tiers that contain the modified data can help to greatly decrease network traffic and thus increase performance. So you should consider it good practice to always utilize these features before passing a DataSet back to a DataAdapter to persist changes.

Tracking and maintaining relationships

Another powerful feature of ADO.NET is the capability to track and maintain consistent relationships between two or more DataTables within a DataSet. This feature allows a DataSet to present a view of data that is very similar to a relational database and provide developers with the tools to maintain those relationships.

All relationships enforced by a single DataSet are maintained by a collection of DataRelation objects available off the root DataSet object directly. With defined relationships, a DataSet can provide you with features that allow you to quickly and easily determine the parent/child relationships between a set of DataRows in one table and the DataRows of another.

Listing 22-15 demonstrates how to programmatically create a relationship between two DataTables and then retrieve a collection of "child" DataRow objects in a related "order" table from a single row in a "person" table based on that relationship:

Listing 22-15: Adding Relationships Between DataTables

```
'Retrieve the 'PersonID' column from the DataColumns collection _
 of our 'Person' DataTable
Dim oPersonID As DataColumn = oDataSet.Tables("Person").Columns(1)

'Retrieve the 'PersonID' column from the DataColumns collection _
 of our 'Orders' DataTable
Dim oOrdersPersonID As DataColumn = _
    oDataSet.Tables("Orders").Columns(2)

'Add the appropriate DataRelation between the 'Person' table _
   and the 'Orders' table
'...also, we wish to add the appropriate constraints to _
  the individual columns
oDataSet.Relations.Add("Person_Orders", oPersonID, _
        oOrdersPersonID, True)

'Retrieve the specific DataRow for person with ID #123
Dim oPerson As DataRow = oDataSet.Tables("Person").Rows.Find(123)

'Use the GetChildRows method to retrieve all the child rows _
   for this particular person row based on the named constraint.
Dim oOrders() As DataRow = oPerson.GetChildRows("Person_Orders")

Dim oOrder As DataRow

'Write the "PersonID" of each child order to the Debug window
'...Note: Each "PersonID" value will be identical
For Each oOrder In oOrders
    Debug.WriteLine(oOrder.Item("PersonID").ToString())
Next
```

As you can see, the DataRelation object provide developers with the ability to allow the DataSet to help enforce database-like constraints on disconnected data housed within a DataSet.

Understanding DataRow versions and states

When working with a DataSet in a disconnected fashion, it is possible that a large number of changes are made to the data in one or many rows. One of the handiest (and most underrated) features of a DataSet lies in its capability to track changes made to specific columns within a DataRow. Each DataRow allows you to view any one of four versions of each field it contains. These four versions are explained in the Table 22-3.

Version	Description
	Table 22-3 **DataRow Versions**
Default	The Default value of the column (as determined by the DataColumn associated with that field).
Original	The value of the field after it was filled from an external source (either loaded from a database or another source). Note that a call to the AcceptChanges method on a DataRow object rewrites the Original values with the current value of the field.
Current	The current value of a field.
Proposed	The proposed value of a field when used with the BeginEdit, CancelEdit, and EndEdit methods.

Listing 22-16 demonstrates how to retrieve a specific version of a field from a DataRow:

Listing 22-16: Examining DataRow Versions

```
Dim oDataRow As DataRow = oDataSet.Tables(0).NewRow()

'Write out the original value of a populated DataRow
Debug.WriteLine(oDataRow.Item("Name_First", _
    DataRowVersion.Original)) '="Alexis" (Original Value)

'Set a new value
oDataRow.Item("Name_First") = "Emily"

'Write the original value
Debug.WriteLine(oDataRow.Item("Name_First", _
    DataRowVersion.Original)) '="Alexis" (Still)

'Write the current value
Debug.WriteLine(oDataRow.Item("Name_First", _
    DataRowVersion.Current)) '="Emily"

'Accept the current changes to the row
oDataRow.AcceptChanges()

'Now that we have called the AcceptChanges method the _
    original version of the field has changed
Debug.WriteLine(oDataRow.Item("Name_First", _
    DataRowVersion.Original)) '="Emily"
```

As Listing 22-16 demonstrates, the item method of each DataRow provides an override that accepts an enumerated constant that specifies which version of the column value is required. This type of functionality (especially the Proposed version), gives you a simple means to develop advanced functionality into your UIs such as dialog boxes that support an OK/Apply/Cancel metaphor for editing data.

At a DataRow level, ADO.NET supports the ability to track the state of any given row. DataTable and DataAdapter use this state, which is updated by performing certain actions against a DataRow or any column within it, when they need to determine which rows need to be added, inserted, or updated against a database. The various states of an individual DataRow are detailed in Table 22-4.

Table 22-4 DataRow States	
State	**Description**
Unchanged	The entire DataRow has not been changed since being populated.
Modified	At least one field has been changed since the DataRow was populated.
Added	This is a new DataRow that did not exist when the DataRow was populated.
Deleted	This row was loaded into the DataSet, and has since been deleted.
Detached	This DataRow has been disconnected from any specific DataTable, or has not yet been added to a DataTable.

During the life of the DataTable, all that is required to determine the state of a specific row is to utilize the RowState property of the DataRow object, as shown in the following line:

```
'Write the state of the oDataRow row to the debug window
Debug.WriteLine(oDataRow.RowState.ToString())
```

Although obvious uses for finding the state of an individual row of data exist, as you see in the next chapter, the true power of the RowState property comes when using DataView objects to allow filtering of data within a specific DataTable.

Filtering and sorting data in DataSets

One of the final features you explore in this chapter regarding DataSets is the DataView object. The DataView object serves as a layer above a DataTable that provides you with the means to filter and sort the data in a specific DataTable. This capability to filter and sort the data on the client (or at least the machine where the DataTable lives) helps minimize any excess calls to the database to perform similar functions. Also, because any control or tool that can bind to a DataTable can also bind to a DataView, you can utilize the DataView object to allow multiple clients to view the same DataSet in different ways.

Each `DataTable` within a `DataSet` contains a default `DataView` object that is what all controls and tools bind to by default when binding to a `DataTable`. As shown in the following code, the `DataView` object provides the ability to sort the data in a `DataTable` and to filter the data:

```
'Create a new DataView object for a specified table
Dim oDataView As New DataView(oDataTable)

'Sort the DataView by the "Name_First" column
oDataView.Sort = "Name_First"

'Filter the dataset by the "Last_Name" column
'...only view rows where the last name starts with 'sm'
oDataView.RowFilter = "Name_First Like 'Sm*'"
```

After the `DataSet` is configured with the appropriate sorting and filtering options, it is possible to bind any data control or object to the `DataView` object directly and take advantage of these features. It is also important to realize that `DataViews` only allow filtering complete rows, and cannot be used to limit the number of columns available to a client.

Another powerful filtering feature of a `DataView` object lies in its capability to filter rows of data based on their `RowState` property (as discussed in the previous section). The following example demonstrates how to build a `DataView` that provides a view of a `DataTable` that shows all new rows that have been added since loading the data from the database:

```
'Only show rows which have been added to the DataSet
oDataView.RowStateFilter = DataViewRowState.Added
```

When filtering by `RowState`, it is important to realize that additional `RowState` values are available to the rows of a `DataView` besides those of a `DataTable`. These additional values, which are specified in Table 22-5, provide developers with a useful set of `RowState` values to be used in most common filtering scenarios.

Table 22-5 RowState Values	
DataView RowState Value	**Description**
Unchanged	`DataRows` that have had no changes made to them (similar to the `DataRow.RowState` value).
OriginalRows	All the rows that were included when the `DataTable` was originally populated. This view also returns each row in its original state.
Added	A view of each row that has been added to the `DataTable` since it was populated.

DataView RowState Value	Description
Deleted	A view of each row that has been deleted from a `DataTable` since it was populated.
ModifiedOriginal	A view of a `DataTable` that presented each `DataRow` that has been modified since the `DataTable` was populated. Each `DataRow` is presented in its original format.
ModifiedCurrent	A view of a `DataTable` that presents all `DataRows` that have been modified in their current format.
OriginalRows	A view of a `DataTable` that contains an exact snapshot of the data as it was when it was loaded into the `DataTable`.

As you can see, with their powerful sorting and filtering capabilities, as well as the capability to use a `DataView` as a source for .NET's powerful data-binding functionality, `DataViews` provide a feature that can greatly simplify most common data-viewing tasks.

Summary

Although the added features of the ADO.NET Framework open the door to a large number of new uses and applications of Data Access technology, the sheer amount of code required to take full advantage of these features could easily outweigh the benefits. To overcome this obstacle, Microsoft has built an enormous amount of tools support for ADO.NET into the Visual Studio .NET development environment. As you see in the next chapter, tools provided in your IDE have automated most of the manual coding you performed in this chapter. Although you want to take advantage of these timesaving features whenever possible, it is important to understand the technologies presented in this chapter and to understand how the ADO.NET objects work together to provide a complete data access solution.

✦   ✦   ✦

Data Access in Visual Studio .NET

by Kevin Grossnicklaus

◆   ◆   ◆   ◆

In This Chapter

A history of Microsoft
data access
technologies

An overview
of ADO.NET

◆   ◆   ◆   ◆

As you saw in previous chapters, ADO.NET provides you
with the tools to build robust and scalable applications
through the use of a very dynamic and extensive object
model. To truly take advantage of the power these objects
provide, without the added overhead of having to write an
enormous amount of plumbing code, Microsoft has built in
first class support for ADO.NET to its Visual Studio .NET
development environment.

The Visual Studio .NET Integrated Development Environment
(IDE) provides you with a large number of wizards and genera-
tors to simplify most of the mundane tasks required to take
full use of the ADO.NET infrastructure. Beyond these timesaving tools, Microsoft has also built powerful database management tools (a.k.a. SQL Server Enterprise Manager) directly
into the IDE to eliminate the need to jump back and forth
between products. Combine these two things with the capability to debug SQL Server stored procedures, version-stored
procedures in SourceSafe, and drag-and-drop connections and
tables into your applications, the Visual Studio .NET environment becomes an extremely attractive suite of tools for any
developer who wants to take advantage of databases from
within an application.

This chapter takes a look at some of these powerful new tools
while walking through some of their uses. Although all the
data features of the IDE can be lumped together, you look at
them in two major sections: those features that provide you
with simplified administration of data sources and those that
provide you with tools to automate the tasks of writing
database applications.

Visual Studio .NET Database Tools

The first set of Visual Studio .NET features provides you with the tools to easily administer data sources. These features allow you to create and manipulate database objects such as tables, views, and stored procedures. Also, developers can use these tools to view and edit the data within data sources to simplify debugging and monitoring of database applications without having to use a separate tool such as SQL Server Enterprise Manager. Although the major tools provided by Visual Studio .NET are only briefly discussed in regards to database administration, each of the tools discussed provides a great deal of power to you when you develop database applications from Visual Studio .NET.

Using Server Explorer

The Visual Studio .NET Server Explorer window serves as a developer's window into not only database objects, but also a myriad of other services that can be accessed on remote machines. The Server Explorer window, like so many other tools in Visual Studio .NET, can be docked and made easily available during regular development (see Figure 23-1).

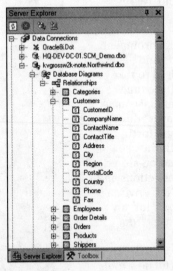

Figure 23-1: You use the Visual Studio .NET Server Explorer to manipulate Database Objects and remoter Servers directly from the Visual Studio .NET IDE.

The nodes in the Server Explorer window are presented in two separate sections: Data Connections and Servers:

✦ The Data Connections section lets you add connections to regularly used data connections. After these data connections are established, the Server Explorer window enables you to manipulate the underlying database objects.

✦ The Servers section allows you to connect to remote servers, and program against a variety of services that may be available, such as Web services.

Adding connections

To add a connection to the Server Explorer, right-click the node and select Add Connection from the pop-up menu. After clicking Add Connection, the Data Link Properties dialog box, which provides all the options available for adding a valid data connection using a variety of available drivers and data sources, opens. As you see later in the chapter, by having this connection available in the Server Explorer, you can easily drag the connections onto forms or components; Visual Studio .NET and the IDE automatically add the appropriate code to configure the connection within that item of a project. Figure 23-2 illustrates some of the options available when configuring a new data connection:

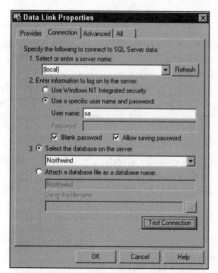

Figure 23-2: You use the Data Link Properties dialog box to add connections to the Server Explorer.

To properly configure a database connection in Visual Studio .NET by using the Data Link Properties dialog box, you must select the appropriate provider and connection information, such as server name, database name, and login credentials. After these settings have been properly configured, you can access this connection information, and manipulate database objects underneath this connection if the datasource supports this, regardless of the Visual Studio .NET solution that is currently open. This feature allows you to add connections to your most commonly used databases and, if required, easily share them across solutions without having to reconnect or configure.

Administering data sources through the Server Explorer

One of the best timesaving features available from within Visual Studio .NET is the capability to completely administer most data sources without leaving the IDE. This administration, similar to that provided by SQL Server Enterprise Manager, allows you to add and configure database diagrams, tables, views, and stored procedures.

Manipulating database tables in Visual Studio .NET

By using the Server Explorer window to expand a specific database connection, you can navigate to the Tables node to gain access to a list of all existing user tables in the database. By right-clicking the Tables node, you can select the New Table option from the resulting pop-up menu to add a new table to the database. Also, by right-clicking an existing table and selecting the Design Table option, you can modify the structure of existing data tables. Figure 23-3 displays the table designer used by Visual Studio .NET to manipulate database table structures.

The table designer provided by Visual Studio .NET allows you to modify the structure of tables by providing complete control over a table's column information. As shown in Figure 23-3, the column information for a table can be easily edited in the grid provided by the table designer. Other features available from within the table designer that can be accessed from the Visual Studio .NET toolbar when the table designer is open include the ability to modify column indexes and foreign key relationships.

Beyond the ability to design tables, the Server Explorer window provides you with the ability to view the data in a table, export all the data to a file, generate the appropriate SQL script to re-create the table on another database, and add a trigger to the database — all from within the standard development environment. Each of these functions is available by right-clicking the appropriate table node in the Server Explorer window.

Manipulating database views in Visual Studio .NET

When working with database views, Visual Studio .NET utilizes a full-featured, built-in query analyzer. This query analyzer allows you to construct or edit SQL statements in a manner very similar to using the query analyzer in SQL Server Enterprise Manager. You spend more time on the query analyzer in the following section that discusses stored procedures. In addition to the query analyzer, Visual Studio .NET provides you with a powerful query builder for graphically designing and constructing SQL statements and views. The Visual Studio .NET query builder gives you the option of building the queries graphically or by manually keying the required SQL statements. Also, by utilizing the query builder, you can verify the validity of the SQL statements against the appropriate data store, and even execute the statement and preview the results, as shown in Figure 23-4.

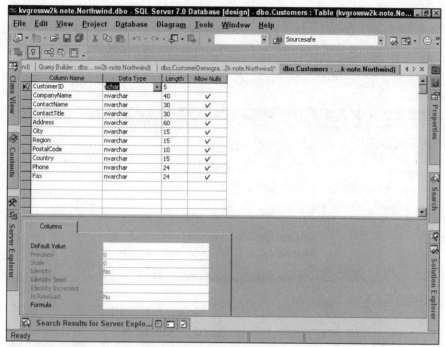

Figure 23-3: The Visual Studio .NET database table designer allows you to manipulate the structure of database tables from directly within the IDE.

The query builder itself is broken into four vertically positioned panes (as shown in Figure 23-4). The following list provides a brief description of each of these panes from top to bottom:

✦ Diagram Pane – Provides a graphical representation of the tables included in a SQL statement and the joins between them. By adding or removing tables from this pane, the query builder automatically makes the appropriate adjustments to the SQL pane (described below). Also, by checking the box next to any column in any table, you can choose to include that particular column in the resulting query.

✦ Grid Pane – Provides you with the ability to see all the columns selected to be returned as a result of executing the current query. This pane also provides you with the ability to enter criteria and filters based on a specific column, and to specify a column alias and sorting information.

✦ SQL Pane – This pane in the query builder displays the current SQL statement as defined by your modifications to the Diagram and Grid panes. You also have the ability to make changes directly to the SQL pane and see them reflected in the above two panes.

✦ Results Pane – It is in this pane that you can view the results of a query executed after clicking the Run button on the toolbar.

As you can see, the query builder provides a number of features to greatly simplify the generation of SQL statements. And as discussed in the next section on manipulating stored procedures, the query builder integrates tightly with the query analyzer in Visual Studio .NET to allow you to quickly build very complex stored procedures made up of a number of logical "blocks" of SQL statements.

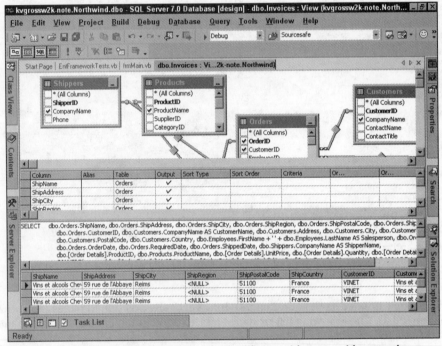

Figure 23-4: The Visual Studio .NET query builder provides you with a number of tools to graphically construct SQL queries and views.

Manipulating database stored procedures in Visual Studio .NET

When working with stored procedures from within Visual Studio .NET, you find a number of powerful new features that can greatly simplify your work

As mentioned in the previous chapter, Visual Studio .NET now provides a built-in query analyzer that provides a powerful editing environment for coding complex SQL statements such as those usually required in stored procedures. The built-in query analyzer has a lot of the same functionality as that provided by the commonly used query analyzers that ship with recent versions of Microsoft SQL Server. One additional feature of the Visual Studio .NET query analyzer lies in its capability to integrate with the SQL query builder to build or modify SQL statements in logical "blocks" of SQL.

When editing a stored procedure, you have a simplified interface that provides the capability to wrap SQL statements into logical blocks that can then be edited by using the query builder presented in the previous section (see Figure 23-5). This level of integration allows logical SQL blocks to be verified and tested independently in an intuitive interface to simplify the creation of the entire stored procedure.

Another powerful new feature available from within Visual Studio .NET when working with stored procedures is the ability to version stored procedures by using Visual SourceSafe or any other source control solution compatible with Visual Studio .NET.

The final and most useful feature to be integrated into the Visual Studio .NET environment for working with stored procedures is the capability to debug SQL Server stored procedures from directly within the IDE.

For large applications that are distributed across multiple tiers, this capability to debug from line to line across multiple projects and down into the underlying stored procedures provides you with a powerful solution to solve the most difficult development problems.

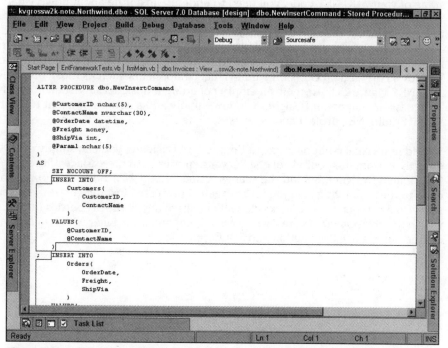

Figure 23-5: The query analyzer in Visual Studio .NET automatically groups SQL statements into logical blocks that can be edited independently by using tools such as the query builder.

Visual Studio .NET and ADO.NET

Now that you have seen a little of the tight integration between data sources and Visual Studio .NET, you see how Microsoft has taken advantage of this integration to provide a number of timesaving features to help write a lot of the standard "plumbing"-type ADO.NET code. These features, which consist of a number of tightly integrated wizards and other tools, allow you to integrate their applications with a data source by simply dragging and dropping the connections, views, or tables directly from the Server Explorer window onto the appropriate form or component. As a result of this drag-and-drop integration, Visual Studio .NET handles the remedial work of generating the underlying code to connect the appropriate ADO.NET objects. To demonstrate this type of integration and how it can be used to quickly and easily build very robust applications, this chapter walks through some of the main points of integration and discusses the features and options available from the wizards they present.

Adding components with the Component Designer

Before you begin your look at the capability for Visual Studio .NET to generate some of your ADO.NET code, you need to understand a little about how Visual Studio .NET adds non-visual components (such as `DataSets` and `DataAdapters`) to components or forms. The Component Designer of Visual Studio .NET provides a blank surface for you to add non-visual components to components. This surface provides you with functionality very similar to dragging a button onto a graphical Windows Form, but accepts only non-visual components such as those provided by ADO.NET. Figure 23-6 presents an empty component designer in Visual Studio .NET. To access a Component Designer window, simply add a new component to your Visual Studio .NET project and view its designer.

To add non-visual components to a Component Designer, you can simply drag and drop them from the Toolbox or the Server Explorer onto the surface of the Component Designer. Behind the scenes, Visual Studio .NET adds the appropriate code to the underlying component to create a protected instance of the selected non-visual component that makes it available from any of the properties or methods within the component. Figure 23-7 shows a Component Designer with two non-visual components: a SQLConnection and SQLCommand.

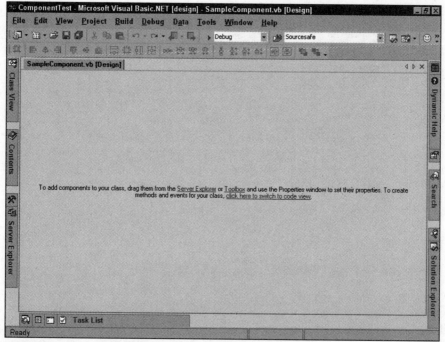

Figure 23-6: To add non-visual components, you drag them into the Visual Studio .NET Component Designer shown here.

The true power of a feature such as the Component Designer gives you the ability to manipulate the properties of these non-visual components at design time by using the Property window or any other available tool (that is, wizards and so on) instead of hand-coding all the properties. When modifying the properties of a component in the Component Designer window, the IDE handles the generation of the appropriate code to set the properties at runtime.

As you see in the next couple of sections, this feature is integral to Microsoft's integration of ADO.NET directly into the Visual Studio .NET environment.

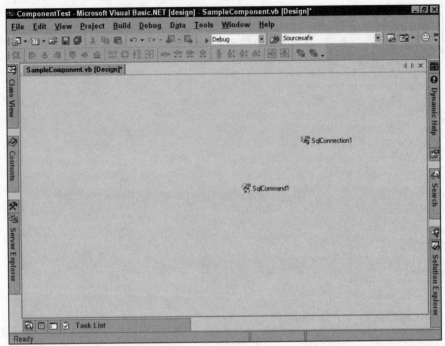

Figure 23-7: Visual Studio .NET Component Designer with two non-visual components.

Adding connections to forms

When working with a graphical user interface (UI) or a Component Designer that supports non-visual components, adding a connection to a database becomes a trivial task. The first step of adding a data connection to an item in a project is to add the connection to the Server Explorer window, as described earlier in this chapter. After the connection has been added to the Server Explorer window, it can be dropped directly onto the appropriate Designer to be made available from within the underlying code.

After the connection has been dropped into the Designer, Visual Studio .NET makes the decision about which type of ADO.NET connection to add. Then either a SQLConnection or an OLEDBConnection object is added as a component-level object, and all the properties, such as connection strings, are set appropriately.

Listing 23-1 shows the results of adding a single SQL Server connection to the Northwind database to a component. Notice that this entire section of code was automatically generated by the Visual Studio .NET IDE when creating the component, and then modified when adding the SQLConnection to the Component Designer:

Listing 23-1: Code Generated by Adding a SQL Server Connection to a Component Designer

```vb
#Region " Component Designer generated code "

    Public Sub New(Container As System.ComponentModel.IContainer)
        MyClass.New()

        'Required for Windows.Forms Class Composition Designer support
        Container.Add(me)
    End Sub

    Friend WithEvents SqlConnection1 As System.Data.SqlClient.SqlConnection

    Public Sub New()
        MyBase.New()

        'This call is required by the Component Designer.
        InitializeComponent()

        'Add any initialization after the InitializeComponent() call

    End Sub

    'Required by the Component Designer
    Private components As System.ComponentModel.Container

    'NOTE: The following procedure is required by the Component Designer
    'It can be modified using the Component Designer.
    'Do not modify it using the code editor.
    <System.Diagnostics.DebuggerStepThrough()> Private Sub _
            InitializeComponent()
        Me.SqlConnection1 = New System.Data.SqlClient.SqlConnection()
        '
        'SqlConnection1
        '
        Me.SqlConnection1.ConnectionString = _
            "data source=kvgrossw2k-note;initial catalog=Northwind; _
            persist security info=False;user id=sa;workstation id= _
            KVGROSSW2K-NOTE;packet size=4096"

    End Sub

#End Region
```

Notice that the IDE handled creating the SQLConnection in the `InitializeComponent` method, and set all the appropriate properties. Thus, if you need to modify a property such as the connection string, it could be done either to the code itself or through the Properties window of the SQLConnection visible on the Component Designer (see Figure 23-8). You can access the Properties window for any non-visual component by right clicking on the desired component in the Component Designer and then selecting Properties.

Figure 23-8: Modifying the properties of a SQLConnection in Visual Studio .NET.

It is important to realize that any change made to the properties of a non-visual class in the Properties window reflects immediately in the underlying code of the form or component. Note that the opposite is also true. Any change in the generated code that sets the initial values of the properties reflects in the Properties window. This is something that holds true for any non-visual component in Visual Studio .NET; it is not specific to any ADO.NET components.

Adding data commands in Visual Studio .NET

Command objects can be added to the appropriate Component Designer or graphical form by dragging a stored procedure node from the Server Explorer onto the designer. After dropping the stored procedure node, the Visual Studio .NET environment automatically generates the appropriate Connection and Command objects, and adds the appropriate configuration code.

It is important to note that the ability to automatically add Command objects applies only to stored procedures, and that the type of Command object (SQLCommand or OLEDBCommand) is determined by the type of connection to which the stored procedure is associated.

Like the Connection object, the Command object exposes all its properties graphically, and modifying them through the UI propagates all changes back to the generated code.

Another key timesaving feature that occurs automatically when generating
Command objects through the IDE is the fact that all the appropriate Parameter
objects are added to the Command object for a specific stored procedure.

Listing 23-2 demonstrates the code generated by Visual Studio .NET when adding
the spCustomersInsert stored procedure to a component. Note that both the
Command and the Connection object were automatically generated when the
stored procedure was dragged on the Component Designer.

Listing 23-2: The Code Generated as a Result of Dragging a Stored Procedure into the Component Designer Window

```
#Region " Component Designer generated code "


    Public Sub New(Container As System.ComponentModel.IContainer)
        MyClass.New()

        'Required for Windows.Forms Class Composition Designer support
        Container.Add(me)
    End Sub

    Friend WithEvents SqlConnection1 As System.Data.SqlClient.SqlConnection
    Friend WithEvents SqlCommand1 As System.Data.SqlClient.SqlCommand

    Public Sub New()
        MyBase.New()

        'This call is required by the Component Designer.
        InitializeComponent()

        'Add any initialization after the InitializeComponent() call

    End Sub

    'Required by the Component Designer
    Private components As System.ComponentModel.Container

    'NOTE: The following procedure is required by the Component Designer
    'It can be modified using the Component Designer.
    'Do not modify it using the code editor.
    <System.Diagnostics.DebuggerStepThrough()> Private Sub _
            InitializeComponent()
        Me.SqlConnection1 = New System.Data.SqlClient.SqlConnection()
        Me.SqlCommand1 = New System.Data.SqlClient.SqlCommand()
        '
        'SqlConnection1
```

Continued

Listing 23-2 *(continued)*

```
'
Me.SqlConnection1.ConnectionString = _
   "data source=kvgrossw2k- note;initial catalog=Northwind; _
    persist security info=Falseuser id=sa;workstation _
    id=KVGROSSW2K-NOTE;packet size=4096"
'
'SqlCommand1
'
Me.SqlCommand1.CommandText = "dbo.spCustomersInsert"
Me.SqlCommand1.CommandType = _
   System.Data.CommandType.StoredProcedure
Me.SqlCommand1.Connection = Me.SqlConnection1

Me.SqlCommand1.Parameters.Add(New _
   System.Data.SqlClient.SqlParameter("@RETURN_VALUE", _
   System.Data.SqlDbType.Int, 4, _
   System.Data.ParameterDirection.ReturnValue, True, CType(10, _
   Byte), CType(0, Byte), "", System.Data.DataRowVersion.Current, _
   Nothing))

Me.SqlCommand1.Parameters.Add(New _
   System.Data.SqlClient.SqlParameter("@CustomerID", _
   System.Data.SqlDbType.NChar, 5, _
   System.Data.ParameterDirection.Input, True, CType(0, Byte), _
   CType(0, Byte), "", System.Data.DataRowVersion.Current, _
   Nothing))

Me.SqlCommand1.Parameters.Add(New _
   System.Data.SqlClient.SqlParameter("@ContactName", _
   System.Data.SqlDbType.NChar, 30, _
   System.Data.ParameterDirection.Input, True, CType(0, Byte), _
   CType(0, Byte), "", System.Data.DataRowVersion.Current, _
   Nothing))

Me.SqlCommand1.Parameters.Add(New _
   System.Data.SqlClient.SqlParameter("@ContactTitle", _
   System.Data.SqlDbType.NChar, 30, _
   System.Data.ParameterDirection.Input, True, CType(0, Byte), _
   CType(0, Byte), "", System.Data.DataRowVersion.Current, _
   Nothing))

Me.SqlCommand1.Parameters.Add(New _
   System.Data.SqlClient.SqlParameter("@Address", _
   System.Data.SqlDbType.NChar, 60, _
   System.Data.ParameterDirection.Input, True, CType(0, Byte), _
   CType(0, Byte), "", System.Data.DataRowVersion.Current, _
   Nothing))
```

```
        Me.SqlCommand1.Parameters.Add(New _
            System.Data.SqlClient.SqlParameter("@City", _
            System.Data.SqlDbType.NChar, 15, _
            System.Data.ParameterDirection.Input, True, CType(0, Byte), _
            CType(0, Byte), "", System.Data.DataRowVersion.Current, _
            Nothing))

        Me.SqlCommand1.Parameters.Add(New _
            System.Data.SqlClient.SqlParameter("@PostalCode", _
            System.Data.SqlDbType.NChar, 10, _
            System.Data.ParameterDirection.Input, True, CType(0, Byte), _
            CType(0, Byte), "", System.Data.DataRowVersion.Current, _
            Nothing))

        Me.SqlCommand1.Parameters.Add(New _
            System.Data.SqlClient.SqlParameter("@Country", _
            System.Data.SqlDbType.NChar, 15, _
            System.Data.ParameterDirection.Input, True, CType(0, Byte), _
            CType(0, Byte), "", System.Data.DataRowVersion.Current, _
            Nothing))

        Me.SqlCommand1.Parameters.Add(New _
            System.Data.SqlClient.SqlParameter("@Select_CustomerID", _
            System.Data.SqlDbType.NChar, 5, _
            System.Data.ParameterDirection.Input, True, CType(0, Byte), _
            CType(0, Byte), "", System.Data.DataRowVersion.Current, _
            Nothing))

    End Sub

#End Region

End Class
```

As you saw in the previous chapter, configuring this type of Command object through coding by hand could be a very tedious task. But the ability for the IDE to generate most, if not all, of the code for use greatly simplifies the use of Command objects when using stored procedures with many parameters.

And, like all the other properties that can be set through the UI, the Parameters collection of a Command object can be edited graphically through the UI, as shown in Figure 23-9. You can accomplish this by clicking the button on the Parameters line of the Properties window. This window allows you to add and remove Parameters for the selected Command object as well as graphically change any of the Parameters properties. Any changes made to the Parameters collection using this window is reflected in the underlying code.

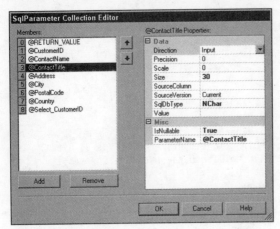

Figure 23-9: Editing command parameters in
Visual Studio .NET.

Also, after a Command object has been added and configured by dragging and
dropping it into a designer from the Server Explorer, you can use the Properties
window to invoke a query analyzer to modify the SQL statement of the Command
object directly by using the query analyzer. From within the query analyzer, you
can modify the SQL statement and also add parameters to the query. You can also
add any new parameters to the underlying code automatically by having the IDE
regenerate the Parameters collection.

Adding DataAdapters in Visual Studio .NET

Adding DataAdapters to components or forms in Visual Studio .NET is done in
much the same way as adding a Command object. When you drag a table or a view
from a data source in the Server Explorer and drop it onto the selected Designer,
Visual Studio .NET automatically adds and configures the appropriate Connection,
DataAdapter, and four Command objects.

Although similar in function to adding a stored procedure through a Command
object, a lot more behind-the-scenes processing occurs when adding a DataAdapter.
First, only the Connection and the DataAdapter objects are visible in the
Component Designer. Each of the four Command objects used by the DataAdapter
(as presented in the last chapter) is available from the properties of the
DataAdapter.

When the IDE attempts to add the DataAdapter to the designer, the first thing it
does is create a basic SQL Select statement, giving the name of the selected table
or view. This Select statement, which simply selects all the columns (that are
explicitly named) from the appropriate table or view, is then used to create the

base `SelectCommand` of the DataAdapter. Given this `SelectCommand`, a `CommandBuilder`, as presented in the last few chapters, is then used to generate the appropriate Insert, Update, and Delete commands. After each of these is generated, the IDE generates the code to reproduce the DataAdapter in code (including the Connection, DataAdapter, and all four Command objects). The simplicity of this design is that after the `CommandBuilder` generates the appropriate SQL statements for the remaining three SQL action commands, the code can be generated to reproduce them at runtime without the needed overhead of the `CommandBuilder`. Listing 23-3 demonstrates the code generated as a result of simply dragging the Customers table node from the Server Explorer window and dropping it onto an empty Component Designer window:

Listing 23-3: The Code Generated as a Result of Dragging a Database Table from the Server Explorer onto a Component Designer

```
#Region " Component Designer generated code "

    Public Sub New(ByVal Container As System.ComponentModel.IContainer)
        MyClass.New()

        'Required for Windows.Forms Class Composition Designer support
        Container.Add(Me)
    End Sub
    Friend WithEvents SqlSelectCommand1 As System.Data.SqlClient.SqlCommand
    Friend WithEvents SqlInsertCommand1 As System.Data.SqlClient.SqlCommand
    Friend WithEvents SqlUpdateCommand1 As System.Data.SqlClient.SqlCommand
    Friend WithEvents SqlDeleteCommand1 As System.Data.SqlClient.SqlCommand
    Friend WithEvents SqlConnection1 As System.Data.SqlClient.SqlConnection
    Friend WithEvents SqlDataAdapter1 As _
            System.Data.SqlClient.SqlDataAdapter

    Public Sub New()
        MyBase.New()

        'This call is required by the Component Designer.
        InitializeComponent()

        'Add any initialization after the InitializeComponent() call

    End Sub

    'Required by the Component Designer
    Private components As System.ComponentModel.Container

    'NOTE: The following procedure is required by the Component Designer
    'It can be modified using the Component Designer.
    'Do not modify it using the code editor.
```

Continued

Listing 23-3 *(continued)*

```
<System.Diagnostics.DebuggerStepThrough()> Private Sub _
        InitializeComponent()
    Me.SqlSelectCommand1 = New System.Data.SqlClient.SqlCommand()
    Me.SqlInsertCommand1 = New System.Data.SqlClient.SqlCommand()
    Me.SqlUpdateCommand1 = New System.Data.SqlClient.SqlCommand()
    Me.SqlDeleteCommand1 = New System.Data.SqlClient.SqlCommand()
    Me.SqlConnection1 = New System.Data.SqlClient.SqlConnection()
    Me.SqlDataAdapter1 = New System.Data.SqlClient.SqlDataAdapter()
    '
    'SqlSelectCommand1
    '
    Me.SqlSelectCommand1.CommandText = "SELECT ShipperID, _
        CompanyName, Phone FROM Shippers"
    Me.SqlSelectCommand1.Connection = Me.SqlConnection1
    '
    'SqlInsertCommand1
    '
    Me.SqlInsertCommand1.CommandText = "INSERT INTO _
        Shippers(CompanyName, Phone) VALUES (@CompanyName, @Phone); _
        SELECT ShipperID, CompanyName, Phone FROM Shippers WHERE _
        (ShipperID = @@IDENTITY)"

    Me.SqlInsertCommand1.Connection = Me.SqlConnection1

    Me.SqlInsertCommand1.Parameters.Add(New _
        System.Data.SqlClient.SqlParameter("@CompanyName", _
        System.Data.SqlDbType.NVarChar, 40, _
        System.Data.ParameterDirection.Input, False, CType(0, Byte), _
        CType(0, Byte), "CompanyName", _
        System.Data.DataRowVersion.Current, Nothing))

    Me.SqlInsertCommand1.Parameters.Add(New _
        System.Data.SqlClient.SqlParameter("@Phone", _
        System.Data.SqlDbType.NVarChar, 24, _
        System.Data.ParameterDirection.Input, True, CType(0, Byte), _
        CType(0, Byte), "Phone", System.Data.DataRowVersion.Current, _
        Nothing))
    '
    'SqlUpdateCommand1
    '
    Me.SqlUpdateCommand1.CommandText = "UPDATE Shippers SET _
        CompanyName = @CompanyName, Phone = @Phone WHERE (ShipperID = _
        @Original_ShipperID) AND (CompanyName = @Original_CompanyName) _
        AND (Phone = @Original_Phone OR @Original_Phone1 IS NULL AND _
        Phone IS NULL); SELECT ShipperID, CompanyName, Phone FROM _
        Shippers WHERE (ShipperID = @Select_ShipperID)"

    Me.SqlUpdateCommand1.Connection = Me.SqlConnection1
```

```
Me.SqlUpdateCommand1.Parameters.Add(New _
   System.Data.SqlClient.SqlParameter("@CompanyName", _
   System.Data.SqlDbType.NVarChar, 40, _
   System.Data.ParameterDirection.Input, False, CType(0, Byte), _
   CType(0, Byte), "CompanyName", _
   System.Data.DataRowVersion.Current, Nothing))

Me.SqlUpdateCommand1.Parameters.Add(New _
   System.Data.SqlClient.SqlParameter("@Phone", _
   System.Data.SqlDbType.NVarChar, 24, _
   System.Data.ParameterDirection.Input, True, CType(0, Byte), _
   CType(0, Byte), "Phone", System.Data.DataRowVersion.Current, _
   Nothing))

Me.SqlUpdateCommand1.Parameters.Add(New _
   System.Data.SqlClient.SqlParameter("@Original_ShipperID", _
   System.Data.SqlDbType.Int, 4, _
   System.Data.ParameterDirection.Input, False, CType(0, Byte), _
   CType(0, Byte), "ShipperID", _
   System.Data.DataRowVersion.Original, Nothing))

Me.SqlUpdateCommand1.Parameters.Add(New _
   System.Data.SqlClient.SqlParameter("@Original_CompanyName", _
   System.Data.SqlDbType.NVarChar, 40, _
   System.Data.ParameterDirection.Input, False, CType(0, Byte), _
   CType(0, Byte), "CompanyName", _
   System.Data.DataRowVersion.Original, Nothing))

Me.SqlUpdateCommand1.Parameters.Add(New _
   System.Data.SqlClient.SqlParameter("@Original_Phone", _
   System.Data.SqlDbType.NVarChar, 24, _
   System.Data.ParameterDirection.Input, True, CType(0, Byte), _
   CType(0, Byte), "Phone", System.Data.DataRowVersion.Original, _
   Nothing))

Me.SqlUpdateCommand1.Parameters.Add(New _
   System.Data.SqlClient.SqlParameter("@Original_Phone1", _
   System.Data.SqlDbType.NVarChar, 24, _
   System.Data.ParameterDirection.Input, True, CType(0, Byte), _
   CType(0, Byte), "Phone", System.Data.DataRowVersion.Original, _
   Nothing))

Me.SqlUpdateCommand1.Parameters.Add(New _
   System.Data.SqlClient.SqlParameter("@Select_ShipperID", _
   System.Data.SqlDbType.Int, 4, _
   System.Data.ParameterDirection.Input, False, CType(0, Byte), _
   CType(0, Byte), "ShipperID", _
   System.Data.DataRowVersion.Current, Nothing))
'
'SqlDeleteCommand1
'
```

Continued

Listing 23-3 *(continued)*

```
Me.SqlDeleteCommand1.CommandText = "DELETE FROM Shippers WHERE _
    (ShipperID = @ShipperID) AND (CompanyName = @CompanyName) AND _
    (Phone = @Phone OR @Phone1 IS NULL AND Phone IS NULL)"
Me.SqlDeleteCommand1.Connection = Me.SqlConnection1

Me.SqlDeleteCommand1.Parameters.Add(New _
    System.Data.SqlClient.SqlParameter("@ShipperID", _
    System.Data.SqlDbType.Int, 4, _
    System.Data.ParameterDirection.Input, False, CType(0, Byte), _
    CType(0, Byte), "ShipperID", _
    System.Data.DataRowVersion.Original, Nothing))

Me.SqlDeleteCommand1.Parameters.Add(New _
    System.Data.SqlClient.SqlParameter("@CompanyName", _
    System.Data.SqlDbType.NVarChar, 40, _
    System.Data.ParameterDirection.Input, False, CType(0, Byte), _
    CType(0, Byte), "CompanyName", _
    System.Data.DataRowVersion.Original, Nothing))

Me.SqlDeleteCommand1.Parameters.Add(New _
    System.Data.SqlClient.SqlParameter("@Phone", _
    System.Data.SqlDbType.NVarChar, 24, _
    System.Data.ParameterDirection.Input, True, CType(0, Byte), _
    CType(0, Byte), "Phone", System.Data.DataRowVersion.Original, _
    Nothing))

Me.SqlDeleteCommand1.Parameters.Add(New _
    System.Data.SqlClient.SqlParameter("@Phone1", _
    System.Data.SqlDbType.NVarChar, 24, _
    System.Data.ParameterDirection.Input, True, CType(0, Byte), _
    CType(0, Byte), "Phone", System.Data.DataRowVersion.Original, _
    Nothing))
'
'SqlConnection1
'
Me.SqlConnection1.ConnectionString = _
    "data source=kvgrossw2k-note;initial catalog=Northwind; _
    persist security info=False;user id=sa;workstation _
    id=KVGROSSW2K-NOTE;packet size=4096"
'
'SqlDataAdapter1
'
Me.SqlDataAdapter1.DeleteCommand = Me.SqlDeleteCommand1
Me.SqlDataAdapter1.InsertCommand = Me.SqlInsertCommand1
Me.SqlDataAdapter1.SelectCommand = Me.SqlSelectCommand1
Me.SqlDataAdapter1.TableMappings.AddRange(New _
    System.Data.Common.DataTableMapping() {New _
    System.Data.Common.DataTableMapping("Table", "Shippers", _
```

```
            New System.Data.Common.DataColumnMapping() {New _
            System.Data.Common.DataColumnMapping("ShipperID", _
            "ShipperID"), New _
            System.Data.Common.DataColumnMapping("CompanyName", _
            "CompanyName"), New _
            System.Data.Common.DataColumnMapping("Phone", "Phone")}}})
        Me.SqlDataAdapter1.UpdateCommand = Me.SqlUpdateCommand1

    End Sub

#End Region
```

Notice that each of the Command objects was added and configured separately by using parameters. This is the same way that adding a Command object was accomplished in the previous section. Also, a collection of DataColumnMappings was added programmatically. These column-mapping objects serve to relate the column names in a DataSet to the actual physical names of the columns in the database. By default, Visual Studio .NET generates a set of column mappings that relates the DataSet to the physical database table using the exact column name defined in the database. The added benefit here is that because all the column mappings are added through code, developers wishing to deviate from the standard column mappings can simply modify the generated code or use the provided Table Mappings editor, which is available from the Properties window of the DataAdapter (see Figure 23-10). For example, if a table column representing the first name of a person is called fname in the table structure, DataAdapter developers could modify the DataAdapter mappings to allow associated DataSets to call the column FirstName. That way, when utilizing the resulting DataSets on the front end, developers can take advantage of much more meaningful names while allowing the DataAdapter to handle the work of manipulating the friendly column names back into the names required by the database.

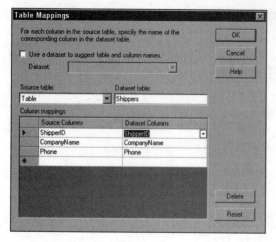

Figure 23-10: You can modify the DataSet column name to database table column name mappings in the Table Mappings editor.

This type of design time configuration and processing of a DataAdapter greatly increases runtime performance by allowing all the performance-intensive processes, such as schema generation, to be done only once. Also, it greatly increases your productivity by not forcing you to write a large amount of code to write this level of DataAdapter integration into your applications.

Additionally, when configuring a DataAdapter, it is possible that the `CommandBuilder` object cannot generate all the associated Command objects due to issues with the generated `Select` statement. This usually occurs when the `CommandBuilder` cannot programmatically determine which column in the `Select` statement serves as the unique identifier for a row. When this occurs, Visual Studio .NET displays a notification similar to the one shown in Figure 23-11. When this screen appears, it usually means that the `CommandBuilder` cannot programmatically determine a primary key for the given table. You can resolve this by verifying that there is a unique, primary key for the table and attempting to drop the table onto the Component Designer again.

After the DataAdapter has been added to a designer, you have the opportunity to perform much of its configuration through a single wizard called the DataAdapter Configuration Wizard. This wizard can be accessed by simply right-clicking the desired DataAdapter in the designer and selecting the Configure Data Adapter option. This wizard allows you to configure existing DataAdapters or to configure newly created DataAdapters. Some of the additional functionality provided by the wizard lies in its capability to create stored procedures to handle all four of the primary Commands required by the DataAdapter, given an appropriate `Select` statement. It then adds them directly to a database. These stored procedures abstract much of the direct SQL out of an individual DataAdapter's Command objects, and simply put the same SQL into stored procedures called with the same parameters. Figure 23-12 shows the frame of the DataAdapter Configuration Wizard, which allows you to specify custom names and options for each of the resulting four stored procedures.

Figure 23-11: DataAdapter configuration error.

Concurrency Checking with the DataAdapter Configuration Wizard

Some of the DataAdapter Configuration Wizard's more advanced features, which are not covered in this section, lie in its capability to automatically generate additions to its stored procedures to handle concurrency checking. This concurrency checking, which would otherwise have to be written manually, helps to assist you in writing database solutions that allow users to work with disconnected data, yet does not immediately overwrite any existing data if it has been modified since being loaded into a DataSet.

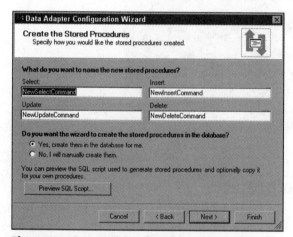

Figure 23-12: You can utilize the DataAdapter Configuration Window to generate stored procedures for interacting with a database table. You can choose to accept the default stored procedure names or provide your own.

Another feature added to assist you in using ADO.NET for your data access needs is the ability to preview the data served up by a DataAdapter. To access this feature, developers can right-click the desired DataAdapter and then select Preview Data from the resulting context menu. Figure 23-13 provides an example of using the DataAdapter preview menu that can be used to preview any of the data returned from a configured DataAdapter. This feature comes in extremely handy when you wish to verify that a DataAdapter has been properly configured to return the correct data and you wish to use it to populate a preconfigured DataSet. From this window, you can choose to preview the results of filling a new DataSet or choose an existing DataSet from those already in the project.

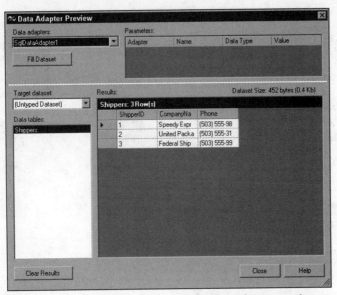

Figure 23-13: You can use the built-in DataAdapter preview window to view the results of using a DataAdapter to fill a DataSet.

Adding DataSets to projects

After a DataAdapter has been added to a designer that supports non-visual components, developers can easily add a new DataSet to the project that is preconfigured with the appropriate XML Schema (as discussed in Chapter 21) to accept any of the data returned by the DataAdapter.

To take advantage of this ability to generate the XML schema for DataSets, you can use the Generate DataSet window that can be accessed through the bottom of a DataAdapter Properties window (see Figure 23-14).

From the following window (see Figure 23-15), you can configure new DataSets or add DataTables to existing DataSets to accept data as defined in the DataAdapter.

After a new DataSet has been configured, a new set of files, containing an XML Schema document and a strongly typed DataSet, which is discussed in the next section, automatically is added to the current project. Figure 23-16 demonstrates how the files appear in the Solution Explorer window. Notice that the primary file has an XSD extension that identifies it as an XML Schema document. This XML Schema document provides the DataSet with a single file to load that configures it to accept data from the DataAdapter. As discussed in the last few chapters, preconfiguring this structure at design time offers a great deal of increased performance at runtime.

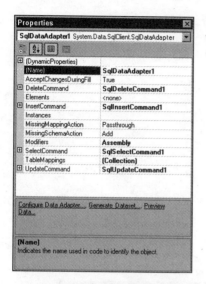

Figure 23-14: Here, the DataAdapter Properties window shows the Generate DataSet command.

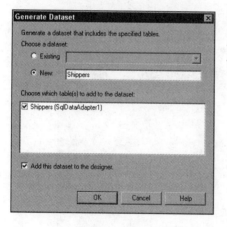

Figure 23-15: You use the Visual Studio .NET Generate DataSet window to specify to which DataSets you wish to add the tables defined by a DataAdapter.

By editing the XML Schema document in the Visual Studio .NET design time environment, you can take advantage of the built-in XML and XML Schema tools provided by the IDE. Figure 23-17 demonstrates the XML Schema editor available in Visual Studio .NET. This editor is available by simple opening any XML Schema document currently in your .NET project.

This editor provides a graphical means to manipulate and build XML Schema, which greatly simplifies a lot of tedious programming for those unfamiliar with the structure of an XML Schema document. The code in Listing 23-4 is the result of the XML Schema generated by Figure 23-17.

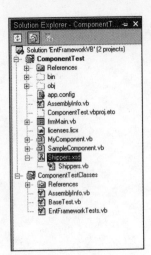

Figure 23-16: You can add XML Schema documents to any .NET project.

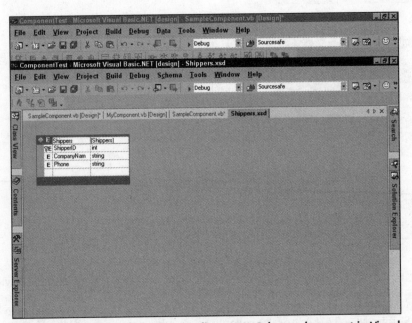

Figure 23-17: When attempting to edit an XML Schema document in Visual Studio .NET, you are taken to the XML Schema Editor and provided with a graphical interface for manipulating the Schema.

Listing 23-4: **The result of XML Schema Generation in Figure 23-18**

```
<xsd:schema id="Shippers"
targetNamespace="http://www.tempuri.org/Shippers.xsd"
  xmlns="http://www.tempuri.org/Shippers.xsd"
  xmlns:xsd="http://www.w3.org/2001/XMLSchema"
  xmlns:msdata="urn:schemas-microsoft-com:xml-msdata"
  attributeFormDefault="qualified"
  elementFormDefault="qualified">

  <xsd:element name="Shippers" msdata:IsDataSet="true">
    <xsd:complexType>
      <xsd:choice maxOccurs="unbounded">
        <xsd:element name="Shippers">
          <xsd:complexType>
            <xsd:sequence>
              <xsd:element name="ShipperID"
                  msdata:ReadOnly="true"
                  msdata:AutoIncrement="true"
                  type="xsd:int" />
              <xsd:element name="CompanyName"
                  type="xsd:string" />
              <xsd:element name="Phone" type="xsd:string"
                  minOccurs="0" />
            </xsd:sequence>
          </xsd:complexType>
        </xsd:element>
      </xsd:choice>
    </xsd:complexType>
    <xsd:unique name="Constraint1" msdata:PrimaryKey="true">
      <xsd:selector xpath=".//Shippers" />
      <xsd:field xpath="ShipperID" />
    </xsd:unique>
  </xsd:element>
</xsd:schema>
```

By having this document available at runtime, DataSets wishing to implement this structure simply need to load this XML Schema document, and they are instantly configured to the appropriate structure.

The remaining file added by the Generate DataSet tool is a code file containing a strongly typed DataSet, which is discussed in the following section.

Using typed DataSets

Strongly typed DataSets provide an added layer of usability to the regular DataSet object. Due to the inherent object-oriented nature of the .NET framework, it is relatively simple to provide abstract layers that inherit their functionality directly from the DataSet objects, but provide an extra layer of typing and usability. For example, rather than having a DataSet and corresponding DataTable that correspond to data out of a table containing Person information, with strongly typed DataSets it is possible to provide an object model that inherits from the DataSet. This object, which inherits from a DataSet, is called Person and provides individual properties for access to the Person data. For example, consider the following line of code:

```
oDataSet.Tables("Person").Rows(1)("Name_First") = "Kevin"
```

By providing a strongly typed "wrapper" around that DataSet, it is possible to have a situation in which the previous line of code could be rewritten with something similar to the following:

```
oPerson.Name_First = "Kevin"
```

This provides for much more readable code, as well as for the added benefit of using Intellisense to help find information about what fields are available.

So how is this accomplished in Visual Studio .NET? Actually, you already did it when you created DataSet using the Generate DataSet tool in the last section. The other file added to the Solution Explorer when you configured your DataSet was a code file containing all the classes necessary to make up a strongly typed DataSet. Now using the previous example, instead of creating a DataSet directly to load your Shipping information, you can instantiate a class of type Shipping. Then you could use the same DataAdapter to fill your Shipping class, and manipulate it by using direct properties and strongly typed (and possibly database-specific) data types.

Actually, when creating the classes that make up a typed DataSet, Visual Studio .NET creates a base named class (Person), and then creates two additional classes. One of these additional classes derives from an individual DataRow to provide the property access to an individual row's fields (PersonRow), and the other provides an event delegate to allow custom events to be raised by the typed DataSet.

To fully understand this type of implementation (without including the entire code in this book), use Visual Studio .NET to generate a typed DataSet and review the resulting code. You should be able to easily discern the structure and idea behind this powerful feature, and begin to see where it can simplify a lot of your code while providing an extremely fast implementation of a DataSet that has been configured to know its structure at design time.

Summary

Now that you have seen how the ADO.NET implementation requires an entirely new "disconnected" mindset for working with data, you can begin to take advantage of the new possibilities this paradigm opens up for you. As you saw in this chapter, Microsoft has gone to great lengths to tightly integrate ADO.NET into the Visual Studio .NET development environment to help simplify some of the more tedious data-access tasks while letting developers focus their efforts on writing business applications and not the underlying data access "plumbing." Another of the key technologies that was not discussed in these few chapters on data access is the powerful data-binding features provided by the .NET framework, as you will see in the next few chapters on Windows Forms and Web Forms. .NET provides an enormous amount of functionality when it comes to binding controls to other objects such as DataSets or DataReaders. By combining the power to easily utilize data binding with Visual Studio .NET's integrated integration with ADO.NET and data source administration, you find that the .NET framework and Visual Studio .NET provide a productive and powerful environment for building almost any type of application that requires data access.

✦   ✦   ✦

Introduction to XML in .NET

by Kevin Grossnicklaus

As you have seen in the last few chapters, and as you have undoubtedly heard elsewhere about .NET, the .NET Framework has a foundation that is built heavily on XML-based technologies. By this, I mean that at its lowest and most basic level, the .NET Framework and the tools provided by Visual Studio .NET understand and can easily manipulate anything that can be represented as XML.

Due to this deep integration with XML, it is important to understand the basic tools provided by the .NET Framework to take advantage of XML and its related technologies. And although a discussion on basic XML is beyond the scope of this book, you get an overview of some of the more useful and available tools and technologies that XML makes possible on the .NET platform.

Visual Studio .NET and XML

The first key tool that is available when working with XML is the Visual Studio .NET design time environment itself. The Visual Studio .NET IDE provides a large number of tools to edit XML documents that also, by default, allow simplified editing of XML Schema documents and XSLT documents.

One key indicator about the level of support that Visual Studio .NET provides in regards to XML is that you can add XML documents, XML Schema documents, or XSL stylesheets directly into the existing project.

When adding XML documents directly into a Visual Studio .NET project, you are taken to a basic XML editor and allowed to enter the XML directly into a text editor, as shown in Figure 24-1.

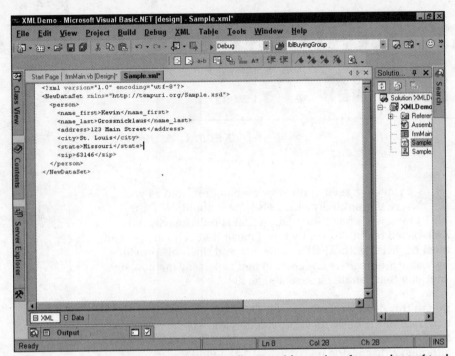

Figure 24-1: The Visual Studio .NET XML editor provides an interface and set of tools to simply enter and manipulate XML documents from within the IDE environment.

Although this editor has the appearance of a basic text editor, it does in fact provide a number of useful features that simplify the entry of XML documents. These features, such as autocompletion of XML element names and automatic formatting and validation of XML documents, are a welcome addition for developers who have used the standard Visual Notepad .NET to modify XML documents in the past. Another feature available in the Visual Studio .NET XML editor is the ever-available real-time underlining of syntax and schema errors when editing an XML document. This type of feature, which is available in most (if not all) of the Visual Studio .NET editors, greatly minimizes the amount of debugging that is usually required to manually enter a properly formatted XML document.

Beyond just the basic XML editing features of Visual Studio .NET, one of the most powerful features of the design time environment is the capability to treat XML as data. This concept is built on the same ideas and technologies that guided the design and architecture of the ADO.NET architecture. After developing the structure of an XML document, either by specifying an XML Schema document or by creating a sample XML document and having the schema inferred, Visual Studio .NET allows developers to build up the XML document by adding "rows" to the "tables," as shown in Figure 24-2. This editing paradigm, available by selecting the Data button at the bottom of the window and switching to the Data view of an open XML document, allows data to be added to XML documents exactly as data is added to SQL tables.

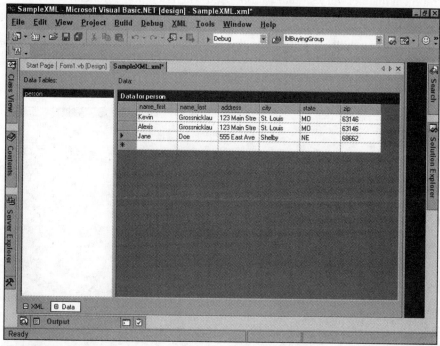

Figure 24-2: Switch to the Data view of an XML document to edit XML documents in a database-like editor.

To provide the ability for you to edit XML data in a manner similar to editing data from a relational database, the structure of the XML document must be either speci-fied directly by providing an XML Schema document or inferred by allowing the Visual Studio .NET IDE to derive the schema directly from the contents. You can take advantage of these powerful inference techniques to generate the XML Schema documents and have them added directly to the current project at design time, which allows you to minimize the amount of runtime inference of schema. To have the Visual Studio .NET environment create an XML Schema document off of an existing XML document, you can simply right-click the XML document editor and select Create Schema.

After an XML Schema document has been added to a project, either by inferring the schema from the structure of an existing XML document or by adding a new XML

Schema document, it can be edited with the built-in Schema editor or as an XML document using the editor discussed previously. You can access the built-in XML Schema editor, as shown in Figure 24-3, simply by attempting to open an XML Schema document from the Solution Explorer window. The XML Schema editor enables developers to define and/or view the structure of XML documents in a graphical manner very similar to that used when defining database schema.

Editing XML schema in Visual Studio .NET, when used in conjunction with ADO.NET's capability to determine the structure of a DataSet from an XML Schema file, can be a powerful tool that enables you to modify the structure and organization of every aspect of a DataSet at design time.

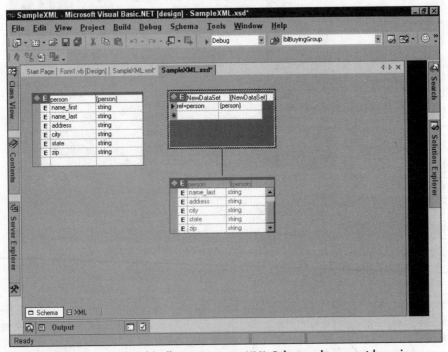

Figure 24-3: You can graphically generate an XML Schema document by using the Visual Studio .NET XML Schema designer.

Manipulating XML in Code

As you saw in the previous section, the Visual Studio .NET environment provides the facilities for you to add and work with XML Schema through various editors and tools provided at design time. Although these tools can prove to greatly increase productivity and truly provide XML support in the .NET Framework, Microsoft has provided a strong set of base classes that allow you to manipulate a consistent set of classes and interfaces with which to work with XML.

These objects, most of which are found in the System.XML namespace, provide you with an enormous amount of options and flexibility as to when a specific tool or technology is appropriate for working with XML. You are not forced to choose between two distinctly different XML development paradigms, as has been available with Microsoft's XML Parser (MSXML) DOM implementation and an event-based Simple API for XML (SAX) implementation.

Note Prior to the availability of the .NET Framework, there were two major technologies available for manipulating an XML document, both of which had implementations provided in Microsoft's COM-based XML Parser, or MSXML. These two technologies consisted of a thick, tree-based object model built around the W3C's Document Object Model (DOM) specification and a forward-only, event-based implementation of the Simple API for XML (SAX) implementation. When working with XML data, you were usually forced to choose between an implementation of one of these two technologies.

With the .NET Framework, you have access to a comprehensive set of classes to work with XML data. Because more options are available, you can choose the correct set of classes to fit a particular programming situation.

As part of the .NET Framework, Microsoft has provided classes to read streams of XML (XMLReader), to write streams of XML (XMLWriter), as well as classes to modify XML documents through a W3C DOM-compliant object model (XMLDocument and XMLNode). Beyond these basic functions, classes are also provided for more advanced XML functions such as manipulating XML Schema documents (XmlSchema), providing encoding and decoding features (XmlConvert), and transforming an XML document by using an XSLT stylesheet (XMLTransform).

Although a number of options do exist for manipulating XML (one you already saw in the ADO.NET DataSet object), most developers who are familiar with XML development prior to the .NET Framework are most familiar with the XMLDocument and XMLNode objects available in the System.XML namespace. These two objects (and those that inherit from them) provide the basic DOM implementation in the .NET Framework. Although the .NET implementation of the DOM has seen great performance increases over Microsoft's prior DOM implementations, it is still important to realize that this structure consists of an in-memory tree structure of XMLNode objects that allow you to navigate and modify an XML document. Although there is certainly a place for this type of control in many development scenarios, when this type of functionality is not needed, most developers can easily make use of the much smaller and faster XMLReaders and XMLWriters to perform most basic XML tasks.

Listing 24-1 provides two sample functions that demonstrate creating a new XML document and writing it directly to a file by using an XMLWriter, as well as reading an XML file back into memory through the use of an XMLReader.

Listing 24-1: Manipulating XML Documents to and from Files Using the XMLReader and XMLWriter Classes

```
Public Function LoadFile(ByVal FileName As String) As _
    String
    'Create a new stream reader to read in the file
    Dim oTextReader As New _
        System.IO.StreamReader(FileName)

    'Create an XMLReader instance to read XML from the _
    text stream
    Dim oXMLReader As New _
        System.Xml.XmlTextReader(oTextReader)

    'Read all the elements from the XML reader until _
    there are none left
    While oXMLReader.Read()
        'Write the values to output
        Debug.WriteLine(oXMLReader.Value.ToString())
    End While

    'Make sure we close the file
    oXMLReader.Close()

End Function

Public Sub WriteFile(ByVal FileName As String)
    'Create a new XML writer to send an XML stream to _
    a file
    Dim oXMLWriter As New Xml.XmlTextWriter(FileName, _
        System.Text.Encoding.ASCII)

    'Using a set of output functions, write our XML _
    document sequentially to the open file
    oXMLWriter.WriteStartDocument(True)
    oXMLWriter.WriteStartElement("Person")
    oXMLWriter.WriteElementString("Name_First", "John")
    oXMLWriter.WriteElementString("Name_Last", "Doe")
    oXMLWriter.WriteElementString("SSN", "123-456-1234")
    oXMLWriter.WriteEndElement()
    oXMLWriter.WriteEndDocument()

    'Flush the contents of the writer to the file
    oXMLWriter.Flush()

    'Make sure we close the stream before continuing
    oXMLWriter.Close()
End Sub
```

One key feature to note about the use of the XMLReader in the previous example is that it is being used to read the XML document in from a file one element at a time by using the Read method. In this example, you simply read the elements in and write their values out to the debug window.

It is also important to note the manner in which the XMLWriter class provides you the ability to write an XML document by using a stream of commands for writing elements and beginning and ending nested sections. When using an XMLWriter to output XML to a file, you'll see the importance of wrapping all your output commands with the appropriate calls to the StartDocument and EndDocument. This same paradigm is then used to nest elements within the entire document by using the appropriate nesting for calls to StartElement and EndElement, as shown in the example.

Although the XMLReader and XMLWriter implementations serve specific purposes and address specific needs when dealing with XML documents, many development situations still require that you use the full DOM implementation to manipulate an XML document. To do this, most developers begin with the XMLDocument object that is an implementation of an XMLNode object that allows developers to work with and manipulate an XMLDocument as a whole while serving as the root of a structured tree of XMLNode objects. Review the code in Listing 24-2 for a basic example of traversing and manipulating an XML document by using the XMLNode tree exposed in the .NET DOM implementation.

Listing 24-2: **Manipulating an XML Document Using the DOM Implementation Provided by the XmlDocument class**

```
'Create a new instance of an XML document
Dim oXMLDocument As New Xml.XmlDocument()

'Fill the instance with a string containing an XML _
  document
oXMLDocument.LoadXml(sXML)

Dim oXMLNode As Xml.XmlNode

'Iterate through each node in the tree and write _
 it's contents to the debug window
For Each oXMLNode In _
    oXMLDocument.DocumentElement.ChildNodes
    'Write out each element at this level's XML _
    value (including nested elements and element _
    names)
    Debug.WriteLine(oXMLNode.OuterXml.ToString())

Next
```

Listing 24-2 utilizes an instance of an `XmlDocument` object to load and manipulate the XML specified in the `sXML` variable. We utilize the `LoadXML` method to populate the `XmlDocument` with the appropriate state, and then simply iterate through the collection of `XmlNode` objects, which represent the various nodes that make up the specified XML document.

As discussed in the last few chapters, the ADO.NET Framework for data access treats data as XML and XML as data. With this paradigm in mind, Microsoft also provided a DOM-based class structure to manipulate XML documents that integrates seamlessly with the ADO.NET `DataSet` object. By utilizing both of these class structures simultaneously, you can achieve real-time, synchronous access to a single set of XML data by using both distinct views of the data. This ability to manipulate the data in both a relational and a hierarchical structure allows you to manipulate XML by using the tools that most readily apply to the situation.

Another key benefit of working with both structures concurrently is that when synchronized with an `XMLDataDocument`, an ADO.NET DataSet retains the original structure of the underlying XML document. When not synchronized with an `XMLDataDocument`, DataSets do little to maintain the underlying structure of the XML document they are manipulating. The standard DataSet does nothing to retain whitespace, to preserve element order, or to keep any parts of an XML document that are not explicitly defined in the DataSet's schema. All these things are maintained when the DataSet is utilized in conjunction with an `XMLDataDocument`, as shown in the following code:

```
'Create a new instance of an XMLDataDocument
Dim oXMLDataDocument As New Xml.XmlDataDocument()

'Fill the DataDocument with XML specified in a string
oXMLDataDocument.LoadXml(sXML)

'Use the DataSet property of the XMLDataDocument _
  to get an ADO.NET DataSet representing the same data
Dim oDataSet As DataSet = oXMLDataDocument.DataSet()

'...at this point oXMLDataDocument and oDataSet _
  share common data and manipulating one or the _
  other will affect both
```

XML serialization

When building VB .NET applications by using the .NET Framework, another powerful use of XML is the capability to serialize an object's state to and from an XML document. This capability allows an object to be persisted into a format that can safely be transferred across the network or between processes, and used to create an identical instance of a given object. This type of serialization is extremely powerful when building distributed applications that need to pass a lot of information between different machines on the network. Picture an application, for example, that needs to pass a `Person` object from the user-interface tier to a middle-tier object to perform the basic data access. This class and all its state can be serialized into an XML format, and the resulting XML document can be passed across the network as a string. After the middle-tier receives this XML document, they can use the same serialization technology to create a new instance of a `Person` object with the appropriate state. This allows developers to build very object-oriented applications and maintain the ability to work with thick, stateful objects while still allowing them to utilize the benefits of XML.

This type of XML serialization is made available by a set of objects in the System.XML.Serialization namespace that make heavy use of the reflection features provided by the .NET Framework to determine the structure of a .NET object and then read its public properties into an XML document. These same reflection features are used when attempting to fill an objects state with data currently in an XML document.

The following example demonstrates a possible implementation of the scenario described previously to demonstrate the power provided by the serialization features made available for XML in .NET. The serialization in Listing 24-3 serializes a basic `Person` class by using a separate `PersonSerialization` class.

Listing 24-3: **Using PersonSerialization to Serialize a Basic Person Class**

```
'A simple Person class to be persisted into XML
Public Class Person
    'These public properties will be persisted to and _
     from XML using the serialization classes
    Public Name_First As String
    Public Name_Last As String
    Public Address As String
    Public City As String
    Public State As String
    Public ZIP As String
End Class

'A seperate class to handle the persistance of Person _
 objects to and from XML
Public Class PersonSerializer
    'A function to return the state of the current object _
     in XML format
    Public Function GetXML(ByVal pPerson As Person) As String
        'Create a new instance of an XMLSerializer object _
         passing a reference to a person type to the _
         constructor
        Dim oSerializer As New _
      System.Xml.Serialization.XmlSerializer(GetType(Person))
```

Continued

Listing 24-3 *(continued)*

```
        Dim oStringWriter As New System.IO.StringWriter()

        'Serialize the current object (Me) into a _
          StringWriter
        oSerializer.Serialize(oStringWriter, pPerson)

        'Return the results
        Return oStringWriter.ToString()
    End Function

    Public Sub LoadXML(ByVal pPerson As Person, _
                       ByVal XML As String)
        'Create another instance of the XMLSerializer _
          object (same as GetXML())
        Dim oSerializer As New _
      System.Xml.Serialization.XmlSerializer(GetType(Person))

        'Create a StringReader instance and instantiate it _
          with the XML parameter
        Dim oStringReader As New System.IO.StringReader(XML)

        pPerson = _
        CType(oSerializer.Deserialize(oStringReader), Person)
    End Sub
End Class
```

Listing 24-3 implements two separate classes: `Person` and `PersonSerializer`.
The `Person` class serves to implement the functionality of a basic object within the
application. The associated `PersonSerializer` class handles the appropriate
serialization to and from XML for a given person object. The `PersonSerializer`
implements two powerful functions to serve its purpose: `LoadXML` and `GetXML`.
The following code demonstrates the usage of the previous two classes:

```
        'Create a new person object
        Dim oPerson As New Person()

        'Set our public properties
        oPerson.Name_First = "John"
        oPerson.Name_Last = "Doe"
        oPerson.Address = "123 Main Street"
        oPerson.City = "St. Louis"
        oPerson.State = "MO"
        oPerson.ZIP = "63146"

        'Instantiate a new serializer object
        Dim oPersonSerializer As New PersonSerializer()
```

```
'Get the entire state of our person object as XML
Dim sXML As String = _
    oPersonSerializer.GetXML(oPerson)

'Create another instance of a person object
Dim oAnotherPerson As New Person()

'Fill it with the same properties as the first _
  Person object
oPersonSerializer.LoadXML(oAnotherPerson, sXML)
```

By using the .NET serialization techniques in Listing 24-3 to retrieve the entire state of a `Person` object into XML format, the following XML document would be the representation of an instance of a `Person` class:

```
<?xml version="1.0" encoding="utf-16"?>
<Person xmlns:xsi="http://www.w3.org/2001/XMLSchema-instance"
    xmlns:xsd="http://www.w3.org/2001/XMLSchema">
  <Name_First>John</Name_First>
  <Name_Last>Doe</Name_Last>
  <Address>123 Main Street</Address>
  <City>St. Louis</City>
  <State>MO</State>
  <ZIP>63146</ZIP>
</Person>
```

This type of serialization lets you manipulate a strongly typed object in a simple manner and then retrieve the results as an XML document. This paradigm essentially hides a lot of the complexities required for XML-based persistence, and allows you to work with object models that you are familiar with while still having the ability to retrieve the results in a standard, definable XML format.

When persisting objects to and from an XML-based format by using .NET's serialization features, you can also provide nested XML elements based on a hierarchical object model. With this feature, you can build complex object structures that contain parent-child relationships and have them persisted to and from XML by using the XML serialization infrastructure of .NET. Listing 24-4 shows how basic `Person` and `Address` objects present a simple object hierarchy with a single parent and a single child.

Listing 24-4: **Creating a Simple Hierarchy Using Nested Classes**

```
'A simple Person class to be persisted into XML
Public Class Person
    'These public properties will be persisted to and _
      from XML using the serialization classes
```

Continued

Listing 24-4 *(continued)*

```
        Public Name_First As String
        Public Name_Last As String
        Public Address As Address
        Public SSN As String

    End Class

    Public Class Address
        'A child instance of an Address object
        Public Line1 As String
        Public Line2 As String
        Public City As String
        Public State As String
        Public ZIP As String
    End Class
```

By using the XMLSerializer object to serialize the nested Person object, as was shown in Listing 24-4, the XMLSerializer automatically recognizes the Address object through reflection, and include it in the XML results as well. The following XML shows an example of a document that might be created:

```
<?xml version="1.0" encoding="utf-16"?>
<Person xmlns:xsi="http://www.w3.org/2001/XMLSchema-instance"
       xmlns:xsd="http://www.w3.org/2001/XMLSchema">
  <Name_First>John</Name_First>
  <Name_Last>Doe</Name_Last>
  <Address>
    <Line1>123 East Main</Line1>
    <Line2>RR 2</Line2>
    <City>St. Louis</City>
    <State>MO</State>
    <ZIP>63146</ZIP>
  </Address>
  <SSN>123-456-7890</SSN>
</Person>
```

As you can see, through the process of reflection, the serialization engine can determine which public elements of a parent object correlate to a child object, and perform the necessary nesting.

By using features such as the XMLSerializer object, .NET developers can take advantage of XML's inherent capability to represent data and state without requiring low-level familiarity with the XML documents themselves. If such fine-tooth control is required in a particular situation, however, the ability to control the output of such objects as the `XMLSerializer` is easily available as well. This makes the serialization features that are available in .NET extremely attractive when dealing with anything from providing thick wrappers around file-based configuration files to handling marshalling of state between applications and tiers of an application. It is this type of low-level integration with XML that has been built into the .NET Framework from the ground up.

Summary

Although this chapter briefly touched on only some of the powerful XML features available in the Visual Studio .NET and the .NET Framework as a whole, it is important to take note that there are a large number of places in the .NET Framework in which XML plays an integral role but is essentially hidden from direct developer interaction. For example, utilizing the powerful Web service-creation features of Visual Studio .NET handles all the XML and SOAP integration code to be written for you. This means that you can take advantage of the interoperability SOAP and XML provide without having to be directly involved with writing that low-level code to make the protocols work.

As with a large number of other protocols, such as HTTP and TCP/IP, the advances in the tools and technologies, such as the .NET Framework, make your reliance on XML greater, but your direct interaction with low-level XML programming decreases greatly.

✦ ✦ ✦

Windows Forms

Introduction to System. Windows.Forms

by Jacob A. Grass

With all the talk about Web Forms, ASP.NET, Web Services, and so on, it is very easy to come to the conclusion that Windows-based application development is dead. This is simply untrue. Marketing is marketing, and the new Windows Forms framework is unbelievable.

The beauty of the Windows Forms framework is undeniable. Gone is the heavy dependence on coding against the Win32 API; gone is the "auto-magical, under-the-covers" plumbing; gone is the inability to transfer acquired skills between languages; gone are the archaic designers and techniques for necessary items, such as menus and ToolTips. This list could go on, but you'll understand soon enough.

Now you have the power of inheritance (or the danger depending on with whom you talk); you have docking and anchoring (that's right, no more annoying resizing code to write); you have a framework that remains constant regardless of the language (yes, the methods, properties and events remain the same); you have significantly smaller need to rely on `WM_XXXX` messages (I know, you miss them). This list could go on, but you'll understand soon enough.

Enough with the celebrating; it's time to get cracking. The most important thing to remember throughout this and the following chapters is that a Form is just a class. Repeat it again, because it should be the mantra of every Visual Basic, rich-client developer:

A Form is just a class.

A Form has properties, methods and events just like every other class. "Wait!" you exclaim, "These were present in previous versions of Visual Basic." This is true. But now, you are able to easily extend the core functionality that Microsoft provides. The chapters in this unit provide many examples of this.

In this chapter, you primarily learn the basics of the Windows.Forms namespace. You understand the class hierarchy and learn some basic techniques for accomplishing your goals. Advanced users find a wealth of information presented so that new techniques and information can be easily gleaned while refreshing the knowledge already possessed.

The Basics of the Window

Just about every task to be accomplished within the System.Windows.Forms framework requires a window of some sort. So, in order to better understand how the framework behaves, you must first understand exactly what it means to be a window.

What constitutes a window?

A window, in its crudest form, is an enclosed, rectangular area of the screen. It is typically defined by a bounding rectangle (visible or not) and often contains data or other windows. By this definition, not only are forms windows, but controls are windows as well.

In the Windows operating system, a handle identifies a window. This is analogous to an online handle, or a CB handle. In the case of windows programming, the handle is unique amongst all windows currently loaded. Furthermore, a window handle remains constant until the window is unloaded.

Visual Basic 4 introduced a type of control called *lightweight* or *windowless*. These were controls (for example, the Line and Shape controls) that did not have a bounding rectangle or a handle. They essentially constituted a set of instructions for the container control to paint.

The introduction of these controls led to many inconsistencies for the developer because windowed and windowless controls had to be handled differently. Furthermore, these controls had significantly reduced functionality due to their lack of a handle.

In .NET, every control is "windowed," which has advantages and disadvantages. The good side is that you now have a thoroughly consistent framework upon which to develop. All controls have a handle and can receive any relevant or necessary message. The downside is that some controls that may not need to receive messages or be identified by Windows now have the overhead of a window.

In short, this means that controls such as the Line and Shape controls, which are no longer present within .NET, can be accomplished only by explicitly composing the painting code. Which, in my opinion, is exactly the way they need to be.

What can a window do?

A window is the primary method of interaction between your software and the end user. Thus, it handles all the input (keyboard, mouse, and so on) from the user, and processes it according to your instructions. Furthermore, it displays any information you instruct it to with any formatting you desire.

The fact that the .NET Framework has now made items such as forms and controls fully inheritable classes almost removes all need to program against the Win32 API. As a developer, you can now get the entire window processing power for free in whatever you wish to accomplish.

It is still possible to deal with the Win32 API directly, though. Methods include calling P/Invoke or overriding the WndProc function. This ability is crucial for accomplishing certain tasks that have not yet been implemented in the framework. However, you will find that your usage of these methods will be minimal.

Other potential pitfalls

Many subtleties related to windows and their properties were in previous versions of Visual Basic. For example, certain Form borders styles could be specified only during the creation of the window rather than at any time in the process.

The old way to handle this problem was to destroy the window, and re-create it so that all existing information was still present with the new border style. The code necessary to accomplish this could lead one to an asylum. Now, the .NET Framework handles these subtleties for you.

Essentially, the .NET Framework serializes all required information to an in-memory buffer, destroys the window, re-creates the window, and then restores the serialized information to the new window.

When the Framework handles these subtleties, there are pitfalls, however. For those of you accustomed to accomplishing tasks via the Win32 API, the Framework can successfully muck up your code. The main reason is that window handles are subject to change. For example, in the NewHandle project, you find the following (see Listing 25-1):

Listing 25-1: **Example of Handle Changing**

```
Private Sub RadioChanged(ByVal sender As System.Object, _
    ByVal e As System.EventArgs) Handles _
    radDropDown.CheckedChanged, _
    radSimple.CheckedChanged, _
    radDropDownList.CheckedChanged
```

Continued

Listing 25-1 *(continued)*

```
  If CType(sender, RadioButton).Checked = True Then
    lblOldHandle.Text = "Old Handle:   " & _
    cmbHandle.Handle.ToString
    Select Case CType(sender, RadioButton).Text
        Case "ComboBox DropDown"
        cmbHandle.DropDownStyle = ComboBoxStyle.DropDown
        Case "ComboBox Simple"
        cmbHandle.DropDownStyle = ComboBoxStyle.Simple
        Case "ComboBox DropDownList"
        cmbHandle.DropDownStyle = ComboBoxStyle.DropDownList
    End Select
    lblNewHandle.Text = "New Handle:   " & _
    cmbHandle.Handle.ToString
  End If
End Sub
```

Very simply, each of the three radio buttons equates to one of the three available combo box drop-down styles. Changing selections changes the combo box to the appropriate style. The `Label` controls display both the old and new handles for the combo box each time the drop-down style changes. As you can see from executing the code in Listing 25-1, the window handle changes every time the value of `ComboBox.DropDownStyle` changes.

Basics of the Windows Form

The Windows Form (see Figure 25-1) is essentially, the most important control in your repertoire as a GUI (Graphical User Interface) developer. The Form is the canvas upon which you paint the controls required for the end users to accomplish their goals of data entry, system administration, software development, or any number of infinite tasks.

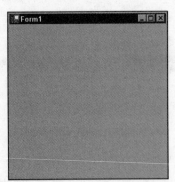

Figure 25-1: The ever-important tabula rasa.

The Form is a control like any other in the toolbox, yet it is so much more. You learn why throughout these chapters.

Where does the Windows Form come from?

The hierarchy of objects from which the Windows Form is derived is shown in Figure 25-2.

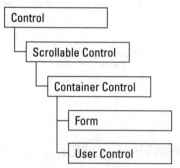

Figure 25-2: The Windows Form class ancestry.

Note

In the past, you may have seen similar diagrams that included a class called Rich Control. From DotNet Beta 2 on, the Rich Control class has been combined with the Control class. Other classes above Control exist, but they go beyond the scope of this unit.

The Control class is the foundation for all of the controls in the System.Windows. Forms namespace. This class handles all of the basic window handle (HWND) functionality such as creation and destruction of windows handles. Control also covers the majority of the basic windows messages (for example, WM_CREATE, WM_WINDOW-POSCHANGED, and so on). Thus, this class provides the basic functionality for user input, pointing devices, and bounding.

The integration of the Control and Rich Control class of yore has also granted even greater functionality to this class. The Control class now handles all of the basic painting of controls. This includes background colors, foreground colors, and text; but not items such as borders.

The ScrollableControl derives from Control to acquire all of the aforementioned capabilities. It adds the capability of a control to scroll vertically and horizontally in the client area of a window. Furthermore, this class adds auto-scrolling capabilities to controls, as well as the capability to house the scroll bars.

The ContainerControl is derived from ScrollableControl, and adds the ability to house other controls along with other functions that are necessary. This includes focus management and tabbing. The ContainerControl can be considered a class that provides logical boundaries for the controls it contains.

This brings us to the form. At this point, the form has all of the capabilities outlined in the class descriptions previously. Added to this functionality is the capability to have caption bars, irregular windowing, system menus, and default controls. This class also introduces the concepts of modality and MDI (Multiple Document Interface).

Also derived from `ContainerControl` is `UserControl`. This class gives you the ability to create controls that can be used and reused throughout any application. Furthermore, by inheriting from `ContainerControl`, all standard positioning, painting, containment, and mnemonics are covered. This class is covered in-depth later in this unit.

Chapter 26 gives extensive coverage to the `Control` object and Chapter 27 provides exhaustive coverage to nearly all controls derived from the `Control` Class. Chapter 28 introduces the concept of creating controls by extending and enhancing the existing controls.

Top 10 Reasons Why a Windows Form Is Better than a Visual Basic 6 Form

The following list delineates 10 items that were previously unavailable or unacceptable in Visual Basic 6 that have been rectified in Visual Basic .NET. Opinions differ on the "best" changes that have occurred. Hopefully, though, this list addresses the majority of the opinions.

10. **A Windows Form has twice as many properties and methods as an old form.** The Windows Form exposes significantly more properties, methods, and events than the Visual Basic 6 form. This means more functionality is available for you to play with. Plus, there is a reduced level of dependency on the Win32 API. Overall, the addition of properties, methods and events further enhances the rapid development experience by exposing significantly more behavior.

9. **A Windows Form can easily contain a dockable toolbar.** The Windows Forms framework introduces handy concepts such as docking, which are easily grasped and implemented by the novice developer. Dockable windows in Visual Basic 6 were virtually impossible to implement. This handy feature can be easily leveraged to create richer GUIs than ever before.

8. **Windows Forms are opaque until they're not.** The Windows Forms framework introduces a property called *opacity*. This is not a particularly new concept because Visual Basic forms have always been opaque. However, rather than use the `SetLayeredWindowsAttributes` API on a layered window to create varying levels of translucency, this property allows you to create a

translucent window by setting a property. (Check out the Search Window in TextPad for a good use of this concept.) This concept can be particularly useful in the development of more graphically oriented applications.

7. **You can capture the mousewheel with the greatest of ease.** It may be a little thing, but darn it, you'll be happy about it. In Visual Basic .NET, when a control has the focus and the user scrolls the mouse wheel, you can respond, if necessary. This was another task for the API in Visual Basic 6. In Microsoft Excel, holding down the CTRL key and scrolling the mousewheel results in the Zoom Factor changing. This type of functionality can be very easily implemented with the inclusion of a mousewheel event.

6. **There is now an object-oriented approach for graphics.** Every window in Visual Basic .NET has an associated Graphics Object. Every form in Visual Basic 6 has a Device Context. In Visual Basic 6, you needed the Device Context to pass to the API calls necessary to draw a polygon. In Windows Forms, you can call the `DrawPolygon` method of the Graphics Object.

5. **All border styles are available to you at any time via the** `FormBorderStyle` **property.** In Visual Basic 6, you were prevented from easily changing the border of a form to certain values. You were required to destroy the form and then redisplay it. Visual Basic .NET now handles all of this for you. You may run into problems regarding changing handles, as outlined in the pitfalls section of this chapter, but how often do you need the handle in Windows Forms?

4. **Autoscroll is not just German parchment.** A Windows Form now supports autoscrolling. Autoscrolling simply means that the scroll bars appear on a form if any of the controls reside outside the visible area of the form. This is a very handy feature for dealing with significant variations in resolution. In Visual Basic 6, you had to develop for the lowest common denominator, 600 x 480.

3. **A Windows Form can anchor like a sailor.** Many important parts of the graphical user interface design involve the little things — the details that make the end user's experience worthwhile. One these little things is resizeable windows. Visual Basic 6 always had resizeable windows, but how do you move the controls in accordance with the form? The only way to handle this in the past was with a fair amount of code that analyzed positions and ratios, and moved the controls to the appropriate place. Windows Forms introduces a concept called anchoring, which grounds the controls in their respective positions in relation to their container. Nothing could be easier.

2. **You don't need no stinking twips.** Few things were more cumbersome in Visual Basic 6 than units of measurement. Okay, some things were more cumbersome, but this one really bugged me. In Windows Forms, everything is measured in pixels. This makes for very consistent interface development.

1. **In the Windows Forms framework, a form is just a class.** The mystical Visual Basic 6 form is gone; it has been replaced by a fully extensible and inheritable class with visual capabilities. One of the most valuable results of this is Visual Inheritance. This feature is fully addressed in Chapter 28.

Summary

As you can see, the power is in your hands. You now have a number of new concepts to try out and play around with, and a number of old habits to forget. The Windows Forms framework is conducive to fast learning and lots of power.

The next few chapters give you a tour of the framework and some detailed information on the classes that are available to the developer.

✦   ✦   ✦

Controls

by Jacob A. Grass

The Form is the canvas upon which you paint your presentation to the user. Yet, what do you use to accomplish this? The user needs to view and modify data, yet the form itself isn't always the best tool for this job — by itself, that is. Controls are the proverbial colors of the palette. But they aren't just pretty, they can do stuff as well — lots of stuff.

This chapter covers the basic control available to you, the .NET developer. You become familiar with the various events, methods, and properties. The purpose of this chapter is to give a foundation for understanding the power of this framework.

The chapter begins by discussing delegates. The concept of delegates is crucial for understanding how events are handled within the new Forms framework.

Ideally, this chapter is not a full rehash of the documentation. It focuses mostly on those properties, methods, and events that are not present in Visual Basic 6. Keep in mind that everything in this chapter relates to all other controls.

This chapter is especially beneficial to the beginner trying to understand how everything in the Windows.Forms Framework fits together. The advanced user finds this chapter a useful reference for syntax and concepts that may not be easily recalled.

Delegates

Delegates are the foundation of events in the .NET Framework. In its simplest form, a delegate is function pointer that allows a function to be called indirectly via a reference to that function. So, what does that really mean?

The concept of delegates can be seen everywhere in normal life. For example, purchasing stocks or bonds typically requires a delegate of some sort. A stockbroker can be considered a delegate because you contact the broker for all sales or purchases you wish to make. In turn, the broker contacts the appropriate exchange or other organization to complete the transaction. As an investor, you do not necessarily know what organization to contact, so the broker handles this for you. In this facility, the broker is acting as a delegate.

Delegates in .NET are designed solely for dealing with events (such as buying and selling). In this example, all the client does is transact. The broker, on the other hand, needs to handle the client's desire to transact. Listing 26-1 shows a simple example from the `DelegateIntro` project to demonstrate this.

Listing 26-1: **Using Delegates**

```
Public Class Investor
```
Defining the delegate in this manner allows for reuse for all events that have the same signature.
```
    Public Delegate Sub Transact( _
        ByVal Quantity As Integer, _
        ByVal StockSymbol As String)

    Event Buy As Transact
    Event Sell As Transact
```

You could also add 600 other events like this if you felt that they were necessary.
```
End Class

Public Class Broker
    Public WithEvents Client As Investor

    Sub New()
        Client = New Investor()
    End Sub

    Private Sub HandleBuy(ByVal Quantity As Integer, _
        ByVal StockSymbol As String) Handles Client.Buy

        'Make the Purchase Here
    End Sub

    Private Sub HandleSell(ByVal Quantity As Integer, _
        ByVal StockSymbol As String) Handles Client.Sell

        'Make The Sale here
    End Sub
End Class
```

System.Windows.Forms.Control

As you saw in the previous chapter, the Control object is integral to windows development. However, you probably never create "just a control." You create controls such as text boxes and labels instead. Listing 26-2, taken from the ControlExample project, demonstrates the creation of a generic control:

> **Listing 26-2: Adding a Generic Control to a Form**

```
Public Class Form1
    Inherits System.Windows.Forms.Form

#Region " Windows Form Designer generated code "

    Public Sub New()
        MyBase.New()
        'This call is required by the Windows Form Designer.
        InitializeComponent()
        'Add any initialization after the _
        InitializeComponent() call
    End Sub

    'Form overrides dispose to clean up the component list.
    Protected Overloads Overrides Sub Dispose _
        (ByVal disposing As Boolean)
        If disposing Then
            If Not (components Is Nothing) Then
                components.Dispose()
            End If
        End If
        MyBase.Dispose(disposing)
    End Sub

    'Required by the Windows Form Designer
    Private components As System.ComponentModel.Container
    Private WithEvents PlainControl As _
      System.Windows.Forms.Control

    'NOTE: The following procedure is required by the _
      Windows Form Designer
    'It can be modified using the Windows Form Designer.
    'Do not modify it using the code editor.
    <System.Diagnostics.DebuggerStepThrough()> _
      Private Sub InitializeComponent()
        components = New System.ComponentModel.Container()
```

Here, the PlainControl is being initialized:

```
        Me.PlainControl = New System.Windows.Forms.Control()
        Me.PlainControl.SuspendLayout()
```

Continued

Listing 26-2 *(continued)*

```
        Me.SuspendLayout()
        '
        'PlainControl
        '
```

The PlainControl is being formatted here:

```
        Me.PlainControl.BackColor = _
        System.Drawing.Color.DarkMagenta
        Me.PlainControl.Size = New Size(20, 20)
        Me.PlainControl.Location = New Point(50, 50)
        '
        'Form1
        '
        Me.Text = "Form1"
        Me.Controls.Add(PlainControl)
        Me.ResumeLayout()
        Me.PlainControl.ResumeLayout()
    End Sub
#End Region
End Class
```

The end result of the code in Listing 26-2 is a purple square on the form. Obviously, not a great deal can be done with this alone. But, as stated previously, the `Control` class is really the foundation for the objects in the System.Windows.Forms namespace.

Properties

The `Control` object is the source of many of the properties available to the developer via other controls. Tables 26-1 through 26-4 give an organized synopsis with enhanced descriptions of the properties that come from the `Control` object. Code examples of some of the more interesting properties follow these tables. Properties with examples are marked with a double asterisk (**).

Public shared properties

A public shared property is a property that is shared between all instances of the class. Essentially, this means that the value of a shared property is the same for instances of the class. In order to understand this better, consider the `DefaultBackColor` property. In a single program, the first instance of the `Control` class would have the same `DefaultBackColor` as any subsequent instance. If it were not a read-only property, the value could be changed and it would be changed for all instances.

Table 26-1
Public Shared Properties of the Control

Property Name	Description
DefaultBackColor	Read-only. Returns what the background color of the control would be if the background color were not explicitly set.
DefaultFont	Read-only. Returns what the font of the control would be if the font were not explicitly set.
DefaultForeColor	Read-only. Returns what the foreground color of the control would be if the foreground color were not explicitly set.
ModifierKeys	Read-only. Returns a bitwise combination of values giving the current state of the Ctrl, Alt, and Shift keys.
MouseButtons	Read-only. Returns a bitwise combination of values giving the current state of the left, middle, and right mouse buttons.
MousePosition**	Read-only. Returns a point giving the current position of the mouse relevant to the upper-left corner of the window.

Public instance properties

A public instance property requires that the class be instantiated. The property values are not shared with any other instances. Thus, if two instances of an object are created, the value of one property of the first instance is not guaranteed to be the same as the value of the same property of the second instance.

Table 26-2
Public Instance Properties of the Control

Property Name	Description
AccessibilityObject	Specifies the AccessibleObject assigned to the control. An AccessibleObject is used by an accessability application that accomodates for users with disabilities.
AccessibleDefault ActionDescription	Specifies the description of the default action of the control when accessed by an accessiblity application.
AccessibleDescription	Specifies the description of the control when used in the context of an accessibity application.
AccessibleName	Specifies the name of the control in the context of an accessibility application.

Continued

Table 26-2 (continued)

Property Name	Description
AccessibleRole	Specifies the role of the control in the context of an accessibility application. The result is a value in the AccessibleRole enumeration; for example, scroll bar and pushbutton.
AllowDrop	Specifies whether the control accepts data that is dragged and dropped into it by the user.
Anchor	Specifies which edges of the control are bound to the edges of its container.
BackColor	Specifies the background color of the control.
BackGroundImage	Specifies the background image of the control.
BindingContext	Specifies the binding context of the control. This manages the BindingManagerBase Collection for the control. Each BindingManagerBase controls binding to one data source. So, if you have three text boxes, each bound to a different column in the same table, the BindingManagerBase guarantees synchronization.
Bottom	Read-only. Returns the y-coordinate of the bottom edge of the control relative to the control's container client area.
Bounds	Specifies the bounding rectangle for the control.
CanFocus	Read-only. Returns whether the control can receive the focus.
CanSelect	Read-only. Returns whether the control can be selected.
Capture	Specifies whether the control has captured the mouse. Capture = True means that the control receives all the mouse messages, regardless of the pointer being in the client area of the control.
CausesValidation**	Specifies whether all controls requiring validation receives it when this control receives the focus.
ClientRectangle	Read-only. Returns the client area of the control. Controls with non-client regions, such as the title bar on a form, do not include these regions in this rectangle.
ClientSize	Read-only. Returns the height and width of the client area of the control.
CompanyName	Read-only. Returns the company name of the application containing the control.
ContainsFocus	Read-only. Returns whether the control or one of its child controls currently has the input focus.

Property Name	Description
ContextMenu	Specifies the context menu object (a.k.a. right-click menu) associated with this control.
Controls	Specifies the collection of controls currently contained within the control.*
Created	Read-only. Returns whether the control has been created. Not to be confused with IsHandleCreated.
Cursor	Specifies the cursor that is displayed when the mouse pointer moves over the control. For example, Cursors.WaitCursor changes the cursor to an hourglass.
DataBindings	Read-only. Returns the collection of simple binding objects for the control.
DisplayRectangle	Read-only. Also returns the client rectangle of the control. However, inherited controls may wish to modify this.
Disposing	Read-only. Returns whether the control is currently in the process of being disposed. Note: When a control is disposed, it is no longer accessible as a valid instance. However, it may remain in memory until the garbage collector reclaims it.
Dock	Specifies to which edge of the container the control is docked. When specified, the resizing of the control is handled automatically. Controls that are "dockable" require code analyzing window movements coupled with the setting of this property.
Enabled	Specifies whether the control is enabled. This also covers items such as receiving focus.
Focused	Read only. Returns whether the control currently has the input focus.
Font	Specifies the current font for the control.
ForeColor	Specifies the foreground color of the control.
Handle	Read-only. Returns the Window handle for the control.
HasChildren	Read-only. Returns whether the control contains children.*
Height	Specifies the full height of the control.
IMEMode	Specifies the Input Method Editor mode supported by this control. The IME is used for allowing users to enter characters needed for Asian languages.
InvokeRequired	Read only. Returns whether Invoke must be used when making method calls on this control. Typically, true only when the handle of the control is on a different thread than the method call.

Continued

Table 26-2 *(continued)*

Property Name	Description
IsAccessible	Specifies whether the control is visible to accessiblity applications.
IsDisposed	Read-only. Returns whether the control has been disposed. If true, the control is no longer accessible as a valid reference.
IsHandleCreated	Read-only. Returns whether a window handle has been associated with this control.
Left	Specifies the x-coordinate of the left edge of the control's window.
Location	Specifies the coordinates of the upper-left corner of the control relative to the upper-left corner of the control's container.
Name	Specifies the name of the control. This value is typically used to refer to the control in code.
Parent	Specifies the parent container of the control.
ProductName	Read-only. Returns the product name of the application containing the control.
ProductVersion	Read-only. Returns the version number of the application containing the control.
RecreatingHandle	Read-only. Returns whether the handle of the control is currently being re-created. The combo box sample in the previous chapter demonstrated how this can occur.
Region	Specifies the elliptical or polygonal area within the window associated with this control. You see many examples of this property in the chapter on irregular forms.
Right	Read-only. Returns the x-coordinate for the right edge of the control relative to the container control's client area.
RightToLeft	Specifies whether the alignment of the control's elements is right-to-left. This property is used to support locales with right-to-left fonts.
Size	Specifies the height and width of the full control.
TabIndex	Specifies this control's place in the tab order of all controls within the same container.
TabStop	Specifies whether the control can receive focus via the Tab key.
Tag	Specifies extraneous data for the control. For example, if a control needs a reference to a specific object for it to suit the programmer's needs, this property could house that object.

Property Name	Description
Text	Specifies the text associated with this control. This is typically, although not always, the text displayed.
Top	Specifies the y-coordinate of the top edge of the control relative to the control's container client area.
TopLevelControl	Read-only. Returns the top-level control that contains the current control. In the instance of a form containing many container controls that in turn contain may other controls, the form is returned for all controls.
Visible	Specifies whether the control is visible.
Width	Specifies the full width of the control.

* These properties make reference to containment by this control; based on the hierarchy, one would conclude that this functionality is incorrect. Table 26-4 covers this in more detail.

Protected instance properties

A protected instance property is accessible from within derived classes only. So you cannot instantiate a control and access the ResizeRedraw property, for example. However, you can create a class that inherits from Control and accesses the property from that class.

Table 26-3
Protected Instance Properties of the Control

Property Name	Description
CreateParams	Read-only. Returns the required creation parameters when the control's handle is created. This typically includes information such as size, caption, and so on.
DefaultIMEMode	Read-only. Returns the default IME mode for this control. Refer to the IMEMode property in Table 26-2 for more information.
DefaultSize	Read-only. Returns what the size of the control would be if a size is not specifically set by the user.
FontHeight	Specifies the height of the Font property of this control.
ResizeRedraw**	Specifies whether the control should repaint after being resized. Specifically, if this is false, only the invalid regions are redrawn; otherwise, the whole control is redrawn.
ShowFocusCues	Read-only. Returns whether the interface is showing focus rectangles.
ShowKeyboardCues	Read-only. Returns whether the interface is showing keyboard accelerators. For example, Ctrl+O to open a file is considered a keyboard accelerator.

Properties inherited from Component

As stated earlier, there are classes in the hierarchy from which Control inherits. However, those classes are covered elsewhere in this book. Component is one of those classes. Table 26-4 outlines these inherited properties and their scope.

Table 26-4
Properties of the Control Inherited from Component

Property Name (scope)	Description
Container (Public Instance)	Read only. Returns the IContainer that contains the component, if any. The IContainer is the interface that accomodates the adding, removing and retrieving of child components.
Site (Public Instance)	Specifies the site of the component. A site essentially binds a component to its container, and enables communication between the two.
DesignMode (Protected Instance)	Read-only. Returns whether the component is currently in Design mode.
Events (Protected Instance)	Read-only. Returns the list of event handlers currently attached to the control. This can be considered a list of delegates.

Listing 26-3 demonstrates the use of the MousePosition property. The code contains three routines for handling three different events related to the movement of the mouse. The entire program fills a list box with information regarding the position and change in position of the mouse pointer.

Listing 26-3: Using the MousePosition Property

```
'This event fires when the mouse enters the control.
Private Sub lblTrackingRegion_MouseEnter(ByVal sender _
    As System.Object, ByVal e As System.EventArgs) _
    Handles lblTrackingRegion.MouseEnter

If blnLogging = True Then
    lstMousePosition.TopIndex = _
        lstMousePosition.Items.Add( _
            "Mouse Has Entered Tracking Region")
End If
End Sub

'This event fires when the mouse leaves the control.
Private Sub lblTrackingRegion_MouseLeave(ByVal sender _
```

```
    As System.Object, ByVal e As System.EventArgs) _
    Handles lblTrackingRegion.MouseLeave

If blnLogging = True Then
    lstMousePosition.TopIndex = _
        lstMousePosition.Items.Add( _
        "Mouse Has Departed Tracking Region")
End If
End Sub

'This event fires when the mouse moves within the control.
Private Sub lblTrackingRegion_MouseMove( _
    ByVal sender As System.Object, ByVal e As MouseEventArgs)
    Handles lblTrackingRegion.MouseMove

If blnLogging = True Then
    lstMousePosition.TopIndex = lstMousePosition.Items.Add( _
    "(" & Me.MousePosition.X.ToString & _
    ", " & Me.MousePosition.Y.ToString & ")")
End If
End Sub
```

Listing 26-4 demonstrates using the CausesValidation property. This listing contains only portions of the code in the project. The code displayed shows the setting of some of the control's properties, and you see two routines and two functions. The two routines handle the validating event, and the two functions are generic methods by which text in a textbox can be determined to be numeric only or alpha only.

Listing 26-4: **Using the CausesValidation Property**

```
'txtNumbers
'
Me.txtNumbers.CausesValidation = True
Me.txtNumbers.Location = New System.Drawing.Point(160, 104)
Me.txtNumbers.MaxLength = 1
Me.txtNumbers.Name = "txtNumbers"
Me.txtNumbers.TabIndex = 1
Me.txtNumbers.Text = ""

'txtText
'
Me.txtText.CausesValidation = False
Me.txtText.Location = New System.Drawing.Point(160, 160)
Me.txtText.MaxLength = 1
Me.txtText.Name = "txtText"
Me.txtText.TabIndex = 2
```

Continued

Listing 26-4 *(continued)*

```
Me.txtText.Text = ""

'txtValidator
'
Me.txtValidator.CausesValidation = True
Me.txtValidator.Location = New System.Drawing.Point(72, 40)
Me.txtValidator.Name = "txtValidator"
Me.txtValidator.Size = New System.Drawing.Size(144, 20)
Me.txtValidator.TabIndex = 0
Me.txtValidator.Text = ""


Private Sub txtNumbers_Validating(ByVal sender As Object, _
ByVal e As System.ComponentModel.CancelEventArgs) Handles _
txtNumbers.Validating
'This code will only be executed if the top textbox is
'clicked.
  If NumericValidatingCode() = False Then
      e.Cancel = True
      txtNumbers.Select(0, txtNumbers.Text.Length)
  End If
End Sub

Private Sub txtText_Validating(ByVal sender As Object, _
ByVal e As System.ComponentModel.CancelEventArgs) Handles _
txtText.Validating
'This Code will never be executed. Because the Causes
'validation property of this textbox is false, not only will
'this code not be executed, but this textbox will not raise
'any other validation events.
  If AlphaValidatingCode() = False Then
      e.Cancel = True
      txtText.Select(0, txtText.Text.Length)
  End If
End Sub

Private Function NumericValidatingCode() As Boolean
  If txtNumbers.Text.Length > 0 Then
      If txtNumbers.Text Like "[!0-9]" Then
       MessageBox.Show("Non numerals in the numeral only")
       Return False
      Else
       Return True
      End If
  Else
      Return True
  End If
End Function

Private Function AlphaValidatingCode() As Boolean
  If txtText.Text.Length > 0 Then
```

```
            If txtText.Text Like "[0-9]" Then
              MessageBox.Show("Numerals in the non numeral only")
              Return False
            Else
              Return True
            End If
      Else
            Return True
      End If
End Function
```

Essentially, the code in Listing 26-5 merely allows the user to toggle the value of the ResizeRedraw property, and shows what areas of the Form get repainted when resized. Notice the routines for handling the Paint and Resize events of the Form.

Listing 26-5: **Using the ResizeRedraw Property**

```
'This is so only the paint messages fired by resize are
'tracked.
Public blnResize As Boolean = False

Private Sub chkRedraw_CheckedChanged( _
    ByVal sender As System.Object, _
    ByVal e As System.EventArgs) _
    Handles chkRedraw.CheckedChanged

    Me.ResizeRedraw = chkRedraw.Checked
End Sub

Private Sub Form1_Resize(ByVal sender As Object, _
    ByVal e As System.EventArgs) Handles MyBase.Resize
    blnResize = True
    End Sub

Private Sub Form1_Paint(ByVal sender As Object, _
    ByVal e As System.Windows.Forms.PaintEventArgs) _
    Handles MyBase.Paint
    If blnResize = True Then
        If Me.ResizeRedraw = True Then
            Me.lstPaintMessages.Items.Add("Entire Form")
        Else
            Me.lstPaintMessages.Items.Add( _
            "Invalid region Only")
        End If
        Me.lstPaintMessages.Items.Add( _
        e.ClipRectangle.ToString)
        blnResize = False
    End If
End Sub
```

Methods

The control is also the source of many of the methods available to you via other controls. Tables 26-6 through 26-9 give an organized synopsis with enhanced descriptions of the methods that come from the `Control` object. Code examples of some of the more interesting methods follow Table 26-9. Methods with examples are marked with a double asterisk (**).

Public static methods

The most important characteristic of a static method is that an instance of the class is not required. Most methods require you to instantiate the class before you can have access to the method you want and then that method only acts on the class that calls it. A static method not only allows you to call it without an instance of the object, but it often modifies a different class or creates a new object altogether. Table 26-5 lists and describes these methods.

<table>
<tr><td colspan="2" align="center">Table 26-5
Public Static Methods of the Control</td></tr>
<tr><td>*Method Name*</td><td>*Description*</td></tr>
<tr><td>FromChildHandle</td><td>Retrieves the control that contains the specified handle. Essentially, this is a more robust version of the FromHandle method because it can accommodate controls that own more than one handle.</td></tr>
<tr><td>FromHandle</td><td>Retrieves the control that is currently associated with the specified handle. There is no guarantee that this method returns the correct control if it owns multiple handles.</td></tr>
<tr><td>IsMnemonic</td><td>Determines if the character is the mnemonic character in a string. The mnemonic character is the character after the first & in a string. For example, a menu item may be named &New. The N is the mnemonic character.</td></tr>
</table>

Public instance methods

A public instance method is the most common type of method you use. These methods are accessible only via an instance of the object. In most cases, these methods act on the calling object instance.

Table 26-6
Public Instance Methods of the Control

Method Name	Description
BeginInvoke	Executes a specific delegate on the thread that owns the control's handle.
BringToFront**	Brings the control to the front of the container's z-order.*
Contains	Returns a value specifying whether the given control is a child member of this control.
CreateControl	Forces the creation of the control. This includes handle creation and any child controls.
CreateGraphics	Creates the graphics object of this control. The graphics object includes items such as region and bounds.
DoDragDrop	Initiates a drag-and-drop operation.
EndInvoke	Terminates the delegate operation initiated due to the BeginInvoke method.
FindForm	Returns the form to which this control belongs. Note that the form is not necessarily the parent of the control or the TopLevelControl of the control.
Focus	Attempts to set the focus to the control. Not all controls can receive the focus as indicated by the CanFocus property.
GetChildAtPoint	Returns the child control that is located at the coordinates specified.
GetContainerControl**	Returns the first-level parent control of this control.
GetNextControl	Retrieves the next control in the tab order of all child controls.
Hide	Makes the control not visible. Equivalent to setting the Visible property of the control to false. Note that this does not unload the control.
Invalidate**	Forces a region of the control to be marked as requiring a repaint. This forces a paint operation only on the specified region of the control. The Refresh method paints the entire control.
Invoke	Equivalent to calling both BeginInvoke and EndInvoke.
PerformLayout	Forces the control to apply layout logic to contained controls.
PointToClient	Converts the specified screen point to client coordinates. When a control is contained in another control, its location is specified relative to the container, not to the screen. Thus, if you have a screen coordinate and want it relative to the client area, this is the method to accomplish this task.

Continued

Table 26-6 *(continued)*

Method Name	Description
PointToScreen	Converts the specified client point to screen coordinates. See PointToClient.
PreProcessMessage	Processes input messages within the message loop before they are dispatched.
RectangleToClient	Converts the screen rectangle to client coordinates. See PointToClient.
RectangleToScreen	Converts the client rectangle to screen coordinates. See PointToClient.
Refresh	Forces the control to repaint all regions of the control and any child controls. See Invalidate.
ResetBackColor	Sets the BackColor property to its default value.
ResetBindings	Sets the DataBindings property to its default value.
ResetCursor	Sets the Cursor property to its default value.
ResetFont	Sets the Font property to its default value.
ResetForeColor	Sets the ForeColor property to its default value.
ResetIMEMode	Sets the IMEmode property to its default value.
ResetRightToLeft	Sets the RightToLeft property to its default value.
ResetText	Sets the Text property to its default value.
ResumeLayout	Immediately resumes normal layout for the control and its children.
Scale	Scales the control and any child controls to the specified ratio. For example, a ratio of 2 doubles the size of this control and its child controls.
Select	Activates the specified control if CanSelect property = True.
SelectNextControl	Activates the next control in the tab order if CanSelect property = true.
SendToBack	Sends the control to the back of the z-order.*
SetBounds	Sets the control's location and size to the specified values.
Show	Equivalent to setting the visible property of the control = true.

Method Name	Description
SuspendLayout	Suspends the layout logic for any child controls.
Update	Forces the control to paint any currently invalid areas. See Invalidate. Similar to Refresh, except that this does not guarantee that the entire control is repainted.

*Z-order is used to define the layering of the controls. Horizontal layout would be considered x-order because the x-axis is horizontal; vertical layout would be considered y-order because the y-axis is vertical. Z-order is the axis that is directed into the screen.

Protected static methods

A protected method behaves similarly to a protected property. It is accessible only to derived objects. The static indicator means that the method does not require an instance of the class for it to be called.

Table 26-7
Protected Static Methods of the Control

Method Name	Description
ReflectMessage	Reflects the specified message to the control that owns the specified handled. Essentially, this is a method used to pass messages to other controls.

Protected instance methods

A protected instance method behaves similarly to a protected instance property. The methods outlined in Table 26-6 are accessible only to derived classes. For example, the CreateHandle method cannot be accessed by an instance of the control. In order to access this method, you must create a class that inherits from control and then you can programmatically access it.

Table 26-8
Protected Instance Methods of the Control*

Method Name	Description
AccessibilityNotifyClients	Notifies child controls of events raised by accessibility devices.
CreateAccessiblityInstance	Creates a new instance of the Accessibility object for this control.

Continued

Table 26-8 (continued)

Method Name	Description
CreateControlsInstance	Creates a new instance of the controls collection, and assigns it to this control.
CreateHandle	Creates a handle for this control.
DefWndProc	Sends the message to the default windows process.
DestroyHandle	Eliminates the handle associated with this control.
Dispose	Releases all resources used by the control. Analogous to Set Obj = Nothing in Visual Basic 6.
GetStyle	Specifies whether the given control style bit is set for this control. Sample control styles include UserPaint, which prevents the operating system from performing any painting of this control.
GetTopLevel	Determines whether the control is a top-level control. Similar to the Parent property being null.
InitLayout	Called after the control is added to a container. Initializes the layout logic for the control.
IsInputChar	Determines whether the character requires preprocessing before being sent to the control. For example, a mnemonic key-code requires preprocessing.
IsInputKey	Similar to IsInputChar. Determines whether the specified key is a regular input key. If it is a special key, for example, PageUp, it first goes through preprocessing.
ProcessCmdKey	Processes a command key. A command key is a key that always takes precedence over normal keys. Examples include Alt and other shortcut keys.
ProcessDialogChar	Processes a dialog character. A dialog character is an input character that the control is not processing. Examples include control mnemonics. Refer to the IsInputChar method.
ProcessDialogKey	Processes a dialog key. A dialog key is an input key that the control is not processing. Examples include Tab and arrow keys. See IsInputKey method.
ProcessKeyEventArgs	This method is called when the control receives a keyboard message. Essentially, this method generates the arguments necessary for the KeyPresses, KeyUp, and KeyDown events and then raises those events.

Method Name	Description
ProcessKeyMessage	This method is called when a control receives a keyboard message. This method calls the control's parent's method of the same name. If the parent does not process the key, the ProcessKeyEventArgs method is called.
ProcessKeyPreview	This method is called before any keyboard events are generated. This method calls the control's parent's method of the same name. This method is called before the ProcessKeyMessage method is called to determine whether the parent processes the message.
ProcessMnemonic	Processes a mnemonic character. Refer to the IsMnemonic method.
RecreateHandle	Forces a re-creation of the handle for the control.
RtlTranslateAlignment	Converts the current alignment to the necessary alignment to support right-to-left text.
RtlTranslateContent	Identical to the previous function, except not in a protected scope.
RtlTranslateHorizontal	Converts the current horizontal alignment to the appropriate horizontal alignment to support right-to-left text.
RtlTranslateLeftRight	Converts the current left-right alignment to the appropriate left-right alignment to support right-to-left text.
ScaleCore	Scales the entire control and any child controls by the ratio specified. This prevents the programmer from having to scale each control individually.
Select	Activates the control if the CanSelect property is true.
SetBoundsCore	Sets the bounds of the control. Saves you from building a rectangle and setting the bounds property.
SetClientSizeCore	Sets the size of the client area of the control. Useful because the clientsize property is read-only.
SetStyle	Sets the specified controlstyle to active or inactive. Control styles include, for example, Fixed Height and Width.
SetTopLevel	Sets the control to be the top-level control. A top-level control cannot have a parent, but may contain children.
SetVisibleCore	Sets the control's state of visibility. Similar to explicitly setting the visible property.

Continued

Table 26-8 *(continued)*

Method Name	Description
UpdateBounds	Updates the bounds of the control. Forces the bounds specified to be applied to the control.
UpdateStyles	Forces the assigned styles to be reassigned. Similar to a refresh.
UpdateZOrder	Reaffirms the z-order for this control amid all sibling controls.
WndProc	Processes Windows messages.

*Not all methods are included in this table. There are a series of methods of the form OnXXXX, in which XXXX is an event. The purpose of these methods is to raise the event specified in XXXX. There are similar methods of the form InvokeXXXX and RaiseXXXX that are not covered at this time. These are covered in detail in the events section of this chapter.

Inherited methods

Table 26-9 lists and describes the methods inherited from the Component class.

Table 26-9
Inherited Methods

Method Name	Description
CreateObjRef	Creates an ObjRef object from the Type Specified. An ObjRef object is used to transfer an object reference between applications.
Dispose	Releases all resources used by the component. See Disposing Property for more information.
Equals	Determines whether the specified object equals the current object. The default version of this method supports reference equality only.
GetHashCode	Returns an integer that represents a hash code for the current object. This is useful for hashing algorithms and data structures.
GetLifeTimeService	Retrieves a lifetime service object that controls the lifetime of this object. A lifetime is analogous to a lease. There is a specified term (can be infinite), and when the term expires, the remote object expires.

Method Name	Description
InitializeLifeTimeService	This method is used when objects need to control their own lease.
ToString	Returns a string that is representative of the specified object. Often, this is equivalent to the value in the name or text property of a control.
Finalize	Allows an object to free resources and other cleanup tasks prior to garbage collection.
GetService	Returns an object representing a service provided by the component. Related to the Site property.
MemberwiseClone	Creates a shallow copy of the current object. A shallow copy handles references and values of the object, but not child objects.

The sample in Listing 26-6 is available in the GetContainerControl example project. Essentially, at the click of a button, a new form with a label is created and placed in the existing form. The TopLevel property is necessary when attempting to host a form inside another form. The GetContainerControl method is very similar to the Parent property.

Listing 26-6: **Using the GetContainerControl and BringToFront Method**

```
Private Sub cmdNewForm_Click(ByVal sender As System.Object, _
ByVal e As System.EventArgs) _
Handles cmdNewForm.Click

If Me.Controls.Count < 7 Then
    Dim frmNew As Form = New Form()
    Dim lblNew As Label = New Label()

    lblNew.BackColor = SystemColors.ControlLightLight

    With frmNew
    .TopLevel = False
    .Text = "This is a form"
    .Name = "Form " & Me.Controls.Count
    . Location = New Point((Me.Controls.Count) * 10, _
    (Me.Controls.Count) * 10)
    .Size = New Size(20, 100)
    .Controls.Add(lblNew)
    End With
```

Continued

Listing 26-6 *(continued)*

```
        lblNew.Text = "ContainerControl: " & _
    CType(lblNew.GetContainerControl, ContainerControl).Name()

        Me.Controls.Add(frmNew)
        frmNew.Show()
```

Without the BringToFront call, the new form would appear behind the others.

```
        frmNew.BringToFront()
    End If
End Sub
```

Listing 26-7 demonstrates the use of the `Invalidate` method. The code contains two routines to handle two events available to the `Label` control. The `Paint` event handles all of the drawing, and the `Click` event occurs when the user clicks on the label. As you can tell by the information displayed by the program, only the invalid areas of the control are repainted.

Listing 26-7: **Using the Invalidate Method**

```
Private Sub Label1_Click(ByVal sender As System.Object, _
    ByVal e As System.EventArgs) Handles Label1.Click

    Dim tempRect As Rectangle = New Rectangle(2, 2, 2, 2)
    'Here, we specifically invalidate the rectangle above.
    Label1.Invalidate(tempRect)
End Sub

Private Sub Label1_Paint(ByVal sender As Object, _
    ByVal e As System.Windows.Forms.PaintEventArgs) _
    Handles Label1.Paint

    'This gives us the bounds of the label
    Dim tempRect As Rectangle = CType(sender, Label).Bounds
    'This gives us the rectangle being repainted.
    Dim tempRectF As RectangleF = e.Graphics.ClipBounds
    If tempRect.Width <> tempRectF.Width Then
        ListBox1.Items.Add("Label Rectangle = " & _
        tempRect.X & ", " & tempRect.Y & ", " & _
        tempRect.Height & ", " & tempRect.Width)

        ListBox1.Items.Add("Invalid Rectangle = " & _
        tempRectF.X & ", " & tempRectF.Y & ", " & _
        tempRectF.Height & ", " & tempRectF.Width)
    End If
End Sub
```

Events

The Control is also the primary source of many of the events available to you via other controls. Table 26-10 gives an organized synopsis with enhanced descriptions of the events that come from the Control object. Note that many of the events are very self-explanatory. Specific examples for events in the following table are not provided. Other samples throughout this chapter use events extensively, and should give an indication as to what they do.

Listings 26-3 through 26-7 demonstrate the use of many events. The most common events you find yourself using are the Click events and the Paint events. The Click event is necessary for handling user responses to buttons and the most common way for a user to interact with any control is to click. The Paint event is used for the display of the control. The most common way that you respond to the user is via painting. The Validating event is also very important in that it gives you a natural segue into analyzing any data that the user has entered.

Listing 26-3 demonstrates the MouseEnter, MouseLeave, and MouseMove events. Listing 26-4 demonstrates the Validating event. Listing 26-5 demonstrates the Paint and Resize events. Listing 26-6 demonstrates the Click event. Listing 26-7 demonstrates the Click and Paint events.

Note   As stated in a footnote in the previous section, each event also has a method in the class designed to raise the event. Typically, these methods are of the form OnXXXX, in which XXXX is the event name. They are not listed here because descriptions of these methods lend no additional insight into the object. Thus, the focus of this section is strictly events.

<table>
<tr><td colspan="2" align="center">Table 26-10
Public Instance Events of the Control</td></tr>
<tr><td>**Event Name**</td><td>**Description**</td></tr>
<tr><td>BackColorChanged</td><td>Occurs when the BackColor property of the control changes.</td></tr>
<tr><td>BackgroundImageChanged</td><td>Occurs when the BackgroundImage of the control changes.</td></tr>
<tr><td>BindingContextChanged</td><td>Occurs when the BindingContext property of the control changes.</td></tr>
<tr><td>CausesValidationChanged</td><td>Occurs when the CausesValidation property changes.</td></tr>
<tr><td>ChangeUICues</td><td>Occurs when Focus or Keyboard cues change.</td></tr>
<tr><td>Click</td><td>Occurs when the control has been clicked.</td></tr>
<tr><td>ContextMenuChanged</td><td>Occurs when the ContextMenu property of the control changes.</td></tr>
</table>

Continued

Table 26-10 (continued)

Event Name	Description
ControlAdded	Occurs when a control has been added to this control.
ControlRemoved	Occurs when a control has been removed from this control.
CursorChanged	Occurs when the Cursor property of this control changes.
Disposed (Inherited from Component)	Represents the method that handles the Disposed event of a component. Occurs when the component's resources are freed.
DockChanged	Occurs when the Dock property of the control changes.
DoubleClick	Occurs when the control has been double-clicked.
DragDrop	Occurs when a drag-and-drop operation has been completed.
DragEnter	Occurs when an object has been dragged to be within the control's bounds.
DragLeave	Occurs when an object has been dragged out of the control's bounds.
DragOver	Occurs when an object has been dragged over a control's bounds. This event covers the DragEnter and DragLeave events.
EnabledChanged	Occurs when the Enabled property of this control changes.
Enter	Occurs when the control is entered.
FontChanged	Occurs when the Font property of this control changes.
ForeColorChanged	Occurs when the ForeColor property of the control changes.
GiveFeedback	Occurs during a drag operation. This is the event that allows the application to change the mouse cursor and so on.
GotFocus	Occurs when the control receives the focus.
HandleCreated	Occurs when the handle for the window is created.
HandleDestroyed	Occurs when the handle for the window is destroyed.
HelpRequested	Occurs when help is requested for a control. For example, by pressing F1.
IMEModeChanged	Occurs when the IMEMode property changes.
Invalidated	Occurs when the control's display is updated. The rectangle that is invalid is available via this event.
KeyDown	Occurs when a key is pressed down while the control has the focus.
KeyPress	Occurs when a key is pressed while the control has the focus.

Event Name	Description
KeyUp	Occurs when a key is released while the control has the focus.
Layout	Occurs when a control lays out its child controls.
Leave	Occurs when the control is left.
LocationChanged	Occurs when the Location property of a control changes.
LostFocus	Occurs when the control loses focus.
MouseDown	Occurs when a mouse button is pressed while the pointer is over a control.
MouseEnter	Occurs when the mouse pointer enters the control.
MouseHover	Occurs when the mouse pointer hovers over a control.
MouseLeave	Occurs when the mouse pointer leaves the control.
MouseMove	Occurs when the mouse pointer moves within the control.
MouseUp	Occurs when a mouse button is released while the mouse pointer is over a control.
MouseWheel	Occurs when the mouse wheel moves when the control has the focus.
Move	Occurs when the control is moved.
Paint	Occurs when the control is drawn or redrawn.
ParentChanged	Occurs when the value of the Parent property of a control has changed.
QueryAccessibilityHelp	Occurs when the Accessible object of the control is providing help to accessibility applications.
QueryContinueDrag	Occurs during a drag-and-drop operation, and allows for the determination of whether the operation should continue.
Resize	Occurs when the control is resized.
RightToLeftChanged	Occurs when the value of the right-to-left property changes.
SizeChanged	Occurs when the size of the control changes.
StyleChanged	Occurs when the style of the control changes.
SystemColorsChanged	Occurs when the system colors change.
TabIndexChanged	Occurs when the tab index of the control change changes.
TabStopChanged	Occurs when the value of the TabStop property change changes.
TextChanged	Occurs when the Text property of the control changes.

Continued

Table 26-10 *(continued)*	
Event Name	**Description**
Validated	Occurs when the control is done validating.
Validating	Occurs while the control is validating.
VisibleChanged	Occurs when the visible property of the control changes.

Many of the events outlined in Table 26-10 are very related, and occur in response to a simple action and in a specific order. Some of these include the MouseEnter, MouseMove, and MouseLeave events. These events can be very handy in responding to user input. The MousePosition property example earlier in this chapter also gives an example of the various mouse movement events.

In fact, the majority of events that you probably use are related to user input. These can be clicks, double-clicks, typing, movement, and mouse activity. The other class of events typically relate to responding to developer input. The chapter on "Visual" Inheritance demonstrates the use of this class of events.

Summary

In this chapter, you received a wealth of information regarding the control. Even if it is a rather dry object, it serves as the foundation for all tasks in Windows Forms development. You also learned about delegates, a very important aspect of development in the .NET Framework. The next chapter goes over the controls individually, and outlines what they bring to the table.

✦   ✦   ✦

Specific Controls

by Jacob A. Grass

In a rapid development environment, the basic Control Object will not be used very frequently. The accomplished coder could easily inherit from the control object and develop the controls necessary for the task at hand. However, not only could this be a tedious task, it could get monotonous.

Thus, you should be thankful that VB .NET gives you a plethora of controls for your development needs. The controls given to you range from a simple text display control to the more complex datagrid. There are a few controls that are beyond the scope of this chapter such as the `Crystal Report Viewer` and the `ActiveX Host` controls.

This chapter provides a comprehensive overview of how controls relate to other controls. The descriptions of each control also give ancestry information to give you a better understanding of their origins. This chapter also outlines the new properties, methods, and events that each control brings to the table. Keep in mind that if a class is derived from control, it has the properties, methods, and events that the control class has. Examples are provided.

The novice user finds a wealth of information detailing how to use each control in the toolbox. The advanced user achieves a better understanding of the ancestry of the controls and fill in any gaps in current knowledge.

The information contained in this chapter and the previous chapter is crucial for understanding the topic of Visual Inheritance covered in Chapter 28.

Base Controls

A number of classes derive from the `Control` object that that, although not able to be instanced, encapsulate behavior that is the foundation of many controls in the Framework. This type of control essentially provides a checkpoint of functionality for inheritance purposes. This section outlines and describes this type of control in detail. Other controls in the framework are the base class for other controls, however, in those instances, the base class can be used as is. Examples aren't provided for this section.

ButtonBase

The purpose of the `ButtonBase` control is to provide all the basic functionality that any button style control requires. This class inherits directly from control. Table 27-1 lists and describes the properties, methods, and events that `ButtonBase` brings to the table.

Table 27-1
Non-Inherited Members of ButtonBase

Member Name (scope and type)	Description
`FlatStyle` (Public Instance Property)	Specfies the `FlatStyle` of the control. Can be one of four values: `Flat`, `PopUp`, `Standard`, or `System`.
`Image` (Public Instance Property)	Specfies the image that is displayed on the `Button` control.
`ImageAlign` (Public Instance Property)	Specifies the alignment of the image displayed on the `Button` control.
`ImageIndex` (Public Instance Property)	Specifies the `Index` value of the image in the image list displayed on the `Button` control. See `ImageList`.
`ImageList` (Public Instance Property)	Specifies the `ImageList` that contains the image displayed on the `Button` control.
`TextAlign` (Public Instance Property)	Specifies the alignment of the text on the `Button` control.
`IsDefault` (Protected Instance Property)	Specifies whether or not the `Button` control is the default button in a container.
`ResetFlagsAndPaint` (Protected Instance Method)	Returns the values of the control's flags to their default values, and redraws the control.

ListControl

The purpose of the `ListControl` is to provide all of the basic functionality that any list style control requires. This class inherits directly from `Control`. Table 27-2 lists and describes the properties, methods, and events that the `ListControl` brings to the table.

Table 27-2
Non-Inherited Members of ListControl

Member Name (scope and type)	Description
DataSource (Public Instance Property)	Specifies the DataSource of a list control. This is typically a collection or array.
DisplayMember (Public Instance Property)	If the list control contains objects that support properties, this indicates which property of the object to display. If unspecified, the result of the ToString method is used.
SelectedIndex (Public Instance Property)	Specifies the index of the selected item in the ListControl.
SelectedValue (Public Instance Property)	Specifies the object selected in the ListControl.
ValueMember (Public Instance Property)	Analogous to DisplayMember. This indicates which property of the object to return.
GetItemText (Public Instance Method)	Similar to a ToString Method. This method, however, takes an object as a parameter and returns the text of that object.
DataSourceChanged (Public Instance Event)	Occurs when the DataSource property changes.
DisplayMemberChanged (Public Instance Event)	Occurs when the DisplayMember property changes.
SelectedValueChanged (Public Instance Event)	Occurs when the SelectedValue changes.
ValueMemberChanged (Public Instance Event)	Occurs when the ValueMember property changes.
DataManager (Protected Instance Property)	Handles management of the BindingContext of the ListControl.
FilterItemOnProperty (Protected Instance Method)	Used for filtering a collection of objects bound to the ListControl.
RefreshItem (Protected Instance Method)	Refreshes the specified item.
SetItemCore (Protected Instance Method)	Changes the item at the specified index to the specified item.
SetItemsCore (Protected Instance Method)	Replaces all existing objects in the ListControl with the objects contained within the specified array.

ScrollableControl

The purpose of the ScrollableControl is to provide all the basic functionality that any scrolling control requires, specifically AutoScroll. This class inherits directly from Control. Table 27-3 lists and describes the properties, methods, and events that the ScrollableControl brings to the table.

Table 27-3 Non-Inherited Members of ScrollableControl	
Member Name (scope and type)	**Description**
AutoScroll (Public Instance Property)	Specifies whether or not the container allows the user to scroll to any items beyond the visible boundaries. Setting this to true essentially creates a virtual space greater than the visible space.
AutoScrollMargin (Public Instance Property)	Specifies the distance from the edge of the container that a control must be for the scrollbars to appear.
AutoScrollMinSize (Public Instance Property)	Specifies the minimum size of the scrollbars.
AutoScrollPosition (Public Instance Property)	Specifies the scroll position of the scrollbar upon appearance. For example, if position = (5,5) and a form is resized to show the horizontal scrollbar, the x-coordinate of the upper left corner of the visible area is 5.
DockPadding (Public Instance Property)	Specifies the number of pixels to pad all docked controls. In other words, the distance between the inside edge of the container and the outside edge of the docked control, in pixels.
SetAutoScrollMargin (Public Instance Method)	Used to set the AutoScrollMargin property.
HScroll (Protected Instance Property)	Specifies whether the horizontal scrollbar is visible.
VScroll (Protected Instance Property)	Specifies whether or not the vertical scrollbar is visible.
AdjustFormScrollBars (Protected Instance Method)	Adjusts the autoscrollbars based on the current positions of the controls and the currently selected control.

Menu

The purpose of the Menu class is to provide all of the basic functionality for menus. This class inherits directly from Component. Table 27-4 lists and describes the properties, methods, and events that the Menu brings to the table.

Table 27-4	
Non-Inherited Members of the Menu Class	
Member Name (scope and type)	*Description*
Handle (Public Instance Property)	ReadOnly. Returns the handle that represents the window of this object.
IsParent (Public Instance Property)	ReadOnly. Returns a value indicating whether or not this menu contains any menu items.
MDIListItem (Public Instance Property)	ReadOnly. Returns a value indicating the menu item that is used to display a list of MDI child forms.
MenuItems (Public Instance Property)	ReadOnly. Returns a collection of menu items associated with this menu.
GetContextMenu (Public Instance Method)	Returns the ContextMenu object that contains this menu.
GetMainMenu (Public Instance Method)	Returns the MainMenu object that contains this menu.
MergeMenu (Public Instance Method)	Merges the menu item collections of two menus.
CloneMenu (Protected Instance Method)	Performs a deep-copy of the current Menu object.

ScrollBar

The purpose of the ScrollBar class is to provide all the basic functionality that any scrollbar control requires. This class inherits directly from Control. Table 27-5 lists and describes the properties, methods, and events that the ScrollBar class brings to the table.

Table 27-5
Non-Inherited Members of the ScrollBar Class

Member Name (scope and type)	Description
LargeChange (Public Instance Property)	Specifies the value to add or subtract from the value property when the scrollbox is moved a great distance.
Maximum (Public Instance Property)	Specifies the upper limit of the scrollbar value.
Minimum (Public Instance Property)	Specifies the lower limit of the scrollbar value.
SmallChange (Public Instance Property)	Specifies the value to add or subtract from the value property when the scrollbox is moved a small distance.
Value (Public Instance Property)	Specifies a numeric value that represents the current position of the scrollbox on the scrollbar.
Scroll (Public Instance Event)	Occurs when the scrollbox has been moved by a mouse or keyboard action.
ValueChanged (Public Instance Event)	Occurs when the value property has changed (typically via a scroll event, or programmatically).

TextBoxBase

The purpose of the TextBoxBase class is to provide all the basic functionality that any Text control requires. This class inherits directly from Control. Table 27-6 lists and describes the properties, methods, and events that the TextBoxBase class brings to the table.

Table 27-6
Non-Inherited Methods of the TextBoxBase Class

Member Name (scope and type)	Description
AcceptsTab (Public Instance Property)	Specifies whether pressing the Tab key inserts a Tab character or shifts focus to the next control in the tab order. Only relevant when the MultiLine property is true.
AutoSize (Public Instance Property)	Specifies whether the height of the control adjusts automatically when the assigned font is changed.
BorderStyle (Public Instance Property)	Specifies the border type of the control. For example, Fixed3D creates a sunken appearance.

Member Name (scope and type)	Description
CanUndo (**Public Instance Property**)	Specifies whether the user can undo the previous operation in a text control.
HideSelection (**Public Instance Property**)	Specifies whether the selected text in a text control remains highlighted when the control loses focus.
Lines (**Public Instance Property**)	Specifies the lines of text in a Text control via a string array.
MaxLength (**Public Instance Property**)	Specifies the maximum number of characters that can be placed in the control.
Modified (**Public Instance Property**)	Specifies whether the control has been modified since its creation or since its contents were set.
MultiLine (**Public Instance Property**)	Specifies whether the Text control accepts more than one line of text.
PreferredHeight (**Public Instance Property**)	ReadOnly. Returns a value based on the FontHeight and BorderStyle of the Text control to ensure that text is displayed properly.
ReadOnly (**Public Instance Property**)	Specifies whether or not the text in the Text control is editable.
SelectedText (**Public Instance Property**)	Specifies the currently selected text within the Text control.
SelectionLength (**Public Instance Property**)	Specifies the number of characters selected in the Text control.
SelectionStart (**Public Instance Property**)	Specifies the starting point of the selected text in the Text control.
TextLength (**Public Instance Property**)	ReadOnly. Returns the length of the text in the Text control.
WordWrap (**Public Instance Property**)	Specifies whether the Text control automatically wraps words to the beginning of the next line when appropriate. Only relevant when the MultiLine property is set to True.
AppendText (**Public Instance Method**)	Combines the specified text to the currrent text within the control.
Clear (**Public Instance Method**)	Removes all text from the Text control.
ClearUndo (**Public Instance Method**)	Removes all information regarding previous operations from the undo buffer.
Copy (**Public Instance Method**)	Copies the currently selected text in the Text control to the Clipboard.

Continued

Table 27-6 *(continued)*

Member Name (scope and type)	Description
Cut (Public Instance Method)	Copies the currently selected text in the Text control to the Clipboard, and removes the selection from the control.
Paste (Public Instance Method)	Replaces the current selection in the Text control with the contents of the Clipboard.
ScrollToCaret (Public Instance Method)	Scrolls the contents of the Text control so that the caret position is visible.
SelectAll (Public Instance Method)	Selects all text within the Text control.
Undo (Public Instance Method)	Undoes the last edit operation in the Text control.
AcceptsTabChanged (Public Instance Event)	Occurs when the AcceptsTab property is changed.
AutoSizeChanged (Public Instance Event)	Occurs when the AutoSize property is changed.
BorderStyleChanged (Public Instance Event)	Occurs when the BorderStyle property is changed.
HideSelectionChanged (Public Instance Event)	Occurs when the HideSelection property is changed.
ModifiedChanged (Public Instance Event)	Occurs when the Modified property is changed.
MultiLineChanged (Public Instance Event)	Occurs when the MultiLine property is changed.
ReadOnlyChanged (Public Instance Event)	Occurs when the ReadOnly Property is changed.

ContainerControl

The purpose of the ContainerControl class is to provide all of the basic functionality that any Container control requires beyond what the Component class offers.
This includes items such as focus management. This class inherits directly from
ScrollableControl. Table 27-7 lists and describes the properties, methods, and
events that the ContainerControl class brings to the table.

Table 27-7
Non-Inherited Members of the ContainerControl Class

Member Name (scope and type)	Description
ActiveControl (Public Instance Property)	Specifies the active control within the container.
ParentForm (Public Instance Property)	ReadOnly. Returns the form that the container control is assigned to.
Validate (Public Instance Method)	Validates the most recently invalidated control and its ancestors up through the current control. Note: does not validate the current control.
ProcessTabKey (Protected Instance Method)	Activates the next available control.

UpDownBase

The purpose of the UpDownBase class is to provide all the basic functionality that any UpDownBase control requires. An UpDownBase control is depicted as a text box with an up arrow button and a down arrow button. It is used for scrolling through values. This class inherits directly from ContainerControl. Table 27-8 lists and describes the properties, methods, and events that the UpDownBase class brings to the table.

Table 27-8
Non-Inherited Members of the UpDownBase Class

Member Name (scope and type)	Description
BorderStyle (Public Instance Property)	Specifies the border style for an UpDown control. For example, Fixed3D creates a sunken appearance.
InterceptArrowKeys (Public Instance Property)	Specifies whether or not values can be selected via the arrow keys.
PreferredHeight (Public Instance Property)	ReadOnly. Returns a value based on the font height and border style of the UpDown control to ensure that text is displayed properly.
ReadOnly (Public Instance Property)	Specifies whether or not the text in the UpDown control is editable.

Continued

Table 27-8 (continued)

Member Name (scope and type)	Description
TextAlign (Public Instance Property)	Specifies the text alignment in the UpDown control.
UpDownAlign (Public Instance Property)	Specifies the alignment of the up and down buttons in the UpDown control.
DownButton (Public Instance Method)	Handles the pressing of the Down button in an UpDown control.
UpButton (Public Instance Method)	Handles the pressing of the Up button in an UpDown control.
ChangingText (Protected Instance Property)	Specifies whether or not the text property is being changed internally or by its parent class.
UserEdit (Protected Instance Property)	Specifies whether or not the value has been entered by the user.
UpdateEditText (Protected Instance Method)	Updates the text in the UpDown control.
ValidateEditText (Protected Instance Method)	Validates the text in the UpDown control.

Derived Controls

The remainder of this chapter covers the controls in the Windows.Forms catalog that inherit from the base controls in the previous section along with the Control class itself. I have organized each control into what I believe is its primary function. Examples are provided for various properties and methods of the controls.

This section outlines all controls that I consider input controls. I define an input control as one that responds to user-input and/or returns a value. Full ancestry information is given as well as descriptions of the properties, methods, and events that the specific control brings to the table. Those controls with code examples provided later in the "Examples" section are marked with an asterisk (*).

Button

This control allows the user to click it and have actions performed. The Enter key also has the same result if the button has focus when the key is pressed. The Button control inherits directly from the ButtonBase class. Table 27-9 lists the properties, methods, and events that the Button class possesses that it did not inherit.

Table 27-9
Non-Inherited Members of the Button Control

Member Name (scope and type)	Description
DialogResult (Public Instance Property)	Specifies the value that is returned to the button's parent form when the button is clicked. Examples of valid values are Ok, Cancel, Retry, Abort.
PerformClick (Public Instance Method)	Generates a click event.

CheckBox

This control is typically used to represent a binary condition such as True/False, Yes/No, or On/Off. This control is commonly used in conjunction with other check boxes to present a list of options to the user. The users can check the box if they want the option, and uncheck the box if they do not want the option. The CheckBox control inherits directly from the ButtonBase class. Table 27-10 lists the properties, methods, and events that the CheckBox class possesses that it did not inherit.

Table 27-10
Non-Inherited Members of the CheckBox Control

Member Name (scope and type)	Description
Appearance (Public Instance Property)	Specifies whether the CheckBox control appears like a standard button or like a standard check box.
AutoCheck (Public Instance Property)	Specifies whether the Checked and CheckState properties are updated when the check box is clicked. Also determines whether the appearance is automatically updated.
CheckAlign (Public Instance Property)	Specifies the horizontal and vertical alignment of the CheckBox control.
Checked (Public Instance Property)	Specifies whether or not the check box is in the checked state.
CheckState (Public Instance Property)	Specifies the current state of the check box. Can be Checked, Unchecked, or Indeterminate.

Continued

Table 27-10 *(continued)*

Member Name (scope and type)	Description
ThreeState (Public Instance Property)	Specifies whether or not the control allows for three different states instead of two. If true, the third state is Indeterminate. The check box area of the control appears shaded in this state.
AppearanceChanged (Public Instance Event)	Occurs when the value of the Appearance property changes.
CheckedChanged (Public Instance Event)	Occurs when the value of the Checked property changes.
CheckStateChanged (Public Instance Event)	Occurs when the value of the CheckState property changes.

CheckedListBox

This control is typically used to list items and display a check box next to them. It has essentially the same functionality as the ListBox control. The CheckedListBox control inherits directly from the ListBox class. Table 27-11 lists the properties, methods, and events that the CheckedListBox class possesses that it did not inherit.

Table 27-11
Non-Inherited Members of the CheckedListBox Control

Member Name (scope and type)	Description
CheckedIndices (Public Instance Property)	ReadOnly. Returns a collection containing the indices of all checked items in the control.
CheckedItems (Public Instance Property)	ReadOnly. Returns a collection containing all checked items in the control.
CheckOnClick (Public Instance Property)	Specifies whether an item should be checked or unchecked when it is selected.
Items (Public Instance Property)	ReadOnly. Returns a collection containing all items in this control regardless of their checked state.

Member Name (scope and type)	Description
ThreeDCheckBoxes (Public Instance Property)	Specifies whether the check boxes appear as three-dimensional.
GetItemChecked (Public Instance Method)	Returns a value indicating whether or not the specified item is checked.
GetItemCheckState (Public Instance Method)	Returns a value indicating the current CheckState of the current item.
SetItemChecked (Public Instance Method)	Sets the CheckState value of the specified item to Checked.
SetItemCheckState (Public Instance Method)	Sets the CheckState value of the item at the specified index.
ItemCheck (Public Instance Event)	Occurs when the CheckState of an item changes.

ComboBox

This control is typically used to list items in a control that has a drop-down style. The first part of the control is a text box that allows the user to type in part of an item in the list. The second part is a ListControl that displays acceptable items. The CheckedListBox control inherits directly from the ListControl Class. Table 27-12 lists the properties, methods, and events that the ComboBox class possesses that it did not inherit.

Table 27-12
Non-Inherited Members of the ComboBox Control

Member Name (scope and type)	Description
DrawMode (Public Instance Property)	Specifies whether the operating system handles the drawing of the control or the code handles the drawing.
DropDownStyle (Public Instance Property)	Specifies the style of the combo box. Can be DropDown, the text portion is editable, and an arrow must be clicked to display the list; DropDownList, which is the same as DropDown, except not editable; Simple, the list is always visible and the text portion is editable.

Continued

Table 27-12 *(continued)*

Member Name (scope and type)	Description
DropDownWidth (Public Instance Property)	Specifies the width of the drop-down portion of the combo box. Very useful due to varying widths of items in the list. Can be used to prevent portions of items from being cut off.
DroppedDown (Public Instance Property)	Specifies whether the control is displaying the drop-down portion of the control.
IntegralHeight (Public Instance Property)	Specifies whether the control should resize to avoid showing partial values.
ItemHeight (Public Instance Property)	ReadOnly. Returns the height of an item within the combo box.
Items (Public Instance Property)	ReadOnly. Returns a collection containing all items within the combo box.
MaxDropDownItems (Public Instance Property)	Specifies the number of items to be shown in the drop-down portion of the control. If the number of items in the list is greater than this number, a vertical scrollbar automatically appears.
MaxLength (Public Instance Property)	Specifies the largest allowable number of characters within the editable portion of the control.
PreferredHeight (Public Instance Property)	ReadOnly. Returns a value based on the border style and the font size used to specifiy the preferred height of an item within the control.
SelectedItem (Public Instance Property)	Specifies the currently selected item within the combo box.
SelectedText (Public Instance Property)	Specifies the currently selected text within the editable portion of the control.
SelectionLength (Public Instance Property)	Specifies the number of characters selected within the editable portion of the combo box.
SelectionStart (Public Instance Property)	Specifies the starting position of the selected text in the editable portion of the combo box.
Sorted (Public Instance Property)	Specifies whether the items in the list portion of the control are sorted.

Member Name (scope and type)	Description
BeginUpdate (**Public Instance Method**)	Suspends painting of the control while items are being added.
EndUpdate (**Public Instance Method**)	Resumes painting of the control after all items are added.
FindString (**Public Instance Method**)	Finds the specified text within the items contained in the combo box. Returns partial matches.
FindStringExact (**Public Instance Method**)	Similar to FindString, but finds only exact matches of the string specified.
GetItemHeight (**Public Instance Method**)	Returns the height of the specified item.
Select (**Public Instance Method**)	Selects the specified range of text within the editable portion of the control.
SelectAll (**Public Instance Method**)	Selects all text within the editable portion of the control.
DrawItem (**Public Instance Event**)	Occurs when a visual aspect of the control changes. Occurs only when the DrawMode property of the control is set to OwnerDraw.
DropDown (**Public Instance Event**)	Occurs when the list portion of the ComboBox control is displayed.
DropDownStyleChanged (**Public Instance Event**)	Occurs when the style of the ComboBox control is changed. As discussed in Chapter 25, changing this property causes the window handle to be re-created.
MeasureItem (**Public Instance Event**)	Occurs when the combo box is created and the sizes of the list items are determined. Valid only when the DrawMode property is set to OwnerDraw.
SelectedIndexChanged (**Public Instance Event**)	Occurs when the index of the selected item has changed.
SelectionChangeCommitted (**Public Instance Event**)	Occurs when the selected item has changed and that change has been committed.
AddItemsCore (**Protected Instance Method**)	Used to add a collection of items to the combo box. Takes an array of items.

ContextMenu

This control is typically used to display frequently used menu items. This is also known as a right-click menu, or a shortcut menu. The ContextMenu control inherits directly from the Menu class. Table 27-13 lists the properties, methods, and events that the ContextMenu class possesses that it did not inherit.

Table 27-13
Non-Inherited Members of the ContextMenu Control

Member Name (scope and type)	Description
RightToLeft (Public Instance Property)	Specifies whether the text displayed in the context menu is from right-to-left.
Show (Public Instance Method)	Displays the shortcut menu at the specified position.
Popup (Public Instance Event)	Occurs before the control is displayed.

DataGrid

The purpose of this control is to display data retrieved via ADO.NET in a scrollable grid. Grid controls are generally considered the most complex category of control and the datagrid is no exception. Table 27-14 is a testament to its customizability. This control inherits directly from the Control class. Table 27-14 lists the properties, methods, and events that the DataGrid class possesses that it did not inherit.

Table 27-14
Non-Inherited Members of the DataGrid Control

Member Name (scope and type)	Description
AutoColumnSize (Public Static Field)	Specifies that the datagrid automatically sizes columns to the maximum width of the first 10 rows. To automatically size the columns, set the PreferredColumnWidth property equal to this constant.
AllowNavigation (Public Instance Property)	Specifies whether navigation is allowed. Navigation refers to traversing tables.
AllowSorting (Public Instance Property)	Specifies whether a column can be sorted by clicking a column header.

Member Name (scope and type)	Description
AlternatingBackColor (Public Instance Property)	Specifies the background color of alternating rows. Typically used to create a ledger-style appearance.
BackgroundColor (Public Instance Property)	Specifies the background color of the datagrid in all portions excluding the data rows.
BorderStyle (Public Instance Property)	Specifies the border style of the datagrid. A value of Fixed3D gives a sunken impression.
CaptionBackColor (Public Instance Property)	Specifies the background color of the caption area within the control.
CaptionFont (Public Instance Property)	Specifies the font of the text in the caption area of the control.
CaptionForeColor (Public Instance Property)	Specifies the foreground color (typically this means the color of the text) for the caption area of the control.
CaptionText (Public Instance Property)	Specifies the text displayed in the caption window of the datagrid.
CaptionVisible (Public Instance Property)	Specifies whether the caption area of the datagrid is visible.
ColumnHeadersVisible (Public Instance Property)	Specifies whether the parent rows of a table are visible.
CurrentCell (Public Instance Property)	Specifies which cell within the datagrid has the focus.
CurrentRowIndex (Public Instance Property)	Specifies the index of the currently selected row.
DataMember (Public Instance Property)	Specifies the list within a DataSource that the datagrid is to display.
DataSource (Public Instance Property)	Specifies the source of the data that the grid is displaying.
FirstVisibleColumn (Public Instance Property)	ReadOnly. Returns the index of the first visible column in a grid.
FlatMode (Public Instance Property)	Specifies whether or not the control displays in FlatMode. FlatMode means that the cells in the grid will appear flat rather than slightly recessed as a 3D-Border would yield.

Continued

Table 27-14 *(continued)*

Member Name (scope and type)	Description
GridLineColor (Public Instance Property)	Specifies the color of the gridlines in the datagrid.
GridLineStyle (Public Instance Property)	Specifies the style of the gridline in the control. Can be Solid or None.
HeaderBackColor (Public Instance Property)	Specifies the background color of all row and column headers.
HeaderFont (Public Instance Property)	Specifies the font of all row and column headers.
HeaderForeColor (Public Instance Property)	Specifies the foreground color of all row and column headers.
Item (Public Instance Property)	Specifies the value of the cell located at the given row and column intersection.
LinkColor (Public Instance Property)	Specifies the color of the text indicating that a click navigates to a child table.
LinkHoverColor (Public Instance Property)	Specifies the color a link changes to when the mouse hovers over it.
ParentRowsBackColor (Public Instance Property)	Specifies the background color of all parent rows.
ParentRowsForeColor (Public Instance Property)	Specifies the foreground color of all parent rows.
ParentRowsLabelStyle (Public Instance Property)	Specifies how the parent row labels are displayed in a datagrid. Can be TableName, ColumnName, Both, or None.
ParentRowsVisible (Public Instance Property)	Specifies whether the parent rows of a table are visible.
PreferredColumnWidth (Public Instance Property)	Specifies the default column width in the datagrid.
PreferredRowHeight (Public Instance Property)	Specifies the default row height in a datagrid.
ReadOnly (Public Instance Property)	Specifies whether the grid is noneditable.
RowHeadersVisible (Public Instance Property)	Specifies whether the row headers are visible.
RowHeaderWidth (Public Instance Property)	Specifies the width of the row headers.
SelectionBackColor (Public Instance Property)	Specifies the background color for cells to display when they are selected.

Member Name (scope and type)	Description
SelectionForeColor (**Public Instance Property**)	Specifies the foreground color for text in cells to display when selected.
TableStyles (**Public Instance Property**)	ReadOnly. Returns the collection of datagrid table styles for the grid.
VisibleColumnCount (**Public Instance Property**)	ReadOnly. Returns the number of visible columns.
VisibleRowCount (**Public Instance Property**)	ReadOnly. Returns the number of visible rows.
BeginEdit (**Public Instance Method**)	Places the grid in a state where editing is allowed.
BeginInit (**Public Instance Method**)	Begins the initialization of the DataGrid control.
Collapse (**Public Instance Method**)	Collapses visible child relations for all rows or for a specified row.
EndEdit (**Public Instance Method**)	Ceases an edit operation taking place on the control.
EndInit (**Public Instance Method**)	Ends the initialization of the control.
Expand (**Public Instance Method**)	Displays child relations for all rows or the specified row.
GetCellBounds (**Public Instance Method**)	Returns the bounding rectangle of the specified cell.
GetCurrentCellBounds (**Public Instance Method**)	Returns the bounding rectangle of the selected cell.
HitTest (**Public Instance Method**)	Returns information describing the region of the datagrid that contains the specified point.
IsExpanded (**Public Instance Method**)	Returns a value detailing whether a specified row is expanded.
IsSelected (**Public Instance Method**)	Returns a value detailing whether a specified row is selected.
NavigateBack (**Public Instance Method**)	Displays the previously displayed table in the grid.
NavigateTo (**Public Instance Method**)	Displays the specified table in the grid.
ResetAlternatingBackColor (**Public Instance Method**)	Restores the AlternatingBackColor property to its default value.
ResetGridLineColor (**Public Instance Method**)	Restores the GrindLineColor property to its default value.

Continued

Table 27-14 *(continued)*

Member Name (scope and type)	Description
ResetHeaderBackColor (Public Instance Method)	Restores the HeaderBackColor property to its default value.
ResetHeaderFont (Public Instance Method)	Restores the HeaderFont property to its default value.
ResetHeaderForeColor (Public Instance Method)	Restores the HeaderForeColor property to its default value.
ResetLinkColor (Public Instance Method)	Restores the LinkColor property to its default value.
ResetLinkHoverColor (Public Instance Method)	Restores the LinkHoverColor property to its default value.
ResetSelectionBackColor (Public Instance Method)	Restores the SelectionBackColor property to its default value.
ResetSelectionForeColor (Public Instance Method)	Restores the SelectionForeColor property to its default value.
SetDataBinding (Public Instance Method)	Sets the DataSource and DataMember properties to the specified values.
UnSelect (Public Instance Method)	Unselects a specified row.
AllowNavigationChanged (Public Instance Event)	Occurs when the value of the AllowNavigation property is changed.
BackButtonClick (Public Instance Event)	Occurs when the Back button on a child table is clicked.
BackgroundColorChanged (Public Instance Event)	Occurs when the value of the BackGroundColor property is changed.
BorderStyleChanged (Public Instance Event)	Occurs when the value of the BorderStyle property is changed.
CaptionVisibleChanged (Public Instance Event)	Occurs when the value of the CaptionVisible property is changed.
DataSourceChanged (Public Instance Event)	Occurs when the datasource of the grid has changed.
FlatModeChanged (Public Instance Event)	Occurs when the value of the FlatMode property is changed.
Navigate (Public Instance Event)	Occurs when the user navigates to a new table.
ParentRowsLabelStyleChanged (Public Instance Event)	Occurs when the value of the ParentRowsLabelStyle property is changed.

Member Name (scope and type)	Description
`ParentRowsVisibleChanged` (Public Instance Event)	Occurs when the value of the `ParentRowsVisible` property is changed.
`ReadOnlyChanged` (Public Instance Event)	Occurs when the value of the `ReadOnly` property is changed.
`Scroll` (Public Instance Event)	Occurs when the user scrolls within the datagrid.
`ShowParentDetailsButtonClick` (Public Instance Event)	Occurs when the `ShowParentDetails` button is clicked.
`HorizScrollBar` (Protected Instance Property)	ReadOnly. Returns the horizontal scrollbar for the datagrid.
`ListManager` (Protected Instance Property)	ReadOnly. Returns the Binding Context Manager for this control.
`VertScrollBar` (Protected Instance Property)	ReadOnly. Returns the vertical scrollbar for the datagrid.
`CancelEditing` (Protected Instance Method)	Cancels the current edit operation, and rolls back all changes.
`ColumnStartedEditing` (Protected Instance Method)	Informs the `DataGrid` control that the user is editing a column.
`CreateGridColumn` (Protected Instance Method)	Creates a new datagrid column to be added to the control.
`ProcessGridKey` (Protected Instance Method)	Processes keys for grid navigation.
`ProcessTabKey` (Protected Instance Method)	Returns a value indicating whether the datagrid should process the Tab key.
`ResetSelection` (Protected Instance Method)	Unselects all selected rows.
`ShouldSerializeAlternatingBackColor` (Protected Instance Method)	Indicates whether the `AlternatingBackColor` property should be persisted. Typically used for custom datagrid designers or derived controls.
`ShouldSerializeBackGroundColor` (Protected Instance Method)	Indicates whether the `BackGroundColor` property should be persisted. Typically used for custom datagrid designers or derived controls.
`ShouldSerializeCaptionBackColor` (Protected Instance Method)	Indicates whether the `CaptionBackColor` property should be persisted. Typically used for custom datagrid designers or derived controls.

Continued

Table 27-14 *(continued)*	
Member Name (scope and type)	**Description**
ShouldSerializeCaptionForeColor (Protected Instance Method)	Indicates whether the CaptionForeColor property should be persisted. Typically used for custom datagrid designers or derived controls.
ShouldSerializeGridLineColor (Protected Instance Method)	Indicates whether the GridLineColor property should be persisted. Typically used for custom datagrid designers or derived controls.
ShouldSerializeHeaderBackColor (Protected Instance Method)	Indicates whether the HeaderBackColor property should be persisted. Typically used for custom datagrid designers or derived controls.
ShouldSerializeHeaderFont (Protected Instance Method)	Indicates whether the HeaderFont property should be persisted. Typically used for custom datagrid designers or derived controls.
ShouldSerializeHeaderForeColor (Protected Instance Method)	Indicates whether the HeaderForeColor property should be persisted. Typically used for custom datagrid designers or derived controls.
ShouldSerializeLinkHoverColor (Protected Instance Method)	Indicates whether the LinkHoverColor property should be persisted. Typically used for custom datagrid designers or derived controls.
ShouldSerializeParentRowsBackColor (Protected Instance Method)	Indicates whether the ParentRowsBackColor property should be persisted. Typically used for custom datagrid designers or derived controls.
ShouldSerializeParentRowsForeColor (Protected Instance Method)	Indicates whether the ParentRowsForeColor property should be persisted. Typically used for custom datagrid designers or derived controls.
ShouldSerializePreferredRowHeight (Protected Instance Method)	Indicates whether the PreferredRowHeight property should be persisted. Typically used for custom datagrid designers or derived controls.

Member Name (scope and type)	Description
ShouldSerializeSelectionForeColor (Protected Instance Method)	Indicates whether the SelectionForeColor property should be persisted. Typically used for custom datagrid designers or derived controls.
RowHeaderClick (Protected Instance Event)	Occurs when a row header is clicked.

DateTimePicker

This control presents a graphical interface for users to view and set date and time information. This class inherits directly from Control. Table 27-15 lists the properties, methods, and events that the DateTimePicker class possesses that it did not inherit.

Table 27-15
Non-Inherited Members of the DateTimePicker Control

Member Name (scope and type)	Description
MaxDateTime (Public Static Field)	ReadOnly. Specifies the maximum date value of the control.
MinDateTime (Public Static Field)	ReadOnly. Specifies the minimum date value of the control.
CalendarFont (Public Instance Property)	Specifies the font in the calendar portion of the control.
CalendarForeColor (Public Instance Property)	Specifies the foreground color of the calendar portion of the control.
CalendarMonthBackground (Public Instance Property)	Specifies the background color of the calendar portion of the control.
CalendarTitleBackColor (Public Instance Property)	Specifies the background color of the title area of the calendar portion of the control.
CalendarTitleForeColor (Public Instance Property)	Specifies the foreground color of the title area of the calendar portion of the control.
CalendarTrailingForeColor (Public Instance Property)	Specifies the color of the days that are part of months not fully displayed within the calendar portion of the control.

Continued

<table>
<tr><td colspan="2" align="center">Table 27-15 *(continued)*</td></tr>
<tr><td>***Member Name (scope and type)***</td><td>***Description***</td></tr>
<tr><td>Checked (Public Instance Property)</td><td>Specifies whether the Value property of the control has been set with a valid value and the displayed value can be updated.</td></tr>
<tr><td>CustomFormat (Public Instance Property)</td><td>Specifies the custom date/time format string.</td></tr>
<tr><td>DropDownAlign (Public Instance Property)</td><td>Specifies the alignment of the drop-down calendar on the control.</td></tr>
<tr><td>Format (Public Instance Property)</td><td>Specifies the format of the date and time displayed in the control.</td></tr>
<tr><td>MaxDate (Public Instance Property)</td><td>Specifies the maximum date and time that can be selected within the control.</td></tr>
<tr><td>MinDate (Public Instance Property)</td><td>Specifies the minimum date and time that can selected within the control.</td></tr>
<tr><td>PreferredHeight (Public Instance Property)</td><td>ReadOnly. Returns the preferred height of the control.</td></tr>
<tr><td>ShowCheckBox (Public Instance Property)</td><td>Specifies whether a check box is displayed next to a selected date.</td></tr>
<tr><td>ShowUpDown (Public Instance Property)</td><td>Specifies whether an UpDown control is used to adjust the value.</td></tr>
<tr><td>Value (Public Instance Property)</td><td>Specifies the date/time value of the control.</td></tr>
<tr><td>CloseUp (Public Instance Event)</td><td>Occurs when the drop-down calendar is dismissed.</td></tr>
<tr><td>DropDown (Public Instance Event)</td><td>Occurs when the drop-down calendar is displayed.</td></tr>
<tr><td>FormatChanged (Public Instance Event)</td><td>Occurs when the Format property has changed.</td></tr>
<tr><td>ValueChanged (Public Instance Event)</td><td>Occurs when the value of the control has changed.</td></tr>
<tr><td>DefaultMonthBackColor (Protected Static Field)</td><td>ReadOnly. Specifies the default value of the MonthBackGround property.</td></tr>
<tr><td>DefaultTitleBackColor (Protected Static Field)</td><td>ReadOnly. Specifies the default background color of the title portion of the control.</td></tr>
</table>

Member Name (scope and type)	Description
DefaultTitleForeColor (Protected Static Field)	ReadOnly. Specifies the default foreground color of the title portion of the control.
DefaultTrailingForeColor (Protected Static Field)	ReadOnly. Specifies the default trailing fore color of the control.

DomainUpDown

This control is typically used to display a list of strings for the user to choose. The DomainUpDown control is very similar to the Simple style of the ComboBox control, however it occupies less space. The DomainUpDown control inherits directly from the UpDownBase class. Table 27-16 lists the properties, methods, and events that the DomainUpDown class possesses that it did not inherit.

Table 27-16
Non-Inherited Members of the DomainUpDown Control

Member Name (scope and type)	Description
Items (Public Instance Property)	ReadOnly. Returns a collection of the objects assigned to this control.
SelectedIndex (Public Instance Property)	Specifies the index of the selected item.
SelectedItem (Public Instance Property)	Specifies the selected item based on the index of the specified item within the items collection.
Sorted (Public Instance Property)	Specifies whether the contents of the control are sorted.
Wrap (Public Instance Property)	Specifies whether the collection of items continues to the first or last item when the user passes the end or beginning of the Items collection respectively.

HScrollBar and VScrollBar

These controls simply represent a standard horizontal and vertical scrollbar. The HScrollBar and VScrollBar controls inherit directly from the ScrollBar class. Neither of these controls have any properties, methods, or events that are not inherited.

ListBox*

This control is typically used to display a list of items from which the user can choose. The Listbox control inherits directly from the ListControl class, and is an ancestor to the CheckedListBox class. Table 27-17 lists the properties, methods, and events that the ListBox class possesses that it did not inherit.

	Table 27-17	
	Non-Inherited Members of the ListBox Control	
Member Name (scope and type)		**Description**
DefaultItemHeight (Public Static Field)		Specifies the default item height for the ListBox control.
NoMatches (Public Static Field)		Specifies that no matching items were found during a search.
ColumnWidth (Public Instance Property)		Specifies the width of the columns in a multicolumn list box.
DrawMode (Public Instance Property)		Specifies whether the operating system handles the drawing of the control or the code handles the drawing.
HorizontalExtent (Public Instance Property)		Specifies the width by which the horizontal scrollbar can scroll.
HorizontalScrollBar (Public Instance Property)		Specifies whether the horizontal scrollbar is displayed on the control.
IntegralHeight (Public Instance Property)		Specifies whether the control should resize to avoid showing partial values.
ItemHeight (Public Instance Property)		ReadOnly. Returns the height of an item within the list box.
Items (Public Instance Property)		ReadOnly. Returns a collection containing all items within the list box.
MultiColumn (Public Instance Property)		Specifies whether this ListBox control supports more than one column.
PreferredHeight (Public Instance Property)		ReadOnly. Returns the combined height of all items within the list box.
ScrollAlwaysVisible (Public Instance Property)		Specifies whether the vertical scrollbar is always visible within the control.
SelectedIndices (Public Instance Property)		ReadOnly. Returns a collection containing the indices of all currently selected items in a multiselect list box.
SelectedItem (Public Instance Property)		Specifies the currently specified item within the control.

Member Name (scope and type)	Description
SelectedItems (Public Instance Property)	ReadOnly. Returns a collection containing the currently selected items in a multiselect list box.
SelectionMode (Public Instance Property)	Specifies the method by which the user can select items in a list box. Valid values are None, One, MultiSimple, and MultiExtended.
Sorted (Public Instance Property)	Specifies whether the items in the list box are sorted alphabetically.
TopIndex (Public Instance Property)	Specifies the top index of the top item visible in the list box.
UseTabStops (Public Instance Property)	Specifies whether the list box can recognize Tab characters when drawing strings.
BeginUpdate (Public Instance Method)	Suspends the painting of the control while items are being added to the items collection.
ClearSelected (Public Instance Method)	Deselects all selected items within the list box.
EndUpdate (Public Instance Method)	Resumes painting of the control after all items are added.
FindString (Public Instance Method)	Finds the specified text within the items contained in the combo box. Returns partial matches.
FindStringExact (Public Instance Method)	Similar to FindString, but finds only exact matches of the string specified.
GetItemHeight (Public Instance Method)	Returns the height of the specified item.
GetItemRectangle (Public Instance Method)	Returns the bounding rectangle for an item in the list box.
GetSelected (Public Instance Method)	Returns a value indicating whether the specified item is selected.
IndexFromPoint (Public Instance Method)	Returns the index of the item in the list box at the specified coordinates.
SetSelected (Public Instance Method)	Toggles the selection for the specified item within the list box.
DrawItem (Public Instance Event)	Occurs when a visual aspect of the control changes. Only occurs when the DrawMode property of the control is set to OwnerDraw.

Continued

Table 27-17 *(continued)*	
Member Name (scope and type)	**Description**
MeasureItem (Public Instance Event)	Occurs when the list box is created and the sizes of the list items are determined. Only valid when the DrawMode property is set to OwnerDraw.
SelectedIndexChanged (Public Instance Event)	Occurs when the index of the selected item has changed.
CreateItemCollection (Protected Instance Method)	Creates a new instance of the items collection.
Sort (Protected Instance Method)	Sorts the items in the list box alphabetically.

ListView

The ListView control is typically used to list items. The four modes of display are LargeIcon, SmallIcon, List, and Details (Report). This control can be used to create an interface similar to the right pane of Windows Explorer. The ListView control inherits directly from the Control class. Table 27-18 lists the properties, methods, and events that the ListView class possesses that it did not inherit.

Table 27-18 **Non-Inherited Members of the ListView Control**	
Member Name (scope and type)	**Description**
Activation (Public Instance Property)	Specifies the use action required to activate an item in the control.
Alignment (Public Instance Property)	Specifies the side of the window to which items are aligned.
AllowColumnReorder (Public Instance Property)	Specifies whether the columns can be repositioned by the user.
AutoArrange (Public Instance Property)	Specifies whether items are automatically arranged according to their alignment property.
BorderStyle (Public Instance Property)	Specifies the border style of the control. Fixed3D provides a sunken appearance.
CheckBoxes (Public Instance Property)	Specifies whether check boxes are displayed next to each item.

Member Name (scope and type)	Description
CheckedIndices (**Public Instance Property**)	ReadOnly. Returns the indices of all items currently checked.
CheckedItems (**Public Instance Property**)	ReadOnly. Returns a collection of all items currently checked.
Columns (**Public Instance Property**)	ReadOnly. Returns a collection of columns in the control.
FocusedItem (**Public Instance Property**)	ReadOnly. Returns the items that currently have the focus.
FullRowSelect (**Public Instance Property**)	Specifies whether selecting an item also selects the entire row to which the control belongs.
GridLines (**Public Instance Property**)	Specifies whether gridlines are drawn between items.
HeaderStyle (**Public Instance Property**)	Specifies the style of the column headers. Can be Clickable, NonClickable, or None.
HideSelection (**Public Instance Property**)	Specifies whether selected items still appear selected when the control loses focus.
HoverSelection (**Public Instance Property**)	Specifies whether an item can be selected by the mouse hovering over it.
Items (**Public Instance Property**)	ReadOnly. Returns the collections of items in the control.
LabelEdit (**Public Instance Property**)	Specifies whether the user can edit the labels of the items in the control.
LabelWrap (**Public Instance Property**)	Specifies whether the item labels wrap when the control is in an Icon view.
LargeImageList (**Public Instance Property**)	Specifies the ImageList object to be used by the control when in LargeIcon mode.
ListViewItemSorter (**Public Instance Property**)	Specifies the object that sorts the items in the control.
MultiSelect (**Public Instance Property**)	Specifies whether the user can select more than one item at a time.
Scrollable (**Public Instance Property**)	Specifies whether the scrollbars are visible in the control.
SelectedIndices (**Public Instance Property**)	ReadOnly. Returns the indices of all currently selected items in the control.

Continued

Table 27-18 *(continued)*

Member Name (scope and type)	Description
SelectedItems (Public Instance Property)	ReadOnly. Returns a collection of all items currently selected in the control.
SmallImageList (Public Instance Property)	Specifies the ImageList object to be used by the control when in SmallIcon mode.
Sorting (Public Instance Property)	Specifies the sort order of the items in the control.
StateImageList (Public Instance Property)	Specifies the ImageList object that is relevant to the current state of the control.
TopItem (Public Instance Property)	ReadOnly. Returns the item that is at the top of the list.
View (Public Instance Property)	Specifies the current view. Can be LargeIcon, SmallIcon, List, Details (Report).
ArrangeIcons (Public Instance Method)	Arranges items in the control when in LargeIcon or SmallIcon view.
BeginUpdate (Public Instance Method)	Suspends painting of the control while items are being added.
Clear (Public Instance Method)	Removes all items from the control.
EndUpdate (Public Instance Method)	Resumes painting of the control after items have been added.
EnsureVisible (Public Instance Method)	Scrolls the control (if necessary) to ensure that the specified item is visible within the viewable area of the control.
GetItemAt (Public Instance Method)	Returns the item in the control located at the specified point.
GetItemRect (Public Instance Method)	Returns the bounding rectangle for the specified item in the List view.
AfterLabelEdit (Public Instance Event)	Occurs after the edit operation on a label has been completed.
BeforeLabelEdit (Public Instance Event)	Occurs immediately prior to a label edit operation.
ColumnClick (Public Instance Event)	Occurs when a column header is clicked. Sorting is usually handled in this event.

Member Name (scope and type)	Description
ItemActivate (Public Instance Event)	Occurs when an item is activated according to the activation property.
ItemCheck (Public Instance Event)	Occurs when an item is checked.
ItemDrag (Public Instance Event)	Occurs when an item is being dragged.
SelectedIndexChanged (Public Instance Event)	Occurs when the index of the selected item changes.
UpdateExtendedStyles(ListView)	Refreshes any style changes that have been made to the control.

MainMenu

This control is typically used to display a menu. The MainMenu control inherits directly from the Menu class. Table 27-19 lists the properties, methods, and events that the MainMenu class possesses that it did not inherit.

Table 27-19
Non-Inherited Members of the MainMenu Control

Member Name (scope and type)	Description
RightToLeft (Public Instance Property)	Specifies whether the text in the control is displayed from right-to-left.
CloneMenu (Public Instance Method)	Creates a new main menu that is a deep-copy of the specified main menu.
GetForm (Public Instance Method)	Returns the form to which this control belongs.

MonthCalendar

This control presents a graphical interface for users to view and set date information. This control is very similar to the DateTimePicker control. This class inherits directly from Control. Table 27-20 lists the properties, methods, and events that the MonthCalendar class possesses that it did not inherit.

Table 27-20
Non-Inherited Members of the MonthCalendar Control

Member Name (scope and type)	Description
`AnnuallyBoldedDates` (Public Instance Property)	Specifies an array of annually recurring dates to be bolded.
`BoldedDates` (Public Instance Property)	Specifies an array of non-recurring dates to be bolded.
`CalendarDimensions` (Public Instance Property)	Specifies the number of columns and rows of months displayed.
`FirstDayOfWeek` (Public Instance Property)	Specifies the day of the week that is first in each row of dates displayed within the control.
`MaxDate` (Public Instance Property)	Specifies the maximum allowable date within the control.
`MaxSelectionDate` (Public Instance Property)	Specifies the maximum number of days that can be selected within the control.
`MinDate` (Public Instance Property)	Specifies the minimum allowable date.
`MonthlyBoldedDates` (Public Instance Property)	Specifies an array of dates to bold within each month.
`ScrollChange` (Public Instance Property)	Specifies the scroll rate for the control. Value is the number of months moved when the control is scrolled.
`SelectionEnd` (Public Instance Property)	Specifies the end date for a selected range of dates.
`SelectionRange` (Public Instance Property)	Specifies the selected range of dates within the control.
`SelectionStart` (Public Instance Property)	Specifies the start date for a selected range of dates.
`ShowToday` (Public Instance Property)	Specifies whether the date contained in the `TodayDate` property is shown at the bottom of the control.
`ShowTodayCircle` (Public Instance Property)	Specifies whether today's date is circled in the control.
`ShowWeekNumbers` (Public Instance Property)	Specifies whether the numbers of the weeks within the year are displayed next to each row of days.
`SingleMonthSize` (Public Instance Property)	ReadOnly. Returns the minimize size necessary to display one month within the control.

Member Name (scope and type)	Description
TitleBackColor **(Public Instance Property)**	Specifies a color for background of the title area.
TitleForeColor **(Public Instance Property)**	Specifies a color for the foreground of the title area.
TodayDate **(Public Instance Property)**	Specifies the date that is considered the current date.
TodayDateSet **(Public Instance Property)**	ReadOnly. Returns a value indicating whether or not the TodayDate property has been explicitly set.
TrailingForeColor **(Public Instance Property)**	Specifies the color of the days that are part of months not fully displayed within the control.
AddAnnuallyBoldedDate **(Public Instance Method)**	Adds a day that is displayed in bold on an annual basis in the control.
AddBoldedDate **(Public Instance Method)**	Adds a day that is displayed in bold in the calendar.
AddMonthlyBoldedDate **(Public Instance Method)**	Adds a day that is bolded monthly in the control.
GetDisplayRange **(Public Instance Method)**	Retrieves date information that represents the limits of the displayed dates.
HitTest **(Public Instance Method)**	Returns an object of the calendar that is at the specified location.
RemoveAllAnnuallyBoldedDates **(Public Instance Method)**	Removes all annual dates that are bolded.
RemoveAllBoldedDates	Removes all non-recurring bolded dates. **(Public Instance Method)**
RemoveAllMonthlyBoldedDates **(Public Instance Method)**	Removes all dates that are bolded on a monthly basis.
RemoveAnnuallyBoldedDate **(Public Instance Method)**	Removes the specified date that is annually bolded.
RemoveBoldedDate **(Public Instance Method)**	Removes the specified non-recurring bolded date.
RemoveMonthlyBoldedDate **(Public Instance Method)**	Removes the specified date that is bolded on a monthly basis.
SetCalendarDimensions **(Public Instance Method)**	Sets the number of columns and rows of months to display.

Continued

Table 27-20 *(continued)*

Member Name (scope and type)	Description
SetDate (Public Instance Method)	Sets the specified date as the current date.
SetSelectionRange (Public Instance Method)	Sets the specified date range as the selected dates.
UpdateBoldedDates (Public Instance Method)	Repaints the list of bolded dates. Used to refresh the lists after they have been modified.
DateChanged (Public Instance Event)	Occurs when the date in the control changes.
DateSelected (Public Instance Event)	Occurs when a date is selected in the control.

NumericUpDown

This control is typically used to display a list of numbers for the user to choose. The NumericUpDown control is very similar to the Simple style of the ComboBox control; however, it occupies less space. The NumericUpDown control inherits directly from the UpDownBase class. Table 27-21 lists the properties, methods, and events that the NumericUpDown class possesses that it did not inherit.

Table 27-21
Non-Inherited Members of the NumericUpDown Control

Member Name (scope and type)	Description
DecimalPlaces (Public Instance Property)	Specifies the number of decimal places displayed in this control.
Hexadecimal (Public Instance Property)	Specifies whether this control should display the current value in hexadecimal format.
Increment (Public Instance Property)	Specifies the amount by which to increment and decrement the value in the control when the Up or Down buttons are clicked.
Maximum (Public Instance Property)	Specifies the maximum value for this control.
Minimum (Public Instance Property)	Specifies the minimum value for this control.

Member Name (scope and type)	Description
ThousandsSeparator (Public Instance Property)	Specifies whether an appropriate thousands separator is displayed within the control when necessary.
Value (Public Instance Property)	Specifies the current value assigned to the control.
ValueChanged (Public Instance Event)	Occurs when the value of this control has changed.
CreateAccessibilityInstance (Protected Instance Method)	Returns the accessible object relevant to this control.
ParseEditText (Protected Instance Method)	Converts the text in the control to a numeric value, and evaluates it.

PropertyGrid*

This control is used to provide an interface for the user to browse the properties of an object. The information displayed is a snapshot of the properties at the time of assignment. New values aren't displayed until the grid is refreshed. Keep in mind that this is equivalent to the property grid in the IDE at design time. This control inherits directly from ContainerControl. Table 27-22 lists the properties, methods, and events that the PropertyGrid class possesses that it did not inherit.

Table 27-22
Non-Inherited Members of the PropertyGrid Control

Member Name (scope and type)	Description
BrowsableAttributes (Public Instance Property)	Specifies a collection of browsable attributes associated with the object to which the grid is attached.
CanShowCommands (Public Instance Property)	ReadOnly. Returns whether the commands pane is made visible for the currently selected objects.
CommandBackColor (Public Instance Property)	Specifies the background color of the commands region of the grid.
CommandsForeColor (Public Instance Property)	Specifies the foreground color of the commands region of the grid.
CommandsVisible (Public Instance Property)	ReadOnly. Returns whether the commands pane is currently visible.

Continued

Table 27-22 *(continued)*

Member Name (scope and type)	Description
CommandsVisibleIfAvailable (Public Instance Property)	ReadOnly. Returns whether the commands pane is available for objects that expose verbs.
ContextMenuDefaultLocation (Public Instance Property)	ReadOnly. Returns the default location for the context menu.
HelpBackColor (Public Instance Property)	Specifies the background color for the help region of the grid.
HelpForeColor (Public Instance Property)	Specifies the foreground color for the help region of the grid.
HelpVisible (Public Instance Property)	Specifies whether the help text is visible.
Largebuttons (Public Instance Property)	Specifies whether the buttons on the grid appear as standard size or large size.
LineColor (Public Instance Property)	Specifies the color of the gridlines and borders of the control.
PropertySort (Public Instance Property)	Specifies the type of sorting used by the control to display properties.
PropertyTabs (Public Instance Property)	ReadOnly. Returns a new collection of property tabs.
SelectedGridItem (Public Instance Property)	Specifies the selected grid item in the control.
SelectedObject (Public Instance Property)	Specifies the currently selected object for which the control displays properties.
SelectedObjects (Public Instance Property)	Specifies a collection of objects for which the grid currently displays properties.
SelectedTab (Public Instance Property)	ReadOnly. Returns the active property tab.
ToolbarVisible (Public Instance Property)	Specifies whether the toolbar is currently visible.
ViewBackColor (Public Instance Property)	Specifies the background color in the grid.
ViewForeColor (Public Instance Property)	Specifies the foreground color in the grid.
ExpandAllGridItems (Public Instance Method)	Fully expands all categories in the grid.
RefreshTabs (Public Instance Method)	Refreshes the property tabs within the specified scope.
ResetSelectedProperty (Public Instance Method)	Resets the selected property to its default value.

Member Name (scope and type)	Description
PropertySortChanged (Public Instance Event)	Occurs when the sort mode has changed.
PropertyTabChanged (Public Instance Event)	Occurs when the currently selected tab changes.
PropertyValueChanged (Public Instance Event)	Occurs when the value of a property changes.
SelectedGridItemChanged (Public Instance Event)changed.	Occurs when the selected grid item is
SelectedObjectsChanged (Public Instance Event)	Occurs when the objects for which properties are displayed has changed.
DefaultTabType (Protected Instance Property)	ReadOnly. Specifies the default tab type. If unspecified, then PropertyTab.
CreatePropertyTab (Protected Instance Method)	Allows for the creation of a new property tab.

RadioButton

This control is typically used to present a set of mutually exclusive choices to the user. This control is always used in conjunction with other radio buttons. Note that checking one radio button automatically deselects all other radio buttons because only one button can be checked at a time. The RadioButton control inherits directly from the ButtonBase class. Table 27-23 lists the properties, methods, and events that the RadioButton class possesses that it did not inherit.

Table 27-23
Non-Inherited Members of the RadioButton Control

Member Name (scope and type)	Description
Appearance (Public Instance Property)	Specifies the current appearance of the RadioButton control.
AutoCheck (Public Instance Property)	Specifies whether the value and appearance of the control automatically change when the control is checked.
CheckAlign (Public Instance Property)	Specifies the alignment of the check box portion of the control.
Checked (Public Instance Property)	Specifies whether the control is checked.

Continued

Table 27-23 *(continued)*	
Member Name (scope and type)	**Description**
PerformClick (Public Instance Method)	Initiates a click on the control as if done by the user.
AppearanceChanged (Public Instance Event)	Occurs after the appearance property of the control has changed.
CheckedChanged (Public Instance Event)	Occurs when the checked value of the control has changed.

RichTextBox

This control is similar to the Textbox control, except it allows for more advanced formatting. This control inherits directly from the TextBoxBase class. As you see in Table 27-24, this control allows for advanced customization. The following table lists the properties, methods, and events that the RichTextBox class possesses that it did not inherit.

Table 27-24 **Non-Inherited Members of the RichTextBox Control**	
Member Name (scope and type)	**Description**
AutoWordSelection (Public Instance Property)	Specifies whether selecting a portion of a word selects the entire word.
BulletIndent (Public Instance Property)	Specifies whether an indentation is used when a bullet style is applied to text.
CanRedo (Public Instance Property)	ReadOnly. Returns a value indicating whether there has been an action applied to the control that can be reapplied.
DetectURLs (Public Instance Property)	Specifies whether the control should automatically format URLs when entered into the box.
RedoActionName (Public Instance Property)	ReadOnly. Returns the name of the action that can be reapplied when the Redo method is called.
RigthMargin (Public Instance Property)	Specifies the size of a single line of text within the control.
RTF (Public Instance Property)	Specifies the text of the control including all Rich Text formatting codes.

Member Name (scope and type)	Description
ScrollBars (Public Instance Property)	Specifies the type of scrollbars to display in the control.
SelectedRTF (Public Instance Property)	Specifies the currently selected RTF text in the control.
SelectionAlignment (Public Instance Property)	Specifies the alignment of the current selection or insertion point.
SelectionBullet (Public Instance Property)	Specifies whether the bullet style is applied to the current selection or insertion point.
SelectionCharOffSet (Public Instance Property)	Specifies if the text in the control should appear as normal, superscript, or subscript.
SelectionColor (Public Instance Property)	Specifies the text color of the currently selected text or insertion point.
SelectionFont (Public Instance Property)	Specifies the font of the currently selected text or insertion point.
SelectionHangingIndent (Public Instance Property)	Specifies the distance of indentation between the first line of text in a paragraph and subsequent lines.
SelectionIndent (Public Instance Property)	Specifies the distance between the left edge of the control and the left edge of the selected text or insertion point.
SelectionProtected (Public Instance Property)	Specifies whether the selected text is protected. This means that the user cannot edit it.
SelectionRightIndent (Public Instance Property)	Specifies the distance between the right edge of the control and the right edge of the selected text or insertion point.
SelectionTabs (Public Instance Property)	Specifies the absolute Tab stop positions in the control.
SelectionType (Public Instance Property)	ReadOnly. Returns the selection type of the control. Used to determine attributes of the currently selected text.
ShowSelectionMargin (Public Instance Property)	Specifies whether the selection margin is displayed within the control. The selection margin is similar to the row header in a datagrid, allowing the user to easily select full lines.

Continued

	Table 27-24 *(continued)*	
Member Name (scope and type)	**Description**	
UndoActionName (Public Instance Property)	ReadOnly. Returns the name of the action that can be undone when the Undo method is called.	
ZoomFactor (Public Instance Property)	Specifies the current zoom level of the control.	
CanPaste (Public Instance Method)	Returns a value indicating whether the current contents of the Clipboard can be pasted into the control.	
Find (Public Instance Method)	Returns the location of the sought text within the control.	
GetCharFromPosition (Public Instance Method)	Returns the character that is closest to the specified location within the control.	
GetCharIndexFromPosition (Public Instance Method)	Returns the index of the character that is closest to the specified position within the control.	
GetLineFromCharIndex (Public Instance Method)	Returns the line number from the specified character position within the control.	
GetPositionFromCharIndex (Public Instance Method)	Returns the location of the specified character index within the control.	
LoadFile (Public Instance Method)	Loads the contents of the specified file into the control.	
Redo (Public Instance Method)	Reapplies the last undone operation in the control.	
SaveFile (Public Instance Method)	Saves the contents of the control to the specified file.	
ContentsResized (Public Instance Event)	Occurs when the contents of the control have been resized.	
HScroll (Public Instance Event)	Occurs when the user clicks the horizontal scrollbar.	
IMEChange (Public Instance Event)	Occurs when the IME device has changed. Applies to Asian Windows only.	
LinkClicked (Public Instance Event)	Occurs when a link in the text of the control is clicked.	
Protected (Public Instance Event)	Occurs when the user attempts to edit protected text.	

Member Name (scope and type)	Description
SelectionChanged (Public Instance Event)	Occurs when the selection within the control has changed.
VScroll (Public Instance Event)	Occurs when the user clicks the vertical scrollbar.
CreateRichEditOLECallBack (Protected Instance Method)	Because the .Net implementation of this control is COM-based versus .Net Framework-based, this method is necessary for COM-based communication.

TextBox

This control is typically used to accept text input from the user or to display text. The Textbox control inherits directly from the TextBoxBase class. Table 27-25 lists the properties, methods, and events that the Textbox class possesses that it did not inherit.

Table 27-25
Non-Inherited Members of the TextBox Control

Member Name (scope and type)	Description
AcceptsReturn (Public Instance Property)	Specifies whether pressing the Enter key in a multiline text box creates a new line of text or activates the default button in the container.
CharacterCasing (Public Instance Property)	Specifies whether the control modifies the case of the text being typed.
PasswordChar (Public Instance Property)	Specifies the character used to mask typing in a single-line text box.
ScrollBars (Public Instance Property)	Specifies which scrollbars should appear in the text box.
TextAlign (Public Instance Property)	Specifies how the text is aligned in the control.
TextAlignChanged (Public Instance Event)	Occurs when the alignment of the text changes.

Timer

This component raises an event at regularly specified intervals. It is very useful for timed, iterative processes. The Timer class inherits directly from Component. Table 27-26 lists the properties, methods, and events that the Timer class possesses that it did not inherit.

Table 27-26 Non-Inherited Members of the Timer Control	
Member Name (scope and type)	*Description*
Enabled (Public Instance Property)	Specifies whether the timer is running.
Interval (Public Instance Property)	Specifies the time, in milliseconds, between ticks of the timer.
Start (Public Instance Method)	Initiates the timer.
Stop (Public Instance Method)	Ceases the timer.
Tick (Public Instance Event)	Occurs when the timer is enabled and the specified interval has elapsed.

ToolBar

This control is typically used to represent a common Windows toolbar. The Textbox control inherits directly from the Control class. Table 27-27 lists the properties, methods, and events that the Toolbar class possesses that it did not inherit.

Table 27-27 Non-Inherited Members of the ToolBar Control	
Member Name (scope and type)	*Description*
Appearance (Public Instance Property)	Specifies the appearance of the toolbar and buttons. Can be Flat or Normal.
AutoSize (Public Instance Property)	Specifies whether the toolbar automatically adjusts its size based on button size and dock style.
BorderStyle (Public Instance Property)	Specifies the border style of the toolbar. Fixed3D provides a sunken appearance.

Member Name (scope and type)	Description
Buttons (Public Instance Property)	ReadOnly. Returns the collection ToolbarButton items on the control.
ButtonSize (Public Instance Property)	Specifies the size of the buttons on the control.
Divider (Public Instance Property)	Specifies whether the toolbar displays a divider.
DropDownArrows (Public Instance Property)	Specifies whether drop-down items on the toolbar display arrows.
ImageList (Public Instance Property)	Specifies the images used on the Toolbar control.
ImageSize (Public Instance Property)	ReadOnly. Returns the size of the images in the image list.
IMEMode (Public Instance Property)	Specifies the IME device supported by this control.
ShowToolTips (Public Instance Property)	Specifies whether the toolbar displays a ToolTip for each button.
TextAlign (Public Instance Property)	Specifies the alignment of the text on the toolbar with respect to the images.
Wrappable (Public Instance Property)	Specifies whether the toolbar wraps to the next line if all buttons cannot be displayed on a single line.
ButtonClick (Public Instance Event)	Occurs when a toolbar button is clicked.
ButtonDropDown (Public Instance Event)	Occurs when a drop-down item on the toolbar is dropped down.

TrackBar

This control is typically used to display a Windows track bar. This control is similar to a scrollbar. An example of this control can be seen in the Options dialog on the Security/Privacy tabs of Internet Explorer. The TrackBar control inherits directly from the Control class. Table 27-28 lists the properties, methods, and events that the TrackBar class possesses that it did not inherit.

Table 27-28
Non-Inherited Members of the TrackBar Control

Member Name (scope and type)	Description
AutoSize (Public Instance Property)	Specifies whether the size of the control should automatically change based on orientation.
IMEMode (Public Instance Property)	Specifies the IME mode of the control.
LargeChange (Public Instance Property)	Specifies the amount the value of the control should change when the scrollbox is moved a large distance.
Maximum (Public Instance Property)	Specifies the maximum allowable value of the control.
Minimum (Public Instance Property)	Specifies the minimum allowable value of the control.
Orientation (Public Instance Property)	Specifies whether the control is positioned horizontally or vertically.
SmallChange (Public Instance Property)	Specifies the amount the value of this control should change when the scrollbox is moved a small distance.
TickFrequency (Public Instance Property)	Specifies the difference between the value of each tick.
TickStyle (Public Instance Property)	Specifies how the tick marks are displayed on the control. Can be on the bottom, top, both, or none.
Value (Public Instance Property)	Specifies the current value of the control.
BeginInit (Public Instance Method)	Begins the initialization of the control.
EndInit (Public Instance Method)	Ceases the initialization of the control.
SetRange (Public Instance Method)	Sets the minimum and maximum values of the track bar to the specified values.
Scroll (Public Instance Event)	Occurs when the user scrolls the control.
ValueChanged (Public Instance Event)	Occurs when the value of the control changes.

TreeView

This control is typically used to display a hierarchy of items. An example of this can be seen in the left pane of Windows Explorer. Each item on the tree is called a node. The TreeView control inherits directly from the Control class. Table 27-29 lists the properties, methods, and events that the TreeView class possesses that it did not inherit.

Table 27-29
Non-Inherited Members of the TreeView Control

Member Name (scope and type)	Description
BorderStyle (Public Instance Property)	Specifies the border style of the control. Fixed3D provides a sunken appearance.
CheckBoxes (Public Instance Property)	Specifies whether check boxes are displayed next to each item.
FullRowSelect (Public Instance Property)	Specifies whether the highlighted area of a selected node expands the width of the control.
HideSelection (Public Instance Property)	Specifies whether the selected region appears selected after the control loses focus.
HotTracking (Public Instance Property)	Specifies whether a node label appears like a hyperlink when the mouse hovers over it.
ImageIndex (Public Instance Property)	Specifies the index in the image list of the default image associated with a node.
ImageList (Public Instance Property)	Specifies the image list that contains all images associated with the nodes.
Indent (Public Instance Property)	Specifies the distance between the left edges of a parent and child node.
ItemHeight (Public Instance Property)	Specifies the height of each tree node within the control.
LabelEdit (Public Instance Property)	Specifies whether the user can edit the labels of each node.
Nodes (Public Instance Property)	ReadOnly. Returns a collection of all nodes within the tree view.
PathSeparator (Public Instance Property)	Specifies the delimiter string used in the tree node path.
Scrollable (Public Instance Property)	Specifies whether the tree view displays scroll bars when needed.
SelectedImageIndex (Public Instance Property)	Specifies the index of the image, of the selected node, in the image list.
SelectedNode (Public Instance Property)	Specifies the node that is currently selected in the control.
ShowLines (Public Instance Property)	Specifies whether lines are drawn between nodes on the tree.

Continued

Table 27-29 *(continued)*

Member Name (scope and type)	Description
ShowPlusMinus **(Public Instance Property)**	Specifies whether + and - symbols are shown next to nodes with children.
ShowRootLines **(Public Instance Property)**	Specifies whether lines are drawn between root (top-level) nodes.
Sorted **(Public Instance Property)**	Specifies whether the tree nodes are sorted by label.
TopNode **(Public Instance Property)**	ReadOnly. Returns the first fully visible node in the tree view.
VisibleCount **(Public Instance Property)**	ReadOnly. Returns the total number of tree nodes that can be fully visible in the control at one time.
BeginUpdate **(Public Instance Method)**	Suspends the painting of the control while nodes are being added.
CollapseAll **(Public Instance Method)**	Collapses all expanded trees and subtrees within the control.
EndUpdate **(Public Instance Method)**	Resumes painting.
ExpandAll **(Public Instance Method)**	Expands all trees and subtrees in the control.
GetNodeAt **(Public Instance Method)**	Returns the tree node at the specified location.
GetNodeCount **(Public Instance Method)**	Returns the number of tree nodes in the tree view.
AfterCheck **(Public Instance Event)**	Occurs after a node with check boxes has been checked.
AfterCollapse **(Public Instance Event)**	Occurs after a node with children has been collapsed.
AfterExpand **(Public Instance Event)**	Occurs after a node with children has been expanded.
AfterLabelEdit **(Public Instance Event)**	Occurs after a user completes editing a label.
AfterSelect **(Public Instance Event)**	Occurs after a node is selected.
BeforeCheck **(Public Instance Event)**	Occurs before a node with check boxes has been checked.
BeforeCollapse **(Public Instance Event)**	Occurs before a node with children has been collapsed.
BeforeExpand **(Public Instance Event)**	Occurs before a node with children has been expanded.

Member Name (scope and type)	Description
BeforeLabelEdit (Public Instance Event)	Occurs before a user completes editing a label.
BeforeSelect (Public Instance Event)	Occurs prior to a node being selected.
ItemDrag (Public Instance Event)	Occurs when an item is dragged into the tree view.

Display Controls

This section outlines all controls that I consider to be Display controls. I define a Display control as one that neither takes user input (beyond standard Windows messages) nor returns a value. Full ancestry information is given as well as descriptions of the properties, methods, and events that the specific control brings to the table. Those controls with code examples provided later in the "Examples" section are marked with an asterisk (*).

Form*

This control is typically used to display various groupings of controls to the user. As described in previous chapters, the Form is by far the control you use the most. The Form control inherits directly from the ContainerControl class. Table 27-30 lists the properties, methods, and events that the Form class possesses that it did not inherit.

Table 27-30
Non-Inherited Members of the Form Control

Member Name (scope and type)	Description
ActiveForm (Public Static Property)	ReadOnly. Returns the currently active form for an application.
GetAutoScaleSize (Public Static Method)	Returns the size of the form after autoscaling based on the specified font.
AcceptButton (Public Instance Property)	Specifies the button on the form that is activated when the user presses the Enter key.
ActiveMDIChild (Public Instance Property)	ReadOnly. Returns the currently active MDI child window.

Continued

Table 27-30 *(continued)*

Member Name *(scope and type)*	Description
AutoScale (Public Instance Property)	Specifies whether the form should adjust its size and the size of contained controls based on the font.
AutoScaleBaseSize (Public Instance Property)	Specifies the base size used for autoscaling the form.
CancelButton (Public Instance Property)	Specifies the button on the form that is activated when the user presses the Escape key.
ClientSize (Public Instance Property)	Specifies the size of the area of the form within the border and under the title bar.
ControlBox (Public Instance Property)	Specifies whether the control box is displayed on the form. The control box comprises the icon and the system menu under the icon.
DesktopBounds (Public Instance Property)	Specifies the size and location of the form relative to the Windows desktop.
DesktopLocation (Public Instance Property)	Specifies the location on the form relative to the Windows desktop.
DialogResult (Public Instance Property)	Specifies the return value of the form when shown and dismissed as a dialog.
FormBorderStyle (Public Instance Property)	Specifies the border style of the form.
HelpButton (Public Instance Property)	Specifies whether or not a Help button should be displayed by the Minimize and Maximize buttons on the title bar.
Icon (Public Instance Property)	Specifies the icon of the form.
IsMDIChild (Public Instance Property)	ReadOnly. Returns whether the form is an MDI child.
IsMDIContainer (Public Instance Property)	Specifies whether the form is an MDI container (whether or not it contains MDI children).
KeyPreview (Public Instance Property)	Specifies whether keypress events should pass through the form before going to the control with focus.
MaximizeBox (Public Instance Property)	Specifies whether or not the Maximize button should appear on the title bar.

Member Name (scope and type)	Description
MaximumSize (**Public Instance Property**)	Specifies the maximum size the form can be.
MDIChildren (**Public Instance Property**)	ReadOnly. Returns an array of forms that this form parents.
MDIParent (**Public Instance Property**)	Specifies the MDI parent form of this form.
Menu (**Public Instance Property**)	Specifies the MainMenu object that is displayed on this form.
MergedMenu (**Public Instance Property**)	ReadOnly. Returns the merged menu for this form.
MinimizeBox (**Public Instance Property**)	Specifies whether or not the Minimize button appears on the title bar.
MinumumSize (**Public Instance Property**)	Specifies the minimum size the form can be.
Modal (**Public Instance Property**)	ReadOnly. Returns whether the form is displayed modally. Modal means that no other aspects of the application can receive user-input until the form is dismissed.
Opacity (**Public Instance Property**)	Specifies the level of transparency of the form.
OwnedForms (**Public Instance Property**)	ReadOnly. Returns an array of forms that are owned by the current form.
Owner (**Public Instance Property**)	Specifies the owner of this form.
ShowInTaskBar (**Public Instance Property**)	Specifies whether the form should appear in the Windows taskbar when minimized.
Size (**Public Instance Property**)	Specifies the size of the form.
SizeGripStyle (**Public Instance Property**)	Specifies the style of size grip to display in the lower-right corner of the form. Can be Auto (Only when necessary), Hide (Never), or Show (Always).
StartPosition (**Public Instance Property**)	Specifies the starting position of the form. Example valid values include CenterParent, CenterScreen, and Manual.

Continued

Table 27-30 *(continued)*

Member Name (scope and type)	Description
Toplevel (Public Instance Property)	Specifies whether this form should be displayed as a top-level window. If this form is to be contained in another form, this needs to be `False`.
TopMost (Public Instance Property)	Specifies whether the form should be displayed as the topmost form in the application.
TransparencyKey (Public Instance Property)	Specifies the color that represents transparent areas of the form.
WindowState (Public Instance Property)	Specifies the form's window state. Can be `Normal`, `Minimized`, or `Maximized`.
Activate (Public Instance Method)	Activates the form and gives it focus.
AddOwnedForm (Public Instance Method)	Adds the specified owned form to this form.
Close (Public Instance Method)	Closes the form.
LayoutMDI (Public Instance Method)	Arranges the MDI children within the form in the specified manner (for example, `Cascade`, `TileHorizontal`).
RemoveOwnedForm (Public Instance Method)	Removes a form owned by this form.
SetDesktopBounds (Public Instance Method)	Sets the bounding rectangle of the form in desktop coordinates.
SetDesktopLocation (Public Instance Method)	Sets the location of the form in desktop coordinates.
ShowDialog (Public Instance Method)	Shows the form as a modal dialog box.
Activated (Public Instance Event)	Occurs when the form is activated.
Closed (Public Instance Event)	Occurs when the form is closed.
Closing (Public Instance Event)	Occurs while the form is closing.
DeActivate (Public Instance Event)	Occurs when the form no longer has the focus.
InputLanguageChanged (Public Instance Event)	Occurs after the input language has changed.
InputLanguageChanging (Public Instance Event)	Occurs while the input language is changing.
Load (Public Instance Event)	Occurs before the form is displayed for the first time.

Member Name (scope and type)	Description
MaximizedBoundsChanged (Public Instance Event)	Occurs when the value of the MaximizedBounds property changes.
MaximumSizeChanged (Public Instance Event)	Occurs when the value of the MaximumSize property changes.
MDIChildActivate (Public Instance Event)	Occurs when an MDI child form is activated.
MenuComplete (Public Instance Event)	Occurs when the menu loses focus.
MenuStart (Public Instance Event)	Occurs when the menu receives focus.
MinimumSizeChanged (Public Instance Event)	Occurs when the value of the MinimumSize property changes.
MaximizedBounds (Protected Instance Property)	Specifies the size of the form when it is maximized.

GroupBox

This control is typically used to logically group controls together inside a frame. However, there is no ownership relationship. A common use is for mutually exclusive groups of radio buttons. The GroupBox control inherits directly from the Control class. Table 27-31 lists the property, method, and event that the GroupBox class possesses that it did not inherit.

Table 27-31
Non-Inherited Member of the GroupBox Control

Member Name (scope and type)	Description
FlatStyle (Public Instance Property)	Specifies the flatstyle appearance of the control.

Label

This control is typically used to display descriptive text. The Label control inherits directly from the Control class. Table 27-32 lists the properties, methods, and events that the Label class possesses that it did not inherit.

Table 27-32
Non-Inherited Members of the Label Control

Member Name (scope and type)	Description
AutoSize (Public Instance Property)	Specifies whether the control automatically resizes to display all contents.
BorderStyle (Public Instance Property)	Specifies the border style of the control. Fixed3D gives a sunken appearance.
FlatStyle (Public Instance Property)	Specifies the flat style of the control. Can be flat or three-dimensional, among others.
Image (Public Instance Property)	Specifies the image that is displayed on the label.
ImageAlign (Public Instance Property)	Specifies the alignment of the image within the control.
ImageIndex (Public Instance Property)	Specifies the index value in the image list of the image displayed in the control.
ImageList (Public Instance Property)	Specifies the ImageList object that contains the image displayed in this control.
IMEMode (Public Instance Property)	Specifies the IME mode supported by this control.
PreferredHeight (Public Instance Property)	ReadOnly. Returns the preferred height of the control based on the font.
PreferredWidth (Public Instance Property)	ReadOnly. Returns the preferred width of the control based on the font.
TabStop (Public Instance Property)	Specifies whether the user can tab to the label. Similar to having the label receive focus.
UseMnemonic (Public Instance Property)	Specifies whether the control acknowledges an ampersand in front of a character to be an access key.
AutoSizeChanged (Public Instance Event)	Occurs when the AutoSize property of the control changes.
TextAlignChanged (Public Instance Event)	Occurs when the text alignment of the control changes.
RenderTransparent (Protected Instance Property)	Specifies whether the background of the label should be the container control background.

Member Name (scope and type)	Description
CalcImageRenderBounds (Protected Instance Method)	Determines the size and location of an image drawn within the control.
DrawImage (Protected Instance Method)	Draws the specified Image within the specified bounds.

LinkLabel

This control is typically used precisely like a label, except that it can display a hyperlink. Each displayed hyperlink can perform a different action. The LinkLabel control inherits directly from the Label Class. Table 27-33 lists the properties, methods, and events that the LinkLabel class possesses that it did not inherit.

Table 27-33
Non-Inherited Members of the LinkLabel Control

Member Name (scope and type)	Description
ActiveLinkColor (Public Instance Property)	Specifies the color in which an active link should be displayed.
DisabledLinkColor (Public Instance Property)	Specifies the color in which a disabled link should be displayed.
LinkArea (Public Instance Property)	Specifies the range of text to be displayed as a link.
LinkBehavior (Public Instance Property)	Specifies the behavior of the link. Used for display purposes only, particularly whether or not underlines should be displayed.
LinkColor (Public Instance Property)	Specifies the color in which to display a normal link.
Links (Public Instance Property)	ReadOnly. Returns the collection of links affiliated with the control.
LinkVisited (Public Instance Property)	Specifies whether the link should be displayed as visited.
VisitedLinkColor (Public Instance Property)	Specifies the color in which a visited link should be displayed.
LinkClicked (Public Instance Event)	Occurs when the link is clicked.
PointInLink (Protected Instance Method)	Returns the link at the specified coordinate.

Panel

This control is typically used to contain other controls. The panel is very similar to the GroupBox, except it has a bit more functionality — given its ancestry. However, there is still no ownership. The Panel control inherits directly from the ScollableControl class. Table 27-34 lists the property, method, and event that the Panel class possesses that it did not inherit.

Table 27-34 Non-Inherited Member of the Panel Control	
Member Name (scope and type)	**Description**
BorderStyle (Public Instance Property)	Specifies the border style of the control. Fixed3D provides a sunken appearance.

PictureBox

This control is used to display an image. The PictureBox control inherits directly from the Control class. Table 27-35 lists the properties, methods, and events that the PictureBox class possesses that it did not inherit.

Table 27-35 Non-Inherited Members of the PictureBox Control	
Member Name (scope and type)	**Description**
BorderStyle (Public Instance Property)	Specifies the border style of the control. Fixed3D provides a sunken appearance.
Image (Public Instance Property)	Specifies the image displayed in the control.
IMEMode (Public Instance Property)	Specifies the IME mode of the control.
SizeMode (Public Instance Property)	Specifies how the picture is displayed within the control. Autosize, CenterImage, Normal, and Stretch are the valid values for this property.
SizeModeChanged (Public Instance Event)	Occurs when the SizeMode property changes.

ProgressBar

This control is typically used to display the progress of a particularly lengthy process. The `ProgressBar` control inherits directly from the `Control` class. Table 27-36 lists the properties, methods, and events that the `ProgressBar` class possesses that it did not inherit.

Table 27-36
Non-Inherited Members of the ProgressBar Control

Member Name (scope and type)	Description
IMEMode (Public Instance Property)	Specifies the IME mode of the control.
Maximum (Public Instance Property)	Specifies the maximum value that the control can achieve.
Minimum (Public Instance Property)	Specifies the value at which the control begins.
Step (Public Instance Property)	Specifies the amount by which to progress the control's value when `PerformStep` is called.
Value (Public Instance Property)	Specifies the current value of the control.
Increment (Public Instance Method)	Increases the value of the control by the specified amount, and refreshes the display.
PerformStep (Public Instance Method)	Increases the value of the control by the amount specified in the step property, and refreshes the display.

Splitter*

This control is typically used to allow resizing of docked controls. An example of this is Windows Explorer. The moveable bar between the left and right panes is considered a splitter. The `Splitter` control inherits directly from the `Control` class. Table 27-37 lists the properties, methods, and events that the `Splitter` class possesses that it did not inherit.

Table 27-37
Non-Inherited Members of the Splitter Control

Member Name (scope and type)	Description
BorderStyle (Public Instance Property)	Specifies the border style of the control. Fixed3D gives a sunken appearance.
IMEMode (Public Instance Property)	Specifies the IME mode of the control.
MinExtra (Public Instance Property)	Specifies the minimum area of the control that is not occupied by docked controls.
MinSize (Public Instance Property)	Specifies the minimum size of the control prior in dock order to the splitter.
SplitPosition (Public Instance Property)	Specifies the position of the splitter.
SplitterMoved (Public Instance Event)	Occurs after the splitter has moved.
SplitterMoving (Public Instance Event)	Occurs while the splitter is moving.

StatusBar

This control is used to represent a common Windows status bar. An example of this control can be seen at the bottom of Microsoft Word. It is essentially used to present low importance, non-editable items to the user. The StatusBar control inherits directly from the Control class. Table 27-38 lists the properties, methods, and events that the StatusBar class possesses that it did not inherit.

Table 27-38
Non-Inherited Members of the StatusBar Control

Member Name (scope and type)	Description
IMEMode (Public Instance Property)	Specifies the IME mode of the control.
Panels (Public Instance Property)	ReadOnly. Returns a collection of StatusBarPanels that are displayed in this control. These panels are completely different from the Panel class because they cannot contain controls.
ShowPanels (Public Instance Property)	Specifies whether the panels should be shown.
SizingGrip (Public Instance Property)	Specifies whether the sizing grip should be displayed on the lower-right corner of the control.
TabStop (Public Instance Property)	Specifies whether the Tab key gives focus to the control.

Member Name (scope and type)	Description
DrawItem (Public Instance Event)	Occurs when an Owner-Drawn status bar changes visually.
PanelClick (Public Instance Event)	Occurs when a panel within the control is clicked.

TabControl

This control is typically used to create a tab-style dialog box. Tabbed dialog boxes are useful for organizing large sets of related controls on a single form. An example of this can be seen in the Options dialog box of Microsoft Word. The TabControl control inherits directly from the Control class. Table 27-39 lists the properties, methods, and events that the TabControl class possesses that it did not inherit.

Table 27-39
Non-Inherited Members of the TabControl Control

Member Name (scope and type)	Description
Alignment (Public Instance Property)	Specifies the area of the control where the tabs are aligned (for example, the top or bottom).
Appearance (Public Instance Property)	Specifies the appearance of the tabs. For example, FlatButtons or NormalButtons.
DrawMode (Public Instance Property)	Specifies the way in which that tabs are drawn. OwnerDrawn indicates that the tabs are drawn by code.
HotTrack (Public Instance Property)	Specifies whether the tabs change appearance when the mouse hovers.
ImageList (Public Instance Property)	Specifies the image list that contains the images to display on the tabs.
ItemSize (Public Instance Property)	Specifies the size of the tabs.
MultiLine (Public Instance Property)	Specifies whether the tabs are displayed as multiple rows.
Padding (Public Instance Property)	Specifies the amount of space around each item on the tab pages.
RowCount (Public Instance Property)	Specifies the number of rows diaplying the tabs on the tab strip of the control.

Continued

Table 27-39 *(continued)*	
Member Name (scope and type)	**Description**
SelectedIndex (Public Instance Property)	Specifies the index of the currently selected tab.
SelectedTab (Public Instance Property)	Specifies the tab that is currently selected.
ShowToolTips (Public Instance Property)	Specifies whether ToolTips should be displayed when the mouse hovers over a tab.
SizeMode (Public Instance Property)	Specifies how the tabs are sized. Can fill the width of the control or be fixed width.
TabCount (Public Instance Property)	ReadOnly. Returns the total number of tabs in the control.
TabPages (Public Instance Property)	ReadOnly. Returns the total collection of tab pages.
GetTabRect (Public Instance Method)	Returns the bounding rectangle for the specified tab.
DrawItem (Public Instance Event)	Occurs when a visual aspect of an Owner-drawn tab control changes.
SelectedIndexChanged (Public Instance Event)	Occurs when the index of the selected tab changes.
RemoveAll (Protected Instance Method)	Removes all tabs in the control.

ToolTip

This control is typically used to display a small window of text when the mouse hovers over a control. The ToolTip control inherits directly from the Component class. Table 27-40 lists the properties, methods, and events that the ToolTip class possesses that it did not inherit.

Table 27-40 Non-Inherited Members of the ToolTip Control	
Member Name (scope and type)	**Description**
Active (Public Instance Property)	Specifies whether the control is currently active.
AutomaticDelay (Public Instance Property)	Specifies the amount of time that passes with the mouse over the control before the ToolTip appears.

Member Name (scope and type)	Description
AutoPopDelay (Public Instance Property)	Specifies the amount of time the ToolTip remains visible before disappearing.
InitialDelay (Public Instance Property)	Specifies the initial delay before the display of the ToolTip.
ReshowDelay (Public Instance Property)	Specifies the amount of time being showings of the ToolTip.
ShowAlways (Public Instance Property)	Specifies whether the ToolTip should display when the associated control is not active.
GetToolTip (Public Instance Method)	Retrieves the text of the ToolTip affiliated to the specified control.
RemoveAll (Public Instance Method)	Removes all ToolTips.
SetToolTip (Public Instance Method)	Associates the ToolTip to the specified control.

Dialog Controls

This section outlines all controls that I consider to be Dialog controls. I define a Dialog control as one that spawns a new window and returns a value. Full ancestry information is given, as well as descriptions of the properties, methods, and events that the specific control brings to the table. Those controls with examples are marked with an asterisk (*).

CommonDialog

This control is the Base class of all Dialog controls. This control is used to create Dialog controls for various tasks. The CommonDialog control inherits directly from the Component. Table 27-41 lists the properties, methods, and events that the CommonDialog class possesses that it did not inherit.

Table 27-41
Non-Inherited Members of the CommonDialog Control

Member Name (scope and type)	Description
Reset (Public Instance Method)	Resets all the properties of a common dialog box to their default values.

Continued

Table 27-41 *(continued)*

Member Name (scope and type)	Description
ShowDialog (Public Instance Method)	Runs the dialog box.
HelpRequest (Public Instance Event)	Occurs when the user submits a help request via the F1 key or another method.
HookProc (Protected Instance Method)	This is the method that a derived class would override to provide specific functionality to the dialog.
OwnerWndProc (Protected Instance Method)	Defines the Owner Window procedure that is overridden in a derived class to provide specific functionality to the dialog.
RunDialog (Protected Instance Method)	Shows the specified dialog box.

ColorDialog

This control is typically used to display windows to allow the user to choose a color or create a color. The ColorDialog control inherits directly from the CommonDialog class. Table 27-42 lists the properties, methods, and events that the ColorDialog class possesses that it did not inherit.

Table 27-42
Non-Inherited Members of the ColorDialog Control

Member Name (scope and type)	Description
AllowFullOpen (Public Instance Property)	Specifies whether the user can define custom colors.
AnyColor (Public Instance Property)	Specifies whether the dialog box displays all available colors.
Color (Public Instance Property)	Specifies the color selected by the user.
CustomColors (Public Instance Property)	Specifies the set of custom colors shown in the dialog box.
FullOpen (Public Instance Property)	Specifies whether the controls necessary to create custome colors are visible when the dialog box is opened.
ShowHelp (Public Instance Property)	Specifies whether the Help button is displayed on the dialog box.
SolidColorOnly (Public Instance Property)	Specifies whether users are restricted to selecting solid colors only.

FileDialog

This control is typically used to display a window from which a user can select a file. The `FileDialog` control inherits directly from the `CommonDialog` class. Table 27-43 lists the properties, methods, and events that the `FileDialog` class possesses that it did not inherit.

Table 27-43
Non-Inherited Members of the FileDialog Control

Member Name (scope and type)	Description
AddExtension (Public Instance Property)	Specifies whether the dialog box should automatically add the extension to the filename if the user omits it.
CheckFileExists (Public Instance Property)	Specifies whether a warning is displayed if the user provides a filename that does not exist.
CheckPathExists (Public Instance Property)	Specifies whether a warning is displayed if the user provides a path that does not exist.
DefaultExt (Public Instance Property)	Specifies the default extension.
DereferenceLinks (Public Instance Property)	Specifies whether the filename returned, if a shortcut selected, is the path to the shortcut or the path that the shortcut references.
FileName (Public Instance Property)	Specifies the string selected in the dialog box.
FileNames (Public Instance Property)	ReadOnly. Returns all the filenames chosen in the dialog box.
Filter (Public Instance Property)	Specifies the filename filter string for the Files of Type box in a File dialog box.
FilterIndex (Public Instance Property)	Specifies the index of the filter currently selected in the dialog box.
InitialDirectory (Public Instance Property)	Specifies the initial directory displayed in the dialog box.
RestoreDirectory (Public Instance Property)	Specifies whether the dialog box restores the current directory to its previous state if the user changed it.

Continued

Table 27-43 (continued)

Member Name (scope and type)	Description
ShowHelp (Public Instance Property)	Specifies whether the Help button is displayed in the dialog box.
Title (Public Instance Property)	Specifies the title of the dialog box.
ValidateNames (Public Instance Property)	Specifies whether the dialog box only accepts valid Windows filenames.
FileOk (Public Instance Event)	Occurs when the user clicks the Open or Save button in a dialog box.

FontDialog

This control is used to display a method by which the user can select font information. The FontDialog control inherits directly from the CommonDialog class. Table 27-44 lists the properties, methods, and events that the FontDialog class possesses that it did not inherit.

Table 27-44
Non-Inherited Members of the FontDialog Control

Member Name (scope and type)	Description
AllowScriptChange (Public Instance Property)	Specifies whether the user can select a different font script.
AllowSimulations (Public Instance Property)	Specifies whether the dialog box supports font simulations.
AllowVectorFonts (Public Instance Property)	Specifies whether the dialog box allows selection of a vector font.
AllowVerticalFonts (Public Instance Property)	Specifies whether the dialog box displays vertical fonts in addition to horizontal.
Color (Public Instance Property)	Specifies the selected font color.
FixedPitchOnly (Public Instance Property)	Specifies whether only fixed-pitch fonts are selectable.
Font (Public Instance Property)	Specifies the selected font.
FontMustExist (Public Instance Property)	Specifies if an error should be thrown if the user selectes a font or style that does not exist.

Member Name (scope and type)	Description
MaxSize (Public Instance Property)	Specifies the maximum selectable font size.
MinSize (Public Instance Property)	Specifies the minimum selectable font size.
ScriptsOnly (Public Instance Property)	Specifies whether the user can select other character sets such as symbols.
ShowApply (Public Instance Property)	Specifies whether to display the Apply button.
ShowColor (Public Instance Property)	Specifies whether the dialog box allows for color selection.
ShowEffects (Public Instance Property)	Specifies whether the user can select special effects such as strikethrough.
ShowHelp (Public Instance Property)	Specifies whether the Help button is displayed.
Apply (Public Instance Event)	Occurs when the user clicks the Apply button in the dialog box.

OpenFileDialog

This control is used to allow the user to select a file to open. The OpenFileDialog control inherits directly from the FileDialog class. Table 27-45 lists the properties, methods, and events that the OpenFileDialog class possesses that it did not inherit.

Table 27-45
Non-Inherited Members of the OpenFileDialog Control

Member Name (scope and type)	Description
MultiSelect (Public Instance Property)	Specifies whether the user can select multiple files.
ReadOnlyChecked (Public Instance Property)	Specifies whether the Read Only check box is checked.
ShowReadOnly (Public Instance Property)	Specifies whether the Read Only check box is visible.
OpenFile (Public Instance Method)	Opens the Selected file with Read Only access.

PageSetupDialog

This control is used to allow the user to manipulate page settings. The PageSetupDialog control inherits directly from the CommonDialog class. Table 27-46 lists the properties, methods, and events that the PageSetupDialog class possesses that it did not inherit.

<table>
<tr><td colspan="2" align="center">Table 27-46
Non-Inherited Members of the PageSetupDialog Control</td></tr>
<tr><td>Member Name (scope and type)</td><td>Description</td></tr>
<tr><td>AllowMargins (Public Instance Property)</td><td>Specifies whether the user can edit the margins of the document.</td></tr>
<tr><td>AllowOrientation (Public Instance Property)</td><td>Specifies whether the user can select a page orientation.</td></tr>
<tr><td>AllowPaper (Public Instance Property)</td><td>Specifies whether the user can modify the paper settings (size and source).</td></tr>
<tr><td>AllowPrinter (Public Instance Property)</td><td>Specifies whether the user is allowed to modify printer settings.</td></tr>
<tr><td>Document (Public Instance Property)</td><td>Specifies the print document from which to get the page settings.</td></tr>
<tr><td>MinMargins (Public Instance Property)</td><td>Specifies the minimum margin size the user is allowed to select.</td></tr>
<tr><td>PageSettings (Public Instance Property)</td><td>Specifies the page settings to modify.</td></tr>
<tr><td>PrinterSettings (Public Instance Property)</td><td>Specifies the printer settings to modify.</td></tr>
<tr><td>ShowHelp (Public Instance Property)</td><td>Specifies whether to display a Help button in the dialog box.</td></tr>
<tr><td>ShowNetwork (Public Instance Property)</td><td>Specifies whether to display the Network button.</td></tr>
</table>

PrintDialog

This control is used to allow the user to select a printer and document fragments to print. The PrintDialog control inherits directly from the CommonDialog class. Table 27-47 lists the properties, methods, and events that the PrintDialog class possesses that it did not inherit.

Table 27-47
Non-Inherited Members of the PrintDialog Control

Member Name (scope and type)	Description
AllowPrintToFile (Public Instance Property)	Specifies whether the user is allowed to print to file.
AllowSelection (Public Instance Property)	Specifies whether the user can specify a range of pages to print via the From...To buttons.
AllowSomePages (Public Instance Property)	Specifies whether the user can specify what pages to print.
Document (Public Instance Property)	Specifies the source of the print settings.
PrinterSettings (Public Instance Property)	Specifies which printer settings to modify.
PrintToFile (Public Instance Property)	Specifies whether the PrintToFile check box is checked.
ShowHelp (Public Instance Property)	Specifies whether the Help button is displayed.
ShowNetwork (Public Instance Property)	Specifies whether the Network button is displayed.

SaveFileDialog

This control is used to allow the user to select a file to save. The SaveFileDialog control inherits directly from the FileDialog class. Table 27-48 lists the properties, methods, and events that the SaveFileDialog class possesses that it did not inherit.

Table 27-48
Non-Inherited Members of the SaveFileDialog Control

Member Name (scope and type)	Description
CreatePrompt (Public Instance Property)	Specifies whether the user should be asked whether the file should be created if a nonexistent file is selected.
OverwritePrompt (Public Instance Property)	Specifies whether the user should be asked whether the file should be overwritten if an existing file is selected.
OpenFile (Public Instance Method)	Opens the selected file with the read/ write permissions specified by the user.

Miscellaneous Controls

This section outlines all controls that I consider to be miscellaneous controls. I define a miscellaneous control as one that does not fit into any of the aforementioned categories. Only the ImageList control is included in this category. Full ancestry information is given, as well as descriptions of the properties, methods, and events that the specific control brings to the table.

This control is used to contain a series of images that are then affiliated to another control. The ImageList control inherits directly from the Component class. Table 27-49 lists the properties, methods, and events that the ImageList class possesses that it did not inherit.

Table 27-49
Non-Inherited Members of the ImageList Control

Member Name (scope and type)	Description
ColorDepth (Public Instance Property)	Specifies the number of colors used to display an image in a control that retrieves images from an ImageList.
Handle (Public Instance Property)	ReadOnly. Returns the handle of the ImageList control.
HandleCreated (Public Instance Property)	ReadOnly. Returns whether the handle for this control has been created.
Images (Public Instance Property)	ReadOnly. Returns a collection of images contained by this object.
ImageStream (Public Instance Property)	Specifies a handle to the data portion of the ImageList control.
TransparentColor (Public Instance Property)	Specifies the color this control should treat as transparent.
Draw (Public Instance Method)	Draws the specified image.
RecreateHandle (Public Instance Event)	Occurs when the handle is re-created.

Examples

The following section contains all the examples of the controls marked with an asterisk (*) in the chapter. All examples use a form in some manner or another. Thus, I don't provide a stand-alone example of the Form object. Each example is from an associated project attached to this chapter.

Listing 27-1 is used to display some of the things that a ListBox can do. The focus of this example is the DisplayMember and DataSource properties. There is also some useful textbox code.

Listing 27-1: Example Using the ListBox

```
Private Sub cmdPeople_Click(ByVal sender As System.Object, _
    ByVal e As System.EventArgs) Handles cmdPeople.Click

'This Routine creates the number of people specified, _
    puts them in a collection that is assigned _
    as the datasource of the ListBox.

Dim PeopleCollection As Collection = New Collection()
Dim i As Integer = 1

If txtNumber.TextLength = 0 Then
    MessageBox.Show("Please enter a numeric value in _
        the textbox before attempting to generate people.")
Else
    For i = 1 To CType(Val(txtNumber.Text), Integer)
        Dim tempPerson As Person = New Person()
            With tempPerson
            .Name = "Person" & i.ToString
            .Age = i
            .Birthday = New Date(Now.Year - i, _
                        Now.Month, Now.Day)
        End With
        PeopleCollection.Add(tempPerson)
    Next
End If
lstPeople.DataSource = PeopleCollection
End Sub

Private Sub cmdClear_Click(ByVal sender As System.Object, _
    ByVal e As System.EventArgs) Handles cmdClear.Click

'This clears the list. Note, a ListBox cannot be cleared _
    while a data source is assigned.

lstPeople.DataSource = Nothing
lstPeople.Items.Clear()

End Sub

Private Sub txtNumber_KeyPress(ByVal sender As Object, _
    ByVal e As System.Windows.Forms.KeyPressEventArgs) _
    Handles txtNumber.KeyPress
```

Continued

Listing 27-1 *(continued)*

```
'This prevents the user from entering anything _
   in the textbox that is not a number.

If Not (e.KeyChar.IsDigit(e.KeyChar)) And _
   e.KeyChar <> ChrW(Keys.Back) Then

    e.Handled = True
End If

End Sub

Private Sub lstProperties_SelectedValueChanged(_
   ByVal sender As Object, _
   ByVal e As System.EventArgs) _
   Handles lstProperties.SelectedValueChanged

'This changes the displaymember of the listbox _
   to the item selected in the smaller listbox.

lstPeople.DisplayMember = lstProperties.SelectedItem.ToString

End Sub
```

Listing 27-2 is used to display some of the aspects of the PropertyGrid. The focus is simply the general use of the grid and how to assign objects to it. Furthermore, it is obvious to see how to edit properties of those assigned objects.

Listing 27-2: **Example Using the PropertyGrid**

```
Private newGrid As PropertyGrid = New PropertyGrid()

Private Sub cmdProperties_Click(_
  ByVal sender As System.Object, _
  ByVal e As System.EventArgs) Handles cmdProperties.Click

If blnGridCreated = False Then
   With newGrid
      .SelectedObject = ObjectToDisplay
      .CommandsVisibleIfAvailable = True
      .Text = "Property Grid Example"
      .Size = New Size(Me.Width \ 2, Me.Height - 20)
      .Location = New Point(360, 5)
   End With
```

```
    Me.Controls.Add(newGrid)
    newGrid.Show()
Else
    newGrid.SelectedObject = ObjectToDisplay
    newGrid.Refresh()
End If

End Sub
```

Listing 27-3 demonstrates how to use a `Splitter` control. This is kind of tricky because items must be added to the container in the correct order. The classic Windows Explorer Interface is created in the `SplitterExample` project.

Listing 27-3: **Example Using the Splitter**

```
'
'TreeView1
'
'Docked to the left because the left edge never moves.
Me.TreeView1.Dock = System.Windows.Forms.DockStyle.Left
Me.TreeView1.Name = "TreeView1"
Me.TreeView1.Size = New System.Drawing.Size(121, 541)
Me.TreeView1.TabIndex = 0

'
'Splitter1
'
Me.Splitter1.Location = New System.Drawing.Point(121, 0)
Me.Splitter1.Name = "Splitter1"
Me.Splitter1.Size = New System.Drawing.Size(3, 541)
Me.Splitter1.TabIndex = 1
Me.Splitter1.TabStop = False

'
'ListView1
'
'Docked to Fill becuase it takes up the rest _
  of the space in the container.
Me.ListView1.Dock = System.Windows.Forms.DockStyle.Fill
Me.ListView1.Location = New System.Drawing.Point(124, 0)
Me.ListView1.Name = "ListView1"
Me.ListView1.Size = New System.Drawing.Size(564, 541)
Me.ListView1.TabIndex = 2
Me.ListView1.View = System.Windows.Forms.View.List
```

Continued

Listing 27-3 *(continued)*

```
'
'Form1
'
Me.AutoScaleBaseSize = New System.Drawing.Size(5, 13)
Me.ClientSize = New System.Drawing.Size(688, 541)

'This is the crucial command. The sequence of the controls _
   in the array is what makes the splitter work.

Me.Controls.AddRange(New System.Windows.Forms.Control() _
         {Me.ListView1, Me.Splitter1, Me.TreeView1})
Me.Name = "Form1"
Me.Text = "Form1"
```

Summary

This chapter presented a wealth of information regarding the common Windows controls available to you, the developer. As you can see, the tools required to make a fantastic user interface are now available to you. The next chapter shows you how to further enhance your toolkit.

✦   ✦   ✦

"Visual" Inheritance

by Jacob A. Grass

Inheritance is the newest object-oriented programming concept introduced into Visual Basic. It has been touted as one of the greatest additions to the Framework, yet it is probably not explicitly used a great deal by the average programmer.

All the while, though, the average programmer is using it extensively.

Nice and paradoxical, eh? The .NET Framework itself uses inheritance extensively. And, for the most part, to use the Framework, a developer must use inheritance. Essentially, the difference is explicit usage versus implicit usage.

Visual Basic 6 handled all the magic of the form in the background. To create a new form, it was necessary to create an instance of the generic Form class and give it a name, for example, "Form1." The .NET Framework allows a form to be created the same way; however, most forms are created via the other method allowed by the Framework—inheritance.

Using inheritance means that a new class is created, called, for example, "Form1" that inherits from the Form object. So, not only does this class get all of the properties, methods, and events detailed in the previous chapter for free, but now the developer can enhance this class very easily.

This chapter explains what "visual" inheritance really means, and when it is appropriate to use this functionality. Furthermore, examples for inheriting forms and controls are provided with an introduction to attributes and designers.

The novice user will find scores of examples for applying some of the techniques presented in this chapter. The advanced user will benefit from an organized presentation of the subject matter to help fill in any gaps in understanding.

In This Chapter

Understanding "visual" inheritance

When is visual inheritance useful?

Understanding forms inheritance

Inheriting from controls

Developing user controls

Enhancing controls with attributes

Customizing the design surface of your control

Why "Visual?"

When I write of "visual" inheritance, I place the "visual" in quotes. There are a couple of reasons for doing this. First, the term "visual inheritance" is essentially a marketing term. There is really no such thing as "visual inheritance." All class-based inheritance is only inheritance. The only difference is that the inheritance covered in this chapter is using base classes with display components, for example, Borders, Background Colors, and so on.

Second, the billing of this feature as being independent from regular old generic inheritance is slightly inaccurate, so it is necessary to differentiate the two concepts in some way from a learning perspective. Breaking up components into "painting" versus "non-painting" seems logical. Consider this more like "Inheritance, Part II."

"Visual" inheritance is essentially inheritance with components that implement painting. The beauty of this fact is that the actual painting is accessible to you, so you can override and control in whatever way you see fit. In doing this, you encounter other objects within the Framework such as the `Pen`, `Brush`, and `Color` objects. These objects do not receive full coverage in this chapter, but, throughout the examples in this chapter, you see many uses of them.

When to Use Visual Inheritance

Even if there are not a great deal of instances in real-world development projects where explicit, non-visual inheritance is recommended, you find visual inheritance to be more and more useful as your familiarity with it grows.

Probably the most helpful usage of visual inheritance is related to controls. Inheriting and extending existing controls become very useful to every GUI developer to the point that each individual has their own "toolkit" of controls.

This, of course, has its advantages and disadvantages. The primary disadvantage is consistency. Suppose that a large-scale development house has 45 different types of text boxes in its toolkits. Who really knows which text box is relevant to which task? And should the code be handed off to someone else? Maintenance could be a nightmare.

Therefore, just as standard inheritance can be considered dangerous, so can visual inheritance. So, it is recommended that you use this functionality only when you really need it. Furthermore, good quality planning should go into the process. For example, rather than creating an e-mail text box, a phone number text box, and a birthday text box, it would make more sense to create a masked text box with definable masks.

Forms

The capability to inherit forms has made rapid GUI development even easier. In Visual Basic 6, you could create a form template and reuse it wherever you needed it. This worked out very well until something needed changing. In short, the techniques in Visual Basic 6 were equivalent to copy-and-paste development.

However, in Visual Basic .NET, this is no longer the case. Now, you can use true inheritance for your forms and, when there is a change, no problem. All you have to do is change what is necessary in the Base Form, and whatever you change propagate to the inherited classes.

As you may or may not have noticed, this process is made even easier by the IDE. One of the options when adding a new item to a project is Add Inherited Form. Choosing this option results in a dialog box allowing you to choose a form from which to inherit.

Wizards

A common interface paradigm in GUI development is that of the wizard. A wizard is basically a series of screens that guides the user through a sequential set of tasks. The important thing about wizard development is to ensure that all the screens are consistent, self-explanatory, and easy-to-use.

Consistency between screens can be somewhat hard to guarantee — especially when more than one developer is working to create it. Inheriting forms, however, makes this task significantly easier. Because all the screens in a wizard should look essentially the same, a form containing all the common elements can be created. Any necessary screens in the wizard can then be created from that. Figure 28-1 shows what a base wizard form may look like.

One of the possible pitfalls of this inheritance approach is that controls that are added to a form have a scope of Friend, meaning that if the base form resides in a DLL, the inherited form does not have access to modify the controls. A situation in which this modification would be desirable is if the text of the buttons on the wizard needs to change based on the page displayed. One way to work around this problem is to modify the scope of the controls to be `Public`. However, you don't necessarily want to open up all the controls to modification such as this. The other option, however, is to `OverLoad` the `Show` method of the form. Listing 28-1, taken from the `WizardExample` project, demonstrates this technique.

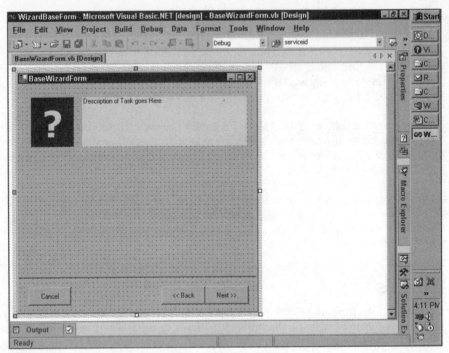

Figure 28-1: A base wizard form from which to inherit

Listing 28-1: **Overloaded Show Method**

```
Public Overloads Sub Show(ByVal Description As String, _
    Optional ByVal Image As System.Drawing.Bitmap = Nothing, _
    Optional ByVal BackEnabled As Boolean = True)

    Me.lblDescription.Text = Description
    Me.PictureBox1.Image = Image
    Me.cmdBack.Enabled = BackEnabled
    Me.Show()

End Sub
```

Now, after you have created an inherited form, and you need to call the Show method, you can pass parameters to modify the state of the controls.

```
Dim FirstForm As Wizard1 = New Wizard1()
FirstForm.Show("This is The First Wizard Form", _
    New Bitmap("C:\Image.Bmp"), False)
```

As you can see, the Show method has been overloaded so that it can take parameters. You can use the parameters to modify the state of the controls on the form. In this case, you only chose three properties to modify. This can be easily enhanced for any additional properties that need to be modified. Keep in mind that any number of parameters can be added to an overloaded Show method.

The other problem that needs to be dealt with is navigation between the forms. This, too, can be a tricky process. The best way to handle this is by first adding two properties to the base wizard form (see Listing 28-2).

The two properties to be added have been called PreviousForm and NextForm. These properties give each form all of the knowledge it needs regarding the sequence of forms throughout the entire wizard. This further allows three routines to handle the actual guts of the navigation process. This approach makes changes and additions to the wizard much easier to cope with.

Listing 28-2: **Added Properties**

```
Private m_NextForm As BaseWizardForm
Private m_PreviousForm As BaseWizardForm

Public Property PreviousForm() As BaseWizardForm
  Get
      Return m_PreviousForm
  End Get
  Set(ByVal Value As BaseWizardForm)
      m_PreviousForm = Value
  End Set
End Property

Public Property NextForm() As BaseWizardForm
  Get
      Return m_NextForm
  End Get
  Set(ByVal Value As BaseWizardForm)
      m_NextForm = Value
  End Set
End Property
```

You use the properties when the user clicks the Next or Back buttons. However, in order for you to do anything with those buttons in the inherited forms, you need to set those events as overridable in the base form. This way, you can add code to these procedures in the inherited forms for validation. Furthermore, you can add the functionality to show the next or previous form in the sequence.

The best general architecture for this process is to have a module that includes three routines: `Sub Main`, `ShowNext`, and `ShowPrevious`. Listing 28-3 shows these routines. The primary benefit of this approach is easier maintenance regarding the flow of the wizard. If a new form needs to be added in the middle of the sequence, modifying the code for this is significantly easier than the other approaches.

Listing 28-3: Module Items

```
Option Strict On

Module Controller
    Sub Main()
        Dim FirstForm As FirstWizardForm = _
         New FirstWizardForm()
        'This section builds the relations between the forms
        'In this example, we only have two forms.
        FirstForm.NextForm = New SecondWizardForm()
        FirstForm.Show("This is The First Wizard Form", _
            ,False)
        Application.Run(FirstForm)
    End Sub

    Public Sub ShowNext( _
    ByVal CurrentForm As WizardBaseForm.BaseWizardForm)
        If CurrentForm.NextForm Is Nothing Then
            'Insert Finishing Code
        Else
            CurrentForm.Hide()
            CurrentForm.NextForm.PreviousForm = CurrentForm
            CurrentForm.NextForm.Show("This is the " & _
                CurrentForm.NextForm.Name & " form", , True)
        End If
    End Sub

    Public Sub ShowPrevious(_
        ByVal CurrentForm As WizardBaseForm.BaseWizardForm)
        CurrentForm.Hide()
        CurrentForm.PreviousForm.Show()
    End Sub
End Module
```

The process, then, to add a new form to this wizard is very simple. The following steps allow you to add as many forms as necessary and maintain the navigable consistency within your wizard.

1. Right-click the project in the Solution Explorer, and select Add Inherited Form.

2. Select the `Inherited Form` object, and name it what you like (see Figure 28-2).

3. Select the existing form that should be the foundation for the form being added (see Figure 28-3).

4. In the Sub Main procedure of the module, add the line `FirstForm.NextForm.`
`NextForm = New YourFormName`. This establishes the form reference necessary for navigation.

5. Copy the `cmdNext` (if necessary) and `cmdBack` procedures to the code of your new form.

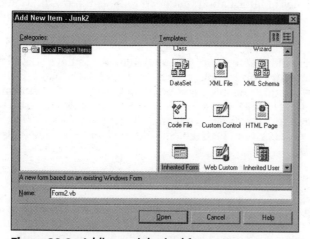

Figure 28-2: Adding an inherited form, step 1

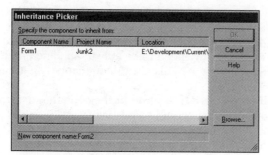

Figure 28-3: Adding an inherited form, step 2

Thus, in mere moments, you can add a new step to a wizard and hook up the navigation accordingly.

Data Entry

Another common GUI development task revolves around data entry applications. Very often, there are tasks that need to be completed that require their own screens; yet the similarity between these tasks is undeniable.

For example, consider a customizable time reporting system. A time reporting system needs to have certain definable objects for reference purposes. These may include Company Departments, Clients, Tasks, and so on. All these items usually have two or three pieces of information that need to be entered—ID, Name, and maybe Description. Furthermore, it is necessary for these items to be edited after their creation.

So, for this task, you could create six forms. Each item would have an Entry form and an Edit form. The Entry form would consist of three labels that describe what should be entered in the three enabled text boxes next to them. It would also have buttons labeled OK, Cancel, and Apply. The Edit form would also have three labels that describe the three text boxes next to them. The text box for the ID field would be disabled, but the others would be enabled. The three buttons would also be there.

This is "Bad Design."

Another approach is to create one form for each item, and use it for the entering and editing. The forms would appear as described previously and, depending on the task at hand, you would just need to toggle the ID field and populate the data if necessary.

"But wait," you say, "I could just use one form, and change the text of the labels and modify the form for the task at hand." That is another possibility. Assume that you go with this approach. You develop the application and deploy it. Then, a big-money client comes to you and says, "We need to be able to add and edit an item called Projects, and we need it tomorrow." This is a "Maintenance Nightmare."

It is plausible that you could accomplish this task, but the code that determines what goes where with that one little field could be problematic.

So, the ideal solution is to use visual inheritance. Create a base form that has the three necessary buttons. And, being the quality designer that you are, you have a data access layer for your system. This base form should thus already have the logic behind those buttons to persist the data entered.

But that isn't all. For a series of similar task, as outlined previously, you create another form derived from the base form with the three buttons. This new form has the descriptive labels and text boxes for data entry. The persistence code already lives behind the buttons, so that isn't an issue. Then, from this second-level form, you can inherit the necessary forms for your application. Then, when that client comes and requests the enhancement, it is very simple for you to inherit a new form and make any other slight modifications necessary.

This sounds somewhat similar to the first approach, but, the main difference is that when that client comes back and wants a fourth field for an item, you only have to add the field in one place.

Listing 28-4, taken from the DataEntryExample project, demonstrates multiple levels of form inheritance.

Listing 28-4: **Data Entry**

```
Public Class BaseDataForm
    Inherits System.Windows.Forms.Form
```

Additional code snipped for brevity.

```
Protected Overloads Sub Show()
End Sub

Protected Overridable Sub cmdOK_Click( _
  ByVal sender As System.Object, _
  ByVal e As System.EventArgs) _
  Handles cmdOK.Click

End Sub

Protected Overridable Sub cmdApply_Click( _
  ByVal sender As System.Object, _
  ByVal e As System.EventArgs) _
  Handles cmdApply.Click

End Sub

Protected Sub cmdCancel_Click( _
  ByVal sender As System.Object, _
  ByVal e As System.EventArgs) _
  Handles cmdCancel.Click

System.Windows.Forms.Application.Exit()

End Class
```

So, you have your base data form that inherits from Form. This form has three buttons: Okay, Apply, and Cancel. As you can see, you have the base signature for overloading the Show method, along with the event signatures for the buttons.

Listing 28-5 inherits this form to create your base, three-field data entry form described previously.

Listing 28-5: **Inherit Again**

```
Public Class BaseThreeField
    Inherits DataEntryBase.BaseDataForm

Protected Overrides Sub cmdOK_Click( _
   ByVal sender As System.Object, _
   ByVal e As System.EventArgs)

    'Insert any data Access code here
End Sub

Protected Overrides Sub cmdApply_Click( _
   ByVal sender As System.Object, _
   ByVal e As System.EventArgs)

    'Insert any data Access code here
End Sub

Protected Overloads Sub Show(ByVal Description As String)
    Me.lblTaskDescription.Text = Description
End Sub

End Class
```

This form now has a label to contain a general description of the task at hand and an overloaded Show method in order to modify that description. This form also has the necessary fields and labels to handle the generic data entry task.

So, you can inherit from this again if you desire to create a form for the specific task. I'll spare the code listing, but the DataEntryExample project demonstrates this as well and Figure 28-4 shows a possible result.

Keep in mind that you are not limited to things covered previously when dealing with inheriting forms. The possibilities are nearly endless.

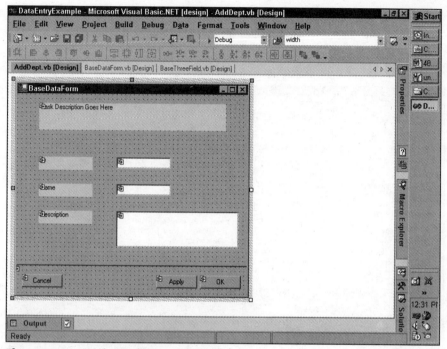

Figure 28-4: An inherited three-field form

Controls

The capability to inherit controls, like forms, has made rapid development even easier. Customized controls in Visual Basic 6 were not easy to create by any stretch of the imagination. Quite frankly, Win32 API functions were the easiest way to accomplish any control development beyond using User controls.

However, in Visual Basic .NET, this is no longer the case. You can now inherit from any existing control, such as the Label or TextBox; or thunk down to the Control class itself and extend it. You also still have User Controls in .NET, but those are covered in the next section.

When you have completed your custom control development, you can then add your creation to the toolbox. The process to do this is as follows:

1. Right-click the Toolbox.
2. Select Customize Toolbox.
3. Click the .NET Framework Components tab (see Figure 28-5).
4. Click the Browse button.

5. Navigate to the DLL containing the control and select it.

6. The control should now appear in the list of available items to check. Check it, and click OK.

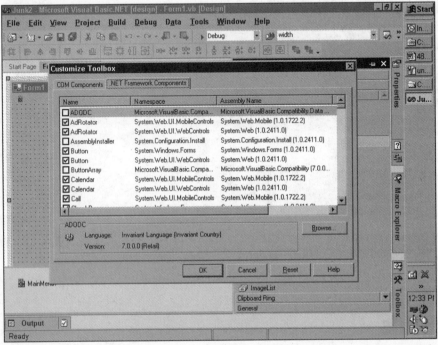

Figure 28-5: The .NET Framework components tab in the Customize Toolbox window

Your customized control now appears on the toolbox. You can drag this control onto a form and set the properties you need. The Designer section, later in this chapter, demonstrates how to write a custom designer to limit or enhance the experience during the design process. I also cover attributes that can enhance the property organization in the Attributes section.

Examples

This section is devoted to showing some examples of custom controls. It shows how to inherit from `Control` and `StatusBar`. Later on in this chapter, you enhance these examples in the "Attributes" and "Designers" sections.

A common graphical effect that appears on many About boxes in software is called drop shadow text. Essentially, this creates a shadow slightly below and underneath the existing text. This can be seen in Figure 28-6. Listing 28-6, taken from the `DropShadowExample` project, accomplishes precisely that. This code has been reconfigured for clarity.

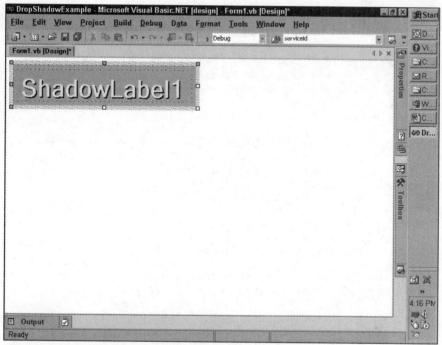

Figure 28-6: An example of a drop shadow

Listing 28-6: **Inheriting from Control**

```
Option Strict On

Imports System.Drawing
Imports System.Drawing.Design
Imports System.Drawing.Drawing2D
Imports System.Windows.Forms
Imports System.Windows.Forms.Design
Imports System.ComponentModel

Namespace ShadowLabelControl

Public Class ShadowLabel

Private m_ShadowColor As Color = Color.Black

Public Property ShadowColor() As System.Drawing.Color
    Get
        Return m_ShadowColor
```

Continued

Listing 28-6 *(continued)*

```
        End Get
        Set(ByVal Value As System.Drawing.Color)
            m_ShadowColor = Value
            Me.Refresh()
        End Set
End Property

Protected Overrides Sub OnPaint(ByVal e As PaintEventArgs)

'This is the Brush to paint the Front Text
    Dim brshForeText As SolidBrush = _
        New SolidBrush(Me.ForeColor)

'This is the Brush to paint the rear text.
    Dim brshRearText As SolidBrush = _
        New SolidBrush(Me.ShadowColor)

'This is the surface we are painting on
    Dim grphSurface As Graphics = e.Graphics

'This is the bounding rectangle of the front text region
    Dim rectForeGround As RectangleF = _
        grphSurface.VisibleClipBounds

'This is the bounding rectangle of the rear text region
    Dim rectBackGround As RectangleF = _
        grphSurface.VisibleClipBounds

'We modify the background rectangle because the text need to
'drop and move to the right.
  rectBackGround.Offset(2, 2)

'This draws the Shadow portion.
    grphSurface.DrawString( _
        Me.Text, Me.Font, brshRearText, rectBackGround)

'This draws the Front Portion.
    grphSurface.DrawString( _
        Me.Text, Me.Font, brshForeText, rectForeGround)

'Clean up
    brshRearText.Dispose()
    brshForeText.Dispose()
    grphSurface.Dispose()

'Call the Base method
    MyBase.OnPaint(e)
End Sub
```

```
Protected Overrides Sub OnFontChanged(ByVal e As EventArgs)
    Me.Refresh
    MyBase.OnFontChanged(e)
End Sub

Protected Overrides Sub OnTextChanged(ByVal e As EventArgs)
    Me.Refresh()
    MyBase.OnTextChanged(e)
End Sub

End Class

End Namespace
```

The previous code begins with the referencing of the necessary libraries for the tasks that need to be accomplished. Then, the necessary properties need to be added to store values that are interesting to the behavior of the control. Because the added property deals with color, the OnPaint routine needs to be overridden to present the opportunity to use the value. The primary properties of this control are the Font and the Text properties. These properties help define how the control paints. In order to notify the control to repaint when these properties change, we have overridden the OnFontChanged and OnTextChanged routines. This code yields the simplest version of this control. After you add it to the toolbox, as described previously, you can drag and drop this control on your container. As you can see, you have leveraged some of the properties that Control gives us (for example, ForeColor, Font, Text, and so on). When you play around with this control, you see that there are some deficiencies, which are covered in the "Attributes" and "Designers" sections.

The next example inherits from StatusBar. In many applications, a progress bar is very useful; however, the necessary screen real estate can cloud the GUI for the user. Thus, a common technique for some applications is to place the progress bar in a status bar. Internet Explorer provides a good example of this type of control. When a page is loading, the status bar at the bottom of the window displays the progress. Unfortunately, .NET does not give you a control such as this. Thankfully, though, it is relatively simple to create your own. Listing 28-7 is taken from the ProgressStatusBarExample project. The code has been reconfigured for clarity.

Creating this control has presented you with an interesting problem, though. The status bar by itself is simply a container for panels. The panels actually handle the text that is displayed. So, you really need to derive a class from StatusBarPanel as well as StatusBar.

Listing 28-7: **Inheriting from StatusBar**

```vbnet
Option Strict On

Imports System.Windows.Forms
Imports System.Drawing

Public Class ProgressPanel
    Inherits StatusBarPanel

Private m_Minimum As Integer = 1
Private m_Maximum As Integer = 100
Private m_Value As Integer = 0
Private m_Step As Integer = 1

Public Property Minimum() As Integer
    Get
            Return m_Minimum
    End Get
    Set(ByVal Value As Integer)
        m_Minimum = Value
    End Set
End Property

Public Property Maximum() As Integer
    Get
            Return m_Maximum
    End Get
    Set(ByVal Value As Integer)
        m_Maximum = Value
    End Set
End Property

Public Property Value() As Integer
    Get
            Return m_Value
    End Get
    Set(ByVal Value As Integer)
        m_Value = Value
        Me.Parent.Refresh
    End Set
End Property

Public Property [Step]() As Integer
    Get
            Return m_Step
    End Get
    Set(ByVal Value As Integer)
        m_Step = Value
    End Set
```

```vb
End Property
Public Sub PerformStep()
   Me.Value += Me.Step
End Sub

Public Sub Increment(ByVal Amount As Integer)
      Me.Value += Amount
End Sub

Private m_Color As Color = Color.Black

Public Property ForeColor() As Color
  Get
      Return m_Color
  End Get
  Set(ByVal Value As Color)
      m_Color = Value
  End Set
End Property

Public Sub New()
  MyBase.New()
  Me.Style = StatusBarPanelStyle.OwnerDraw
End Sub

End Class

Public Class ProgressStatusBar
    Inherits StatusBar

Public Sub New()
      MyBase.New()
      Me.SizingGrip = False
      Me.ShowPanels = True
End Sub

Protected Overrides Sub OnDrawItem( _
  ByVal e As StatusBarDrawItemEventArgs)
'This checks to see if the panel being painted is one of
'ours.
If e.Panel.GetType Is _
  Type.GetType("ProgressStatusBarExample.ProgressPanel") _
Then
    Dim ProgressPanel As ProgressPanel = _
      CType(e.Panel, ProgressPanel)

   If ProgressPanel.Value > ProgressPanel.Minimum Then

   'This calculates the width of the region we need to
paint
      Dim NewWidth As Integer = _
      CType(((ProgressPanel.Value / _
```

Continued

Listing 28-7 (continued)

```
        ProgressPanel.Maximum) * ProgressPanel.Width), _
        Integer)

        Dim NewBounds As Rectangle = e.Bounds
            Dim PaintBrush As _
             New SolidBrush(ProgressPanel.ForeColor)

        NewBounds.Width = NewWidth
'This method call actually fills the Progress region with
'the color specified
        e.Graphics.FillRegion( _
             PaintBrush, New [Region](NewBounds))
        PaintBrush.Dispose()
    Else
        MyBase.OnDrawItem(e)
    End If
Else
    MyBase.OnDrawItem(e)
End If
End Sub

End Class
```

Because the control above essentially combines the behavior of two existing controls, the decision needs to be made as to which control is inherited. In the case, the easier route seemed to be inheriting the StatusBarPanel and implementing custom ProgressBar behavior.

The class begins by specifying the properties common to a ProgressBar. As seen in the last chapter, the ProgressBar has properties to accommodate minimum, maximum, value, and step values. These properties have been mimicked here. The ProgressBar also has methods to perform a step operation and a standard increment. Methods to accomplish these tasks with this control have been included as well.

In the constructor of the class, it is necessary to specify that this control is OwnerDrawn. An OwnerDrawn control specifies that the code to draw the control is provided rather than the default behavior. This is required because the actual progress indicator needs to be drawn. Not setting this property results in the progress indicator not being drawn.

A second class then needs to be created in order to house the panel. Because a standard StatusBar houses a standard StatusBarPanel, this class inherits from StatusBar as the first class inherited from StatusBarPanel. The primary task of this class is to actually handle the painting of the ProgressBarPanel. In order to accomplish this, the OnDrawItem method needs to be overridden. As you can see, the EventArgs passed into the method provides the panel that needs to be drawn. It is easy to test if the panel is a ProgressBarPanel, and the painting can thus be handled by the provided code.

To use this control, simply add it to the form in the Form's constructor. The example project demonstrates how to accomplish this.

User Controls

The primary purpose of a UserControl is to act as a container for other controls. In this respect, it is very similar to a UserControl in Visual Basic 6. This designer allows for multiple controls and components to be grouped together and code to be applied to each control.

A UserControl is analogous to a Form in this respect. Furthermore, the UserControl is derived from the ContainerControl class, like the Form. However, it does have reduced functionality.

A UserControl is most useful when a piece of software or multiple pieces of software require some similar tasks that do not warrant their own form. An example may be a class of software that requires Address data to be entered. Rather than rewrite or cut and paste the same controls and code into each piece of software to accomplish this task, you can create a User Control.

The UserControlExample project demonstrates a UserControl fashioned after entering address data. There is no code affiliated to the individual controls, but this is a perfect scenario for the CausesValidation property that was demonstrated in Chapter 26. Each of the text boxes may require to be a certain format and this property could be used to raise such events.

Attributes

As you have seen in previous sections, the .NET Framework exposes significant methods by which you can enhance the tools at hand. However, this isn't all you can do. Microsoft has exposed the Design Time Framework for full integration with the controls you develop.

You may have noticed that when examining the DropShadowExample, the ShadowColor property appeared in the Property Browser in the IDE when the control was active in the design surface. This is one big leap for the control developer. No longer is it necessary to require properties to be set in code or proprietary licenses to take advantage of some of the IDE features.

This integration with the Property Browser can be further enhanced with the use of attributes. The goal of an attribute is to give descriptive information about the properties of your control and enhance the design time experience for the developer. An attribute is really all about Metadata. There are about 150 existing attributes in the .NET Framework, along with the ability to create your own. This section merely highlights a couple of the more interesting ones.

In the Property Browser, you may have noticed that the bottom of the grid has a region that gives the description of the selected property. This is accomplished via an attribute. Furthermore, items such as the category also are controlled by attributes.

Listing 28-8 demonstrates a few attributes, and is taken from the DropShadowExampleEnhanced project.

Listing 28-8: **Attributes**

```
<Description("Choose a color to specify the color _
    of the text shadow"), _
  Category("Appearance")> _
Public Property ShadowColor() As System.Drawing.Color
    Get
        Return m_ShadowColor
    End Get
    Set(ByVal Value As System.Drawing.Color)
        m_ShadowColor = Value
        Me.Refresh()
    End Set
End Property

<Editor("BitmapEditor", "UITypeEditor"), _
Description("Specify the bitmap with which _
        to texturize the text"), _
Category("Appearance")> _

Public Property TextureImage() As Bitmap
    Get
        Return m_TextureImage
    End Get
    Set(ByVal Value As Bitmap)
        m_TextureImage = Value
        Me.Refresh()
    End Set
End Property
```

The attributes on the first property in the previous code allow the Description and the Category of the property to be set. These attributes apply to how and where the property appears in the Property Browser. Figure 28-7 demonstrates how these attributes set the behavior of the property in the Property Browser.

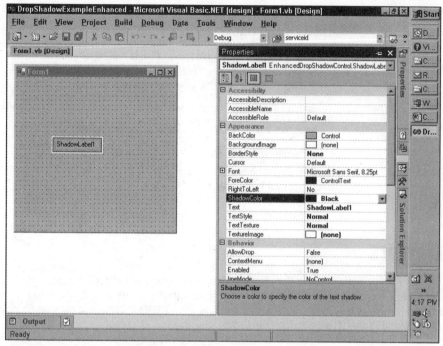

Figure 28-7: The property ShadowColor appears in the Appearance category with a description displayed at the bottom.

The second property in the listing is used to specify the image to be used if painting the text in the control with a gradient. The `Editor` attribute tells the Property Browser to display an ellipsis next to the property value. Clicking on the ellipsis displays a FileOpen dialog box. The first parameter of the Editor attribute specifies which type of FileOpen dialog box to display. In this instance, specifying BitmapEditor restricts the dialog box to display only image files.

Some of the more useful attributes with descriptions are listed in Table 28-1.

Table 28-1
Useful Property Attributes and Descriptions

Attribute Name	Description
Browsable	Specifies whether the property is displayed in the browser.
Category	Specifies the category in the Property Browser to which the property belongs.

Continued

Table 28-1 *(continued)*

Attribute Name	Description
Description	Specifies the text to be displayed in the bottom of the Property Browser to describe the property when activated.
DesignOnly	Specifies whether the property can be modified only at design time.
Editor	Specifies the editor used to modify the property value.
Help	Specifies the Help file and topic for the property.
PersistContents	Specifies whether the property value appears in the Windows Forms generated code region.

Designers

Just as attributes enhance the design time experience for the developer, so can designers. To help you understand what a designer is, consider the following task. Place a label on the form, and resize the Label. The item that allows you to resize the control is the designer for the Label.

The base designer for control should handle the majority of your needs as a developer. However, there may be an instance in which some common task needs to be restricted. For example, you may want to restrict the size of your control on a form because the size is derived from the values of other properties.

In order to further modify the design time experience, the .NET Framework gives you the ControlDesigner class. This class exposes a significant amount of functionality, some of which is detailed in Table 28-2.

Table 28-2
The ControlDesigner Class

Member Name (scope and type)	Description
SelectionRules (Public Instance Property)	Specifies the resize, move, and visible capabilities of the control. The following values are valid for this property by themselves or via a bitwise combination. AllSizeable, BottomSizeable, LeftSizeable, Locked, Moveable, None, RightSizeable, TopSizeable, Visible.

Member Name (scope and type)	Description
Verbs (Public Instance Property)	ReadOnly. Returns the collection of designer verbs associated with this control. A designer verb is a menu command that is linked to an event handler. Verbs appear on the right-click context menu of the control designer. For example, right-clicking a label brings up a menu including items such as View Code and Properties. This allows you to add other commands.
EnableDragRect (Protected Instance Property)	Specifies whether drag rectangles can be drawn on the designer.
OnPaintAdornments (Protected Instance Method)	This method gets called when the control is done painting in design time. This gives the component developer the opportunity to add any additional painted features to the control.

These are just a few of the enhancements available to the developer via modifying a designer. Listing 28-9 shows a simple designer for the DropShadowEnhanced control. This is available in the DropShadowEnhancedExample Project.

Listing 28-9: **A Custom Designer**

```
Public Class ShadowLabelDesigner
Inherits ControlDesigner

Public Overrides ReadOnly Property SelectionRules() As
SelectionRules
    Get
        Return SelectionRules.Moveable Or _
        SelectionRules.Visible
    End Get
End Property
End Class
```

To use the designer, you simply set an attribute on the control:

```
<Designer(_
GetType(ShadowLabelControl.Design.ShadowLabelDesigner))> _
Public Class ShadowLabel
```

The `ShadowLabel` control draws text based on the Font property of the control. This value, coupled with length of the text, is used to determine the size of the control. Because the size of the control is crucial, it is necessary to restrict the developer from resizing the control programmatically or otherwise. This, of course, requires you to provide your own resizing code.

Summary

This chapter provided a wealth of information useful to any developer. The focus was inheritance, and you learned the proper techniques for creating applications based on inherited forms as well as a framework for a common task such as wizards. Inheriting controls was explained and demonstrated in detail and you learned that every aspect of the Framework is available to you. Couple this with the capability to use attributes and designers, and the Framework really starts to open up for your enjoyment. The flexibility of the Framework and the IDE really comes out with these modifications.

✦   ✦   ✦

Irregular Forms

by Jacob A. Grass

I chose to write a chapter on irregular forms because, quite frankly, I think they are a lot of fun. In previous chapters, you received information necessary to create standard GUIs for applications. This chapter focuses mainly on nonstandard GUIs.

As the .NET Framework gains in popularity and distribution, you will probably see a wider range of applications developed with Visual Basic than ever before. Games, of course, are probably the most popular task to complete.

This chapter is not a "how-to" in good GUI design and, as the adage says, "Just because you can, doesn't mean you should." Irregular forms are not the answer to every difficult issue in GUI development, but they are exciting and entertaining.

The majority of items covered in this chapter are things such as rectangles, ellipses, polygons, regions, graphics, graphics paths, points, and brushes. Other issues such as how to deal with a form that has no caption bar are also addressed.

The novice user will find this chapter to be entertaining, and will learn a great deal about window manipulation. The advanced user will discover how to leverage certain objects within the framework that they may not have otherwise had time to investigate.

I have provided examples to cover the more interesting techniques in irregular form creation.

Shapes

There are really only a handful of shapes in the toolkit of irregular forms creation. Thankfully, though, you only need a few. Nearly every shape can be created from an ellipse or a polygon. Shapes such as circles and triangles are really only special cases or combinations of these two figures. Other items that can be drawn include arcs, Beziers, curves, and lines. This chapter primarily deals with closed shapes.

Graphics

Drawing an irregular form, like drawing anything, requires four things: a surface, a stylus, a color, and something to draw. This section details what objects in the Framework equate to these required items. Special care is given to those objects that are complex or used frequently.

Surface

The surface upon which you draw is equivalent to two different objects within the Framework: the Graphics object and the Region object. The Graphics object provides the methods for drawing to the device context. A device context is analogous to a coordinate system laid on top of the form. Useful items such as position can be extrapolated from this object. This essentially means that the drawing surface of the form, as represented by the Graphics object, can be directly used by your application.

The Graphics object uses what is known as vector graphics, which are drawings that exist on a coordinate system and are ideal for 2-D creations. Thus, the bounds of the Graphics object are always defined by a rectangle. The available drawing surface, though, may not be a rectangle (more on this later in the chapter). To draw a figure with the Graphics object, it is necessary to provide certain key information about the figure with reference to the coordinate system. Thus, to draw a rectangle, you need to provide the coordinates of the four corners.

As indicated previously, the Graphics object has a bounding rectangle that you can access via the ClipBounds property. You access the actual drawing area via the Clip property. This property returns a Region object that is not required to be rectangular. Listing 29-1, taken from the IntroGraphicsExample, demonstrates this.

Listing 29-1: **Intro to Graphics**

```
Private Sub Form1_Click(ByVal sender As Object, _
    ByVal e As System.EventArgs) Handles MyBase.Click

        Dim grphTemp As GraphicsPath = New GraphicsPath()
        Dim pntPath(4) As PointF
        Dim grphSurface As Graphics
        Dim rgnSurface As Region
```

Next, you show the bounds of the ClientRectangle before changing the surface:

```
        With Me.ClientRectangle
            MessageBox.Show(.X & ", " & .Y & _
                ", " & .Width & ", " & .Height)
        End With

        Me.BackColor = Color.Black
```

The following five points define the path around the new region:

```
pntPath(0) = New PointF(0, 0)
pntPath(1) = New PointF(80, 80)
pntPath(2) = New PointF(80, 40)
pntPath(3) = New PointF(200, 200)
pntPath(4) = New PointF(0, 0)
```

Next, you create the region and change the region of your form to be equivalent to it:

```
grphTemp.AddPolygon(pntPath)
rgnSurface = New Region(grphTemp)
Me.Region = rgnSurface
```

The following shows the bounds of the ClientRectangle after changing the surface:

```
With Me.ClientRectangle
    MessageBox.Show(.X & ", " & .Y & _
        ", " & .Width & ", " & .Height)
End With

grphTemp.Dispose()
rgnSurface.Dispose()
End Sub
```

You should have noticed that the ClientRectangle coordinates didn't change, but the painting surface did. The shape that appears on your screen is defined by the five points mentioned in Listing 29-1, thereby limiting the painting surface to that region. However, the bounding rectangle of the form remains the same.

As you can see, the Region object describes the interior of a Graphics object. This region is the actual available drawing surface. It can be a rectangle or any polygonal area. This object is typically used to limit the drawing capabilities on a form, for example.

Stylus

The stylus is the tool with which you draw. The .NET Framework gives you tools with which to draw: the pen and the brush. The purpose of the pen is to draw lines and curves. Thus, the pen can be used to draw borders, graphs and outlines of regions or shapes.

The DashStyle of a pen determines how the lines are drawn. They can be dashed, dotted, solid, or a combination of the three. The pen object also allows for custom DashStyle. This gives you the ability to create a full range of line appearances for any task at hand.

The pen also allows for capping, which essentially defines what the line looks like at the beginning of the line and at the end. This functionality makes drawing an object such as an arrow as simple as drawing a line.

The other stylus in your toolkit is the brush. Specifically, there are five types of brushes: HatchBrush, LinearGradientBrush, PathGradientBrush, SolidBrush, and TextureBrush. You may have seen a couple of these in the enhanced DropShadow control last chapter. All of the following examples and listings come from the Brushes project.

The HatchBrush is designed to paint a Weave style pattern. There is a Foreground color defining what color the lines are, and a Background color defining what color the gaps between the lines are. Currently, there are 56 different hatch styles available. This brush is very useful when you want to draw a pattern such as Plaid (I won't ask if you won't). Figure 29-1 demonstrates this effect and Listing 29-2 provides the code to accomplish this.

Figure 29-1: Drawing in plaid with the HatchBrush

Listing 29-2: **The HatchBrush**

The color and the pattern are specified in the constructor:

```
Dim brsh As HatchBrush = _
    New HatchBrush(HatchStyle.Plaid, Color.Aqua)
```

Next, draw the string on the graphic's surface:

```
grph.DrawString("EXAMPLE", Surface.Font, brsh, 5, 5)
```

Finally, clean up the brush:

```
brsh.Dispose()
```

The LinearGradientBrush is used to paint along a line (or within a rectangle) using two colors. The brush begins at the right side of the line with the first color and, while painting across the area, the color morphs into the second color. Figure 29-2 demonstrates this effect and Listing 29-3 provides the code to accomplish this.

Figure 29-2: Example of a linear gradient

Listing 29-3: **The LinearGradientBrush**

Here, you are specifying the bounds that the brush can paint in, the two colors, and the gradient type:

```
Dim brsh As LinearGradientBrush = _
    New LinearGradientBrush(grph.VisibleClipBounds, _
    Color.Red, Color.Blue, LinearGradientMode.Horizontal)

grph.DrawString("EXAMPLE", Surface.Font, brsh, 5, 5)
brsh.Dispose()
```

The `PathGradientBrush` is a more complicated brush than the others. This brush takes a `GraphicsPath`, and fills in the encapsulated area with a gradient. You can modify such items as blending and the speed at which the shades change among other things. Figure 29-3 shows what a `PathGradientBrush` looks like, and Listing 29-4 provides the code to accomplish this.

Figure 29-3: A PathGradientBrush with colors Red, BlueViolet, and Black

Listing 29-4: **The PathGradientBrush**

First, you define the path along which the brush will paint:

```
Dim pnt(4) As PointF

pnt(0) = New PointF(0, 0)
pnt(1) = New PointF(200, 50)
pnt(2) = New PointF(200, 100)
pnt(3) = New PointF(100, 100)
pnt(4) = New PointF(0, 0)
```

You define the colors here. If you wish, you could add more to the SurroundColors property:

```
Dim brsh As PathGradientBrush = New PathGradientBrush(pnt)
brsh.CenterColor = Color.BlueViolet
brsh.SurroundColors = New Color() {Color.Black, Color.Red}
```

Continued

Listing 29-4 *(continued)*

Next, you fill the path in with the brush:

```
grph.FillPolygon(brsh, pnt)
brsh.dispose()
```

The `SolidBrush` is the simplest brush of the group. This brush is single color only and is used to fill polygons, ellipses, or text. Figure 29-4 shows the simplicity of the `SolidBrush` and Listing 29-5 provides the code to accomplish this task.

Figure 29-4: The SolidBrush in ForestGreen

Listing 29-5: Using the SolidBrush

This is just too easy:

```
Dim brsh As SolidBrush = New SolidBrush(Color.ForestGreen)
grph.DrawString("EXAMPLE", Surface.Font, brsh, 5, 5)
brsh.Dispose()
```

The fifth and final brush is the `TextureBrush`. This brush uses an image to fill a region, polygon, or text. Figure 29-5 demonstrates the capabilities of the `TextureBrush`, and Listing 29-6 provides the code to accomplish this.

Figure 29-5: The TextureBrush using the DefaultThumbnail.bmp from Donkey.Net

Listing 29-6: Using the TextureBrush

Here, you need to specify the image that makes up the ink on the TextureBrush:

```
Dim brsh As TextureBrush = _
   New TextureBrush(New Bitmap _
   ("Insert Path To BitMap Here."))
grph.DrawString("EXAMPLE", Surface.Font, brsh, 5, 5)
brsh.Dispose()
```

Color

As you can see in the previous code listings, colors are used quite frequently for different effects. Luckily, the .NET Framework gives you a nice batch of colors from which to choose.

The colors available in the Framework are categorized under two headings: KnownColor and SystemColors. A KnownColor is essentially a color with a warm and fuzzy name. For example, in this enumeration, you find treasures such as Bisque, AliceBlue, PapayaWhip, and PeachPuff. Under the SystemColors class, you find the system-level settings for items in the operating system such as WindowFrame, ActiveBorder, and Desktop.

You can also specify new colors not already defined. This is commonly done via the FromARGB method. This method requires the Alpha component; and the Red, Green, and Blue components. In Visual Basic 6, colors were represented by a Long value. To transfer any colors you may have created in Visual Basic 6 to .NET, use the technique shown in Listing 29-7:

Listing 29-7: Translating a Color

```
Dim newColor As Color = _
System.Drawing.ColorTranslator.FromOle(&H996600&)
```

Object to draw

After everything is said and done, nothing in the previous section does you any good if you don't have something to draw. So, experiment and play around. If you find something you are interested in depicting programmatically, take a cubist approach, and see what happens. That's what I did. The following code listings are taken from the StreetSigns project, and are designed to demonstrate some of the capabilities of the Graphics and Regions objects, along with brushes and colors.

In all instances, I overrode the OnPaint method of the form and performed all of the painting myself (see Listing 29-8).

Listing 29-8: **The StopSign**

The purpose of this code is to draw a crude stop sign.

```
Protected Overrides Sub OnPaint(ByVal e As PaintEventArgs)
        Dim grphPath As GraphicsPath = New GraphicsPath()
        Dim grphSurface As Graphics
        Dim rgnSurface As Region
        Dim rectText As RectangleF
        Dim octArray(8) As PointF
        Dim fntText As Font

        Me.BackColor = Color.Red
```

The following is the point array for the octagon:

```
        octArray(0) = New PointF(70, 0)
        octArray(1) = New PointF(170, 0)
        octArray(2) = New PointF(240, 70)
        octArray(3) = New PointF(240, 170)
        octArray(4) = New PointF(170, 240)
        octArray(5) = New PointF(70, 240)
        octArray(6) = New PointF(0, 170)
        octArray(7) = New PointF(0, 70)
        octArray(8) = New PointF(70, 0)
```

This turns the form itself into the octagon:

```
        grphPath.AddPolygon(octArray)
        rgnSurface = New Region(grphPath)
        Me.Region = rgnSurface
```

The following handles the borders. The polygon is the same, but rather than fill it, I simply draw it. And I simply changed the width and color of the pen to handle having one border inside of the other:

```
        grphSurface = Me.CreateGraphics()
        grphSurface.DrawPolygon(New Pen(Color.White, 5), _
         octArray)
        grphSurface.DrawPolygon(New Pen(Color.Black, 3), _
         octArray)
```

The next section handles the text. The rectangle for the region in which the text shoud be written. The font specifies the font in which you would like it to be written:

```
        rectText = New RectangleF(8, 80, 240, 100)
        fntText = New Font(Me.Font.FontFamily, _
          55, FontStyle.Bold)
```

```
grphSurface.DrawString("STOP", fntText, _
    New SolidBrush(Color.Black), rectText)
```

Clean up!!

```
        fntText.Dispose()
        grphSurface.Dispose()
        grphPath.Dispose()
        rgnSurface.Dispose()
    End Sub
```

Listing 29-9 outlines the techniques for creating a railroad crossing sign. The most important shapes in this exercise are the circle and the rectangle. Take notice of the technique for creating the "X" on the sign. Figure 29-6 displays the result of this code.

Figure 29-6: A railroad crossing sign

Listing 29-9: **The Railroad Crossing Sign**

```
Protected Overrides Sub OnPaint(ByVal e As PaintEventArgs)
        Dim grphSurface As Graphics
        Dim grphPath As GraphicsPath = New GraphicsPath()
        Dim rgnSurface As Region
        Dim rectText As RectangleF
        Dim fntText As Font
        Dim XPoints1(3) As PointF
        Dim XPoints2(3) As PointF

        Me.BackColor = Color.Goldenrod
```

The following are the diagonal rectangles to create the X in the center. Unfortunately, actual rectangle objects cannot be angled:

```
        XPoints1(0) = New PointF(10, 0)
        XPoints1(1) = New PointF(0, 10)
        XPoints1(2) = New PointF(Me.Width - 10, Me.Height)
        XPoints1(3) = New PointF(Me.Width, Me.Height - 10)
```

Continued

Listing 29-9 *(continued)*

```
        XPoints2(0) = New PointF(Me.Width - 10, 0)
        XPoints2(1) = New PointF(Me.Width, 10)
        XPoints2(2) = New PointF(10, Me.Height)
        XPoints2(3) = New PointF(0, Me.Height - 10)
```

The following turns the form into the circle that the sign is. You'll notice that ellipses are drawn inside the specified bounding rectangle:

```
    grphPath.AddEllipse(Me.ClientRectangle)
    rgnSurface = New Region(grphPath)
    Me.Region = rgnSurface

    With Me.ClientRectangle
        rectText = New RectangleF(.X + 3, .Height \ 3, _
            .Width + 3, .Height \ 2)
    End With

    fntText = New Font(Me.Font.FontFamily, 55, _
    FontStyle.Bold)

    grphSurface = Me.CreateGraphics
```

This is to draw the border:

```
    grphSurface.DrawEllipse(New Pen(Color.Black, 10), _
    Me.ClientRectangle)
```

This section actually draws the X and handles the text:

```
    grphSurface.FillPolygon( _
    New SolidBrush(Color.Black), XPoints1)

    grphSurface.FillPolygon( _
    New SolidBrush(Color.Black), XPoints2)

    grphSurface.DrawString("R       R", fntText, _
    New SolidBrush(Color.Black), rectText)
```

Clean up!!!!

```
    fntText.Dispose()
    grphSurface.Dispose()
    grphPath.Dispose()
    rgnSurface.Dispose()
  End Sub
```

Listing 29-10 outlines the techniques for creating a Yield sign. This is a particularly difficult sign to create because the mathematics can get a bit awkward. This process breaks the triangle into pieces, and draws the pieces separately.

Listing 29-10: **The Yield Sign**

This task is a little more difficult. Rather than try and draw a triangle within another a triangle, I broke the figure up into three trapezoids:

```
Protected Overrides Sub OnPaint(ByVal e As PaintEventArgs)
        Dim grphPath As GraphicsPath = New GraphicsPath()
        Dim grphSurface As Graphics
        Dim rgnSurface As Region
        Dim rectText As RectangleF
        Dim pntOuterOuter(3) As PointF
        Dim fntText As Font
        Dim Trap(4) As PointF
        Dim Trap2(4) As PointF
        Dim Trap3(4) As PointF

        Me.BackColor = Color.White
```

Next, you define the three trapezoids, each one representing a side of the triangle:

```
        Trap(0) = New PointF(0, 0)
        Trap(1) = New PointF(200, 0)
        Trap(2) = New PointF(150, 40)
        Trap(3) = New PointF(50, 40)
        Trap(4) = New PointF(0, 0)

        Trap2(0) = New PointF(0, 0)
        Trap2(1) = New PointF(50, 40)
        Trap2(2) = New PointF(100, 123.2)
        Trap2(3) = New PointF(100, 173.2)
        Trap2(4) = New PointF(0, 0)

        Trap3(0) = New PointF(200, 0)
        Trap3(1) = New PointF(150, 40)
        Trap3(2) = New PointF(100, 123.2)
        Trap3(3) = New PointF(100, 173.2)
        Trap3(4) = New PointF(200, 0)
```

This is the border:

```
        pntOuterOuter(0) = New PointF(-2, -2)
        pntOuterOuter(1) = New PointF(202, -2)
        pntOuterOuter(2) = New PointF(100.5, 175.2)
        pntOuterOuter(3) = New PointF(-2, -2)

        grphPath.AddPolygon(pntOuterOuter)
        rgnSurface = New Region(grphPath)
        Me.Region = rgnSurface
```

Continued

Listing 29-10 *(continued)*

This is drawing the trapezoids and the text:

```
    grphSurface = Me.CreateGraphics()
    grphSurface.FillPolygon( _
     New SolidBrush(Color.OrangeRed), Trap)
    grphSurface.FillPolygon( _
     New SolidBrush(Color.OrangeRed), Trap2)
    grphSurface.FillPolygon( _
     New SolidBrush(Color.OrangeRed), Trap3)

    rectText = New RectangleF(65, 50, 140, 30)
    fntText = New Font(Me.Font.FontFamily, _
     18, FontStyle.Bold)

    grphSurface.DrawString("Yield", fntText, _
     New SolidBrush(Color.OrangeRed), rectText)
```

Clean up!!!

```
    fntText.Dispose()
    grphSurface.Dispose()
    grphPath.Dispose()
    rgnSurface.Dispose()
  End Sub
```

User Interactivity

Designing irregular forms is fun, and the forms can be pretty, but the ability of the end-user to actually use the interface is still at issue. Using irregular forms can very easily confuse, annoy, and frustrate your user. As I have stated throughout these chapters, consistency is key. For example, how annoyed would you be if, in the next version of Windows Explorer, the Tree view and List view switched positions?

"Just because you can, doesn't mean you should."

If, after careful consideration and deliberation, you decide that irregular forms are the right interface for your software, the following section is helpful to ensure that the user has a quality experience.

User interactivity with the form, if not with the controls of the form, takes place with the title bar and borders. The title bar is used to move, minimize, maximize, and close the form. The borders of the form are used for resizing purposes. But your irregular forms have removed the title bar and conventional borders.

The question then becomes the following: How does the user move or close the form? There are a number of different possible approaches, including tying tasks to events (such as clicking) or placing large buttons on the form (which kind of ruins the fun). In Visual Basic 6, a common way to resolve the moving problem was to use the Win32 API. When the user clicked the form, you could send a message to the form with parameters WM_NCLBUTTONDOWN and HTCAPTION. This tells the form that even if the mouse appears in the client area of the form, it should treat it like the user is clicking the caption.

Unfortunately, the .Net Framework gives you nothing to work with the non-client areas of the form. So, you can either move down to the API, or use another little technique (which also works in Visual Basic 6). Listing 29-11 demonstrates how to allow the user to move a form without a title bar.

Listing 29-11: **Non-Client Movement in the Client**

Use these three variables to tell you whether the mouse is moving, and where it is moving from:

```
Private blnMoving As Boolean = False
Private MouseDownX As Integer
Private MouseDownY As Integer

Private Sub MouseDown(ByVal sender As Object, _
    ByVal e As System.Windows.Forms.MouseEventArgs) _
    Handles MyBase.MouseDown
```

When the user clicks the left mouse button, you automatically assume that the intention is to move the form. So, you store the current location of the mouse at the time the button was clicked:

```
If e.Button = MouseButtons.Left Then
    blnMoving = True
    MouseDownX = e.X
    MouseDownY = e.Y
End If

End Sub
```

Obviously, you don't want the form to be moving when the user doesn't have the button depressed:

```
Private Sub MouseUp(ByVal sender As Object, _
    ByVal e As System.Windows.Forms.MouseEventArgs) _
    Handles MyBase.MouseUp

If e.Button = MouseButtons.Left Then
    blnMoving = False
End If
```

Continued

Listing 29-11 *(continued)*

```
End Sub

Private Sub MouseMove(ByVal sender As Object, _
    ByVal e As System.Windows.Forms.MouseEventArgs) _
    Handles MyBase.MouseMove

If blnMoving Then
    Dim temp As Point = New Point()
```

This is where you actually move the form. You take the difference between the current mouse location and the stored mouse location, and modify the Form's location by that amount:

```
    temp.X = Me.Location.X + (e.X - MouseDownX)
    temp.Y = Me.Location.Y + (e.Y - MouseDownY)
    Me.Location = temp
End If
End Sub
```

Chances are that you don't want to let the user resize the form, or you wouldn't go to so much trouble to create the fancy shape in the first place. But you do need to worry about closing the form. The simplest way to handle this is to create a context menu with one item on it called Close. In the code behind this menu item, close the form. Very simple.

Summary

In this chapter, you learned a fair amount about how graphics and irregular forms work within the Framework. We covered shapes, styles, and colors — among other things. There were also a couple of little tips for handling some of the more common tasks an end-user might expect to be able to do. Most of all, though, this chapter should have instilled mantra number two of this unit: "Just because you can, doesn't mean you should."

✦   ✦   ✦

Other Namespaces and Objects in the Catalog

By Jacob A. Grass

CHAPTER 30

The Windows.Forms framework has a significant amount of functionality built into it as you have already seen. Believe it or not, however, that is not all the functionality there is. There are a handful of additional objects and namespaces that further enhance the development experience. Previous chapters talked a bit about custom control designers. The designers have their roots in the Windows.Forms.Design namespace. This chapter addresses some aspects of this namespace in a little more detail.

Throughout some of the sample code, you may have seen items such as the `Application.Exit`. This references the `Application` object. The `Application` object provides some important properties and methods necessary to control an application. These techniques are covered in this chapter.

You may have yet to see anything related to retrieving information about the current user or the Operating System they are using. As .NET gains in distribution, these tasks become more and more necessary. The `SystemInformation` object provides most of this for you. This object is covered in this chapter.

Despite all the powers of forms, there are invariably some tasks that they cannot accomplish. Yet, these tasks may be accessible through other means. In order to provide interface functionality of the rawest form, the .NET Framework possesses a `NativeWindow` class, which is covered in this chapter.

Globalization, localization, and internationalization have all been thorns in the sides of developers. Accomplishing these goals in previous versions of Visual Basic have never been incredibly easy, nor logical. The .NET Framework now provides you with the System.Resources namespace to tackle these tasks. This chapter gives brief coverage to this namespace.

System.Windows.Forms.Design

Chapter 28 briefly covered the concept of a custom designer for inherited controls. The source of that information is this namespace. In fact, the entire purpose of this namespace is to extend the design-time support of the Windows.Forms Framework.

Developing custom designers for controls really places a power in your hands. No longer is it necessary to lock down properties or require modification only in code. The IDE, as you have seen in earlier chapters, has really opened itself up for modification and customization. The design-time experience becomes almost as grand as the runtime experience you create with it.

The .NET Framework exposes the `ControlDesigner` in order to modify how the control behaves in a design environment. As grand as this is, this capability would not be complete without being able to modify how the properties of your objects behave in the Properties window. Thankfully, the Framework also exposes the `UITypeEditor`.

In the `DropShadowEnhanced` Project in Chapter 28, we discussed the `Editor` attribute, specifically `BitmapEditor`. `BitmapEditor` is derived from `UITypeEditor`. The `UITypeEditor` not only provides the foundation for many existing property editors, it allows you to create your own.

There are five Type editors derived from the `UITypeEditor` that this chapter covers. They are outlined in Table 30-1:

Table 30-1
Select Derived Classes From UITypeEditor

Editor Name	Description
AnchorEditor	A graphical drop-down control to specifiy the value of the Anchor property for a control. A picture of this can be seen in Figure 30-1.
CollectionEditor	A standalone dialog box that allows you to edit the contents of almost any collection.
FontEditor	A standalone dialog box (similar to the Font dialog box from Chapter 27) that allows the developer to select a font.

Editor Name	Description
ImageEditor	A standalone File dialog box with a filter applied for image files from which you can select a file.
FileNameEditor	A standalone dialog box for file selection and renaming.

Figure 30-1: The AnchorEditor

In order to create your own Type editor, you need to perform the following steps:

1. Create a class that inherits from UITypeEditor.

2. Override the EditValue and GetEditStyle methods.

3. Override the GetPaintValueSupported and PaintValue methods.

The EditValue method actually launches the interface for property value editing. GetEditStyle returns the type of editing that is allowed by the particular editor. The valid values are DropDown, Modal, and None. None allows for the standard text editing. Modal creates the Ellipsis button next to the property, and displays a dialog box for editing. DropDown allows for an editor similar to the Anchor editor.

The GetPaintValueSupported method indicates whether the Property editor actually paints anything. The AnchorEditor would return true when this function is called because the dialog box is custom painted. The PaintValue method is simply a Paint routine. Code to create the custom picture should be handled within this routine. It seems complicated, but the most difficult aspect of the ordeal is ensuring that your painting code is correct.

When all is said and done, you can assign the editor to the property in your class, which is similar to the way you assigned the ImageEditor in the DropShadowEnhanced example. This allows you to easily create fancy-type editors such as the AnchorEditor.

Unfortunately, this still does not handle all the modifications you want to make to the Property window. What about the complex properties that appear as one item, yet expand to show that they comprise multiple properties? A good example of this can be seen with the Font property in Figure 30-2. These, too, can be yours.

The class that you need to use to accomplish this is called TypeConverter. The purpose of the TypeConverter is to obviously convert from one type to another. The most common conversion is to and from a string. Thankfully, TypeConverter gives you many methods to assist you in this endeavor. Table 30-2 describes the Public methods of TypeConverter.

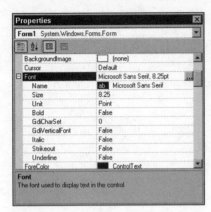

Figure 30-2: A complex property that comprises multiple properties

Table 30-2
Public Instance Methods of TypeConverter

Member Name	Description
CanConvertFrom	Returns whether the converter can convert an object of the specified type to the type of this converter.
CanConvertTo	Returns whether the converter can convert the type of this converter to an object of the specified type.
ConvertFrom	Converts the given value to the type of this converter.
ConvertFromInvariantString	Converts the given string to the type of its converter without respect to culture or localization issues.
ConvertFromString	Converts the given string to the type of its converter.
ConvertTo	Converts the given value to the specified type.
ConvertToInvariantString	Converts the specified value to a string representation, irrespective of culture.
ConvertToString	Converts the specified value to a string representation.
CreateInstance	Re-creates an object, given a set of valid property values for the object.
GetProperties	Returns a collection of properties for the type.
GetPropertiesSupported	Returns whether this type supports properties.
GetStandardValues	Returns a collection of standard values for type of this converter.
GetStandardValuesExclusive	Returns whether the set of values returned from the GetStandardValues method is an exclusive list.

Member Name	Description
GetStandardValuesSupported	Returns whether the standard set of values can be picked from a list.
IsValid	Returns whether the given value object is valid for this type.

The subproperties that get exposed in the property browser and the editing of their values are controlled by the TypeConverter class. So, in short, a TypeConverter, custom ControlDesigner, and custom UITypeEditor are all that is needed to make a marvelous design-time experience for your component.

System.Resources

In Visual Basic 6, when developers needed a storehouse of strings or images for an application, a resource file was often used. This namespace replaces the concept of a resource file with significantly more flexible and comprehensible classes and techniques. Localization has never been so easy.

A resource is defined as a non-executable data file that logically belongs with the application. This resource may contain error messages, images or persisted objects. One of the key benefits of using resources is that changing data in a resource file does not require recompilation of the application. The most common use of a resource file, though, is for internationalization. Resource files often contain all of the necessary strings for an application, which then loads the appropriate information for the culture in which it is running.

There are currently 12 classes in this namespace. The classes that get used most frequently are the ResourceManager, ResourceReader, ResourceWriter, and ResourceSet. There are also equivalent classes for ResX-Resources that represent external resources. For example, the ResXFileRef class represents a link to an external resource file like a bitmap.

ResourceManager

The purpose of the ResourceManager class is to provide a unified way for looking up localized resources for the necessary culture and bringing them into the application.

Note   A culture is essentially a grouping of items such as language, country/region, calendar, and cultural conventions for a particular country or user-group in the world. An example is French or Russian. The globalization formats available in the .NET Framework are dictated by the standards RFC 1766, ISO 639-1, and ISO 3166. The text of these standards can be found at www.ietf.org and www.unicode.org.

This class exposes three very important methods: GetString, GetObject, and GetResourceSet. GetString allows you to pass culture information and the desired KeyString to the method and receive the appropriate string in return. A simple example would be the text in a label. If in Spain, return Spanish, and so on. Of course, this requires that the Spanish resource exists. If not, this method accesses the default resource, which is probably in the language of the developer. The GetObject method functions in much the same way.

The GetResourceSet method is used to retrieve a whole range of resources for a specific culture. In a successfully internationalized application, there are usually a slew of resources in an assembly. Each resource should be named and organized so that only items of the same culture exist in that assembly. For example, in developing an application that functions in Spain, the associated resource file may be named "AppResource.esp.resources." This would be considered a resource set. If all resources for that particular culture exist together in a set, the entire application can be localized from the same assembly.

The Application Object

The Application object exposes a significant number of static properties and methods that make controlling an application a breeze. Among the capabilities of this object is to start and stop an application as well as process Windows messages. This section details the capabilities of this object.

Many tasks in application development require funky logic and potentially error-prone code. Simple tasks such as shutting down an application can cause memory leaks if not done correctly. The Application object takes care of the tedium for you. Table 30-3 provides a reference for the Application object.

Table 30-3
Members of the Application Object

Member Name (scope and type)	Description
AllowQuit (Public Static Property)	Returns whether or not the Calling object can quit the application. Returns false only if being accessed via a control in a browser.
CommonAppDataPath (Public Static Property)	Returns the path that stores all data shared by all users. An example can be seen at the following path: c:\documents and settings\all users\application data\microsoft
CommonAppDataRegistry (Public Static Property)	Returns the Registry key that houses data shared by all users.

Member Name (scope and type)	Description
CompanyName **(Public Static Property)**	Returns the name of the company associated with the application.
CurrentCulture **(Public Static Property)**	Specifies the current culture on the current thread.
CurrentInputLanguage **(Public Static Property)**	Specifies the current input language for the current thread.
ExecutablePath **(Public Static Property)**	Returns the path for the executable that started the application.
LocalUserAppDataPath **(Public Static Property)**	Returns the path for data of a local user.
MessageLoop **(Public Static Property)**	Returns a value indicating whether or not a message loop exists on the current thread.
ProductName **(Public Static Property)**	Returns the Product Name associated with this application.
ProductVersion **(Public Static Property)**	Returns the Product Version Number associated with the application.
SafeTopLevelCaptionFormat **(Public Static Property)**	Specifies the format string to apply to top-level captions when they are displayed with a warning banner.
StartUpPath **(Public Static Property)**	Returns the path for the executable file that started the application.
UserAppDataPath **(Public Static Property)**	Returns the path at which to store data for the roaming user.
UserAppDataRegistry **(Public Static Property)**	Returns the Registry key in which data is stored for the roaming user.
AddMessageFilter **(Public Static Method)**	Method used to add a filter to the message loop of the application. This allows Windows messages to be intercepted and rerouted.
DoEvents **(Public Static Method)**	Processes all Windows messages currently in the queue.
Exit **(Public Static Method)**	Terminates all message pumps after messages have been processed then terminates all windows.
ExitThread **(Public Static Method)**	Terminates the message loop on the specified thread and the terminates all windows existing on the thread.
OLERequired **(Public Static Method)**	Initializes OLE on the current thread.

Continued

Table 30-3 *(continued)*

Member Name (scope and type)	Description
RemoveMessageFilter (Public Static Method)	Removes the specified message filter from the message loop of the application.
Run (Public Static Method)	Begins a standard application message loop on the current thread.
ApplicationExit (Public Static Event)	Occurs when the application is about to shut down.
Idle (Public Static Event)	Occurs when the application is about to enter an idle state.
ThreadException (Public Static Event)	Occurs when an un-caught thread exception is thrown.
ThreadExit (Public Static Event)	Occurs when a thread of the application is about to be shut down. If it is the main thread, this event is raised before the ApplicationExit event.

The Application object is specifically useful for the Exit and Run methods. It is very easy now to add a module to a project; you simply include a subroutine called Main, and place the following code in it (see Listing 30-1):

Listing 30-1: **Application.Run and Exit**

This places control of the application in the hands of the instance of Form1. If Form1 ceases to exist, the rest of the application also terminates:

```
Sub Main()
   Dim StartingForm As Form1 = New Form1()
   Application.Run(StartingForm)
End Sub
```

Visual Basic 6 had the dreaded End command, which was a bad idea. It left scores of holes and memory leaks. Now, you have an alternative:

```
Private Sub Form1_Closing(ByVal sender As Object, _
   ByVal e As System.ComponentModel.CancelEventArgs) _
   Handles MyBase.Closing

Application.Exit()

End Sub
```

The `Application` object handles any loose ends you may have. This is not to say that you should exit all of your applications this way; it is still good practice to release all of your resources beforehand.

Another exciting aspect of the `Application` object is the capability to insert a message filter. The purpose of a message filter is to "pre-process" all Windows messages sent to the application, and determine whether they need to be sent on. This can be very handy if, for whatever reason, you do not want your application to receive certain messages. Typical messages that you may want to filter include messages generated from user interaction with the non-client area of the form. Listing 30-2 demonstrates how to filter out double-click messages.

 Note   Adding a message filter can seriously degrade the performance of your application.

Listing 30-2: **Using a Message Filter**

This creates our message filter:

```
Public Class DoubleClickMessageFilter
   Implements IMessageFilter

   Public Function PreFilterMessage( _
      ByRef m As System.Windows.Forms.Message) As Boolean _
      Implements IMessageFilter.PreFilterMessage

   If m.Msg = &H203 Or m.Msg = &H206 Or m.Msg = &H209 Then
          Debug.WriteLine("Filter: " & m.Msg)
          Return True
   Else
          Return False
   End If
   End Function
End Class
```

To add the filter to the application, we simply need to do the following:

```
Application.AddMessageFilter(DoubleClickMessageFilter)
```

Removing the filter is just as easy:

```
Application.RemoveMessageFilter(DoubleClickMessageFilter)
```

Thus, it is easy to see the benefits we receive from the `Application` object within the Framework.

The NativeWindow Object

The `NativeWindow` class provides a low-level encapsulation of the items that make a window what it is. The standard `Form` class exposes a lot of functionality, but sometimes we don't need all of that functionality. This is a situation for the `NativeWindow` class. A perfect example of the need for this class would be creating your own context menus, which is a window with a few strings representing the menu items. A `Form` provides significantly more functionality than is necessary for this task.

Amid the loss of functionality, though, are key things such as automatic handle destruction. These types of things need to be handled by the developer. The `NativeWindow` class is, essentially, an equivalent to the result of a CreateWindowEx API call from Visual Basic 6.

Table 30-4 provides a reference for the `NativeWindow` class.

Table 30-4 The NativeWindow Object	
Member Name (scope and type)	*Description*
`Handle` (Public Instance Property)	ReadOnly. Returns the Handle associated with this object.
`AssignHandle` (Public Instance Method)	Assigns the specified Handle to this window.
`CreateHandle` (Public Instance Method)	Creates a Handle for the Window. Requires a `CreateParams` object containing information regarding the initial state of the window. The information in the `Params` is analogous to the `Parameters` passed to the CreateWindowEx Procedure.
`DefWndProc` (Public Instance Method)	Invokes the default window procedure for this window in order to process a Windows message.
`DestroyHandle` (Public Instance Method)	Destroys the Handle associated with this window. This is necessary after the window has outlived its usefulness so the Garbage Collector can retrieve the resources.
`ReleaseHandle` (Public Instance Method)	Releases the Handle associated with the window. The procedure is called when Windows destroys the Handle.

The SystemInformation Object

The purpose of this class is to provide information about the operating system upon which the program is running. In Visual Basic 6, it was necessary to thunk down to the Win 32 API to access this information. The Windows.Forms Framework wraps those APIs into this object to open up system information to the developer. Every property of this object has a static scope.

Table 30-5 provides a reference and description of the static properties of the SystemInformation object.

<table>
<tr><td colspan="2" align="center">Table 30-5
Members of the SystemInformation Object</td></tr>
<tr><td>Member Name</td><td>Description</td></tr>
<tr><td>ArrangeDirection</td><td>Returns how the operating system arranges minimized windows. Can be Down, Up, Left, or Right. This value is combined with the ArrangeStartingPosition property.</td></tr>
<tr><td>ArrangeStartingPosition</td><td>Returns how the operating system arranges minimized windows. Can be BottomLeft, BottomRight, Hide, TopLeft, or TopRight. This value is combined with the ArrangeDirection property.</td></tr>
<tr><td>BootMode</td><td>Returns how the system was started. Can be Normal, FailSafe, or FailSafeWithNetwork.</td></tr>
<tr><td>Border3Dsize</td><td>Returns the dimensions of a 3-D border.</td></tr>
<tr><td>BorderSize</td><td>Returns the dimensions of a standard window border.</td></tr>
<tr><td>CaptionButtonSize</td><td>Returns the size of a button on the title bar. This is useful for sizing additional buttons.</td></tr>
<tr><td>CaptionHeight</td><td>Returns the height of the normal title bar on a window.</td></tr>
<tr><td>ComputerName</td><td>Returns the name of the current system. This is the same name that appears to other computers on a network.</td></tr>
<tr><td>CursorSize</td><td>Returns the dimensions of a cursor.</td></tr>
</table>

Continued

Table 30-5 (continued)

Member Name	Description
DbcsEnabled	Returns whether or not the OS supports double byte character sets (Dbcs). Note, even if the OS does support Dbcs, this is not enough information to assume that the user runs a culture that uses this character set.
DebugOS	Returns whether or not the current OS is a debug version.
DoubleClickSize	Returns the dimensions in which a user must click for two clicks to be considered a Double-Click. To conceptualize this, assume that every first mouse click is at (0, 0). If this value returns (2, 2) and the user clicks a second time at (1,1), it constitutes a Double-Click.
DoubleClickTime	Returns the number of milliseconds in which two clicks must occur to be considered a Double-Click.
DragFullWindows	Returns whether or not the user has enabled FullWindowDrag. If true, this means that the contents of windows are displayed while being dragged.
DragSize	Returns the dimensions that a drag operation must extend to be considered a drag operation.
FixedFrameBorderSize	Returns the width of the border for a window that is not resizable, but has a caption.
FrameBorderSize	Returns the width of the border on a resizable window.
HighContrast	Returns whether or not the system is running in High Contrast mode.
HorizontalScrollBarArrowWidth	Returns the width of the arrow bitmap on a horizontal scrollbar.
HorizontalScrollBarHeight	Returns the height of the horizontal scrollbar.
HorizontalScrollBarThumbWidth	Returns the width of the scrollbox on the horizontal scrollbar.
IconSize	Returns the default dimensions of an icon.

Member Name	Description
IconSpacingSize	Returns the dimension of the grid used to lay out icons in a LargeIcon view.
KanjiWindowHeight	Returns the height of the window used for displaying Kanji (Asian pictographic characters).
MaxWindowTrackSize	Returns the default maximum dimensions of a window with a caption bar and a border.
MenuButtonSize	Returns the dimensions of a menu bar button.
MenuCheckSize	Returns the default size of a menu check mark.
MenuFont	Returns the system font used for menus.
MenuHeight	Returns the height of a single line in a menu.
MidEastEnabled	Returns whether or not the current OS can handle Hebrew and Arabic script.
MinimizedWindowSize	Returns the dimensions of a normal minimized window.
MinimizedWindowSpacingSize	Returns the dimensions of the grid upon which multiple minimized windows are placed.
MinimumWindowSize	Returns the minimum allowable dimensions of a window.
MinWindowTrackSize	Returns the default minimum allowable size for a sizable window with a caption bar.
MonitorCount	Returns the number of monitors being used for display.
MonitorsSameDisplayFormat	Returns whether or not all attached monitors have the same display format.
MouseButtons	Returns the number of buttons of the mouse. The wheel is not included in this count.
MouseButtonsSwapped	Returns whether or not the user has flipped the left and right mouse buttons.
MousePresent	Returns whether or not a mouse is installed.

Continued

Table 30-5 *(continued)*

Member Name	Description
MouseWheelPresent	Returns whether or not an installed mouse has a wheel.
MouseWheelScrollLines	Returns the number of lines to scroll when the mouse wheel is rotated.
NativeMouseWheelSupport	Returns whether or not the OS offers native support for the mouse wheel.
Network	Returns whether or not the user is connected to a network.
PenWindows	Returns whether or not the extensions for PenComputing are installed.
PrimaryMonitorMaximizedWindowSize	Returns the dimensions of a maximized window on the primary monitor.
PrimaryMonitorSize	Returns the dimensions of the primary display monitor.
RightAlignedMenus	Returns whether or not drop-down menus are right-aligned with corresponding menu-bar items.
Secure	Returns whether or not SecurityManager is present on the system.
ShowSounds	Returns whether or not Accessibility settings necessitate visual feedback in situations that would typically require audible feedback.
SmallIconSize	Returns the default dimensions of a small icon.
ToolWindowCaptionButtonSize	Returns the dimensions of a button of the caption bar of a tool window.
ToolWindowCaptionHeight	Returns the height of the title bar on a tool window.
UserDomainName	Returns the domain name of the current user.
UserInteractive	Returns whether or not the current process is in a user-interactive mode.
UserName	Returns the name of the user currently logged in.
VerticalScrollBarArrowHeight	Returns the height of the arrow bitmap on a vertical scrollbar.

Member Name	Description
VerticalScrollBarThumbHeight	Returns the height of the scrollbox in a vertical scrollbar.
VerticalScrollBarWidth	Returns the width of the vertical scrollbar.
VirtualScreen	Returns the bounds of a Virtual Screen. A Virtual Screen is the entire viewable area on a multimonitor system.
WorkingArea	Returns the dimensions of the working area of the display. The working area takes into account items such as the systray and the task bar.

Many of the properties of the SystemInformation object can come in handy when doing window manipulation, either up at the Form level or down at the NativeWindow level. But, beyond that, it simply is a very, very easy object to use and understand.

Furthermore, items such as Authentication, in which it is necessary to retrieve the user's network login, are very handy. The code in Listing 30-3 demonstrates how to use a few of these properties.

Listing 30-3: **Using the SystemInformation Object**

```
MessageBox.Show(SystemInformation.UserDomainName _
             & "\" & SystemInformation.UserName)

MessageBox.Show(SystemInformation.ComputerName & _
             " -- " & SystemInformation.MonitorCount)
```

So, as you can plainly see, the SystemInformation object even further enhances the capabilities we have in our application, while completely avoiding the Win32API.

Note Another option to obtain the current user name is to use System.Threading. Thread.CurrentPrincipal.Identity.Name. The primary difference between these two approaches is that the SystemInformation.UserName property retrieves the name of the User logged into the computer. The Threading technique retrieves the name of the User currently authenticated on a thread. This is not necessarily the same value.

Summary

Overall, the System.Windows.Forms Framework gives you the capability to make an incredibly robust and powerful application. The repository of controls is significant enough to the point that developing one is almost unnecessary. Yet, when we do, it is the easiest control development experience we have ever had.

The capability to enhance the usage of controls via custom designers and full integration with the property browser greatly enhances the design-time experience. As you saw above, the Design Framework exposes many aspects of the IDE you may have taken for granted in the past.

The Resources library finally gives the developer an easier path to Localization. With ResourceManagers, Readers, and Writers, access and modification of the files necessary for a quality end-user experience is closer than ever before.

The Application, SystemInformation, and NativeWindow classes wrap up nearly all of the Win32API functions that we used to wrap in our own classes. Our code can finally stop looking like a garbled mess with hundreds of Declare statements and WM_ constants.

And finally, the grandest aspect of the entire Framework:

A Form is just a Class.

✦   ✦   ✦

VB .NET and the Web

Introduction to Web Development

by Bill Evjen

The decade-long evolution of Visual Basic has finally and truly met Web application development with VB .NET — and it couldn't come at a better time! This object-oriented language brings to Web development the capability to provide rich applications that other client/server scripting languages of the past couldn't provide. With the introduction of VB .NET into the Web arena, the next step of the Internet revolution has begun.

Web development has dramatically changed since people started doing static brochure sites in the mid-1990s, and has branched out to now include dynamic Internet applications. Once reserved for Win16 and Win32 Visual Basic applications, companies are now turning to the Internet to deliver these robust applications. The browser has actually turned out to be a great medium to deliver applications.

If you think about it, it makes plenty of sense. Imagine that you are a company that wants to build an application that 3,000 employees will use on a daily basis. You could build a Win32 Visual Basic application, but this requires you to install the application on every employee's computer (assuming that they have the proper hardware configurations needed to run the application). You must then train them to use this new program. Beyond that, every time you need a bug fix or an upgrade to the application, someone needs to go out and apply these changes to each instance of the program. That can be a daunting task!

This is exactly why Internet-based applications have become so popular, and continue to increase in popularity each and every day.

Internet applications use the browser as the container of the application. This is a great advantage. There really aren't that many computers out there that do not have a browser installed, and there aren't many users who do not know how to use a browser (greatly reducing any training that may be required). Using the browser also makes the need to install the program on users' computers (as well as any upgrades) obsolete. Users always see the latest and greatest version of the application because only one instance of the application is sitting on the server.

As time goes on, these Internet applications become more and more robust, and allow parties to work with each other in ways they never dreamed of in the past. Even with these changes in application development underway, there is still a need on the Web for brochure, commercial, and informative sites. Some sites require only a simple form, whereas others may connect to a simple database table to provide up-to-date information. The great thing about all this is that these sites can use the same advantages of .NET development that the largest browser-based applications use.

It is important to understand that VB .NET is only one part of Web development. It is true now, as it was in the past, that Internet application development involves a mixing of multiple languages and requires a special understanding of browser behaviors. Although VB .NET makes this easier for the programmer, it is still important to understand how all the pieces fit together.

Languages and Technologies of the Web

The number of Web pages on the Internet is enormous, and the languages that built these pages are numerous as well. Even the untrained observer can see it in the URL extensions that are out there. Some of the extensions include html, asp, jsp, cgi, perl, js, php, and many more. This is due to the plethora of languages out there that a programmer can use to build a Web page.

In the past, the choice of language was really dependent on what you knew, what languages the server accepted, and what sort of functionality you wanted the page to perform. You wouldn't build a page purely in HTML if you wanted the page to perform some calculation on-the-fly or to store the user's name in a database. This required other languages to work alongside the HTML. Due to this fact, it is important to learn and understand some of the other languages that play an important role in VB .NET development.

HTML

Hypertext Markup Language (HTML) is a language used to present information to the browser for display. HTML is not a true programming language—it won't allow you to apply any logic. It is basically a collection of tags that browsers interpret to apply styles to text. HTML can also provide links to other pages, show images, and present basic forms. The tags in HTML are enclosed within an opening less-than sign (<) and a closing greater-than sign (>). It is important to note that different browsers interpret HTML differently, and not all the tags are equally identified in each of the various browsers. An example of HTML can be seen in Listing 31-1.

Listing 31-1: HTML Code Example

```
<html>
  <head>
      <title>My Homepage</title>
  </head>

  <body>
      <font size=2 color=red><b>Hello World!</b></font>
  </body>
</html>
```

Cross-Reference For an entire book written on the subject, take a look at *HTML 4 Bible* (published by Hungry Minds, Inc.) by Bryan Pfaffenberger and Bill Karrow.

Cascading Style Sheets (CSS)

Cascading Style Sheets (CSS) is an outstanding addition to HTML that allows you to apply a certain style to a particular HTML tag. For instance, if you want each <h1> tag in your page to be bold, be in Arial font, and have a font size of 15, you can apply HTML <font> tags around each instance. This can sometimes be very time-consuming, and can make for some messy code. By applying a *style sheet* to the page, you can specify how every <h1> tag is formatted, which saves time and allows for cleaner code. An example is shown in Listing 31-2.

Listing 31-2: Cascading Style Sheets Code Example

```
<html>
  <head>
      <title>My Homepage</title>
          <style type="text/css">
            body {
                font-family: Arial, Helvetica, sans-serif;
                font-size : smaller;
                 color : Red;
                 font-weight : bold;
                 }
          </style>
```

Continued

Listing 31-2 *(continued)*

```
  </head>

  <body>
        Hello World!
  </body>
</html>
```

These style sheets can also be included into an HTML file by referring to a particular Cascading Style Sheet file (`<!--#include file="filename.css"-->`) within the page.

JavaScript

JavaScript is an outstanding programming language that allows you to program both client- and server-side actions. Most developers use JavaScript to perform actions on the client-side, which allows them to program for certain events the user makes on the page.

For instance, you may have noticed that if you hover your cursor over an image (usually a button), it changes to a different image. This is called a *rollover*, and this functionality is usually done in JavaScript. It is based on an event (the hovering of the cursor over the image). You can usually program for a number of different events on the same page, such as button clicks, mouseovers, page loads, and more. Listing 31-3 provides a code example of JavaScript.

Listing 31-3: **JavaScript Code Example**

```
<html>
  <head>
        <title>My Homepage</title>
  </head>

<body>

<script language="JavaScript" type="text/javascript">
<!--
  document.write("You are using " + navigator.appName + " " +
    navigator.appVersion);
// -->
</script>

</body>
</html>
```

The JavaScript code between the `<script>` tags tells users which browser and browser version they are using. Every user sees something different, depending on the particular browser type. What is output to the user's browser is generated the moment the page is called into the browser.

Cross-Reference For an outstanding book on JavaScript, see *JavaScript Bible* (published by Hungry Minds, Inc.) by Danny Goodman and Brendan Eich.

Transact-SQL

Yes, there is an SQL Server program to build databases, but there is also a programming language that allows you to program transactions against this database. It is called *Transact-SQL* (or T-SQL). To program against an Oracle database, you would use *PL-SQL*, which is similar to T-SQL, but with slightly different syntax (it's more like C).

Using T-SQL, you can send a wide variety of commands to the database. Here is a short list of some examples:

✦ To select the entire table of data from the database, use `Select * from Customers`.

✦ To select only a selected row of data, use `Select * from Customers where customerid = 11`.

✦ To select only certain information and then reorder the data based upon selected parameters, use `Select firstname, lastname from Customers order by lastname`.

The last example selects the first name and the last name of each person in the Customers table. T-SQL then rearranges this data based on the customers' last names.

With T-SQL, it is also possible to use various other commands to perform the actions needed in the database. Table 31-1 lists the main commands to use in T-SQL statements.

	Table 31-1 T-SQL Commands	
T-SQL Command	**Description**
`Select`	Selects specified data from the chosen table. The programmer can then use this data in a number of different ways.
`Insert`	Inserts a row of data into the database. It basically creates a new row of table data.

Continued

Table 31-1 *(continued)*

T-SQL Command	Description
Update	Updates a chosen number of rows of data. By updating table data, data is changed permanantly within a field.
Delete	Deletes a specified number of rows. It is possible to delete from one row of data to every row in the database.

ADO 2.6 and ADO.NET

Microsoft's ADO.NET, the latest version after ADO 2.6, is a collection of objects that programmers use to manage data.

ADO stands for *ActiveX Data Objects*. This latest version is called ADO.NET, but if you watched Visual Studio .NET install, you may have noticed that Windows Components Install needed to install ADO 2.7. Basically, ADO.NET is ADO 2.7. It was at one time called ADO+ as well. It has a lot of different names, but it is the same product.

It is important to note that ADO 2.6 is not gone. The .NET Framework includes support for ADO 2.6 alongside ADO.NET. Therefore, you may still use ADO 2.6 in data access, but you may find ADO.NET to be a simpler alternative.

ASP.NET

Don't let this name fool you. ASP.NET is not Active Server Pages 4.0. VB .NET Internet programming is the next step for the traditional ASP 3.0 programmer, but it is a huge generational change.

Cross-Reference   For a more complete discussion of ASP.NET, see Chapter 32.

In its simplest form, ASP.NET is a new technology available with the .NET Framework that allows you to build Web Forms and Web Services. ASP.NET contains a collection of controls that you can program. Although it contains a collection of built-in controls, it enables you to develop your own controls. ASP.NET allows you to develop Web-based applications in the same manner as a Visual Basic .NET Windows Form. This new technology also has some outstanding new features that were not available in classic ASP such as ways to manage state as well as numerous options that are available in the configuration of your applications.

In programming these controls, you can currently use VB .NET, C#, or JScript. All these languages offer you more control than VBScript ever did.

Browser Issues

The issue with browsers is that you can find more than one browser out there to which you can program. Yes, it is a great thing when you have more than one choice when you go to the store to buy a particular item. This also holds true for the person who sits at home surfing the Internet, and who wants a certain browser for a specific reason. But this democracy in action does make the life of the Internet programmer rather difficult at times.

Programmers can be quite certain that pages they have designed won't appear the same way in Netscape Navigator 3.0 as in Internet Explorer 5.0. It doesn't only have to do with version numbers, either. Pages also sometimes present differently in Netscape Navigator 4.0 and Internet Explorer 4.0 because of the way each browser interprets the HTML.

When you program, you can never be sure of the browser type the user will view the site with (unless you are programming for an enclosed environment, in which the browser and its version numbers are controlled). Due to this problem, programmers have always had to program for the least-common denominator. Other times, development would draw a line for the smallest browser version they would build for (usually versions 4.0 and above). This limited the programmer's ability to build the best sites by using the latest and greatest browser features available at that moment.

Traditionally, Web developers developed their Internet applications and then tested the applications in a wide variety of browsers. How did they do this? Basically, they had two or three browsers open on their machine at the same time, and looked at each page in each of the browsers to make sure that the page they developed rendered properly. After it passed this test, they usually figured it was ready to go. Then, there was usually someone who came along later to say that he or she looked at the new site that was developed in an AOL 2.0 browser, and it appeared strange.

In their contracts to build a Web site, most developers specified that they would build for a specific version of browser just for this reason; otherwise, the job became rather difficult.

The most frustrating part about the whole thing is that although each new iteration of a browser brought with it some great new features to program, developers were unable to use these new features in a public site because they constantly needed to program for the guy who came to the site with Internet Explorer 3.0 or something similar. All Web developers who can relate to this problem are in for a pleasant surprise in the way .NET handles this situation.

.NET to the rescue!

A lot of these browser issues have now become a thing of the past, especially in regards to using JavaScript. Applications built using the .NET framework now contain a browser sniffer that first tries to detect what browser the user is using, and build the appropriate code based upon the results attained.

Do not depend too heavily on this new functionality, however. It is still important to understand the different browser behaviors and how they play a role in the presentation of the page you are building. For example, forgetting to close a table cell (`</td>`) tag causes havoc in Netscape Navigator, and breaks the page. At the same time, however, you'll find Internet Explorer more forgiving—it makes the assumption for you that the table includes a closing tag.

Another browser concern—resolution

Some other browser concerns arise when developing Internet sites that go beyond the browser version issue. You must also take into consideration the issue of appropriate screen resolution in developing sites.

Note   Every user's monitor is made up of pixels. These pixels are lined up in rows and columns, and each pixel displays a certain number of colors. A monitor that is set to 800 x 600 is therefore showing 800 pixels horizontally and 600 pixels vertically. The higher the resolution setting, the more screen real estate is available.

Back in the mid-1990s, almost all development was intended for users viewing Web sites at 640 x 480 resolution. Over time, as monitors got bigger, so did the resolution sizes that programmers developed for. Today, you can find some public sites that are best viewed with 1024 x 768 resolution (see Figure 31-1). Figures 31-2 and 31-3 show the same page at 800 x 600 and 640 x 480.

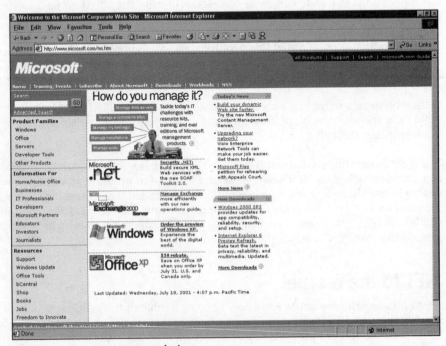

Figure 31-1: 1024 x 768 resolution

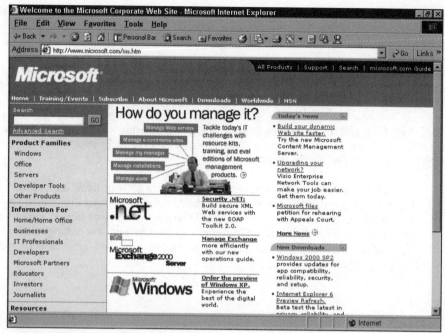

Figure 31-2: 800 x 600 resolution

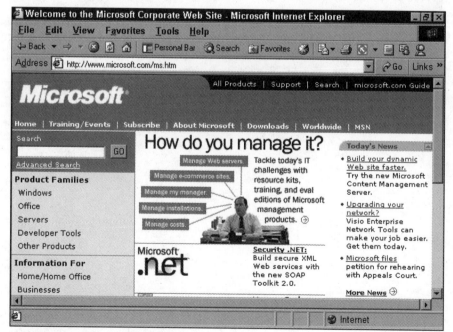

Figure 31-3: 640 x 480 resolution

As with browser versions, everyone who surfs the Internet is not necessarily using a monitor with a 1024 x 768 resolution. In fact, some people are still quite happy browsing the Internet with their 640 x 480 resolution monitors.

What happens is as follows: If you are building a site for larger resolution sizes and users view your page at 640 x 480, they are forced to scroll not only up and down, but also left to right.

So, once again, you are forced to draw a line with your development and decide what the smallest resolution you will develop for is. Presently, most sites are built with an 800 x 600 resolution in mind.

Tip
To change the resolution of your monitor, minimize all your open applications so that you can see the desktop. Right-click the desktop, and select Properties. Select the last tab in the window, Settings. You'll see the Screen Area box, in which you can change the resolution of your monitor. It displays only the settings that your monitor can handle. If you don't see the resolution you want, get a new monitor and/or graphics card.

Summary

The Internet is constantly changing. It is evolving into a dynamic communications tool for people to interact with each other and with remote applications.

The changes are so dramatic that it is still an Internet revolution, and VB .NET is the next step in that revolution. VB .NET brings a powerful and needed language to the development table, and changes the scope of Internet applications for a long time to come.

✦   ✦   ✦

Introduction to ASP.NET

by Bill Evjen

ASP.NET is built upon the .NET Framework, which means that the entire framework is available for your ASP.NET application. Don't let the ASP.NET name fool you, though. This is not Active Server Pages 4.0, but a new and exciting way of populating data and controls onto Web pages. ASP.NET is used to build Web Forms and Web Services.

When Microsoft introduced ASP 3.0 with Windows 2000 and Internet Information Server 5.0, it was a small extension from ASP 2.0. With this introduction of ASP 3.0, there were some additional objects added (for example, `ASPError` object). There were also some changes made to performance, as well as new commands such as `Server.Execute` and `Server.Transfer`.

ASP 3.0 used VBScript 5.0 or JScript 5.0, and this confined developers to the limited capabilities of these scripting languages.

With ASP.NET, Microsoft set aside VBScript, and allowed developers to use richer languages to develop server-side code. Developers can now use VB .NET, C#, or JScript .NET to code their Web pages. This chapter will focus on using VB .NET for Web development.

Why ASP.NET?

Previously in Web application development, programmers developed in a restricted environment. This was mainly due to the stateless nature of the Internet and the limiting languages that were available to develop the truly robust applications that were being demanded by the companies and organizations that wanted to use the Internet and the browser to deliver a new generation of rich applications. Now, ASP.NET has arrived on the scene answering the problems that have limited you in the past.

ASP.NET is an integrated Web development platform that allows you to use various tools to build rich Web applications. This new technology offers great new advances in state management, scalability, caching, deployment, security, performance and support for a Web services infrastructure. ASP.NET also contains a collection of controls to use and build on within the context of a Web page. ASP.NET is not replacing ASP 3.0. There isn't an ASP.NET component replacing the ASP 3.0 component on the server when you do the install. In fact, the server can run both ASP.NET pages, as well as ASP 3.0 pages, side by side. At an application level, ASP and ASP.NET do not share sessions.

ASP.NET was developed by Microsoft as Active Server Pages Plus (ASP+), and later got a name change to ASP.NET and became part of the .NET family.

ASP.NET controls

ASP.NET includes a number of controls to program. These controls are used within a Web Form to produce forms with the exact functionality that you require.

For use within the Web Form are a number of new available controls such as HTML controls, Web controls, Validation controls, and User controls. It is possible for you to program these controls using VB .NET to provide specific functionality.

In the past, you could produce some of this functionality by using JavaScript or some other language. One example was the ability to provide client-side validation of the forms before the server processed them. In the past, this was done by intermingling JavaScript within the HMTL page itself. Since the JavaScript that is supported varies from browser to browser and also from specific browser versions to others (for example, from IE 3.0 to IE 4.0), developers always had to plan on developing for the lowest common denominator — the browser with the least JavaScript support that they thought might come to their site.

Now, ASP.NET has a set of Validation controls that allow you to specify client-side validation rules. ASP.NET will take care of the JavaScript, and will code the JavaScript based on the browser the user is viewing the page with.

ASP.NET compared to ASP 3.0

ASP.NET provides a number of new and exciting features. By making some basic comparisons of ASP.NET to ASP 3.0, you will see why ASP.NET provides a better way to build Web pages. ASP.NET in the end will make for easier and faster development, and the applications built on this will be better and faster.

Page extensions

The first noticeable difference is that pages built using ASP.NET use the `aspx` extension instead of the `asp` extension that is used in ASP 3.0. With traditional ASP, whenever the server came to an `asp` page, it sent the page to be processed by the `asp.dll`, whereas the aspx pages of ASP.NET are sent to the `xspisapi.dll`.

As stated earlier, traditional ASP pages can run side-by-side with ASP.NET pages. Based on the extensions, they will be sent to the appropriate DLL for processing.

It is not possible to just change the extension name of the file to magically create an ASP.NET page. You would create an ASP.NET page only by extension, and you will get a page full of errors if you try.

Language neutrality

A majority of traditional ASP developers used VBScript as the scripting language to program their ASP pages. With ASP.NET, VBScript is no more. ASP.NET does not limit itself to which language it needs. ASP.NET allows you to use any of the .NET languages to use when programming your ASP.NET pages (for example, VB .NET and C#). ASP.NET is a set of controls that you can place on a page to provide specific functionality, and you use other languages to program a richer set of functionalities and attribute changes. No matter which .NET language you use when you build an ASP.NET application, you have access to the same controls and features that everyone else has access to. You can even plug pieces into your application and not be concerned about which .NET language they were programmed in — because it won't make any difference. All these languages work together under the same set of rules.

ASP.NET will work with any .NET-compliant language. Presently, these include VB .NET, C#, and JScript .NET. There are other languages that are being adapted to join this .NET family. For example, you can use COBOL to develop .NET applications and even Java is becoming .NET-compliant There are plans for other languages to join this .NET family, and there is even talk of COBOL and Java becoming .NET-compliant. So, it will be possible to sit on a developer team and have a COBOL programmer create a User control that you can plug into your VB .NET form. Sounds exciting, doesn't it?

Code separation

ASP.NET includes a great new feature called CodeBehind. When developing ASP pages, the developer would traditionally intermingle a number of languages within one page (I recently developed a page that contained HTML, ASP, DHTML, JavaScript, and some CSS). The page, when called by a browser, would be processed through the `asp.dll` in a linear fashion, one line at a time — starting at the top of the page. With this number of languages on a single page, the developer could have a really complicated page to maintain and update. Some developers call this *spaghetti code,* and with good reason!

There were also many situations in which you could have multiple developers working on one ASP page. You could have an HTML developer and an ASP developer working on distinct sections of the page. Then, the JavaScript wizard of the group would jump in and start programming some client-side code. With everyone coding his own sections, the code would sometimes get rather messy.

However, ASP.NET provides the means for providing the page's logic, the VB .NET code, within a separate file: the CodeBehind file (see Figure 32-1). This allows people to work in their own settings, and not bump into one another as the page develops. This is also the part of the page in which the developer can program event-driven routines. The authors will be doing all the CodeBehind files in VB .NET, even if it is also possible to code them in C#.

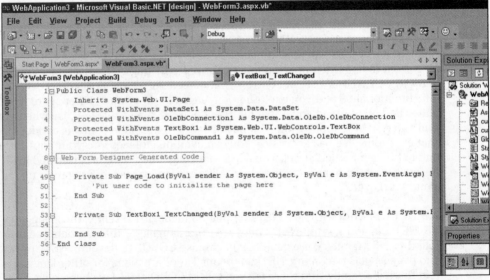

Figure 32-1: An example of a CodeBehind page. Notice that the page is written as WebForm3.aspx.vb on the tab.

Each control that is in the presentation layer can be controlled in the CodeBehind page. Even events that have nothing to do with the Web controls can be placed in the CodeBehind page, such as events for when the page initializes or is posted.

Note   *Postbacks* occur when the page and its contents are posted back to the same ASP.NET page whenever the user interacts with any of the controls on the page.

This CodeBehind feature makes maintenance and upgrading easier as the code is separated into its display and logic pieces.

Cleaner code

ASP.NET provides a cleaner coding environment. As you build Web Forms, you will find that the code required to build the build-specific functionality is a lot less than it would if you did the same thing in traditional or classic ASP (sometimes many *pages* less code are required).

Let's say that you have a customer who is building an online reservation system. The customer wants to be presented with a calendar in which a user can select a date. The user would see the calendar laid out in a table and be able to scroll through the months to find the date that is wanted. How would you do this in ASP 3.0? I have done this many times in many ways. One way was to build a COM component, and register the component on the server to use within the application. The other was to develop it straight on the page using ASP. Using the second method, every time the user needed to change months, I had to go back to the server and parse the page again through the `asp.dll`. So the user would click the arrow to take them to the next month, sit for five to ten seconds, and be presented with the next month of the calendar. Not the greatest solution, but it worked.

How would you do it ASP.NET? It is quite easy, actually. All it takes is just one line of code! That's it. It is an ASP.NET control.

```
<asp:calendar id="calendar1" runat="server" />
```

This functionality is slimmed down to just one line. Now *that* is cleaner code!

Code compilation

One of the greatest features in ASP.NET is that the code is compiled. With traditional ASP pages, each time the page was called by the browser, it was interpreted. Even if none of the information on the page changed, it was interpreted.

With ASP.NET, the code is compiled the first time into an Assembly containing MSIL and cached. The next time a user requests the page, the ASP.NET page's compiled class is sent to the user. This greatly increases overall speed. You will notice this actually happening. After you build an ASP.NET page, hit it for the first time. You will notice the browser working away and then you will finally get the page (duration depends on the server's capabilities, of course). After this first compilation of the code, you will notice that the pages usually appear so quickly that they seem to be straight HTML!

State management

Traditional ASP could deal with sessions as a means of state management, although this got rather difficult when dealing with a Web Form. If a user requests an ASP page from Server A, at the same time creating a session, and then requests an ASP page served from Server B, the session was impossible to pass between the servers.

ASP.NET provides a complete and robust means of providing state management, however. Table 32-1 describes various ASP.NET session objects.

Table 32-1
ASP.NET Session Objects

Session Type	Description
In-process mode	A session that runs in-process. This is the default setting and is the same as the ASP 3.0 session.
Out-of-process mode	This session management runs out-of-process, and stores the session information on the same server or an entirely different server.
SQL Server mode	Allows for the storing of sessions in a backend database.
Cookieless state	For clients who chose not to take advantage of the ASP.NET session state.

Cross-Reference   A more complete discussion on state management can be found in Chapter 37.

Application configuration

ASP.NET enables you to store application settings in a XML file called the web.config file. This file is composed of readable XML tags that apply certain configuration settings for the entire application. Within the web.config file, you can apply settings for the way your application handles security, sessions, and a number of other things.

The IDE

One thing that makes ASP.NET so great is Visual Studio .NET! This development environment was specially made to code ASP.NET pages as quickly and efficiently as possible.

In the past, ASP was tough to use within Visual InterDev. This was obvious by a lot of developers' preferences to use other environments, such as Notepad or Allaire's Homesite.

The Integrated Development Environment (IDE) is what the developer uses to build Web applications. In developing ASP.NET applications, you are not limited to using just Visual Studio .NET (although I recommend this). You can build your applications and pages in any text-based editor.

Visual Studio .NET will quickly provide you with the tools you need to produce the pages needed. Visual Studio .NET provides you with the drag-and-drop capabilities that other development environments presently don't have. There is also the great feature, called IntelliSense, which provides drop-down lists of possible selections — based on what you already entered.

If Visual Studio .NET is too big to install on your local machine, however, and you really want to get started with developing great Web pages using ASP.NET and VB .NET, there are other options.

Notepad

Good old trusty Notepad has been around a long time, and it is still one of the greatest coding environments available. It sure doesn't mess with your code and enables you to develop most Web pages today.

You can find Notepad by clicking Start ➪ Programs ➪ Accessories ➪ Notepad. An example of an ASP.NET page written with Notepad is shown in Figure 32-2.

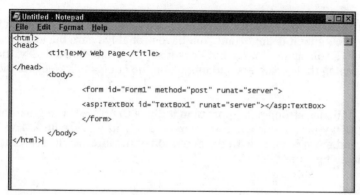

Figure 32-2: An ASP.NET page written with Notepad.

Be sure to save your code as `"FileName.aspx"`. You need to include the quotes when you save the file; otherwise, Notepad will save the file as `Filename.aspx.txt`, and that won't work.

Web Forms

Web Forms consist of the traditional forms you can build in any HTML page. Web Forms are used whenever there is some interaction with the user on the page. Some examples include any of the form elements, such as text boxes, radio buttons, and check boxes. These elements demand interaction, and therefore need to be encapsulated within a Web Form. With Web Forms, you can really get down to detail and make each aspect of the form function as you see fit. You will be building a large number of forms in the chapters that follow.

Developing Web Forms is fairly straightforward, and can be done in a couple of different ways. The first way is the method that most ASP programmers use: coding each of the elements straight into the code window of the page (HTML mode). The second way is more familiar to traditional Visual Basic 6.0 developers: using Visual Studio .NET to simply drag and drop the items onto the page, thereby building the form (Design mode).

Web Services

Although this part of the book describes everything you need to know to get started building VB .NET Web Forms using ASP.NET, it is also possible to build ASP.NET Web Services.

Cross-Reference Web Services are discussed in detail in Part VII of this book.

Web Services are used to remotely call a specific functionality across the Internet using XML to transport the data. We won't be discussing Web Services within this section of the book.

XML

Everyone is talking about XML today. Even if they don't know what it is or what it does, people do know that it is important. You have probably heard business managers asking their IT colleagues, "Yeah, but does it support XML?" (Ironically, they had problems opening their browsers and pulling up the company's Web site the day before.)

Within ASP.NET, XML has stronger support than it did with ASP 3.0. The great thing is that with ASP.NET, you can now read, write, or edit XML as you see fit. XML is becoming more and more popular with the evolution of the Internet. It is a great tool to use for handling data.

Browser sniffing

One of the greatest features of ASP.NET is that it detects what browser the user is using and then generates the HTML code based from the controls to work with that specific browser. This one functionality alleviates the headaches of many of today's developers.

Cross-Reference Browser sniffing is covered in more detail in Chapter 35.

Security

ASP.NET offers a tremendously better security feature set. With the `web.config` file, you can now modify security settings in one spot in your system, and those changes will take effect immediately without stopping and starting IIS. With ASP.NET, you can use a wide variety of authentication and authorization models, such as Windows, Forms, and Passport authentication.

Summary

This chapter was just a brief introduction to ASP.NET and some of the things you can look forward to in developing your ASP.NET applications.

✦   ✦   ✦

Page Framework

by Bill Evjen

If you are new to Internet application development, it is important to understand the page framework and what is required as far as page construction when you build your ASP.NET pages.

As with most Web pages, ASP.NET uses a considerable amount of HTML to lay out pages. The ASP.NET controls that you have at your disposal are placed within the framework of the HTML page tags.

There will be pages that are pure VB .NET code because the page will be just performing some back-end server functions and routines, but your presentation pieces (the pages that show up in the user's browser window) will be based on an HTML layout.

Understanding HTML

HTML stands for *Hypertext Markup Language* and that is exactly what it is — a markup language that marks up text to the browser. With HTML, you can specify the way the text is laid out on the page as well as create basic forms using HTML form elements.

But before getting into how to alter text with HTML, this chapter will discuss the framework that HTML will provide you in order to build your pages.

Using HTML, you will be able to lay out your ASP.NET pages within two sections of the document. Both sections are enclosed within opening and closing <html> tags, as follows:

```
<html>
          <!--Both Sections go between these
tags-->
</html>
```

Notice that the opening tag is enclosed within brackets, and the closing tag starts with a forward slash after the opening bracket.

Note   HTML tags are case-insensitive. This means that `<html>`, `<HTML>`, and `<HTml>` are the same tags.

Each of the sections that HTML provides for the development of your ASP.NET pages is discussed as follows.

Head section

The head section is the first section within the HTML document. It is not required (most things aren't in HTML), but it is recommended. The head section of the document can contain a number of items; most importantly, it contains your VB .NET scripts.

The head section of the document is constructed with an opening and closing `<head>` tag as shown here:

```
<html>
  <head>
        <!--The documents head data goes here-->
  </head>
</html>
```

All the document's header information is put in between these two tags. Some of the information that can be placed within the `<head>` tags include title information, script tags, Meta information, and document style sheets.

Listing 33-1 shows a sample of an HTML head section.

Listing 33-1: HTML **<head>** Sample

```
<html>
  <head>
    <title>My First Document</title>

    <!--Client side comments go here-->

    <meta http-equiv="Description" content="This is my site
    description.">
    <meta http-equiv="Keywords" content="Keywords go here
    for search engines">

    <script language="vb" runat="server">
        <!--VB .NET page code goes here-->
    </script>
```

```
<style type="text/css">
    <!--CSS Style Sheet goes here-->
</style>
</head>
</html>
```

First of all, this is just a sample header section of a HTML document, and everything here is optional. The first tag within the head section is the page title, which is enclosed within `<title>` tags. It is always a good habit to include a title for your page. The contents of this tag are placed in the top bar of the browser to help the user navigate your site.

The next line is the comment tag. This is a client-side comment, meaning that anyone who views the source of your page can see this comment embedded within the code. So don't include information that you don't want the users to see. Client-side comments are a good spot to place technical contact information, technical help, and any other information that you want clients to see if they are browsing through your Web page's code.

It is good habit to include comments (whether they are client-side or server-side comments) within your code to explain what is going on with the code and what sort of functionality the page provides. This is necessary because after you finish building the page, you will probably not be the one who maintains the page and its code years from now. Including comments make it a lot easier on the next developers who are told to add or fix something. With proper comments, they won't have to spend so much time trying to figure out what you were doing.

The Meta tags follow the HTML comments. There are a number of Meta tags, but two in particular are important for getting your site listed on search engines: the Meta description tag and the keywords tag. Did you ever wonder how some search engines provide all that page information, or how they even find the pages you are looking for when you type **"VB .NET"** into the search engine? They do it with the help of these tags. The search engines look for these tags when they parse the page, and log both the page's description and keywords to use within their search engine. So it is important to craft these tags with some thought if getting into a search engine is important for the page's promotion.

After the Meta tags are the script tags. For your script tag, you chose the language of the script to be VB .NET, but you can also choose a number of other languages to use for your script. You are also telling the server that you want to process this particular script on the server before the page is rendered. In your page construction, you would put all of our VB .NET code between these scripts. You will see this in action in the next chapter.

The final tag in the sample head section is the style tag. In this example, you use Cascading Style Sheets to set style attributes to particular HTML tags.

Body section

The second section is the body section of the document. It is necessary because the page you build won't display anything without it.

The body section is constructed using opening and closing `<body>` tags.

```
<html>
   <head>
   </head>

   <body>
        <!--Body Section goes here-->
   </body>
</html>
```

The document's presentation piece is placed between the body tags. One of the simplest ways to provide content to display within the body section is to put static text between the tags. In most cases, though, you will mark up the text with some formatting to make it a little more presentable to the user who is coming to your page.

A number of tags are used to change the format of the text that you place within the body tags. If you are unsure about which tags to use, there are plenty of excellent books on this subject that you can refer to.

It is important to understand that these formatting HTML tags are constructed using the same principles that are used to lay out the head and body sections of the document. For most HTML opening tags, there is a closing tag.

```
<b>Hello</b> John!
```

In this example, you use the HTML bold tag to bold the `Hello` text. This simple example shows the following:

```
Hello John!
```

Now that is pretty simple.

The body section is also where you place all the ASP.NET controls. The HTML Server controls, Web controls, and Validation controls are placed within the body section to create user interfaces and presentation pieces. These controls can interact with VB .NET code that is in-between the script tags in the head section or with VB .NET code that is in the CodeBehind page.

Understanding Internet Infrastructure

The pages that you view on the Internet through your browser are single pages that are part of a larger *Internet application*. An Internet application is a collection of files and components that work together to use the browser as the portal of a presentation piece or a full-blown application.

These Internet applications are then placed on a computer that has software on it that allows remote requests (requests for the Web page). For these purposes, you will deal with Microsoft's servers, such as Microsoft's Internet Information Server (IIS). Active Server Pages 3.0 was part of IIS 5.0.

When you are on the Internet, you pull up your browser and type in an URL. This URL makes an HTTP request to the appropriate server, which can be on your own network or thousands of miles away. The server takes your request, renders the page you requested, and then sends it back as an HTTP reply. Not bad, eh?

Based upon the extension of the file that you request, the server will act accordingly. If it is an HTML file with the `html` or `htm` extension, IIS sends the contents of the file to the browser, where the browser in turn interprets the HTML tags and presents your document.

If the file is an ASP 3.0 page with the `asp` extension, IIS takes this file and sends it to the `asp.dll` on the server. The `asp.dll` then parses through the file and executes all of the server-side code.

IIS treats the `aspx` files the same way, except that it sends them to the `xspisapi.dll`, and renders the controls in the appropriate way.

Setting Up Your Server in Windows 2000

You can turn your Windows 2000 computer into a server and work through all the Web examples presented in this section of the book. Not all Windows 2000 servers come configured with IIS already to go, but it is easy to do.

If you are unsure whether your Windows 2000 Professional operating system is already configured to act as a server, open up Windows Explorer and look on your hard drive (usually `Local Disk (C:)`). Double-click this drive; if you see an `InetPub` folder with a `wwwroot` folder contained within, you already have it installed and don't need to go any further (an example of this can be seen in Figure 33-1). If you don't see these two folders, you have to install IIS on your machine.

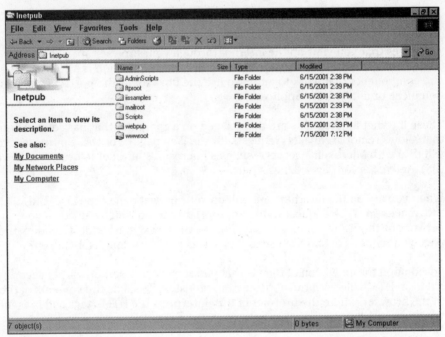

Figure 33-1: The Inetpub folder. The last folder (with the hand holding the folder) is the wwwroot folder.

To install IIS:

1. Pull up your Control Panel (Start ➪ Settings ➪ Control Panel).

2. Click Add/Remove Programs.

3. Click Add/Remove Windows Components, which is located on the left side of the dialog box.

   The Windows Components Wizard is displayed (see Figure 33-2).

4. Check the Internet Information Services (IIS) box.

5. Click Next (located at the bottom of the dialog box).

   The wizard installs IIS.

After you install IIS, go to your local hard drive and look for the InetPub folder. Double-click this folder; you will see the wwwroot folder. When you build Web pages, you place the files within the wwwroot folder. You can then gain access to the files through your browser, just as if you were surfing on the Internet.

Place one of the simple HTML files within the wwwroot folder, and pull up your browser. Type the following URL: http://localhost/default.html.

`Default.html` is the name of the file. This will pull up the file in the browser window as if you were on the Internet. You are, in effect, because you make your HTTP request to a server (local server) and then IIS sends back an HTTP reply (to your browser).

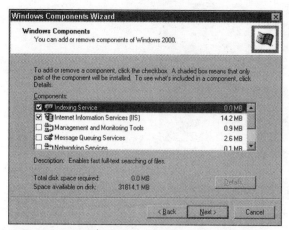

Figure 33-2: The Windows Components Wizard

Using Visual Studio .NET to Build Your Web Forms

In the previous chapter, you learned about the different Integrated Development Environments (IDEs) you can use, including Visual Studio .NET. VS .NET is presently the best choice for developing your VB .NET Web applications.

Cross-Reference

Visual Studio .NET is covered in detail in Part III of this book.

Even though VS .NET was covered in detail earlier in the book, the following sections discuss setting up your first Web application.

Creating your first Web application

Pull up VS .NET. Depending on how you have the IDE configured, you should see the Start Page, as well as the Solution Explorer and the empty Properties Box.

The Start Page lists any applications that you may have already started. To build your new application, click New Project within the Start Page. The New Project dialog box displays (see Figure 33-3).

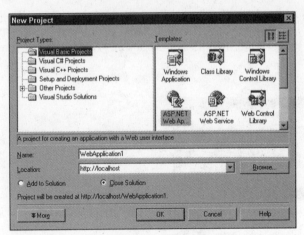

Figure 33-3: The New Project dialog box

For the purposes of this book, select the Visual Basic Projects folder. You see a selection of templates in the right window of the dialog box. The list of dialog boxes include the following:

✦ Windows Application

✦ Class Library

✦ Windows Control Library

✦ ASP.NET Web Application

✦ ASP.NET Web Service

✦ Web Control Library

✦ Console Application

✦ Windows Service

✦ Empty Project

✦ Empty Web Project

✦ New project in existing folder

You should select ASP.NET Web Application, which is a project for creating an application with a Web user interface. Name the application whatever you want, and the location where the application will reside should be `http://localhost/`. After you configure this dialog box, click Open.

VS .NET then creates an application folder within your `wwwroot` folder. Within the folder, it places a number of files that are important for your application. You can view all these files that are created within the Solution Explorer box in VS .NET (see Figure 33-4).

Figure 33-4: The Solution Explorer allows you to view all the files within your solution.

VS .NET will have created the following files for your application:

✦ References: This is a folder that contains application references to .NET Framework namespaces. If you open the folder within the Solution Explorer window (click once on the plus sign next to the folder), you will notice what namespaces are there at that moment. At this point your application is referencing only System, System.Data, System.Drawing, System.Web, System.Web.Services, and System.XML.

✦ AssemblyInfo.vb: This VB .NET file contains all the information for your assembly, such as versioning and dependencies.

✦ Global.asax: Similar to the Global.asa file from ASP 3.0. This is the ASP.NET application file in which you can place code to respond to application-level events.

✦ Styles.css: A Cascading Style Sheet file that applies styles to your documents.

✦ Web.Config: The configuration file that contains the application settings. This is an XML-based file that is easy to understand.

✦ WebApplication1.vsdisco: This is an XML file that contains informational links about an ASP.NET Web Service.

✦ WebForm1.aspx: This is the first Web Form ASP.NET page for your application. If you want, right-click the file and rename it default.aspx.

Working with your first Web Form

Now that you have your first Web Form open, notice that you see a page that contains a lot of dots throughout the page. This means that you are working within the GridLayout mode. To change to the FlowLayout mode, click anywhere within the design area. Notice that a long list of properties now appears within the Properties box (see Figure 33-5). Scroll down until you find the pageLayout property, and change it there.

FlowLayout means that all the controls will be laid out in a left-right and up-down manner. GridLayout lays out the controls based upon XY positioning, similar to the way it was in Visual Basic 6.0. ASP developers will be more familiar with the FlowLayout mode, and Visual Basic 6.0 developers will be more familiar with the GridLayout mode.

Figure 33-5: Changing the PageLayout property

Notice two tabs at the bottom of the page at the bottom of the code window. The tab on the left is the Design tab (you are presently in Design mode). The right tab is the HTML tab. Clicking the HTML tab displays the code page. Feel free to work in any view that you desire, and switch back and forth between the views. Changes that are made in one of the views are reflected in the opposing view.

Throughout this part of the book, you build Web Form applications in HTML mode because it offers the greatest understanding of what is happening in the code. This may not be the fastest way of developing your page, but it does offer you the most understanding. However, you can also code these examples by using the Design mode. It is recommended that you work in HTML mode until you truly understand how all the controls and your VB .NET code work together. After gaining this insight, feel free to switch over to Design mode.

Working in Design mode

If you work in Design mode, you see the Toolbox on the left side of the VS .NET application. Clicking the Web Forms tab within the Toolbox displays all the Web controls and Validation controls. The HTML tab shows you a large list of HTML elements that can be converted to HTML Server controls.

To build a form within Design mode, just drag-and-drop your selected controls onto the page. To apply any VB .NET code to the control, just double-click the control. You will see the CodeBehind page, which is a separate container for all your server-side code. It already created a Page_Load routine for you as well as a routine for the control that you just clicked.

Note   The Page_Load event is fired each time the page is loaded or reloaded.

Using the tabs at the top, you can switch between your CodeBehind page and the Presentation page with ease. Double-clicking any control returns you to the CodeBehind page.

After you finish building your application, right-click the file within the Server Explorer box, and choose Build and Browse. This saves the file and runs the file through a browser, but all within VS .NET. If there are errors on the page, VS .NET will inform you of those errors.

Working with controls

You can also work with the control's properties or attributes within the Design mode of VS .NET. Click once on the control that you want to work with, and notice that all the control's properties appear in the Properties box. Changing any of the properties here will be reflected back to the control. After changing the properties so that the control is as you want it, click HTML mode and see how VS .NET altered the code to reflect the changes you made in Design mode.

Adding more files

It is quite rare when an Internet application contains only one page. You usually need a number of pages. To create another page within VS .NET, right-click your application within the Server Explorer box and select Add. Scroll down and choose Add New Item. You will be presented with the Add New Item dialog box (see Figure 33-6).

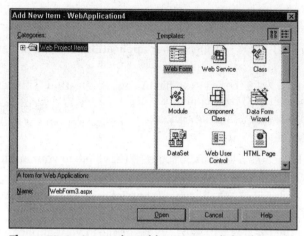

Figure 33-6: Access the Add New Item dialog box to create another item.

You see the following items, all of which can be added to your application:

✦ **Web Form:** Creates a `WebForm.aspx` file in your application. This is the form for Web applications.

✦ **Web Service:** Creates a `Service1.asmx` file in your application. This is a visually designed class for creating a Web Service.

✦ **Class:** Creates a `Class1.vb` file in your application. This is an empty class declaration.

✦ **Module:** Creates a `Module1.vb` file in your application. This is a file for storing groups of functions.

✦ **Component Class:** Creates a `Component1.vb` file in your application. This is a class for creating components using the visual designer.

✦ **Data Form Wizard:** Creates a `DataWebForm1.aspx` file in your application. This is a data form for Web applications.

✦ **DataSet:** Creates a `Dataset1.xsd` file in your application. This is a file for creating an XML schema with DataSet classes.

✦ **Web User Control:** Creates a `WebUserControl1.ascx` file in your application. This is an ASP.NET server control created using the visual designer.

✦ **HTML Page:** Creates an `HTMLPage1.htm` file in your application. This is an HTML page that can include client-side code.

✦ **Frameset:** Creates a `Frameset1.htm` file in your application. This is an HTML file that hosts multiple HTML pages.

✦ **Style Sheet:** Creates a `StyleSheet1.css` file in your application. This is a cascading style sheet used for rich HTML-style definitions.

✦ **XML File:** Creates an `XMLFile1.xml` file in your application. This is basically a blank XML file.

✦ **XML Schema:** Creates an `XMLSchema1.xsd` file in your application. This is a file for creating a schema for XML documents.

✦ **XSLT File:** Creates an `XSLTFile1.xslt` file in your application. This is a file used to transform XML documents.

✦ **Web Custom Control:** Creates a `WebCustomControl1.vb` file in your application. This is a class for creating an ASP.NET server control.

✦ **Code File:** Creates a `CodeFile1.vb` file in your application. This is basically a blank code file.

✦ **Dynamic Discovery File:** Creates a `Disco1.vsdisco` file in your application. This is a file used to publish information about a Web Service.

✦ **Static Discovery File:** Creates a `Disco1.disco` file in your application. This is a file used to publish information about a Web Service.

✦ **Global Application Class:** Creates a class for handling Web application events.

✦ **Web Configuration File:** Creates a file used to configure Web application settings.

✦ **Text File:** Creates a `TextFile1.txt` file in your application. This is a blank text file.

✦ **Installer Class:** Creates an `Installer1.vb` file in your application. This is a class to be invoked at setup time.

✦ **Crystal Report:** Creates a `CrystalReport1.rpt` file in your application. This is a Crystal Report file that publishes data to a Windows or Web Form.

✦ **Bitmap File:** Creates a `Bitmap1.bmp` file in your application. This is a Win32 bitmap file.

✦ **Cursor File:** Creates a `Cursor1.cur` file in your application. This is a Win32 cursor file.

✦ **Icon File:** Creates an `Icon1.ico` file in your application. This is a Win32 icon file.

✦ **Assembly Resource File:** Creates a `Resource1.resx` file in your application. This is a .NET resource file.

✦ **Assembly Information File:** Creates an `AssemblyInfo1.vb` file in your application. This is a file containing general assembly information.

✦ **JScript:** Creates a `JScript1.js` file in your application. This is a script file containing JScript code.

✦ **VBScript:** Creates a `VBScript1.vbs` file in your application. This is a script file containing VBScript code.

✦ **Windows Host Script:** Creates a `WindowsScript1.wsf` file in your application. This is a file containing script that is run as a Windows program.

As you can tell, there are a large number of files that can be added to your Web applications. For the example in the following chapters, you will mainly be dealing with creating Web Forms (the first choice).

To create a Web Form, just select it from the list, and click Open. The new Web Form will then be created, opened, and displayed in VS .NET.

Using page directives

Page directives are very similar to application directives in the `global.asax` file. Page directives are commands to the compiler to use when the page compiles. Although there are only three application directives available for use, there are eight page directives available for use. Page directives are meant to be used with ASP.NET pages (`aspx`) and within User controls (`ascx`).

Before each of the page directives is discussed, it is important to understand how to write a directive within your ASP.NET pages or User controls. The directive is written in the following format:

```
<%@ [Directive] [Attribute=Value] %>
```

The best bet is to put all your page directives at the top of the page. It isn't required, but it makes the code more manageable and readable. The directive is opened and closed with brackets that are the same as they are in classic ASP — with the opening <% and closing %>. The directive allows for as many attribute/ value pairs as you want. If you have more than one attribute, the directive would be written as follows:

```
<%@ [Directive] [Attribute=Value] [Attribute=Value] %>
```

Table 33-1 describes the page directives that are available for use within your pages.

Table 33-1
Page Directives

Page Directive	Description
@Page	Enables you to specify page-specific attributes and values for use when the page parses or compiles.
@Control	Defines control-specific attributes and values to use when the page parses or compiles.
@Import	Imports namespaces into the Page or User control.
@Implements	Implements a specified .NET Framework interface.
@Register	Associates aliases with namespaces and class names for notation in custom server control syntax.
@Assembly	Links an assembly to the Page or User control.
@OutputCache	Controls the output caching policies of a Page or User control.
@Reference	Links a Page or User control to the current Page or User control.

In the following sections, you run through the page directives and see what you can do with them.

@Page

The @Page directive allows you to specify page attributes and the values that are used when the page is parsed or compiled. There are a large number of @Page attributes available for use within the page directive.

Table 33-2 briefly describes each of the @Page attributes that are available.

Table 33-2 @Page Directive Attributes	
Attribute	**Description**
AspCompat	When set to True, AspCompat permits the page to be executed on a single-threaded apartment thread. Default setting is False.
AutoEventWireup	When set to True, specifies whether the pages events are autowired. Default setting is True.
Buffer	When set to True, it enables HTTP response buffering.
ClassName	Specifies the name of the class that will be bound to the page when the page is compiled.
ClientTarget	Specifies the target user agent the page will render content for.
CodePage	Indicates the code page value for the response.
CompilerOptions	A compiler string that indicates compilation options for the page.
ContentType	Defines the HTTP content type of the response as a standard MIME type.
Culture	Specifies the culture setting of the page.
Debug	When set to True, compiles the page with debug symbols.
Description	Provides a text description of the page. It is ignored by the ASP.NET parser.
EnableSessionState	When set to True, session state for the page will be enabled. The default setting is True.
EnableViewState	If left on the default setting of True, view state will be maintained across pages.
EnableViewStateMac	When set to True, the page runs a machine authentication check on the page's view state when the page is posted back from the user. The default is False.
ErrorPage	Specifies a URL for all unhandled page exceptions.
Explicit	When set to True, Visual Basic Option Explicit is enabled. The default setting is False.
Inherits	Specifies a CodeBehind class for the page to inherit.
Language	Defines the language that is being used for any inline rendering and script blocks.
LCID	Defines the locale identifier for the Web Forms page.

Continued

Table 33-2 *(continued)*

Attribute	Description
ResponseEncoding	Specifies the response encoding of page content.
Src	Points to the source file of the CodeBehind class of the page being rendered.
Strict	When set to True, compiles the page using the Visual Basic Option Strict mode. The default setting is False.
Trace	When set to True, page tracing will be enabled. The default setting is False.
TraceMode	Specifies how the trace messages are displayed when tracing is enabled. The settings are either SortByTime or SortByCategory. The default setting is SortByTime.
Transaction	Specifies whether transactions are supported on the page. The settings for this attribute are either NotSupported, Supported, Required, and RequiresNew. The default is NotSupported.
WarningLevel	Specifies the compiler warning level at which to stop compilation of the page. Possible values are 0 through 4.

It is important to note that the @Page directive can be used only in your ASP.NET pages, and it isn't possible to place these directives within any User control.

An example of using the @Page directive with multiple attributes is as follows:

```
<%@ Page Language="VB" Tracing="True"
TraceMode="SortByCategory" Description="This is a page for
updating the Project Management System."%>
```

@Control

The control directive is the same as the @Page directive, except that you use the @Control directives within User controls. The control directive allows you to specify User control attributes, and their values are used in the User control as the page is parsed or compiled. The number of available attributes for the User control is a little less than the @Page control, but you have 12 attributes at your disposal.

Table 33-3 describes the control directive attributes that are available.

Table 33-3
Control Directive Attributes

Attribute	Description
AutoEventWireup	When set to True, specifies whether the User control's events are autowired. Default setting is True.
ClassName	Specifies the name of the class that will be bound to the page when the page is compiled.
CompilerOptions	A compiler string that indicates compilation options for the page.
Debug	When set to True, compiles the page with debug symbols.
Description	Provides a text description of the User control. It is ignored by the ASP.NET parser.
EnableViewState	If set to the default setting of True, view state is maintained across pages.
Explicit	When set to True, Visual Basic Option Explicit is enabled. The default setting is False.
Inherits	Specifies a CodeBehind class for the User control to inherit.
Language	Defines the language that is being used for any inline rendering and script blocks
Strict	When set to True, this compiles the User control using the Visual Basic Option Strict mode. The default setting is False.
Src	Points to the source file of the CodeBehind class of the User control being requested.
WarningLevel	Specifies the compiler warning level at which to stop compilation of the User control. Possible values are 0 through 4.

The important point about control directives is that they are meant to be used only in User controls (ascx).

An example of using the control directive with multiple attributes is as follows:

```
<%@ Control Language="VB" Explicit="True" Description="This
is the calculator user control for Intertech." %>
```

@Import

The import directive specifies the namespaces to be imported into the page or User control, thereby making all classes and interfaces available to the page. This directive supports only one attribute: Namespace.

The Namespace attribute directly specifies the namespace to be imported. It is important to note that with the import directive, the import directive cannot contain more than one attribute/value pair.

An example that imports two different namespaces using the import directive is as follows:

```
<%@ Import Namespace="System.Data" %>
<%@ Import Namespace="System.Net" %>
```

The important thing to understand is that there are already a number of namespaces being automatically imported into the page and the application. The following namespaces are already imported:

```
System
System.Collections
System.Collections.Specialized
System.Configuration
System.IO
System.Text
System.Text.RegularExpressions
System.Web
System.Web.Caching
System.Web.Security
System.Web.SessionState
System.Web.UI
System.Web.UI.HtmlControls
System.Web.UI.WebControls
```

Importing a namespace into your page or User control gives you the opportunity to use the classes without fully identifying the class name. For instance, by importing the namespace System.Data.OleDB into the ASP.NET page, you can then refer to classes within this namespace by just expressing the singular class name (for example, OLEDBConnection instead of System.Data.OleDB.OLEDBConnection).

@Implements

The implements directive specifies the page that will implement a specified .NET Framework interface. This directive supports only one attribute: Interface.

The Interface attribute directly specifies the .NET Framework interface. When the Page or User control implements an interface, it has direct access to all its events, methods, and properties.

An example of the implements directive is as follows:

```
<%@ Implements Interface="System.Web.UI.IValidator" %>
```

@Register

The `register` directive associates aliases with namespaces and class names for notation in custom controls. One example of using the `register` directive is to register your User controls onto your ASP.NET page. This directive supports a number of different attributes, as described in Table 33-4.

<table>
<tr><td colspan="2" align="center">Table 33-4
Register Directive Attributes</td></tr>
<tr><td>*Attribute*</td><td>*Description*</td></tr>
<tr><td>`tagprefix`</td><td>The alias to relate with the namespace.</td></tr>
<tr><td>`tagname`</td><td>The alias to relate to the class name.</td></tr>
<tr><td>`Namespace`</td><td>The namespace to relate with `tagprefix`.</td></tr>
<tr><td>`Src`</td><td>The location of the User control.</td></tr>
<tr><td>`Assembly`</td><td>The assembly of the namespace you are associating with the tagprefix is located.</td></tr>
</table>

An example of using the register directive to import a User control to an ASP.NET page is as follows:

```
<%@ Register Tagprefix="MyTag" Namespace="MyName:MyNameSpace"
Assembly="MyAssembly" %>
```

Cross-Reference See Chapter 34 for more information on User controls.

@Assembly

The `assembly` directive attaches assemblies to a Page or User control as it compiles, thereby making all the assembly's classes and interfaces available to it. This directive supports two attributes: `Name` and `Src`.

✦ `Name`: This `assembly` directive attribute allows you to specify the name of an assembly. This assembly is the one that will be used to attach to the page files. The name of the assembly should include only the file name, not the file's extension. For instance, if the file is `MyAssembly.vb`, the value of the name attribute could be `MyAssembly`.

✦ `Src`: This application directive attribute allows you to specify the source of the assembly file to use in compilation.

An example of the `assembly` directive is as follows:

```
<%@ Assembly Name="MyAssembly" %>
<%@ Assembly Src="MyAssembly.vb" %>
```

@OutputCache

The `outputcache` directive controls the output caching policies of a Page or User control. This directive supports six attributes, as described in Table 33-5.

<table>
<tr><th colspan="2">Table 33-5
OutputCache Directive Attributes</th></tr>
<tr><th>Attribute</th><th>Description</th></tr>
<tr><td>Duration</td><td>The duration of time in seconds that the Page or User control is cached in the system.</td></tr>
<tr><td>Location</td><td>OutputCacheLocation enumeration value. The default is Any.</td></tr>
<tr><td>VaryByCustom</td><td>A string specifying the custom output caching requirements.</td></tr>
<tr><td>VaryByHeader</td><td>A semicolon-separated list of HTTP headers used to vary the output cache.</td></tr>
<tr><td>VaryByParam</td><td>A semicolon-separated list of strings used to vary the output cache.</td></tr>
<tr><td>VaryByControl</td><td>A semicolon-separated list of strings used to vary the output cache.</td></tr>
</table>

An example of the `outputcache` directive is as follows:

```
<%@ OutputCache Duration="180" VaryByParam="none" %>
```

The `Duration` attribute in this tag specifies that the page or control should be cached for 180 seconds.

@Reference

The `reference` directive declares that another Page or User control should be compiled along with the active page or control. This directive supports two attributes: `Page` and `Control`.

✦ `Page`: The name of the page that should be compiled along with the present page or control.

✦ `Control`: The name of the control that should be compiled along with the present page or control.

An example of the `reference` directive is as follows:

```
<%@ Reference Control="MyControl.ascx" %>
```

Summary

This chapter took a look at the basic structure you need to follow when creating ASP.NET pages that use VB .NET. You also learned how to create a local server on your Windows 2000 computer, and how to create your first Web application. You also learned about directives that are available to use on your ASP.NET page and your User controls.

✦   ✦   ✦

HTML Server Controls

by Bill Evjen

In This Chapter

Understanding HTML
Server controls

Building XHTML-
compliant code

Common tag
attributes

Programming against
HTML Server controls

Creating an HTML
Server control in
Design mode

Using VB .NET and ASP.NET together, you can get programmatic access to a number of HTML elements. By default, ASP.NET treats HTML elements as they have always been treated in the past — as literal text that is used as traditional HTML markup. But by adding a bit of code, programmers open the door to these elements and can easily manipulate them in a number of ways.

Note HTML stands for *Hypertext Markup Language*. The latest version is presently HTML 4.0.

HTML elements are HTML tags. Some examples include the <a>, <font>, <button>, and <input> tags.

Though HTML is not covered in this book in too much detail, it is quite vital that you understand HTML in order to adequately develop Web pages.

When you wish to program HTML elements, you need to write your HTML to comply with XHTML standards as well as include various attributes within the tags themselves.

This chapter covers everything that you need to know to program HTML controls for your ASP.NET Web applications and the most common attributes that you might use in developing these controls. You find HTML controls simple and very easy to work into your applications.

XHTML-Compliant Code

When writing HTML Server controls to program, it is very important to write the controls so that they are XHTML-compliant.

The rules are few and fairly straightforward. The first rule to follow is that tags are nested properly. To nest tags properly, you need to open and close them in a specific order. The rule is to close the tags in the reverse order in which you open them. For instance, if you open Tag A and then you open Tag B, you cannot close Tag A until you close Tag B.

INCORRECT:

```
<a href="somepage.aspx"><b>Hello World!</a></b>
```

As you can see from the following example, you open the `<a>` tag and then open the `<b>` tag to make the link bold, but you closed the `<a>` tag before you closed the `<b>` tag. This is not XHTML-compliant code. This code should instead be written as follows:

CORRECT:

```
<a href="somepage.aspx"><b>Hello World!</b></a>
```

It is also important to note that for every opening tag, there must be a closing tag for all tags that have closing tags. So make sure that whenever you open any of these HTML tags, you also close the tag in the proper place within the document.

For tags that are singular elements, you now need to end the tag with a `/>` to close the tag in order to be XHTML-compliant. For instance, the `<hr>` tag does not have opening and closing tags, instead, it is a singular element. With XHTML, you would now display the `<hr>` tag as `<hr/>` when you are programming it.

Common Tag Attributes

In order for traditional HTML elements to work as HTML Server controls, you have to add some common attributes to work against in order to change the element's functionality.

The first attribute that every HTML Server control must contain is a `runat=server` within the tag itself. The attribute `runat=server` tells the processing server that the tag is processed on the server, and is not to be considered as a traditional HTML element. Also, the tag must contain an ID attribute in order for the server to identify it and for you to program it. The following example is a HTML Server control.

```
<a id="FirstLink" runat="server">Click Me!</a>
```

This `<a>` tag has been turned into an HTML Server control by its inclusion of the ID and the `runat=server` attributes.

Overview of HTML Server Controls

ASP.NET Server controls are group of new controls provided by .NET. HTML Server controls are one type of control now available. Other types include Web Server controls and Validation controls.

Figure 34-1 shows the hierarchy of HTML server controls in the System.Web. UI.HtmlControls namespace.

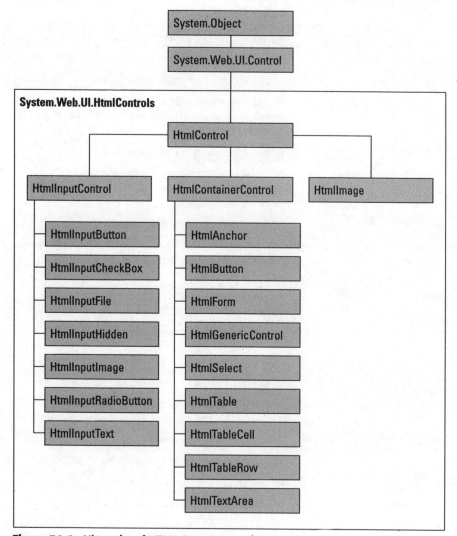

Figure 34-1: Hierarchy of HTML Server controls

HTML Server controls map directly to their corresponding HTML elements. When converting ASP 3.0 pages to ASP.NET pages, using HTML Server controls is a less-painful solution than using ASP.NET's Web controls (discussed in the next chapter).

Table 34-1 describes these controls in more detail.

Table 34-1
HTML Server Controls Quicklist

Control	Related HTML Tag
HTMLAnchor	Allows access to program against the `<a>` tag.
HTMLButton	Allows access to program against the `<button>` tag.
HTMLForm	Allows access to program against the `<form>` tag.
HTMLGeneric	This control allows access to HTML tags that are not represented by any HTML Server control specifically; for example, the `<span>`, `<div>`, and `<font>` tags.
HTMLImage	Allows access to program against the `<img>` tag.
HTMLInputButton	Allows access to program against the `<input type=button>`, `<input type=submit>`, and `<input type=reset>` tags.
HTMLInputCheckbox	Allows access to program against the `<input type=checkbox>` tag.
HTMLInputFile	Allows access to program against the `<input type=file>` tag.
HTMLInputHidden	Allows access to program against the `<input type=hidden>` tag.
HTMLInputImage	Allows access to program against the `<input type=image>` tag.
HTMLInputRadioButton	Allows access to program against the `<input type=radio>` tag.
HTMLInputText	Allows access to program against the `<input type=text>` and `<input type=password>` tags.
HTMLSelect	Allows access to program against the `<select>` tag.
HTMLTable	Allows access to program against the `<table>` tag.
HTMLTableCell	Allows access to program against the `<td>` and `<th>` tags.
HTMLTableRow	Allows access to program against the `<tr>` tag.
HTMLTextArea	Allows access to program against the `<textarea>` tag.

Descriptions of the HTML Server Controls and How to Program Them

The following pages describe in more detail what each Server control is and, more importantly, how to actually program them in your code. The great thing about these controls is that all the normal attributes you would have in the tags are now dynamic and under your control. You see how to control them in some of the following examples.

HTMLAnchor control

The `HTMLAnchor` control allows access to program the HTML `<a>` tag. This is the tag used to create links within HTML documents.

Listing 34-1 is an example of how to control this tag programmatically. An example of how this code renders out to the browser can be seen in Figure 34-2.

Listing 34-1: **HTMLAnchor Example**

```
<html>
  <head>
          <title>HTMLAnchor</title>

<script language=VB runat=server>
  Sub Page_Load(sender As Object, e As EventArgs)
          PageLink.href = "http://www.hungryminds.com/"
  End Sub
</script>

  </head>
  <body>
  Here is an example of using the HTMLAnchor Control<p>
  <a id=PageLink runat=server>Click Me!</a>
  </body>
</html>
```

As stated in previous chapters, you can tell right away that this simple page is constructed quite differently from the way it would be constructed in ASP 3.0. First of all, there are no delimiters. Instead of traditional `<%` tags that enclosed ASP code, you now define all your server-side code within `<script>` tags. Within the script tag itself you define the language that you are going to use in the code using attributes. For this book, you always use `language=VB`, but you could also use `language=C#`. The other attribute that you need to make sure is within the script tag is the `runat=server` attribute. This attribute informs the ASP.NET processor that this script is processed on the server.

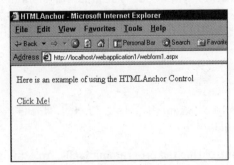

Figure 34-2: The HTMLAnchor control where the href attribute is set at runtime

The server-side code is within the `<head>` part of the code. This code is processed before the page is sent to the browser. Using VB .NET, you specify in the `Page_Load` subroutine that the `PageLink`'s `href` attribute is equal to `http://www.hungryminds.com/`. If you look further in the code, the `<a>` tag has the ID `PageLink`, and that is how the tag gets referenced. You also ensure that this tag is processed on the server by using the `runat=server` attribute.

Note   To reference any tag's attribute, reference the tag's ID, followed by a period and then by the attribute's name. The reference should be constructed in the following manner: `IDName.Tag_Attribute`. For example, to reference the `href` attribute in the `<a>` tag, it would be `IDName.href`, and to reference the `target` attribute in the same tag, it would be `IDName.target`.

HTMLButton control

The `HTMLButton` control allows access to program the HTML `<button>` tag. This is the tag used to place clickable buttons within HTML documents. The only event that you can program for this element is if someone clicks the button. For this, you can provide custom code for the `ServerClick` event.

Listing 34-2 shows an example of how to control this tag programmatically. In this example, you use a little of what you learned from the `HTMLAnchor` control and build upon that. See Figure 34-3 to see how this example should appear in the browser.

Listing 34-2: **HTMLButton Control Example**

```
<html>
  <head>
          <title>HTMLButton</title>

<script language=VB runat=server>
  Sub Page_Load(sender As Object, e As EventArgs)
        PageLink.href = "http://www.hungryminds.com/"
  End Sub

  Sub Button1_onclick(sender As Object, e As EventArgs)
        PageLink.href = "http://www.hungryminds.com/"
        Span1.InnerHtml = "You chose Hungry Minds"
  End Sub

  Sub Button2_onclick(sender As Object, e As EventArgs)
        PageLink.href = "http://www.microsoft.com/"
        Span1.InnerHtml = "You chose Microsoft"
  End Sub
</script>

  </head>

  <body>

  <form runat="server">
  Here is an example of using the HTMLButton Control<p>
  <button id="button1" runat="server"
  OnServerClick="Button1_OnClick">
  Change Link to Hungry Minds
  </button>
  <p>
  <button id="button2" runat="server"
  OnServerClick="Button2_OnClick">Change Link to
  Microsoft</button>
<p>
  <a id=PageLink runat=server>Click Me!</a> 
  <span id="span1" runat="server"/>
  </form>

  </body>
</html>
```

Once again, the CodeBehind feature was not used here in order to show you how all the code works together a little better. The server-side code in Listing 34-2 is between the <script> tags. Within this are three subroutines. The first one is the Page_Load event. This is the code that the server processes when it is first rendering the page.

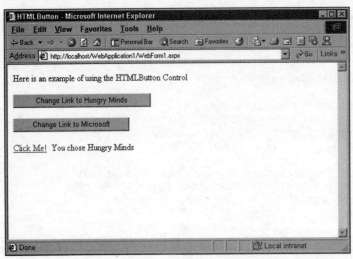

Figure 34-3: An example of the HTMLButton Control in action. This is what the user would see after pressing the Change Link to Hungry Minds button.

The code in the `Page_Load` event assigns the `<a>` tag's `href` the address of the Hungry Minds' Web site. After this subroutine, the following two subroutines dictate what happens if the user clicks either of the buttons. Clicking one of the buttons fires the appropriate subroutine, which in turn assigns the URL and, at the same time, assigns the text that the `<span>` tag displays.

Within the body of the code, you display your two buttons. The `<button>` tag contains an ID, as well as a specification that this tag is to be processed on the server. You also include an `OnServerClick` event instead of the customary `OnClick` because you are concerned here with server events.

It is important to note that all the form code is displayed between `<form>` tags. This is important because the code errors out without the `<form>` tags in place. Within the `<form>` tag, this form is run on the server.

The end result is that when the user clicks a button, the link is dynamically changed. Within ASP 3.0, you wouldn't have seen that change without reloading the page, but with ASP.NET using VB .NET, all these changes are happening without any trips back to the server. This saves a considerable amount of time and resources.

HTMLForm control

The `HTMLForm` control allows access to program the HTML `<form>` tag. This is the tag used to place a wrap around other controls and to provide direction on what should be done with the user data after it has been submitted.

To take advantage of programming any of the other controls by using the postback feature, any control must be within the `HTMLForm` control tags:

```
<form runat=server>
   ... other controls here ...
</form>
```

By default, the `method` attribute of the `HTMLForm` control is set to `post`, and the action is set to the URL of the source page. But like any other HTML Server control, you can dynamically change any of the attributes of a tag by programming them using VB .NET.

Note Unfortunately, the .NET Framework does not allow more than one `HTMLForm` control per page.

HTMLGeneric control

The `HTMLGeneric` control allows access to program the HTML tags that are not represented by any of the specified controls. Examples of these tags include `<span>`, `<div>`, `<body>`, `<p>`, and `<font>`. Like any of the other controls, you can program these controls by relating an ID attribute to the tag.

Listing 34-2 showed an example of programming the `<span>` tag. Listing 34-3 shows you how to program the `<body>` tag using the `HTMLGeneric` control. See Figure 34-4 to see the code's results.

Listing 34-3: **HTMLGeneric <body> Tag Example**

```
<html>
  <head>
        <title>HTMLGeneric Using the Body Tag</title>

  <script language=VB runat=server>
  Sub ChangeButton_click(Source As Object, e As EventArgs)
      BodyID.Attributes("bgcolor") = PageColor.Value
  End Sub
  </script>

  </head>

  <body id="BodyID" runat="server">

  <form runat="server">
  Here is an example of the HTMLGeneric Control.<p>
  Select a background color for this page:<p>
```

Continued

Listing 34-3 *(continued)*

```
<select id="PageColor" runat="server">
        <option value="#ffffff">White</option>
        <option value="#ff0000">Red</option>
        <option value="#bfbfbf">Silver</option>
        <option value="#ffff10">Yellow</option>
</select>
<p>
<input type="submit" runat="server" id="submit1"
value="Change Background Color"
OnServerClick="ChangeButton_Click">
</form>

</body>
</html>
```

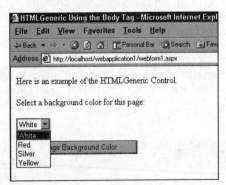

Figure 34-4: Using the HTMLGeneric
control to dynamically change the font size

In the VB .NET section of the code, notice that the attributes of the `<body>` tag are declared differently from other controls. This is because this control can be used for multiple elements and isn't tied to one particular element, such as the `HTMLAnchor` control.

Because it isn't tied to a particular element, there isn't an understanding of which attributes are possible to list. So, instead of using the typical `IDName.AttributeTitle`, you write the `HTMLGeneric` control as `IDName.Attributes("AttributeTitle")`. In the code example in Listing 34-3, the `<body>` tag's attribute `bgcolor` is assigned by using `BodyID.Attributes("bgcolor") = PageColor.Value`.

Listing 34-4 shows another example using the HTMLGeneric control, using the <font> tag. Figure 34-5 shows how the code appears in the browser.

```
<html>
  <head>
        <title>HTMLGeneric Using the Font Tag</title>

  <script language=VB runat=server>
  Sub ChangeButton_click(Source As Object, e As EventArgs)
      SpainText.Attributes("size") = FontSize.Value
  End Sub
  </script>

  </head>

  <body>

  <form runat="server">
  Here is an example of the HTMLGeneric Control.<p>
  <font id="SpainText" runat="server">
  The rain in Spain stays mainly in the plains.
  </font><p>
  <select id="FontSize" runat="server">
        <option value=1>Small</option>
        <option value=2>Medium</option>
        <option value=4>Large</option>
        <option value=5>Extra Large</option>
  </select>
  <p>
  <input type="submit" runat="server" id="submit1"
  value="Change Font Size"
  OnServerClick="ChangeButton_Click">
  </form>

  </body>
</html>
```

Listing 34-4 works off of the <font> tag, and changes the font size of the line of text based upon what the user submits in the drop-down list of choices. Once again, you did not make a round-trip to the server to reload the page in order to display the text, but instead the text changed without the page refreshing! Figure 34-6 shows how the page appears.

Listing 34-5 uses the HTMLGeneric control to code the <p> tag to place specified text within the browser.

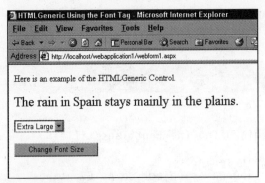

Figure 34-5: Changing the font size attribute
by dynamically changing the <font> tag with
the HTMLGeneric control

Listing 34-5: **HTMLGeneric <p> Tag Example**

```
<html>
  <head>
        <title>HTMLGeneric Using the Paragraph Tag</title>

  <script language=VB runat=server>
  Sub SubmitButton_click(Source As Object, e As EventArgs)
      PText.InnerHTML = "Welcome to our page " & _
      NameField.Value & ". Come Again!"
  End Sub
  </script>

  </head>

  <body>

  <form runat="server">
  Here is an example of the HTMLGeneric Control.<p>
  What is your name?<p>
  <input type="text" id="NameField" runat="server">
  <p>
  <input type="submit" runat="server" id="submit1"
  value="Submit"
  OnServerClick="SubmitButton_Click">
  </form>

  <p id="PText" runat="server" />

  </body>
</html>
```

Figure 34-6: Using the HTMLGeneric control with the paragraph tag to add personalized text to the page

This is a great and simple example that shows how a user can input some information through a form and then have that information display on the page. The user enters his name within the `NameField` text field, and within the `SubmitButton_ click` subroutine you assign that value with a concatenated text string to `PText.InnerHTML`.

The `InnerHTML` is a specification concerning the content that goes in between the opening and closing `<p>` tags. The choices are either `InnerHTML` or `InnerText`. The `InnerHTML` choice allows the browser to interpret the HTML that is assigned to it. For instance, in the example, type `<b>William Evjen</b>` and you notice that the text becomes bold due to the fact that it is assigned with the bold tags. Now change the `PText.InnerHTML` to `PText.InnerText`, and type `<b>William Evjen</b>` in the text field. This time, you notice that the browser doesn't interpret the bold tags, but instead displays the HTML tags as text. It is all a matter of what you want to display in your document when deciding on which choice to use.

HTMLImage control

The `HTMLImage` control allows access to program the HTML `<img>` tag. This is the tag used to display images within HTML documents.

Listing 34-6 shows an example of how to use the `HTMLImage` control to switch images that are displayed in the browser based upon the user's request.

Listing 34-6: **HTMLImage Control Example**

```
<html>
  <head>
        <title>HTMLImage Control</title>
```

Continued

Listing 34-6 *(continued)*

```vb
<script language=VB runat=server>
  Sub Page_Load(sender As Object, e As EventArgs)
        PicTitle.InnerHTML = "<b>First Image</b>"
  End Sub

  Sub SubmitButton_click(Source As Object, e As EventArgs)
      Dim PicChoice as Integer
      PicChoice = PicSelect.Value

      If (PicChoice = 1) then
        PicTitle.InnerHTML = "<b>First Image</b>"
        Image1.src = "image1.jpg"
        Image1.width = 200
        Image1.height = 200
        Image1.border = 1
        Image1.align = "center"
      Else If (PicChoice = 2) then
        PicTitle.InnerHTML = "<b>Second Image</b>"
        Image1.src = "image2.jpg"
        Image1.width = 250
        Image1.height = 250
        Image1.border = 1
        Image1.align = "center"
      Else If (PicChoice = 3) then
        PicTitle.InnerHTML = "<b>Third Image</b>"
        Image1.src = "image3.jpg"
        Image1.width = 175
        Image1.height = 175
        Image1.border = 1
        Image1.align = "center"
      End If
  End Sub
</script>

</head>

<body>

<form runat="server">
Here is an example of using the HTMLImage Control<p>
Choose an image to view:<p>
<select id="PicSelect" runat="server">
   <option value=1>First Image</option>
   <option value=2>Second Image</option>
   <option value=3>Third Image</option>
</select>
<p>
<input type="submit" runat="server" id="submit1"
```

```
        value="View Image Choice"
        OnServerClick="SubmitButton_Click">
        <p>
        <p id="PicTitle" runat="server" />
        <img src="image1.jpg" width=200 height=200 align="center"
        runat="server" id="Image1">
        </form>

        </body>
    </html>
```

From the code in Listing 34-6, you display an image (the first image) and then allow the user to view other images based upon a choice within the drop-down list of images.

Using VB .NET, you use some logic to run through the possible choices of images to view, and based upon that choice, you define a number of attributes. You assign values to the image source: width, height, border and alignment. In addition, you assign a title for the image that you display above the image with the paragraph tag.

HTMLInputButton control

The `HTMLInputButton` control allows access to program the HTML `<input type="submit">`, `<input type="reset">`, and `<input type="button">` tags. These tags are used to display functional buttons within HTML documents.

Note   These controls do not require closing tags.

After a user clicks an input button within a form, the form's data is sent to the server for processing.

Listing 34-7 authenticates a user based upon the user name and password.

Listing 34-7: **HTMLInputButton Control Example**

```
<html>
  <head>
        <title>HTMLInputButton Example</title>

    <script language=VB runat=server>
    Sub SubmitButton_click(Source As Object, e As EventArgs)
        If (Username.Value = "Guest") then
```

Continued

Listing 34-7 *(continued)*

```
            If (Pass.Value = "Abracadabra") then
                Span1.InnerHTML = "<b>Correct!</b><P>"
            End If
        Else
            Span1.InnerHTML = "<b>Sorry .. Not Correct!</b>"
        End If
    End Sub

    Sub ResetButton_click(Source As Object, e As EventArgs)
            Username.Value = ""
            Pass.Value = ""
    End Sub
    </script>

    </head>

    <body>

    <form runat="server">
    Here is an example of the HTMLInputButton Control.<p>
    <span id="Span1" runat="server" />
    User Name:<br>
    <input type="text" id="Username" runat="server">
    <br>
    Password:<br>
    <input type="Pass" id="Password" runat="server"><p>
    <input type="submit" runat="server" id="submit1"
    value="Submit"
    OnServerClick="SubmitButton_Click"> 
        <input type="reset" id="reset1" runat="server"
    value="Reset" OnServerClick="ResetButton_click">
        </form>

        </body>
    </html>
```

As you notice within the code, after the user enters a user name and password, you check on it using an if then statement. If the user enters the correct user name and password, the user is informed using the HTMLGeneric control off of the <span> tag.

A subroutine is also activated when the user clicks the Reset button. With a click of this button, the fields are emptied.

HTMLInputCheckBox control

The HTMLInputCheckBox control allows access to program the HTML <input type="checkbox"> tag. This is the tag used to display a check box form element within HTML documents. A check box is either checked or unchecked.

Listing 34-8 shows how to use the HTMLInputCheckBox and the HTMLButton controls to check whether the check box is either checked or not. Figure 34-7 shows the page as it appears in the browser.

Listing 34-8: **HTMLInputCheckBox Control Example**

```
<html>
  <head>
        <title>HTMLInputCheckBox Example</title>

  <script language=VB runat=server>
  Sub SubmitButton_click(Source As Object, e As EventArgs)
      If (ChBox.Checked = True) Then
         Ptext.InnerHTML = "CHECKED!"
      Else
         Ptext.InnerHTML = "NOT CHECKED!"
      End If
  End Sub
  </script>

  </head>

  <body>

  <form runat="server">
  Here is an example of the HTMLInputCheckBox Control.<p>
  CheckBox: 
  <input type="checkbox" id="ChBox" runat="server">
  <p>
  <input type="submit" runat="server" id="submit1"
  value="Check Checkbox Status"
  OnServerClick="SubmitButton_Click">
  </form>

  <p id="PText" runat="server" />

  </body>
</html>
```

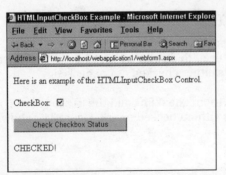

Figure 34-7: Using the HTMLInputCheckBox control to check the status of a check box.

The `<script>` tags check to see whether the check box is checked or not using the check box's ID and the attribute you are checking against—`ChBox.Checked`. If a check box is checked, the value is `True`. An unchecked check box's value is `False`.

You could also apply the same technique when rendering a page for the first time. The following code piece puts the check box checked based upon the type of user:

```
If (UserType = 1) Then
    ChBox.Checked = True
Else If (UserType = 2) Then
    ChBox.Checked = False
End If
```

HTMLInputFile control

The `HTMLInputFile` control allows access to program the HTML `<input type="file">` tag. This is the tag used to work with file data within a HTML form. In the past, using traditional ASP, many programmers worked with third-party components to upload files from the client to the server. Now, with .NET, it is taken care of for you, and it couldn't be simpler.

Listing 34-9 shows how to upload a file to the server.

Listing 34-9: **HTMLInputFile Control Example**

```
<html>
  <head>
        <title>HTMLInputFile Example</title>

  <script language=VB runat=server>
  Sub SubmitButton_click(Source As Object, e As EventArgs)
      If Not (File1.PostedFile Is Nothing) Then
```

```
        Try
          File1.PostedFile.SaveAs("c:\temp\uploadedfile.txt")
          Span1.InnerHtml = "Upload Successful!"
        Catch exc As Exception
          Span1.InnerHtml = "Error saving file <b>c:\\temp\\"
          & File1.Value & "</b><br>" & exc.ToString()
        End Try
      End If
    End Sub
    </script>

    </head>

    <body>

    <form runat="server" enctype="multipart/form-data">
    Here is an example of the HTMLInputFile Control.<p>
    File to Upload: 
    <input type="file" id="File1" runat="server">
    <p>
    <input type="submit" runat="server" id="submit1"
    value="Upload File"
    OnServerClick="SubmitButton_Click">
    </form>

    <span id="Span1" runat="server" />

    </body>
  </html>
```

This is a great feature that ASP 3.0 programmers always wished for! Now, with just a few lines of code, you can upload documents to the server.

One very important thing to notice within the code is that within the `<form>` tag we have used the `enctype` attribute to be `"multipart/form-data"`. Without this attribute, the Web page errors out.

The Submit button causes an `OnServerClick` event that uploads the file and displays a message if the upload was successful. If unsuccessful, the page displays an error message about why the upload failed.

By using the `<input type="file">` tag, the browser automatically places a Browse button next to the text field, so you don't need to do anything for that to happen. When the users click the Browse button, they can navigate through their file system on their computer to find the file that they wish to upload (see Figure 34-8). Clicking Open places that filename and the file's path within the text field.

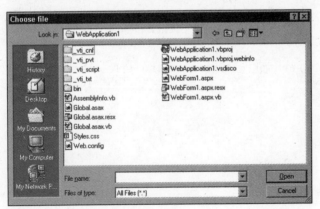

Figure 34-8: Choosing a file

HTMLInputHidden control

The `HTMLInputHidden` control allows access to program the HTML `<input type="hidden">` tag. This is the tag used to store data within an HTML document. The hidden tag is hidden, of course, but can be viewed by right-clicking within the browser window and choosing to view the HTML source code. Within the code, you can view the hidden tag and its value.

Listing 34-10 is an example of how to use the `HTMLInputHidden` and the `HTMLButton` controls to change the value of the hidden tag. Figure 34-9 shows how the code appears in the browser.

Listing 34-10:   HTMLInputHidden Control Example

```
<html>
  <head>
        <title>HTMLInputHidden Example</title>

  <script language=VB runat=server>
  Sub Button1_onclick(sender As Object, e As EventArgs)
        Hidden1.Value = 1
        Span1.InnerHtml = "The value is now 1"
  End Sub

  Sub Button2_onclick(sender As Object, e As EventArgs)
        Hidden1.Value = 2
        Span1.InnerHtml = "The value is now 2"
  End Sub
  </script>

  </head>

  <body>
```

```
<form runat="server">
Here is an example of the HTMLInputHidden Control.<p>
Change the hidden tag's value by pressing a button.<p>
<button id="button1" runat="server"
OnServerClick="Button1_OnClick">Value = 1</button>
<p>
<button id="button2" runat="server"
OnServerClick="Button2_OnClick">Value = 2</button>
</form>
<input type="hidden" id="hidden1" runat="server">
<span id="Span1" runat="server" />

</body>
</html>
```

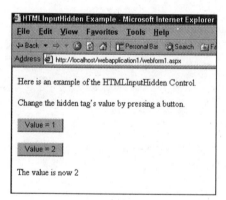

Figure 34-9: Using the HTMLInputHidden control after the second button is clicked

This page displays two buttons, and the value of the hidden tag is changed depending on which button is clicked. Clicking one of the buttons fires the OnServerClick event for that button. It is possible to see the value of the hidden tag in two places. It is displayed in the browser with the <span> tag and also by right-clicking in the browser and viewing the source code, you can view the value of the hidden tag.

HTMLInputImage control

The HTMLInputImage control allows access to program against the HTML <input type="image"> tag. This control is very similar to the HTMLInputButton control, but allows the same button functionality for an image. Using this control would allow a user to click a custom Submit button that is an image file type (for example, jpg or gif).

Note   DHTML events can be used within this control without causing any conflicting errors. For instance, it is possible to use the onmouseover and onmouseout DHTML events for browsers that are HTML 4.0-compliant.

Listing 34-11 shows an example of how to use the HTMLInputImage control.

Listing 34-11: HTMLInputImage Control Example

```
<html>
  <head>
         <title>HTMLInputImage Example</title>

  <script language=VB runat=server>
  Sub Button1_click(Source As Object, e As
    ImageClickEventArgs)
         Para1.InnerHtml = "You clicked button 1"
  End Sub

  Sub Button2_click(Source As Object, e As
  ImageClickEventArgs)
         Para1.InnerHtml = "You clicked button 2"
  End Sub
  </script>

  </head>

  <body>

  <form runat="server">
  Here is an example of the HTMLInputImage Control.<p>
  Click on either of the buttons.<p>
  <input type="image"
  id="button1"
  runat="server"
  src="/images/image1.jpg"
  OnServerClick="Button1_click">
  <p>
  <input type="image"
  id="button2"
  runat="server"
  src="/images/image2.jpg"
  OnServerClick="Button2_click">
  </form>

  <p id="Para1" runat="server" />

  </body>
</html>
```

This page has two <input type="image"> tags. Each one displays an image that acts as a button and can be clicked. After it is clicked, it triggers an event; in this case, a Button#_click event. Then using the HTMLGeneric control, you publish which button was pressed.

HTMLInputRadioButton control

The `HTMLInputRadioButton` control allows access to program against the HTML `<input type="radio">` tag. This tag allows the user to make a selection within an HTML document. Unlike the check box, in which the user can make multiple selections, the radio button allows only one choice within a grouping.

Listing 34-12 shows an example of how to use the `HTMLInputRadioButton` control. Figure 34-10 shows how the code appears in the browser.

Listing 34-12: HTMLInputRadioButton Control Example

```
<html>
  <head>
        <title>HTMLInputRadioButton Example</title>

  <script language=VB runat=server>
  Sub SubmitButton_click(Source As Object, e As EventArgs)
     If Radio1.Checked = True Then
         Para1.InnerHTML = "You like green "
     Else If Radio2.Checked = True Then
         Para1.InnerHTML = "You like yellow "
     Else If Radio3.Checked = True Then
          Para1.InnerHTML = "You like red "
     End if

     If Radio4.Checked = True Then
         Para1.InnerHTML = Para1.InnerHTML & "apples."
     Else If Radio5.Checked = True Then
          Para1.InnerHTML = Para1.InnerHTML & "bananas."
     End If
  End Sub
  </script>

  </head>

  <body>

  <form runat="server">
  Here is an example of the HTMLInputRadioButton Control.<p>
  Make your selection and then press Submit.<p>
  What color do you like?<br>
  <input type="radio" runat="server" id="radio1"
  name="radio1" checked>Green
  <input type="radio" runat="server" id="radio2"
  name="radio1">Yellow
  <input type="radio" runat="server" id="radio3"
  name="radio1">Red
  <p>
```

Continued

Listing 34-12 *(continued)*

```
What type of fruit do you like best?<br>
<input type="radio" runat="server" id="radio4"
name="radio2">Apples
<input type="radio" runat="server" id="radio5"
name="radio2">Bananas
<p>
<input type="submit" runat="server" id="submit1"
value="Submit"
OnServerClick="SubmitButton_Click">
</form>

<p id="Para1" runat="server" />

</body>
</html>
```

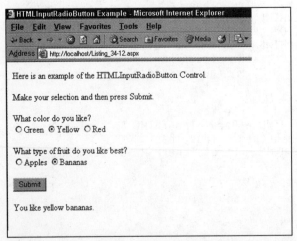

Figure 34-10: Using the HTMLInputRadioButton control to dynamically add personalized text based upon the user's choices

First of all, after reviewing the code, it is important to note that you group radio buttons based upon the name. Listing 34-12 has two radio groups. The first one is called radio1. So each radio button that needs to be in that group must have the attribute `name="radio1"`. The second radio group is called radio2. Each radio button that belongs to this group must have the attribute `name="radio2"`.

Within the <script> tags, you check whether each of the radio buttons is checked. If one of the buttons is checked, you apply the proper text to the paragraph tag that you are building and display this text at the bottom of the page.

HTMLInputText control

The HTMLInputText control allows access to program against the HTML <input type="text"> or the <input type="password"> tags. These tags allow the user to input data within a text field that is contained within a form. Programming these items allows dynamic changes to set the MaxLength, Size, and Value attributes.

The password field is different from the text field in that when the user enters text into this field, the characters entered are hidden and replaced with an asterisk (*).

Listing 34-13 shows an example of how to use the HTMLInputText Control. (Another example can be seen in Listing 34-7.) Figure 34-11 shows how this code appears in the browser.

Listing 34-13:   HTMLInputText Control Example

```
<html>
  <head>
        <title>HTMLInputText Example</title>

  <script language=VB runat=server>
  Sub SubmitButton_click(Source As Object, e As EventArgs)
      Dim TextSize as Boolean
      TextSize = IsNumeric(First.Value)

      If TextSize = True then
          Third.Size = First.Value
          Third.Value = Second.Value
          Para1.InnerHTML = ""
Else
    Para1.InnerHTML = "You must enter a number!"
      End If
  End Sub
  </script>

  </head>

  <body>

  <form runat="server">
  Here is an example of the HTMLInputText Control.<p>
  Select the size of the bottom text field<br>
  <input type="text" id="First" runat="server">
  <p>
```

Continued

Listing 34-13 *(continued)*

```
Select the value to place within the bottom text field.
<br>
<input type="text" id="Second" runat="server">
<p>
Result<br>
<input type="text" id="Third" runat="server">
<p>
<input type="submit" runat="server" id="submit1"
value="Submit"
OnServerClick="SubmitButton_Click">
</form>

<font color="red"><b>
<p id="para1" runat="server" />
</b></font>

</body>
</html>
```

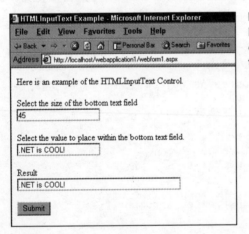

Figure 34-11: Using the HTMLInputText control to dynamically change the text box

Listing 34-13 changed the text field's size and value attributes based upon what is entered in the other two text fields. Within the code, you first check to see whether the user entered in a valid number. If they did, you then change the third text field's attributes dynamically based upon what the user entered. If the user entered in some text or some other character besides a valid number, you do not change the text field, but instead display an error message at the bottom of the page.

HTMLSelect control

The HTMLSelect control allows access to program against the HTML <select> tag as well as any <option> tags nested within. This tag creates drop-down lists within HTML documents.

Listing 34-14 is an example of how to use the HTMLSelect control.

Listing 34-14: HTMLSelect Control Example

```
<html>
  <head>
            <title>HTMLSelect Example</title>
 <script language="VB" runat="server">
Sub SubmitButton_click(Source As Object, e As EventArgs)
  Dim Count as Integer
  Count = SelectTag.Items.Count
  Para1.InnerHTML = "There are " & Count & _
  " items in the Select Tag."
End Sub

Sub SubmitButton2_click(Source As Object, e As EventArgs)
  SelectTag.Items.Add(OptionAdd.Value)
  Dim Count as Integer
  Count = SelectTag.Items.Count
  Para1.InnerHTML = "There are " & Count & _
  " items in the Select Tag."
End Sub
</script>

  </head>

  <body>

  <form runat="server">
  Here is an example of the HTMLInputText Control.<p>
  <select id="SelectTag" runat="server">
   <option>CA</option>
   <option>MO</option>
   <option>WA</option>
   </select>
  <p>
  <input type="text" id="OptionAdd" runat="server">
  <p>
  <input type="submit" runat="server" id="Submit2" value="Add
  Another State" onserverclick="SubmitButton2_Click"
  name="Submit2">
  <input type="submit" runat="server" id="submit1"
```

Continued

Listing 34-14 *(continued)*

```
value="Submit" onserverclick="SubmitButton_Click">
</form>

<b><p id="para1" runat="server" /></b>

</body>
</html>
```

In this example (shown in Figure 34-12), you can count the number of items that are contained within the drop-down list, as well as add items to the list. The great part about all of this is that you were able to do this without many lines of code.

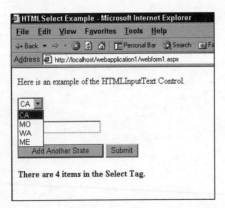

Figure 34-12: Using the HTMLSelect control. Here, you added a control and counted the number of items in the control.

By specifying `SelectTag.Items.Count`, you are asking for the count of items within the tag you are using the ID of. In this case, `SelectTag` is the ID of your `<select>` tag.

There are various other functions you can use with the `<select>` tag. Table 34-2 describes some of the available methods.

Table 34-2
Various Methods to Use with the <select> tag

Methods	Written Out As	Description
Add	IDName.Items.Add	This method adds a specified item to the list. For instance, within the <select> tag, there are a number of <option> tags. Each option is one item in the drop-down list. Using this method adds another <option> item to the end of list.
Clear	IDName.Items.Clear	This method clears all the <option> tags from the <select> tag.
Contains	IDName.Items.Contains	This method returns a True/False value, depending on whether the list of items contains a specified item. A True statement means that the list contains the item in question.
Count	IDName.Items.Count	This property returns the number of items within the drop-down list of the <select> tag.
IndexOf	IDName.Items.IndexOf	This method returns an ordinal index value that represents the position of the specified item.
Insert	IDName.Items.Insert	This method inserts the specified item to the list at the specified index location.
Remove	IDName.Items.Remove	This method removes the specified item from the list.
RemoveAt	IDName.Items.RemoveAt	This method removes an item from the collection at the specified index location.

HTMLTable, HTMLTableCell, and HTMLTableRow controls

The HTMLTable, HTMLTableCell, and HTMLTableRow controls allow access to program against the HTML <table>, <tr>, <th>, and <td> tags. These tags generate tables within HTML documents.

Like the other HTML Server controls, it is possible to dynamically change the attributes that are contained within these tags. It is also possible to dynamically add and rows and cells to tables.

Listing 34-15 shows how to change some of the table's attributes from a selection of drop-down lists.

Listing 34-15:   HTMLTable, HTMLTableCell and HTMLTableRow Control Example

```
<html>
  <head>
        <title>HTMLTable, HTMLTableCell, HTMLTableRow
        Example</title>

<script language="VB" runat="server">
Sub SubmitButton_click(Source As Object, e As EventArgs)
  Table1.Bgcolor = Select1.Value
  Table1.Border = Select2.Value
  Table1.Cellpadding = Select3.Value
  Table1.Cellspacing = Select4.Value

  If Select5.Value = "1" Then
        Tr1.Bgcolor = Select6.Value
  Else If Select5.Value = "2" Then
        Tr2.Bgcolor = Select6.Value
  Else If Select5.Value = "3" Then
        Tr3.Bgcolor = Select6.Value
  End If
End Sub
</script>

  </head>

<body>

<form runat="server">
Here is an example of the HTMLTable, HTMLTableCell and
HTMLTableRow Controls.<p>

<table runat="server" id="table1" cellspacing=3
cellpadding=3 border=1>
    <tr runat="server" id="Tr1">
        <td>Team 1</td>
        <td>Seattle Mariners</td>
    </tr>
    <tr runat="server" id="Tr2">
      <td>Team 2</td>
        <td>St. Louis Cardinals</td>
    </tr>
    <tr runat="server" id="Tr3">
      <td>Team 3</td>
      <td>New York Yankees</td>
    </tr>
```

```
   </table>

   <p>
   Table Backgroud Color:<br>
   <select id="Select1" runat="server">
    <option>White</option>
    <option>Yellow</option>
    <option>Red</option>
    <option>Blue</option>
   </select><br>
   Table Border:<br>
   <select id="Select2" runat="server">
    <option>0</option>
    <option>1</option>
    <option>2</option>
    <option>3</option>
   </select><br>
   Table Cellpadding:<br>
   <select id="Select3" runat="server">
    <option>0</option>
    <option>1</option>
    <option>2</option>
    <option>3</option>
   </select><br>
   Table Cellspacing:<br>
   <select id="Select4" runat="server">
    <option>0</option>
    <option>1</option>
    <option>2</option>
    <option>3</option>
   </select><br>
   <p>
   Select a Row:<br>
   <select id="Select5" runat="server">
    <option>1</option>
    <option>2</option>
    <option>3</option>
   </select><br>
   Row Color:<br>
   <select id="Select6" runat="server">
    <option>White</option>
    <option>Yellow</option>
    <option>Red</option>
    <option>Blue</option>
   </select><br>
   <input type="submit" runat="server" id="submit1"
   value="Submit" onserverclick="SubmitButton_Click">
   </form>

   </body>
</html>
```

In this example (as shown in Figure 34-13), you can change all the attributes of the table elements dynamically as you can change the other attributes of the other HTML elements. In this example, note that when you establish a row color, you are not overriding that color by changing the table's background color.

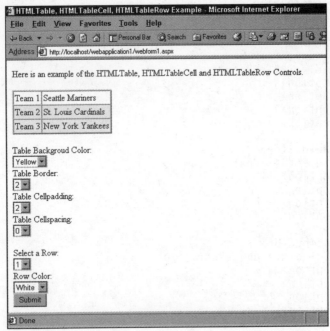

Figure 34-13: Using the HTMLTable control to dynamically change the table's properties

HTMLTextArea control

The HTMLTextArea control allows access to program against the HTML `<textarea>` tag. This is similar to the text field, but the HTML `<textarea>` element allows the area to type in to be set by assigning the width and height of the area. Assigning a value to the `cols` attribute sets the width and assigning a value to the `rows` attribute sets the height.

Listing 34-16 shows an example of how to use the HTMLTextArea Server control.

Listing 34-16:   HTMLTextArea Control Example

```
<html>
<head>
    <script language="VB" runat="server">
     Sub SubmitButton_click(Source As Object, e As EventArgs)
        Para1.InnerHtml = "You wrote: <br>" & TextArea1.Value
     End Sub
    </script>
</head>
<body>
    Here is an example of the HTMLTextArea Control.<p>
    <form runat="server">
        Tell me your life story: <br>
    <textarea id="TextArea1" cols=40 rows=4 runat=server />
        <input type="submit" runat="server" id="submit1"
        value="Submit" onserverclick="SubmitButton_Click">
        <p>
        <p id="Para1" runat="server" />
    </form>
</body>
</html>
```

In this example, after the user enters any information into the text area field and submits a response, this information is then displayed on the same page. This is done without returning to the server and regenerating the page.

Creating HTML Server Controls — Another Way

You have been creating all the HTML Server controls by entering all the text straight into the code window (by clicking the HTML tab at the bottom). The other way of creating these pages is to use the Design mode (by pressing the Design tab at the bottom, shown in Figure 34-14). Creating your pages in the Design mode is a simple process that is familiar to Visual Basic application developers.

Design   HTML   **Figure 34-14:** The Design and HTML tabs

The previous examples of this chapter used the code mode to show you how the code works. You will now build a prior example in the Design mode to learn another way to construct your pages.

By creating pages using the Design mode, you also create a CodeBehind page that keeps the VB .NET code separate from the HTML and the controls that you build on your page.

Constructing a page with HTML controls or Web controls (covered in the next chapter) in Design mode is very similar to creating a VB form in Visual Basic 6.0. The controls that you place on the page are similar in nature to the VB controls that you placed on your forms.

The first step is to open Visual Studio .NET and start a new Web application.

1. Right-click your Web application's name within the Solution Explorer, and add a new item (Add ➪ Add New Item). You are then presented with a list of various templates to choose from. For this example, choose Web Form. Feel free to name the Web Form whatever you wish with the .aspx extension.

Note   For a full description of Visual Studio .NET, see Part III. Also, for a brief description on creating Web applications with Visual Studio .NET, see Chapter 33.

2. Click Open, and you see that Visual Studio .NET created your page within the Solution Explorer and opened the page within the code window. You can tell what page you are working on within Visual Studio .NET by the page tab at the top of the window. The tab has the name of the page that is open at the moment. While working on multiple pages at the same time, you see a number of tabs at the top of the window. To switch between pages, just click the represented tab.

3. Your document opens in Grid Layout mode. For this example, you need to switch to Flow Layout mode. To do this, change the property in the Properties box on the right side of the window. Scroll down until you find the pageLayout property. It says GridLayout. Click the box that contains the GridLayout text, and you see an arrow appear that allows you to open a drop-down list of options. Select FlowLayout.

   You now build the example from Listing 34-2, which builds a small page that used the HTMLAnchor, HTMLButton, and HTMLGeneric controls that allow the user to change the link based upon the button they click.

4. From the left side of the Visual Studio .NET application, bring up the HTML controls in the Toolbox. If you do not see the Toolbox, you can bring it up by clicking View ➪ Toolbox or by pressing Ctrl+Alt+X (at the same time).

5. From the Toolbox, drag and drop a Button control onto your page. The button is highlighted with some white squares around the button (see Figure 34-15). This means that this is the selected control on the page (even if it is the only control on the page at this time).

6. Selecting the Button control displays the control's properties in the Properties box on the right side of the screen (see Figure 34-16). You can change any of the buttons properties here.

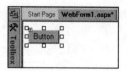

Figure 34-15: A selected Button control

Figure 34-16: The Button control's properties

7. Before you write any code for the button, you add your other controls. Bring the curser to the right side of the button. Press Enter. Add another button control at this point and then press Enter again.

8. Type the text of the link here. Type **Click Me!** to put the text on the page. To turn this text into a clickable link, highlight the text. Press Insert ➪ Hyperlink to open the Hyperlink dialog box (see Figure 34-17). Within this dialog box, you can build your hyperlink for the text that you highlighted. Keep the hyperlink Type set at http:, but you can see a number of different choices if you view all the available choices in the drop-down list. Type `http://www.hungryminds.com/` in the URL text field and click OK, or just press Enter. Now the text on the screen has changed to a link.

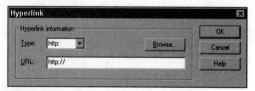

Figure 34-17: The Hyperlink dialog box

9. To add some text at the bottom when the user clicks on one of the buttons, press Insert ➪ Div. This adds a square box to your page with the word `Div` written in the box. Right-click the box, and choose the Run As Server control from the context menu. You don't want to have any text on the page when the user first pulls the page up. Therefore, remove the word `Div` from the box. Then highlight the box and while holding your left mouse button down, click and drag the lower-right corner of the Div box to form the area in which you

want your message to display. Notice the ID attribute within the Properties box. In this case, it is DIV1.

10. Next, you work on the hyperlink. Right-click the link, and choose Run As Server Control from the context menu. You can also change any of the properties for this control within the Properties box. Make a note of the control's ID (in this case, A1).

11. Right-click both buttons and also turn them into Server controls. If you don't do this, you can't put any code behind the buttons because the server would treat them as traditional HTML buttons. After the controls are converted to server controls, you notice that a green arrow in a green box appears in the upper-left part of the control. This means that the control is a Server control.

12. Highlight the first button, and change the properties of this control. Make the ID Button1, and change the value to Change Link toHungry Minds. Highlight the second button and do the same, except the ID is Button2, and the value is Change Link to Microsoft. Your page should be similar to what is shown in figure 34-18.

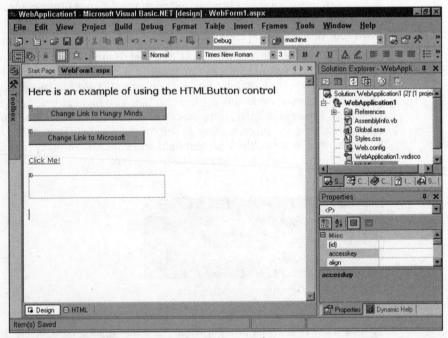

Figure 34-18: Building a page in the Design mode

The code that is generated from the page made in the Design mode isn't that much different from the code you used to build the page yourself. The main difference is the @Page directive that at the top of the page that references the CodeBehind page, and calls the Page class. The @Page directive looks like the following:

```
<%@ Page Language="vb" AutoEventWireup="false"
Codebehind="WebForm1.aspx.vb"
Inherits="WebApplication1.WebForm1"%>
```

Now comes the fun part!

13. Double-click the first button, and another page (with a new tab) is pulled up. In this case, the page's title is WebForm1.aspx.vb. This is the VB .NET CodeBehind page for your ASP.NET page. The CodeBehind page has already generated a lot of code for you, as you can tell. There should be two subroutines already in place on the CodeBehind page. One is the `Page_Load`, and the other is for the `Button1_ServerClick` button.

14. To the `Button1_ServerClick` event, add the following code:

```
A1.href = "http://www.hungryminds.com/"
DIV1.InnerHTML = "You chose Hungry Minds"
```

The great thing that you notice is that as you type, IntellisSense is at work for you. After you type A1, IntelliSense gives you a drop-down list of choices that might follow.

15. Now go back to the ASP.NET page by clicking the WebForm1.aspx tab. Double-click the second button. You are presented with another subroutine on your CodeBehind page.

16. For the `Button2_ServerClick` event, add the following code:

```
A1.href = "http://www.microsoft.com/"
DIV1.InnerHTML = "You chose Microsoft"
```

That is pretty much it. The complete code from the CodeBehind page can be seen in Listing 34-17. Right-click the page within the Solution Explorer, and choose Set As Start Page. Then, click the blue Debug arrow at the top of the page to run through all the files within your application, and look for errors and compile your application.

After you are through all of this, you can pull the page up in a browser, and you see that it is the same as the page you built earlier in the chapter. It also was very easy to do, and it is even easier to manage now that the event code is contained within a separate page.

Listing 34-17: The Generated CodeBehind Page WebForm1.aspx.vb

```
Public Class WebForm1
    Inherits System.Web.UI.Page
    Protected WithEvents Button1 As
System.Web.UI.HtmlControls.HtmlInputButton
    Protected WithEvents DIV1 As
System.Web.UI.HtmlControls.HtmlGenericControl
    Protected WithEvents A1 As
```

Continued

Listing 34-17 *(continued)*

```
System.Web.UI.HtmlControls.HtmlAnchor
    Protected WithEvents Button2 As
System.Web.UI.HtmlControls.HtmlInputButton

#Region " Web Form Designer Generated Code "

    'This call is required by the Web Form Designer.
    <System.Diagnostics.DebuggerStepThrough()>
 Private Sub InitializeComponent()

    End Sub

    Private Sub Page_Init(ByVal sender As System.Object,
ByVal e As System.EventArgs) Handles MyBase.Init
        'CODEGEN: This method call is required by the Web
Form Designer
        'Do not modify it using the code editor.
        InitializeComponent()
    End Sub

#End Region

    Private Sub Page_Load(ByVal sender As System.Object,
ByVal e As System.EventArgs) Handles MyBase.Load
        'Put user code to initialize the page here
    End Sub

    Private Sub Button1_ServerClick(ByVal sender As
System.Object, ByVal e As System.EventArgs) Handles
Button1.ServerClick
        A1.HRef = "http://www.hungryminds.com/"
        DIV1.InnerHtml = "You chose Hungry Minds"
    End Sub

    Private Sub Button2_ServerClick(ByVal sender As
System.Object, ByVal e As System.EventArgs) Handles
Button2.ServerClick
        A1.HRef = "http://www.microsoft.com/"
        DIV1.InnerHtml = "You chose Microsoft"
    End Sub
End Class
```

All the events that you call on are this page. Keeping this in a separate file makes this quite easy to manage and work with later.

Summary

In this chapter, you saw what is possible in Web application development using HTML Server controls. Very much like traditional VB controls, HTML Server controls can be programmed to dynamically change a number of attributes.

In the next chapter, you look at a different, but similar type of control—the Web control. As you notice, the Web control gives you even greater control over the Web page.

✦   ✦   ✦

Web Controls

by Bill Evjen

Within ASP.NET Server controls, Web controls are one type of control that is now available. Other types include HTML Server controls and Validation controls.

Between Web controls and HTML Server controls, Web controls are the more sophisticated control type. They allow a higher level of functionality that is not found in HTML Server controls.

Unlike HTML Server controls, which map directly to their corresponding HTML elements, Web controls generate HTML code based upon functionality and the visiting client's browser type. With Web controls, you might say that you want a text box in your Web Form. You can change the style of the text box by just changing the properties of the text box control itself. By changing these properties, you can specify whether the control should output a regular text box, a password text box or a text area. When someone hits that particular page, ASP.NET sends to the client the code that is appropriate for that browser. Each browser may see different HTML code, depending on what their browser supports. ASP.NET takes care of all the browser detection and the work that goes with this for you.

Not only are there Web controls for common Web Form components, but also for other common (yet more advanced) Web page functionality — such as displaying data in tables, paging through information and data, and creating templates to display information. One example of a rich control that is now available in ASP.NET is the calendar control. In classic ASP, it would be a time-consuming task to develop a calendar that would work in all the major browsers. Though ASP.NET provides you with a completely modifiable calendar that can be placed within Web Forms by just using one simple line of code.

As you see in this chapter, Web controls make your Internet applications easier to develop and manage.

Browser Sniffing

Web controls generate HTML code based upon specified functionality and the client's browser type and version. Not all browsers are made the same way. All browsers support a specified level of HTML, but both Microsoft and Netscape found it in their best interests to develop tag specifications beyond what HTML offered. Because it wasn't always the case that the other companies followed suit in adopting these extensions, you could never be sure if the page you generated would render the same in the other browser.

When developing Web pages with Web controls, you are not developing specific HTML that the browser reads and interprets; instead, you are developing controls for the server. The server then detects the browser and renders the appropriate code for that specific browser.

Traditionally, the developers would develop their Web page for the lowest common denominator — the lowest browser version that would possibly come to their site. This isn't a concern when developing a site with Web controls now, however. The server always renders the appropriate code. Today, developers can build for the latest and greatest browser, and include the functionality they always wanted to include in their pages, but didn't because they had to build for older browser versions.

HTML Server Controls versus Web Controls

If you read through the previous chapter, you are now wondering which is better: HTML server controls or Web controls? What it really comes down to is the exact functionality you require within your page.

It is also important to realize that you don't have to choose one or the other. It is possible to have both HTML Server controls and Web controls on the same page and within the same Web application.

When creating a Web control, you are creating a control for the server and not for the client. The server takes this control and renders the appropriate HTML based upon the specified functionality within the control itself.

A Web control looks like this:

```
<asp:Label [attributes] >Hello World!</asp:Label>
```

One important difference between HTML Server controls and Web controls is that the attributes in HTML Server controls are specific to that HTML element, but the attributes within Web controls are specific for the control itself, not for the HTML that is generated based upon the control.

When deciding what type of control to use, you should base your choice on what control offers the specific functionality that you require. Table 35-1 summarizes when to use HTML Server controls and when to use Web controls.

Table 35-1
HTML Server Controls versus Web Controls

Control Type	When to Use This Control
Web control	When you require a richer set of functionality to perform complicated page requirements.
	When you are developing Web pages that will be viewed by a mutitude of browser types that would require different code based upon these types.
	When you prefer a more Visual Basic-type programming model that is based on the use of controls.
HTML Server control	When converting traditional ASP 3.0 Web pages to ASP.NET Web pages, and speed is a concern. You'll find that it is a lot easier to change your HTML elements to HTML Server controls rather then changing them to Web controls.
	When you prefer a more HTML-type programming model.
	When you wish to explicitly control the code that is generated for the browser.

There really aren't any hard and fast rules for this. You may come to realize that you are using one type of control more than the other, though it is important that you don't become too dependent on only one type of control, and that you truly have an understanding of both types in order to build the best Web pages and forms possible.

Web Controls and How to Program for Them

In the following pages, you see a good description of each of the Web controls and, more importantly, how to program for them and add their rich functionality to your Web pages.

Web controls can be as simple and as complex as you want them to be, but in general, they are very easy to use within your pages.

Figure 35-1 shows the hierarchy of Web controls in the System.Web.UI.WebControls namespace.

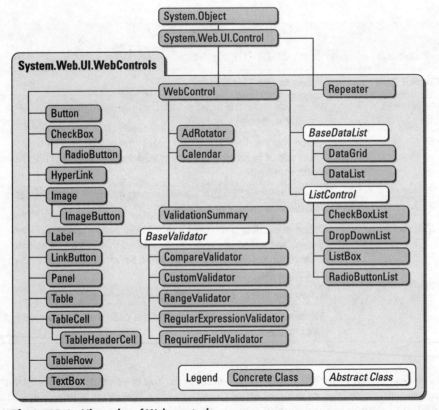

Figure 35-1: Hierarchy of Web controls

You need to code Web controls in an XHTML-compliant way, meaning that you must properly nest tags. Close the tags that are singular elements with />. For instance, you can write the Label control as the following:

```
<asp:label runat="server" id="label1"></asp:label>
```

Or, you can write the Label control as the following:

```
<asp:label runat="server" id="label1" />
```

Either way is fine.

Table 35-2 gives a brief description of the controls that are covered in this chapter.

Table 35-2 **Web Controls**	
Web Control	**Description**
`<asp:adrotator>`	Similar to the traditional ASP `adrotator` component. This control displays a specified order of images. It is also possible to set the sequence of images to be random.
`<asp:button>`	Used to perform a task or initiate an event. Used to submit forms to the server.
`<asp:calendar>`	A rich control that displays a graphical calendar, and allows the user to select a date that can initiate an event on the page.
`<asp:checkbox>`	Displays a traditional HTML check box that allows users to click it on or off.
`<asp:checkboxlist>`	A group of check boxes that allow for mutiple selections.
`<asp:datagrid>`	A list control that allows data-bound information to be displayed in tables. The tables can be constructed to allow for editing and sorting.
`<asp:datalist>`	A list control that allows data-bound information to be displayed. Construction of the display is done by using a customizable template.
`<asp:dropdownlist>`	Displays a traditional HTML select tag that allows users to select an item from a drop-down list of items.
`<asp:hyperlink>`	Displays a traditional HTML hyperlink that users click to perform an event (such as going to a new page).
`<asp:image>`	Displays an image.
`<asp:imagebutton>`	The same as a Button control, but allows an image to be used for the button.
`<asp:label>`	Displays text that the user cannot edit directly.
`<asp:linkbutton>`	The same as a Button control, but looks like a hyperlink.
`<asp:listbox>`	Similar to the drop-down list control, but instead of seeing just one list item, the user can see multiple list items. It also optionally allows for mutiple selections.
`<asp:literal>`	Displays static text.
`<asp:panel>`	Creates a borderless division on the form that serves as a container for other controls.

Continued

	Table 35-2 *(continued)*
Web Control	**Description**
`<asp:placeholder>`	Reserves a location in the page control hierarchy for controls that are added programmatically.
`<asp:radiobutton>`	Displays a traditional HTML radio button.
`<asp:radiobuttonlist>`	Displays a group of traditional HTML radio buttons. The user can select only one choice from the group.
`<asp:repeater>`	A list control that allows for data-bound information to be displayed using any number of controls as a template.
`<asp:table>`	Displays a traditional HTML table.
`<asp:textbox>`	Displays a traditional HTML text box.
`<asp:xml>`	Displays XML documents, and allows XSL documents to transform them.

Text display controls

The following controls displays text within the browser. The Label control allows for programmatic access to its properties, whereas the Literal control is meant to display static text:

<asp:label>

The Label control allows you to place text blocks on a Web page, and program against them. Within the code of the document, the Label control is written as `<asp:label>`, and examples are shown in the following blocks of code:

```
<asp:Label id="Label1"
     Text="label"
     runat="server"/>
```

or

```
<asp:Label id="Label1"
     runat="server">
   Text
</asp:Label>
```

If you want to place static text on a page, you don't need to use the Label control; you should use HTML to format and present your static text within the document. You also have the option of using the Literal control (discussed later in this chapter).

The Label control (shown in Figure 35-2) allows you to change text at runtime and to change text on events, such as button clicks. You use this control a lot within list bound controls (DataList, DataGrid, and Repeater). Think of the Label control as a placeholder for text.

The example in Listing 35-1 shows how to change some text on the page when a button is clicked.

Listing 35-1: <asp:label> Code Example

```
<html>
  <head>
        <title>Using the Label Control</title>

  <script language=VB runat=server>
        Sub Page_Load(Sender As Object, E As EventArgs)
              Label1.Text = "Hello World!"
        End Sub

        Sub Button1_Click(Sender As Object, E As EventArgs)
              Label1.Text = "How are you doing today?"
        End Sub
  </script>

  </head>

  <body>
    <form runat="server">
        <asp:label id="label1" runat="server" />
        <p>
        <asp:button id="button1" runat="server"
        onclick="Button1_Click" Text="Change Text" />
    </form>
  </body>
</html>
```

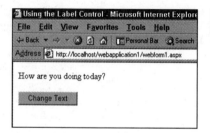

Figure 35-2: Changing the Label control with a button click

This is a simple page, but it shows what you can do with the Label control. You could also build the page by grabbing and dropping a Label control from the Toolbox in Visual Studio .NET onto your page.

Looking at the code, you notice that the controls are placed between form tags. The form needs to have the attribute `runat=server` in order to work properly.

Within the script tags at the top of the page are two subroutines. The first subroutine, `Page_Load`, is fired when the page loads. In this routine, the `Label` control contains the text `"Hello World!"` The second routine is a click event for the button on the page called `Button1_click`. For this event, you change the `Label` control text by establishing the text the same way as you did in the `Page_Load` event. All you are doing is reassigning a new value to the `Label` control in the button click event.

Notice that the script tag has two required attributes. The first establishes the language the script uses. In this case, you are using `language=VB`, but you could have used `language=C#` (for the purposes of this book, you should stick to VB .NET). The second attribute is `runat=server`, which specifies that this script is to run on the server, not on the client.

You are building controls that the server interprets and generates the appropriate HTML for the browser that is viewing the page. In this way, you are always assured of downward compatibility for your pages.

So, for the page with the `Label` control that you just created, the code generated looks like that in Listing 35-2 for Microsoft Internet Explorer 6.0 (which you should have if you installed Visual Studio .NET on your machine).

Listing 35-2: **Code Generated from Listing 35-1 Controls**

```
<html>
  <head>
          <title>Using the Label Control</title>
  </head>
  <body>

  <form name="ctrl0" method="post" action="webform4.aspx"
  id="ctrl0">
  <input type="hidden" name="__VIEWSTATE"
value="dDwtMTA2MDQwMDUyMDtOPDtsPGk8Mj47PjtsPHQ8O2w8aTwxPjs+O2
w8dDxwPHA8bDxUZXh0OO0z47bDxIZWxsbyBXb3JsZCE7Pj47Pjs7Pjs+Pjs
+Pjs+" />

  <span id="label1">Hello World!</span>
  <p>
  <input type="submit" name="button1" value="Change Text"
  id="button1" />
  </form>

  </body>
</html>
```

As you can tell from Listing 35-2, your controls were turned into a `<span>` tag and an `<input type="submit">` tag.

Be aware that a number of attributes are available for your controls. By placing the control directly on the page by dragging and dropping it from the Toolbox within Visual Studio .NET and then highlighting the control, you get a complete list of attributes in the Properties window. If you are just typing the code directly into the code page, place your cursor on the control, and a list of available attributes appears. The third (and best) way to discover the available attributes is when you are typing in the code. You can view the list that IntelliSense provides of the available attributes to include for that control (see Figure 35-3). For instance, you could customize the Label control with the following attributes: `AccessKey`, `BackColor`, `BorderColor`, `BorderStyle`, `BorderWidth`, `CssClass`, `Enabled`, `EnableViewState`, `Font-Bold`, `Font-Italic`, `Font-Name`, `Font-Names`, `Font-Overline`, `Font-Size`, `Font-Strikeout`, `Font-Underline`, `ForeColor`, `Height`, `ID`, `Runat`, `TabIndex`, `Visible`, and `Width`. The events that are available include `ondatabinding`, `ondisposed`, `oninit`, `onload`, `onprerender`, and `onunload`.

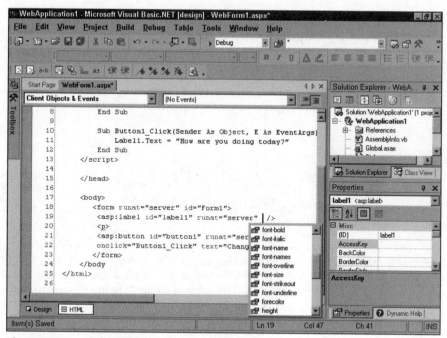

Figure 35-3: Using IntelliSense to help write code

As you can see, you can do a lot to just this simple control. Please keep this in mind as you work through the other controls because this chapter does not talk about every possible attribute.

<asp:literal>

The Literal control allows you to place static text on a Web page and program against them. Within the code of the document, you write the Literal control as <asp:literal> and is shown in the following code:

```
<asp:Literal id="Literal1"
    Text="Text"
    runat="server"/>
```

The big disadvantage of the Literal control (or perhaps the advantage to others) is that unlike the Label control, you cannot apply any styles to this control. Hence the name—Literal control. It is a literal representation of the text.

Input controls

The controls in this section allow the user to input specific information to the server by various form elements.

<asp:textbox>

The TextBox control (shown in the following code) allows you to place text boxes on a Web page within a form, and program for them. Within the code of the document, the TextBox control is written as <asp:textbox>.

```
<asp:TextBox id=value
    AutoPostBack="True|False"
    Columns="characters"
    MaxLength="characters"
    Rows="rows"
    Text="text"
    TextMode="Single | Multiline | Password"
    Wrap="True|False"
    OnTextChanged="OnTextChangedMethod"
    runat="server"/>
```

The TextBox control can be used to create three different types of HTML elements. The first is the single line text box, which is a text box that is allows only one line of text to be entered in. With the single-line text box, it is possible to modify the size and number of characters accepted. The second element is the password text box, shown in Figure 35-4. This text box is similar to the first one, except that it uses asterisks (*) to mask all the characters the user inputs into it.

Figure 35-4: TextBox Control with the TextMode set to Password

The third type of element that you can create with the TextBox control is the HTML text area element, which is a text box that can expand to a set width and height by specifying the columns and rows of the text box (see Figure 35-5).

The default setting of the TextBox control is the single-line mode.

In the following example (Listing 35-3), you build a page that uses the Textbox control in a couple of different ways.

Listing 35-3: **<asp:textbox>** Code Example

```
<html>
  <head>
        <title>Using the TextBox Control</title>

  <script language=VB runat=server>
        Sub Page_Load(Sender As Object, E As EventArgs)
              Label1.Text = "Hello, what is your name?"
        End Sub

        Sub Button1_Click(Sender As Object, E As EventArgs)
              Label1.Text = "Thank you " & Text1.Text & _
              "<br>You live at:<br>" & Text2.Text
        End Sub

        Sub Text1_Change(Sender As Object, E As EventArgs)
              Label2.Text = "User Entered Their Name."
        End Sub
  </script>

  </head>

  <body>
     <form runat="server">
         <asp:label id="label1" runat="server"
         font-name="verdana" font-bold="true"/>
         <p>
         Name:<br>
         <asp:textbox id="Text1" runat="server"
         font-name="verdana" autopostback="True"
         ontextchanged="Text1_Change"/>
         <p>
         Address:<br>
         <asp:textbox id="Text2" runat="server"
         font-name="verdana" columns="65" rows="5"
         textmode="MultiLine" />
         <p>
         <asp:button id="Button1" runat="server"
         text="Submit Information" onclick="button1_click" />
         <p>
         <asp:label id="label2" runat="server"
         font-name="verdana" />
     </form>
  </body>
</html>
```

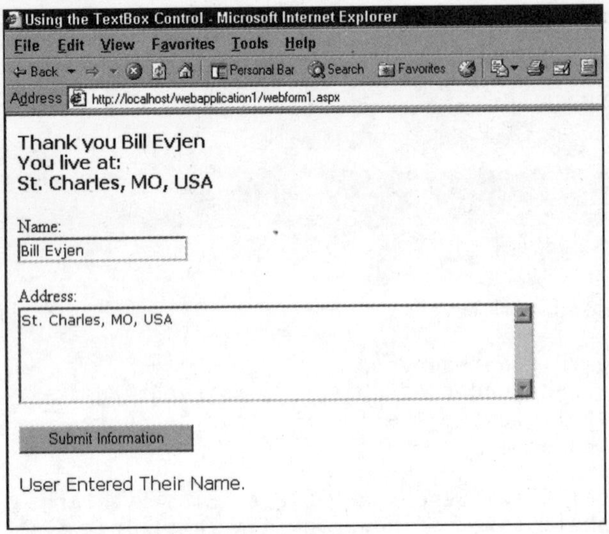

Figure 35-5: Using the TextBox control

This example uses the `TextBox` control in two ways: The first is to create a traditional HTML text box, and the second is to create an HTML text area. By default, the `TextBox` control uses a single-line control, so in order to switch the control to a multiline control, you must specify `textmode="MultiLine"` as an attribute of the control.

This page uses a single `Label` control to display both the greeting message and the message that gives the user's name and address. This is changed with a button click event. The second `Label` control informs you when an event is initiated. This event is tied to the `Text1` `TextBox` control. `OnTextChange` raises an event when the user leaves the control. In order to use this, you need to set the `autopostback` to `True` as well.

It is also possible to set the value of the `TextBox` control so that when the page renders for the first time, there is a message within the box itself. There are two ways of assigning the value. The first way is within the `Page_Load` event:

```
Text1.Text = "Enter your name here."
```

The other way of doing this is to assign it with an attribute within the control itself:

```
<asp:textbox id="text1" runat="server"
text="Enter your name here." />
```

`<asp:checkbox>` and `<asp:checkboxlist>`

The two CheckBox controls (shown in the following code) allow you to place check boxes on a Web page within a form and program against them. Within the code of the document, the CheckBox control is written as `<asp:checkbox>`, whereas the CheckBoxList control is written as `<asp:checkboxlist>`.

```
<asp:CheckBox id="CheckBox1"
    AutoPostBack="True|False"
    Text="Label"
    TextAlign="Right|Left"
    Checked="True|False"
    OnCheckedChanged="OnCheckedChangedMethod"
    runat="server"/>

<asp:CheckBoxList id="CheckBoxList1"
    AutoPostBack="True|False"
    CellPadding="Pixels"
    DataSource='<% databindingexpression  %>'
    DataTextField="DataSourceField"
    DataValueField="DataSourceField"
    RepeatColumns="ColumnCount"
    RepeatDirection="Vertical|Horizontal"
    RepeatLayout="Flow|Table"
    TextAlign="Right|Left"
    OnSelectedIndexChanged="OnSelectedIndexChangedMethod"
    runat="server">

<asp:ListItem value="value"
    selected="True|False">
  Text
</asp:ListItem>

</asp:CheckBoxList>
```

Check boxes are HTML elements that allow you to specify on/off, yes/no, or true/false settings. For example, if you ask the users what their favorite books are, and list 10 books with check boxes next to the titles, the users either like the books or they don't. The check boxes are either checked or not.

`<asp:checkbox>` and `<asp:checkboxlist>` are similar in nature. Some of the main differences are that `<asp:checkbox>` allows for customization and event handling for individual check boxes on the page. Alternatively, the `<asp:checkboxlist>` control only allows for customization and event handling for a group of related check boxes.

In Listing 35-4, you create a page that uses both the CheckBox and the CheckBoxList controls. The page is shown in Figure 35-6.

Listing 35-4: `<asp:checkbox>` and `<asp:checkboxlist>` Code Example

```
<html>
  <head>
        <title>Using the CheckBox and CheckBoxList
        Controls</title>

    <script language=VB runat=server>
    Sub CheckBox1_CheckedChanged
        (Sender As Object, E As EventArgs)
            Label1.Text = "What authors do you like?"
            CheckBox1.Visible = False
            CheckBoxList1.Visible = True
    End Sub

    Sub CheckBoxList1_SelectedIndexChanged
        (Sender As Object, E As EventArgs)
            Label2.Visible = True
            Dim msg As String
            Dim li As ListItem
            msg = "You Like:"
            For Each li In CheckBoxList1.Items
                If li.Selected = True Then
                   msg = msg & "<BR>" & li.Text
                End If
            Next
            Label2.Text = msg
    End Sub
    </script>

  </head>

  <body>
    <form runat="server">
        <asp:Label id="Label1" runat="server">
        Do you like any authors?</asp:Label>
        <p>
        <asp:CheckBox id="CheckBox1" runat="server"
        Text="Yes I like some authors" AutoPostBack="True"
        oncheckedchanged="CheckBox1_CheckedChanged">
        </asp:CheckBox>
        <p>
<asp:CheckBoxList id="CheckBoxList1" runat="server"
Visible="False" Font-Names="Verdana" Font-Size="X-Small"
autopostback="True" Font-Bold="True"
onselectedindexchanged="CheckBoxList1_SelectedIndexChanged
">
        <asp:ListItem Value="author1">
        Stephen King</asp:ListItem>
        <asp:ListItem Value="author2">
```

```
            Ernest Hemingway</asp:ListItem>
            <asp:ListItem Value="author3">
            John Steinbeck</asp:ListItem>
            <asp:ListItem Value="author4">
            Michael Crichton</asp:ListItem>
            <asp:ListItem Value="author5">
            Jackie Collins</asp:ListItem>
    </asp:CheckBoxList>
            <p>
            <asp:Label id="Label2" runat="server"
            visible="False">You Like:</asp:Label>
    </form>
  </body>
</html>
```

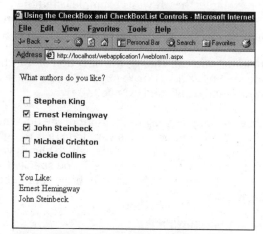

Figure 35-6: The second set of displayed controls. This shows the output of a CheckBoxList control and a Label control.

This example really shows you some of the power of Web controls, and what you can do with them. Everything that is happening here is happening on one page, without any trips back to the server to render the page again. In fact, running through the program, it looks as if you reached to a new page altogether, but it is just .NET at work all on one page.

You accomplished this by turning controls on and then off again. When users come to the page for the first time, they are asked a question, and there is a single check box on the page. If they check the check box, a number of events are fired off at the same time. First, you make that singular check box invisible by setting the visible attribute to False. Then you display other controls by switching their visible attributes to True.

Everything you are doing is based on `Click` events. When the user clicks any of the check boxes, an event fires. In this example, you have two different types of check boxes on the page: an `<asp:checkbox>` and an `<asp:checkboxlist>`. It is important to note that each control has a different `Click` event, because the `<asp:checkbox>` is concerned only with a single check box, whereas the `<asp:checkboxlist>` is watching over any number of check boxes.

The event for the `<asp:checkbox>` control is `OnCheckedChanged`, and the event for the `<asp:checkboxlist>` control is `OnSelectedIndexChanged`.

Another important setting for these controls is `TextAlign`. This attribute is either set to `Left` or `Right`. Setting this attribute to `Left` means that the text displays on the left side of the check box. Setting it to `Right` means that the text displays on the right side of the check box. The default setting is `Right`.

When using the `<asp:checkboxlist>` control, the check boxes within the group are aligned vertically by default. For example, the previous example listed the check boxes and the authors' names in a stacked appearance. However, you can customize the alignment of a group of check boxes.

By using the `RepeatDirection` attribute, you can change the direction of the check boxes. The choices for this attribute are `Horizontal` or `Vertical`. If you chose a `Horizontal` setting, the check boxes would be aligned from left to right.

But you may not want the check boxes to keep flowing to the right of the document. What would happen if you had 50 items? It would become a very long (left to right) page! To work with this, you have the `RepeatColumns` attribute, which allows you to specify the number of rows or columns allowed. For instance, if you specify the `RepeatDirection` to be `Horizontal` and the `RepeatColumns` to be 3, your check boxes would lay out in the following manner:

CheckBox1	CheckBox2	CheckBox3
CheckBox4	CheckBox5	CheckBox6
CheckBox7		

However, if you had the `RepeatDirection` set to `Vertical` and the `RepeatColumns` set to 3, your check boxes would lay out in the following manner:

CheckBox1	CheckBox4	CheckBox7
CheckBox2	CheckBox5	
CheckBox3	CheckBox6	

Another important attribute to be aware of when working with the `RepeatDirection` and `RepeatColumns` is the `RepeatLayout` attribute. This attribute can be either set to `Flow` (the default setting) or to `Table`. By using the `Table` setting, the check boxes are placed within a table, one check box in one cell. This lines up the layout of the check boxes.

<asp:radiobutton> and <asp:radiobuttonlist>

These two radio controls allow you to place radio buttons on a Web page within a form and program against them. Within the code of the document, the RadioButton control is written as `<asp:radiobutton>`, whereas the RadioButtonList control is written as `<asp:radiobuttonlist>`. A code example follows:

```
<asp:RadioButton id="RadioButton1"
    AutoPostBack="True|False"
    Checked="True|False"
    GroupName="GroupName"
    Text="label"
    TextAlign="Right|Left"
    OnCheckedChanged="OnCheckedChangedMethod"
    runat="server"/>

<asp:RadioButtonList id="RadioButtonList1"
    AutoPostBack="True|False"
    CellPadding="Pixels"
    DataSource="<% databindingexpression %>"
    DataTextField="DataSourceField"
    DataValueField="DataSourceField"
    RepeatColumns="ColumnCount"
    RepeatDirection="Vertical|Horizontal"
    RepeatLayout="Flow|Table"
    TextAlign="Right|Left"
    OnSelectedIndexChanged="OnSelectedIndexChangedMethod"
    runat="server">

    <asp:ListItem Text="label"
        Value="value"
        Selected="True|False" />

</asp:RadioButtonList>
```

Radio buttons are similar to check boxes in that they enable the user to make a selection from a choice of items. However, radio buttons are different in that they only allow a single choice from a group. For instance, if you wanted to know a user's choice for President in an online vote, you wouldn't give options with check boxes in which the user could select more than one choice. Instead, you would list options with radio buttons. With radio buttons, the user could make only one selection from a list of candidates.

The `<asp:radiobutton>` and the `<asp:radiobuttonlist>` are similar to each other. Some of the main differences are that the `<asp:radiobutton>` allows for customization and event handling for individual radio buttons on the page. Alternatively, the `<asp:radiobuttonlist>` control only allows for customization and event handling for a group of related radio buttons.

Note Radio buttons are usually in groups of two or more radio buttons. It doesn't make much sense to have a singular radio button because the user can't make a yes/no choice from only one element. A check box is better in that situation.

There really isn't much difference between the `<asp:radiobutton>` and the `<asp:radiobuttonlist>` controls. Like the `<asp:checkbox>` and the `<asp:checkboxlist>` controls, the RadioButton controls have different Onclick events. With these Click events, the `<asp:radiobutton>` control determines if a user clicks singular radio buttons (with the CheckChanged event), and the `<asp:radiobuttonlist>` control watches a group of radio buttons for the Click event (with the SelectedIndexChanged event). It is important to remember that if you want to watch for a Click event while it happens, you need to set the attribute autopostback=true.

The `<asp:radiobutton>` control does allow for non-radio button text to be inserted between radio buttons, whereas the `<asp:radiobuttonlist>` control does not allow this functionality.

In Listing 35-5, you create a page that uses both the RadioButton and the RadioButtonList controls. Figure 35-7 shows the output.

Listing 35-5: `<asp:radiobutton>` and `<asp:radiobuttonlist>` Code Example

```
<html>
  <head>
    <title>Using the RadioButton and RadioButtonList
    Controls</title>

<script language="VB" runat="server">
Sub RadioButton1_CheckedChanged
        (Sender As Object, E As EventArgs)
                if radiobutton1.checked then
                        RadioButtonList1.visible = true
                        RadioButtonList2.visible = false
                        Label2.visible = false
                else if radiobutton2.checked then
                        RadioButtonList2.visible = true
                        RadioButtonList1.visible = false
                        Label2.visible = false
                end if
        End Sub

Sub RadioButtonList1_Changed
        (Sender As Object, E As EventArgs)
                Label2.Visible = True
                Label2.Text = "You say you are using:<br>" &_
                RadioButtonList1.SelectedItem.Text
        End Sub
```

```
    Sub RadioButtonList2_Changed
          (Sender As Object, E As EventArgs)
                  Label2.Visible = True
                  Label2.text = "You say you are using:<br>" &_
                  RadioButtonList2.SelectedItem.Text
    End Sub
</script>

    </head>

    <body>
          <form runat="server">
    <asp:label id="Label1" runat="server" font-bold="True"
    font-names="Arial"> What browser are you
    using?</asp:label>
    <p>

    <asp:radiobutton runat="server" id="Radiobutton1"
    autopostback="true" backcolor="#cccccc" font-
    name="verdana" groupname="br_choice1" text="Microsoft
    Internet Explorer" font-size="X-Small" font-
    names="verdana" width="205px"
    oncheckedchanged="RadioButton1_CheckedChanged" /><br>

    <asp:radiobutton runat="server" id="Radiobutton2"
    autopostback="true" backcolor="#cccccc" font-
    name="verdana" groupname="br_choice1" text="Netscape
    Navigator" font-size="X-Small" font-names="verdana"
    width="205px"
    oncheckedchanged="RadioButton1_CheckedChanged" /></p>
    <p>

    <asp:RadioButtonList id="RadioButtonList1" runat="server"
    Font-Size="XX-Small" Font-Names="Verdana" Width="205px"
    BackColor="#FFEOCO" ToolTip="Select a browser version"
    Visible="False"
    onselectedindexchanged="radiobuttonlist1_Changed"
    autopostback="true">
          <asp:ListItem Value="Internet Explorer 3.0">Internet
          Explorer 3.0</asp:ListItem>
          <asp:ListItem Value="Internet Explorer 4.0">Internet
          Explorer 4.0</asp:ListItem>
          <asp:ListItem Value="Internet Explorer 5.0">Internet
          Explorer 5.0</asp:ListItem>
          <asp:ListItem Value="Internet Explorer 6.0">Internet
          Explorer 6.0</asp:ListItem>
    </asp:RadioButtonList></p>
    <p>

    <asp:RadioButtonList id="RadioButtonList2" runat="server"
    Font-Size="XX-Small" Font-Names="Verdana" Width="205px"
```

Continued

Listing 35-5 *(continued)*

```
BackColor="#FFE0C0" ToolTip="Select a browser version"
Visible="False"
onselectedindexchanged="radiobuttonlist2_Changed"
autopostback="true">
        <asp:ListItem Value="Netscape Navigator
        3.0">Netscape Navigator 3.0</asp:ListItem>
        <asp:ListItem Value="Netscape Navigator
        4.0">Netscape Navigator 4.0</asp:ListItem>
        <asp:ListItem Value="Netscape Navigator
        6.0">Netscape Navigator 6.0</asp:ListItem>
</asp:RadioButtonList></p>
<p>

<asp:label id="Label2" runat="server" Font-Size="X-Small"
Font-Names="Verdana" visible="False"></asp:label></p>

</form>
</body>
</html>
```

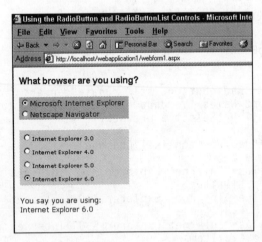

Figure 35-7: Using both the RadioButton and RadioButtonList controls

When users first pull up the page, they only see the two sets of radio buttons. When they make a selection, one of the two available groups of radio buttons shows up in the browser. Then, when the user selects a browser version from one of the RadioButtonList controls, text displays at the bottom of the page and informs them of their choice.

Like the CheckBox controls, the attribute TextAlign dictates what side of the radio button the text displayed. The default setting is Right, and it means that the text is displayed to the right of the radio button. A setting of Left means that the text displays on the left side of the radio button.

Also, like the CheckBox controls, you can customize the layout of the RadioButton controls using RepeatDirection, RepeatColumns, and RepeatLayout.

<asp:dropdownlist>

The DropDownList control allows you to place an HTML select box on a Web page within a form and program against it. Within the code of the document, the DropDownList control is written as <asp:dropdownlist>. A coding example follows:

```
<asp:DropDownList id="DropDownList1" runat="server"
    DataSource="<% databindingexpression %>"
    DataTextField="DataSourceField"
    DataValueField="DataSourceField"
    AutoPostBack="True|False"
    OnSelectedIndexChanged="OnSelectedIndexChangedMethod">

    <asp:ListItem value="value" selected="True|False">
        Text
    </asp:ListItem>

</asp:DropDownList>
```

The drop-down list allows the user to select one item from a drop-down list of items (see Figure 35-8). Only one item displays at a time (the selected item). When the user clicks the arrow button within the control, the drop-down list opens up and displays all the available choices. Depending on the number of choices, users may have to scroll through the list to find their choice.

Note   It is impossible to control how many items in the drop-down list are displayed when the list opens up. This is controlled by the browser, and is different based upon the browser type.

The DropDownList control is similar to the ListBox control, but the ListBox control allows the user to make multiple selections.

In the following example, you use the DropDownList control (see Listing 35-6) and then the following text works through what you built. You can see the result of the following code in Figure 35-8.

Listing 35-6: <asp:dropdownlist> Code Example

```html
<html>
  <head>
        <title>Using the DropDownList Control</title>

    <script language=VB runat=server>
        Sub DropDownList1_Changed
             (Sender As Object, E As EventArgs)
             Label1.Visible = True
             Label1.text = "Have fun in " & _
             DropDownList1.selecteditem.value & "!"
        End Sub
    </script>

  </head>

  <body>
    <form runat="server">
        <font size=3 face=arial><b>
        What country do you want to visit for your vacation?
        </b></font>
        <p>

        <asp:DropDownList id="DropDownList1" runat="server"
        Font-Names="Verdana" AutoPostBack="True"
        onselectedindexchanged="DropDownList1_changed">

        <asp:ListItem Value="Canada">Canada</asp:ListItem>
        <asp:ListItem Value="Finland">Finland</asp:ListItem>
        <asp:ListItem Value="Russia">Russia</asp:ListItem>
        <asp:ListItem Value="Germany">Germany</asp:ListItem>
        <asp:ListItem Value="China">China</asp:ListItem>

        </asp:DropDownList>
        <br></p>

        <p>
<asp:Label id="Label1" runat="server" Font-Size="X-Small"
Font-Names="Verdana" Visible="False"></asp:Label></p>
    </form>
  </body>
</html>
```

This page has only two controls. The first control is the DropDownList control. With this control, you list five possible selections. Each selection is an <asp:ListItem> item. It is important that you set the AutoPostBack to True. This allows the OnSelectedIndexChanged event to take place after the user selects one of the items in the drop-down list. If you leave the AutoPostBack setting on False (the default setting), a change to the selection or a first-time selection wouldn't fire off the event until the form was sent to the server. You want the `OnSelectedIndexChanged` event to fire right when users make their selections.

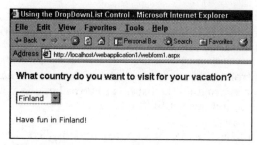

Figure 35-8: Using the `DropDownList` control

After the user makes a selection from the drop-down list, you turn the `Label` control from invisible to visible by changing the attribute `Visible="False"` to `Visible="True"`. When you want to print out what the user selected, you use `DropDownList1.selecteditem.value`, but you could also use `DropDownList1.selecteditem.text`. The difference is that by using `Text`, you mean whatever is between the `<asp:listitem>` tags, and by value you mean the value of the selected `<asp:listitem>` tag.

This example added a little more style to the controls than previous examples. For instance, it assigns Verdana font to all the controls, and changes the font size on the `Label` control.

<asp:listbox>

The `ListBox` control allows you to place an HTML select box on a Web page within a form and program against it. Within the code of the document, the `ListBox` control is written as `<asp:dropdownlist>`. (See the following code.)

```
<asp:ListBox id="Listbox1"
    DataSource="<% databindingexpression %>"
    DataTextField="DataSourceField"
    DataValueField="DataSourceField"
    AutoPostBack="True|False"
    Rows="rowcount"
    SelectionMode="Single|Multiple"
    OnSelectedIndexChanged="OnSelectedIndexChangedMethod"
    runat="server">

    <asp:ListItem value="value" selected="True|False">
        Text
    </asp:ListItem>

</asp:ListBox>
```

The `ListBox` control allows the user to select one or more items from a group of items (see Figure 35-9). The `ListBox` control is different from the `DropDownList` control in that it allows more than one selection if the `SelectionMode` is set to `Multiple`. The default setting is `Single`, meaning that the user can only make a single selection from the list.

Note To select mutiple items, the user must hold down the Ctrl or Shift key while clicking the item with the mouse to make the selection.

Also, unlike the `DropDownList` control, the `ListBox` control can show more than one selection at a time. In fact, you can program the list box to be as large as you want it to be and to show any amount of items within the box.

In Listing 35-7, you build a page that uses the `ListBox` control and displays the user's selections within a `Label` control. The result of the code can be seen in Figure 35-9.

Listing 35-7: `<asp:listbox>` Code Example

```
<html>
  <head>
        <title>Using the ListBox Control</title>

<script language=VB runat=server>
    Sub ListBox1_Change(Sender As Object, E As EventArgs)
        Label2.Visible = True
        Label2.Text = " You want to go to:<p><ol>"

        Dim li as ListItem
        For Each li in ListBox1.Items
                If li.Selected Then
                        Label2.text += "<li>" & li.Text & _
                        "</li>"
                End If
          Next
        Label2.Text += "</ol>"
    End Sub
</script>

  </head>

<body>
    <form runat="server">
        <font size="3" face="arial"><b>
        What countries do you want to visit for your
        lifetime?
```

```
</b></font>
<p>

<asp:ListBox id="ListBox1" runat="server"
SelectionMode="Multiple" Rows="5" Width="250px"
Height="60px" autopostback="True"
onselectedindexchanged="listbox1_change">

<asp:ListItem Value="Canada">Canada</asp:ListItem>
<asp:ListItem Value="Finland">Finland</asp:ListItem>
<asp:ListItem Value="Russia">Russia</asp:ListItem>
<asp:ListItem Value="Germany">Germany</asp:ListItem>
<asp:ListItem Value="China">China</asp:ListItem>
<asp:ListItem Value="Mexico">Mexico</asp:ListItem>

</asp:ListBox>

</p><p>
<asp:Label id="Label2" runat="server" Font-Size="X-
Small" Font-Names="Verdana" Visible="False"
backcolor="#E0E0E0" width="250"></asp:Label>
</p>
</form>
</body>
</html>
```

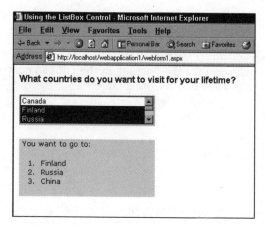

Figure 35-9: Using the `ListBox` control

This example uses a `ListBox` control and a `Label` control to display the user's selections. Within the `ListBox` control, you allow the user to choose more than one country by making the `SelectionMode` attribute equal to `Multiple`.

One interesting point is that you set the Rows attribute within the ListBox control to equal 5. This means that the control should show five countries; if there were more than five countries within the control, there would be a vertical scrollbar so the user could scroll down to see all the choices. If you typed in this code and ran the page, you would notice that there are only three countries shown within the control (with the scrollbar). The reason for this is because you made a setting to the Height attribute of the control. You specified that the height of the control should be 60 pixels. If you set the Height attribute, this attribute takes precedence over the Rows attribute.

You also listed out the user's choices in an ordered-list, and the list would dynamically change based upon the choices selected within the ListBox control.

This example also added some style attributes to the mix. You set the width of the ListBox control to 250 pixels, as well as the Label control's width. Then, you added a background color to the output of the Label control.

Form submission controls

The following controls support form submission. It is usually the case, that within a form, there are a number of form elements that allow the user to enter or modify data. Then at the bottom of the form, there is the means for the user to submit this information to the server or to the page.

Cross-Reference For a detailed description on connecting to a database and inserting data, see Part IV.

<asp:button>

The Button control allows you to place an HTML button on a Web page within a form and program against it. Within the code of the document, the Button control is written as <asp:button>, and is shown in the following code:

```
<asp:Button id="MyButton"
    Text="label"
    CommandName="command"
    CommandArgument="commandArgument"
    OnClick="OnClickMethod"
    runat="server"/>
```

The Button control can be used to initiate events, as well as to submit a form to the server (see Figure 35-10). By default, the Button control is a submit button. You can control the button's actions by responding to the button's click events.

Listing 35-8 builds a page that has a number of buttons. Each button changes the value of a number.

Listing 35-8: **<asp:button> Code Example**

```
<html>
  <head>
        <title>Using the Button Control</title>

  <script language=VB runat=server>
        Sub Page_Load(Sender As Object, E As EventArgs)
              If Not IsPostback Then
                    Dim OurNumber as Integer
                    OurNumber = 100
                    Label1.Text = Label1.Text & _
                     " <b>100</b>"
                    Hidden1.Value = OurNumber
              End If
        End Sub

        Sub CommandBtn_Click
              (sender As Object, e As CommandEventArgs)
           Dim OurNumber As Integer
           OurNumber = Hidden1.Value
           Select Case e.commandname
              Case "add"
                    OurNumber = OurNumber + 5
              Case "subtract"
                    OurNumber = OurNumber - 5
              Case "multiply"
                    OurNumber = OurNumber * 5
              Case "divide"
                    OurNumber = OurNumber / 5
           End Select
           Hidden1.Value = OurNumber
           Label1.Text = "Present Value: <b>" & OurNumber & _
              "</b>"
        End Sub
  </script>

  </head>

  <body>
     <form runat="server">
        <font face="Verdana" size="2">
        The original value is <b>100</b>
        </font><p>
        <asp:Label id="Label1" runat="server" Font-
        Names="Verdana" Font-Size="X-Small">Present
        Value:</asp:Label></p>

        <p><asp:Button id="Button1" runat="server" Text="Add
        5" commandname="add"
        oncommand="commandbtn_click"></asp:Button>
```

Continued

Listing 35-8 *(continued)*

```
 <asp:Button id="Button2" runat="server"
Text="Subtract 5" commandname="subtract"
oncommand="commandbtn_click"></asp:Button>

 <asp:Button id="Button3" runat="server"
Text="Multiply by 5" commandname="multiply"
oncommand="commandbtn_click"></asp:Button>

 <asp:Button id="Button4" runat="server"
Text="Divide by 5" commandname="divide"
oncommand="commandbtn_click"></asp:Button></p>

        <input type="hidden" id="hidden1" runat="server">
    </form>
  </body
</html>
```

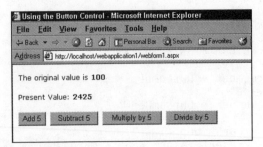

Figure 35-10: Using the `Button` control

There is a lot going on here, so start from the top. The first item is the script section of the code. The first subroutine is the `Page_Load` event:

```
Sub Page_Load(Sender As Object, E As EventArgs)
            If Not IsPostback Then
            Dim OurNumber as Integer
            OurNumber = 100
                Label1.Text = Label1.Text & _
    " <b>100</b>"
                Hidden1.Value = OurNumber
            End If
End Sub
```

This is a good introduction to the `PostBack` event. Whenever a page is rendered for the first time, it loads up the `Page_Load` subroutine. Also, when the page is rendered again from a button click, a form submission, or any other event, it runs through the `Page_Load` routine again. To differentiate between rendering the very first time and any subsequent times, you can check for the `PostBack` event.

In this case, you wanted to run through this VB .NET code only the first time the page was rendered, so you were checking to see if the page was not a `PostBack`. So, for other pages, you can follow this example:

```
Sub Page_Load(Sender As Object, E As EventArgs)
        If Not IsPostback Then
                'Do code for first time rendering here.
        Else
                'Do PostBack code here.
        End If
End Sub
```

Notice that on one of the last lines of the routine from the code example, it sets the value of a `<input="hidden">` HTML Server control. As stated earlier, you can mix Web controls and HTML Server controls. In this case, the code assigns the initial value of 100 to the HTML control.

The second subroutine looks as follows:

```
Sub CommandBtn_Click
            (sender As Object, e As CommandEventArgs)
        Dim OurNumber As Integer
        OurNumber = Hidden1.Value
        Select Case e.commandname
            Case "add"
                OurNumber = OurNumber + 5
            Case "subtract"
                OurNumber = OurNumber - 5
            Case "multiply"
                OurNumber = OurNumber * 5
            Case "divide"
                OurNumber = OurNumber / 5
        End Select
        Hidden1.Value = OurNumber
        Label1.Text = "Present Value: <b>" & OurNumber & _
        "</b>"
End Sub
```

The first difference is that this code is not loading up the System.EventArgs name-space within this subroutine. Instead, it loads the System.CommandEventArgs, which gives you access to the member CommandName.

You then grab the value of the hidden HTML Server control and then, based on which button was pressed, you add, subtract, multiply, or divide from the value. Using `e.commandname`, you could check which button was pressed. Within the `<asp:Button control>`, you have an attribute `CommandName="Something"` and you can check against the name used.

After refiguring the value of `OurNumber`, you then rewrite the value into the `Label` control.

<asp:linkbutton>

The LinkButton control (shown in the following examples) is a variation of the Button control. The LinkButton control allows you to place a text on a Web page within a form, and program against it so that it acts as a Button control. Within the code of the document, the LinkButton control is written as <asp:linkbutton>.

```
<asp:LinkButton id="LinkButton1"
    Text="label"
    Command="Command"
    CommandArgument="CommandArgument"
    OnClick="OnClickMethod"
    runat="server"/>
```

or

```
<asp:LinkButton id="LinkButton1"
    Command="Command"
    CommandArgument="CommandArgument"
    OnClick="OnClickMethod"
    runat="server" >
  Text
</asp:LinkButton>
```

The LinkButton control looks as if it is the Hyperlink control, but think of it as a textual version of the Button control.

You now build an example (see Listing 35-9) that uses the LinkButton control.

Listing 35-9: <asp:linkbutton> Code Example

```
<html>
  <head>
        <title>Using the LinkButton Control</title>

    <script language=VB runat=server>
        Sub Page_Load(Sender As Object, E As EventArgs)
                If Not IsPostback Then
                        LinkButton1.Text = "You have not
                        clicked this button yet"
                End If
        End Sub

        Sub LinkButton1_Click
                (sender As Object, E As EventArgs)
                LinkButton1.Text = "You have now clicked this
                button"
        End Sub
    </script>

  </head>
```

```
<body>
  <form runat="server">
    <asp:LinkButton id="LinkButton1" runat="server"
    font-bold="True" font-names="Verdana" font-size="X-
    Small" onclick="LinkButton1_Click"></asp:LinkButton>
  </form>
</body>
</html>
```

Using the `onclick` event, you were able to tell when the user clicked the textual button you created. Based on the `Click` event, you then changed the text of the button.

Also, like the `Button` control, you can use the `oncommand` event for this button in the same way:

`<asp:imagebutton>`

The `ImageButton` control is another variation of the `Button` control. The `ImageButton` control allows you to place an image on a Web page within a form, and program against it so that it acts as a `Button` control. Within the code of the document, the `ImageButton` control is written as `<asp:imagebutton>`. (See the following code.)

```
<asp:ImageButton id="ImageButton1"
    ImageUrl="string"
    Command="Command"
    CommandArgument="CommandArgument"
    OnClick="OnClickMethod"
    runat="server"/>
```

When placed on a Web page, the `ImageButton` control looks as if it is a regular image, although it is programmed to perform the same as any `Button` control. Many developers like to build their own style of submit buttons, and by using the `ImageButton` control, you can perform this type of functionality.

Listing 35-10 shows an instance of the `ImageButton` control.

Listing 35-10: `<asp:imagebutton>` Code Example

```
<html>
  <head>
      <title>Using the ImageButton Control</title>

  <script language=VB runat=server>
```

Continued

Listing 35-10 *(continued)*

```
      Sub ImageButton1_Click
         (sender As Object, E As ImageClickEventArgs)
            Label1.Visible = true
            Label1.Text = "<p>You have clicked the image
            button!</p>"
   End Sub
</script>

</head>

<body>
   <form runat="server">
      <asp:ImageButton id="ImageButton1" runat="server"
      BorderStyle="Solid" BorderColor="Black"
      BorderWidth="1px" AlternateText="Submit the Form"
      ImageUrl="button1.gif" onclick="imagebutton1_click">
      </asp:ImageButton>

      <asp:label id="Label1" runat="server"
      visible="False" />
   </form>
</body>
</html>
```

This short example shows that you can use images as buttons within your .NET Web pages with little work on your part. Within the body of the code, you place one `ImageButton` control and a `Label` control. The `Label` control is not visible until the user presses the image button.

For the `ImageButton` control, you specify the location of the image using the `ImageUrl` attribute. In this example, you added a little style to the button by placing a border around the image button, and gave it a black solid border that is one pixel wide.

Navigation controls

The `Hyperlink` control displays a hyperlink within the browser, and allows for programmatic access to its properties.

<asp:hyperlink>

The `Hyperlink` control allows you to place an HTML hyperlink on a Web page within a form and program against it (see Figure 35-11). Within the code of the document, the `Hyperlink` control is written as `<asp:hyperlink>`. Examples of the `Hyperlink` control follow:

```
<asp:HyperLink id="HyperLink1" ""
    NavigateUrl="url"
    Text="HyperLinkText"
    ImageUrl="url"
    Target="window"
    runat="server"/>
```

or

```
<asp:HyperLink id="HyperLink1"""
    NavigateUrl="url"
    ImageUrl="url"
    Target="window"
    runat="server">
  Text
</asp:HyperLink>
```

The Hyperlink control is used to allow users to move from page to page within a Web application. You can set the text of the hyperlink using the Text attribute. It is also possible to create an image hyperlink by using the ImageUrl attribute and setting it to a specified image.

In Listing 35-11, you build a page that allows you to dynamically change the destination of the hyperlink.

Listing 35-11: **<asp:hyperlink> Code Example**

```
<html>
  <head>
        <title>Using the HyperLink Control</title>

  <script language=VB runat=server>
  Sub RadioButtonList1_Change
    (sender As Object, E As EventArgs)
    HyperLink1.Visible = True
    HyperLink1.Text = "<p>Click here to go to " & _
    RadioButtonList1.SelectedItem.Text & "</p>"
    HyperLink1.NavigateURL =
    RadioButtonList1.SelectedItem.Value
  End Sub
  </script>

  </head>

  <body>
     <form runat="server">
         <p><font face="Verdana">
         <b>Where do you want to go today?</b>
         </font></p>
```

Continued

Listing 35-11 *(continued)*

```
            <p>
            <asp:RadioButtonList id="RadioButtonList1"
            runat="server" Font-Names="Verdana" Font-Size="X-
            Small"
            onselectedindexchanged="RadioButtonList1_Change"
            autopostback="true">

            <asp:ListItem Value="http://www.hungryminds.com/">
            Hungry Minds
            </asp:ListItem>
            <asp:ListItem Value="http://www.microsoft.com/">
            Microsoft</asp:ListItem>
            <asp:ListItem Value="http://www.cnn.com/">CNN
            </asp:ListItem>
            <asp:ListItem Value="http://www.usatoday.com/">
            USA Today</asp:ListItem>
            <asp:ListItem Value="http://www.yahoo.com/">
            Yahoo!</asp:ListItem>

            </asp:RadioButtonList></p>

            <p>
            <asp:HyperLink id="HyperLink1" runat="server" Font-
            Names="Verdana" Font-Size="X-Small" ToolTip="Click
            on this link to go to your desired page."
            Visible="False" Target="_blank"></asp:HyperLink>
            </p>
        </form>
    </body>
</html>
```

This example uses the Hyperlink control with the RadioButtonList control. When the user makes a selection from the group of radio buttons, the appropriate link displays at the bottom of the page.

After the user makes a selection, the RadioButtonList1_Change event, as shown in the following code snippet, is fired.

```
Sub RadioButtonList1_Change
    (sender As Object, E As EventArgs)
    HyperLink1.Visible = True
    HyperLink1.Text = "<p>Click here to go to " & _
    RadioButtonList1.SelectedItem.Text & "</p>"
    HyperLink1.NavigateURL =
    RadioButtonList1.SelectedItem.Value
End Sub
```

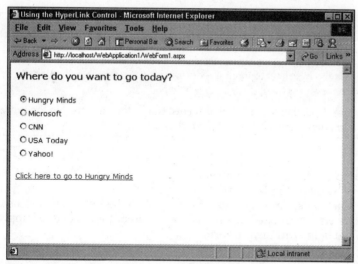

Figure 35-11: Working with the HyperLink control

Within this event, the first thing you do is make the `Hyperlink` control visible by
setting the `HyperLink1.Visible = True`. Then, you assign a string value to the
`HyperLink1.Text` because before the user clicks one of the radio buttons, there is
no text assigned to the `Hyperlink` control. You add to the text by using the
`RadioButtonList1.SelectedItem.Text`, and assign the `href` of the hyperlink by
`HyperLink1.NavigateURL = RadioButtonList1.SelectedItem.Value`.

Within the `Hyperlink` control itself, you set the `Target` attribute to `_blank`, meaning that when the user clicks the link, it opens a new browser window to display the
page. Table 35-3 lists the available hyperlink targets.

Table 35-3
Available HyperLink Targets

Target	Destination
_blank	Has the hyperlink open a new blank window. Some developers like to keep users on their site. One way to do this is to have all external links open in a new browser window.
_parent	For use within framed HTML documents. Opens the document in the current frameset.
_search	Has the hyperlink open the document in Microsoft Internet Explorer's Search frameset.

Continued

Target	Destination
_self	Causes the hyperlink to open the document in the same window as the hyperlink. This is the default setting of hyperlinks.
_top	For use within framed HTML documents. Opens the document in the browser window, but is independent of the rest of the frameset.

Table 35-3 *(continued)*

Also within the Hyperlink control, you use the `ToolTip` property. You set the `ToolTip` property by using the `ToolTip=Click on this link to go to your desired page`. When a user mouses over the control on the Web page, a delayed yellow box appears with your specified text. This is a great tool to use to supply quick help to all the fields within your forms.

Image controls

The `Image` control displays an image within the browser, and allows for programmatic access to its properties.

<asp:image>

The `Image` control allows you to place images on a Web page within a form, and program against them. Within the code of the document, the `Image` control is written as `<asp:image>`. An example of the `Image` control is shown in the following code:

```
<asp:Image id="Image1" runat="server"
     ImageUrl="string"
     AlternateText="string"
     ImageAlign="NotSet|AbsBottom|AbsMiddle|BaseLine|
               Bottom|Left|Middle|Right|TextTop|Top"/>
```

Images are generally used throughout HTML documents in order to make the pages more attractive and more presentable to users. The `Image` control allows developers to display and manage images within their Web Forms.

You can generate images either at design time—when you are building the page—or you can dynamically generate the images at runtime by specifying the `ImageUrl` attribute of the `Image` control.

It is also possible to bind the `ImageUrl` to a datasource so that images are based on some data within the database.

Cross-Reference   Data Binding of controls is discussed in the ListBound controls section of this chapter.

Unfortunately, the `Image` control does not support the user clicking the image. If you want to program events based on clicks, use the `ImageButton` control.

The code in Listing 35-12 shows a page that allows you to dynamically change some of the images attributes.

Listing 35-12: `<asp:image>` Code Example

```
<html>
  <head>
        <title>Using the ImageButton Control</title>

  <script language=VB runat=server>
  Sub Button1_Click(source As Object, E As EventArgs)
        Image1.ImageUrl = Server.MapPath("button2.gif")
  End Sub
  </script>

  </head>

  <body>
     <form runat="server">
        <p>
        <asp:image id="Image1" runat="server"
        imagealign="Left" forecolor="White"
        ImageUrl="button1.gif"></asp:image></p>
        <br clear="all">

        <p><asp:Button id="Button1" runat="server"
        Text="Change Image"
        onclick="Button1_Click"></asp:Button>

     </form>
  </body>
</html>
```

This is a pretty simple example, mainly because the `Image` control is a pretty simple control. It is very easy with this control to change images on the fly, and the source of your images can be almost anything. You can get them from the code or from a database source.

Although the example in Listing 35-12 doesn't, you can also dynamically set and change the `AlternateText` attribute of the `Image` control. The alternate text is the text that displays in place of an image if the download is too slow and the image hasn't yet displayed, or if the user is unable to view images. It is also possible to change the alignment, height, and width of the image.

Layout controls

The following controls support Web page presentation. The `<asp:panel>`, `<asp:table>`, and `<asp:placeholder>` controls play an important role in the lay-out of the page and the way the page is presented as a whole.

`<asp:panel>`

First of all, the `Panel` control is a great control because of the time it saves you in your programming and code organization. The `Panel` control is basically a wrapper for other controls. It allows you to take a group of controls and turn them into a sin-gle unit. The `Panel` control is shown in the following example:

```
<asp:Panel id="Panel1"
    BackImageUrl="url"
    HorizontalAlign="Center|Justify|Left|NotSet|Right"
    Wrap="True|False"
    runat="server">

(Other controls declared here)

</asp:Panel>
```

The advantage of using the `Panel` control to encapsulate a set of controls is that as a single unit of controls, you are then able to control the same attribute in one place (the `Panel` control), and it changes the same attribute in all of the controls contained within.

For instance, sometimes you want to turn controls on or off. By using the `Panel` control, you can turn on or off all the controls declared within the `Panel` control itself. You also can control the styles of the controls within the `Panel` control (see Figure 35-12).

Tip   Don't use the `Panel` control to group radio buttons or check boxes together. It does not force the radio buttons and check boxes to function together as a group. Instead, use the `RadioButtonList` and the `CheckBoxList` controls to perform this functionality.

As far as style goes, you can create unique areas within your Web pages by giving the `Panel` control a specified background color or border as well.

Listing 35-13 shows a page that makes use of the `Panel` control. You can see the results of this in Figure 35-12.

Listing 35-13: **<asp:panel>** Code Example

```
<html>
  <head>
        <title>Using the Panel Control</title>

  <script language=VB runat=server>
  Sub Page_Load(sender As Object, e As EventArgs)

     If Checkbox1.Checked Then
         Panel1.Visible = False
     Else
         Panel1.Visible = True
     End If

   Dim TextBoxNumber As Integer = _
   Int32.Parse(DropDownList1.SelectedItem.Value)
   Dim i As Integer
     For i = 1 To TextBoxNumber
        Dim NewTextBox As New TextBox()
        NewTextBox.Text = "New TextBox" & i.ToString()
        NewTextBox.ID = "TextBox" & i.ToString()
        Panel1.Controls.Add(NewTextBox)
        Panel1.Controls.Add(New LiteralControl("<br>"))
     Next i

   Dim LabelNumber As Integer = _
   Int32.Parse(DropDownList2.SelectedItem.Value)
     For i = 1 To LabelNumber
        Dim NewLabelControl As New Label()
        NewLabelControl.Text = "This is new label number"
        + i.ToString()
        If i=1 Then
             NewLabelControl.Text = "<p>This is new label
             number " + i.ToString()
   End If
        NewLabelControl.ID = "Label" + i.ToString()
        Panel1.Controls.Add(NewLabelControl)
        Panel1.Controls.Add(New LiteralControl("<br>"))
     Next i

    End Sub
  </script>

  </head>

  <body>
    <form runat="server">
        <p><font face="Verdana" size="2">
        Here is an example using the Panel Control.
        </font></p>
```

Continued

Listing 35-13 *(continued)*

```
<p>
<asp:Label id="LabelControlOutside" runat="server"
Font-Names="Verdana" Font-Size="X-Small" Font-
Bold="True">This is a Label Control outside of the
Panel.</asp:Label></p>

<p><asp:panel id="Panel1" runat="server" Font-
Names="Verdana" Font-Size="X-Small"
BackColor="Silver" Width="400px" Height="20px"
BorderColor="#404040" BorderWidth="1px"
BorderStyle="Solid">

<p>This is the Panel Control.<br></p>

</asp:panel>

<p><font face="Verdana" size="2">Specify
Textboxes:<br>

<asp:dropdownlist id="DropDownList1" runat="server"
Font-Names="Verdana">
        <asp:ListItem Value="0">0</asp:ListItem>
        <asp:ListItem Value="1">1</asp:ListItem>
        <asp:ListItem Value="2">2</asp:ListItem>
        <asp:ListItem Value="3">3</asp:ListItem>
        <asp:ListItem Value="4">4</asp:ListItem>
        <asp:ListItem Value="5">5</asp:ListItem>
</asp:dropdownlist></p></font>

<p><font face="Verdana" size="2">
Specify Labels:<br>

<asp:DropDownList id="DropDownList2" runat="server"
Font-Names="Verdana">
        <asp:ListItem Value="0">0</asp:ListItem>
        <asp:ListItem Value="1">1</asp:ListItem>
        <asp:ListItem Value="2">2</asp:ListItem>
        <asp:ListItem Value="3">3</asp:ListItem>
        <asp:ListItem Value="4">4</asp:ListItem>
        <asp:ListItem Value="5">5</asp:ListItem>
</asp:DropDownList></font></p>

<p><asp:CheckBox id="CheckBox1" runat="server"
Text="Panel Control ON/OFF" Font-Names="Verdana"
Font-Size="X-Small"></asp:CheckBox></p>
```

```
<p><asp:Button id="Button1" runat="server"
Text="Reformat Panel Control"></asp:Button></p>

        </form>
    </body>
</html>
```

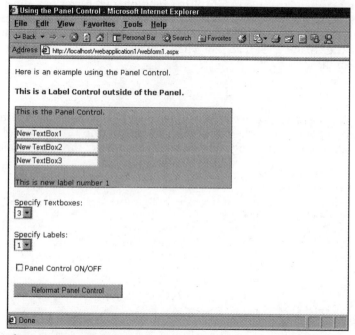

Figure 35-12: Wrapping other controls in the Panel control

Listing 35-13 shows a Panel control that contains a specified number of controls within. The great thing about this example is that it applies a singular style to this control by specifying that the font of the Panel control be Verdana. Doing this made every control placed within the Panel control inherit that font, so you don't need to go into every control and specify the font.

The coding also added a background color to the Panel control. This caused every control placed within the control to be on top of that background color. It is also possible to add an image as the background to the Panel control as well.

One control exists outside of the Panel control. This is noticeable if you turn the Panel control on and then off again. By doing this, you should notice that there is a Label control at the top of the page that is there and not changing, no matter what is done to the Panel control. This is because that particular Label control is sitting outside of the Panel control and it is not affected by any changes the Panel control makes. The Panel control specifically controls only the controls that it is encapsulating.

At first, the Panel control is pretty empty until you add controls to it. From a selection of drop-down lists, you are able to add either multiple text boxes or Label controls. Selecting a number from the drop-down list adds the specified number of controls. It is important to note that the control outside of the Panel control must have a unique ID other than Label1, so that when you generate new Label controls, the names don't conflict.

<asp:table>

The Table control allows you to place HTML tables on a Web page within a form and program against them. Within the code of the document, the Table control is written as <asp:table>. The following code shows an example of the Table control:

```
<asp:Table id="Table1"
     BackImageUrl="url"
     CellSpacing="cellspacing"
     CellPadding="cellpadding"
     GridLines="None|Horizontal|Vertical|Both"
     HorizontalAlign="Center|Justify|Left|NotSet|Right"
     runat="server">

<asp:TableRow>

    <asp:TableCell>
        Cell text
    </asp:TableCell>

</asp:TableRow>

</asp:Table>
```

The <asp:tabelrow> and <asp:tablecell> controls, which are discussed here, are within the Table control.

Cross-Reference This book does not discuss HTML tables. If you are new to the concept of tables and want to learn the basics, refer to *HTML 4.0 Bible,* by Bryan Pfaffenberger and Bill Karrow (Hungry Minds Inc.).

Tables are used within HTML documents for presentation and organization. Almost every Web page uses tables to place items in desired locations. Using the Table control gives you powerful control for doing this.

Tables are made up of rows and cells. Therefore, rows are created as `TableRow` controls and cells are created as `TableCell` controls (see Figure 35-13).

It is best to use the `Table` control to specify table properties at runtime. However, if you are presenting a static table within your Web page, it is best to just use the HTML `<table>` tag.

Listing 35-14 shows how to create a table that allows the user to add and remove rows and columns from the table.

Listing 35-14: `<asp:table>` Code Example

```
<html>
  <head>
        <title>Using the Table Control</title>

  <script language=VB runat=server>
  Sub Page_Load(sender As Object, e As EventArgs)
        Dim NumRows As Integer
        Dim NumCells As Integer
  For NumRows = 1 To
     Int32.Parse(DropDownList1.SelectedItem.Value)
        Dim tRow As New TableRow()
        For NumCells = 1 To
                Int32.Parse(DropDownList2.SelectedItem.Value)
         Dim tCell As New TableCell()
         tCell.Text = "Row " & NumRows & ", Cell " &
     NumCells
         tRow.Cells.Add(tCell)
        Next
Table1.Rows.Add(tRow)
  Next
End Sub
  </script>

  </head>

  <body>
    <form runat="server">
        <p><font face="Verdana" size="2">
        Here is an example using the Table Control.</font>
        </p><p>

        <asp:Table id="Table1" runat="server"
        BorderColor="#404040" BorderWidth="1px"
        BorderStyle="Solid" cellpadding="5">
                <asp:TableRow>
                        <asp:TableCell></asp:TableCell>
                </asp:TableRow>
```

Continued

Listing 35-14 *(continued)*

```
        </asp:Table>
      </p>

      <p>
      <font face="Verdana" size="2">Rows:</font>
      <br>

      <asp:DropDownList id="DropDownList1" runat="server">
              <asp:ListItem Value="1">1</asp:ListItem>
              <asp:ListItem Value="2">2</asp:ListItem>
              <asp:ListItem Value="3">3</asp:ListItem>
              <asp:ListItem Value="4">4</asp:ListItem>
              <asp:ListItem Value="5">5</asp:ListItem>
      </asp:DropDownList>

      </p><p><font face="Verdana" size="2">
      Columns:<br>

      <asp:DropDownList id="DropDownList2" runat="server">
              <asp:ListItem Value="1">1</asp:ListItem>
              <asp:ListItem Value="2">2</asp:ListItem>
              <asp:ListItem Value="3">3</asp:ListItem>
              <asp:ListItem Value="4">4</asp:ListItem>
              <asp:ListItem Value="5">5</asp:ListItem>
      </asp:DropDownList>

      </font></p>
      <p><asp:Button id="Button1" runat="server"
      Text="Reformat Table"></asp:Button></p>

    </form>
  </body
</html>
```

Listing 35-14 starts by displaying a table with one row and one cell. There are two drop-down lists, in which the user can change the number of rows and columns after pressing the button to refresh the table.

Changing the rows and columns happens immediately and within each cell of the table is the row and cell description. There is a little style added to the table in this example by specifying the border and border color.

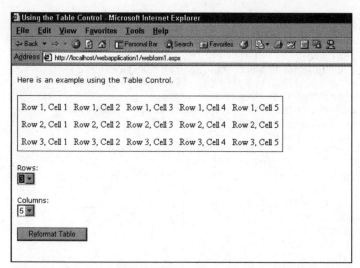

Figure 35-13: Using the Table control to specify rows and columns

<asp:placeholder>

The PlaceHolder control is very similar to the Panel control in that it allows you to use this control as a wrapper for other controls. Within the code of the document, the PlaceHolder control is written as <asp:placeholder>. However, unlike the Panel control, the PlaceHolder control doesn't allow the developer to apply any inheritable styles to the controls contained within the control. An example of the PlaceHolder control appears in the following code:

```
<asp:PlaceHolder id="PlaceHolder1"
    runat="server"/>
```

Intrinsic controls

Now you are getting to some fun controls that Microsoft developed to make the lives of developers easier. Intrinsic controls are controls that add specific functionality that in the past, when using traditional ASP, took quite a bit of programming or the use of COM components to work. In the following sections, you find descriptions of both the <asp:calendar> and the <asp:adrotator> controls.

<asp:calendar>

The Calendar control allows you to place a rich calendar on a Web page within a form and program against it. Within the code of the document, the Calendar control is written as <asp:calendar>. The following example shows the use of the Calendar control:

```
<asp:Calendar id="Calendar1"
     CellPadding="pixels"
     CellSpacing="pixels"
     DayNameFormat="FirstLetter|FirstTwoLetters|Full|Short"
     FirstDayOfWeek="Default|Monday|Tuesday|Wednesday|
                     Thursday|Friday|Saturday|Sunday"
     NextMonthText="HTML text"
     NextPrevFormat="ShortMonth|FullMonth|CustomText"
     PrevMonthText="HTML text"
     SelectedDate="date"
     SelectionMode="None|Day|DayWeek|DayWeekMonth"
     SelectMonthText="HTML text"
     SelectWeekText="HTML text"
     ShowDayHeader="True|False"
     ShowGridLines="True|False"
     ShowNextPrevMonth="True|False"
     ShowTitle="True|False"
     TitleFormat="Month|MonthYear"
     TodaysDate="date"
     VisibleDate="date"
     OnDayRender="OnDayRenderMethod"
     OnSelectionChanged="OnSelectionChangedMethod"
     OnVisibleMonthChanged="OnVisibleMonthChangedMethod"
     runat="server">

<TodayDayStyle property="value"/>
<DayHeaderStyle property="value"/>
<DayStyle property="value"/>
<NextPrevStyle property="value"/>
<OtherMonthDayStyle property="value"/>
<SelectedDayStyle property="value"/>
<SelectorStyle property="value"/>
<TitleStyle property="value"/>
<TodayDayStyle property="value"/>
<WeekendDayStyle property="value"/>

</asp:Calendar>
```

The basic functionality of the Calendar control is that it places a one-month calendar on your Web page that allows the user to select a date (see Figure 35-14.) There is also functionality for the user to move forward or backward to other months.

By setting the SelectionMode attribute, you can specify whether the user can select a single day, a week, or a month, or you can disable date selection entirely.

This is quite a useful control for those Web sites that need users to choose dates to either make appointments, specify reservation dates, or to inform the site about their birthday.

There are a number of things you can do to customize the style of the calendar, but this first example builds a page that shows the date that the user selects within a Label control (see Listing 35-15).

Listing 35-15: `<asp:calendar>` Code Example

```
<html>
  <head>
          <title>Using the Calendar Control</title>
  <script language=VB runat=server>
Sub Calendar_Change(sender As Object, e As EventArgs)
     Label1.Visible = True
     Label1.text =
     "You selected: " & _
     Calendar1.SelectedDate.ToShortDateString
End Sub
  </script>

  </head>

  <body>
    <form runat="server">
        <p><font face="Verdana" size="2">
        Here is an example using the Calendar
        Control.</font></p>

        <p>
        <asp:Calendar id="Calendar1" runat="server"
        onselectionchanged="calendar_change"></asp:Calendar>
        </p>

        <p><asp:Label id="Label1" runat="server"
        Visible="False"></asp:Label></p>
    </form>
  </body>
</html>
```

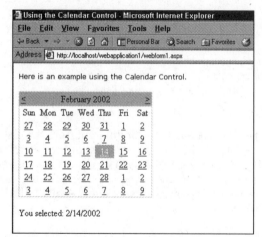

Figure 35-14: Basic Calendar control

This is a very simple example of the `Calendar` control. Here, the default `Calendar` control displays a basic calendar, and when the user clicks one of the dates within the control, you write to the `Label` control using the date they selected. Not bad! Imagine how many lines of code would have been needed to create this in ASP 3.0.

Now, you change this calendar around a little so that the user can select a week, not just a day. In order to do this, use the same page, but rewrite the subroutine so that it is like this:

```
Sub calendar_change(sender As Object, e As EventArgs)
   Label1.Visible = True
   Label1.Text = "You selected the week of: " & _
     Calendar1.SelectedDate.ToLongDateString & " to " & _
   Calendar1.SelectedDate.AddDays(6).ToLongDateString
End Sub
```

Now the user selects a date, and you can add six days to the date to create the final day of their week choice. The dates were converted to the long date format (it says September 01, 2001 instead of 10/1/2001).

There are many things you can do to create a unique style to your `Calendar` control. In this next example, you make the calendar more presentable (though it is all a matter of taste, isn't it?).

In this case, instead of the `Calendar` control in the previous code example, use this `Calendar` control:

```
<asp:Calendar id="Calendar1" runat="server"
    onselectionchanged="calendar_change"
firstdayofweek="Sunday"
daynameformat="Full"
backcolor="#FFE0C0"
bordercolor="#404040"
borderstyle="Solid"
font-names="Verdana"
font-size="X-Small"
forecolor="Black"
showgridlines="True"
cellpadding="3">
<selecteddaystyle font-bold="True"
    backcolor="#FF8080"></selecteddaystyle>
<weekenddaystyle backcolor="#FFFFC0"></weekenddaystyle>
</asp:Calendar>
```

There is a lot going on here style-wise. First of all, it is a lot different from the original control. You specified the `daynameformat` to be `Full`, meaning that the calendar should show the full name of the day of the week (`Tuesday`) instead of the default `Tue` (see Figure 35-15). You also changed a lot of colors and the border of the calendar. You changed the color of the weekend days so the users could easily tell the difference between weekdays and weekends.

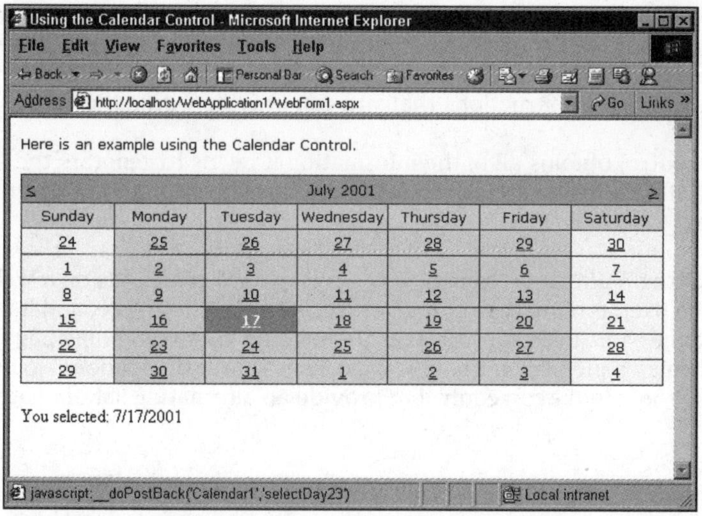

Figure 35-15: Calendar control with some style applied

The default is to have the calendar start on a Sunday. Many European countries start their calendars with a Monday, so you can change this at runtime, depending on your users' locale.

<asp:adrotator>

The AdRotator control allows you to place a component on your page that displays and rotates banner ads to your specifications. Within the code of the document, the AdRotator control is written as <asp:adrotator>, and is shown in the following code:

```
<asp:AdRotator
      id="Value"
      AdvertisementFile="AdvertisementFile"
      KeyWordFilter="KeyWord"
      Target="Target"
      OnAdCreated="OnAdCreatedMethod"
      runat="server"/>
```

The AdRotator control in ASP.NET is quite similar to the AdRotator component from ASP 3.0, but you find that this new AdRotator control is easy to use and manage within your applications.

Everywhere you go on the Internet, you see advertisements in the form of various sized banner ads. Almost every commercial page has them, whether they are advertising other products and services from other companies, or advertising products and services found within their own site. Usually, clicking one of these banner ads take you to a different location on the Internet.

The AdRotator control plays well with this type of functionality. You can display advertisements on your Web page with very little programming. Each time users refresh the page, they are presented with another banner ad. The banner ads can rotate based upon specific instructions that you can provide within the code.

The AdRotator control obtains all of the information it needs to generate the images from an XML file. There are other ways to obtain the information, but this is the preferred way.

Keep in mind that the AdRotator control was developed to rotate ads on a Web page, but it can be used for any type of images that you want to rotate, and it is not limited to just banner ads. Let's say that you are building your own home page, and you wanted to display a picture on the first page from your last vacation. Wouldn't it be better to use the AdRotator control to provide an alternating list of images instead?

Jump right in and create an AdRotator control and the associated XML file. See Listing 35-16.

Listing 35-16: <asp:adrotator> Code Example

```
<html>
  <head>
        <title>Using the AdRotator Control</title>
  </head>

<body>
    <form runat="server">
        <p><font face="Verdana" size="2">
        Here is an example using the AdRotator
        Control.</font></p>

        <p><asp:AdRotator id="AdRotator1" runat="server"
        Width="468px" Height="60px"
        advertisementfile="AdRotator.xml"></asp:AdRotator>
        </p>
    </form>
  </body>
</html>
```

That is pretty simple and straightforward. It is only one control, though you do specify the width and the height of the image that you are placing within the control. Most importantly, you specify where the control can find the associated XML file. The control needs this file in order to display the images.

Go to the XML file (see Listing 35-17), and see what you need to do in order to make the two pieces work together.

Listing 35-17: **AdRotator.XML File**

```xml
<?xml version="1.0" encoding="utf-8" ?>
<Advertisements
    xmlns="http://schemas.microsoft.com/AspNet/AdRotator-
      Schedule-File">
  <Ad>
        <ImageUrl>
              http://www.somewhere.com/images/banner1.gif
        </ImageUrl>
        <AlternateText>First Image</AlternateText>
        <Impressions>100</Impressions>
  </Ad>
  <Ad>
        <ImageUrl>
              http://www.somewhere.com/images/banner1.gif
        </ImageUrl>
        <AlternateText>Second Image</AlternateText>
        <Impressions>100</Impressions>
  </Ad>
</Advertisements>
```

This is the XML file that you are using for your AdRotator control. There are some other tags you can use to specify specific functionality. Table 35-4 describes each of the tags you can use within the AdRotator XML file.

Table 35-4
XML Attributes to Use within an AdRotator XML File

XML Attribute	Description
`<ImageUrl>`	Location of the image to use for the control.
`<NavigateUrl>`	The URL to go to when the user clicks the image.
`<AlternateText>`	The text that is displayed if the image is unavailable.
`<Keyword>`	A keyword to use so you can filter for specific ads.
`<Impressions>`	A number that tells how often the image should be displayed compared to the numbers of the other images within the XML file.

Visual Studio .NET makes it easy to create this XML file in order to use it with the AdRotator control. Follow these steps in order to create your AdRotator XML file:

1. In your open application, right-click the application within the Solution Explorer window.

2. Choose Add ⇨ Add New Item.

3. From the list of templates, choose the XML file. Name the file, and click Open.

4. Place your cursor within the code window.

   You see the Properties of the document display within the Properties window on the right side of the screen.

5. Within the Properties box, change the `targetSchema` property to **Ad Rotator Schedule File**.

6. Type <Ad> for each image that you want to place within the control.

7. Use any of the attribute tags for each ad to complete the document.

As you can tell, it is quite simple to add a rotation of images, whether they are banner ads or just generic images, to your Web page.

Data Binding

Before discussing the final three Web controls, you need to understand Data Binding and how to bind data to a control.

 Cross-Reference   See Part IV of this book for information on Data Binding.

Data is very important to almost every Web application. Today, it is quite rare to present only static text and images within your Web documents. It is data from a variety of sources that is driving current Web pages.

This was the great thing about ASP 3.0. You could develop pages that would render when the user pulled up the page in the browser. As it was rendering, the page would grab data from all sorts of sources, and place this data in appropriate places within the document for presentation.

It is important to note that with Data Binding, the control is not connected to the data source. Instead, what you are doing is making a *copy* of the data and then binding this copy with the Server control.

With Data Binding, not only can you connect to traditional data sources such as relational databases, but you can also make connections to a wide variety of other data sources. You can connect to any of the following data sources and more:

   ✦ DataSets

   ✦ XML files

   ✦ Array lists

✦ Hash tables

✦ Properties

✦ Expressions

✦ Functions

✦ Collections and lists

To bind to data sources to be used in complex controls such as the `<asp:datalist>`, `<asp:datagrid>`, and `<asp:repeater>` controls, you use the `DataBind()` method (which is discussed shortly). But first, you need to learn some of the other basic forms of binding data within Web pages using VB .NET.

Listing 35-18 shows how to bind to a page's property.

Listing 35-18: **Binding to a Page Property**

```
<html>
<head>
    <script language="VB" runat="server">
        Sub Page_Load(sender As Object, e As EventArgs)
            Page.DataBind
        End Sub

        ReadOnly Property FirstName() As String
            Get
                Return "William"
            End Get
        End Property

        ReadOnly Property Age() As Integer
            Get
                Return 31
            End Get
        End Property
    </script>
</head>
<body>
    <font face="Verdana" size=2>
        DataBinding to a Property on the Page
    </font>

    <form runat=server>
        Name: <b><%# FirstName %></b><br>
        Age: <b><%# Age %></b>
    </form>

</body>
</html>
```

In this example, you use the traditional ASP delimiters to display the data that you are binding to. Instead of just the <% %>, however, you need to put a pound sign there so that it reads as follows: <%# property_name %>.

Listing 35-19 shows how to bind directly to a Web control (see Figure 35-16).

Listing 35-19: **Binding to a Web Control**

```
<html>
<head>
    <script language="VB" runat="server">
        Sub SubmitBtn_Click(sender As Object, e As EventArgs)
            Page.DataBind
        End Sub
    </script>
</head>
<body>
  <font face="Verdana" size=2>
    DataBinding to the DropDownList Control<P>
    <b>What is your favorite Color?</b><P>

  <form runat=server>
        <asp:DropDownList id="Colors" runat="server">
          <asp:ListItem>White</asp:ListItem>
          <asp:ListItem>Red</asp:ListItem>
          <asp:ListItem>Blue</asp:ListItem>
          <asp:ListItem>Green</asp:ListItem>
          <asp:ListItem>Brown</asp:ListItem>
          <asp:ListItem>Yellow</asp:ListItem>
          <asp:ListItem>Orange</asp:ListItem>
          <asp:ListItem>Purple</asp:ListItem>
        </asp:DropDownList>

        <asp:button Text="Submit" OnClick="SubmitBtn_Click"
        runat=server/>

        <p>

        Your Favorite Color is: <asp:label
        text='<%# Colors.SelectedItem.Text %>'
        runat=server/>
        </font>
    </form>
</body>
</html>
```

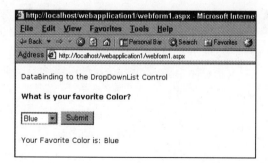

Figure 35-16: Data Binding to a DropDownList control

In this example, after the user makes a selection and then clicks the Submit button, the `SubmitBtn_Click` event is called. This event binds all the page's form data at that moment by using `Page.DataBind`. Then, you can bind this data and use it in the `Label` control at the bottom of the page by using `<%# Colors.SelectedItem. Text %>`.

Another example is Data Binding to an array list, as shown in Listing 35-20.

Cross-Reference   For information on arrays, see Chapter 6.

Listing 35-20: **Binding to an Array List**

```
<html>
<head>

    <script language="VB" runat="server">
        Sub Page_Load(sender As Object, e As EventArgs)
            If Not IsPostBack Then
                Dim OurArray as ArrayList= new ArrayList()
                OurArray.Add ("White")
                OurArray.Add ("Red")
                OurArray.Add ("Blue")
                OurArray.Add ("Green")
                OurArray.Add ("Brown")
                OurArray.Add ("Yellow")
                OurArray.Add ("Orange")
                OurArray.Add ("Purple")

                DropDownList1.DataSource = OurArray
                DropDownList1.DataBind
            End If
        End Sub

        Sub SubmitBtn_Click(sender As Object, e As EventArgs)
            Label1.Text = "You chose: " +
```

Continued

Listing 35-20 *(continued)*

```
                DropDownList1.SelectedItem.Text
        End Sub

    </script>

</head>
<body>
    <font face="Verdana" size=2>
        <b>DataBinding to an Array</b></font>

    <form runat=server>

        <asp:DropDownList id="DropDownList1" runat="server" />

        <asp:button Text="Submit" OnClick="SubmitBtn_Click"
        runat=server/>

        <p>

        <asp:Label id=Label1 font-name="Verdana" font-
        size="10pt" runat="server" />
    </form>
</body>
</html>
```

This is a pretty simple and straightforward example. When the page is rendered for the first time, it creates an array. Then `DropDownList1.DataSource = OurArray` specifies that the `DataSource` for the control with the ID of `DropDownList1` is equal to `OurArray`. In this case, `OurArray` is holding your array! Then, `DropDownList1.DataBind` binds `OurArray` to your control. It is that simple.

In other examples in this chapter, you see more complex forms of Data Binding, such as from a Microsoft Access table and an XML file.

List Bound controls

There are three List Bound controls to use within your applications: `<asp:datal-ist>`, `<asp:datagrid>`, and `<asp:repeater>`. All three controls offer outstanding programming functionality to your Web pages by allowing you to specify the layout and appearance of rows of data. The data that these controls present is data that you would bind the control to for displaying, updating, inserting and/or deleting.

`<asp:datalist>`

The `DataList` control allows you to display data on a Web page using custom templates and styles that you define. Within the code of the document, the `DataList` control is written as `<asp:datalist>`. There are options within the `DataList` control that allow users to edit and delete data as well. The following example shows the use of the DataList control:

```
<asp:DataList id="DataList1"
     CellPadding="pixels"
     CellSpacing="pixels"
     DataKeyField="DataSourceKeyField"
     DataSource='<% databindingexpression %>'
     ExtractTemplateRows="True|False"
     GridLines="None|Horizontal|Vertical|Both"
     RepeatColumns="ColumnCount"
     RepeatDirection="Vertical|Horizontal"
     RepeatLayout="Flow|Table"
     ShowFooter="True|False"
     ShowHeader="True|False"
     OnCancelCommand="OnCancelCommandMethod"
     OnDeleteCommand="OnDeleteCommandMethod"
     OnEditCommand="OnEditCommandMethod"
     OnItemCommand="OnItemCommandMethod"
     OnItemCreated="OnItemCreatedMethod"
     OnUpdateCommand="OnUpdateCommandMethod"
     runat="server">

<AlternatingItemStyle property="value"/>
<EditItemStyle property="value"/>
<FooterStyle property="value"/>
<HeaderStyle property="value"/>
<ItemStyle property="value"/>
<SelectedItemStyle property="value"/>
<SeparatorStyle property="value"/>

<HeaderTemplate>
    Header template HTML
</HeaderTemplate>
<ItemTemplate>
    Item template HTML
</ItemTemplate>
<AlternatingItemTemplate>
    Alternating item template HTML
</AlternatingItemTemplate>
<EditItemTemplate>
    Edited item template HTML
</EditItemTemplate>
<SelectedItemTemplate>
    Selected item template HTML
</SelectedItemTemplate>
<SeparatorTemplate>
    Separator template HTML
</SeparatorTemplate>
<FooterTemplate>
    Footer template HTML
</FooterTemplate>

</asp:DataList>
```

The custom templates you create to display the data can contain both HTML traditional elements (such as `<b>`, `<table>`, `<select>` tags) and any of the controls that were discussed in this section.

Think of templates as wrappers for presentation for certain sections of the code. The `DataList` control supports the templates shown in Table 35-5.

<table>
<tr><td colspan="2" align="center">Table 35-5
Templates Used in the DataList Control</td></tr>
<tr><td>*Template*</td><td>*Description*</td></tr>
<tr><td>ItemTemplate</td><td>This is the only required template. The ItemTemplate is rendered one time for each row of data.</td></tr>
<tr><td>AlternatingItemTemplate</td><td>If this template is provided within the DataList control, it renders for every other row of data. Use this template if you want to provide alternating colors for the rows of your table.</td></tr>
<tr><td>SelectedItemTemplate</td><td>This template displays when the user selects an item that is in the ItemTemplate or the AlternatingItemTemplate. You can change the background color or even show additional information.</td></tr>
<tr><td>EditItemTemplate</td><td>The template that is displayed when the user is editing one of the rows of data.</td></tr>
<tr><td>HeaderTemplate</td><td>If this template is provided, it is the first row before the ItemTemplate is rendered. You can display column headings and introductions with this template.</td></tr>
<tr><td>FooterTemplate</td><td>Similar to the HeaderTemplate, although this is the last row after all the data is displayed.</td></tr>
<tr><td>SeparatorTemplate</td><td>This template is rendered between each ItemTemplate or AlternatingItemTemplate. It is useful to provide some sort of visual separation of rows of data. In one of its simpler forms, the SeparatorTemplate can contain just an `<hr>` tag.</td></tr>
</table>

The next example uses the `DataList` control to show you what it is capable of doing. In this example, you create a table based upon your own style.

First, however, you need to create a Microsoft Access table. You can basically create any kind of table in Access that you want. For this example, a table was created (Customers) that is comprised of just three fields (see Figure 35-17). The first field is the CustomerID field, which is where you can keep track of the customer number. No two numbers are the same, and this keeps customers unique, even if they have the same name. The next field is the `CustomerName` field, which is pretty self-explanatory. The last field is the `NumPurchases` field, which is where you can keep track of the number of purchases this particular customer has made from the imaginary online store. The content of this field is just a number.

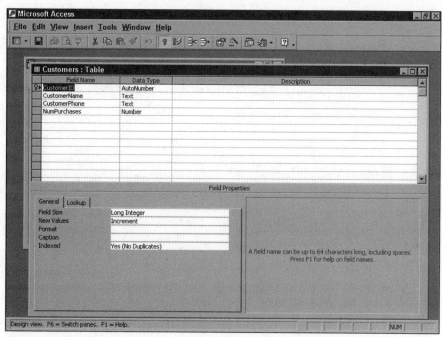

Figure 35-17: The Microsoft Access Customers table in Design view

Cross-Reference For a complete description of Microsoft Access, please see the book *Access Bible,* by Cary N. Prague and Michael R. Irwin (Hungry Minds, Inc.).

Next, fill your database with content (as shown in Figure 35-18). In this table, only 11 rows of data were inserted. Save it as `db1.mdb`, and place the file in the root directory of your application. Listing 35-21 shows you how to build the page.

Listing 35-21: `<asp:datalist>` Code Example

```
<%@ Import Namespace="System.Data.OLEDB" %>
<html>
<head>

    <script language="VB" runat="server">
```

Continued

Listing 35-21 *(continued)*

```
Sub Page_Load(sender As Object, e As EventArgs)
    Dim strConn as string =
      "PROVIDER=Microsoft.Jet.OLEDB.4.0;DATA SOURCE=" & _
      server.mappath("db1.mdb") & ";"
    Dim strSQL as string = "select * from customers "
    Dim Conn as New OLEDBConnection(strConn)
    Dim Cmd as New OLEDBCommand(strSQL,Conn)
    Conn.Open()
    DataList1.DataSource =
      Cmd.ExecuteReader(system.data.CommandBehavior.Close
      Connection)
    DataList1.DataBind()
End Sub
</script>

<style language="text/css">
        table, tr, td, body {
        font-size: x-small;
        font-family : Verdana, Geneva, Arial,
        Helvetica, sans-serif; }
</style>

</head>
<body>
  <font face="Verdana" size="2">
        Using the DataList Control
  </font></p>

  <form runat="server">
  <p>
  <asp:datalist id="DataList1" runat="server">
        <itemtemplate>
                <tr bgcolor="Gainsboro">
                <td><%# DataBinder.Eval(Container.DataItem,
                "CustomerID")%></td>
                <td><%# DataBinder.Eval(Container.DataItem,
                "CustomerName")%></td>
                <td><%# DataBinder.Eval(Container.DataItem,
                "NumPurchases")%></td>
                </tr>
        </itemtemplate>
        <alternatingitemtemplate>
                <tr bgcolor="AliceBlue">
                <td><%# DataBinder.Eval(Container.DataItem,
                "CustomerID")%></td>
                <td><%# DataBinder.Eval(Container.DataItem,
                "CustomerName")%></td>
                <td><%# DataBinder.Eval(Container.DataItem,
                "NumPurchases")%></td>
```

```
                        </tr>
                <//alternatingitemtemplate>
                <headertemplate>
                        <table align="center" cellpadding="4"
                        cellspacing="0" border="0" width="400">
                        <tr bgcolor="#000000">
                        <td><font color="#ffffff">Customer
                        ID</font></td>
                        <td><font color="#ffffff">Customer
                        Name</font></td>
                        <td><font color="#ffffff"># of
                        Purchases</font></td>
                        </tr>
                </headertemplate>
                <footertemplate>
                        </table>
                </footertemplate>
        </asp:datalist>
        </form>
</body>
</html>
```

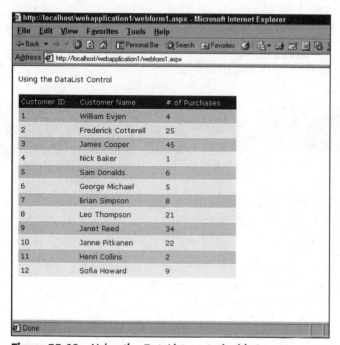

Figure 35-18: Using the DataList control with Access

There is a lot to go over in this file, so start at the beginning. The following code declares a `Namespace` to use in the document, which allows you to use the OLEDB types:

```
<%@ Import Namespace="System.Data.OLEDB" %>
```

Within the script at the top of the page, VB .NET connects to an Access database (the one you created) to bind the Customers table to your control.

```
<script language="VB" runat="server">
    Sub Page_Load(sender As Object, e As EventArgs)
        Dim strConn as string =
        "PROVIDER=Microsoft.Jet.OLEDB.4.0;DATA SOURCE=" & _
        server.mappath("db1.mdb") & ";"
        Dim strSQL as string = "select * from customers"
        Dim Conn as New OLEDBConnection(strConn)
        Dim Cmd as New OLEDBCommand(strSQL,Conn)
        Conn.Open()
        DataList1.DataSource =
        Cmd.ExecuteReader(system.data.CommandBehavior.Close
        Connection)
        DataList1.DataBind()
    End Sub
</script>
```

This is your `Page_Load` subroutine. Right away, you are declaring where the script can find your database by declaring a provider. You are using the Microsoft Jet Provider to access your Access database. There are a number of different providers that are available for use, as Table 35-6 describes.

Table 35-6
Providers as Used in the Connection String

Provider	What Can it Access?	Connection String Example
Microsoft OLE DB Provider for Microsoft Active Directory Service (ADSI)	LDAP-compliant directory services	`"Provider= ADSDSOObject; User ID=userName; Password= userPassword;"`
Microsoft OLE DB Provider for Internet Publishing	HTML files or Windows 2000 Web Folders	`"Provider= MSDAIPP.DSO; Data Source= ResourceURL;User ID= userName;Password= userPassword;"`

or

Provider	What Can it Access?	Connection String Example
		```"URL=ResourceURL; User ID= userName;Password= userPassword;"```
Microsoft OLE DB Provider for Microsoft Indexing Service	File system and Web data indexed by Microsoft Indexing Service	```"Provider= MSIDXS;Data Source=myCatalog; Locale Identifier= nnnn;"```
Microsoft OLE DB Provider for Microsoft Jet	Microsoft Jet Databases (for example, Access)	```"Provider= Microsoft.Jet. OLEDB.4.0;Data Source=databaseName; User ID=userName; Password= userPassword;"```
Microsoft OLE DB Provider for ODBC	Most databases available today, including Microsoft SQL, Access, FoxPro, and even Oracle	```"Provider= MSDASQL;DSN= dsnName;UID= userName;PWD= userPassword;"```
Microsoft OLE DB Provider for Oracle	Oracle databases	```"Provider= MSDAORA;Data Source=serverName; User ID=userName; Password= userPassword;"```
Microsoft OLE DB Provider for SQL Server	Microsoft SQL Server	```"Provider= SQLOLEDB;Data Source=serverName; Initial Catalog= databaseName; User ID=userName; Password= userPassword;"```

After declaring a provider, you then make a SQL string. This string is a command to the database you are connecting to about what data you want to retrieve. It is not always the best case to grab every field from the table of data if you only need one field. In this case, however, you use a SQL string that grabs all the data from all the fields of your Customers table, as follows:

```
Select * From Customers
```

In this statement, you are saying that you need to select all (*) from the Customers table. But if you want only one of the fields, you would write the SQL string as follows:

```
Select CustomerName From Customers
```

In this case, you want only the `CustomerName` field. To specify only one row, use the following select statement:

```
Select * From Customers Where CustomerID = "2"
```

This select statement grabs only the fields from the customer in the table who has the `CustomerID` of 2. For the last select example, you can also organize your original table by alphabetizing the customers by their names with the following select statement:

```
Select * From Customers Order by CustomerName
```

This would change the order of the table by listing out all the customers alphabetically from A to Z.

Within the rest of the script, you are establishing your connection and then binding the data from the connection and select statement to the control `DataList1`.

The `DataList` control itself is made up of four templates. The only template that you need to use is the `<itemtemplate>`, but in this case, you want to build a table in which the alternating rows are different colors. So, you use the `<alternating-itemtemplate>` tag. You also have to start the table, so you use the `<header-template>` and create the table along with the first row, in which you build the column headers. The `<footertemplate>` closes the table.

Next, you alter the body of the example that you created so that the `DataList` control presents the same data (but in a different format) by using the templates that the control provides you with (see Listing 35-22).

Listing 35-22: `<asp:datalist>` with Different Format

```
<form runat="server">
  <font face="Verdana" size="2">
        Using the DataList Control
  </font></p>

  <p>
  <asp:datalist id="DataList1" runat="server">
        <itemtemplate>
                <li><asp:label id="label1" runat="server"
                text='<%# DataBinder.Eval(Container.DataItem,
                "CustomerName")%>' /></li>
```

```
                    </itemtemplate>
                    <separatortemplate>
                            <hr>
                    </separatortemplate>
                    <headertemplate>
                            Customers by name:<p>
                            <ol>
                    </headertemplate>
                    <footertemplate>
                            </ol>
                    </footertemplate>
            </asp:datalist>
        </form>
```

This example takes the customers' names and then presents their names within a list with a `<hr>` tag in-between each name. In this example, you also displayed the customer's name within another control, the `Label` control. This example shows that you can place whatever you want within the templates of the `DataList` control, whether they are other controls or just straight HTML.

<asp:datagrid>

The `DataGrid` control allows you to display data in a grid format on a Web page using custom templates and styles that you define. Within the code of the document, the `DataGrid` control is written as `<asp:datagrid>`. There are options within the `DataGrid` control that allow users to edit and delete data as well, as shown in the following example:

```
<asp:DataGrid id="programmaticID" runat=server
     DataSource='<%# DataBindingExpression %>'
     AllowPaging="True|False"
     AllowSorting="True|False"
     AutoGenerateColumns="True|False"
     BackImageUrl="url"
     CellPadding="pixels"
     CellSpacing="pixels"
     DataKeyField="DataSourceKeyField"
     GridLines="None|Horizontal|Vertical|Both"
     HorizontalAlign="Center|Justify|Left|NotSet|Right"
     PagedDataSource
     PageSize="ItemCount"
     ShowFooter="True|False"
     ShowHeader="True|False"
     VirtualItemCount="ItemCount"
     OnCancelCommand="OnCancelCommandMethod"
     OnDeleteCommand="OnDeleteCommandMethod"
     OnEditCommand="OnEditCommandMethod"
     OnItemCommand="OnItemCommandMethod"
```

```
        OnItemCreated="OnItemCreatedMethod"
        OnPageIndexChanged="OnPageIndexChangedMethod"
        OnSortCommand="OnSortCommandMethod"
        OnUpdateCommand="OnUpdateCommandMethod">

    <AlternatingItemStyle property="value"/>
    <EditItemStyle property="value"/>
    <FooterStyle property="value"/>
    <HeaderStyle property="value"/>
    <ItemStyle property="value"/>
    <PagerStyle property="value"/>
    <SelectedItemStyle property="value"/>

</asp:DataGrid>
or
<asp:DataGrid id="programmaticID" runat=server
    DataSource='<%# DataBindingExpression %>'
    AutoGenerateColumns="False"
    (other properties)>

    <AlternatingItemStyle property="value"/>
    <EditItemStyle property="value"/>
    <FooterStyle property="value"/>
    <HeaderStyle property="value"/>
    <ItemStyle property="value"/>
    <PagerStyle property="value"/>
    <SelectedItemStyle property="value"/>

    <Columns>
        <asp:BoundColumn
            DataField="DataSourceField"
            DataFormatString="FormatString"
            FooterText="FooterText"
            HeaderImageUrl="url"
            HeaderText="HeaderText"
            ReadOnly="True|False"
            SortField="DataSourceFieldToSortBy"
            Visible="True|False"
            FooterStyle-property="value"
            HeaderStyle-property="value"
            ItemStyle-property="value"/>

        <asp:ButtonColumn
            ButtonType="LinkButton|PushButton"
            Command="BubbleText"
            DataTextField="DataSourceField"
            DataTextFormatString="FormatString"
            FooterText="FooterText"
            HeaderImageUrl="url"
            HeaderText="HeaderText"
            ReadOnly="True|False"
            SortField="DataSourceFieldToSortBy"
            Text="ButtonCaption"
            Visible="True|False"/>
```

```
    <asp:EditCommandColumn
        ButtonType="LinkButton|PushButton"
        CancelText="CancelButtonCaption"
        EditText="EditButtonCaption"
        FooterText="FooterText"
        HeaderImageUrl="url"
        HeaderText="HeaderText"
        ReadOnly="True|False"
        SortField="DataSourceFieldToSortBy"
        UpdateText="UpdateButtonCaption"
        Visible="True|False"/>

    <asp:HyperLinkColumn
        DataNavigateUrlField="DataSourceField"
        DataNavigateUrlFormatString="FormatExpression"
        DataTextField="DataSourceField"
        DataTextFormatString="FormatExpression"
        FooterText="FooterText"
        HeaderImageUrl="url"
        HeaderText="HeaderText"
        NavigateUrl="url"
        ReadOnly="True|False"
        SortField="DataSourceFieldToSortBy"
        Target="window"
        Text="HyperLinkText"
        Visible="True|False"/>

    <asp:TemplateColumn
        FooterText="FooterText"
        HeaderImageUrl="url"
        HeaderText="HeaderText"
        ReadOnly="True|False"
        SortField="DataSourceFieldToSortBy"
        Visible="True|False">

    <HeaderTemplate>
        Header template HTML
    </HeaderTemplate >
    <ItemTemplate>
        ItemTemplate HTML
    </ItemTemplate>
    <EditItemTemplate>
        EditItem template HTML
    </EditItemTemplate>
    <FooterTemplate>
        Footer template HTML
    </FooterTemplate>

    </asp:TemplateColumn>
  </Columns>

</asp:DataGrid>
```

One of the great advantages of the `DataGrid` over the other list bound controls is that the `DataGrid` allows you to easily build paging into your presentation pages.

In this first example of the `DataGrid` control, connect to the same Access database that you created in the previous example, and build a simple `DataGrid` control (see Listing 35-23).

Listing 35-23: `<asp:datagrid>` Code Example

```
<%@ Import Namespace="System.Data.OLEDB" %>
<html>
<head>

    <script language="VB" runat="server">
    Sub Page_Load(sender As Object, e As EventArgs)
        Dim strConn as string =
        "PROVIDER=Microsoft.Jet.OLEDB.4.0;DATA SOURCE=" & _
        server.mappath("db1.mdb") & ";"
        Dim strSQL as string = "select * from customers "
        Dim Conn as New OLEDBConnection(strConn)
        Dim Cmd as New OLEDBCommand(strSQL,Conn)
        Conn.Open()
        DataGrid1.DataSource =
        Cmd.ExecuteReader(system.data.CommandBehavior.Close
        Connection)
        DataGrid1.DataBind()
    End Sub
    </script>

</head>
<body>
  <form runat="server">
  <font face="Verdana" size="2">
        Using the DataGrid Control
  </font></p>

  <p>
  <asp:datagrid id="datagrid1" runat="server" />
    </form>
</body>
</html>
```

Now, that is pretty simple! The `DataGrid` control is one simple line in this example, and it generated a simple table with even column headings (see Figure 35-19). Now, think of how many lines of code that would take to write in traditional ASP.

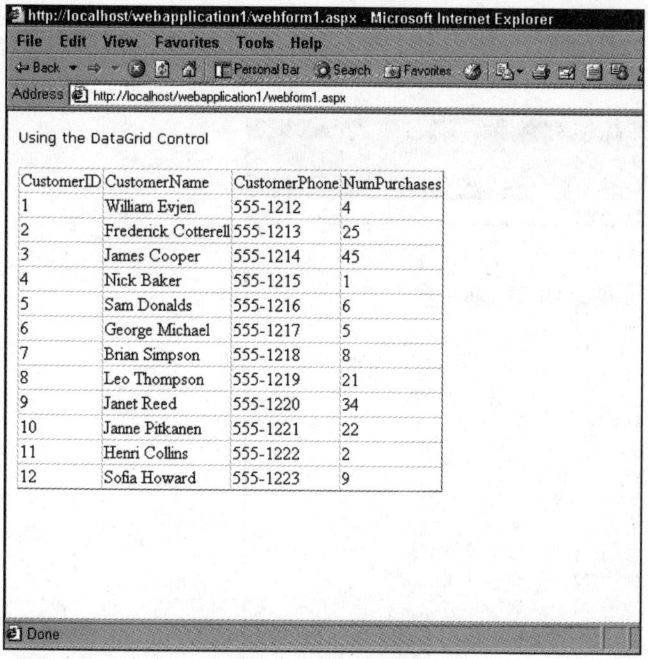

Figure 35-19: A simple DataGrid control

In this example, you connected to the Access database as you did in the DataList example, but instead bound the data to the DataGrid1 control. The DataGrid control then took care of the rest.

Now, you can add a little style to the table. Replace the one-lined <asp:datagrid> control with the control shown in Listing 35-24.

Listing 35-24: **DataGrid Control with Some Styles**

```
<asp:datagrid id="datagrid1" runat="server" bordercolor="Tan"
borderwidth="1px" cellpadding="2" gridlines="None"
backcolor="LightGoldenrodYellow" forecolor="Black">

<footerstyle backcolor="Tan"></footerstyle>

<headerstyle font-bold="True" backcolor="Tan"></headerstyle>

<alternatingitemstyle backcolor="PaleGoldenrod">
</alternatingitemstyle>
</asp:datagrid>
```

With a little bit more code, some style to the grid layout of the data is added. What a difference! (See Figure 35-20.)

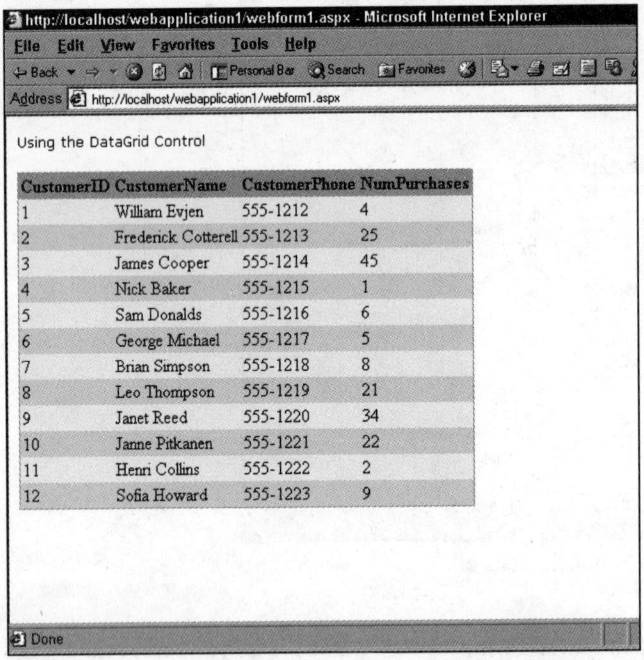

Figure 35-20: A DataGrid control with some styles added

The next thing you do with the `DataGrid` is connect to an XML file, and use the data from the XML to populate your `DataGrid`. Listing 35-25 is your `WebForm1.aspx` file.

Listing 35-25: **Using a DataGrid with an XML File**

```
<%@ Import Namespace="System.IO" %>
<%@ Import Namespace="System.Data" %>
<html>
  <head>

        <title>DataGrid and XML File</title>
        <script language="VB" runat="server">

    Sub Page_Load(Sender As Object, E As EventArgs)
        Dim DS As New DataSet
        Dim FS As FileStream
        Dim Reader As StreamReader
```

```
    FS = New FileStream(Server.MapPath("Customers.xml"),
FileMode.Open,FileAccess.Read)
        Reader = New StreamReader(FS)
        DS.ReadXml(Reader)
        FS.Close()

        Dim Source As DataView
        Source = new DataView(ds.Tables(0))

        DataGrid1.DataSource = Source
        DataGrid1.DataBind()
    End Sub

</script>
</head>
<body>
        <font face="Verdana" size="2">
            Using the DataGrid Control with an XML File.
        </font></p>

        <asp:datagrid id="DataGrid1" runat="server"/>
</body></html>
```

Now, you really can't do much with this until you also have your XML file ready. Listing 35-26 shows the content for Customers.xml.

Listing 35-26: **Customers.xml File**

```
<NewDataSet>
  <xsd:schema id="NewDataSet" targetNamespace="" xmlns=""
  xmlns:xsd="http://www.w3.org/2001/XMLSchema"
  xmlns:msdata="urn:schemas-microsoft-com:xml-msdata">
    <xsd:element name="Customer">
    <xsd:complexType>
  <xsd:sequence>
        <xsd:element name="CustomerID" type="xsd:int"
        minOccurs="0" />
        <xsd:element name="CustomerName" type="xsd:string"
        minOccurs="0" />
        <xsd:element name="NumPurchases" type="xsd:int"
        minOccurs="0" />
    </xsd:sequence>
    </xsd:complexType>
    </xsd:element>
  <xsd:element name="NewDataSet" msdata:IsDataSet="true">
```

Continued

Listing 35-26 *(continued)*

```
<xsd:complexType>
  <xsd:choice maxOccurs="unbounded">
   <xsd:element ref="Customer" />
     </xsd:choice>
       </xsd:complexType>
 </xsd:element>
</xsd:schema>
<Customer>
        <CustomerID>1</CustomerID>
        <CustomerName>William Evjen</CustomerName>
        <NumPurchases>4</NumPurchases>
</Customer>
<Customer>
        <CustomerID>2</CustomerID>
        <CustomerName>Frederick Cotterell</CustomerName>
        <NumPurchases>25</NumPurchases>
</Customer>
<Customer>
        <CustomerID>3</CustomerID>
        <CustomerName>James Cooper</CustomerName>
        <NumPurchases>45</NumPurchases>
</Customer>
<Customer>
        <CustomerID>4</CustomerID>
        <CustomerName>Janne Pitkanen</CustomerName>
        <NumPurchases>22</NumPurchases>
</Customer>
<Customer>
        <CustomerID>5</CustomerID>
        <CustomerName>Henri Collins</CustomerName>
        <NumPurchases>2</NumPurchases>
</Customer>
</NewDataSet>
```

After you get both files into the system and you run the page, you should have a page that displays the data from the XML file. This data is presented in a simple DataGrid control, but you can apply styles to format the control as you wish.

The following example loads an XML file that contains both the XML data as well as the XML Schema within one document. This isn't always the case because sometimes you may have these items in two separate files. In order to do this, you have to use the Page_Load event, shown in Listing 35-27, in your page.

Listing 35-27: **Alternate Page_Load Event**

```
Sub Page_Load(Sender As Object, E As EventArgs)
    Dim DS As New DataSet
    Dim FS As FileStream
    Dim Schema, Reader As StreamReader

 FS = New FileStream(Server.MapPath("schema.xml"),
 FileMode.Open,FileAccess.Read)
    Schema = new StreamReader(FS)
    DS.ReadXmlSchema(Schema)
    FS.Close()

 FS = New FileStream(Server.MapPath("data.xml"),
 FileMode.Open,FileAccess.Read)
    Reader = New StreamReader(FS)
    DS.ReadXml(Reader)
    FS.Close()

    Dim Source As DataView
    Source = new DataView(ds.Tables(0))

    DataGrid1.DataSource = Source
    DataGrid1.DataBind()
End Sub
```

In this example, you load both the schema text and the XML file very easily.

<asp:repeater>

The Repeater control allows you to display in any format you desire on a Web page using custom templates and styles that you define. Within the code of the document, the Repeater control is written as <asp:repeater>, as shown in the following code:

```
<asp:Repeater id="Repeater1"
    DataSource="<% databindingexpression %>"
    runat=server>

  <HeaderTemplate>
    Header template HTML
  </HeaderTemplate>
  <ItemTemplate>
    Item template HTML
  </ItemTemplate>
  <AlternatingItemTemplate>
    Alternating item template HTML
  </AlternatingItemTemplate>
```

```
<SeparatorTemplate>
    Separator template HTML
</SeparatorTemplate>
<FooterTemplate>
    Footer template HTML
</FooterTemplate>
```

```
<asp:Repeater>
```

The `Repeater` control is based upon a template system that is very much like the `DataList` control. There are templates for `ItemTemplate`, `AlternatingItemTemplate`, `HeaderTemplate`, `FooterTemplate`, and the `SeparatorTemplate`. These templates act in the same way that they do in the `DataList` control.

Using the `Repeater` control, along with the templates, you can create data displays using the following:

- ✦ Tables
- ✦ Comma-delimited data
- ✦ Numbered or unordered lists

For the next example (Listing 35-28), you use the `Repeater` control to display a list of comma-delimited items from a SQL Server database.

Listing 35-28: <asp:repeater> Code Example

```
<html>
<head>

    <script language="VB" runat="server">
    Sub Page_Load(sender As Object, e As EventArgs)
        Dim strConn as string
        ="server=servername;uid=username;pwd=password"
        Dim strSQL as string = "select * from customers"
        Dim Conn as New SQLConnection(strConn)
        Dim Cmd as New SQLCommand(strSQL,Conn)
        Conn.Open()
        Repeater1.DataSource =
Cmd.ExecuteReader(system.data.CommandBehavior.Close
    Connection)
        Repeater1.DataBind()
        End Sub
    </script>

</head>
<body>
    <font face="Verdana" size=2>
        <b>Using the Repeater control</b></font><P>
```

```
<form runat=server>

<asp:repeater id="repeater1" runat="server">

<ItemTemplate>
<%# DataBinder.Eval(Container.DataItem, "FName")%>
 
<%# DataBinder.Eval(Container.DataItem, "LName")%>
</ItemTemplate>

<SeparatorTemplate>, </SeparatorTemplate>

</asp:repeater>

    </form>
</body>
</html>
```

This page generates a list of customers that are separated by commas. It is fairly simple, but shows you that you can generate controls to perform whatever task you throw at them.

`<asp:xml>`

The XML control allows you to display XML on a Web page. You can also include an XSL file to transform the XML data. Within the code of the document, the XML control is written as `<asp:xml>`, and is shown in the following example:

```
<asp:Xml id="Xml1"
     Document="XmlDocument object to display"
     DocumentContent="String of XML"
     DocumentSource="Path to XML Document"
     Transform="XslTransform object"
     TransformSource="Path to XSL Transform Document"
     runat="server">
```

Go through each of the three files that you use to make the XML control display your XML data. The first is shown in Listing 35-29.

Listing 35-29: **Customers2.xml File**

```
<Base>
   <Customer>
        <CustomerID>1</CustomerID>
        <CustomerName>William Evjen</CustomerName>
        <NumPurchases>4</NumPurchases>
```

Continued

Listing 35-29 *(continued)*

```
        </Customer>
        <Customer>
              <CustomerID>2</CustomerID>
              <CustomerName>Frederick Cotterell</CustomerName>
              <NumPurchases>25</NumPurchases>
        </Customer>
        <Customer>
              <CustomerID>3</CustomerID>
              <CustomerName>James Cooper</CustomerName>
              <NumPurchases>45</NumPurchases>
        </Customer>
        <Customer>
              <CustomerID>4</CustomerID>
              <CustomerName>Janne Pitkanen</CustomerName>
              <NumPurchases>22</NumPurchases>
        </Customer>
        <Customer>
              <CustomerID>5</CustomerID>
              <CustomerName>Henri Collins</CustomerName>
              <NumPurchases>2</NumPurchases>
    </Customer>
</Base>
```

This is basically the same file that you used in the `DataGrid` example, except there isn't any schema data in the file.

The next file you will use for the `XML` control example is the XSL file (see Listing 35-30). This is a file that transforms the appearance of the XML file so that you can present the data in a more readable format with a style that is more user-friendly.

Listing 35-30: XSL File

```
<xsl:stylesheet version="1.0"
        xmlns:xsl="http://www.w3.org/1999/XSL/Transform">
    <xsl:template match="/Base">
       <xsl:apply-templates select="Customer" />
    </xsl:template>

    <xsl:template match="Customer">
       <table width="50%" border="1">
          <tr>
             <td width="10%">
                <b>
                   <xsl:value-of select="CustomerID" />
                </b>
             </td>
```

```
            <td width="60%">
                <xsl:value-of select="CustomerName" />
            </td>
            <td>
                <xsl:value-of select="NumPurchases" />
            </td>
        </tr>
    </table>
</xsl:template>
</xsl:stylesheet>
```

Now that you have an XSL file that takes the XML data and then transforms the data into something more presentable, you now need to turn your attention to the WebForm1.aspx page that you create. It uses these two files within the context of an XML control (see Listing 35-31).

Listing 35-31: <asp:xml> Code Example

```
<%@ Import Namespace="System.Xml" %>
<%@ Import Namespace="System.Xml.Xsl" %>
<html>
    <script language="VB" runat="server">
        Sub Page_Load(sender As Object, e As EventArgs)
            Dim doc As XmlDocument = New XmlDocument()
            doc.Load(Server.MapPath("customers2.xml"))

            Dim trans As XslTransform = new XslTransform()
            trans.Load(Server.MapPath("customersSchema.xsl"))

            xml1.Document = doc
            xml1.Transform = trans
        End Sub
    </script>
<body>
    <font face="Verdana" size=2>
    <b>Using the XML control</b></font><P>
    <form runat=server>
        <asp:Xml id="xml1" runat="server" />
    </form>
</body>
</html>
```

After running the ASP.NET page, notice that the XML control used both files together to display a collection of tables with the customer data. Working with XSL, you can transform your XML data into presentable Web data.

Within the `Page_Load` event, you load the XML document and bind it to the XML control by specifying the `xml1.Document = doc`. You then specify the XSL document by also binding it to the `XML` control with `xml1.Transform = trans`.

Using Visual Studio .NET and Web Controls

You built all these controls by typing code directly into the code window (the HTML tab) of Visual Studio .NET. However, you could have very easily used Visual Studio .NET's drag-and-drop capabilities.

After a control is placed on the page in the Design mode (the Design tab), highlighting the control makes the control *active* and allows you to change the control's properties (or attributes) within the Properties window.

Double-clicking any of the controls brings you to a CodeBehind page. This is a separate page that allows you to keep the VB .NET code in a location other than the presentation piece of the code. Doing this helps you keep your Web applications organized and easy to manage.

Also, using this process of page development allows IntelliSense to work to its fullest. You then notice that Intellisense works great on the CodeBehind page.

Summary

This was a long chapter, but it showed you that there are a lot of powerful and rich controls at your disposal. These controls alleviate a lot of the problems that traditional ASP programmers of the past had to deal with. Now, with Web controls, you can build database-driven Internet applications with ease. You now know that even if they build for the highest common denominator (the highest level of browser available to the user), the user who is still running around the Internet with Microsoft Internet Explorer 3.0 can still view the page because the controls generate the appropriate code for the appropriate browser.

As you see in the following chapters, you are not done with controls! There are still Validation controls and User controls. Beyond this, Microsoft has also promised that more controls are on the way.

✦   ✦   ✦

Validation Controls

by Bill Evjen

◆ ◆ ◆ ◆

In This Chapter

Introduction to
Validation controls

How to use
Validation controls
within Web Forms

How to use regular
expressions

◆ ◆ ◆ ◆

In the past two chapters, you learned about the controls
needed to build forms of all kinds, but how do you validate
the information that the user types into these controls? That
is where Validation controls come into play.

What Validation Means

First of all, you need to understand what validating data
means. Validating does not mean that if John Doe types an
alias into a form field, the computer sends an alert to inform
you that the data is untruthful. No, we still do not have the
ability to find out if this is a true statement or not.

Validation is testing to determine whether the user entered
something into the field. After you determine that something
was entered, you can also check to see whether what was
entered is either a number or a character, and also compare
user input between different fields. There is a lot of other
information you can check for, as you will find out in the rest
of the chapter.

Data collection on the Internet is one of the most important
features available, and it is important to make sure that the
data you collect has value and meaning. The way to do this is
to make sure that you eliminate any chances that the information collected does not abide by the rules you outline.

Server-Side/Client-Side Validation

There are a couple of ways that validation took place within traditional Active Server Pages. The first was after users entered their information in the Web Form: They clicked the Submit button and then this information was sent to the server. You could then test the validity of the information by using ASP code.

On the server, if something were wrong with what the user entered, you could go back to the form, and ask the user to correct the information in that particular field of the form. Sometimes, you carried the correct input from the other fields back to the form page, and populated the fields for the users so they didn't have to re-enter the same information again. There are sites on the Internet that don't carry this inputted information back to the form page, and the user is then required to enter in all the information back into the form for a second time. As you might realize, this quickly causes people to leave your site for another.

The bad thing about server-side validation is that it requires trips back and forth to the server, and this takes a lot of resources and makes for a slower-paced form for the user. There is nothing more annoying for a user who is on a dial-up connection than clicking the Submit button on their form and then waiting for 20 seconds to find out that they didn't enter their password correctly.

The other option for form validation was to put some client-side JavaScript at the top of the ASP page that checked the information that the user inputted into the fields was correct. This took care of the problem of making unnecessary trips to the server, but it required another language to learn and manage. JavaScript is a great language, but takes a lot of time to master, and there are always problems getting your JavaScript code to work on different browsers. Listing 36-1 shows an example of one simple form check using JavaScript.

Listing 36-1: **Client-side JavaScript Code Example**

```
<script language="javascript">
<!--
Function CheckForm(form)
{
   for(var intCtr = 0; intCtr <= (form.elements.length - 5);
++intCtr)
   {
        var temp = form.elements[intCtr];
        if(temp.type == "text" && temp.value == "")
        {
        alert("Please Enter All Information!");
            temp.focus();
            return false;
        }
```

```
    }
    return true;
}
//-->
</script>
```

This sample piece of JavaScript does some validation, but it doesn't check for all the information that you might need on the form you are building. This piece of code determines only whether the user entered *anything* at all in all of the five fields within the form. It does *not* determine whether the user entered an e-mail address within the e-mail address text box, whether the user entered a number between two set numbers, or whether the password and the confirm password text boxes match. After awhile, you can see that you would need a large number of JavaScript functions to truly get into some serious form validation.

.NET to the Rescue!

There are presently six different Validation controls to use in your ASP.NET documents to perform all the validation that you might need — *and they couldn't be easier to use!*

The validation controls at your disposal include the following:

✦ Compare **Validator**

✦ Custom **Validator**

✦ Range **Validator**

✦ Regular Expression **Validator**

✦ Required Field **Validator**

✦ Validation **Summary**

Not only can you validate all sorts of information from your forms, but also you can customize validation for your own needs. Then, if there are any errors in the form data, these Validation controls allow for you to customize the display of error information back on the browser.

You place Validation controls on your page the same way as any other type of controls. After the user submits the form, the user's form information is sent to the appropriate Validation control, where it is evaluated. If the information inputted doesn't validate, the control sets a page property that indicates this. After all the form information is sent to all the Validation controls, if one or more of the Validation controls can't validate the information sent to it, the entire form input is found to be invalid, and the user is notified of this action.

Table 36-1 describes each of the six Validation controls.

Table 36-1
Validation Controls

Validation Control	Description
`<asp:comparevalidator>`	A Validation control that allows for comparisons between the user's input and another item using a comparison operator (equals, greater than, less than, and so on).
`<asp:customvalidator>`	A Validation control that checks the user's entry using custom-coded validation logic.
`<asp:rangevalidator>`	A Validation control that checks the user's input based upon a lower- and upper-level range of numbers or characters.
`<asp:regularexpressionvalidator>`	A Validation control that checks that the user's entry matches a pattern defined by a regular expression. This is a good control to use to check e-mail addresses and phone numbers.
`<asp:requiredfieldvalidator>`	A Validation control that ensures that the user does not skip a form entry field.
`<asp:validationsummary>`	A Validation control that displays all the error messages from the validators in one specific spot on the page.

Before you get into each of these different Validation controls, you need to build a Web Form to validate against (see Listing 36-2). You use this same Form with every one of the Validation controls.

Listing 36-2: **WebForm1.aspx**

```
<html>
  <head>
      <title>St. Louis .NET User Group</title>

      <script language="vb" runat="server">
      Sub Button1_Click(Sender As Object, E As EventArgs)
          Label1.Visible = True
          Label1.Text = "Welcome to the group!"
      End Sub
      </script>
```

```
</head>
<body>

<form runat="server" id="Form1">

<table cellspacing="1" cellpadding="3" width="300"
border="0">
      <tr>
      <td bgcolor="navy">
      <p align="center">
      <font face="Verdana" color="#ffffff" size="4">
      <b>St. Louis .NET User Group<br>
      Membership Signup</b></font></p>
      </td>
      </tr>
</table>

<p align="left">
<font face="Verdana" size="2">
<b>Name<br>
<asp:TextBox id="TextBox1" runat="server"
columns="35"></asp:TextBox><br>

Email Address<br>
<asp:TextBox id="TextBox2" runat="server"
columns="35"></asp:TextBox><br>

Age<br>
<asp:TextBox id="TextBox3" runat="server" columns="3"
maxlength="3"></asp:TextBox><br>

Profession<br>
<asp:DropDownList id="DropDownList1" runat="server" Font-
Names="Verdana" Font-Size="X-Small">
      <asp:ListItem Value="--- Select Profession ---">
      --- Select Profession ---</asp:ListItem>
      <asp:ListItem
      Value="Programmer">Programmer</asp:ListItem>
      <asp:ListItem Value="Senior Programmer">Senior
      Programmer</asp:ListItem>
      <asp:ListItem
      Value="Developer">Developer</asp:ListItem>
      <asp:ListItem Value="Web Master">
      Web Master</asp:ListItem>
</asp:DropDownList><br>

Password<br>
<asp:TextBox id="TextBox4" runat="server" columns="35"
textmode="Password"></asp:TextBox><br>

Confirm Password<br>
```

Continued

Listing 36-2 *(continued)*

```
<asp:TextBox id="TextBox5" runat="server" columns="35"
textmode="Password"></asp:TextBox>
</font></b></p>

<p align="left">
<asp:Button id="Button1" runat="server" Text="Submit"
OnClick="Button1_Click"></asp:Button></p>

<p>
<asp:label id="Label1" runat="server" visible="False"
font-names="Verdana" font-bold="True" font-size="X-Small"
/></p>

</form>
</body>
</html>
```

Now, after typing the code for this, or building this page within Visual Studio .NET by just dragging and dropping the appropriate controls onto the page, you notice that the user can enter any information they wish, submit the form, and get a welcome message (see Figure 36-1).

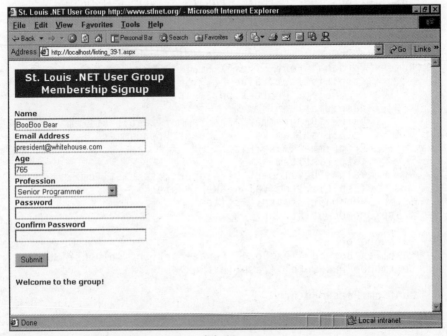

Figure 36-1: The form without any validation

But you want to make sure that you collect real information within your form and not allow people to just enter in arbitrary info. You can begin the validation process with the `RequiredFieldValidator` control.

\<asp:requiredfieldvalidator\>

The `RequiredFieldValidator` control makes sure that the user enters *something* into the field that it is associated with in the form. You need to tie the `RequiredFieldValidator` to each control that is a required field in the form. What happens is that the `RequiredFieldValidator` control fails if the user does not enter something that is different from the initial value of the control. The `RequiredFieldValidator` looks as follows:

```
<asp:RequiredFieldValidator
     id="RequiredFieldValidator1"
     runat="server"
     ControlToValidate="DropDownList1"
     InitialValue="--- Select Profession ---"
     ErrorMessage="You must select a profession"
     ForeColor="Red" BackColor="Grey">
</asp:RequiredFieldValidator>
```

For instance, the `InitialValue` attribute of the `DropDownList` control in your form has to be set to `"--- Select Profession ---"`; otherwise, the Validation control thinks that this is the choice. For text boxes, however, you don't need to specify the `InitialValue` of the control (unless you have some text you put in there on rendering). The `InitialValue` in this case is considered nothing or empty.

Listing 36-3 shows how to add a `RequiredFieldValidator` control to your form. Next to the `DropDownList1` control, you place the following code:

Listing 36-3: \<asp:requiredfieldvalidator\> Code Example

```
<asp:RequiredFieldValidator id="RequiredFieldValidator1"
runat="server" Font-Names="Verdana" Font-Bold="True" Font-
Size="X-Small" ErrorMessage="* Please enter a profession!"
initialvalue="--- Select Profession ---"
controltovalidate="DropDownList1">
</asp:RequiredFieldValidator>
```

After placing this code within your form, right-click the file within the Solution Explorer in Visual Studio. NET, and choose Build and Browse. The page then saves itself and runs in a browser window within Visual Studio. NET. Don't change any of the fields. Click the Submit button. You are then presented with a validation error message, as shown in Figure 36-2.

Figure 36-2: Validation error based upon the drop-down list

What happened was that after you clicked the Submit button, the `RequiredFieldValidator` control went into action, and validated what you entered into the `DropDownList1` control (the select box with the list of professions). Because you didn't enter a profession, it was returned with the error message. Pretty outstanding! It would have taken considerably more code to do this by writing your own JavaScript function, and you would have to also develop the JavaScript code to be browser-independent. Isn't it easier to let ASP.NET worry about all of that?

Listing 36-4 shows the code that it generates for us (Note: I am using Microsoft's Internet Explorer 6.0 to view the code and different browsers may show different code based on what the browser supports). Open a fresh version of the page, right-click on the page and select View Source.

Listing 36-4: **Page Code Generated by ASP.NET Using a Validation Control**

```
<html>
  <head>
        <title>St. Louis .NET User Group
        http://www.stlnet.org/</title>

  </head>
  <body>

  <form name="Form1" method="post"
  action="listing_36-2.aspx" language="javascript"
  onsubmit="ValidatorOnSubmit();" id="Form1">
  <input type="hidden" name="__VIEWSTATE"
  value="dDwtOTAyMTQzMTMxOzs+" />

  <script language="javascript"
  src="/aspnet_client/system_web/1_0_2914_16/WebUIValidation
  js"></script>

  <table cellspacing="1" cellpadding="3" width="300"
  border="0">
        <tr>
          <td bgcolor="navy">
            <p align="center">
              <font face="Verdana" color="#ffffff"
              size="4">
```

```
        <b>St. Louis .NET User Group<br>
        Membership Signup</b></font></p>
      </td>
      </tr>
  </table>

  <p align="left">
  <font face="Verdana" size="2">
  <b>Name<br>
  <input name="TextBox1"
  type="text" size="35" id="TextBox1" />

  <br>
  Email Address<br>
  <input name="TextBox2" type="text"
  size="35" id="TextBox2" />

  <br>
  Age<br>
  <input name="TextBox3" type="text"
  maxlength="3" size="3" id="TextBox3" />

  <br>
  Profession<br>
<select name="DropDownList1" id="DropDownList1" style="font-
family:Verdana;font-size:X-Small;">
  <option value="--- Select Profession ---">
  --- Select Profession ---</option>
  <option value="Programmer">Programmer</option>
  <option value="Senior Programmer">Senior
  Programmer</option>
  <option value="Developer">Developer</option>
  <option value="Web Master">Web Master</option>
</select>

<span id="RequiredFieldValidator1"
controltovalidate="DropDownList1" errormessage="* Please
enter a profession!"
evaluationfunction="RequiredFieldValidatorEvaluateIsValid"
initialvalue="--- Select Profession ---"
style="color:Red;font-family:Verdana;font-size:X-Small;font-
weight:bold;visibility:hidden;">* Please enter a
profession!</span>

  <br>
  Password<br>
  <input name="TextBox4" type="password" size="35"
  id="TextBox4" />

  <br>
  Confirm Password<br>
```

Continued

Listing 36-4 *(continued)*

```
<input name="TextBox5" type="password" size="35"
id="TextBox5" />
</font></b></p>

<p align="left">
<input type="submit" name="Button1" value="Submit"
onclick="if (typeof(Page_ClientValidate) == 'function')
Page_ClientValidate(); " language="javascript"
id="Button1" /></p>

<script language="javascript">
<!--
var Page_Validators =  new
Array(document.all["RequiredFieldValidator1"]);
// -->
</script>


<script language="javascript">
<!--
var Page_ValidationActive = false;
if (typeof(clientInformation) != "undefined" &&
clientInformation.appName.indexOf("Explorer") != -1) {
    if (typeof(Page_ValidationVer) == "undefined")
        alert("Unable to find script library
'/aspnet_client/system_web/1_0_2914_16/WebUIValidation.js'.
Try placing this file manually, or reinstall by running
'aspnet_regiis -c'.");
    else if (Page_ValidationVer != "121")
        alert("This page uses an incorrect version of
WebUIValidation.js. The page expects version 121. The script
library is " + Page_ValidationVer + ".");
    else
        ValidatorOnLoad();
}

function ValidatorOnSubmit() {
    if (Page_ValidationActive) {
        ValidatorCommonOnSubmit();
    }
}
// -->
</script>


        </form>
</body>
</html>
```

You notice a lot of code that you didn't put in there! There are now a number of JavaScript functions that take care of the validation for you. This code was generated to comply with the browser you viewed the page with.

Back on the page in the browser, this time select a profession and then click the Submit button. This time, validation occurs, and you see the welcome message.

This example added a `RequiredFieldValidator` control to a `DropDownList` control. It is pretty much the same to add one to a `TextBox` control, as shown in Listing 36-5.

Listing 36-5: Using the RequiredFieldValidator on a TextBox Control

```
<asp:RequiredFieldValidator id="RequiredFieldValidator2"
runat="server" Font-Names="Verdana" Font-Bold="True" Font-
Size="X-Small" ErrorMessage="* Please enter your name!"
ControlToValidate="TextBox1">
</asp:RequiredFieldValidator>
```

Now, add this `RequiredFieldValidator` control next to the `TextBox1` control that asks the users for their name. Notice that this time, you didn't specify the `InitialValue` attribute because the field is empty when the user first sees it. It is also vital with all Validation controls to specify the `ControlToValidate` attribute or else the Validation control won't be tied to anything, and you get a page error.

<asp:comparevalidator>

The `CompareValidator` compares the value entered into the form field to another field, a database value, or a value that you specify. When comparing against data types, you just set the `Operator` = `DataTypeCheck`. After that is done, you can set the `Type` attribute to `String`, `Integer`, `Double`, `Date`, or `Currency` in the `CompareValidator` control to make sure that what the user enters into the field falls into the specified type. The `CompareValidator` control looks as follows:

```
<asp:CompareValidator
    id="programmaticID"
    runat="server"
    ControlToValidate="ID of Server Control to Validate"
    ValueToCompare="104.5"
    Type="Double"
    Operator="LessThan"
    ErrorMessage="Temperature must not exceed 104.5"
    ForeColor="Red"
    BackColor="Grey">
</asp:CompareValidator>
```

In this case, you want to compare what the user enters in the password field to the entry in the confirm password field to see whether they are the same. This is a common practice when a form asks for a password to make sure that the user didn't mistype the password (see Listing 36-6).

Listing 36-6: <asp:comparevalidator> Code Example

```
<asp:CompareValidator id="CompareValidator1" runat="server"
ControlToValidate="TextBox5" ErrorMessage="* Passwords do not
match!" Font-Size="X-Small" Font-Bold="True" Font-
Names="Verdana" ControlToCompare="TextBox4">
</asp:CompareValidator>
```

Within the form you are building, place this next to TextBox4 (the password field) to compare what is entered into TextBox4 with what is entered into TextBox5. You are making sure that they are equal strings when compared to each other. If they are not equal, the page returns an error message (see Figure 36-3). If they are equal, your page submits valid.

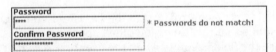

Figure 36-3: Here, the user typed in mismatched passwords, and the page didn't validate.

For another example of how the CompareValidator control works, you use this control next to the age field (TextBox3), as shown in Listing 36-7.

Listing 36-7: <asp:comparevalidator> Code Example 2

```
<asp:CompareValidator id="CompareValidator2" runat="server"
ControlToValidate="TextBox3" ErrorMessage="* You must be
younger than 95!" Operator="LessThan" Type="Integer"
ValueToCompare="95">
</asp:CompareValidator>
```

Let's say that in order to gain membership to the St. Louis .NET User Group, you have to be younger than 95 years old (this is a hypothetical situation; anyone can join!). If you want to make sure that everyone joining is younger than 95, you can check for it when the prospective members enter their information into your form by using the `CompareValidator` control. Figure 36-4 shows the resulting error message if the user does not enter a valid age.

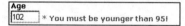

Figure 36-4: With your validation, the user is too old.

In this situation, you are not comparing two fields in the form; instead, you are comparing one field against a value that you have specified. There are three important attributes to be aware of for this kind of validation. The first is the `ValueToCompare` attribute. For this attribute, you put in 95 because that is the value you want to compare against. The next is the `Operator` attribute, which has the following operators:

✦ `Equal`

✦ `NotEqual`

✦ `GreaterThan`

✦ `GreaterThanEqual`

✦ `LessThan`

✦ `LessThanEqual`

✦ `DataTypeCheck`

You want the person to be younger than 95 years old, so the operator you want to use is the `LessThan` operator. The last attribute is the `type` attribute, and in this case you specified the type to be an `integer`.

<asp:rangevalidator>

The `RangeValidator` is similar to the `CompareValidator`, but the `RangeValidator` compares what is entered into the form field with two values, and makes sure that what was entered by the user is between these two specified values. `RangeValidator` appears as follows:

```
<asp:RangeValidator
     id="RangeValidator1"
     runat="server"
     ControlToValidate="Temperature"
     MinimumValue="98.5"
     MaximumValue="104.5"
     Type="Double"
     ErrorMessage="Temperature cannot exceed 104.5"
     ForeColor="Red"
     BackColor="Grey">
</asp:RangeValidator>
```

For instance, imagine that the user group now accepts members between the ages of 10 and 95, and nobody else. So, for your entry form, you want to add a `RangeValidator` control to the age field in your form (`TextBox3`). You already have a `CompareValidator` control there, so remove that and put the code shown in Listing 36-8 in its place. The error message that this code creates is shown in Figure 36-5.

Listing 36-8: `<asp:rangevalidator>` Code Example

```
<asp:RangeValidator id="RangeValidator1" runat="server"
ControlToValidate="TextBox3" ErrorMessage="* You must be
between 10 and 95 to join!" Font-Size="X-Small" Font-
Bold="True" Font-Names="Verdana" Type="Integer"
MaximumValue="95" MinimumValue="10">
</asp:RangeValidator>
```

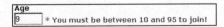

Figure 36-5: This user did not enter a number in the valid range.

The important attributes to take notice of here are the `Type` attribute, which you have set to `Integer`, and the `MaximumValue` and `MinimumValue` attributes, in which you specify your range. In this case, the range you are looking for is between 10 and 95. Using this `RangeValidator` control ensures that the user enters a number between 10 and 95.

`<asp:regularexpressionvalidator>`

The `RegularExpressionValidator` control is a Validation control that allows you to check the user's input based on a pattern defined by a regular expression. This is a great control to use to check if the user has entered in an e-mail address or a telephone number. These kinds of validations in the past took a considerable amount of JavaScript coding. With ASP.NET, however, it is now so easy that it can only make you smile! The `RegularExpressionValidator` control looks as follows:

```
<asp:RegularExpressionValidator
     id="Validator1"
     runat="server"
     ControlToValidate="ZipCode"
     ValidationExpression="\d{5}"
     ErrorMessage="Zip code must be 5 digits"
     ForeColor="Red"
     BackColor="Grey" ... >
</asp: RegularExpressionValidator>
```

Regular expression can be a little tricky, but Visual Studio .NET helps you find the expression that you may need for your control. Within the Properties window for the `RegularExpressionValidator` control, click the button within the `ValidationExpression` box, and Visual Studio.NET provides you with a short list of expressions to use within your form (see Figure 36-6).

Figure 36-6: The Properties window showing the button in the ValidationExpression box

Table 36-2 lists some of the expressions (you can also, of course, create your own expressions):

Table 36-2
Regular Expressions

Description	Expression
U.S. Phone Number	`((\(\d{3}\) ?)|(\d{3}-))?\d{3}-\d{4}`
U.S. Social Security Number	`\d{3}-\d{2}-\d{4}`
U.S. Zip Code	`\d{5}(-\d{4})?`
Internet Email Address	`\w+([-+.]\w+)*@\w+([-.]\w+)*\.\w+([-.]\w+)*`
Internet URL	`http://([\w-]+\.)+[\w-]+(/[\w-./?%&=]*)?`
French Phone Number	`(0( \d|\d ))?\d\d \d\d(\d \d| \d\d )\d\d`
French Postal Code	`\d{5}`
German Phone Number	`((\(0\d\d\) |(\(0\d{3}\) )?\d )?\d\d \d\d \d\d\d|\(0\d{4}\) \d \d\d-\d\d?)`
German Postal Code	`(D-)?\d{5}`

Continued

<table>
<tr><th colspan="2">Table 36-2 (continued)</th></tr>
<tr><th>Description</th><th>Expression</th></tr>
<tr><td>Japanese Phone Number</td><td><code>(0\d{1,4}-|\(0\d{1,4}\)
?)?\d{1,4}-\d{4}</code></td></tr>
<tr><td>Japanese Postal Code</td><td><code>\d{3}(-(\d{4}|\d{2}))?</code></td></tr>
<tr><td>P.R.C. Phone Number</td><td><code>(\(\d{3}\)|\d{3}-)?\d{8}</code></td></tr>
<tr><td>P.R.C. Postal Code</td><td><code>\d{6}</code></td></tr>
<tr><td>P.R.C. Social Security Number (ID Number)</td><td><code>\d{18}|\d{15}</code></td></tr>
</table>

Go through the Internet Email Address example here to understand how the regular expression is compared to our form inputs. The Internet Email Address regular expression is written as follows:

```
\w+([-+.]\w+)*@\w+([-.]\w+)*\.\w+([-.]\w+)*
```

This is how to read the code:

- ✦ `\w+` is any number of text characters. This can be either letters or numbers.

- ✦ `([-+.]\w+)` is an expression saying that it may or may not contain a period followed by any number of text characters. This expression is in parentheses because they are grouped together. For instance, if it were written without the parentheses, the user could enter `William.@idg.com`, and that is not a valid e-mail address.

- ✦ `*@\w+` means that there has to be a @ sign within the text (an "at" sign), followed by any number of text characters.

- ✦ `([-.]\w+)` means that after the @ sign, there can be another instance of a period followed by more text.

- ✦ `*\.\w+` means that it most have a period followed by more text.

- ✦ `([-.]\w+)*` means that it can have an undisclosed amount of periods followed by text.

If you are thinking about e-mail addresses, the typical e-mail address is just *name@ server.com*. But there are more complicated e-mail addresses out there (for instance, government e-mail addresses can be rather long beasts!).

For the form you are building for the user group, you need to validate that the user entered in a valid e-mail address, as shown in Listing 36-9.

Listing 36-9: `<asp:regularexpressionvalidator>` Code Example

```
<asp:RegularExpressionValidator
id="RegularExpressionValidator1" runat="server"
ControlToValidate="TextBox2" ErrorMessage="* You must enter
in a valid email address!" Font-Size="X-Small" Font-
Bold="True" Font-Names="Verdana" ValidationExpression="\w+([-
+.]\w+)*@\w+([-.]\w+)*\.\w+([-.]\w+)*">
</asp:RegularExpressionValidator>
```

In this example, it is important to notice that you placed the Internet Email Address regular expression within your `ValidationExpression` attribute. Place this code next to the e-mail address textbox (`TextBox2`). Use the Build and Browse feature, and test the e-mail validation. Pretty simple, and it took hardly any code at all! Figure 36-7 shows the error message that results if a user enters an invalid e-mail address.

Email Address
William@Evjen   * You must enter in a valid email address!

Figure 36-7: Invalid e-mail address

`<asp:customvalidator>`

The `CustomValidator` control allows you to develop your own custom server or client-side validations. At times, you want to compare the user's input based upon a value in the database, or determine whether their input conforms to some arithmetic validation that you are looking for (for instance, if the number is even or odd). The `CustomValidator` control is as follows:

```
<asp:CustomValidator id="CustomValidator1"
    runat="server"
    ControlToValidate="ID of Server Control to Validate"
    ClientValidationFunction="ClientValidateID"
    OnServerValidate="ServerValidateID"
    ErrorMessage="Invalid user id"
    ForeColor="Red"
    BackColor="Grey">
</asp:CustomValidator>
```

By using the `OnServerValidate` event, you can call a subroutine within your code that may open a database and grab an item to compare to what the user entered. In the following subroutine (see Listing 36-10), you check to see whether the number the user entered into the text box was an even number.

Listing 36-10: `<asp:customvalidator>` Code Example

```
Sub ServerValidation
    (source As object, args As ServerValidateEventArgs)
    Try
        Dim Num As Integer = Integer.Parse(args.Value)
        args.IsValid = ((Num mod 2) = 0)
    Catch ex as Exception
        args.IsValid = False
    End Try
End Sub
```

In this case, you can work your `ServerValidation` routine to perform almost any kind of comparison that you wish.

For your form example that you are building in this chapter, you will not use the `CustomValidator` control.

`<asp:validationsummary>`

The `ValidationSummary` control is a great control that works with all the controls on the page. What it does is take all the error messages that the other Validation controls may send back to the page, and puts them all in one spot that you specify on the page. These error messages can be displayed in a list, bulleted list, or paragraph. You specify this in the `DisplayMode` attribute. The `ValidationSummary` control is as follows:

```
<asp:ValidationSummary
    id="prgrammaticIDforValidationSummaryControl"
    runat="server"
    DisplayMode="BulletList | List | SingleParagraph"
    EnableClientScript="true | false"
    ShowSummary="true | false"
    ShowMessageBox="true | false"
    HeaderText="TextToDisplayAsSummaryTitle"/>
```

In Listing 36-11, you put all the error messages in one spot above all the form fields, and customize it a bit so it fits in with the page you are building. Figure 36-8 shows the resulting form.

Listing 36-11: `<asp:validationsummary>` Code Example

```
<asp:ValidationSummary id="ValidationSummary1" runat="server"
Font-Size="X-Small" Font-Bold="True" Font-Names="Verdana"
HeaderText="<P>Please correct the following errors:">
</asp:ValidationSummary>
```

Place this control right under the banner of the form. Test it, and notice how it is displaying the page errors. Feel free to switch the Display mode to both List and Paragraph to see how it lays out. Also, another great feature of this control is that it can display the errors in a pop-up message box for Level 4 browsers and above.

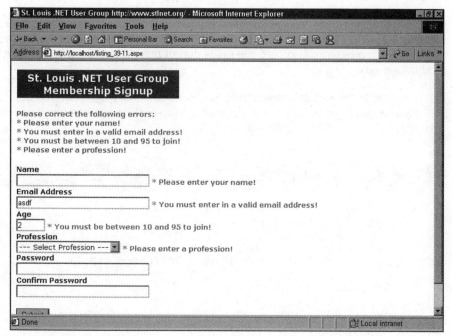

Figure 36-8: The validation summary is at the top of the page in this form.

Finishing the form

Now, there are just a few more steps to finish your form for the user group. First, you want to compare the age of the users when they enter in an age in your form. But you don't have a control there to make this text box a required field. Can a control have more than one Validation control associated with it? Yes it can; in most cases, the controls you build will have more than one Validation control. For example, in this case, you want the user to enter in an age *and* you want to compare the age entered with two values. So go ahead and add a `RequiredFieldValidator` control to the form, and validate against the age text box (`TextBox3`).

The problem with the password validation is that it is also not a required field. Presently, it validates only if the user enters a password for it to compare with. Because you want the user to enter a password, you need to also make this text box a required field.

You don't need to do this to the Compare password text box (`TextBox5`) because if the user enters in a password in the Password text box and doesn't enter anything in the Confirm password text box, the fields do not match, and the page generates a validation error.

The final field is the e-mail address field; you need to make this a required field as well. Finally, you need to add some script at the top of the page if you will use this data after is validated (see Listing 36-12).

Listing 36-12: **Script if Page IsValid**

```
Sub Page_Load(Source As Object, E As EventArgs)
   If Page.IsPostBack Then
            If Page.IsValid Then
                'You can submit data to the database here
                    Response.Redirect("ValidForm.aspx")
            End If
   End If
End Sub
```

In this script, you can add some database access and place your data in a table. You get to this point by checking the `Page.IsValid` event. If the page passes all the validation checks, the page is valid.

Summary

Validation controls make a developer's life a lot easier than in the past (when in order to develop the same type of functionality, a developer had to go sometimes to extreme JavaScript coding measures).

The great thing about using these Validation controls is that they are very simple and easy to implement. Modifying them is a piece of cake, and you can easily check for all sorts of parameters on the input generated from our forms.

Using Validation controls along with Web controls make an outstanding combination in building smart forms.

✦   ✦   ✦

User Controls

by Bill Evjen

User controls are encapsulated chunks of code that you can place in the middle of your ASP.NET application and reuse. The goal is to build commonly used but generic sections of Web documents and just place them in your Internet applications wherever you need them.

User controls make your life a lot easier because they provide you with an almost "plug-and-save" development environment. All you need to do is plug them into your application and save it, and you have immediate access to everything the control has to offer. They bring developers closer to the holy grail of coding—*code reuse*. You will find that User controls are used quite frequently in your applications. Basically, they're mini-versions of an ASP.NET page that you can use anywhere within your ASP.NET application. In fact, originally they were called *pagelets*.

This chapter introduces you to User controls and shows you how to build and use them within your applications.

Embracing Code Reuse

No developer likes to sit down at a computer and reinvent the wheel every time he does a new page or starts a new project. Yes, it's nice to have enough development work to do, but instead of building a part of a Web page that you've built a 100 times in the past, your time could be better spent making the application more bulletproof.

The goal is to have sections of code that you can reuse wherever you wish, whenever you need to call it. There are ways to get closer and closer to this nirvana, and User controls are another step in that direction.

In classic Active Server Pages (ASP), developers could do one of two things to achieve code reuse. First, they could open up a document that contained code that was used in the past, highlight the desired code, copy it, and then paste it into their new document. Then they could go through the code, changing it as necessary to fit in with the new development environment. Presto! Code reuse, eh?

This approach was okay, but it had many disadvantages. The first was that developers couldn't always remember where they put the old code. Also, they never really knew what other developers did in their own code, or which code was out there for them to use within their own applications. There was also the problem of carrying over code that shouldn't have been moved over, as a lot of code contains application and server specific items. This approach was very error-prone. After a while, it just turned out to be easier for developers to sit down and retype what they did before.

The other approach to code reuse in classic ASP was to use *include files,* which developers would call into their applications within any point in the code. The include files would look as follows:

```
<!--#INCLUDE FILE="myIncludeFile.inc"-->
```

The number one problem with include files was that they were always called before the ASP code was processed, so developers couldn't pass any arguments to them. This made them rather difficult to deal with.

The trick is to design ASP.NET User controls so that they're generic enough to be used anywhere. For example, you wouldn't want to make a User control that used the text "Company ABC Online Registration Form" everywhere within the control and then try to use it for Company XYZ. If you need to make significant changes to a User control to get it to work within your application, you're defeating the whole purpose of User controls.

So the idea is to build a generic control and then control its properties in order to set them at runtime. To accomplish this, you need a solid understanding of the various parts of a User control.

Understanding the Benefits of User Controls

A User control can be made up of the following components:

✦ Static text

✦ Other controls

✦ Events

There isn't that much difference between an ASP.NET page and a User control page. The main distinction is that since the User control is going to be placed within the ASP.NET document at any point and will never act as a standalone page, the User control cannot have any of the page framework tags such as <html>, <head>, or <body>. If a User control contained any of these tags, the page would encounter these tags twice and would error out.

The User control is going to be a section of the ASP.NET page that has some interface to it (text or control) and will then be placed within the main ASP.NET page's <body> tags. The User control can have any number of events associated with any of the controls. However, these events need to be written out within the User control itself and cannot be contained in the main ASP.NET page.

 Events are discussed in Chapter 38.

There are a number of great benefits to using User controls within your application. The first is that it will cut down on your development time and allow you to focus on other aspects of the site, rather than redoing some section of the site that you've done on other pages. When you place a User control file into your application, you can use the control on any of your Web pages that are in the same application.

For instance, let's say that there's a simple form that asks the User for his contact information, and you use this form on almost every application that you develop. Instead of rebuilding this form over and over again, you can build the form as a User control file, place that file within your document, and then call the form in the appropriate spot.

The other great benefit of using User controls is that they're language-independent, which is true of many aspects of .NET. You can place a C# User control right into your VB .NET application and it won't have any adverse effects on any other part of the application. This is an outstanding advantage to a multi-developer team. One developer can contribute sections of complicated or repetitive code, and it won't make any difference what language it's in. Then another developer can take that code as a User control and use it within his site as many times as he likes.

Building a Simple User Control

The first User control that you build will be the simplest one possible — straight static text with a heading and a line of text that says it isn't part of the User control. You build it in the design mode of Visual Studio .NET. Follow these steps:

1. Open up Visual Studio .NET and start a new ASP.NET application called UserControlTestApp, as shown in Figure 37-1.

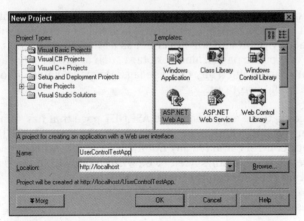

Figure 37-1: Creating an ASP.NET application for your User control test

2. Once you've created the application, change the `PageLayout` property from `pageLayout` to `FlowLayout`.

3. Next you need to create the page that incorporates a User control that you build later in the chapter. There is a blank `WebForm1.aspx` file open in the Design Mode. Type **My First User Control Page** and **This line of text is not part of the User control**, as it appears in Figure 37-2.

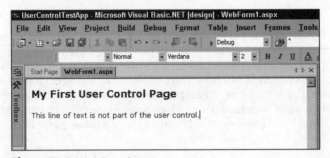

Figure 37-2: `WebForm1.aspx`

4. Now you're going to create a User control to use within this page. Right-click on the application in the Solution Explorer and select Add ➪ Add New Item. You will then be given a list of available items that you can add to the application. For the User control, you're going to be adding a Web User control, as shown in Figure 37-3.

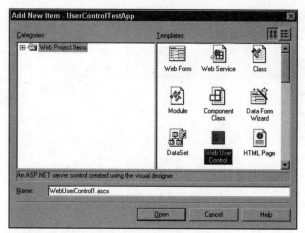

Figure 37-3: Adding a Web User control

Visual Studio .NET has now created a new file in the sample application. User controls use the extension .ascx. You created a User control called WebUserControl1.ascx, and the control page should now be open within Visual Studio .NET as if you're creating a new ASP.NET application.

5. Type **This is the User Control** within the Design Mode of the WebUserControl1.ascx page and save the file. Then, since this is a static User control and you're not going to be incorporating any code behind in this control, click on the HTML tab of the User control page. There will be a directive line at the top of the page highlighted in yellow:

```
            <%@ Control Language="vb"
AutoEventWireup="false"
Codebehind="WebUserControl1.ascx.vb"
Inherits="WebApplication1.WebUserControl1" %>
```

Delete this line of code and then resave the page.

6. Go back to the WebForm1.aspx page and add the User control that you just created. Within the Solution Explorer window, you will see the User control that you just created. Click and drag the file into your Web Form. You've just added a User control to your page. It was that simple.

Figure 37-4 displays what you will see in the Design mode of your page.

The User control is shown in the Web Form as a gray bar with the ID of the control (in this case, WebUserControl11). Save and run the WebForm1.aspx page by right-clicking on the WebForm1.aspx file within the Solution Explorer and choosing Build and Browse. This produces the result shown in Figure 37-5.

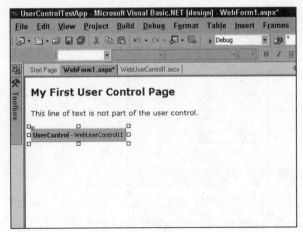

Figure 37-4: The User control as part of the
`WebForm1.aspx` **page**

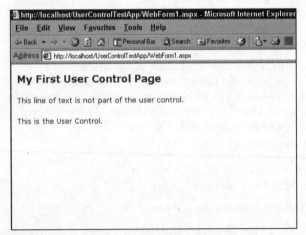

Figure 37-5: The `WebForm1.aspx` page with the
User control

When you go back to Visual Studio .NET and look at the HTML mode of the
`WebForm1.aspx` page, notice that there's now a page directive at the top of the
page:

```
<%@ Register TagPrefix="uc1" TagName="WebUserControl1"
Src="WebUserControl1.ascx" %>
```

The register directive is registering the control onto your page. The three following attributes register the control:

✦ `TagPrefix`

✦ `TagName`

✦ `src`

The `TagPrefix` attribute specifies the tag's prefix that will be used for the control within the page. In this case, it's `uc1`. To give you an example of what this means, all the Web controls use the tag prefix of `asp`, so whenever you use a Web control on your page, you use `<asp:` to start the control off. You'll be doing the same thing and starting your control as `<uc1:`.

Tip

If you're going to use multiple controls on your page, I suggest that you keep the tag prefixes organized. For example, you can keep the tag prefixes based upon your company name (`<MyCompany:`) or the project itself (`<ProjectX:`).

The second attribute in this directive is the `TagName` attribute, which specifies the name of the tag. To compare it to a Web control, in `<asp:TextBox>`, `TextBox` is the `TagName` attribute's value. Name your controls so that you can understand them later. In this example, the value of the `TagName` attribute is the ID of the control, `WebUserControl1`. I don't recommend this, but it's done automatically by Visual Studio .NET if you built this in design mode.

The final attribute, `src`, specifies the virtual path of the User control file. In this case, it's `WebUserControl1.ascx`.

The control in this User control example is written on the page as

```
<uc1:WebUserControl1 id=WebUserControl1
runat="server"></uc1:WebUserControl1>
```

Notice that the control also has an `id` and a `runat="server"` attribute/value pair. These attributes were added automatically by Visual Studio .NET. The `id` attribute specifies the `id` tag of the control, and `runat="server"` signals that this control will need to be processed on the server.

Working with User Control Properties

To make User controls generic enough to be usable in a number of different situations, you need to be able to pass the control properties to use within the control itself. The User controls that you build may not have all the parameters that it needs at coding time. Instead you assign these parameters at runtime by passing properties to the control. For instance, if your User control displays the user's favorite color, you don't even know this information until the user actually gets to the page. Then you can take their favorite color, or any other information that you're storing, and pass that information by setting the control properties or the attribute/value pair within the control itself. Fortunately, it's simple to pass a property to a User control. If I were going to pass the name of a user to the control to use within a greeting message, my User control would include the property within the control:

```
<ucl:WebUserControl1 id=WebUserControl1 runat="server"
UserName="William Evjen"></ucl:WebUserControl1>
```

Notice the addition of a new attribute/value pair to the control. You're specifying that the UserName property has the value of "William Evjen". The full code of the Web Form page that contains the User control appears in Listing 37-1.

Listing 37-1: **WebForm1.aspx File with User Control**

```
<%@ Register TagPrefix="ucl" TagName="WebUserControl1"
Src="WebUserControl1.ascx" %>

<html>
  <head>
    <title></title>
    <meta name="GENERATOR" content="Microsoft Visual
    Studio.NET 7.0">
    <meta name="CODE_LANGUAGE" content="Visual Basic 7.0">
    <meta name=vs_defaultClientScript content="JavaScript">
    <meta name=vs_targetSchema
    content="http://schemas.microsoft.com/intellisense/ie5">
  </head>
  <body>

  <form id="Form1" method="post" runat="server">
<h1><font face=Verdana size=4>My First User Control
Page</font></h1>
<p><font face=Verdana size=2>This line of text is not part
of the User control.</font></p>
<p>
<ucl:WebUserControl1 id=WebUserControl1 runat="server"
UserName="William Evjen"></ucl:WebUserControl1></p>

  </form>

  </body>
</html>
```

Now you have to change the `WebUserControl1.ascx` file (the User control) as it is shown in Listing 37-2. You're changing the control so that it accepts a property assignment.

Listing 37-2: **WebUserControl1.ascx**

```
<script language="VB" runat="server">
  Public UserName As String
</script>


<font face=Verdana size=2>This is the User Control.
<P>
Greetings <%=UserName%>!</font>
```

The script

This file is made up of two parts. The first part is the script of the page where you place all of your VB .NET code. The only thing you're going to do is declare the `UserName` variable as a string. This will allow developers to use the `UserName` attribute within the control to pass a property to the User control.

Be aware that you declared the variable as a public variable. This allows you to use the variable outside of the User control. If you wanted to use a variable only within the User control itself and prevent access to it outside of the control, you would declare the variable as a `Private` variable. `Private` variables cannot display their values in the Web Form.

The file display

The second part of your User control file is the display part of the file. You're writing a few lines of text and then displaying the variable that was passed from the control on the Web Form page. To do the latter, you use the same opening and closing brackets that are used in classic ASP (`<% %>`). The equal sign (=) directly after the opening bracket means to write out the variable.

Testing the User control

Now you need to test out the User control to see how good it will be for code reuse. Within the code of `WebForm1.aspx`, add some `<br>` tags and then another User control. You're going to call the same control that you just used, as follows:

```
<uc1:webusercontrol1 id="Webusercontrol2" runat="server"
Username="Friend"></uc1:webusercontrol1>
```

Figure 37-6 shows the results.

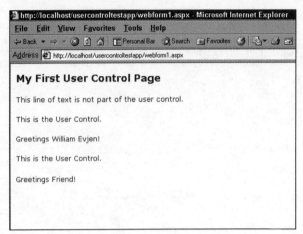

Figure 37-6: Calling the User control twice

As you can see, you were able to call the User control twice in the same page, but you can also call this control as many times as you wish throughout your application.

Using Web Form events to change User control properties

In the last example, you changed the User control's properties by specifying an attribute/value pair within the control itself. The other way to programmatically pass properties to the User control is based upon events within the script part of the Web Form page.

Start a by adding a new Web Form to your application. Click the HTML tab this time and type your own code (see Listing 37-3).

Listing 37-3: **WebForm2.aspx**

```
<%@ Register TagPrefix="HMI" TagName="Greeting"
Src="WebUserControl2.ascx" %>

<html>
  <head>
    <title>User Controls</title>

    <script language=VB runat=server>
```

```
    Sub Button1_Click(Sender As Object, E As EventArgs)
        WebUserControl1.IntroText = "Come to our site again!"
        WebUserControl1.UserName = ""
    End Sub
    </script>

</head>
<body>

    <form id="Form1" method="post" runat="server">
    <h1><font face=Verdana size=4>User Control
    Properties</font></h1>
    <p><font face=Verdana size=2>This line of text is not
    part of the User control.</p>
    <p>
    <HMI:Greeting id="WebUserControl1" runat="server"
    UserName="William Evjen"
    Color="Blue"></HMI:Greeting></font></p>
     <p>
    <asp:button id="button1" runat="server" text="Click
    button to change" onclick="Button1_Click" />
    </p>
    </form>

</body>
</html>
```

First of all, the register directive in this example is a bit different from the one at the beginning of "Building a Simple User Control." It specifies that the `TagPrefix` is `"HMI"` and that the `TagName` is `"Greeting"` because this is the greeting tag that you're playing with here.

Because a few of the values of some of the attributes have changed, you need to format how you refer to the User control within your code, as follows:

```
<HMI:Greeting id="WebUserControl1" runat="server"
   UserName="William Evjen"
   Color="Blue"></HMI:Greeting>
```

You're passing a few properties as well within the User control. You're sending a value for `UserName` and `Color` to be used on your User control page. However, next you'll see what happens in your User control if the developer doesn't specify anything for these values.

You've placed a button control on the page, and there's a button click event within the script. When the button is clicked, you change some of the properties of the User control. You set the `IntroText` attribute and empty the `UserName` attribute.

Let's take a look at the User control page (see Listing 37-4).

Listing 37-4: **WebUserControl2.ascx**

```
<script language="vb" runat="server">
    Public IntroText As String = "Welcome to our site"
    Public UserName As String = "Friend"
    Public Color As String = "Black"
</script>

<font face="Verdana" color="<%=Color%>" size="2">
    <%=IntroText%> <%=UserName%>
</font>
```

The code for this User control accomplishes several things. First of all, it declares a few public variables. The first is IntroText. This will be the text that first appears before the button is clicked. The next is UserName. Even though you wrote out the control on the Web Form page and gave a value to UserName, you give a value here as well. The value you gave to UserName back in WebForm2.aspx (see Listing 37-3) overrode the original UserName value of Friend. If you're going to use the User control in a lot of different places, it's good habit to give values to important properties (just in case the developer doesn't give a value for some reason). You also gave a value to Color, even though that's the default also.

Then, you write out the greeting and the User's name within the body of WebUserControl2.ascx, as shown in Figure 37-7.

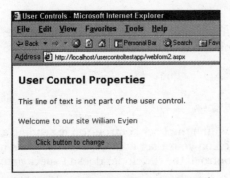

Figure 37-7: The greeting User control

Passing properties back to the Web Form

Now that you've passed some properties to the User control and changed some initial properties, it's time to pass some variables from the User control back to your

Web Form. You're going to work through a form that's built within your User control, and this form will pass the form results back to the Web Form page after the user clicks the Submit button.

If you have a number of similar forms throughout an application, it would be wise to put this form in a User control and then call it whenever it's needed.

Listing 37-5 contains the code for your Web Form page.

Listing 37-5: **WebForm3.aspx**

```
<%@ Register TagPrefix="HMI" TagName="WebUserControl3"
Src="WebUserControl3.ascx" %>

<html>
  <head>
    <title>User Control Form</title>
        <script language=vb runat=server>
         Sub Page_Load(Sender As Object, E As EventArgs)
             If ((Page.IsValid) and (Page.IsPostBack)) Then
                 Label1.Text = "You Submitted the Following
                 Information:<p>" & _
                 "Name: " & MyForm.Name & "<br>" & _
                 "Address: " & MyForm.Address & "<br>" & _
                 "Phone: " & MyForm.Phone & "<br>" & _
                 "Email: " & MyForm.Email & "<br>" & _
                 "Sex: " & MyForm.Sex & "<br>" & _
                 "Position: " & MyForm.Position & "<P>"
             End If
         End Sub
        </script>
  </head>
<body>

<form id="Form1" method="post" runat="server">
 <p><strong><font face=Verdana size=2>Registration
 Form</strong></p>
 <p>
 <HMI:WebUserControl3 id=MyForm
 runat="server"></HMI:WebUserControl3></p>
 <p>
 <asp:label id=label1 runat=server /></font>
</form>

   </body>
</html>
```

On this Web Form, there are only a few items to note. The first is that the body of the page contains the User control, which must reside between the form tags.

The second item to note is the Page_Load event at the top of the page. This checks whether the page is posted back and if the page is valid after a form submittal. You know that your User control is a form, so you're going to make sure that the form is valid before you take anything from it.

Now take a look at the User control shown in Listing 37-6.

Listing 37-6: WebUserControl3.ascx

```
<script language="VB" runat="server">
   Public FormTitle As String = "Company XYZ Registration"

   Public Property Name As String
     Get
        Return TextBox1.Text
     End Get
     Set
        TextBox1.Text = Value
     End Set
   End Property

   Public Property Address As String
     Get
        Return TextBox2.Text
     End Get
     Set
        TextBox2.Text = Value
     End Set
   End Property

   Public Property Phone As String
     Get
        Return TextBox3.Text
     End Get
     Set
        TextBox3.Text = Value
     End Set
   End Property

   Public Property Email As String
     Get
        Return TextBox4.Text
     End Get
     Set
        TextBox4.Text = Value
     End Set
   End Property
```

```
      Public Property Sex As String
         Get
            Return RadioButtonList1.SelectedItem.Value
         End Get
         Set
            RadioButtonList1.SelectedItem.Value = Value
         End Set
      End Property

      Public Property Position As String
         Get
            Return DropDownList1.SelectedItem.Value
         End Get
         Set
            DropDownList1.SelectedItem.Value = Value
         End Set
      End Property

      Public Sub Page_Load(Sender As Object, E As EventArgs)
         If Page.IsPostBack Then
            Label1.Text = "This is a postback event in the User
            control."
         End If
      End Sub
   </script>

   <p><font face=Verdana size=2>
   <table cellspacing=0 cellpadding=5 bgcolor=silver border=0>
     <tr bgcolor=#ffffff>
       <td valign=center colspan=2>
         <p align=center><strong><font
   size=2><%=FormTitle%></font></strong></p></td></tr>
     <tr>
       <td valign=center>
         <p align=right><font size=2>Name</font></p></td>
       <td>
   <asp:TextBox id=TextBox1 runat="server"
   columns="35"></asp:TextBox></td></tr>
     <tr>
       <td valign=center>
         <p align=right><font size=2>Address</font></p></td>
       <td>
   <asp:TextBox id=TextBox2 runat="server"
   columns="35"></asp:TextBox></td></tr>
     <tr>
       <td valign=center>
         <p align=right><font size=2>Phone</font></p></td>
       <td>
   <asp:TextBox id=TextBox3 runat="server"
```

Continued

Listing 37-6 *(continued)*

```
columns="35"></asp:TextBox></td></tr>
  <tr>
    <td valign=center>
      <p align=right><font size=2>Email</font></p></td>
    ·<td>
<asp:TextBox id=TextBox4 runat="server"
columns="35"></asp:TextBox></td></tr>
  <tr>
    <td style="HEIGHT: 37px">
      <p align=right><font size=2>Sex</font></p></td>
    <td style="HEIGHT: 37px">
<asp:RadioButtonList id=RadioButtonList1 runat="server" Font-
Size="X-Small" Width="149px" Height="19px"
RepeatDirection="Horizontal">
<asp:ListItem Value="Male"
Selected="True">Male</asp:ListItem>
<asp:ListItem Value="Female">Female</asp:ListItem>
</asp:RadioButtonList></td></tr>
  <tr>
    <td>
      <p align=right><font size=2>Position</font></p></td>
    <td>
<asp:DropDownList id=DropDownList1 runat="server" Font-
Size="X-Small" width="150px">
<asp:ListItem Value="-- Select --">-- Select --
</asp:ListItem>
<asp:ListItem Value="Manager">Manager</asp:ListItem>
<asp:ListItem Value="Programmer">Programmer</asp:ListItem>
<asp:ListItem Value="Developer">Developer</asp:ListItem>
</asp:DropDownList></td></tr>
  <tr bgcolor=#ffffff>
    <td colspan=2 align=middle>
<asp:Button id=Button1 runat="server" Text="Submit
Information"></asp:Button></td></tr></table></p></FONT>
<P>
<asp:Label id="Label1" runat="server" font-size="X-Small"
font-bold="True" font-names="Verdana"/></P>
```

The WebForm3.aspx and WebUserControl3.ascx pages together produce the results you see in Figure 37-8.

This User control contains a form even though this code doesn't contain any <form> tags. This is because the form tags are already in WebForm3.aspx. There's nothing different about building the form in a User control. It's built exactly the same way you would build any form within any ASP.NET page.

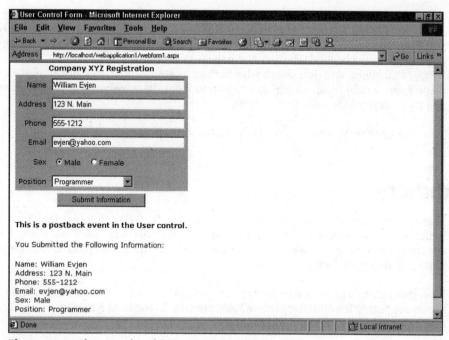

Figure 37-8: The completed form created with a User control

Within the script code at the top of the page, you're using VB .NET to get and set all of the form's values:

```
Get
    'The code for getting the property goes here
End Get

Set
    'The code for setting the property goes here
End Set
```

You get all the properties from the form and then return them to the Web Form page. Notice that when you declare the property, it's Public. You also specify the name of the property. This name will be used within the Web Form page.

Another interesting point is that you have the following Page_Load event in the User control:

```
Public Sub Page_Load(Sender As Object, E As EventArgs)
    If Page.IsPostBack Then
        Label1.Text = "This is a postback event in the User
            control."
    End If
End Sub
```

This is the Page_Load event for the User control, and it won't interfere with the Page_Load event in your .aspx page. If this were going to be production code of any kind, you would have included some Validation controls within the form, and you would have checked whether the page was valid. Each page contains a Page_Load event, and you check whether each one is a postback or not. Either of these spots would be also ideal to connect to a database, record the form values, and then redirect the user to another page.

Cross-Reference See Chapter 36 for a discussion of Validation controls.

Summary

User controls are fairly simple and straightforward to create if you're familiar with building ASP.NET pages and with HTML or Web controls. User controls allow you to encapsulate code and reuse it on other pages within the application, or in different applications altogether.

It's a good idea to predict which parts of applications will be reused often and then incorporate that functionality into a User control. In the long run, this will create a more organized and efficient application.

✦   ✦   ✦

Events

by Bill Evjen

An *event* occurs when an object on the page sends a message to the server that some sort of action has taken place. Understanding event-driven programming is essential to programming Visual Basic .NET Web applications. Visual Basic .NET is built on this principle that the page you develop is full of objects, and these objects sometimes react to events from the user, system events, or other events you program. So your event may be a user clicking on a button, the time of the day being after 6:00 p.m., or a user who is the 6,000th visitor to the page.

This chapter covers how to program for these events and use them properly within your applications.

Placing Events in Your Controls

Controls are objects that wait for specific events and notify the server when those specified events take place. The act that initiates the notification is called a *trigger,* and the object that sends the trigger is called an *event sender.* The code that runs when an event is triggered is called an *event handler.*

A common example of an object triggering an event is a button on a page. The button is the object, and the user clicking on it initiates the trigger (the OnClick event) that is then sent to the appropriate event handler. If you've worked through the chapters on the various controls that you can place on your page (Chapters 34, 35, and 36), you've already worked with a number of page events and even programmed functionality against these events.

Placing an event in your control is fairly straightforward. You only have to think about the exact event you're going to be looking for, such as a button click or the page loading in the browser. After you put a control on your page, Intellisense will offer a large number of attributes that can be used within that control. Within these lists of attributes are a number of events that you can also use with the control. For instance, `<asp:button>` allows the following events to be used:

- ✦ `OnClick`
- ✦ `OnCommand`
- ✦ `OnDataBinding`
- ✦ `OnDisposed`
- ✦ `OnInit`
- ✦ `OnLoad`
- ✦ `OnPrerender`
- ✦ `OnUnload`

IntelliSense displays lightning-bolt icons next to events, as shown in Figure 38-1.

Cross-Reference See Chapter 17 for a discussion of IntelliSense.

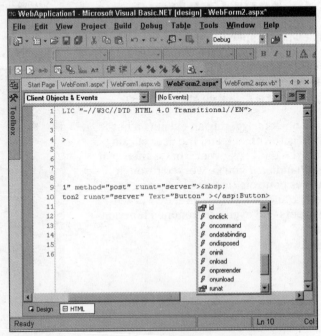

Figure 38-1: IntelliSense showing the available events for the Button Web control

Building Events

After you've specified the event within the control, you need to give the event call a value. This value will be the name of the event handler for that particular event. For instance, if you wanted the button to monitor click events, you would use the OnClick event and then make the event handler, Button1_Click, perform the functionality you wanted based on that event.

The sample event handler has the following format:

```
Sub Button1_Click(Sender As Object, E As EventArgs)
    Button1.Text = "The button text has changed!"
End Sub
```

This subroutine will be an event handler. The Click event isn't the only one there is for this control; your application can watch for a number of other events. For instance, the button control will also allow you to program for when the button is loaded, databound, unloaded from the browser, and other events.

The code for event handlers must be either in a code-behind page (WebForm1. aspx.vb) or between <script> tags on the Web Form page. It's possible to have more than one event associated with a control. For instance, in addition to the button Click event, you may want to assign text to the button at runtime by using the button's onload event.

Note   Application event handlers must be placed between the script tags within the global.asax file or within the global.asax.vb file.

You're going to build a page that will use a number of the events that are available for a button Web control. You will program for the button's onload, oninit, onprerender, onunload, ondisposed and onclick events. The page will print to the screen as each event is fired, thereby showing you an order of execution. The code you use to build your page can be seen in Listing 38-1.

Listing 38-1: **Button Events Web Form**

```
<html>
  <head>
    <title>Monitoring Button Events</title>
      <script language=vb runat=server>
      Dim Message As String = "The Message String has
      started!<br>"

        Sub Page_Load(Sender As Object, E As EventArgs)
          Label1.Text = Message
        End Sub
```

Continued

Listing 38-1 *(continued)*

```
     Sub Button1_Click(Sender As Object, E As EventArgs)
       Message += "The button has been clicked.<br>"
       Label1.Text = Message
     End Sub

     Sub Button1_Init(Sender As Object, E As EventArgs)
       Message += "The button has been initialized.<br>"
       Label1.Text = Message
     End Sub

     Sub Button1_Load(Sender As Object, E As EventArgs)
       Message += "The button has been loaded.<br>"
       Label1.Text = Message
     End Sub

      Sub Button1_Prerender(Sender As Object, E As
        EventArgs)
       Message += "The button has been prerendered.<br>"
       Label1.Text = Message
     End Sub

     Sub Button1_Unload(Sender As Object, E As EventArgs)
       Message += "The button has been unloaded.<br>"
       Label1.Text = Message
     End Sub

     Sub Button1_Disposed(Sender As Object, E As
        EventArgs)
       Message += "The button has been disposed.<br>"
       Label1.Text = Message
     End Sub
   </script>
</head>
<body>

  <form id="Form1" method="post" runat="server">
  <asp:button id=button1 runat=server
   onclick="button1_click" text="Button1"
   oninit="button1_init" onload="button1_load"
   onprerender="button1_prerender"
   onunload="button1_unload"
   ondisposed="button1_disposed"/>
      <p>
  <asp:label id=label1 runat=server font-names="Verdana"
   font-size="X-Small"/>
  </form></P>

  </body>
</html>
```

Figure 38-2 shows you the order in which some of these events take place on the server, allowing you to program any sequential functionality that you might need.

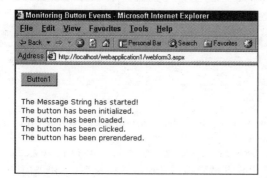

Figure 38-2: Multiple button events.

`Button1_Init` is fired when the control is initialized, `Button1_Load` is fired when the control is loaded, and `Button1_Prerender` is fired right when the button is about to be rendered onto the screen.

Based upon this knowledge, you can now put code in the appropriate event handler.

Using Web Form Events

Events in Web Forms are considerably different than events within desktop applications. Within a typical desktop application, the event's trigger and the event handler are both happening client-side. Events within a Web Form are triggered client-side, but in most cases they need to be handled on the server. ASP.NET uses HTTP Post to manage these server-side event-handling situations. The ASP.NET framework then determines which method needs to take care of handling the event.

ASP.NET takes care of all of this for you behind the scenes, but it's important to understand what's going on here. Since Web applications need to make round-trips to the server to perform server-side events, using a large number of server controls that contain a substantial number of server-side events can have a definite impact on the performance of your Web application.

Event arguments

The event handlers that you build for Web Form applications contain two arguments, `sender As Object` and `e As EventArgs`. Table 38-1 describes these two arguments.

Table 38-1 Event Arguments	
Parameters	**Description**
`sender As Object`	An object that represents the object that raised the event.
`e As EventArgs`	Contains all the event specific data that the event sender passes along.

In most cases, these two arguments will be the typical arguments used within any event handler. The second argument will typically use the type `System.EventArgs`, but there are certain controls that require a specific type to pass along any data pertinent to the control that's sending the event. Table 38-2 lists some other possible types of arguments that you can use in place of `EventArgs`.

Table 38-2 Other Types of Arguments	
EventArgs (System.TypeName)	**Description**
`FileSystemEventArgs`	Provides information on directory events, such as `Created`, `Changed`, and `Deleted`.
`ImageClickEventArgs`	Provides information on when a user clicks on an image.
`KeyEventArgs`	Provides information on keyboard events, such as `KeyUp` and `KeyDown`.
`CommandEventArgs`	Provides information on the command event.

A lot of other types of arguments are available. This is just to give you a taste of the different ones you might use in your event handler.

Event postbacks

When you're using HTML and Web controls throughout your pages, there are many event triggers that cause an event to be sent to the server to be handled. For instance, the button `OnClick` is sent to the server for processing once the user clicks on the button. However, there are also events that are triggered on a Web Form that are deposited and saved until there's a postback to the server for processing.

Note A postback is when the page is sent back to itself on the server after a specified event occurs. A postback is *not* when the page is loaded for the first time. If you want to run some code when the page loads — but only the first time the page loads — check to see if `Page.IsPostback` in an `If Then` statement is false.

One example of this is the `TextBox` control. If you have a `TextBox` control in your Web Form, you can place an `OnTextChanged` event within the control. This will tell you if the user placed any text within the text box. However, the event handler that will take care of this trigger won't react until the form's Submit button sends the information to the server. The reason is that the `TextBox` control stores and holds onto the event trigger until there's a postback to the server.

It's possible to change this situation by changing the `AutoPostBack` property to `True`. This will cause the event to be triggered once the user leaves the text box field. Once the event is triggered, the event sender will send the event to be handled by the server the instant it happens.

Caution Be forewarned that multiple trips to the server for processing are resource-intensive.

Creating Event Handlers in Design Mode

Now we're going to go through the process of creating event handlers within the design mode of Visual Studio .NET. Visual Studio .NET lets you create a number of different event handlers easily.

Default event handlers

Follow these steps to create an application that allows you to build events for the button control.

1. Start a new application called `EventHandlerApp`. This will be an ASP.NET Web application. On the page, place a button and a label control. Figure 38-3 shows what your page should look like.

2. Double-click on the Button control to create a page called `WebForm1.aspx.vb`. Within this page, your cursor will be placed within a freshly created event handler, a button click handler. Your page should resemble Figure 38-4.

   Visual Studio .NET chose the click event handler for the button because that's the Button control's *default event*. Each control has its own default event. For instance, the DropDownList control's default event is the `SelectedIndexChanged` event.

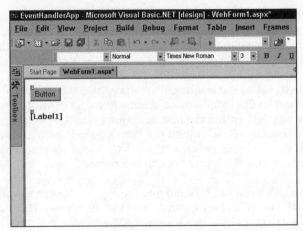

Figure 38-3: Your WebForm1.aspx page

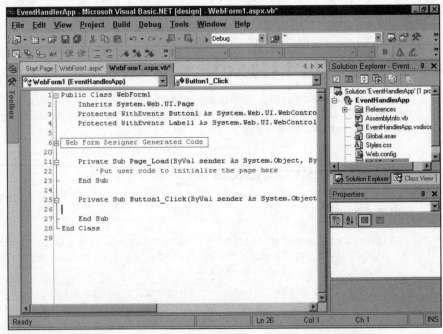

Figure 38-4: WebForm1.aspx.vb and your Button1_Click event handler

3. Next, add the following code for the `Button1_Click` event:

`Label1.Text = "The button has been clicked!"`

When you right-click on `WebForm1.aspx` within the Solution Explorer and select Build and Browse, you're presented with the newly created page.

4. Click the button and you get the text within the Label control that informs you that you clicked the button, initiating an event. This was all based upon the event handler executing code based upon a trigger (the button click). The result can be seen in Figure 38-5.

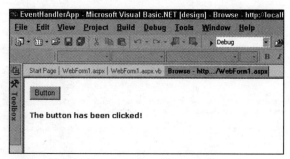

Figure 38-5: Your event handler in action!

Non-default event handlers

What if you want to add more event handlers based upon your Button control? Visual Studio .NET makes it quite easy. Simply follow these steps:

1. Get back to the code-behind page by clicking on the `WebForm1.aspx.vb` file tab. There are two drop-down boxes at the top of the page. The one on the left is the Class Name drop-down box. The other is the Method Name drop-down box.

The Class Name drop-down box contains a list of the controls that are on the page. By selecting one of the controls, you can specify specific event handlers for the selected control.

2. Select the Button1 control, and then you can pull down a large list of events you can use against the Button control within the Method Name drop-down box. The default event, `Click`, is in bold. You should see a list of events, as shown in Figure 38-6.

3. Select the `Load` event. The subroutine for this event is then created instantly in the code-behind page, with the proper arguments.

4. Add the following code:

```
Label1.Text = "The button has loaded!"
```

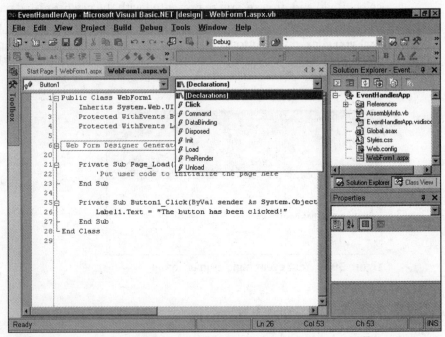

Figure 38-6: A list of available events to program against

5. Right-click on the file and choose Build and Browse. Notice that once the Button control is loaded, it displays what it had in the Label control. Pressing the button changes the text within the Label control based upon the `Button1_Click` event. The results can be seen in Figure 38-7.

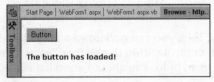

Figure 38-7: When the page is loaded, the Button1_Load event is triggered.

Visual Studio .NET lets you program for your control's default events as well as the non-default events, as you just did in the previous example.

Summary

Event-driven programming is an important part of Visual Basic .NET, and understanding it is vital to Visual Basic .NET Web application development.

This chapter introduced you to a couple of ways of creating events within your application. The first is to hard-code the events right into your Web Form pages. These events need to be between script tags in order to work. The other way of creating event handlers is in the code-behind page, in which Visual Studio .NET makes creating events as easy as selecting your event choice from a drop-down box.

✦   ✦   ✦

Cascading Style Sheets

by Bill Evjen

Cascading Style Sheets, or *CSS*, lets you assign formatting properties to HTML tags throughout your document. Applying *styles* to your Web documents can save you considerable time in development.

This chapter goes over everything you need to quickly and easily apply stylesheets to the Web pages you develop in .NET. It covers placing your style blocks inline, as well as applying the styles from a separate stylesheet.

The Benefits of Using CSS

There are two methods to use when applying styles to any text that is displayed in the browser. The first is to apply the appropriate HTML tags that format the text, such as `<font>`, `<b>`, and `<i>`. The other method is to apply a stylesheet, either inline or attached as a separate file, that applies changes to the text directly. In the latter method, the stylesheet is a separate file with a `.css` extension that you reference in the page that's applying the styles.

Tip

Name your CSS files appropriately. Stylesheets play an important role in *code reuse* and are easily transported from one application to another. Therefore, you should name your stylesheets based upon the standard that's being applied. For instance, you might use `CompanyName.css` for a stylesheet that's used on all company applications.

The other great thing about using stylesheets within your application is that they're easy to change globally. Applying a document style that's located in a central place has a definite advantage over applying styles manually throughout the document.

For example, let's say you've built a Web application that encompasses over 200 pages of forms and information that you're displaying. You've applied fonts and formatted the code to give the documents a uniform look and feel that's in line with your company's image.

Then one day, the company changes its image and the guys from marketing want you to change all sorts of things within the application—font styles, font sizes, and even font colors. Can you imagine the hardship of going through all the code for 200 pages? It would take you a fair amount of time to accomplish this task.

Now imagine the same situation, but instead you have the formatting and general styles for all the applications contained within one file, `style.css`. Instead of going to all the pages to change the formatting of the text, you only go to one page and alter a few lines of code. After this, the style is instantly applied to all 200 pages of the application. Then, with all the time you just saved, you and the marketing guys go out for a game of golf. Not bad, eh?

Creating and Applying Styles

Before you learn how to create a stylesheet and apply it to the page, you should know that there are several ways to apply styles to the text and objects that you're presenting in the browser. You can create styles in the following ways:

✦ HTML tags

✦ Style Builder

✦ Internal stylesheets

✦ External stylesheets

These methods are described in the following sections.

Creating styles directly in your HTML tags

The first and simplest way to apply styles is to put formatting HTML tags directly around the text that you want to format, as shown in this example.

```
<font face="verdana"><b><i>Hello World!</i></b></font>
```

But this is exactly what you're trying to avoid doing. One simple way to get away from this is to apply a style directly in the tag of the document. For instance, let's say that you want all the text between the opening and closing `<p>` tags in your page to be of a certain font style and type. You could apply the style right in the tag very easily.

```
<p style="color:red;font-style:bold">
Here is the text that we want to change
</p>
```

This would change the line of text to bolded red. By applying two styles within the paragraph tag, you've changed the appearance of everything between the opening and closing tags.

Let's take a look at the stylesheet code that you used to change the text. First of all, you used the attribute `style` in the HTML tag. You then placed the styles within quotation marks. The first style you applied was `color:red`. This is your *style definition*. Style definitions are separated by semicolons, and you can apply as many styles as you wish.

There are so many different types of style definitions that you might think you'd need a reference book next to you at all times. However, with Visual Studio .NET, applying styles has become a lot easier because it takes care of creating the style definitions for you.

Style Builder

Style Builder is Microsoft's way to quickly apply styles to your Web documents. It's a dialog box with a number of screens that allow you to modify the appearance of text and objects in your Web documents (see Figure 39-1).

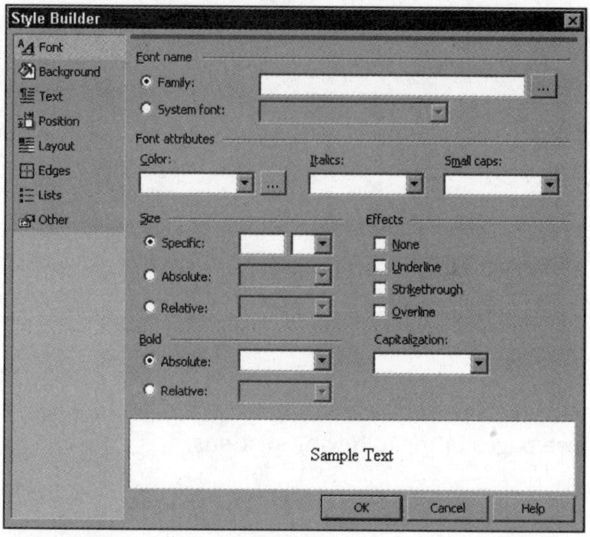

Figure 39-1: The Style Builder dialog box allows you to modify your style definitions easily.

First, you want to apply a style to an individual item on your Web page. Within Visual Studio .NET, start a new Web Form page (an `.aspx` file) and type in a line of text at the top of the page. Do *not* apply any formatting styles to the text by using the toolbar. Instead, after highlighting the text, right-click on your selection and choose Build Style. You are presented with the Style Builder.

> **Note**   Applying styles by using the toolbar in Visual Studio .NET doesn't apply any CSS style blocks to your documents, but instead formats the text with HTML tags. For instance, highlight some text in the Design mode and then click the Bold button on the toolbar. Visual Studio .NET places HTML `<b>` tags around your selected item.

Applying styles using the Style Builder

It's easy to apply a style block to an item that you have selected on your Design page:

1. Highlight the item where you want to apply the style.

2. Right-click on the highlighted item and select Build Style.

3. Change the style settings to any desired setting within the Style Builder. For instance, you can change the color of the selected text to blue by selecting Blue from the color drop-down list in the Font Attributes section. You can also switch the text to uppercase by selecting UPPERCASE in the Capitalization drop-down list.

4. Select OK and your highlighted item changes accordingly. It's as simple as that.

Style Builder is very straightforward and easy to use. The dialog box has the following eight types of styles that you can apply to your selected item:

Font

Background

Text

Position

Layout

Edges

Lists

Other

You find out more about these pages in the following sections.

Font page

The Font page of Style Builder allows you to specify the font names and/or families. Other font characteristics that can be changed on this page include font color and size. You can make text italic, bold, uppercase, or lowercase.

Background page

The Background page allows you to change the background color of the selected item. If the item you're applying the style to is the `<body>` tag, for example, it would be a page-wide background color. If you're applying the background style to a selection of text, however, it would only apply the background color for the text and not for the rest of the document. It's also possible to apply a background image to your page. Once an image is selected within the dialog box, you can then dictate the background image's behavior. Although it's not required, the background image can be tiled in a horizontal or vertical direction and can also be set to scroll with the page or to consistently remain fixed in the browser window.

Text page

The Text page allows you to change text alignment (left, center, right, or justified), as well as make the text subscripted or superscripted. You can change the spacing between letters and lines on the page, as well as apply indentation.

Position page

By using the Position page, you can move the selected item anywhere in the browser window by selecting the item's coordinates within the page. To use the Position page, follow these steps:

1. Type **I Love ASP.NET** in the Design mode of Visual Studio .NET in one of your Web Forms.

2. Highlight and right-click on the text. Select Build Style.

3. Select the Position page.

4. Select Absolutely Position from the Position Mode drop-down list.

5. Type **100** in both the Top and Left text boxes and click OK.

6. Save and run the file. Notice that the text "I Love ASP.NET" is 100 pixels down from the top and 100 pixels to the left of the browser window.

When you look at the code, you see your style directly applied to the text. For instance, I am using Internet Explorer 6.0 and the code came out as follows:

```
<P style="LEFT: 100px; POSITION: absolute; TOP: 100px">
          I Love ASP.NET
</P>
```

Layout page

The Layout page allows you to define how elements are positioned in the flow of the HTML stream. Another interesting thing that the layout page allows you to do is set a print break before or after the selected item. This means that when the user prints what's in her browser, the printer stops printing and start printing on a new page wherever you've applied these breaks.

One thing you can do with the Layout page is select the visibility of the selected item to be hidden:

1. Type in some text within the Design mode of Visual Studio .NET in a new Web Form page, such as "VB .NET Rocks!"

2. Highlight and right-click on the text. Select Style Builder.

3. Click on the Layout page tab and change the Visibility drop-down list to Hidden.

4. Click OK. Save and run the page. Notice that the text is not shown in the browser.

When you look at the source code of the page, the text that you typed in is indeed there, but it has a style applied to it so that it's invisible. The following code is what you would see in IE 6.0:

```
<P style="VISIBILITY: hidden">
VB .NET Rocks!
</P>
```

Edges page

The Edges page allows you to put a border around your selection. You can modify the border by selecting its color, width, and style. You can also set a margin around the item, as well as establish padding within the box that the border creates. Follow these instructions to create a box around your selected item:

1. Place some text in the Design window of Visual Studio .NET in one of your Web Form files.

2. Highlight and right-click on the text. Select Style Builder.

3. Click on the Edges page tab. Change the Style drop-down box to Solid.

4. Select OK. Save and run your file.

Notice that your selected text now has a boxed border around it.

Lists page

The Lists page allows you to apply styles to any bulleted or unbulleted lists in your selection. You can select the style of the bullet used, as well as your own image bullet that you might want to use.

Other page

The Other page is just a collection of the other style attributes that are left over, such as cursor style, table border, and layout attributes, and the ability to link to DHTML behavior files. The first style available to modify on this page is the cursor style. When a user hovers the mouse over your selection, the cursor changes to the type that you've specified here.

This page of the Style Builder also allows for customization of any table borders that might be in your selection. You can specify whether the table cells all have their own individual borders or not. You can also collapse table cell borders.

You can also link your selected item directly to a DHTML behaviors file (.hta, .htc). Behaviors files specify dynamic attributes to change the appearance of HTML elements in response to the user's input.

Internal Stylesheets

Another option for creating specific styles within your Web documents is to place an *internal stylesheet* within the documents. An internal stylesheet is very similar to an *external stylesheet* (discussed in the next section), but as its name implies, it's placed right in the document itself.

If you really only have to apply styles to a single page or a small number of styles to a small number of pages, using an internal stylesheet might be the answer for you. If you were going to apply styles to multiple documents throughout your application, though, using an external stylesheet would be better.

Listing 39-1 provides an example of applying an internal stylesheet to a Web document.

Listing 39-1: Styles1.html – Applying an Internal Stylesheet

```
<html>
  <head>
        <title>Internal Stylesheet</title>

<style type="text/css">
<!--
  Table, Tr, Td {
        Background:silver;
        font-family: Arial, Helvetica, sans-serif;
        font-size: 1em;
  }
```

Continued

Listing 39-1 *(continued)*

```
A:link {
        Text-decoration:none;
        Color:blue;
}
A:hover {
        Text-decoration:underline;
        Color:red;
}
A:visited {
        Text-decoration:none;
        Color:blue;
}
-->
</style>

</head>

<body>
        Here is a line without any style.
<P>
<Table>
        <Tr>
                <Td>
                Here is some text in the table
                that has some style!
                </Td>
        </Tr>
</Table>
<P>
<A Href="http://www.idg.com/">Visit IDG</A>
</body>
</html>
```

First, note that an internal stylesheet needs to be placed within the head tags of the document. The stylesheet is composed of CSS code that is placed between `<style>` tags. Within the opening style tag, specify the type of style as `text/css`.

HTML comment tags exist within the stylesheet because even though most browsers support stylesheets, some older browsers don't. Applying HTML comments around the CSS stylesheet definitions hides them from these older browsers.

The ways in which styles are defined are fairly simple and straightforward. Take a look at this basic example:

```
Table, Tr, Td {
        Background:silver;
        font-family: Arial, Helvetica, sans-serif;
        font-size: 1em;
    }
```

When defining styles, you don't have to do each style separately. Instead, you can select the HTML tags to be defined in one line and then apply one set of style definitions to all the tags. Selected HTML tags are separated by commas in this definition. Style definitions follow this pattern:

```
Definition:Value;
```

Note   Remember to always include a semicolon after a definition, even if there's only one style definition. It's part of CSS's language syntax.

What if you want to define a style for only the text within a table that's between bold tags (<b>)? Put the parent tag and the child tag on one definition line, but only separated by a space instead of a comma. The following is a style for all the bold tags within a table:

```
Table B {
        Background:silver;
        font-family: Arial, Helvetica, sans-serif;
        font-size: 1em;
    }
```

Please note that CSS requires you to put all the style definitions between curly brackets as per the languages syntax.

External Stylesheets

When you create a Web application in Visual Studio .NET, it makes a number of different files. One of these files is the `Styles.css` file that you see in Listing 39-2. This listing contains part of the code in `Styles.css`.

Listing 39-2: Default Styles.css

```
/* Default CSS Stylesheet for a new Web Application project
   */

BODY
{
    BACKGROUND-COLOR: white;
    FONT-FAMILY: Verdana, Helvetica, sans-serif;
```

Continued

Listing 39-2 *(continued)*

```
        FONT-SIZE: .8em;
        FONT-WEIGHT: normal;
        LETTER-SPACING: normal;
        TEXT-TRANSFORM: none;
        WORD-SPACING: normal
}

H1, H2, H3, H4, H5, TH, THEAD, TFOOT
{
        COLOR: #003366;
}
H1 {
    font-family: Verdana, Arial, Helvetica, sans-serif;
    font-size: 2em;
    font-weight: 700;
    font-style: normal;
    text-decoration: none;
    word-spacing: normal;
    letter-spacing: normal;
    text-transform: none;
    }

H2 {
    font-family: Verdana, Arial, Helvetica, sans-serif;
    font-size: 1.75em;
    font-weight: 700;
    font-style: normal;
    text-decoration: none;
    word-spacing: normal;
    letter-spacing: normal;
    text-transform: none;
    }
```

This code continues on for quite a bit, but you get the idea. Visual Studio .NET uses this default stylesheet, which can be applied throughout the application. This stylesheet can work in a lot of situations, but in most cases you're going to want to create your own customized stylesheet.

Note   Placing this default stylesheet within your application doesn't automatically make all your pages apply this style. In fact, no page applies this stylesheet unless you specifically add it.

Referencing stylesheets in Web documents

You must reference stylesheets in Web documents, which is quite easy. Simply follow these steps:

1. Open up any Web document. It doesn't matter if the document is in the design or HTML mode.

2. Drag-and-drop the `Styles.css` file over to your open document. This automatically creates a reference to the stylesheet within the code for your page.

3. If you're in Design mode, go over to the HTML mode. Notice the new line added to the page:

```
<link rel="stylesheet" type="text/css"
href="http://localhost/WebApplication1/Styles.css">
```

This line references a stylesheet specifying the type and location of the file. With this line in the code for your page, the page is now formatted to the specifications in the `Styles.css` file. You need to add this file to each and every page within the application to which you want to apply this style.

Having an external stylesheet makes it possible to change an application-wide style with few problems. Just make the change within the CSS file and save the file back into the application, and then all pages that reference this file instantly reflect the changes.

Creating your own external stylesheet

In most cases, you're going to want to create your own stylesheet to use throughout your application. Although you can have more than one external stylesheet within an application, it's a lot easier to manage your styles if they all reside in one file.

Visual Studio .NET makes creating your own external stylesheet rather easy:

1. Right-click on your application within the Server Explorer and select Add ⇨ Add New Item.

2. Select Style Sheet.

   You're presented with an empty stylesheet with only one HTML element, the body element, specified on the page. On the left side of Visual Studio .NET is the CSS Outline, as shown in Figure 39-2.

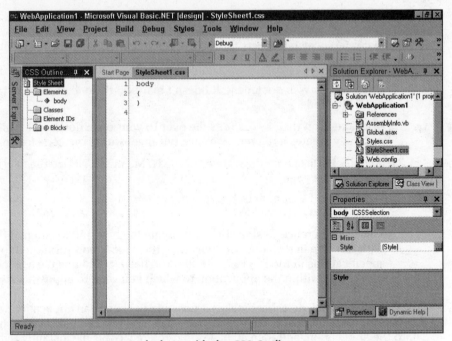

Figure 39-2: Your new stylesheet with the CSS Outline open

There are a number of ways to create the CSS Outline file. One option is to code your styles directly into the code window of your `.css` file. The easier option is to work with the CSS Outline window and Style Builder to create your stylesheet.

The CSS Outline contains the following four folders:

✦ Elements

✦ Classes

✦ Element IDs

✦ @ Blocks

The first three of these folders are discussed in the following sections.

Elements folder

The Elements folder allows you to map styles to specific HTML elements. Presently, the body tag is the only element listed in the folder. If you don't see any elements listed, click on the plus sign next to the folder to expand the folder and expose the elements.

Within the Elements folder, you can map to as many different HTML elements as you wish. Before you start adding some more elements, though, add some styles to your body tag:

1. Right-click on the body element in the Elements folder. Choose Build Style to launch Style Builder, as shown in Figure 39-3.

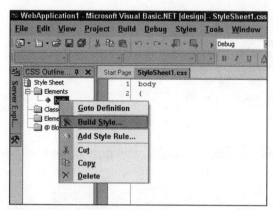

Figure 39-3: Selecting Build Style

You can then go through all of the pages of the dialog and create the style for the body tag. By creating a style for the body tag, you're saying that this is the style for everything on the page, unless the style is overridden by another style specific to the element that's being displayed.

2. After selecting styles for the body tag, you can then start creating styles for other elements within your application. Right-click on the Elements folder and select Add Style Rule.

3. The Add Style Rule dialog box appears, as shown in Figure 39-4. This dialog box allows you to create another association to a HTML element in the stylesheet.

4. The Add Style Rule dialog box contains a large Element drop-down list of elements. After selecting the desired element, click the arrow key to select that element. Click OK and the element is added to the stylesheet. You can then pull up the Style Builder for that element and create a style. Keep doing this until you've worked through all the elements.

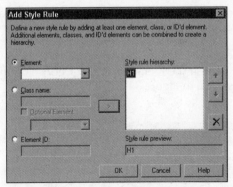

Figure 39-4: The Add Style Rule dialog box allows you to easily apply styles to your stylesheets.

Some of the interesting elements listed in the Element drop-down box include the following:

```
A:active

A:hover

A:link

A:visited
```

These are great elements to apply styles to in your documents. They're all associated with the anchor tag, `<a>`, which is responsible for creating hyperlinks. With these four elements, it's possible to modify the behavior of how the hyperlinks are presented.

A:active

This is an active hyperlink. A hyperlink is active the moment that it's clicked and activated. On very fast Internet connections, you won't see the active link's style because the link isn't active for very long before the page moves on to the selected destination. For slow connections, the active link can be presented for a couple of seconds or more.

Here is an example of an `A:active` style definition:

```
A:active {
  text-decoration:none;
  color:blue;
  }
```

Notice that for this definition, you specify the color to be `blue` and the text decoration to be `none`. A text decoration of `none` means that when the hyperlink is in an active state, it won't have the traditional line underneath it.

A:hover

This element pertains to when the user brings the mouse cursor over the link, which is called *hovering*. When the user moves the mouse cursor so it isn't on top of the link any longer, the `A:Hover` style is turned off.

Here is an example of an `A:Hover` style definition:

```
A:hover {
   text-decoration:underline;
   color: red;
   }
```

This is a common style. Notice that the style color is red in this definition. If all the other anchor behavior styles are blue, when the user hovers over the link, it turns from blue to red. This is a great feature to implement for sites that contain a lot of links. The user has an easier time navigating through those links to make a selection.

A:link

This element pertains to when the item is just a link. For this behavior, the user isn't hovering over the link, the link isn't active, and the user hasn't been to this destination in the user's browser history (it's different for each browser). Traditionally, the fresh link is blue.

A:visited

This element pertains to when the user has this link in their browser history. This means that they've been there recently and you can change the style of the link to let the user know. Traditionally, the visited hyperlink is purple.

Classes folder

Classes allow you to create a style definition that doesn't relate to a specific HTML element. Instead, they pertain to any tag or set of tags that you later specify. For example, if you have an application with 100 pages but three of the pages are going to be of a completely different style, or if you have one section of your page that really breaks off from the style of the rest of the page, creating a style class is the way to go.

Follow these steps to create a style class:

1. Open the Style Builder by right-clicking anywhere in the CSS Outline box and selecting Add Style Rule. The Add Style Rule dialog box appears (see Figure 39-5).

2. The default setting in the Style Builder is to create a style for an element, so click the Class name radio button. Then give your class a name and click OK.

3. You have now created a new style class. Notice that you can see the class definition in the code window at the bottom of the `style.css` file. To create the style for this class, type the style definitions straight into the code page. You can also create it with the Style Builder, which is easier.

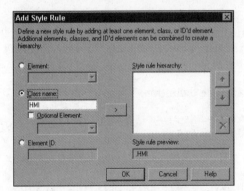

Figure 39-5: Creating a style class

4. Within the CSS Outline window, open up the Classes folder to see the class that you just created, as shown in Figure 39-6.

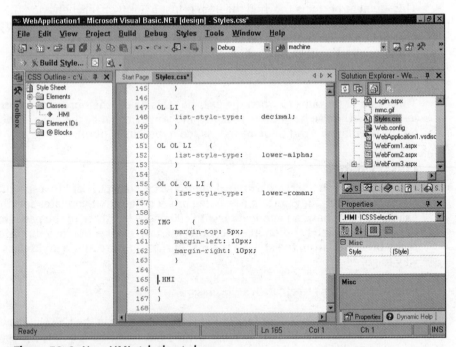

Figure 39-6: Your HMI stylesheet class

5. Right-click on the class and select Build Style.

After pulling up the Style Builder, you can go through and create the style you want to use just as you would for any HTML element. But instead, you're going to apply this style to any element that you want in your Web document.

6. Within the Web document, make sure you have a reference in the file to the stylesheet. If you want to use your class within any HTML element, use the `class` attribute. Therefore, if you wanted to apply this style to the `table` tag, you could do the following:

```
<table class="HMI">
```

Anything within the `table` tag now has the style you created in your class applied to it. Let's say you wanted to apply this style to a Web control. Instead of using the `class` attribute, you would apply the reference to your class by using the `cssclass` property. For instance, if you wanted to apply your style class to a Label control, you would do it in the following manner:

```
<asp:label id=label1 runat=server cssclass=HMI />
```

This would apply our style class to the control. Now let's look at how to use the style class to also apply a style definition to a specific HTML element type.

7. To apply a style class to specific HTML element types, right-click on the Classes folder and select Add Style Rule. In this case, you want to create a definition for the `HMI` class for every hyperlink. Therefore, create another `HMI` class, but this time click the Optional Element check box to add an optional element.

8. Choose an element, such as the A tag, from the drop-down box. The style rule is shown as A.HMI (see Figure 39-7).

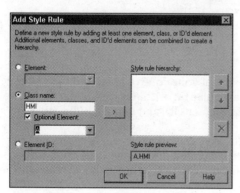

Figure 39-7: Creating a style class for a specific HTML element type

9. Now you can write your hyperlink in the following manner:

```
<a href="somewhere.aspx" class="HMI">Go Here</a>
```

This won't take the style definition from the parent, `HMI`, but it takes its style definition from the subclass, `A.HMI`.

Element ID folder

It's also possible to work with ASP.NET and create a style for a specific control on the page. For instance, if you were using an `<asp:label>` control to display a title on your Web document, you could then apply a style to this particular control by defining it within the stylesheet using the `Element ID` style definition:

1. Right-click on the Element ID folder and select Add Style Rule.

2. Click the Element ID radio button and type in the ID of the control for which you want to define a style. In this case, define the style of the title Label control, `Label1`, as shown in Figure 39-8.

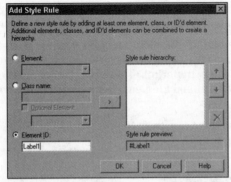

Figure 39-8: Creating a style definition for a specific ASP.NET control

3. The style rule title is the name of your control preceded by a pound sign (#). To create a style for this particular tag within Style Builder, open the Element ID folder, right-click on your Element ID, and choose Build Style.

By using the Element ID style rule, you don't have to put anything in the control itself to apply the style. The style is applied directly without any attribute or property defined, as long as there's a control with that specific ID in the Web Form.

Summary

By using Visual Studio .NET's Style Builder, you can now build truly robust style definitions. It's possible to apply these styles application-wide as well as just to a particular element on a particular page.

Applying styles is recommended over formatting the style definitions directly into your Web documents. Creating style definitions in one file allows developers to quickly change existing styles and apply new styles.

✦   ✦   ✦

State Management

by Bill Evjen

Developing an application on the Internet presents some special challenges. One of the major obstacles is persisting state throughout the application.

This chapter discusses how, in the disconnected world of the Internet, it is possible to maintain state between pages as the user clicks through your applications.

Understanding State

Traditional Win32 applications consistently maintained state as the user worked through the program. The state of the user was consistently known to the application. Basically, *state* is what the application knows about the user. That includes who the user is, where he is in the process of the application, and what he has entered into the application to that point.

Having an application on the Internet is a different story entirely.

The Internet is *stateless* in nature. Basically, the whole thing works with HTTP requests and responses. The server receives an HTTP request for a particular page and sends the browser the requested page. The server makes no distinction about the browser it just sent the page to. Every browser is equal in the server's eyes.

When the browser makes a request for a second page, the server gives it the second page and doesn't have any information about this requesting browser. It truly doesn't know that the browser is the same one that just recently requested a different page. To the server, it could be any browser. This creates a problem if you want the server to remember information about the browser so that the user on this browser can work through an application in a meaningful way.

The way to fix this problem is to remember who the user is, their preferences, or any other pertinent information about them from one request to the next as they work through the pages of your application. This is accomplished by various techniques that you can apply throughout the application's code.

ASP.NET includes the following features and techniques to apply when you're working with state management:

✦ ViewState

✦ Querystrings

✦ Sessions

✦ Cookies

You may already be using most of the techniques discussed in this chapter within Active Server Pages 3.0.

ViewState

ViewState is the latest ASP.NET feature that wasn't available in ASP 3.0. With ViewState, you can easily maintain the state of your controls between round trips to the server. ASP.NET required this capability because you can program your Web forms with multiple round trips to the server. It's possible to program your Web controls so that each control forces the page to make a round trip to the server every time the control is changed in order to perform an event.

As the page makes this trip to the server and back, it remembers what the state of each control is and populates each control's status back into the control as the page is redrawn. It does this by including a hidden form field element within your form page. If you look at the source of your Web form page, notice that there's a ViewState model right at the beginning of the form.

Listing 40-1 displays the beginning of one of your Web forms.

Listing 40-1: **ViewState of a Form**

```
<html>
  <head>
        <title>ViewState Display</title>
  </head>
```

```
<body>
<form name="Form1" method="post" action="WebForm1.aspx"
language="javascript" onsubmit="ValidatorOnSubmit();"
id="Form1">

<input type="hidden" name="__VIEWSTATE"
value="dDwtMTA3MTIxNjQxMTtOPDtsPGk8Mj47PjtsPHQ8O2w8aTwyNj47Pj
tsPHQ8cDxwPGw8VGV4dDtWaXNpYmx1Oz47bDxXZWxjb211IHRvIHRoZSBncm9
1cCFcPGJyXD4x0288dD47Pj47Pjs7Pjs+Pjs+Pjs+" />
```

This unreadable mess within the hidden form field is the state of all the controls on the Web form page. Instead of listing out the state of the controls directly, it's put into a format that's not readable to you and me, but is readable to the ASP.NET parser.

The parser takes this data and repopulates that page's controls. This is wonderful because this task usually took a lot of coding with ASP 3.0. However, you can probably tell that it takes some processing on the server to persist this state and to repopulate the controls after the page is redrawn.

Toggling ViewState on and off

Keeping the ViewState functionality on isn't always going to be a priority with every Web form you create. For this reason, you can turn the ViewState off, thus saving server resources and increasing the speed of your application. You can turn this functionality off in two ways. The first is to disable ViewState on the page level, and the other is to disable it on the control level. To disable ViewState for the entire page, turn off this functionality within the page directive.

Cross-Reference

Page directives are discussed in Chapter 33.

To turn off the ViewState functionality for the entire page, just add the following attribute to the page directive at the top of the page.

```
<%@ Page EnableViewState="False" %>
```

It's also possible to disable ViewState on the control level. If maintaining a control's state is not an important feature of that control, turn it off. This mildly increases the performance of the page overall. To turn off ViewState for a control, add the EnableViewState attribute to the control:

```
<asp:Label id="Label1" Runat="Server"
EnableViewState="False" />
```

Tip

Paying attention to which pages and controls are ViewState-enabled leads to better overall application performance.

Extending ViewState

There are times when you might want to carry user specific information in your Web forms that needs to be carried across server round trips but is beyond the state of the control. In this case, it's possible to piggyback onto the ViewState functionality. In a sense, you're adding your own set of name/value pairs to ViewState. Listing 40-2 shows a simple example of this.

Listing 40-2: **Adding onto ViewState**

```
<html>
  <head>
    <title>ViewState Example</title>

    <script language=vb runat=server>
        Sub Page_Load(sender As Object, e As EventArgs)
                If not Page.IsPostBack Then
                        ViewState("PageCount") = 1
                Else
                        ViewState("PageCount") += 1
                End If
        End Sub
    </script>

  </head>
  <body>
  <form id=form1 runat=server>
    The ViewState("PageCount") is equal to:
    <%= ViewState("PageCount") %>

    <p><asp:button id=button1 runat=server
        text="Cause PostBack" /></p>
</form>
  </body>
</html>
```

In the past, you would perform this operation either using sessions or to making your own hidden tags within the code. (The Sessions feature is discussed later in this chapter.) Using this ViewState functionality is a great way to keep data relatively private and to pass it with the ease of sessions.

In this example, when the page is first drawn, you create a name/value pair named PageCount and give it a value of 1:

```
ViewState("PageCount") = 1
```

It's possible to create as many name/value pairs as you want, but in this case, you've only created one.

In the example page, you also refer to the name/value pair by calling it in much the same way that you created it. Within the body part of the page, you print the `ViewState("PageCount")` directly onto the screen. Another option would have been to create a Label control and set the `Text` property of the control as follows:

```
Label1.Text = ViewState("PageCount")
```

Clicking the Button control causes the page to postback, and your code adds 1 to the value of `PageCount`.

```
ViewState("PageCount") += 1
```

Querystrings

Querystrings are an easy way to pass data from one page to the next within a Web application. They place a created name/value pair and append it onto the URL to be passed to the next page.

Here is how the URL looks when passing the name of a user from one page to the next:

```
http://www.hmi.com?username=Bill
```

This example appends a variable called `username` and gives it a value of `Bill`. You did this by ending the URL string with a question mark, followed by the variable name.

It's possible to pass more than one querystring along with the URL. To pass more than one name/value pair, separate the name/value pairs with an ampersand (&). For example, if you were passing the username and the employee's ID number, you could do it in the following manner:

```
http://www.hmi.com?username=Bill&employeeid=9040777
```

Creating querystrings

There are a number of different ways to create querystrings. One of the simpler ways is to directly place the name/value pairs with the URL. For example, you can create a hyperlink with a querystring attached, as shown here:

```
<a href="WebForm2.aspx?username=Bill&employeeid=9040777>
Registration Page</a>
```

Wherever there is a URL in your page, you can place querystrings along with that URL. For example, you can work them into your events on the code-behind page as follows:

```
Response.Redirect("WebForm2.aspx?username=Bill")
```

It's also possible to create the values of the querystrings as the page is parsed on the server by concatenating the values to the URL:

```
Response.Redirect("WebForm2.aspx?user=" & TextBox1.Text & _
   "&employeeid=" & TextBox2.Text & "")
```

If you're allowing the user to dictate the value of the querystrings that you're creating, be sure that the querystrings are passed in a manner that is readable on the receiving page. For instance, if the value of one of the querystring variables contains a space, there will be problems on the other end in some versions of Netscape. Some of these browsers will only read the value of the querystring up until the space.

To get past that, you can apply one of Visual Basic.NET's built-in functions, Server.URLEncode. You could correct your querystring by using this function:

```
Response.Redirect("WebForm2.aspx?user=" & _
   Server.URLEncode(TextBox1.Text) & _
   "&employeeid=" & _
   Server.URLEncode(TextBox2.Text) & "")
```

This encodes all the characters contained within the URL, so this example produces the following result:

```
http://localhost/webform2.aspx?user=Bill%20Evjen&employeeid=
9040777
```

In this case, the function replaces the single space between the first and last name with a %20.

Retrieving querystrings

It's easy to grab querystring variable names and their values on the receiving page. Use something similar to the following statement:

```
Dim UserName As String
UserName = Request.Querystring("user")

Dim EmployeeID As Integer
EmployeeID = Request.Querystring("employeeid")

Label1.Text = "Hello " & UserName
Label2.Text = "Your Employee ID is: " & EmployeeID
```

With the preceding code, you now have two page variables you can use in your controls that contain the values of the querystring variables that you sent to the page. In this example, you assign the values to two Label controls.

You could also write a statement to the text property of your Label control that lists out both the name of the querystring variable and the value of the variable. You'll build two pages and use this example (see Listing 40-3 and Listing 40-4) in the page that receives the querystrings. The first page is a typical form page that collects the values from a couple of text boxes and then passes those values as a querystring to the next page.

Listing 40-3: **WebForm1.aspx**

```
<html>
  <head>
        <title>QueryString Example</title>

  <script language="vb" runat="server">
     Sub Page_Load(sender As Object, e As EventArgs)
        If Page.IsPostBack Then
         Response.Redirect("WebForm2.aspx?UserName=" &__
         TextBox1.Text & "&Occupation=" &__
         TextBox2.Text & "")
        End If
     End Sub
  </script>

  </head>
  <body>
  <form id="form1" runat="server">

  <p>Name <asp:TextBox id="TextBox1"
  runat="server"></asp:TextBox>

  <p>Occupation <asp:TextBox id="TextBox2"
  runat="server"></asp:TextBox>

  <p><asp:button id="button1" runat="server" text="Submit"
  /></p>

  <p><asp:Label id="Label1" runat="server"
  Visible="False"></asp:Label></p>

  </form>
  </body>
</html>
```

The second page (see Listing 40-4), the receiving page, takes the querystring and lists out both the querystring variable names and their values. It does this by using a for each statement, listing out each variable name and value of the entire querystring.

Listing 40-4: **WebForm2.aspx**

```
<html>
  <head>
        <title>QueryString Receiving Page</title>

  <script language="vb" runat="server">
    Sub Page_Load(sender As Object, e As EventArgs)
        Dim key As String
        For Each key in Request.Querystring
            Label1.Text += "The " & key & " Querystring
            variable has a value of " & _
            Request.Querystring(key) & "<br>"
Next
    End Sub
  </script>

  </head>
  <body>

        <form id="Form1" method="post" runat="server">
            <asp:label id="label1" runat="server" />
        </form>

  </body>
</html>
```

When you enter some values on the first form page, the values of the text boxes and the variable names that are associated with them are then presented on the second page (see Figure 40-1).

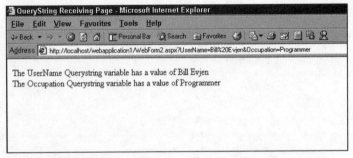

Figure 40-1: Passing variables by querystring from one page to another

The Pros and Cons of Using Querystrings

Querystrings provide an easy way to pass data and application state from one page to the next, but there are some definite disadvantages to using querystrings over other methods. The worst thing about querystrings is that they're the least effective way to pass sensitive or secure data. The reason for this is right in front of your eyes — with querystrings, you can see everything. In the worst-case scenario, the user could just change some of the values in the URL, click Submit, and then gain access to another user's account or other private information. Also keep in mind that most browsers have a 255-character limit on URL length. Therefore, the total sum of the URL and the attached querystrings cannot be longer than 255 characters. However, querystrings *can* be advantageous if used properly.

Sessions

Similar to ViewState name/value pairs, sessions within an ASP.NET application allow users to easily maintain application state. Sessions remain with the user as the user works through the pages of a Web application for a defined period of time.

You can create sessions easily, and it's just as simple to retrieve information from them. Creating a session for the user that can be accessed later in the application is done just like it was in ASP 3.0:

```
Session("EmployeeID") = TextBox2.Text
```

This assigns what was placed in `TextBox2` to the `EmployeeID` session. To retrieve this information from the session and then use it on your page, you can use the following code:

```
Label1.Text = Session("EmployeeID")
```

In classic ASP, a session would timeout on the user after 20 minutes. This meant that if the user opened up a page within a Web application (thereby creating a session) and then took a coffee break, the session wouldn't be there to continue on with the application when the user came back. It was possible to go into the server and change the time allotted to the session timeout property, but this was cumbersome and required the server to be stopped and then started again for the changes to take effect. It also wasn't good to make this timeout property too long. Sessions are resource-intensive, and you wouldn't want to be storing too many for too long.

With ASP.NET, it's now possible to change the session timeout property quite easily. On the application level, it's now stored in the `web.config` file. The `machine.config` file stores the default timeout setting for the entire server. By changing the setting in the `web.config` file, you can effectively change the timeout property of sessions within the application. The great thing about changing this property within this XML application file is that the server doesn't have to be stopped and started for the changes to take effect. Once the `web.config` file is saved with its changes, those changes take effect immediately.

The part of the `web.config` file that deals with session state management is the `sessionState` node, as shown here:

```
<sessionState
   mode="InProc"
   stateConnectionString="tcpip=127.0.0.1:42424"
   sqlConnectionString="data source=127.0.0.1;user
      id=sa;password="
   cookieless="false"
   timeout="20"
   />
```

The `sessionState` node of the `web.config` file is where session state is managed. The property that you're going to learn about now is the `timeout` property.

The default setting of the `timeout` property is 20 minutes. Therefore, if you wanted the user's sessions to last for one hour, you would set the timeout property to 60.

Running sessions in-process

Presently, the default setting for sessions in ASP.NET is that they're stored in the *in-process* mode. This is the same as it was in classic ASP. Running sessions in-process means that they're stored in the same process as the ASP.NET worker process. Therefore, if IIS is shut down and then brought back up again, all sessions are destroyed and unavailable to users who are in the middle of using them. On mission-critical Web applications, this can be a nightmare.

To set the sessions to run in-process, set the mode property in the `sessionState` node to `InProc`. Running sessions in-process provide the application with the best possible performance.

Table 40-1 describes all the available session modes.

Table 40-1 Session State Modes	
Mode	**Description**
InProc	Session state is in-process with the ASP.NET worker process. Running sessions InProc is the default setting.
Off	Session state is not available.
StateServer	Session state is using an out-of-process server to store state.
SQLServer	Session state is using an out-of-process SQL Server to store state.

Running sessions out-of-process

It's possible to run sessions out-of-process. This means IIS can be stopped and then restarted and the user's sessions are maintained. The .NET Framework includes a Windows service called ASPState that allow you to run sessions out-of-process. Follow these steps to start ASPState so you can use it to use it to manage sessions:

1. Open up the Command Prompt (Start ➪ Programs ➪ Accessories ➪ Command Prompt). On the Command Prompt line, type the following command:

   ```
   cd WINNT\Microsoft.NET\Framework\v1.0.2914
   ```

2. Press Enter to change the directory of the command prompt.

> **Note** The version number of the .NET Framework you're running may be different than the one in this example. To find out your version number, use Windows Explorer to navigate through the folders. Within the Framework folder is a folder with the version number you're running.

3. After typing that line at the command prompt, type this:

   ```
   net start aspnet_state
   ```

   This turns on the session out-of-process capabilities, displayed in Figure 40-2.

```
Command Prompt                                          _ □ X
Microsoft Windows 2000 [Version 5.00.2195]
(C) Copyright 1985-2000 Microsoft Corp.

C:\>cd WINNT\Microsoft.NET\Framework\v1.0.2914

C:\WINNT\Microsoft.NET\Framework\v1.0.2914>net start aspnet_state
The ASP.NET State service is starting.
The ASP.NET State service was started successfully.

C:\WINNT\Microsoft.NET\Framework\v1.0.2914>
```

Figure 40-2: Turning the ASP.NET State Service on

4. To turn on the ASP.NET State Service through the Services console, start by opening the console (Start ➪ Settings ➪ Control Panel ➪ Administrative Tools ➪ Services). You're presented with a list of available services on the server (see Figure 40-3). Right-click on the ASP.NET State Service to either stop or start it.

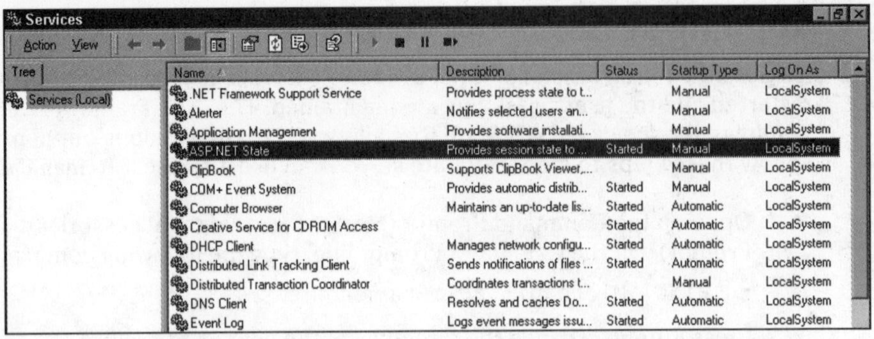

Figure 40-3: Starting the ASP.NET State Service from the Services console

Now that the out-of-process mode is enabled, you can change the settings in the `sessionState` node of the `web.config` file so that all the user's sessions are then run in this manner. You do this by setting the `mode` to `StateServer`, as follows:

```
<sessionState
    mode="StateServer"
    stateConnectionString="tcpip=127.0.0.1:42424"
    sqlConnectionString="data source=127.0.0.1;user
        id=sa;password="
    cookieless="false"
    timeout="20"
    />
```

Now IIS can be turned off and then on again, and the user's sessions remain intact. However, this is a little more resource-intensive than running the sessions in-process.

If the mode is set to `StateServer`, the server looks to the `stateConnectionString` property to assign the sessions to a specified server and port. In this case, which uses the default setting, it's set to the local server. You could easily change this so that the sessions are stored on a completely separate server.

Running sessions out-of-process is a great advantage of ASP.NET over classic ASP. This is a great advantage when you're running Web applications in a Web farm and you're unsure which server the user will navigate to. You can now move users from one server to another and maintain the user's state.

Maintaining sessions on SQL Server

Another way to run sessions out-of-process is to use SQL Server to store the user sessions. This also allows users to move from one server to another and maintain their state. It's the same as the `StateServer` mode, but instead it stores the sessions straight into SQL Server.

If you installed the .NET Framework, you also installed a mini-version of SQL Server on your server. This version allows you to store your sessions to use for state management. However, you should use a full-blown version of SQL Server, such as SQL Server 2000. This is a more dependable solution.

In order to use SQL Server as a repository of your sessions, you must create the database within SQL that ASP.NET can use. Included in the version folder of ASP.NET (found at `C:\WINNT\Microsoft.NET\Framework\v1.0.2914`) are two scripts that work with SQL Server session management. The first is the install script, `InstallSqlState.sql`. This is a script that instructs SQL Server on the database tables and procedures to create. You can look at the script instructions, which are quite readable, by opening up the script in Notepad.

The other script is the uninstall script you'll use if you ever want to remove this feature. Running `UninstallSqlScript.sql` removes the tables and procedures from SQL Server.

If you want to use SQL Server to manage your sessions, you first need to run the install script. Open up the command prompt again and navigate to the version folder of ASP.NET that you're running. On the command line, type

```
OSQL -S localhost -U sa -P <InstallSqlState.sql
```

This creates the tables and procedures needed to run the SQL Server session management option. The `-S` option on the command line is specifying the location of the server that is to be used. In this case you're using `localhost`, meaning your local server. The `-U` option is the SQL Server's assigned username to gain access. In this case, it's just the typical `sa`. The `-P` option is for the SQL Server's password, if required. It isn't required in this case, so it's blank.

Following the SQL Server's settings specifications, you then specify the script that you want to install, `InstallSqlState.sql`. This installs what is necessary to run SQL Server session management.

After you've created the necessary tables and procedures, you then need to change the `sessionState` node of the `web.config` file, as follows:

```
<sessionState
    mode="SQLServer"
    stateConnectionString="tcpip=127.0.0.1:42424"
    sqlConnectionString="data source=127.0.0.1;user
        id=sa;password="
    cookieless="false"
    timeout="20"
    />
```

To use SQL Server to manage sessions, the mode of the sessionState node needs to be set to SQLServer. ASP.NET then looks to the sqlConnectionString property to find the SQL Server to connect to. The value of this property should be set so that the data source is the server where SQL is located, as well as any needed login information.

Deciding on the state of sessions

Determining which mode to use to run sessions within your ASP.NET Web application is an important decision. It makes a considerable difference in the performance, functionality, and reliability of your Web application. Table 40-2 describes the benefits of choosing one mode for session state management over another.

Table 40-2
Differences in Session State Management Choices

Mode	When Best Used
InProc	This option is similar to the way it was done in classic ASP. The session is run in the same process as the ASP.NET worker process. Therefore, this option should be used when maintaining sessions is *not* mission-critical to the application. This option has the best performance possible out of all the choices.
StateServer	This Windows Service option runs the sessions out-of-process, and therefore it's best when used on mutliple servers or when sessions need to be maintained if IIS is stopped and then restarted. This option is the best in performance when compared to the other out-of-process option, SQLServer.
SQLServer	This out-of-process option is the most relable choice because the sessions are stored directly in SQL Server. However, it's the worst choice in performance.

Cookieless session state

All of the options mentioned so far also allow you to set the sessions so that they employ a cookieless option. This is for visitors to your site who choose to have cookies disabled in their browsers. You enable the cookieless session state environment by setting the cookieless property in the sessionState node of the web.config file to true, as shown here:

```
<sessionState
    mode="StateServer"
    stateConnectionString="tcpip=127.0.0.1:42424"
```

```
sqlConnectionString="data source=127.0.0.1;user
    id=sa;password="
cookieless="True"
timeout="20"
 />
```

ASP.NET embeds the user's session directly into the URL. When a page is rendered, all the page's URLs are rendered to contain the user's session ID in the middle of the URL itself.

Figure 40-4 refers to the querystring example in Figure 40-1. In this case, you set the cookieless property to `True` in the web.config file.

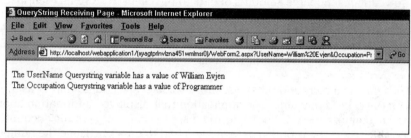

Figure 40-4: Cookieless session state

The URL in the browser's address box now contains the session ID right in the middle:

```
http://localhost/webapplication1/(xyagtprlnvlzna451wmlmsr0)/
WebForm2.aspx?UserName=William%20Evjen&Occupation=Programmer
```

Since you set the web.config file to perform cookieless sessions, it gave the user a session ID of (xyagtprlnvlzna451wmlmsr0). ASP.NET uses this to identify the user on any subsequent pages in the application. The drawback is that the user could change the contents of his session, thus destroying the session.

Cookies

Cookies are key/value pairs that are stored on the client computer. Using cookies to persist information is a simple and easy option in ASP.NET. Cookies are passed along with the HTTP request to the server and are used to identify the user upon receipt.

Advantages to using cookies

There are many advantages to using cookies within your applications to store simple data. First of all, it doesn't require server resources because none of the cookies are stored on the server. Secondly, you can set cookies to expire when the browser is shut down or for any date in the future. Therefore, it's possible to remember the user upon return visits weeks or months later.

Disadvantages to using cookies

There are also some negatives to using cookies, and for some applications they can account for some serious security flaws. One negative is that cookies need to be small. You cannot send large amounts of data to the client to store on their machine. Generally, there's a 4,096-byte limit to the size of a cookie, so the types of data that you can store are limited. The biggest negative is that cookies are easy for knowledgeable users to change. This can be a major problem if you're using cookies for users to gain access to private information.

I knew of a financial institution that was storing a user's account number as a cookie on the client's machine. The application that displayed information about the user's accounts used this cookie for the user to gain access to the account. You might be able to see the problem here. All you had to do was change the numbers in the cookie and you were in someone else's account.

Listing 40-5 shows an example of creating and displaying a pair of cookies.

Listing 40-5: **Creating and Displaying Cookies**

```
<html>
  <head>
        <title>Cookies Example</title>

<script language="vb" runat="server">
Sub Page_Load(sender As Object, e As EventArgs)
      If Page.IsPostBack Then
        Dim MyCookie As HttpCookie
        MyCookie = New HttpCookie("UserType")
        MyCookie.Values.Add("UserName", TextBox1.Text)
        MyCookie.Values.Add("Occupation", TextBox2.Text)
        Response.AppendCookie(MyCookie)

        Label1.Visible = True
        Label1.Text = "Cookies Set<p>" & _
        "<b>UserName:</b> " & MyCookie.Item("UserName") & _
        "<br><b>Occupation:</b> " & _
        MyCookie.Item("Occupation")
     end if
```

```
      End Sub
      </script>

      </head>
      <body>
            <form id="form1" runat="server">
            <p>Name <asp:TextBox id="TextBox1"
            runat="server"></asp:TextBox>

            <p>Occupation <asp:TextBox id="TextBox2"
            runat="server"></asp:TextBox>

            <p><asp:button id="button1" runat="server"
            text="Submit" /></p>

            <p><asp:Label id="Label1" runat="server"
            Visible="False"></asp:Label></p>
      </form>
        </body>
      </html>
```

This example is similar to the querystring example (see Listing 40-3), except that you're recording the results of the form into client-side cookies. On your page post-back, you take the values of the two text boxes and place those values into your cookies. First, though, create your cookie as follows:

```
Dim MyCookie As HttpCookie
MyCookie = New HttpCookie("UserType")
```

After creating HTTPCookie, you assigned it the name UserType. UserType can contain multiple name/value pairs. In this example, you assign these two name/value pairs to the cookie:

```
MyCookie.Values.Add("UserName", TextBox1.Text)
MyCookie.Values.Add("Occupation", TextBox2.Text)
```

Then you append the name/value pairs to your cookie:

```
Response.AppendCookie(MyCookie)
```

Writing the cookie to the browser is simple. You just refer to the name/value pair you want to display:

```
Label1.Text = "Cookies Set<p>" & __
      "<b>UserName:</b> " & MyCookie.Item("UserName") & __
      "<br><b>Occupation:</b> " & __
MyCookie.Item("Occupation")
```

Summary

This chapter showed you that maintaining state within your Web applications is an important process. There are a number of options for managing the user's state as he works through the pages of your application.

Some state management options are better than others, but it all really depends on the situation. Choose wisely.

✦   ✦   ✦

ASP.NET Applications

by Bill Evjen

CHAPTER

41

♦ ♦ ♦ ♦

In This Chapter

Creating an
application

Using the
Global.asax file

Understanding
web.config

♦ ♦ ♦ ♦

A *Web application* may consist of a collection of ASP.NET files and the `Global.asax` file. (The `Global.asax` file is discussed in its own section of this chapter.) When you type a URL into your browser (such as `http://www.somewhere.com/`), you're calling a Web application and firing any application events that go along with it. Locally on the server, the Web application resides in a virtual directory that you specify, typically within the `C:\Inetpub\wwwroot` directory.

This chapter covers how to create and modify your applications as well as everything that you need to know and understand to control the settings and configuration of the application through the `web.config` file.

Creating a Web Application

With classic ASP, you could create a Web application by having a collection of `.asp` files and a `global.asa` file within the root directory. It's important to note that these classic files can reside in the same virtual directory as your `.aspx` pages with the `global.asax` file and they won't interfere with each other. These two applications won't share state or events. In the usual fashion, when people upgrade from one version of a product to another, the new version ususally overrides the older one. But in this case, ASP.NET doesn't override the classic ASP dynamic link library (DLL). Instead, files run side-by-side. However, intermingling the two may prove problematic because the two versions don't share state or events.

With the growth of the Internet and the wide acceptance of the Web browser as a way to port information and applications around the world, more and more emphasis is being placed upon Web applications. It's now becoming a stronger necessity in development to make a group of pages work together just as a group of forms can work together in a Win32 application. The increasing popularity of the Internet as a portal for Web application development is directly related to the growth of the Internet as a whole. It is becoming far easier for companies and organizations to use a browser to port their applications, instead of forcing users to install a certain version of an application on their machines at home or at work. Porting their applications through the browser guarantees users the latest version of the application. Users are also quite knowledgeable these days about working in forms that are in a browser. It is also far better not to worry about the end user's hardware situation and push the data, as opposed to pulling data in a Win32 application.

Probably the biggest concern with Web application development for programmers is *state management*, or the applications' ability to pass the value of variables from one page to another. How you handle this matter also addresses issues with security and server resources.

See Chapter 40 for a discussion of state management.

The other concern with Web applications is application events, such as firing events when the user first starts up the application or leaves it. There are a number of different application-level events that can be used with your applications, and they are covered briefly in this chapter.

For a full description of application events, please see Chapter 38.

With Visual Studio .NET, creating a Web application is an easy and straightforward process. To do so, follow these steps:

1. From the Start Page that's displayed when you pull up Visual Studio .NET for the first time, open any existing applications that you've created in the past, or start a new application. If you do not see the Start Page when you open up Visual Studio .NET, click Help ➪ Show Start Page. The Start Page is shown in Figure 41-1.

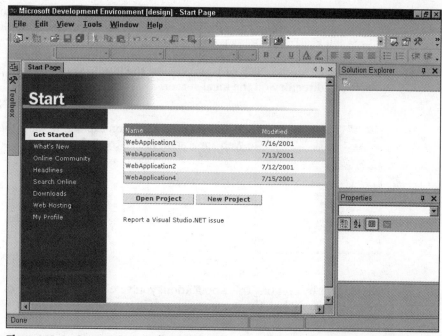

Figure 41-1: Start a new application in Visual Studio .NET from the Start Page and select New Project.

2. To start a new application, click on the New Project button. This displays the dialog box you see in Figure 41-2. It has a large list of various applications that you can create with Visual Studio .NET.

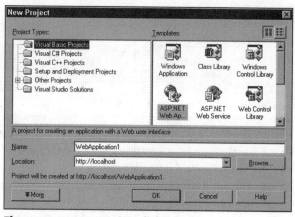

Figure 41-2: New Project dialog box.

3. Choose ASP.NET Web Application and click OK. Visual Studio .NET automatically creates the application for you, as well as the appropriate application files (such as `global.asax`). After Visual Studio .NET creates the application, you can see all the files in the Solution Explorer window (see Figure 41-3) within Visual Studio .NET, or you can view the files in your `C:\Inetpub\ wwwroot\` directory on the local server.

Figure 41-3: The Solution Explorer displays the entire Web application you've created.

Notice that by creating this application, you've created a number of other items as well. Not all the items are shown in the Solution Explorer at this point, though.

4. Look at the files that are listed in the Solution Explorer, and then go to `C:\ Inetpub\wwwroot\WebApplication1` and compare what's different. There are some extra files and folders in the Windows Explorer view. Visual Studio .NET doesn't show you all the files that are actually within the application, but only the ones that you need to work with on a regular basis.

5. To show more of the files and folders that are at your disposal within the Solution Explorer, click on the Show All Files button located at the top. This shows a larger list of available items. The most important of these application items are described in Table 14-1.

Table 41-1
Application-Specific Items

Item Created	Description
`\bin` **Folder**	This folder is used for .NET assemblies that are used by the application.
`Global.asax`	This is a file where you can specify application events and variables. This is the next version of the classic ASP `global.asa` file.
`web.config`	This is an XML file that allows the developer to set application settings such as security, state, and a number of other items.

Deleting an Application

Deleting or destroying an application is just as easy as creating it was. Within the Solution Explorer window in Visual Studio .NET, right-click on the application and select Remove. This removes the application from the server and deletes all the files.

global.asax

The `global.asax` file is used by the application to hold application-level events, objects, and variables. It's the next version of the `global.asa` file that was used in classic ASP 3.0, so if you were comfortable with that, you'll feel quite at home with `global.asax`.

There can only be one `global.asax` file for an application. However, it's possible for a `global.asax` file to reside next to a `global.asa` file without any concerns. Just realize that running them side-by-side won't allow you to share sessions or events between the two. In this situation, your `.asp` pages within the application use the `global.asa` file, and the `.aspx` pages use its application file, `global.asax`.

The `global.asax` file supports a number of items:

✦ **Directives** — Very much like the directives that are used in ASP.NET pages, user controls, and Web Services, these directives allow you to specify instructions to the application.

✦ **Declarations** — These allow you to declare specific items such as scripts and includes.

✦ **Application events** — These are events that can be initiated on an application level.

Application directives

Application directives are very much like the directives that you can use within ASP.NET pages and Web Services. The `global.asax` file supports the three following types of directives:

✦ `@ Application`

✦ `@ Import`

✦ `@ Assembly`

Before exploring each of these, it's important that you understand how to write an application directive within your `global.asax` file. The directive is written in the following format:

```
<%@ [Directive] [Attribute=Value] %>
```

The directive goes at the top of the page in the `global.asax` document. The directive is opened and closed with the same brackets used in classic ASP, with the opening `<%` and closing `%>`. The directive allows for as many attribute/value pairs as you wish. So if you had more than one attribute, the directive would be written as follows:

```
<%@ [Directive] [Attribute=Value] [Attribute=Value] %>
```

@ Application

The `@ Application` directive defines application-specific attributes. This directive supports the two following types of attributes:

- ✦ `Inherits` allows developers to specify the base class that `global.asax` uses.
- ✦ `Description` allows developers to specify a description for the entire `global.asax` file.

Here's an example that uses both attributes within one directive:

```
<%@ Application Inherits="PM.Object" Description="The Project
Management Application for the Sales Department." %>
```

Note The ASP.NET parser ignores the description directive at runtime. This is important if you have a lengthy description.

@ Import

The `@ Import` directive specifies the namespaces to be imported into the application, thereby making all classes and interfaces available to the pages of the application. This directive only supports *one* attribute — `Namespace`.

The `Namespace` attribute directly specifies the namespace to be imported. Note that with the `@Import` directive, it cannot contain more than one attribute/value pair.

Here's an example that imports two different namespaces using the `@Import` directive:

```
<%@ Import Namespace="System.Data" %>
<%@ Import Namespace="System.Net" %>
```

The important thing to understand is that there are already a number of namespaces being imported into the application automatically. The following namespaces are already imported:

```
System

System.Collections

System.Collections.Specialized

System.Configuration

System.IO

System.Text

System.Text.RegularExpressions

System.Web

System.Web.Caching

System.Web.Security

System.Web.SessionState

System.Web.UI

System.Web.UI.HtmlControls

System.Web.UI.WebControls
```

There's no need to re-import these items because they're already there. It's also possible to import namespaces into your applications within the web.config file, which are discussed later in the chapter.

Importing a namespace into your application allows you to use its classes without fully identifying their names. For instance, if you import the namespace System. Data.OleDB into the application or into the ASP.NET page, you can then refer to classes within this namespace by just expressing the singular class names. You could refer to OLEDBConnection instead of System.Data.OleDB.OLEDBConnection, for example.

@ Assembly

The @ Assembly directive attaches assemblies to a page as it compiles, thereby making all the assembly's classes and interfaces available to the page. This directive supports the two following attributes:

✦ Name allows developers to specify the name of an assembly. This assembly is the one that is attached to the page files. The name of the assembly should only include the filename and not the file's extension. For instance, if the file is MyAssembly.vb, the value of the name attribute could be MyAssembly.

✦ Src allows developers to specify the source of the assembly file to use in compilation.

Note The Src (source) attribute is an optional attribute that specifies the file of the code that you want to include within the script block.

An example of the @ Assembly directive is as follows:

```
<%@ Assembly Name="MyAssembly" %>
<%@ Assembly Src="MyAssembly.vb" %>
```

Note that the source attribute can contain the complete path as well. Also, any assemblies that are placed within the \bin directory are automatically available to the page.

Declarations

Code declarations within a global.asax file work in the same manner as they do within your ASP.NET pages. Code is declared between <script></script> tags, and you can define any number of variables, event handlers, and methods. Here is an example of using code declaration:

```
<script runat="server" language="LanguageType"
            src="FilePath">
Write your code out here.
</script>
```

The <script> tag must contain a runat=server attribute/value pair, and then you can specify two other attributes within the tag itself—the language and src attributes.

The language attribute specifies the language that is used in the script. For the purposes of this exercise, use the language="VB" attribute/value pair. You don't need to declare this attribute within the <script> tag if you've declared the language in either the application or page directive, or if it's declared in the web.config file.

The following code demonstrates how to use the <script> tags within a global.asax file to define an event handler:

```
<script language="VB" runat=server>
    Sub Application_OnStart()
        ' Application startup code goes here...
    End Sub
</script>
```

Application-level events

Application-level events are held in the `global.asax` file between the `<script>` tags. There are a number of different application-wide events that you can call, including `Application_OnStart`, `Application_OnEnd`, `Session_OnStart`, and `Session_OnEnd`.

See Chapter 38 for a more complete discussion of events.

Understanding web.config

`web.config` is an application file that allows you to set application-wide settings from one convenient file. This file is created for you when you create an application. If you wanted to change any of the application settings in classic ASP, it was done in the IIS Microsoft Management Console (MMC). The administrator had to stop and start your application for the settings to take place. With ASP.NET, you just need to open the `web.config` file in any text editor, change the settings, and resave the file. ASP.NET can then detect when there are new configuration settings for your application, and it doesn't need to stop and start the application. Instead, ASP.NET lets current users finish with the application under the old settings, and any new users are directed to the application with the new settings applied.

The `web.config` file is an XML file, which makes it quite readable and understandable. Feel free to open it up and change the settings.

The `web.config` file is created when you start an application. After doing so, you are presented with the code shown in Listing 41-1.

Listing 41-1: **web.config**

```
<?xml version="1.0" encoding="utf-8" ?>
<configuration>

  <system.web>

  <!-- DYNAMIC DEBUG COMPILATION
  Set compilation debug="true" to insert debugging symbols
  (.pdb information) into the compiled page. Because this
  creates a larger file that executes more slowly, you should
  set this value to true only when debugging and to
  false at all other times. For more information, refer to
  the documentation about debugging ASP.NET files.
  -->
  <compilation defaultLanguage="vb" debug="true" />
```

Continued

Listing 41-1 *(continued)*

```
<!-- CUSTOM ERROR MESSAGES
Set customErrors mode="On" or "RemoteOnly" to enable
custom error messages, "Off" to disable.
Add <error> tags for each of the errors you want to handle.
-->
<customErrors mode="RemoteOnly" />

<!-- AUTHENTICATION
This section sets the authentication policies of the
application. Possible modes are "Windows",
"Forms", "Passport" and "None"
-->
<authentication mode="Windows" />

<!-- AUTHORIZATION
This section sets the authorization policies of the
application. You can allow or deny access
to application resources by user or role. Wildcards: "*"
mean everyone, "?" means anonymous(unauthenticated) users.
-->
<authorization>
        <allow users="*" /> <!-- Allow all users -->
        <!--  <allow users="[comma separated list of
                users]"
        roles="[comma separated list of roles]"/>
        <deny users="[comma separated list of users]"
        roles="[comma separated list of roles]"/>
        -->
</authorization>

<!-- APPLICATION-LEVEL TRACE LOGGING
Application-level tracing enables trace log output for
every page within an application.
Set trace enabled="true" to enable application trace
logging.  If pageOutput="true", the
trace information will be displayed at the bottom of each
page.  Otherwise, you can view the
application trace log by browsing the "trace.axd" page from
your web application root.
-->
<trace enabled="false" requestLimit="10"
pageOutput="false" traceMode="SortByTime" localOnly="true"
/>

<!-- SESSION STATE SETTINGS
By default ASP.NET uses cookies to identify which requests
belong to a particular session.
If cookies are not available, a session can be tracked by
adding a session identifier to the URL.
```

```
To disable cookies, set sessionState cookieless="true".
-->
<sessionState
      mode="InProc"
      stateConnectionString="tcpip=127.0.0.1:42424"
      sqlConnectionString="data source=127.0.0.1;user
          id=sa;password="
      cookieless="true"
      timeout="20"
/>

<!-- PREVENT SOURCE CODE DOWNLOAD
This section sets the types of files that will not be
downloaded. As well as entering
a httphandler for a file type, you must also associate that
file type with the xspisapi.dll
in the App Mappings property of the web site, or the file
can be downloaded.
It is recommended that you use this section to prevent your
sources being downloaded.
-->
<httpHandlers>
      <add verb="*" path="*.vb"
       type="System.Web.HttpNotFoundHandler,System.Web" />
      <add verb="*" path="*.cs"
       type="System.Web.HttpNotFoundHandler,System.Web" />
      <add verb="*" path="*.vbproj"
       type="System.Web.HttpNotFoundHandler,System.Web" />
      <add verb="*" path="*.csproj"
       type="System.Web.HttpNotFoundHandler,System.Web" />
      <add verb="*" path="*.webinfo"
       type="System.Web.HttpNotFoundHandler,System.Web" />
</httpHandlers>

<!-- GLOBALIZATION
This section sets the globalization settings of the
application.
-->
<globalization requestEncoding="utf-8"
 responseEncoding="utf-8" />

</system.web>

</configuration>
```

Because this is an XML file, you don't have to go through a wizard to change application-wide settings. Instead, you just make the appropriate changes to this file and save it in the root directory of your application. The changes take effect for all new requests immediately.

<configuration> node

The following lines from the first part of the web.config file inform you that this is an XML file and open up the main node of the file:

```
<?xml version="1.0" encoding="utf-8" ?>
<configuration>
  <system.web>
              ... SETTINGS HERE ...
  </system.web>
</configuration>
```

You need to open and close the web.config file with <configuration> tags. Within these <configuration> tags are your <system.web> tags. Forgetting one of these tags causes an exception.

<compilation> node

The <compilation> node allows you to directly affect how your ASP.NET application compiles. The following shows the structure of the <compilation> node:

```
<compilation debug="true|false"
    defaultLanguage="language"
    explicit="true|false"
    batch="true|false"
    batchTimeout="number"
    numRecompilesBeforeAppRestart="number"
    strict="true|false" >

    <compilers>
        <compiler language="language"
            extension="ext"
            type=".NET Type"
            warningLevel="number"
            compilerOptions="options" />
    </compilers>

    <assemblies>
        <add assembly="assembly" />
        <remove assembly="assembly"  />
        <clear />
    </assemblies>

    <namespaces>
        <add namespace="namespace" />
        <remove namespace="namespace" />
        <clear />
    </namespaces>
</compilation>
```

The compilation section of the web.config file allows you to configure how the ASP.NET application compiles, as shown here:

```
<compilation defaultLanguage="vb" debug="true" />
```

Note As you work through all these examples, remember that these settings are applied application-wide unless you override them directly within your page code.

The <compilation> tag takes a number of attributes, but there are two important ones. The first is the defaultLanguage attribute, which specifies the default compiler you use to compile all server side code. In this case it's "vb", so you don't need to specify the language=vb in your scripts. The second attribute is the debug attribute. Setting this to true turns on the debug compilers. This results in slower performance, but it's necessary in development. When your application is released, change this setting to false.

The compilation node can contain three sub nodes: <compilers>, <assemblies>, and <namespaces>.

<customerrors> node

The <customerrors> node allows you to directly place instructions in your application about how it deals with errors that it encounters. The following example shows the structure of the <customerrors> node:

```
<customErrors
    defaultRedirect="url"
    mode="On|Off|RemoteOnly">
    <error statusCode="statuscode"
        redirect="url"/>
</customErrors>
```

The <customerrors> node allows you to control how the application deals with errors. Instead of just allowing the application to display errors to users, it's more beneficial to forward the client to another page. The <customerrors> node allows you to specify the page where users are redirected in case of any errors. The mode can be set to On, which causes the <customerrors> rules to be applied to all users, even local users. The second value of the mode attribute is Off, which turns off this feature. The final possible value is RemoteOnly, which applies the rules of the <customerrors> settings to all users, except for users who are using the local server.

The <customerrors> node can take sub nodes as well. The error node within the <customerrors> node can specify specific errors for which you might want to make a special case in your application. This node takes two attributes. The first is `statusCode`. With this attribute, you can specify the particular error by its error code:

```
<error statusCode="500" redirect="ErrorInPage.aspx?er=500" />
```

The `redirect` attribute of the error node points to the page where users are redirected when the specified error occurs.

`<authentication>` node

The `<authentication>` node allows you to directly control all the authentication aspects of your application. The following code shows the structure of the `<authentication>` node:

```
<authentication mode="Windows|Forms|Passport|None">

    <forms name="name" loginUrl="url"
        protection="All|None|Encryption|Validation"
        timeout="30" path="/" >

        <credentials passwordFormat="Clear|SHA1|MD5">
            <user name="username" password="password" />
        </credentials>

    </forms>

    <passport redirectUrl="internal"/>

</authentication>
```

When you're developing applications for the Internet, there are many times when you don't want to allow every public user to gain access. You want to build an authentication system so users can identify themselves before entering the application. You could build a page that checks for names in a database before allowing users to continue, but ASP.NET gives you a number of different authentication options.

It's possible to configure ASP.NET authentication in the four modes listed in Table 41-2.

Table 41-2
Authentication Options

Authentication Mode	Description
Windows	Use this mode with any form of Internet Information Services (IIS) authentication, such as Basic, Digest, Integrated Windows authentication (NTLM/Kerberos), or certificates.

Authentication Mode	Description
Forms	This mode uses ASP.NET forms-based authentication.
Passport	Uses Microsoft Passport authentication.
None	No authentication.

Cross-
Reference   Chapter 43 covers ASP.NET authentication in more detail.

\<authorization\> node

The \<authorization\> node works with the \<authentication\> node in the web.
config file to apply an authorization model to your ASP.NET applications. The following code shows the structure of the \<authorization\> node:

```
<authorization>

    <allow users="comma-separated list of users"
        roles="comma-separated list of roles"
        verb="comma-separated list of verbs" />

    <deny users="comma-separated list of users"
        roles="comma-separated list of roles"
        verb="comma-separated list of verbs" />

</authorization>
```

The \<authorization\> node allows for two sub nodes, \<allow\> and \<deny\>. You
can allow individual users by using the users attribute and separating the values
with a comma. It's also possible to allow groups or members by using the roles
attribute:

```
<allow users="Bill, Jim, Keven" roles="Admins" />
```

The \<deny\> sub node works in the same way, except it denies users access. For
either the \<allow\> or \<deny\> node, an asterisk means to apply that particular functionality to all users. A question mark applies that functionality to all anonymous
users. So if you wanted to allow all users to your resource, but at the same time
deny anonymous users, here's how it would look:

```
<allow users="*" />
<deny users="?" />
```

The verb attribute allows you to specify the HTTP transmission methods that are
used for allowing or denying users to the resource. The values of the verb attribute
include GET, POST, HEAD, and DEBUG.

\<trace> node

The \<trace> node allows you to work with debugging an ASP.NET application. The following code structure shows how to configure an application with tracing:

```
<trace
    enabled="true|false"
    requestLimit="integer"
    pageOutput="true|false" />
```

The \<trace> node allows you to specify tracing settings for your application. You can turn tracing on or off by setting the enabled attribute to true or false. You can also output the tracing document to each page by setting the pageOutput attribute to either true or false.

Cross-Reference   Tracing is covered in more detail in Chapter 42.

\<sessionState> node

The \<sessionState> node allows you to configure how your ASP.NET application handles sessions. The following code snippet shows how to structure this node within the web.config file:

```
<sessionState
    mode="Off|Inproc|StateServer|SqlServer"
    cookieless="true|false"
    timeout="number of minutes"
    connectionString="server name:port number"
    sqlConnectionString="sql connection string" />
```

The \<sessionState> node is a great new way to manage your sessions in ASP.NET. It's now possible to manage sessions in a separate process than the ASP.NET worker process, which wasn't possible in classic ASP.

Now you can store a user's sessions in an out-of-process mode that's separate from the ASP.NET worker process, even if it's on a separate server from the application. For maximum reliability, it's now possible to store sessions in SQL Server. With these options, you can maintain a Web farm, and users can switch between servers and still maintain their sessions.

Table 41-3 lists the four modes for session management in ASP.NET.

<table>
<tr><th colspan="2">Table 41-3
Session State Modes</th></tr>
</table>

Mode	Description
InProc	Session state is in-process with the ASP.NET worker process. Running sessions InProc is the default setting.
Off	Session state is not available.
StateServer	Session state is using an out-of-process server to store state.
SQLServer	Session state is using an out-of-process SQL Server to store state.

If you use the cookieless attribute, the user maintains his sessions within a cookie that's placed within the URL itself. The timeout attribute is the value in minutes that the sessions should be maintained.

 Cross-Reference See Chapter 40 for more information on maintaining sessions within a Web application.

<globalization> node

The <globalization> node allows you to directly control how your application configures culture settings. The following code shows how to structure the <globalization> node:

```
<globalization
    requestEncoding="any valid encoding string"
    responseEncoding="any valid encoding string"
    fileEncoding="any valid encoding string"
    culture="any valid culture string"
    uiCulture="any valid culture string" />
```

Because the Internet is global, it's important to to code applications that are internationally aware. For instance, when an application prints the date to the screen, it should be formatted in the fashion that's expected by the viewing user, no matter which country he's in.

By using the <globalization> node in the web.config file, you can establish how the server should treat certain elements, such as dates. Listing 41-2 displays a page that shows the date in a Label control.

Listing 41-2: Global Dates

```
<html>
  <head>
        <script language="vb" runat="server">
        Sub Page_Load(sender As Object, e As EventArgs)
            Label1.Visible = True
            Label1.Text = DateTime.Now.ToString("D")
        End Sub
        </script>
  </head>

  <body>
        <asp:label id="label1" runat="server" />
  </body>
</html>
```

By default, the date is printed out in the United States date format (Saturday, August 4, 2001). By using the `<globalization>` node of the `web.config` file, however, you can change the output format of the date in your applications as follows:

```
<globalization requestEncoding="utf-8"
responseEncoding="utf-8" culture="fi-FI" uiCulture="fi-FI" />
```

This sets the `web.config` file to print server-side outputs in Finnish:

```
4. elokuuta 2001
```

`<appSettings>` node

The `<appSettings>` node allows you to store key/value pairs within the `web.config` file to use anywhere within your ASP.NET application. The following code shows the structure of the `<appSettings>` node to use within the `web.config` file:

```
<appSettings>
        <add key="key" value="value"/>
</appSettings>
```

The `<appSettings>` node allows you to define custom application settings that can be used throughout your application. This node allows for one type of sub node, `<add>`, which specifies a key/value pair. You can have as many `<add>` nodes as you want.

One good example is storing your database connections and commonly used SQL strings within the `<appSettings>` node, as shown here:

```
<appSettings>
  <add key="DSN"
   value="server=localhost;uid=sa;pwd=;database=customers"
  />
  <add key="SQL1"
  value="Select * From CustomerOrders" />
</appsettings>
```

This allows you to change the connection easily because the change is in one spot and not scattered throughout the application. You can use the following code to retrieve these settings within your pages later:

```
Dim DSN As String
Dim SqlString As String

DSN = ConfigurationSettings.AppSettings("DSN")
SqlString = ConfigurationSettings.AppSettings("SqlString")
```

It's quite simple now to include these key/value pairs and refer to them throughout your pages. Once it's changed, the application resets itself and immediately starts using the new key/value pairs.

Summary

When you're developing an ASP.NET page, it's important to understand the page's place within the entire application. The application has the Global.asax and web.config files, which allow application events and configurations to be applied easily.

Coding these files correctly contributes to an all-around better application, no matter how many pages it encompasses.

◆　　◆　　◆

Tracing

by Bill Evjen

Agreat new feature of ASP.NET is the ability to trace the information that's passed from requests and responses. This plays a great role in the error-checking and debugging of applications.

The tracing feature in ASP.NET is a new means of debugging a Web application. One of the more important steps in developing applications for the Web is understanding which information is being sent from one page request to the next. With tracing turned on in your ASP.NET application, you can closely follow all the variables and conditions within your pages in unprecedented ways.

This chapter works through all the options that are at your disposal when you are working with tracing in your ASP.NET applications. You also learn how to customize the tracing feature to follow the information about what's happening in your application.

Understanding the Benefits of ASP.NET Tracing

Everyone makes mistakes, and programmers are no exception. These mistakes could be in the code, or how the browser interprets the code. They could even be in the communications between components. Classic ASP didn't allow developers to easily trace information in requests and responses. So instead, many developers built their own types of tracing directly into the code. For example, many programmers would litter their applications with `Response.Write` statements to see how their page's state was working.

Note Response.Write is a means of writing content to the browser window. For example, writing Response.Write("ASP.NET is cool!") causes the specified text to be printed to the browser when the user calls the page.

Carrying sessions around from page to page, and in many cases changing the value of these sessions, is vital to the proper functioning of your applications. Therefore, placing these Response.Write statements allowed developers to see what was happening with the sessions and other elements as they progressed through the application. Although this worked, there were many problems. It took time to place these statements in the application on the pages that needed them. Then, it took time to either comment them all out or remove them from the application altogether.

This situation was also a problem whenever you needed to debug a live application. You couldn't write the information you needed directly to the screen because you wouldn't want your users to see that information. You could write them either to a text file or to a database, but this took away from the performance of the application.

This type of tracing and debugging in classic ASP didn't do anything in terms of performance monitoring. It only allowed you to see the values of different items being passed around from page to page.

ASP.NET has changed all that, and now you can easily use its built-in tracing abilities to trace all this information going back and forth.

Enabling Tracing

You can configure your ASP.NET applications to enable tracing in two places. The first is at the application level, and the second option is at the page level. Note that you can have both options turned on at once.

Enabling tracing at the application level

It's quite easy to enable tracing within your ASP.NET applications at either the application level or the page level. To enable tracing application-wide, open the web.config file and make some modifications there. You can find the web.config file within the root of your application.

Cross-Reference For more information on the web.config file, please see Chapter 41.

When you open the web.config file, you see the following line of code that deals with tracing in the application:

```
<trace enabled="false" requestLimit="10" pageOutput="false"
traceMode="SortByTime" localOnly="true" />
```

To turn tracing on, change the `enabled` attribute to true. This turns tracing on, but nothing is viewable on the pages themselves yet. Table 42-1 lists what these attributes mean in the modification of the tracing environment.

Table 42-1 Attributes in the \<trace> Node	
Attribute	**Description**
Enabled	Turns the tracing on or off. The default is false.
RequestLimit	This is the number of HTTP requests that will be recorded. The default setting is 10. As the requests build up, ASP.NET tracing keeps track of the last specified number of requests.
PageOutput	A setting of true means that the tracing information is shown on each page as it's rendered, in addition to being recorded in the `trace.axd` file. The default is false.
TraceMode	This attribute specifies the display order of the tracing information. Options include `SortByTime` or `SortByCategory`. `SortByTime` is the default setting.
LocalOnly	Indicates whether the trace information is shown only on the local server or is shown to remote clients also.

Now that you've changed the setting of the `enabled` attribute within the tracing node of your `web.config` file to true, tracing has been switched on. Tracing information won't show up yet in your pages (although you can show it by switching the `pageOutput` attribute to true), but instead is stored for easy access. Next, let's take a look at enabling page-level tracing.

Enabling page-level tracing

Enabling page-level tracing is just as easy as enabling it on the application level. In order to change your pages so that they start giving you tracing information, you need to add a page directive at the top of the page in which you want to enable tracing.

 Page directives are covered in more detail in Chapter 33.

Just include the following page directive at the top of the page you want to add tracing to:

```
<%@ Page Trace="True" %>
```

That's all there is to it. When the page is rendered, all the tracing information appears at the bottom of the page.

Caution   If you turn tracing on by using a page directive, the tracing feature is turned on for any browser that requests the page. When you're moving the application to a production server, be sure to disable tracing at the page level within this directive.

Viewing Tracing Output

After enabling tracing on the application level, ASP.NET starts keeping track of all the HTTP requests that are happening. It logs all the tracing information automatically for you and only stores the last 10 HTTP requests to the application. You can change the number of requests that are stored by changing the `requestLimit` attribute to the desired number of requests.

These requests aren't shown on the page themselves unless the `pageOutput` attribute is set to true. In any case, tracing is still stored in a tracing log that is accessible through the browser.

To view the tracing log using your browser, navigate to your application and to the file `trace.axd`. This file is located in the root directory. Type in the following URL to see the application tracing page:

```
http://localhost/webapplication1/trace.axd
```

Note   If you used Windows Explorer to view the file in the root directory, you will not find it there. The file is *only* viewable through the browser.

The `trace.axd` file lists all the requests that have been made to the application and give you some basic information about the requests, such as the time of the request and the file requested (see Figure 42-1).

In the upper-left corner of the `trace.axd` file, you can clear the trace log by clicking the Clear Current Trace link. It's possible to view the details of the each HTTP request made by clicking the View Details link. This displays a new page that contains all the tracing information for that request (see Figure 42-2).

The important thing to note about Figure 42-2 is that not all the tracing information is displayed on the screen. There's quite a bit more if you just scroll down the page. The depth of information that's available is quite staggering, and you did all this simply by changing a few settings within the `web.config` file.

The other great thing about tracing is that whether you're just using application-level tracing or enable tracing down to the page level, the information is the same and in the same format.

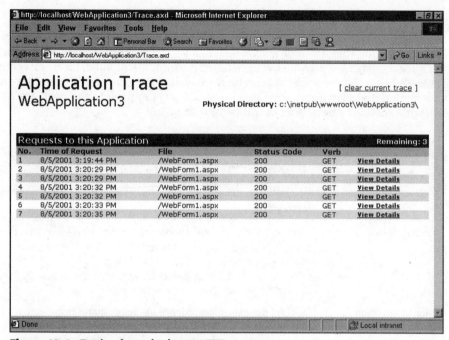

Figure 42-1: Tracing from the latest HTTP requests

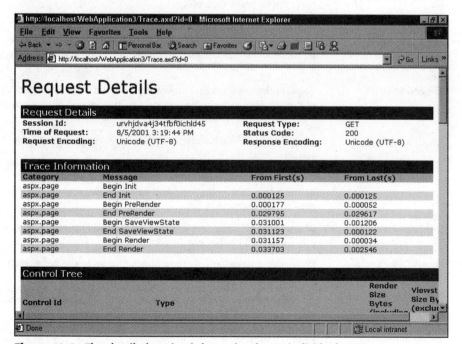

Figure 42-2: The detailed tracing information for an individual request

Reading and Customizing the Trace Log

The information that ASP.NET gives you when you have tracing enabled is called the *trace log*. This log provides very detailed information about each HTTP request. Table 42-2 lists the sections that can be displayed in the trace log. Depending on the information that you are working with from one page request to the next, any of the following sections can be shown within your trace log.

Table 42-2 Trace Log	
Section	**Description**
Request Detail	Displays the generic information about the request, such as the session ID of the request, the time the request was made, the character encoding of the request, the request type (GET or POST), the status code value associated with the response, and the character encoding for the response.
Trace Information	Displays the execution order of the request and response. Information provided includes the category of the event, the message to display for the event, and the time in seconds from when the first message or event took place to when the last message or event took place.
Control Tree	Displays a list of all the controls on the page. Specific items include the ID of the control, the type of the control, the byte size of the rendered control, and the byte size of the control's view state.
Session State	Displays the sessions that are available to the page. The specifics of the sessions include the session key, the session type (such as System.String), and the value of the session.
Application State	Similar to the session state, but keeps track of all application variables.
Cookies Collection	Displays information about the page's cookies, including the name of the cookie, the keys and values of the cookie, and the byte size of the cookie.
Headers Collection	Displays the HTTP header information, such as the name and value of each header item.
Forms Collection	Displays the form variable data that is passed to the page, such as the name of the variable and its value.
QueryString Collection	Displays the querystring variable data that is passed to the page, such as the name of the querystring and its value.
Server Variables	Displays any available server variables.

You can customize the trace log so that you can place your own messages within the log itself. For instance, if you want to record a specific event that's taking place in the page, you can place a trace message within the event and it appears in the trace log once the page is requested.

Along with the `Response` and `Request` objects that have been available in ASP since the very beginning, you now can use the `TraceContext` object to trace certain pieces of information within your pages or applications.

Simply place some code in the event you want to trace, as shown here:

```
Sub Page_Load(Sender As Object, E As EventArgs)
   Trace.Write("Page_Load", "The Page Has Loaded!")

   Dim a As Integer = 2
   Dim b As Integer = 20

   a = a + b

   If a = 22 Then
        Trace.Write("A", "A is True")
   Else
        Trace.Write("A", "A is False")
   End If
End Sub
```

When this page is loaded, you're writing two items to the trace log (see Figure 42-3). First, you're writing that the `Page_Load` event took place, and second, you're writing whether your statement is either true or false. The structure of the `Trace.Write` statement is that the values need to be contained within parentheses. The first value in the parentheses is the category, and the second is the message. They need to be separated by a comma.

You can even change your `Trace.Write` statements to `Trace.Warn`. This makes custom traces appear in red so that they stand out more on the page, which is quite useful if there are a lot of events taking place. For example, the Page_Load and A categories shown in Figure 42-4 appear in red on your screen.

It's now possible to enable tracing on a live application, and your users won't see the tracing output on the screen if you have the `localOnly` attribute set to true in the `web.config` file. The following code shows this in action:

```
<trace enabled="true" requestLimit="10" pageOutput="false"
traceMode="SortByTime" localOnly="true" />
```

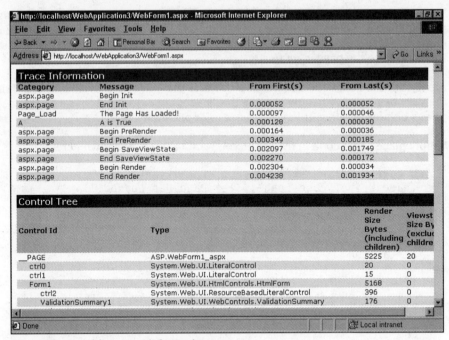

Figure 42-3: Adding trace information

Category	Message	From First(s)	From Last(s)
aspx.page	Begin Init		
aspx.page	End Init	0.000079	0.000079
Page_Load	The Page Has Loaded!	0.001298	0.001219
A	A is True	0.001371	0.000074
aspx.page	Begin PreRender	0.001419	0.000048

Figure 42-4: Trace.Warn enabled

Summary

In this chapter, you learned a new way of debugging your Web applications. You can use the trace feature to follow information easily as it moves from page to page. Trace logs track information so that you can monitor it and optimize your applications based on the results.

✦   ✦   ✦

Security

by Bill Evjen

You're more than likely to build pages to which you want to restrict access. Not every Web page or application is built for the public. Many applications are built for a selected audience. Some examples of this include intranets, extranets, and subscription-based sites.

There are many ways to keep certain individuals out of an application but let certain other individuals in. This chapter doesn't cover all the ways to do this, but it does get into a few of the more popular ones that you might use in your application development.

Authentication and Authorization

The way to make security work in your applications is with authentication and authorization. Each one plays an important role in the development of the security model that you build into your site.

Authentication

Authentication is the process of determining the identity of the user. Once the user has been authenticated, you can use his identity to determine if he has *authorization* to proceed.

You can really never authorize a user to proceed to the resource if you haven't applied an authentication program to the process. There are different means of obtaining authentication, and some of them are better than others. The ones you use within your applications should directly reflect upon the level of security that you want to achieve.

There are many different modes of authentication to use within your applications. Some of these modes include basic authentication, digest authentication, forms authentication, Passport, Integrated Windows authentication (such as NTLM or Kerberos), or authentication methods that you might develop yourself.

One of the more standard ways to authenticate users is to ask for a login and password. Asking for two pieces of information from the user before he can proceed is usually a secure method of authenticating the user. Or you can ask for a single password that's the same for all users. For instance, let's say you're building a Web site for a private club that wants to allow only club members to have access. You can require every member to use a login and password to access the site, but you can also just use a one-word password that everyone uses to gain access. Either way is fine, as long as the user is authenticated.

The `web.config` file has three different authentication modules that you can use in the development of your Web applications:

✦ Windows

✦ Forms

✦ Passport

Table 43-1 describes the differences in these forms of authentication.

Table 43-1
Authentication Providers

Authentication Provider	Description
Windows	Windows authentication is used together with IIS authentication. Authentication is performed by IIS in the following ways: basic, digest, or Integrated Windows Authentication. When IIS authentication is complete, ASP.NET uses the authenticated identity to authorize access.
Forms	Requests that are *not* authenticated requests are redirected to an HTML form using HTTP client-side redirection. The user provides his login information and submits the form. If the application authenticates the request, the system issues a form that contains the credentials or a key for reacquiring the identity.
Passport	A centralized authentication service provided by Microsoft that offers a single login and core profile services for member sites.

Change the setting of the authentication provider within the `web.config` file itself, as shown here:

```
<authentication mode="Windows|Forms|Passport|None" />
```

Notice that four possible choices are used in determining the mode of authentication. The default setting is Windows.

Windows-based authentication

Windows-based authentication exists between the Windows server and the client's browser. Windows-based authentication goes to IIS to provide the authentication module. Using this kind of authentication is quite useful in an intranet environment, where you can let the server deal with the authentication process.

Windows-based authentication first tries to use the user's credentials from the domain login. If this fails, it then pops up a dialog box so the user can re-enter his login information. When Windows-based authentication is used, the user's password isn't passed from the client to the server. If a user has logged on as a domain user on a local computer, the user won't need to be authenticated again when accessing a network computer in that domain.

The next step is to configure the sample application so that it uses a Windows-based authentication system. Before doing so, play around a little with creating users and groups. You use these users and groups to give access to the application to only the people that you specify in your `web.config` file.

Creating users

Follow these steps to create users on the local server:

1. Within Windows 2000 Professional, open up the Computer Management utility (Start ➪ Control Panel ➪ Administrative Tools ➪ Computer Management). You can also open up the utility by right-clicking on the My Computer icon on your desktop and choosing Manage.

Note   The Computer Management utility manages and controls resources on the local or remote servers. There are many things that you can do within the Computer Management utility, but you want to focus on creating users. Open up the Local Users and Groups branch.

After expanding this branch, two folders are displayed, Users and Groups.

2. Right-click on the Users folder and select New User, as shown in Figure 43-1. The New User dialog box appears (see Figure 43-2).

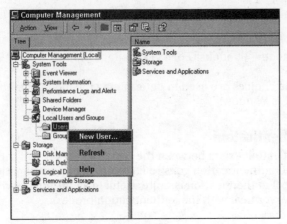

Figure 43-1: Selecting a new user

Figure 43-2: Give the user a name in this dialog box.

3. Give the user a name, such as Jdoe. You can provide his full name and description.

4. Give the user a password and uncheck the User must change password at next logon check box. This is just a test on your part, but it's best to force the user to do this when you create a real user in the system.

5. Once you've filled in all the necessary information, click Create. Your user now appears in the list of users in the Computer Management utility.

Authenticating and authorizing a user

Next, arrange for IIS to authenticate users once you provide the *authorizations* based upon these authentications. In order to accomplish this, open up the web.config file and change some of the application settings within the file. You find the web.config file within the root directory of your application. Once it's open, navigate down to the <authentication> node. Directly after this node, place the following code:

```
<identity impersonate="true" />
```

It doesn't need to be directly after the <authentication> node, but it's shown that way here for file readability. They're related in terms of the functionality you're working with now.

This code changes the impersonate attribute to true so that you don't have to deal with authentication and authorization issues in the ASP.NET application code. Instead, you're relying on IIS to either authenticate the user and pass an authenticated token to the ASP.NET application or, if it's unable to authenticate the user, pass an unauthenticated token.

Next, change the <authorization> node to suit your needs. The authorization element allows for two subelements, <allow> and <deny>. You can have as many of these two subelements within the authorization element as you see fit.

Both the <allow> and <deny> nodes can contain the attributes users, roles, and verbs. users specifies individual users to allow or deny access to the application, roles is for groups, and verbs specifies how the user came to the application. (Groups are discussed in the next section.) This chapter won't be showing any examples using the verbs attribute, but basically, you can allow or deny users based on whether they came to the application using GET, POST, HEAD, or DEBUG methods.

For example, let's say you've created the user, Jdoe, and now you want to allow Jdoe to access the application. Before you do that, make it so that nobody can gain access. Add the <identity impersonate="true" /> line of code, as you were instructed earlier, and change the <authorization> node so that it reads as follows:

```
<authorization>
  <deny users="*" />
</authorization>
```

A "*" refers to all users, and a "?" refers to anonymous users. So you just instructed the application to deny all users, even if they're authenticated.

Next, type in the URL. You're asked to log on to the application, even though nobody is allowed (see Figure 43-3). You're given three chances to type in your login information.

Because you're not letting any user access the application after the third try, you're informed that you were denied access (see Figure 43-4).

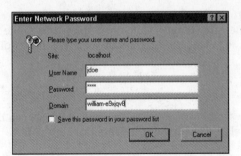

Figure 43-3: Request to log on to the application

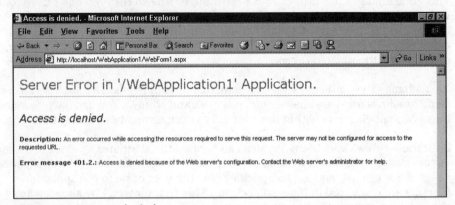

Figure 43-4: Access denied

You've now successfully locked out everyone, but this is usually never the case. You'll tend to want to let people into the application, even if it's only yourself.

Back in the web.config file, within the <authorization> node, you can allow your user Jdoe to access the application by adding an <allow> subnode to the document:

```
<authorization>
  <allow users="william-e9xjqv8\jdoe" />
  <deny users="*" />
</authorization>
```

Remember to replace william-e9xjqv8 with the name of your own computer domain. Remember that if you changed the web.config file to allow Jdoe, you have to be logged into the computer as Jdoe. Refreshing the browser page allows you to gain access to the application instantly.

Note   To add multiple users, separate them with commas.

Creating groups

Creating groups is just as easy as it was to create a user:

1. Open up the Computer Management utility by right-clicking on the My Computer icon on your desktop and choosing Manage.

2. Right-click on the Groups folder under Local Users and Groups. Select New Group. This is shown in Figure 43-5. You're presented with the New Group dialog box, shown in Figure 43-6.

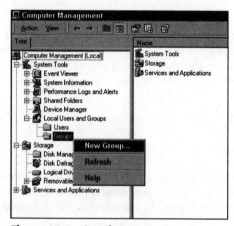

Figure 43-5: Creating a new group

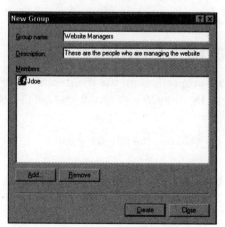

Figure 43-6: New Group dialog box

3. Give your group a descriptive name and a description.

4. To add members to the group, click the Add button and select a user from the list. Select as many members for the group as you wish. After you're finished, click the Create button.

Authenticating and authorizing a group

Now you're going to change the settings in the web.config file to authorize your group to access the application. IIS authenticates your user and makes sure that the user belongs to the group.

For example, let's say you've created the user, Jdoe, and added Jdoe to the group Website Managers. You now want to allow Website Managers to access the application. Add the `<identity impersonate="true" />` line of code as you were instructed earlier, and change the `<authorization>` node so that it reads as follows:

```
<authorization>
  <allow roles="william-e9xjqv8\Website Managers" />
  <deny users="*" />
</authorization>
```

Remember to change the domain name so that it's the same as the domain name on your computer. If you are not part of a domain, you need to include the computer name. You can add more groups to the list by separating them with commas.

When Jdoe logs onto the site, the server authenticates Jdoe, checks that he is a member of the Website Manager group, and then grants him access to the application.

Accessing Authentication Properties

It's possible to access authentication properties and use them within your code. For instance, directly in the code, it's possible to access the user's login name and find out if he's an authenticated user.

To check the user's login name, you would use the following code:

```
Dim UserName As String
UserName = User.Identity.Name
```

To check if the user is authenticated, use the following code:

```
Dim UserAuth As Boolean
UserAuth = User.Identity.IsAuthenticated
```

This returns True if the user is authenticated and False if he's not. One example is to use this statement directly in an `If Then` clause, as shown here:

```
If User.Identity.IsAuthenticated Then
    ' do something
Else
    ' do something else
End If
```

You can use the `WindowsIdentity` object to get more information about the user's login credentials. First you need to create a reference to the `System.Security.Principal` namespace, and then you can create your `WindowsIdentity` object. Listing 43-1 is an example of this process.

Listing 43-1: **Web Form1.aspx**

```
<%@ Import Namespace="System.Security.Principal" %>
<html>
  <head>
        <title>WindowsIdentity</title>

    <script language="vb" runat="server">

    Sub Page_Load(sender As Object, e As EventArgs)

    Dim UserIdentity = CType(User.Identity, WindowsIdentity)
    Dim UserCurIdentity = UserIdentity.GetCurrent()
    Label1.Text = "Name: " & UserCurIdentity.Name & "<br>" & _
        "AuthenticationType: " & _
        UserCurIdentity.AuthenticationType & "<br>" & _
"IsAnonymous: " & UserCurIdentity.IsAnonymous & _
        "<br>" & _
"IsAuthenticated: " & _
        UserCurIdentity.IsAuthenticated & "<br>" & _
        "IsGuest: " & UserCurIdentity.IsGuest & "<br>" & _
        "IsSystem: " & UserCurIdentity.IsSystem & "<br>"
    End Sub

    </script>

  </head>
  <body>

        <form id="Form1" method="post" runat="server">
                <asp:label id="label1" runat="server" />
        </form>

  </body>
</html>
```

Implementing the code in Listing 43-1 imported the `System.Security.Principal` namespace at the top of the page and then created an instance of the `WindowsIdentity` object. You related the current user session to this object. The listing then displayed information about the current user's credentials, such as if the user was authenticated, anonymous, a guest account, or a system account, as well as the user's authentication type and login name. This is shown in Figure 43-7.

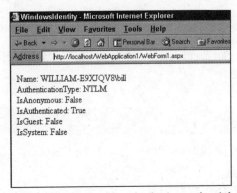

Figure 43-7: Checking the login credentials

Performing Forms-Based Authentication

Another popular way to authenticate and authorize users to have access to application resources is to have them type in their credentials into HTML forms. When a user attempts to enter the application but is unauthenticated, he's redirected to a specified login page. Here he can type in his username and password to get authenticated. Once he's authenticated, the user receives a HTTP cookie to use on subsequent requests.

To activate forms-based authentication, you first need to change the `web.config` file as follows:

```
<authentication mode="Forms">
        <forms name="MyForm" path="/" loginUrl="login.aspx"
        protection="ALL" timeout="30">

        <credentials passwordFormat="Clear">
                <user name="Jdoe" password="Password" />
                <user name="Bill" password="Obiwan" />
        </credentials>

        </forms>
</authentication>
```

```
<authorization>
      <allow users="Jdoe, Bill" />
      <deny users="?" />
</authorization>
```

The preceding code changed the mode of the authentication to Forms within the Mode attribute. This allows you to use a couple of new elements within the web. config file. The first is the forms element, shown here:

```
<forms name="name" loginUrl="url"
    protection="All|None|Encryption|Validation"
    timeout="30" path="/" >
```

The attributes of the forms element are defined as follows:

✦ name — This is the name that is assigned to the cookie. The default value is .ASPXAUTH.

✦ loginUrl — Specifies the URL to which the request is redirected for login if no valid authentication cookie is found. The default value is default.aspx.

✦ protection — Specifies the amount of protection you want to apply to the cookie. There are four available settings: All, None, Encryption, and Validation.

✦ All — Specifies that the application uses both data validation and encryption to protect the cookie. All is the default (and recommended) value.

✦ None — Applies no encryption to the cookie. This isn't the best setting to use, but it could be used for personalization and for settings that don't require any amount of true security. This option is the least resource-intensive of the four choices.

✦ Encryption — This is a setting where the cookie is encrypted but data validation isn't performed on it. Cookies used in this way might be subject to chosen plain text attacks.

✦ Validation — This is the opposite of Encryption. Data validation is performed, but the cookie is not encrypted.

✦ path — Specifies the path for cookies issued by the application. In most cases you want to use "/", which is the default setting.

✦ timeout — Specifies the amount of time, in minutes, after which the cookie expires. The default value is 30.

The form element can take one subelement, <credentials>. This element allows you to specify valid user/password pairs that allow access to the application through the forms-based authentication process.

The <credentials> element takes one attribute, passwordFormat. This attribute allows you to specify the format in which the password is stored. The options are Clear, MD5, and SHA1. Table 43-2 lists the password formats that are available to use within ASP.NET.

Password Format	Description
Clear	Passwords are stored in clear text. The user password is compared directly to this value without further transformation.
MD5	Passwords are stored using a Message Digest 5 (MD5) hash digest. When credentials are validated, the user password is hashed using the MD5 algorithm and compared for equality with this value. The clear-text password is never stored or compared when using this value. This algorithm produces better performance than SHA1.
SHA1	Passwords are stored using the SHA1 hash digest. When credentials are validated, the user password is hashed using the SHA1 algorithm and compared for equality with this value. The clear-text password is never stored or compared when using this value. Use this algorithm for best security.

Table 43-2
Password Formats

Then, using a user element, store the user's name and password to use within the authentication process. Within the authorization process, specify the users that are allowed into the application after authentication. You also want to deny all unauthenticated users, forcing users to log on with their credentials. Do this by using the question mark (?), a symbol for unauthenticated users.

Now build the first of two pages that you need (see Listing 43-2).

Listing 43-2: Default.aspx

```
<html>
  <head>
        <title>Welcome!</title>
  </head>

  <body>
  Welcome <%= User.Identity.Name %><br>
  You used the authentication type of
  <%= User.Identity.AuthenticationType %>
  to access the site.
  </body>

</html>
```

This is the main page of your application and the page that the users are directed to after they've been authenticated to access the site. Once they're authenticated and forwarded to this page, you give them a little introduction and print some of their login credentials to the screen.

Now let's take a look at your login page. See Listing 43-3.

Listing 43-3: **Login.aspx**

```
<html>
  <head>
    <title>Login Page</title>

    <script language="vb" runat="server">
    Sub LoginUser(sender As Object, e As EventArgs)
     If FormsAuthentication.Authenticate(TextBox1.
          Text,TextBox2.Text) Then


FormsAuthentication.RedirectFromLoginPage(TextBox1.
          Text,False)


        Else

          Label1.Visible = True
          Label1.Text = "Invalid Login ... Please Re-Enter!"

        End If
End Sub
  </script>

  </head>

  <body>

    <form id="Form1" method="post" runat="server">
        <p>Username:
        <asp:TextBox id=TextBox1 runat="server">
        </asp:TextBox>
        </p>
        <p>Password:
        <asp:TextBox id=TextBox2 textmode="Password"
        runat="server">
        </asp:TextBox>
        </p>
        <p>
        <asp:Button id=Button1 runat="server" Text="Submit"
        onclick="LoginUser">
        </asp:Button>
        </p>
```

Continued

Listing 43-3 *(continued)*

```
        <p>
        <asp:Label id=Label1 runat="server" Visible="False">
        </asp:Label>
        </p>
    </form>

    </body>
</html>
```

The login page has a traditional login interface. It contains a place for the user to enter his username and password (see Figure 43-8). If he types in the wrong credentials, you tell him by attributing text to a Label control and making the text visible in the browser.

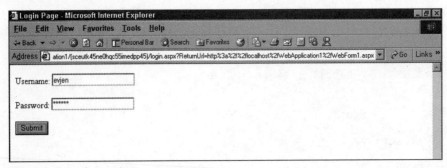

Figure 43-8: The Login.aspx page

On the `submit button click` event, ask if the user is authenticated. If he is, redirect him to the page that he's calling. The `FormsAuthentication.RedirectFromLoginPage` method takes two arguments. The first argument is the name of the user for cookie authentication purposes. This argument doesn't need to map to an account name and is used by URL Authorization. The second argument specifies whether or not a durable cookie (one that is saved across browser sessions) should be issued.

All these examples have been great, but what if you have thousands of users who want to access the application? Putting all their names and passwords in the `web.config` file won't work. (Well, it would work, but you would have to spend a significant time entering all those users into the file!) The best option, of course, is to store all the usernames and passwords in a database and look to that database when the user types in his credentials.

First, create a table in Microsoft Access that stores your usernames and passwords (see Figure 43-9).

AccessTable : Table

	ID	UserName	Password
▸	1	evjen	obiwan
	2	quilogy	firm
	3	henri	test
	4	sofia	test
*	(AutoNumber)		

Figure 43-9: A sample table of usernames and passwords

Then use the same default page from the previous example, but redo the `Login.aspx` page so that it looks to an Access table to authenticate the user (see Listing 43-4).

Listing 43-4: **Login2.aspx That Connects to Access**

```
<%@ Import Namespace="System.Data.Oledb" %>
<%@ Import Namespace="System.Data" %>

<html>
  <head>
    <title>Login Page</title>

    <script language="vb" runat="server">
         Sub LoginUser(sender As Object, e As EventArgs)
            Dim blnUserAuthenticated As Boolean = False

            Dim strConn as string =
            "PROVIDER=Microsoft.Jet.OLEDB.4.0;DATA SOURCE=" & _
            Server.Mappath("db1.mdb") & ";"
            Dim strSQL as string =
            "Select Password from AccessTable Where Username ='" & _
            TextBox1.Text & "' And Password = '" & TextBox2.Text & "'"
           Dim Conn as New OLEDBConnection(strConn)
           Dim Cmd as New OLEDBCommand(strSQL,Conn)
           Conn.Open()

           Dim ObjDataReader As OleDbDataReader
           objDataReader = Cmd.ExecuteReader()

           If objDataReader.Read() Then
               blnUserAuthenticated = True
           End If

           If blnUserAuthenticated Then

           FormsAuthentication.RedirectFromLoginPage(TextBox1.Text, False)
```

Continued

Listing 43-4 *(continued)*

```
            Else
                Label1.Visible = True
                Label1.Text =
                "Invalid Login ... Please Re-Enter!"
            End If
        End Sub
    </script>
</head>
    <body>

        <form id="Form1" method="post" runat="server">
            <p>Username:
            <asp:TextBox id=TextBox1 runat="server">
            </asp:TextBox>
            </p>
            <p>Password:
            <asp:TextBox id=TextBox2 runat="server" textmode="Password">
            </asp:TextBox>
            </p>
            <p>
            <asp:Button id=Button1 runat="server" Text="Submit"
            onclick="LoginUser">
            </asp:Button>
            </p>
            <p>
            <asp:Label id=Label1 runat="server" Visible="False">
            </asp:Label>
            </p>
        </form>

    </body>
</html>
```

The beginning of the Login2.aspx file imports the namespaces required to connect to the Access table, as shown here:

```
<%@ Import Namespace="System.Data.Oledb" %>
<%@ Import Namespace="System.Data" %>
```

Then, on the button click event, you connect to the table AccessTable and check to see if there's a username/password pair that match what the user has entered in the text boxes. Next, you use the DataReader to see if there's at least some data that has been returned, as shown here:

```
Dim ObjDataReader As OleDbDataReader
objDataReader = Cmd.ExecuteReader()
```

```
If objDataReader.Read() Then
   blnUserAuthenticated = True
End If
```

If there's a match, you execute your statement in the If Then clause and make your user authentication variable true. Then you can run through an If Then clause that allows the user to continue on his way if the authentication variable is set to true. If it's false, the user stays on the login page and can't proceed.

Summary

This chapter covered everything you need to get started securing the applications that you build and maintain. You learned about various authentication and authorization models, such as Windows-based and Forms-based authentication, and how to protect your site from unwanted visitors. Also covered was how to use authentication properties within your applications and how to authorize users and groups based on data in a database.

In most situations, security in Web applications is very important. Sometimes you want to lock down applications and keep them off-limits to all but certain selected individuals. Authentication and authorization of the users is a vital step in this process, and it's possible to authenticate in a number of different ways. This chapter showed you a couple of the more popular ways, but you should explore other opportunities that are available.

✦   ✦   ✦

Web Services

Introduction to Web Services

by Jim Chandler

This chapter covers some of the limitations of today's Internet as a backbone for application integration, and how Web Services promise to be an effective platform for delivering the next generation of distributed, integrated applications to the Web. It discusses the fundamental elements of Web Services and the infrastructure that enables them to be built and consumed. Finally, it explains some of the Web Services being planned by Microsoft, which you can use in your own Web Service implementations.

The Next-Generation Internet

The next generation of the Internet is upon us. Many talented and energetic people are working very hard to deliver the infrastructure that will make the Internet a platform for doing business in ways that were unimaginable only a few years ago. This Internet of the future holds great potential for allowing businesses to collaborate and integrate data and applications as never before. It promises to pull together islands of information into a transparently coordinated whole and deliver that information to all kinds of devices, including cell phones, personal digital assistants, handheld devices, laptops, pagers, and others.

The heart and soul of these next-generation services are Extensible Markup Language (XML), Hypertext Transfer Protocol (HTTP), and Web Services. XML is a World Wide Web Consortium standard that permits data to be portable and self-describing, so it can be exchanged easily between applications and devices on many platforms. *Web Services* allow users to programmatically exchange structured data encoded as XML over the Internet via HTTP. You can think of Web Services as programmable URLs. Stated another way, a Web Service is an application component that can be called remotely. Thus, any system that supports these basic, standard protocols is capable of supporting Web Services.

Understanding the Need for Web Services

Web Services solve a basic but pervasive problem that many of us experience with today's Internet. Although there are literally billions of pages of useful data and information on the Web, it's typically difficult to extract, examine, and use that data programmatically. Much of this difficulty arises from the fact that the Web (at least as it exists today) is designed for human consumption. Consequently, data is presented in a form that's easy for people to read but relatively difficult and error-prone for applications to read and process reliably.

As an example, many e-commerce sites need to calculate shipping charges based on a variety of shipping options. Typically, such a site might maintain a set of database tables that describe the shipping options and charges for each shipping company. Obviously, this can become a time-consuming process because the data is likely to change often and someone must update the tables repeatedly.

A more sophisticated approach might incorporate a process called *screen scraping*, which analyzes the data in a page for certain patterns and extracts this data for further processing. Suppose that one of the shipping companies maintains a Web site that conveniently lists the various shipping options and associated charges. By using screen scraping, a program can examine the Web page and extract the shipping information from that page.

At first glance, this might appear to be an effective solution. In fact, it's used relatively frequently and with some success today. But what happens if the Web master at the shipping company decides to change the layout or otherwise reformat the data on the page? This might be necessary if a new shipping option is introduced, for example. Suddenly and unexpectedly, your screen scraper may no longer be able to locate the data that you need.

Now, let's say this same e-commerce site programmatically calls a Web Service provided by the shipping company on their Web site. It automatically calculates shipping costs based on the shipping method and package weight that you specify in your request and returns the resulting charge to you in real time.

While this is admittedly a simple example, it clearly illustrates the power and potential of Web Services to transform the Web from a passive, interactive information display medium into a platform for truly distributed computing. Essentially, Web Services extend the capabilities of classic distributed applications and services to the heterogeneous platform that is the Internet.

Of course, there are many other potentially valuable applications of Web Services. Some examples of these services include the following:

✦ **Credit card validation, financial account management, stock quotes, and so on**. These are services that might be too difficult or too expensive to implement yourself.

✦ **User authentication, usage billing, usage auditing, and so on**. These services provide commonly needed functionality for other services.

✦ **Travel booking**. This type of service aggregates distributed, discrete services into an orchestrated whole.

✦ **Accounts receivable, accounts payable, invoicing, purchase orders, and so on**. These services provide the ability to integrate your business systems with your partners (or other business systems within your own organization).

Packaging application code into reusable components that can be called across process and machine boundaries isn't a new concept. Today, we have technologies such as the Component Object Model (COM), the Common Object Request Broker Architecture (CORBA), Internet Inter-ORB Protocol (IIOP) and Remote Method Invocation (RMI), to name a few. A key limitation of these technologies is that they're not easily interoperable between the tremendous number of heterogeneous systems that make up the Internet. This is due, in part, to dependencies on particular operating systems, programming languages, or object-model-specific protocols. Consequently, this limits their effectiveness as standard methods for programming the Web. Clearly, what's needed for Web Services to succeed on the Internet is a platform that doesn't depend on a specific operating system, object model, or programming language.

What sets Web Services apart from these prior-generation middleware technologies is that they're built upon widely accepted Internet standards that can interoperate seamlessly across the Web. Web Services use a text-based messaging model to communicate, allowing them to operate effectively on many different platforms.

If you're familiar with creating and consuming COM components to create distributed applications, you'll find creating and consuming Web Services a natural extrapolation of what you already know. The remainder of Part VII of *VB .NET Bible* will give you a solid introduction to the technologies for building and consuming Web Services.

As this book is being written, major platform and software vendors (including Microsoft, IBM, Sun, Hewlett Packard, and others) have all begun delivering technologies and tools that enable software developers to easily create Web Services on those platforms. Here we'll be concerned with creating Web Services by using the Microsoft .NET Framework, Visual Basic .NET, and Visual Studio .NET.

Basic Elements of Web Services

Now that you have an idea of what Web Services are and how they can be used, let's examine the key technologies that you'll encounter when working with Web Services.

Microsoft provides an excellent platform for building and consuming Web Services with the .NET Framework, which virtually eliminates the need to learn about the "plumbing" involved in building and consuming Web Services. If things worked right all the time, there would be no need to even discuss this plumbing. But of course, things don't always work right, so it's useful to have a basic understanding of the foundation upon which Web Services are built.

Note This section won't go into excruciating detail in describing any of these technologies. The only goal here is to give you enough knowledge to effectively troubleshoot any problems you might encounter when working with Web Services.

The key to the broad-reaching capabilities of Web Services on the Internet is a software infrastructure built on Internet standards that doesn't rely on any platform-specific technology. This infrastructure supplies standards-based services that provide the following capabilities to Web Services:

✦ Describing data in a structured, portable manner

✦ Communicating requests and responses by means of an extensible message format

✦ Describing the capabilities of Web Services

✦ Discovering available Web Services

✦ Determining which sites provide Web Services

The following sections will help you to understand why these issues are important and will introduce you to the technologies that provide these capabilities to the Web Services platform.

Describing data

Web Services enable consumers to programmatically request and obtain structured data. But how is this data encoded so that it can be exchanged between service and consumer? How do you ensure a consistent and accurate interpretation of the data when the service and consumer may reside on different platforms, operating systems, object models, and/or programming languages?

To enable Web Services to communicate their data unambiguously, efficiently, and effectively, you must use a common, portable, and standard method for describing data. The simple (and logical) answer is XML.

XML is used extensively in every aspect of Web Services. It's a standards-based method for describing data (also known as metadata). XML can describe data by using a simple grammar that is highly interoperable between the many heterogeneous systems that are connected to the Internet. Using the basic elements of the XML language, you can describe both simple and complex data types and relationships.

XML has several key strengths that have helped it to become the de facto method for describing data (especially compared to HTML and other binary formats). These include the following:

✦ It's a text-based language, which makes it easily readable and more portable than binary data formats.

✦ You can define your own tags to describe data and its relationships to other data (hence the word "extensible" in its name).

✦ It strictly enforces its language syntax, unlike HTML.

✦ Parsers are widely available to accurately parse and validate XML structures that you define, which means you don't have to do it yourself!

The following sections briefly examine the syntax and structure of XML documents.

XML syntax and document structure

XML is a markup language that, at first glance, looks very much like HTML. In fact, XML and HTML are both derived from the Standard Generalized Markup Language (SGML). Like HTML, XML uses a set of human-readable tags and declarations to create a document. The major difference is in the meanings implied by these tags and declarations. Whereas HTML is concerned with describing how to format information on a page, XML is concerned with describing data and its relationships to other data.

XML uses tags enclosed in angle brackets (<>) to define elements that form element structures and hierarchies within an XML document. An XML document consists of a prolog, document elements, and optional attributes that model a logically related set of data. An invoice is one example of such an information model. The prolog contains information that applies to the document as a whole, and it appears at the top of the document before the first document tag. The prolog usually contains information about the character encoding and document structure, as well as other possible information. XML parsers use the prolog to correctly interpret the contents of an XML document.

The following example is a simple XML document that describes the weather conditions in the city of St. Louis:

```
<?xml version="1.0" encoding="UTF-8"?>
<weather>
  <location city="St. Louis, MO USA">
    <forecast date="2001-07-15">
<temperature units="F">80</temperature>
      <humidity units="%">55</humidity>
      <skies>Cloudy, 40% chance of showers</skies>
</forecast>
  </location>
</weather>
```

This example describes the weather conditions in St. Louis, Missouri. The indentation applied to elements isn't required, but it makes reading the document and understanding the relationship between elements easier.

You can see that the `<weather>` element serves as a container for a collection of city-based weather conditions (in this case, for St. Louis). The weather conditions for a specific city are contained within a `<location>` element. Within the `<location>` element are child elements that describe a date-based weather forecast.

Note that several of the elements contain a `"units"` attribute. In XML, attributes are used to further describe or qualify information related to the element in which they are contained. In this example, the `"units"` attribute is used to define the numeric units of the air temperature described by the `<temperature>` element. Other examples of attributes are `"city"` and `"date"`.

As this simple example shows, XML lets you define your own tags for describing data. The XML standard does *not* define the meaning of the `<weather>` tag. It will, however, enforce the grammatical rules, which are required to create a well-formed XML document.

Specifically, when you're creating an XML document, it's very important that you follow these basic rules:

> ✦ All elements must have an end tag.
>
> ✦ All elements must be cleanly nested (no overlapping).
>
> ✦ All attribute values must be enclosed in quotation marks.
>
> ✦ Each document must have a unique first element (the document root).

Unlike HTML, syntax errors and other mistakes in an XML document will cause the XML parser to halt processing of the document. This is important because you're relying on XML to accurately describe your data. When dealing with data, there's no room for the ambiguities and loose interpretation that HTML allows in its syntax.

XML namespaces

When you're developing XML documents, it's common to refer to element and attribute names that share a common context as a *vocabulary*. Thus, you might say that your previous example XML document belongs to a weather vocabulary.

Given that an XML document consists of a vocabulary that you define, an element or attribute in that vocabulary may have a name that's identical to an element or attribute used by someone else in a different vocabulary. What's worse, what if someone else also defined a weather vocabulary that used some of the same names, but whose elements meant something quite different or arranged the elements in a different hierarchy?

Let's take the case of the fictional weather example in the preceding section. The `<temperature>` element you used to define the current air temperature might also be used to define the temperature of a liquid or the surface temperature on Mars. How do you distinguish one type of temperature from another? Or, stated another way, how do you determine the vocabulary to which the `<temperature>` element belongs?

XML solves this ambiguity problem by referencing an explicit *namespace* in elements and attributes of an XML document. A namespace associates a unique name with all the elements and attributes of a particular XML vocabulary. An XML namespace is declared by using the `xmlns` attribute.

For example, you can slightly change the weather example as follows:

```
<?xml version="1.0" encoding="UTF-8"?>
<weather xmlns="http://mydomain.com/xml/weather">
   <location city="St. Louis, MO">
     <forecast date="2001-07-15">
<temperature units="F">80</temperature>
        <humidity units="%">55</humidity>
        <skies>Cloudy, 40% chance of showers</skies>
</forecast>
   </location>
</weather>
```

In this example, the `<weather>` element includes a namespace declaration specified by the standard `xmlns` attribute. This defines a namespace by using a URI with the name `"http://mydomain.com/xml/weather"` for the `<weather>` element and all of the elements contained within.

It's worth pointing out here that the Uniform Resource Identifier (URI) used to define the namespace can be a completely abstract name. This is unlike a URL, which serves as a pointer to a physical endpoint or resource. The URI is simply a method to differentiate your weather vocabulary from all others. Therefore, typically you'll want to define namespaces by using names that you own or have control over.

Generally, Internet domain names are used because they're already guaranteed to be unique (and also identify the entity defining the namespace). But when you're using the XML Schema Definition language (XSD), this URI can point to the XSD file, which defines the schema for the XML document. The fundamental features of XSD are covered later in this chapter under "The XSD schema."

You can use a default declaration for a namespace (as in the example), or you can specify an explicit declaration. A *default declaration* defines a namespace whose scope includes all elements contained within the element where the declaration was specified. Typically, a default declaration is used when a document contains elements from a single namespace. The weather example used a default namespace declaration because all the elements shared the same context or vocabulary (that is, none of the elements referred to elements from other namespaces).

An *explicit declaration* defines a shorthand reference to an existing namespace. This method is used when referencing an element or attribute from other namespaces. For example, you could combine the elements from several namespaces into another XML document by using explicit namespace declaration, as follows:

```
<weather:temperature
    xmlns:weather="http://md.com/xml/weather">
  80
</weather:temperature>
<liquid:temperature
    xmlns:liquid="http://md.com/xml/liquid">
  150
</liquid:temperature>
```

The name preceding the colon is called the *prefix*. It serves as a shorthand notation so that references to the actual namespace URI don't need to be repeated every-where an element or attribute is used within the document. Instead, you simply use the prefix to refer to the namespace. The only requirement for the shorthand name is that it must be unique within the context of the document that you're using.

Using namespaces in this way eliminates naming conflicts and guarantees that any two elements that have the same name must come from the same vocabulary. For example, the weather temperature is clearly distinguished from the liquid temperature.

You'll find explicit namespace declarations used in many places within the XML documents that are an integral part of the Web Services architecture.

The XSD schema

Recall that the XML parser uses strict rules to ensure that the XML document is well-formed. Also remember that a well-formed XML document follows the rules for properly closing tags, nesting tags, enclosing attributes in quotes, and using a unique first element. But this doesn't address the issue of validating that an XML document contains the proper assortment of elements and that they're in valid combinations. What's needed is a language that will allow a generic XML parser to determine that the document conforms to these additional user-defined rules.

The XML Schema Definition language (XSD) defines rules for describing the valid combinations and relationships of elements, attributes, and types that can appear in an XML document. This enables authors as well as consumers to validate that the document is formed correctly according to the schema definition.

An XSD schema document contains a top-level schema element. The schema element must define the XML schema namespace, as in the following:

```
<xsd:schema xmlns:xsd="http://www.w3.org/2001/XMLSchema">
```

The `schema` element contains type definitions and element/attribute declarations. XSD allows you to use built-in data types (such as `integer` and `string`) as well as user-defined data types when specifying the valid types of data that can be specified for particular elements in the schema definition. To define the elements and attributes for an XML grammar, you use the `element` and `attribute` tags.

In addition to the built-in types, user-defined types are built by using the `simpleType` and `complexType` tags. All elements that contain child elements and attributes are defined as complex types. Simple types can be represented purely as strings (they have no elements or attributes) and are used to describe the children of attributes and text-only elements.

To illustrate these features of the XSD language, let's examine the schema definition for the sample weather XML document that you have seen in previous examples. This schema is shown in Listing 44-1.

Listing 44-1: **XSD Schema for the Weather Forecast Grammar**

```xml
<?xml version="1.0" encoding="utf-8"?>
<xsd:schema xmlns:xsd="http://www.w3.org/2001/XMLSchema">

    <xsd:element name="skies" type="xsd:string" />
    <xsd:attribute name="city" type="xsd:string" />
    <xsd:attribute name="units" type="xsd:string" />
    <xsd:attribute name="date" type="xsd:date" />

    <xsd:element name="temperature">
        <xsd:complexType>
            <xsd:attribute ref="units" />
        </xsd:complexType>
    </xsd:element>
```

Continued

Listing 44-1 *(continued)*

```
        <xsd:element name="humidity">
            <xsd:complexType>
                <xsd:attribute ref="units" />
            </xsd:complexType>
        </xsd:element>

        <xsd:element name="forecast">
            <xsd:complexType>
                <xsd:all>
                    <xsd:element ref="temperature" />
                    <xsd:element ref="humidity" />
                    <xsd:element ref="skies" />
                </xsd:all>
                <xsd:attribute ref="date" />
            </xsd:complexType>
        </xsd:element>

        <xsd:element name="location">
            <xsd:complexType>
                <xsd:all>
                    <xsd:element ref="forecast"
                        minOccurs="1" maxOccurs="unbounded" />
                </xsd:all>
                <xsd:attribute ref="city" />
            </xsd:complexType>
        </xsd:element>

        <xsd:element name="weather">
            <xsd:complexType>
                <xsd:all>
                    <xsd:element ref="location"
                        minOccurs="1" maxOccurs="unbounded" />
                </xsd:all>
            </xsd:complexType>
        </xsd:element>

    </xsd:schema>
```

The schema begins by declaring the `<xsd:schema>` root element.

The next several lines of the schema declare simple type elements and attributes, such as the `<skies>` element and the `<city>` attribute. As in regular programming, it is good practice to declare variables before they are referenced. This same practice is followed in defining XML schemas. All elements, whether simple or complex, should have their constituent types declared before they are referenced by other element declarations.

Following the simple type declarations are the complex type declarations, indicated by the `<complexType>` tag. The first of these is the `<temperature>` element declaration. Recall that any elements that contain attributes or other elements are defined as complex types. Because the `<temperature>` element has an associated `"units"` attribute, the declaration uses the `<complexType>` tag to form the declaration of this element. This same structure is used to declare the `<humidity>` element as well.

Note that this is the first use of the XSD schema `"ref"` attribute. This attribute is used to refer to a previously declared element in the schema. In this instance, you're referring to the `"units"` attribute that was declared earlier in the schema document.

The next part of the schema declares the `<forecast>` element. This is also a complex type declaration, as indicated by the `<complexType>` tag. The `<all>` tag indicates that the child elements can appear in any order within the `<forecast>` element.

The declaration of the `<location>` element closely resembles that of the `<forecast>` element. The major difference is the inclusion of the `"minOccurs"` and `"maxOccurs"` attributes in the declaration of the `<forecast>` element reference. These attributes control how many times a particular element can occur. The declaration states that at least one `<forecast>` element must appear within a `<location>` element. The term `"unbounded"` indicates that there is no upper limit to the number of `<forecast>` occurrences.

This brings us to the final declaration of the root `<weather>` element. As you can see, the `<weather>` element consists of at least one occurrence of a `<location>` element with no upper limit. This declaration is nearly identical to that of the `<location>` element preceding it.

By using the basic XML schema building blocks, you can describe the required vocabulary and structure for any arbitrary XML grammar and document derived from that grammar.

In the context of Web Services, given an XML document and a schema, an XML parser can validate the document against the schema and report any problems that it finds. This mechanism is a simple way to determine that a particular document conforms to a specified XML grammar. This allows Web Services to provide reliable and deterministic results when using XML to describe such items as data, service contracts, SOAP messages, and so on.

Note   Prior to XSD, the Document Type Definition language (DTD) was used to describe the valid syntax of XML documents. Unfortunately, the DTD language has several drawbacks, which makes it unsuitable for use with Web Services. If you're familiar with DTDs, you should be aware that they've been retired in favor of XSD.

In short, XML is at the heart of Web Services. As you'll soon see, XML is used to describe the data for many of the Web Service technologies. To learn more about all of the XML standards discussed in this book (as well as many others), you can visit the Worldwide Web Consortium at `www.w3.org`.

Communicating requests and responses

Web Services communicate in the form of messages. A *request message* delivers information about a function to be executed and any data required to carry out that function. Request messages flow from clients to Web Services. A *response message* delivers information about the results of the function execution. Response messages flow from Web Services to clients.

Communication via messages is an extremely effective method for insulating Web Service consumers from the implementation details of the service. Of course, it's necessary to define the rules for how these messages should be formatted and what they can contain.

The HTTP protocol is an example of a message-based request/response protocol. Specifically, the HTTP-GET and HTTP-POST protocols can be used to transport Web Service request and response messages.

Message exchange with HTTP-GET and HTTP-POST

Web Services can exchange messages by using the HTTP-GET and HTTP-POST protocol. These are standard messages of the HTTP protocol that enable the exchange of information as name/value pairs. HTTP-GET passes name/value pairs as UUencoded text appended to the URL of a request. This method of passing parameters is referred to as a *query string*. Figure 44-1 shows an example of a URL with a query string.

In the figure, a question mark separates the base URL from the list of name/value pairs. Following the ? delimiter, each name/value pair is encoded as follows:

```
Name=value
```

Multiple name/value pairs are separated by the & character. In Figure 44-1, the name/value pairs are

```
Temperature=98.6
FromUnits=F
ToUnits=C
```

HTTP-POST also passes name/value pairs as UUencoded text, except that the parameters are passed within the actual request header rather than as a query string appended to the URL. Typically, this method enables you to transport larger amounts of data. The data is encoded in the body of the request rather than as an adjunct to the URL in the form of a query string.

Tip Because HTTP-GET and HTTP-POST use name/value pairs to encode data, fewer data types can be supported than with SOAP. Generally, using SOAP will provide for more flexibility in passing complex data types such as classes, DataSets, and XML documents.

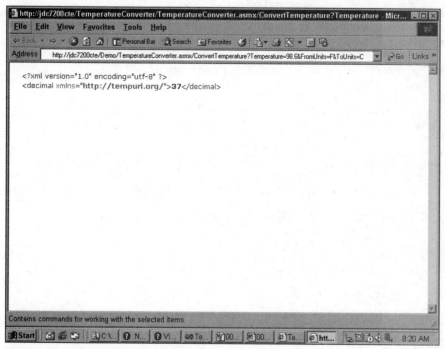

Figure 44-1: An HTTP-GET request with a query string

Message exchange with SOAP

The Simple Object Access Protocol (SOAP) is a standard message format that enables message-based communication for Web Services. SOAP implements a message format based on XML to exchange operation requests and responses. Using XML as the basis for SOAP messages makes them understandable and transportable by any system that implements basic Internet communications services.

SOAP simply defines a message format. It doesn't impose a specific transport protocol for exchanging these messages. Thus, it's possible to transport SOAP messages over many widely available transport protocols, such as HTTP, SMTP, and FTP. The HTTP POST command, however, is the default method for transporting SOAP requests and responses.

Tip SOAP uses the term *binding* when referring to a specific protocol that is used to transport SOAP messages.

A SOAP request is an HTTP POST request with a SOAP message payload, as opposed to an HTML name/value pair payload. An HTTP POST request (like all HTTP commands) consists of human-readable text that contains one or more headers followed by the command payload. The payload is separated from the headers by a blank line.

A SOAP request over HTTP uses the payload section of the HTTP POST request to contain the encoded SOAP envelope. The following code shows the structure of a simple SOAP message using HTTP POST as the transport mechanism:

```
POST /TemperatureConverter/TemperatureConverter.asmx HTTP/1.1
Host: jdc7200cte
Content-Type: text/xml; charset=utf-8
Content-Length: {length}
SOAPAction: "http://tempuri.org/ConvertTemperature"

<?xml version="1.0" encoding="utf-8"?>
<soap:Envelope xmlns:xsi="http://www.w3.org/2001/XMLSchema-instance"
               xmlns:xsd="http://www.w3.org/2001/XMLSchema"
               xmlns:soap="http://schemas.xmlsoap.org/soap/envelope/">
  <soap:Body>
    <ConvertTemperature xmlns="http://tempuri.org/">
      <Temperature>{decimal}</Temperature>
      <FromUnits>{string}</FromUnits>
      <ToUnits>{string}</ToUnits>
    </ConvertTemperature>
  </soap:Body>
</soap:Envelope>
```

As shown in this example code, SOAP messages must use the `text/xml` content type. Note that named placeholders are substituted where the SOAP message would normally contain the actual content length and specific argument values associated with the request.

The example also illustrates the basic structure of a SOAP message. The outermost element in a SOAP payload is the envelope, which encapsulates the various parts of the SOAP message. Within the envelope are elements that define SOAP headers (not present in this example), and the SOAP body, which defines the specific request or response message.

Because SOAP uses XML to encode commands and data, this message format can pass any kind of data that can be described in XML! This includes classic scalar and array data types, as well as complex document types such as invoices, purchase orders, and so on. For this reason, SOAP is the preferred method of Web Service communications, rather than the HTTP-GET and HTTP-POST protocols.

Cross-Reference   SOAP is discussed in more detail in Chapter 46. To learn more about the SOAP protocol and standard, you can visit www.soap.org or www.w3.org/soap.

Describing Web Service capabilities

Now that you have a standard method to encode data (XML) and a standard method to exchange Web Service requests and responses via messages (SOAP), you need a standard way to describe the specific message exchanges (or capabilities) that a Web Service supports. Recall that SOAP defines a message format based on XML to enable exchange of method requests and responses. But SOAP doesn't define the specific methods and results that a Web Service may offer.

If you're familiar with COM programming, you know that COM components use interfaces to describe their capabilities to a potential consumer. This is done by using a language called IDL (Interface Definition Language). Compiling an IDL file results in the creation of a Type Library (TLB). A Type Library in COM contains all of the information necessary to query the specific capabilities of the COM component (the objects, methods, attributes, events, and anything else that it supports).

Similar to the Type Library concept in COM, Web Services must have a method to tell potential consumers about the specific capabilities that the service offers. Otherwise, consumers wouldn't know how to request a particular operation of the Web Service or what to expect as a response.

A Web Service description is an XML document that defines the Web Service's capabilities. This document provides essential information in a structured form that tells a consumer how to interact with a Web Service. The Web Service Description Language (WSDL) defines a standard, extensible XML grammar that's used to define these Web Service descriptions in the form of an XML document.

The WSDL document defines the message formats and message exchange patterns that a Web Service can process. In addition to these definitions, the WSDL document contains the address of each Web Service entry point, formatted according to the protocol used to access the service (for example, a URL for HTTP or an e-mail address for SMTP).

A WSDL document defines services as a collection of network endpoints, or ports, using the XML elements listed in Table 44-1.

Table 44-1
WSDL XML Elements

Element	Description
Types	A container for data type definitions using some type system (such as XSD)
Message	An abstract, typed definition of the data being communicated
Operation	An abstract description of an action supported by the Web Service

Continued

Table 44-1 (continued)	
Element	**Description**
Port Type	An abstract set of operations supported by one or more endpoints
Binding	A concrete protocol and data format specification for a particular port type
Port	A single endpoint defined as a combination of a binding and a network address
Service	A collection of related endpoints

Let's take a look at an example WSDL document that describes the capabilities of a Web Service named CTemp. (You'll build this Web Service in an upcoming chapter.) The CTemp Web Service converts temperature values between various units. Listing 44-2 displays the WSDL document for this service.

Listing 44-2: **WSDL document for the CTemp Web Service**

```
<?xml version="1.0" encoding="utf-8" ?>
<definitions xmlns:s="http://www.w3.org/2001/XMLSchema"

xmlns:http="http://schemas.xmlsoap.org/wsdl/http/"

xmlns:mime="http://schemas.xmlsoap.org/wsdl/mime/"

xmlns:tm="http://microsoft.com/wsdl/mime/textMatching/"

xmlns:soap="http://schemas.xmlsoap.org/wsdl/soap/"

xmlns:soapenc="http://schemas.xmlsoap.org/soap/encoding/"
                    xmlns:s0="http://tempuri.org/"
                      targetNamespace="http://tempuri.org/"
                      xmlns="http://schemas.xmlsoap.org/wsdl/">
<types>
<s:schema
attributeFormDefault="qualified"elementFormDefault="qualified"
                    targetNamespace="http://tempuri.org/">
<s:element name="CTemp">
<s:complexType>
<s:sequence>
   <s:element minOccurs="1" maxOccurs="1"name="Temperature"
                      type="s:decimal" />
   <s:element minOccurs="1" maxOccurs="1"name="FromUnits"
nillable="true"
                      type="s:string" />
   <s:element minOccurs="1" maxOccurs="1"name="ToUnits"
nillable="true"
                      type="s:string" />
```

```
      </s:sequence>
      </s:complexType>
      </s:element>
  <s:element name="CTempResponse">
  <s:complexType>
  <s:sequence>
      <s:element minOccurs="1" maxOccurs="1"name="CTempResult"
  type="s:decimal" />
      </s:sequence>
      </s:complexType>
      </s:element>
      <s:element name="decimal" type="s:decimal" />
      </s:schema>
      </types>
  <message name="CTempSoapIn">
      <part name="parameters" element="s0:CTemp" />
      </message>
  <message name="CTempSoapOut">
      <part name="parameters" element="s0:CTempResponse" />
      </message>
  <message name="CTempHttpGetIn">
      <part name="Temperature" type="s:string" />
      <part name="FromUnits" type="s:string" />
      <part name="ToUnits" type="s:string" />
      </message>
  <message name="CTempHttpGetOut">
      <part name="Body" element="s0:decimal" />
      </message>
  <message name="CTempHttpPostIn">
      <part name="Temperature" type="s:string" />
      <part name="FromUnits" type="s:string" />
      <part name="ToUnits" type="s:string" />
      </message>
  <message name="CTempHttpPostOut">
      <part name="Body" element="s0:decimal" />
      </message>
  <portType name="TempConverterSoap">
  <operation name="CTemp">
      <input message="s0:CTempSoapIn" />
      <output message="s0:CTempSoapOut" />
      </operation>
      </portType>
  <portType name="TempConverterHttpGet">
  <operation name="CTemp">
      <input message="s0:CTempHttpGetIn" />
      <output message="s0:CTempHttpGetOut" />
      </operation>
      </portType>
  <portType name="TempConverterHttpPost">
  <operation name="CTemp">
      <input message="s0:CTempHttpPostIn" />
      <output message="s0:CTempHttpPostOut" />
```

Continued

Listing 44-2 *(continued)*

```
    </operation>
    </portType>
<binding name="TempConverterSoap" type="s0:TempConverterSoap">
  <soap:binding
transport=http://schemas.xmlsoap.org/soap/httpstyle="document"
/>
<operation name="CTemp">
  <soap:operation soapAction=http://tempuri.org/CTemp
style="document"
/>
<input>
  <soap:body use="literal" />
  </input>
<output>
  <soap:body use="literal" />
  </output>
  </operation>
  </binding>
<binding name="TempConverterHttpGet"
type="s0:TempConverterHttpGet">
  <http:binding verb="GET" />
<operation name="CTemp">
  <http:operation location="/CTemp" />
<input>
  <http:urlEncoded />
  </input>
<output>
  <mime:mimeXml part="Body" />
  </output>
  </operation>
  </binding>
<binding name="TempConverterHttpPost"
type="s0:TempConverterHttpPost">
  <http:binding verb="POST" />
<operation name="CTemp">
  <http:operation location="/CTemp" />
<input>
  <mime:content type="application/x-www-form-urlencoded" />
  </input>
<output>
  <mime:mimeXml part="Body" />
  </output>
  </operation>
  </binding>
<service name="TempConverter">
<port name="TempConverterSoap" binding="s0:TempConverterSoap">
  <soap:address
location="http://jdc7200cte/Services/Ctemp/CTemp.asmx"
```

```
  />
    </port>
  <port name="TempConverterHttpGet"
  binding="s0:TempConverterHttpGet">
    <http:address
  location="http://jdc7200cte/Services/Ctemp/CTemp.asmx"
  />
    </port>
  <port name="TempConverterHttpPost"
  binding="s0:TempConverterHttpPost">
    <http:address
  location="http://jdc7200cte/Services/Ctemp/CTemp.asmx"
  />
    </port>
  </service>
  </definitions>
```

As shown in this example, the `CTemp` Web Service supports a single method named `CTemp` that accepts the three input arguments shown in Table 44-2.

Table 44-2
CTemp Method Arguments and Data Types

Argument	Data Type
Temperature	Decimal
FromUnits	String
ToUnits	String

In addition, `CTemp` returns a result of type Decimal. You can also see that the Web Service supports the HTTP-GET, HTTP-POST, and SOAP protocols for transporting the request and response messages.

 Note

As of this writing, the WSDL specification had been submitted to the World Wide Web Consortium (W3C) as a note for review. For its part, the W3C has created a group called the XML Protocol Activity, whose mission is to define and formalize standards for using XML to communicate between distributed applications on a peer-to-peer basis. This includes the WSDL specification as well as several others.

For more information about the WSDL specification, you can visit `www.w3.org/TR/WSDL`. For more information about the XML Protocol Activity, you can visit `www.w3.org/2000/xp`.

Discovering available Web Services

Now that you have a standard way to describe the capabilities of a Web Service via the WSDL document, you must now consider how a potential consumer of a Web Service will locate a WSDL document on a target Web server. Recall that in order to consume a service, a client must be able to determine how to interact with that Web Service. This means that the consumer must follow the message formats and message exchange patterns described for the Web Service in the WSDL document.

Of course, if you're both the author and consumer of the Web Services, you probably won't need help in locating the WSDL document. But if you'll be consuming Web Services from other authors, you may not know where the services are located on a target Web server. Web Service authors use a discovery (DISCO) document to publish their Web Services. The DISCO document is an XML document that contains pointers to such things as the WSDL file for a Web Service. Web Service consumers employ a discovery process to learn that a Web Service exists and where to find its WSDL document. Web Service consumers enact this discovery process on a target Web server by providing a URL to a discovery tool. The discovery tool attempts to locate DISCO documents on the target server and informs the consumer of the locations of any available WSDL documents.

Recall that the DISCO document is encoded as an XML document, which allows you to programmatically discover information about Web Services. This technique has enabled the creation of tools that a consumer can use to locate Web Services. The Microsoft .NET Framework provides a tool named `disco.exe` to enable Web Service discovery. In addition, Visual Studio has integrated support for Web Service discovery by using Web References. You'll learn more about these tools and their capabilities in upcoming chapters.

The following example illustrates the structure of a DISCO document:

```
<?xml version="1.0" ?>
<disco:discovery
xmlns:disco="http://schemas.xmlsoap.org/disco"
xmlns:wsdl="http://schemas.xmlsoap.org/disco/wsdl">
    <wsdl:contractRef

ref="http://jdc7200cte/Services/CTemp/CTemp.asmx?WSDL"/>
</disco:discovery>
```

In this example, a pointer to the WSDL document is contained in a `contractRef` element, which contains the URL that points to the WSDL document.

An interesting feature of the DISCO document is that it doesn't need to physically reside alongside the Web Service description document or other Web Service implementation files. This is because the DISCO document provides information about these resources via pointers. Thus, it's possible to distribute DISCO documents to centralized Web Service directories, which can be used to locate Web Services more easily.

Enabling discovery of your Web Service is optional. You may not wish to enable discovery if you're providing a Web Service for restricted and/or private use, or if you've delegated the discovery process to a dedicated directory server instead of the host Web server.

At the time of this writing, the DISCO technology has been submitted to the W3C XML Protocol Activity for consideration. You can find out more about DISCO in the Microsoft .NET Framework documentation, as well as the Visual Studio documentation.

Determining which sites provide Web Services

As more and more Web Services are created and deployed by numerous companies on the Internet, it will become increasingly difficult for consumers to find these services. Imagine how difficult it would be to find a specific page of information among the billions of pages on the Web if there were no search engines.

Similar to the search engine approach that is used to query and locate Web pages, the Universal Description, Discovery, and Integration (UDDI) specification defines a logically centralized but physically distributed, XML-based registry database and API that allows companies to find each other and the Web Services that they offer. The UDDI registry API offers support for querying as well as updating the registry database. The UDDI Web site (located at www.uddi.org) provides a browser-based interface for registering your company and services, as well as the capability to look up potential business partners.

The true power of the UDDI business registry lies in the UDDI Web Service (that's right, UDDI is itself a Web Service), which provides a mechanism for ad hoc discovery of potential business partners and dynamic integration of Web Services. Visual Studio .NET support for UDDI is built into the Web Reference metaphor used to locate and consume Web Services.

UDDI defines, classifies, and stores three basic types of information:

- ✦ **White Pages** describes address, contact, and other standard business demographic information.
- ✦ **Yellow Pages** describes industrial categorizations for businesses based on standard categories.
- ✦ **Green Pages** describes the technical specification for Web Services.

Collectively, these three types of data provide a flexible and effective method for locating Web Services.

In July 2001, version 2.0 of the UDDI specification was released, and several registry databases are currently operational. You can see the latest list of registries by visiting www.uddi.org. As of the writing of this book, both IBM and Microsoft had registries operational at the UDDI Web site. If you want to find potential Web Service providers, you can browse to `www.uddi.org/find.html` or click the Find tab on the UDDI home page. Figure 44-2 displays this Find page.

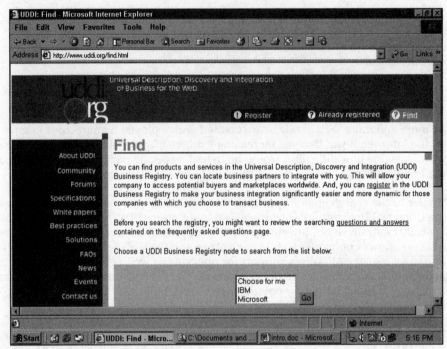

Figure 44-2: The UDDI Find page

If you want to register your business and any Web Services that you offer, you can browse to `www.uddi.org/register.html` or click the Register tab on the UDDI home page. Figure 44-3 displays the Register page.

More than 280 companies have now come aboard to support the specification, and the outlook is good that UDDI will become the standard method for locating business partners and Web Services on the Internet. In addition, the service is free to use.

Searching the UDDI database from the UDDI Web site is free and doesn't require registration or authentication. But if you want to register your company in the database, you must first obtain a username/password from the registry site. This is necessary so that you can control who can change your company's information in the database.

For its part, Microsoft is using UDDI (or has plans to use it) as a core building block in the .NET platform. There are plans to integrate UDDI into such products as

Microsoft BizTalk Server, Microsoft PassPort, Microsoft bCentral, and the Microsoft .NET Framework. And, as mentioned earlier, support for UDDI is already built into Visual Studio .NET. For more information about UDDI, you can visit `www.uddi.org`.

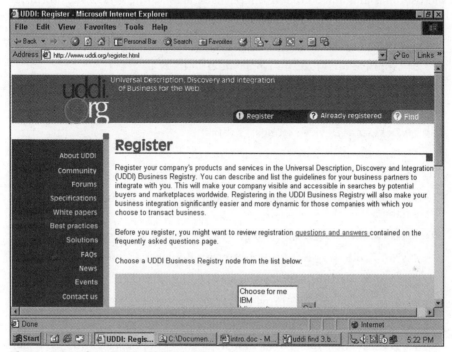

Figure 44-3: The UDDI Register page

Microsoft HailStorm

With the creation of such an important and far-reaching technology as Web Services, it's not surprising that major software vendors are planning to deliver a horizontal set of useful Web Services that will be needed by many next-generation Web-based applications. Microsoft itself has announced that it will deliver a set of Web Services based on the .NET technologies, codenamed HailStorm. These services will collect and store personal information that can be shared with other applications and services, based entirely on your consent and control.

Nearly all of us have dealt with the frustration of having multiple usernames, passwords, and profiles for the myriad sites and services that we visit on the Web. What's more, it seems like each site that retains this personal information has a different privacy policy and procedure for sharing this information with partners.

HailStorm promises to eliminate this frustration and lack of control over your personal information and replace it with a single source for this data that's under your complete control.

Microsoft has announced that it will release the following sets of HailStorm services initially:

✦ **MyAddress**—Electronic and geographic address for an identity

✦ **MyApplicationSettings**—Application settings

✦ **MyCalendar**—Time and task management

✦ **MyContacts**—Electronic relationships/address book

✦ **MyDevices**—Device settings, capabilities

✦ **MyDocuments**—Raw document storage

✦ **MyFavoriteWebSites**—Favorite URLs and other Web identifiers

✦ **MyInbox**—Inbox items like e-mail and voice mail, including existing mail systems

✦ **MyLocation**—Electronic and geographical location and rendezvous

✦ **MyNotifications**—Notification subscription, management, and routing

✦ **MyProfile**—Name, nickname, special dates, picture

✦ **MyServices**—Services provided for an identity

✦ **MyUsage**—Usage report for the preceding services

✦ **MyWallet**—Receipts, payment instruments, coupons, and other transaction records

Of course, one of the most important issues related to these technologies is personal data security. Because all of these services store personal information of some nature, it's imperative to protect this information according to your wishes. Consequently, other people will require your explicit authorization to access your personal data. You'll be able to determine which services can access your data, and you can revoke or deny these privileges at will or on a timed basis.

Unfortunately, there's not a lot of information available about HailStorm as of this writing. By the time you read this, however, a broadly available beta version of these initial HailStorm services is expected. For more information about HailStorm, you can visit www.microsoft.com/net and http://msdn.microsoft.com/net.

Summary

Providing a foundation for the creation and consumption of Web Services based on standards such as XML, SOAP, WSDL, DISCO, and UDDI makes Web Services capable of being supported on any platform that implements XML and HTTP. What's more, having an infrastructure that supports these standards makes it possible for development platforms such as Visual Studio .NET to supply these capabilities to your Web Services automatically, greatly simplifying and accelerating the Web Service development process. You'll see the fruits of this labor as you begin working in Visual Studio to create a Web Service.

✦　　✦　　✦

Web Services Infrastructure

by Jim Chandler

✦ ✦ ✦ ✦

In This Chapter

Microsoft Web
Services platform

The Microsoft .NET
Framework

Web Services
infrastructure

Leveraging ASP.NET
features in Web
Services

Inside an ASP.NET
Web Service

✦ ✦ ✦ ✦

In this chapter, you learn about the Microsoft technologies for executing, creating, and consuming Web Services on the Microsoft platform. Although it's possible to build or consume Web Services on a platform with support for only the core technologies (XML, TCP/IP, HTTP, and SOAP), it's certainly not a task suited for the beginning programmer or the easily intimidated. But the power of Web Services is in the basic design principle that they should be simple to create and easy to call.

Rather than waste your time writing Web Service infrastructure code, you should be able to focus your time and energy on the actual functionality of your application and let the platform do the rest. The Microsoft .NET Framework and Visual Studio .NET do just that. They provide an excellent, easy-to-use platform for building and consuming Web Services, as you'll soon find out.

Microsoft Web Services Platform

In the last chapter, you learned that Web Services are built on the foundation of eXtensible Markup Language (XML), Hypertext Transfer Protocol (HTTP), and Simple Object Address Protocol (SOAP). Using these technologies, Web Services enable the creation of distributed applications that can easily leverage the size and diversity of the Internet.

One of the primary motivations behind the creation of the Web Services architecture was the inadequacy of the existing distributed object model technologies, such as the Distributed Component Object Model (DCOM), the Common Object Request Broker Architecture (CORBA), and the Internet Inter-Orb Protocol (IIOP) for Internet-based applications. Although each of these technologies worked well in a controlled, homogeneous environment, this obviously cannot be guaranteed for systems on the Internet. What's more, these legacy object technologies could also be extremely large and complex (some more than others). Again, this makes it difficult to rely on these older technologies as a foundation for distributed computing on the Internet.

The major advantages of the Web Services foundation are its simplicity and its reliance on existing (or emerging) Internet standards. This ensures that Web Services can be implemented all across the Internet.

Although the Web Services foundation does a great job of enabling a programmable Internet composed of distributed building blocks, there's really much more to creating scalable, robust, distributed applications. Each individual platform must supply these services because the Web Services foundation doesn't attempt to address these issues. The Microsoft .NET platform is specifically designed to provide these essential services that make it easy to create world class Web Services. Figure 45-1 illustrates the Microsoft Web Services platform architecture.

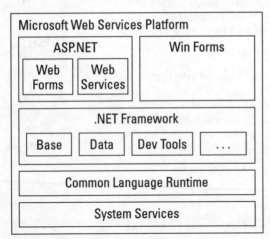

Figure 45-1: The Microsoft Web Services platform architecture

As shown in Figure 45-1, the Common Language Runtime (CLR) is built on top of the system services platform (such as Windows 2000). Layered on the CLR is the .NET Framework Class Library, which provides a large set of services via a hierarchically arranged collection of classes and types. On top of this base are the ASP.NET Web platform and Windows Forms environments. This chapter looks at most of these architectural pieces, as they relate to the development and consumption of Web Services.

One of the primary goals of the Microsoft Web Services platform is to make it easy to build Web Services that can solve complex, business-critical problems. The following sections will take a look at the Web Services platform features that make it easy to create these types of applications.

The Microsoft .NET Framework

The .NET Framework is Microsoft's premier platform for building and deploying robust Web Services. It provides built-in support for creating and consuming Web Services in three key areas:

✦ The Common Language Runtime (CLR)

✦ The .NET Framework Class Library

✦ ASP.NET

Let's examine some of the features of these key .NET Framework pieces, which provide a robust environment for the creation and execution of world-class Web Services.

The Common Language Runtime

The CLR provides the foundation for the .NET Framework. It's responsible for managing code at execution time and provides the following services:

✦ *Automatic memory management* — Garbage collection is handled by the runtime, relieving the programmer from managing memory. This improves the reliability and stability of applications.

✦ *Code safety and security* — Code can be "locked down" to prevent unauthorized, or untrusted access. This security infrastructure is highly flexible and configurable.

✦ *Code versioning and deployment support* — Multiple versions of code can be run in side-by-side mode, thus providing more reliable operation for older applications that rely on older versions of code libraries.

✦ *Cross-language integration* — Enables all programming languages to share data consistently via a common type system.

✦ *Remoting* — Extends the calling of components across process and machine boundaries using an extremely efficient wire protocol.

✦ *Self-describing objects* — Metadata that describes an object's capabilities is stored with the object, making it easy to dynamically determine how to interact with an object.

✦ *Thread management* — A simple yet flexible thread management infrastructure makes it easy to create multi-threaded applications.

Code that targets the CLR is called *managed code*. Compatible language compilers generate code that enables the runtime to manage the execution of your applications. To do this, compilers generate *Microsoft Intermediate Language (MSIL)*. This intermediate code is platform-independent and can be hosted on any processor architecture supported by the CLR. A Just-In-Time (JIT) compiler is used to convert MSIL into processor-specific code at runtime. During execution, CLR-managed code automatically receives the benefits of memory management, cross-language debugging support, security, and many other features.

Managed code is packaged into units called *assemblies*. These are the building blocks of .NET Framework applications and form the fundamental unit of deployment, version control, reuse, and security. An assembly contains all of the information necessary for the CLR to provide its services.

A major design goal of the CLR (as is true of all the pieces in the Web Services architecture) is to make the development process easier. As you can see, the CLR provides an excellent execution environment for Web Services. The developer doesn't need to provide and manage these features himself, making it quick and easy to build and deploy robust Web Service applications that take advantage of the CLR.

Now that you know a little about the CLR and its contribution to the Web Services platform, let's take a few moments to look into the next layer of the architecture: the .NET Framework Class Library.

The .NET Framework Class Library

The *.NET Framework Class Library* is a collection of classes that are organized into a single hierarchical tree of namespaces. The class library provides access to system features via classes, interfaces, and value types that greatly enhance programmer productivity and simplify the development process. The class library is built on top of the Common Language Runtime, which was just discussed. Therefore, it's also managed code that receives all the benefits provided by the CLR.

At the root of the class library hierarchy is the System namespace. This namespace contains over 100 core types and classes that are used by all .NET applications. In addition to the System namespace, the class library contains namespaces for abstract base classes and derived class implementations. This includes file I/O, messaging, networking, security, and access to the Internet. You can use these classes as-is or derive from them to create your own implementations.

The .NET Framework uses a dot-based naming scheme to represent grouped classes and types that make up a namespace. Namespaces make it easier to search for and reference classes and types. The namespace name includes everything from the beginning of the name up to the last dot in the name. The remaining part of the name identifies the type name. For example, the System.Web namespace defines the Web type, which belongs to the System namespace. Table 45-1 lists some of the namespaces that implement features of Web Services on the .NET platform.

Table 45-1
.NET Web Service Namespaces

Namespace	Purpose
System.Web.Services	Contains classes that enable you to build and consume Web Services.

Namespace	Purpose
System.Web.Services.Description	Contains classes that enable you to describe a Web Service via the Web Service Description Language (WSDL).
System.Web.Services.Discovery	Contains classes that implement the discovery process used by Web Service consumers to locate available Web Services.
System.Web.Services.Protocols	Contains classes that implement the protocols used to exchange Web Service messages between Web Services and Web Service consumers.

These are just the Web Service-specific namespaces. As you'll learn in the next section, the ASP.NET platform provides a robust framework and application environment for developing and executing Web applications (including Web Services) that is built on top of the .NET class library and the CLR.

ASP.NET

ASP.NET is a unified Web development platform that provides advanced services for building Web applications and Web Services. It provides a new programming model and infrastructure that allows you to create powerful Web applications with unprecedented speed, flexibility, and ease. ASP.NET is fully supported by the .NET Framework, allowing you to take full advantage of the Common Language Runtime (CLR), type safety, inheritance, and all of the other features of that platform.

ASP.NET offers two programming models: Web Forms and Web Services. Developers can use Web Forms to create the more traditional type of Web application where users interact with individual pages and input forms. Web Services, of course, is the focus of this part of the book.

Both of these programming models offer two techniques for coding Web pages and Web Services. Using embedded implementation code, the logic for a Web page or Web Service is embedded in the page itself (much like that of the traditional ASP programming environment). Contrast this technique with the code-behind file approach. Using code-behind, the logic for a Web page or Web Service is stored in a separate file from the user interface of a Web page or the entry point declaration of a Web Service.

By default, Visual Studio creates ASP.NET Web Forms and Web Services by using the code-behind technique. This creates a clear distinction between the definition of the user interface (or Web Service) and the code that implements its behavior.

The next few sections survey some of the features of the ASP.NET platform that are available to ASP.NET Web Services.

ASP.NET applications

An ASP.NET *application* consists of all the files, pages, handlers, modules, and executable code in a Web server virtual directory (and any subdirectories). Web Services are also ASP.NET applications and therefore are governed by the same configuration rules as any other ASP.NET application.

Each ASP.NET application can include an optional `Global.asax` file in the root virtual directory. This file contains handlers for application-level events that can be raised by ASP.NET. For example, you can handle such events as `Application_OnStart` and `Application_OnEnd` in the `Global.asax` file.

In addition to these events, you have access to any events exposed by HTTPModules. An HTTPModule is a class that can process information from any HTTP requests made to your ASP.NET application. You can customize or extend modules supplied by ASP.NET or create your own. Any events raised by HTTPModules are handled within the `Global.asax` file.

Web Service projects created with Visual Studio automatically create a `Global.asax` file. This employs a code-behind file to contain the code that handles the aforementioned events. The code-behind file is declared in the `Global.asax` file by using the ASP.NET `Application` directive:

```
<%@ Application Codebehind="Global.asax.vb"
Inherits="CTemp.Global"
%>
```

This declaration identifies `Global.asax.vb` as the code-behind file and instructs the compiler to create an ASP.NET application class that extends the `CTemp.Global` class contained in `Global.asax.vb`. The contents of this file are shown here:

```
Imports System.Web
Imports System.Web.SessionState

Public Class Global
    Inherits System.Web.HttpApplication

    Public Sub New()
        MyBase.New()
        'This call is required by the Component Designer.
        InitializeComponent()
        'Add any initialization after the InitializeComponent() call
    End Sub


    'Required by the Component Designer
    Private components As System.ComponentModel.Container
    'NOTE: The following procedure is required by the Component Designer
    'It can be modified using the Component Designer.
    'Do not modify it using the code editor.
    <System.Diagnostics.DebuggerStepThrough()> Private Sub InitializeComponent()
        components = New System.ComponentModel.Container()
    End Sub
```

```
    Sub Application_BeginRequest(ByVal sender As Object, ByVal e As EventArgs)
        ' Fires at the beginning of each request
    End Sub

    Sub Application_AuthenticateRequest(ByVal sender As Object, ByVal e As
        EventArgs)
        ' Fires upon attempting to authenticate the use
    End Sub

    Sub Application_Error(ByVal sender As Object, ByVal e As EventArgs)
        ' Fires when an error occurs
    End Sub
End Class
```

This file contains the declaration of the Global class, as well as empty template event handling routines for such events as BeginRequest, AuthenticateRequest, and Application_Error. To enable any of these events, simply add the code to the event handling template. If you want to handle an event such as Application_OnStart, simply add the procedure template and fill in the code to handle the event in the manner that you require.

ASP.NET applications also support a hierarchical application configuration architecture. Application configuration settings are stored in an XML file named web.config. The settings stored in these files are applied hierarchically as follows:

✦ Web.config files supply their settings to the directory in which they are located, as well as all subdirectories.

✦ Configuration settings for a Web resource are supplied by the Web.config file located in the same directory as the resource, and by all configuration files in all parent directories.

The default, global configuration file is named machine.config and is stored at %SYSTEM_ROOT%\Microsoft.NET\Framework\{version}\CONFIG. If no developer-supplied configuration files are found, the settings in this file apply to your Web application.

Web Service projects created with Visual Studio automatically add a Web.config file to the application virtual root. This file contains settings that control the code compilation process, authorization policies for the application, session state settings, and HTTP handler declarations, among others. A sample Web.config file is shown here:

```
<?xml version="1.0" encoding="utf-8" ?>
<configuration>
  <system.web>
    <!-- DYNAMIC DEBUG COMPILATION -->
    <compilation defaultLanguage="vb" debug="true" />
    <!-- CUSTOM ERROR MESSAGES -->
```

```
        <customErrors mode="RemoteOnly" />
        <!-- AUTHENTICATION -->
        <authentication mode="Windows" />
        <!-- AUTHORIZATION -->
        <authorization>
            <allow users="*" /> <!-- Allow all users -->
                <!-- <allow     users="[comma separated list of users]"
                               roles="[comma separated list of roles]"/>
                    <deny      users="[comma separated list of users]"
                               roles="[comma separated list of roles]"/>
                -->
        </authorization>
        <!-- APPLICATION-LEVEL TRACE LOGGING -->
        <trace enabled="false" requestLimit="10" pageOutput="false"
               traceMode="SortByTime" localOnly="true" />
        <!-- SESSION STATE SETTINGS -->
        <sessionState
               mode="InProc"
               stateConnectionString="tcpip=127.0.0.1:42424"
               sqlConnectionString="data source=127.0.0.1;user
id=sa;password="
               cookieless="false"
               timeout="20"
        />
        <!-- PREVENT SOURCE CODE DOWNLOAD -->
        <httpHandlers>
               <add verb="*" path="*.vb"

type="System.Web.HttpNotFoundHandler,System.Web" />
               <add verb="*" path="*.cs"

type="System.Web.HttpNotFoundHandler,System.Web" />
               <add verb="*" path="*.vbproj"

type="System.Web.HttpNotFoundHandler,System.Web" />
               <add verb="*" path="*.csproj"

type="System.Web.HttpNotFoundHandler,System.Web" />
               <add verb="*" path="*.webinfo"

type="System.Web.HttpNotFoundHandler,System.Web" />
        </httpHandlers>
        <!-- GLOBALIZATION -->
        <globalization requestEncoding="utf-8" responseEncoding="utf-8"
/>
    </system.web>
</configuration>
```

The first section of the `Web.config` file controls compilation behavior. You can set `compilation debug="true"` to insert debugging symbols (`.pdb` information) into the compiled page. Because this creates a larger file that executes more slowly, you should set this value to true only when debugging.

The next section controls custom error messages. You can set `customErrors mode="On"` or `"RemoteOnly"` to enable custom error messages, or `"Off"` to disable. You add `<error>` tags for each of the errors you want to handle. This process is described further in the.NET online documentation.

The next section sets the authentication policies of the application. Possible modes are `"Windows"`, `"Forms"`, `"Passport"`, and `"None"`, corresponding to the authentication policies supported by the IIS Web server, as well as the custom `"Forms"` and `"Passport"` policies supported by ASP.NET.

The next section sets the authorization policies of the application. You can allow or deny access to application resources by user or role. Wildcards are supported in this section. An asterisk means everyone, and a question mark means anonymous (unauthenticated) users.

The next section controls application-level tracing. This controls trace log output for every page within an application. Set `trace enabled="true"` to enable application trace logging. If `pageOutput="true"`, the trace information is displayed at the bottom of each page. Otherwise, you can view the application trace log by browsing the `"trace.axd"` page from your Web application root.

The next section controls the use of cookies to identify which requests belong to a particular session. By default, ASP.NET uses cookies to identify sessions. If cookies are not available, you can track a session by adding a session identifier to the URL. To disable cookies, you can set `sessionState cookieless="true"`.

Finally, the remaining sections of the `Web.config` file set the types of files that will not be downloaded, as well as controlling globalization parameters. To control the download behavior for different types of files, you must include an `httphandler` for a file type and associate that file type with the `xspisapi.dll` in the App `Mappings` property of the Web site. Otherwise, the file can be downloaded. Use this section to prevent your sources from being downloaded. As you can see, the default `Web.config` file is a comprehensive, straightforward, and flexible mechanism for configuring Web Services quickly and easily. Still, there are even more ASP.NET application parameters that you can control via this mechanism. Refer to the .NET Framework online documentation for more information on the `Web.config` file.

ASP.NET versus ASP

Unlike Active Server Pages (ASP), ASP.NET is a compiled, .NET-based platform. ASP.NET applications can be built by using any .NET-compatible programming language. Also, because ASP.NET is built on top of the .NET Framework, your ASP.NET applications have access to the entire range of functionality provided by the framework.

Among the major advantages of the ASP.NET environment are the following:

✦ Applications are fully compiled .NET applications, providing superior performance characteristics.

✦ It supports WYSIWYG HTML editors and programming environments such as Visual Studio .NET. This allows you to be very productive when developing ASP.NET applications and enables you to leverage the many features of these tools.

✦ Applications support extensive configuration capabilities based on XML configuration files.

✦ It has flexible, advanced, and easy-to-use application and session state management features that can be extended or replaced with custom schemes.

✦ It implements multiple authentication and authorization schemes that can be extended or replaced with custom schemes.

ASP.NET provides two programming models that can be used to create Web applications: Web Forms and Web Services. Web Forms allow you to build forms-based Web applications by using a technology called *server controls*. You can create user interfaces from common UI elements such as text boxes, list boxes, and so on.

ASP.NET Web Services can take advantage of all ASP.NET features, as well as those of the .NET Framework and CLR. You're likely to interact with many of these features when implementing your Web Service applications. ASP.NET leverages the classes found in the .NET Framework Class Library to support Web Services and the many other capabilities that this environment provides to developers.

Note   As you read through the following overview of ASP.NET features, remember that all of these features can be leveraged by your Web Service applications. As you'll see, having these capabilities at your fingertips makes developing world-class Web Services much easier.

State management

HTTP is a *stateless protocol*. This means that it doesn't retain any information from one request to the next, even though those requests may come from the same user session and may even be related to each other. Of course, if you're building Web applications that need to retain state between requests, the lack of such state information can make Web application development difficult at best.

ASP.NET provides both application state and session state management capabilities for Web applications. *Application state* is used to store data that applies to the application as a whole and is available to all sessions using the application. *Session state* is used to store data that is specific to each browser session using the application. Session state is not visible across different sessions (unlike application state).

Both application and session state information is stored in key/value dictionary objects. Access to this information is supplied through an Application object (for application state) and a Session object (for session state).

Essentially, application state is a global variable storage mechanism for ASP.NET applications. Experienced developers know that global variables come with specific issues and must be used sparingly. This is even more important in a server-based scenario such as an ASP.NET application. In particular, you should be aware of the following when considering the use of application state in ASP.NET applications:

✦ **Memory used by application variables is not released between requests**. Thus, it can have extended effects on server memory use. You should be a good custodian of application state memory.

✦ **Application variables have concurrency and synchronization issues**. Since multiple requests can be executing simultaneously, any changes to application-scoped variables must be synchronized. This can cause concurrency issues and slow down server performance.

✦ **Application state is not shared across a Web farm or Web garden**. *Web farms* host applications on multiple servers, and *Web gardens* host applications on multiple processes on a single server.

None of this is meant to scare you away from using application state. On the contrary, it can be a very valuable tool for Web applications when used properly. But you need to clearly understand the capabilities and limitations of application state within ASP.NET, and the typical applications in which application state can be used effectively.

Session state permits you to identify requests that come from the same browser client automatically, as well as store information specific to that session. ASP.NET session state provides the following features:

✦ It can survive Internet Information Server (IIS) and worker-process restarts without losing information.

✦ It can be used in both Web farm and Web garden configurations.

✦ It can be used if the client browser doesn't support cookies. (Cookies are discussed later in this chapter.)

ASP.NET session state can be fully configured to meet your specific needs via the `config.web` configuration files. For Web applications that require session state, ASP.NET provides excellent, reliable, and scalable support for maintaining session state.

Caching

One of the most important factors in creating highly scalable, high-performance Web applications is *caching*. Essentially, caching lets the Web application supply the results of a previous request to any other requests for the same information without involving the server in regenerating that information. This can greatly increase the performance of your Web application.

ASP.NET provides two types of caching:

✦ *Output caching* supplies the output of previous requests from the output cache instead of executing the server code necessary to generate the output a second time.

✦ *Application cache* is a programmatic cache that applications can use to store objects and other resources that can take a lot of time to re-create.

Transactions

A *transaction* is a set of related tasks that either succeed or fail as a unit. By combining a set of related operations into a unit that either completely succeeds or completely fails, you can simplify error recovery and make your application more reliable.

ASP.NET Web Services support declarative, attribute-based transaction support at the method level. This means that you can use a property of the `WebMethod` attribute to specify which type of transaction support (if any) is required for your Web Service method. Subsequently, any resource managers that you interact with during the execution of the Web method (such as SQL Server, Message Queue Server, SNA Server, Oracle Server, and so on) are transacted.

Security

ASP.NET provides a comprehensive, flexible, and extensible security framework that allows you to secure your Web Services. The security framework addresses four fundamental security needs:

✦ Authentication determines that a user is who he claims to be.

✦ Authorization controls access to resources based on the identity of a user.

✦ Impersonation assumes the identity of the requesting user when accessing resources.

✦ Code access security restricts the operations that a piece of code can perform.

Fundamentally, ASP.NET uses Internet Information Services (IIS) to obtain requests for pages or Web Services. Thus, it can use the security features of IIS. Currently, ASP.NET is hosted by IIS 5.0 and relies on its basic security features. IIS 5.0 supports three authentication mechanisms: basic, digest, and Integrated Windows authentication.

In addition to the IIS authentication services, ASP.NET supports two additional types of authentication: Forms and Passport. Forms authentication enables custom authentication via support provided by the application. For example, you can use a custom SQL Server database of defined users and passwords to identify users. Passport authentication is a centralized authentication service provided by Microsoft that offers a single sign-on feature, along with basic profile services.

ASP.NET security is configured in the ASP.NET application configuration file (named `Web.Config`). Using this configuration file, you can specify how users are authenticated, control access to resources via authorization settings, and determine impersonation settings.

Web Services Infrastructure

In the last chapter, you learned about these four primary pieces of the Web Services infrastructure:

✦ Web Service Directories

✦ Web Service Discovery

✦ Web Service Description

✦ Web Service Wire Formats

In the next few sections, you'll learn how this infrastructure is provided on the Microsoft .NET Web Services platform.

Web Service directories

Recall that *Web Service directories* provide a centralized, Internet-accessible location that consumers can use to find Web Services that have been offered by other companies or organizations. You can think of a Web Service directory as a type of Web portal or "Yellow Pages" specifically suited for listing and locating Web Services.

You can search for Web Services by using a variety of structured criteria, such as business type, industry, type of goods produced, services offered, and so on. For example, if you were looking for a credit card validation Web Service, you could search the directory using personal credit companies as the criteria.

Currently, the Universal Description, Discovery, and Integration (UDDI) specification is the de facto standard for cataloging and finding Web Services. The UDDI organization (located on the Web at `www.uddi.org`), composed of several hundred industry participants, has created a directory schema, distributed repository, and APIs for manipulating and querying the repository.

As of this writing, Microsoft and IBM both had cooperating UDDI directories operational and available for general use. These sites include operational Web Services, which can be called to programmatically manipulate and query the UDDI registry database.

If you're using Microsoft Visual Studio .NET to create your Web Services or Web Service consumer applications, you can use the Web Reference feature to search these online UDDI directories automatically. In fact, the Visual Studio .NET Web Reference feature is itself a consumer of the UDDI Web Services.

Alternatively, if you're not using Visual Studio .NET, you can use the UDDI Web site to search for Web Services. The Web site contains interactive forms for manipulating and querying the registry database.

If neither of these methods suits your needs, you can also download a UDDI SDK from either Microsoft or IBM and use it to create your own custom search tool.

Cross-Reference   You'll learn how to use these services in Chapter 49 and Chapter 50.

Web Service discovery

Web Service discovery is the process of locating one or more related documents that describe a specific Web Service. Recall that Web Services are described in terms of the request messages they can process and the response messages (if any) that they return. These capabilities are described in a standard way by using the Web Service Description Language (WSDL), which is an XML grammar specifically designed for this purpose.

Before you can submit requests to a Web Service, you must know how to format a request for a particular service. It must be in the form of a message that encodes the operation requested (such as converting a temperature from one unit to another), as well as any data required to carry out the operation (such as the input temperature, the source units, and the target units). In addition, you must know whether or not to expect a response message from the Web Service and what format this response will take (such as the converted temperature value).

The Web Service discovery process permits a consumer to search for and locate the WSDL document for a Web Service. A consumer must have the WSDL document before any requests can be properly formatted and delivered to the Web Service.

The DISCO specification defines an XML-based grammar and algorithm for discovering the existence of Web Services and locating their WSDL documents. Using DISCO, you can define search trees that are processed according to the DISCO algorithm to locate Web Service descriptions. Of course, if you already know the location of the WSDL document for a specific Web Service, this discovery process isn't needed.

Cross-Reference   See Chapter 44 for a discussion of DISCO.

Discovery documents are XML files that have a file type of `.disco` or `.vsdisco` (when automatically generated by Visual Studio). A discovery document is a container for two types of elements: pointers to WSDL documents, and pointers to other discovery documents. These pointers take the form of URLs and can be absolute or relative. The `<contractRef>` element is used to link to Web Service WSDL documents, whereas the `<discoveryRef>` element is used to link to other discovery documents. The following sample illustrates the format of a `disco` document:

```
<?xml version="1.0" encoding="utf-8"?>
<discovery xmlns:xsi="http://www.w3.org/2001/XMLSchema-instance"
           xmlns:xsd="http://www.w3.org/2001/XMLSchema"
           xmlns="http://schemas.xmlsoap.org/disco/">
  <contractRef ref="http://localhost/CTemp/CTemp.asmx?wsdl"
               docRef="http://localhost/CTemp/CTemp.asmx"
               xmlns="http://schemas.xmlsoap.org/disco/scl/" />
  <soap address="http://localhost/CTemp/CTemp.asmx"
        xmlns:q1="http://mydomain.com/CTemp" binding="q1:TempConverterSoap"
        xmlns="http://schemas.xmlsoap.org/disco/soap/" />
</discovery>
```

This sample includes a `<contractRef>` element that points to the WSDL document for a Web Service named `CTemp`. In addition, a `<soap>` element defines the SOAP-based entry point to the `CTemp` Web Service.

If you're using Microsoft Visual Studio .NET to create your Web Services or Web Service consumer applications, you can use the Web Reference feature to locate Web Services automatically by using the discovery process. To do this, you simply type the URL of a discovery document in the address bar of the dialog box. This will initiate the discovery process starting at the requested URL.

Alternatively, if you're not using Visual Studio .NET, you can use the .NET Framework's `disco` tool to search for Web Service description files. The `disco` tool is a command-line utility that accepts one parameter: the URL to initiate the search process. In addition, command-line switches can be used to further control the discovery process.

The `disco` tool copies the WSDL documents of any Web Services that it finds and also creates several other files (including a discovery document that refers to the Web Service descriptions that it finds, as well as a `discomap` file) on the hard drive where you ran the `disco` tool. These files can be input into the .NET Framework's `wsdl` tool to create Web Service client proxy classes.

Note   You must know at least the URL to a Web server in order to initiate the discovery process. If you don't have such a URL, you may wish to use the UDDI search mechanisms to locate Web servers that implement one or more Web Services.

The implementation of the discovery process is also embodied in the .NET Framework's System.Web.Services.Discovery namespace. This namespace contains the classes that implement the .NET Web Service discovery process and can be leveraged programmatically by your applications. Or you can replace it with your own implementation.

Cross-Reference   You can look at Web Service discovery using these tools in greater detail in Chapters 49 and 50.

Web Service description

A *Web Service description* is an XML document that defines the capabilities of a Web Service. Using the Web Service Description Language (WSDL) XML grammar, you can clearly and unambiguously define the Web-addressable entry points, the request messages that a Web Service will accept, and the response messages a Web Service can return. Also included in this description are the supported protocol bindings and a description of the data types processed by the Web Service.

Recall that the .NET Framework supports self-describing assemblies. This is accomplished by storing metadata with the assembly that describes the interfaces, data types, and other information about the classes in the assembly. Using the self-describing nature of .NET assemblies, the .NET Framework can generate WSDL documents to describe Web Service capabilities from the .NET assemblies that contain ASP.NET Web Service code.

Describing Web Service capabilities in ASP.NET

From the Web Service perspective, ASP.NET supports the dynamic generation of WSDL documents from the Web Service assembly when it's requested. This eliminates any issues related to keeping a separate WSDL document in sync with the Web Service assembly that implements the service. In a nutshell, this process works as follows:

1. The client requests the WSDL document by using a URL of the form `http://server/webservicepath/entrypoint.asmx?WSDL`.

2. The Web server maps the request for the `.asmx` file to the ASP.NET runtime.

3. The ASP.NET runtime uses an instance of the `WebServiceHandlerFactory` class (found in the System.Web.Services.Protocols namespace) to process the URL.

4. The `WebServiceHandlerFactory` class obtains the query string and uses classes from the System.Reflection namespace to obtain the Web Service assembly metadata.

5. The metadata is then used with classes from the System.Web.Services. Description namespace to generate and return the WSDL document to the client.

This process makes it simple for a Web Service to describe its capabilities to a requesting or potential consumer. The .NET platform automatically generates the WSDL for you, relieving you of this hassle. You can view the WSDL document for any ASP.NET Web Service by using your Web browser. Simply enter a URL of the form shown in Step 1. The ASP.NET runtime returns the WSDL document to the Web browser in the form of an XML document. Using this technique, you can quickly examine the WSDL structure of any ASP.NET Web Service. In addition, you can save the WSDL to a file for later use in generating a proxy class that can be used to consume the Web Service.

Proxy classes

The standard method of interacting with a Web Service is through a *proxy class*. From the consumer perspective, Visual Studio and ASP.NET make it easy to generate Web Service proxy classes given a Web Service description. From an interface standpoint, the proxy class serves as a mirror image of the actual Web Service, but it doesn't contain the actual implementation of the service. It's a local resource (local to the consumer, that is) that accepts method calls and then forwards them to the actual Web Service via HTTP and SOAP. Results are gathered from the Web Service method and returned to the consumer. This way, a Web Service method call looks like it's interacting entirely with a local class.

Visual Studio .NET automatically generates proxy classes from WSDL documents when you use the Web Reference feature to locate Web Services that you want to call from within your application. After you've located a WSDL document, you can use the Add Reference button on the dialog box to generate the proxy class.

If you don't (or can't) use Visual Studio to develop your consumer application, the .NET Framework supplies a tool named `wsdl` that you can use to generate .NET Web Service proxy classes from a supplied WSDL document. The `wsdl` tool is a command-line utility that accepts a URL pointing to the WSDL document that's used to generate the proxy class. There are a number of switches that you can use to control this process, such as specifying the target language for the generated proxy class. For example, you can create a Web Service proxy class for the `CTemp` Web Service in the Visual Basic language using a command line similar to the following:

```
WSDL /out:CTempProxy.vb /language:vb
http://localhost/CTemp/CTemp.asmx?WSDL
```

This command specifies that the generated Visual Basic proxy class should be saved to a file named `CTempProxy.vb`. Note that the WSDL service contract is obtained from the ASP.NET runtime on the server hosting the Web Service (in this case, your local Web server).

 Cross-Reference You can examine the use of these tools in greater detail in Chapter 50.

Web Service wire formats

The final piece of the ASP.NET Web Services infrastructure is the *Web Service wire formats*, which define the method by which Web Service request and response messages are encoded and transported between the Web Service and any consumer. To maximize the reach of Web Services on the Internet, standard Internet protocols are used.

ASP.NET Web Services support three wire formats:

✦ HTTP-GET

✦ HTTP-POST

✦ HTTP-SOAP

Traditional Web applications have used HTTP-GET and HTTP-POST to deliver Web Forms-based data to the Web server for processing. These same protocols are used to deliver Web Service operation requests, along with any necessary arguments, to the Web Service for processing. The HTTP-SOAP wire format is a new format that has been developed exclusively to enable Web Services to communicate by using very rich data types.

 Caution   The HTTP-GET and HTTP-POST protocols cannot support all data types that can be described in ASP.NET Web Services. For this reason, you should use HTTP-SOAP to call all Web Service methods.

Each of these wire formats finds its implementation in the System.Web.Services. Protocols namespace of the .NET Framework Class Library. Let's take a look at how these wire formats are implemented for ASP.NET Web Services.

HTTP-GET

The HTTP-GET protocol encodes Web Service operation requests and arguments in the URL to the Web Service. The operation is coded as part of the URL string, and any arguments are coded as query string parameters appended to the base URL. For example:

```
http://localhost/ctemp/ctemp.asmx/ctemp?Temperature=32&FromUnits=
F&ToUnits=C
```

This URL specifies the Web-addressable entry point for the CTemp **Web Service** (ctemp.asxm), including the method to be called (also named ctemp). The arguments to the ctemp method are passed as query string arguments to the method request.

Similar to the way WSDL documents are generated and returned to requests for such information via a URL to the Web Service entry point file (the .asmx file), the HTTP-GET method of calling Web Service methods is handled by the WebService HandlerFactory class. This class takes the URL and query string parameters as input and translates them into a method call on the appropriate Web Service class implementation.

HTTP-POST

The HTTP-POST protocol encodes Web Service operation requests and arguments within the payload area of the HTTP-POST request as name/value pairs. From an ASP.NET perspective, this technique of invoking a Web Service method is identical in operation to the HTTP-GET method, except in the way the Web Service call arguments are passed to the server. Once again, the .NET Framework's WebService HandlerFactory class is responsible for extracting the method name and arguments from the request and calling the appropriate Web Service method found in the Web Service class implementation.

HTTP-SOAP

HTTP-SOAP is the default ASP.NET Web Service wire format. It's based on the SOAP specification (currently submitted to the W3C as a note) and supports the widest range of simple and complex data types (including document-oriented operations).

Web Service request and response messages are encoded into SOAP messages that are included in the payload area of an HTTP-POST message. SOAP messages are encoded in XML using the SOAP vocabulary defined in the specification.

Because SOAP is really XML, it's possible to describe nearly any type of data. This makes SOAP an excellent choice for passing rich data types between Web Services and their consumers. For example, it's possible to pass very complex types, including entire XML documents such as an invoice or purchase order.

Although these are the default wire formats, ASP.NET lets you replace or add to them. For example, you can implement additional wire formats that allow Web Services to communicate using FTP or SMTP.

 Cross-Reference These supported Web Service wire formats are covered in greater detail in Chapter 47.

Leveraging ASP.NET Features in Web Services

So far, this chapter has outlined the broad support provided by the .NET platform and ASP.NET for building and consuming Web Services. The next few sections will look at more specific details of how to leverage some of these features within your ASP.NET Web Service applications:

✦ Supporting transactions

✦ Enabling session state

✦ Caching Web Service data

✦ Buffering server responses

Supporting transactions

ASP.NET Web Services are capable of supporting transactions, just like the automatic transaction support provided for classic COM+ components. When working with databases and data access, often you'll want to use transactions to simplify and maintain the integrity of updates to your database.

The major difference between the transaction support features in classic COM+ and those in ASP.NET is that ASP.NET transactions cannot be started by another application and then flowed into the Web Service method. In other words, Web Services only support transactions that are started by the Web Service method itself.

To enable transaction support for a Web Service method, you must add the `TransactionOption` property to the `WebMethod` attribute that's used to identify Web-callable methods in your Web Service classes. For example:

```
<WebMethod(TransactionOption:=Required)> Public Function
CTemp...
```

This property accepts an enumerated type that specifies the type of transaction support desired for the Web method. Table 45-2 describes the supported transaction property options.

	Table 45-2
	TransactionOption Property Values

Option	Description
Disabled	The method doesn't participate in transactions.
NotSupported	The method doesn't run within the scope of a transaction, even if one is currently pending.
Supported	The method participates in any pending transaction. If a transaction isn't pending, the method will execute without one.
Required	If a transaction is pending, this method participates in the transaction. If a transaction isn't pending, a new transaction is started.
RequiresNew	Regardless of the current transaction state, a new transaction is started for the method.

The default option is `Required`. If you're familiar with COM+ transaction support, you were required to use the `SetComplete` or `SetAbort` methods to signal the completion state of the transaction. This is no longer required for .NET classes. The successful completion of a method call implies a call to `SetComplete`, whereas if the method call raises an exception, this implies a call to `SetAbort`.

 Cross-Reference For more information about transaction support in ASP.NET Web Services, please refer to the .NET Framework online documentation.

Enabling session state

As discussed earlier in this chapter, session state allows Web Service methods to maintain contextual information between calls. To use the built-in session state support provided for ASP.NET Web Services, the Web Service class must inherit from either the `WebService` base class or use the `HttpContext` class.

Session state support for Web Services is bound to the HTTP protocol because it relies on the *cookies* feature of HTTP. HTTP cookies permit a Web application to save and recall information specific to a particular user between visits to a Web site. You may recall that the design of SOAP is purposely transport-independent, allowing SOAP messages to be piggybacked on other transport protocols such as FTP or SMTP. But if you rely on the HTTP transport for session state support, you can no longer bind your SOAP messages to another transport without losing session state support.

Session state support for Web Services is disabled by default because it incurs additional overhead that you may not want or need to use. To enable session support, you must add the `EnableSession` property to the `WebMethod` attribute that's used to identify Web-callable methods in your Web Service classes. For example:

```
<WebMethod(EnableSession:=True)> Public Function CTemp...
```

This property accepts a true or false value and specifies whether or not to enable session support for the Web method. Again, the default value of this property is false.

Session state uses temporary cookies to track a session. This means that the cookie is never saved to the hard drive. So, for the session state to remain valid, the same session ID must be used between requests. The session ID is normally supplied by the proxy class and therefore only exists as long as the proxy class exists. This means that the lifetime of the proxy class normally determines the lifetime of the session. If this default behavior is unacceptable, it's possible to change it so that the cookie can be persisted and will survive across proxy class instances.

 For more information about maintaining session state with ASP.NET Web Services, please refer to the .NET Framework online documentation.

Caching Web Service data

ASP.NET Web Services support *output caching*. This permits the result of a previous method request to be saved in a memory cache that can be recalled on subsequent requests, without having to execute the logic of the method again. Output caching is convenient and useful in situations where the data being returned doesn't change very often. This can result in large performance gains for the Web Service when many consumers make requests for the same information.

To enable output caching, you must add the `CacheDuration` property to the `WebMethod` attribute that's used to identify Web-callable methods in your Web Service classes. For example:

```
<WebMethod(CacheDuration:=120)> Public Function CTemp...
```

This property accepts an integer value that specifies the length of time (in seconds) that the output will remain in the cache after the first execution of the method has returned the result. Subsequent requests will immediately return the result to the call from the output cache until the specified time period expires. When this occurs, the method will be executed again, repopulating the cache and restarting the cache expiration countdown.

Output caching works correctly even if the method requires one or more arguments that can vary between requests. In this case, the output is cached for each unique combination of arguments supplied to the method. If the method has been called with identical parameters to a previous request, the response is obtained from the output cache. Otherwise, the method is executed normally.

Finally, output caching can be a very valuable tool in dramatically increasing the performance of your application. But the effectiveness of this technique must be balanced against the memory used and the type of data being cached. If the data changes frequently or isn't accessed often, output caching will only degrade server performance. Carefully examine your situation before deciding whether to use output caching to increase server performance.

Buffering server responses

Response buffering allows the Web server to return the response to the consumer all at once, after the response has been completely generated, rather than transmitting it in multiple chunks. By default, ASP.NET Web Services buffer the response before sending it. Sometimes, however, it may be appropriate to change this default behavior. For example, it may be beneficial for long-running methods to transmit the response as it's generated.

To disable response buffering for Web Services, you must add the `BufferResponse` property to the `WebMethod` attribute that's used to identify Web-callable methods in your Web Service classes. For example:

```
<WebMethod(BufferResponse:=false)> Public Function CTemp...
```

This property accepts a true or false value that specifies whether or not output buffering is enabled. The default for this property is true, which enables output buffering.

If you choose to disable response buffering, you must balance the potential benefits of this against the additional resources required to transmit the response in multiple requests.

Inside an ASP.NET Web Service

So far, you've learned a lot about the motivation behind Web Services and the technologies that enable us to build and consume Web Services. But how does a Web Service work, exactly? To wrap up this chapter on Web Service infrastructure, let's walk through what happens during the execution lifetime of a Web Service. This will bring together all of the elements of Web Services you've learned about and how they fit together to enable the Web Service execution model.

Now that you have a complete picture of the technologies and tools used to build and consume ASP.NET Web Services, let's take a conceptual but detailed look at the execution flow and lifetime of a fictional Web Service named CTemp.

The CTemp Web Service converts temperature values from one unit to another. The service supports a single method that accepts three input arguments: the temperature value, the source units, and the destination units. The Web Service method takes these input arguments, converts the specified temperature to the destination units, and returns the new temperature value to the caller.

The following walkthrough begins at the point where the consumer sends a properly formatted SOAP message to the target server requesting the CTemp method of the CTemp Web Service:

1. The IIS Web server hosting the CTemp Web Service receives the request message (technically, an HTTP-SOAP request).

2. The URL is interpreted by the Web server to determine which ISAPI filter is responsible for handling the request (based on the file type). The URL points to the Web Service entry point file (the .asmx file), so the request is passed along to the ASP.NET ISAPI filter.

3. The ASP.NET ISAPI filter passes the request to an instance of the .NET HTTPRuntime class, which is hosted within an IIS application process. The movement of the request from the ISAPI filter to the HTTPRuntime class completes a transition from unmanaged to managed code.

4. The ASP.NET HTTPRuntime class is responsible for handling all incoming HTTP requests. The runtime resolves the URL to a specific application and then dispatches the request to that application. Web Services are handled by the .NET WebServiceHandlerFactory class.

5. The WebServiceHandlerFactory class deserializes the SOAP payload from the request, creates an instance of the CTemp Web Service implementation class, and executes the CTemp method, passing the input arguments.

6. Finally, the ASP.NET runtime takes the result of the CTemp method call and serializes it into a SOAP response message. This message is then added to the payload of an HTTP response and delivered back to the client (in this case, the proxy class).

As you can see, a lot goes on behind the scenes of a Web Service method request. Although this overview gives you an idea of what happens to a Web Service request while it's being processed, it's by no means a complete picture. There are many details within each of these steps that have been left out for brevity (and clarity). This short tour, however, should make it easier to see how the various pieces of the puzzle fit together. Upcoming chapters will further refine these details and go into the step-by-step procedures for building and consuming ASP.NET Web Services.

Summary

This chapter covered the elements of the Microsoft Web Services platform, which is based on the Common Language Runtime, the .NET Framework Class Library, and the ASP.NET Web application environment. These architectural elements provide broad and extensive support for building and consuming world-class Web Services that can incorporate the platform's advanced features with very little effort. You used these architectural elements to examine the execution flow and lifetime of a typical Web Service.

✦   ✦   ✦

SOAP

by Jim Chandler

In this chapter you learn more about the Simple Object
Access Protocol (SOAP), which is one of the foundational
elements of Web Services. Although you don't need to have
a detailed understanding of SOAP to build or consume Web
Services based on ASP.NET, you should at least be familiar
with it. That knowledge will be useful in debugging situations,
as well as when you're dealing with specialized interoperability issues that might arise when exchanging SOAP messages
with services on other platforms.

This chapter discusses the major features of SOAP, the data
types that are supported, and the SOAP features provided by
the .NET Framework, including capabilities for extending or
modifying the behavior of SOAP-based Web Services.

What Is SOAP?

The Simple Object Access Protocol (SOAP) is a lightweight,
XML-based protocol for exchanging information in a decen-
tralized, distributed environment such as that offered by the
Internet. In other words, SOAP enables two processes (possibly on different machines) to communicate with each other
regardless of the hardware and software platforms on which
they're running.

One of the greatest benefits of SOAP is that it's part of an open
process that has been embraced at an unprecedented level by
most of the major hardware and software vendors. The SOAP
specification is an open technology (having been submitted to
the W3C) that provides the basis for application-to-application
integration known as Web Services.

Benefits of using XML with SOAP

The fundamental building block of SOAP is XML. SOAP defines a specialized yet flexible XML grammar that standardizes the format and structure of messages. Messages are, in turn, the fundamental method for exchanging information between Web Services and Web Service consumers. Using XML to encode SOAP messages provides several benefits, such as the following:

✦ It's human-readable, making it easier to understand and debug.

✦ Parsers and related technologies are widely available.

✦ It's an open standard.

✦ Many related technologies that can be leveraged in SOAP are included.

Thus, XML is a natural choice for encoding SOAP messages, and it contributes to the simplicity of the specification (at least in relation to more complex binary protocols such as COM and CORBA).

Transporting messages

Typically, a Web Service consumer will send a message to a Web Service, requesting a specific operation to be performed. The Web Service processes this request and typically (but not necessarily) returns the results in a response message. This request/response model is conceptually akin to the Remote Procedure Call (RPC) model.

To transport SOAP messages, you need a transport protocol. The obvious choice for a transport protocol is HTTP because it's used on so many systems today. In addition, HTTP is allowed through most firewalls, making it easy to get up and running without requiring administrators to open more ports through their corporate firewalls.

Although HTTP is an obvious choice for a transport protocol (and the one that most major vendors are implementing), the SOAP specification doesn't require a specific transport protocol. It's quite possible to transport SOAP messages over other transport mechanisms, such as SMTP and FTP. However, the default transport protocol for ASP.NET Web Services based on SOAP is HTTP.

So, in a nutshell, SOAP provides the following capabilities:

✦ Enables interoperability between systems using standard, widely available protocols such as XML and HTTP.

✦ Allows systems to communicate with each other through firewalls without having to open up additional, potentially unsafe ports.

✦ SOAP fully describes each data element in the message, making it easier to understand and troubleshoot problems that may occur.

Arguably, as important as what SOAP does to enable interoperability is what it *doesn't* do. Specifically, SOAP doesn't do any of the following:

✦ Attempt to define how objects are created or destroyed.

✦ Impose any specific security mechanism or implementation.

✦ Define an authentication scheme.

At first glance, these might seem to be serious shortcomings. However, in reality, they allow each platform to address these issues in a way that best suits its needs. For example, SOAP messages can also be exchanged over SSL to provide a secure, encrypted connection between the client and server.

Now that you have a basic understanding of SOAP, let's take a closer look at some of the fundamental parts of the SOAP specification.

The SOAP Specification

The SOAP protocol specification is a W3C-submitted note that's now under the umbrella of the XML Protocols working group. Version 1.2 of the specification (the follow-up to version 1.1) was under development as a working draft at the beginning of July 2001. The .NET Framework and ASP.NET Web Services produce and consume SOAP messages that are compliant with version 1.1 of the SOAP protocol specification.

The SOAP protocol specification has four primary parts, each of which has a specific purpose:

✦ A definition for a mandatory, extensible message envelope that encapsulates all SOAP data. The SOAP envelope is the fundamental message carrier that forms the basis for SOAP message exchange between SOAP-aware endpoints. This is the only part of the SOAP specification that's mandatory.

✦ A set of data encoding rules for representing application-defined data types, and a model for serializing data that appears within the SOAP envelope.

✦ A definition for an RPC-style (request/response) message exchange pattern. SOAP doesn't require two-way message exchanges, but Web Services typically implement such RPC-style request/response patterns when used with HTTP as the transport protocol. Thus, the request/response RPC-style protocol is a function of HTTP and not of SOAP.

✦ A definition for a protocol binding between SOAP and HTTP. This describes how SOAP messages are transmitted using HTTP as the transport protocol.

Since the SOAP envelope is the only mandatory part of the specification, let's first take a look at the elements that make up a SOAP message.

Elements of a SOAP Message

A SOAP message is composed of the three following primary elements, each of which performs a special purpose:

✦ **Envelope** — Serves as a container for the remaining SOAP message elements.

✦ **Header** — Contains optional data that a consumer may or may not be required to understand in order to process the message properly. This is the primary extensibility mechanism of SOAP.

✦ **Body** — Contains the actual encoding of a method call, and any input arguments or an encoded response that contains the results of the method call.

The next few sections look at these message elements in detail.

The SOAP envelope

The SOAP envelope element is a required part of a SOAP message. It serves as a container for all remaining SOAP message elements. Typically, this includes the SOAP header and body elements. In addition, the envelope defines the namespaces used by these elements. Figure 46-1 depicts the structure of a complete SOAP message.

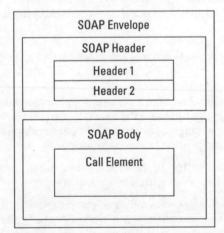

Figure 46-1: The SOAP message structure

To deliver a SOAP message to an endpoint, addressing information that's specific to the transport protocol binding is used to ensure that the message is delivered to the correct endpoint. It's much like putting a recipient's name and address on a real envelope so a postal authority can deliver it. In the case of HTTP, a custom HTTP header named SOAPAction is used to direct the message to the proper endpoint.

One of the major reasons that message addressing is implemented this way is so systems administrators can configure firewall software to filter traffic based on this header information, without requiring parsing of the XML.

The following example illustrates the format of a SOAP request message envelope:

```
<soap:Envelope xmlns:xsi="http://www.w3.org/2001/XMLSchema-instance"
           xmlns:xsd="http://www.w3.org/2001/XMLSchema"
           xmlns:soap="http://schemas.xmlsoap.org/soap/envelope/">
  <soap:Body>
    <!-- The Soap body elements are inserted here -->
  </soap:Body>
</soap:Envelope>
```

The SOAP envelope is identified by the soap:Envelope element. This particular example contains a soap:Body element, but no soap:Header element.

Now that you know about the SOAP envelope, let's discuss SOAP headers.

The SOAP header

The SOAP header element is an optional part of a SOAP message. It defines additional information that can be related to the method request in the body element. Or, more likely, it defines information independent of the method request that's required or otherwise useful to your application. SOAP doesn't define the specific contents or semantics for a SOAP header.

SOAP headers are quite similar in concept to the META tags found in HTML documents. They define metadata that can be used to provide context to, or otherwise direct the processing of, the message. The following example shows a SOAP header named Authentication that passes user credentials as part of a Web Service method request:

```
<soap:Envelope xmlns:xsi="http://www.w3.org/2001/XMLSchema-instance"
           xmlns:xsd="http://www.w3.org/2001/XMLSchema"
           xmlns:soap="http://schemas.xmlsoap.org/soap/envelope/">
  <soap:Header>
    <Authentication xmlns="http://tempuri.org">
      <Username>JDC</Username>
      <Password>unknown</Password>
    </Authentication>
  </soap:Header>
  <soap:Body>
    <!-- The SOAP body elements are inserted here -->
  </soap:Body>
</soap:Envelope>
```

Each direct child element of the header element is defined as a separate SOAP header. A typical use of SOAP headers is in the area of authentication, as shown in this example, where the credentials required to access the method are encoded in a SOAP header. The implementation code of the method can use the credentials obtained from the SOAP header to invoke an authentication service provided by the underlying platform, rather than having to implement this functionality itself.

If a header element is specified within a SOAP envelope, it must be the first element to appear after the opening envelope tag. In addition, SOAP headers (header subelements) must use XML namespaces to qualify their names, as you did with the `Authentication` SOAP header example.

SOAP header elements also support an optional `MustUnderstand` attribute. This attribute accepts a true or false setting, which is used to specify whether or not the message recipient must understand the data within the header. If the `MustUnderstand` attribute is set to true, the recipient must acknowledge the header by setting the `DidUnderstand` attribute on the header to true. If this is not done, a `SoapHeaderException` is generated.

That's enough about SOAP headers until later in the chapter. Now let's look at the SOAP body.

The SOAP body

The SOAP body element is a required part of a SOAP message that contains the data specific to a particular method call, such as the method name and any input/output arguments or the return values produced by the method. The contents of the SOAP body depend on whether the message is a request or a response. A request message contains method call information, whereas a response message contains method call result data.

The following example illustrates a SOAP body for a request to a temperature conversion method named `CTemp`:

```
<soap:Envelope xmlns:xsi="http://www.w3.org/2001/XMLSchema-instance"
            xmlns:xsd="http://www.w3.org/2001/XMLSchema"
            xmlns:soap="http://schemas.xmlsoap.org/soap/envelope/">
  <soap:Body>
    <CTemp xmlns="http://tempuri.org/">
      <Temperature>32</Temperature>
      <FromUnits>F</FromUnits>
      <ToUnits>C</ToUnits>
    </CTemp>
  </soap:Body>
</soap:Envelope>
```

The example shows the method name encoded as the CTemp element. Within this element are the encoded input arguments required to call the CTemp method.

The SOAP body for the response message to the CTemp method request is shown here:

```
<soap:Envelope xmlns:xsi="http://www.w3.org/2001/XMLSchema-instance"
               xmlns:xsd="http://www.w3.org/2001/XMLSchema"
               xmlns:soap="http://schemas.xmlsoap.org/soap/envelope/">
  <soap:Body>
    <CTempResponse xmlns="http://tempuri.org/">
      <CTempResult>0</CTempResult>
    </CTempResponse>
  </soap:Body>
</soap:Envelope>
```

Here you can see that the body of the response message contains a single result element named CTempResult that encodes the numeric result of the temperature conversion. Of course, if the method call were to fail for some reason, the response message wouldn't contain the expected results. Instead, it would contain exception (or fault) information describing the error that occurred. This possibility is discussed in the next section.

SOAP Data Type Support

The SOAP specification defines data type support in terms of XSD, the XML Schema specification. This specification defines standards for describing primitive data types, as well as complex, hierarchical structures. As you would expect, there's support for integers, strings, floats, and many other primitive types, as well as lists (or arrays) of these primitive types.

In addition to primitive types, user-defined structures can be represented. This paves the way for describing complex, hierarchical data relationships such as those found in an invoice or purchase order. The bottom line here is that it's possible to describe any type of data using XSD. Thus, SOAP can support any data type, from the built-in primitives defined by XSD all the way to any arbitrary user-defined structure. This is one of the primary reasons that SOAP is the preferred protocol for exchanging Web Service request and response messages. It enables Web Services to accept as well as return any type of data that can be represented by an XSD schema.

The Common Language Runtime (CLR) within .NET supports a wide variety of the common data types. All of these data types are shared equally across all of the .NET languages and also have a well-defined mapping to XSD data types, as shown in Table 46-1.

Table 46-1
XSD Data Types vs. CLR Data Types

XML Schema Definition	Common Language Runtime
boolean	Boolean
byte	N/A
double	Double
datatype	N/A
decimal	Decimal
enumeration	Enum
float	Single
int	Int32
long	Int64
Qname	XmlQualifiedName
short	Int16
string	String
timeInstant	DateTime
unsignedByte	N/A
unsignedInt	UInt32
unsignedLong	UInt64
unsignedShort	UInt16

In addition to complete primitive data type support, complex structures can be represented within .NET using classes. For example, you can define a class named Invoice that describes the data elements of an invoice document. The .NET Framework and ASP.NET automatically serialize and deserialize user-defined classes into XML-encoded element hierarchies that can be carried in the SOAP message body. This makes it possible to pass very complex structures as a single argument to a Web Service method!

As you can see, the data type support provided by XSD and SOAP is very powerful and enables the development of complex applications. Although there's a great deal of information related to data types and structures as defined within XSD and SOAP, there's just not enough space to go into it here. What's more, you really don't have to know much about how your Web Service parameters or results are serialized into XML because ASP.NET and the .NET Framework classes handle it for you automatically.

Cross-Reference If you want to learn more about describing data, examine the XML Schema Definition and SOAP specifications at the W3C web site, located at www.w3.org. There's also Visual Studio and .NET Framework online documentation related to this subject.

SOAP Exceptions

If Web Service methods were guaranteed to work at all times, you wouldn't need any form of error notification or processing capabilities. Unfortunately, things can go wrong (and often do). As such, errors or exceptions that occur in a Web Service method call need to be communicated back to the consumer of the Web Service in some manner. This is where SOAP *exceptions* come into play. They're used to return error or exception information to the consumer of a Web Service as the result of a failed method call.

Note The SOAP specification uses the term *faults* rather than *exceptions*. This chapter uses the latter to maintain consistency with the terminology used within the .NET Framework classes and documentation. This terminology is also reflected in the SOAP classes within .NET.

SOAP exceptions can occur at various stages of processing a Web Service request. For example, an error can occur at the HTTP level before the method call can actually be delivered to the Web Service. In this case, an HTTP response must be returned, using the standard HTTP status code numbering conventions. If the message makes it past the HTTP layer, it must be translated and dispatched to the actual implementation code that executes the method request. If an error occurs here, the server must return a fault message.

The following is an example of a SOAP exception message that returns an application-defined exception as the response message:

```
<soap:Envelope xmlns:xsi="http://www.w3.org/2001/XMLSchema-instance"
          xmlns:xsd="http://www.w3.org/2001/XMLSchema"
          xmlns:soap="http://schemas.xmlsoap.org/soap/envelope/">
  <soap:Body>
    <soap:Fault>
      <faultcode>400</faultcode>
      <faultstring>
        Divide by zero error
      </faultstring>
      <runcode>Maybe</runcode>
      <detail>
        <t:DivideByZeroException xmlns:t="http://tempuri.org">
          <expression>x = 2 / 0;</expression>
```

Continued

```
        </t:DivideByZeroException>
      </detail>
    </soap:Fault>
  </soap:Body>
</soap:Envelope>
```

As shown in this example, the exception is contained within the soap:Fault element. The faultcode element specifies the SOAP fault that occurred. Currently, there are four defined fault codes, which are listed in Table 46-2.

Table 46-2
SOAP Fault Codes

Value	Name	Meaning
100	Version Mismatch	The call used an unsupported SOAP version.
200	Must Understand	An XML element was received that contained an element with the "mustUnderstand=true" attribute, but the receiver didn't understand it.
300	Invalid Request	The receiver didn't process the request because it was malformed or wasn't supported.
400	Application Faulted	The receiving application faulted when processing the request. The detail element contains information about the fault.

The faultstring element contains a string description of the error that occurred. The runcode element indicates whether or not the requested operation was performed before the error occurred. This must contain either Yes, No, or Maybe.

The detail element is optional and specifies an application-defined exception object (in this case, a DivideByZeroException object).

ASP.NET implements a SoapException class that can be used with the CLR's structured exception handling capabilities to catch SOAP exceptions and handle them using try...catch blocks. This means that your ASP.NET applications have a robust, natural mechanism for handling errors within a Web Service, as well as within a consumer application, that's identical to handling any other type of exception within the CLR.

HTTP as a SOAP Transport

To deliver messages encoded as SOAP requests or responses, you need a transport protocol. This transport protocol must be widely available in order to maximize the reach of your Web Services. The obvious choice of HTTP as the transport protocol makes SOAP a highly available message format. In addition, the request/response nature of HTTP gives SOAP its RPC-like behavior when piggybacking this transport protocol. Another advantage of HTTP as the primary transport protocol is that it's human-readable, just like the SOAP message itself. Figure 46-2 depicts the structure of a SOAP message within the payload section of an HTTP Post request.

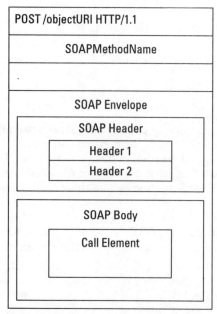

Figure 46-2: An HTTP Post message with a SOAP payload

The POST command contains a request uniform resource identifier (URI) that specifies the object endpoint ID. The server is responsible for mapping this URI to the implementation of the Web Service, and is also responsible for activating the proper code for the platform on which it's running.

The SOAP request also must specify which method is to be called. This is done via a custom HTTP header (signified by SoapMethodName in Figure 46-2) that specifies the namespace-qualified method name to be invoked. Following the HTTP header is the actual payload of the POST request. The payload is always separated from the last header by a single empty line.

The following example code shows a complete SOAP request message in the payload section of an HTTP POST request.

```
POST /ctemp/ctemp.asmx HTTP/1.1
Host: localhost
Content-Type: text/xml; charset=utf-8
Content-Length: length
SOAPAction: "http://tempuri.org/CTemp"

<?xml version="1.0" encoding="utf-8"?>
<soap:Envelope xmlns:xsi="http://www.w3.org/2001/XMLSchema-instance"
            xmlns:xsd="http://www.w3.org/2001/XMLSchema"
            xmlns:soap="http://schemas.xmlsoap.org/soap/envelope/">
  <soap:Body>
    <CTemp xmlns="http://tempuri.org/">
      <Temperature>32</Temperature>
      <FromUnits>F</FromUnits>
      <ToUnits>C</ToUnits>
    </CTemp>
  </soap:Body>
</soap:Envelope>
```

Notice that the POST request URI specifies the object endpoint ID. This is used by ASP.NET to locate and activate the Web Service code. The method call being requested is specified by the HTTP SOAPAction header. In this instance, the CTemp method is the requested function to be called. Finally, the body of the SOAP message contains the input arguments to the CTemp method call. In this case, there are three arguments.

Similar to the SOAP request message bound to the HTTP POST command, a SOAP response message uses the HTTP response command to indicate the results of the method call:

```
HTTP/1.1 200 OK
Content-Type: text/xml; charset=utf-8
Content-Length: length

<?xml version="1.0" encoding="utf-8"?>
<soap:Envelope xmlns:xsi="http://www.w3.org/2001/XMLSchema-instance"
            xmlns:xsd="http://www.w3.org/2001/XMLSchema"
            xmlns:soap="http://schemas.xmlsoap.org/soap/envelope/">
  <soap:Body>
    <CTempResponse xmlns="http://tempuri.org/">
      <CTempResult>0</CTempResult>
    </CTempResponse>
  </soap:Body>
</soap:Envelope>
```

In this example, you can see the result of the CTemp method call returned in the payload section of the HTTP response message. The SOAP rules for encoding the response element use the same name as the call element from the request message, with the `Response` suffix concatenated to it. In this case, this results in a response element named `CTempResponse`.

Although SOAP doesn't require HTTP as a transport binding, it's the default and preferred binding for SOAP messages. However, it's also possible to create bindings for SOAP messages over such protocols as SMTP and FTP. ASP.NET Web Services transport SOAP messages using HTTP.

This brief overview of the SOAP specification should help you to feel comfortable working with SOAP messages if it's necessary. If you need more information about SOAP, read the SOAP specification available at `www.w3.org`.

Now that you have a basic understanding of SOAP, let's take a look at the SOAP support built into the .NET Framework and how you can use it in building your Web Service applications.

SOAP in the .NET Framework

Fortunately, everything that you've learned about SOAP up to this point is largely unnecessary with respect to implementing simple ASP.NET Web Services. This is because ASP.NET and the .NET Framework automatically generate and process SOAP messages for your Web Service, leaving you to focus on writing the logic of your Web Service application using a familiar object-oriented design approach.

However, more sophisticated Web Services may require access to the SOAP messages in order to add custom headers, examine incoming/outgoing SOAP messages, or otherwise alter the default format of messages generated by the .NET XML serializer when interoperating with SOAP message processors on other platforms.

If SOAP message customization becomes necessary for a particular Web Service that you want to implement, the .NET Framework and ASP.NET can give you access to the SOAP messages. This section will look at the following features provided by ASP.NET for customizing the default SOAP message formats and contents:

- ✦ SOAP headers
- ✦ SOAP extensions
- ✦ SOAP exceptions

Using SOAP headers

SOAP headers are the chief extensibility mechanism offered by the SOAP specification. This feature allows you to piggyback metadata, along with a method request or response message that can be used by the receiver to control, or add additional context to, the method call. For example, user credentials are often added as a SOAP header to enable a Web Service method to authenticate a user before allowing the method call to be executed. In this example, the SOAP header is added by the consumer application and processed by the Web Service method.

> **Note** The SOAP specification doesn't define the contents of SOAP headers. The content and semantics associated with a SOAP header are completely defined by the application that adds the header and the recipient that processes it.

ASP.NET Web Services use SOAP as the default protocol for exchanging messages. This makes it possible for applications to add SOAP headers for their own use. Adding SOAP headers to ASP.NET Web Services is as simple as adding a SoapHeader attribute onto a Web Service method.

The .NET SoapHeader class

The .NET Framework provides a SoapHeader base class (found in the System. Web.Services.Protocols namespace), which you can inherit from in order to create and use a SOAP header. Drawing on the previous discussion of user credentials and authentication, here's an example of a custom SOAP header class:

```
Imports System.Web.Services.Protocols
Public Class AuthenticationSoapHeader
   Inherits SoapHeader
   Public Username as String
   Public Password as String
End Class
```

This example creates a class named AuthenticationSoapHeader that inherits from the SoapHeader base class. Within this class are two public member variables named Username and Password. These member variables can be set by applications that want to pass this data within the SOAP header.

Once you've defined your SOAP header class, you can add it to your Web Service implementation and reference it within the method declaration by adding an attribute to that declaration. Although we haven't covered the details of coding Web Services and Web Service methods, let's take a quick look at the basic syntax involved in this process.

The following code snippet shows the use of your AuthenticationSoapHeader class:

```
Public Class MyWebService
   Public AuthSoapHeader As AuthenticationSoapHeader
   <WebMethod, SoapHeader("AuthSoapHeader")> _
   Public Function MyWebMethod() As Integer
```

This example declares a class named `MyWebService` that's the implementation class for your Web Service. Within this class you declare a public member variable named `AuthSoapHeader`, which is an instance of your custom SOAP header class. This class instance is used to set the values contained in the SOAP header.

The next line decorates the `MyWebMethod` method declaration with two attributes (the string that's enclosed in angle brackets). The `WebMethod` attribute indicates that this will be a Web-callable method. The simple addition of this attribute causes ASP.NET to add all of the additional features required to make your method callable via the Web. Otherwise, your code continues to look and function like a normal class. The `SoapHeader` attribute is used to specify that a SOAP header should be added to the `MyWebMethod` method. The parameter of this attribute is used to identify the specific header information to be added to this header, and it's the name of the member variable you previously declared for your SOAP header instance.

The result of this work is that a SOAP header will be added to the SOAP message that contains two SOAP header elements, the username and password. These elements will have values that are specified by the consumer of the Web Service.

Recall that there are two attributes named `MustUnderstand` and `DidUnderstand` that are used with a SOAP header to indicate whether it's mandatory or optional for a recipient to process the header entry. The .NET `SoapHeader` class implements these SOAP attributes as two Boolean properties of the base class. Therefore, you can set these properties to the desired Boolean value, which will automatically generate the appropriate SOAP attribute when the SOAP message is generated by ASP.NET.

The .NET SoapHeader attribute

As you saw in the last example, the `SoapHeader` attribute is used to enable support for SOAP headers on specific Web Service methods that are declared with the `WebMethod` attribute. Specifically, the `SoapHeader` attribute is supplied with the name of a member variable that's an instance of your custom `SoapHeader` class. Technically, this syntax is setting a property of the `SoapHeader` attribute, namely the `MemberName`-property. The `SoapHeader` attribute supports these three properties:

✦ `MemberName`

✦ `Direction`

✦ `Required`

The `MemberName`-property of the `SoapHeader` attribute identifies the name of the class variable that determines the type of the SOAP header. In this example, the type of the SOAP header is obtained from the `AuthSoapHeader` member variable within the `MyWebService` class.

The Direction property of the SoapHeader attribute is used to specify in which direction the header is expected to be supplied. By default, SOAP headers are attached to method requests only and are said to be inbound to the Web Service. Using this property, you can change this default behavior. The Direction property accepts an enumeration named SoapHeaderDirection that supports the following three values:

✦ SoapHeaderDirection.In: Declares that the SOAP header is expected to be supplied to request messages generated by the Web Service consumer.

✦ SoapHeaderDirection.Out: Declares that the SOAP header is expected to be supplied by response messages generated by the Web Service.

✦ SoapHeaderDirection.InOut: Declares that the SOAP header is expected to be supplied by both the request and response messages.

Here's an example of the Direction property in VB .NET:

```
<SoapHeader("AuthSoapHeader", Direction:=SoapHeaderDirection.Out>
```

Finally, the Required property of the SoapHeader attribute is a Boolean property that controls whether or not the SOAP header is required. By default, this property is set to true. This means that if the header isn't supplied, a Soap exception will be raised. Setting this property to false makes the header optional, as in the following example:

```
<SoapHeader("AuthSoapHeader", Required:="false")>
```

These are the basics for using SOAP headers in ASP.NET Web Services. But how does a consumer access the SOAP header to set the values that needed to be passed? Fortunately, these details are handled for you by ASP.NET when the Web Service proxy class is created. This makes setting SOAP header values as simple as setting a property on the proxy class instance. You'll learn all about Web Service proxy classes (the primary means by which a consumer interacts with a Web Service) in the chapter about consuming Web Services.

Now, let's look at a slightly more advanced feature of ASP.NET called SOAP extensions.

Using SOAP extensions

One of the more advanced features of SOAP within the .NET Framework is the SOAP extensions technology. This lets you inspect or modify a SOAP message at specific stages in message processing on either the client (the consumer of the Web Service) or server (the Web Service itself). Of course, this assumes that the client and server are both based on the .NET Framework.

This is a powerful feature because it allows you to implement some very interesting applications that can be leveraged by Web Services and/or their clients in a completely transparent manner. For example, you can create extensions that

✦ Encrypt messages to protect the contents while in transit.

✦ Compress messages to reduce the size of the transmission stream.

✦ Log messages for auditing or tracing message activity (especially useful in debugging).

✦ Process SOAP attachments.

These are just a few examples of the useful applications of SOAP extensions.

The .NET Framework exposes this functionality through the following base classes that you can derive from in order to create custom SOAP extensions:

✦ `System.Web.Services.Protocols.SoapExtension`

✦ `System.Web.Services.Protocols.SoapExtensionAttribute`

The `SoapExtension` class is the base class for all SOAP extensions. This class defines a method named `ProcessMessage` that's called several times at various stages of message processing. These stages are listed in Table 46-3.

Table 46-3
SOAP Extension Message Processing Stages

Stage	Description
BeforeSerialize	During `SoapClientMessage` processing, the `BeforeSerialize` stage occurs after a client calls a Web Services method, but prior to the call being serialized.
	During `SoapServerMessage` processing, the `BeforeSerialize` stage occurs after the Web Services method returns results, but prior to those results being serialized.
AfterSerialize	During `SoapClientMessage` processing, the `AfterSerialize` stage occurs after a client call to a Web Services method is serialized, but prior to the network request for the call being made.
	During `SoapServerMessage` processing, the `AfterSerialize` stage occurs after the results for a Web Services method are serialized, but prior to the network response sending the results to the client.

Continued

Table 46-3 *(continued)*	
Stage	*Description*
BeforeDeserialize	During `SoapClientMessage` processing, the `BeforeDeserialize` stage occurs after the network response for a Web Services method has been received, but prior to the response being deserialized.
	During `SoapServerMessage` processing, the `BeforeDeserialize` stage occurs after a network request for a Web Services method is received, but prior to the request being deserialized.
AfterDeserialize	During `SoapClientMessage` processing, the `AfterDeserialize` stage occurs after the network response for a Web Services method has been deserialized, but prior to the client receiving the results.
	During `SoapServerMessage` processing, the `AfterDeserialize` stage occurs after a network request for a Web Services method is deserialized, but prior to the Web Services method being called.

To create a SOAP extension, you simply derive a class from the `SoapExtension` class and implement your extension code in the `ProcessMessage` method. The SOAP message is supplied to you as an input argument to the method. You can examine the SOAP message to determine which stage of message processing is in effect (using the `Stage` property) and then perform the appropriate processing for that stage. For example, a SOAP extension that's applied to a Web Service client could gain access to the SOAP request message at the `AfterSerialize` stage. To gain access to the SOAP response message, the extension would wait for the `BeforeDeserialize` stage to occur.

Note   You don't have to implement code for all SOAP extension message stages.

In addition to implementing the `SoapExtension` class, you must also derive a class from the `SoapExtensionAttribute` base class. You use this class to create and apply a custom SOAP extension attribute to a method. When the custom extension attribute is added to a Web Service method or a proxy class method, the associated extension is invoked at the appropriate time.

In summary, to implement a SOAP extension, you must derive classes from the .NET `SoapExtension` and `SoapExtensionAttribute` base classes, and then you must implement the code in these derived classes to intercept SOAP messages at the message processing stages you're interested in handling.

Cross-Reference   For specific examples of SOAP extensions, you can refer to the Microsoft .NET online documentation or the Visual Studio online documentation. The MSDN library also contains information about SOAP extensions in the .NET Framework.

Handling SOAP exceptions

Recall that SOAP defines a mechanism for Web Services to return a SOAP exception message in the face of a failed method call. Handling SOAP exceptions within .NET applications (including ASP.NET applications) is a simple, straightforward process. The .NET Framework implements a class named `SoapException` (contained within the System.Web.Services.protocols namespace). The ASP.NET runtime converts SOAP exceptions into instances of the .NET `SoapException` class. This means that you can use `try...catch` blocks within your calls to Web Service methods to catch SOAP exceptions. The following example illustrates how this is done:

```
Imports System.Web.Services
Public Class MyWebService
  <WebMethod()> Public Function _
              Divide(x as Integer, y as Integer) as Integer
    Return x / y
  End Function
End Class
```

You can catch divide-by-zero exceptions that occur when calling the `Divide` Web method by using code similar to the following fragment:

```
Dim div As New MyWebService
Dim z as Integer
Try
   Z = div.Divide(1, 0)
Catch err As SoapException
   StrError = "Web method caused an exception"
End Try
```

The structured exception handling offered by the CLR makes error handling efficient and effective. All you need do is use `try...catch` blocks to trap errors that may occur in your calls to Web Service methods.

Generally speaking, you should always wrap Web Service method calls in `try...catch` blocks. Since Web method calls are at least cross-process (and typically, cross-machine or even cross-network), there's always the possibility that something within the underlying network may go wrong. Unlike local procedure calls that are within a single process, there are many other factors that could cause a remote Web method invocation to fail. It's better to be safe than sorry when it comes to recognizing and handling these types of errors.

The Microsoft SOAP Toolkit

As you might expect, it's entirely possible to create and consume Web Services without the infrastructure and services provided by the .NET Framework and Visual Studio .NET (although it's much easier to do so with their support). Since Web

Services are based on XML, HTTP, and SOAP, all you need to create or consume Web Services are implementations of these technologies. This is precisely what Microsoft has done with the Microsoft SOAP toolkit.

The Microsoft SOAP toolkit supplies the technologies and tools needed to build and deploy Web Services using Visual Studio 6.0 as the development environment, along with the familiar COM programming model. In addition to building Web Services that can run on Windows NT 4.0 SP6 and Windows 2000, you can build Web Service consumers that will run on Windows 98, Windows ME, Windows NT 4.0 SP6, or Windows 2000 SP1.

The toolkit is a free and fully supported SDK that you can download from the MSDN Web site. If you cannot deploy .NET or want to address legacy platforms with Web Services, the Microsoft SOAP Toolkit will prove to be a valuable resource for you.

Although this chapter won't go into great detail, let's briefly look at the features of the toolkit in case you ever need to use it. If that happens, you'll want to refer to the documentation that comes with the toolkit for more detailed information on system requirements, installation instructions, code samples, and the like.

Toolkit Features

The toolkit contains both client-side and server-side COM components, as well as development tools that enable you to build or consume Web Services using Visual Studio 6.0 as the development environment. The technologies and tools included in the SOAP toolkit are as follows:

+ A server-side component that maps Web Service requests to COM object method calls described by WSDL and Web Service Meta Language (WSML) documents.

+ A client-side component that enables a consumer to call Web Services described by a WSDL document.

+ Components that generate, transport, and process SOAP messages.

+ A WSDL/WSML document generator tool.

+ A Visual Basic add-in that simplifies the processing of XML documents contained in SOAP messages.

+ Additional APIs, utilities, and sample applications that illustrate how to use the SOAP Toolkit to build Web Service and consumer applications.

It's worth noting here that Web Service consumers created with the SOAP toolkit can invoke any Web Service, whether it's based on the SOAP toolkit, ASP.NET, or some other Web Service implementation. Likewise, Web Services that are created with the SOAP toolkit can be invoked by any Web Service client, regardless of implementation. This illustrates one of the most powerful features of the Web

Services model: implementation independence. The way in which a Web Service or Web Service consumer is implemented is unimportant, just as long as they can communicate via XML, HTTP, and SOAP, and implement the standards in an equivalent manner.

The remainder of this chapter describes the SOAP Toolkit technologies that you can use to do the following:

✦ **Create a Web Service**. This discussion covers the proper selection of a Web Service request listener, as well as the use of a server-side component that maps Web Service requests to COM object method calls described by WSDL and Web Service Meta Language (WSML) documents.

✦ **Consume a Web Service**. This discussion covers the use of a client-side component that uses a Web Service WSDL document to enable a consumer to call methods of Web Services.

✦ **Troubleshoot Web Services.** This task will be accomplished with the SOAP Trace utility.

Let's take a quick look at some of these SOAP Toolkit features that enable you to create Web Services and Web Service consumers.

Creating a Web Service

To enable Web Service capabilities on the server, first and foremost you must be able to listen for Web Service requests (SOAP messages) that are delivered to the server. This means that the Web server must be configured to listen for and process Web Service request messages. The Soap Toolkit provides two choices for providing a SOAP listener for the IIS Web server: an Internet Server API (ISAPI) listener and an Active Server Pages (ASP) listener. After making your choice, you must edit the WSDL document to specify the appropriate URL of the Web Service endpoint. For the ASP listener, you should specify the URL to the ASP file. To use the ISAPI listener, you specify the URL to the WSDL file.

ISAPI listener

In most cases, you can choose the ISAPI listener. The advantages of the ISAPI listener are that it's faster than the ASP listener and doesn't require you to implement any code. You simply need to supply the WSDL and WSML files that describe the Web Service and the mappings to COM server methods. The disadvantage of the ISAPI listener is that you have no control over the invocation of Web Service methods (this is done automatically).

ASP listener

If you need to parse or validate input arguments, perform security checks, or perform similar actions on an incoming request, you must use an ASP listener. The advantage of the ASP listener is that you can perform special message processing on the server before invoking the Web Service method. The drawbacks of the ASP listener are that it's slower than the ISAPI listener and you must implement custom code in an ASP page to invoke the Web Service methods.

Web Service message processing

If you're using the ISAPI listener, Web Service message processing is automatic. When an incoming SOAP request is detected, the ISAPI listener is invoked to handle the message. The ISAPI listener loads the WSDL and WSML files, executes the request, and returns the results in a response message. In this scenario, you only need to provide the WSDL and WSML files.

If you're using the ASP listener, you must create an ASP page that uses the SOAPServer COM component to process incoming Web request messages.

Note Both the ISAPI and ASP listeners use the SOAPServer component. So regardless of listener choice, the SOAP messages are handled identically once the SOAPServer component receives the request.

The SOAPServer component

The SOAPServer component enables Web Service request messages to call methods on COM components. The component exposes several properties and methods that permit an ASP page to pass a Web Service request to the component for execution (via the request stream) and supply the results to the caller (via the response stream). Using this component, the ASP page doesn't have to understand how to process SOAP messages.

To use the SOAPServer component, you specify the WSDL and WSML documents as input arguments to the initialization method. This allows the component to create the mappings between Web Service requests and COM method calls.

After you've initialized the SOAPServer object, you can call its invoke method, passing the ASP input stream and output stream as arguments to the method. When you call the invoke method on the SOAPServer object, the following steps occur:

1. The SOAPServer object deserializes the SOAP request message supplied to it via the invoke method.

2. The request is then examined to locate the COM component and method to be called from the WSDL and WSML documents that were loaded when the SOAPServer object was initialized.

3. An instance of the identified COM object is created and the appropriate method is called, using the arguments obtained from the request message.

4. The result is obtained from the method call and serialized into a SOAP response message.

5. The SOAP response message is returned to the caller via an output argument of the invoke method.

Creating a Web Service consumer

The SOAPClient COM component enables Web Service consumers to call Web Services. This component leverages the features of the SOAP Toolkit to provide properties and methods that a Web Service consumer can use to call Web Service methods without having to deal with SOAP messages directly. In this way, the SOAPClient component acts as a proxy object for the Web Service.

To use the SOAPClient component, you must have access to the WSDL document that describes the Web Service. When you call the initialization method on the component, you pass in the location of the WSDL document. This causes all of the operations defined in the WSDL document to be dynamically bound to the SOAPClient component. Once this has been completed, you can invoke the methods defined in the WSDL document via the SOAPClient object.

When you invoke a Web Service method bound to the SOAPClient object, the following steps occur:

1. The SOAPClient object serializes the method call into a SOAP request message and delivers it to the server.

2. The server deserializes the SOAP request message and processes the request.

3. The server serializes the result into a SOAP response message and delivers it to the client.

4. The SOAPClient object deserializes the SOAP response message and returns the result to the caller.

The SOAPClient object also exposes SOAP fault properties so that you can examine error information in case a method call fails for some reason.

To summarize, the SOAPClient object makes it easy to consume Web Services in a COM-like manner. The consumer needs only to supply the WSDL document that describes the Web Service to the SOAPClient object in order to call the operations exposed by the Web Service. The SOAPClient object takes care of translating COM method calls into SOAP requests and then translating the SOAP response into a COM method return value. If an error occurs in the method call, the SOAPClient object exposes properties that give a consumer access to the SOAP fault information that's returned.

The WSDL/WSML generator tool

The WSDL/WSML generator tool is used to automatically generate WSDL and WSML documents from COM type libraries. The graphical version of the tool (named wsdlgen.exe) walks you through the process of generating these documents. It will request the type of listener you want to use, the location of the COM type library, which methods you want to expose from the available interfaces in the type library, the folder in which to write the WSDL and WSML documents, and a few other details. After you answer these questions, the tool will generate the files for you.

If you want to script the generation of these files, a command-line version of the tool, `wsdlstb.exe`, is also supplied. You can use the `/?` switch on the command line to get help information on valid command parameters and switches.

The bottom line here is that the WSDL/WSML generator tool can be a great time-saver when you're preparing your COM components for accessibility as Web Services.

The SOAP trace utility

One final utility that ships with the Microsoft SOAP Toolkit is the SOAP trace utility. Using this graphical utility, you can view SOAP request and response messages transported over HTTP between a Web Service and Web Service consumer. The trace utility can be configured to run on either the client or the server.

To run the trace utility on the server, first you must make a small modification to the WSDL document that specifies the URL to the SOAP endpoint. Then you can start the trace utility to begin a tracing session.

To run the trace utility on the client, you must copy the WSDL document to the client machine, make a similar modification to the WSDL document, and start the trace utility. After starting the utility, you need to specify the name of the host where the actual Web Service is running. Then you'll be able to begin a tracing session.

Summary

SOAP is a major element of the Web Services infrastructure and a critical factor in its ability to reach across platforms, operating systems, object models, and programming languages. This greatly increases the interoperability of distributed computing components built on this model.

SOAP ends the language and object model wars by permitting component interoperability at a message level. This allows the user to implement his Web Service code in any way he wants, using tools and technologies that are familiar and native to the platform on which he works.

Relatively speaking, SOAP is still a young technology. Although it has been submitted to the W3C as a note, the specification hasn't made it through the W3C's standardization process. Rest assured, though, that the major vendors driving and implementing SOAP will keep pace with any changes that occur through the standards process, and hopefully they'll be able to insulate developers from the subtle changes that may occur.

✦   ✦   ✦

Building a Web Service

by Jim Chandler

This chapter teaches you how to build a simple Web Service using Visual Basic .NET in Microsoft Visual Studio. It goes step-by-step through the process of creating a Web Service that converts given temperatures between Fahrenheit, Celsius, Kelvin, and Rankine. Along the way, I'll describe some of the Visual Studio implementation options related to building Web Services.

Creating the Temperature Conversion Web Service

The temperature conversion Web Service converts specified temperature values from Fahrenheit or Celsius to either Fahrenheit, Celsius, Kelvin, or Rankine. Each of these unit conversions is defined by a well-known arithmetic formula that can be easily represented in Visual Basic and doesn't require a lot of code. This chapter keeps it simple so that you can focus more on the various architectural elements of ASP.NET Web Services, rather than the details of the algorithm implemented by the code.

Before you start building this service, you should know a little about the following components of this example:

✦ Temperature conversion formulas

✦ Method descriptions

✦ Method arguments

✦ Method behavior

Temperature conversion formulas

Table 47-1 shows the conversions that are supported by the service and the corresponding formulas used to perform the conversion:

From/To	Fahrenheit (F)	Celsius (C)	Kelvin (K)	Rankine (R)
Celsius	((C * 9) / 5) + 32	N/A	C + 273.15	F + 459.67
Fahrenheit	N/A	((F - 32) * 5) / 9	C + 273.15	F + 459.67

Table 47-1
Temperature Conversion Formulas

As you can see from the table, some of the conversions are specified assuming an initial conversion to another unit. For example, to convert a Celsius temperature to Rankine, the temperature value is first converted to Fahrenheit and then the remaining conversion rules are applied.

Finally, in keeping with the goal of code simplicity and brevity, the service only supports temperature conversions from Celsius or Fahrenheit to any of the other applicable units.

Method description

The temperature conversion Web Service supports a single method named CTemp, which is modeled along the lines of the classic Visual Basic type conversion functions such as CBool, CLng, CDbl, etc. The obvious difference, of course, is that you're converting to other numeric units instead of converting to other data types.

Method arguments

The temperature conversion method accepts the three arguments that are summarized in Table 47-2.

The method returns a Decimal result, which is the value of the conversion to the units specified in the ToUnits argument.

Table 47-2
Temperature Conversion Method Arguments

Argument Name	Data Type	Comments
Temperature	Decimal	Any numeric value that can be specified by the Decimal data type.
FromUnits	String	Valid values are C for Celsius or F for Fahrenheit.
ToUnits	String	Valid values are C for Celsius, F for Fahrenheit, K for Kelvin, and R for Rankine.

Method behavior

If the FromUnits and ToUnits arguments are the same, the method call is success-ful and the Temperature argument is returned unchanged. If the FromUnits and/or ToUnits don't specify valid unit identifiers, an ArgumentException exception is thrown. Likewise, if the conversion specified by the FromUnits and ToUnits argu-ments isn't supported, an ArgumentException exception is thrown.

Building the Web Service in Visual Studio

The Visual Studio Integrated Development Environment (IDE) is a highly productive tool for building Web Services. As you learned in the previous chapters of Part VII, Web Services require an addressable entry point file, an assembly that implements the functionality of the service, a Web Service Description (WSDL) document, an optional Discovery (DISCO) document, and an optional UDDI registration. Fortunately, the .NET Framework and Visual Studio implement much of this infrastructure for you, allowing you to focus your efforts on the features of the Web Service.

Web Services built with Visual Studio are ASP.NET Web Services. This means that a Web Service built in Visual Studio leverages the ASP.NET infrastructure, tools, and runtime. Of course, ASP.NET itself is built upon the foundation of the .NET Framework and the Common Language Runtime (CLR), providing all of the benefits of these technologies to your Web Service implementation.

These relationships are also important because they affect the physical structure of Web Services within the Visual Studio environment. The power of this model is quite evident as you begin to dissect the various pieces of a Web Service on the .NET platform and understand their features. This chapter covers these points as you work your way through the temperature conversion Web Service implementation.

Before you start working with Visual Studio to build a Web Service application, you must consider a few environmental factors related to your software and network configuration. These considerations directly affect how you build, debug, and deploy Web Services using Visual Studio. They fall into two categories:

✦ **Web Service Development Environment**—Describes the software environment necessary for developing a Web Service.

✦ **Web Service Project Access Methods**—Describes the methods for managing the Web Service project files on a Web server.

ASP.NET Web Service development environment requirements

The typical development environment for an ASP.NET Web Service application usually consists of the following elements:

✦ A personal workstation containing the Visual Studio development software and .NET framework SDK used to design and build your Web Service.

✦ A development Web server that's configured to host and run a development (non-release) version of your Web Service.

✦ A production Web server that's configured to host the final runtime (release) version of your Web Service.

Often, the personal workstation and development Web server are combined on a single computer. This makes design, implementation, and debugging easier during the early development stages of your Web Service. However, if you intend to develop Web Services using this configuration, you must be running Windows 2000 or later as your operating system.

If you intend to develop Web Services on a remote Web server that doesn't have Visual Studio installed, you should consider installing the Server Components portion of Visual Studio on the target Web server. Perform the following steps:

1. Run the Visual Studio .NET setup on the Web server computer and choose Step 1 to install the Windows Component Update (this installs the .NET Framework and other software updates).

2. After the Windows Component Update installation has been completed, choose Step 2 to begin the installation of Visual Studio.

3. In the left-hand pane of the Visual Studio installation window, clear the selection of all components except for Server Components.

4. Expand the Server Components node and select the Web Development and Remote Debugger options.

5. Click Install Now to proceed with the installation.

You should also make sure that the FrontPage Server Extensions are installed and configured on the Web server. The FrontPage Server Extensions are a component of the IIS installation group, which is a part of the Windows 2000 components.

The preceding process installs the necessary runtime files and creates the proper file shares, security groups, etc. required to develop Web Service applications on the Web server. If you don't want to install the server components of Visual Studio on a server, you have to manually configure the Web server to enable it to support Web Services that you develop in Visual Studio.

You should refer to the Visual Studio installation guide and release notes for more information related to installation requirements and other issues.

Web Service project access methods

Recall that ASP.NET Web Service applications require access to an IIS Web server that hosts the project files and provides the execution environment for your application. Visual Studio provides two Web access methods for managing the project files on a Web server: FrontPage Server Extensions and Windows File Share. It's important that you understand these access methods and choose a method based on your specific network environment.

FrontPage Server Extensions

FrontPage Server Extensions use HTTP to manage your Web Service project files on the server. The advantage of this method is that you don't need local access to the Web server that's hosting your application (as you do with the Windows File Share method). However, there's no integrated source code control.

The disadvantages of this method are as follows:

+ File access is slower.
+ Source code control is limited.
+ The FrontPage Server Extensions must be installed on the server.

Of course, if your Web server is resident on the Internet or otherwise unavailable via local access, you have no choice but to use this access method.

Windows File Share

The Windows File Share method permits you to manage your Web Service project files using a file share on the Web server. To use this method, you must have local access to the Web server that's hosting your application.

The advantages of this method are as follows:

+ File access is faster.
+ There's complete support for the integrated source code control features in Visual Studio.
+ The FrontPage Server Extensions don't have to be installed on the server.

The major disadvantage of this method is that Windows File Shares typically are limited to intranet-only access. Therefore, this method isn't suited to Web servers that are located outside a firewall and accessible to the Internet at large.

When Visual Studio is installed on your computer, a file share named `wwwroot$` is added to the `inetpub/wwwroot` folder. The share permissions specify a group named VS Developers that provides every member of this group full control capabilities on the Web server.

Choosing a Web access method

By default, Visual Studio uses the Windows File Share Web access method for Web Service projects. This method is suitable when you have local access to your Web server, which is typically the case in an intranet scenario (or if you're using your local computer's Web server). This method provides the fastest file access and integrated support for source code control. You need the proper access rights on the Web server in order to create the file structure that contains your Web Service project files.

However, if you don't have local access to your Web server (as might be the case if you're building your Web Service on an Internet Web server), you can't use the Windows File Share access method to manage your Web Service project files. Under these conditions, you must use the FrontPage Server Extensions method. Since this isn't the default Web access method, you need to explicitly set FrontPage Server Extensions as your preferred access method.

Caution

After you set the Web access method and place your files under source code control, you can't change the setting for your project.

Setting the default Web access method

To set the default Web access method for all Web Service projects, follow these steps:

1. Start Visual Studio.

2. From the Tools menu, choose Options.

3. In the Options dialog box, select the Projects folder.

4. Click the Web Settings category. The Options dialog box should look similar to Figure 47-1.

5. Choose your preferred access method by clicking on the appropriate radio button.

6. Click the OK button to save your changes.

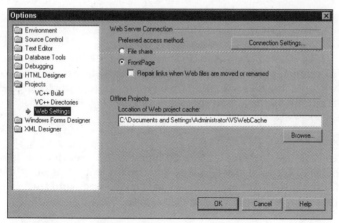

Figure 47-1: Setting the default Web access method

The Visual Studio Start Page

When you start the Visual Studio IDE, the Start Page is displayed, as shown in Figure 47-2.

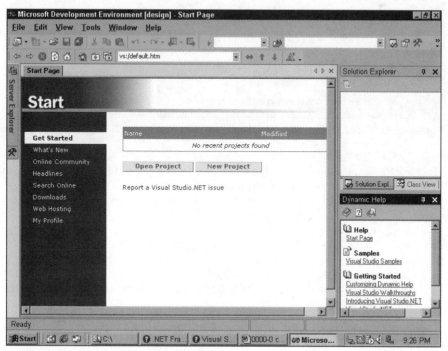

Figure 47-2: The Visual Studio .NET Start Page

The Start Page provides links to general information about Visual Studio, such as What's New and Downloads.

One of the first things you may want to do is customize the Visual Studio IDE to your particular level of development experience and individual taste. You can do this by clicking the My Profile link and adjusting the settings to your personal preferences from the list of options displayed on the resulting page.

Creating a Web Service project

The first step to building the temperature conversion Web Service outlined at the beginning of this chapter is to create a Web Service project in Visual Studio. After you've started Visual Studio, choose New from the File menu and then choose Project from the submenu. Visual Studio displays the New Project dialog shown in Figure 47-3.

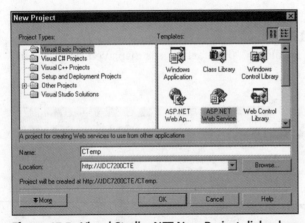

Figure 47-3: Visual Studio .NET New Project dialog box

The New Project dialog box is where you can create many different types of projects based on preconfigured project templates. These templates define such things as the basic structure of a project, the files to be included, and the parameters necessary to build and deploy your project.

To create a Visual Basic .NET Web Service project, follow these steps:

1. Choose the Visual Basic Projects folder from the list of project types on the left. Next, choose the ASP.NET Web Service icon from the list of templates on the right.

2. Specify a name for your project. The sample project is named CTemp, so enter **CTemp** in the Name text box. Notice that as you type into the text box, Visual Studio automatically fills out the project location, showing you where your project files will be stored.

3. The project location text box defines which Web server you use to store and execute your Web Service project files during development in Visual Studio.

By default, the project location points to the local Web server on your computer. My computer name is `JDC7200CTE`, which results in a root location of `http://jdc7200CTE`. Your name will be different, of course. Usually, you should develop and test your Web Service using your local computer's Web server because that's the simplest configuration.

Underneath the Location text box, the dialog box displays the complete path to your new Web Service. This is the path that consumers of your Web Service can use when calling your service (at least while it's under development).

4. Click the OK button to create the project. At this point, Visual Studio connects to the Web server you specified in the Location text box and creates the Web Service project file structure. Visual Studio also creates a solution file on your local computer.

Note If the Web server you specified isn't on your local computer, the solution file is the only file that's stored locally.

When you've finished building and testing your Web Service, Visual Studio makes it easy to specify a different Web server when it comes time to deploy your Web Service to a production Web server.

Cross-Reference Web Service deployment is discussed in more detail in Chapter 48.

When Visual Studio has finished creating the project, the IDE looks similar to Figure 47-4.

Notice that the Solution Explorer window has been added to the IDE, and it lists the files that were created for your project. Underneath the Solution Explorer is the Properties window, which lists the properties for the currently selected object (in this case, the `Service1.asmx` file). By default, the component designer surface is displayed in the main part of the Visual Studio window.

Setting the Web Service name

The next step you need to complete to construct your Web Service is to change the name of your Web Service declaration file, currently named `Service1.asmx` (the default name given by Visual Studio).

You may recall that ASP.NET uses a file with an `.asmx` extension to identify a Web Service. This file serves as the Web-addressable entry point for your Web Service and defines the class that implements the functionality of the Web Service. The Web Service declaration can specify that the class implementation is embedded in the `.asmx` file itself, or that the class is contained in an external assembly. This latter type of declaration is also called a *code-behind file* and is the type of Web Service implementation created by Visual Studio.

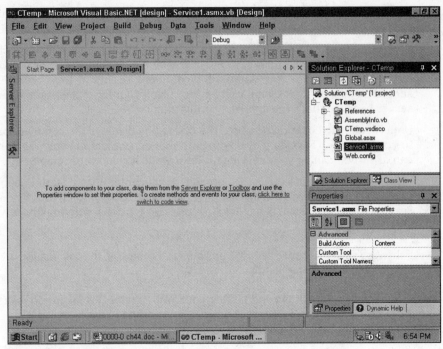

Figure 47-4: Visual Basic .NET Web Service project in Visual Studio

To change the name of the Web Service entry point file, follow these steps:

1. Right-click on the `Service1.asmx` file in the Solution Explorer window shown in Figure 47-4.

2. Choose Rename from the pop-up menu.

3. Type **CTemp.asmx** in the text box.

4. Press the Enter key.

This renames the Web Service entry point file. Note that since Visual Studio uses code-behind files for a Web Service, you've only changed the name of the entry point file. The actual implementation class still has the name of `Service1`. You'll correct this shortly when you add the implementation code discussed in the upcoming section, "Writing the Implementation Code."

Web Service project files

When you create a Web Service project in Visual Studio using the Web Service project template, a project file structure is created on the target Web server and a Visual Studio Solution file is created on your local computer. The files listed in Table 47-3 are created by Visual Studio automatically and placed in the file structure on the target development Web server.

Tip

By default, some of the files in your Web Service project are hidden in the Solution Explorer. To view all of the files in your project, choose Show All Files from the Project menu. Or, you can use the Show All Files button at the top of the Solution Explorer window.

Recall that Web Services on the .NET platform are based on ASP.NET. The files listed in Table 47-3 include files associated with a typical ASP.NET Web application (such as `Web.config` and `Global.asax`). In addition to these files, the `{service name}.asmx` and `{service name}.asmx.vb` files define the entry point and code-behind file for the ASP.NET Web Service, respectively.

Table 47-3	
Visual Studio Web Service Project Files	
Project File	**Description**
`{service name}.asmx`	This file serves as the Web-accessible entry point for the Web Service. It contains the Web Service processing directive, which declares information about the implementation of the Web Service.
`{service name}.asmx.vb`	This file contains the code-behind class that implements the functionality of the Web Service. This file is referenced by the `Service1.asmx` file in its Web Service processing directive.
`AssemblyInfo.vb`	This file contains information about the assemblies within the Web Service project.
`Web.config`	This XML file contains ASP.NET application configuration information for the Web Service.
`Global.asax`	This file is responsible for handling ASP.NET application-level events.
`Global.asax.vb`	This file contains the code-behind class that handles the ASP.NET application-level events. This file is referenced by the `Global.asax` file in its ASP.NET application directive. By default, this file doesn't appear in the Solution Explorer.
`{project name}.vbproj`	This file contains project metadata, such as the list of project files, build settings, and so on.
`{project name}.vbproj.webinfo`	Identifies the project Web server and any configuration information. This file is created only for Web type projects.
`{project name}.vsdisco`	This file contains links (URLs) to the discovery (DISCO) information available for the Web Service.

Continued

Table 47-3 *(continued)*	
Project File	**Description**
`Bin\{project name}.dll`	This file is the assembly package for the classes that implement the functionality of the Web Service.
`Bin\{project name}.pdb`	This file contains the debug symbols for the Web Service. It's only built when the Debug configuration is selected for a project build.
`{solution name}.sln`	This file contains solution metadata, such as project dependencies, global build configurations, etc. Note that if you're using a remote Web server to develop your Web Service, this is the only file that's stored locally on your computer.

Visual Studio relies on the `sln (solution)` file to define the projects and properties associated with the entire solution you are writing. In addition, Visual Studio automatically maintains a Web Service discovery document (the `.vsdisco` file), as well as the language project files (such as `{project name}.vbproj`).

The files located in the `Bin` folder are generated by Visual Studio when you build your project. These include the .NET assembly that implements the functionality of the Web Service, as well as any debugging symbols generated during the build process.

Now let's take a look at how the build process organizes project output files into separate debug and release configurations.

Viewing project configuration settings

Visual Studio creates and maintains separate debug and release configurations for your ASP.NET Web Service project. The Debug configuration is used to build the project for the purposes of testing and debugging your Web Service. The Release configuration is used when you're ready to release and deploy your Web Service to a production Web server.

Visual Studio creates these configurations by default when the project is created. Each of these configurations also contains default settings that you can change, if you find it necessary. To view the configuration settings, follow these steps:

1. Right-click on the Web Service project file in the Solution Explorer, shown in Figure 47-4.

2. Choose Properties from the pop-up menu.

3. In the <Project> Property Pages dialog box, choose the configuration you want to view from the Configuration list box.

4. Click on the Configuration Properties folder to open it.

All of the user-changeable configuration settings are available from the list of settings categories under the Configuration Properties folder.

Debug configuration

The Debug configuration causes Visual Studio to compile your Web Service with full symbolic debug information and no compiler optimizations. This configuration maximizes your ability to debug the Web Service at the expense of performance. This is the default configuration when Visual Studio creates a Web Service project.

Release configuration

The Release configuration causes Visual Studio to compile your Web Service with full code optimization and no symbolic debug information. This configuration maximizes the performance of the Web Service at the expense of debugging.

Changing the project configuration

When you're ready to release your Web Service, you should change the project configuration before you build your Web Service for the final time. To do this, choose Release from the Solution Configurations list box on the Standard toolbar in Visual Studio. When you build your Web Service, Visual Studio creates a highly optimized version that's suitable for deployment to a production Web server.

Writing the Implementation Code

You're now ready to write the code that implements your temperature conversion service. To view the code-behind file specified in your Web Service .asmx file, simply double-click on the component design surface. This displays the template code that Visual Studio generated in the code-behind file of CTemp.asmx, as shown in Figure 47-5.

The code view enables you to edit the Visual Basic implementation code for your Web Service. As shown in Figure 47-5, Visual Studio has already generated a skeleton class to contain your Web Service implementation. All you have to do now is fill in the details of your implementation. Begin this process by slightly modifying the class declaration to match some of the changes you made to your project in earlier in this chapter.

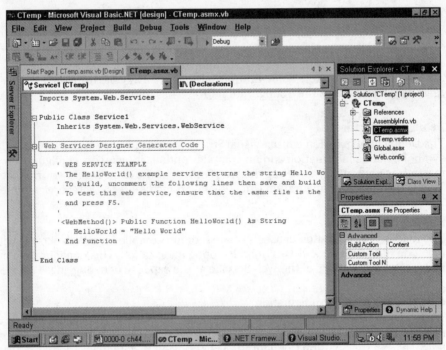

Figure 47-5: Code-behind template for the CTemp Web Service

The class declaration

Before you add your implementation code, you need to change the class name that contains the implementation for your Web Service from `Service1` to `TempConverter`. Do that now by typing the new name in the code window.

In addition to changing the class name within your code-behind file, you also need to update the Web Service declaration contained in the Web Service entry point file. Follow these steps to do so:

1. Right-click on the `CTemp.asmx` file in the Solution Explorer and choose Open With... from the pop-up menu.

2. Choose Source Code (Text) Editor from the Open With dialog box and click the Open button.

3. Locate the `class=` attribute in the Web Service declaration and change `Service1` to `TempConverter`.

Note   Before you move on to the next step, you may also want to remove the commented-out code in the class that refers to HelloWorld. This is a sample Web method declaration that's added by Visual Studio as a part of the ASP.NET Web Service project template.

The `WebService` attribute is an optional attribute that can be added to the Web Service class declaration to configure various properties for the class. The `WebService` attribute can be added to the front of the class declaration as follows:

```
<WebService()> Public Class TempConverter
```

Table 47-4 lists the properties that you can add to the `WebService` attribute.

Table 47-4
WebService Attribute Properties

Property Name	Description
Description	Provides a brief description of the functionality of the Web Service as a whole.
Namespace	Provides a unique XML namespace for the WSDL document that describes the capabilities of the Web Service.
Name	Overrides the Web Service name, normally taken from the class name. The name is typically used when generating proxy classes from the WSDL document of the Web Service.

You don't use these properties in your `TempConverter` class declaration, but you use the `Namespace` property later when you learn about Web Service deployment and publishing in an upcoming chapter.

Creating Web methods

Now that you've updated the class name, you're ready to insert the implementation code for your Web Service. Begin by entering the following method declaration into the code window inside your `TempConverter` class:

```
<WebMethod()> Public Function CTemp(_
            ByVal Temperature As Decimal, _
            ByVal FromUnits As String, _
            ByVal ToUnits As String) As Decimal
```

The first thing that you should notice (and also appreciate) is that the method declaration looks quite similar to the function or method declarations you're already used to writing in previous versions of Visual Basic.

But perhaps more important is what's *missing* from this declaration. Note that there's no reference to SOAP, XML, HTTP or any of the other technologies required for Web Services. All of these details are buried in the plumbing provided by the ASP.NET runtime and the .NET Framework!

The WebMethod attribute

The only part of your method declaration that's remotely different from traditional component programming in Visual Basic is the `<WebMethod()>` attribute. The simple addition of this attribute to a public method declaration instructs Visual Basic to make this method a Web method. This results in additional support for serialization/deserialization of XML, the mapping of data types to XML, and the formatting/exchange of SOAP-based messages.

> **Note** The `WebMethod` attribute can also be applied to public properties of a class, making these Web-callable as well.

Notice that the `WebMethod()` attribute also has room (within the parentheses) for attribute properties. Attribute properties allow you to override default behavior or enable Web methods with additional functionality. Table 47-5 lists the properties that you can add to the `WebMethod` attribute.

Table 47-5
WebMethod() Attribute Properties

Property Name	Description
Description	Provides a brief description of the functionality of the Web method.
EnableSession	Enables session state so that state can be maintained between method calls.
MessageName	Provides an alias name for Web methods. This is typically required when implementing polymorphic methods in a class.
TransactionOption	Allows the Web method to support transactions (similar to the transaction support provided by MTS and COM+).
CacheDuration	Enables output caching so that the results of a particular method call can be saved to a cache and reused, rather than regenerated.
BufferResponse	Permits the server to buffer the response and transmit it only after the response has been completely generated.

You won't use these optional properties in your `CTemp` Web Service method. To learn more about these properties, refer to the .NET Framework or Visual Studio online documentation.

Adding the implementation code

After you've added the Web method declaration, you're ready to insert the code that actually performs the temperature conversions. Enter the code from Listing 47-1 into the code window underneath the `CTemp` Web method declaration.

Listing 47-1: Temperature Conversion Code

```
    Select Case FromUnits.ToUpper.Chars(0)
      Case "F" 'Fahrenheit
        Select Case ToUnits.ToUpper.Chars(0)
          Case "F" 'No conversion necessary
            Return Temperature
          Case "C" 'Convert Fahrenheit to Celsius
            Return ((Temperature - 32) * 5) / 9
          Case "K" 'Convert Fahrenheit to Kelvin
            Return (((Temperature - 32) * 5) / 9) + 273.15
          Case "R" 'Convert Fahrenheit to Rankine
            Return Temperature + 459.67
          Case Else
            'Throw exception
            Throw New ArgumentException("Bad ToUnits arg.")
        End Select
      Case "C" 'Celsius
        Select Case ToUnits.ToUpper.Chars(0)
          Case "C" 'No conversion necessary
            Return Temperature
          Case "F" 'Convert Celsius to Fahrenheit
            Return ((Temperature * 9) / 5) + 32
          Case "K" 'Convert Celsius to Kelvin
            Return Temperature + 273.15
          Case "R" 'Convert Celsius to Rankine
            Return (((Temperature * 9) / 5) + 32) + 459.67
          Case Else
            'Throw exception
            Throw New ArgumentException("Bad ToUnits arg.")
        End Select
      Case Else
        'Throw exception
        Throw New ArgumentException("Bad FromUnits arg.")
    End Select
End Function
```

Handling errors

The .NET framework, via the Common Language Runtime (CLR), provides excellent support for handling errors via exceptions. Applications built on the .NET Framework can throw and catch exceptions to handle all types of runtime errors. This support is also available to Web Services.

Generally, you want to use exceptions to communicate runtime errors back to Web Service consumers for conditions that your service cannot handle effectively. As you can see in your implementation of the CTemp Web method, in some cases you must throw exceptions based on invalid input obtained from the consumer in the method call.

Web Services communicate exceptions to consumers via SOAP exception messages. A SOAP exception is represented by the `SoapException` class in the .NET Framework's System.Web.Services.Protocols namespace. As a Web Service consumer, you can wrap calls to Web Service methods within `try...catch` blocks to intercept exceptions thrown by Web Services.

Referring back to your `CTemp` implementation, arguments that cannot be processed as specified by the consumer cause the Web Service to throw an `Argument Exception` exception. This exception is serialized into a `SOAPException` message and returned to the consumer.

Note that communicating exceptions to Web Service consumers is only supported via SOAP. Therefore, if you use HTTP-GET or HTTP-POST to call a Web Service method (as is the case when you're using a Web browser to test and invoke Web Services), you cannot get exceptions transported back to the browser. In this case, the exception within the Web Service is handled by the Web server, which results in the transmission of a server error page back to the consumer.

 Cross-Reference See Chapter 44 for discussions of SOAP, HTTP-GET, and HTTP-POST.

Building the Web Service

Now that you've added all of the implementation code for your CTemp Web Service, you're ready to build it. When you build a Visual Studio ASP.NET Web Service project, the following occurs:

1. Visual Studio saves all of the files in the project you modified since the last build.

2. Visual Studio copies the `{service name}.asmx` file and the default project files to the development Web server.

3. The `{service name}.asmx.vb` class file and the `Global.asax` class file are compiled into the project `.dll` file, which is then copied to the server in the default `\Bin` directory of the target virtual directory. If the project is set to compile a debug version, Visual Studio creates a project `.pdb` file in the `\Bin` directory.

To build the `CTemp` Web Service, choose Build from the Build menu. Visual Studio displays the Output window to show the progress and final results of the build process for your project, as shown in Figure 47-6.

Now that you've successfully built your Web Service, you're ready to test it. The next section covers Web Service testing.

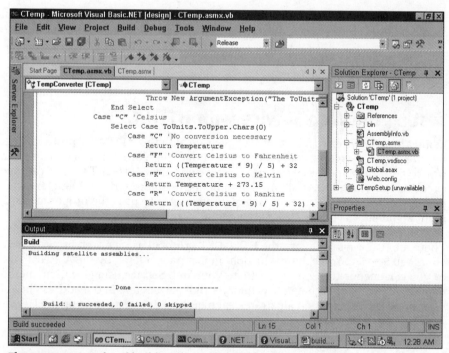

Figure 47-6: Results of building the Web Service in Visual Studio

Testing the Web Service

Visual Studio and the .NET Framework provide several methods you can use to test your Web Service. The simplest and quickest method to test your Web Service is to use a Web browser using the HTTP-GET protocol. This technique doesn't require developing a consumer application.

Note   This technique works only for the HTTP-GET protocol support that's provided by the browser. By default, an ASP.NET Web Service built in Visual Studio supports the HTTP-GET, HTTP-POST, and HTTP-SOAP protocols.

In addition to using a Web browser with HTTP-GET, you can also test your Web Service using a Web browser with HTTP-POST, with a slight modification to the default ASP.NET page used to view Web Services. Finally, you can test your Web Service by developing a custom consumer application.

Cross-Reference   This technique is discussed in Chapter 50, where you build a consumer application to invoke the CTemp Web Service.

The following sections describe how to use the HTTP-GET, HTTP-POST and Visual Studio methods to test your Web Service.

See Chapter 44 for discussions of HTTP-GET and HTTP-POST as message encoding and transport mechanisms for Web Services.

Testing the Web Service with HTTP-GET

Using a Web browser to test your Web Service with the HTTP-GET protocol doesn't require you to develop a consumer application. Therefore, this is a quick and easy way to perform some initial testing of your Web Service. The HTTP-GET protocol encodes data (in this case, method arguments) as query string parameters when posting to the server. This encoding method is used to pass the proper method input arguments as query string arguments.

There are two ways to invoke the HTTP-GET protocol using a Web browser to test your Web Service. You can use the built-in test page offered by the ASP.NET runtime or you can encode the complete URL to your Web Service using location, method name and any input arguments as query string parameters in the address bar of your browser. This section illustrates each of these techniques using the CTemp Web Service as an example.

Using the Web Service test page

The ASP.NET runtime provides excellent support for interactive viewing of Web Service information and capabilities as well as basic HTML forms for performing interactive tests using the HTTP-GET protocol support built into your browser. ASP.NET provides this capability via a Web Service help file template named `DefaultWsdlHelpGenerator.aspx`. By default, this file is located in the `\Winnt\ Microsoft.NET\Framework\{version}\CONFIG` folder. Note that this is just an ordinary ASP.NET page, so you can customize this page to suit your particular needs. What's more, you can copy this file to your Web Service virtual application folder to provide custom capabilities for each Web Service application that you create! You learn how to do this in the section "Testing the Web Service with HTTP-POST."

To use the Web Service help template to view Web Service information, simply enter the URL to your Web Service entry point file (the .asmx file) into the address bar of your browser.

To view the help page for your CTemp Web Service, type the following URL in your Web browser address bar (this example assumes that the Web Service is available on your local machine): `http://localhost/services/ctemp/ctemp.asmx`. Doing so causes the Web server to execute the help file template and return a page similar to the one shown in Figure 47-7.

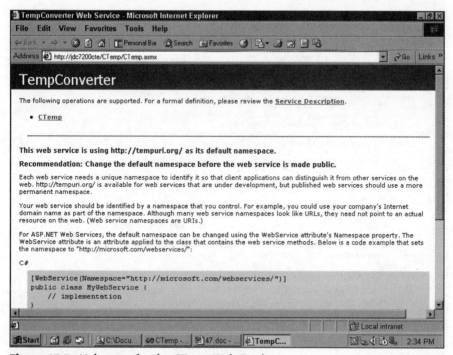

Figure 47-7: Help page for the CTemp Web Service

This page shows the name of the Web Service (TempConverter), the methods that it supports (the single method named CTemp), and a link to the Web Service WSDL document.

The second part of this page includes a warning regarding the use of the temporary namespace URI http://tempuri.org/ for your service. This namespace is used to uniquely identify your Web Service from all others, and you should change it before deploying your Web Service for public consumption. During initial development, however, it isn't necessary to change this URI.

Cross-Reference   The Web Service namespace URI is covered in Chapter 48.

Let's continue exploring the Web Service help page by following some of the links found on the page. First, let's look at the WSDL service contract.

Viewing the WSDL service contract

Take a quick look at the WSDL service contract document for the CTemp Web Service. To view the WSDL service contract, simply click the Service Description hotlink on the Web Service help page. This displays the WSDL XML file contents, as shown in Figure 47-8.

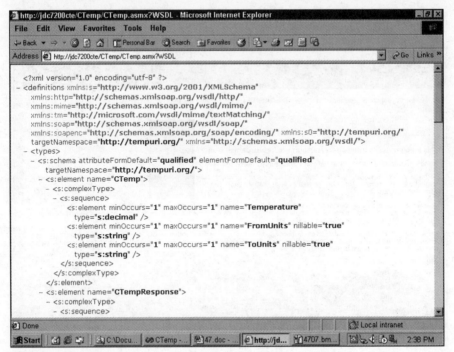

Figure 47-8: WSDL service contract for the CTemp Web Service

Note the URL in the address bar of the browser window. The base URL is the same (it points at your .asmx file), but the URL now also includes a query string:

```
http://jdc7200cte/CTemp/CTemp.asmx?WSDL
```

This query string instructs ASP.NET to generate and display the WSDL service contract for the specified Web Service.

You may be wondering how this process works, since there's no actual WSDL file stored in the virtual directory of your Web Service application. The .NET Framework supports a feature called *reflection*. Basically, this means that a .NET class can be queried to obtain information about the properties, methods, events, and other features it offers via its programmatic interfaces. Reflection is a great feature because you don't have to worry about keeping a separate WSDL file in sync with the actual class that implements the capabilities of the Web Service. Simply let ASP.NET use runtime reflection to query the Web Service class and dynamically generate the WSDL contract all at once!

Now that you've had a chance to look at the WSDL service contract for your Web Service, let's take a look at the help page provided for the CTemp Web method.

Viewing Web method help

If you followed the instructions in the last section to view the WSDL service contract, click the Back button in the browser window to return to the main Web Service help page. Then click the `CTemp` method hotlink. Your browser displays the page that you see in Figure 47-9.

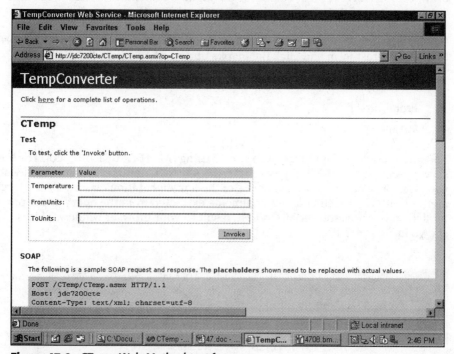

Figure 47-9: CTemp Web Method test form

Note the URL that appears in the address bar of the browser window. The base URL is the same as before (it points at your .asmx file), but it now includes a new query string as follows:

    http://jdc7200cte/CTemp/CTemp.asmx?op=CTemp

This query string instructs the IIS Web server (or, more specifically, the ASP.NET runtime) to display a page that contains detailed information about the Web Service method specified as the value part of the query string argument (in this case, the `CTemp` method).

The first part of the Web method help page contains a hotlink that returns you to the main Web Service documentation page. Underneath this link is a simple form that permits you to invoke the Web Service method.

The second part of the Web method documentation page contains sample SOAP, HTTP-GET, and HTTP-POST request and response message definitions. These are the messages that are exchanged between the Web Service and the consumer for this method call for the three supported message transports.

On this page, you can test your CTemp method by interacting with a form in your browser! You can enter test values for the input arguments and click the Invoke button to execute the CTemp method using the HTTP-GET protocol.

Go ahead and test the service with some sample input. Enter the following information into the test form and click the Invoke button when you're finished.

Temperature: 78

FromUnits: F

ToUnits: C

The form data is posted to the Web server using the HTTP-GET protocol. The Web server receives the URL and passes it to the ASP.NET runtime. The runtime locates your Web Service, creates an instance of the implementation class, calls the target method with the specified input arguments extracted from the query string parameter list, and returns the serialized XML result to your browser window. This is shown in Figure 47-10.

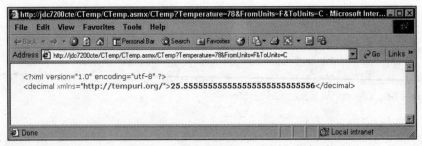

Figure 47-10: XML result returned by the CTemp Web method

The XML lists the return type in the element name and displays the return value of 25.5 within this element. Note the URL that's displayed in the browser address bar. The query strings are formatted to specify the input arguments required by the method that appears as the last component of the base URL.

Manually invoking a Web Service method

In addition to using the Web Service test page to test your CTemp method using the HTTP-GET protocol, you can also manually enter a properly formatted URL into the address bar of your browser. It encodes the method name and input arguments as query string parameters, as follows:

```
http://localhost/ctemp/ctemp.asmx/CTemp?

Temperature=78&FromUnits=F&ToUnits=C
```

Entering this URL into your browser results in the same XML-encoded response from the Web server as the one you obtained in the preceding section, testing the Web Service using the test form generated by the DefaultWsdlHelpGenerator.aspx page.

Testing the Web Service with HTTP-POST

Just like the HTTP-GET protocol, you can use a Web browser to test your Web Service with the HTTP-POST protocol without going to the trouble of writing a consumer application. The HTTP-POST protocol encodes data as name/value pairs within the body of the HTTP request when posting to the server, rather than encoding data in the form of query strings as HTTP-GET does.

See Chapter 44 for a discussion of the HTTP-GET and HTTP-POST as message encoding and transport mechanisms for Web Services.

With only a few minor modifications to the default Web Service help page and your application configuration file, you can test your CTemp Web Service using the HTTP-POST protocol. To do this, follow these steps:

1. Copy Winnt\Microsoft.NET\Framework\{version}\CONFIG\ DefaultWsdlHelpGenerator.aspx to your CTemp Web Service application virtual directory.

2. Rename the file CTemp.aspx.

3. Import this file into Visual Studio by choosing Add Existing Item... from the Project menu and selecting CTemp.aspx from the file dialog box. If Visual Studio asks you whether or not to create a class file for this file, click No.

4. In the Visual Studio editor window, change the showPost flag to true.

5. Save the changes to the file.

6. Open the Web.config file from the Project Explorer.

7. Navigate to the end of the file and locate the closing </system.web> tag.

8. Just above this tag, add the following new XML tags:
   ```
   <webServices>
     <wsdlHelpGenerator href="CTemp.aspx" />
   </webServices>
   ```

9. Save the changes to the file.

You can now test your `CTemp` method using the HTTP-POST protocol. To do this, enter the URL to the `CTemp` entry point file into your browser's address bar as follows:

```
http://localhost/ctemp/ctemp.asmx
```

When the test page is displayed, click the `CTemp` method link once again and enter test values into the form. Click the Invoke button and you should see the XML-formatted results returned to a new browser window (identical to testing with the HTTP-GET protocol).

The only difference between the two methods is revealed in the URL that's displayed in the browser address bar in the results window. Note that the method name is the last segment of the URL, and no query string arguments are visible.

Now you know how easy it is to perform initial testing of your Web Service using your Web browser and the help generator template provided by ASP.NET. Now let's take a look at testing your Web Service using similar methods from within the Visual Studio IDE.

Test using Visual Studio

Visual Studio lets you test Web Services using the same help generator template described earlier in this chapter. The behavior and method for invoking this feature are only slightly different than the testing procedures just described. However, the most significant benefit of testing in this scenario is that you can do it right from the Visual Studio IDE.

To test your `CTemp` Web Service within Visual Studio, follow these steps:

1. Start Visual Studio and load the `CTemp` Web Service solution file.

2. Choose Start Without Debugging from the Debug menu.

Visual Studio builds your Web Service project, automatically launches a Web browser, and displays the Web Service help page. When you're finished testing your Web Service, you can close the browser window. Of course, Visual Studio also contains extensive support for interactive debugging of your Web Services. Now let's look at how to debug your Web Service.

Debugging the Web Service

Sometimes, testing your Web Service reveals flaws in your implementation or other unexpected results. If this occurs, you may need to debug your Web Service using the Visual Studio debugger. If you've debugged ASP applications before, you'll find that Visual Studio has excellent support for testing and debugging your Web

Service applications that is far superior to the relatively primitive and inflexible debugging methods offered by the older ASP technology.

When you start the debugger using your Debug build configuration, Visual Studio automatically launches Internet Explorer and generates the test page that allows you to test your Web Service. This test page provides access to the Web Service contracts, as well as a Web Form for entering values to interact with your Web Service.

To illustrate the general debugging process, let's set a breakpoint in the CTemp method code and start the debugger so that you can examine what happens during a call to this method.

Setting a breakpoint

To set a breakpoint in the Web Service code, simply place your mouse in the left-hand margin of the code window and click on the line where you would like to set a breakpoint. For the purposes of this test, set a breakpoint at the first line of the CTemp method, as shown in Figure 47-11.

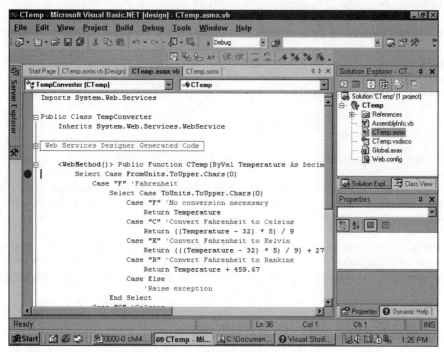

Figure 47-11: Setting a debugger breakpoint in the CTemp Web method

Visual Studio represents a breakpoint using a solid red circle in the code margin adjacent to the appropriate line of code. You can toggle the breakpoint on and off by clicking in the code margin repeatedly. Visual Studio also provides menu options to manage breakpoints and other debugger features.

Starting the debugger

Having set a breakpoint, you're now ready to start the Visual Studio debugger:

1. Choose Start from the Debug menu. Note that Visual Studio automatically builds the necessary pieces of your Web Service. If that's successful, it starts an instance of Internet Explorer that once again displays the help page for your Web Service.

2. Click on the CTemp method link to display the Web Service method help page.

Testing Web Service methods

The Web Form displayed in the Web Service method help page contains text entry boxes for each of the input arguments defined by the method in the WSDL file. Follow these steps to test the functionality of a method:

1. Enter values in each of the input argument text boxes and click the Invoke button.

2. For this example, enter the following argument values:

   Temperature: 74

   FromUnits: F

   ToUnits: C

3. Click the Invoke button to execute the CTemp method.

If you examine the HTML source of the Web method documentation page, notice that the test form uses the HTTP-POST method to post the request and argument values to the CTemp Web Service method.

Since you previously set a breakpoint in your CTemp method code, Visual Studio is activated and halts execution at your breakpoint. If the Immediate window isn't displayed, choose Windows from the Debug menu and then choose Immediate from the Windows submenu.

Examining program variables

You can use the Immediate window in debug mode to quickly examine the values of variables in your Web Service method. One of the first places to look when debugging new Web Service methods is to examine the values of all input arguments.

To examine the values supplied to the `CTemp` method input arguments within Visual Studio, follow these steps:

1. Click in the Command window and type **? Temperature**.

2. Press Enter. This causes the debugger to print the value of the input argument named `Temperature`. The result of these examinations is shown in Figure 47-12.

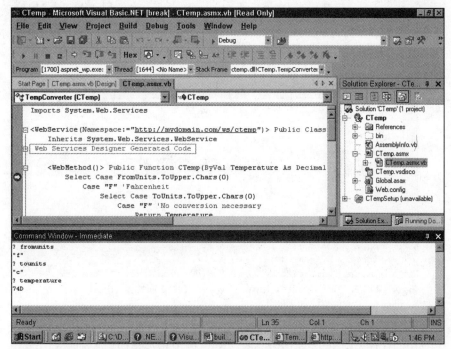

Figure 47-12: Examination of input arguments in the Visual Studio debugger

Note that the temperature value is displayed as 74D, where D signifies that the quantity is a Decimal data type and is not a part of the actual value.

To gain some more experience with examining variables, repeat this process to examine all of the input arguments supplied to the Web Method.

Resuming method execution

After you've examined program variables and performed the other actions necessary to debug your Web Service, you can resume execution of the method call within Visual Studio by pressing the F8 key. Or, you can choose **Continue** from the **Debug** menu.

When the method completes execution, a new browser window is loaded and displays the results of the method call as shown in Figure 47-13.

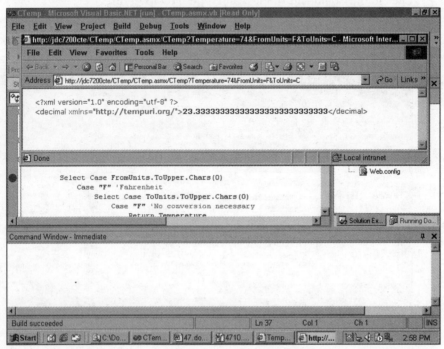

Figure 47-13: XML results returned by the CTemp Web method

Recall that the Web Form that's a part of the Web method documentation page uses the HTTP-GET request/response protocol to invoke the CTemp Web Service method. However, you changed this method to HTTP-POST in a previous section of this chapter. This is evident when you examine the URL in the address bar of the browser window that displays the result of the method call. Note that the result format conforms to the sample HTTP-POST request/response protocol messages displayed in the Web method documentation page.

Summary

In this chapter, you learned the basics of building a Web Service using Visual Basic .NET in the Visual Studio IDE, including how to test and debug the service during development. Now that you've successfully built and tested your first Web Service, you're ready to learn how to deploy your service to a production-quality Web server. The next chapter explores how to do this.

✦   ✦   ✦

Deploying and Publishing Web Services

by Jim Chandler

Deploying a Web Service enables it to execute on a specific host Web server, whereas publishing a Web Service enables potential consumers to locate and interrogate the capabilities of the Web Service before actually calling any methods of the service. This chapter discusses what you need to do before deploying a Web Service, the options for deploying and publishing a Web Service using .NET techniques, and the support built into Visual Studio.

Deployment Preparation

Before you deploy a Web Service, you must make sure that the Web Service specifies a unique XML namespace. This namespace is used within the Web Service WSDL document to uniquely identify the callable entry points of the service. As mentioned in Chapter 47, the default Web Service namespace is set to `http://tempuri.org/` when you're building a Web Service in Visual Studio. Now that you are ready to deploy and publish your Web Service, you must change this temporary namespace designator to a permanent value.

The namespace that you choose to identify your Web Service must be unique. In general, it is recommended that you choose a namespace URI that is owned or otherwise under your control. Typically, using your Internet domain name as part of the Web Service namespace will guarantee uniqueness and also more readily identify the owner of the Web Service.

ASP.NET Web Services support a `Namespace` property as part of the `WebService` attribute used to identify the class that implements the functionality of the Web Service. For example, the `WebService` attribute for the `CTemp` Web Service looks like this:

```
<WebService(Namespace:="http://mydomain.com/ws/ctemp/")>
    Public ClassTempConverter
      ' implementation
    End Class
```

Changing the Web Service namespace is even more important for Web Services created using Visual Studio because a default namespace of `http://tempuri.org/` is used. Unfortunately, this makes it even more likely that you will have namespace conflicts with other Web Services, unless you change this default.

Before you deploy the `CTemp` Web Service, you need to change the default name-space to a more suitable value. To do this, follow these steps:

1. Start Visual Studio.

2. Load the `CTemp` project.

3. If the implementation code in the `CTemp.asmx.vb` file is not displayed, open it by right-clicking on the file in the Solution Explorer window and choosing Open.

4. On the `TempConverter` class declaration line, add the `<WebService>` attribute along with the `Namespace` property and set it to the appropriate value.

The new class declaration line should look as follows:

```
<WebService(Namespace:="http://mydomain.com/ws/ctemp")>
    Public Class TempConverter
      Inherits System.Web.Services.WebService
```

Save your changes and rebuild your project when you are finished. You are now ready to deploy your Web Service!

Deploying Web Services

Generally speaking, the deployment process for a Web Service involves copying the Web Service entry point file (the `.asmx` file), the Web Service assembly along with any dependent assemblies (excluding the .NET framework assemblies), and related support files (such as the Web Service contract file) to an appropriately configured virtual directory file structure on the target Web server.

In sharp contrast from deploying previous-generation Windows applications, Web Services typically are easy to deploy. Visual Studio makes this process even easier by providing several deployment options that are available directly within the Visual Studio environment.

A typical Web Service built in Visual Studio consists of the Web Service entry point file (the `.asmx` file), the `Web.config` file, the WSDL file, the DISCO file, the Web Service assembly that contains the implementation classes for the Web Service, and any dependent assemblies the Web Service references (excluding the .NET Framework). Table 48-1 summarizes the standard file structure for deploying the `CTemp` Web Service built with Visual Studio.

Table 48-1 Files Deployed with a Web Service		
Folder	**File**	**Description**
\inetpub\wwwroot\CTemp	CTemp.asmx	The Web Service entry point file. The folder containing this file should be configured as a Web application directory in IIS.
	Global.asax	The ASP.NET application startup file.
	Web.config	The ASP.NET application configuration file.
\inetpub\wwwroot\CTemp\bin	CTemp.dll	The Web Service assembly that contains the implementation classes for the Web Service, as well as any dependent assemblies that aren't part of the .NET Framework.

The files listed in Table 48-1 are the typical files that you will deploy from an ASP.NET Web Service built with Visual Studio .NET. However, you may need to deploy additional files, such as a Web Service discovery document. At a minimum, you will need to deploy the `.asmx` file and its associated code-behind .NET assembly stored in the `bin` folder.

Web Service deployment tools

There are several choices for tools you can use to deploy a Web Service, depending on the complexity and circumstances of that particular project. These choices are

✦ Visual Studio Web Setup Project

✦ Visual Studio Project Copy

✦ DOS XCOPY Command

✦ Generic File Transfer Method

The following sections describe these options so that you can choose the proper deployment model for Web Services that you have built in Visual Studio.

Deployment using a Web Setup Project

Visual Studio provides a Web Setup Project template that uses the services of the Microsoft Windows Installer technology to create a deployment package for your Web Service. A Web Setup Project creates an .msi file (also called an installation package) that creates and configures a virtual directory on the Web server, copies the files required to execute the Web Service to the virtual directory, and registers any additional assemblies needed by the Web Service.

One of the advantages of using a Web Setup Project is that the installation package automatically handles any registration and configuration issues that your Web Service may depend upon, relieving you of this burden.

In general, the basic steps required to deploy a Web Service using the Web Setup Project method are as follows:

1. Create a Web Setup Project using the Web Setup Project template in Visual Studio.

2. Build the project.

3. Copy the installation package to the target Web server.

4. Run the installation package on the target Web server.

 Note   You must have administrative privileges on the target Web server computer in order to successfully install the Web Service using the installation package.

To teach you the basic steps necessary to deploy a Web Service using the Visual Studio Web Setup Project method, you will create an installation package for the CTemp Web Service you built in Chapter 47. To create the installation package, follow these steps:

1. Start Visual Studio.

2. Open the CTemp Web Service solution file.

3. If you intend to deploy your Web Service to a production-quality Web server, make sure that you have built a release-quality version of your Web Service using the Release configuration.

 Note   For more information about build configurations, refer to the "About Project Configurations" section in Chapter 47.

4. Choose Add Project from the File menu, and then choose New Project from the submenu. Visual Studio displays the Add New Project dialog box, as shown in Figure 48-1.

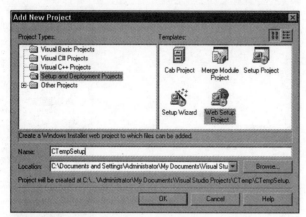

Figure 48-1: The Visual Studio Add New Project dialog box

5. Select Setup and Deployment Projects from the Project Types pane.

6. Select Web Setup Project from the Templates pane.

7. Type **CTempSetup** in the Name text box.

8. Click the OK button to create the project.

Visual Studio creates the Web Setup Project using the template, adds the project to the Solution Explorer, and opens the file system editor window, as shown in Figure 48-2.

Note that the `CTempSetup` project file is now selected in the Solution Explorer window, and its properties are viewable in the Properties window. The File System Editor window that is displayed in the main workspace area of the Visual Studio window models the file system of a target computer. But instead of using specific folder paths (such as `c:\inetpub\wwwroot`), the File System Editor uses abstract names (such as Web Application Folder) to represent file deployment locations on a target computer. This ensures that no matter where folders are located or what they are named on a target computer, your files will be installed where you expect them to be. For example, the virtual Desktop folder can be used to install files to the Desktop folder on a target computer.

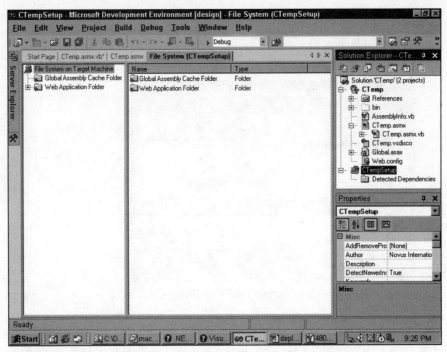

Figure 48-2: The Visual Studio File System Editor window

Using the File System Editor, you specify the files that you want to include in the deployment and where they should be located on the target computer. For more information about the File System Editor in Setup and Deployment Projects, refer to the Visual Studio documentation.

Now that you have a brief overview of the File System Editor, let's continue the construction of the Web Service Setup project:

1. Select the `ProductName` property in the Properties window and type **CTemp Web Service**. This property specifies the product name that will be displayed during the setup process when the setup file is executed.

2. Select the Web Application folder in the File System Editor window.

3. Add the appropriate project files from your `CTemp` Web Service to the File System Editor.Choose Add from the Action menu and then choose Project Output from the submenu. This displays the Add Project Output Group dialog box shown in Figure 48-3.

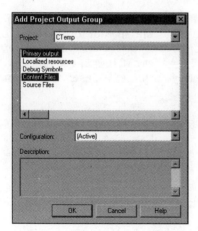

Figure 48-3: The Visual Studio Add Project Output Group dialog box

4. If CTemp is not the currently selected project, select it from the dropdown list.

5. Select the Primary Output and Content Files groups from the list. The Primary Output group includes the project DLL and any dependencies. The Content Files group includes the remaining files for the Web Service, such as the `.asmx` file, the `.config` file, etc.

Tip To select multiple items in a list, hold down the Ctrl key while clicking on each item you want to select.

6. Click the OK button to add the specified file groups to your deployment project. These files are now deployed to the Web application folder on any target computer from which the setup program is executed.

Now that you have specified which files you want to deploy, you need to specify the target virtual directory to which the Web Service files are deployed, as well as the default document for the virtual directory. Follow these steps:

1. Select the Web Application folder in the File System Editor window.

2. Select the `VirtualDirectory` property in the Properties window and type **CvtTemp**. This property specifies the name of the virtual directory that is created on the target computer.

3. Select the `DefaultDocument` property in the Properties window and type **CTemp.asmx**. This property specifies the default document to be executed if the URL to the virtual directory does not explicitly specify a document.

4. Choose Build Solution from the Build menu.

Visual Studio uses the structure and settings you created in the Web Setup Project to create a standard installation package (`.msi` file) in your local project folder. By default, this folder is located at `\documents and settings\`*yourloginname*`\ my documents\visual studio projects\CTemp\CTempSetup\debug\ CTempSetup.msi`. You can copy this file to your target Web server and double-click it to install your Web Service.

It is important to remember the following facts about the setup packages created by Web Setup Projects in Visual Studio:

✦ The user can specify an alternate virtual directory target during the setup process.

✦ The setup process creates a new virtual directory and configures the virtual directory for the Web Service.

In summary, although the Web Setup Project method of deployment requires more up-front work to create and configure properly, the result is a setup package that provides a solid, repeatable, and reliable installation.

Deployment using project copy

Copying a Web Service project in Visual Studio is a simpler deployment method than using a Web Setup Project to deploy your Web Service to a target Web server. However, copying your Web Service project files does not perform such tasks as virtual directory configuration or file registrations that may be necessary for your Web Service to function correctly. In more complex scenarios, the Web Setup Project method described in the previous section is a superior and more reliable choice (although somewhat more complex to set up and configure). Be that as it may, you can use the Project Copy feature in Visual Studio to deploy simple Web Services to target Web servers with very little effort.

To deploy a Web Service to a target Web server using the Visual Studio Project Copy method, follow these steps:

1. Start Visual Studio.

2. Open your Web Service solution file.

   If you intend to deploy your Web Service to a production-quality Web server, make sure that you have built a release-quality version of your Web Service using the Release configuration.

Note   For more information about build configurations, refer to the About Project Configurations section in Chapter 47.

3. Choose Copy Project... from the Project menu. This displays the Copy Project dialog box, as shown in Figure 48-4.

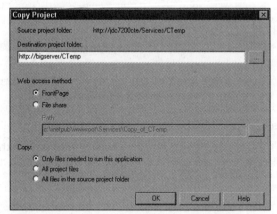

Figure 48-4: The Visual Studio Copy Project dialog box

4. Specify the URL of the target virtual directory in the Destination project folder text box. This example specifies that the Web Service should be deployed to the `CTemp` virtual directory on the `bigserver` Web server (within the intranet).

   Of course, it is also possible to deploy your Web Service to a Web server on the Internet, as long as you have the FrontPage Server extensions installed on the target Web server. If you were deploying your Web Service to a server on the Internet, your URL might look more like this: `www.mydomain.com/ws/CTemp`.

5. Select the appropriate access method for the target Web server.

   Your choice here depends on which access methods are available on the target Web server. Typically, the FrontPage method is used when the Web server is on the Internet or hidden behind a firewall. The File share method, on the other hand, usually is available only for Web servers that are resident on an intranet. However, you can still use the FrontPage method for intranet Web servers.

Note

For more information about Web access methods, refer to the Web Service Project Access Methods section in Chapter 47.

6. Choose the appropriate option for the project files you want to copy. These three options are available for copying files:

- **Only files needed to run this application** copies all .dll files with references in the /bin folder, as well as any files marked with a BuildAction of Content.

- **All project files** copies all project files created and managed by Visual Studio.

- **All files in the source project folder** copies all Visual Studio project files, as well as other files that reside in the project folders.

The default option is to copy only the files needed to run the application.

7. Click the OK button to begin copying the files. Visual Studio copies the appropriate Web Service files to the target Web server using the specified access method.

After the files have been copied, you may want to test the deployment by using your Web browser. This test method is described in detail in the "Testing the Web Service" section in Chapter 47.

Deployment using XCOPY

The DOS XCOPY command is perhaps the simplest method for deploying a Web Service to a target Web server. However, as is the case with the Visual Studio Copy Project feature, XCOPY simply copies files from one location to another. It does not create or configure virtual directories for your Web Service, nor does it register or configure any dependent assemblies outside of the .NET Framework.

You can type **XCOPY /?** at a Windows command prompt to get help on the XCOPY command-line syntax and available options.

Deployment using other file transfer methods

Of course, it is also possible to deploy your Web Service files to a properly configured ASP.NET Web server using other generic file transfer methods.

For example, you can use FTP to copy your Web Service solution files to your Web server. In this case, your Web server must also maintain an FTP server to which the Web Service files will be copied.

The bottom line here is that you can use any file transfer mechanism that is compatible with Windows 2000 Web servers configured to support ASP.NET Web Services.

Publishing Web Services

Publishing a Web Service enables potential consumers to locate and interrogate service descriptions that instruct the consumer on how to interact with the Web Service. The process of locating and interrogating Web Service descriptions is referred to as the *discovery* process. The two methods for enabling discovery of a Web Service are DISCO and UDDI. You may choose to use one or both of these methods based on the consumer audience you are trying to reach.

Cross-Reference   See Chapter 44 for discussions of DISCO and UDDI.

If your consumer population is fairly small (or well-known), such as a software development department of 5-10 people, you could simply point them to the target Web server and deploy the DISCO file on that server. In this case, the consumers invoke the discovery process against the URL of the target server to locate your Web Service description. In this situation, you only need to deploy your DISCO documents to the proper server and inform the consumers of the URL to the server. You may find that discovery through DISCO is sufficient for publishing your Web Services in this scenario. On the other hand, if your consumer population is relatively large or unknown, such as distributed corporate developer groups that may number in the hundreds, or even the Internet developer community at large, it's impractical to provide the consumers with a pointer to the target Web server where the service is located. You need to provide a mechanism for the consumers to find where your DISCO and/or Web Service descriptions are located, just as Web users use search engines to find Web pages. In this situation, you need to publish your Web Service through UDDI. You may decide to use the public UDDI registries on the Internet (if you will be exposing your Web Services to the Internet at large), or you may implement your own internal UDDI registry just for company-specific Web Services.

At any rate, the DISCO and UDDI tools offer a great deal of flexibility in structuring the discovery process for your specific needs.

The DISCO document and the UDDI business registry provide the mechanisms to solve these issues. This is covered in Chapter 44. The next section explores how to enable potential consumers to locate the essential information they need in order to use your Web Service.

Publishing with DISCO

Consumers of Web Services enact a discovery process to locate those services. The discovery process searches for XML-encoded discovery documents that contain pointers to other resources that describe the Web Service. Encoding discovery documents in XML enables tools such as Visual Studio to programmatically discover the availability of Web Services (if you know the URL to the server). This is how the Web Reference metaphor works in Visual Studio when you provide it with a specific discovery URL. Alternatively, you can use the `disco.exe` tool that comes with the .NET Framework SDK to discover Web Services.

Web Service discovery via Visual Studio's Web Reference feature or the NET Framework SDK's `disco.exe` tool is useful when the consumer knows the URL to the server that's hosting the Web Service or the application virtual directory.

Visual Studio automatically creates a DISCO file when you create a Web Service project. This file has a type of `.vsdisco` and is stored in the main application virtual directory (along with the `.asmx` file). As an example, your `CTemp` Web Service project contains a file named `CTemp.vsdisco`. This file contains links to the resources that describe the `CTemp` Web Service.

Note If you do not want to enable discovery for a particular Web Service, simply eliminate the `.vsdisco` file from the deployment process.

If you are not using Visual Studio to create your Web Services, you need to manually create the DISCO document. In this case, you must create an XML file containing DISCO elements that can be used to find your Web Service description documents. The following is a sample DISCO document for your `CTemp` Web Service:

```
<?xml version="1.0" ?>
<disco:discovery
xmlns:disco="http://schemas.xmlsoap.org/disco/">

xmlns:scl="http://schemas.xmlsoap.org/disco/scl">
  <scl:contractRef
ref="http://mydomain.com/CTemp/CTemp.asmx?WSDL"/>
  <disco:discoveryRef ref="SomeFolder/default.disco" />
</disco:discovery>
```

The DISCO document consists of a `discovery` element that serves as a container for the `contractRef` and `discoveryRef` elements. You can specify as many `contractRef` and `discoveryRef` elements as you desire. This makes it possible to provide information for more than one Web Service from within a single DISCO document.

The `contractRef` element is used to provide a pointer to the WSDL document that describes the message formats and exchanges supported by the Web Service. In the preceding example, you can see that a single `contractRef` element has been included that provides a pointer to the WSDL document for the CTemp Web Service. The `contractRef` element is optional.

Note URLs specified by the `ref` attribute can be absolute or relative. An absolute URL specifies a complete path to a resource, whereas a relative URL specifies a partial path to a resource that is relative to the location of the referring resource. If you specify a relative URL, the reference is relative to the folder in which the DISCO document resides.

The discoveryRef element is used to provide a pointer to other DISCO documents. This allows you to logically link the discovery process to several Web Services, which may have independent DISCO documents. In the preceding example, a single discoveryRef element has been included that provides a pointer to another DISCO document. The discoveryRef element is optional.

Since a DISCO document simply contains pointers to the resources that describe a Web Service, you can physically deploy your DISCO documents anywhere you want. They don't have to be physically deployed with the Web Services that they describe. This lets you enable discovery of any set of Web Services that may be physically distributed on your network, but allows users to browse to a single point at which to begin the discovery process.

Note   If you want to deploy your DISCO documents in a different location from the Web Service itself, you should be very careful when using relative references.

To make it easier for consumers to find your Web Service, create a DISCO file in the root directory of your Web server that then links to the various Web Service DISCO files that you have implemented. That way, a consumer can simply browse to the root directory of the server to begin the discovery process.

For more information about DISCO documents and the disco.exe tool, refer to the .NET Framework documentation. Chapters 49 and 50 cover the Web Reference feature in Visual Studio, as well as the disco.exe tool, when you learn to build a consumer for the CTemp Web Service.

Publishing with UDDI

Discovery of Web Services via DISCO is sufficient if you know the URL to the Web server or the application virtual directory that hosts the Web Service. However, in cases where this information is unavailable, you must use a more generalized search tool. Universal Description, Discovery, and Integration (UDDI) enables a Web Service consumer to search for and locate Web Services, even if the consumer is unaware of the exact location, owner, or author of those Web Services.

UDDI is to Web Services what Lycos and AltaVista are to Web pages. UDDI helps consumers locate Web Services based on a logically centralized, globally available registry of businesses accessible via the Internet. UDDI consists of two basic parts:

✦ An XML schema that describes and categorizes a business and the Web Services that it offers.

✦ The business registry (or database) that contains all known information about businesses and Web Services based on the XML schema.

The business registry is accessible interactively via the www.uddi.org Web site, as well as programmatically through the UDDI Web Services. These Web Services are used by Visual Studio's Web Reference feature to locate and create proxy classes that interact with Web Services.

Although you're not publishing the CTemp Web Service through UDDI, let's look at the basic features and procedures for getting your Web Services published to the UDDI business and Web Service registry via the UDDI.org Web site. The UDDI home page, www.uddi.org, is shown in Figure 48-5.

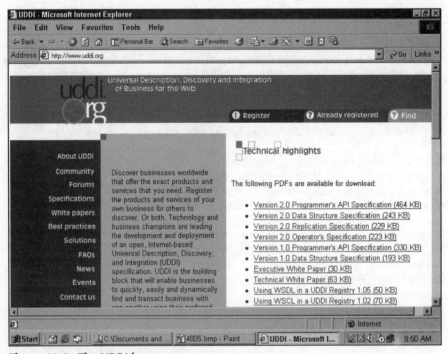

Figure 48-5: The UDDI home page

You can register your business by clicking on the Register tab at the top of the home page. Or you can go directly to the page by typing www.uddi.org/register.html into your Web browser.

On the other hand, if you have already registered your business and want to maintain your business and/or Web Service information (including adding new Web Services), click on the Already registered tab at the top of the home page. Or you can go directly to the page by typing www.uddi.org/alreadyregistered.html in your Web browser.

In either case, next you're asked to choose which registry you want to use to add or update your information. As of the writing of this book, IBM and Microsoft were both maintaining UDDI business registry sites. The examples presented here use the Microsoft site, but you could just as easily use the IBM site with the exact same results.

Although there are multiple distributed registries (and more expected to come online), the UDDI architecture uses replication techniques to keep all of the registries synchronized. Therefore, you don't have to worry about which online registry you use to search or maintain your business information.

If you have not registered your business yet, you must obtain a username/password before adding any information to the UDDI business registry. This is necessary so that your particular business information can be protected from any unauthorized changes. Although the specific methods for obtaining a username and password differ between the IBM and Microsoft sites, the end result is the same. On the Microsoft site, you're asked to create a Passport account. If you already have a Passport account, you can use that account instead of creating another one.

1. Choose Microsoft from the list and submit the form. Then you must log in to the site using your username and password. If you don't have a username and password yet, create one and then log in.

2. After you have successfully logged into the site, you see the personal registration page shown in Figure 48-6. Fill in your personal contact information here. This information is used for private registration purposes so that you can add and update entries in the business registry database. It's not published within the public business registry database.

Figure 48-6: The UDDI personal registration form

3. Confirm your acceptance of the terms and conditions. A confirmation page is displayed.

4. Click on the Continue button and you are ready to register your business. The screen in Figure 48-7 is displayed.

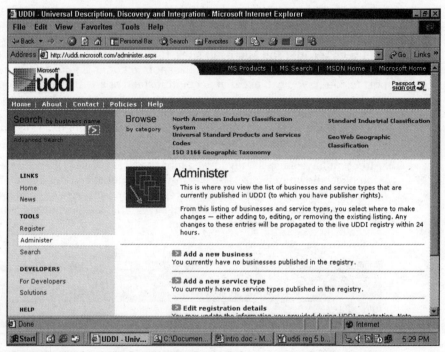

Figure 48-7: The UDDI business registration form

5. Click on the Add a new business link and enter the details regarding your business. You can add and maintain the following categories of information about your business:

- **Business Detail Information** specifies the name, address, and other details about your company.

- **Contacts** specifies company contact information.

- **Services** is where you publish your Web Services, among other things. Details include the specifics of these applications, such as location, supported bindings, and other details.

- **Business Identifiers** are pieces of data that are unique to an individual business, such as a company register listing number.

- **Business Classifications** are pieces of data that classify the field of operation of a business or a service, such as a geographic location or an industry sector.

- **Discovery URLs** provide a location where details about a particular entity can be found.

Each of these categories can contain one or several entries. The ultimate goal of this variety of information is to make it quick and simple for consumers to find your Web Services using various criteria, such as industry, geographic location, and others.

Note   Typically, any changes you make to your business information are updated to the live registry within 24 hours.

Adding a Web Service to your business registration

Finally, let's walk through the process of adding a Web Service to your business registration:

1. Scroll the browser window to the Services section within the business details page. This is where all of your published Web Services reside in the business registry.

2. Next, click on the Add a service link. Specify the name of your Web Service and a brief description, as shown in Figure 48-8.

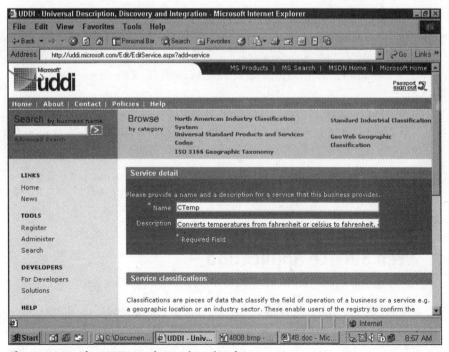

Figure 48-8: The UDDI service registration form

3. Click the Continue button and then add the appropriate classification categories for your service, as well as the bindings that your service supports. This screen is shown in Figure 48-9.

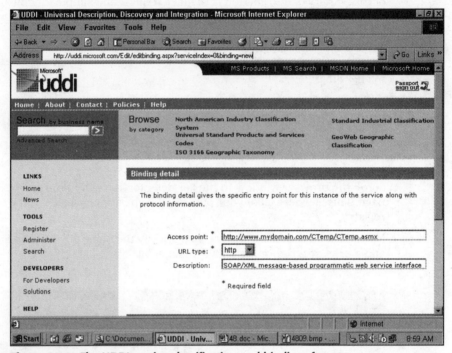

Figure 48-9: The UDDI service classification and bindings form

The classifications are similar to those that you specified when you registered your company information using the UDDI Business Registration Form. This helps potential consumers locate Web Services more easily.

Note   This chapter won't go through the classification process, but you should consider using classifications so that it is easier for consumers to find your Web Services.

Defining a new binding for the Web Service application

Let's define a new binding for your Web Service publication:

1. Click on the Define new binding link in the Bindings section of the page. This displays the binding detail page shown in Figure 48-10.

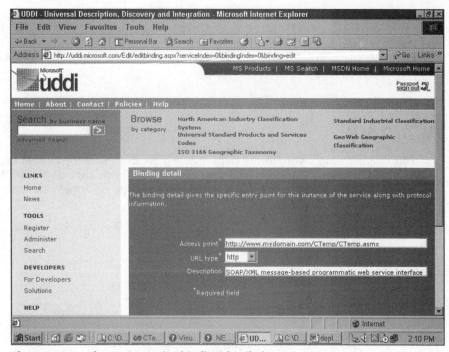

Figure 48-10: The UDDI service binding details form

2. In the Access Point text box, enter the URL to your Web Service entry point (.asmx) file. In this example, you can see the pseudo-URL for the CTemp Web Service.

3. Next, select HTTP as the URL type from the drop-down list. In the Description text box, enter a description for the binding. Typically, you want to mention the protocol details for the entry point you specified. For ASP.NET Web Services (which is what you build using Visual Studio or the .NET Framework), you should specify HTTP and SOAP. Note the description that was specified for the CTemp Web Service.

4. Click the Continue button. This returns you to the Service Details page. Click the Continue button on this page to return to the Business Detail page, where you can further administer your business information.

Tip

You may find it easier to supply the appropriate information for your business and Web Services if you examine business registry information from other companies, such as Microsoft and IBM.

That, in a nutshell, is the basic process for getting your Web Services published via UDDI. You can learn a lot more about UDDI by visiting the UDDI Web site at `www.uddi.org` and browsing the existing registry, as well as the available help information. This will help you create the necessary information that makes it easier for consumers to find your Web Services.

Summary

This chapter taught you how to deploy a Web Service using the built-in support provided by Visual Studio, as well as alternative methods such as XCOPY. In addition, you learned how to publish a Web Service so that potential consumers can locate it via DISCO and/or UDDI.

✦   ✦   ✦

Finding Web Services

by Jim Chandler

Previous chapters discussed the tools used to publish Web Services from the perspective of a Web Service author. This chapter examines the tools used to find Web Services from the perspective of a Web Service consumer. This process includes locating where a Web Service resides, as well as interrogating the WSDL document to determine how to interact with the Web Service. This chapter examines the support built into Visual Studio for finding Web Services, as well as the tools in the Microsoft .NET Framework that can be used to locate Web Services.

Web Service Discovery

As you learned in Chapter 48, there are several ways for a consumer to locate a Web Service. Visual Studio combines these methods into a single tool via the Add Web Reference feature. If you decide to use the .NET tools to locate Web Services, the tool you use depends on how much you know about the location of the Web Service before you start. These tools include disco and Universal Description, Discovery, and Integration (UDDI), which are examined in this chapter.

If you already know the URL of a Web server where one or more Web Services are deployed, you can locate these Web Services by using a *discovery tool*, a software utility that automates the discovery process. (If Web Service discovery has been enabled by placing one or more discovery documents on the Web server.) The .NET Framework provides a command-line tool named `disco.exe` that can be used to locate discovery documents against a specified URL. In addition to the .NET disco tool, Visual Studio supports the ability to locate Web Services via discovery documents by using the Add Web Reference feature.

If you don't know anything about where a Web Service is located (or even if it exists), you need the services of UDDI. Essentially, this technology is a universal search engine for Web Services, and it's available via the Internet as both an interactive Web site and a set of programmable Web Services. UDDI consists of two parts:

✦ An XML-based schema that describes attributes of businesses, including basic demographic information and specialized information related to industry affiliations, types of goods or services provided, and other taxonomies.

✦ A Web-based distributed database consisting of multiple, synchronized nodes that can be accessed via a Web browser, as well as programmable Web Services.

> **Note**   As of the writing of this book, two UDDI nodes were available at IBM and Microsoft. It is expected that other nodes will come online over time. You can read more about UDDI on the UDDI web site at `www.uddi.org`. Although there are multiple registry nodes, the UDDI architecture maintains data synchronization between all of the nodes so that you do not have to worry about which particular node services your search requests.

Because UDDI supports programmable Web Services, tools such as Visual Studio can provide support for finding Web Services automatically. Visual Studio also supports Web Service discovery via UDDI through the Add Web Reference feature, which is discussed later in this chapter under "Finding Web Services with Visual Studio."

Ultimately, you're searching for Web Services because you intend to consume them programmatically. To consume a Web Service, you must locate the Web Service description document (the WSDL file). Therefore, once you locate a Web Service, you use the Web Service description document to create one or more proxy classes from the description. A proxy class is a software component that provides access to the remote Web Service as if it were a local resource. Essentially, the proxy class hides the details of the request/response protocols and underlying network transport from the consumer. Web Service proxy classes are discussed later in this chapter.

Now, let's take a look at how `disco`, UDDI, and Visual Studio discovery tools can be used to help you locate and consume Web Services.

Finding Web Services with the disco tool

The .NET Framework provides a tool named `disco.exe` to locate Web Services at a given URL and copy the Web Service descriptions that it finds to your local hard drive. The output of the `disco` tool is typically used as input to the `wsdl` tool to create a proxy class with which to consume the Web Service. The next section discusses the `wsdl` tool in more detail. By default, the `disco` tool is located at `Program Files\Microsoft.NET\FrameworkSDK\Bin`.

The `disco` tool is a console application, so you need to start it from within a command window.

 Tip   You may want to add the path to the .NET Framework Bin folder to your system's PATH environment variable so that the tools can be located without typing the paths to them on the command line.

The general format of the `disco` command line is

```
disco [options] URL
```

Here, URL specifies the HTTP address of the target Web server that you want to search for discovery (`.disco`) documents.

The `disco` tool supports the command-line options listed in Table 49-1.

<table>
<tr><th colspan="2">Table 49-1
Disco Tool Command-Line Options</th></tr>
<tr><th>Option</th><th>Description</th></tr>
<tr><td>/d[omain]:domain</td><td>Specifies the domain name to use when connecting to a proxy server that requires authentication.</td></tr>
<tr><td>/nosave</td><td>The discovered documents or results (.wsdl, .xsd, .disco, and .discomap files) are not saved to disk. The default is to save these documents.</td></tr>
<tr><td>/nologo</td><td>Suppresses the Microsoft startup banner display.</td></tr>
<tr><td>/o[ut]:directoryName</td><td>Specifies the output directory in which to save the discovered documents. The default is the current directory.</td></tr>
</table>

Continued

Table 49-1 *(continued)*

Option	Description
/p[assword]:password	Specifies the password to use when connecting to a proxy server that requires authentication.
/proxy:URL	Specifies the URL of the proxy server to use for HTTP requests. The default is to use the system proxy setting.
/proxydomain:domain or /pd:domain	Specifies the domain to use when connecting to a proxy server that requires authentication.
/proxypassword:password or /pp:password	Specifies the password to use when connecting to a proxy server that requires authentication.
/proxyusername:username or /pu:username	Specifies the user name to use when connecting to a proxy server that requires authentication.
/u[sername]:username	Specifies the user name to use when connecting to a proxy server that requires authentication.
/?	Displays command syntax and options for the tool.

Let's look at an example using the `disco` tool to locate the Web Service description files for your `CTemp` Web Service. First, let's assume that you only know the name of the Web server that is hosting your `CTemp` service, but you need the complete URL to it. You can do this by typing the following at the command prompt:

```
disco /nosave http://localhost
```

This command initiates the discovery process against the local Web server, searching for all discovery documents and related files that are referenced in these discovery documents. Note that you are not saving any of the results yet (because of the /nosave option).

When dynamic discovery is enabled at the root of the Web server (the default), the `disco` tool searches hierarchically through all Web server folders. Running the previous command against my Web server produces the results you see in Figure 49-1.

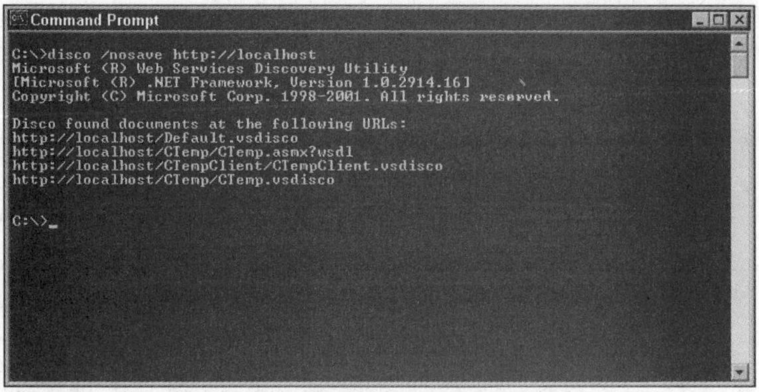

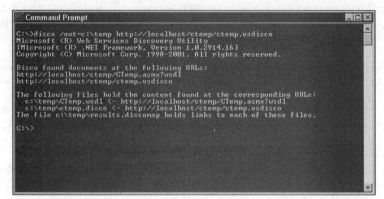

Figure 49-1: Using disco to find Web Services.

Notice that the `disco` tool has listed all the `disco` documents it found on the Web server, as well as a reference to a single WSDL document for your `CTemp` Web Service.

Now that you know the complete URL to the `CTemp` Web Service, let's use the `disco` tool one more time to discover information specific to the `CTemp` Web Service. This time, you save the results to a temporary folder, using the following command:

```
disco /out=c:\temp http://localhost/ctemp/ctemp.vsdisco
```

This initiates the discovery process against the `disco` document of the `CTemp` Web Service located on your local Web server. Executing this command on my Web server produces the results you see in Figure 49-2.

Figure 49-2: Using disco to retrieve the WSDL for the CTemp Web Service.

Note that the disco tool has saved three files to your local computer. These files are summarized in Table 49-2.

Table 49-2
Files Created by the disco Tool

File	Description
CTemp.wsdl	The WSDL document for the CTemp Web Service.
ctemp.disco	The discovery document for the CTemp Web Service.
results.discomap	A discovery document that contains references to the local copies of the CTemp.wsdl and ctemp.disco files.

In actual practice, you would save the results of the discovery process to the project folder where you were building the client application that consumes the Web Service just discovered.

Armed with the information and files copied to your system by the disco tool, you could use the wsdl tool to generate a proxy class for the CTemp Web Service, which could be used to consume the service in a client application. This process is discussed later in this chapter under "Creating a Proxy Class with the WSDL Tool."

Finding Web Services with UDDI

While the disco tool is an effective means of locating Web Service descriptions, it requires you to know either the URL to a specific target server where the Web Service is deployed or the URL to a specific Web Service virtual directory on a Web server. In any case, you won't be able to find any Web Services using disco without knowing a URL.

As mentioned previously, UDDI is a more generalized search tool for locating Web Services. Using UDDI, you can specify search terms that allow you to pinpoint Web Services you want to use based on company, industry, service types, and many other classifications. Using these more generalized search terms, UDDI can return in a list of URLs with information about specific Web Services, including the WSDL document that you are searching for.

This section explores how to find Web Services by using the interactive UDDI Web site. This Web site provides search forms for locating Web Services (and Web Service descriptions).

Examining the search process

To illustrate the search process, let's search for Web Services that are published by Microsoft. Start by browsing to the UDDI Web site at `www.uddi.org`. Click the Find link at the top of the page. This displays the Find page. On that page, choose the Microsoft UDDI node from the list box and click GO. This brings you to the Microsoft UDDI node search page, as shown in Figure 49-3.

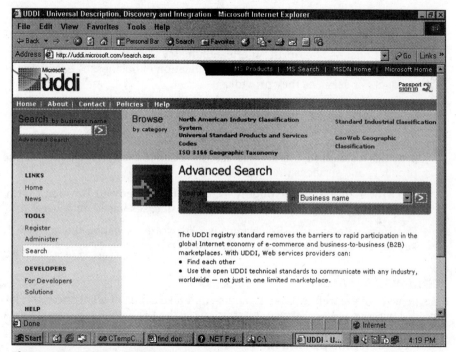

Figure 49-3: Microsoft UDDI search page.

Notice that the search page provides category-based browsing that allows you to locate Web Services based on various company classifications, including ISO 3166 Geographic Taxonomy and Standard Industrial Classification, among others.

In the middle of the page is the Advanced Search form. From here, you can enter text in the Search For text box to perform a custom search of various fields within the database. You can locate Web Services in this manner by searching any one of the following field types:

✦ **Business name** — Use this field to search within registered business names. For example, you could search for services provided by IBM.

✦ **Business location** — Use this field to search by geographic location. For example, you could search for companies that provide services within the St. Louis area.

✦ **Service type by name** — Use this field to search services submitted by a company by the service name.

✦ **Business identifier** — Identifiers are pieces of data that are unique to an individual business, such as the standard D-U-N-S(r) Number. There are several standard identifiers, as well as custom ones, that a company can register.

✦ **Discovery URL** — Provides a location with details about a particular entity, such as the URL to a company Web site or a particular Web Service.

✦ **GeoWeb Taxonomy** — Provides a standard, hierarchical classification of geographic locations by which to search.

✦ **NAICS Codes** — The North American Industry Classification System (NAICS) provides a standard, hierarchical classification of businesses based on the products or services they provide.

✦ **SIC Codes** — Standard Industrial Classification (SIC) provides a standard, hierarchical classification of businesses based on industry.

✦ **UNSPSC Codes** — Universal Standard Products and Services Codes (UNSPSC) provides a standard, hierarchical classification of businesses based on the products and services they provide.

✦ **ISO 3166 Geographic Taxonomy** — Similar to the GeoWeb Taxonomy, provides a standard, hierarchical classification of businesses based on geography.

✦ **RealNames Keyword** — RealNames is a keyword-like name, similar to AOL keywords, that is registered to a specific company.

Performing a search

Let's do a simple search by business name and take a look at what Microsoft has provided in terms of Web Service registrations to the UDDI database (see Figure 49-4).

Follow these steps to perform the search:

1. Choose Business Name from the drop-down list, type **Microsoft** in the Search for text box, and submit the form. The search facility looks for any businesses with the name Microsoft in the business name field and returns a list of hits. In this example, you should see a single listing.

2. Click the Microsoft Corporation link.

3. Scroll down the page until you see the list of services offered. Here you find an entry named Web Services for Smart Searching. Click this link and the browser displays a service detail page. Scroll down this page until you find the Bindings section. Your browser window should look similar to Figure 49-5.

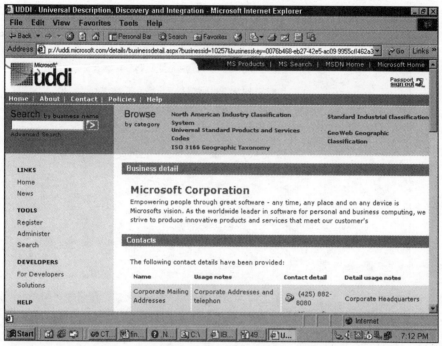

Figure 49-4: UDDI business registration information for Microsoft.

The interesting information displayed here is supplied by the Access point link. Note that the URL points to the entry point of two categorized Web Service interfaces:

- A Vocabulary service
- A Best Bets service

4. Each service shares a common URL. Go ahead and click one of the entry point links. By now you know that pointing your browser to an .asmx file returns the ASP.NET Web Service description page. From this page, you can access the WSDL contract, which can be saved to your local hard drive and then interrogated by the wsdl tool to create a Web Service proxy class. This process is covered in more detail shortly.

Congratulations! You have just located your first Web Service from the UDDI business registry! Of course, there are myriad ways to search the registry. Which one you choose depends on what you are looking for and how much information you have related to the Web Service.

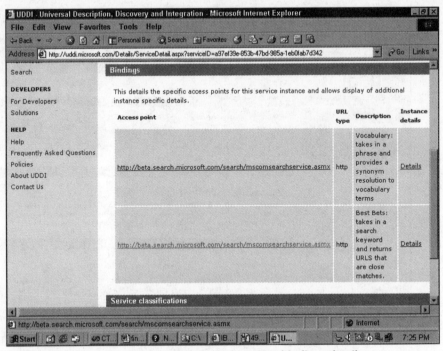

Figure 49-5: Microsoft Smart Searching Web Service bindings detail.

Caution

While this book was being written, the UDDI nodes at Microsoft and IBM were still very immature. The search capabilities on the Microsoft node had several bugs, and both sites had few businesses registered. This is a new technology, and it appears that some patience will be required before these registries become truly useful to the average developer.

If you are not using Visual Studio to build or consume Web Services, you should become familiar with the facilities provided by the UDDI business registry nodes. Over time, these sites will provide one-stop-shopping for high-quality Web Services that you can incorporate into your custom solutions.

Finding Web Services with Visual Studio

Visual Studio provides integrated support for finding Web Services via the Add Web Reference dialog box (available from the Project menu), and it can find Web Services (and, ultimately, Web Service descriptions) using `disco` or UDDI.

When you add a Web reference, Visual Studio copies the Web Service discovery documents and the WSDL document to your local project folder. Then it generates a Web Service proxy class automatically, adding the results to a Web References section in the Solution Explorer window.

A Web Service proxy class exposes the methods of the Web Service and handles the marshalling of appropriate arguments back and forth between the Web Service and your application. Visual Studio uses the WSDL document of the Web Service to generate the proxy class in the same language as the rest of your project.

Visual Studio automatically creates and maintains discovery documents (using the .vsdisco extension) for Web Service projects that you create in Visual Studio. In addition to the discovery document that is created in the virtual directory of the Web Service, Visual Studio creates a discovery document in the Web server root directory named Default.vsdisco. As you create Web Services, Visual Studio updates this discovery document with references to your project-specific Web Service discovery documents.

To open the Add Web Reference dialog box, choose Add Web Reference from the Project menu in Visual Studio. The Add Web Reference dialog box appears, as shown in Figure 49-6.

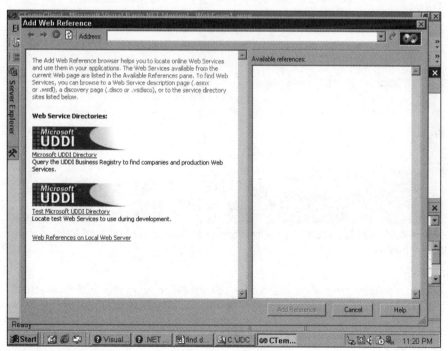

Figure 49-6: The Visual Studio Add Web Reference dialog box.

Using this dialog box, you can add Web references from your local Web server or the Microsoft UDDI directory, or manually enter the URL to a Web server in the address bar. These options are covered in the following sections.

Adding a Web reference from the local Web server

To locate Web Services on your local Web server, simply click the Web References on Local Web Server link. Visual Studio examines the `default.vsdisco` discovery document located in the local Web server root directory and displays its contents in the left pane of the dialog box. The available Web Services, along with any linked reference groups, are listed in the Available References pane of the dialog box, as shown in Figure 49-7.

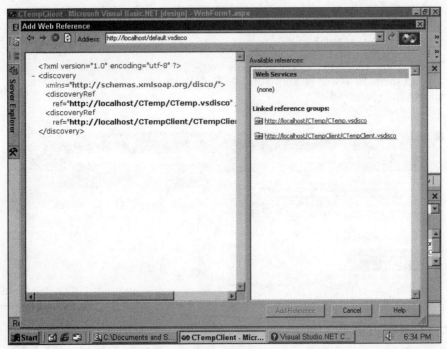

Figure 49-7: Finding Web Services on your local Web server in the Add Web Reference dialog box.

Linked reference groups are references to other discovery documents. In this example, there are no Web Services described in the discovery document, but there are two linked reference groups. One of these linked reference groups is a pointer to your `CTemp` sample. Clicking the `CTemp` link displays the information shown in Figure 49-8.

The left pane of the Add Web Reference dialog box now displays the contents of the `CTemp` Web Service discovery document (`CTemp.vsdisco`) that resides in the `CTemp` virtual directory. The right pane contains links to the WSDL file (the View Contract link) and the help page (the View Documentation link) for the `CTemp` Web Service. Note that the Add Reference button is now enabled, indicating that Visual Studio has recognized the information necessary to add this Web Service to your project.

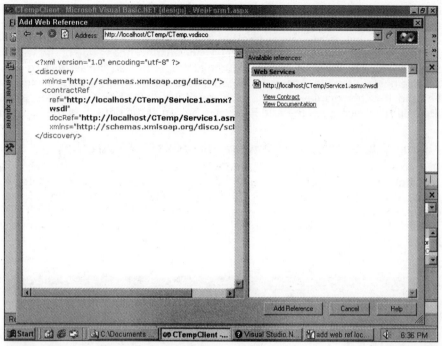

Figure 49-8: Discovery results for the CTemp Web Service in the Add Web Reference dialog box.

As you can see, adding a Web reference to your Visual Studio project from Web Services that reside on your local Web server is quick and easy. Of course, using the local Web server link to locate Web Services is useful only in cases where you have developed the Web Service you want to consume. In the more general case, you need to enter the URL to a remote Web server that hosts the Web Services you want to consume. This scenario is discussed in the next section.

Adding a Web reference from a known URL

If you know the URL of an `.asmx`, `.wsdl`, `.disco`, or `.vsdisco` document associated with a Web Service you are interested in using, you can enter that URL into the Address bar at the top of the Add Web Reference dialog box. Visual Studio displays the results of your search in a manner similar to that described in the preceding section.

If you specify the address of an `.asmx` or `.wsdl` file, Visual Studio attempts to load the associated Web Service description file. If this file is valid, it is displayed in the left pane of the dialog box. To add the Web reference, click the Add Reference button located in the bottom-right corner of the dialog box.

If you specify the address of a .disco or .vsdico document, Visual Studio lists all the Web Service descriptions it finds according to the instructions found in the disco file, as well as references to other disco documents. If more than one Web Service is displayed in the Available References pane, choose one of the Web Services listed by clicking it. Visual Studio attempts to load the associated Web Service description file. Again, if the Web Service description is parsed and found to be valid, it will be displayed in the left pane of the dialog box. Once again, to add the Web reference, click the Add Reference button at the bottom of the dialog box.

Adding a Web reference from the Microsoft UDDI Directory

Of course, if you do not know where to begin a search for a particular Web Service (you don't have a URL to a particular Web server or Web Service-related document), you can click the Microsoft UDDI Directory link in the Add Web Reference dialog box. This will allow you to browse for Web Services in the Microsoft UDDI directory. Clicking the Microsoft UDDI Directory link displays the page shown in Figure 49-9.

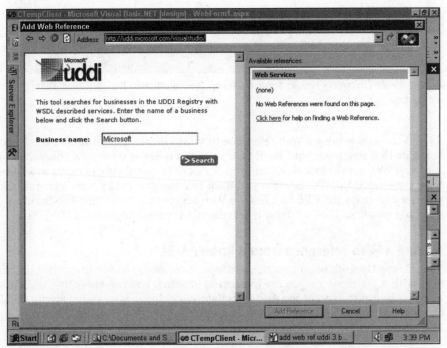

Figure 49-9: Searching for Web Services by using UDDI in the Add Web Reference dialog box.

This page allows you to search the Microsoft UDDI directory by matching any portion of a business name. Enter Microsoft into the text box (as shown in Figure 49-9) and click the Search button. Visual Studio will respond by calling UDDI Web Service methods published on the Microsoft UDDI Web site to search the directory for any matching entries based on the name you entered. In addition, the search will be limited to Web Services that are published by the companies that meet your business name criteria.

After the search has been completed, you should see a page similar to Figure 49-10.

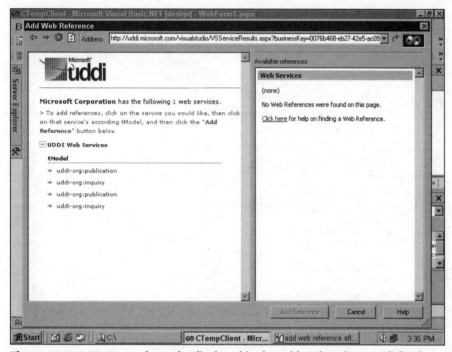

Figure 49-10: UDDI search results displayed in the Add Web Reference dialog box.

In this window, you can see that Microsoft has published one Web Service titled UDDI Web Services. Under this title is a list of four Web Service bindings that are available for this Web Service. These bindings are links to the WSDL document for each specific binding. Clicking the `uddi-org:inquiry` link displays the page shown in Figure 49-11.

As shown in Figure 49-11, the WSDL document is displayed in the left pane and the Add Reference button is now enabled, making it possible to add a reference to this Web Service in your Visual Studio project.

As you have seen, the Add Web Reference feature in Visual Studio makes it fairly simple to find and add references to other Web Services, whether you have a URL to a specific service, a URL to a Web server, or no URL with which to begin your search.

Although this is a simple and effective solution for finding Web Services, sometimes you may not be able to use Visual Studio's Web Reference feature, such as when the Web Service is not accessible from the machine on which you are using Visual Studio. Under these circumstances, you can use the Web Service Description Language Tool (Wsdl.exe) to generate a Web Service client proxy class. This tool is covered in the next section.

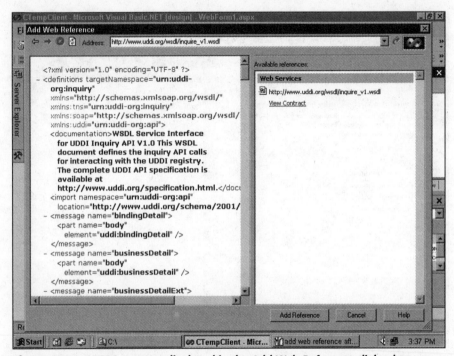

Figure 49-11: WSDL contract displayed in the Add Web Reference dialog box.

Web Service Interrogation and Proxy Classes

Web Service interrogation is the process of examining a Web Service description to determine how to interact with the Web Service as a consumer. As you have learned, a Web Service communicates with consumers by using messages encoded in XML and encapsulated in SOAP. You have also seen that these messages can be transported over one of several protocols (such as HTTP and SMTP). Lastly, the Web Service description defines the message formats and exchange patterns for the particular methods, arguments, and return values that the Web Service supports.

If you were required to code directly to these technologies, calling Web Services would be a time-consuming (and probably painful) process. What's worse, you would be spending time writing what is essentially plumbing code to consume a Web Service, rather than focusing on the actual task you were attempting to accomplish.

Fortunately, you do not have to worry about creating and formatting SOAP messages, or understanding how to exchange messages with various transport protocols. All of this plumbing is hidden from you via the Web Service proxy class. Instead, you simply instantiate an instance of the proxy class and make calls to its methods in a completely object-oriented fashion.

Recall that the .NET Framework provides the Web Service Description Language (WSDL) tool for parsing Web Service description files. But in addition to interrogating these files, the wsdl tool can generate a proxy class, which provides an object-oriented interface for calling methods on the Web Service and returning the results to the caller.

Visual Studio automatically creates Web Service proxy classes for you when you use the Add Web Reference dialog box to create a reference to a Web Service. If you are unable to use Visual Studio's Web Reference feature, however, you can create the proxy class manually by using the wsdl tool. Let's take a look at the tool and how it can be used to create Web Service proxy classes that can be used by Web Service consumers.

Creating a proxy class with the WSDL tool

The .NET Framework provides a tool named wsdl.exe to parse Web Service descriptions and generate proxy classes, which can be used by a consumer to call methods on a Web Service. The wsdl tool is capable of generating proxy classes given any one of the following types of files as input:

✦ .wsdl files

✦ .xsd (XML Schema Definition) files

✦ .disco files

✦ .discomap files

Note that these files are all outputs of .NET's disco tool. By default, the wsdl tool is located in the same place as the disco tool:

```
Program Files\Microsoft.NET\FrameworkSDK\Bin
```

The wsdl tool is a console application, so you will need to start it from within a command window, just like the disco tool discussed in the last section.

Tip   You may want to add the path to the .NET Framework Bin folder to your system's PATH environment variable so that the tools can be located without typing the path to them on the command line.

The general format of the `wsdl` command line is

```
wsdl [options] {URL | Path}
```

Here, URL specifies the HTTP address of a target Web server that you want to search for any of the supported file types (excluding `.discomap` files), and Path specifies the local file path to any of the supported file types.

The `wsdl` tool supports the command-line options listed in Table 49-3.

Table 49-3
WSDL Tool Command-Line Options

Option	Description
`/appsettingurlkey:key` or `/urlkey:key`	Specifies the configuration key to use in order to read the default value for the URL property when generating code. This allows you to obtain the URL of the Web Service from the ASP.NET configuration file, rather than having it hard-coded in the proxy class.
`/appsettingbaseurl:baseurl` or `/baseurl:baseurl`	Specifies the base URL to use in conjunction with the `/appsettingurlkey` option. The tool calculates the URL fragment by converting the relative URL from the baseurl argument to the URL in the WSDL document. You must specify the `/appsettingurlkey` option with this option.
`/d[omain]:domain`	Specifies the domain name to use when connecting to a server that requires authentication.
`/l[anguage]:language`	Specifies the language to use for the generated proxy class. You can specify CS (C#; default), VB (Visual Basic), or JS (JScript) as the language argument. You can also specify the fully qualified name of a class that implements the `System.CodeDom.Compiler.CodeDomProvider` class. The default language is C#.
`/n[amespace]:namespace`	Specifies the namespace for the generated proxy or template. The default namespace is the global namespace. As an example, setting the namespace to TempConverter would permit you to reference your CTemp proxy class as `TempConverter.CTemp`.
`/nologo`	Suppresses the Microsoft startup banner display.
`/o[ut]:filename`	Specifies the file in which to save the generated proxy code. The tool derives the default file name from the Web Service name. The tool saves generated datasets in different files.

Option	Description
/p[assword]:*password*	Specifies the password to use when connecting to a server that requires authentication.
/protocol:*protocol*	Specifies the protocol to implement. You can specify SOAP (default), HttpGet, HttpPost, or a custom protocol specified in the configuration file.
/proxy:*URL*	Specifies the URL of the proxy server to use for HTTP requests. The default is to use the system proxy setting.
/proxydomain:*domain* or /pd:*domain*	Specifies the domain to use when connecting to a proxy server that requires authentication.
/proxypassword:*password* or /pp:*password*	Specifies the password to use when connecting to a proxy server that requires authentication.
/proxyusername:username or /pu:username	Specifies the user name to use when connecting to a proxy server that requires authentication.
/server	Generates an abstract class for a normal (server-side) Web Service based on the contracts. The default is to generate client proxy classes. This option will probably rarely be used, but it's useful when you have defined a standard interface for a Web Service but want to create several separate implementations.
/u[sername]:*username*	Specifies the username to use when connecting to a server that requires authentication.
/?	Displays command syntax and options for the tool.

The following example illustrates the use of the wsdl tool to generate a proxy class for your CTemp Web Service:

```
wsdl /lang:vb /out:CTempProxy.vb
http://localhost/services/ctemp/ctemp.asmx?wsdl
```

This example creates a proxy class in the Visual Basic language and saves it to a file named CTempProxy.vb. The proxy is generated from the WSDL provided by the URL specified on the command line.

The output of the wsdl tool in the command window should look similar to Figure 49-12.

Figure 49-12: Creating a proxy class for the CTemp Web Service by using the WSDL tool.

The Visual Basic proxy class source code generated by the `wsdl` tool is shown in Listing 49-1.

Listing 49-1: **CTemp Web Service Proxy Class Source Code**

```vb
Option Strict Off
Option Explicit On

Imports System
Imports System.Diagnostics
Imports System.Web.Services
Imports System.Web.Services.Protocols
Imports System.Xml.Serialization


'This source code was auto-generated by wsdl, Version=1.0.2914.16.
'

<System.Web.Services.WebServiceBindingAttribute( _
      Name:="TempConverterSoap",
      [Namespace]:="http://mydomain.com/ws/ctemp")>
Public Class TempConverter
    Inherits System.Web.Services.Protocols.SoapHttpClientProtocol

    <System.Diagnostics.DebuggerStepThroughAttribute()> _
    Public Sub New()
        MyBase.New
        Me.Url = "http://jdc7200cte/services/ctemp/ctemp.asmx"
    End Sub

    <System.Diagnostics.DebuggerStepThroughAttribute(), _
```

```
       System.Web.Services.Protocols.SoapDocumentMethodAttribute( _
       "http://mydomain.com/ws/ctemp/CTemp", _
       RequestNamespace:="http://mydomain.com/ws/ctemp", _
       ResponseNamespace:="http://mydomain.com/ws/ctemp", _
       Use:=System.Web.Services.Description.SoapBindingUse.Literal, _
       ParameterStyle:= _
          System.Web.Services.Protocols.SoapParameterStyle.Wrapped)>
       Public Function CTemp(ByVal Temperature As Decimal, _
                            ByVal FromUnits As String, _
                            ByVal ToUnits As String) As Decimal
          Dim results() As Object = _
Me.Invoke("CTemp", New Object() {Temperature, FromUnits, ToUnits})
          Return CType(results(0),Decimal)
       End Function

       <System.Diagnostics.DebuggerStepThroughAttribute()>  _
       Public Function BeginCTemp(ByVal Temperature As Decimal, _
                           ByVal FromUnits As String, _
                           ByVal ToUnits As String, _
                           ByVal callback As _
                               System.AsyncCallback, _
                           ByVal asyncState As Object) _
                           As System.IAsyncResult
          Return Me.BeginInvoke("CTemp", New Object() _
             {Temperature, FromUnits, ToUnits}, callback, asyncState)
       End Function

       <System.Diagnostics.DebuggerStepThroughAttribute()>   _
       Public Function EndCTemp(ByVal asyncResult As _
                           System.IAsyncResult) As Decimal
          Dim results() As Object = Me.EndInvoke(asyncResult)
          Return CType(results(0),Decimal)
       End Function
End Class
```

At this point, you are ready to add the class to your project so that it can be compiled and used to call the methods of the Web Service from a consumer application. Chapter 50 covers this proxy class, when you create a complete consumer application for the CTemp Web Service.

Creating a proxy class with Visual Studio

As mentioned, Visual Studio automatically creates Web Service proxy classes by using the Add Web Reference feature. All you need is the ability to locate the WSDL document for the Web Service. Visual Studio silently takes care of the rest for you, locating the WSDL for a selected Web Service, validating the contents, and then generating the proxy class.

Although this is by far the simplest method for obtaining a Web Service proxy class, you could also use the `wsdl` tool in the .NET Framework to accomplish the same thing.

Summary

Finding Web Services and generating proxy classes that you can use to consume them is a simple process when you use the tools built into .NET and Visual Studio. Instead of having to worry about the implementation details of how to communicate with a Web Service, you can interact with the proxy class in an object-oriented fashion and rely on the proxy to handle the details. This greatly simplifies creating applications that consume Web Services and permits you to focus on creating the application logic, rather than coding the necessary plumbing.

✦   ✦   ✦

Consuming Web Services

by Jim Chandler

This chapter teaches you how to use Visual Studio and VB .NET to write a consumer application for the `CTemp` Web Service that you built in previous chapters. Many different types of applications can consume Web Services, including traditional desktop applications, Web applications, or even other Web Services. The example in this chapter illustrates how to call the `CTemp` Web Service from an ASP.NET Web application by using Visual Studio as the development environment.

In addition to covering the details of creating Web Service consumers, this chapter takes a fairly detailed look at execution flow between your Web Service and consumer applications. This is to help you understand how Web Services work in ASP.NET, as well as to appreciate the great many details related to Web Service implementation that are handled for you automatically by the ASP.NET and Visual Studio tools.

Web Service Consumer Overview

A Web Service *consumer* is any application that references and uses a Web Service. It can take many forms: a client application, a server application, a component, or even another Web Service. It does not matter, as long as it can call Web Services by using HTTP and SOAP.

To consume a Web Service, you need to do the following:

✦ Find the Web Service.

✦ Obtain its WSDL service contract.

✦ Generate a proxy class with which to call the Web Service.

✦ Create an instance of the proxy class.

✦ Call the methods exposed by the proxy.

Previous chapters have covered how to find Web Services by using various tools, including Visual Studio. You've also seen how to obtain the WSDL document and generate a proxy class by using the wsdl tool from the .NET Framework SDK, as well as Visual Studio's Add Web Reference feature. Armed with this knowledge, you are now ready to create a client application that is capable of calling the methods of any Web Service that you can locate and generate a proxy class from.

Recall that communication with a Web Service is accomplished via messages that are delivered by a transport protocol. With no assistance from the platform, you would have to understand how to create and format SOAP messages, as well as handle the delivery and receipt of these messages via HTTP, just to interact with a Web Service.

Ideally, the platform should provide this support for you. Even more beneficial would be the ability to create an instance of a class that represented the Web Service and the ability to call the methods, which in turn would carry out the necessary SOAP message generation and transportation activities required to communicate with the actual Web Service.

Fortunately, this is exactly what happens when you create a Web Service proxy class within the .NET Framework. The proxy class mimics the interfaces of the actual Web Service and takes care of formatting appropriate SOAP messages to deliver requests to the Web Service, as well as processing the responses that come back. Calling a Web Service is boiled down to the simple process of calling a method on a .NET class! This makes using Web Services easy.

An interesting attribute of ASP.NET Web Services is that they can be referenced and called both as native .NET classes as well as Web Services. You could, for example, build and deploy the CTemp Web Service assembly to an application's \bin folder, create an instance of the class, and call its methods directly.

By generating and using a proxy class, however, you can reach your Web Service via HTTP and SOAP. The benefit of the proxy class is that you can create an instance of the class and call its methods, just like the native .NET assembly. The HTTP and SOAP plumbing required to call Web Service methods is completely hidden from you within the proxy class (as it should be).

Why would you want to do this? Simple . . . you can distribute your Web Service to any remote server, and all that you need is XML, HTTP, and SOAP to communicate with it! This greatly broadens the reach of your component to many different platforms, not just Windows platforms.

Of course, the remoting of Web Service method calls across process and machine boundaries introduces additional opportunities for error. As an example, the network link between the consumer and the Web Service may be temporarily unavailable, causing a timeout error to be thrown. This illustrates the need to be aware of these additional error scenarios and have plans to handle them accordingly. In the case of SOAP-based Web Services, you will want to bracket the method calls of your proxy class using structured exception handling techniques so that you can trap SOAP-specific errors that can occur.

Let's take a look at how easy it is to create an ASP.NET application that can consume your `CTemp` Web Service by using Visual Studio and VB .NET.

Creating the Web Application Project

Recall that any type of application can be a Web Service consumer, including other Web Services. This is possible because all an application needs in order to consume a Web Service is the ability to communicate with that Web Service via HTTP and SOAP.

In this chapter, you will create an ASP.NET Web application to interact with the `CTemp` Web Service. Visual Studio provides an ASP.NET Web application project template so you can create the files for this type of application quickly and easily.

Let's begin by using Visual Studio to create the project files for your Web Service consumer application:

1. If you have not already done so, start Visual Studio now and choose New from the File menu, and then choose Project from the submenu. This displays the New Project dialog box, as shown in Figure 50-1.

2. In the New Project dialog box, select the Visual Basic Projects folder from the list of project types on the left side of the dialog box. Then choose ASP.NET Web Application from the list of templates on the right side of the dialog box.

3. Next, type **CTempClient** in the Project Name text box. Note that, by default, the project files are located on your local Web server in a virtual folder named `CTempClient`.

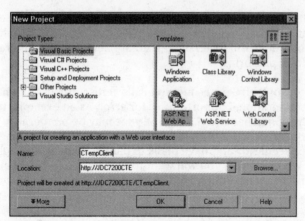

Figure 50-1: The Visual Studio New Project dialog box.

4. After you have entered this information, click the OK button to create the project. Visual Studio automatically creates the project and all of the related project files necessary to create an ASP.NET Web application on your local Web server. After you've created, loaded, and built the project, the Visual Studio window should resemble Figure 50-2.

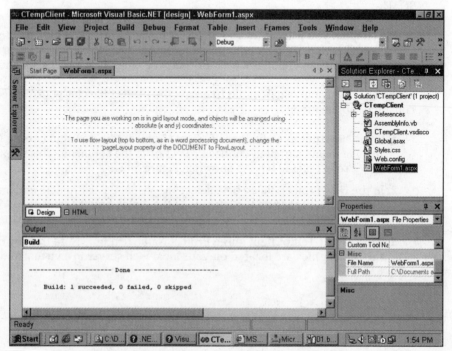

Figure 50-2: ASP.NET Web application skeleton in Visual Studio.

Visual Studio displays the form designer surface of the default ASP.NET Web Form (named `WebForm1.aspx`). Eventually, this form will display the user interface for requesting temperature conversions in a Web browser. This is discussed later in this chapter.

When you create an ASP.NET Web application project in Visual Studio by using the Web application project template, a project file structure is created on the target Web server and a Visual Studio Solution file is created on your local computer.

The files listed in Table 50-1 are automatically created by Visual Studio and placed in the file structure on the target development Web server.

Tip   Some of the files in your Web application project are hidden by default in the Solution Explorer. To view all of the files in your project, choose Show All Files from the Project menu or click the Show All Files tool button at the top of the Solution Explorer window.

Table 50-1 Visual Studio Web Application Project Files	
Project File	**Description**
Webform1.aspx	This file contains the form definition, user interface controls, and so on that make up the Web Form. WebForm1.aspx is the default name given to the page by Visual Studio when the Web application project is first created.
WebForm1.aspx.vb	This file contains the code-behind class that handles the events and related functionality represented by the Web Form.
AssemblyInfo.vb	This file contains information about the assemblies within the Web Service project.
Web.config	This XML file contains ASP.NET application configuration information for the Web Service.
Global.asax	This file is responsible for handling ASP.NET application-level events.
Global.asax.vb	This file contains the code-behind class that handles the ASP.NET application-level events. This file is referenced by the Global.asax file in its ASP.NET application directive. By default, this file does not appear in the Solution Explorer.
{project name}.vbproj	This file contains project metadata such as the list of project files, build settings, and so on.

Continued

Table 50-1 *(continued)*	
Project File	**Description**
`{project name}.vbproj.webinfo`	This file contains a pointer to the Web server virtual directory that hosts your Web application project files.
`{project name}.vsdisco`	This file contains the links (URLs) to the discovery (`disco`) information for this application.
`Licenses.licx`	This file contains licensing and version information for the controls used in any Web Forms (`.aspx`) files.
`Styles.css`	This file contains stylesheet settings used by the display elements of your application.

Caution These project files are important to the proper operation of your application, as well as Visual Studio. Therefore, you should be very sure of what you are doing before changing or deleting any of these files. In addition, Visual Studio may unexpectedly (and silently) overwrite these files with any changes you may have made to them manually. Thus, it's a good idea to use a hands-off policy when it comes to these files.

Before you develop the user interface for your Web Service consumer application, you need to walk through the procedure for finding and adding a reference to the `CTemp` Web Service that you're calling from within your application.

Locating the CTemp Web Service

Recall that in Visual Studio, the Add Web Reference dialog box is used to locate and create references to Web Services. Because you are interested in consuming the `CTemp` Web Service, let's take a look at how to use the Add Web Reference dialog box to create a reference to the `CTemp` Web Service.

If you have followed the examples in this book, the `CTemp` Web Service was developed on your local Web server. In this case, you can use the Web References on Local Web Server link in the Add Web Reference dialog box to find the `CTemp` Web Service.

Follow these steps to locate the `CTemp` Web Service:

1. To locate the `CTemp` Web Service on your local Web server, choose Add Web Reference from the Project menu in Visual Studio. This displays the Add Web Reference dialog box. In the left pane of the dialog box, click the Web

References on Local Web Server link to search your local Web server for any published Web Services.

2. Visual Studio searches the local Web server for any Web Services it can find, as directed by `disco` documents that are stored in the virtual directories of the Web server. When this process has been completed, the Add Web Reference dialog box should resemble Figure 50-3.

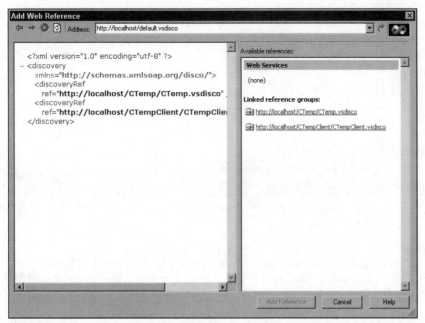

Figure 50-3: Finding local Web Services by using the Add Web Reference dialog box.

As shown in Figure 50-3, Visual Studio has searched the local Web server and found a document named `default.vsdisco`, which contains discovery references to two other discovery documents: one for your `CTemp` Web Service and one for your `CTempClient` Web application. These references are represented as links on the right side of the dialog box.

3. Click the first link (the reference to the `CTemp` `disco` document). Visual Studio processes the contents of the `CTemp` `disco` document and displays the results, as shown in Figure 50-4.

The left side of the dialog box now displays the contents of the `CTemp` discovery document. This document contains a WSDL contract reference, as well as a link to documentation for the `CTemp` Web Service. Note that the documentation reference uses the features of the ASP.NET runtime to display the Web Service help page by referencing the `.asmx` file.

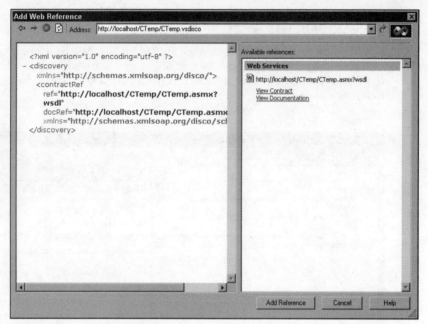

Figure 50-4: CTemp Web Service discovery by using the Add Web Reference dialog box.

If you want to view the WSDL contract document or the Web Service help page, click either link on the right side of the dialog box. This causes Visual Studio to display the contents of these documents on the left side of the dialog box.

Note that Visual Studio has discovered the location of the WSDL contract file via the disco document and has enabled the Add Reference button in the dialog box. This is your indicator that Visual Studio has found the WSDL contract file, has recognized it, and is ready to process it.

Now that you have successfully located the CTemp Web Service, let's add a reference to it.

Adding a Web Reference

When you located the CTemp Web Service by using the Add Web Reference dialog box, Visual Studio recognized the reference to the WSDL contract (which is needed in order to create the proxy class) and enabled the Add Reference button.

Follow these steps to add a Web reference to the CTemp Web Service:

1. To add the reference to the `CTemp` Web Service, click the Add Reference button now. Visual Studio creates a new section in your `CTempClient` project (located on the target Web server) named Web References that holds information about all of the Web Service references in your project. In addition, Visual Studio copies the `CTemp` discovery and WSDL documents to the local Web server project virtual directory of your `CTempClient` application. Then a proxy class is generated from the WSDL document.

2. To view this file in Solution Explorer, choose Show All Files from the Project menu in Visual Studio. The proxy class (named `CTemp.vb`) is listed as a child node of the WSDL document, as shown in Figure 50-5.

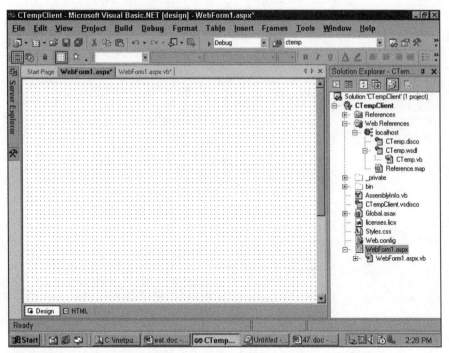

Figure 50-5: Web Service references in the Solution Explorer window of Visual Studio.

Now that you have a reference to the `CTemp` Web Service, you can call methods on the service by using the proxy class generated for you by Visual Studio.

Before you move on to the next step in writing your Web Service consumer application, let's take a brief look at the code for the proxy class. To view the proxy class source code, double-click the CTemp.vb file listed in the Solution Explorer window. A partial code snippet for the CTemp proxy class is shown in Listing 50-1.

Listing 50-1: **CTemp Proxy Class Source Code**

```
Public Class CTemp
    Inherits System.Web.Services.Protocols.SoapHttpClientProtocol

    <System.Diagnostics.DebuggerStepThroughAttribute()> _
    Public Sub New()
        MyBase.New
        Me.Url = "http://localhost/CTemp/CTemp.asmx"
    End Sub

    <System.Diagnostics.DebuggerStepThroughAttribute(), _
    System.Web.Services.Protocols.SoapDocumentMethodAttribute _
        ("http://tempuri.org/CTemp", _
        Use:=System.Web.Services.Description.SoapBindingUse.Literal, _
        ParameterStyle:= _
System.Web.Services.Protocols.SoapParameterStyle.Wrapped)>
    Public Function CTemp(ByVal Temperature As Decimal, _
                        ByVal FromUnits As String, _
                        ByVal ToUnits As String) As Decimal
        Dim results() As Object = _
                        Me.Invoke("CTemp", New Object() _
                            {Temperature, FromUnits, ToUnits})
        Return CType(results(0),Decimal)
    End Function

    <System.Diagnostics.DebuggerStepThroughAttribute()> _
    Public Function BeginCTemp(ByVal Temperature As Decimal, _
                        ByVal FromUnits As String, _
                        ByVal ToUnits As String, _
                        ByVal callback As _
                            System.AsyncCallback, _
                        ByVal asyncState As Object) _
                            As System.IAsyncResult
        Return Me.BeginInvoke("CTemp", New Object() _
        {Temperature, FromUnits, ToUnits}, callback, asyncState)
    End Function

    <System.Diagnostics.DebuggerStepThroughAttribute()> _
    Public Function EndCTemp(ByVal asyncResult As _
                        System.IAsyncResult) As Decimal
        Dim results() As Object = Me.EndInvoke(asyncResult)
        Return CType(results(0),Decimal)
    End Function
End Class
```

Note that the CTemp proxy class inherits from the .NET class named System. Web.Services.Protocols.SoapHttpClientProtocol, which implies that the CTemp proxy uses HTTP and SOAP as the communications protocol to invoke the CTemp Web Service.

Now direct your attention to the declaration and implementation of the CTemp method in Listing 50-1. As you can see, the proxy method declaration is identical to the CTemp Web Service method, using the name number, order, and type of arguments. But the actual implementation is quite different. The proxy class does not perform any conversion of temperature units, as does the actual Web Service. Instead, the proxy method contains just a few lines of code, as follows:

```
Dim results() As Object = Me.Invoke("CTemp", New Object()
    {Temperature, FromUnits, ToUnits})
Return CType(results(0),Decimal)
```

The first line of code calls the Invoke method of the proxy class to synchronously call the CTemp Web Service and return the result. The second line of code converts the result to the proper type (Decimal) and returns this result to the caller.

Of course, your call to the CTemp proxy and its call to the actual CTemp Web Service method are all marshaled on your local Web server by using XML, HTTP, and SOAP. Your proxy class, however, could just as easily have been calling the CTemp Web Service on a machine in another room, across the country, or even halfway across the world! This distinction is completely hidden from the consumer of the Web Service, as is the fact that the proxy is exchanging SOAP messages with the CTemp Web Service. All you have to do is create an instance of the proxy class and invoke its methods as if it were a local class. What could be easier?

Note that in addition to the CTemp method implementation, the proxy class also contains two additional method implementations named BeginCTemp and EndCTemp. These methods provide the support necessary to invoke the CTemp method asynchronously.

These and other features of the proxy class are covered a little later in this chapter. For now, let's get back to building your client application by creating a simple user interface form that can be used to interact with your CTemp Web Service.

Building the Web Form

Now that you've created the base project files for your consumer application and added a Web Reference to the CTemp Web Service, you're ready to build a form that allows you to enter values that can be passed to the CTemp Web Service and display the results after a call is made.

If the designer surface for the WebForm1.aspx page is not currently displayed, click the tab in the main window area of Visual Studio corresponding to this file. The Web

Form designer allows you to drag and drop controls onto the designer surface and manipulate them in a WYSIWYG manner.

This application uses the following controls:

✦ Two text boxes, one for the input temperature and one for the output temperature

✦ Two radio button lists, one to select the input temperature units and one to select the output temperature units

✦ One command button to execute the units conversion

Drag and drop these controls onto the designer surface of the form. The controls are available in the control toolbox from the left side of the main Visual Studio window. If the control toolbox is not visible, choose Toolbox from the View menu. You should be able to find the controls that you need within the Web Forms section of the control toolbox.

After you have added the controls to the designer surface, you need to set some control properties. Make sure the Properties window appears by choosing Properties Window from the View menu.

Follow these steps to initialize the control properties of each control on the Web Form:

1. Click one of the text boxes to select it.

2. In the Properties window, erase any text in the `Text` property and change the `ID` property to `txtInputTemp`. This text box allows the user to enter an input temperature value. Note that the text stored in the `ID` property is used to reference this control within your form code at runtime.

3. Click the remaining text box to select it.

4. In the Properties window, erase any text in the `Text` property, change the `ReadOnly` property to `True`, and change the `ID` property to `txtOutputTemp`. This text box is used to display the temperature conversion value. The `ReadOnly` property prevents users from modifying the text in the text box (since this is set to the appropriate value by the form after obtaining the results of the unit conversion).

5. Click the command button to select it.

6. In the Properties window, change the `Text` property to `Converts To` and change the ID property to `btnConvert`. Clicking this button executes the units conversion based on the settings chosen by the user in the other controls. The `Text` property is used to display a string on the face of the button.

7. Click one of the option button lists to select it.

8. In the Properties window, change the `ID` property to `optFromUnits`. Next, select the `Items` property and click the details button (the button with the ellipsis). This displays the ListItem Collection Editor dialog box, as shown in Figure 50-6.

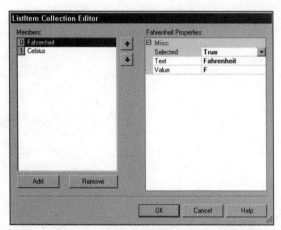

Figure 50-6: Visual Studio ListItem Collection Editor dialog box.

9. Add two entries to the list: one named Celsius with a value of C and one named Fahrenheit with a value of F. Set the Fahrenheit item's `Selected` property to `True` so that this entry is selected by default when the form is displayed for the first time. When you are finished adding the option button list items, close the ListItem Collection Editor dialog box by clicking the OK button.

10. Click the remaining option button list to select it.

11. In the Properties window, change the `ID` property to `optToUnits`. Next, select the `Items` property and click the details button. This displays the ListItem Collection Editor dialog box once again.

12. Repeat the steps you used to populate the `optFromUnits` option button list to add the various output unit items to this list. You should add options for Fahrenheit (value F), Celsius (value C), Kelvin (value K), and Rankine (value R). Set the Celsius item's `Selected` property to `True` so that this entry is selected by default when the form is displayed for the first time. When you are finished adding the option button list items, close the ListItem Collection Editor dialog box by clicking the OK button.

After you have completed these steps, rearrange the controls on the form so that they resemble the form layout shown in Figure 50-7.

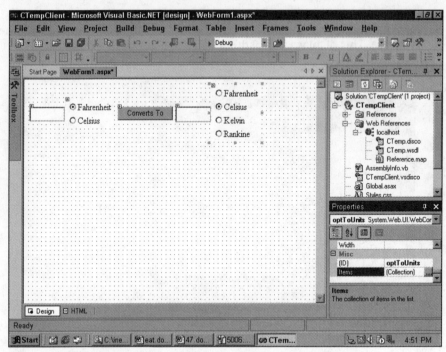

Figure 50-7: Arrangement of user interface controls on the Web Form.

Now that you have your Web Form created and initialized, you are ready to add the code to the form that creates an instance of the CTemp proxy class so you can interact with the proxy class to perform temperature unit conversions.

Creating an Instance of the CTemp Proxy

In order to call methods of the proxy class that represents the Web Service, you must create an instance of the proxy class. As it turns out, creating an instance of a Web Service proxy is identical to creating an instance of any other .NET class, which is quite easy.

When creating an instance of the Web Service proxy, you must reference the namespace assigned to the proxy in order to qualify the class instance you want to create uniquely. As part of the Add Web Reference functionality built into Visual Studio, the default namespace of the CTemp proxy is set to localhost (your local Web server). If you want to change this namespace, rename the localhost container found under the Web References section of the Solution Explorer window.

So, to create an instance of the CTemp proxy class, you simply reference the class as localhost.CTemp in your declaration. Let's illustrate this process by adding some code to the consumer application you have been building.

Double-click the command button you added to your Web Form on the designer surface. This displays the code window for the Web Form, as shown in Figure 50-8.

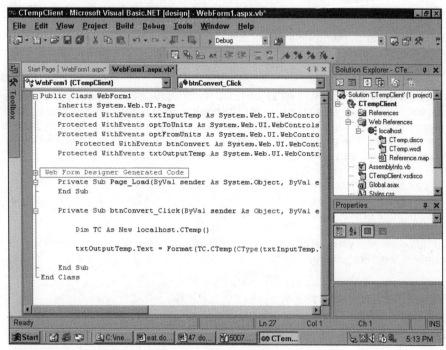

Figure 50-8: Web Form code view in Visual Studio.

Visual Studio has created a template event handling procedure for the `Click` event of the button control for you. All you have to do is fill in the code to handle the event. Add the following code to the `Click` event handler for the button:

```
Dim TC As New localhost.CTemp()

txtOutputTemp.Text = _
    Format(TC.CTemp(CType(txtInputTemp.Text, Decimal), _
                optFromUnits.SelectedItem.Value, _
                optToUnits.SelectedItem.Value), "Fixed")
```

As shown in the preceding example, the `TC` variable is declared to be an instance of the `CTemp` proxy class denoted by the `localhost.CTemp` namespace designator. Following this declaration is a single line of code that extracts the input arguments from the Web Form, calls the `CTemp` method on the proxy class (the synchronous form), formats the results, and inserts the value into the output text box.

Let's take a closer look at the code that actually invokes the `CTemp` method on the proxy class.

Calling CTemp Proxy Methods

ASP.NET Web Services can be called both *synchronously* and *asynchronously*. In a synchronous method call, the caller waits for a response from the Web Service before continuing execution. An asynchronous method call, on the other hand, permits the caller to continue with other work while the call is in progress. A notification mechanism (or *callback*) is then used to inform the consumer that the Web Service call has been completed.

ASP.NET Web Services use HTTP as the default transport protocol and SOAP as the messaging format. This provides for the exchange of a much larger family of data types, as well as complex XML-based document types between the Web Service and the consumer. The proxy class eliminates these details from the caller, of course, making it quick and easy to call Web Service methods.

To call a Web Service method on your proxy class, all you need to do is specify the name of the method to call (along with any arguments) by using the reference to the instance of the proxy that you declared.

In this example, you are calling the synchronous form of the `CTemp` Web method to convert temperature units as follows:

```
txtOutputTemp.Text = _
    Format(TC.CTemp(CType(txtInputTemp.Text, Decimal), _
                    optFromUnits.SelectedItem.Value, _
                    optToUnits.SelectedItem.Value), "Fixed")
```

Let's break down this statement so that you can thoroughly examine everything that is occurring at this stage.

The proxy object reference (`TC`) is used to call the `CTemp` method (`TC.CTemp`).

The first argument to the `CTemp` method specifies the input temperature. This value is obtained from the text box on the Web Form by referring to the `Text` property of the text box control (`txtInputTemp.Text`).

The `CTemp` method expects the input temperature argument to be of type `Decimal`, so the `CType` function is used to convert the text obtained from the text box control to the `Decimal` data type.

The second argument to the method specifies the source units of the temperature value. This value is obtained from the option button list by using the `SelectedItem` property to reference the currently selected option button and then referencing the `Value` property of that result (`optFromUnits.SelectedItem.Value`). This returns a single character string that encodes the source units as either F (for Fahrenheit) or C (for Celsius).

The third argument to the method specifies the target units of the temperature conversion. This value is obtained from the option button list by using the `SelectedItem` property to reference the currently selected option button and then referencing the `Value` property of that result (`optToUnits.SelectedItem.Value`). This returns a single character string that encodes the target units as F (for Fahrenheit), C (for Celsius), K (for Kelvin), or R (for Rankine).

Lastly, the `Decimal` result that is returned by the method call is converted to a formatted text string by using the `Format` function and the built-in `"Fixed"` format specifier. This results in a text string that displays at least one digit to the left of the decimal separator and two digits to the right. This string is then assigned to the `Text` property of the output text box (`txtOutputTemp.Text`).

This single line of code handles the entire process: gathering the input from the Web Form controls, converting that input to the proper data types expected by the `CTemp` method call, calling the method, formatting the result, and assigning it to the text box control on the Web Form that displays the results of the call.

If you are familiar with programming forms in Visual Basic 6 (or earlier), you should have noticed by now that programming Web Forms in Visual Studio .NET is strikingly similar to programming Windows forms in previous versions of Visual Basic. What's more, interacting with Web Services is very much like interacting with traditional COM automation components.

The simple addition of two lines of code to your consumer application now gives you everything you need to test your application. Let's take a look at that process in the next section.

Testing the Consumer Application

Now that you have created the consumer application, designed the Web Form, and added the code to the `Click` event of the button control, you are ready to test your application.

To test your application, simply choose Start Without Debugging from the Debug menu within Visual Studio. This causes Visual Studio to save your project files, compile your application, and start a new instance of your Web browser pointing to the Web Form page, as shown in Figure 50-9.

To test the application, enter a temperature value in the first text box, select the source units, select the target units, and then click the Converts To button. The Web Form is submitted to the server, where the `Click` event code of the button is executed. This code creates an instance of the `CTemp` proxy class, calls the `CTemp` method, and outputs the conversion results to the target temperature text box.

Having now seen your consumer application in action, let's take a look at the larger picture of what really happens when you run your application to interact with the CTemp Web Service.

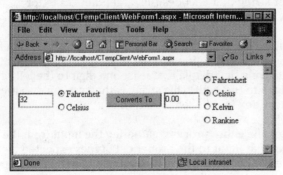

Figure 50-9: CTempClient Web application user interface in Internet Explorer.

Handling SOAP Exceptions

Web Service method calls can fail for any of a number of reasons. The method itself may throw an exception due to missing or invalid arguments, a runtime execution error (such as divide by zero), or other types of logic errors. In addition to method-specific exceptions, the framework itself may cause an exception to be thrown, such as when a communication failure occurs or a request message is malformed.

In either case, it is extremely important that Web Service consumers bracket all Web Service method calls inside try/catch blocks. When consuming Web Services using the SOAP protocol, ASP.NET will throw SOAP exceptions to indicate the occurrence of runtime errors.

The .NET Framework defines a SOAPException class in the System.Web.Services. Protocols namespace that Web Service consumers use when calling Web Service methods over SOAP.

When an exception occurs in a Web Service, ASP.NET determines whether or not the client called the Web Service method using SOAP. If SOAP is identified as the message protocol, ASP.NET wraps the exception that occurred into a SOAPException and sets the Actor and Code properties accordingly.

The VB .NET code snippet shown in Listing 50-2 provides an example usage of the SOAPException class:

Listing 50-2: **Catching SOAP Exceptions**

```
Try
    math.Divide(3, 0)
Catch err As System.Web.Services.Protocols.SoapException
    LogError err.Code.Namespace, err.Code.Name, err.Actor, err.Message
    Return
End Try
```

In this example, the `Divide` method of the math Web Service is called with a divisor of zero. Of course, this will cause a divide-by-zero runtime exception to occur. Since this method is being called via SOAP, the exception is wrapped in a `SOAPException` by the ASP.NET runtime.

As shown in the example, you can access the details of the exception via various properties of the `SOAPException` class. The `Code` property is perhaps the most important attribute of the `SOAPException`, as it identifies the type of exception that has occurred.

Currently, the `Code` property of the `SOAPException` class can be set to any one of the values listed in Table 50-2.

Table 50-2
SOAP Fault Codes

SOAP Fault Code	Description
VersionMismatchFaultCode	An invalid namespace for a SOAP envelope was found.
MustUnderstandFaultCode	Not all SOAP elements require processing. However, if a SOAP element is marked with the `MustUnderstand` attribute with a value of 1, it is required. Failure to process the element generates this exception.
ClientFaultCode	A client call was not formatted correctly or did not contain the appropriate information. For example, the client call could have lacked the proper authentication or payment information. It is generally an indication that the message should not be re-sent without change.

Continued

SOAP Fault Code	Description
ServerFaultCode	An error occurred during the processing of a client call on the server, however the problem was not due to the message contents. For example, an upstream server couldn't respond to a request due to network problems. Typically, with this type of exception, the client call may succeed later.
	If a Web Service throws an exception, other than SoapException and the client is calling via SOAP, ASP.NET converts the exception to a SoapException, setting the Code property to ServerFaultCode and throws it back to the client.

Table 50-2 *(continued)*

Again, it is highly recommended that you get in the habit of enclosing Web Service method calls in try/catch blocks. Getting in this habit early will pay great dividends later as your consumer application will be much more resilient and capable of recovering from a number of errors that are beyond your control.

Application Execution Model

Seeing how simple it was to create a consumer for your CTemp Web Service, you might be tempted to forget all that is actually taking place when calling a Web Service method. The real value of the .NET framework and the Visual Studio IDE is quite evident when you examine some of the details behind the operation of your simple consumer application and Web Service as it processes a single temperature conversion request.

Recall that both Web Services and Web applications are really ASP.NET applications and run under the control of ASP.NET and the Common Language Runtime. As such, both applications are contained in a virtual directory on a Web server, with the appropriate files for each application stored in the root of the virtual directory along with any needed assemblies, which are stored in the bin folder of the virtual directory.

The consumer application is started when a user requests the main form of the application:

1. A user requests the main form of the CTempClient application, such as http://localhost/CTempClient/WebForm1.aspx.

2. The IIS Web server on localhost receives the request (technically, an HTTP GET request) and hands it off to the ASP.NET runtime for execution of the

page (because the requested page has an .aspx extension). This hand-off occurs via an ISAPI filter extension that is registered within IIS to handle all of the ASP.NET file types.

3. The ASP.NET runtime creates an instance of the page class that represents the Web Form and executes the page.

4. The page class generates the HTML and sends it to the browser, causing the form to be rendered in the user's browser window.

5. The page class is then destroyed by the ASP.NET runtime along with any other necessary request cleanup processing. (Remember, HTTP is a stateless protocol, so there is no need to keep the page class around after the HTML has been transmitted to the client.)

6. The user enters information into the form and clicks the Convert To button. This causes the form to be posted back to the Web server.

7. Again, the Web server hands off the request (technically, an HTTP POST request) to the ASP.NET runtime, which creates a new instance of the page class that implements the Web Form and executes the page.

8. Because this is a postback request, the server-side button control's Click event code is executed. Recall that this is where you added your code to create and call the CTemp Web Service.

9. The Click event code creates an instance of the CTemp Web Service proxy class. This class inherits from the System.Web.Services.Protocols.SoapHttpClientProtocol class. This provides the foundation for communicating the method request and response via SOAP messages over the HTTP transport.

10. The Click event code now calls the synchronous CTemp method on the proxy object, passing the input arguments obtained from the postback data of the form (via server-side control properties).

11. The Web Service proxy calls the Invoke method, passing along the input arguments. This method serializes the CTemp method call into a SOAP message that matches the method signature defined in the WSDL document. The SOAP message is then added to the payload of an HTTP request and delivered to the Web Service endpoint (the URL of the .asmx file).

12. The IIS Web server that hosts the CTemp Web Service (in this specific case, localhost) receives the request (technically, a SOAP POST request) and hands it off to the ASP.NET runtime to execute the requested page.

13. The ASP.NET runtime deserializes the SOAP payload from the request, creates an instance of the CTemp Web Service implementation class, and executes the CTemp method, passing the input arguments.

14. Next, the ASP.NET runtime takes the result of the CTemp method call and serializes it into a SOAP response message. This message is then added to the payload of an HTTP response and delivered back to the client (in this case, your proxy class).

15. The `Invoke` method of the proxy class deserializes the result from the SOAP response message into a generic .NET Object type. This type is then explicitly cast to the return data type expected by the caller (in this case, a `Decimal` temperature value) and returned to your consumer application.

16. The `Click` event code in your consumer application takes the result, converts it to a string data type, and assigns the result to the output text box in the Web Form, formatted to two decimal places. The event code processing is now completed and page execution continues.

17. The page executes through its rendering phase to generate the HTML that is returned to the user's browser. Just as before, the page class is then torn down by the ASP.NET runtime, and any other cleanup processing that is necessary is executed.

Whew! That was a handful! Hopefully, this simulated flow of execution between a Web Service and its consumer gives you a solid foundation for further exploration into the underpinnings of how Web Services work. This information is also useful as you build Web Services and/or consumers and need to troubleshoot problems that might arise.

Summary

As demonstrated in Part VII, Web Services are poised to become the programmable building blocks for the next generation of the Internet. The wide adoption of XML, HTTP, and SOAP has made it possible to create an object middleware infrastructure that can be leveraged on the many types of systems attached to the Internet, regardless of hardware platform, operating system, or object model. Even more importantly, there finally exists a consistent and simple way to interact with these programmable components.

Having this new level of interoperability at a programming level enables many new and innovative solutions to problems that were once difficult, if not impossible, to address in the past. It is only a matter of time before you will have a huge library of these programmable building blocks at your fingertips, from which to construct truly distributed applications that can interoperate with all kinds of systems.

In many respects, it is up to you, the professional programmer, to create these building blocks. Web Services give you a powerful tool to construct these building blocks in a way that greatly expands the potential population of consumers that can leverage these services. The future awaits us. I hope that you welcome it and enjoy the ride, as it's sure to be an interesting one!

✦   ✦   ✦

Globalization

by Jason Beres

In today's global community, it is more and more likely that your applications will be used by people who do not consider U.S. English to be their first language. This appendix teaches you how to use the tools provided by VB .NET and the .NET Framework to ensure that your applications can handle multiple applications and cultures correctly.

Globalizing Applications

By *globalizing* your applications, you ensure that the user interface and functionality you provide makes sense to users all over the world. When designing applications, most developers use their native language. Not just for the code, but for the user interface elements such as labels and other descriptive features. This is fine 99.99% of the time because most work is done for in-house use, and beyond the doors of their offices, their applications are never used by anyone else.

If there is a chance, however slight, that an application could be used in a market that doesn't understand your language, it is a good idea to design globalization in the application from the beginning.

The Windows operating system comes in many languages. If you have ever received the MSDN Universal subscription with the International Pack option, you know that there are tons of flavors of each OS for any language you need to test on. Each one of these installations contains DLLs that tailor the user interface to the locale of the user. If you install the Italian version of Windows, all the dialog boxes, screens, options, and so on are geared toward the Italian language and Italian culture.

The word "culture" is important. The U.S. version of Windows is geared towards English-speaking America. The Great Britain version of Windows is geared towards the Queen's English. Each language has different characters that represent different words, and there are terms or slang in one language that could mean something completely different in the other language (and it could be offensive). By designing your applications to handle multiple cultures and languages, you are globalizing it.

Localization

On any version of Windows, the Control Panel has a Regional and Language Settings applet that allows you to modify how items are displayed on your screen (see Figure A-1). This applet allows you to change your *locale*, which is a set of rules for a given geographical area, including the following:

✦ Date and time formatting

✦ Currency and numeric formatting

✦ Weight and measure formatting

✦ Character classification

✦ Sorting rules

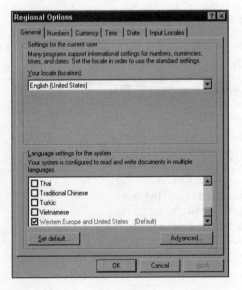

Figure A-1: Regional options in the Control Panel

When you change the locale of your computer, the formatting defined by the control panel takes over and your computer functions in terms of that locale. Numbers, dates, times, and other items are presented to the user they would be in that locale. This does not mean that all of a sudden your dialog boxes and labels are displayed in Italian or Greek; it means that the formatting is correct for the selected locale. In order to use another language in your application correctly, you must define resource files that are used to display the correct language based on the locale of the computer. The user's locale is not a language setting; you can consider it a formatting setting.

True localization is possible only if your application has been designed to include globalization. This means that the user interface string resources are separate from the actual code, allowing the application to determine which resources to display based on the locale. Although numbers and formatting can be changed with the click of a button in the Control Panel, true localization requires careful planning.

Resource Files

Resource files allow you to separate the code from the user interface string resources. In .NET, a resource file is an XML text file that contains language-specific resources. When designing an application to support globalization, you need to decide how you are going to implement language-specific resources. In VB .NET, you have two choices:

+ Build separate XML files for each locale and load them through the Resource Manager at runtime.

+ Use the Forms designer to specify language-specific strings at design time. Based on the culture of the operating system, the resource loads automatically at runtime.

The following sections teach you how to use both methods, but using the separate XML files is better than the built-in Forms designer method. The separate XML files are more flexible and easier to use. The Forms designer is less work, but it's sort of a hokey interface.

How you implement resource files also affects the application when it is compiled. If you are using separate XML files, the compiler builds an additional satellite assembly for each language you are targeting. If you use the built-in Forms designer tool, the resource files are compiled with the main assembly, and satellite assemblies aren't generated.

Follow these steps to use separate resource files in your application:

1. Create a regular Windows application.

2. After the project is loaded, right-click the project and select Add New Item. From the list, select Assembly Resource File, as shown in Figure A-2.

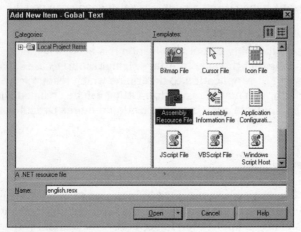

Figure A-2: Add New Item dialog box.

3. Name the file english.resx, all lowercase. In your Solution Explorer, you now see a .resx file. The way this works is that you create a separate resource file for each language that you want to support. The files all have the same prefix, and they need to indicate the locale for the resource that the file represents. Your initial file is called english.resx, so in order to support German and Italian, you would have two additional files named English.de-DE.resx for German and English.it-IT.resx for Italian. The original file is the *fall-back* file. If at runtime the resource manager cannot find what it needs in a locale specific file, it uses the fall-back file to load the resources.

This naming formula is based on the RFC 1766 standard for language and country code. The first part, the language code, must always be lowercase and is derived from ISO 639-1. The second part, the country/region code, must be uppercase and is based on ISO 3166. In the .NET Framework, these combinations are used in the CultureInfo class of the System.Globalization namespace.

Table A-1 is a partial list of CultureInfo names. The framework supports around 200 of them, ranging from Afrikaans to Vietnamese, so make sure to look up CultureInfo in the SDK to get a comprehensive list. The next section covers the members of the CultureInfo class. There is more to this class than just the language code, including regions' code pairings.

Table A-1 **CultureInfo Names**	
Culture	**Language-Country/Region**
en-AU	English – Australian
en-CA	English – Canada
en-US	English – United States
fr-BE	French – Belgium
fr-CA	French – Canada
fr-MC	French – Monaco
de-DE	German – Germany
de-CH	German – Luxembourg
it-IT	Italian – Italy
it-CH	Italian – Switzerland
es-MX	Spanish – Mexico
es-ES	Spanish – Spain

After the resource file is added, you can edit the values in the resource editor that Visual Studio provides. Double-click a .resx file in the Solution Explorer to bring up the resource editor in the main window. Figure A-3 shows the resource file for the English.resx file that you added to your project.

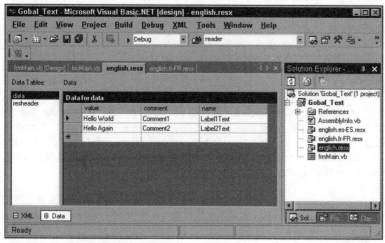

Figure A-3: Resource file editor.

The three columns of the resource editor, value, comment, and name, represent the string resources that you need to display on a form. The value is the actual data that is displayed, and the name is how you determine in your code what to display. Notice that I added two values and names in Figure A-3. To get your project up to speed, do the following:

1. Add two label controls to the default form and clear the `Text` property.

2. Add two more Assembly Resource Templates, named `english.fr-FR.resx` and `english.es-ES.resx`. The first one is French, the second is Spanish.

3. Modify the French resource file to contain the following values:

Value	Name
French Hello World	Label1Text
French Hello Again	Label2Text

4. Modify the Spanish resource file to contain these values:

Value	Name
Spanish Hello World	Label1Text
Spanish Hello Again	Label2Text

Now you need to use these resource files in your application. You use the `CultureInfo` class and the `ResourceManager` class in the `System.Globalization` namespace.

CultureInfo Class

The `CultureInfo` class can be used to obtain culture-specific details for the current culture setting. This class can be used to set or retrieve a culture on the current system. Using the `ResourceManager` class in conjunction with the `CultureInfo` class, you can determine which string resources should be displayed on your forms. The next section looks at the `ResourceManager`.

The `CultureInfo` constructor takes a single string argument, which is the RFC 1766 format for language and region. After this is set for the current thread, you can use the `ResourceManager` class to manipulate form objects by using your resource files. The `CultureInfo` class has members that can be used to determine information about the current culture. Tables A-2 through A-4 list the members of the `CultureInfo` class.

Table A-2
CultureInfo Static Properties

Name	*Description*
`CurrentCulture`	Gets the `CurrentCulture` instance that represents the culture used by the current thread.
`CurrentUICulture`	Gets the `CurrentUICulture` instance that represents the current culture used by the resource manager to look up culture-specific resources at runtime.
`InstalledUICulture`	Gets the `CurrentUICulture` instance that represents the default culture used by the resource manager to look up culture-specific resources at runtime.
`InvariantCulture`	Gets the `CultureInfo` instance that is not culture-dependent.

Table A-3
CultureInfo Static Methods

Name	*Description*
`CreateSpecificCulture`	Creates a `CultureInfo` instance.
`GetCultures`	Gets the list of supported cultures.

Table A-4
CultureInfo Instance Properties

Name	*Description*
`Calendar`	Returns the default calendar.
`CompareInfo`	Returns the `CompareInfo` instance that defines how to compare and sort strings for the culture.

Continued

Table A-4 (continued)

Name	Description
DateTimeFormat	Returns or sets the `DateTimeFormatting` instance that defines the culturally appropriate format for displaying dates and times.
DisplayName	Returns the culture name in the format `"<languagefull><country/regionfull>"` in the .NET Framework language.
EnglishName	Returns the culture name in the format `"<languagefull><country/regionfull>"` in English.
IsNeutralCulture	Determines whether the current culture instance is neutral.
IsReadOnly	Returns whether the current instance is read-only.
LCID	Returns the culture identifier for the current instance.
Name	Returns the culture name in the format `"<languagecode2>-<country/regioncode2>"`.
NativeName	Returns the culture name in the format `"<languagefull><country/regionfull>"` in the language that the culture is set to display.
NumberFormat	Returns or sets the `NumberFormatInfo` instance that defines the culturally appropriate format for displaying numbers.
OptionalCalendars	Returns or sets the list of optional calendars that can be used by the culture.
Parent	Returns the `CultureInfo` instance that represents the parent culture of the current `CultureInstance`.
ThreeLetterISOLanguageName	Returns the ISO 639-2 three-letter code for the language of the current culture instance.
ThreeLetterWindowsLanguageName	Returns the three-letter code for the language as defined by the Windows API.
UseUserOverride	Returns a value indicating whether the current instance uses the user-selected culture settings.
TwoLetterISOLanguageName	Returns the ISO 639-1 two-letter code for the language of the current culture instance.

All of these properties allow you to find anything out about the culture of the system your application is running on. In the following code, you can see the output of creating a new culture instance (Spanish) and retrieving some of the properties about the culture:

```
Dim ci As New CultureInfo("es-ES")
  With ci
      ' Delcare a string array to hold the days
      ' of the week and and short counter
      Dim str As String(), intX As Short
      Console.WriteLine(.Calendar)
      ' Fill the array with the days of the week
      str = (.DateTimeFormat.DayNames)
      For intX = 0 To str.Length - 1
          Console.WriteLine("Day " & intX.ToString _
              & " = " & str(intX))
      Next
      WriteLine("Display Name = " & .DisplayName)
      WriteLine("English Name = " & .EnglishName)
      WriteLine("LCID = " & .LCID)
      WriteLine("Name = " & .Name)
      WriteLine("Native Name = " & .NativeName)
      WriteLine("Currency Symbol = " _
              & .NumberFormat.CurrencySymbol)
      WriteLine(.OptionalCalendars.Length)
      WriteLine("ISO Lang Code = " _
              & .ThreeLetterISOLanguageName)
      WriteLine("Windows Lang Code = " _
              & .ThreeLetterWindowsLanguageName)
      WriteLine("2 Letter ISO Code = " _
              & .TwoLetterISOLanguageName)
  End With
```

This code produces the following output to the console:

```
System.Globalization.GregorianCalendar
Day 0 = domingo
Day 1 = lunes
Day 2 = martes
Day 3 = mièrcoles
Day 4 = jueves
Day 5 = viernes
Day 6 = sãbado
Display Name = Spanish (Spain)
English Name = Spanish (Spain)
LCID = 3082
Name = es-ES
Native Name = español (España)
Currency Symbol = ¤
1
ISO Lang Code = spa
Windows Lang Code = ESN
2 Letter ISO Code = es
```

Based on the different properties available, you can determine all culture-specific information of the system your application is running on.

ResourceManager Class

The ResourceManager class allows you to access resources for a specific culture on the current thread by using the information obtained from the current instance of the CultureInfo class. All culture-specific information is based on the current thread running, so to specify a specific culture code, you need to set the CurrentUICulture property of the current thread that is executing.

In order to set the correct culture for a form, you need to place code in the Sub New procedure. Consider the following code, which sets the U.S. English culture for the default form:

```
Public Sub New()
  MyBase.New()
  Thread.CurrentThread.CurrentUICulture = _
        New CultureInfo("en-US")
  'This call is required by the Windows Form Designer.
  InitializeComponent()
  'Add any initialization after the InitializeComponent() call
End Sub
```

After the culture is set, you create an instance of the ResourceManager to look up values in the resource files that you created earlier. Then the methods GetString and GetObject are used to access specific resources that need to be displayed.

In the following code, you create an instance on the ResourceManager in the form load event and fill in the Text property of the labels on your form:

```
Dim rm As New ResourceManager _
              ("Gobal_Text.english", _
               GetType(Form1).Module.Assembly)
        Label1.Text = rm.GetString("Label1Text")
        Label2.Text = rm.GetString("Label2Text")
```

The name of the resource file, english.resx, is the fall-back resource. Remember that if the specified resource cannot be found, the Resource Manager looks at the fall-back file to get the correct string information.

After you run your code, you see output that reflects the Label1Text and Label2Text values in your resource file.

Note Keeping in mind that the culture is based on the current thread, you should be able to set or retrieve different culture values if you create additional threads.

In your project, create two new sub-procedures for the form, one called Do_French and one called Do_Spanish. In these procedures, you need to write code that uses a new thread to specify the current culture, and use the other resource files that you created earlier. The end goal is to display the French and Spanish resources in other labels, so add four more labels to the main form also. The code for the procedure should look like the following:

```
Sub Do_French()
  ' Set the French culture setting for this thread
  t.CurrentUICulture = New CultureInfo("fr-FR")
  Dim rm As New ResourceManager _
      ("Gobal_Text.english", GetType(Form1).Module.Assembly)
  Label3.Text = rm.GetString("Label1Text")
  Label4.Text = rm.GetString("Label2Text")
End Sub

Sub Do_Spanish()
  ' Set the Spanish culture setting for this thread
  t1.CurrentUICulture = New CultureInfo("es-ES")
  Dim rm As New ResourceManager _
      ("Gobal_Text.english", GetType(Form1).Module.Assembly)
  Label5.Text = rm.GetString("Label1Text")
  Label6.Text = rm.GetString("Label2Text")
End Sub
```

Notice that you do not specify a resource file by name; you just use the fall-back name of the original file. Based on the current culture for the thread, the resource manager figures it out.

The threads you are using need to be created as global to the form. After the Public Class Class1 statement, type the following code:

```
Dim t As New Thread(AddressOf Do_French)
Dim t1 As New Thread(AddressOf Do_Spanish)
```

If you recall, the Thread constructor expects the address of a procedure. In this case, send the threads to your newly created procedures.

Now that you have the procedures written and the threads created, you need to start the threads. You can do this in the form load event. Your new form load looks something like this:

```
Private Sub Form1_Load(ByVal sender As System.Object,_
          ByVal e As System.EventArgs) Handles MyBase.Load

    Dim rm As New ResourceManager _
        ("Gobal_Text.english", GetType(Form1).Module.Assembly)
    Label1.Text = rm.GetString("Label1Text")
    Label2.Text = rm.GetString("Label2Text")

    ' Start both threads
    t.Start()
    t1.Start()
    ' wait until they are done
    t.Join()

End Sub
```

Now, when you run the application, you should see something like Figure A-4 on the screen.

Figure A-4: Output from multithreaded culture application.

Windows Forms Designer Globalization

The second method of globalizing forms is to use the built-in properties of the Windows Forms Designer. This method requires less work, but its behavior is a little inconsistent.

1. To start, you need to create a new Windows Forms application. After the application is loaded, add two labels to the default form. You can leave the default properties for everything.

2. Set the Localizable property to true on the form. Then you can modify the Language property of the form to add additional resource files to your form, based on the language you choose. The resource files are not displayed unless

you click the Show All Files button on the Solution Explorer toolbar. By default, the resources for the application are in the language of your system, so all text properties that you set are for the default resource file.

3. To add French, select French (France) from the Language drop-down on the Form properties. Notice that two new resource files have been added to your form, the default French language and the French – French resource file.

From this point forward, your form will use the French culture. Now you can change the text properties of the labels to indicate that you are using the French resources. Change the following properties through the Properties window:

```
Label2.Text = "French Label1"
Label2.Text = "French Label2"
```

Now your `Language` property is set to French, and you are manipulating objects on the forms for this specific culture.

If you need to go back to English, change the `Language` property on the form back to Default. This sets you back to your default culture.

When you run the application, the form displays the original label texts, as shown in Figure A-5.

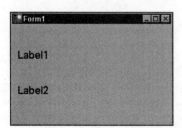

Figure A-5: Original labels on the default form.

If you modify the language of your operating system to French, reboot, and then run the application again. The French labels display the correct output. That is a lot of work. Instead, do the following to test the French strings:

✦ Import the System.Globalization namespace to your form.

✦ Import the System.Threading namespace to your form.

The top of your code should look like this:

```
Imports System.Threading
Imports System.Globalization
```

Set the current culture of your form to French. If you recall, you set this in the Sub_New event of the form by setting the current thread to a specific culture. Your Sub_New code should look like this:

```
Public Sub New()
    MyBase.New()
    Thread.CurrentThread.CurrentUICulture = _
      New CultureInfo("fr-FR")
    ' This call is required by the Windows Form Designer.
    InitializeComponent()
    ' Add any initialization after _
    ' the InitializeComponent() call
End Sub
```

That should do it. Now, when you run your application, you see results similar to Figure A-6.

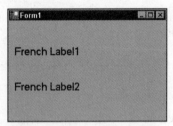

Figure A-6: Form after setting current culture to French.

The major advantage to using the tools provided by the forms designer is that less code is required. The disadvantages are that the hotkey interface is awkward, it's easy to make mistakes, and it's difficult to manage multiple languages. You might find yourself setting the French text when the form language is set to Finnish.

✦   ✦   ✦

VB6 Upgrade Wizard

by Jason Beres

Visual Basic .NET is the first version of VB in which your old Visual Basic code has only a 50-50 chance of working. Sure, you are probably still maintaining an old VB3 app because of its robust support for VBXs, which were not supported in 32-bit Visual Basic. But when you moved from VB3 to VB4 to VB6, the core of your hard work still worked 100% in the next version. VB developers expected this to be the case.

Well, all that has changed with the introduction of VB .NET. There are some major code changes, and a lot of your VB6 code will not work in VB .NET. In fact, not just the code is different, but the whole execution engine, the whole framework in which your code runs, is different.

This sounds a little scary, but the code changes are not impossible. They are actually rather exciting. You have new doors to walk through as a VB .NET developer.

If you are not thrilled and do not want to rewrite everything, you are in luck. An upgrade wizard exists that will take your existing projects and attempt to make them VB .NET-compatible. Well, the wizard does make some of your code VB .NET-compatible, but not 100% .NET Framework-compatible. The upgrade wizard scans your existing project, reads through the dependencies, forms, and code, and changes what it can to VB .NET by using a compatibility library. For code that is not upgradeable, the wizard generates a handy HTML report with what you need to change manually.

This appendix explores why you should not use the upgrade wizard process, and it contains code listings before and after the upgrade process.

Why You Should Not Upgrade

When I first got hooked into VB .NET, I realized that upgrading any of my existing work through a wizard would be a really bad idea. This is not because the wizard does a bad job, but because I would be writing VB6 code in VB .NET, and that is not what I wanted to accomplish. I encourage you to consider the same thing before you attempt to wizardize your existing applications and run them in VB .NET.

Cross-Reference Chapter 2 goes through the differences between the two languages, and some are quite significant. Make sure that you've read Chapter 2 before reading this appendix. It explains the changes that have been made to major parts of the Visual Basic language, and in many cases, things that are just plain obsolete.

Here are some other issues regarding what it takes to upgrade to VB .NET:

✦ **File IO** — The new `System.IO` objects offer more robust IO services than previous VB versions.

✦ **Error Handling** — The Structure Exception Handling (SEH) in VB .NET is more robust and CLS-compliant than the old `On Error Goto` statement.

✦ **Data Access** — ADO.NET is a reworking of how you will access data in the future. It is syntactically similar to ADO, but under the hood, it is a complete reworking of how data is accessed.

✦ **Forms and Controls** — The Forms model has completely changed, along with the controls you are used to putting on your forms. Many intrinsic controls from previous VB versions are obsolete, and there is no upgrade path.

When you run your application through the upgrade process, it takes your existing code and converts it to VB .NET syntax by using something called the Visual Basic Compatibility Library. The DLL allows outdated statements and functions to run inside of the .NET Framework. Note that this compatibility layer may not be around forever. Future versions of VB might deep-six the library, and your old VB6 code running in VB .NET won't work.

I know I sound negative, but run the wizard and just see what happens to your code. After going through this book, I think you will see that using the new features of VB .NET and the .NET Framework for your next project will probably be the best idea. VB .NET is way too much fun not to use, with all its new classes and name-spaces that offer such great functionality. (I just received my check from Microsoft's marketing department today.)

The Upgrade Wizard

If you plan on upgrading, you need to prepare first. Again, you should read through Chapter 2 before running the wizard. Some major points from Chapter 2 include the following:

✦ `Variant` data type is not supported.

✦ `Currency` data type is not supported.

✦ `Date$` and `Date` are not supported.

✦ Line and Shape controls are not supported.

✦ Print methods and graphics controls are not supported.

✦ DAO is not supported.

✦ RDO is not supported.

✦ Data binding is not supported.

✦ User controls are not supported.

✦ WebClasses, DHTML Projects, and ActiveX Document projects are not supported.

Now that we have that out of the way, let's run the Upgrade wizard:

1. Make a backup copy of your project. The wizard does not modify your existing application, but you need to be safe. Anything can happen, and you do not want to be the first person to report it to Product Support.

2. Open Visual Studio .NET and select the Open Project button.

3. Browse to your previous version's .VBP project file, select it from the directory list, and click the OK button.

4. Step 1 of 5 is an introduction to the wizard, so click the Next button.

5. Step 2 of 5 (see Figure B-1) lets you determine what type of project you would like to upgrade to. If the project can only be upgraded to an EXE project, all other options will be disabled.

6. Step 3 of 5 allows you change the output directory.

7. Step 4 of 5 is the actual upgrade process. When you click Next on Step 3, the wizard starts its job and it suddenly changes itself into Step 5 of 5. So Step 4 really just says Click Next to Continue. Your hard drive will be churning anywhere from a few minutes to a few hours, depending on how big your application is.

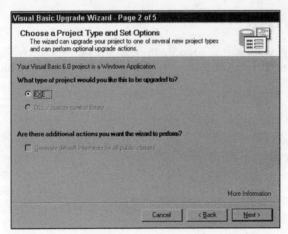

Figure B-1: Step 2 of 2 in the Upgrade wizard.

Visual Studio .NET is now open with your newly upgraded project.

That was painless. In the Solution Explorer of your newly upgraded project, you have an HTML document called _UpgradeReport.htm. Figure B-2 gives you an idea of what this report looks like.

List of Project Files

New Filename	Original Filename	File Type	Status	Errors	Warnings	Total Issues
⊟ (Global Issues)				0	0	0
Global update issues: None						
⊟ frmMyForm.vb	frmMyForm.frm	Form	Upgraded with issues	5	2	7

Upgrade Issues for frmMyForm.frm:

#	Severity	Location	Object Type	Object Name	Property	Description
1	Compile Error	Form_Load	Screen	Screen	vbNormal	Unable to determine which constant to upgrade vbNormal to.
2	Compile Error	Get_Authors	TextBox	Text1	DataField	TextBox property Text1.DataField was not upgraded.
3	Compile Error	Get_Authors	TextBox	Text1	DataSource	TextBox property Text1.DataSource was not upgraded.
4	Compile Error	Get_Authors	TextBox	Text2	DataField	TextBox property Text2.DataField was not upgraded.
5	Compile Error	Get_Authors	TextBox	Text2	DataSource	TextBox property Text2.DataSource was not upgraded.
6	Runtime Warning	Form_Load	Screen	Screen	MousePointer	Screen property Screen.MousePointer has a new behavior.
7	Runtime Warning	Form_Load	Screen	Screen	MousePointer	Screen property Screen.MousePointer has a new behavior.

| 1 File(s) | | Forms: 1 | Upgraded: 1 Not upgraded: 0 | 5 | 2 | 7 |

Click here for help with troubleshooting upgraded projects

Upgrade Settings

GenerateInterfacesForClasses: 0
LogFile: SimpleClient.log
MigrateProjectTo: WinExe
OutputDir: C:\Documents and Settings\Administrator\My Documents\Simple Upgrade Client\SimpleClient.NET

Figure B-2: Upgrade report from SimpleClient.vbp.

SimpleClient.VBP

Listing B-1 is a simple client that I wrote in VB6 and then ran through the upgrade process.

Listing B-1: Input to the Upgrade Wizard

```
Option Explicit
Dim rs As ADODB.Recordset
Dim cn As ADODB.Connection
Private Sub Get_Authors()
    Set rs = New ADODB.Recordset
    rs.Open "Select * from Authors", cn
    ' Use Data Binding
    Text1.DataField = "au_fname"
    Set Text1.DataSource = rs
    Text2.DataField = "au_lname"
    Set Text2.DataSource = rs
End Sub
Private Sub Get_Connection()
    Set cn = New ADODB.Connection
    With cn
        .ConnectionString =
            "uid=sa;pwd=;database=pubs;server=."
        .CursorLocation = adUseClient
        .Provider = "sqloledb"
        .Open
    End With
End Sub
Private Sub cmdMove_Click(Index As Integer)
    Select Case Index
        Case 0
            rs.MovePrevious
        Case 1
            rs.MoveNext
    End Select
End Sub
Private Sub Form_Load()
    Screen.MousePointer = vbHourglass
    ' Set the Form caption
    Me.Caption = "Simple Upgrade Client"
    ' Set some button properties
    With Command1
        .Caption = "Get Authors"
        .FontSize = 14
        .FontName = "Verdana"
        .ToolTipText = "Click to do nothing"
```

Continued

Listing B-1 *(continued)*

```
    End With
    ' Clear the boxes
    Text1 = ""
    Text2 = ""
    ' Make same size
    Text2.Width = Text1.Width
    ' Set Font Size
    Text1.Font.Size = 12
    Text2.Font.Size = 12
    ' Set Font Name
    Text1.Font.Name = "Tahoma"
    Text2.Font.Name = "Tahoma"
    'Get Connection to Database
    Get_Connection
    ' Fill the Recordset
    Get_Authors
    ' Set mouse back to normal
    Screen.MousePointer = vbNormal
End Sub
```

SimpleClient.NET

After the upgrade process was completed, I had a new output directory with a VB .NET solution and all the upgraded goodies from the wizard.

Listing B-2 is the new project that was created.

Listing B-2: **Output from the Upgrade Wizard**

```
Option Strict Off
Option Explicit On
Friend Class frmMyForm
Inherits System.Windows.Forms.Form

Dim rs As ADODB.Recordset
Dim cn As ADODB.Connection

Private Sub Get_Authors()
    rs = New ADODB.Recordset
    rs.Open("Select * from Authors", cn)
    ' Use Data Binding
    'UPGRADE_ISSUE: TextBox property
```

```
        'Text1.DataField was not upgraded.
        'Click for more:
        'ms-help://MS.MSDNVS/vbcon/html/vbup2064.htm
        Text1.DataField = "au_fname"
        'UPGRADE_ISSUE: TextBox property
        'Text1.DataSource was not upgraded.
        'Click for more:
        'ms-help://MS.MSDNVS/vbcon/html/vbup2064.htm
        Text1.DataSource = rs
        'UPGRADE_ISSUE: TextBox property
        'Text2.DataField was not upgraded.
        'Click for more:
        'ms-help://MS.MSDNVS/vbcon/html/vbup2064.htm
        Text2.DataField = "au_lname"
        'UPGRADE_ISSUE: TextBox property
        'Text2.DataSource was not upgraded. _
        'Click for more:
        'ms-help://MS.MSDNVS/vbcon/html/vbup2064.htm
        Text2.DataSource = rs
End Sub

Private Sub Get_Connection()

    cn = New ADODB.Connection

    With cn
        .ConnectionString = _
            "uid=sa;pwd=;database=pubs;server=."
        .CursorLocation = _
            ADODB.CursorLocationEnum.adUseClient
        .Provider = "sqloledb"
        .Open()
    End With

End Sub

Private Sub cmdMove_Click(ByVal eventSender _
    As System.Object, ByVal eventArgs _
    As System.EventArgs) Handles cmdMove.Click

    Dim Index As Short = cmdMove.GetIndex(eventSender)

    Select Case Index
        Case 0
            rs.MovePrevious()
        Case 1
            rs.MoveNext()
    End Select

End Sub
```

Continued

Listing B-2 *(continued)*

```
Private Sub frmMyForm_Load(ByVal eventSender _
        As System.Object, ByVal eventArgs _
        As System.EventArgs) Handles MyBase.Load

    'UPGRADE_WARNING: Screen property
    'Screen.MousePointer has a
    'new behavior. Click for more:
    'ms-help://MS.MSDNVS/vbcon/html/vbup2065.htm

    System.Windows.Forms.Cursor.Current = _
        System.Windows.Forms.Cursors.WaitCursor
    ' Set the Form caption
    Me.Text = "Simple Upgrade Client"
    ' Set some button properties
    With Command1
        .Text = "Get Authors"
        .Font = VB6.FontChangeSize(.Font, 14)
        .Font = VB6.FontChangeName(.Font, "Verdana")
        ToolTip1.SetToolTip(Command1, "Click to do nothing")
    End With
    ' Clear the boxes
    Text1.Text = ""
    Text2.Text = ""
    ' Make same size
    Text2.Width = Text1.Width
    ' Set Font Size
    Text1.Font = VB6.FontChangeSize(Text1.Font, 12)
    Text2.Font = VB6.FontChangeSize(Text2.Font, 12)
    ' Set Font Name
    Text1.Font = VB6.FontChangeName(Text1.Font, "Tahoma")
    Text2.Font = VB6.FontChangeName(Text2.Font, "Tahoma")
    'Get Connection to Database
    Get_Connection()
    ' Fill the Recordset
    Get_Authors()
    ' Set mouse back to normal
    'UPGRADE_ISSUE: Unable to determine
    'which constant to upgrade
    'vbNormal to. Click for more:
    'ms-help://MS.MSDNVS/vbcon/html/vbup2049.htm
    'UPGRADE_WARNING: Screen property
    'Screen.MousePointer has a
    'new behavior. Click for more:
    'ms-help://MS.MSDNVS/vbcon/html/vbup2065.htm
    System.Windows.Forms.Cursor.Current = vbNormal
End Sub
End Class
```

By looking at the code that could not be upgraded and the syntax changes, you get a good idea of what might happen when you run the wizard.

After running through the code, you can see that the wizard is pretty smart. It's an extremely useful feature, both in the comments in the new code and in the upgrade report, and it has hyperlinks to the help files where you can learn more about any issue the wizard encounters. Overall, it did upgrade 95% of my stuff, but it is not really VB .NET code. It is VB6 code running in VB .NET. Notice the ADO code in the Get_Authors method call. The wizard just added the MDAC 2.6 Type Library as a reference and left it as is. This is not good. I want to use ADO.NET, and so should you.

The larger the project that you attempt to upgrade, the more complex the code. Keep in mind that the most complicated thing I did in SimpleClient was to change the fonts at runtime. Just remember to use caution if you decide to use the wizard.

✦　　✦　　✦

Index

Symbols & Numbers

Continued

C

C# language, VB .NET vs., 13–14
CacheDuration property, 1049–1050
caching
  ASP.NET, 1040, 1049–1050
  defined, 1039
  Web Services and, 1039–1040, 1049–1050
CalculateDiscount procedure, 138–139
Calendar control, 833–837
  asp:calendar code example, 835–836
  described, 793, 833–834
  styles, 836–837
  uses for, 834
Call keyword for Sub procedures, 134
Call Stack window, 366, 384–385
calling
  CTemp proxy methods, 1164–1165
  debugging and, 384–385
  functions, 139
  Sub procedures, 134
  VB6 vs. VB .NET, 24–25
Cancel buttons, multithreading for, 311–312
CanConvertFrom method, 694
CanConvertTo method, 694
CanFocus property, 562
CanSelect property, 562
capping lines, 679
Caption property (VB6), 28
Capture property, 562
caret (^)
  in exponentiation assignment operator (^=),
    94–95
  as exponentiation operator, 54, 88, 89
Cascading Style Sheets (CSS), 919–936
  A:active style definition, 932
  Add Style Rule dialog box, 931–932, 933–934,
    935, 936
  A:hover style definition, 933
  A:link style definition, 933
  alternative methods for styles, 920–922
  A:visited style definition, 933
  benefits of, 919–920
  body tag styles, 931–932
  Classes folder for, 933–935
  code example, 711–712
  creating, 929–936
  CSS Outline window, 930
  default Styles.css file, 927–928
  Element ID folder for, 936
  Elements folder for, 930–933
  external stylesheets, 927–936
  internal stylesheets, 925–927

  overview, 711
  referencing in Web documents, 929
  style class creation, 933–935
Case statements, 123–124. See also Select...Case
    statement
Catch statement. See Try...Catch...Finally
    block
Category attribute, 673
CausesValidation property, 562, 567–569
Chandler, Jim, 1003, 1029, 1053, 1077, 1107,
    1127, 1149
Char data type, 60, 72
check boxes, checking state of, 765–766
Check In dialog box, 439
Check Out dialog box, 438
CheckBox control
  asp:checkbox code example, 802–804
  attributes, 804
  checkboxes described, 801
  CheckBoxList control vs., 801
  click events and, 804
  described, 593, 793
  non-inherited members, 593–594
  for Web Forms, 793, 801–804
  for Windows Forms, 593–594
CheckBoxList control, 801–804
  asp:checkboxlist code example, 802–804
  attributes, 804
  CheckBox control vs., 801
  checkboxes described, 801
  click events and, 804
  described, 793
CheckedListBox control, 594–595
checking in files (SourceSafe), 428, 439, 446
checking out files (SourceSafe), 428, 438, 446
Chr function, 151
Circle method (VB6), 28
Class1.vb file, 271–272
Class statement, 290–291
Class View window, 360
classes, 281–304
  associating aliases with, 745
  Class block, 290–291
  Component Classes, 288–290
  constructors, 302
  creating, 285–290
  data types as, 63
  destructors, 303–304
  events in, 297–298
  fields in, 296–297
  Forms as, 549–550
  garbage collection, 9, 303–304

Continued

Continued

Continued

Continued

Continued

Continued